Nineteenth-Century Literature Criticism

Guide to Thomson Gale Literary Criticism Series

For criticism on	Consult these Thomson Gale series
Authors now living or who died after December 31, 1999	*CONTEMPORARY LITERARY CRITICISM (CLC)*
Authors who died between 1900 and 1999	*TWENTIETH-CENTURY LITERARY CRITICISM (TCLC)*
Authors who died between 1800 and 1899	*NINETEENTH-CENTURY LITERATURE CRITICISM (NCLC)*
Authors who died between 1400 and 1799	*LITERATURE CRITICISM FROM 1400 TO 1800 (LC)* *SHAKESPEAREAN CRITICISM (SC)*
Authors who died before 1400	*CLASSICAL AND MEDIEVAL LITERATURE CRITICISM (CMLC)*
Authors of books for children and young adults	*CHILDREN'S LITERATURE REVIEW (CLR)*
Dramatists	*DRAMA CRITICISM (DC)*
Poets	*POETRY CRITICISM (PC)*
Short story writers	*SHORT STORY CRITICISM (SSC)*
Literary topics and movements	*HARLEM RENAISSANCE: A GALE CRITICAL COMPANION (HR)* *THE BEAT GENERATION: A GALE CRITICAL COMPANION (BG)* *FEMINISM IN LITERATURE: A GALE CRITICAL COMPANION (FL)* *GOTHIC LITERATURE: A GALE CRITICAL COMPANION (GL)*
Asian American writers of the last two hundred years	*ASIAN AMERICAN LITERATURE (AAL)*
Black writers of the past two hundred years	*BLACK LITERATURE CRITICISM (BLC)* *BLACK LITERATURE CRITICISM SUPPLEMENT (BLCS)*
Hispanic writers of the late nineteenth and twentieth centuries	*HISPANIC LITERATURE CRITICISM (HLC)* *HISPANIC LITERATURE CRITICISM SUPPLEMENT (HLCS)*
Native North American writers and orators of the eighteenth, nineteenth, and twentieth centuries	*NATIVE NORTH AMERICAN LITERATURE (NNAL)*
Major authors from the Renaissance to the present	*WORLD LITERATURE CRITICISM, 1500 TO THE PRESENT (WLC)* *WORLD LITERATURE CRITICISM SUPPLEMENT (WLCS)*

ISSN 0732-1864

Volume 173

Nineteenth-Century Literature Criticism

Criticism of the
Works of Novelists, Philosophers, and Other
Creative Writers Who Died between 1800
and 1899, from the First Published Critical
Appraisals to Current Evaluations

Jessica Bomarito
Russel Whitaker
Project Editors

Detroit • New York • San Francisco • New Haven, Conn. • Waterville, Maine • London

Nineteenth-Century Literature Criticism, Vol. 173

Project Editors
Jessica Bomarito and Russel Whitaker

Editorial
Kathy D. Darrow, Jeffrey W. Hunter, Jelena O. Krstović, Michelle Lee, Thomas J. Schoenberg, Noah Schusterbauer, Lawrence J. Trudeau

Data Capture
Frances Monroe, Gwen Tucker

Indexing Services
Factiva®, a Dow Jones and Reuters Company

Rights and Acquisitions
Margaret Abendroth, Emma Hull, Jackie Jones

Imaging and Multimedia
Dean Dauphinais, Robert Duncan, Leitha Etheridge-Sims, Lezlie Light, Michael Logusz, Dan Newell, Kelly A. Quin, Denay Wilding

Composition and Electronic Capture
Tracey L. Matthews

Manufacturing
Rhonda Dover

Associate Product Manager
Marc Cormier

LIBRARY OF CONGRESS CATALOG CARD NUMBER 84-643008

ISBN-13: 978-0-7876-8657-4
ISBN-10: 0-7876-8657-3
ISSN 0732-1864

Printed in the United States of America
10 9 8 7 6 5 4 3 2 1

Contents

Preface vii

Acknowledgments xi

Literary Criticism Series Advisory Board xiii

William Blake 1757-1827 ... 1
English poet and essayist
Entry devoted to the poem Milton *(1804?)*

Francis James Child 1825-1896 ... 164
American editor, critic, and librettist

Nikolai Mikhailovich Karamzin 1766-1826 ... 248
Russian historian, short story writer, poet, essayist, editor, and translator

Literary Criticism Series Cumulative Author Index 363

Literary Criticism Series Cumulative Topic Index 469

NCLC Cumulative Nationality Index 483

NCLC-173 Title Index 487

Preface

Since its inception in 1981, *Nineteeth-Century Literature Criticism* (*NCLC*) has been a valuable resource for students and librarians seeking critical commentary on writers of this transitional period in world history. Designated an "Outstanding Reference Source" by the American Library Association with the publication of is first volume, *NCLC* has since been purchased by over 6,000 school, public, and university libraries. The series has covered more than 450 authors representing 33 nationalities and over 17,000 titles. No other reference source has surveyed the critical reaction to nineteenth-century authors and literature as thoroughly as *NCLC*.

Scope of the Series

NCLC is designed to introduce students and advanced readers to the authors of the nineteenth century and to the most significant interpretations of these authors' works. The great poets, novelists, short story writers, playwrights, and philosophers of this period are frequently studied in high school and college literature courses. By organizing and reprinting commentary written on these authors, *NCLC* helps students develop valuable insight into literary history, promotes a better understanding of the texts, and sparks ideas for papers and assignments. Each entry in *NCLC* presents a comprehensive survey of an author's career or an individual work of literature and provides the user with a multiplicity of interpretations and assessments. Such variety allows students to pursue their own interests; furthermore, it fosters an awareness that literature is dynamic and responsive to many different opinions.

Every fourth volume of *NCLC* is devoted to literary topics that cannot be covered under the author approach used in the rest of the series. Such topics include literary movements, prominent themes in nineteenth-century literature, literary reaction to political and historical events, significant eras in literary history, prominent literary anniversaries, and the literatures of cultures that are often overlooked by English-speaking readers.

NCLC continues the survey of criticism of world literature begun by Thomson Gale's *Contemporary Literary Criticism* (*CLC*) and *Twentieth-Century Literary Criticism* (*TCLC*).

Organization of the Book

An *NCLC* entry consists of the following elements:

- The **Author Heading** cites the name under which the author most commonly wrote, followed by birth and death dates. Also located here are any name variations under which an author wrote, including transliterated forms for authors whose native languages use nonroman alphabets. If the author wrote consistently under a pseudonym, the pseudonym will be listed in the author heading and the author's actual name given in parenthesis on the first line of the biographical and critical information. Uncertain birth or death dates are indicated by question marks. Single-work entries are preceded by a heading that consists of the most common form of the title in English translation (if applicable) and the original date of composition.

- The **Introduction** contains background information that introduces the reader to the author, work, or topic that is the subject of the entry.

- The list of **Principal Works** is ordered chronologically by date of first publication and lists the most important works by the author. The genre and publication date of each work is given. In the case of foreign authors whose works have been translated into English, the list will focus primarily on twentieth-century translations, selecting those works most commonly considered the best by critics. Unless otherwise indicated, dramas are dated by first performance, not first publication. Lists of **Representative Works** by different authors appear with topic entries.

- Reprinted **Criticism** is arranged chronologically in each entry to provide a useful perspective on changes in critical evaluation over time. The critic's name and the date of composition or publication of the critical work are given at the beginning of each piece of criticism. Unsigned criticism is preceded by the title of the source in which it appeared. All titles by the author featured in the text are printed in boldface type. Footnotes are reprinted at the end of each essay or excerpt. In the case of excerpted criticism, only those footnotes that pertain to the excerpted texts are included. Criticism in topic entries is arranged chronologically under a variety of subheadings to facilitate the study of different aspects of the topic.

- A complete **Bibliographical Citation** of the original essay or book precedes each piece of criticism.

- Critical essays are prefaced by brief **Annotations** explicating each piece.

- An annotated bibliography of **Further Reading** appears at the end of each entry and suggests resources for additional study. In some cases, significant essays for which the editors could not obtain reprint rights are included here. Boxed material following the further reading list provides references to other biographical and critical sources on the author in series published by Thomson Gale.

Indexes

Each volume of *NCLC* contains a **Cumulative Author Index** listing all authors who have appeared in a wide variety of reference sources published by Thomson Gale, including *NCLC*. A complete list of these sources is found facing the first page of the Author Index. The index also includes birth and death dates and cross references between pseudonyms and actual names.

A **Cumulative Nationality Index** lists all authors featured in *NCLC* by nationality, followed by the number of the *NCLC* volume in which their entry appears.

A **Cumulative Topic Index** lists the literary themes and topics treated in the series as well as in *Classical and Medieval Literature Criticism, Literature Criticism from 1400 to 1800, Twentieth-Century Literary Criticism,* and the *Contemporary Literary Criticism* Yearbook, which was discontinued in 1998.

An alphabetical **Title Index** accompanies each volume of *NCLC*, with the exception of the Topics volumes. Listings of titles by authors covered in the given volume are followed by the author's name and the corresponding page numbers where the titles are discussed. English translations of foreign titles and variations of titles are cross-referenced to the title under which a work was originally published. Titles of novels, dramas, nonfiction books, and poetry, short story, or essay collections are printed in italics, while individual poems, short stories, and essays are printed in roman type within quotation marks.

In response to numerous suggestions from librarians, Thomson Gale also produces an annual paperbound edition of the *NCLC* cumulative title index. This annual cumulation, which alphabetically lists all titles reviewed in the series, is available to all customers. Additional copies of this index are available upon request. Librarians and patrons will welcome this separate index; it saves shelf space, is easy to use, and is recyclable upon receipt of the next edition.

Citing *Nineteenth-Century Literature Criticism*

When citing criticism reprinted in the Literary Criticism Series, students should provide complete bibliographic information so that the cited essay can be located in the original print or electronic source. Students who quote directly from reprinted criticism may use any accepted bibliographic format, such as University of Chicago Press style or Modern Language Association style.

The examples below follow recommendations for preparing a bibliography set forth in *The Chicago Manual of Style,* 14th ed. (Chicago: The University of Chicago Press, 1993); the first example pertains to material drawn from periodicals, the second to material reprinted from books:

Franklin, J. Jeffrey. "The Victorian Discourse of Gambling: Speculations on *Middlemarch* and *The Duke's Children*." *ELH* 61, no. 4 (winter 1994): 899-921. Reprinted in *Nineteenth-Century Literature Criticism*. Vol. 168, edited by Jessica Bomarito and Russel Whitaker, 39-51. Detroit: Thomson Gale, 2006.

Frank, Joseph. "*The Gambler*: A Study in Ethnopsychology." In *Freedom and Responsibility in Russian Literature: Essays in Honor of Robert Louis Jackson,* edited by Elizabeth Cheresh Allen and Gary Saul Morson, 69-85. Evanston, Ill.: Northwestern University Press, 1995. Reprinted in *Nineteenth-Century Literature Criticism*. Vol. 168, edited by Jessica Bomarito and Russel Whitaker, 75-84. Detroit: Thomson Gale, 2006.

The examples below follow recommendations for preparing a works cited list set forth in the *MLA Handbook for Writers of Research Papers,* 6th ed. (New York: The Modern Language Association of America, 2003); the first example pertains to material drawn from periodicals, the second to material reprinted from books:

Franklin, J. Jeffrey. "The Victorian Discourse of Gambling: Speculations on *Middlemarch* and *The Duke's Children*." *ELH* 61.4 (Winter 1994): 899-921. Reprinted in *Nineteenth-Century Literature Criticism*. Eds. Jessica Bomarito and Russel Whitaker. Vol. 168. Detroit: Thomson Gale, 2006. 39-51.

Frank, Joseph. "*The Gambler*: A Study in Ethnopsychology." *Freedom and Responsibility in Russian Literature: Essays in Honor of Robert Louis Jackson.* Eds. Elizabeth Cheresh Allen and Gary Saul Morson. Evanston, Ill.: Northwestern University Press, 1995. 69-85. Reprinted in *Nineteenth-Century Literature Criticism*. Eds. Jessica Bomarito and Russel Whitaker. Vol. 168. Detroit: Thomson Gale, 2006. 75-84.

Suggestions are Welcome

Readers who wish to suggest new features, topics, or authors to appear in future volumes, or who have other suggestions or comments are cordially invited to call, write, or fax the Associate Product Manager:

Associate Product Manager, Literary Criticism Series
Thomson Gale
27500 Drake Road
Farmington Hills, MI 48331-3535
1-800-347-4253 (GALE)
Fax: 248-699-8054

Acknowledgments

The editors wish to thank the copyright holders of the criticism included in this volume and the permissions managers of many book and magazine publishing companies for assisting us in securing reproduction rights. Following is a list of the copyright holders who have granted us permission to reproduce material in this volume of *NCLC*. Every effort has been made to trace copyright, but if omissions have been made, please let us know.

COPYRIGHTED MATERIAL IN *NCLC*, VOLUME 173, WAS REPRODUCED FROM THE FOLLOWING PERIODICALS:

Blake Studies, v. 1, 1968-69. Copyright © 1968, Kay Long and Roger R. Easson. Reproduced by permission.—*Colby Library Quarterly*, v. 13, June, 1977. Reprinted by permission of the publisher.—*College English*, v. 66, May, 2004. Copyright © 2004 by the National Council of Teachers of English. Reproduced by permission of the publisher.—*European Romantic Review*, v. 8, summer, 1997 for "Locating the Satanic: Blake's *Milton* and the Poetics of 'Self-Examination'" by Kevin D. Hutchings. Copyright © 1997 by Logos Press. Reproduced by permission of Taylor & Francis, Ltd., http// :www.tandf.co.uk/journals, and the author.—*Folk Music Journal*, v. 4, 1981; v. 7, 1996. Copyright © The English Folk Dance and Song Society 1981, 1996. All rights reserved. Both reproduced by permission.—*Forum for Modern Language Studies*, v. 5, January, 1969 for "N. M. Karamzin's *Messenger of Europe* (*Vestnik Yevropy*), 1802-03" by A. G. Cross. Copyright © 1969 Oxford University Press. Reproduced by permission of Oxford University Press and the author.— *Journal of English and Germanic Philology*, v. 81, January, 1982 for "Typology, History, and Blake's *Milton*" by Albert J. Rivero. Copyright © 1982 by the Board of Trustees of the University of Illinois. Used with permission of the University of Illinois Press and the author.—*Journal of Folklore Research*, v. 31, January-December, 1994. Copyright © Indiana University Press. Reproduced by permission.—*Milton Studies*, v. 11, 1978. Copyright © 1978, University of Pittsburgh Press. All rights reserved. Reproduced by permission.—*Nineteenth-Century Contexts*, v. 19, 1995 for "Blake's *Milton*: The Metaphysics of Gender" by Marc Kaplan. Copyright © 1995 O. P. A. (Overseas Publishers Association). Reproduced by permission of Taylor & Francis, Ltd., http//:www.tandf.co.uk/journals, and the author.—*Religion and Literature*, v. 25, spring, 1993. Copyright © 1993 by the University of Notre Dame English Department. Reprint permission granted by the University of Notre Dame.—*Romantic Russia*, v. 1, 1997. Reproduced by permission.—*Scando-Slavica*, v. 27, 1981 for "Metafiction in Russian 18th Century Prose: Karamzin's *Rycar' nasego vremeni* or *Novyj Akteon, vnuk Kadma i Garmonii*" by Gitta Hammarberg. Reproduced by permission of Taylor & Francis AS, http//:www.tandf.no/scandoslavica, and the author.—*SEL: Studies in English Literature, 1500-1900*, v. 30, autumn, 1990. Copyright © 1990 The Johns Hopkins University Press. Reproduced by permission.—*Slavic and East European Journal*, v. 29, summer, 1985. Copyright © 1985 by AATSEEL of the U.S., Inc. Reproduced by permission.—*South Central Bulletin*, v. 31, winter, 1971. Copyright © 1971 *South Central Bulletin*. Reprinted with permission of The John Hopkins University Press.—*Studies in Romanticism*, v. 20, spring, 1981; v. 36, spring, 1997. Copyright © 1981, 1997 by the Trustees of Boston University. Both reproduced by permission.—*Studies on Voltaire and the Eighteenth Century*, v. 151, 1976 for "Nicholas Karamzin and the Dilemma of Luxury in 18th Century Russia" by J. L. Black. Copyright © Theodore Besterman 1976. Reproduced by permission of the publisher and author.—*Western Folklore*, v. 47, October, 1988. Copyright © 1988 by the Western States Folklore Society. Reproduced by permission.

COPYRIGHTED MATERIAL IN *NCLC*, VOLUME 173, WAS REPRODUCED FROM THE FOLLOWING BOOKS:

Bradford, Gamaliel. From *As God Made Them: Portraits of Some Nineteenth-Century Americans*. Houghton Mifflin Company, 1929. Copyright © 1929 by Gamaliel Bradford. Renewed 1956 by Sarah Bradford Ross. All rights reserved. Reprinted by permission of Houghton Mifflin Company.—Emerson, Caryl. From *Boris Godunov: Transpositions of a Russian Theme*. Indiana University Press, 1986. Copyright © 1986 by Caryl Emerson. All rights reserved. Reproduced by permission.—Howard, John. From *Blake's* Milton: *A Study in the Selfhood*. Fairleigh Dickinson University Press, 1976. Copyright © 1976 by Associated University Presses, Inc. All rights reserved. Reproduced by permission.—Kisljagina, L. G. From "The Question of the Development of N. M. Karamzin's Social Political Views in the Nineties of the Eighteenth Century: N. M. Karamzin and the Great French Bourgeois Revolution," in *Essays on Karamzin: Russian Man-of-Letters, Political Thinker, Historian, 1766-1826*. Edited by J. L. Black. Mouton, 1975. Copyright © 1975 in the Netherlands by

Thomson Gale Literature Product Advisory Board

Milton

William Blake

English poet and essayist.

The following entry presents criticism of Blake's poem *Milton* (1804?). For criticism devoted to *Songs of Innocence and of Experience: Shewing the Two Contrary States of the Human Soul* (1794), see *NCLC,* Volume 37; for criticism devoted to *The Marriage of Heaven and Hell* (1793), see *NCLC,* Volume 57; for criticism devoted to *Jerusalem: The Emanation of the Giant Albion* (1820), see *NCLC,* Volume 127; for information on Blake's complete career, see *NCLC,* Volume 13.

INTRODUCTION

Most scholars recognize Blake's *Milton* as one of the poet's most imaginative, and challenging, literary works. First published circa 1804, the poem captures Blake's besieged mental state during the years 1800 to 1803, when he worked as an engraver for the poet William Hayley in the quiet coastal town of Felpham. At first Blake welcomed the slower pace of life in the countryside, after years of struggling to survive as an artist in London. Eventually, however, Blake became frustrated by the drudgery of his labor, as well as by Hayley's failure to appreciate his unique genius, and in 1803 he returned to the capital. Although Blake wrote much of *Milton* at Felpham, he completed it in London, while also executing a series of illuminated plates to accompany the long poem. Along with *The Four Zoas* (composed between 1796 and 1807; published in 1963 as *Vala, or The Four Zoas*) and *Jerusalem* (1820), *Milton* is one of Blake's three Prophetic Books, longer poems that seek to create a new mythology of human history, while exploring themes of apocalypse and renewal in the face of the corrosive spiritual effects of the Enlightenment age. The poem's complex structure, its use of arcane symbolism and obscure terminology, and its intensely vivid imagery make it one of the strangest and most difficult to interpret works of the Romantic era. On one level, *Milton* offers an allegorical retelling of Blake's difficult years in Felpham; it contains numerous references to his work, his living arrangements, and his troubled relationship with Hayley. In a broader sense, however, the poem dramatizes the plight of the artist in a society dominated by industrialization and science, and it calls on the heroic figure of the poet, personified

by the resurrected John Milton, to deliver humanity to the heavenly kingdom of Jerusalem. Interpreted in this light, Blake's portrayal of Milton's redemption symbolizes the triumph of inspiration over the cold logic of reason, as well as the ascendancy of a true Christian spirituality (one that is rooted in self-sacrifice and the courage to confront evil) over the selfish material worldview of natural religion, or faith rooted in empirical knowledge.

PLOT AND MAJOR CHARACTERS

Milton is comprised of two books, a preface, and a series of illustrations. In the preface, Blake calls upon all artists to join together in establishing a "New Age," one in which poetic inspiration will supplant scientific inquiry as the dominant intellectual and creative force in human society. In Blake's view, the artist must repudiate the "Stolen and Perverted Writings" of Greek and Roman antiquity, works founded on the artificial precepts of human ingenuity, and instead embrace the purely inspiring texts of the Bible as a means of reaching "those Worlds of Eternity in which we shall live forever in Jesus our Lord." Book One of the poem opens with the "Bard's Song," an apocalyptic retelling of the Fall of Man and the subsequent creation of the universe. This section of the poem recapitulates portions of Blake's earlier work, *The First Book of Urizen* (1794)— even reprinting several lines verbatim—while recasting the figure of Urizen as Satan, whose primary purpose is to thwart the poet Milton's return to earth. After establishing the mythological context of the work, the Bard recounts the ongoing struggle between Satan and Palamabron, a humble artisan representing Blake himself. As an unwitting minion of Satan, Palamabron finds his creativity stifled in the service of fruitless ends, a circumstance that provokes sympathy among the deities of Eternity. Among these deities are Los, a prophet who helps guide mortals in their creative acts; Los's female incarnation, Enitharmon; and Rintrah, a god of political and social upheaval. In order to liberate Palamabron from Satan's charge and in the process restore positive creative energy to the universe, the deities call forth the figure of John Milton. Dead for more than a hundred years, Milton returns to earth to support Palamabron in his battle with Satan. As Milton enters the consciousness of Palamabron in the form of a prophetic vision,

Satan gathers his earthly forces, among them commerce and industry, in order to oppose him. The remainder of Book One chronicles the warlike awakening of Albion, which symbolizes both England and industrial society in general, in anticipation of Milton's arrival; Blake's description of the mounting conflict is replete with images of destruction and chaos. These events all occur within a single moment of poetic vision and reveal the divide between spiritual power, emblematic of humanity's ideal state, and natural power, which embodies the man-made laws of the earth and "continually seeks & tends to Destruction / Ending in death."

Book Two, which is roughly half the length of Book One, opens with the descent to earth of Milton's poetic emanation, the female spirit Ololon. Ololon reveals to Palamabron the inherently corrupt and self-destructive nature of human society, while instructing him in the ways of seeing the world as a true poet. While Ololon embodies many of the virtues necessary for prophecy, she is also tainted, a product of Milton's earthly transgressions. For Blake, Milton's sins lay in his faith in the power of human reason rather than the power of inspiration and in his dogmatic repudiation of human sexuality, something Blake regarded as a healthy manifestation of spirituality. At this point the poem's central drama, in which the heroic figure of the poet must annihilate himself in order to destroy the selfish and false ways of the world, begins to take shape. Milton descends into himself so that he can come to terms with his erroneous thinking; Ololon, fearing her own destruction, transforms herself into Rahab, a virgin deity embodying the selfish, power-lusting attributes of the material world. As Milton experiences his revelation, recognizing the inherent falseness of his earlier convictions, Ololon becomes penitent and is restored to her previously selfless form. This annihilation of the self, far from representing the destruction of human consciousness, in fact represents the liberation of the creative individual from the repressive forces of society, opening the imagination to the healing power of "Jesus the Savior." Milton's act of self-annihilation has saved the earth from chaos and destruction; at the same time, he has effected his own reformation as a poet.

MAJOR THEMES

Milton explores the rift between two facets of human existence: the material world, represented by manufacturing, commerce, and government; and the spiritual world, embodied in the inspired works of great artists. Blake announces his central theme in the poem's preface: he invokes a day in the future when "the Daughters of Memory shall become the Daughters of Inspiration"—in other words, when the kingdom of heaven will reign on earth, history will end, and humanity will

be restored to a state of eternal bliss. On one level, the idea of redemption had deep personal meaning for Blake as he struggled to extricate himself from an unfulfilling professional situation and reassert his literary talents. Blake also viewed the redemptive act as a means of reforming John Milton, whose great poetic works had been corrupted, in Blake's view, by his failure to recognize the inherent evils of rationalism and natural religion. Blake dramatized these individual struggles within the larger allegorical framework of the world, where a more protracted and menacing battle between the forces of reason and inspiration takes place. By making Milton the protagonist of his poem, Blake established a connection between his own personal redemption, the redemption of his hero-poet, and the redemption of society in general. Milton's central role in the poem also invests the work with a certain literary authority; in *Milton,* as in his other poems, Blake acknowledged Milton's primacy among English poets, even as he leveled scathing critiques at Milton's intellectual beliefs.

While the poem is rich in symbolism and metaphoric language, Blake intended it to be read literally, as a work of prophecy akin to the Book of Revelations. Blake's personal correspondence from this period attests to the visionary aspects of the poem's composition; in a letter to Thomas Butts dated April 25, 1803, Blake claims to have written *Milton* "from immediate dictation . . . without premeditation, and even against my will." In this sense, the poem's ideal of artistic creation, unmediated by rational thought, finds an echo in Blake's own writing methods.

CRITICAL RECEPTION

Like most of Blake's writings, *Milton* failed to attract much attention at the time of its original publication. Even as interest in Blake's work increased toward the end of the nineteenth century, readers remained perplexed by the convoluted symbolism and unusual diction found in *Milton* and his other prophetic works. For years, scholars puzzled over the poem's complex structure and meaning. Alfred T. Story, in his 1893 study *William Blake,* provides an early examination of the visionary elements in Blake's poetry. While Story had great admiration for Blake's *Milton,* he nevertheless admitted to understanding very little of it and described Blake's later poetry in general as containing a "vast overplus of words utterly without meaning." With the rise of Freudian psychology in the early twentieth century, some commentators began to interpret the poem's visionary imagery and unorthodox language within the context of Blake's mental state during the work's composition. Algernon Charles Swinburne asserted in his *William Blake,* published in 1906, that *Milton* bore "the stamp of an over-heated brain, and of nerves too in-

tensely strung." Even Blake's defenders conceded that the poem was the product of a difficult period for the poet; Edwin J. Ellis, author of *The Real Blake,* which appeared in 1907, referred to Blake's "jarred nerves" and "distracted mind," while Hubert J. Norman, writing in the *Journal of Mental Science* in 1915, associated the poem's "wild welter of verbiage" with Blake's high level of emotional stress. With the rise of Blake scholarship in the years after World War I, however, more meaningful critical interpretations of *Milton* began to emerge. Renowned Blake scholar Samuel Foster Damon, in his 1924 study *William Blake,* was among the first to provide an in-depth reading of *Milton,* while Northrop Frye's *Fearful Symmetry,* published in 1947, explores the poem's symbolic framework. Harold Bloom offered a thorough analysis of the poem's narrative structure in his 1963 study *Blake's Apocalypse,* praising *Milton* as "a poem worthy of a place beside the Book of Job and *Paradise Regained.*" The essay collection *Blake's Sublime Allegory,* edited by Stuart Curran and published in 1973, contains a range of critical interpretations of the work, while John Howard's 1976 study, *Blake's* Milton: *A Study in the Selfhood,* provides an exhaustive examination of the poem's philosophical, psychological, and symbolic underpinnings. More recently, scholars have begun to explore the poem outside of conventional interpretive models, reading the work as an expression of what Paul Youngquist called the "drama of Blake's poetic empowerment." Other, more specialized readings of the poem have emerged since the 1990s, examining such issues as Blake's representations of gender, his attitude toward nature, and the relationship between his vision of the world and the rise of Great Britain in the early nineteenth century.

PRINCIPAL WORKS

Poetical Sketches (poetry) 1783

**All Religions Are One* (poetry) 1788

**There Is No Natural Religion* (poetry) 1788

The Book of Thel (poetry) 1789

Songs of Innocence (poetry) 1789; revised and enlarged as *Songs of Innocence and of Experience: Shewing the Two Contrary States of the Human Soul,* 1794

America: A Prophecy (poetry) 1793

For Children: The Gates of Paradise (poetry) 1793; revised as *For the Sexes: The Gates of Paradise,* 1818?

**The Marriage of Heaven and Hell* (poetry and prose) 1793

Visions of the Daughters of Albion: The Eye Sees More than the Heart Knows (poetry) 1793

Europe: A Prophecy (poetry) 1794

The First Book of Urizen (poetry) 1794

The Book of Ahania (poetry) 1795

The Book of Los (poetry) 1795

The Song of Los (poetry) 1795

**Milton* (poetry) 1804?

A Descriptive Catalogue of Pictures, Poetical and Historical Inventions, Painted by William Blake in Water Colours, being the Ancient Method of Fresco Painting Restored: and Drawings for Public Inspection, etc. (prose and criticism) 1809

†*Jerusalem: The Emanation of the Giant Albion* (poetry) 1820

The Poetical Works of William Blake, Lyrical and Miscellaneous (essays, poetry, and prose) 1874

‡*The Works of William Blake, Poetic, Symbolic, and Critical.* 3 vols. (essays, poetry, and prose) 1893

The Letters of William Blake (letters) 1906

The Writings of William Blake (poetry, essays, criticism, prose, journals, and letters) 1925; revised as *The Complete Writings of William Blake,* 1957; revised, 1966

#*The Note-Book of William Blake* (journal) 1935

The Portable Blake (essays, poetry, and prose) 1946

Selected Poetry and Prose (poetry and prose) 1953

The Complete Poetry and Prose of William Blake (poetry and prose) 1965; revised, 1982

‖*Tiriel* (poetry) 1967

*Dating the original publication of many of Blake's works is difficult, for he alternately printed and revised some of his individual writings over a long period of time and left few plates and copies of books for bibliographers to examine as evidence.

†The date on the title page of this work is 1804, but it was not distributed in its modern form until 1820. A few of the plates from *Jerusalem* may have been exhibited in 1812.

‡This work contains the first published version of *The Four Zoas: The Torments of Love and Jealousy in the Death and Judgment of Albion the Ancient Man,* originally created between 1796-1807. It was published under the title *Vala* in this edition.

#The *Note-Book* is also referred to as the *Rossetti Manuscript.* It contains *A Vision of the Last Judgment,* composed around 1810, which is thought to have been intended to form part of a second *Descriptive Catalogue.*

‖*Tiriel,* written c. 1789, was not printed during Blake's lifetime.

CRITICISM

William Blake (letter date 25 April 1803)

SOURCE: Blake, William. "To Thomas Butts." In *The Letters of William Blake,* edited by Archibald G. B. Russell, pp. 113-16. London: Methuen & Co., 1906.

[*In the following excerpt from a letter dated April 25, 1803, Blake describes his spiritual and psychological state during the composition of* Milton. *The letter is regarded by scholars as the earliest known reference to the poem.*]

And now, my dear sir, congratulate me on my return to London, with the full approbation of Mr. Hayley and with promise. But, alas! now I may say to you—what perhaps I should not dare to say to anyone else: that I can alone carry on my visionary studies in London un-annoyed, and that I may converse with my friends in eternity, see visions, dream dreams, and prophesy and speak parables unobserved, and at liberty from the doubts of other mortals; perhaps doubts proceeding from kindness; but doubts are always pernicious, especially when we doubt our friends. Christ is very decided on this point: "He who is not with Me is against Me." There is no medium or middle state; and if a man is the enemy of my spiritual life while he pretends to be the friend of my corporeal, he is a real enemy[1]; but the man may be the friend of my spiritual life while he seems the enemy of my corporeal, though not *vice versa.*

What is very pleasant, every one who hears of my going to London again applauds it as the only course for the interest of all concerned in my works; observing that I ought not to be away from the opportunities London affords of seeing fine pictures, and the various improvements in works of art going on in London.

But none can know the spiritual acts of my three years' slumber on the banks of ocean, unless he has seen them in the spirit, or unless he should read my long poem [*Milton*][2] descriptive of those acts; for I have in these years composed an immense number of verses on one grand theme, similar to Homer's *Iliad* or Milton's *Paradise Lost*; the persons and machinery entirely new to the inhabitants of earth (some of the persons excepted). I have written this poem from immediate dictation, twelve or sometimes twenty or thirty lines at a time, without premeditation, and even against my will. The time it has taken in writing was thus rendered nonexistent, and an immense poem exists which seems to be the labour of a long life, all produced without labour or study. I mention this to show you what I think the grand reason of my being brought down here.

Notes

1. cp. *Milton*, p. 3*, l. 26: "Corporeal Friends are Spiritual Enemies."

2. The *Milton* (dated 1804, but not given to the world until about 1808) deals especially with the acts at Felpham: cp. *Public Address* (Gilchrist, 1880, vol. ii. p. 175), "The manner in which I have rooted out the nest of villains will be seen in a poem concerning my three years' herculean labours at Felpham, which I shall soon publish"—(he is speaking of the attack made upon him in *The Examiner*). From the title-page we learn that Blake's original intention was to publish twelve books of this poem. Two only, however, were engraved; and a good deal of the material seems to

have been transferred to *Jerusalem*. The latter is also dated 1804, but seems not to have been ready for publication until about 1818 (see note 1, p. 223).

Alfred T. Story (essay date 1893)

SOURCE: Story, Alfred T. *William Blake: His Life Character and Genius,* pp. 127-37. London: Swan Sonnenschein & Co., 1893.

[*In the following excerpt, Story offers a close reading of* Milton, *examining some of the work's central themes.*]

The two remaining Prophetic Books, which we shall examine, are separated from what we may term the Cycle of the Four Continents by a broad space of years. During that time Blake's ideas developed, or else, to use his own form of speech, the visions became more angry, and made greater demands upon him. It may be that the change of air, and scene—the one quickening the blood in his veins, the other kindling to renewed vigour the fiery vehemence of his brain—gave a fresh impetus to his creative and prophetic powers, and was thus largely instrumental in the production of the *Milton* and *Jerusalem,* which, in their way, form as marvellous a piece of writing as is to be met with in our literature. I do not know that we have any precise information as to which of these books was first in point of time. Both were issued in 1804. But from internal evidence, I should judge that *Milton* was the earlier of the two, and that it was completed before the author left Felpham. . . .

There is another reason for thinking that the *Milton* was composed first, namely, that it is the less obscure of the two. This is perhaps not saying a great deal when there is so much that is dark and enigmatic in both; but taking them bulk for bulk, one finds more in the *Milton* that rewards the unaided intellect than in the *Jerusalem.* There are not wanting indications, that the poet was inspired to this effort by a renewed perusal of *Paradise Lost.* In the following lines, for instance, we find several Miltonic echoes:

> Say first, what moved Milton, who walked about in
> Eternity
> One hundred years, pondering the intricate mazes of
> Providence?
> Unhappy tho' in heaven, he obeyed, he murmured
> not, he was silent,
> Viewing his six-fold Emanation scattered through the
> deep
> In torment. To go into the deep her to redeem and
> himself to perish?
> What cause at length moved Milton to this unex-
> ampled deed?
> A Bard's prophetic song: for sitting at eternal tables,

Terrific among the Sons of Albion in chorus solemn
 and loud,
A Bard broke forth; all sat attentive to the awful man.

But we ought not to pass amid the shadows and mist of
the poem with its Titanic forms and thunderous rever-
berations, without first giving something more than a
glance at the preface, which is worth quoting in full.

"The stolen and perverted writings of Homer and Ovid,
of Plato and Cicero, which all men ought to contemn,
are set up by artifice against the sublime of the Bible;
but when the New Age is at leisure to pronounce, all
will be set right, and those grand works of the more an-
cient and consciously and professedly inspired men will
hold their proper rank; and the daughters of memory
shall become the daughters of inspiration. Shakespeare
and Milton were both curbed by the general malady and
infection from the silly Greek and Latin slaves of the
sword. Rouse up, O young men of the New Age! Set
your foreheads against the ignorant hirelings! For we
have hirelings in the camp, the court, and the univer-
sity; who would, if they could, for ever prolong corpo-
real war. Painters! on you I call! Sculptors! Architects!
suffer not the fashionable fools to depress some powers
by the prices they pretend to give for contemptible
works, or the expensive advertising boasts that they
make of such works: believe Christ and His Apostles,
that there is a class of men whose whole delight is in
destroying. We do not want either Greek or Roman
models if we are but just and true to our own imagina-
tions, those words of eternity in which we shall live for
ever, in Jesus our Lord."

And did those feet in ancient time
 Walk over England's mountains green,
And was the holy hand of God
 On England's pleasant pastures seen?

And did the Countenance Divine
 Shine forth upon our clouded hills?
And was Jerusalem builded here,
 Among these dark Satanic mills?

"Bring me my bow of burning gold;
 Bring me my arrows of desire;
Bring me my spear: O clouds, unfold
 Bring me my chariot of fire.

"I will not cease from mental fight,
 Nor shall my sword sleep in my hand,
Till we have built Jerusalem
 In England's green and pleasant land."

This striking prelude is closed with the words from
Numbers (xi. 29): "Would to God that all the Lord's
people were prophets," from which we may gather
something of the sense in which Blake uses the word
"prophet." At first sight it would seem as though not
much meaning were to be got out of the poet's appeal
from the "artifice" of the old classical writers to the
pure and fresher spirit of the New Age. But there is
both sense and truth in what he says, though, like all
that the poet advances, it is touched with the vagueness,
if not with the delirium, of the oracular or prophetic ut-
terance.

After this strange preface, the poem opens with charac-
teristic Blakeian splendour of diction and quaintness of
mysticism:—

Daughters of Beulah! Muses who inspire the Poet's
 Song!
Record the journey of immortal Milton thro' your
 realms
Of terror and mild moony lustre, in soft sexual delu-
 sions
Of varied beauty, to delight the wanderer, and repose
His burning thirst and freezing hunger!

Of the poem itself let it suffice to say that it purports to
tell of the incarnation and descent into hell of Milton,
his task being that of redemption through inspiration,
which cannot be effected in less than six thousand years.
But to state this is to give but the scantiest possible de-
scription of the Prophecy, in which, what with his won-
drous cosmogony, his gigantic myths, and his theology,
we soon find ourselves travelling through regions of in-
choate darkness and dim moony mist, amid giant shad-
ows and forms for ever fluid and changing; perplexed,
too, by—even though often admiring—his heterodox
views and striking imaginations. We find here thoughts
and ideas repeated that are never far to seek in Blake's
works; but we also encounter new ones, or the re-
instatement of old ones in more startling guise. After
the **"Song of the Bard,"** in which we have the magnifi-
cent but almost formless myth of Palamabron's harrow
and horses, Milton states his purpose in these words:—

I go to Eternal Death! The nations still
Follow after the detestable Gods of Priam; in pomp
Of warlike selfhood, contradicting and blaspheming.
When will the Resurrection come, to deliver the sleep-
 ing body
From contemptibility? O when, Lord Jesus, wilt Thou
 come?
Tarry no longer, for my soul lies at the gates of death.
I will arise and look forth for the morning of the grave;
I will go down to the sepulchre and see if morning
 breaks;
I will go down to self-annihilation and eternal death,
Lest the Last Judgment come and find me unannihi-
 late,
And I be seized and given into the hands of my own
 Selfhood.
The Lamb of God is seen through mists and shadows,
 hovering
Over the sepulchres in clouds of Jehovah and winds
 of Elohim,
A disk of blood distant; and heavens and earths roll
 dark between.
What do I here before the Judgment without my Ema-
 nation?

With the daughters of memory, and not with the
 daughters of inspiration?
I in my Selfhood am that Satan; I am that Evil One!
He is my Spectre! in my obedience to loose him from
 my Hells,
To claim the Hells, my Furnaces, I go to Eternal
 Death.

The poet then describes how, "on the verge of Beulah,
he saw his own shadow," and "entered into it." The ac-
companying illustration, depicting Milton entering his
shadow, is one of the grandest to be found in the whole
of these Prophetic Books. Space will not permit us to
follow the shadow as it "kept its course among the
spectres in a trail of light as of a comet," till it came to
the "Mundane Shell," in the account of which we have
a piece of Blake's strange cosmogony; nor to describe
the enormous strife between Milton and Urizen, the one
typifying inspiration, the other reason, which, as we
have seen, always stands for error and wrong in Blake's
mystical philosophy. As little can we tarry to take note
of the temptation by the sons and daughters of Rahab
and Tirzah, when

The Two-fold form Hermaphroditic, and the Double-
 sexed,—
The Female-male, and the Male-female, self-dividing
 stood
Before him in their beauty, and in the cruelties of ho-
 liness,
Shining in darkness, glorious upon the deeps of Entu-
 thon.

Very beautiful is the self-sacrifice of Ololon for Milton,
as again setting forth one of Blake's greatest and most
characteristic thoughts, the necessity of eternal self-
sacrifice, by way of redemption from eternal selfish-
ness.

And Ololon said, 'Let us descend also, and let us give
Ourselves to death in Ulro among the Transgressors.'

But the myth—for it is more myth than allegory—is so
involved and obscure that it were vain to attempt expla-
nation here; nor will there be found many with patience
enough to toil through the remainder of the poem, bril-
liant and scintillating with gems though much of it is. It
is interesting to know, albeit we do not obtain much by
the knowledge, that "Bowlahoola is named Law by
mortals," that "Golgonooza is named Art and Manufac-
tures" (though elsewhere Golgonooza is London), and
that "in Bowlahoola Los's Anvils stand and his Fur-
naces rage."

Thundering the Hammers beat and the Bellows blow
 loud.
. .
The Bellows are the Animal Lungs, the Hammers the
 Anvil Heart,
The Furnaces the Stomach for digestion.

It would help us, too, in our attempts to understand
Blake's gigantic mythology or demonology if he gave

us an insight into the meaning of his vast and too often
enigmatic forms, as here into those of Los and Enithar-
mon.

Los is by mortals named Time; Enitharmon is named
 Space;
But they depict him bald and aged who is in eternal
 youth
All-powerful, and his locks flourish like the brows of
 morning;
He is the Spirit of Prophecy, the ever-apparent Elias.
Time is the mercy of Eternity; without Time's swift-
 ness,
Which is the swiftness of all things, all were eternal
 torment.

The rest of the first book is mainly taken up with a de-
scription of Nature, the like of which was never before
conceived by mortal man, in which is included a vision
of the gathering of the harvest of Time and of the tread-
ing of the winepress of War, when all are put "into the
press, the oppressor and the oppressed." Not much is
there in the whole of Blake's writings wherein such
splendour of thought and thorough earnestness of con-
viction cause each line, as it were, to palpitate with vi-
tal energy like those that follow.

How red the sons and daughters of Luvah! Here they
 tread the grapes,
Laughing and shouting, drunk with odours; many fall
 o'erwearied;
Drowned in the wine is many a youth and maiden;
 those around
Lay them on skins of Tigers and of the spotted Leop-
 ard and the Wild Ass
Till they revive, or bury them in cool grots, making
 lamentation.
This Winepress is called War on Earth; it is the
 Printing-Press
Of Los: there he lays his words in order above the
 mortal brain,
As cogs are formed in a wheel to turn the cogs of the
 adverse wheel.

Every living thing takes part in the vintage, "the earwig
armed, the tender maggot—emblem of immortality—
the flea, louse, bug, the tapeworm, all the armies of dis-
ease, visible or invisible." These and all living things
else "throw off their gorgeous raiment," and "rejoice
with loud jubilee around the winepresses of Luvah, na-
ked and drunk with wine." But it is different with man:

. . . in the Winepresses, the Human grapes sing not
 nor dance;
They howl and writhe in shoals of torment, in fierce
 flames consuming,
In chains of iron and in dungeons circled with cease-
 less fires,
In pits and dens and shades of death, in shapes of tor-
 ment and woe.
. .
They dance around the dying, and they drink the howl
 and groan;

> They catch the shrieks in cups of gold; they hand
> them to one another;
> These are the sports of love, and these the sweet de-
> lights of amorous play,
> Tears of the grape, the death-sweat of the cluster, the
> last sigh
> Of the mild youth who listens to the luring songs of
> Luvah.

One might go on quoting gem after gem; but only one more selection shall be given here, and that from the second book, which, taken as a whole, is much more obscure and difficult of comprehension than the first. The following, however, considering the poet's symbolical style, is plain enough, and needs little by way of gloss or explanation.

> In the Eastern porch of Satan's Universe Milton stood
> and said:
> "Satan, my Spectre! I know my power thee to annihi-
> late
> And be a greater in thy place, and be thy Tabernacle,
> A covering for thee to do thy will, till one greater
> comes
> And smites me as I smote thee, and becomes my cov-
> ering.
> Such are the Laws of thy false Heavens; but Laws of
> Eternity
> Are not such. Know thou that I come to Self-
> Annihilation:
> Such are the Laws of Eternity, that each shall mutu-
> ally
> Annihilate himself for others' good, as I for thee.
> Thy purpose, and the purposes of the Priests and of
> thy Churches,
> Is to impress on men the fear of death, to teach
> Trembling and fear, terrors, constriction, abject self-
> ishness;
> Mine is to teach men to despise death and to go on
> In fearless majesty annihilating Self, laughing to scorn
> Thy Laws and terrors, shaking down thy Synagogues
> as webs.
> I come to discover before Heaven and Hell self-
> righteousness
> In all its hypocritic turpitude, opening to every eye
> These wonders of Satan's holiness, shewing to the
> earth
> The Idol Virtues of the Natural Heart, and Satan's
> Seat
> Explore in all its Selfish Natural Virtue, and put off
> In Self-annihilation all that is not of God alone:
> To put off Self and all I have ever and ever. Amen."

One needs not to insist upon the splendour and noble quality of the thought here presented; it is evident to all, notwithstanding Blake's peculiar method of expressing himself. He seems to hold in especial disdain the particularly Christian virtue of thinking for ever of self and of the safety of self, setting the consideration of personal salvation above everything else, in it forgetting or neglecting the higher duty of thinking of and doing for others. This to him is "self-righteousness in all its hypocritic turpitude," and constitutes "Satan's Seat," which can only be conquered by the mutual an-

nihilation of self for others' good. The thought is essentially heretical, but therein lies Blake's peculiar characteristic and strength, that he cannot hypocritically pretend to believe in a thing that is alien to his thought.

One would like, before finally finishing with the *Milton,* to quote the almost unapproachable lines, commencing—

> Thou hearest the nightingale begin the song of spring;
> The lark, sitting upon his earthly bed, just as the morn
> Appears, listens silent; then, springing from the wav-
> ing cornfield, loud
> He leads the choir of day;

but the temptation must be resisted, else we might be led on to quote gem after gem from these incomparable compositions that, like the world, are full of dark and inscrutable things, though illumined here and there with beauties that redeem and, as it were, sanctify the whole.

E. R. D. MacLagan and A. G. B. Russell (essay date 1907)

SOURCE: MacLagan, E. R. D., and A. G. B. Russell. "Introduction." In *The Prophetic Books of William Blake:* Milton, edited by E. R. D. MacLagan and A. G. B. Russell, pp. v-xvi. London: A. H. Bullen, 1907.

[*In the following excerpt, MacLagan and Russell examine the central thematic and stylistic concerns of* Milton, *discussing the poem within the context of Blake's life circumstances during its composition.*]

When, in the autumn of the year 1800, Blake withdrew from London into the country, he seemed to see the dawn of another life, in which he was to emerge at last from the confusion and unrest of his past existence into a state of freedom and spiritual felicity. He believed that the generosity of his new patron would for ever redeem him from that servile necessity of soul-destroying drudgery which had hitherto been imposed upon him by the fear of starvation, and that he would be able to pursue the arts of imagination, unfettered and uninterrupted. The atmosphere of Felpham appeared to his liberated perceptions to be a "more spiritual" one than that of London. "Heaven," he wrote, on arriving, to Flaxman, "opens here on all sides her golden gates; . . . voices of celestial inhabitants are more distinctly heard, and their forms more distinctly seen." He dreamed of becoming the prophet of a new era of visionary creation when men should again "converse in heaven and walk with angels," upon earth. But he was quickly to be disillusioned. It was soon clear that his patron was not at all disposed to bestow, with his benevolence, a free hand. Besides this, he was wholly out of sympathy with the visionary character of Blake's inventions, both in

poetry and painting, and irritated him beyond measure by the "genteel ignorance and polite disapprobation," with which he was content to receive them. "He is as much averse," Blake bitterly complained in a letter to Butts, "to my poetry as he is to a chapter in the Bible," and "approves of my designs as little as he does of my poems." Miniature painting, engraving of a despicable sort and the decoration of Hayley's library with a frieze of poets' heads were by no means the most grievous of the tasks set; and the worst of them was far more tolerable than the habit of reading Klopstock aloud with which his patron sought to improve the brief hours of recreation. No wonder at the expressions of unconcealed disappointment which we find in some of Blake's letters. He discovered immediately and to his cost that in the country there is no peace at all and that it is only in the midst of a great city that the artist can be truly alone with his own soul. "I do assure you," he wrote afterwards to Butts, "that, if I could have returned to London a month after my arrival here, I should have done so"; and in another letter, "I can alone carry on my visionary studies in London unannoyed, and converse with my friends in eternity, see visions, dream dreams, and prophesy and speak parables unobserved, and at liberty from the doubts of other mortals."

But in spite of the truly "Herculean labours" which, he tells us, were imposed upon him at Felpham, Blake was at the same time fully conscious of a considerable debt of gratitude. He also speaks of his "three years slumber on the banks of Ocean." "O lovely Felpham," he affectionately exclaims, writing to Hayley, "parent of immortal friendship, to thee I am eternally indebted for my three years' rest from perturbation and the strength I now enjoy." The mere fact of the entire change of environment and the respite which he obtained from all the cares and worries which his life in London had accumulated, gave him a sense of rest and freedom, and he found in "the sweet air and the voices of winds, trees and birds, and the odours of the happy ground" an influence soothing and refreshing to the brain. The three years at Felpham were in this way years of retreat, during which he was enabled to devote himself to bringing to an end the period of mental war; and the conflict was there fiercest because it had passed into the ultimate world of vision. It became possible for him to effect the clarification of his ideas both upon religion and art. "One thing of real consequence," he himself observes, in one of his letters, "I have accomplished by coming into the country, which is to me consolation enough: namely, I have recollected all my scattered thoughts on art . . . which in the confusion of London I had very much obliterated from my mind." It was a time of personal introspection and analysis, and of the final purging away from his imagination of all that was not pure vision; and, with the passing of this period of trial and probation, came the return of all his youthful enthusiasm. "I am drunk," he wrote to Hayley from London,

"with intellectual vision whenever I take a pencil or graver into my hand, even as I used to be in my youth, and as I have not been for twenty dark, but very profitable years. I thank God that I courageously pursued my course through darkness"; and again, six weeks later, "I have indeed fought through a hill of terrors and horrors (which none could know but myself) in a divided existence; now, no longer divided nor at war with myself, I shall travel on in the strength of the Lord God, as poor Pilgrim says."

The events of this final struggle at Felpham, together with its triumphant issue, are recorded by Blake in the book of **Milton**. The poet had from his earliest days made a strong appeal to his imagination. In the lines (enclosed with a letter to Flaxman dated 12th September, 1800) where he gives a brief summary of the various influences which had entered into his life, he places Milton first in the list of his spiritual instructors: "Now my lot in the heavens is this, Milton lov'd me in childhood and shew'd me his face." In *The Marriage of Heaven and Hell* Blake criticizes, it is true, *Paradise Lost,* because in it the restrainer of reason, (Urizen-Jehovah) who is by Milton called Messiah, is made to cast out desire or energy (Satan), which "is the only life"; for, as he contemptuously observes, "those who restrain desire, do so because theirs is weak enough to be restrained," and, as he further explains, in *A Vision of the Last Judgment,* "Men are admitted into heaven, not because they have curbed and governed their passions, or have no passions, but because they have cultivated their understandings. The treasures of heaven are not negations of passion, but realities of intellect, from which all the passions emanate, uncurbed in their eternal glory. . . . Those who are cast out are all those who, having no passions of their own, because no intellect, have spent their lives in curbing and governing other people's by . . . cruelty of all kinds." But at the same time he points out that Milton was none the less "a true poet and of the Devil's party without knowing it"; for, in spite of himself, Satan became the hero of his poem and he found himself writing "in fetters when he wrote of Angels and of God, and at liberty when of Devils and Hell."

The substance of the poem is almost entirely autobiographical. Blake himself tells us, in one of his letters, that it is descriptive of "the spiritual acts" of his "three years' slumber on the banks of ocean." Both the characters and the action have their counterparts in the drama which had been enacted at Felpham. The disguise is often a close one: but we are told that it is a "sublime allegory," and "allegory addressed to the intellectual powers, while it is altogether hidden from the corporeal understanding," is Blake's "definition of the most sublime poetry." The writing was "from immediate dictation, twelve or sometimes twenty or thirty lines at a time, without premeditation, and even against" his

"will." "Thus," he writes, "the time it has taken in writing was rendered non-existent, and an immense poem exists . . . all produced without labour or study." The purpose of the book [*Milton*] is clearly stated on p. 36, ll. 21-25:

> . . . When Los join'd with me he took me in his fiery whirlwind:
> My vegetated portion was hurried from Lambeth's shades:
> He set me down in Felpham's vale and prepar'd a beautiful
> Cottage for me, that in three years I might write all these visions,
> To display Nature's cruel holiness: the deceits of natural religion.

Blake had already issued, some years earlier, two little tracts containing aphorisms on the subject of natural religion [*There Is No Natural Religion* (1788) and *All Religions are One* (1788)]. They had doubtless been called forth by Hume's *Dialogues concerning Natural Religion,* written 1751 but not published until 1779, three years after the author's death. In *The Song of Los* again he speaks of the laws and religions which had bound men more and more to earth, "Till a philosophy of five senses was complete," which Urizen, weeping, had given "into the hands of Newton and Locke." In *Milton* the subject is more comprehensively dealt with. The author's intention "to justify the ways of God to man" is stated on the title-page. The Muses whom he invokes in the Preface are not the classical "Daughters of Memory"; they are the daughters of "Imagination" or "Inspiration"; for his appeal is for the restoration of purely imaginative art, based upon biblical and not upon classical models. The Bible he held to be directly and consciously derived from the source of all inspiration, while the art of the Greeks and Romans he believed to be a mere perverted copy, derived from ancient originals. He has another charge against Milton here, that he also was corrupted by the general infection and submitted to learn of the classics, when he should have resorted to the Bible alone. Blake wished to restore the authority of imagination, and to substitute an intellectual war for that which arises from the corporeal understanding. He adjures us, instead of disputing over science and religion and morality, to fight for an eternal kingdom and to engage ourselves in the rebuilding of Jerusalem in our own land, where now she lies in ruins. He would have us beware also of "the False Tongue," which is the origin of all the error and ignorance by which our eternal portion is fettered. It is elsewhere connected with "the Western Gate" and we learn that it denotes the sense of touch; that is to say, it is the sense by which we become conscious of the phenomenal world and are deceived by its apparent solidity into endowing it with a material existence. It is the cause of natural religion, empirical philosophy, evolutionary eth-

ics and the hundred other follies by which our vision is obscured. The earlier pages of the book are occupied with the story of the interference and oppression to which Blake (Palamabron) had to submit from Hayley (Satan). The news of his sufferings had reached the dwellers in eternity, with the result that the poet Milton received a heavenly command to return to earth to deliver him from the tyranny of his oppressors. This was the fulfilment of an ancient prophecy "in Eden recorded that Milton of the land of Albion should up ascend, forwards from Ulro, from the Vale of Felpham, and set free Orc from his chain of jealousy." The person of Orc is used by Blake to represent "the fires of youth," which were by nature free and untamed, until they were riveted to a rock by Los and Enitharmon, acting under the influence of the "jealous" God. It must be remembered that throughout his writings Blake adopts the Gnostic view of Jehovah; as Irenaeus says of Marcion, "blasphemans eum, qui a lege et Prophetis annunciatus est deus: malorum factorem, et bellorum concupiscentem, et inconstantem quoque sententia, et contrarium sibi ipsum dicens." He is Blake's Urizen, who had separated himself from the fourfold "Divine Family" and exalting his own self-hood, and usurping sovereignty, had endeavoured to impose upon man his iron laws which "no flesh nor spirit could keep one moment." Before Milton could enter upon his work of emancipation, it was necessary for him to wrestle with this "darkened" Urizen in his own person. He is described by Blake standing before him "as the sculptor silent stands before his forming image," giving life to him who would give death and preparing him for his reunion with the Divine Body. Thus the return of Milton was not only to effect the deliverance of Blake but the redemption of his own imagination from the state of bondage into which it had fallen during his lifetime owing to the detestable nature of his religion. He was to put off the "hypocritic holiness" and to embrace the forgiveness of sins; for "every religion that preaches vengeance for sin is the religion of the enemy or avenger." The doctrine of the forgiveness of sins and of "the mutual annihilation of each for another's good" is one of the principal themes of the poem. Evil must only be imputed to the various states into which the individual may enter. Those states were especially created by Divine mercy for "the deliverance of individuals." We are told that Milton descended to redeem his emanation, as it is only through our emanative or imaginative portion that it is possible for us to learn both to refrain from judging other people and ourselves to steer a right course among the states which environ us. Imagination and love are the two central facts of Blake's teaching. "The Imagination" he tells us, "is not a state: it is the human existence itself. . . . Love becomes a state when divided from imagination."

Edward J. Rose (essay date fall 1968)

SOURCE: Rose, Edward J. "Blake's *Milton*: The Poet as Poem." *Blake Studies* 1, no. 1 (fall 1968): 16-38.

[*In the following essay, Rose analyzes the prophetic elements in Blake's* Milton. *In Rose's reading, the poem represents a symbolic transfiguration of the poet John Milton into Blake's own poetic vision.*]

The purpose of this essay is to discuss *Milton* as a creative "state" by examining how Blake uses the figure of Milton as a symbol of the active and prophetic imagination, how he answers aesthetic questions by dramatizing them, and how he relates Milton's quest to Los's labors to restore man's real humanity according to the "Divine Image." In writing *Milton*, Blake took Milton at his word: "He who would not be frustrate of his hopes to write well hereafter in laudable things, ought himself to be a true poem, that is, a composition and pattern of the best and honourablest things."[1] Blake, therefore, made Milton, the poet, into *Milton*, the poem.

I

Karl Kiralis has said that "*Jerusalem* is Blake's *Divine Comedy, Paradise Lost,* and *Paradise Regained* in condensed form,"[2] a comment he makes as an aside when forgiving Blake his failures. This estimate, however, ignores internal thematic and structural principles relative to both *Milton* and *Jerusalem.* Although any one of Blake's three major poems contains subject matter for any one of the "three districts," as Eliot in *Little Gidding* calls Hell, Purgatory, and Paradise, the themes and structures of the three poems indicate that *The Four Zoas, Milton,* and *Jerusalem* are, if any parallel can be drawn at all, Blake's *Inferno, Purgatorio,* and *Paradiso.* And they are so because in general thematic terms they are concerned respectively, despite their common apocalyptic conclusions, with despair, purgation, and fulfillment. If paradise is lost or regained in Blake's work, it is lost or regained after the manner of Samson's experience in Milton's poem, for fallen man merely *thinks* or *reasons* about paradise when he should be imagining or, perhaps, *imaging* it.

While Blake gave up *The Four Zoas* as a finished work never to be engraved and illuminated in the highly finished style of the colored copy of *Jerusalem,* he did complete and color *Milton,* purging and mining his abandoned inferno for both of his later long poems. Like Shelley and Keats, he turned his attention from the "gods" as heroes to the poet as hero, and like Wordsworth wrote about the growth of the poet's soul in a very un-Wordsworthian way. It is significant that Blake, who is closer in spirit to Milton than he is to Dante, should have had to turn Milton himself into a Dantean poet-hero on his way to paradise, for by merging the

Miltonic epic with the Dantean, he reconceived the narrative structure of *The Four Zoas* in terms, first, of the dramatic experience of the individual poet, and second, of the symbolic struggle of the imagination itself. In the process he condensed the nine night nightmare of *Vala* into the one long night of the soul of the primary poet-prophet of English literature and of the imagination in man. Perhaps this is Kiralis's point. If so, a linear analysis of any one of Blake's poems is doomed to failure, since the structure of each breaks down when subjected to a critical commentary that searches for a sequential framework.[3] It is as much a mistake to read *Milton* or *Jerusalem* as a narrative poem as it would be to read any one of the lyrics from the *Songs* as a narrative poem. Blake, in fact, calls *Jerusalem* a "Song." Essentially all of his poems are conceived as dramatic lyrics, written after the manner of biblical rhapsodies, which is how Blake viewed the epic form. All of his poems are spoken by an "Inspired Man" whose words are of "eternal salvation," as he says in *Milton.*[4] In addition, Blake is a visual artist and his songs are also water-color paintings ("frescos"), which are to be *seen* as well as heard "Within a Moment"—the period in which they were conceived (*M* [*Milton*] 29: 516).

The content of each of Blake's major poems can be identified with Orc, Milton, and Jesus (or Los)—the "first" and the "last" of Los's sons[5] and the divine body who is "The Imagination" and who is of the "likeness & similitude of Los."[6] The power of Satan and the Reason is confronted in a different way by the dominant spirit of each poem: Orc, who as energy and desire or thwarted creativity, expends himself; Milton, who as poetic inspiration and vision, reveals reality in and to himself; and Jesus, who as fulfilled energy and desire, brings about, through the labor of Los, the reintegration and apocalypse of fourfold man in the "Eternal Body of Man," which he is and which is imagination. Each appears as an *apparent* Satan, who is a state that must be put off continually.

Orc is an "apparent" Satan because he is the archetypal rebel. Throughout the shorter prophetic works, most of the epithets and metaphors associated with him are those traditionally assigned to the conventional dark power. These are repeated in *The Four Zoas.* In *Milton,* Milton is, in fact, mistaken for Satan by those who see him fall perpendicular like the "son of the morning" in Isaiah, a traditional reading of the biblical text which Blake accepted.[7] Milton, in fact, acknowledges his spectre or selfhood to be SATAN (*M* 14: 496). To Urizenic Christianity whose God is the God of this World (Satan or the Accuser), Blake's Jesus appears also to be "Satan" in several ways. And so far as Blake is concerned such a reversal is to be expected. It is a reversal in keeping with the reversed roles of the devil and angel in *The Marriage of Heaven and Hell* and with the ironic worship of those who worship Satan "by the

Names Divine of Jesus & Jehovah." Blake's Jesus is imagination, the real man, not a crucified Luvah.

Satan is the "last" of Los's sons before generation. This is why he is listed as the fifteenth among the Sons of Los in **The Four Zoas** (viii, 359: 350) before Har and the remaining generated sons who postdate *in time* or *history* the garden of Genesis. In the opening lines of **Milton,** Satan is "At last . . . brought forth . . . Refusing form in vain" (**M** 3: 483), but these lines record a non-temporal event or struggle for power *outside* the revolution of six thousand years. The **"Bard's Song"** tells of this quarrel and thereby supplies the background necessary for the establishment *inside* the revolution of six thousand years of the three classes of men who are then subject to the generated sons of Los in space-time from Har and Adam through to Paul, Constantine, Charlemagne, Luther, and finally, Milton. Thus, both Satan and Milton appear to be the "last" of Los's sons. Both are also *states,*

> . . . thou, O Milton, art a State about to be Created,
> Called Eternal Annihilation, that none but the Living shall
> Dare to enter, & they shall enter triumphant over Death
> And Hell & the Grave: States that are not, but ah!
> Seem to be.
>
> (**M** 32: 521-22)

Milton the state is, in fact, **Milton** the poem. Milton "judges" himself, explores his own "Eternal Lineaments" and therefore frustrates the Accuser, Judge, and Executioner of this dark world and wide. That is how Blake's poem **Milton** functions in Blake's imaginative life at the time of Hayley and Schofield. As a state of self-discovery and recovery, Milton does not reptilize into the State of Satan as Orc does, but, instead, purges himself of his selfhood. Like Jesus, Milton puts off Holiness (that is, he puts off the State of Satan continually), which Los proclaims in **Jerusalem** (**J** [**Jerusalem**] 91: 739) is necessary and puts on Intellect; the "Mathematic Holiness" of Satan is redesigned by the "Divine Saviour" with "Los's Mathematic power" (**M** 29: 517).[8] As Jerusalem is **Jerusalem,** so Milton is **Milton.** Bloom seems to have an inkling of Blake's intention when he says that "Palamabron's movement toward a confrontation with Satan is itself the act of writing a poem."[9] If Blake is to be identified with Palamabron, as many critics have said,[10] then **Milton** is that poem.

In **Milton,** Milton is baptized by Urizen as Jesus was by John; but, then, Milton's task is, like Jesus's, to rebuild fallen reason or to re-establish vision by exalting reason, to rebuild the fallen temple not according to ratiocinative or analytical ideas but according to imagination. Abstract forms are made concrete.

> Silent they met and silent strove . . .
> . . . when with cold hand Urizen stoop'd down

> And took up water from the river Jordan, pouring on
> To Milton's brain the icy fluid from his broad cold palm.
> But Milton took of the red clay of Succoth, moulding it with care
> Between his palms and filling up the furrows of many years,
> Beginning at the feet of Urizen, and on the bones
> Creating new flesh on the Demon cold and building him
> As with new clay, a Human form in the Valley of Beth Peor.
>
> (**M** 19: 500)

Milton is creating a mental form, a sculpture for Los's Halls. He gives human form to the abstract and the indefinite, and his act is motivated indirectly by Los, the spirit of prophecy. By clothing the ratiocinative skeleton that is fallen reason with new clay, Milton's labor is a "Divine Analogy." The artist's task is to make abstract ideas concrete by lending form and giving body.

> . . . Silent Milton stood before
> The darken'd Urizen, as the sculptor silent stands before
> His forming image; he walks round it patient labouring.
>
> (**M** 20: 502)

Milton is creating a mental form, a sculpture for Los's Halls. He walks around it because he is "Vehicular" (like Los) and must be on all sides of his work continually; that is, he must see with fourfold vision.

> Thus Milton stood forming bright Urizen, while his Mortal part
> Sat frozen in the rock of Horeb, and his Redeemed portion
> His real Human walk'd above in power and majesty,
> Tho' darken'd, and the Seven Angels of the Presence attended him.
>
> (**M** 20: 502)

The clay is fired in the crucible that Milton as **Milton** has become, and "darken'd Urizen" becomes "bright Urizen." The Milton who is all selfhood or Satan is frozen by his baptism as one of the Elect. The Milton who is Redeemed or Palamabron resists the ironic intent of reason's baptism and is at work as the poet-prophet of English literature, for within that Redeemed portion is Milton the Reprobate who reappears in Blake's poem once again one with imagination in order to complete the labor he had begun.

Neither the identification of "Urizenic law" with the "Body of Moses," nor a phrase like "Urizen-Jehovah's covenant with Moses," nor a compound like "Urizen-Satan" is meaningful for the study of **Milton** or **Jerusalem.**[11] Milton's struggle with Urizen, with vain reasoning—his own selfhood—makes simplified equations of

a parabolic sort useless for a study of the subtle symbolism in Blake's work. As a point of view or isolated region of man's mental life, Urizen perverts what he (or it) beholds. In *Jerusalem,* the words "Building the Body of Moses in the Valley of Peor" and "the Body of Divine Analogy" are in apposition, not opposition.[12] Jehovah is God as father and Satan is a state. From the point of view that is Urizen, Satan is God as father and can be worshiped by many names, even Jesus, as Bloom recognizes.[13] In fact, Satan is the state of this world, psychologically, politically, economically, and in every way. Milton's action is art against empire. At this point in *Milton,* the poet-hero is himself building the body of Divine Analogy both *in* the poem and *as* the poem. Just as he uses fourfold vision, so he can draw upon the eyes of God, the "lamps" of the "Almighty," the angels of the Divine Presence.[14] With greater facility than his own Samson, Milton, the seemingly blind yet inspired bard, is able to put vain reason down because he no longer wrestles with it. He creates, instead, a new form, "Mental" and "Human." He is truly "illumined" from within where walks "above in power and majesty" what Blake calls "His real Human," that which is to be associated with imagination since "The Imagination is not a State: it is the Human Existence itself."

A creative man *is* creativity itself. A man who acts *is* act. Blake's symbolism *is* the symbolic process dramatizing itself, for the process is simultaneously being used and described. Just before Milton begins his "awful precipitate descent," Blake cries out for the power to express adequately his vision of Milton's experience within the creative moment, for Milton falls "thro' Albion's heart."

> O how can I with my gross tongue that cleaveth to the
> dust
> Tell of the Four-fold Man in starry numbers fitly
> order'd,
> Or how can I with my cold hand of clay! But thou, O
> Lord,
> Do with me as thou wilt! for I am nothing, and vanity.
> If thou chuse to elect a worm, it shall remove the
> mountains.
>
> (*M* 20: 502)[15]

Milton passes through the human heart to become one with Blake, just as Blake enters the "state" of Milton. This union of Blake and Milton in Los and Blake's call for creative power in the lines just quoted from plate 20 is what Blake means when he says that he is no more "than the Secretary" of his poems and that "The Authors are in Eternity."[16] Blake enters his own poem just as Los enters *Jerusalem* and Milton and he become one in Albion when Los enters fourfold man.

There is an "old Prophecy in Eden," Los recalls, "That Milton of the Land of Albion should up ascend" by going "Forwards from Ulro" to "set free Orc from his Chain of Jealousy" (*M* 20: 503), which means that the once thwarted creativity and rebellion of Orc is finally realized. Milton's role as a poet-prophet is clear. He is an architect or sculptor of eternity or imagination as opposed to Urizen, who as the architect of reason, is the point of view of those who have entered the state of Satan. Milton sets free creativity, energy, desire, and rebellion—Orc. Milton labors to complete the *revolution* of six thousand years that man wages against Nobodaddy-tyranny.

In *Milton,* Blake achieves an effect similar to the one achieved by Dante in the *Purgatorio* (cantos xxi-xxxiii), and at the end of each poem our point of view is paradisal. As Dante has three poets climb the mount together after the descent into Hell, each poet representing the poet under different conditions, so Blake has three persons in one nature (poets of imagination) "up ascend." The trinity of bards in the *Purgatorio*—Dante, Statius, and Virgil—are paralleled in *Milton* by Blake, Milton, and Los. In both poems, the third figure is the master of the first two and identifiable with poetic imagination or inspiration. Both Virgil and Los also dwell in the rocky inferno of man—earth. They are equally shut out (or in) in a kind of isolated Limbo. Milton, like Statius, is in the process of ridding himself of his sins or his error. While Statius mounts Purgatory, Milton must "up ascend" in order to free Orc. Milton and Statius are deceased mortals close to Blake and Dante in time. Virgil, like Los, belongs to another age or sphere of being. Blake and Milton, like Dante and Statius, are within the historical era of Christianity. The parallels between Blake and Dante are clear enough. Both are authors of and actors in their respective poems. They are both conducted and are, so far as their readers are concerned, conductors. Being led by their brother poets they then lead us. They bear witness respectively to the acts of Milton and Statius. Their visions occur during their mortal existence, that is, both Blake and Dante are privileged to be simultaneously in time and in eternity, in space and in infinity. Of course, it is their perception and their consciousness that makes this possible. They possess visionary power. Blake and Dante bear similar relationships as disciples to their respective masters, Los and Virgil. *Milton* is very much Blake's *Purgatorio.* Like Dante, Blake also has the bride-emanation (the anima) greet the poet at the climax of his experience and the poem. Ololon is like Beatrice, the symbol of his experience as a member of the Redeemed. The relation between Milton and Ololon is echoed by that between "Blake" and his "Sweet Shadow of Delight" in the *garden* at Felpham. The structural and thematic parallels between Blake's *Milton* and Dante's *Purgatorio,* despite the differences there are, are important for an understanding of Blake's achievement in *Milton.*

Milton is a poem about purgation. It is, as Bloom says, "a study in gathering self-awareness . . . Blake's Milton recognizes himself as God or imaginative Man and proceeds to purge from himself everything opposed to that recognition."[17] Writing of *The Four Zoas* as Blake's *Purgatorio,* Fisher comments on its "tragic vision of man's fallen condition,"[18] but while this "tragic vision" is certainly in evidence the purgatorial characteristics are not. If any of Blake's poems can be called a purgatory, then it must be *Milton.* As Fisher says, "*Milton* introduced his Paradiso." Bloom describes *Milton* as a "Prelude to Apocalypse" and Fisher describes it as a "'Preludium' to *Jerusalem.*" So far as a general linear analysis of Blake's work is concerned, there can be little argument with these descriptions as simplified characterizations, but they are deceptive. *Milton* is about Milton, who is a *state* "Called Eternal Annihilation." And its successor, *Jerusalem,* is about an emanation called Jerusalem. In this way, *The Four Zoas* is about the four fractured faces of man who are divided in "torments of love and jealousy," a kind of cosmic nervous breakdown, but who are reunited in the structure *and* in the mythic resolution of *Jerusalem.*

The Four Zoas is about the four Zoas, who in "Attempting to be more than Man . . . become less," the fundamental rule of conduct for those who dwell in infernos rather than in purgatories. Even while Blake's first long poem was in its first version and still titled *Vala,* it clearly was no purgatory, either in theme or structure. Like Young's *Night Thoughts,* it was a nightmare poem. The healthy split personality of Los in *Jerusalem* is the outcome of the two major poems that preceded it, but those poems have each a structure and a center of orientation of their own distinct from that of a preludium.

It is as wrong to approach Blake on "divisionist" principles as it is to divide his radicalism from his Christianity, for the "curse" which Frye says will be "on any critic who tries to see the Christianity and the radicalism of Blake as a dichotomy instead of a unity"[19] will also be on the critic who tries to see Blake at any given point in his career to be radically different from the whole Blake. Though it would be impossible to make a better case for the whole Blake than is made in *Fearful Symmetry,* Blake criticism has failed to accept wholeheartedly Blake's conception of the relation of the part to the whole. Blake's works are indeed one work, but each work and each plate in his engraved works are also each one work. Were Blake not a visual artist I should not make the claim for him with such emphasis as I do. But, then, I should not have this claim for him in any case had he not made it himself. If "Every Poem" is, "must necessarily be," a "perfect Unity,"[20] and we still choose to call it a "Preludium,"[21] we run the risk of not seeing it as a distinct and complete whole. *Milton,* like any one of Blake's works or any one of his individual designs, has a form, theme, and structure of its own. That is why "one Central Form composed of all other Forms being Granted, it does not therefore follow that all other Forms are Deformity."[22] Frye's estimate of *Milton* as "Blake's longest, greatest and most elaborate 'Preludium'"[23] is the source, no doubt, for Bloom's and Fisher's approaches to the poem, but Frye's opinion is part of his approach to Blake's work as a "unified scheme," a view which has invited fundamentally hostile and erroneous interpretation and appreciation of Blake's achievement as an artist.[24] The *coherence* of any poem or design does not depend on logical constructs made after the fact, even when they are based upon sensitive and intelligent critical rapport and certainly not when they are fundamentally the product of less acute concerns. An incomplete or abandoned work is as much a whole as any other work of art, as Blake himself repeatedly asserts. Any artist's work, especially Blake's, is simultaneously finished and unfinished, but it is always at any given point a complete whole, even if the artist succumbs to late revisions of hitherto supposedly "completed" works. And this judgment applies to an artist's individual works and also to the whole body of his work. For a visual artist, this point is of special importance. If *Milton* is a "Preludium" it is a very special kind of prelude and should help us to understand that the illustrations to Dante are not incomplete or *The Four Zoas* a confused totality which Blake erroneously believed was a "controlled, cohesive, and coherent poem."[25] Blake's individual achievements as an artist must always be judged in the "state" in which he left them.

As a visual artist Blake was forever scratching away at his work, as textual detective work reinforces.[26] This was the way he worked as an engraver *and* as a poet. Each plate was a separate work of art and each draft, too. Melville writes, "For small erections may be finished by their first architects; grand ones, true ones, ever leave the copestone to posterity. God keep me from every completing anything. This whole book is but a draught—nay, but the draught of a draught."[27] This is a lesson for critics that should never go unheeded. "The reasoning historian, turner and twister of causes and consequences, such as Hume, Gibbon, and Voltaire, cannot with all their artifice turn or twist one fact or disarrange self evident action and reality. . . . To suppose that Art can go beyond the finest specimens of Art that are now in the world, is not knowing what Art is; it is being blind to the gifts of the spirit."[28] Blake applied this judgment even to "remains." His view of art was that it was, indeed, as Melville says, "the draught of a draught." Caught up in the whirlwind of the Lord with Los, the poet-prophet breathes what the authors in eternity dictate even if his "gross tongue . . . cleaveth to the dust," be he Milton or Blake. In *Milton,* Blake focussed on the aesthetic problem raised by a "gross tongue that cleaveth to the dust" (his own and

Milton's), whose prophecies were simultaneously finished and unfinished, complete yet incomplete, and still susceptible to *REvision*.

Milton is about Milton, a poet whose work is complete and whole, but unfinished. As such it is a poem about Blake or any artist. The purgation in *Milton* is aesthetic purgation as much as any other kind, which in Blake's terms is not to be separated from the process of recreation. Just as *Jerusalem* is based upon the fourfold imagery of Blake's inferno (dramatized in *The Four Zoas*), *Milton* is based upon the experience of the creative man confronted by that inferno. *The Four Zoas* is about the building of "Heaven in Hell's despair" and the building of "Hell in Heaven's despite." *Milton* is about the casting out of that selfhood which must result in either clod or pebble love. Once the selfhood is annihilated, Milton is no longer forced to choose between two insufficiencies, clod or pebble love, Cromwell or Charles, the past or the future, political or social reform, the protectorate or the empire. Frye writes that Milton "wants to re-enter the world and gain a new vision. This vision will do two things for him: it will enable him to see the physical world as Satanic rather than divine, and it will enable him as a result to see his 'emanation,' or totality of the things he loves, as part of himself and not as a remote and objective 'female will.' The former is the climax of the first book of *Milton*; the latter is the climax of the second."[29] Though this is indeed the case, Milton learns also "To cast aside from Poetry all that is not Inspiration"; he also learns that he "who publishes doubt & calls it knowledge" creates a "science" that "is Despair" (*M* 41: 533). He learns that the epic poem is truly the dramatic (something which Milton long suspected), and that a poet's work is done in terms of prophetic time, in a moment, and not in terms of clock-time. Milton returns in order to get the *artistic* job done.

Fisher is certainly correct in saying that Blake "was also purging himself of the urge to justify his view of life as a compensation for personal disappointment."[30] That is why *Milton* is Blake's *Purgatorio* and that is why biographical criticism of Blake runs great risks. However, *Milton* is not concerned with justice and the quality of mercy, but is, instead, about the aesthetic of vision. Milton's long speech on plates 40 and 41 is a proclamation of Blake's theory of art and vision and an everlasting warning to poets who are tempted to become governmental secretaries, instead of secretaries to eternal authors, a warning, perhaps, not to engage in political or physical battles at the expense of "Mental Fight."[31] Without discounting in anyway Blake's all-inclusive commitment to radicalism, we must understand, as he did, that Jerusalem cannot be built in "England's green & pleasant Land" unless all the Lord's people are prophets and not self-righteous spectres. Milton was a prophet who forsook his calling in order

to justify, but prophets prophesy the ways of God to man, they do not justify them. The authors of Milton's work, like the authors of Blake's, are in Eternity, not in Westminster. Milton's famous line, which Blake uses for a subtitle in a supremely ironic way, introduces us to the ironic description of eighteenth century England as a "pleasant Land" with "pleasant pastures." Milton's rebellion in Blake's poem is like Blake's, a fourfold revolution, and is a new vision, not simply a change of opinion within the framework of the old vision.

Blake recreates Milton as a state or poem called "Eternal Annihilation" which makes Milton "triumphant over Death and Hell & the Grave" because it is a work of art through which "The Imagination," "the Human Existence itself," can be seen as Los sees his way through Albion, as the spectator can "Enter into . . . Images in his Imagination."[32] A poet's work, Milton's and Blake's included, is complete yet never finished because it is the shape of vision expanding.[33] Milton, that is, *Milton,* is the *twenty-eighth* church, not a justification of any of the previous twenty-seven churches or heavens or states, because, like the twenty-eighth lark, Los's messenger, Milton brings about the reintegration of the self purged of selfhood and the freedom of art from all kinds of empire. As the twenty-eighth church, Milton is Blake's *Milton,* the art of Los, who is "the fourth," "the twenty-eight & is four-fold," having as his source "The true Man, . . . he being the Poetic Genius."[34]

II

The words of the inspired man are of salvation. Los's descent (like Milton's) makes him the agent of Jerusalem in the fallen giant, for the "ever apparent Elias" is the "Spirit of Prophecy" and is the manifestation of Jesus in the fallen world (*M* 24: 510; *J* 44 [39]: 674). Jesus is in "the likeness & similitude of Los" (*J* 96: 743). Through Los, Jesus prepares an abode, which is an analogy not an allegory, for his city-bride through his prophets who maintain the Divine Vision. Los stands watch over this analogy. He is the imagination in man and in the poem he makes. That poem is the process of his ascent.

> Fearing that Albion should turn his back against the
> Divine Vision,
> Los took his globe of fire to search the interiors of Albion's
> Bosom, in all the terrors of friendship entering the
> caves
> Of despair & death to search the tempters out, walking among
> Albion's rock and precipices, caves of solitude & dark
> despair,
> And saw every Minute Particular of Albion degraded
> & murder'd,
> But saw not by whom; they were hidden within in the
> minute particulars
> Of which they had possess'd themselves, and there
> they take up

The articulations of man's soul and laughing throw it
down
Into the frame, then knock it out upon the plank, &
souls are bak'd
In bricks to build the pyramids . . .

(*J* 31 [45]: 656-57)

The individuality of the "real Human" is usurped by the
general and thrust into institutional tombs.

Every Universal Form was become barren mountains
of Moral
Virtue, and every Minute Particular harden'd into
grains of sand.

(*J* 31 [45]: 657)

Instead of windows into Eden, the art of Blake's time
produces opaque bricks. "The articulations of man's
soul" are thrown into frames which confine instead of
frames which expand.

Universal forms, mental forms, are organic; they are
energyzing symbols that create continually.[35] Every
minute particular is unique, an "articulation." The poet-
prophet must preserve them, must redeem them, from
the general law, the abstract and indefinite, as Milton
redeems his emanation from its virginity. Los, like Mil-
ton, must build amidst the murdered and the murderers,
must create amidst destruction. Los, the one unslain
Zoa (*J* 42: 670), prepares for the apocalypse with his
art, but he cannot, must not, prevent the consolidation
of error. The symbolic city-woman is twofold. Against
Jerusalem, the bride, is Vala, the whore of Babylon.
Against art is nature and empire. Man's city stands op-
posed to Nature's city (the city of God against the city
of Cain), just as man's buildings, his sculpture and ar-
chitecture of the mind, stands opposed to the stony
temples of the Druids, the allegory of reason, whose ar-
chitect is Urizen.

The sacrifice and torment that are described throughout
Jerusalem and against which Los speaks in the verse
on plates 43 [38] and 44 [39] alludes to Mexican and
Druidian human sacrifice and the imagery of grinding
wheels and bloody altars. Echoed again in Part Three,
they recall *The Four Zoas* and the Satanic miller of
Milton. The world-man seems intent on self-destruction.
Plate 43 [38] is especially pertinent to the character of
fallen man's point of view. Blake described Ezekiel's
wheels *fallen,* the four beasts in bestial war, the main
elements of the inferno which play so large a part in his
final draft of *The Four Zoas.*

They saw their Wheels rising up poisonous against
Albion:
Urizen cold & scientific, Luvah pitying & weeping,
Tharmas indolent & sullen, Urthona doubting & de-
spairing,

Victims to one another & dreadfully plotting against
each other
To prevent Albion walking about in the Four Com-
plexions.

(*J* 43 [38]: 671)

The perversion of the Zoas characterizes the disunity or
disintegration of man.

Swell'd bloated General Forms repugnant to the Di-
vine—
Humanity who is the only General and Universal
Form,
To which all Lineaments tend & seek with love &
sympathy.

(*J* 43 [38]: 672)

The struggle and search of Los for true art and science
is perverted.

And the two Sources of Life in Eternity, Hunting and
War,
Are become the Sources of dark & bitter Death &
corroding Hell.

(*J* 43 [38]: 672)

The search or hunt ceases to be spiritual or mental and
becomes physical. The struggles of the mind become
the wars of the body, as in *Milton* (35: 525). "General-
izing Art & Science till Art & Science is lost" is basic
to "A World in which Man is by his Nature the Enemy
of Man (*J* 43 [38]: 673). "Instead of the Mutual For-
givenesses, the Minute Particulars," are the "Pits of bi-
tumen ever burning" and the worlds of crusted snow
and ice, that is, Orc and Urizen (*J* 43 [38]: 673). The
inspirational wheels of Ezekiel—the arts of life—are
demonically parodied. They become the rational wheels
of Satan's mills at which Jerusalem labors as a harlot
and against which Los strives—the arts of death. These
are the mills of fate and the "gods" that grind exceed-
ing slow and against which the "Inspired Man" speaks
in *Milton.*

The limiting influence of the fallen world serves as an
important functional idea in the overall pattern of
Blake's symbolism from the early poetry onwards. The
image of the sealed furnace is always ironic, for through
the fiery furnace which by analogy becomes a crucible
of the self, the self must go. Through generation man
many be regenerated, and through art nature may be re-
deemed. The furnace imagery and symbolism dramatize
the limitations of the fallen world, but also express the
possibilities open to an over-expanding vision that has
not yet reached the limits of opacity and contraction.

Los open'd the Furnaces in fear, the Spectre saw to
Babel & Shinar
Across all Europe & Asia, he saw the tortures of the
Victims.

He saw now from the outside what he before saw &
 felt from within;
He saw that Los was the sole, uncontroll'd Lord of
 the Furnaces.

(*J* 8: 627)

The fiery furnace of the Book of Daniel in which the
three Hebrew children become *fourfold* with the appear-
ance of the angel of the Lord (This mighty angel is
identifiable with the Lark who is Los's messenger, *M*
35-36: 526-27), achieves an ironic result so far as Neb-
uchadnezzar is concerned, since he helps to bring about
the opposite of what he intended.

Nebuchadnezzar's intent is the same as that of the
"Shadowy Female." In *Milton,* she takes on "the Hu-
man Form" and the "Image of God," but her "clothing"
is Cruelty" (*M* 18: 499), as in the song of experience,
"The Human Abstract." "Cruelty has a Human Heart"
and that heart is the "hungry Gorge" of "The Human
Face" which is "a Furnace Seal'd." It is Los's function,
as it is Milton's, to break the seal and restore the Four
Faces of Man in Eternity (*M* 27: 517), which are in
Eternity "the Four Arts, Poetry, Painting, Music and Ar-
chitecture."[36] Milton's self-recreation in *Milton* is paral-
lel to Los's dialogue with the Spectre in *Jerusalem.*
Both Los and Milton do battle with the shadowy female
will who is Nebuchadnezzar's goddess to whom the
Hebrew children of Albion are sacrificed. By tending
the furnace himself from within the Mundane Shell,
Los breaks the "brazen fetters" or "mind-forg'd
manacles" on man's imagination and his poetry.[37]

Blake's poetic theory and his conception of imagination
are embodied in the imagery and iconography of almost
all of his work, even in the songs. Throughout, the di-
vine *image* is contrasted with the human *abstract,* that
is, the imagination is contrasted with the reason as a
poetic image is contrasted by implication with a discur-
sive description. In Blake's *Songs of Innocence and of
Experience,* **"The Divine Image"** and **"The Human
Abstract"** reflect the contrary states of the human soul
through their parody of one another. **"The Divine Im-
age"** says that Mercy, Pity, Peace, and Love *is* God and
is man (second stanza), and that where they dwell God
dwells. Both dwell in the love of the human form, and
in the human form divine which is the divine image. In
"The Human Abstract" the same qualities are used by
human beings to dominate and enslave one another. In
human relations we exist by relative proportion and by
ratio. Fallen existence is allegorical. The first three
stanzas describe fallen man in imagery associated later
in Blake's work with fallen Albion. Under his spectre's
power, man is the picture of selfhood. He entraps and
despairs while the Polypus grows in the deep, its roots
feeding upon his humility.

Pity would be no more
If we did not make somebody Poor;

And Mercy no more could be
If all were as happy as we.

And mutual fear brings peace,
Till the selfish loves increase:
Then Cruelty knits a snare,
And spreads his baits with care.

He sits down with holy fears,
And waters the ground with tears;
Then Humility takes its root
Underneath his foot.

(*SE* [*Songs of Experience*]: 217)[38]

These are the arts of death, producing mutual fear in-
stead of mutual forgiveness. The Covering Cherub-like
image of the fourth stanza introduces Blake's consistent
"Mystery" imagery: the "dismal shade" and the "Catter-
piller" and the fly. The title page of *Jerusalem,* it will
be recalled, has as its design the butterfly-caterpillar
cycle which describes the natural and the fallen world.
The Gates of Paradise is controlled by the same image.
It has a two-fold importance because, besides describ-
ing the natural cycle, it indicates that through genera-
tion there is the possibility of regeneration. The cater-
pillar on the leaf reminds us of our mother's grief
because the womb and the tomb are the same. The tree
image, its root underfoot, is the cross and oak of the
later poems. The Druid oak grows in the human
brain—a not unusual place in the fallen giant domi-
nated by the reasoning spectre—especially since it is
watered with the tears of holy fears.

"The Divine Image" and the additional poem in *The
Song of Experience,* **"A Divine Image,"** carry the con-
trast a step further in its ironic development by empha-
sizing the reversal in the passage from the state of inno-
cence to the state of experience. In the song of
innocence, **"The Divine Image,"**

. . . Mercy has a human heart,
Pity a human face,
And Love, the human form divine,
And Peace, the human dress.

(*SI* [*Songs of Innocence*]: 117)

This is the unfallen condition. However, in the fallen
state, the same *four* human elements mask the opposites
of mercy, pity, love, and peace:

Cruelty has a Human Heart,
And Jealousy a Human face;
Terror the Human Form Divine,
And Secrecy the Human Dress.

(*SE*:221)

In the second stanza of this two stanza poem, Blake
completes a dialectic pattern that appears throughout
his work, and in imagery consistently characteristic of
it. Los, the smith of the arts of life, rebuilds the image

of mercy from cruelty, the image of pity from jealousy, the image of love from terror, the image of peace from secrecy. Only the imagination could accomplish such a re-reversal, for mercy, pity, love, and peace are in the fallen world, like hunting and war, not what they are in eternity. It is secrecy (mystery) that creates the false peace of natural religion. Man is merciful and feels pity and love only when he feels superior, craves attention, and is frightened. Through another reversal in order, Blake, using the human metaphor, sees the "Human Dress," peace made secretive, as "Forged Iron"; the "Human Form," love made terrifying, as a "fiery Forge"; the "Human Face," pity made jealousy, as "a Furnace seal'd"; and the "Human Heart," mercy made cruelty, as the furnace's "hungry Gorge."

> The Human Dress is forged Iron,
> The Human Form a fiery Forge,
> The Human Face a Furnace seal'd,
> The Human Heart its hungry Gorge.[39]

Blake achieves several effects with this imagery. The "Human" under the shadowy female is fallen, hence the change of cruelty for mercy, but is described in terms of the smith's material and tools which allow the smith to reclaim his own. Both the *need* for recreation and the *process* of recreation co-exist in the imagery of the human heart, face, form divine, and dress (body or clothing) which *is* the imagery of the gorge, furnace, forge, and iron. Los labors to complete the metaphor in terms of his quest and in terms of a recreation of man's "real humanity." And he achieves this recreation with the tools, material, and human characteristics already identified in the metaphor. By this dramatization of the process of recreation in imagination, Blake describes the way in which allegory is changed into analogy and describes how "Allegoric Generation" is related to imaginative regeneration. Furthermore, with Milton as his hero he shows how the poet's passage or pilgrimage, for Milton is a "pilgrim of eternity," affects the imagery of the poet's verse according to the states through which he passes. The "Song" or "Voice" of the "Ancient Bard" in *Milton* ["The Bard's Song"] and in the song which completes the *Songs of Innocence* ["Voice of the Ancient Bard"] calls Milton to "the attempt" (*M* 21: 504). One with Los, Milton understands that metaphors are not pretence, that "The Ancients did not mean to Impose when they affirm'd their belief in Vision & Revelation." That is why Plato and Milton were in "Earnest." "They believ'd that God did Visit Man Really & Truly and not as Reynolds pretends."[40] Milton supplants the "writings written" at the command of the Shadowy Female in "Human words" (*M* 18: 469) with the "Words" and "Writing" described elsewhere in the poem (*M* 27: 513; *M* 42: 534).

III

The ancient bard of *Milton* and the *Songs of Innocence* also introduces the *Songs of Experience*. His meta-phors are the metaphors of the prophets, the way in which God visits man "Really & Truly." The "Writing" that "Is the Divine Revelation in the Litteral expression" is the kind of writing to which Milton must return, since he, like Shakespeare, was "curb'd by the general malady & infection from the silly Greek & Latin slaves of the Sword . . . We do not want either Greek or Roman models if we are but just & true to our own Imaginations . . ." (*M* 1: 480). The "iron pillars of Satan's Throne" are "Temperance, Prudence, Justice, Fortitude, the four pillars of tyranny," which are Puritan virtues ironically portrayed in terms of Classical architecture.[41] Satan's fourfold parody expresses the puritanical and classical ideals of the Elect, for the throne of the Divine Humanity is also fourfold. Los and Milton attempt fourfold reintegration. Milton goes to the center of Los's "Egg form'd World," passing through the point where the "Chaotic" universes of Luvah and Urizen intersect. The "Egg form'd World" is imagination's effort to reintegrate the four Zoas, the four arts, the four faces, of fourfold man who is the throne of the Divine Humanity. Viewed from above as a diagrammatic cross-section, the four circles on plate 33 are pillars, but they are also globes in a fiery furnace since the illustration *is* flame-enclosed. They are described in the verse on plate 34. The second book of *Milton* is devoted to Milton's effort to open the "Center" of "these Ruin'd Universes" which have sunk "downward in dire Ruin."[42] The diagram on plate 33 is really a map or plan for the second book of the poem and is to that part of *Milton* what the "Bard's Song" is to Book One. Thus *Milton* is a combination of two modes of expression, the aural and the visual, sound and sight, the song and the vision, the Divine Voice and the Divine Vision, which are presented as a mythopoeic narrative that does not depend on time and is therefore not a narrative but a single dramatic act of self-illumination.[43]

The second book of *Milton* is concerned with the contraries at war beneath "Negation's banner." The opening plate defines contraries as "positives" that are "equally true" in Beulah and thereby prepares the reader for Milton's final speech which is the climax of the poem. In that speech he reveals that he has learned to recognize the relation of contraries to one another and to the negation. Milton's speech is really a kind of prophetic editorial addressed to those who dwell within Los's tent. That tent, which is immortal and which is their sky (*M* 29: 516), is destined to be in a transfigured form a garment around the limbs of Jesus. Blake develops a gigantic metaphorical relation through the image of six thousand years as a woven fabric. The image recurs throughout his work, but in *Milton* it serves an extremely important structural and thematic purpose. The first book ends with a picture of the weaving of six thousand years, "Such is the World of Los, the labour of six thousand years" (*M* 29: 518), and the second book draws to a close with the description of that woof

of six thousand years as a Divine Revelation (*M* 42: 534).[44] The tent is in fact the fabric, but so is the poem. Both are the labor of Los "Written within & without in woven letters." The tent is identified in Blake's work with the tabernacle or temple which Jesus rebuilds, as prophesied, and which is contrasted with Vala's or Nature's temple. Before his apocalyptic self-illumination, Milton, like man, can only read that revelation from within. At the end of the poem he is able to read it from without, too. The "Divine Revelation in the Litteral expression" is a garment of mental war now revealed as the clothing of imagination because he has cast off the "rotten rags of Memory by Inspiration" (*M* 41: 533). Los's "Egg form'd World," which is the central event of the poem linking the **"Bard's Song"** with "Milton's Track" (a nice pun on Miltonic *tracts*), is finally hatched. From that egg man emerges reborn. "The Microscope knows not of this nor the Telescope" because they are instruments invented by men who have resigned themselves to living in "Spaces called Earth" forever. They "alter The ratio of the Spectator's Organs, but leave Objects untouch'd." They are useless "If the Spectator" should want to "Enter into . . . Images in his Imagination," as Blake says he must in *A Vision of the Last Judgement* (82-84: 611). He must approach them in the "Fiery Chariot of his Contemplative Thought," as Los-Milton-Blake does (Blake calls for this "Chariot" in the prefatory poem.) "For every Space larger than a Globule of Man's blood Is visionary, and is created by the Hammer of Los," while "every Space smaller than a Globule of Man's blood opens Into Eternity." The whole of *Milton* is a single visionary act dramatized by Milton's return and is descriptive of Blake's theory of art as visions of imagination.

Milton is really composed of three parts, the first two of which form Book One. The **"Bard's Song"** ends when the Bard takes "refuge in Milton's bosom" and Milton begins his descent-ascent in the "World of Los," the "labor of six thousand years." (These two phrases are in apposition.) Milton's movement into the mundane shell or egg is described twice, at the beginning of the second part of the poem in Book One (plate 17) and near the beginning of the third part of the poem in Book Two (plate 34).[45] In part two in Book One, Milton must get past Urizen, as Satan in *Paradise Lost* must get past Sin and Death which, so far as Blake is concerned, are the creations of reason. In part three in Book Two, we see him on his way from the point of view of his own emanation. One with Blake in Los's world, Milton recreates reason. From plate 21 to the end of the first book (plate 29), Los *is* Milton-Blake and his sons and the brothers of Milton-Blake. I do not believe many readers take these identifications as seriously as they should, nor do they take special note of just when in the poem the identifications take place. (Some critics, like Bent-

ley, scoff at Blake's claims about divine dictation.) Not only is Milton joined with Blake (plates 15 and 21), Blake with Los (plate 22), and Milton with Los (plate 23), but earlier the Bard with Milton (plate 14). This fourfold unity is one person. The "perfect Unity" of a poem depends upon the perfect unity of the poet and imagination. If *Milton* recalls any single Miltonic expression, and I suggest that this is in essence the heart of Blake's poem, then it recalls Milton's words in the "Apology for Smectymnuus" which I quoted at the beginning of this essay, "He who would not be frustrate of his hopes to write well hereafter in laudable things, ought himself to be a true poem," like *Milton.* The structure of *Milton,* like the structure of *Jerusalem,* is fourfold, but, then, these fourfold structures are also the thematic and mythic content of each poem. Milton is himself, the Bard, Blake, and Los *as* poem. Milton finally sees Golgonooza, the spiritual fourfold London, in the only way possible: "It is viewed on all sides round by a Four-old Vision."[46] The "Allergoric Generation" of six thousand years when viewed from "within & without" and "on all sides round" turns out to be a Divine Analogy that is the "Divine Revelation in the Litteral expression."

If it is possible to summarize Blake's achievement in *Milton,* I think it can best be done in terms of Blake's effort to "dress" Milton in imagery that dramatizes his own vision and theory of art, the major point that I have tried to emphasize throughout this essay. Milton, who is of the spirit of Los, recreates the human form, face, heart, and dress in his imagination. Milton-Los-Blake, a composite bard, like Statius-Virgil-Dante, reaches a kind of imaginative paradise which climaxes his temporal endeavours as Milton the seventeenth-century poet. Blake, like Dante in the *Purgatorio,* records in *Milton* his own version of man's effort to purge himself of error. Without the traditional Catholic symbolic context, the English Protestant-Romantic poet develops his own myth of self-illumination. Actually prophetic or intellectual pride, like Satan's in *Paradise Lost,* so far as Blake is concerned, is reconceived by Blake in Romantic terms as a *positive* or "Contrary" force in contest with that which is not a contrary but the power which "Negatives" everything. Milton is Los's agent within the mundane shell or egg, for he is Los's most recent son.

> The Mundane Shell is a vast Concave Earth, an immense
> Harden'd shadow of all things upon our Vegetated Earth,
> Enlarg'd into dimension & deform'd into indefinite space,
> In Twenty-seven Heavens and all their Hells, with Chaos

And Ancient Night & Purgatory. It is a cavernous
 Earth
Of labyrinthine intricacy, twenty-seven-folds of opa-
 keness,
And finishes where the lark mounts . . .

(*M* 17: 498)

This is what Los's "Egg form'd World" is from the
point of view of reason, that is, Urizen. This picture
ushers in the Satanic Milton, who is "unloos'd upon Al-
bion." He appears as the Romantic Satan, rebelling
against the false heavens while also overcoming his
selfhood or spectre who is the State of Satan and who
is the God of these heavens and this world. To those
struggling for freedom within the establishment he ap-
pears to be a leader, if not *the* leader, of that establish-
ment. But Milton the redeemer who was of the Re-
deemed is not now of the Elect but of the Reprobate. It
is not long before he is properly recognized as the
"Awakener" (*M* 21: 504) and embraced by Los (*M* 23:
507).

Blake's "Purgatorio" is clearly a Romantic one. Mil-
ton's quest is through eternity and is instantaneous.
Like Goethe's Faust, Blake's Milton is saved because
he is perpetually striving while his Gretchen (Ololon)
awaits his return.

> Wer immer stebend sich bemüht
> Den Konnen wir erlösen.

(Faust, II, v, 7)

With Los in *Jerusalem,* Milton is eternally "Striving
with Systems to deliver Individuals from those Sys-
tems" (*J* 11: 630). As the crucible-furnace-blacksmith
imagery, Los's quest within the fallen human form, and
Milton's exploration of his eternal lineaments all indi-
cate, Blake's purgatory is to be found in man's vision
of his own interior life. If he reaches paradise, it will
have been achieved only through an intense and imagi-
native effort of self-recreation or illumination. *Milton*
records this experience by being this experience.

The main drift of Milton's remarks on plates 40 and 41
is directed towards aesthetic concerns. This is why Los
refuses "To throw him into the Furnaces" (*M* 22: 505).
Milton cannot be renewed (*M* 21: 504) because he is
going to Eternal Death "in that which can never Die"
(*M* 32: 521). He is clothed with imagination and is
about to have a state created for him, which will be-
come identical with him, "Called Eternal Annihilation,"
and which, because it is the poem *Milton,* will be a
unique identity not divided from imagination. In that
state Milton learns that "All that can be annihilated
must be annihilated" so "that the Children of Jerusalem
may be saved from slavery." He learns to "cleanse the
Face" of his "Spirit by Self-examination":

> To cast aside from Poetry all that is not Inspiration,
> That it no longer shall dare to mock with the asper-
> sion of Madness

Cast on the Inspired by the tame high finisher of pal-
 try Blots
Indefinite, or paltry Rhymes, or paltry Harmonies,
Who creeps into State Government like a catterpiller
 to destroy;
To cast off the idiot Questioner who is always ques-
 tioning
But never capable of answering, who sits with a sly
 grin
Silent plotting when to question, like a thief in a cave,
Who publishes doubt & calls it knowledge, whose
 Science is Despair, . . .
These are the destroyers of Jerusalem, these are the
 murderers
Of Jesus, who deny Faith & mock at Eternal Life,
Who pretend to Poetry that they may destroy Imagina-
 tion
By imitation of Nature's Images drawn from Remem-
 brance.

(*M* 41: 533)[47]

It would be easy enough to cite in repetition passages
from *Milton* which other critics have already estab-
lished as references to Hayley or other personal disap-
pointments in Blake's life up to the time he was com-
pleting *Milton,* but Milton's final speech, which begins
with a discussion of the nature of contraries, is directed
at the same aesthetic concerns, thoughts, opinions, and
persons that Blake castigates throughout his work. The
speech editorializes in the same fashion as much of his
other verse, or his letters, or the annotations to the
works of Reynolds, Bacon, or Wordsworth. The similes
recall recurrent patterns of imagery, such as the cater-
pillar and the cave (the cycle of generation and the
cavern-cocoon of the five senses),[48] while also recalling
the questioner-accuser, paltry harmonies and rime, the
indefinite, blots and blurs, aspersions of madness, na-
ture and memory. *Milton* is as much a quasi-critical
poem as *Jerusalem.* And the destroyers of Jerusalem
are also the would-be destroyers of Blake's *Jerusalem.*
These would-be destroyers of poetry and painting past,
present, and future are the enemies of art in all ages
which the Bard can see because he "Present, Past & Fu-
ture sees." "To cast off Bacon, Locke & Newton from
Albion's covering" is to reject the threefold accuser of
English philosophical thought and his hired knaves, like
Reynolds, Hayley, or anybody, who try to hide the
"real" Milton that is Blake's.[49]

Notes

1. "An Apology for Smectymnuus," *Milton's Prose
 Writings* (London, 1958), p. 69.

2. "The Theme and Structure of William Blake's
 Jerusalem," in *The Divine Vision* (London, 1957),
 p. 162. *Cf.* Northrop Frye, "Notes for a Commen-
 tary on *Milton,*" in *The Divine Vision,* p. 103.

3. The unsatisfactory character of narrative readings
 of his poems has dogged Blake criticism from

Yeats to the present day. For two recent efforts to read Blake's major poems as narratives, see Harold Bloom, *Blake's Apocalypse* (New York, 1963), and William R. Hughes, *Jerusalem by William Blake* (London, 1964). Among other less recent efforts, see, also, J. H. Wicksteed, *William Blake's Jerusalem* (London, 1954), and W. H. Stevenson, "Blake's *Jerusalem*," *Essays in Criticism,* IX (1959), pp. 254-264. See, also, Bloom's "Commentary," *The Poetry and Prose of William Blake,* ed. D. V. Erdman (New York, 1965).

As a parallel development to his Dantean literary turn of mind (I am not speaking of theology), it is important to remember that after illustrating Milton's poems off and on over several decades, Blake finally at the end of his life also illustrated Dante. It may be also that Blake's literary critics could profit from the commentary of some objective and non-Blakean critics of his painting, and set aside *temporarily,* at least, the text to which the illustrations to Milton and Dante are assigned. Once this is done, Blake's imaginative achievement can be fully appreciated, for the water-colors can be placed side by side according to "pictorial form." For one critic who presses this point, see R. H. Wilenski, *English Painting* (London, 1954), pp. 258-59. Blake's water-colors to Young's *Night Thoughts,* which in bulk constitute about one-fourth of his major designs, also take on new meaning and greater significance when freed from the narrative pattern of Young's poem. Though Wilenski does not mention the Young designs, his point about the illustrations to *Paradise Lost, Comus,* and the *Divine Comedy* is, I think, indisputable. None of Blake's "epics" are essentially narrative since they occur in the moment of vision and are simultaneous in part and whole rather than sequential.

4. *Cf.,* for example, the words of Los (*J* [*Jerusalem*] 8, ll. 14-17: 627) with the refrain of the Bard and the command of Milton: "Mark well my words! they are of your eternal salvation" and "Obey thou the Words of the Inspired Man." All references to Blake's work are from *The Complete Works,* ed., Geoffrey Keynes (London, 1966).

5. *FZ* [*The Four Zoas*] v: 307; *BU* [*The Book of Urizen*] VI-VII: 231-34; *FZ* viii, 362: 350. For Orc's birth, see, also, *M* [*Milton*] 3: 483. Orc is born "first" and both Milton and Satan "last." In *FZ* viii: 350, Satan is fifteenth and Milton last. This is another illustration of why it is not only a mistake to try to supply a linear narrative to Blake's poems but also to his myths which are instantaneous rather than sequential in the usual sense. Blake resists *mythological* criticism and systemization as effectively as he does criticism geared to sequen-

tial events. Since "all the Great Events of Time start forth & are conceiv'd . . . Within a Moment," temporal sequence loses its relevance in myth and narrative alike. Most important is where the event takes place, such as in "fixed space," or from what point of view, such as that of the "*Spectre* of Prophecy" or the "*Spirit* of Prophecy" (my italics). Of course, Milton as Spectre *is* Satan. Milton himself says, "I in my selfhood am that Satan. . . . He is my Spectre."

6. "The Laocoon": 776; *J* 96: 743.

7. See the Epilogue to [*For the Sexes*:] *The Gates of Paradise,* 1. 7: 771.

8. *Cf.* "Notes for a Commentary on *Milton,*" p. 127, where Frye says "The building of the Mundane Shell and 'mathematic power,' associated with Urizen in *The Four Zoas,* are transferred in Milton." They are transferred because Urizen has then become a part of Los's universe, sculptured by Milton who is inspired by Los. *Cf.* [Frye,] *Fearful Symmetry* (Princeton, 1947), pp. 332-33. See, also, *J* 12: 631.

9. [Bloom,] *Blake's Apocalypse* (New York, 1963) p. 350.

10. See, for example, *Fearful Symmetry,* p. 333.

11. *Blake's Apocalypse,* pp. 361-72.

12. *Cf. J* 49, ll. 57-58: 680. See *J* 98 for the Jehovah of the Covenant and compare him to the Jehovah of *J* 49: 680.

13. *Blake's Apocalypse,* pp. 482-84.

14. "The Laocoon" identifies Jehovah as an angel of the Divine Presence, that is, an idea of God, and *Milton* cites Lucifer as one of the seven angels (*M* 32: 521) while also naming him as the first of the seven eyes; Jehovah appears as the sixth (*M* 13: 494). All the eyes or ideas and the angels (perhaps, *angles* of vision) are affected by point of view and even, as in *M* 32: 521, the doctrine of states under the power of Satan, who is himself a state. "Jah" in "The Laocoon" is said to have "two Sons, Satan & Adam" as copied and misapplied under Priam's Covenant (see *J* 98: 746). It is important to remember that Satan and Adam are the limits of opacity and contraction *and* sons of Los. They are also states. Jesus creates states in order to deliver individuals from them (*J* 25: 648).

15. The "mountains" are, of course, "The Atlantic Mountains where Giants dwelt in Intellect, / Now given to stony Druids and Allegoric Generation" (*J* 50: 681). They are the "terrible Surfaces" which must be removed from Albion.

16. Letter to Butts, 6 July 1803: 825.

17. *Blake's Apocalypse,* p. 400.

18. [Vardis Fisher,] *The Valley of Vision* (Toronto, 1961), p. 247.

19. *Fearful Symmetry,* p. 346.

20. "On Homer's Poetry": 778. Unity becomes a "cloke of folly" and like Morality is a "secondary" consideration belonging to "Philosophy & not to Poetry" when confined exclusively to one *supposedly* finished work of art. This is not the case when as an aesthetic consideration rather than a philosophical abstraction, unity is the vision of the artist himself. Then it is "a perfect Whole" in all its "Minute Particulars" (*J* 91: 738).

21. See *BU* plate 2: 222 for the word "preludium" as used by Blake.

22. "Annotations to Reynolds' *Discourses*," 60: 459.

23. *Fearful Symmetry,* p. 323.

24. *Cf.* recently, for example, E. D. Hirsch, Jr., *Innocence and Experience: An Introduction to Blake* (New Haven, 1964). See, also, W. H. Stevenson, "Blake's *Jerusalem*," *Essays in Criticism,* IX (1959), pp. 254-64.

25. G. E. Bentley, Jr., *William Blake, Vala, or The Four Zoas* (Oxford, 1963), p. 167. *Cf.* "The Laocoon": 777, "Without Unceasing Practice nothing can be done. Practice is Art. If you leave off you are Lost." See, also, Blake's comment on Raphael's Cartoons, *DC* [*A Descriptive Catalogue of Pictures, Poetical and Historical Inventions*] XV: 584. Coherence, control, or cohesiveness, like unity, is a matter of vision, "so he who wishes to see a Vision, a perfect Whole," *must* not only be able to envision, he "Must see it in its Minute Particulars, Organized . . ." (*J* 91: 738).

26. See David V. Erdman, "The Suppressed and Altered Passages in Blake's *Jerusalem*," *Studies in Bibliography,* 17 (1964), pp. 1-54. Even the master-polisher, Henry James, revised early work in his later manner.

27. *Moby-Dick,* Ch. XXXII. "Draft" or "draught" is also, of course, a term in masonry, which Melville knew and which Blake, could he have read this sentence, would certainly have appreciated, since he, too, uses technical terms literally and metaphorically.

28. *DC* V: 579. The entire passage is worth careful perusal and raises a point which Frye never loses sight of in *Fearful Symmetry.*

29. *Fearful Symmetry,* p. 336.

30. *The Valley of Vision,* p. 247.

31. *Cf. PA* [*Public Address*] 18-19: 600.

32. *Cf. M* 32: 522; *VLJ* [*Vision of the Last Judgment*] 82-84: 611.

33. See Blake's letter to Butts, 26 October 1800, 11. 45-48 especially: 804-06.

34. *M* 35-36: 526-27; *ARO* [*All Religions Are One*] 7: 98. *Cf. M* 13-14, 11. 51 and 1-3: 495. The Milton of Blake's poem is the *vision of Milton,* as the risen Albion is the "Vision of Albion" (*J* 97: 744). He is the spiritual man, not the natural man (Blake's "Adamah," see "The Laocoon": 776).

35. See my essay, "Visionary Forms Dramatic: Grammatical and Iconographical Movement in Blake's Verse and Designs," *Criticism,* 8: 2 (Spring, 1966), 111-125.

36. *Ibid.*

37. *Cf.* "London" and "A Divine Image" in *Songs of Experience*: 210; 221. See, also, *J* 10: 629-30; *J* 3: 621.

38. *Cf.* Milton's "fibrous left foot" (*M* 22: 506).

39. *SE* [*Songs of Experience*]: 221. The Shadowy Female's "Clothing," her allegorical robe or veil (her deception) is reclaimed or rent and revealed by imagination. The sealed furnace appears in *The Four Zoas,* too. *Cf.,* also, *Fearful Symmetry,* pp. 349; 364.

40. "Annotations to Reynolds' *Discourses*," 195: 473. *Cf. DC* IV: 576-77.

41. *M* 29: 517. *Cf.* Annotations to Bacon's *Essays,* 66: 402.

42. *M* 34: 524 should be compared to *M* 19: 500 and *J* 59: 691. *J* 59 brings in the throne imagery, explicitly associating "Verulam, London, York & Edinburgh" with Urthona, Urizen, Luvah, and Tharmas. *Cf.,* also, *J* 12-13: 631-34.

After describing the diagram, Blake also poses several rhetorical questions which help to interpret its meaning. Our point of view is Ololon's. We look "down into the Heavens of Ulro." The "Wars of man, which in Great Eternity Appear around in the External Spheres of Visionary Life" (as in the diagram) are "Here render'd Deadly within the Life & Interior Vision" (as in the diagram) because "Ideas themselves (which are The Divine Members)" are sacrificed in Albion, an inevitable chain of events for any nation where poetry is fettered (*M* 34-35: 524-25; *cf. J* 43 [38]: 672; *J* 3: 621). Note that in a spatial context Blake calls the circles "Spheres" and says "ideas" (when not abstracted) are "Divine Members." *Cf.* "The Laocoon": 776.

43. *Cf. Fearful Symmetry,* p. 316.

44. Frye suggests that "the tent is the symbol of the fact that the City of God is movable." See "Notes for a Commentary on *Milton,*" p. 136.

45. Milton's track runs from right to left. (See my essay mentioned in notes 35 and 36.) The diagram on plate 33 makes this direction unmistakable. Blake's sense of the structure or balance of the poem is suggested by the almost even division of the poem into equal thirds.

46. *M* 35: 525. See my essay "'Mental Forms Creating': 'Fourfold Vision' and the Poet as Prophet in Blake's Designs and Verse," *Journal of Aesthetics and Art Criticism,* 23:2 (Winter, 1964), 173-183.

47. *Cf.* "The Laocoon" where Blake says "There are States in which all Visionary Men are accounted Mad men" (777).

48. See my article, "Blake's Human Insect," in *Texas Studies in Literature and Language,* X: 2 (Summer, 1968), 215-232.

49. *Cf.* [David V. Erdman,] *Blake: Prophet Against Empire* [(Princeton, 1954)], p. 406, note 11: "Aware of all [the] Miltonic labors of Cowper, Fuseli, Hayley, and a shoal of engravers from 1790 on (Barry too had 'in good forwardness' in Dec. 1794 a project 'to dress Milton'). Blake naturally chose to write, illustrate, and 'print' his own *Milton*; nor is it improbable that the early draft of *M.,* comparable in symbolism to *F.R.* and *A.,* was begun early in the 1790's." In the first two decades of the nineteenth century, Blake continued "to dress Milton" by illustrating much of Milton's work, his own *Milton* being the focal point of all these illustrations.

I think Bloom is correct in stressing the image of the garment in *Milton* because the garment is the poem itself, Blake's effort "to dress Milton" in the clothing of imagination—"the Divine Revelation in the Litteral expression." See *Blake's Apocalypse,* p. 396. *Cf.* not only *M* 42: 534, but also *M* 26: 512, especially 11. 10-12. For past, present, and future, see also, *J* 15, 11. 6-13 (especially 11. 8-10): 635.

John Howard (essay date 1976)

SOURCE: Howard, John. "The Spiritual World." In *Blake's* Milton: *A Study in the Selfhood,* pp. 25-55. Rutherford, N.J.: Fairleigh Dickinson University Press, 1976.

[*In the following essay, Howard examines the symbolic framework of Blake's* Milton *through a discussion of the poem's diverse historic, artistic, and philosophical sources.*]

I. MATERIALISTS AND SPIRITUALISTS

Upon examining the cosmic framework within which the action of *Milton* occurs, one finds Blake's characteristic two-edged sword carving out the lineaments of the spiritual world and revealing the current delusion of materialism used by the selfhood to control mankind. With the burin of prophetic vision Blake exposes Bacon, Newton, and Locke as representatives of this delusion.[1] Bacon, Newton, and Locke share the assumptions that matter has an independent existence, and that, like a machine, it is governed by mechanical causation that is discoverable and knowable. Bacon's inductive method, which assumes that matter is independent and understandable, aims at the dissection of nature into its parts "as did the school of Democritus."[2] Blake must have sensed something sinister in Bacon's preference for "the school of Leucippus and Democritus."[3] Not only is Bacon's favoring of these materialistic philosophers a key to his own philosophy's easy conjoining with the philosophy of atomism in the *Novum Organon,* but, in his essay "of atheisme," he attempts to make the point that the philosophy of Democritus and Epicurus is not at odds with religion. But Blake saw the Baconian science as another manifestation of that earthly delusion which manifested itself in Bacon's materialistic forebears and pointed to its further manifestation in Newton. Bacon's attempts to find the forms of nature were no other than attempts to find a cause-and-effect relationship in matter[4] that would make the natural world self-sufficient under a few simple laws. The rules of reasoning in this attempt are set out in Book III of Newton's *Mathematical Principles of Natural Philosophy.* These rules include the rules of natural cause and effect, and the rule of precedence of the inductive method, based on observations of phenomena, over hypotheses not based on phenomena.[5] It is the observation of phenomena as a source of truth that implies the reality of matter. The latest manifestation of delusion, Locke's empiricism, asserts, in Locke's distinction between primary and secondary ideas, the assumption of the independent existence of matter. Primary ideas exist in matter itself. Locke writes: "The particular bulk, number, figure, and motion of the parts of fire, or snow, are really in them,—whether any one's senses perceive them or not and therefore they may be called real qualities, because they really exist in those bodies."[6] In all three philosophers, matter has the real, independent existence upon which knowledge is based.

The delusion of Bacon, Newton, and Locke is also manifest in the thought of Hartley and Priestley. Hartley, the follower of Locke, traces thought to the mechanical workings of the vibratiuncles in the brain, as though thought were governed by a mechanical cause-and-effect relationship.[7] Priestley, though attempting to

rid Christianity of various corruptions such as the belief in the duality of matter and spirit, gives the most obvious support to the high valuation of matter:

> It has been the opinion of many philosophers, and among others of Mr. Locke, that, for any thing that we know to the contrary, a capacity of thinking might be given to matter. Dr. Hartley, however, notwithstanding his hypothesis would be much helped by it, seems to think otherwise. He also supposes that there is an intermediate *elementary body* between the mind and the gross body; which may exist, and be the instrument of giving pleasure or pain to the sentient principle, after death. But I own I see no reason why his scheme should be burdened with such an incumbrance as this.
>
> I am rather inclined to think that, though the subject is beyond our comprehension at present, man does not consist of two principles so essentially different from one another as *matter* and *spirit,* which are always described as having not one common property, by means of which they can affect or act upon each other; the one occupying space, and the other not only not occupying the least imaginable portion of space, but incapable of bearing relation to it; insomuch that, properly speaking, my mind is no more *in my body* than it is in the moon. I rather think that the whole man is of some *uniform composition,* and that the property of *perception,* as well as the other powers that are termed mental, is the result (whether necessary or not) of such an organical structure as that of the brain. Consequently, that the whole man becomes extinct at death, and that we have no hope of surviving the grave but what is derived from the scheme of revelation.[8]

In Priestley the ultimate implication is made. Man, both mind and body, is matter, and the extinction of his body is the extinction of his mind. Here, hope for eternal life is removed to faith, while reason reports only of death. The farther this hope is removed from man, the closer comes the sinister and gripping fear that there is no spiritual existence at all, and ultimately that death is the final eclipse of the individual. In such a philosophic world view, man's fear drives him to any servility to avoid death, making him an easy prey to the survival-determined selfhood.

But the century's materialism had not gone without its opponents, both direct and oblique. In his *Essay on Spirit,* Robert Clayton saw nature as a result of direct spiritual causation,[9] and Abraham Tucker, in *The Light of Nature,* imagined a kind of cosmic assembly line of pure spirits working on gravity and other laws of nature.[10] But a more direct opponent, Thomas Taylor, launched more than one attack against materialism. To pursue matter "through its infinite divisions and wander in its dark labyrinths is the employment of the philosophy in vogue," wrote Taylor in his introduction to Plotinus's *Concerning the Beautiful.*[11] "All modern sects are in a state of barbarous ignorance: for Materialism, and its attendant Sensuality, have darkened the eyes of the *many,* with the mists of error."[12] Matter is for Taylor a

"nonentity."[13] But the most philosophic attack on materialism came from Berkeley, who insisted that "the very notion of what is called matter or *corporeal substance,* involves a contradiction in it."[14] There are conclusive proofs "against the existence of material substance."[15] Berkeley's attack on material substance was part of an attack on the Lockean notion that ideas are derived from the senses reacting to the material world. For Berkeley no ideas exist anywhere but in the perceiving mind. "Their *esse* is *percepi,* nor is it possible they should have existence out of the mind of thinking things which perceive them."[16] It is spirit that perceives.[17] "The cause of ideas is an incorporeal active substance or spirit."[18]

But Berkeley took pains not to deny the existence of a world exterior to the mind of the individual. His attack essentially was directed against the notion "of absolute or external existence of unperceiving substances,"[19] but since he could not disbelieve in the existence of exterior reality, he postulated a divine mind that at all times perceives the infinite universe. This perception is an archetype in the divine mind. The individual's perception of the forms of the archetype is ectypal.[20] Thus things do exist, but not as material objects independent of mind. Matter cannot account for causation.[21] The "substratum" of matter is an unnecessary and delusory invention.[22]

Blake's visionary cosmos is the symbolic embodiment of the anti-materialist principle that matter cannot have its own independent system of cause and effect. Matter is brought into motion by spiritual cause. When Blake writes "every Natural Effect has a Spiritual Cause" ([*The Poetry and Prose of William Blake*] 26.44), he is on the side of Berkeley, but with a visionary's allegiance.

II. TIME AND SPACE

Blake countered the concepts of materialism by his picture of the cosmos as a spiritually animated, nonmechanistic, visionary creation that functions in accordance with the purposes of eternity.[23] His picture is heavily detailed and sometimes confusing, but its basic patterns remain clear. It directly denies the temporal and spatial concepts of the universe of Newton's astronomy, for in Blake's universe space is a symbolic creation of the mind, figuring forth in the objectification of the exterior world the inner rooms and framework of the psyche. And in this universe, time is a sequential cover, a separation from eternity that will disappear.[24]

Blake conceives of time as the sequence of events extending from the fall of man from eternity into the physical creation, which has the absolute limit of six thousand years,[25] to his eventual return to eternity.[26] He embodied this concept in the myth of the fall of Albion,

"when Albion was slain upon his Mountains" (3.1). The mythic Albion, on a cosmic level, represents all of the life of eternity that is fallen into the physical world. To bring that life back to eternity is the purpose of creation. Throughout **Milton** Albion sleeps on his couch; and though Blake dramatizes Albion's rousing himself at the end of the poem, Albion relapses, his relapse suggesting that man refuses to return to eternity because he refuses to relinquish the delusions of the selfhood. Blake's many references to sleeping, couches, and waking suggest that temporal existence is merely a brief episode of sleep in the eternal world. But this sleep has been changed to death by Satan (29.32-33), that is, the delusion that the material world has independent, real existence turns the "sleep" of this life into a potential everlasting death.[27] On a psychological level this condition of Albion represents a psychic malfunction of the mind caused by the selfhood's domination of the whole personality.

Blake's sequencing of time runs as follows: Albion's fall into a deathlike sleep preceded the initial episode of the poem, the shaping of Urizen by Los, which is Los's characteristic attempt to stop the degenerative process begun in the fall. Blake describes the seven passing ages of Los's formation of Urizen (3.6-27), which are to be taken as events prior to the formation of the world of time and space. When the formation of Urizen was complete, Los viewed his semi-successful attempt with terror (3.28), recognizing his own defensive posture in the inadequacy of his achievement. This recognition led to the separation of Enitharmon and Los's Spectre from Los's bosom and back (3.29-36). Among these three, the process of creation was then taken up as a serious pursuit. They built the looms of generation and Golgonooza (3.38-39), which symbolize the spiritual machinery that brings about material formation and process. In essence Los's pursuit constitutes the spiritual causation that leads to all natural effect. Blake then tells how Los's power was subdivided among all his children, from Orc to Satan, all of whom have been given form: "First Orc was Born then the Shadowy Female; then All Los's Family / At last Enitharmon brought forth Satan Refusing Form, in vain" (3.40-41).

Satan's formation coincides with the beginning of man as it is recorded in the Bible, for in **Milton** Satan and Adam occur at the same interval in the temporal sequence: "The Divine hand found the Two Limits: first of Opacity, then of Contraction / Opacity was named Satan, Contraction was named Adam" (13.20-21).[28] The limit is a limit to the fall from eternity, a kind of absolute end of degeneration beyond which mankind cannot go.[29] This merciful act occurred during the six thousand years of time, following the sending of two guards to the world to time. These two, Lucifer and Molech, had themselves fallen, and the degenerative process would have gone on had it not been limited. The formation of Adam preceded the descent of Elohim, Shaddai, Pahad, and Jehovah, whom Blake sees as guards also subject to corruption. Jehovah, the perfection of "hypocritic holiness" (13.25), without corrupting Jesus, formed a false body (a church) around him, which perverted his teachings (13.22-26).

Milton's descent to Blake marks the nearing of the end of the six thousand years of time. Los himself announces this end: "Fellow Labourers! The Great Vintage & Harvest is now upon Earth" (25.17). The harvest and vintage stand for the spiritual life that will proceed after the end of time, also symbolized in the awakening of Albion (25.23). In psychological terms, the end of temporal existence is really an end to the delusion that independent matter constitutes reality. The consummation of the creation, leading to the awakening of Albion (25.61-2), occurs when man acquires spiritual vision. Each individual may experience this vision during his lifetime and all of mankind will experience it at the last judgment. At any time, an individual may transcend his narrow sensual view and acquire spiritual vision, thus causing the world of time and space to be consumed for that individual. When all men accomplish this change, then Albion, who represents sleeping, collective man, will truly awake, not simply rouse himself and relapse, as he does at the end of the poem (39.32-52).

The spread of time thus can be a psychic spectrum as well as cosmic. Blake's description of infinity as a vortexlike projection from the individual which changes with time but includes all the individual's experience within it or behind it (15. 21-35), suggests that time is an illusion of sequence caused by the selfhood. Moreover, Blake's mundane shell is, in part, a psychological time-space continuum where place, or events of place, are essentially past time. Late in the poem the twenty-seven heavens of the mundane shell are given in temporal sequence from Adam to Luther, suggesting a sequential ordering of the past in space, the oldest in time being the most distant in space, the youngest the closest (37.35-43). That "All these are seen in Milton's Shadow" (37.44) suggests that the history of cosmic man can be contained within the confines of a single individual. This past time in the mind is the individual's memory, yet it can aid the delusion of independent material existence, since men may think, with Locke, that nothing enters the mind except from the exterior world of phenomena. But past time has its real existence only within the mind, for personal consciousness is the human imagination itself, which has no beginning or end, merely different manifestations. The individual personality has "destin'd lineaments permanent for ever & ever" (22.25), and "can never Die" (32.24). Death as the eclipse of identity, and time as the inevitable sequence of events for the personality, are delusions. Time is, in essence, a visionary construction, a mercy to the fallen soul. When one delves below the smallest par-

ticle of time, he is in touch with eternity and has in his possession the sum of time, of "Six Thousand Years" (28.63).

Space is a series of symbolic constructs that deny the normal spatial relationships that one dwelling in a spatial world customarily accepts. For Blake, space, like time, is essentially "visionary" (29.20). The Newtonian notion of space, limiting "existence" to external, sensuous objects, neglects the unsensed existence of eternity. For Blake, events in the exterior world are really manifestations of spiritual, interior causes. Their existence is not only not limited by an exterior spatial world, but their existence itself is caused by an internal vision of man. The laws, therefore, of spatial relationship, so important in a Newtonian universe of "Length Bredth Highth" (4.27), are illusions in Blake's universe of mental space.[30] Rather, the spatial relationships in **Milton** are indicators of spiritual relationships. Thus the opposing points of the compass, the inner and outer view of man, above and below, within and without, represent not spatial, but psychological opposites. An example of this symbolism can be seen in the relationship between inner and outer, and within and without. In the statement "travellers to Eternity pass *outward* to Satan's seat, / But travellers to Eternity pass *inward* to Golgonooza" (17.29-30; italics mine) the directions reflect not spatial paths but flows of psychic energy. *Within* the mind is eternal vision. That vision lies *within* the nerves of the eye that is spiritually open, "and *in this hallowed center* holds the heavens of bright eternity" (28.38; italics mine) while "Spectrous cunning" (28.41) waits *without*. "*Within* the Center [of the Flower] Eternity expands" (31.48; italics mine) When the fallen vision assumes reality to exist only in the exterior world, it is turning *outward* to Satan's seat, that is, it is being deluded by the selfhood that spatial existence alone is real. To turn *inward* to the imagination is to put the visionary existence on a higher plane of reality and thus to become spiritual. To attempt to deduce knowledge about God from the *outward* natural world is to deduce knowledge only of Satan. The empirical philosophy of five senses is traveling *outward*; traveling *inward* is the philosophy of the visionary.

III. EDEN, BEULAH, ULRO

Recognizing that portions of space symbolize psychological reality, we can examine the places known as Eden, Beulah, and Ulro to see their meaning.[31] Blake's universe, the supreme, timeless part of it, is called eternity or Eden. It contains God, the spiritual life, and is God. It can expand to become a single entity or contract and divide into multitudes. In eternity the individual identity exists as a part of the whole, at the same time retaining the capability of individuality. Psychologically, expanded eternity is that selfless harmony with others which allows one to identify with a group.

Eternity is known also as the Divine Body of Jesus as well as the Human Imagination. The connection of eternity with the imagination implies that the essence of human life is spiritual existence; it also implies that the individual's imagination is the spiritual essence of the individual, while his body, senses, and reason are merely enclosures of the spirit, keeping it from contact with eternity.

The life of eternity seems characterized by strenuous, excessive, unwearying mental strife. So exceedingly active is eternity that the "female" portion of eternity is unable to withstand it and fades away. Therefore a temporal region of rest and sleep is provided, called Beulah. It is not eternity, but not exactly time either. Beulah is a sleep of eternity that *may* lead into a fall, but not inevitably. The active portions of eternity turn to Beulah for rest and for correction of error. There they have an "emanation" to repose in before they return to eternity.

The masculine nature of eternity is intended to suggest the selflessness that underlies Blake's whole ethical point of view. Eternity is a place where there is nothing for the comfort of the self. From each individual a constant outpouring of creative energy flows in a selfless stream of activity. Though **Milton** gives us brief pictures of the eternal tables, and of a bard before a divine assembly, suggesting a calm, Lucretian existence, the brief hints of the earlier **Book of Urizen**—where eternity seems conceived as a place of joy mixed with pain, of constant death of the self in creation, and metaphorically of "unquenchable burnings" (**BU** [**Book of Urizen**] 4.13)—help us to see what Blake means by "the great Wars of Eternity in fury of Poetic Inspiration, / To build the Universe stupendous: Mental forms Creating" (30.19-20). This is life "too exceeding unbounded" (30.22), a terrible joy that consumes the "weak & weary" (31.1). It is a life of selfless creative activity.[32] The presence of terror and pain in eternity is inevitable, because the individual is without his defenses. It is the desire to avoid the inevitable pain of selflessness that leads the weak and weary to a land of rest and, potentially at least, to the selfhood. Yet, despite its terrors, eternity is not deadly. The wars of eternity are changed to fixity and finality only when the fall into the world of Ulro occurs. They are then turned from a state of flux to "a frozen bulk subject to decay and death" (34.54). In eternity what are manifested in the physical world as war and hunting are the fluxile "fountains of the River of Life" (35.2). This fall from the freedom of eternity results from the selfhood's reaching for fixity because it believes fixity to give unthreatening permanence and stability. But what exists in defenseless freedom then becomes enclosed in a fortress, which is really a prison.

The world of eternity, where mental forms are continuously being created, thus stands also for creativity.[33] In

eternity form and shape are created. Eternity is selfless in that it refuses to concern itself with survival, always turning the attention to the shaping of creation. Eternity exists when man builds the universe, that is, creates mental form (30.19-20). The psychological truth of this idea becomes clear when one reflects on his own experience. Anyone who has painted, written, composed, built, constructed a work of art, architecture, or artifact subsequently becomes aware of the timelessness of the act. What seemed to be experienced as a few minutes may actually have taken hours. Man experiences creativity as timelessness or eternity. Eternity is thus a symbolic place representing a combination of the individual creative urges of the imagination with the nonself-centered impulses.

Around eternity, and between eternity and this world, is the realm of Beulah. It is a realm of dream, of contrariety, where contrariety is truth. It is a pleasant rest. It is a land of sexual delusion. It is the realm of the daughters who inspire. Beulah is certainly suggested by the Beulah in *Pilgrim's Progress,* which is a land adjacent to the celestial city (Blake's eternity) where weary pilgrims (Blake's mental warriors in eternity) may rest and be refreshed. Here is renewed the contract between bride and bridegroom (Blake's male and emanation; contrarieties). It is beyond the valley of the shadow of death (not in the lower world of time and space). From Blake's Beulah an individual may fall away from eternal life just as the soul, crossing the river from Bunyan's Beulah, may itself yet be lost. Thus Blake's Beulah's pleasant connotations must be balanced against the fact that Beulah is the place from which souls are drawn down into spiritual death, to generation. It is an intermediary between eternity and the world as it appears to us. The sleepers of Beulah may be lured down "the River Storge (which is Arnon) into the Dead Sea" (34.30); that is, the sleeping individual may be lured into a great delusion. Just as the Arnon flows into the Dead Sea, souls descend to embodiment in flesh. Parental appetite (Storge) wishes to lure the souls into the worlds of the flesh. But just as the flowing Arnon and souls fall into the Dead Sea and into flesh, so does the unwary and over-relaxed soul fall into delusion.

It is the tinge of the selfhood inherent in Beulah that leads potentially to the delusion of this world. A place "where no dispute can come" (30.3), a place of shade and sleep (30.2), a place protected like an infant cradled in its mother's arms (30.11-12), a place of "mild & pleasant Rest" (30.14) is created essentially for those who cannot withstand absolute selflessness. It is a bounded, nonexcessive place, representing the need for protection. It was founded originally to give a place of rest to those who might "consume" (30.27). This kind and merciful motive for its foundation, however, does not cancel the ambivalence of Beulah, for in its own extremes Beulah can become the world of Ulro. This "lovely Shadow" (30.2) is a "Temporal Habitation" (30.29), the first step of the descent to the delusion of time and space. It is the first time-structuring act of the mind anxious to avoid feelings of insecurity. It is a shadow into which the eternals go, a dovelike covering (31.3), a child in its mother's arms. In essence it is the first bit of protective covering from selflessness that can become the incrustation of the selfhood. No creativity is said to exist in Beulah, though it may be a place of inspiration. The daughters of Beulah may inspire a poet's song (2.1), but they are not themselves the creators. As a land of rest and inspiration Beulah may function as a place of dreams where the weary may rest and restore their creative energies. But if it becomes a permanent haven, then the individual has begun the fall into Ulro.

Beulah as a place thus symbolizes that mental state of noncreativity wherein the weary mind seeks refreshment; the strife of creativity is relaxed so that the paradoxical, the contrary, the apparently illogical is not disputed. In its relaxed ambience the pursuit of creation is dropped for the refreshment of pleasure. This mental state, though there is no exact word for it, is a state between creative struggle and delusory stasis. It is between eternity and Ulro.

The symbol *Ulro* represents delusion in many forms but, particularly in **Milton,** the delusion that the material universe had independent and exclusive reality. This empirical delusion appears in Blake's occasional equations of spatial existence with Ulro. As space, Ulro is mentioned when Los sees the world without Bowlahoola and Allamanda as a visionless polypus that would tremble "thro all the Ulro space" (24.39). This equation is also suggested by the "watchers of Ulro" (20.50), who behold the spatial world, and by the fact that the spatially visible wild Thyme is "Los' messenger . . . in Ulro dark" (35.54-55). But more frequently Ulro means not space but the delusion of the mind that equates space with total reality. As delusion, Ulro is mentioned when Satan falls into a "World of deeper Ulro" (9.34), when "the shades of Death & Ulro" (14.12) appear in Milton's visage, or when Milton's wives and daughters must remain in the "dark Ulro till the Judgement" (17.5). Its destructive qualities appear when Blake thinks of it as a nether region of Beulah (21.6-7; 22.46; 27.45; 37.16). It is a result of the delusive Tirzah at the end of Book I: "The Three Heavens of Ulro, where Tirzah & her Sister / Weave the black Woof of Death" (29.55-56). Here the three heavens, usually associated with Beulah in the poem, are associated with Ulro and given over to Tirzah's perverting influence. Tirzah's weaving carries the meaning of materialization, and death here represents the delusion that the physical world has independent reality. Thus Ulro in **Milton** becomes a symbol for the same delusion of materialism as that attacked by Berkeley.

The connection between the senses as agents of delusion and Ulro as a state of delusion is suggested when Satan grows "Opake against the Divine Vision" (9.31) and falls into "a World of deeper Ulro" (9.34), opacity being later referred to as a possible condition for the eye (28.34) and ear (29.35-37). It is Hartley, following Newton, who calls the nerve fibers of the brain pellucid, because "Opacity of any Body . . . [is] an argument that its Pores are so large and irregular, as to disturb and interupt the vibration of the Aether."[34] Blake has ironically substituted opacity for the pellucid quality of the nerves assigned to them by Hartley. Associated with Satan, opacity stands for the limited Lockean view of reality that grows in thought divided from vision.[35] This deceptive potentiality of the senses is suggested in the symbol the *False Tongue* (2.10), which appears in: "Ulro, Seat of Satan, / Which is the False Tongue beneath Beulah: it is the Sense of Touch" (27.45-46). The false tongue symbolizes the sense that *may* delude one into believing that what it detects is alone real. The delusive false tongue is also the part of materialism which has changed the belief in Christ's mercy to a belief in retribution.

> Tell also of the False Tongue! vegetated
> Beneath your land of shadows: of its sacrifices. and
> Its offerings; even till Jesus, the image of the Invisible
> God
> Because its prey; a curse, an offering. and an atonement,
> For Death Eternal in the heavens of Albion, & before
> the Gates
> Of Jerusalem his Emanation, in the heavens beneath
> Beulah.

> (2.10-15)

Thus Ulro, along with its associated symbols, is the spatial equivalent of the particular delusion of the selfhood that the material universe has independent reality, a delusion that leads eventually to a belief in retribution. It is the work of the rational philosophy of Bacon, Newton, and Locke.

IV. Space as Mental Form

There are several other spatial relationships in *Milton,* but these do not fit neatly into the structure of Eternity-Beulah-Ulro. However, as psychological states of mind they make abundant sense. Blake had Swedenborg as an example in using spatial relationships to symbolize mental states. Swedenborg insisted that space belongs only to the natural world and that heaven is indeterminate and unmeasurable. For Swedenborg it is a gross absurdity to apply the idea of space to heavenly things.[36] The progression through space in the spiritual world represents a change of the mental interior: "Motions, progressions, and changes of place, in the other [spiritual] life are changes of the state of the interior of life [i.e., the states of psychic being] and nevertheless it re-

ally appears to spirits and angels as if they actually existed."[37] This is also Blake's meaning in his spatial concepts. They are spiritual relationships, and the indeterminate and unmeasurable spatial relations between these symbolic states is of no consequence in determining their meaning.[38]

The diagram of the cosmic world on plate thirty-three of *Milton,* though not containing all of Blake's spatial symbols (e.g., Beulah), is itself a picture of the various psychic elements. The flames surrounding the four globes are the flames of eternity. As such they represent creativity and selflessness. The globes of the fallen Urizen, Urthona, Tharmas, and Luvah constitute chaos (34.32). Chaos traditionally holds the primal matter of all creation, but in Blake's view these globes are the dire ruin that constitute a spatial world (34.39). Traditionally, chaos exists before creation. But for Blake, these globes are ruins after a fall. Thus Blake's chaos is really a fallen mental perception resulting from the delusion of the independent existence of matter. Since the independent existence of primal matter is not an acceptable idea for Blake, that matter is not only a chaos, but a ruin, without form or order. Psychologically, Blake is denying that our sensations of a natural world have the power to shape thought. Within the chaos, however, is the mundane shell or, as Blake calls it here, the "Egg form'd World of Los" (34.33). It is proper here to imagine chaos as the external world and the mundane shell as part of the internal mind of man. The mundane shell is a twenty-sevenfold creation, but it is an interior, not exterior creation. It is a "Concave Earth" (17.21), a "shadow of all things upon our Vegetative Earth / Englarg'd into dimension & deform'd into indefinite space" (17.22-23). The mundane shell is the world of memory within the vegetated man.[39] When projected into space, that is, when it is assumed to have independent existence, it is deformed. Then it is seen as the outer sphere of a limited spatial world, much like the eighth sphere in the Ptolemaic universe, which contains the fixed stars (37.47-55). As a shadow it is human memory. The "shadow" is described in the culmination of the poem when Blake describes the twenty-seven churches associated with "Milton's Shadow" (37.44). Conceived solely as objective events in historical sequence, these churches are delusion. Though they exist in the memory, they can become delusions when they are assumed to have had independent existence. They are delusory coverings of the true vision when so perverted, though they all have sprung from an impulse of the creative imagination.

In Blake's diagram the mundane shell encloses a strange design appearing as tongues of flame, but if viewed upside down, one can see the flames as tentaclelike projections. This is the polypus "of living fibres down . . . [in] the Sea of Time & Space" (34.25). This polypus, without the shaping function of Los, would constitute

the fallen world. It would be a "Fibrous Vegetation / A Polypus of soft affections without Thought or Vision" (24.37-38). In essence it would represent sensation without thought. It may appear to be the flame of thought, but it is only an inverted delusion. The polypus is said to be the abode of the five females (here representing the five senses) whose amorous songs lure souls into the flesh (34.27-30). As a symbol of affection, pleasure, or appetite, the polypus is a place of sensation. It seems perplexing at first that the "Heads of the Great Polypus" are also "Cities of the Levites" (38.1-3), but when one recollects that the Levites are the priestly caste of the Hebrews and that sensation, empirical philosophy, natural religion, deism, and druidism were also associated with the "churches" as attempts to deny spirituality, then one begins to accept Blake's unusual double meaning for polypus. It represents the sensory apparatus on the individual level and the delusory apparatus on the cosmic level of meaning. That Blake equates it with Ulro (34.24) makes its delusory nature clear.

Blake's design shows the names of Satan and Adam within the mundane shell, signifying that the mundane shell contains the stated limits of the fall: opacity and contraction. Man can go no farther from eternity, and at this limit Los begins his creative work that leads to a return to eternity. Sensation and memory are in the mundane shell, but the truly saving process is imaginative creativity: to create, or to give form, is the function of Los.

V. LOS'S WORLD

From the time of the fall of Urizen to the present of Milton's descent, form-giving is Los's central function, but form-giving has a large scope of meaning. It is the entire process of birth, growth, and fruition. In terms of Blake's myth of the fall, form-giving is an attempt to give a solid form to that which would endlessly disorganize in its fall from eternity. That form, moreover, is the step back toward eternity. In that form what has fallen is, like a seed, being dropped into the world for growth into spiritual existence. The world of growth is a world of process carried on by Los's sons. The words of St. Paul (used by Blake in **"To Tirzah"** in *Songs of Experience*) "it is raised a spiritual body," derive from St. Paul's implied comparison between soul and seed. This is the function of Los: to give the form that the spiritual seed will take in the process of moving toward the great harvest, the last vintage, or spiritual vegetation of the soul. The whole process should also be taken as a symbol of mental activity. The work of Los is to give images to ideas, to create forms of thought. Here Blake is giving the imagination a central place in his psychological picture of man. Sensation is a dangerous polypus. Memory can be a construct of delusion. But imagination is the magnificent work of Los.[40]

Unfortunately, the form-giving of Los becomes an elaborate allegory that drifts back and forth across the basic ground of the psychological analogue between space and mind as it develops its theme: "every Natural Effect has a Spiritual Cause, and Not / A Natural" (26.44-45). Blake's world of Los becomes a fanciful extension of the thesis that Los is the spiritual cause of all natural effects. This mythic explanation of natural phenomena accounts for events in ways other than scientific, and its details are so elaborated as to render the picture paradoxical at times. Blake, however, in elaborating the thesis in such detail is only extending an idea that has occurred before in the eighteenth century. Swedenborg's spiritual world constitutes the groundwork for Blake's thesis, but Blake proceeds exhaustively to give substance to such suggestions as those of Robert Clayton: "All Nature, therefore, seems to be animated, or alive; and this whole World to be replete with Spirits formed with different Kinds and Degrees of abilities, according to the various Ends and Uses, for which they were designed by their Creator"[41]; or the more elaborate ideas of Abraham Tucker, whose *mundane soul* is in part the spiritual cause of natural events. For Tucker the mundane soul is the spatial repository for spirits after they have left their vehicular state. Like an ocean, it is everywhere. Spirits exist in this ocean as individuals, yet there is a telecommunication between them that makes awareness universal. Moreover, each spirit has its own function, in which it finds great satisfaction, as an effective cause in the material world.[42] Blake's ornate, mythical world of Los is similar in that the individual spirits associated with Los are seen as the spiritual causes of natural events.

The complications of the thesis of spiritual causation appear generally in such oblique and unclear statements as this: that the four arts—poetry, painting, music, and architecture, which is science—in eternity are the four faces of man; but in time and space only science exists, and its function is to make manifest the other three arts (27.55-62). Blake's statement here, unpoetic and jumbled beyond complete explication, rests on the thesis that eternity (spirituality) is manifested in time and space (nature). Yet Blake's successful elaborations of spiritual causation over-balance his failures. The thesis lies behind the grand comparison of the black storm and the face of Los:

> Like the black storm, coming out of Chaos, beyond
> the stars:
> It issues thro the dark & intricate caves of the Mundane Shell
> Passing the planetary visions, & the well adorned Firmament
> The Sun rolls into Chaos & the stars into the Desarts;
> And then the storms become visible, audible & terrible,
> Covering the light of day, & rolling down upon the
> mountains,

Deluge all the country round. Such is a vision of Los;
When Rintrah & Palamabron spoke; and such his
 stormy face
Appeared, as does the face of heaven, when covered
 with thick storms
Pitying and loving tho in frowns of terrible perturba-
 tion.

(23.21-30)

The natural world of storm, stars, sun, light, mountains, and country are the sensational phenomena corresponding to the spiritual event of Los's frown, and in this brilliant passage the phenomenal and spiritual are so interconnected that the thesis is exemplified as well as stated. The same thesis lies behind the two magnificent pictures of nature in the lamentations of Beulah. The nightingale, lark, and choir of birds; the thyme and all the spring flowers are visions of the lamentation of Beulah insofar as the spiritual event can be seen as a sensational phenomenon (31.28-64). The constellations in their grand course through the sky, the calm ocean, the gorgeously clothed fly, and the wind-swept trees on mountains are visions of eternity if seen with the imagination (25.66-26.10). "But we see only as it were the hem of their garments / When with our vegetative eyes we view these wond'rous Visions" (26.11-12).[43] The spiritual cause can be seen only after we realize that our imprisoning sensation perceives only a mere portion, and that portion a small one, of the totality of existence, which is mainly spiritual and always spiritually caused.

Time and space are spiritually caused. The sons of Los build up time: like a castle expanding from the couch of sleep to the towers and outworks, time is expanded by building blocks of moments into ages.[44] Space, like the moment of time, is built from the smallest structure, the globule of blood. The world we inhabit is thus a series of visionary creations of the sons of Los. But the senses themselves without imagination cannot report the essential spirituality of that vision. They give only a partial report. The notions of material science, based on the extension of the senses by the telescope and microscope,[45] cannot give that vision, and it is therefore a delusion to think that the limited capability of mere sensation can give an all-inclusive view even of the spatial world (29.15-18).

Blake's elaboration of spiritual causation also illustrates creativity's function as guardian against the destructive urges. The sons of Los are spiritual causes, both good and bad. After Los's separation from Enitharmon, he begot a series of sons, all of whom work on the building of Golgonooza (3.39-42). Orc, Palamabron, Rintrah, Antamon, and Ozoth are workers helping Los to give form to chaos. Yet Los's fallen sons and daughters, Satan, Tirzah, Rahab, and others, are trying to destroy

Los's forms. In this struggle Los and his unfallen sons act the role of guardians, and their role is associated with the role of the prophet. As the prophet in the Old Testament is the guardian of the truth of Israel against the evil practice of the Israelites, so Los is the guardian against evil. Furthermore, his function of guardian is associated with the guardianship of the seven eyes of God.[46] The seven eyes (Lucifer, Molech, Elohim, Shaddai, Pahad, Jehovah, and Jesus; Milton himself is the eighth) are sequentially sent to guard the world of time and space, presumably from destruction (13.12-25). Blake does not clearly explain why they become fallen, but their connection to Los makes it clear that their mission is to guard against destruction. The seven eyes are connected to Los in their common source, Revelation. When Blake says that Los is the "Fourth Zoa, that stood around the Throne Divine" (24.76), he is referring to the vision of the throne of God in Revelations 4, where the divine throne is surrounded by twenty-four elders, and "four beasts" (Rev. 4:6), or *zoa* in Greek. The fourth beast, an eagle, which in Swedenborgian correspondence represents prophecy, is an appropriate symbol for Los, the "Spirit of Prophecy" (24.71). But in Revelation the throne divine is also fronted by the "seven Spirits of God" (4:5), who are seen in chapter 5 of Revelation as the seven eyes of the Lamb of God. These are Blake's "Seven Eyes of God [who] continually / Guard round . . . the Generations of Tirzah / Because of Satan" (24.6-7). They share the duty of Los who, as the "Fourth Zoa . . . [is] also set / The Watchman of Eternity" (24.8-9). Though fallen, as the seven eyes are fallen, Los prevents the destruction of any event of time and space (22.15-25) through his prophetic or imaginative function. "They vanish not from me & mine, we guard them first & last" (22.23). Los bends his force against the east to prevent destruction (26.18-20), and he gives safe conduct to "the Spirits to be vegetated" (29.47). As a prophet he walks "up and down" (22.18) in the six thousand years of time, preserving the eternal lineaments of all the generations of men (22.18-25). They are preserved in Los's halls, where the mercy of time as a preserver against chaotic destruction allows all Los's fallen sons, who are sons of the spirit of prophecy, to work against eternal destruction (24.68-76). Los, as time, is a guard against the eternally destructive urges, and is merciful in the same sense that Enitharmon's decision to give space to Satan is a kind decision (13.16). Psychologically, the guardian-prophet embodies the imaginative creativity that, through its insistence on giving form to the formless, keeps in check the selfhood's destructiveness, which is manifested externally in a class of men who are destroyers. Historically, Los's guardianship manifests itself as faith in the preservative power of vision and imagination against reason, science, and Lockean epistemology. Religiously, it causes a reliance on the in-

spired but personally interpreted word of the Bible, as opposed both to the rationalism of deism and to the dogma of orthodoxy.

Los's guardianship, however, has its dark side. One remembers that the seven eyes of God are in some degree fallen, and Los himself is a fallen zoa. His attempts to recreate Urizen have been only partially successful and his effort leaves him terrified and weeping. As a preserver from chaos he succeeds, but as a restorer to eternity he is doomed to failure. His work, the mundane shell, has this double aspect. It is a form that preserves from chaos, but it is also a hardened shell that restricts. The eternal vision is given shape in the material world to prevent the chaotic dissolution of man, but the manifested vision becomes "frozen to unexpansive deadly destroying terror" (35.1). In the world of time and space, the perfection of eternity does not exist and the material product of creativity inevitably will be imperfect. Los's fallibility is part of the reason for Palamabron's and Rintrah's distrust (22.27-28). Los himself, after Satan slays Thullough, alters his world with rage (9.12-18). He also mistakenly resists Milton's journey at first (17.35-36).

The larger meaning of this potential fallibility of the creative side of the mind suggests a discrimination to be made between intention and achievement. Creativity is thought of as producing something new. But there is always an analogue in the past for every new venture; nothing comes to flower without its roots. Newness is only the slightly different manifestation of an eternal archetype, a manifestation that can never equal the archetype in perfection. Yet, though inevitably incomplete and imperfect in achievement, creativity's imperfection does not hurt its saving power; in fact, it can be viewed as a cause of that power. Because of its imperfection in achievement, creativity can never cease. After all, eternity, for Blake, is a life of ceaseless creativity. Perfect creation is never promised, and the dark aspects of Los are warning that the products of creativity are not its final goal.

Moreover, and perhaps paradoxically, the past cannot become a conscious determinant in man's creativity. To permit such would be to exchange creativity for imitation. Imitation of nature is the preservation of chaos. One must give form not to the material world, but to the eternal vision that resides in the imagination. The product will be flawed because form-giving in the material world cannot be perfect. But unless the imagination's visions are given form, the world remains a chaos. Here the psychological implications are clear. The fall into chaos, the necessity of form to stop the fall, and the necessity of a process to return what is fallen to eternity are most appropriate as symbolic treatment for an idea in consciousness. If the idea is not given form, it will fall away from consciousness and be lost, never

to be in the eternity of another's mind. The idea, like the spirit and like the seed, must be given form to ensure the "glorious spiritual / Vegetation" (25.60-61).

Blake uses varying symbols for the processes of spiritual embodiment. The process of Los's form-giving is described in the symbols of building and producing: "The Passions & Desires descend upon the hungry winds . . . / The Sons of Los clothe them & feed & provide houses & fields" (26.28-30). The passions and desires, the souls, the spirits, are unembodied creatures seeking forms provided by the sons of Los. At times Blake refers to the souls as spectres choosing their forms (26.38; 28.10-43), but he reverts to calling them "Spirits to be Vegetated" (29.47).[47] The use of spectre here merely as a synonym for spirit is not entirely inconsistent with the spectre's meaning as rational power (40.34). The spectre is the rational power of man seeking form just as desires and passions seek form. These mental functions are being vegetated just as spirits are, and the shape they take, human form or otherwise, is a matter of choice. The sleeper is another symbol for the spirit to be vegetated (26.29). This symbol is derived from the part of Blake's myth that sees the spirit as a sleeper of Beulah falling away from eternal vision. The sleeper then must have a form so that he can begin the process of return. Still another symbol for the process is that of the gateway. The souls descend and ascend to and from the body by a north and south gate (26.12-17). Though not consistent in itself (at first all souls descend through both gates; later they are said to ascend through the north gate) the conception is based on the myth of the gates from Porphyry's *Concerning the Cave of the Nymphs*. In Porphyry the northern gate is "the gate through which souls descend,"[48] while the southern gates "are . . . avenues . . . of souls ascending to the Gods."[49] Blake seems to have reversed the two gate's directions, but the essential meaning remains. The gates are the entrance ways of the spirits to be vegetated. The process of being vegetated may, however, suggest limitation. Although the spirit is said to be given inner form, like a garden (26.31-32), (i.e., given an inner spiritual shape), or given sexual texture (4.4) (i.e., put into the body as either male or female), it is really enclosed in the five senses (5.19-26) (i.e., limited from eternal vision). Blake's strangest symbolic formulation of the embodiment process is in the use of the term *vehicle*. Twice Blake uses Abraham Tucker's strange conception of the vehicular state. Tucker had fantasized about the vehicular body as a very tiny, elastic, material husk that contains the spiritual essence. The vehicle, as he called it, can travel from one state, or life, to another after death. It travels through several existences before it dissolves, permitting the soul to rejoin the sea of spirit. It implants on the soul the character derived from its past experience. Picking up Tucker's notion, Blake uses it to suggest the transformation of identity. In ***Milton***, Lazarus is the "Vehicular Body of Albion the

Redeem'd" (24.27), and Los is a "Vehicular Terror" (17.31). Los is the vehicular, or present state of the transformed Urthona, even as Lazarus is a state of the transformed Albion. In all of these symbols, Blake is depicting the spiritual essence receiving material form so that essence, or soul, may avoid chaos and return to eternity.

The process of creation Los has performed in part, but part has been performed by his sons. As a direct agent Los has given form to the fallen Urizen (3.6-27) and still creates the sun each morning (29.41), but the processes of creativity are spread among a minutely articulated hierarchy of spirits. Los is father and ruler of these spirits. Some are in opposition to him, such as Satan. Some have fallen into vegetation in past time and are no longer part of Los's processes: "Twelve Sons successive fled away in that thousand years of sorrow" (23.62). Among Los's remaining sons are Rintrah, Palamabron, Sotha, Theotormon, Orc, Bromion, Ozoth, and Antamon, who are each manifested in Los's processes in different ways. Rintrah and Palamabron, scantly depicted as governors "over Day & Night" (29.27), are also the operators of the plow and harrow in the symbol of spiritual growth and vegetation (4.1-2). Sotha and Theotormon have direct involvement in giving material form to the spirit,[50] when they induce the unwilling spirits, or spectres, to choose a material form.[51] Like Rintrah and Palamabron, they are agents effecting a transformation (28.21-28).

Orc, however, insofar as he constitutes the nervous system of each human, is not so much an efficient as a material cause of the embodiment in form. As the means of sensation in material form, he is associated with the polypus. His identity is also slightly confused when he is said to be a manifestation of Satan, who is a manifestation of Urizen, and simultaneously to be a manifestation of Luvah. But this confused set of identifications is merely an attempt to suggest that the vision of man (Luvah as an eternal) usurped by his reason (Satan) degenerates to become mere sensation (Orc) (29.28-39). Orc is imprisoned in the nerves, which are falsely assumed to be the only connecting links between the senses and the seat of awareness: "Orc incessant howls burning in fires of Eternal Youth" (29.29); Orc's freedom symbolizes the removal of the delusion that passive sensation constitutes awareness. Orc is also the pleasure principle. The fire of eternal youth is the pleasurable sensation of the nerves, which is good in itself, but deadly when considered the only pleasure. The danger of being imprisoned in the materialistic delusion is expressed in the vague statement that "sleep [i.e., being born into this world] was transformed / To Death" (29.32-3) in the "optic vegetative Nerve" (29.32) and in the equally vague statement about the "Nerves of the Nostrils" and opacity (29.35-39). The sons of Ozoth work within the eye, in a still different fashion. They do not create the eye, which is a material manifestation of Orc, but they create the vision of the eye. They give various delights in two ways. To those who possess artificial riches (i.e., the wealthy) they give scorn, hardening the optic nerve and thereby shutting out natural beauty, so that the eye becomes "opake" like a black pebble. But to the poor they give internal vision, which allows them to see internally even as a diamond is clear within. This internal vision enables them to behold eternity (28.37-38).

The symbolism associated with Orc and Ozoth is not always perspicuous, but in Blake's best depictions of Los's spiritual agents, he makes the agent take on several layers of meaning. Antamon exemplifies this success:

> And sometimes two Spectres like lamps quivering
> And often malignant they combat (heart-breaking sorrowful & piteous)
> Antamon takes them into his beautiful flexible hands,
> As the Sower takes the seed, or as the Artist his clay
> Or fine wax, to mould artful a model for golden ornaments.
> The soft hands of Antamon draw the indelible line;
> Form immortal with golden pen; such as the Spectre admiring
> Puts on the sweet form; then smiles Antamon bright thro his windows
> The Daughters of beauty look up from their Loom & prepare.
> The integument soft for its clothing with joy & delight.
>
> (28.11-20)

Here Antamon is the spiritual agent as a painter, a sculptor, and a sower. His skill is such that the beautiful form he creates entices the spectre or spirit to take the form. On another level he is a true sower of seeds, for like a phallus producing semen, he permits the spirit to take embodiment in the human seed. The looms of the daughters of beauty, which are wombs, provide the bodily integument that is a clothing or garment of the spirit. Thus the artistic creative process and the biological procreative process are manifestations of the same spiritual cause. Blake derived this concept from the interpretation of generation found in Porphyry's *Concerning the Cave of the Nymphs.*[52] In Porphyry's view the humid soul is "insnared by corporeal love"[53] and descends "into generation and the tenacious vestment of the body,"[54] where the nymphs weave on the bodily bones the purple garment of flesh. Like Porphyry's nymphs, Blake's daughters of beauty weave the body for the enticed soul, but Blake has changed the emphasis of Porphyry by making the beauty of the form rather than corporeal love the enticement, and by adding Antamon as the spiritual and artistic agent. Blake has kept the paradigm of Porphyry's myth, but used it in his own meaning, making the process a universal creative process on both biological and artistic levels.

The work of creation is notably the work of both male and female. Enitharmon, like Los's sons, has her place. She is the creator of space and of the body. The space created for Satan is an act of mercy (13.12-13), and Enitharmon herself, like Orc, constitutes space: "By mortals . . . Enitharmon is nam'd Space" (24.68). As such she is the emanated ground for the creative activity to work. With her daughters, she constitutes the female procreativity that gives flesh to bare form (29.51-53).

The instruments used for the processes described in the world of Los are interconnected. Los's forge, with its associated chains, anvil, furnace, hammer, bellows, and iron ladles, has a double function: to furnish the instruments necessary for the harvest (6.8-13) and to give shape to the spectres (26.38). The harvest is the spiritual harvest that is being grown from the labors of Rintrah and Palamabron, whose plow and harrow are its preparatory forerunners. Los's winepress is associated with his harvest as well as Satan's mills. Satan's mills are the places where the husks of the harvest are ground away. Thus, Satan, the destroyer, yet has a function in the process of spiritual growth, though he does not comprehend it. The forge-harvest series of metaphors represents the process of spiritual birth and maturation. The same kind of meaning exists in the picture of Enitharmon's looms, which are called the looms of Cathedron. From the material point of view, Cathedron's looms are the womb where the garment of flesh is woven. From a spiritual point of view, the loom of Cathedron is a couch where the sleeper reposes until his awakening ($\kappa\alpha\theta\epsilon\delta\rho o\nu$ means throne and can be a place of idle sitting or reclining, i.e., a couch). Thus the death couch of eternity is a loom where spirits are woven flesh for the world of time and space. However, the weaving symbol, along with the mills of Satan, and the concept of space, is also a potential source of evil wherein the selfhood works. In fact, the garment woven on the looms is a hood or covering that must eventually be put off. The body must die; the selfhood must be put off.

Just as the symbolic instruments function in the process of spiritual birth and maturation, so do the locations of Los's world, but because of the multiplicity of meaning Blake puts on some locations, they sometimes seem rather obscure symbols. The world of Los is distinct from either eternity, the Ulro vision, or Beulah; for as Blake makes Milton's identity divide, he shows Milton's redeemed portion traveling in the mundane shell, which is the egg-formed world of Los; while Milton's eternal human portion resides in eternity, his elect portion becomes the rock Sinai as part of the Ulro delusion, and his shadow portion remains visible to Blake. Los's mundane shell holds the various locations of Los's world, such as Bowlahoola, Allamanda, Udan Adan, and Entuthon Benython. Bowlahoola on one level is the place where the soul enters the material form, choosing the form it desires.[55] Los's forge is in Bowlahoola (24.51). Allamanda is the cultivated land, the place where souls are matured appropriately.[56] Away from these are the lake of Udan Adan,[57] which is a destructive area belonging to Satan's camp ($\alpha\delta\upsilon\nu\alpha\tau\epsilon\iota\nu$ means to be unable), Satan's mills, and Entuthon Benython ($\epsilon\nu\tau\upsilon\theta\epsilon\nu$ means thenceforth, $\beta\epsilon\nu\theta o\varsigma$ means the depths of the sea),[58] which suggests the nonentity of matter.[59] From Blake's spiritual viewpoint, matter is the nonentity that must be given a unique name. The locations of these places in relation to Eternity, Beulah, and Ulro are not detailed, but it is necessary only to see them as places associated with Los and his functions to see that as places they are symbols for spiritual ideas that take shape in many forms. Bowlahoola is also law and the human stomach (24.48, 67). As spiritual idea, it is the principle of form manifested in human relationships as law and in the human digestive system as stomach. Allamanda is the principle of cultivation that in human relationships is commerce (27.42), in human economy the growing wheat field. Golgonooza is the principle of conception in the human body as the skull, in human history as a new Golgotha where a birth of the new conception of self-annihilation will occur.[60]

Perhaps Blake's symbolic universe would not be too confusing if all these place-symbols remained in this unfamiliar context. But Blake also attempts to relate the symbolic places with the familiar surroundings of England and the Holy Land of the Bible. This represents Blake's attempt to integrate the spiritual and cosmic world with the phenomenal existence of common experience. The implication is that great action of cosmic significance can and does occur in the homely places of everyday life. Moreover, the place names of England become parallels to places in the Holy Land. Tyburn is Calvary, Lambeth is Jerusalem. The banks of Cam are Rephaim's vale. Yet not all the places are equivalent. However, Carmel, Ephraim, the deserts of Midian, and the other biblical places, take on a familiar atmosphere because of the general admixture. The first effect is a shock to our normal sense of time and place, but the ultimate effect is a recognition that spiritual action is repeated at different temporal intervals with the same import, the same problem, the same goal. The sacrifice of Calvary, with its implications of oppression from worldly men, is now the sacrifice at Tyburn.

The English place names are involved in further complexities through Blake's tendency to see analogy between geographic entities and the human body. Thus the material form of the British Isles is seen as the giant Albion, asleep. Parts of his body are locations in the British Isles, Tyburn, for instance, being the resting place of his left foot. The myth of Albion's fall is seen as the formation of the material form of the British Isles. The myth of the sleep of Albion and his awaken-

ing represents the awakening of the people of England from that sleep. Thus the analogy of body to geography tends to lose its distinct boundary and Albion becomes a symbol for the spiritual condition of the people of England. But the rockiness and hardness of the material entity is indeed an appropriate symbol for what Blake saw as the spiritual condition of his fellow men.

These, then, are the main elements of Blake's mythic world. The spiritual and psychological condition—Eternity, Beulah, and Ulro; Los and Enitharmon and their progeny; and the complex mixture of various places in biblical and English geography and times—are all indicative of the anti-materialistic, essentially spiritual and imaginative belief that drove Blake to mental warfare against those he considered agents of the selfhood. Los's creation of form can be seen as the creation of form for fallen spirits. But this myth is also a way of saying that the imagination gives shape to perception.[61] The world of Los symbolizes mental process.[62] Embodiment represents a putting off of the less definite and becoming more definite. This is the process of evolving thought.

Notes

1. Voltaire, Blake's target for other reasons, had extolled men of reason, who penetrate the hidden secrets of nature and the universe, far above the warrior or the divine. He singles out for praise "the Bacons, the Lockes, and the Newtons," *Essay on Chancellor Bacon* in *The Works of Voltaire,* trans. W. F. Fleming, 22 vols. (New York: Dumont, 1901), 19: 27. Frye recognizes the connection in the similarity of Locke's substratum of nature, the atomism of Democritus and Epicurus as found in Bacon, and Newton's corpuscular theory of light ([Northrop Frye,] *Fearful Symmetry* [(1947)], p. 17). Asloob Ansari, *Arrows of Intellect* (Aligarh, India: Noya Kilabghar, 1965) devotes a chapter to the "infernal trinity," pp. 1-34.

2. Francis Bacon, *Novum Organon,* (trans. unknown), ed. Joseph Devey (New York: P. F. Collier, 1902), p. 29.

3. Ibid., p. 30.

4. Israel Levine, *Francis Bacon* (London: Parsons, 1925), p. 121.

5. Isaac Newton, *The Mathematical Principles of Natural Philosophy,* trans. Andrew Motte, 2 vols. (London, 1729; rpt. London: Dawson, 1968), 2: 202-5.

6. *Essay Concerning Human Understanding,* 2: 8.17. In *The Works of John Locke,* 10 vols. (London: Otridge, 1812).

7. David Hartley, *Observations on Man,* 2 vols. (London, 1749: Gainesville, Fla: Scholars' Facs. rpt. 1966), 1: 58-64.

8. Joseph Priestley, *The Theological and Miscellaneous Works of Joseph Priestley,* ed. J. T. Rutt, 25 vols. (London: Hackney, 1817-32), 3: 181-82.

9. (London, 1751), pp. 12-25 and throughout.

10. *The Light of Nature Pursued,* 7 vols. (London, 1768-1778; rev. London: Foulder, 1805), 3: 384-400.

11. *Selected Writings* [*Thomas Taylor the Platonist: Selected Writings.* Edited by Kathleen Raine and G. M. Harper. (New York: Bollingen, 1969)], p. 138.

12. Ibid., p. 159.

13. Ibid., p. 147.

14. *Principles of Human Knowledge,* Part I, par. 9, in *Works* [*Works of George Berkeley, Bishop of Cloyne.* Edited by A. A. Luce and T. E. Jessop. 9 vols. (London: T. Nelson, 1948-1957)], II.

15. Ibid., par. 23.

16. Ibid., par. 3.

17. Ibid., par. 7.

18. Ibid., par. 26.

19. *Three Dialogues, Works,* 2: 246.

20. Ibid., pp. 212-13.

21. Ibid., p. 216.

22. In considering Blake's conception of matter we can find two distinct ideas which, superficially similar, logically lead to different conclusions affecting the meaning of parts of *Milton.* The conceptions are (1) that material existence is purely delusion, and (2) that material existence separate from mind does not exist. From the first, followed by Hazard Adams, (*Blake and Yeats: the Contrary Vision* [(Ithaca, N.Y.: Cornell University Press, 1955; rpt. New York, 1968)]; see, e.g., pp. 25, 30, 33, 37), it follows that all things exist only in man's mind. Past time and memory are not the result of passing experience, but an illusion contained in the mind alone. In the second proposition, real experience, memory, and physical objects such as flowers, constellations, etc. are real insofar as they can exist without the thought of an individual. According to Berkeley, who follows this second proposition, these things exist in the archetypal perception of God. Blake, it seems to me, is much closer to the second proposition. The difference between Blake and Berkeley, however, is that in Blake the perception of the individual mind is not constrained by the archetypal world, which in fact is highly modified by the shaping imagination of the perceiver. But the thing

perceived has an archetypal existence, not an existence independent of mind. [Kathleen] Raine, *Blake and Tradition* [2 vols. (New York: Bollingen, 1968)], 2: 102, 119, and 145 (incorrectly), and Frye, *Fearful Symmetry*, p. 14, have suggested Blake's "debt" to Berkeley. T. W. Herzing correctly claims, without giving any treatment of eighteenth-century philosophy, that Blake only rejects the "Urizenic assumption that materiality is everything," in "Book I of Blake's *Milton*: Natural Religion as an Optical Fallacy," *Blake Studies* 6 (Fall 1973): 29.

23. Raine finds *Milton* Blake's best expression of the ideas of "space and time and all appearances as creation of mind" (2: 142). See T. W. Herzing for a similar view, p. 32.

24. In Leutha's words: "Till two Eternities meet together" ([*The Poetry and Prose of William Blake*] 13.11). Boehme sees diversity as unity manifested temporally as two opposites; "it goes from Eternity to Eternity into Two Essences." These two eternities are evil and good, the two making an eternal enmity. Only when the individual turns from the evil to the good can he return to God (Signature of All Things, XVI. 20), *The Works of Jacob Behmen*, 4 vols. [London, 1763-81], 4: 135.

25. Cf. Emanuel Swedenborg, *Earths in the Universe*, par. 126, in *Miscellaneous Theological Works* (New York, 1928). All references to Swedenborg, except where noted, are to the standard editions of the Swedenborg Foundation. References are made to Swedenborg's works always by paragraph number.

26. In *Three Dialogues* Berkeley conceives of the creation in a way that Blake might accept. Since God has eternally perceived all things, then creation seems to have had no beginning. Berkeley answers this point by suggesting that "things, with regard to us, may properly be said to begin their existence, or be created, when God decreed they should become perceptible to intelligent creatures." *Works*, 2: 253.

27. Cf. Boehme: "the Self-Will of Man rent itself off from the Will of the Word; . . . and was thereupon weak and blind as to God, and fell down into sleep, and laid between God and the kingdom of the World" (Mysterium Magnum, LXXVI. 14), *Works*, 3: 487-88.

28. Cf. Raine, 2: 78, who finds this source of opacity and contraction in Fludd's *Mosaicall Philosophy*.

29. For an extended discussion of Blake's use of the term *limit* as borrowed from Boehme, see Raine, 1: 404.

30. It is notable that, in Renaissance studies of the art of perspective in drawing, the trick of depicting spatial relationships depended on the postulation of a horizon, which is a line drawn across the picture. This line is labeled variously *orizon* or *ourizen*; see e.g., Erwin Panofsky, *The Codex Huygins and Leonardo DaVinci's Art Theory* (London: Warburg Institute, 1940), plates 49, 50, 51, 54. It is the basis for the illusion of the spatial, three-dimensional world. It also limits the possibility of the picture to a single view of reality. Only one spatial world fits the picture. This suggests that Urizen, perhaps derived from orizon, is a limiter who causes the delusion of the spatial world. It is single vision, Newton's sleep.

31. Cf. Susan Fox, ["The Structure of a Moment: Parallelism in the Two Books of Blake's *Milton*," *Blake Studies* 2 (Fall 1969): 21-35,] p. 34, who points out the change of this scheme from its form in the *Four Zoas*.

32. R. L. Grimes ("Time and Space in Blake's Major Prophecies," *BSA* [*Blake's Sublime Allegory*. Edited by Stuart Curran and Joseph Anthony Wittreich. (Madison: University of Wisconsin Press, 1973)], p. 64) expresses this notion clearly when he writes that Blake's concern is "not creation but creativity."

33. Boehme writes of God's creation: "The Creation is the same sport out of himself" (Signature, XVI. 2), *Works*, 4, which recalls the "Divine Vision / and . . . the sports of Wisdom in the Human Imagination" of *Milton* (3.3-4). J. J. McGann, without reference to Boehme, suggests the same thing in "The Aim of Blake's Prophecies and the Uses of Blake Criticism" *BSA*, p. 14.

34. [David Hartley,] *Observations* [*Observations on Man*], 1: 18.

35. Cf. Frye, *Fearful Symmetry*, p. 349.

36. [*A Treatise Concerning*] *Heaven and Hell*, par. 94-95.

37. *Earths In the Universe*, par. 125n [See note 25].

38. Cf. Raine, 2: 145-46.

39. Cf. Frye, *Fearful Symmetry*, p. 348. Rose equates the mundane shell with inner space, in "Los, Pilgrim of Eternity," *BSA*, p. 92.

40. Cf. Raine, 2: 202.

41. *Essay* [*Essay on Spirit* (London: J. Noon, 1751)], p. 12.

42. [*The Light*] *of Nature* [*Pursued*], 3: 384-97.

43. Cf. Boehme: "Thou must learn to distinguish well betwixt the Thing, and that which only is an image thereof. . . . But if thou have left the *imagi-*

nary Life, and quitted the low imaged condition of it; then art thou come into the super-imaginariness, . . . which is a State of living *above Images,* Figures, and Shadows" ("Of the Supersensual Life"), *Works,* 4: 75.

44. Raine finds sources for Blake's concept of the moment in Locke, Boehme, and Swedenborg. See 2: 144, 147, 154-55.

45. Berkeley mentions the telescope and microscope in *Three Dialogues, Works,* 2: 211, 245.

46. Cf. Frye, *Fearful Symmetry,* p. 343.

47. Cf. ibid., p. 18. Frye traces the spectre to Locke's "reflection." Also see Raine, 1: 25, 237. I feel that in *Milton,* as in the other epics, Blake refers to an aspect of identity as the spectre. Indeed, he equates the spectre with reason (see [S. Foster] Damon, *A Blake Dictionary,* [(Providence, R. I.: Brown University Press, 1965)] p. 380), but he is using the term to represent the visible form of man that is perceived by sensation. *Spectre* was the term used by the Epicurean school (mentioned in Thomas Reid, *Essays on the Intellectual Powers of Man* [Edinburgh, 1785; rpt. New York: Garland, 1971], p. 26) to represent images or semblances that emanate from corporeal things. Each object gives off continuous images, or spectres, of itself, through its fluxile atoms, which are received by the senses. In places in *Milton,* the word *spectre* seems to mean only *aspect.*

48. [Thomas Taylor,] *Selected Writings,* p. 309.

49. Ibid., pp. 310-11.

50. The numbers of Sotha and Theotormon, as well as the sons of Ozoth, indicate that they are an aggregation of spiritual causes having a vast field in which to work, but the precise numbers (7,007,700 and 8,000,008) seem unimportant as specific numbers.

51. Raine, 1: 253, points to a passage in McPherson's *Introduction to the History of Great Britain and Ireland* dealing with the crested cock of Odin who calls the heroes to war. It is interesting that the spectres in *Milton* are terrified by the cock and flee (28. 24-26).

52. Raine, 1: 242.

53. [Thomas Taylor,] *Selected Writings,* p. 304.

54. Ibid., p. 305.

55. Cf. Eve Teitelbaum, "Form as Meaning in Blake's *Milton,*" *Blake Studies* 2 (Fall 1969): 56.

56. Cf. ibid., pp. 55-56.

57. Raine (1: 250) sees Udan Adan as space-time.

58. Raine, 2: 296.

59. Entuthon Benython seems much like Berkeley's definition of matter: "nothing but the general abstract idea of entity" of "those miserable refuges, whether in an eternal succession of unthinking causes and effects, or in a fortuitous concourse of atoms . . . in a word, the whole system of materialism" (*Works,* 2: 213).

60. Cf. Adams, *Blake and Yeats,* p. 111.

61. Cf. [Florence] Sandler ["The Iconoclastic Enterprise: Blake's Critique of Milton's Religion," *Blake Studies* 5 (Fall 1972): 13-57], p. 21.

62. Cf. Adams, *Blake and Yeats,* pp. 5, 25.

John H. Sutherland (essay date June 1977)

SOURCE: Sutherland, John H. "Blake's *Milton*: The Bard's Song." *Colby Library Quarterly* 13, no. 2 (June 1977): 142-57.

[*In the following essay, Sutherland examines the complex interplay between* Milton*'s psychological, spiritual, and symbolic elements. Sutherland argues that although the poem functions on several levels of meaning, it primarily represents an expression of Blake's troubled personal life at the time of its composition.*]

There are at least three basic levels of meaning in ***Milton.*** One of these is the level of the archetypes, representing universal psychological forces, and acted by god-like figures in and out of "Eternity." Since these figures are presented as personified fragments of the psyche of the fallen giant Albion, this connects with a second level where historical and biographical allegory is important. On this level, archetypal figures are perceived as sometimes acting through, sometimes representing, individual historical persons, countries, and events. On a third level, these same archetypal figures may be seen as acting within the psyche of William Blake, and as being personifications of parts of his psyche. In the following paper I shall trace the interworking of these three levels through selected parts of the Bard's song. I shall give particular attention to the third level in an attempt to demonstrate its importance.

All three levels interact because the same forces which motivate individuals motivate nations. As David Erdman has pointed out, "From his earliest interest in kings as accusers of adultery, Blake looked upon psychology as a phase of politics and upon politics as an acting out of mental strife."[1] Sometimes a kind of magical correspondence seems to be asserted when, by writing about the interaction of archetypes, Blake refers simultaneously to the outworking of these forces in history, and in his own life.

I believe the focus of *Milton* is most directly and literally on events within Blake's own mind at a time of personal crisis. *Milton* is a very introverted work, but in no sense is it claustrophobic. Blake believed that his vision expanded when he looked within himself, using the eye of imagination. He believed that his "great task" (as he identified it in *Jerusalem*) was

> To open the Eternal Worlds, to open the immortal
> Eyes
> Of Man inwards into the Worlds of Thought: into Eter-
> nity
> Ever expanding in the Bosom of God, the Human
> Imagination[.][2]

Blake's fulfillment of this task—his descriptions of many inhabitants, and important parts of the geography, of the "Eternal Worlds"—is a major theme in *Milton,* and a connector between the various levels of meaning.

Blake seems to have believed that all men are interconnected through the imagination. Thus, at a crisis in the poem, Blake reports:

> But Milton entering into my Foot; I saw in the nether
> Regions of the Imagination; also all men on Earth,
> And all in Heaven, saw in the nether regions of the
> Imagination
> In Ulro beneath Beulah, the vast breach of Miltons
> descent.

> (*M* [*Milton*] 21:4-7, E [*The Poetry and Prose of William
> Blake,* edited by David V. Erdman] 114)

Blake also believed that the imagination is largely unconscious, accessible primarily in dream and in moments of inspiration; therefore he continues:

> But I knew not that it was Milton, for man cannot
> know
> What passes in his members till periods of Space and
> Time
> Reveal the secrets of Eternity. . . .

I imagine Blake writing and engraving *Milton* over a period of years, first at Felpham, then in his rooms on South Molton Street, trying to understand and put in order psychological experiences which had nearly overwhelmed him.

Milton may be summarized as a series of crises. The first major crisis is when Milton enters into Blake's foot, and, in the vegetative world of time and space this occurs while the Blakes are still in Lambeth. The next crisis, when Los binds on Blake's sandals and becomes "One Man" with him, also happens while Blake is "Standing in the Vale / Of Lambeth" (*M* 22:10-11; E 116). After this, as Blake tells us later in the poem,

> . . . when Los joind with me he took me in his firy
> whirlwind
> My Vegetated portion was hurried from Lambeths
> shades

> He set me down in Felphams Vale & prepared a beau-
> tiful
> Cottage for me that in three years I might write all
> these Visions[.]

> (*M* 36:21-24, E 136)

The final crisis, when Milton confronts Satan in sacrificial "Self-Annihilation" (*M* 38:34, E 138), and then is triumphantly reintegrated with his emanation, Ololon, intersects with this world in Blake's consciousness while Blake is in the garden of his cottage at Felpham.

(The reference to writing "all these visions" in his "three years" at Felpham seems to have been written after the event, and thus is itself evidence that Blake did not finish writing *Milton* while at the shore. Other passages, also, seem to have been written later. For example, the reference on Plate 4 to the place "Between South Molton Street and Stratford Place: Calvarys foot / Where the Victims were preparing for Sacrifice . . ." probably was suggested to him when he lived on South Molton Street, near the approaches to Tyburn Gallows.)[3]

The poem centers around an "old Prophecy in Eden" which is twice recalled by Los:

> That Milton of the Land of Albion should up ascend
> Forwards from Ulro from the Vale of Felpham; and
> set free
> Orc from his Chain of Jealousy. . . .

> (*M* 20:59-61, E 114)

Presumably this prophecy is fulfilled at the end of the poem, and at the end of the Blakes' stay at Felpham, when

> Immediately the Lark mounted with a loud trill from
> Felphams Vale
> And the Wild Thyme from Wimbletons green & im-
> purpled Hills
> And Los & Enitharmon rose over the Hills of Surrey
> Their clouds roll over London. . . .

> (*M* 42:29-32, E 142)

Presumably, also, William and Catherine Blake return at this time with Los and Enitharmon to London, where Blake will continue his prophetic tasks, his strength augmented by the spirit of the reintegrated Milton.

Most of the time sequence of the poem covers Blake's three years at Felpham; however, time sequences cannot be taken too seriously in a poem in which so much of the action is outside of time. For example, Milton is inspired by the song of a "Bard" to descend from Eternity into the Ulro, and, as it happens, into Blake, while Blake is still living in Lambeth. Yet, as we read the Bard's song, it seems apparent that many of the events indirectly referred to therein took place during Blake's residence at Felpham, probably a year or more after he had

left Lambeth. There are two possible resolutions to this apparent anachronism. First: although the duration of Milton's sojourn in Eternity is identified as "One hundred years" (*M* 2:17, E 95), while he was in Eternity he should have been free from the tyranny of time and space, and able to respond to a song which, from the point of view of time, had not yet been sung. Second (a less metaphysical suggestion): perhaps all the indirect references to temporal events in the Bard's song were not meant to be picked up. Perhaps the quarrel with Hayley, for example, may be more properly regarded as a private source of inspiration than as an obscure theme in a kind of satiric allegory.

In examining part of the Bard's song as examples of Blake's method, it should be noted that the Bard himself seems to represent Blake at his most inspired. At the end of the song, when some of the audience in Eternity question the song's truth, the Bard replies:

> . . . I am Inspired! I know it is Truth! for I sing
> According to the inspiration of the Poetic Genius
> Who is the eternal all-protecting Divine Humanity
> To whom be Glory & Power & Dominion Evermore
> Amen
>
> (*M* 13:51-14:3, E 107)

This affirmation is surely also Blake's, and tells us why he believed that he had won through to an understanding of some of "the secrets of Eternity."

If the Bard has something of Blake in him, so also does Los, the archetype of imagination and inspiration. In fact, as has already been noted, Blake becomes "One Man" with Los slightly later in the poem. In much of *The Four Zoas,* and in *Jerusalem,* Blake seems to identify with Los; however, in the Bard's song he seems to identify with Palamabron (who is, of course, one of the sons of Los).

Los has many sons and many daughters; "myriads" according to a passage in *The Four Zoas* (*FZ* [*The Four Zoas*] 115:10, E 365). In the Bard's song,

> First Orc was Born then the Shadowy Female: then all
> Los's Family
> At last Enitharmon brought forth Satan Refusing
> Form, in vain[.]
>
> (*M* 3:40-41, E 97)

Thus all the principal actors in the poem are sons or daughters of Los, and, insofar as Los represents Blake, may be considered (among other things) to be personifications of parts of Blake's makeup. As integration proceeds through the poem, some of them are explicitly gathered back into Blake, and into Los.

However, to claim that Los's family is quite so widespread may approach apocalyptic excess on Blake's part. Los identifies the four sons of whom he feels sure on Plate 24:

> Still my four mighty ones are left to me in Golgo-
> nooza
> Still Rintrah fierce, and Palamabron mild & piteous
> Theotormon filld with care, Bromion loving Science
> You O my sons still guard round Los. . . .
>
> (*M* 24:10-13, E 118)

These four basic sons are an analysis of Los in the same sense that the four Zoas are an analysis of the giant Albion. And when, in the Bard's song, Blake identifies primarily with Palamabron, he is confessing to a falling off in power which will only be regained when he can identify consciously again with all of Los.

The conflict between Hayley and Blake was certainly an important stimulus to Blake's imagination in writing the Bard's song. However, he carefully wrote in terms of archetypes, so that the events at Felpham may be seen as a particular outworking of universal forces.

Blake's partially ironic use of Calvinistic terminology is important to the perception of Satan as the appropriate name for the force which animated Hayley. Satan is identified as an example of "the Elect from before the foundation of the world" (*M* 7:1, E 99). The paradox which this presents to orthodox usage not only alerts us to Blake's satiric intentions, but also gives edge to the satire as it develops. Palamabron is given as an example of "the Redeem'd" with the ironic explanation "For he is redeem'd from Satans law" (*M* 11:23, E 104). Here orthodox usage ironically implies redemption from orthodox law. (Rintrah's classification as an example of the "Reprobate" will be discussed later.)

Blake perhaps felt that he was too gentle and yielding in his relationship with Hayley. Thus it seems appropriate that he associates himself with the "mild & piteous" Palamabron. Blake must at that time have been subject to conflicting emotions, and led by his emotions to yield to the Satan/selfhood within himself, as well as to Satan/Hayley's "intreaties." (Los is the one who actually yields, and is said also to have been "blamable." Palamabron "fear'd to be angry lest Satan should accuse him of / Ingratitude. . . .")[4] That Blake should for a time be ruled by his feelings is not surprising; Palamabron is identified as "the strongest of Demons" (*M* 7:45, E 100).

On the political level, Erdman suggests that "though the clues are slight, it is possible that the strife between Satan and Palamabron derives from the struggle between Cromwell and Parliament." He goes on to suggest that Blake saw a parallel between the careers of Cromwell and Napoleon.[5] While the confirmation of this depends (as does the more widely accepted identification of Hayley as Satan) upon the development of a pattern of corroborating detail, it is at least consistent that Blake/Palamabron should initially have had exaggerated hopes for the pseudo-revolutionary, Napoleon, as he had for the pseudo-artist, Hayley.

Palamabron is in charge of the harrow, which in the Bard's song seems to represent an artist's engraving tool. However, it is noteworthy that the Bard himself (clearly a less fragmented artist than Palamabron) uses a plow. ("Follow with me my plow!" [*M* 7:3, E 99] says the Bard fiercely, as he explains the "Three Classes of Men.") Both plow and harrow are forged by all four of the basic sons of Los (or by the reintegrated Los/Blake) in London.[6] The plow, as the edge which cuts deeper and more definitively, is assigned to the "fierce" Rintrah. The harrow as an archetypal symbol of pity (compare the medieval myth of the harrowing of hell) may seem more appropriate for the "mild" Palamabron. Thus the harrow may be thought of as the engraving tool when it is used to convey feeling. Perhaps the plow/burin cut the hard outlines, while the same tool may be called a harrow when it is used for cross-hatching and shading. Or perhaps Palamabron/Blake used the harrow altogether when he was illustrating Hayley's sentimental ballads, or doing portraits. (Rintrah could not appropriately use his fierce plow in such genteel enterprises.)

The harrow, of course, is at the center of the controversy with Satan, since Satan wishes to drive it. When Satan "with most endearing love / . . . soft intreated Los to give him Palamabrons station" (*M* 7:5-6, E 99), we may imagine Hayley attempting to direct a particular artistic enterprise which Blake/Palamabron is executing for him. Perhaps we may imagine Cromwell trying to take over the function of Parliament. (On the political level, Erdman suggests that the harrow may represent "the leveling function of revolutionary legislation: it is abused in the tyrant's hands.")[7] However, we must also imagine Satan as Blake's own selfhood: as that part of Blake which wishes to follow Hayley's directions, and thus to follow what he hopes is the main chance for commercial success. (This last reading seems particularly likely because, as we have seen, Satan is a son of Los. And Milton himself, shortly before he enters into Blake, recognizes, "I in my Selfhood am that Satan: I am that Evil One! He is my Spectre!" [*M* 14:30-31, E 107]. Thus, insofar as Blake identifies in this poem with Los and with Milton, Satan is a recognized part of his own makeup.)

However, the harrow proves an unmanageable tool for Satan. When he first asks to drive it, Los refuses in language which illuminates the forces at work:

> Anger me not! thou canst not drive the Harrow in
> pitys paths
> Thy work is Eternal Death. . . .
>
> (*M* 4:16-17, E 97)

And when Satan finally is allowed to drive it, Phaeton-like he makes a disastrous mess of the situation. The reason why Satan fails is complicated, and involves forces which Blake personifies as emanations.

Palamabron, as an aspect of Los, represents the conjunction of imagination and emotion. Elynittria, the emanation of Palamabron, seems to represent the principle of living harmony which can control imagination and emotion. Elynittria, in a sense, is Blake's answer to those rationalists who fear that such powers cannot be controlled except by repression. Elynittria's character as a representative of "living proportion," or harmony, is made explicit when Satan (representing, among other things, repressive "Mathematical Proportion") falls in love with her:

> Charles calls on Milton for Atonement. Cromwell is
> ready
> James calls for fires in Golgonooza. for heaps of
> smoking ruins
> In the night of prosperity and wantonness which he
> himself Created
> Among the Daughters of Albion among the Rocks of
> the Druids
> When Satan fainted beneath the arrows of Elynittria
> And Mathematical Proportion was subdued by Living
> Proportion
>
> (*M* 5:38-44, E 98)

This episode contributes to the archetypal drama by helping to explain Satan's motivations in his desire to take over from Palamabron. It may suggest the kind of erotic attraction felt by tyrants like Cromwell or Napoleon for the "Living Proportion" of the revolutionary institutions which they destroyed in the act of possession. It may allegorize the attraction felt by a would-be artist for principles of living art. And, on the biographical level, the lines may suggest Blake's suspicion that Hayley was sexually attracted to Catherine Blake.[8]

When Satan fails in his attempt to drive Palamabron's horses and harrow, he fails because he does not have Elynittria's humanizing and civilizing powers to help him. Emotions and imagination can be terrifying when unrestrained. The Bard suggests this by reporting that ". . . Palamabrons horses. / Rag'd with thick flames redundant, & the Harrow maddend with fury" (*M* 7:43-44, E 100). Leutha attempts to help Satan, but, as an archetypal power, she is involved with his sexual desires, not with his artistic powers. She reports:

> I sprang out of the breast of Satan, over the Harrow
> beaming
> In all my beauty! that I might unloose the flaming
> steeds
> As Elynittria use'd to do; but too well those living
> creatures
> Knew that I was not Elynittria, and they brake the
> traces
>
> (*M* 12:10-13, E 105)

At this point, Satan may easily be imagined as the force within Blake which wishes to cooperate with Hayley. This Satan attempts to deal with runaway emotional and creative energies by means of repression. He

Compell'd the Gnomes to curb the horses, & to throw banks of sand
Around the fiery flaming Harrow in labyrinthine forms.
And brooks between to intersect the meadows in their course.

(*M* 12:17-19, E 105)

Next Leutha tells how the "thick flames" of passion from "the fiery Harrow" "orb'd us round in concave fires." The result is to close Leutha and Satan together into what Leutha calls "A Hell of our own making" (*M* 12:21-23, E 105). Both Hayley, and Blake's selfhood, may be imagined as inhabitants of this hell.

All this throws further light on Blake's techniques of irony. There is nothing ironic in his identification of the ambitious, rational selfhood as Satan. He means it. And he is serious, too, in his identification of hell as the experience of that selfhood when it is overwhelmed by the dark flames of repressed emotion and imagination. The word *irony* can appropriately be used only to describe his technique of deliberately echoing, and reversing, the language of more orthodox writers—such as the historical Milton.

Satan was deeply disturbed by his inability to control Palamabron's horses and harrow. However, he was equally disturbed when he returned to his own "Mills," where Palamabron had been working, to find "all confusion." He called Los, who came to see

The servants of the Mills drunken with wine and dancing wild
With shouts and Palamabrons songs, rending the forests green
With ecchoing confusion. . . .

(*M* 8:8-10, E 101)

As Damon points out, this may suggest, biographically, that "Hayley finds the work he has given Blake quite disrupted with Blake's own ideas."[9] However, perhaps Blake went too far in reaction to Hayley's outraged dullness. Both Blake/Palamabron and Hayley/Satan are upset by the quarrel: "all the Elect and all the Redeem'd mourn'd one toward another." Los—who, among other things, represents Blake's potentially more fully integrated psyche—calls for a day of "solemn mourning" (*M* 8:25,12; E 101).

Blake was severely divided against himself. Two of his four basic functions were on the side of Satan, Hayley, Napoleon, and his own selfhood. For when

. . . Satan wept over Palamabron
Theotormon & Bromion contended on the side of Satan
Pitying his youth and beauty; trembling at eternal death

(*M* 8:29-31, E 101)

Palamabron was sentimental, and too open to persuasion. Only Rintrah held out against the blandishments of Satan:

But Rintrah who is of the reprobate: of those form'd to destruction
In indignation. for Satans soft dissimulation of friendship!
Flam'd above all the plowed furrows, angry red and furious

(*M* 8:34-36, E 101)

However, Blake never loses his perspective on Rintrah as a universal archetypal force. Thus, when Hayley (or Napoleon?) hypocritically suppressed anger, Blake was able to allegorize this by saying that Satan flamed "with Rintrah's fury hidden beneath his own mildness." He also tells us that

. . . Rintrah and his rage:
. . . flam'd high & furious in Satan against Palamabron
Till it became a proverb in Eden, Satan is among the Reprobate.

(*M* 9:10-12, E 102)

Erdman has suggested that Rintrah is also used to stand for Pitt in the Bard's song. This seems to me unlikely. Morton Paley has argued convincingly that Rintrah stands for revolutionary wrath in the "Argument" to *The Marriage of Heaven and Hell.*[10] I believe the same identification holds for *Milton.* I suggest that Rintrah's anger at Satan represents, among other things, revolutionary anger at Satan/Napoleon's betrayal of the revolution.

This identification of Rintrah helps to explain his classification as "Reprobate." Again, Blake's irony is subtle, and reflects feelings which were no doubt mixed. If Rintrah is revolutionary wrath, he is the very force within himself which the respectable world had too often described as "Reprobate." Blake's self-division was genuine, and he no doubt sometimes condemned this part of himself. However, as the inspired Bard he knew that Rintrah was an essential component of the integrated Los.

After things had gone very wrong, Blake turned inward and debated the issue in his imagination, in the presence of all the archetypal forces concerned, and in the light of eternity. This seems to have been the sort of process by which Blake maintained and strengthened his psychic balance, in spite of all the stresses brought about by his great imaginative sensitivity. Instead of continuing the quarrel, Palamabron calls down "a Great Solemn Assembly," after which, it is asserted, "all Eden descended into Palamabrons tent" (*M* 8:46,9:1; E 102).

This represents an important spiritual experience for Blake. However, he was not able to achieve it, and the

insights which came from it, until Satan showed that he was something other than imperviously "Elect." As we are told later:

> . . . Palamabron dared not to call a solemn Assembly
> Till Satan had assum'd Rintrahs wrath in the day of
> mourning

(*M* 11:24-25, E 104)

I would agree with Erdman that this probably means that Blake dared not discuss the guilt of Napoleon/Satan until after the failure of the Peace of Amiens.[11] However, I suggest that the wrath that flared up in Satan was the wrath of the old revolutionary movement—the wrath of the spirit of Voltaire, Rousseau, and others whom Blake was now coming to blame for starting the whole violent process.

Blake's attitude toward Rintrah is too equivocal—contains too much grudging approval—to apply to as cold a villain as Pitt. When Palamabron appeals for judgment to "all Eden," the judgment falls first "on Rintrah and his rage" (*M* 9:10, E 102). Blake/Los's sympathy for Rintrah betrays the fury of disappointment and betrayal: "Los in wrath curs'd heaven & earth, he rent up Nations," and caused many other catastrophes. But, insofar as Los represents Blake, he seems to have maintained some of the proprieties, for "he clos'd up Enitharmon from the sight of all these things" (*M* 9:13-18, E 102). This and other references suggest that Catherine was not always informed of the complexities of William's doubts and conflicts.

Hayley may have been superior and moralistic in his response to the outward situation; the spirit of Blake's old revolutionary loyalties may have caused inner conflict:

> For Satan flaming with Rintrahs fury hidden beneath
> his own mildness
> Accus'd Palamabron before the Assembly of ingrati-
> tude! of malice:
> He created Seven deadly Sins drawing out his infernal
> scroll,
> Of Moral laws and cruel punishments upon the clouds
> of Jehovah
> To pervert the Divine voice. . . .

(*M* 9:19-23, E 102)

Satan's assumption of rational, moral superiority involves an unsatisfactory attempt to repress wrath, and to cultivate pity. We have seen that his repression of emotional and imaginative fires has condemned him to hell. He is not able to repress wrath, but only to separate it:

> . . . Satan not having the Science of Wrath, but only
> of Pity:
> Rent them asunder, and wrath was left to wrath, &
> pity to pity.

(*M* 9:46-47, E 103)

The result for him is "dreadful Death," since it is implied that either of these emotions, undiluted by the other, is too much to bear. Satan's difficulty with pity, and his creation of a moralistic religion, both are reminiscent of Urizen's difficulties in *The Book of Urizen*. It is little wonder that, after seeing Satan's failure to manage Rintrah's rage, "Los and Enitharmon knew that Satan is Urizen" (*M* 10:1, E 103), and that Satan is the God of this world (*M* 11:10-14, E 104). Satan's torment is depicted in a full-page illumination which shows him writhing in flames while Rintrah and Palamabron look on. I suggest that it is Rintrah who is communicating the energy of his fury into Satan, by touching Satan's right foot with his own left foot. Rintrah enters into Satan through the foot, as Milton later enters into Blake through the foot.[12]

The initial decision to blame Rintrah made a kind of rational sense—which may be part of what so enraged Blake/Los. It is not difficult to imagine Blake bottling up mixed feelings, while agreeing with Hayley that he should not have lost his temper. However, Blake seems to have persuaded himself that it also made a kind of imaginative sense. Hayley could not openly be condemned because he would not admit that he was angry. Napoleon could not be condemned without betraying many of Blake's past loyalties. Blake's own selfhood could not be condemned until Blake was ready to give up all his ambitions for commercial success. And, on the archetypal level, Satan *should* not be condemned—as Blake discovered from the "Great Assembly" within himself—because "If the Guilty should be condemn'd, he must be an Eternal Death" (*M* 11:17, E 104). The Elect (including Hayley, Napoleon, and Blake's own ego) could only continue by being "new Created continually moment by moment," since their status depended upon their own self-esteem and the cooperative ego-support provided by the belief of the Redeemed: that is, upon what might be described in negative analysis as little more than a massive confidence trick.

All this, however, was not enough to save Satan from guilt by association. For, as we have seen, Blake/Palamabron was unwilling even to call a "Great Assembly" until after "Satan had assum'd Rintrah's wrath in the day of mourning." However, as soon as Satan is threatened with condemnation, Leutha appears before the "Great Solemn Assembly" in order to offer "herself a ransom for Satan, taking on her, his Sin." Leutha is the archetype of the attractive principle in female sexuality. She is described as "glowing with varying colours immortal, heart-piercing / And lovely," and as having "moth-like elegance" (*M* 11:29-30, 32-33; E 104). Her introduction into the story represents, among other things, another attempt by Blake to understand Hayley's motivations, and perhaps to forgive him.

Leutha tells the "Great Assembly" that she loved Palamabron, but could not approach him because of the jealousy of Palamabron's emanation, Elynittria. In order to get her way, she plays the part of Sin in a variation on Milton's allegory of Satan, Sin, and Death. Leutha's character as an archetypal motivating force becomes explicit when she tells how she entered

> . . . the doors of Satans brain night after night
> Like sweet perfumes I stupified the masculine perceptions
> And kept only the feminine awake. hence rose his soft
> Delusory love to Palamabron: admiration join'd with envy
> Cupidity unconquerable!
>
> (*M* 12:4-8, E 104-105)

That Satan's love is sexual in origin is made clear by identifying Leutha as the arousing agent.[13] However, Hayley/Satan apparently expressed this love only in statements which Blake believed stemmed from artistic jealousy, and by attempting to drive Blake/Palamabron's harrow "in Pitys paths"—where, of course, the gnomes revolted, and Satan failed dismally.

After Leutha's failure to control "the flaming steeds" of Palamabron, and after Satan's failure to repress the flames of the harrow, then (as we have seen) both Satan and Leutha are plunged into "A Hell of [their] own making." While in this hell, Leutha "form'd the Serpent / Of precious stones and gold turned poisons . . ." (*M* 12:29-30, E 105). This bit of allegory is explained immediately:

> To do unkind things in kindness! with power armd, to say
> The most irritating things in the midst of tears and love
> These are the stings of the Serpent!
>
> (*M* 12:32-34; E 105)

It is not difficult to imagine Hayley, in conscious innocence, acting the part of this serpent.

The rest of the allegory is acted out in a manner far different from that of *Paradise Lost* (or of *James*, I, 15). Leutha springs from the head of Satan "with Blandishments" after the gnomes (Hayley/Satan's repressed energies) "refus'd to labour more." These energies (although probably not Hayley, himself, consciously) recognize the source of his motivation, and name her "Sin" (*M* 12:37-39, E 105). Sexual desire, of course, is no substitute for a sense of aesthetic proportion. Thus love is blamed for the disaster, as wrath and pity were before.

Leutha's true nature is still ambiguous. She is "a Daughter of Beulah" (*M* 11:28; E 104) who is sincerely repentant after the event, even though Satan is not repentant:

> O Divine Vision who didst create the Female: to repose
> The Sleepers of Beulah: pity the repentant Leutha. My
> Sick Couch bears the dark shades of Eternal Death infolding
> The Spectre of Satan. he furious refuses to repose in sleep.
> I humbly bow in all my Sin before the Throne Divine.
> Not so the Sick-one; Alas what shall be done him to restore?
>
> (*M* 12:49-13:4, E 105-106)

Nonetheless, as soon as Leutha saw that Enitharmon, in pity, "had / Created a New Space to protect Satan from punishment; / She fled to Enitharmon's Tent & hid herself" (*M* 13:12-14, E 106). Thus she chose limitation, and life in Generation. Afterwards, Elynittria "met Leutha in the place where she was hidden." Elynittria is nice to her, and brings her without jealousy "to Palamabron's bed," where the allegory of Satan, Sin, and Death is completed:

> In moments new created for delusion, interwoven round about
> In dreams she bore the shadowy Spectre of Sleep, & namd him Death.
> In dreams she bore Rahab the mother of Tirzah & her sisters
> In Lambeths vales; in Cambridge & in Oxford, places of Thought
> Intricate labyrinths of Times and Spaces unknown, that Leutha lived
> In Palamabrons Tent, and Oothoon was her charming guard.
>
> (*M,* 13:39-44, E 106)

It is noteworthy here that Palamabron, rather that Satan, seems to be the father of Death. Yet Death in one sense is "Eternal Death"—the natural cycle of birth and death—and perhaps the vital flux of this cycle seemed to Blake to need a more vigorous male parent than the essentially sterile Satan/Urizen. It is also significant that all this happens in a world of "delusion" and "dreams"—which most probably is Beulah. What is being said in part is that the vegetative cycle of life and death owes its origin and continuation to the repeated conjunctions of female sexual allure and human emotion. This presents an interesting parallel to the banishment of Luvah and Vala to "the place of seed" in *The Four Zoas* (126:6-8, E 380). (Palamabron is the son of Los most directly influenced by the archetype of the emotions—Luvah. Leutha is the mother of Rahab, who is "Vala drawn down into a Vegetated body" [*FZ* 105:13, E 364].) However, Palamabron and Leutha are not exact equivalents of Luvah and Vala, thus another nuance of meaning is implied. The spirit of Palamabron might well inspire an imaginative theologian, and Leutha might well represent his idea of female sexuality. Thus the pair make particularly appropriate parents to Death and his troublemaking sisters, when these offspring are

viewed as distorted archetypes, conceived by theologians in such places as the bishop's palace at Lambeth, and in the colleges of Oxford and Cambridge.

That Oothoon should be Leutha's "charming guard" during the time "Leutha lived / In Palamabrons Tent" is noteworthy. This conjunction of sexual appetite and allure, represented by Leutha, and the idealistic spirit of free love, represented by Oothoon, does not happen often in Blake. Oothoon is more characteristically represented by her role in *Visions of the Daughters of Albion,* where she seems to represent the inevitable frustration of idealistic freedom in a world in which most people are crippled by inhibition and jealousy. The time in Palamabron's tent does not have happy results, since Leutha's offspring represent forces which lead mankind further into delusion and despair. Nonetheless, as we have noted, the affair seems to take place in Beulah, and Oothoon is said to be "charming."

Perhaps the relationship between Oothoon and Leutha is suggested most clearly in a passage following shortly after the Bard's song, where the two emanations, as components of the "Shadowy Female," hover over Orc:

> So spoke Orc when Oothoon & Leutha hoverd over
> his Couch
> Of fire in interchange of Beauty & Perfection in the
> darkness
> Opening interiorly into Jerusalem & Babylon shining
> glorious
> In the Shadowy Females bosom. . . .
>
> (*M* 18:39-43, E 111)

Here both Oothoon and Leutha enjoy "Beauty & Perfection," since they "interchange" these qualities. However, I suggest that parallel word order is important in the listing of Jerusalem and Babylon. Leutha's beauty, taken alone, can connect her only with the glories of Babylon, where the power and wealth of empire exploit female beauty. On the other hand, the true freedom of Oothoon, "the soft soul of America" (*VDA* [*Visions of the Daughters of Albion*] 1:3, E 44), is always in rebellion against empire. She may be raped and then frustrated (as in *Visions of the Daughters of Albion*), or she may be forced by human jealousy to find her freedom only in secret (as in *Milton* and *Jerusalem*). However, she stands for the proposition that freedom can lead to the final integration represented by Jerusalem. For, as we learn from Jerusalem, 26, "JERUSALEM IS NAMED LIBERTY AMONG THE SONS OF ALBION."

It is interesting that Elynittria cooperates with Leutha. Shortly before, Los had reproved her for her jealousy:

> Elynittria! whence is this Jealousy running along the
> mountains
> British Women were not Jealous when Greek & Roman were Jealous

> Every thing in Eternity shines by its own Internal
> light: but thou
> Darkenest every Internal light with the arrows of thy
> quiver
> Bound up on the horns of Jealousy to a deadly fading
> Moon
>
> (*M* 10:14-18, E 103)

Yet obviously she conquers her jealousy, since she brings Leutha to Palamabron's bed.

Ocalythron is the emanation of Rintrah. She is often coupled with Elynittria, just as Rintrah and Palamabron are often mentioned together. Like Elynittria, she is jealous, but unlike Elynittria, there is no evidence that she ever conquers her jealousy. When Los reproves Elynittria for her jealousy, he goes on to complain that

> . . . Ocalythron binds the Sun into a Jealous Globe
> That every thing is fixd Opake without Internal light.
>
> (*M* 10:19-20, E 103)

Elynittria and Ocalythron may represent two aspects of Catherine Blake/Enitharmon's psyche. When they are jealous, they can cut off both sun and moon—essential sources of "Internal Light" by which the dark stirrings of Blake/Los's imagination may be perceived and brought to expression in art or action.[14]

The extent to which all this is either a political allegory, or an allegory of events in Blake's life, is debatable. Elynittria may represent the spirit of Marie Antoinette, as Erdman suggests, but his argument does not seem to me to be convincingly corroborated by textual evidence. It seems to me likely, at least, that she represents one aspect of the character of Catherine Blake, just as Palamabron represents one aspect of William's character. Yet both William and Catherine are more complete when they comprehend all the basic sons and daughters of Los, and thus may be seen, themselves, as Los and Enitharmon. The whole episode may refer to Catherine's theoretical acceptance of Blake's ideas concerning sexual freedom. The unexpected cooperation of Elynittria with Leutha may even have been suggested by Catherine's acceptance of some of the attributes of Leutha within herself. In any event, Elynittria's cooperation with Leutha is appropriate for an emanation who represents "living proportion," and thus should have exceptional resistance to Urizenic "mathematical proportion," prescriptive morality, and jealousy.

The Bard's song ends with the episode of Elynittria, Leutha, Oothoon, and Palamabron. The reaction in Eternity is mixed:

> . . . many condemn'd the high tone'd Song
> Saying Pity and Love are too venerable for the impu-
> tation

Of Guilt. Others said. If it is true! if the acts have
 been perform'd
Let the Bard himself witness. . . .

 (*M* 13:47-50, E 107)

After this, as we have seen, the Bard claims that he
must be right because he is inspired by "the Poetic Ge-
nius." However, his unsubstantiated assertion does not
convince all those in "the Heavens of Albion" where

 . . . there was great murmuring . . .
 Concerning Generation & the Vegetative power &
 concerning
 The Lamb the Saviour. . . .

 (*M* 14:8-9, E 107)

It is in response to his sudden accession of the spirit of
the Bard that Milton rises and announces his decision
to return to incarnation in this world of "Eternal Death."
Apparently the Bard's song has reminded him, first of
all, that

 . . . the Nations still
 Follow after the detestable Gods of Priam; in pomp
 Of warlike selfhood, contradicting and blaspheming.

 (*M* 14:14-16, E 107)

However, the song also suggests that the Resurrection
may be coming, and that it is high time that he come to
terms with his own emanation:

 What do I here before the Judgment? without my Ema-
 nation?
 With the daughters of memory, & not with the daugh-
 ters of inspiration[?]
 I in my Selfhood am that Satan: I am that Evil One!
 He is my Spectre! in my obedience to loose him from
 my Hells
 To claim the Hells, my Furnaces, I go to Eternal
 Death.

 (*M* 14:28-32, E 107)

Milton, first of all, has recognized in the Satan of the
Bard's song the same rational spirit which he deified in
Paradise Lost. He also recognizes in the "Hell" of cre-
ative energy which torments Satan, the "Furnaces"
within which he created his own best work. He sees in
the various shifts adopted by "the Redeem'd" Blake/
Palamabron, in his efforts to love and forgive "the
Elect" Satan, some of the principles which he must
adopt in order to come to terms with his own Spectre.
Moreover, he may see in the self-sacrificing conquest of
jealousy exhibited by Elynittria, a model of the kind of
behavior which will be required of Ololon, if he and his
emanation are ever to be reconciled. For all these rea-
sons, and because aspects of Blake's own spirit are rep-
resented by both Palamabron and the Bard, Blake's
body is a natural target for Milton's spirit.

Milton's finding in the Bard's song evidence of con-
temporary wars is a reminder of the probable impor-
tance of political allegory in the song. Erdman com-

ments that "Milton with surprising ease, considering the
failure of modern readers to find political meaning here,
understands him [the Bard] to have said that the persis-
tence of corruption and war in the world of the nine-
teenth century is an indictment of the revolution for
which Milton bears bardic responsibility."[15] Blake art-
fully obscured the political implications of his work.
We may be sure that political allegory is present; unfor-
tunately, we have not yet identified enough positive ref-
erences to be as sure of meaning on this level, as we
are of meaning on the level of biographical allegory.

There is much more in the first fourteen plates of *Mil-
ton* than I have managed to comment on, even in pass-
ing. However, I hope I have demonstrated a little of
how the figures in the poem reach in all directions: how
they may represent real persons in history and in
Blake's own life, and simultaneously how they repre-
sent the psychological forces which animated those per-
sons, and which Blake knew intimately and wrestled
with, because they were component parts of his own
psyche.

All the implications of the event which Blake allego-
rized by saying that Milton entered into his foot must
have been extremely traumatic for Blake. The kind of
psychological crisis he underwent is conveyed to us by
parallel full page pictures: one labelled "William" show-
ing a falling star approaching a man's left foot, and an-
other, much darker, labelled "Robert," showing a falling
star approaching a man's right foot.[16] The pictures are
very nearly mirror images of each other, and both men
are collapsing backward as if struck dead. Since we
know Robert did die, the pictures seem to imply that
the inward events symbolized by the descent of Milton
struck William Blake with a critical intensity like that
of death.

However, death is necessary to rebirth. After this expe-
rience Blake could begin again. He could condemn, and
yet forgive, men whom he had once revered—such as
Hayley and Napoleon. Without abandoning his earlier
libertarian ideals, he could abandon hope for their
achievement through violence. And he could develop
his growing conviction that only through combining ar-
tistic vision with the continuous mutual forgiveness of
sins could salvation be found.

Notes

 1. *Blake: Prophet Against Empire* (New York:
 Doubleday Anchor, 1969), p. 422.

 2. William Blake, *Jerusalem*, Pl. 5, ll. 18-20, as re-
 printed in *The Poetry and Prose of William Blake*,
 ed. David V. Erdman (New York, 1965), p. 146.
 All subsequent references to this edition are indi-
 cated by the letter E. Other abbreviations used in
 this essay: *Milton: M*; *Visions of the Daughters of
 Albion: VDA*; *The Four Zoas: FZ.*

3. For a detailed discussion of the problems of dating *Milton,* see E, pp. 727-730.

4. *M* 7:10-12; E, pp. 99-100. My interpretation of these lines has been aided by John E. Grant, who pointed out that the period (full stop) after "Palamabron" in l. 11 of the Erdman text is not to be found in the originals.

5. *Prophet Against Empire,* p. 424.

6. See *M* 6:8-13; E, p. 99.

7. *Prophet Against Empire,* p. 424.

8. Cf. the near-paranoid conclusion of Blake's epigram "On Hayley's Friendship": "And when he could not act upon my wife / Hired a Villain to bereave my life" (E 497).

9. S. Foster Damon, *William Blake, His Philosophy and Symbols* (London, 1924, 1969), p. 407.

10. *Energy and the Imagination* (Oxford, 1970), Appendix A.

11. *Prophet Against Empire,* p. 425.

12. Plate 10, William Blake Trust facsimile (London, 1967); see also David V. Erdman, *The Illuminated Blake* (New York, 1974), p. 226, for a black and white reproduction, and for contrasting identifications.

13. Blake may have suspected that Hayley was bisexual. See n. 8, above. Also, cf. the following epigram from his notebook: "Of His birth this was the happy lot / His Mother on his Father him begot" (E 497).

14. Cf. S. Foster Damon, *A Blake Dictionary* (Brown U. P., 1965), p. 305.

15. *Prophet Against Empire,* p. 426.

16. Plates 32 and 37, Blake Trust facsimile; also see *The Illuminated Blake,* pp. 248, 253.

Joseph Anthony Wittreich, Jr. (essay date 1978)

SOURCE: Wittreich, Joseph Anthony, Jr. "Blake's *Milton*: 'To Immortals, . . . a Mighty Angel.'" *Milton Studies* 11 (1978): 51-82.

[*In the following essay, Wittreich discusses aspects of prophetic revelation in Blake's poem. Wittreich asserts that John Milton's* Paradise Lost *and* Paradise Regained *exerted a profound influence on Blake's own poetic process.*]

> The time is arriv'd when Men shall again converse in
> Heaven & walk with Angels.
> I am the companion of angels.
>
> —William Blake

Miltonists all know that Pope disliked Milton's God for being a "school divine"; and most of them presume that Blake liked Milton's Satan, and Milton too—to the extent that he could be numbered among "the Devils party." What they forget (or what perhaps they do not know) is that Thomas Butts, Blake's friend and patron, visited the poet's home, walked into his garden, and found there Blake and his wife, both nude, reading aloud not Books I and II of *Paradise Lost* but Book IV. The poet so widely known for his criticism of Milton in *The Marriage of Heaven and Hell* should also be remembered as the poet who, attentive not to the Satanic but to the visionary books of *Paradise Lost,* wrote an epic to which Milton gave his name. That epic is both a criticism and a celebration. The poem itself points to those moments in Milton's life and art where Blake saw (as he had seen in Wordsworth) "the Natural Man rising up against the Spiritual Man." In such moments, Milton, like Wordsworth, is "No Poet" but "a Heathen Philosopher at Enmity against all true Poetry or Inspiration" (p. 654).[1] In the illuminations accompanying Blake's poem, however, Milton is shown undertaking a journey . . . , encountering his selfhood . . .—this journey, this encounter, enabling the Spiritual Man to triumph over the Natural Man. In that moment of victory, Milton becomes like Jesus, all Vision, all Imagination. . . .

The first poem, and still the only one, in which one poet elevates another to the rank of epic hero, Blake's *Milton* records the poet's struggle and his triumph—a struggle that involved Milton for most of his life and a triumph that occurred when he set down the vision of *Paradise Regained.* In this poem, having developed a refined sense of mental revolution, Milton embraces a radical theology. This pattern of development Blake extrapolates from Milton's life and art, mythologizing it into a story in which Milton, having wandered through eternity for a hundred years, determines to descend into the world of generation, in this moment of decision casting off his errors: the doctrine of chastity that disfigured the vision of *Comus,* the politics of violence that scarred the prose works, and the dark cloud of religion that hovered oppressively over the vision of *Paradise Lost.* Annihilating these errors, Milton joins first with his female counterpart Ololon and thereupon with Blake, energizing his successor and, with him, leading the way into Jerusalem. Without a precursor—*without Milton*—Blake's own epic vision would have had no vehicle.

I

> All the prophets prophesied by virtue of some influence raying forth from the spirit of some other prophet into them.
>
> —John Smith

Milton is, for Blake, the model of the true prophet; and the Revelation of Saint John the Divine, the culmina-

tion of scriptural prophecy, is a model for his art. These two sources contribute to the poem called *Milton,* the poet providing the poem with its heroic substance and the Bible supplying it with a design, both structural and iconographic. Appropriately, a poem portraying the apotheosis of Milton takes as its context Revelation, which depicts "the Apotheosis of Christ."[2] Without Milton the poem would lack a hero; and without Revelation, Blake's idea of Milton would be, at best, amorphously defined.

Blake accomplishes Milton's elevation to the rank of epic hero by identifying him with various angels of St. John's Apocalypse. In the process, he subscribes to the prophetic tradition of Joachim of Fiore which, acknowledging three ages of the world, finds each of them governed by a prophet who descends to mankind from heaven. Moses presides over the first age and Elijah over the second. The last age has its angel-prophet too, who is identified with various historical figures by commentators on Revelation, and with Milton by Blake. This tradition, to which Blake's poem is firmly tied, receives important modification in the hands of Joachim's successors, and that modification works to the same end as Blake's poem. Joachim's successors made Christ the transitional figure between the first and second ages; and correspondingly, two historical figures in whom Christ will manifest himself will make the transition from the second into the third age, presiding over it as Christ did over the second. One of those figures Blake identifies as Milton, and the other he associates with himself. It is Milton's role, however, that concerns Blake most; and his function in the renovative process is best explained in terms of an analogy developed between the poet and various angels of the Apocalypse. According to a long tradition of commentary on Revelation, the apocalyptic angels are all reproved by St. John for one fault or another; yet even as their vices are condemned their virtues are commended.[3] Whatever their failings, these angels, figured as stars, "give light unto men"; held in Christ's hand, they share in his glory, but they also bring other men into that glory.

Milton, from Blake's point of view, is like the apocalyptic angels, three of them in particular: he falls into error like the third and fifth angels but, upon his transfiguration, resembles the Mighty Angel who instigates the building of Jerusalem. Believing that empire follows art and that poets are the architects of a renovated society, Blake subscribes to the tradition of commentary on Revelation that conceives of Jerusalem not outside, but within history; and he thus conceives of Milton as a *renovator mundi*—a view of him that is pictorialized in four plates associating Milton with angels of the Apocalypse . . . and that is confirmed by four others portraying Milton, emblematically, as a falling star. . . . Doubly significant, these emblematic portrayals, even as they focus the apocalyptic thrust of Blake's designs,

capture their ambiguity, alluding simultaneously to Prometheus, who brought fire down from heaven, thereby enlightening the human race, and to the falling Lucifer, who is regarded by interpreters of Revelation as representative of any one of the great religious heretics or as an emblem for all of them collectively. The star trailing light as a comet conveys both Blake's tribute to Milton and his criticism of him.

The importance of plate 32 . . . to the underlying conception for Blake's poem is suggested by the fact that Blake here magnifies the interlinear design of plate 17 into a full-page illumination for his poem. Both plates, emblematizing Milton as a star, symbolizing through him the light of conversion and of deliverance, carry an allusion to Acts—to the stories of both Saul's conversion and Peter's deliverance. The story of Saul, however, is probably not, as David Erdman argues,[4] the primary referent of Blake's star image; but that story, in its following aspects, is at least incidentally relevant to Blake's poem. First of all, Saul (who is known after his conversion as Paul) goes forth with Barnabas to witness for Christ, and there is eventually sharp contention between the two prophets. This story thus provides a New Testament example of the pairing of prophets and a precedent, too, for the contention that may exist between two prophets as they accept their respective callings. Second, an episode in Paul's life explains the detail of Milton's bald head in plate 18 . . . and, simultaneously, reinforces the thematic content of that plate. In Acts, the shearing of hair is part of the purification rite that Paul undergoes as he is about to enter Jerusalem where he dies for Jesus—dies metaphorically, that is, just as Milton does in plate 18 of Blake's poem (see Acts xii, 25; xv, 39; xviii, 18; xxi, 13, 24).

Yet, even as Blake invites, through these details, recollection of Saul's story, he subordinates that story to that of St. Peter's deliverance, for this episode provides a biblical analogue more in keeping with the accents of Blake's poem. *Milton* is not, as the analogy with Paul would suggest, an account of Blake's conversion. Rather, it recounts Milton's conversion, which makes possible Blake's, and subsequently mankind's, deliverance. Accordingly, the allusion to Paul's conversion becomes an analogue for Milton's experience within Blake's poem: like his biblical prototype, Blake's hero, while under the power of his specter, may be said to have "made havock of the church" (Acts viii, 3); and, like Paul—at times overly zealous of Christian orthodoxy—Milton stretched its dark cloud over England. Such a criticism may be leveled against the Milton of *Comus* and *Paradise Lost,* from Blake's point of view, but not against the Milton of *Paradise Regained.* This Milton, like Paul after his conversion, preaches against blood sacrifice and, adopting an aesthetic of testimony, witnessing to the doctrine of the Resurrection, proceeds to open the eyes of his countrymen (see Acts xiii, 50;

xxvi, 13-18). This is also the Milton whom Blake acknowledges to be the agent in his own deliverance; he is the bright light that, shining upon Blake during the Felpham years, releases him from Hayley's prison, just as a comparable light descended upon St. Peter as he lay in prison, chained and sleeping. Paul, then, analogizes Milton's situation, and Peter analogizes Blake's. Like his prototype, Blake falls into a death sleep, becoming "a slave bound in a mill" (p. 703); but also like his prototype, Blake triumphs over the "spectrous Fiend" (p. 702), emerging from his experience with a renewed capacity for vision. Unsurprisingly, then, in their moments of deliverance, Peter and Blake act identically: each prophet, rising out of his death sleep, binds on his sandals and enters the city's gates; thereupon, like Los in plate 1 of **Jerusalem,** each prophet finds a door that he opens and enters, the door signifying Christ, the Crucifixion, the state of self-annihilation. Entering the door which is Christ and the state of self-annihilation that he signifies, each prophet steps into the divine vision, becoming infused with the breath and finer spirit of true prophecy.

Noteworthy, too, is the fact that Peter accomplishes the healing of a man named Aeneas: through Jesus, he "maketh [him] whole" (Acts ix, 33-34). Blake, of course, has been said to perform the same kind of healing operation on his epic hero, Milton. Yet it is probably because Blake wished to discourage such a reading that he subordinated the Peter analogy to those, already pointed to, which are drawn from Revelation. In the process, Blake challenges the view that Milton recanted his precursor's errors rather than his own. Through the fiction of his poem, Blake has Milton recant errors that the poet recognized and cast off during his own lifetime; and in accordance with the pattern established by various angels of John's Apocalypse, Milton is thus shown journeying within and there discovering and divesting himself of those errors which disfigured his vision. Since the primary referents of the star image in plate 32 . . . are to be found in Revelation and because this plate, along with plates 1 and 16 . . . , is so dependent upon an iconography deriving from the Apocalypse, we should now pursue, in greater detail, the debt that Blake owes to John of Patmos for his Milton designs.

Revelation provides three sources for Blake's star image. There is, first of all, the third angel of the Apocalypse, the star called Wormwood, who focuses the negative meaning in Blake's image. This star, falling from heaven, "burning as it were a lamp," signifies man's falling away from true religion; and it is called Wormwood because it is known by its effects, by the "pestilent institutions" it creates through the perversities of its doctrines.[5] This star, according to Emanuel Swedenborg's commentary on Revelation, symbolizes "all those who are in the love of self" and who thus "falsify the

Word."[6] Blake develops this association to suggest that Milton has clouded the divine vision with errors deriving from the selfhood that, in this poem, Milton is poised to destroy. . . .

But in Revelation there are two other stars that emphasize the positive elements in Blake's image. The fifth angel of the Apocalypse, the Angel of the Bottomless Pit, also appears as a falling star; and the Mighty Angel of chapter 10 is referred to as the Morning Star. In the first instance, the star again signifies the divine vision that is perverted by those who fall away from it. But now the meaning of the image is complicated, for the star is identified with an angel who is about to explore and expose a universe of error. One commentator calls this angel who descends into the pit Reason, who is said to release all those errors which are reason's perversities, errors manifesting themselves in the shape of a beast that the angel then subdues.[7] Swedenborg specifically identifies these errors with "dense falsities . . . originating in the evils of earthly and corporeal loves."[8] Within this context, Blake, by appropriating the star image, chastises Milton for his cruelties to both his wives and daughters. Yet, as Swedenborg explains, the pit this angel is entering—a place of fire, throwing off clouds of smoke—is entered voluntarily; and it has its reference points not in the external world but in "the interiors of the mind," the world within that is being opened, that is ready to be explored.[9] The very act of entering this universe of error, because it is undertaken willingly, promises the exposure of falsities; and this exposure culminates in their annihilation. Like the Angel of the Bottomless Pit, Milton descends into error in order to confront and consolidate it, in order then to cast it off. When Milton completes this act, his prototype changes; Blake identifies him with the Mighty Angel, the Morning Star, the source of true light and of John's divine vision, who is described as an "angel come down from heaven," clothed with a cloud, and having a face that blazes "as it were the sun." This angel, says St. John, "set his right foot upon the sea, and *his* left *foot* on the earth . . . and lifted up his hand to heaven" (x, 1-2, 5).[10] These three angels, then, all of them emblematized as stars, stand behind Blake's portrayals of Milton.

Within Revelation, there are various apocalyptic angels whom some commentators would distinguish, but whom some would identify with one another. Blake, in his portrayals of Milton, holds these two traditions of commentary in dynamic tension. Both the third and fifth angels, commonly understood to be the source of innumerable errors who effect the decay of religion, contrast with the Mighty Angel who is Christ. The contrast is observed by Blake, who allows these different angels to impinge upon his portrayals of Milton. In their associations with Milton, the third and fifth angels epitomize the poet's intellectual faults, and the Mighty Angel serves as a measure of what, by annihilating his errors,

Milton becomes. With the coming of the Mighty Angel, "prophecy is restored" as Satan, the Angel of the Bottomless Pit, the enemy within, is overthrown.[11] This triumph is the subject of plate 18 of Blake's *Milton* . . . , which draws upon the common understanding that the Mighty Angel of the Apocalypse is Satan's binder.

Yet Blake, apparently cognizant of the other tradition of commentary, blurs this contrast between the Mighty Angel and the other angels of the Apocalypse, observing the idea that all these angels are finally one and the same, distinguished from one another only to define the process whereby errors are purged and renovation accomplished. In plate 1 . . . , two images are superimposed, the figure itself recalling, through gesture, the Mighty Angel of the Apocalypse, and the iconography of the design recalling the pit into which the fifth angel of the Apocalypse descends. In this plate, we see Milton, with one foot firmly planted, the other about to enter the sea of time and space, as he lifts up his hand to heaven, dispelling the "erroneous doctrine" that hides his glory and majesty.[12] The errors signified by the clouds are twofold, pointing on the one hand to the sterilities of vision that Milton in his own lifetime overcame and on the other to the disfigurations of his vision caused by obfuscating commentaries of the eighteenth century—commentaries committed, for the most part, to deradicalizing Milton's vision by harnessing it to orthodoxy. Yet it is also in plate 1 that the equation between Milton and the Angel of the Bottomless Pit is made explicit. The flames of fire, the billows of smoke, remind us that when this angel entered the world within "there arose a smoke . . . as the smoke of a great furnace" (ix, 2), the smoke signifying the intellectual failings of those who have perverted the divine vision, as well as the evils that derive from the pride of selfhood and one's attendant failings in earthly love. The effect of the rising smoke is to darken the air and the sun, isolating the erring figure from the divine vision.[13] However, by entering the pit, the figure indicates an awareness of his failings and a desire to effect his regeneration by exposing himself to the fires of purgation.

Blake's *Milton* is the story of a poet's journey, of his pilgrimage; and therefore both plates 1 and 16 depict Milton as a mental traveler. If Revelation's commentators provide one gloss on the clouds in plate 1, Blake provides another, explaining that "those who are in Eternity" appear in clouds "when any thing of Creation Redemption or Judgment are the Subjects of Contemplation." Moreover, says Blake, the reason they so appear is that they are in the act of "Humiliating . . . Selfhood & . . . Giving up all to Inspiration" (p. 553). *Giving up all to inspiration*—that is just what the Milton of *Paradise Lost* would do. There he represents himself as surrounded by clouds that, through the agency of celestial light, will be "Purge[d] and disperse[d]" (III, 45-46, 51-54). In plate 1, as elsewhere

then, Blake portrays Milton as Milton portrayed himself; thus, pushing aside the billowing clouds, Milton is enveloped by purifying flames that enable him both to don white raiment and to shine like a sun. Having begun his prayer that introduces the third book of *Paradise Lost* with the hope that he, like other prophets, would be invested with a mantle, Milton suggests how he might be portrayed, once his journey is over—a suggestion that Blake pursues in plate 16. Where Milton is depicted, as is Jesus in Blake's *Vision of the Last Judgment,* "surrounded by Beams of Glory." In his commentary on that painting, Blake suggests why: in the Divine Humanity, "the Nature of Eternal Things [is] Displayed," all things "beam[ing] from him," because *"as he himself has said All dwells in him"* (pp. 551-52). The resurrected Milton of plate 16, then, is a type of Christ, the Mighty Angel and true visionary. . . . And if any line associated with *Milton* glosses plate 16, it is the one inscribed on the last plate of Blake's poem—"I return from flames of fire tried & pure & white"—a line which, closely paraphrasing a verse from the Book of Daniel ("Many shall be purified, and white, and tried"), includes a promise that those who are purified shall, like Milton, shine "like the stars" (xii, 3, 10).

In plate 16, Milton shines radiantly, as his black garments are transformed into white ones unmistakably stained with blood. This detail reminds us that when Ololon, in the climactic moments of *Milton,* "descended to Felphams Vale / In clouds of blood, in streams of gore," the Starry Eight, the last of whom is Milton, "became / One Man Jesus the Saviour" and "round his limbs / The Clouds of Ololon folded as a Garment dipped in blood" (42 [49]: 7-8, 11-13). These white garments, rather than draping Milton's body, are held in his hand, Blake's point being that the garments, signifying "Christ himself," now cover "the nakednesse of the soul."[14] To possess them is to have put on Christ, to be wrapped in his perfection and glory, the white raiment being an emblem of the heroes who through intellectual warfare release themselves and thereby their civilizations from the powers of darkness. It is therefore fitting that a poem celebrating Milton as a Christian warrior should begin with a lyric poem that celebrates "Mental Fight" (just as Milton did in his two defenses of the English people) as the only form of warfare truly appropriate to man, seeing as its effect the building of Jerusalem in England's green and pleasant land.

A prophet's resemblance to Jesus was said to authenticate him as a prophet; and thus nowhere in the *Milton* designs is the poet more like Jesus than in plate 16 . . . , which incorporates, in all its details, the iconography of transfiguration. The clouds of plate 1 have disappeared, the sun rises behind Milton, and a sun circles the poet's head, seeming to radiate from it; Milton's

head turned upward, like Christ's both in the vision of the candlesticks and in his appearance as a mighty angel, shows as a sun. In these corresponding moments between Blake's poem and John's prophecy, "the Divine Humanity . . . [is] seen."[15] Christ, who appears in white, with white hair, is the conspicuous reference of plate 16, where Milton, hair streaked with white, holds white raiments in each hand, signifying as they do in the Apocalypse "the divine proceeding, which is divine truth, united with divine goods, which fills the universal heaven, and enters into the interior of the mind." "This," says Swedenborg, "is what is understood by being clothed with white garments."[16] This is a part of the meaning of Blake's design, and its implications are drawn out by Blake himself when he writes, "Naked we come here . . . & naked we shall return. but while clothed with the Divine Mercy" (p. 689).

Another part of Blake's meaning is invested in the image of the sun, its function being to dispel darkness, to enlighten the world, and "to warm and comfort dead . . . bodies, . . . to revive them."[17] Again Blake offers a gloss, this time as he speaks of "Heavenly Men beaming bright" and appearing as "One Man . . . / In . . . beams of gold" (p. 684). Here, in plate 16, not only does the sun radiate upon Milton; but in accordance with Blake's insistence that "Every thing in Eternity shines by its own Internal light" (10 [11]: 16), it radiates from Milton, the suggestion being that one aspect of the poet's struggle involves reception of the divine vision, while another involves its extension. Only in the act of transmitting the vision—making the Word into flesh, hammering it into form—does the poet become the Awakener, and only after his triumph is the apocalyptic moment, involving the renovation of history, able to occur.

II

Joachim [of Fiore] had seen various angels of the Apocalypse as symbols of the new spiritual men. . . . These disciples were brought up into the high mountain and shown both the Promised Land and the crossing of the Jordan which must first be accomplished. Then they saw their own calling: on the one hand, to embody the true spiritual life of the future, and, on the other, to lead the pilgrimage toward the Age of the Spirit. . . . [Thus, through these angels of apocalypse, Joachim] summoned men to . . . spiritual adventure:

Clear the eyes of the mind from all dusts of the earth; leave the tumults of crowds and the clamour of words; follow the angel in spirit into the desert; ascend with the same angel into the great and high mountain; there you will behold high truths hidden from the beginning of time and from all generations. . . . For we, called in these latest times to follow the spirit rather than the letter, ought to obey, going from illumination to illumination, from the first heaven to the second, and from

the second to the third, from the place of darkness into the light of the moon, that at last we may come out of the moonlight into the glory of the full Sun.

—Marjorie Reeves

When Blake described his portrayals of Nelson and Pitt in *A Descriptive Catalogue,* he set them within the apotheosis tradition, which he traced to classical antiquity. To this tradition Blake's portrayals of Milton also belong. They are a supreme example of Blake's effort "to emulate the grandeur" of classical and Christian heroes "seen in his vision, and to apply it to modern Heroes" (p. 522); yet once the apotheosis tradition is noted, it should be acknowledged that Blake's portrayals of Milton, though they possess ties with this tradition, involve a radical reassessment of it. Not the first visionary to attempt a portrayal of Milton's apotheosis, Blake, intentionally or not, takes up where one popular rendering of Milton's apotheosis terminated. Once attributed to Dr. Johnson, this earlier rendering, first published in the *Gentleman's Magazine* in 1738, describes the appearance of a figure "girded with white," arm raised, who causes a visionary named William Gutherie to fall to his feet, after which Gutherie, in resistless motion, flies with the figure through air. They come upon a great hall, with a great assembly, on the night Milton is to be admitted to the pantheon of poets; however, what Gutherie witnesses is not Milton's apotheosis but the assembly's denial of it to a poet who is judged defective in character for having been the architect of "black Designs" against the king and state and for having then "varnish[ed] and defend[ed] the most inhuman Action."[18] Blake's *Milton* begins with a judgment of Milton that is no less harsh, scoring him, not for being a revolutionary, but for allowing contradictions in his ideology to impede the revolutionary cause. In plate 1 of *Milton,* the poet walks naked, Blake exposing Milton's faults, so that by overcoming them Milton can be clothed in white. . . . The apotheosis tradition is thus invoked, but at the same time that Blake observes its literary and artistic conventions he criticizes the philosophy, the morality, that the tradition usually enshrines.

As John Steadman explains, the apotheosis of the hero is a conventional motif whose purpose is to trace a figure's progress toward heroic knowledge, a knowledge that has the status of a divine orthodoxy. The apotheosis tradition, signaled by a flight or by an ascent, depicts a hero, literally or fictively, in a period after his death—a hero who is shown in a region of dark clouds, cleansing himself of error, "of the contagion of earthly sins," and inuring himself "to withstand the pure flames of heaven." This tradition, with its strong apocalyptic overtones, is generally confined "to a handful of verses"; it constitutes "a brief episode" in a long poem.[19] Connections between such a tradition and Blake's poem should be obvious: Blake's *Milton* is about an epiphany

that, bringing the poet to illumination, freeing him from his death sleep, causes him to cast off his previous errors.

But besides the parallels between the apotheosis tradition and Blake's poem, there are important deviations from the tradition that are integral to the poem's meaning. The hero's journey is neither a flight nor an ascent; it is a descent into the self and into the world of generation. The apotheosis motif, rather than being relegated to a brief episode, is expanded into the central episode of a brief epic poem. These inversions of tradition point to Blake's reassessment of it, his purpose being to rid a literary and artistic tradition of its usual philosophical underpinnings. Ordinarily the hero's apotheosis is the result of his adopting an attitude of contempt for this world; only by divorcing his soul from his body, only by freeing himself of worldly concerns by taking on the cloak of chastity, is he able to achieve his apotheosis. Blake's point is otherwise. Precisely because Milton exhibited contempt for this world, precisely because he donned the robes of chastity, holding his soul distinct from his body, Milton remained isolated, for most of his life, from the divine vision, from the fiery city of Jerusalem. Milton's errors, then, are the errors of the philosophical tradition behind the apotheosis motif; and so Milton undertakes his descent into this world, not a flight from it, which begins with his reentering his body and which culminates in his union with Ololon, "a Virgin of twelve years" (36 [40]: 17). This descent finally enables Milton to achieve an altitude of ascent higher than other poets because he penetrates and unveils the errors with which other poets tried to wing their way to Jerusalem.

The pattern of experience represented in Blake's *Milton* is derived from Milton's own life, a life replete with "signs of pattern" (to use the words of Milton's most recent biographer).[20] The poet who lost God in his childhood returned to him in old age, presumably in the act of setting forth the vision of *Paradise Regained*. This observation Blake makes to Henry Crabb Robinson, but it is also implicit in Blake's reference to Milton's "bright pilgrimage of sixty years" (15 [17]: 52). Milton, born in 1608, had reached "sixty years" in 1668, the year after *Paradise Lost* was first published and the year in which he was contemplating, if not writing, *Paradise Regained*. In his brief epic, Milton breaks away from the terrifying theology that clouded the vision of his earlier epic; he returns to the Christocentric theology of his early poems—a return made possible by an understanding Milton acquired while living and writing under the stress of revolution and, in a very real sense, experiencing that revolution in his own mind. Milton thus accomplished his own redemption; and the pattern set down for it in his own lifetime and preserved in his art became the pattern by which Blake and his contemporaries could achieve theirs. In this

sense, Milton may be called England's awakener and redeemer; and in this sense, Milton may be seen within the lineage of Christ, who created a similar pattern for man's redemption out of his experience in the wilderness.

The primary analogues for Blake's Milton myth are provided, then, by Milton's own life and by the resemblances Blake observed between it and Christ's experience in the wilderness. Yet one suspects that Blake perceived yet other analogues that lent support to the correspondences he had already drawn between Milton and Christ. His Milton myth, like the Christ myth, involves a pattern of descent, which may be comprehended metaphorically (as a descent into the self) but which is portrayed literally (as a descent into the world of generation). Not only does Christ descend into this world for the Incarnation, but he undertakes another descent, after his death, just before his Resurrection, which is motivated, as Milton's is, by the desire to rescue Adam *and his sons* from hell, from their death sleep. The source for Milton's descent can be traced to eighteenth-century poetry and commentary; and the source for Christ's descent is the Gospel of Nicodemus. In each case, the tradition exists in order to accentuate its protagonist's commitment to the human race, his determination to return it to paradise.

These analogues, especially, help to focus (or to refocus) the meaning of Blake's poem. The idea of Milton's returning as England's savior, dramatized in plates 1 and 16, is anticipated by Cowper and Hayley, by Wordsworth and Coleridge. For example, Cowper speaks of Milton as a giant who, now arising from slumber, takes his place among those who are privileged to sleep no more; and Hayley imagines Milton revisiting earth in his mortal character. Wordsworth, in his famous sonnet, cries out: "Milton, thou shouldst be living at this hour / England hath need of thee"; and Coleridge, in a seldom quoted aside, regards Milton as one of the sages and patriots who, though dead, continues to wander through his native country. But this idea of Milton returning to England, which is central to Blake's epic, extends even further back into the eighteenth century than these analogues might suggest. It informs the poetry of Collins and Gray, and the 1738 stage adaptation of *Comus* carries the following prefatory lines:

> Like some bless'd spirit he [Milton] *to-night descends,*
> *Mankind he visits, and their steps befriends;*
> *Thro' mazy error's dark perplexing wood,*
> *Points out the path of true and real good.*[21]

These lines, predictably, have not an easy, but an ironic, relationship to the poem Blake has written. They depict "Mankind" wandering "Thro' mazy error's dark perplexing wood," which is where mankind still is when Blake writes his epic, partly because Milton himself is

shown, through the fiction of Blake's poem, still lost in error. Thus, it is Milton whom Blake depicts as "a wanderer lost in dreary night" (15 [17]: 16); and it is also Milton who, as a redeemed prophet, finally leads mankind back to the path. Connections of this sort between Milton commentary and Blake's poem proliferate and, in their proliferation, emphasize that the poem called **Milton** is the culmination of a tradition of eighteenth-century criticism that is still too little known, as well as the culmination of a tradition of illustration that depicts "episodes of national history, especially those concerning a struggle for liberty," many of which are "based on scenes from Milton's life." Those which are, as Marcia Pointon explains, result in "the crystallization of the concept of Milton the man as a great revolutionary, nonconformist protagonist of liberty,"[22] which, current in the early nineteenth century, is espoused by Blake in his poem.

There is no more evident link between Blake's idea of Milton and the Milton of the other Romantic poets than their eagerness to elevate their precursor and themselves into the eschatological position of angels of apocalypse, these angels symbolizing the spiritual men who will usher in a new order and a new age: like many of their predecessors, these poets saw their calling as to embody the spiritual life of the future and to lead the pilgrimage toward it. All these poets wrote epics, and each of their epics is infused with the spirit of prophecy whose master theme, whether we are talking about **Milton** or **Jerusalem**, *The Prelude* or *Prometheus Unbound*, is the Natural Man becoming the Spiritual Man, his apotheosis being a prelude to the apotheosis of history. The correlative to the centuries-old tradition of historicizing Antichrist, of seeing him as pope or high priest, as monarch or ruler, is the historicizing and secularizing of Christ, which involves the belief that he will reign over the new age in spirit, through the angels of apocalypse, the poets and prophets who rather than predicting the future help to create it.[23]

III

To be loved for what one is, is the greatest exception. The great majority love in another only what they lend him, their own selves, their vision of him.

—Goethe

Blake's portrayals of Milton tell us much about his idea and about the Romantics' idea of Milton; but they tell us much too about how all these poets approached Milton: not in an attitude of contention but in a spirit of collaboration. Yet, recently, a different story of the Romantics' encounters with Milton has been related. In *The Anxiety of Influence*, Harold Bloom writes:

Poetic Influence—when it involves two strong, authentic poets,—always proceeds by a misreading of the prior poet, an act of creative correction that is actually and necessarily a misinterpretation. The history of fruitful poetic influence, which is to say the main tradition of Western poetry since the Renaissance, is a history of anxiety and self-saving caricature, of distortion, of perverse, wilful revisionism without which modern poetry as such could not exist.[24]

This proposition is advanced by a critic who, watching Blake square off against Milton, finds in these two poets a historical example of the eternal enmity that exists between God and Satan in *Paradise Lost*.

Such a theory of poetic influence is mounted upon a misunderstanding of the Blake-Milton relationship—a relationship that finds its historical models in the involvement of Elisha with Elijah, of Daniel with Jeremiah, and of John of Patmos with Daniel, and that finds its mythic model in *Paradise Lost*, in the relationship of the Father and the Son, the Father shining "Most glorious . . . / Substantially express'd," "without cloud / Made visible," in his son (III, 139-40, 385-86). Like the eternal son, the poetic son enables us to behold "visibly" what is there "invisibly" in his poetic father (VI, 681-82); and like the eternal son of *Paradise Regained*, he provides "glimpses of his Father's glory" (I, 93), helping to establish in history what the poetic father decrees. The poetic son, then, manifests the qualities, clarifying and concretizing the vision of his precursor. His objective, his achievement, is not the malforming of his predecessor's vision, but the reforming of it in such a way that the precursor's vision is released from the malforming operation performed on it by those who did not understand it or by those who, understanding it, did not wish to countenance it.

As the Son relates to his Father in Milton's epics, so Spenser relates to Chaucer and Milton to Spenser. That Blake imagined himself relating to Milton in a similar fashion finds confirmation in Bloom's contention that the opposing aspects of poetic influence may be emblematized by the negative image of "the flowing in of an occult power exercised by humans . . . upon humans" or by the positive image of "stars [operating] upon humans."[25] Given these terms, it is noteworthy that when Blake chooses in **Milton** to verbalize, even to pictorialize, his relationship with his hero, he chooses the image of a star . . . , fully conscious of one commonplace of prophetic literature: "Stars are ministers not masters";[26] rather than darkening the prophet's vision they cast light upon it. The proof text is found in Revelation, where Christ appears as the Morning Star because, according to one student of prophecy, "he illuminates mens wills and understandings," he gives to men "perfect illumination and lightning."[27] Blake's point is that Christ revived revelation rather than caused its cessation, and the last poet to possess it was Milton; hence Blake's willingness to subject himself to Milton's influence in full sympathy with the prophetic dic-

tum that the precursor, even if sometimes mistaken, is not an oppressor but a liberator, that, as the popular expositor of prophetic literature, John Smith, puts it, "under the beams of the greater," the prophet submits to his "irradiations and influence."[28]

Blake's commitment to such a view of poetic influence is openly stated in the poem **Milton,** where the Seven Angels of the Presence weep over Milton's shadow and then, as the Seven Eyes of God, enter the poet's sleeping body, causing Milton to arise and walk with them through Eden "as an Eighth Image Divine" (14 [15]: 42-15 [17]: 1-7; see also 20: 14). Milton, by the end of the poem, is therefore designated as one of "The Eight Immortal Starry-Ones" (34: 4) and, with the other seven, becomes "One Man Jesus the Saviour" (42 [49]: 10-11). The seven angels, the seven spirits, the seven eyes of God—all this imagery finds its source in Revelation. There the seven eyes, referring both to the seven epistles and the seven angels, relate to the cleansing process whereby the doors of perception are successively opened. Appropriating this imagery and then elaborating upon it, Blake represents Milton as the eighth eye, signifying through him the final stage of human consciousness and thereby making him into "a direct emblem of apocalypse."[29] This complex of images, S. Foster Damon once observed, represents "the whole course of human thought in its search for an ideal."[30] For Blake, that search culminates in the poetry of Milton: Milton is the last in a line of prophets before Blake and symbolizes for him the highest peak of imaginative development. In Blake's epic, Milton is repeatedly portrayed out of the same impulse that led Blake to depict Moses and Abraham in *The Vision of the Last Judgment.* As Blake explains in his lengthy commentary on that painting, these biblical figures are to be understood as "the States Signified by . . . [their] Names, the Individuals being representatives or Visions of those States" (p. 546). Since man, through Milton, passes from the seventh eye of Jesus to the eighth eye of his Second Coming, Milton epitomizes, for Blake, the "inward-turning" process that culminates in apocalypse, in the highest state of mental freedom which is finally no state but human existence itself.[31] The seven eyes, the seven spirits, the seven angels of John's Apocalypse were traditionally associated with Christ's ministers who are charged with the building up of Jerusalem. By adding Milton to this assemblage, Blake makes clear that Milton is the city's master-builder, crediting his precursor with being the last, the most capacious, and thus, potentially, the most effectual of the apocalyptic angels.

Revelation, then, provides Blake with a precedent for his eighth apocalyptic angel and, so doing, enables Milton to enter into the same relationship with Blake that Revelation's eighth angel enjoys with John of Patmos. Of that angel we are told that "the earth was lightened with his glory" and that, upon proclaiming himself as

John's fellow prophet, the two together give "the testimony of Jesus" (xviii, 1; xix, 10). The figure of the eighth angel, through his relationship with John, is thus irrevocably linked to the story of the "two Witnesses"—a story that provides still further insight into Blake's alliance with Milton, yielding a biblical model for it.

St. John's account of the two witnesses is invoked in Blake's **Milton** by references to two sets of historical types—Whitefield and Wesley, Milton and Blake—and is accompanied by the suggestion that their prototype is the Bard ("Let the Bard himself *witness*," Blake says in plate 13). Even more directly, the story is the undoubted reference of the inscription Blake writes on the final plate of his poem: "I return from flames of fire tried & pure & white." That inscription has been explained as a cryptic reference to the conclusion of Milton's *Comus,* a poem Blake was illustrating as he was conceiving, if not writing, his own poem.[32] But, more to the point, Blake's inscription, as we have already observed, is a near quotation of a passage from the Book of Daniel, a passage often recalled marginally in exegesis of the story of John's two witnesses. Belonging to the last age and generally thought to be two particular men, the witnesses had been identified with various historical personages. Blake identifies them with Milton and himself, his point being that it is not the priests of the church but the poet-prophets who are the fullest approximations of these biblical models. To know who the witnesses are and what they represent is to understand more fully Blake's idea of Milton, as well as his idea of himself in relation to Milton. Their story, as told by St. John, epitomizes the meaning of Blake's poem and, at the same time, confirms the meaning we have already assigned to the iconography of plates 1 and 16.

The two witnesses of Revelation, dying and reviving after three and one-half days (that is, years), are called "two prophets" because they bear witness to the truth of a new life. These witnesses, as Henry More explains, are not naturally dead; instead John's reference is to "their Moral and Political Life and Resurrection"—they are "*alive,* or *slain,* either in a *Political,* or *Moral* sense." No sooner do the two witnesses "begin to perform their office of witnessing to the truth," says More, than they are "assaulted, suppressed, kept out of power, and *politically* killed"; but just as their death is political so too is their resurrection.[33] Their rising is a prelude to apocalypse, with England providing the stage on which it can be enacted.

The witnesses in Revelation recall all the famous pairs of prophets in the Old Testament: Moses and Aaron, Elijah and Elisha, Zerubbabel and Joshua. Builders of Jerusalem, they are charged with measuring, constructing, and finishing the temple; and their authenticity is established by their apparel, by their exchanging filthy

garments for white ones. It was understood by commentators on Revelation such as Joseph Mede and also Samuel Hartlib (Milton's friend who helped to popularize Mede's commentary) that white garments stained with blood are evidence that a hero, having undergone Christ's sacrifice (metaphorically through the annihilation of selfhood), has been redeemed by it.[34]

The changing of the garments thus occurs in a moment of symbolic death. Christ may have been crucified literally; but Milton and Blake, conforming to his pattern, are crucified metaphorically—Milton by succumbing to the politics of violence through his defense of regicide and Blake by acquiescing in the politics of withdrawal through his retreat to Felpham. In this sense, both poets are self-crucified, but they are both politically crucified as well, by a society that would distort, confuse, and even suppress their respective visions. Each poet dies, then, but each is also resurrected, both in his own lifetime and in his successors. In his own lifetime, Milton rises up, most notably, with the publication of *Paradise Regained*; and in his lifetime, Blake rises up on two occasions: first, when having fallen into a three-day death sleep following his brother's death, he awakened from it into the divine vision[35]; and later, when returning to London, after his three and one-half years' stay in Felpham, he renewed his commitment to visionary art. (In *Milton,* quite evidently, Blake mythologizes not only experiences from Milton's life but experiences from his own, an understanding that goes a long way toward explaining why, besides the eleven portrayals of Milton, there are portrayals of both Blake and his brother.) Both poets are also resurrected in their successors: Milton rising up in Blake and the other romantic poets, and Blake rising up in various modern poets who, like Yeats, set out to define his system just as Blake attempted to lay open Milton's. In this respect, both poets are like Elijah, who was said to rise up in John the Baptist, who, in turn, seemed to rise up again in Christ. In each instance, the rising witnesses represent a "great turn of things," a "hastening to the New Jerusalem," and their subsequent ascents into heaven are translated into a symbol both of their apotheosis and of the apotheosis of history they are expected to accomplish.[36] As mankind's deliverers from tyranny and servitude, the two witnesses, Milton and Blake, "pull downe errours and wicked vices."[37] They are revolutionaries who, like Christ, "confoundeth all traditions, and subverteth all constitutions,"[38] and whose story Blake invokes, believing with various commentators on Revelation that "God stirs up many of the English spirits . . . to finish what was before left incomplete."[39] And Blake appears to be committed, with these same commentators, to the idea that those who "receiveth a Prophet in the name of a Prophet shall receive a Prophet's reward."[40] So it is that Blake receives Milton and that he invites us to receive not just Milton but also himself.

In his portrayals of Milton, Blake remembers that the prophet's reward is a halo, which, shining like the sun, symbolizes his transcendent glory and special office; that the prophet, though called a star, is not just any star but the brightest in the firmament. According to Joseph Mede, the fallen prophet rolls great clouds through the heavens; yet fallen prophets rise again, and we know when their resurrection commences for they appear as stars breaking through the clouds, and we know, too, when their resurrection is completed for then they appear as the sun, signifying that the Word eventually pierces the dark cover that would conceal it.[41] Milton's resurrection begins in plate 1 . . . of Blake's poem: this is made clear by the fact that at exactly the point where Milton's hand rolls back the clouds (in the upper right-hand corner), a star shoots forth on the next plate; and Milton's resurrection is completed in plate 16 . . . , where the poet, holding white garments in both hands, has his head encircled by a sun.

Blake's *Milton,* then, rather than corroborating a theory of poetic influence predicated upon "anxiety," serves as a check upon it. And a similar check may be found outside this poem, in a response Blake makes to one of Lavater's aphorisms—a response that shows Blake standing in defiance of those who believe with Harold Bloom that St. Paul's admonition, "let each esteem others better than themselves," delineates "a pattern that no poet whatever could bear to emulate."[42] When Lavater writes, "*Who seeks those that* are greater *than himself, their greatness* enjoys, *and forgets his greatest* qualities *in their greater ones, is* already *truly great,*" Blake responds, "I hope I do not flatter my self that this is pleasant to me" (p. 577). The notion that Blake suffered under the anxiety of influence, that he was obsessed by a drive to transcend Milton, even at the cost of misrepresenting and misinterpreting him, is antithetical not only to the spirit of Blake's rejoinder to Lavater but to the principle of art that Blake enunciates in *A Descriptive Catalogue*: "To suppose that Art can go beyond the finest specimens of Art that are now in the world," says Blake, "is not knowing what Art is; it is being blind to the gifts of the spirit"—a principle, let it be noted, that follows upon Blake's remark that Milton represents "the extent of the human mind" (p. 535). Indeed, Harold Bloom's theory of influence negates the message that Blake allows to climax first *The Marriage of Heaven and Hell* ("The worship of God is. Honouring his gifts in other men each according to his genius, and loving the greatest men best" [plates 22-23]) and then *Jerusalem,* where in almost identical words he appeals, "Go, tell them that the Worship of God, is honouring his gifts / In other men: & loving the greatest men best, each according / To his Genius" (91: 7-9).

Blake, his own words testify, was not psychologically crippled by Milton; rather, he admits to having had the joy of seeing the divine countenance more distinctly in

him than in any other hero. The donning of the bright sandal in Blake's **Milton** occurs at a crucial moment—the moment of union between Blake and Milton. It should be understood in terms of the convention of prophecy which, recognizing that walking without sandals is a sign of great poverty or deep mourning, asserts that, conversely, strapping on the sandal signifies that the prophet, no longer impoverished, has achieved an integrated personality, is about to throw his entire being into his prophecy, making not his lips only, but his whole personality, the vehicle for the divine Word. Milton, in the full possession of all his prophetic faculties, is the ideal that Blake aspires to become, that he does become in this moment of union. In this moment, Blake does what Dante would not do.

Dante had taken Virgil as his guide in the *Commedia*; by taking Milton as his own guide in **Milton,** Blake introduces an analogy only to violate it. As a guide, Virgil was abandoned at the moment when Dante came to the threshold of paradise. In contrast, it is at exactly the moment when Blake is ready to enter eternity that Milton joins him: grasping Milton, in the form of "a bright sandal," becoming energized by him, Blake is now ready to walk with his mentor "forward thro' Eternity." The contrasting status that Blake here assigns to Dante and Milton is underscored by the eagle that figures so prominently in both the *Commedia* and Blake's **Milton.** In the *Commedia,* the eagle awakens Dante; but in Blake's epic, the eagle *as* **Milton**[43] is poised to awaken Albion, to ready England for Apocalypse. . . . This idea, if not this very figure, stands behind most Romantic criticism of Milton.

In their idea of Milton, the Romantics found a motive for their criticism. Milton set out to rescue men from the oppressive orthodoxies of civilization; and the Romantics, in turn, none more notably than Blake, undertook to release Milton from the prisons of critical orthodoxy that had manacled his vision. Unveiling the Miltonic vision, these poets could assist Milton in the task with which they charged him. Their criticism, to be sure, is pointed, yet usually judicious; but it is also orchestrated as a symphony of praise, honoring not Milton alone but the whole tradition of poetry that, because he perfected and popularized it, Milton may be said to have fathered.

The Milton tradition, I should say in conclusion, is what Blake understood it to be, the tradition of prophecy; and that tradition is rich indeed, involving a way of seeing and a way of writing—indeed, a whole system of aesthetics. In addition, prophecy involves a way of relating: it postulates a theory of influence and provides a paradigm for intrapoetic relationships. But a word of caution: prophecy does not explain *all* poetic relationships; and it certainly does not provide, as Harold Bloom attempts to do, a paradigm for all "fruit-

ful poetic influence . . . since the Renaissance."[44] Instead, prophecy sustains a view of poetry, like Shelley's, that emphasizes its interconnectedness, its progressive character—a view of poetry that pertains not to poets who approach their precursors as if they were grab bags to steal from or Nobodaddys they must run away from, but to those who encounter their predecessors in an attitude of cooperation. In *The Arte of Prophecying,* William Perkins makes the point admirably well, observing, in accordance with 1 Corinthians xiv, 31-32, that "Prophets . . . are not to be reprooved of other Prophets," for they "prophesy one by one," each new prophet being "subject to" his predecessors.[45] Prophecy, then, is creation, not *ex nihilo* but out of pre-existent matter; accordingly, prophets study old prophecies by way of creating new ones, old prophecy, as one commentator on Revelation puts it, providing "the frame" from which new prophecy "is fetched."[46] Visionary art is thus marked by interdependence, by a "multifarious Allusivenesse"[47] that establishes continuity between prophecies and communion among prophets. Such communion Blake sought with Milton and many moderns have sought with both poets.

The collective influence of Milton and Blake is evident in many quarters, some unexpected. Much has already been said about how modern poets have echoed Milton and Blake—their words, phrases, even their ideas. What needs to be said is that this echoing process, operating in accordance with prophetic tradition, does not imply a paucity of poetic talent. Rather, its purpose is to indicate a relationship, to authenticate it, by confirming old prophecy anew and by throwing new light on its import. This process, because it yokes together the old and the new, also punctuates the interdependence of visionary art. Christopher Wordsworth understood this principle well and, in fact, traced it to Revelation, where, he explains, repeated words and phrases "serve to connect one portion with another," showing that the Apocalypse is interwoven with the prophecies of the Old Testament to form "a compact whole with them."[48] Authenticated by scriptural prophecy, the same process is operative in English poetry, joining the poems of Chaucer, Spenser, and Milton with those of the Romantics and moderns. Their various poems, to appropriate words from Shelley's *Defence of Poetry,* are "episodes to that great poem which all poets, like the cooperating thoughts of one great mind, have built up since the beginning of the world." The lesson in the poetics of influence to be learned from Shelley is the same one that Milton, through his poetry and prose, taught Blake and that Blake, through **Milton,** delivered to future generations of artists—to those, that is, with the eyes to see and the ears to hear.

Notes

1. All quotations of Blake, the sources of which are given parenthetically within the text, are from *The*

Poetry and Prose of William Blake, rev. ed., ed. David V. Erdman (New York, 1970). My observations on the illuminations for *Milton* are based upon Copy D of the poem, owned by Lessing J. Rosenwald, which is now in the Library of Congress. Because Erdman does not number full-page designs, his numbering of plates does not correspond with Copy D; I have therefore inserted in brackets the corresponding plate number of Copy D. Thus 15 [17]: 47-48 means plate 15, lines 47-48, in the Erdman edition, which corresponds with plate 17 in Copy D. For a full discussion of the different versions of the plates reproduced with this essay, see my *Angel of Apocalypse: Blake's Idea of Milton* (Madison, Wis., 1975), pp. 13-48. The present essay develops a number of perceptions that are scattered through my book.

2. Henry More, *Apocalypsis Apocalyseos; or the Revelation of St. John the Divine Unveiled* (London, 1680), p. xvii.

3. For the tradition behind Blake's identification, see Marjorie Reeves, *The Influence of Prophecy in the Later Middle Ages: A Study of Joachimism* (Oxford, 1969), pp. 143, 154, but also pp. 193, 209, 232-33, 354, 443; and see also George Gifford, *Sermons upon the Whole Booke of the Revelation* (London, 1599), p. 33.

4. *The Illuminated Blake* (New York, 1974), pp. 217, 248.

5. David Pareus, *A Commentary upon the Divine Revelation of the Apostle and Evangelical John,* tr. Elias Arnold (Amsterdam, 1644), pp. 161-64.

6. *The Apocalypse Explained According to the Spiritual Sense,* 5 vols. (New York, 1846-47), nn. 517-19.

7. Ludowick Muggleton, *A True Interpretation of the Eleventh Chapter of St. John* (1662; rpt. ed., London, 1833), p. 118.

8. *The Apocalypse Explained,* n. 533.

9. Ibid., n. 536.

10. The Mighty Angel of the Apocalypse, because his hand is raised, is customarily associated with the Angel in the Book of Daniel; see, for example, William Fulke, *Praelections upon the Sacred and Holy Revelation of S. John,* tr. George Gifford (London, 1573), p. 64; and Henry Bullinger, *A Hundred Sermons upon the Apocalypse of Jesu Christ* (London, 1573), pp. 130 ff. The contrast between the Angel of the Bottomless Pit and the Mighty Angel of John's Apocalypse is interestingly developed by William Guild, *The Sealed Book Opened* (London, 1656), p. 100: the Mighty Angel comes down with a face like a sun (that is, bringing light with him), whereas the Angel of the Bottomless Pit, enveloped by smoke and clouds, brings darkness; the Mighty Angel is thus charged with dispelling the errors, with rolling back the dark clouds created by his adversary. Blake sees Milton as his own adversary, and thus in plate 1 . . . Milton is shown overcoming (that is, dispersing) the errors of the Natural Man. Blake's conception is in keeping with Guild's belief that Christians "mis-know" Antichrist: "the seduced Christian looks for an individual Antichrist" in history; the true Christian finds the Antichrist within and thereupon extirpates him (sig. A4).

11. See Patrick Forbes, *An Learned Commentarie upon the Revelation of Saint John* (Middleburg, 1614), p. 81.

12. *His glory, his majesty*—these are the qualities, judging from inscriptions that accompany Milton portraiture of the eighteenth century, that artists before Blake attempted to capture in their portrayals of the poet. Many eighteenth-century portraits of Milton carry Dryden's famous epigram, which represents Milton as surpassing both Homer and Virgil in "loftiness of thought" and "Majesty"; another epigram by Jonathan Richardson, Jr., accompanying a portrait by his father, represents Milton as a "Fierce Dazling light," calling Milton "Another Sun" (the tradition is charted by John Rupert Martin, *The Portrait of Milton at Princeton and Its Place in Milton Iconography* [Princeton, 1961], see esp. plates 7, 8, 11, and 13).

13. These associations are developed by Swedenborg in *The Apocalypse Explained,* n. 533. In *The Influence of Prophecy in the Later Middle Ages,* Reeves provides a useful gloss on the idea behind Blake's title-page design, explaining that "in the development of the Sibylline prophecies we see the desire for a human triumph in history struggling with the conviction that only divine intervention can overcome the inherent evil in man. From this conflict of ideas" (and I would argue that precisely this conflict of ideas stands behind Blake's poem) emerges the figure of a human savior (in Blake's poem, Milton), "a Last Emperor who achieves a partial triumph before the final onset of evil and the final spiritual intervention" (p. 299). That figure, Reeves notes, appears in clouds . . . at the moment just before his triumph. . . .

14. William Perkins, *Lectures upon the Three First Chapters of the Revelation* (London, 1604), p. 323. Blake here toys with the paradox prominent in commentary on Revelation: that a body clothed conceals a naked soul; that, conversely, a naked body reveals a soul clothed in Christ. It should be noted as well that, while the coloration of the gar-

ments in Copy D suggests the blood-stained garments in both Revelation and the final plates of *Milton,* another detail, Milton's foot on the garment, reminds us that the poet is able to assume white garments (to become clothed with Christ and with Ololon) only because, and only after, he casts off his filthy garments. Plate 16 gathers both moments into a single illumination.

15. Swedenborg, *The Apocalypse Explained,* n. 65.

16. Ibid. The rending of the garment in two pieces, as it appears in plate 16 . . . , involves an allusion to 2 Kings ii, 12; and the rending occurs at the moment that the mantle of prophecy is passed from Elijah to Elisha—in Blake's poem at the moment it is passed from Milton to Blake. Correspondingly, that moment signals for Milton, as it does for Elijah, his transfiguration, his apotheosis.

17. Perkins, *Lectures,* pp. 105-06.

18. See "The Apotheosis of Milton, A Vision," *Gentleman's Magazine,* VIII (1738), 223-35, 469, 521-22; IX (1739), 20-21, 73-75. John Hawkins included this piece in volume 11 of *The Works of Samuel Johnson* (London, 1787-88). On the attribution, see *Monthly Review,* LXXVII (1787), 69.

19. *Disembodied Laughter: Troilus and the Apotheosis Tradition* (Berkeley and Los Angeles, 1972), pp. 37-38.

20. William Riley Parker, *Milton: A Biography,* 2 vols. (Oxford, 1968), II, 1065.

21. I quote from *Comus: A Masque* (London, 1750), p. 5.

22. *Milton and English Art* (Manchester, 1970), p. xxvii; see also n. 12 of this essay.

23. On the historicizing of Satan, see Christopher Hill, *Antichrist in Seventeenth-Century England* (London, 1971), but also Reeves, *Influence of Prophecy;* on the secularizing of Christ, see M. H. Abrams, *Natural Supernaturalism: Tradition and Revolution in Romantic Literature* (New York, 1971).

24. (New York, 1973), p. 30. Bloom applies his theory, not to Blake, but to a number of other poets including Spenser and Milton, Wordsworth and Shelley, in *A Map of Misreading* (New York, 1975). Here the Spenser-Milton relationship replaces the Milton-Blake relationship of *The Anxiety of Influence,* becoming a new paradigm for the operation of poetic influence. It is noteworthy that in *A Map of Misreading* Blake is scarcely mentioned, one suspects because he is too much the idealist: "Poets, supposedly defending poetry, idealize their relationship to one another," writes

Bloom, "and the magical Idealists among critics follow the poets in this self-deception. Northrop Frye idealizes more powerfully than ever Blake does" (p. 199). Nonetheless, we must conclude, as Bloom seems to do, that Blake does *idealize:* specifically, he idealizes his relationship with Milton in *Milton;* then he writes *Jerusalem* under Milton's sway.

25. *Anxiety of Influence,* p. 39. In *A Map of Misreading,* Bloom observes that "poets tend to think of *themselves* as stars because their deepest desire is to be an influence, rather than to be influenced, but even in the strongest, whose desire is accomplished, the anxiety of having been formed by influence still persists" (pp. 12-13; italics added). In *Milton,* it should be emphasized, Blake depicts Milton, not himself, as a star, thereby celebrating rather than retreating from the poet whose vision helps to shape his own. Analogously, in his famous sonnet, "London, 1802," Wordsworth represents Milton as "a Star" (9): Milton, he says, is "Pure as the naked heavens, majestic, free" (11). *Pure,* one supposes, and *free* from the anxieties that Bloom ascribes to him and to his Romantic successors.

26. William Lilly, *Merlinus Anglicus Junior: The English Merlin Reviv'd,* 2d ed. (London, 1644), sig. [A1ᵛ].

27. Perkins, *Lectures,* p. 250.

28. "Of Prophecy," in *A Collection of Theological Tracts,* ed. Richard Watson, 6 vols. (London, 1785), IV, 362.

29. Harold Bloom, *Blake's Apocalypse: A Study in Poetic Argument* (New York, 1963), p. 441.

30. *A Blake Dictionary: The Ideas and Symbols of William Blake* (Providence, R.I., 1965), p. 134.

31. See Andrew Wright, *Blake's Job: A Commentary* (Oxford, 1972), p. 3; and for what is still the finest exposition of this symbolism as it is used by Blake, see also Northrop Frye, *Fearful Symmetry: A Study of William Blake* (1947; rpt. ed., Boston, 1962), esp. pp. 360-61 and 448-49.

32. See Irene Tayler, "Say First! What Mov'd Blake? Blake's *Comus* Designs and *Milton,*" in *Blake's Sublime Allegory: Essays on The Four Zoas, Milton, and Jerusalem,* ed. Stuart Curran and Joseph Anthony Wittreich, Jr. (Madison, Wis., 1973), p. 257. The position that the inscription has no real bearing on this design has been taken, most recently, by John E. Grant in an essay that comments helpfully on designs not attended to in my own essay. See "The Female Awakening at the End of Blake's *Milton*: A Picture Story, with Ques-

tions," in *Milton Reconsidered: Essays in Honor of Arthur E. Barker,* ed. John Karl Franson (Salzburg, 1976), pp. 95, 97.

33. *Apocalypsis Apocalypseos,* pp. 105-08; and see also Thomas Goodwin, *An Exposition of the Revelation* (1639), in *The Works of Thomas Goodwin,* 12 vols. (Edinburgh, 1861-66), III, 158-59, 189, 190-91.

34. See Mede's *Key of the Revelation,* tr. Richard More, 2d ed. (London, 1650), p. 112; and Hartlib et al., *The Revelation Reveled by Two Apocalyptical Treatises* (London, 1651), pp. 57, 67.

35. See Kaethe Wolf-Gumpold, *William Blake: Painter, Poet, Visionary,* tr. Ernest Rathgeben (London, 1969), p. 26.

36. Goodwin, *Exposition,* in *Works,* III, 149, 182, 192; see also Mede, *Key of the Revelation,* p. 23.

37. Gifford, *Sermons,* p. 197.

38. Bullinger, *A Hundred Sermons,* p. 46.

39. See, for example, Mede, *Key of the Revelation,* p. 110.

40. Ibid.

41. "Discourse XLII," in *The Works of Joseph Mede,* 2 vols. (London, 1664), I, 314-15; and also in *Works,* see "Discourse XXIII," I, 110-13.

42. *Anxiety of Influence,* p. 91.

43. The eagle, it should be noted, is a component of the iconography that develops around Milton portraiture in the eighteenth century.

44. *Anxiety of Influence,* p. 30.

45. In *The Works of Mr. W. Perkins,* 3 vols. (Cambridge, 1613), II, 664.

46. Richard Bernard, *A Key of Knowledge for the Opening of the Secret Mysteries of St. Johns Mysticall Revelation* (London, 1617), p. 89.

47. I borrow the phrase from Henry More, *An Exposition of the Seven Epistles to the Seven Churches* (London, 1669), p. 143.

48. *The Apocalypse* (London, 1849), p. xii.

Andrew M. Cooper (essay date spring 1981)

SOURCE: Cooper, Andrew M. "Blake's Escape from Mythology: Self-mastery in *Milton.*" *Studies in Romanticism* 20, no. 1 (spring 1981): 85-110.

[*In the following essay, Cooper analyzes representations of Blake's personal mythology in the poem.*]

The central problem of this essay is epitomized by the printing-house in ***The Marriage of Heaven and Hell*** depicting "the method in which knowledge is transmitted from generation to generation."[1] Blake here does not exalt the creation of art-forms, as is usually claimed,[2] but shows with characteristic dead-pan irony how unimaginatively people use them, and hence their deficiency and liability to perversion. The passage portrays a journey through the author's mind, a five-chambered zoo inhabited by the Senses.[3] These creatures, although mystifying to the reader (the brain and its operations can be surgically exposed to view without rendering any less elusive the phenomena of mind), are nonetheless clearly engaged in a common pursuit; despite their wildness, it appears they all labor submissively at some larger enterprise (mind). At this point, then, the creative process remains unified and continuous. However, once the "living fluids" of this forge-like brain are "cast into the expanse" and there "receiv'd by Men," they harden into metal books and become punctiliously "arranged in libraries." The forms for transmitting knowledge—books—prove to be most tame compared to the fantastic bestial energies that begot them.

I

This rather Gnostic view of the written word as entailing fragmentation of the mind's creative unity is not unique to Blake. It is shared in some measure by anybody who has ever felt that the thought is greater than its expression. Still, there is a vast difference between writers who enjoy an invigorating disquietude toward their finished *oeuvres* ("the next will be better"), and those who must struggle with a genuinely anxious ambivalence about the value of writing at all. ***The Marriage of Heaven and Hell***'s exuberance notwithstanding, it appears the works of the mid-1790's, especially their attempted résumé and consolidation in ***The Four Zoas,*** carry Blake further and further in the direction of the second attitude. The supernatural mythology merely implicit in ***The Marriage*** because volatilized for the most part by the author's intense personal Energy—it emerges chiefly through the Blake-Devil's Memorable Fancies, flippant public renditions of his still largely unrevealed, more seriously private imaginings[4]—now begins to calcify into a cluster of self-isolated individuals. Spinning outwards and down from their life-source in the poetic mind, Blake's miserable titans assume concrete form only at the very limit of entropy, Earth. Thus the same Fall that reduces the poet's boundless inner Energy to a set of discrete figures also furnishes, via this externalization, a comprehensive means of locating and identifying those figures: a grand mythology of the uncreating word. One sees from this that Blake's mythologizing is a compensation; but an insidious compensation, for the control it supplies him is largely illusory. Manipulate it as he may, especially in ***The Four Zoas,*** Blake's elaborate "grammar of the Imagination"

never quite offsets the debilitating realities of fallen self-expression so much as gesture back at them with reemphasis.

The Four Zoas represents a deliberate attempt at confronting this dilemma. It fails mainly through its shapelessness, reflecting too honestly the author's divided motives. The poem's huge bulk and scope, its consolidation of the Prophetic Books, above all its basic acceptance of the Christian model of fall and redemption, suggest an enormous effort at affirmation. Yet what the narrative affirms is the parodic view of form as springing from fall and fragmentation; Creation only gratifies the Zoas' megalomania and shields them from Eternity. Thus Blake's attempt to surmount the problem of fragmentation by writing a poem about it becomes itself part of the problem. One reads his perplexity in the story of Los. Like the mythologist, Los fabricates lifeforms. Although he knows his creations are merely provisional (come the apocalypse, all things will be one), circumstances compel Los to ignore this truth. Since Earth lies in imminent peril of Eternal Death, he cannot take time to assess his work but must forge on blindly without rest. And yet this blind urgency is itself potentially disastrous; for if Los loses sight of the main end, Eternity, his misguided industry will serve to usher in Eternal Death just as well as torpor would have done. Indeed, Los's endowing the Spectres with bodies makes them more not less capable of evil, so that he must refashion them all over again. Apparently he is defeating himself; hence his racking self-doubt.

It is no coincidence that the composition of *The Four Zoas* evinces the same floundering on the part of Blake. Written piecemeal, perhaps as largely unpremeditated reportage of contemporary military-political events,[5] the poem was evidently intended to capture history in the making, even to become itself a direct part of the upheavals it records. The question here is, how to end such a poem? Most likely, considering his inflamed millennialism, Blake expected the end of history would shortly end it for him. But it didn't, and so the poet toiled on, increasingly disturbed by lack of direction (as his extensive revisions suggest).[6] Like Los, Blake becomes lost in immediate labors of organization and alienated from their ultimate goal. A collapse of perspective ensues: the poet's personal strivings toward unity (namely, a completed poem) gradually displace those of the Universal Man, not dissimilar yet vastly more important. Blake avails himself little of the dramatic irony which, as the successful presentation of Urizen goes to show, could make us identify with his titans while recognizing that their pathetic efforts at self-integration only underscore their dehumanization. In consequence, he seems throughout *The Four Zoas* to be implicitly claiming the giant warriors as evidence of his own imaginative strength, when after all their size is primarily ironic: it indicates the monumental propor-

tions of man's misery and self-conflict. Similarly, the constant multiplication of mythological personae attests not the author's prolificness, as Blake enthusiasts tend to think, but the anxiety of the Universal Man compulsively struggling to conceal the inner void made by his fragmentation—a labor of evasion which fragments him all the more.

Blake's evident abandonment of *The Four Zoas*— whether or not he ultimately intended to engrave it, the existing MS is plainly something less (or more) than a finished copy—no doubt rescued the poem from the process of calcification depicted in *The Marriage of Heaven and Hell*; but of course a rescue so desperate is failure by any other name. Ultimately Blake did make Los succeed, but only through a paradox. In the Eighth Night abruptly enters Satan, Lord of Spectres, who soon hypostatizes so much darkness that he bursts the Limits of Contraction and Opacity within which the narrative takes place, and falls out of the poem. The reifying Selfhood actually reifies itself out of the personality; his epiphany is suicide. Ostensibly, Satan's defeat leaves Los victorious. But if Satan defeats himself, Los could hardly find his *post facto* victory personally very satisfying; his sudden transformation into Luvah renders such satisfaction moot, anyway. So instead of an encounter between the antagonists Satan and Los, the poem offers only their separate epiphanies. Yet Blake had good reason for avoiding this encounter. Face-to-face with Satan, Los might not have withstood his archenemy. After all, what is Satan but a mass of spectrous forms which Los himself created? Blake's evasion is even more telling in view of his identification with Los. For may we not suppose that Los's specious consummation of his long-suffering labors accurately reflects the factitiousness of Blake's apocalyptic Night the Ninth, a finale imposed without real mastery of his poem's complexities?[7]

II

Nevertheless, it is only by countenancing such ambiguities that one can overcome them. Self-doubt thrives on the effort to pretend it does not exist. In actuality, says Blake, self-doubt cannot exist, being a contradiction or Negation,[8] but evidently one must look hard at it in order to make it disappear. This we do at the end of *Milton,* where Satan forfeits his illusive existence acquired through *The Four Zoas* and stands fully exposed as the formless "Trembling & fear, terror, constriction; abject selfishness" (38:39) lurking about Milton's and Blake's and every man's "outline of identity" (38:10). Thus *Milton* strives toward an unqualified affirmation of concrete human life. In the closing scene Blake repossesses his mythology as direct personal vision, thereby returning to a new form of the vigorous self-expression of *The Marriage of Heaven and Hell.* And as we shall see, the entire preceding course of the poem works to

make possible this final scene in all its passionate apprehension of particularity.

The circumstances of *Milton*'s composition are well-known.[9] Suffice to say that Blake's dilemma vis-à-vis patron Hayley, critical as it was to Blake's material welfare, seems to have assumed even greater proportions for him privately. The letter to Butts of January 10, 1802 reveals grave anxieties intensified by the poet's fear of having compromised his artistic, and therefore spiritual, integrity. Breaking away from the dangerous security of Hayley's patronage thus could represent for Blake a triumph over internal doubts having little to do with Hayley or Felpham in direct fact. "I have indeed fought thro a Hell of terrors & horrors (which none could know but myself.) in a Divided Existence," he told Hayley himself on December 4, 1804; "now no longer Divided. nor at war with myself I shall travel on in the strength of the Lord God as Poor Pilgrim says." In overcoming Felpham's temptation of corporeal ease, Blake had asserted as in earlier days the autonomy of Imagination and the precedence of his artist's calling: "I have proved that I am Right & shall now Go on with the Vigor I was in my Childhood famous for. . . . My Enthusiasm is still what it was only Enlargd and confirmd."[10]

Yet the characteristic exuberance of these letters is expressed in quite new tones of brotherliness and humility. As his last remark suggests, Blake's recovered enthusiasm necessarily differed from the enthusiasm that had been lost, for the struggle of recovery had altered the man himself. Perhaps not by coincidence, Blake now begins to develop a doctrine of provisional States through which the individual passes on pilgrimage to renewed unity.

> Distinguish therefore States from Individuals in those States.
> States change: but Individual Identities never change or cease:
> You cannot go to Eternal Death in that which can never Die.
>
> Judge then of thy Own Self; thy Eternal Lineaments explore
> What is Eternal & what Changeable? & what Annihilable!
> The Imagination is not a State: it is the Human Existence itself.
>
> (32:22-32)[11]

Although his youthful Devil's repudiation of external form cannot be sustained, it remains for Blake to master the corollary development of a flexible, human relation to form. In *Milton* he turns upon himself the dramatic irony merely latent in *The Four Zoas*. Through a series of mergings, the various mythological figures belie their apparent autonomy and ultimately reveal themselves to be extruded personae of the man William Blake. Thus re-integrated into a human being, the poet, for all his mortal weakness, is literally seen to surpass his wildest imaginings. *Milton* is Blake's exploration of his own mythological "lineaments," culminating in his arrival at the "Individual Identity" that underlay them all and indeed made the whole exploration possible. The poem comprises a series of States of mythological non-being finally leading to disclosure of "the Human Existence itself": the inspired Blake living in Felpham who has just completed *Milton*.

Recent studies of *Milton*'s structure tend to distinguish several different narratives within the poem, each of which is considered to repeat a fundamental pattern of prophetic awakening and descent. As James Rieger observes: "Rhetorically, *Milton* exists on four levels of discourse, corresponding to the four worlds of Blake's myth. . . . The utterances of any higher realm are only partially intelligible to the inhabitants of the worlds below it. That is the central stylistic problem of the poem."[12] This needs a caveat. For what the visionary finale of *Milton* suggests is that none of the worlds of Blake's myth is fully real, precisely *because* they all entail "style." How to expose the Logos underlying actual everyday human life and indeed all human expression, poetry included, without simply reducing it to these mundane appearances: *that* is the central stylistic problem of the poem. Hence Susan Fox's emphasis on the poem's basic "structural principles" is perhaps slightly, but crucially, misplaced. Fox quotes Riffaterre summarizing Jakobson: "the recurrence of equivalent forms, parallelism, is the basic relationship underlying poetry." Then she one-ups him: "Parallelism is more than that in *Milton*; it is the theme of the poem realized concretely as its narrative structure."[13] But if the arrangement of *Milton* shows anything, it is that the poem's recurrent "forms" ("the four worlds of Blake's myth," presumably) are *not* genuine logical equivalents. The emphasis falls on their non-identicality and non-convertibility. Strictly speaking, then, parallelism is not "the theme of the poem" but only a technique. It is Blake's provoking *use* of parallelism that enables him to dramatize his real theme, Self-annihilation, a theme paradoxical to earthly sense and thus expressible only indirectly.

I am suggesting that *Milton* progressively "uses up" its various styles so as to unveil its theme without ever actually embodying it. Each style merely serves as means to the next, until finally style itself is called into question and, as W. J. T. Mitchell sees, *Milton* the poem self-annihilates just like Milton the character.[14] *Milton*'s "parallelism" is purely functional. It is the rehearsal of a single prophetic pattern on several different levels which serve, first, to expose the animating truth behind the pattern (the Logos of the conclusion), but then also serve to signal the falseness of reducing this truth to

any of the vehicles that shadow it forth (the mythopoeic Bard, the mythological Los, the various spiritual figures of Milton, or the historical character William Blake in Felpham garden circa 1800). Such parallelism we might term "sublime allegory" according to Blake's definition: "Allegory address'd to the Intellectual powers, while it is altogether hidden from the Corporeal Understanding."[15]

Hence *Milton*'s narrative is as paradoxically incorporeal as its theme. The different journeys of the Bard, Milton, Los, and Blake link up through the progressive merging together of these protagonists, yet the single extended journey which results doesn't go anywhere at all. *Milton* ends in the same Felpham garden that Damon showed to be allegorically concealed within the **"Bard's Song."**[16] Meanwhile, though, the stylistic context becomes changed utterly, from obscure mythology to a comparatively detailed naturalistic presentation of human life. What kind of journey returns to its starting-point, only on a new level? A spiral. Unlike "The Greater Romantic Lyric," however, *Milton* spans not years but a single moment. This flattens the spiral, precluding spacious open-ended meditation back and forth through time such as M. H. Abrams finds in Coleridge and Wordsworth.[17] Yet as we've seen, the result for Blake is not circular repetition of the journey. Since the mythic cosmology of the **"Bard's Song,"** the poem's point of departure, is of much vaster scope than the concluding particularized depiction of the author's house and grounds in Felpham, it appears the path of *Milton* forms an eddy. Moreover, since Felpham was in reality the place where Blake composed the poem, as eventually he tells us at 36:21-24, *Milton* eddies toward a center which is also its source. In sum, the poem describes a Vortex:

> The nature of infinity is this: That every thing has its
> Own Vortex; and when once a traveller thro' Eternity
> Has passed that Vortex, he perceives it roll backward
> behind
> His path, into a globe itself infolding; like a sun:
> Or like a moon, or like a universe of starry majesty,
> While he keeps onwards in his wondrous journey on
> the earth
> Or like a human form, a friend with whom he lived
> benevolent.

(15:21-27)

The Vortex is a process. It delineates the coming to grips with and mastering of ordinary fragmented experience. Even as the mental traveller circles involvedly about some local "thing" (such as a poem), he also progresses steadily toward an apex that will free him to continue his life journey. He thus avoids entrapment within the products of his "concentration"; these come to be regarded merely as means of continuing the journey. Although a Vortex seems engulfing at the open end ("infinity"), it appears in retrospect a solid object, that

portion of ourselves we have lived through and can never re-enter ("a human form"). As the afterthought of the last line insists, the sense of loss is great. Yet there is a corresponding gain in self-perception. "For man cannot know / What passes in his members till periods of Space & Time / Reveal the secrets of Eternity: for more extensive / Than any other earthly things, are Mans earthly lineaments" (21:8-11). The configuration of the poem works to dramatize this basic law of providence. Whether or not we agree with J. A. Wittreich that *Milton* progresses from shadowy types to truth specifically by virtue of belonging to the genre of "epic prophecy,"[18] passage through the *Milton* Vortex clearly does generate a crystallization of awareness, as the cosmic **"Bard's Song"** is discovered in retrospect to be the projection of a quite particular bard, William Blake. If the human poet cuts a modest figure alongside the sublime Bard, nevertheless he is not belittled; the contrast arises only because man is sometimes unequal to his own desires. So Eternity, which at first seemed a vast self-enclosed universe, is found to concentrate within the author's mind.

The course of *Milton,* then, is a progressive compression of form leading to the internalization of form as vision, thus liberating the poet from his work.[19] What we could call *Milton*'s "Living Form"[20]—its symbiosis of style and narrative—appears literally as a form of subjectivity. The poem's growth in self-expressiveness suggests ineluctably that the figure who comes into focus as William Blake was present imperceptibly throughout the rest of the poem as well. That is, when Blake suddenly appears in Felpham garden repossessing his mythology as personal vision, we can only conclude that for the whole preceding course of the poem he must have been lost *within* the mythology. Lacking "outline of identity," he couldn't possibly have entered the narrative as an individual possessing mental acts of his own. Yet he was all the while struggling to do and be just this. The author, we realize, had succumbed to the entropy of "becoming what you behold." *Milton* was his means of getting back inside his visionary self.[21]

* * *

If *Milton* shows the poet progressively becoming himself, logically the beginning of the poem should show him furthest from his goal. "He," however, must be taken figuratively in this case: if the poet has scarcely begun to become himself, who, or what, is he? The question defines our experience of plates 3-7. Far from viewing the author Blake assimilated into his poem as a distinct human figure ("a human form . . ." such as the conclusion presents), here one apprehends merely unmediated intention, an inchoate "authority" gesticulating *through* the broken verse paragraphs, not expressing itself by means of them. These plates represent the engulfing end of the *Milton* vortex. Yet the effect is not

simple confusion but rather darkness visible, inarticulateness made explicit. The narrative disjunctions thwart the narrative, and all critical attempts to make sense of it as well,[22] yet they do communicate an unmistakable force of will. What we seem to confront is a kind of stammering, the speech act reduced to physical impulse. In light of the author's palpable absence from his text, it is perhaps appropriate we call in a surrogate to help establish a basis of understanding. Consider Nietzsche's analysis of the experience of "willing":

> Willing seems to me to be above all something complicated. . . . In all willing there is, first, a plurality of sensations, namely, the sensation of the state "away from which," the sensation of the state "towards which," the sensations of this "from" and "towards" themselves, and then also an accompanying muscular sensation. . . . [Also,] in every act of the will there is a ruling thought—let us not imagine it possible to sever this thought from the "willing," as if any will would then remain over! Third, the will is . . . above all an affect, and specifically the affect of the command. That which is termed "freedom of the will" is essentially the affect of superiority in relation to him who must obey: "I" am free, "he" must obey. . . . But we are accustomed to disregard this duality, and to deceive ourselves about it by means of the synthetic concept "I" . . . to such a degree that he who wills believes sincerely that willing suffices for action.[23]

Broadly speaking, *Milton* reveals a development similar to the one outlined here. The poem progresses from a confusing plurality of sensations entailing gradual disclosure of a ruling thought—namely, "William Blake"—to a triumphant sense of self-mastery and renewed power. The opening plates primarily exhibit obscure first-stage "sensations." But they do so in a manner as highly specific as Nietzsche's analysis would suggest.

The passages comprising plates 3-7 form two sets: 1) pieces of an epic narrative which subsequently becomes the **"Bard's Song"** (4:1-20, 5:1-4), and 2) everything else. The second set is not random, however, but has two defining characteristics: first, the identifiability of the material, which presents either scenes from London (4:21-28, 5:38-6:35) or interpolations of Blake's previous mythologizing (3, 5:5-37); second, the material's apparent total irrelevance to the proposed theme of the narrative, the Three Classes of Men. In set 2, then, is represented Nietzsche's "sensation of the state 'away from which'": the selfhood of accumulated past experience (the historical Blake's life in London, his previous literary writings) which is to be overcome through self-annihilation (hence the passages' irrelevance to the work at hand). Set 1, the narrative bits, gives on the other hand "the sensation of the state 'towards which'": the new poem, whose successful performance will revitalize the poet's identity. The narrative disjunctions embody "the sensation of this 'from' and 'towards' themselves" and its "accompanying muscular sensation." They manifest the disruptiveness of the speech act *as* an act, the effort needed to wrest oneself out of oneself and so create possibilities for growth—possibilities which are not actualized until plate 7, when the Bard begins to sing in earnest.

The success of this effort is measured by the seven-times repeated "Mark well my words! they are of your eternal salvation."[24] Is this the Bard addressing his epic audience, or the author warning baffled readers not to throw the book down? Initially (2:25) there is no way of telling; the line lacks a determining context. Yet by plate 7 it has occurred no fewer than three times. Such insistence is necessary presumably because the poem's words indeed do *not* appear of our eternal salvation. The abrupt injunction only makes us more forcibly aware how far *Milton* is from containing a persona who might plausibly be speaking with such self-assurance. However, once the **"Bard's Song"** becomes continuous (plate 7), the phrase is henceforth heard as his. If we continue to hear in it the author's personal voice, it is only indirectly, *via* the Bard's (just as we learn of Blake's residence at Felpham *via* the Bard's epic allegory). So it appears the author has finally submerged himself in the Bard persona. Previous "Mark well my words!" tended to sound self-important, like a parody of the somewhat firmer admonitions of Milton's epic voice. By contrast, the final two repetitions seem to reveal a distinctly new tone of seriousness and authority. They evince the growth in self-mastery that Nietzsche sees as springing from a successful act of the will: "'I' am free, 'he' must obey." It is by some such development as this that the inchoate would-be author of plates 3-7 evolves into the Bard, a collective entity more resembling Homer than the supremely individualistic Milton, but one who can at least speak and be recognized.

But why should *Milton*'s initial speech act entail an effort of will so much more conspicuous than that of any other poem? Most simply, because *Milton* takes place within a single moment of inspiration; the poem scrutinizes at length mental acts occurring in a flash. A more detailed reply is suggested by the ambiguities of the invocation. As Harold Bloom noticed, the Daughters of Beulah "delight" but they also offer "delusions" (2:1-5).[25] Like patrons, the Daughters are a necessary evil. By refreshing the pilgrim's hunger and thirst they enable him to continue his spiritual journey; yet these refreshments are also temptations to abandon the journey. The poet's capsule history of Beulah can therefore be seen to summarize the mythology leading up to and necessitating *Milton*:

> . . . Come into my hand
> By your mild power; descending down the Nerves of my right arm

> From out the Portals of my Brain, where by your ministry
> The Eternal Great Humanity Divine. planted his Paradise,
> And in it caus'd the Spectres of the Dead to take sweet forms
> In likeness of himself. Tell also of the False Tongue! vegetated
> Beneath your land of shadows: of its sacrifices, and
> Its offerings; even till Jesus, the image of the Invisible God
> Became its prey; a curse, an offering. and an atonement.
>
> (2:5-13)

The agents of Eternal Great Humanity Divine are modestly unnamed, but lines 2:8-10 clearly refer to Los's labors in **The Four Zoas** "to fabricate embodied semblances in which the dead May live,"[26] and by extension to Blake's own attempt at forming a mythological pantheon. The poet appears fully aware of the greenhouse effect to which his mental garden is liable. "The False Tongue" is evidently a run-away mythological language which has usurped the human realities meant to be its inspiration ("even Jesus") and destroyed itself as a result (thus becoming a curse *and* an atonement).

The invocation tells not simply that **Milton** is to be the product of misleading Muses, Bloom's point. It indicates further that the poet acknowledges these Muses' necessity to himself. Either he must accept his unreliable mythological tongue, at least provisionally, or forever hold his peace, for it seems the tongue cannot be made true but by process of use. The inarticulateness of plates 3-7 reflects the poet's not unanxious search for a viable mythology with which to begin the new poem, a search complicated by his consciousness of the potential falsity of mythology. We see him attempting a variety of styles recalling the **Books of Los and Urizen** (3), **Visions of the Daughters of Albion** (5:19-37), also **Jerusalem** Chapter One (6). And yet they all prove false starts, a fact which suggests the poet is not comfortable with any. Hence Blake cut the Preface when he added plates 3, 4 and 5 to the two previously completed versions of **Milton**; its aggressive self-confidence clashes with the effect of stammering anxiety which was evidently the reason for these plates. Modern editors are wrong to put the two together.[27]

Finally, on plate 7 the narrative disjunctions cease and the Bard takes control of **Milton.** Evidently the Muses of Beulah approve of his Song. So they should, for the style of the **"Bard's Song"** is the style of **The Four Zoas,** their most recent inspiration: hermetic mythology concealing autobiographical material within a cosmic narrative. The run-away False Tongue of **The Four Zoas** is where Blake left off before beginning **Milton**; by now accepting this Tongue as the only one he's got, Blake will perhaps be able to make it speak true, thus recovering poetic self-control. The story of Leutha, an apparent digression little regarded by most commentators, implies as much.[28] Calling herself "the Author" (11:35) of Satan's sin, Leutha claims she alone is responsible for Satan's losing control of the Harrow and Phaeton-like razing of Earth. Damon has shown that the Blakean Harrow can be seen as a vehicle of poetry: it plows "lines" into the poet's mental garden, enabling the spectres to vegetate into mythology. Leutha would therefore seem to be allegorizing a failure of authorship we have already noticed. It is moving to regard as the Blake of **The Four Zoas** her brave but cupidinous Satan struggling to master a self-imposed task that only gets harder the more he resists it, until finally he defeats himself, blackening the Earth he desired to glorify (the sun he pulls ought to be life-giving).

Yet this comparison, set up after all by the Blake of **Milton,** is also ironic. The allegory of Satan and his muse Leutha (a Daughter of Beulah) parodies the inspiration of *Paradise Lost.* Having followed his muse "Into the Heav'n of Heav'ns," the Miltonic poet in Book VII requests her for a safe journey home:

> Return me to my Native Element:
> Lest from this flying Steed unrein'd, (as once
> Bellerophon, though from a lower Clime)
> Dismounted, on th' Aleian Field I fall,
> Erroneous there to wander and forlorn.
> .
> Standing on Earth, not rapt above the Pole,
> More safe I sing with mortal voice.
>
> (VII, 16-24)[29]

Satan-Blake suffers just such a dismount, with consequences fully as damaging as Milton suggests: for the author of **Milton,** the run-away False Tongue of **The Four Zoas** is a form of wandering erroneous and forlorn. Yet this fall is not irreversible. In the end, **Milton** displays its author standing on Earth, not lost within the vastnesses of the **"Bard's Song,"** and singing more securely with mortal voice. Thus the falling Blake reaches the same destination Milton reached without falling; he only takes a more roundabout route. This twisting fortunate fall is Blake's passage through the vortex of the poem **Milton** itself.

Meantime, the Leutha-muse's nocturnal temptation of Satan-Blake is a mere travesty of Milton's "Celestial Patroness, who deigns / Her nightly visitation unimplor'd, / And dictates to me slumb'ring, or inspires / Easy my unpremeditated Verse" (IX, 21-24). In a quite different context, Erdman concludes that unpremeditation was precisely the cause of **The Four Zoas'** foundering. Each new narrative sequence necessitated painstaking revision of all the rest of the narrative before the two could be brought into alignment.[30] One step forward, two steps back: inspiration in this case is perhaps more facile than "easy." There is further irony in the

fact that Milton's lines accompany a demand for "answerable style" with which to complete the last, most directly human part of his argument, the eating of the apple; whereas the mythology of the uncompleted *Four Zoas,* we have seen, is a style unanswerably oblique. The thrust of these Miltonic parodies is to stress the provisionality of the Bard's Song; the style of *The Four Zoas* is adopted but then made to discredit itself. Evidently the poet of *Milton* is *using* the style as means to an identity beyond the Bard persona, who of course is unaware of the parodies, and its obliqueness enables him to avoid exposing his intentions prematurely.

* * *

The cosmos of the **"Bard's Song"** is an inner space. As Bloom in particular recognizes,[31] Los, Palamabron, Rintrah and Satan, whatever else they may be (*pace* Damon and Erdman), personify universal aspects of the poetic mind. In terms of the concomitant psychological allegory, Satan's fall is a purging of preoccupying self-doubts; it establishes the minimum of imaginative unity needed in order for the poet to look beyond himself to the announced story of Milton. Out of sight, out of mind: the obstreperous Satan actually disappears through his own breach in the psychic decorum (9:19-52). To avoid lobotomy, however, Satan is not destroyed but repressed, thus becoming cathected as remote but omnipresent anxiety. His fall is an apparent rise to power over the Earth created to sustain him in his Eternal Death (10:6-9). These events recapitulate the penultimate Eighth Night of *The Four Zoas,* but in *Milton* they are merely preliminary. The function of the Bard's Song is to externalize Satan from the poet's mind in order that he may then be discovered by Milton. Thus the Satan of corrupted Puritanism which the dead poet goes to redeem we see to be the living poet Blake's Satan of personal self-doubt. If the poetic mind behind the **"Bard's Song"** is too uncertain of himself to embrace Satan directly, he may yet do so indirectly by embracing Milton.

But not without struggle, as plates 14-22 show. The story of Milton's descent to Earth demands relinquishing the egocentric mythology of the **"Bard's Song."** No longer able to hide behind his titans, the author is simply thrust naked into the narrative, generating a crisis of confidence which threatens to end not just the **"Bard's Song"** but the poem itself. Milton's objective, we are told, is "Albions land: / Which is this earth of vegetation on which now I write" (14:40-41). Instantly the mythological curtain falls back—too late, though, to prevent a comparison of the two poets hardly reassuring for Blake. When the above-cited passage on the vortex next appears (15:21-27), it only re-emphasizes the author's need of humility. The "human form, a friend with whom [the traveller thro' Eternity] livd benevolent" recalls Hayley, and Blake's rueful realization that "Corporeal Friends are Spiritual Enemies"[32] who obstruct one's spiritual journey unless abandoned. In context, however, the traveller is Milton; Blake merely watches him from Earth below. So as Hayley was to Blake, now Blake is to Milton; like Hayley, Blake has become an expedient in a greater poet's mission. Hence when he again breaks into the narrative to declare how Milton entered his left foot (15:47-49), the account of the consequences focuses exclusively on Milton: his heightened self-awareness, his confrontations of the Shadowy Female, Urizen, and Rahab-Tirzah. Blake, evidently none the wiser for this merging, is ignored. So, although one might expect Blake as a poet to identify with Milton, there follows a startling outburst of despair in which he explicitly associates himself with Urizen's freezing clay:

> O how can I with my gross tongue that cleaveth to the dust,
> Tell of the Four-fold Man, in starry numbers fitly orderd
> Or how can I with my cold hand of clay! . . .
>
> Here, in the dead waste and middle of the poem, the poet apparently
> too feeble to pen another word, comes an about-face.
>
> . . . But thou O Lord
> Do with me as thou wilt! for I am nothing, and vanity.
> If thou chuse to elect a worm, it shall remove the mountains.
>
> (20:15-19)

The difference between the two passages is the difference between looking back toward a lost world (the Bard's mythological cosmos) and looking ahead to whatever might eventually replace it (Earth). Like Phoebus' reply to the despairing poet of *Lycidas* (". . . But not the praise"), Blake's tone shift is all the more abrupt for arriving at a line-ending; and yet it also serves manifestly to complete the line and continue the poem, thus seeming necessary and providential. The device in both cases makes the poet appear to discover, in his moment of need, an answering voice at some deeper stratum of himself. For Blake, the virtue of this voice is its unHomeric, unBard-like humility. By thus reconciling himself to an outwardly restricted role in the poem—a role heroic only in the passive Miltonic sense of "uprightness," "standing firm"[33]—Blake here begins to accept his Urizenic necessity to be remade in Milton's image. In a quite unprecedented style of direct address, he intimately enjoins us to share his awareness of the redeeming vulnerability of the life-principle:

> Seest thou the little winged fly, smaller than a grain of sand?
> It has a heart like thee; a brain open to heaven & hell,
> Withinside wondrous & expansive; its gates are not clos'd,
> I hope thine are not: hence it clothes itself in rich array;

Hence thou art cloth'd with human beauty O thou
 mortal man.
Seek not thy heavenly father then beyond the skies:
There Chaos dwells & ancient Night & Og & Anak
 old.

(20:27-33)

What dwells beyond the skies is mythology, "the Seat Of Satan" (20:37-38), an unregenerate disguising of the human which Blake now casts off. By contrast, the microcosmic fly stands at the other end of the *Milton* vortex, the infinitely small point at the tip where the mind repossesses its projections as lively acts of vision. Restricted Blake's role may be, but at least it is now overt, unvitiated. In a crucial affirmation, he tells how "all this Vegetable World appear on my left foot / As a bright sandal . . . / I stooped down & bound it on to walk forward thro' Eternity" (21:12-14). Blake's difficulties in reaching this resolution recall Satan on the last leg of his journey from Hell in *Paradise Lost*:

Satan now in prospect of Eden, and nigh the place
where he must now attempt the bold enterprise which
he undertook alone against God and Man, falls into
many doubts with himself, and many passions, fear,
envy, and despair; but at length confirms himself in
evil, [and] journeys on to Paradise. . . .

(The Argument, Bk IV)

Having survived his crisis of confidence, Blake—who with Milton appears as Satan to the now obviously impeded perception of Palamabron and Rintrah—can commence his final descent to Earth for the unmasking of the "real" Satan, the anxious Usurper of whom the Bard sang.

The description of Los's world (plates 22-30) consolidates *Milton*'s new style of direct address. It is a return to mythologizing after the disjunctions of plates 14-21, but mythologizing now in service of personal prophecy by Blake as author telling how poems get written. The redemptive Moment in which "the Poets Work is Done" (29:1) extends systematically the vision of sportive Minute Particulars that became available in the fly-passage of plate 20. Blake is no longer the Sons of Los but Los himself; thus from 25:66 to the close of Book One, the Father's exhortations to his Sons are simultaneously seen to be mythological explications controlled by the author directly. Unlike the **"Bard's Song,"** however, the mode of these plates is not autobiographical concealment. The Los persona does positively serve as a vehicle of self-expression. As the prophetic statement of their merging plainly shows—it begins as Blake's but ends by being attributed to Los (22:12-26)—Blake speaks not delphically through Los but rather *as* Los. This evidently is an improvement over the **"Bard's Song"**; yet the ultimate goal is for Blake to speak directly as himself.

For despite its splendors, Los's world can only be provisional. Although his Sons's ingenious artistry makes them masters of mundane time and space (28:44-29:36), the Sons are themselves limited and their realm of artistry is therefore insufficient. Los's apocalyptic Winepress operates with a distinct indifference to human life; occasionally in their exuberance the pressers trample and drown one another. Conversely, the merciful artisans who fashion forms for the doubting Spectres appear ignorant of their charges' fates: Rahab simply weaves them back into "the veil of human miseries" (29:62). If Los's world supplies the means of redeeming human life, as almost all readers agree it does, nevertheless Blake's point would seem to be that except in certain supreme Moments of vision one cannot actually dwell there and be human. Rather the place for ordinary human dwelling is, apparently, Earth.

Hence Blake-Milton's discovery that he must modify his journey of self-annihilation to include the more positive act of bringing Ololon to life. Ultimately, Ololon is the intimacy which John Milton, and implicitly William Blake, denied expression in their relationships on Earth, particularly with women.[34] Union with Blake teaches Milton that "the Three Heavens of Beulah were beheld / By him on earth in his bright pilgrimage of sixty years / In those three females whom his Wives, & those three whom his Daughters / Had represented and contained . . . / . . . also Milton knew: they and / Himself was Human" (15:51-17:6). Milton's new knowledge is the prerequisite for his eventual transformation. One can look back on one's public life as a Rintrah prophet-reformer, see its errors and decide, still in character, to reform them too; this is to be just before the Law. But the conscious desire to realize a portion of one's humanity which one never knew to exist even potentially, much less erroneously, implies a change of the character itself; this is Self-annihilation in the radical sense of conversion, the transformation of oneself through love into Christ, as the conclusion reveals.[35] Milton therefore cannot already know at the outset of his descent that there is something missing from his pilgrimage of sixty years which needs redemption. Gradually, his approach to Earth opens his eyes.

Thus the arousal of Ololon, the poet's human potential, is also gradual. *Milton* is arranged to present her phenomenologically: she is an event occasioned by the poet's awakening and meaningful solely in terms of it. So our first sight of Ololon, on plate 21, is just a glimpse. "A sweet River, of milk & liquid pearl. Namd Ololon" (21:15-16) groggily decides to descend into Beulah; the significance of this is unclear, but plainly it follows somehow from the union of Blake and Milton immediately preceding. Then comes Blake-Milton's further union with Los and journey through his realms of Imagination (plates 22-29). Our perceptions thus heightened, when plates 30-36 shift back to Ololon she appears proportionately more distinct. Here, Ololon is the collective personality of all her Sons and Daughters.

When finally she steps out the other side of Beulah into Felpham garden, "as One Female, Ololon and all its mighty Hosts / Appear'd: a Virgin of twelve years" (36:16-17). Like the poet himself, Ololon is becoming a progressively more human being. She has passed through a series of mythological lineaments—States—which are not themselves her Individual Identity but yet means to it.

The editing of *Milton* resembles a D. W. Griffith movie climax. Across a great Space (Earth) the pair of estranged lovers are seen straining with one instinct towards an embrace; meanwhile the poem cuts back and forth between them, looking through the eyes of each at the other figure coming into view, ever more urgently desired. Milton and Ololon, it seems, are converging on a single point. As the curiously prosaic illustration to plate 36 (**"Blake's Cottage at Felpham"**) shows, their inspired reunion takes place, finally, as nothing more or less than a moment of vision in the brain of the historical William Blake, who walked in the garden one spring dawn while his wife, "sick with fatigue" (36:32), remained indoors. So it appears that *every* day is a means of gathering in human potential (35:42-47); and every day, therefore, a type of the apocalypse to which it actually brings us one step closer (42:16-43:1).

What makes possible such exuberant mundaneness is the final dispersal of *Milton*'s mythology, revealing with enhanced beauty the concrete particulars that evidently stood behind it all along. The "Vision of the lamentation of Beulah over Ololon" (31:45, 63) derives from nothing more exotic than actual birds and flowers of an English spring morning. Like the pagan gods of the "Nativity Ode," or the pastoral tribute of flowers in *Lycidas*—gods and flowers to which Ololon is deliberately compared[36]—Blake's similarly unredeemed Tongue of Beulah burgeons most plangently while in process of falling silent. Yet despite this ironic awareness of suffering and loss, *Milton*'s lyricism here is primarily an exultant survey by the author, in person, of the brave new world he is about to inhabit. We are *told* that Ololon's music, a glad Song of Spring to the clogged ears of men, is for the virgin herself a lament of her impending womanhood; but what the poem actually presents to our hearing is the glad Song of Spring. The Tongue of *Milton,* then, is evidently no longer Beulah's but the mortal author's own.

* * *

Pointedly, Blake reports that when the virgin Ololon entered his garden he "address'd her as a Daughter of Beulah" (36:27). In other words she is his Muse, the invocation's generalized Daughters of Beulah compressed into human form. Evidently they are obeying his summons to come into his physical person from out the portals of his mythologizing brain (2:1-15); simply,

Blake then had no idea how arduous that journey might prove to be, and how tremendously important for himself.[37] Thus it appears the whole of *Milton* has taken place within the poet's single dawning moment of insight into the human truth behind the myth of his muses. The poem itself was only a means to this realization. So when Blake writes Butts from Felpham, April 25, 1803, disclosing "the Grand Reason of my being brought down here," he barely mentions the "long poem" which it seems he has just accomplished for the most part but instead stresses the "spiritual Acts" embodied in its composition:

> I have written this Poem from immediate Dictation twelve or sometimes twenty or thirty lines at a time without Premeditation & even against my Will. the Time it has taken in writing was thus renderd Non Existent. & an immense Poem Exists which seems to be the Labour of a long Life all producd without Labour or Study.

Such a poem is a vortex: it is provisional, merely a means to life. Or more precisely, considering the apparent time and labor required to produce it, we should say that such a poem is like the vortex a potential barrier to life which succeeds, paradoxically, through the poet's attaining enough inspiration to surmount it. After all, necessary as *Milton* seems to have been for Blake in retrospect, the task was quite voluntarily, even defiantly, chosen: materially speaking, Blake's efforts could have been much better employed in service to Corporeal Friend Hayley, as both well knew. Like any freely willed challenge, therefore, what the poem provided was an opportunity for self-mastery—and also its converse, self-annihilation.

With his muse so close at hand, Blake is able to experience the action of *Milton* directly as personal vision, thus taking control of the narrative *in propria persona*. Since there is no doubting his inspiration now, his concealment of anxieties by mythology is no longer necessary, and so mythology—indeed *Milton* itself—is sloughed off as one more Satanic covering of the human which the poet must annihilate in order to become fully himself. "This is a False Body: an Incrustation over my Immortal Spirit," Milton tells Ololon and points to Satan (40:35). So, "collecting all his fibres into impregnable strength" (38:5), Milton compresses himself into his actual seventeenth-century "outline of identity," steps out from Satan's bosom and exposes him as the Usurper, self-contradiction itself, a mere parody of humanity (39:25-27). Somewhat less grandly, the small figure of Blake achieves a similar victory with respect to his own mythology. He explodes it—literally, almost: the machinery at 38:50-39:9 and 42:7-12 combines the thunder and lightning of epiphanies with that of opera and fireworks[38]—and the energy released by this combustion instead of being lost is then repossessed as Ololon, unmediated inspiration. To put it an-

other way: what Blake experiences, walking in his garden, is quite simply the concussive "impact" of the poem's exploding mythology, the charged significance of its annihilation for himself as author (it literally knocks him to his senses). He sees not a hallucination but, in his own phrase (my emphasis), an *"Intellectual Vision."* That is, the explosion is a "realization" in both main senses of the word. It is Blake's *recognition* of his personal Satan, self-doubt cloaked in mythology; and, what follows from this, it is also the repossession of the poet's emanation, Ololon, Blake's *actualization* of the mythologically projected portion of himself.

Yet the Miltonic repossession produces an apotheosis; Blake's, merely a reawakening. Being already dead, Milton is a step ahead of Blake, who can recover Ololon in a provisional way until tomorrow but cannot altogether redeem her. For the struggle toward full self-integration is one that can never be final while we are still in life. The point is enforced most dramatically. Milton ascends to Eternity the same instant fainting Blake hits solid earth, there to continue the life pilgrimage which his predecessor just completed. But henceforth Blake must be his own guide. For, once the two poets appear in the garden as distinct figures, it is plain that their union is over. Milton's merging with Ololon is mildly reflected in Blake's life when he collapses and awakens reconciled with his own "sweet Shadow of Delight" (42:28), his hitherto refractory wife; but for the most part, says Blake, the "wondrous acts" of the great pair remained "by me unknown Except remotely" (40:2-3).

Yet if Milton now abandons Blake in order to become Jesus, we also see that Blake no longer needs Milton because he has finally become, by great effort, himself. Evidently Blake has been in Felpham throughout the poem; the long journey he undertook was only to get there more fully. So where Milton leaves off, Blake begins; and the effect is mixed. Denied a Miltonic apotheosis, wistfully Blake sees that the alternate route to Eternity, apocalypse, is also at present unavailable. In a very major respect, then, unfulfillment is the order of the day. Prophecy can become actual in the sense of being explicit, these last plates show, but it cannot become actuality. Albion's awakening will doubtless prove most inspiring, when it happens; but a proleptic narrative of the event at this point would only falsify the poem, which concludes by humbly entering history as a document in the life of its author. For if Blake let Albion walk forth now, he would equally have to allow all the rest of the mythology which Albion comprises, so throwing the poem back to the **"Bard's Song."** Staunchly, *Milton* lets him slumber. But though Albion's time is not yet, the final paragraph and accompanying illustration (42:36-43:1) make it plain that Blake's time, and the *beginning* of the time for apocalypse, is now.[39] In the end, therefore, Blake's difficult submission

to earthly life confers a subdued fulfillment of its own: namely, a *vision* of Milton's much greater fulfillment, in which Blake cannot share.

The one goal which everybody has been striving towards, and, considering its stylistic metamorphoses, even the poem itself, is briefly attained when Milton embraces Ololon and becomes

> One Man Jesus the Saviour. wonderful! round his
> limbs
> The Clouds of Ololon folded as a Garment dipped in
> blood
> Written within & without in woven letters: and the
> Writing
> Is the Divine Revelation in the Litteral Expression.
>
> (42:11-14)[40]

Ololon's consummation redeems Milton from her demonic parody Rahab's rigid cloak of Puritan errors. "My Garments shall be woven of sighs & heart broken lamentations," crows Rahab; "I will have Writings written all over it in Human Words / That every Infant that is born upon the Earth shall read / And get by rote as a hard task of a life of sixty years" (18:6-14). Like the interweaving narratives of **The Four Zoas,** Rahab's writings, which include even the living word of God once it is made matter for Memory merely, do not serve human life but entangle and bind it. By contrast, Ololon's cloudy garment is virtually intangible; it interpenetrates the wearer and spells with his blood. Like **Milton** itself, then, Ololon's paradoxical covering of words only reveals the more explicitly the naked human truth in which, for Blake, all imagination essentially subsists: Christ as Logos, here seen to be the vital principle of human being which every individual identity innately strives to express through its own particular life and works, and yet also strives to become in spite of itself (poets only more deliberately so than others).

Finally, Blake collapses. For an anticlimactic "moment" (small "m", now) he appears in his "mortal state" (42:26) outstretched upon the garden path, the path Milton has just trod. Then **Milton** ends and the author, it seems, actually passes beyond his poem into the daily realities awaiting him just outside the last line, "To go forth to the Great Harvest & Vintage of the Nations" (43:1).[41] Having emerged from his mythological Vortex through an apex of vision, Blake thus resumes his earthly pilgrimage. Ultimately even the visionary remains divided from Jesus, the object of vision, by his own body; through certain inspired Moments he may surmount this last of all Satanic "coverings," but short of suicide he could hardly annihilate it for good. Hence the reintegration of Blake's human self at the end of **Milton** is really an escape from the poem and readiness to write another. Of all its peculiarities, perhaps the strangest thing about **Milton** is that it self-destructively gets itself out of the way as it proceeds, so clearing the way for the thoroughly Logocentric **Jerusalem.**

III

A mythological poem which proceeds by annihilating mythology neatly supplies its own conclusion—but where does one go from there? The next poem, if there is to be one, somehow must be made to self-annihilate continually from the start. Having realized through *Milton* that the creative process entails a perpetual sending forth of new "emanations" even though its ultimate aim is to repossess them all, Blake in *Jerusalem* strives to write in full face of this perplexity. His solution is characteristically strenuous: it is continually to recreate his continually self-annihilating mythology. *Jerusalem* is therefore a return to mythology, but mythology now tempered and qualified by Los's need to subjugate his Spectre and remain personally self-unified before he can attempt to awaken Albion, the unified humanity that is the end of every artist's labors.

The reason this struggle particularly dominates Chapter One is that the poet of *Jerusalem* must confront self-doubt fully at the outset of writing. Possessed, now, of the unavoidable awareness that he also stands in Satan's bosom, Blake cannot repeat the gradual lifting of mythological veils that made *Milton* essentially just a preparing for this confrontation. Hence Los's struggle, unlike the earlier combat between Palamabron and Satan which it resembles, is not preliminary to his main endeavor but a constant part of it. The smithy hammering away at the dread furnaces of vision, patiently "measuring out" "minute particulars" with "beats" upon his anvil,[42] is a picture never far from view—a patent allegory of Blake himself composing *Jerusalem* and contending, as Chapter One tells, with the nightmare of solipsistic isolation in a London made paranoid by years of war and repression. He is "Striving with Systems to deliver Individuals from those Systems" (11:5), the paradox being that since he strives both *against* systems and *by means of* them (for the "with" is ambiguous), what endures is not the systems but only the striving itself.

Such running in order to stand still is reflected in the form of the poem, heterogeneous yet broadly unified. *Jerusalem* takes the different styles through which *Milton* evolved and presents them all simultaneously: Albion and Los jostle alongside Biblical figures, personified British cities, great men of European intellectual history, as well as obscure contemporary individuals such as Scofield whose significance in the poem is purely autobiographical. The result is ceaseless ferment, mythology expanded to bursting. So, for example, those lengthy catalogues matching British counties with Hebrew tribes (15:30-16:60, 70:10-72:52), tedious as they may seem, actually comprise systematic demonstrations of the versatility of *Jerusalem*; they represent mythology in the act of self-annihilation, that extreme limit of formlessness where personification verges apocalyptically on pure naming. Such passages are evidently poetry's closest approach to the redeemed Zoas' conversation "in visionary forms dramatic which bright / Redounded from their Tongues . . . / . . . & every Word & Every Character / Was Human" (98:28-36): the language of the indwelling Logos, a plastic mythology of spontaneous self-expression in which creative word and act are one.

Yet, despite the protean formlessness of its mythology, *Jerusalem* is not a chaos. On the contrary, the poem has a distinctly human shape, only "human" in a sense so thoroughgoing as to obliterate mere individuality. With the poet's mythology now exploded through its implied contrast with that of the Universal Man we inevitably look *through* the mythology to its actual source, the historical William Blake. Clearly, *he* is the organizing central presence behind the poem's assemblage of so many passages otherwise unrelated. Yet what, after all, is this entity, "William Blake"? Only an idea, we see, for in reality no one, no matter how isolated or visionary, is ever quite cut off from the root circumstances of experience. *Jerusalem*'s directly autobiographical material (Los at the anvil, the fight with Scofield and ensuing trial for sedition, the quarrel with Hayley) is therefore only the limiting "outline of identity" of a life-experience ultimately inseparable from the vast surrounding contours of Albion himself—that is, the overall life-experience (social, political, intellectual) of late eighteenth-, early nineteenth-century England.

Thus Blake, having in *Milton* repossessed his mythology as direct personal vision, is able to go on projecting it despite its internalization. *Jerusalem* takes up and inverts the *Areopagitica*'s vision of a London filled with warfaring Christian humanists whose industrious mental activity must eventually rouse the whole nation (this is the passage beginning, "Behold now this vast City: a city of refuge . . ."). Milton's city swarms with thoughtful men; Blake's is a man swarming with citified thoughts. "I behold London," he answers Milton, "a Human awful wonder of God! / He says . . . / Awake Albion, awake! and let us awake up together. / My Houses are my Thoughts: my Inhabitants; Affections, / The children of my thoughts . . ." (34:29-34). *Jerusalem*'s humanized universe springs from its free-form mythology, no longer calcified but returned to its original molten state in *The Marriage of Heaven and Hell* as "living fluids" of the poet's mind. Yet, as I hope this essay has served to show, the return is not a simple one. The poet has recovered the self-expressive vigor he lost through the entropy of creation only because his mind has, in effect, turned inside out. Whereas the young Blake-Devil's living fluids circulated within a private cavern surrounded by an "expanse" full of Devourers, those of the *Jerusalem* poet wash easily back and forth across the expanse itself—all 6,000 years of it, from London to Jerusalem—swallowing the Devourers in vi-

sion. If the **Milton** Vortex supplied Blake the provisional means to concrete human life, **Jerusalem,** expanding inwards from the earlier poem's apex, serves to embrace the new world of visionary experience in all its diverse plenitude. "I rest not from my great task!" the poet exclaims at the new poem's outset,

> To open the Eternal Worlds, to open the immortal
> Eyes
> Of Man inwards into the Worlds of Thought: into Eternity
> Ever expanding in the Bosom of God. the Human
> Imagination.

<div align="right">(5:17-20)</div>

Notes

1. Plate 15, in *The Poetry and Prose of William Blake* ed. David V. Erdman, with Commentary by Harold Bloom, 4th ed. (Garden City, N.Y.: Doubleday, 1970), p. 39. All Blake quotations are from this edition; henceforth, page or plate numbers are given in the text.

2. E.g. Bloom in *Poetry & Prose,* p. 812, believes the men to be of the class "Prolific," and not "Devourers." Yet the men do not create, they only "receive" endlessly.

3. Cf. J. M. Murry on the first Memorable Fancy (plates 6-7): "the Devil whom Blake sees is Blake. The flat-sided steep . . . is the copper-plate on which he is writing at this very moment. He traces with corroding fires 'the sentence now perceived by the minds of men, and read by them on earth.' Blake is simply describing what he is actually doing." *William Blake* (1933; rpt. New York: McGraw Hill, 1964), pp. 67-68.

4. In view of Blake's constant attacks on Memory and Fancy, the term "Memorable Fancy" is evidently one of disparagement.

5. See David V. Erdman, *Blake: Prophet Against Empire* (1954; rev. Garden City, N.Y.: Doubleday, 1969), pp. 286-403 *passim.*

6. See *Poetry & Prose,* Textual Notes, pp. 737-39. Cf. the letter to Hayley of October 23, 1804: "O the distress I have undergone, and my poor wife with me: incessantly labouring and incessantly spoiling what I had done well. Every one of my friends . . . knew my industry and abstinence from every pleasure for the sake of study, and yet—and yet—and yet there wanted the proofs of industry in my works." Such misapplied industry precisely characterizes *The Four Zoas.*

7. Cf. Northrop Frye: "Gorgeous as it unquestionably is, one comes to wonder, in studying it, how far this night Ninth is the real climax of the vision, and how far it has been added as an effort of

will, perhaps almost of conscience." *Fearful Symmetry* (Princeton: Princeton U. Press, 1947), p. 308. Cf. also Harold Bloom, *Blake's Apocalypse* (Ithaca, N.Y.: Cornell U. Press, 1963), pp. 283-84.

8. E.g. "Auguries of Innocence": "If the Sun & Moon should doubt / They'd immediately Go out." Or, more ponderously, *Jerusalem* 32:51-54: "What seems to Be: Is: To those to whom / It seems to Be, & is productive of the most dreadful / Consequences to those to whom it seems to Be: even of / Torments, Despair, Eternal Death."

9. For *Milton*'s dates of composition, see *Poetry & Prose,* pp. 727-28. For the quarrel with Hayley see Frye, pp. 327-32. The best biographical account remains Mona Wilson, *The Life of Blake* (1927; rev. London: Oxford U. Press, 1971), pp. 145-79 *passim.*

10. Letter to Butts of November 22, 1802 [in *The Poetry and Prose of William Blake*].

11. Blake enforces his doctrinal point by making the speaker of these lines the Devil himself. Lucifer's essential human identity, reposing strengthless on its Death Couch in Beulah while the State of Satan prevails on Earth, still pronounces uncorrupted wisdom.

12. James Rieger, "'The Hem of Their Garments': The "Bard's Song" in *Milton,*" in *Blake's Sublime Allegory,* ed. Stuart Curran and J. A. Wittreich, Jr. (Madison: U. of Wisconsin Press, 1973), p. 277.

13. Susan Fox, *Poetic Form in Blake's Milton* (Princeton: Princeton U. Press, 1976), p. 24.

14. W. J. T. Mitchell, "Blake's Radical Comedy: Dramatic Structure as Meaning in *Milton,*" in *Sublime Allegory,* p. 307.

15. Letter to Butts, July 6, 1803.

16. S. Foster Damon, *William Blake: His Philosophy and Symbols* (1924; rev. Gloucester, Mass.: Peter Smith, 1958), p. 175.

17. M. H. Abrams, "Structure and Style in the Greater Romantic Lyric," in *From Sensibility to Romanticism: Essays Presented to Frederick A. Pottle,* ed. Frederick W. Hilles and Harold Bloom (New York: Oxford U. Press, 1965), pp. 527-60. Rpt. in *Romanticism and Consciousness,* ed. Harold Bloom (New York: Norton, 1970), pp. 201-29.

18. Joseph Antony Wittreich, Jr., "Opening the Seals: Blake's Epics and the Milton Tradition," in *Sublime Allegory,* pp. 23-58. See also his *Blake: Angel of Apocalypse* (Madison: U. of Wisconsin Press, 1975), pp. 221-50, 167-70.

19. See Harold Bloom, "The Internalization of Quest-Romance," in *The Yale Review,* (Summer 1969). Rpt. in *Romanticism and Consciousness,* pp. 3-24.

20. "Living Form is Eternal Existence." "On Virgil," [in *The Poetry and Prose of William Blake*].

21. *Milton* culminates a long line of 18th-century progress-poems about inspiration anxieties. Most conclude in melancholy acquiescence to a determinism insisting that the possibilities for poetry have already been exhausted by the giant bards of the past, most recently Milton; it remains only for the modern poet to recognize this fact and accordingly end his poem. Blake had parodied such despondency as early as "To the Muses"; in *Milton* he undermines it from within. For the ending of *Milton* is not necessitated by the precursor poet as by some inexorable external force, rather it develops as Blake's long-sought affirmation of personal choice. Cf. W. J. Bate: "Finally why, in our dissatisfactions, do we so strongly clutch at deterministic explanations that relieve us from the burden of deciding not only what we most want but what we can and should do about it? Could this not be the real 'burden' after all—not determinism, but the burden of choice?" *The Burden of the Past and the English Poet* (New York: Norton, 1970), pp. 66-67.

22. The most dynamic analysis to date of *Milton*'s opening plates is Christine Gallant's, although it is marred by excessive Jungianism; see her *Blake and the Assimilation of Chaos* (Princeton: Princeton U. Press, 1978), pp. 119-23.

23. Friedrich Nietzsche, *Beyond Good and Evil,* trans. Walter Kaufmann (New York: Random House, 1966), "On the Prejudices of Philosophers," pp. 23-24.

24. The line appears at 2:25, 3:5, 4:20, 7:16, 9:7 and 11:31.

25. *Poetry & Prose,* pp. 823-24.

26. *The Four Zoas,* 90:9-10.

27. See *Poetry & Prose,* pp. 727-29.

28. Leutha's origins seem distinctly Homeric. The letter to Butts of April 25, 1803 describes a poem which is evidently *Milton,* and then mentions that it centers around "One Grand Theme Similar to Homers Iliad." Clearly the warfare at 8:38-41 is modelled on passages in the *Iliad* where an injured warrior is suddenly made invisible and rescued by his guardian deity. Leutha's story reads like a psychologized version of the Anger of Achilles, with herself as a Briseis usurped from Satan-Achilles by Palambron-Agamemnon. Also as in Homer, Los-Priam convenes a Great Assembly to judge between the two warriors and it wrongly condemns the enraged Satan, who retaliates, like Achilles, by withdrawing himself from the other heroes, thereby weakening their forces.

29. *John Milton: Complete Poems and Major Prose,* ed. Merrit Y. Hughes (New York: Odyssey, 1957), p. 346. All Milton quotations are from Hughes.

30. See *Prophet Against Empire,* pp. 294, 298, 286-403 *passim.*

31. See *Poetry & Prose,* p. 823.

32. 4:26. The slogan also appears, again with reference to Hayley, in the letter to Butts of April 25, 1803.

33. See Stanley E. Fish, *Surprised by Sin: The Reader in Paradise Lost* (Berkeley: U. of California Press, 1971), Chap. 4, "Standing Only: Christian Heroism," pp. 158-207.

34. Cf. Bloom in *Poetry & Prose,* pp. 832-33. Similarly, Erdman terms Ololon "history-as-it-should-have-been." *Prophet Against Empire,* p. 423.

35. Hence Milton does not finally defeat Urizen, the tyrant of Law, until he embraces Ololon and becomes Jesus. The letter to Butts of November 22, 1802 intimates that Blake's resolution of his personal crisis at the time of Felpham entailed an evangelical awakening: "Tho' I have been very unhappy, I am so no longer. I am again Emerged into the light of day; I still & shall to Eternity Embrace Christianity and Adore him who is the Express image of God; but I have travel'd thro' Perils & Darkness not unlike a Champion." Not unlike Milton, that is, or not unlike the Blake-poet of *Milton.*

36. Compare 31:12-27 with the Nativity Ode sts. 21-22, and 31:46-64 with *Lycidas* ll. 132-51.

37. *The Book of Thel* similarly shows a young virgin progressing through different States of being (Lily, Cloud, Worm, Clay) toward womanhood. But self-growth entails self-annihilation—Thel's way to maturity lies through the grave of her childhood—and this Thel cannot accept; recoiling from her Couch of Death, she flees back to Innocence, Thel is the prototypical Daughter of Beulah, just as *The Book of Thel,* the earliest of the engraved Prophetic Books, represents Blake's first effort under supervision of the anxious Beulah muse. Thus when the Ololon of *Milton* returns to her Death Couch in "humiliation and sorrow" (35:33) and, unlike her predecessor, bravely confronts "the Void Outside of Existence, which if enter'd into / Becomes a Womb" (41:37-42:1), we are in a sense witnessing Blake's annihilation and reinception of some fifteen years of mythologizing.

38. See Martha W. England, "Apprenticeship at the Haymarket?" in *Blake's Visionary Forms Dramatic,* ed. David V. Erdman and John E. Grant (Princeton: Princeton U. Press, 1970), pp. 3-29.

39. E.g., the standard formula of the New Dispensation, as in John 7.6: "My time is not come, your time is always ready."

40. The lines literalize their meaning through a revealed pun: "the Litteral Expression" is both "actual, non-allegorical" and "comprised of letters"—as well as "littoral." Blake's visions occur for the most part "upon mild Felpham shore" (38:13).

41. The line recalls several Milton conclusions, especially "Tomorrow to fresh Woods, and Pastures new" and "The World was all before them, where to choose. . . ." See Christopher Grose, *Milton's Epic Process* (New Haven: Yale U. Press, 1973), pp. 188-201, 245-63: "the laborer, 'homeward returning' less than twenty lines from the end of the poem appears to confirm . . . that the reader is ultimately made another Adam in *Paradise Lost*. It is he who in concluding the poem most clearly returns homeward, back to the familiar creatural realm now also about to receive Adam and Eve" (p. 192). *Milton* similarly seems to supersede its poetic context and open out directly into the reader's immediate locus of experience, Earth.

42. Among several such passages, see 56:18-24.

Albert J. Rivero (essay date January 1982)

SOURCE: Rivero, Albert J. "Typology, History, and Blake's *Milton*." *Journal of English and Germanic Philology* 81, no. 1 (January 1982): 30-46.

[*In the following essay, Rivero examines Blake's concept of poetic perception in* Milton, *paying particular attention to his notion of a series of actions happening simultaneously, "within a moment" in the poet's consciousness. Rivero argues that in order to convey a sense of several phenomena occurring at once, Blake must translate his ideas into a more traditional framework of space and time—in other words, the poem itself—in order to make it comprehensible to the reader.*]

In *A Blake Dictionary*, concluding his summary of the action of Blake's *Milton* (ca. 1800-1810), S. Foster Damon remarked that

The act of the poem is one, but the causes are so complex that Blake had to invent an original structure, to suggest the simultaneousness of all the material. He introduced material without any preparation, abruptly changing the subject over and over. Thus the lark, who is the idea of the poem, and whose song marks the mystical ecstasy (42:29), first is mentioned in 17:27; he sings in 31:29; his nest is located in 35:58; he is a messenger in 35:63-67; and (with material about the other larks) he meets Ololon (36:10). The universe of Los, which is the setting for the poem, is thus introduced at considerable length, while the astronomical universe is described and related to man.

Had Blake taken time to introduce his material in logical sequence, he would have ruined the effect of culminating immediacy.[1]

Because Damon intended his remarks to be nothing more than a suggestive coda to his brief summary, he did not feel compelled to substantiate his claims with more than the most general (and sometimes actually misleading) documentation; nevertheless, he succeeded in singling out the crucial facts about the complex structure of the poem. His remarks, however, need qualification. If the poem, as Damon suggests, portrays a single and simultaneous action, one must begin by redefining what is intended by "single" and "simultaneous." For it is fairly obvious, from even the most superficial reading of the poem, that certain events precede others. The **"Bard's Song,"** for example, clearly comes before Milton's decision to "go into the deep . . . to redeem" his Sixfold Emanation.[2] It may be argued, of course, that the **"Bard's Song"** is not part of the action proper, but only that which triggers the action. This is a useful line of argument because there is some evidence, especially in the central plates of the poem, to suggest that all the events that follow the **"Bard's Song"** happen at the same time. Indeed, one could go further and argue that all these events are versions of the same event, viewed from different perspectives.[3] The only problem with this approach is that, in order to be completely successful, it must dispense with one third of the poem. One must look, then, for a more comprehensive scheme, a scheme that will somehow account for the "simultaneity" of certain events within the poem which appear, at least to the corporeal understanding, to occur sequentially.

Perhaps the best way to start the search for a more comprehensive scheme is to examine several passages, both within and without the poem, in which Blake attempts to distinguish between modes of apprehending reality. For the issue here is clearly one of perception: that is, whether a poem whose action appears to unfold sequentially in space and time can in any way be grasped or understood as occurring in one imaginative, visionary instant, as a "Flash of lightning but more quick" (36:19). As usual with Blake, one must begin by making an intuitive leap from the natural world into the realm of the eternal. For a poet who could profess

To see a World in a Grain of Sand
And a Heaven in a Wild Flower
Hold Infinity in the palm of your hand
And Eternity in an hour

("Auguries of Innocence" [1803-1804], ll. 1-4)

such a leap was not difficult or out of the ordinary. Blake's tendency to see the eternal in the temporal, the infinite in the circumscribed, pervades all his works, but

it occupies a position of singular importance in his prophecies.[4] In his invocation to the "Divine Spirit" in *Jerusalem* (1804-1819), for instance, he confidently declared, "I see the Past, Present & Future, existing all at once / Before me" (15:8-9). Blake is speaking here of the true (i.e., prophetic, visionary) poet's ability to collapse all of history into one intense moment of vision. Like God, he sees all events before him, freed from their historical time and space, yet (and this is a crucial point) within them.

This Godlike perception of the true poet manifests itself in his works. For Blake—to paraphrase Robert Graves— there was one story and one story only, and every poet worthy of the name from the Bible onward has told this story, modifying it only in so far as such modification has been required by his own particular historical situation. Writing on "Sir Jeffery Chaucer and the nine and twenty Pilgrims on their journey to Canterbury" in *A Descriptive Catalogue* (1809), Blake observed that

> The characters of Chaucer's Pilgrims are the characters which compose all ages and nations: as one age falls, another rises, different to mortal sight, but to immortals only the same; for we see the same characters repeated again and again, in animals, vegetables, minerals, and in men; nothing new occurs in identical existence; Accident ever varies, Substance can never suffer change nor decay.
>
> (E [*The Poetry and Prose of William Blake,* edited by David V. Erdman], p. 523)[5]

The surface or accidents of history change, but the underlying pattern or substance does not; the actors and settings come and go, but the action always remains one and the same.

The view of history as the repetition of an unchanging pattern—a pattern that can be discerned only by men of vision, by prophets, or, as Blake believed, by true poets—had a long and distinguished tradition behind it. Although space limitations do not permit anything like a fully documented account of the origins and development of Biblical typology, ways can nevertheless be suggested in which this method of Biblical exegesis was employed to interpret both political and personal history throughout the Christian centuries.[6] Briefly, typology establishes connections between persons, objects, or events (type) of Old Testament history and persons or things (antitype) revealed under the new dispensation. Thus, Adam (or Moses or Joshua) is a type of Christ, Israel a type of the Christian Church, and the Israelites' forty years in Egyptian captivity a type of Christ's forty days in the desert. At first, typology was confined solely to events within Scripture, but soon (owing perhaps to several passages in the New Testament which point in that direction) it expanded its frame of reference to include not only the spiritual life of every Christian, but also the political history of whole nations. In this expanded typology, the whole historical movement from Adam to Christ was believed to be recapitulated within the soul of every individual Christian as he strives to free himself from sin and achieve salvation, while the history of the Chosen People in Scripture was understood to be duplicated by the temporal history of the Church or, more specifically, by the particular history of one Christian nation (in this case, England).

Although typology did not become a coherent system of Biblical exegesis until developed by the early Fathers of the Church to defend the New Testament from the charges of Gnostics and Jews, its origins date back to the Biblical writers' own understanding of history.[7] For them, history was a progressive chain of events leading up to man's final deliverance from the misery of his fallen state. For the authors of the Old Testament, this deliverance was to be accomplished by a Messiah, whose advent would signal a new era of peace and prosperity for God's chosen people. The writers of the New Testament claimed that Jesus Christ was this expected Messiah, and that all the Messianic promises of the Old Testament had been fulfilled in his person. To substantiate their claim, they began to look for similarities between occurrences in Old Testament history and events in the life of Christ. This effort finds its most complete expression in the Epistle to Hebrews, a work which was obviously written to justify the new religion to the members of the old. Here words like SKIA, HYPODEIGMA (pattern), PARABOLE, and TYPOS describe those events in Old Testament history which foreshadowed or prefigured the earthly life of Christ.[8]

The *locus classicus* for the typological interpretation of the Bible is found, not in Hebrews, but in St. Paul's Epistle to the Romans. As St. Paul explains the curious relationship between Adam and Christ in the most heroic drama of human redemption,

> Nevertheless death reigned from Adam to Moses, even over them that had not sinned after the similitude of Adam's transgression, who is the figure of him that was to come. But not as the offence, so also is the free gift. For if through the offence of one many be dead, much more the grace of God, and the gift by grace, which is by one man, Jesus Christ, hath abounded unto many. . . . For as by one man's disobedience many were made sinners, so by the obedience of one shall many be made righteous.[9]

The word translated in the first sentence as "figure" is the Greek noun *Typos,* or "type." The relationship between Adam and Christ, then, is "typical," or, in more recent terminology, "typological." Adam, by his transgression, lost for man Eden and all its bliss, casting him into the wilderness of this world, where he is heir to woe and death. Christ, the new and antithetical Adam, by his perfect obedience to God's command to sacrifice

his life on the cross, has restored man to his rightful place in a heavenly paradise, whose bounty far surpasses that of the original Garden of Eden, its Old Testament type. Furthermore, as St. Paul hints in Romans 6:6, this historical movement from Adam to Christ is recapitulated within the soul of every Christian as he attempts to extricate himself from the bonds of sinfulness and win his way back onto the path of redemption.

St. Paul's statement about Adam and Christ also helps to illustrate some of the most salient features of typology. First, St. Paul limits his typological identification to an Old Testament character (Adam) and his fulfillment in Christ. Typology, in its narrowest sense, is christocentric. As Benjamin Keach writes, "divines understand nothing else by types, but . . . the actions and histories of the Old Testament, respecting such as prefigured Christ our Saviour in his actions, life, passion, death, and the glory that followed."[10] The language of types, however, as noted above, expanded its frame of reference later on, to encompass not only the private internal life of the individual Christian, but also the public history of whole nations. In the words of Samuel Mather, the "Types relate not only to the Person of Christ, but to his Benefits, and to all Gospel Truths and Mysteries, even to all New-Testament Dispensations."[11] Second, the independent actions of Adam and Christ acquire their profound meaning for salvation history only when yoked together in St. Paul's typological equation. That is, the significance of one event is enhanced by the existence of the other; without either one of them the redemptive cycle would be incomplete and meaningless. Finally, though Adam and Christ are thus related, they nonetheless retain their identities as real historical figures. As Keach observes, "types are only historical . . . look only to matter of fact, and compare one fact with another."[12] Typological interpretation, then, is deeply rooted in history. And since the author of history is God, it follows that "God is the only Author of the Types."[13] Typology, therefore, is, before all else, God's own language. Thus the writer who chooses to use typology as his vehicle of expression is, in a very real sense, imitating God's way of writing; and, as the scribe of the Lord, he unveils for his readers the age-old patterns of salvation that lie buried underneath the seemingly chaotic surface of daily experience, thus reassuring them of God's constant presence among His chosen people, of His paternal concern for their welfare, until the end of time.[14]

During the Middle Ages, typology became mingled with allegory. On the origins of allegory, G. W. H. Lampe has written: "Allegory must be referred to Hellenistic ideas about the correspondence of the earthly order as the shadow with the intelligible sphere as the reality, to the Alexandrian tradition of the moralizing allegorization of the Homeric poems, and to a lesser extent to Rabbinic exegesis with its disregard of the context and

the original meaning of proof-texts."[15] Its mixture with typology resulted in the gradual disappearance of one of the most important characteristics of the typological method: its regard for historical fact. Begun by Philo and fully developed by Origen and his successors, Jerome and Augustine, the new approach tended to dismiss the historical-literal sense for the sake of the spiritual meanings couched under it. Origen, for instance, claimed that every scriptural passage must be read allegorically, in its moral and spiritual senses. To attain this goal, he seldom paid attention to the facts of the text. St. Augustine, though he made the historical-literal sense the basis of his fourfold method of exegesis, repeatedly ignored the historical statement in his pursuit of aetiological, analogical, and allegorical meanings; and though typology was central to his analysis of Scripture, it was quite often subordinated to the search for extraliteral meanings. This allegorizing tendency persisted right up to the time of the Reformation, when it was not so much rejected as transformed.[16]

For Reformation theologians, the union of typology and philosophical allegory was an error introduced by the Alexandrians and perpetuated by the Schoolmen, and therefore something far removed from the original intention of the Biblical writers. For this reason, they sought to recover the pure typology of the New Testament, especially that of the Pauline Epistles. In order to effect this recovery, they devoted all their energies to stressing the importance of the literal sense of Scripture. William Ames in *The Marrow of Sacred Divinity* (1643) articulates what is perhaps the most extreme argument for this position. As he puts it, "there is only one sence to one place of Scripture; because otherwise the sence of Scripture should be not only not cleare and certaine but none at all: for that which doth not signifie one thing, signifieth certainly nothing."[17] These words are aimed directly at Origen's claim for multiple scriptural meanings. For Calvin, Origen was also the culprit. In a famous passage in his "Commentary on Corinthians," Calvin argues that St. Paul's distinction between the letter and the spirit should not be viewed as a key for expounding Scripture, but rather as a statement about different kinds of preaching. As he writes,

> The exposition contrived by Origen has got into general circulation—that by the *letter* we ought to understand the grammatical and genuine meaning of Scripture, or the *literal* sense (as they call it), and that by the *spirit* is meant the allegorical meaning, which is commonly reckoned to be the *spiritual* meaning. Accordingly during several centuries, nothing was more generally received, than this—that Paul here furnishes us with a key for expounding Scripture by allegories, while nothing is farther from his intention. For by the term *letter* he means outward preaching, of such a kind as does not reach the heart; and, on the other hand, by *spirit* he means living doctrine, of such a nature as *worketh effectually* . . . on the minds of men, through the grace of the Spirit.[18]

Despite their emphasis on the letter, most Reformation theologians were willing to admit that certain texts can only be understood figuratively, and that in fact Scripture itself sometimes employs similitudes and parables to elucidate the literal sense.[19] But they regarded these "allegories" as inextricably bound up with the all-important literal sense, not something detached from it. Valid scriptural interpretation, they believed, must begin and end with the text and should never violate the "fair probabilities agreeable to the analogy of faith."[20] As Samuel Mather warns, "men must not *indulge their own Fancies,* as the Popish Writers used to do, with their Allegorical Senses . . . except we have some Scripture ground for it."[21] In this manner, the Reformers managed to have their allegorical cake and to eat it, too. The message, however, was loud and clear: the multilevel edifice of Medieval exegesis, so far as the Reformers were concerned, had finally collapsed. Tradition and the Catholic Church were no longer the interpreters of the Bible; the text itself was its own best exegete. Paradoxically enough, as the subsequent history of Biblical hermeneutics amply testifies, what began as a movement to eradicate one species of interpretive excess, gave rise to another. Because of its disavowal of tradition, the new mode of scriptural exegesis tended to emphasize not only the autonomy of the Biblical text, but also that of the *individual* interpreter. The Anglican Church solved the problem in part by establishing its own exegetical tradition. But the sheer proliferation of religious sects after the initial impetus of the Reformation, both on the Continent and in England, bears eloquent testimony to the fragmentation that the new approach encouraged. Blake's peculiar reading of Scripture, then, clearly lies within the individualistic tradition of Reformation hermeneutics.

Perhaps the single most important consequence of the Reformers' emphasis on the literal sense of Scripture was the recovery of the history of the Old Testament people for the Church. Medieval allegoresis, with its reluctance to dwell on the letter of the text, had tended to deny the existential reality of the Old Testament by regarding it as a mere shadow which the light of Christ's coming had finally dispersed. As James Samuel Preus has phrased it, "one would not exaggerate too much in saying that, in this view, redemption history really begins only with the coming of Christ. Everything before it is figura."[22] The return to Pauline typology changed all this. Because of its customary concern for historical fact, typology made the Reformation theologian aware, in a most striking manner, of the daily life of the Hebrew people and, what is even more important, of their resemblance to today's faithful, especially in their knowledge about, and expectation of, the true Messiah.[23] In the words of Samuel Mather, "Christ and the Heavenly Things of the Gospel were Preached . . . to the People of God of Old."[24] They too had "the glad Tidings of Man's Recovery by Jesus Christ . . . into a State of Life and Happiness . . . sounded in their Ears."[25] Otherwise, Mather argues with impeccable logic and Senecan brevity, they were not saved—or if saved, saved without Christ, which is, of course, impossible.[26] The only difference between ancient Hebrews and contemporary Christians is that the latter are living after the one historical coming of Christ, but since Christ's advent is always happening (within each man's soul) and always to be expected (at the end of time), both Old Testament and New Testament faithful share the same hope for a future coming, and both, while in the wilderness of this world, are subject to the same temptations to backslide and despair.

Another way to account for this change in historical perspective is to see it in terms of the two dominant modes of Christian historiography from Augustine to the Reformation.[27] The first mode—the Augustinian— tended to consider worldly events important only in so far as they related to the spiritual reality of God's heavenly kingdom. Because of the prospect of Satan's supremacy until the end of time, secular history made sense only if understood spiritually as a record of personal salvation. For Augustine and his followers, Christ's Second Coming was only a spiritual happening, occurring daily within the souls of the regenerate and at the end of historical time. The second mode— the Eusebian—stressed God's redemptive work within history, connecting one worldly event with another in a meaningful causal chain leading up to mankind's final deliverance, and focusing therefore not on the private life of the individual Christian, but on the public salvation history of whole nations. Furthermore, lurking beneath this progressivist theory of history was the possibility that God's second kingdom would be an earthly, rather than a spiritual, reality.[28] Both modes of Christian historiography influenced the Reformers, but the latter had the larger share in helping to shape their peculiar understanding of history.

Briefly stated, Reformation theologians from Luther onward believed that Christ's Second Coming was close at hand—that His thousand-year reign, foretold in Revelation 20:1-5 (cf. Daniel 7:9, 22, 29), was an imminent *earthly* reality. That is to say, unlike Augustine and his successors, they envisioned the resounding victory of Christ and His chosen ones over the forces of Satan as happening within time, not at the end of it. For one thing, the end of the rule of Antichrist, which Revelation 12 postulates as the immediate forerunner of Christ's final triumph, had already come about with the Reformation's "overthrow" of the Catholic Church—an overthrow that Samuel Mather, reflecting a common view, saw as the antitype of Israel's deliverance out of Egypt and Babylon.[29]

By the seventeenth century, the millenarian view of history had become "canonical" with Protestant theologians in both England and New England, and it contin-

ued to hold its appeal long after all hopes for the theocracy had vanished.[30] One of the ways to measure the extent of a nation's progress toward this millenarian fulfillment was by drawing analogies between contemporary events and episodes in Old Testament history. Puritans in New England, for example, saw the New World as an antitype of the wilderness and the desert, and the Israelites' journey to the Promised Land then as "foreshadowing . . . the journey now by a *Christian* Israel to the long-awaited 'new heavens and a new earth.'"[31] For Puritans in England, who saw their persecution by the High Church as an antitype of the captivity of the ancient Israelites by the Egyptians, the myth of the American wilderness was no less powerful.[32]

The concept of the elect nation, though more pronounced with the Puritans, was by no means limited to them.[33] The tendency to see England as the antitype of Israel and her ruler as the antitype of David or Christ was common to all Englishmen, regardless of religious affiliation, at least until the first few decades of the eighteenth century, though by then the idea had lost much of its original power. This loss is reflected in the steady decline of Biblical imagery in connection with political events in the prose and poetry of the period. The Biblical types which had greeted the rise of Cromwell and the subsequent restoration of the monarchy under Charles II begin to fade out by the end of the seventeenth century, to be replaced by figures from classical history and mythology: England was no longer Israel but Rome or Mount Olympus, and her king not David or Christ, but Caesar, Jove, or Hercules.[34] But the "old" tradition did not die out completely. It survived, among other places, in popular homiletic tradition, most prominently in the Martyr's Day sermons of the first sixty years of the eighteenth century. Typological language also emerges later on in the century, in a more clearly secular and political context, in connection with the American and French revolutions, both of which were widely interpreted as harbingers of the "new" millennium.

By Blake's time, however, thanks to the persuasive arguments of the proponents of Deism and natural religion, typology had become thoroughly discredited as a valid way of interpreting personal and national history. It was simply too irrational; it did not conform to the rules of Cartesian, Baconian, or Lockean reason. Blake's intense dislike of Deism and natural religion, of Descartes, Bacon, and Locke, and all their followers and predecessors, is well documented.[35] If, as Frye has suggested, Blake wrote **Milton** and **Jerusalem** partly to combat the rampant Deism and rationalism of his day, it should not seem strange to us that he chose as his weapon a method of interpreting history which, though it had ceased to be effective for almost a century, had proved particularly troublesome to earlier Deists.[36] Suitably modified to answer his poetic needs, Blake's ver-

sion of typology helped him to transcend the rationalists' world of mere accidents by revealing a world of everlasting substance behind it, a world of immutable forms which, as he never failed to emphasize in his works, ultimately exists nowhere but "in the human breast" (***The Marriage of Heaven and Hell*** [1790-1793], Plate 11). Blake's genius for perceiving the permanent behind the evanescent, the eternal in the temporal, was precisely what allowed him to view his quarrel with Hayley in the cosmic context of universal history, as yet another retelling of the ancient and ongoing struggle between the tyrannical and the oppressed, between Satan and Christ, between the conventional rationalist and the uncompromising prophet or poet.[37] And since this struggle, as Blake saw it, reflected an aspect of the eternal story sung by all true poets or prophets, it was only natural for him to turn to the prophetic-poetic tradition, especially to the Bible and Milton, in his search for an appropriate analogue to his personal situation.[38] By attaching himself to this "eternal" literary tradition, then, by looking at his private difficulties from the dispassionate perspective of eternity, Blake was able to exorcise the Satan in Hayley, in Milton, and in himself, and to clear the way for the "Great Harvest & Vintage of the Nations" prophesied in the last line of **Milton** and fulfilled at the end of **Jerusalem.**

With this excursus on Blake's view of history and the poetic tradition as background, we can now turn to **Milton** and briefly see how these ideas appear in the poem. Since the poem burgeons with pronouncements on the difference between eternal and temporal modes of perception, it is to our advantage to be selective and to focus our attention on only two representative passages.[39] The first passage (21:4-11) deals with the question of perception in the context of Milton's "reincarnation" in Blake.[40] This is actually the second time in the poem that we hear about this event (the first time being in 15:47-49). This repetition is significant in at least two ways. First, the reenactment six plates later of what appears to be an earlier occurrence, when the reader has perhaps begun to assume that the poem has made some spatial and temporal progress, serves to indicate that the movement of the poem is far from linear. We are, after all, as the text makes sufficiently clear, back where we started, though with a better appreciation of the event being described. The recurrence of this apparently earlier event suggests not only the oneness of the poem's action, but also its independence from the strictures of time and space. Second, and this point may help to elucidate what has been said so far in this connection, in this passage Blake tells of the way in which the eternal must be perceived in the temporal:

> But Milton entering my Foot; I saw in the nether
> Regions of the Imagination; also all men on Earth,
> And all in Heaven, saw in the nether regions of the
> Imagination

In Ulro beneath Beulah, the vast breach of Miltons
descent.
But I knew not that it was Milton, for man cannot
know
What passes in his members till periods of Space &
Time
Reveal the secrets of Eternity: for more extensive
Than any other earthly things, are Mans earthly linea-
ments.

(21:4-11)

Because of man's fallen perception, the "secrets of Eter-
nity" must be revealed in "Space & Time." A moment
of vision, to be comprehended by the corporeal under-
standing, must be unfolded in time and space. The slow-
ness and difficulty of this comprehension are illustrated
by the movement of the poem from the fifteenth to the
twenty-first plate. In 15:47-49, Milton's descent into
Blake is merely described: "Then first I saw him [Mil-
ton] in the Zenith as a falling star / Descending perpen-
dicular, swift as the swallow or swift; / And on my left
foot falling on the tarsus, enterd there." In 21:4-11, as
we have seen, an explanation for this descent is offered.
It is only by reconstructing in his temporal and spatial
mind what he experienced then in a visionary trance
that Blake begins to apprehend with his fallen intellect
the full import of his eternal vision. The writing (and
reading) of poetry thus becomes a way of understand-
ing corporeally what has been grasped in an instant by
the Imagination.

The second passage (28:44-29:65) completes the po-
em's first book and the account of "the World of Los
the labour of six thousand years" (29:64). Los, as Bloom
has succinctly put it, "is the father of any civilizing im-
pulse, of every attempt to build the City of Art."[41] He is
the eternal prophet-poet who, while contending with his
own flawed intellect, seeks to redeem mankind by re-
storing the Imagination to its original supremacy. After
the fall of Albion, as related in *The Four Zoas* (ca.
1795-1804) and *Milton,* Los created the world as an
"Act of Mercy" to prevent further deterioration. One of
the peculiar features of Los's fallen world is its narrow
conception of space and time. In it "every Space that a
Man views around his dwelling-place: / Standing on his
own roof, or in his garden on a mount / Of twenty-five
cubits in height, such space is his Universe" (29:5-7).
Blake, however, underscores not the limitations—"that
false appearance which appears to the reasoner"
(29:15)—but the imaginative and redemptive possibili-
ties of this human-centered view of the "Universe" by
making his garden at Felpham the starting point and
setting of his vision. In other words, the rebuilding of
Jerusalem must take place in "Englands green & pleas-
ant Land" (1:16); it must begin in "Lambeths Vale"
(6:14) or not at all.

Similarly, time is composed of "Moments & Minutes &
Hours / And Days & Months & Years & Ages & Peri-
ods" (28:44-45). This is the earthly illusion of clock
and calendar time. To free himself from this temporal
maze, a man must understand that "A Moment equals a
pulsation of the artery" (28:47) and that

Every Time less than a pulsation of the artery
Is equal in its period & value to Six Thousand Years.
For in this Period the Poets Work is Done: and all the
Great
Events of Time start forth & are concievd in such a
Period
Within a Moment: a Pulsation of the Artery.

(28:62-63; 29:1-3)

In short, a man must be able to see "Eternity in an
hour," in his own "earthly lineaments," to apprehend
the whole through the intense perception of one part. If
he does so, he can then see why the poet's work, which
must unfold itself in space and time in the six thousand
years of human history, can be understood as occurring
"Within a Moment." Yet, as Blake shows in *Milton,* if
the poet wishes to communicate this moment of vision
to other men he must reveal it sequentially in space and
time, he must expand it again to something akin to "Six
Thousand Years," and suggest in passages like those ex-
amined here that his temporal and spatial text depicts
an instantaneous and eternal action. One might go fur-
ther and argue that *Milton* portrays not so much an ac-
tion as a visionary moment within which that action is
apprehended. Paradoxically, in order to sketch out that
visionary moment, the poet must resort to describing
that action as it appears to the discursive intellect, as an
action revealed in space and time.

* * *

To sum up, *Milton* does indeed portray a single and si-
multaneous action, but only if that single and simulta-
neous action is understood as occurring "Within a Mo-
ment" of intense visionary perception. That Blake had
to expand this moment into a poem of nearly two thou-
sand lines is only a measure of the limitations of post-
lapsarian man. What the Imagination perceives as one
single moment must be unfolded sequentially in space
and time in order to be grasped by the corporeal under-
standing. It is the reader's task, then, as he reads the
poem, to put on *his* Imagination and try to re-enact
within himself that single moment of vision from the
spatial and temporal text before him. To the ordinary
reader, this may appear as an unreasonable demand
upon his intellectual faculties. And so in a sense it is.
But, as critics from Edwin J. Ellis and W. B. Yeats to
Northrop Frye and Harold Bloom have demonstrated,
Blake always requires this kind of imaginative coopera-
tion from those who dare enter his visionary universe.
To understand the poetry and art of a man who could in
all seriousness declare,

Now I a fourfold vision see
And a fourfold vision is given to me

Tis fourfold in my supreme delight
And three fold in soft Beulahs night
And twofold Always. May God us keep
From Single vision & Newtons sleep,[42]

we must obviously discard, or radically modify, our conventional, "rational" ways of apprehending reality. But, as this essay has attempted to suggest, we need not always remain on such unorthodox ground. For Blake's peculiar ideas about the perception of space and time, about the relations between the temporal and the eternal, make perfect sense, become eminently "rational," when studied in the context of Protestant Biblical hermeneutics. Seemingly arcane poetic meanings and procedures lose some of their mystery and "irrationality" when we examine the conceptual links among typology, history, and Blake's **Milton.**

Notes

1. S. Foster Damon, *A Blake Dictionary: The Ideas and Symbols of William Blake* (Providence, R.I.: Brown Univ. Press, 1965), p. 280. In working my way through the intricate mazes of Blake's system, I have often resorted to this invaluable guide. I have also become indebted to several other Blake scholars in preparing this essay. Specific borrowings from their works will be acknowledged in these notes. To the following studies, however, I owe a more general debt, for they have both corroborated and, to an extent I find difficult to ascertain after long acquaintance, shaped my reading of Blake's *Milton*: Harold Bloom, *Blake's Apocalypse: A Study in Poetic Argument* (Garden City, N.Y.: Doubleday, 1965), esp. pp. 334-402; Bloom's "Commentary" on *Milton,* in *The Poetry and Prose of William Blake,* ed. David V. Erdman (Garden City, N.Y.: Doubleday, 1965), pp. 822-43; Bloom, *The Visionary Company: A Reading of English Romantic Poetry,* rev. ed. (Ithaca: Cornell Univ. Press, 1971), esp. pp. 97-108; S. Foster Damon, *William Blake, His Philosophy and Symbols* (Boston and New York: Houghton Mifflin, 1924); Damon, "Blake and Milton," in *The Divine Vision: Studies in the Poetry and Art of William Blake,* ed. Vivian de Sola Pinto (New York: Haskell House, 1968), pp. 91-96; Northrop Frye, *Fearful Symmetry: A Study of William Blake* (Princeton: Princeton Univ. Press, 1947), pp. 313-55, *passim*; and Frye, "Notes for a Commentary on *Milton,*" in *The Divine Vision,* ed. Vivian de Sola Pinto, pp. 99-137.

2. *Milton* 2: 20. All quotations of Blake are from Erdman's edition (Garden City, N.Y.: Doubleday, 1965).

3. The textual evidence is scanty and less satisfactory than one would wish it to be. Briefly, Blake's introduction of material without regard for logical sequence hardly makes the action simultaneous. Damon's remarks, in this respect, are misleading. So is his evidence. The several appearances of the lark suggest not so much a sense of simultaneity as one of disjointedness. In the middle plates, however, thanks to Milton's four bodies (20:7-24), Blake can manage to have Milton on one level searching for his Emanation, on another entering Blake's foot, on another discoursing with the Seven Angels of the Presence and resting on his couch, and on yet another wrestling with Urizen—an action that runs from the nineteenth to the thirty-ninth plate, so that in this sense all the events that occur between these plates may be said to happen simultaneously. This theory of correspondences, if extended to other characters in the poem, might well vindicate Damon. In this scheme, Albion is the fallen Blake, who must be awakened by the fallen but not completely stupefied Los, who is Blake in his role as poet. Los, Milton, and Blake are versions of the man who recognizes his mistakes, who passes a Last Judgment upon himself, and as poet attempts to rectify these mistakes. (For Blake's concept of the Last Judgment, see Erdman, p. 551.) So whatever happens to one character happens to another. Indeed, they may all be undergoing the same experience, but at different levels of perception. Thus, the "Bard's Song," which seems to precede the "main action," can become part of it if read as another retelling, in "a finer tone," of that action. But, on a strictly textual basis, this last hypothesis is not entirely persuasive. The "Bard's Song," though a rehearsal of the central action of the poem, is by no means conterminous with it. Perhaps the evidence for simultaneity of action does exist, but, after several close readings of the poem, I fail to see how all these separate pieces of evidence can cohere into a convincing whole. For further discussion of Blake's notions of simultaneity, see W. J. T. Mitchell, "Poetic and Pictorial Imagination in Blake's *The Book of Urizen,*" *Eighteenth-Century Studies,* 3 (1969), 83-107.

4. The most concise analysis of Blake's distinction between the eternal and the temporal is that offered by Frye in *Fearful Symmetry* (pp. 45-48, 251-53). John Beer shows the relevance of this distinction to the poet's "developing mythology" in an illuminating chapter in his *Blake's Visionary Universe* (Manchester: Manchester Univ. Press, 1969), pp. 101-13.

5. A corollary of this belief in the permanence of substance and the changes wrought upon this substance by accidents (one recalls the use of this distinction in the arguments for and against transubstantiation during the Reformation) is found in

Milton (Plate 32) in the Seven Angels' discourse on Forms (permanent) and States (changeable).

6. A small introductory list of critical studies on typology may include the following: A. C. Charity, *Events and Their Afterlife: The Dialectics of Christian Typology in the Bible and Dante* (Cambridge: Cambridge Univ. Press, 1966); Northrop Frye, "The Typology of *Paradise Regained*," *MP* [*Modern Philology*], 53 (1956), 227-38; Barbara K. Lewalski, "*Samson Agonistes* and the 'Tragedy of the Apocalypse,'" *PMLA*, 85 (1970), 1050-62; H. R. MacCallum, "Milton and the Figurative Interpretation of the Bible," *UTQ* [*University of Toronto Quarterly*], 31 (1961-1962), 397-415; William G. Madsen, *From Shadowy Types to Truth: Studies in Milton's Symbolism* (New Haven: Yale Univ. Press, 1968); Steven N. Zwicker, *Dryden's Political Poetry: The Typology of King and Nation* (Providence, R.I.: Brown Univ. Press, 1972). An indispensable tool for the student of typology is Sacvan Bercovitch's "Selective Checklist on Typology," in *Typology and Early American Literature*, ed. Sacvan Bercovitch (Amherst: Univ. of Massachusetts Press, 1972), pp. 249-337.

7. See Jean Daniélou, S.J., *From Shadows to Realities: Studies in the Biblical Typology of the Fathers*, trans. Wulstan Hibberd (London: Burns and Oates, 1960), and K. J. Woollcombe, "The Biblical Origins and Patristic Development of Typology," in *Essays on Typology*, ed. G. W. H. Lampe and K. J. Woollcombe (London: SCM Press, 1957), pp. 39-75.

8. Other typological passages in the New Testament include Matthew 12:40-42, 17:1-5; John 3:14-17; I Peter 3:20-21; Galatians 6:16; I Corinthians 10:6, 10; 15:47.

9. Romans 5:14-15, 19. All Biblical quotations are from the Authorized King James Version.

10. Benjamin Keach, *Tropologia: Or a Key to Open Scripture Metaphors* (London, 1681; rpt. Grand Rapids, Mich.: Kregel, 1972), p. 226.

11. Samuel Mather, *Figures or Types of the Old Testament*, 2nd ed. (London, 1701), p. 56.

12. Keach, pp. xi-xii. For this aspect of typological interpretation, see the seminal essay by Erich Auerbach, "*Figura*," in *Scenes from the Drama of European Literature*, trans. Ralph Manheim (New York: Meridian Books, 1959), pp. 11-76. See also his *Mimesis: The Representation of Reality in Western Literature*, trans. Willard R. Trask (Princeton, Princeton Univ. Press, 1953), pp. 16, 48-49, 73-76, 116, 156-62, 194-202, 247, 317-18, 555.

13. Mather, p. 53.

14. On this aspect of typology, see Charity, *Events and Their Afterlife*.

15. G. W. H. Lampe, "The Reasonableness of Typology," in Lampe and Woollcombe, *Essays on Typology*, p. 32.

16. The most comprehensive study of medieval exegesis to date still remains Henri DeLubac's *Exégèse Médiévale: Les Quatre Sens de L'Écriture*, 4 vols. (Paris: Aubier, 1959-1964). On the origins of typology, see Vol. I, Ch. 5, "Les deux testaments," pp. 305-63. See also his "Typologie et allégorie," *Recherches de Science Religieuse*, 34 (1947), 180-226. For other works on medieval exegesis, typology, and related subjects, see Jean Daniélou, *Origène* (Paris: La Table ronde, 1948); Charles Donahue, "Patristic Exegesis," in *Critical Approaches to Medieval Literature*, ed. Dorothy Bethurum (New York: Columbia Univ. Press, 1960), pp. 61-82; R. M. Grant, *The Letter and the Spirit* (New York: Macmillan, 1957); R. P. C. Hanson, *Allegory and Event* (London: SCM Press, 1959); Beryl Smalley, *The Study of the Bible in the Middle Ages* (Oxford: Clarendon Press, 1941); *Essays on Old Testament Hermeneutics*, ed. Claus Westermann (Richmond, Va.: John Knox Press, 1963). On Augustine as exegete, see *De Doctrina Christiana*, trans. D. W. Robertson, Jr. (New York: Liberal Arts Press, 1958), esp. Robertson's Introduction, pp. ix-xxi; *The City of God*, trans. Marcus Dods (New York: Modern Library, 1950); and *The Enchiridion on Faith, Hope, and Love*, trans. Ernest Evans (London: S. P. C. K., 1953).

17. William Ames, *The Marrow of Sacred Divinity* (London, 1643), p. 151.

18. Jean Calvin, *Commentary on Corinthians*, trans. John Pringle (Edinburgh: Calvin Translation Society, 1848-1849), I, 175. For similar utterances, see Calvin's *Institutes of the Christian Religion*, ed. John T. McNeill, trans. Ford Lewis Battles, 2 vols. (Philadelphia: Westminster Press, 1960), *passim*.

19. On this point, see Thomas M. Davis, "The Exegetical Tradition of Puritan Typology," in *Typology and Early American Literature*, ed. Bercovitch, pp. 11-45, esp. pp. 29-45.

20. Keach, p. 232.

21. Mather, p. 55.

22. James Samuel Preus, *From Shadow to Promise: Old Testament Interpretation from Augustine to the Young Luther* (Cambridge, Mass.: Belknap Press of Harvard Univ. Press, 1969), p. 20.

23. Preus has credited Luther with this "peculiar appropriation of the Old Testament" (p. 6) and traced its origins to Luther's commentaries on the Psalms.

24. Mather, title page.

25. Mather, p. 3.

26. Mather, p. 7.

27. For fuller treatments of this distinction, see Sacvan Bercovitch, "Typology in Puritan New England: The Williams-Cotton Controversy Reassessed," *American Quarterly,* 19 (1967), 166-91; and Zwicker, *Dryden's Political Poetry,* pp. 6-8.

28. I am here thinking of the last book of the *Ecclesiastical History* (trans. G. A. Williamson [New York: New York Univ. Press, 1966]), in which Eusebius sees the reign of Constantine, the perfect Christian emperor, as the fulfillment of God's promises to His people, as the earthly triumph of His elect (pp. 380-82), as the beginning of an era of harmony and joy for all believers (pp. 413-14). Ernest Lee Tuveson, however, argues in *Millennium and Utopia: A Study in the Background of the Idea of Progress* (Berkeley: Univ. of California Press, 1949) that Eusebius opposed the notion of an earthly kingdom, citing Eusebius' attacks on Cerinthus (apparently a notable sensualist) to support his claim (p. 15). What Tuveson has failed to observe is that at this point in the narrative (p. 309), Eusebius is quoting from the epistles of Dionysus, Bishop of Alexandria, so that these attacks on Cerinthus do not necessarily reflect Eusebius' own opinions on the matter. For a short but comprehensive account of the life and work of Eusebius, see Colm Luibhéid's Introduction to his edition of *The Essential Eusebius* (New York: New American Library, 1966), pp. 9-31.

29. Mather, p. 54.

30. See Ernest Lee Tuveson, *Redeemer Nation: The Idea of America's Millennial Role* (Chicago: Univ. of Chicago Press, 1968), p. 17, *et passim*; *The American Puritan Imagination: Essays in Revaluation,* ed. Sacvan Bercovitch (Cambridge: Cambridge Univ. Press, 1974), esp. Bercovitch's Introduction, pp. 1-16; and *Puritans, the Millennium and the Future of Israel: Puritan Eschatology, 1600 to 1660,* ed. Peter Toon (Cambridge: Cambridge Univ. Press, 1970).

31. Bercovitch, *American Puritan Imagination,* p. 9.

32. See, for example, Andrew Marvell's "Bermudas." Frank Kermode, in a note to this poem in his *The Selected Poetry of Marvell* (New York: New American Library, 1967), writes: "John Oxenbridge, in whose house at Eton Marvell lived in 1653, had twice been to the Bermudas, first in 1635 as a result of the ecclesiastical persecutions. The islands, thus associated with Puritan exile, had for long been celebrated as a kind of earthly paradise, and the traditional attributes of that place associated with them. They were sometimes known as the Somers Islands, in memory of the captain whose shipwreck gave rise to pamphlets on which Shakespeare drew in *The Tempest*. These already suggest that the islands were a paradise, with continuous spring and summer together, rich in natural resources and reserved for the godly English" (Kermode, p. 59).

33. Indeed, one may trace the origins of this concept to the Venerable Bede's *Church History of the English People,* in which he stresses the special mission of the English race while relating the story of its conversion to Christianity. See *Venerabilis Bedae Opera Historica,* ed. Charles Plummer, 2 vols. (Oxford: Clarendon Press, 1896). There is a good translation of this work in Everyman's Library (#479). For the importance of the concept in Elizabethan times, see William Haller, *Foxe's Book of Martyrs and the Elect Nation* (London: J. Cape, 1963).

34. See J. A. Mazzeo, "Cromwell as Davidic King," in *Renaissance and Seventeenth-Century Studies,* ed. J. A. Mazzeo (New York: Columbia Univ. Press, 1964), pp. 29-55; and Gerard Reedy, S.J., "Mystical Politics: The Imagery of Charles II's Coronation," in *Studies in Change and Revolution: Aspects of English Intellectual History, 1640-1800,* ed. Paul J. Korshin (Menston, Yorkshire: Scolar Press, 1972), pp. 19-42. For the brief revival of the David-King of England (in this case, George II) parallel in the 1760's and the resulting controversy over this identification, see Moira Dearnley, *The Poetry of Christopher Smart* (London: Routledge and Kegan Paul, 1968), pp. 173-74.

35. See, for example, Blake's *There is No Natural Religion* (1788) and *All Religions are One* (1788) in Erdman, pp. 1-2; also *Jerusalem,* Plate 52, "To the Deists."

36. Frye, *Fearful Symmetry,* p. 320.

37. Aside from Blake's own writings on the subject, which range from the excoriating to the witty to the forgiving, there are four major critical assessments of the nature of the quarrel between the poet and Hayley; all four must be read to arrive at a balanced view of the affair. On the pro-Blake side, see Damon, *Blake, His Philosophy and Symbols,* pp. 172-82, and Frye, *Fearful Symmetry,* pp. 327-32. Morchard Bishop in *Blake's Hayley* (London: V. Gollancz, 1951) has—in the words of

the half repentant, half tongue-in-cheek Damon (*A Blake Dictionary*, p. 176)—"rectified considerably our estimate of that really estimable gentleman" by underscoring Hayley's unselfishness and good intentions (as Blake himself realized) in his dealings with both Blake and Cowper. Finally, in what is perhaps the most comprehensive discussion of the relations between the two men, *Angel of Apocalypse: Blake's Idea of Milton* ([Madison: Univ. of Wisconsin Press, 1975], esp. pp. 229-36), Joseph Anthony Wittreich, Jr., has argued for Blake's indebtedness to Hayley's *An Essay on Epic Poetry* (1782) for his epic theory and practice.

38. In addition to Frye's magisterial treatment of the English prophetic epic tradition in connection with *Milton* in *Fearful Symmetry* (pp. 318-25), I refer the reader to Joseph Anthony Wittreich, Jr., "'Sublime Allegory': Blake's Epic Manifesto and the Milton Tradition," *Blake Studies*, 4:ii (1972), 15-44. This article—the best I have seen on the subject—provides a useful corrective to T. S. Eliot's view that Blake's "genius . . . sadly lacked a framework of accepted and traditional ideas which would have prevented him from indulging in a philosophy of his own, and concentrated his attention upon the problems of the poet" (Eliot, "Blake" [1920], *Selected Essays* [New York: Faber and Faber, 1961], pp. 279-80).

39. Other passages on the subject in *Milton* include 10:1-11:26; 13:36-44; 15:21-52; 22:15-25; 24:68-76; 26:10-12; 27:8-63; 35:42-67; and 36:13-37:19.

40. On the question of "reincarnation" and its relevance to the concept of the poetic tradition, see Frye, *Fearful Symmetry*, pp. 322-23.

41. Bloom, *The Visionary Company*, p. 101.

42. Letter to Thomas Butts (22 November 1802); in Erdman, p. 693.

David Riede (essay date 1987)

SOURCE: Riede, David. "Blake's *Milton*: On Membership in the Church Paul." In *Re-Membering Milton: Essays on the Texts and Traditions*, edited by Mary Nyquist and Margaret W. Ferguson. 1987. Reprint, pp. 257-77. New York: Methuen, 1988.

[*In the following essay, Riede evaluates how Blake interpreted Milton's attitudes toward religion and creative expression.*]

Perhaps no poet has responded to the works of another in fuller, more complex, and more radically revisionary ways than William Blake responded to the writings of John Milton. Throughout his career, Blake continually returned to Milton, from his critical attack in **The Marriage of Heaven and Hell** to his usurpation of the Miltonic sublime in **Milton** and the other prophetic writings. Blake's response to Milton's influence has been much discussed by theorists of literary tradition and poetic influence, but as Blake said of the Judeo-Christian tradition, "this history has been adopted by both parties."[1] For Harold Bloom it magnificently illustrates a theory about anxiety and discontinuity in the tradition of "strong poets," while for Joseph Anthony Wittreich it demonstrates confidence and continuity in the "Miltonic tradition," the "line of vision."[2] Such opposed positions might seem to be the very stuff of Blakean mental warfare, but they have not produced a very informative debate. Wittreich, dismissive of Bloom's position, has continued as the spokesman for a relatively unproblematic Miltonic and Blakean tradition of prophecy, and Bloom, disdainful of explanation, has declined to argue his position in any detail. In fact, Bloom's psychoanalytic model for the transmission of the tradition continues to romanticize the unconscious as a realm of imaginative inspiration. I would like to propose a reading that supports some of Bloom's views about combative reading, but without the Bloomian apparatus of strong fathers and strong sons. My reading will call into question the whole idea of a "line of vision" by rejecting such fundamental romantic mystifications as "inspiration" and "vision." Blake himself established the terms for his romantic critics by insisting on the authority of his inspiration, the truth of his vision, but I will argue that his own accounts of that inspiration in **Milton** undermine themselves and subvert the very idea of authoritative inspiration. A close look at his oddly neglected account of precisely how Milton's spirit entered into him and at his parody of Milton's invocation of the muse in *Paradise Lost* will reveal that side by side with Blake's suggested "line of vision" are not quite compatible signs of a very different tradition descending from St Paul. Drawing out the neglected threads of Pauline allusion in **Milton** leads, I think, to a fresh perspective on Blake and on the idea of a Miltonic tradition. I will suggest in particular that the very idea of "visionary" poetry ought to be looked at more critically than it usually has been, and that we may need to reconsider the received doctrine concerning a "line of vision" descending from John of Patmos through Milton and Blake. It may be that Milton and Blake must be understood instead in a "line of reading" descending from St Paul.

Blake's analysis of Milton's accomplishment involves, most obviously, a radical critique of Milton's Puritan (and essentially Pauline) Christianity, and consequently of the idea of Christian inspiration that enabled Milton to write with dogmatic authority by transcribing the word of God. As Blake saw it, such a claim for inspiration made Milton akin to Moses, not as a prophet, but as the founder of an absolute and tyrannical moral law.

To attack this monolithic authority, Blake associated it not only with Moses but with the equally authoritarian teachings of the "Church Paul," the morally repressive institution of Christianity. In Blake's subtle and complex analysis, however, the Church Paul is not to be confused with the St Paul who wrote the epistles. Rather it represents the hardening of Paul's discourse into dogmatic authority by passive, obedient readers who take the letter as law. Blake had earlier associated Milton with the doctrines of the Church Paul—in **The Four Zoas** his list of the fallen sons of prophecy ends with "Paul Constantine Charlemaine Luther Milton" (pl. 115, l.6). Milton's acceptance of a vast gulf between human and divine, which Blake associates with the Church Paul, is attacked already in **The Marriage of Heaven and Hell**; there, Blake criticizes *Paradise Lost* for accepting and promulgating the "Pauline" doctrine "That Man has two real existing principles Viz: a Body & a Soul" (pl. 4) and that the body, representing energy and inspiration, must be chastened to elevate the soul, a repressive moral governor.

Paul can become the "Church Paul" and Milton can become the "Church Milton" if their fierce writings are not encountered by fierce readers. Part of Blake's argument in **Milton** will be that too much deference to a writer's claimed inspiration, or authority, will result in reducing that author to a "church," a mere codifier of repressive moral laws. Blake associates Milton with Paul, however, not merely to attack the false authority of the Miltonic "vision," but also to redeem a new kind of Miltonic and Pauline sublime. Both Milton and Paul are to be admired not as prophets uttering the authoritative word of God, but as combative readers who shattered and usurped the authority of earlier prophets. Paul's transformative typological readings of the Old Testament and Milton's combative utterances in *Areopagitica* become models for a Blakean mode of mental warfare that replaces the divinely authoritative voice of *Paradise Lost* with a contentious heteroglossia in which Blake, Milton, and Paul contend with and against one another, with and against the myriad voices of the living Judeo-Christian tradition. Such a view, of course, supports Bloom's idea of Blake as a strong reader who wrestles with Milton's works in a radically revisionary way, and even supports Wittreich's sense of Blake's confidence in the continuity of a tradition, but it removes the notion that transcendent vision and authoritative prophecy necessarily privilege *the* tradition. In a sense, Blake attempts to replace the univocal Miltonic sublime with a kind of dialogic sublime of spiritual strife in which *vision* is always combative *revision*. As we shall see, however, Blake himself runs into difficulty when he attempts to transcend this sublime combat, to meld dissonance into visionary, inspired, and therefore authoritative univocity—as if the tumult of his Babel were actually an inspired speaking in tongues.

The famous lyric that introduces **Milton** significantly summons the combative, revolutionary Milton of *Areopagitica* rather than what Blake saw as the authoritarian author of *Paradise Lost*:

> And did those feet in ancient time,
> Walk upon Englands mountains green:
> And was the holy Lamb of God,
> On Englands pleasant pastures seen!
>
> .
>
> I will not cease from Mental Fight,
> Nor shall my Sword sleep in my hand:
> Till we have built Jerusalem,
> In Englands green & pleasant Land.
>
> Would to God that all the Lords people were Prophets.
>
> Numbers XI. ch. 29 v.

The motto, as has often been noted, refers not only to the Bible but also to Milton's defense of "Mental Fight," of "sects and schisms" in *Areopagitica*: "For now the time seems come, wherein Moses, the great prophet, may sit in heaven rejoicing to see that memorable and glorious wish of his fulfilled, when not only our seventy elders, but all the Lord's people, are become prophets." But what has not generally been noted is how fully the surrounding discussion in *Areopagitica* anticipates the symbolism of Blake's major prophecies.[3] Working within the typological traditions of Puritanism, Milton precedes Blake in equating Sion, or Jerusalem, with England's green and pleasant land, and the symbolic rebuilding of the temple with the establishment of Truth. And most important, he anticipates Blake in his adoption of the Pauline body of Christ imagery. Milton's famous description of the body of Christ as the "perfect shape" of Truth, of its mutilation and gradual restoration by the "sad friends of Truth," is recapitulated in Blake's central epic symbol of the "Human Imagination / Which is the Divine Body of the Lord Jesus" (**Milton**, pl.3). Further, Blake's dormant Albion, a figure whose awakening will symbolize the spiritual awakening of the nation, is prefigured in Milton's ostentatiously "visionary" prophecy: "Methinks I see in my mind a noble and puissant nation rousing herself like a strong man after sleep, and shaking her invincible locks."[4]

The presence of *Areopagitica* in the background of Blake's **Milton** is not surprising. *Areopagitica* was written in response to Parliament's licensing ordinance, which threatened to silence dissent from received opinion and put an end to mental combat, and Blake's **Milton** was written, in part, for similar reasons. Under the patronage of William Hayley, Blake was being strongly urged to make money, not war, with art. Hayley pressured him to paint fashionable miniatures instead of writing and illustrating revolutionary epics. Blake was

to conform to conventions as an artist, to stifle his in-spiration, and silence his imagination. Consequently *Milton,* the epic Blake wrote in response to this pres-sure, quite naturally draws on Milton's proclamations of mental warfare. Perhaps inevitably Blake's particular debt to *Areopagitica* led him to adopt the stance of a combative writer with whom he is rarely associated. Milton's Biblical authority in defence of free expres-sion is, more than anyone else, the pugnacious St Paul—Milton repeatedly alludes to Pauline doctrines of char-ity and restraint from judging one another in his defence of "this Christian liberty which Paul so often boasts of."[5] It is with this combative Paul, and combative Mil-ton, that Blake aligns himself in *Milton.*

Blake scorned the "Church Paul," but the embattled apostle was, with Milton, a major influence on his epics about influence and inspiration. His comments about the composition of *The Four Zoas* and *Milton* reflect his sense of a joint Pauline/Miltonic idea of inspiration, and passages from *Milton* demonstrate a curious con-flation of Paul and Milton as the very sources of Blake's own inspiration. In an 1803 letter to Butts, Blake de-scribed his inspiration for the nearly completed *The Four Zoas* and *Milton* (evidently still meant to be inte-grated into one poem): "I have written this Poem from immediate Dictation twelve or sometimes twenty or thirty lines at a time without Premeditation & even against my Will."[6] The passage plainly echoes Milton's inspiration by his "Celestial Patroness" who "dictates to me slumb'ring, or inspires / Easy my unpremeditated Verse" (*PL* [*Paradise Lost*] IX.21-4). Although Blake's comments to Butts cannot be taken at face value, the statement certainly seems to indicate that Blake was at this point disposed to accept a Miltonic notion of inspi-ration. Nevertheless, the phrase "even against my Will" may suggest some reservations about such a notion, since it indicates that the author lacks control over his own imagination, is unable to combat successfully the imposition of an authoritarian will beyond his own. The desire to avoid such passivity is apparent in the motto prefixed to *The Four Zoas.* The motto, from Paul's Epistle to the Ephesians, reveals Blake's identification with the apostle's commitment to spiritual combat:

> For we wrestle not against flesh and blood, but against principalities, against powers, against the rulers of the darkness of this world, against spiritual wickedness in high places.
>
> (Eph. 6.12)

In *Milton* the Pauline reference is subtler, but is of fun-damental importance because it directly links Blake, Milton, and Paul. The crucial passage describes Mil-ton's descent from Eternity back into time and space to be incorporated in Blake:

> Then first I saw him in the Zenith as a falling star,
> Descending perpendicular, swift as the swallow or swift;

> And on my left foot falling on the tarsus, entered there;
> But from my left foot a black cloud redounding spread over Europe.
>
> (pl.15, ll.47-50)

The passage is, to say the least, peculiar, but it would seem to conflate the entrance of Milton into Blake with the dramatic conversion of Saul of Tarsus on the road to Damascus (Acts 9:1-18).[7] Indeed, though this has not been previously noted, the startling image was very likely influenced by a passage in Milton's *The Reason of Church-Government* in which Blake would have seen his struggle of contraries and the Miltonic warfare of "sects and schisms" conflated with the sudden conver-sion of St Paul:

> For if we look but on the nature of elementall and mixt things, we know they cannot suffer any change of one kind, or quality into another without the struggl of con-trarieties. And in things artificiall, seldome any elegance is wrought without a superfluous wast and refuse in the transaction. No Marble statue can be politely carv'd, no fair edifice built without almost as much rubbish and sweeping. Insomuch that even in the spirituall conflict of S. *Pauls* conversion there fell scales from his eyes that were not perceav'd before.[8]

Blake's almost ludicrous pun on "tarsus" as the locus of conversion and of the convergence of visionary poets is so bizarre that it seems to open an ironic gap between Milton and Blake even as it brings the two poets to-gether. The peculiar anatomical precision is sufficiently explained by the pun on "tarsus," but Blake may also be punning on yet another meaning of the word, for "tarsus" means not only sole, but also the "rim of the eyelid" (*OED*), perhaps here the corporeal scales that prevent spiritual vision. The conversion of Saul of Tar-sus to St Paul, of the vehement defender of Jewish law to the Apostle of Jesus Christ, is the type for both Mil-ton and Blake of the triumph of spiritual warfare, both emphasizing the rubbish and debris of false vision that must be swept away. Blake's extraordinarily complex pun may, however, imply that Milton himself failed to recognize the hardening of the Church Paul into scales, a hindrance to vision.

The rubbish in Milton's vision is evident in the "black cloud" that "redounding spread over Europe" when Mil-ton entered into Blake. It is the same as the rubbish in Saul's (and Paul's) vision, a continued adherence to the old law that Jesus had come to sweep away. The "black cloud" is Milton's spectre, or selfhood, identified throughout the poem with Satan, who "is Urizen" (pl.10, l.1), the Miltonic God of "Moral laws and cruel punish-ments" (pl.9, l.22) who perverts the "Divine voice in its entrance to the earth" (pl.9, l.23). When the "black cloud" becomes "the Cherub on Sinai" (pl.20, l.23), moreover, it emphatically associates Milton with Paul,

for the "Covering Cherub" is both "Miltons Shadow" (pl.37, 1.44) and, in part, the "Church Paul." Both Paul and Milton are associated with the repressive moral law that blocks imaginative vision, for it is the Covering Cherub who prevents the return to Eden with a flaming sword (notably at the end of *Paradise Lost*) and who adorns the curtains of the ark to prevent vision of the divine presence.

Blake's criticism of his predecessor's inspiration in *Milton* is essentially a repudiation of his dualistic separation of human and divine, his denial of human energy and imagination as he attempted to find inspiration from a far removed, non-human, law-giving God. In fact, *Milton* significantly locates Milton's "Spectrous body" on Horeb and Sinai (pl.20, ll.20-3), thereby mocking the inadequacies of Milton's sources of inspiration in an ironic allusion to the invocation of *Paradise Lost*:

> Sing Heav'nly Muse, that on the secret top
> Of *Oreb*, or of *Sinai*, didst inspire
> That Shepherd.
>
> (I.6-8)

It is true that Milton goes on to seek the spiritual inspiration of the New Testament as well, but Blake is concerned to point out an excessive emphasis in *Paradise Lost* on a religion of secrecy ("the secret top"), a hidden God, and a repressive Mosaic law. Immediately after Milton's descent into Blake's tarsus, the real sources of Milton's inspiration are described from a Blakean perspective. Milton is another Moses in the desert, writing on the "iron tablets" that Blake always associates with the ten commandments and the restraints of religion. Further, taking dictation from God and dictating in turn to his "Wives & Daughters," Milton becomes so hardened in his repressive, patriarchal character that "his body was the Rock Sinai" (pl.17, ll.9-14). Blake says in **"The Song of Los"** that "Moses beheld upon Mount Sinai forms of dark delusion," and in **"The Book of Ahania"** he says that "Mount Sinai, in Arabia" is a poisoned rock used by Urizen to slay a Christ-like figure and to become the source of a religion of mystery and a "book of iron."

The phrase "Mount Sinai, in Arabia," a reference not to the Old Testament but to the New, begins to suggest how in Blake's view a different way of reading the New Testament might have redeemed Milton from the bondage of the old law. The phrase occurs in Paul's Epistle to the Galatians, in a passage that became the basis of St Augustine's, and Blake's, typological vision of the eternal City:[9]

> Tell me, ye that desire to be under the law, do ye not hear the law? For it is written, that Abraham had two sons, the one by a bondmaid, the other by a freewoman. But he who was of the bondwoman was born after the flesh; but he of the freewoman was by promise. Which

> things are an allegory: for these are the two covenants; the one from the mount Sinai, which gendereth to bondage, which is Agar. For this Agar is mount Sinai in Arabia, and answereth to Jerusalem which now is, and is in bondage with her children. But Jerusalem which is above is free, which is the mother of us all. . . . Now we, brethren, as Isaac was, are the children of promise.
>
> (Gal. 4:21-6, 28)

Like Paul, Milton read the Old Testament typologically, and saw that it prefigures its fulfillment in the New, but for Blake Milton's reading was not radical enough. Milton did not free himself from the bondage of the law because, like Paul, he continued to see the human condition in terms of separation from a transcendent kingdom that is inaccessibly above ("Jerusalem which is above") and in terms of an indefinite period of waiting for the fulfillment of "promise," in which, at last, Jesus will

> bring back
> Through the world's wilderness long wander'd man
> Safe to eternal Paradise of rest.
>
> (*PL* XII.312-14)

But although Milton interpreted the Old Testament typologically, in Blake's view he read the New Testament "in the letter." Consequently he accepted as law the Pauline distinction between Flesh and Spirit, and therefore perpetuated the religion of fear (though "filial" now rather than "servile" (*PL* XII.305-6)). Blake, in contrast, read both books typologically, or "in the spirit," rather than passively submitting to their literal authority. As Blake read the passage from Paul, the new Jerusalem is here and now if we have the imaginative vision to see it, and it frees us from bondage to the vegetative natural world, from natural law. For him the basic failure in Milton's vision was his acceptance of a dualistic universe in which God is above and eternal and humanity is below, wandering in time under conditions of enforced obedience, humility, chastity and, especially, patience in order to await the eventual fulfillment of the promise. This dualism has everything to do with Milton's limitations as a visionary poet because his assumption that inspired poetry is dictated from a divine source outside of humanity separates inspiration from imagination, which is Jesus Christ—the Eternal Human Form Divine. For Blake, Milton's poetry is too much a wandering and a waiting for vision, rather than an imaginative revisioning of earlier texts. The most important single lesson that Milton can learn is to "Seek not thy heavenly father then beyond the skies" (pl.20, ll.31-2), and the first step he must take to be redeemed in Blake's poem is to engage in spiritual warfare by breaking the covenant: "He took off the robe of the promise, & ungirded himself from the oath of God" (pl.14, l.13). Blake's revision of Milton, then, uses Pauline typology to attack Pauline and Puritan dualism, the separation of spirit and flesh, God and humanity, in-

spiration and imagination. In order to combat the Church Paul in Milton, Blake simply reads Milton as Paul read the Old Testament.

The full complexity of Blake's response to Milton's peculiarly Pauline inspiration is implicit in the densely cryptic invocation to **Milton.** Blake's invocation is in some ways a parodic revision of Milton's invocation in *Paradise Lost,* and is consequently a critique of Milton's inspiration. The most crucial, and most obvious difference between Blake's and Milton's invocations is that Blake fully internalizes the muses:

> Daughters of Beulah! Muses who inspire the Poets Song
> Record the journey of immortal Milton thro' your Realms
> Of terror & mild moony lustre, in soft sexual delusions
> Of varied beauty, to delight the wanderer and repose
> His burning thirst & freezing hunger! Come into my hand
> By your mild power; descending down the Nerves of my right arm
> From out the Portals of my Brain, where by your ministry
> The Eternal Great Humanity Divine. planted his Paradise,
> And in it caus'd the Spectres of the Dead to take sweet forms
> In likeness of himself.

<div align="right">(pl.2, ll.1-10)</div>

Unlike Milton, who seemed to Blake to seek inspiration from a God beyond the skies, Blake seeks it in his own imagination, which is the "Eternal Great Humanity Divine." The invocation, then, does not simply place Blake in a "line of vision" with Milton, but establishes a wholly new idea of the imagination to displace the earlier poet's profound—and significantly Pauline—distrust of the imagination.

The tendency of modern romantic criticism has been to gloss over this obvious distinction between a Blakean and a Miltonic sublime by obscuring Milton's very un-Blakean antagonism to imagination. Wittreich, for example, attempts to illustrate Milton's commitment to a Blakean mental warfare with a quotation from *The Reason of Church-Government* that describes a "warfare, not carnall, but mighty through God to the pulling down of strong holds, casting down imaginations, and every high thing that exalteth it selfe against the knowledge of God." Wittreich does not note, however, that the passage is a direct quotation from St Paul, and that it is plainly an attack on the unaided imagination, on spiritual pride.[10] For Milton (and Paul) divine inspiration made one "mighty through God," and was therefore radically different from idolatrous "imaginations." As we know from Eve's dream, imagination is the province of the toad-like Satan, who assays "his Devilish art

to reach / The Organs of her Fancy" (*PL* IV.801-2). For Milton, inspiration and imagination are not only different from one another, but are opposed in mutual warfare. The one is of God, the other of Satan.

Blake regarded Milton's Pauline separation of the "carnall" and the spiritual as the root of his error. For Blake, body and soul must be one; imagination must be incarnate. Consequently he attempts to redeem his predecessor's inspiration by summoning female muses. In **Jerusalem** Blake directly invokes the Divine Humanity within himself, his own imagination, but in **Milton** he calls upon the sexual "Daughters of Beulah" because it is they who are missing from Milton's vision. Milton had utterly rejected his fallen sexual nature, but now he must be redeemed by passing through the sexually liberated, female land of Beulah. Though the female sexuality he will experience there will lead him into "soft sexual delusions," it will destroy his worse delusion that spiritual inspiration comes from subjugating the "carnall" imagination. The sexual nature, though not an end in itself, is a source of creative energy that Milton had repressed, but that ought to minister to the higher powers of the imagination. In other words, Blake's Milton must recognize that true inspiration comes not from subduing the flesh to the spirit and taking dictation from a distant God, but from accepting the creative energies of the senses as a part of the Eternal Great Humanity Divine.

Because Milton must be separated from the false inspiration that misled him, Blake's invocation asks the Daughters of Beulah to "Tell also of the False Tongue! vegetated / Beneath your land of shadows" (pl.2, ll.10-11). The False Tongue is Blake's Satan (pl.27, ll.45-6) but Milton's God, the source of a religion that sacrifices even Jesus, the Divine Imagination, to its fallen and corrupt moral laws. The "False Tongue" that Milton mistook for inspiration is the lying tempter who perverts and frustrates moral vision. As the poem proceeds, Blake's characterization of this vegetated tongue shows what is wrong with Milton's inspiration, and exposes much that is false in visionary language. It is the fleshly tongue of fallen nature that, perceived as separate from the realm of spirit, can speak only in the terms of the law that abases the flesh to exalt the spirit:

> The Tongue a little moisture fills, a little food it cloys
> A little sound it utters & its cries are faintly heard
> Then brings forth Moral Virtue.

<div align="right">(pl.5, ll.25-7)</div>

The vegetable tongue can only speak of its incapacity to speak spiritual truths: "Can such a Tongue boast of the living waters?" (pl.5, l.34). Consequently the immediate effect on Blake as Milton enters into his foot and his "Spectrous body" redounds over his sources of inspiration on Horeb and Sinai is to make him doubt the ability of his tongue to speak:

> O how can I with my gross tongue that cleaveth to the
> dust,
> Tell of the Four-fold Man, in starry numbers fitly or-
> dered
> Or how can I with my cold hand of clay! But thou O
> Lord
> Do with me as thou wilt! for I am nothing, and vanity.
> If thou chuse to elect a worm, it shall remove the
> mountains.
>
> (pl.20, ll.15-19)

The lines parody Milton's view, frequently reiterated in *Paradise Lost,* that human (or even angelic) speech cannot adequately describe the works of the Almighty. As even the angelic chorus sings: "what thought can measure thee or tongue / Relate thee?" (VII.603-4). The limitations of language reflect, in Raphael's words, the mortal limits of "Human imagination" separated by an infinite distance from the "highth / Of Godlike Power" (VI.300-1). To Blake the idea that human faculties are incapable of divine utterance only reflects the Pauline belief that humanity is merely natural or vegetative. And fallen humanity is just that; it is the slain "Human Imagination . . . the Divine Body of the Lord Jesus" deformed by jealousy and Urizenic "doubt & reasoning" until the imagination is confined to a "stony hard" skull, the eyes are rolled into "two little Orbs & closed in two little Caves," the ears are "petrified" in spiraling "close volutions," and the tongue is a mere organ of natural appetite, "a Tongue of hunger & thirst" (pl.3, ll.1-23). The fragmentation of the speaker's being into the various bodily parts re-enacts the dismemberment of Truth or Christ described in *Areopagitica,* but Blake's point is that the unified body of Truth, the "Four-fold Man," is only perceived as fragmented by those who see themselves as fragments, as assemblages of various members. The fragmented consciousness results in "Differences between Ideas, that Ideas themselves, (which are / The Divine Members) may be slain in offerings for sin" (pl.35, ll.5-6), as Christ was. The disjointed carnal senses are of course incapable of imaginative perception, of perceiving the Divine Body as whole. The vegetated body is, Florence Sandler points out, the "body of this death" that St Paul prays to be delivered from (Rom. 7:24),[11] but it is also the "fleshly tabernacle" with which the Church Paul obscures the divine vision. One of Milton's first utterances in *Milton* assimilates him to the Pauline sense of entrapment within this body:

> When will the Resurrection come; to deliver the sleep-
> ing body
> From corruptibility: O when Lord Jesus wilt thou
> come?
>
> (pl.14, ll.17-18)

But Milton—like Paul—remains entrapped within the body of death because he believes himself helpless and utterly dependent upon God for his release. Because he passively accepts the vegetative, shrunken state of his senses, he is incapable of the imaginative vision that would be, in fact, the savior he awaits, Jesus Christ.

Blake saw that at the heart of Milton's concern about the limitations of language is his sense of the vast gulf between a God who is outside of time and a language that must move sequentially in time. The need for language to unfold itself in time is the basis of Raphael's comment on the inadequacy of human speech or comprehension to understand God's timelessness:

> Immediate are the Acts of God, more swift
> Than time or motion, but to human ears
> Cannot without process of speech be told,
> So told as earthly notion can receive.
>
> (*PL* VII.176-9)

Blake, of course, denied that God is inexpressibly other than man, but more specifically he denied that human speech and comprehension are trapped in time. For Blake, after all, it is only the dualistic corporealization of the body that reduces the receptiveness of the spirit to the "petrified close volutions of the ears." Similarly, "process of speech," trapped in time, is the function of the "gross tongue." Indeed, the *disjecta membra* of the Pauline body of death are paradoxically incapable of following the Pauline injunction to understand the matter-moulded forms of speech in the spirit, not in the letter. Milton's—or Raphael's—idea that comprehension is necessarily confined to narrative "process of speech" must have struck him as one more consequence of the deluded belief constantly reiterated in *Paradise Lost* that mankind, fallen into materiality, is exiled from eternity and so must learn to wait meekly and patiently in time.

Blake's impatience with Milton's patience emerges fully, if cryptically, in the final part of his invocation, a direct parody of various passages in *Paradise Lost:*

> Say first! what mov'd Milton, who walkd about in
> Eternity
> One hundred years, pondring the intricate mazes of
> Providence
> Unhappy tho in heav'n, he obey'd, he murmur'd not.
> he was silent
> Viewing his Sixfold Emanation scatter'd thro' the
> deep
> In torment! To go into the deep her to redeem & him-
> self perish?
> What cause at length mov'd Milton to this unexampled
> deed?
> A Bards prophetic Song!
>
> (pl.2, ll.16-22)

The most obvious target of these lines is the second part of Milton's opening invocation:

Say first, for Heav'n hides nothing from thy view
Nor the deep Tract of Hell, say first what cause
Mov'd our Grand Parents in that happy State,
Favor'd of Heav'n so highly, to fall off
From thir Creator, and transgress his Will
For one restraint, Lords of the World besides?
Who first seduc't them to that foul revolt?
Th'infernal Serpent;

(*PL* I.27-34)

Blake ironically parallels Milton with Adam and Eve to contrast their aboriginal "happy State" with his unhappiness in the false heaven of his religious vision. Adam and Eve, however, were happy as long as they obeyed God, while Milton is unhappy even though "he obey'd, he murmur'd not. he was silent." From the start Blake's theme is that passive, obedient acceptance of restraint by a mysterious Providence is inimical to imaginative vision and prophetic utterance. Appropriately, the parallel invocations also equate the temper of Adam and Eve, "Th'infernal Serpent," with the tempter of Milton, "A Bards prophetic Song!" The point is not far different from that made in *The Marriage of Heaven and Hell*— the true bard in Milton is in Milton's sense "Satanic," but in Blake's he represents the "true Poet." Milton was tempted to his "unexampled deed," by a creative impulse antithetical to quiet obedience—and the "unexampled deed," of course, is his departure from the false heaven to rewrite the cosmic scheme of *Paradise Lost*: "Things [still] unattempted yet in Prose or Rhyme."

Blake's lines mock Miltonic patience not only in the invocation to *Paradise Lost* but in other passages as well. Milton asks "what cause / Mov'd our Grand Parents . . . Who first seduc't them . . . ?" but Blake adds a note of impatience: "what mov'd Milton . . . What cause at length mov'd Milton . . . ?" The addition of "at length" implies that Milton has been rather slow, but it also echoes a later passage from *Paradise Lost* to show the source of his hesitation in his belief that Providence decrees the role of humanity to be an indefinite waiting in a vegetative state until

by degrees of merit rais'd
They open to themselves at length the way
Up hither, under long obedience tri'd,
And Earth be chang'd to Heav'n, and Heav'n to Earth,
One Kingdom, Joy and Union without end.

(VII.157-61)

The apocalyptic union projected in these lines is admirable, but from Blake's perspective it should take place here and now, in the human imagination, not in the indefinite future and beyond the skies. Milton's patient "long obedience" merely forestalls imaginative apocalypse, rather than bringing it about. Like the devils in Hell, whose discussion of Providence finds "no end, in wand'ring mazes lost" (*PL* II.561), Milton in heaven can only endlessly ponder "the intricate mazes of Providence."

Milton's heaven is a hell because it retains the notion of a separation between the human and the divine. Milton, in heaven, is still separated from his essential humanity, his imagination. Blake's invocation strongly implies that Milton's vision failed because his imitation of a patriarchal sky-god destroyed his human integrity, separating a masculine soul from feminine senses. Milton is "Unhappy tho in heav'n" because he has destroyed his senses by casting out female sexuality. He is separated from his "Sixfold Emanation" which is "scatter'd thro' the deep / In torment." As Blake sees it, Milton's false heaven is an illusion that mires humanity more deeply in the corrupt senses simply by insisting on their corruption. The false heaven is created by a maiming of the integrated human imagination, a dismembering of the Divine Body that splits it into repressive male and thwarted female fragments. As Blake saw it, Milton's misogynistic, literally dictatorial, treatment of his wives and daughters reflected his own divided nature. The Sixfold Emanation, in fact, represents the three wives and three daughters who "wrote in thunder smoke and fire / His dictate" (pl.17, ll.13-14). It is this dictatorial Milton who "was the Rock Sinai" of the Church Paul, and who therefore also represents the Pauline body of death: "his body was the Rock Sinai; that body, / Which was on earth born to corruption" (pl.17, ll.14-15). Dictating law to a subjugated female will, Milton covers over the divine vision of Jesus, thus re-enacting the tyranny of the leprous Jehovah, whose stony law created the "Body of Death . . . / Around the Lamb, a Female Tabernacle" (pl.13, ll.25-6). Evidently Milton's unredeemed emanation is also a "Body of Death," a repressive church of Paul and other patriarchs, a "Female Tabernacle:"

A Male within a Female hid as in an Ark & Curtains,
Abraham, Moses, Solomon, Paul, Constantine, Charlemaine
Luther, these seven are the Male-Females, the Dragon Forms
Religion hid in War, a Dragon red & hidden Harlot
All these are seen in Miltons Shadow who is the Covering Cherub.

(pl.37, ll.40-4)

To put the matter simply, by dictating law to a subordinate female will, Milton becomes just another patriarch, and his writings just another church. The unredeemed Shadowy Female, indeed, declares that she

will have Writings written all over [her garments] in Human Words
That every Infant that is born upon the Earth shall read
And get by rote as a hard task of a life of sixty years.

(pl.18, ll.12-14)

As soon as he "took off the robe of the promise, & ungirded himself from the oath of God," Milton recognized that his unredeemed emanation was "the daugh-

ters of memory, & not . . . the daughters of inspiration" (pl.14, ll.28-9). As his Preface to **Milton** makes clear, Blake's intention is to bring about a "New Age" in which "the Daughters of Memory shall become the Daughters of Inspiration" (pl.1), so in the invocation he indicates that Milton's vision can only be salvaged if Milton goes "into the deep . . . to redeem" his emanation, to replace remembered law with imaginative inspiration.

The historical Milton, the revolutionary iconoclast, had claimed that his inspiration would not come from "Dame Memory and her Siren Daughters, but by devout prayer to that eternall Spirit who can enrich with all utterance and knowledge."[12] To Blake, however, Milton's devout prayer to a remote law-giver was quite insufficiently revolutionary. It left Milton still constrained by the traditional authority most closely associated with the Church Paul, able only to *remember* past utterances, not to *redeem* them in the present as living, contentious, perhaps fallible voices that could be engaged in the spiritual warfare of the revisionary imagination. Though Milton had read the Old Testament creatively, he had made a church of the New Testament, and of his own writings. In the prescribed Pauline manner, he read the Old Testament in the spirit, but he read the New in the letter, and so remained a slave to law—remembering, not creating.

But as Blakean commentators point out, Blake's objections are not to Milton, but to Milton's Shadow, the Covering Cherub described by Bloom: "that something that makes men victims and not poets, a demon of discursiveness and shady continuities, a pseudo-exegete who makes writings into Scriptures."[13] Blake's purpose, and the character Milton's purpose, is to cast off this shadow, to annihilate it and so redeem Milton's inspiration, his genuine poetic genius. To do this Milton must redeem his emanation, and at the end of the poem he succeeds in separating his true emanation from the "Sixfold Miltonic Female" who destroys

> Imagination;
> By imitation of Natures Images drawn from Remembrance
> These are the Sexual Garments, the Abomination of Desolation
> Hiding the Human Lineaments as with an Ark & Curtains.

> (pl.41, ll.23-6)

The Daughters of Memory are replaced by "Ololon," a Daughter of Beulah. Since the Daughters of Beulah are Blake's own muses in **Milton,** it would seem that Blake has made Milton's redeemed inspiration his own. The difficulty, however, is that in a sense one veil over the Divine Vision is only replaced with another as Ololon descends over the "One Man Jesus the Saviour:"

> round his limbs
> The Clouds of Ololon folded as a Garment dipped in blood
> Written within & without in woven letters: & the Writing
> Is the Divine Revelation in the Litteral expression:
> A Garment of War, I heard it namd the Woof of Six Thousand Years.

> (pl.42, ll.11-15)

The "Divine Revelation" appears, but not as vision. It appears only in writing, not in the spirit, but in the letter, the "Litteral expression." What is saved, in the end, is not a fully liberated visionary imagination, but the combative words that both conceal and somehow protect the imagination, words that are a "Garment of War." For Blake, as for Milton, inspiration must come from the six thousand years of human writing, and must therefore depend on the contentious *reading* of fallible writings, not the *vision* of immortal truths. To some extent, at least, the muses must be the Daughters of Memory.

Blake, however, resisted accepting these implications about the impossibility of authoritative inspiration and genuinely visionary poetry, and his resistance drew him into a dualism as disturbingly sexist as that he attempted to rectify in Milton. His feminine muses can supply him with the "Litteral expression," but that expression conceals more than it reveals of the purely masculine imagination that is, unfortunately, quite inexpressible, quite beyond the realm of a language bound in space and time. The "weak & weary / Like Women & Children" remain always in the "soft sexual delusions" of Beulah, but "every Man" goes forward into a realm without Error, in the patriarchal "Bosom of the Father in Eternity on Eternity" (pl.31, ll.1-5). Blake redeems sexual love in Beulah from the religion of chastity, but he retains a Pauline dualism that separates male intellect from female sensuality, soul from sense, and vision from language. In fact, Blake's continuation of Milton's phallocentrism is strangely, and presumably accidentally, suggested in his bizarre pun on "tarsus." Milton descends into Blake's lowest member in one more sense than we have considered, for yet another pun on "tarsus" plays on the plural of "tarse," an archaism for phallus (*OED*).

Nevertheless, as Blake saw it, and as his critics continue to see it, his mental warfare with Milton had annihilated Milton's Shadow, the Covering Cherub, and so redeemed the essential Milton. Milton's Poetic Genius can join Blake, apparently, in the "line of vision." After Milton enters into his foot, Blake binds his "sandals / On; to walk forward thro' Eternity" and the composite Blake-Milton, joined at the tarsus, is joined there also by Los, the spirit of prophecy: "he also stoop'd down / And bound my sandals on" (pl.22, ll.4-9). With appar-

ent justice, Wittreich sees this moment as evidence that Blake does not anxiously spurn his predecessor, but joins with him in the tradition of prophecy.[14] Blake is evidently more ambivalent than Wittreich, however, since the source for his image is not any of the usual figures in the "line of vision," but is once again St Paul. The Pauline passage used as a motto for **The Four Zoas** continues with an exhortation to the peculiarly Miltonic heroism of *standing*:

> Wherefore take unto you the whole armour of God, that ye may be able to withstand in the evil day, and having done all, to stand. Stand therefore, having your loins girt about with truth, and having on the breast-plate of righteousness; And your feet shod with the preparation of the gospel of peace.
>
> (Eph. 6:13-15)

But Blake may well have intended this ironically: Milton stood still with the gospel of peace, not advancing it beyond Paul. He needed Blake's aid to "walk forward thro' Eternity." In any case, the relation is surely not as benign as Wittreich repeatedly suggests—without Blake's aid, Milton is not only unshod, but "his feet bled sore / Upon the clay now changed to marble" as he journeyed on in a hellish fallen landscape, just as Milton's own Satan's "unblest feet" suffered on the "burning Marl" of Hell's floor (*PL* I.238, 296). Even at the end of the poem, as the redeemed Milton re-enacts Christ's annihilation of Satan in *Paradise Regained,* he does so by parodying central doctrines of *Paradise Lost* (pl.38, ll.28-33). Further, when Satan is defeated, it is in terms that once again echo the conversion of Saul to St Paul. Struck down on the road to Damascus, Saul, "trembling and astonished," heard the voice of the Lord. So Satan is described twice as trembling "with exceeding great trembling & astonishment" (pl.39, ll.17, 31). The passage reflects the ambivalence of Milton's earlier incarnation in Blake. Once again the preparation of Milton (and of Blake) for prophecy involves a violent conversion in which Milton must be delivered from the body of death as Paul is delivered from Saul.

Blake's characterization of Milton—at least as expressed in **Milton**—does coincide in some ways with both Bloom's and Wittreich's theory of poetic influence and literary history. Blake reads Milton with remarkable critical acuity, and he shows no particular anxiety in taking what he wants and rejecting the rest, though he does follow the Bloomian pattern to the extent that he deceives himself into believing that he is "tougher-minded" than his precursor.[15] And in his uses of Milton and other "prophets" he is of course, as Wittreich argues, working within a tradition of some kind. Nevertheless, his critique of Milton is more coolly reasoned than Bloom's idea of psychologically induced misprision would lead one to expect, and Blake's total rejection of Milton's inspiration, doctrines, and poetic style

make it difficult to place him in a "Miltonic tradition," let alone to use him in establishing *the* Miltonic tradition, as both Wittreich and Bloom attempt to do. Blake cannot even establish a Blakean sublime as a mode of visionary poetry that would redeem a dualistic universe in a monistic vision. Indeed, by continuing to privilege such terms as "vision" and "inspiration," modern criticism establishes an authoritative institutionalized literature, a Church Milton and Church Blake. Academic criticism, of course, has an interest in sacralizing literature in this way, but a full understanding of the Blake—Milton relationship ought to teach us to question the authoritarian claims not only of Milton, but of any discourse, including Blake's.

The problem at the center of Blake's "visionary" epics is that Blake, like Milton, does emphatically claim authoritative inspiration even as he teaches us to suspect such claims. Blake and Milton are the most extreme examples in the English language of major poets claiming such authority—both present themselves as secretaries taking dictation from a source of eternal truth. Yet Blake repudiates Milton's source, and strongly suggests that Milton failed because he did not read the New Testament correctly. Milton must learn to read St Paul as St Paul read the Old Testament. And despite his often transcendent language, Blake's inspiration comes from the works of human imagination, from a creatively combative reading of those works, so that every new text becomes a scene of battle as well as of continuity. Blake's demystification of divine inspiration is made economically explicit in a definition of the "Eternal Great Humanity:"

> As the breath of the Almighty. such are the words of man to man
> In the great Wars of Eternity, in fury of Poetic Inspiration,
> To build the Universe stupendous: Mental forms Creating.
>
> (pl.30, ll.18-20)

Blake, then, humanizes the sacred, and sacralizes the human imagination—and from a high Romantic perspective, one could end the discussion there, with general commendations. Yet Blake's demystification of the language of transcendence does not go far enough, and his excision of God from the sacred language he continues to use raises vexing problems about poetic authority.[16] In the spiritual warfare of imagination, no one voice should, presumably, be privileged as authoritative, or the spiritual conflict would end, superseded by a "body" of dogma. Yet Blake clearly wants to establish an authoritative, prophetic voice, wants to describe a timeless vision. He wants to establish a voice that *is* the "breath of the Almighty," though he knows that the result would be yet another authoritative patriarchal church. The problem is evident in all of his prophetic

works: cut off from a transcendent, authoritative God, his language wanders endlessly in labyrinthine mazes as it attempts to develop contexts in which to accrete sacred meanings. Indeed, his mythic language, particularly when he sacralizes the "divine" imagination as Jesus, creates only an illusion of permanent truth and authority, though it is an illusion that he needs to cling to. The prophecies, with their extraordinarily allusive language and symbolism, plainly depend for their meaning on the past "words of man to man," on the long history of religious and poetic language, but in so doing they inevitably demonstrate the fallen condition of language that Blake desperately wanted to overcome. Not surprisingly, then, the various claims of inspiration throughout the poem ring rather hollow. For example, when the Bard is asked for the origins of his song, he asserts his inspiration in a fully sacralized language:

> The Bard replied. I am Inspired! I know it is Truth!
> for I Sing
> According to the inspiration of the Poetic Genius
> Who is the eternal all-protecting Divine Humanity
> To whom be Glory & Power & Dominion Evermore
> Amen.
>
> (pl.13, l.51-pl.14, ll.1-3)

But bald assertion in a largely demythologized idiom is less than convincing. It is a wish for inspiration, not the thing itself.

The extraordinary stridency of much of Blake's writing—the constant howling, and weeping, and shrieking, and lamentation—is generated, I think, by a profound sense of uncertainty underlying his extreme claims of inspiration. Decentered, with no transcendent origin, his language and vision sometimes seem to spin wildly, out of control. William Kerrigan is right, I think, in saying that after the Word of God lost its authority, after Milton, poet-prophets began to spin their wheels off-center: "The new 'poet-prophet,' defining his prophetic tradition with increasing eccentricity, spoke his fiery words from the margins of culture."[17] Eccentric to be sure—in his lifetime and long after, many thought Blake mad. And in fact one of his motives in writing *Milton* was to prove to himself and others that he was not insane but inspired. At the conclusion of the poem, Milton, now inspired in a Blakean way, commands (of all things) obedience: "Obey thou the Words of the Inspired Man." The primary purpose of the "Inspired Man" is to annihilate conventional, non-inspired thought so

> That it no longer shall dare to mock with the asper-
> sion of Madness
> Cast on the Inspired.
>
> (pl.41, ll.8-9)

In 1801, possibly during the writing of *Milton,* Blake wrote to a patron to apologize for his "want of steady perseverance" in terms that seem to equate his "vision" with insanity. He could not get his work done because

my Abstract folly hurries me often away while I am at work, carrying me over Mountains & Valleys which are not Real in a Land of Abstraction where Spectres of the Dead wander. This I endeavour to prevent & with my whole might chain my feet to the world of Duty & Reality. but in vain! the faster I bind the better is the Ballast for I so far from being bound down take the world with me in my flights.[18]

Blake's whimsy is not without a degree of seriousness and the letter throws a peculiar light on the symbolism of the sandals in *Milton*:

> And all this Vegetable World appeared on my left
> Foot,
> As a bright sandal formd immortal of precious stones
> & gold:
> I stooped down & bound it on to walk forward thro'
> Eternity.
>
> (pl.21, ll.12-14)

The sandal—the prophetic and literary tradition, including the work of Milton—is evidently ballast. It does not raise Blake above humanity in visionary song, but restrains him from the excesses of his own decentered, unauthorized imagination. The image betrays a profound distrust of the unfettered imagination, and suggests that the poet must remain encumbered by his predecessors. He is restricted to the "Litteral expression," and his "vision" is obscured by the soiled garment of language.

Some of the implications of Blake's confrontation with Milton can be summed up briefly. In order to establish his own poetic authority, Blake needed to subvert Milton's, to establish a difference between himself and Milton. He attempted to overcome Milton's dualism, to repudiate what Milton saw as the essential structure of differences that constituted his cosmos and his text, the differences between God and man, soul and body, reason and sensuality, inspiration and imagination, man and woman. But Blake is the inheritor of Milton's language, the language of a western tradition built on dualisms, and he has no other language to express, or even imagine, a monistic "vision." Blake cannot transcend Milton's dualism if only because language itself, based on a structure of differences, cannot present "godman-soul . . ." as a seamless whole. Inevitably, Blake's poem does not end with seamless vision, but with a woven garment of language that prevents, or defers, revelation. Ultimately *all* Blake can do is establish his difference from Milton, and so generate yet another duality: Blake/Milton.

But as we have seen, establishing this ultimate duality is no small matter. It re-establishes the act of reading as a form of combat, and turns the subservient reader into a revolutionary reader/writer. In fact, Blake's insistence on destroying the Church Paul and the Church Milton,

in subverting their authority, has a peculiarly modern ring. It is akin to the post-structuralist criticism most clearly represented in the writings of Barthes, whose distinction between the authoritative, classic, "readerly" text and the decentered "writerly" text is precisely analogous to Blake's distinction between the Church Paul and Paul, the Church Milton and Milton, the classic Milton and Blake himself. For Blake as for Barthes, the classic text imposes itself on the passive, obedient reader, but the contentious reader transforms the "readerly" to the "writerly," and so creates his own text. Blake does indeed insist on his own visionary authority, but at the same time his confrontation with Milton shows us how to subvert that authority, by insisting not on a truer vision, but on a different reading, a contrary reading that combats the author's authority, and so preserves the difference between author and reader that makes continual intellectual activity possible. Establishing this difference, the reader avoids passive receptivity, and engages in active "mental warfare."

Notes

1. *The Marriage of Heaven and Hell,* pl.5, in *The Poetry and Prose of William Blake,* ed. David Erdman, with a commentary by Harold Bloom (New York, Doubleday, 1965). All further citations from Blake's works will refer to plate and line numbers in this edition.

2. See Harold Bloom, *The Anxiety of Influence: A Theory of Poetry* (New York, Oxford University Press, 1973), 29-30. For Wittreich's extensive discussions of the "line of vision" see *Angel of Apocalypse: Blake's Idea of Milton* (Madison, University of Wisconsin Press, 1975), "Opening the seals: Blake's epics and the Milton tradition," in *Blake's Sublime Allegory: Essays on The Four Zoas, Milton, Jerusalem,* ed. Stuart Curran and Joseph Anthony Wittreich (Madison, University of Wisconsin Press, 1973), 23-58, and "'A poet amongst poets': Milton and the tradition of prophecy," in *Milton and the Line of Vision,* ed. Joseph Anthony Wittreich (Madison, University of Wisconsin Press, 1975), 97-142.

3. Northrop Frye, however, long ago pointed out that "It is in *Areopagitica* that Milton is nearest to Blake." See *Fearful Symmetry: A Study of William Blake* (Princeton, Princeton University Press, 1947), 159. But subsequent critics have not followed up Frye's comment.

4. Quotations are from *John Milton: Complete Poems and Major Prose,* ed. Merritt Y. Hughes (New York, Odyssey, 1957), 744, 741-2, 745.

5. ibid., 747.

6. In *The Poetry and Prose of William Blake,* 728-9.

7. As David Erdman has noted, Blake's illustrations make the point still more emphatically by showing the poet thrown backwards with his face towards heaven as the star approaches his foot—the posture is a variant of that in Blake's watercolor drawing of Saul. *The Illuminated Blake* (New York, Anchor Press, 1974), 233, 248, 253.

8. *The Reason of Church-Government urg'd against Prelaty,* ed. Henry Morgan Ayres, in *The Works of John Milton* (New York, Columbia University Press, 1931), vol. III, pt 1, 223-4.

9. See Northrop Frye, op. cit., 341-2.

10. Wittreich, *Angel of Apocalypse,* 241. Wittreich quotes Milton from *The Reason of Church-Government,* but Milton is quoting 2 Cor. 10:4-5.

11. Florence Sandler, "The iconoclastic enterprise: Blake's critique of Milton's religion" (*Blake Studies,* 5, 1972, 15). See also Thomas W. Herzing, "Book I of Blake's *Milton*: Natural religion as an optical fallacy" (*Blake Studies,* 6, 1973, 19-34).

12. *The Reason of Church-Government,* 241.

13. Bloom, op. cit., 35.

14. Wittreich, *Angel of Apocalypse,* 250.

15. Bloom, op. cit., 69.

16. See John Guillory, *Poetic Authority: Spenser, Milton, and Literary History* (New York, Columbia University Press, 1983). Guillory argues that "The 'imagination' names for the post-Miltonic poet an 'internal vision,' a source of poetry, but it does not name the sacred text so much as a desire for such a text. As a name for poetic power, the word preserves both the visionary longing, and the failure of that longing. The authority of the poet is henceforth more problematic, and requires an ever more complex defense" (22).

17. William Kerrigan, *The Prophetic Milton* (Charlottesville, University Press of Virginia, 1974), 14.

18. *The Poetry and Prose of William Blake,* 716.

Paul Youngquist (essay date autumn 1990)

SOURCE: Youngquist, Paul. "Criticism and the Experience of Blake's *Milton*." *Studies in English Literature, 1500-1900* 30, no. 4 (autumn 1990): 555-71.

[*In the following essay, Youngquist analyzes Blake's representations of his own writing process in* Milton.

Youngquist argues that the poem ultimately represents Blake's efforts to come to terms, psychologically and intellectually, with the power of his own creative visions.]

I cannot deny that there is truth in prophecies.

—Herodotus

William Blake's **Milton,** for all its grandeur, presents interpreters with a formidable task. Although praised as "a poem worthy of a place beside the Book of Job and *Paradise Regained,*"[1] it resists easy explication and lacks the cultural status of those comparable works. In the effort to understand **Milton,** critics have approached it from a variety of angles, interrogating its systematic symbolism, innovative narrative, or critique of metaphysics.[2] But still the poem awaits a criticism adequate to its rigors. Its most inspired readings to date have been those that focus on the drama of Blake's poetic empowerment.[3] For **Milton** is a poem about the ordeal of writing a major poem, one that dramatizes its author's experience of the vision it depicts. Poetry of this sort requires a criticism firmly grounded in the world of experience. The leading candidate for such a criticism, the line of reading that descends from Freud, cannot accommodate a poem like **Milton** precisely because it underestimates the importance of that world. In what follows I hope to take a step toward the kind of criticism **Milton** requires, looking closely at the Bard's song, the poem's biographical opening movement, and showing how Blake therein anticipates the limits of his Freudian readers.

Thomas Vogler calls the **"Bard's Song"** "a pure example of poetic inspiration" and suggests that it functions as a stimulus for the very vision it presents.[4] So essential to Blake and his sense of prophetic calling is the experience of vision that he organizes **Milton** around two instances of it, the descent in Book I of Milton from eternity and the appearance in Book II of Ololon, Milton's emanation. The strange power of these events derives from their literal presentation. "Then first I saw him in the Zenith as a falling star / Descending perpendicular," Blake says of Milton, whose emanation appears similarly unannounced: "Walking in my Cottage Garden, suddenly I beheld / The Virgin Ololon."[5] Reading Blake, one grows accustomed to expecting the unexpected, but what is one to make of his claim to have *seen* Milton, *beheld* Ololon?

Because he makes it in a poem, critics generally take it metaphorically; **Milton** is not so much about vision as about symbols rendered in a visionary setting. Thus Northrop Frye insists that "the two great illuminations portrayed in that poem do not describe events in Blake's life, but form a visionary drama."[6] And yet Blake places

himself conspicuously at the center of this drama. To overlook his presence is to edit his poem by half. More recent criticism senses that further discussion of **Milton** must restore the poet to his poem. Andrew Cooper argues that "**Milton** shows the poet progressively becoming himself" as he sloughs off his old mythology to emerge in the end fully identified and inspired.[7] On the issue of vision, however, Cooper too pleads metaphor: the descent of Ololon is not a vision at all, but a dawning insight, "the concussive impact of the poem's imploding mythology."[8] All vision is mere projection, and Blake ends a good Freudian, mastering a self whose only disequilibrium was internal.

While I readily agree that Blake ends his poem with himself, conscious and restored to his "mortal state" (42:26), I must insist that he presents Ololon's appearance as a confrontation in the world with something wholly other. On plate 36 of **Milton,** in a rare display of realism, Blake shows himself walking in his garden while a diaphanously clad female hovers above him. Ololon appears here as something—or someone—other than himself, and frankly enough to elicit from Cooper the following caveat: "He sees not a hallucination but, as he puts it elsewhere, an 'Intellectual Vision'."[9] Blake's graphic testimony argues against this distinction, however, depicting literally the hallucinatory character of his vision. If criticism is to be equal to the task of interpreting **Milton,** it must give up the old fiction of a difference between Blake's visions and hallucination. However intellectual, those visions are the fruits of a pathological distortion of consciousness, an experience that reveals a world, or more precisely, elements of *this* world, hitherto closed from sight and mind.[10] Blake has *seen* Milton, *beheld* Ololon, and his poem is in part an attempt to come to terms with these experiences. Pathology becomes a subject for poetry when Blake places these visions at the center of **Milton.**

But does this mean that Blake was mad—or near it—during the years he composed his poem? Harold Bloom maintains that "Blake's triumph over this madness is in one sense the biographical foundation of **Milton,**"[11] and the poem itself suggests that madness, though not victorious, posed a real threat to Blake during this period of his life. The **"Bard's Song"** is all about madness, its origins and possible outcomes. The word "mad" appears in various forms six times in the **"Bard's Song,"** enough to suggest that madness is a thematic preoccupation in a poem whose aim is to proclaim Blake's poetic empowerment.

The action of the **"Bard's Song"** centers upon a wily usurpation.[12] Satan, the "Miller of Eternity," wheedles from his brother Palamabron a day's labor at the harrow of civilization. Satan's entreaty is ostensibly just,

but its ultimate effect is disastrous, for by operating the harrow he drives the source of its power—its "horses"—mad. Palamabron returns to find his whole project run amok:

> Next morning Palamabron rose: the horses of the Harrow
> Were maddend with tormenting fury, & the servants of the Harrow
> The Gnomes, accus'd Satan, with indignation fury and fire.
>
> (7:17-19)

The word "maddend" carries the weight of these lines, for with it Blake confesses his extreme disequilibrium during the stay at Felpham. The conventional biographical reading of this episode has Blake chafing beneath the bridle of his patron William Hayley. The madness of those horses guiding the harrow is a literary correlative for the derangement of Blake's own motivating passions.

The whole purpose of the **"Bard's Song,"** however, is not simply to describe this madness but to investigate its origins. And in doing so Blake advances an implicit theory of madness that has important implications for literary criticism, for it locates the problem not merely in the individual but in his or her relationship as well to the world. Blake identifies two components to the origin of madness, one internal and one external. The episode of Satan's usurpation of the harrow and the maddening of Palamabron's horses begins internally, in a personal act of repression, the refusal of Palamabron to speak his mind regarding Satan's unctuous entreaty. Blake suggests as much in his own voice early in the **"Bard's Song"**: "If you account it Wisdom when you are angry to be silent, and / Not to shew it: I do not account that Wisdom but Folly" (4:6-7). Two plates later Blake shows us Palamabron concealing his true feelings about Satan's importunings: "Palamabron fear'd to be angry lest Satan should accuse him of / Ingratitude" (7:12-13). The maddening of Palamabron's horses begins partly in this internal act of repression, the concealment of anger from view by another. It is worth noting at this point that for Blake repression is never an unconscious process, but rather a willful, conscious hypocrisy in the style of **"A Poison Tree"**: "I was angry with my foe: / I told it not, my wrath did grow" (p. 28). The personal beginnings of madness involve intentionally stifling strong passions like anger.

But madness does not menace all secretly angry people. Correlative to this internal cause is an external one; Blake calls it "oppression." In his marginal **"Annotations to Reynolds's *Discourses*,"** Blake quotes Solomon's dour remark that "Oppression Makes the wise Man Mad" (p. 658). Something of the same dark wis-

dom guides the drama of the **"Bard's Song."** For Palamabron's decorous hypocrisy (or Blake's own genteel obeisance) amounts to an act of complicity with an oppressive social regime:

> You know Satans mildness and his self-imposition,
> Seeming a brother, being a tyrannt, even thinking himself a brother
> While he is murdering the just; . . .
> .
> My horses hath he maddend! and my fellow servants injur'd
> How should he [,] he [,] know the duties of another?
> O foolish forbearance.
>
> (7:21-28)

Satan here represents not merely the individual oppressor, Hayley to Blake's Palamabron. He figures as well for the social regime that authorizes such relations between individuals. In either case Blake locates part of the origin of an incipient madness in something other than the individual. Repression and oppression are both constituents in a coming madness. Both warp the creative relationship between an individual and the world in a way that reduces inspired activity to trembling confusion, as Blake's poetry amply illustrates:

> Palamabrons horses
> Rag'd with thick flames redundant, & the Harrow maddend with fury.
> Trembling Palamabron stood, the strongest of Demons trembled:
> Curbing his living creatures; many of the strongest Gnomes,
> They bit in their fury, who also madden'd like wildest beasts.
>
> (7:43-47)

Madness turns creative activity against itself, inspiring a retreat from the pressures of the world. The **"Bard's Song"** is Blake's attempt to account symbolically for this menacing derangement.

Blake does not stop, however, with an easy indictment of social circumstance and psychic history. He pursues the problem much further, seeking to explain *how* relations between individual and world got so confused in the first place. The question shifts from why Satan and Palamabron are at odds to how Satan came to find Palamabron's activity worth usurping. This concern leads Blake to examine and to critique poetically all economic theories of human behavior, for it turns out that in Blake's view Satan's trouble starts when he submits himself to a wholly internal economy of drives. What we shall witness here is Blake criticizing Freud, long before our age ever canonized Freud's economics of human experience.

Before Palamabron represses his wrath, before Satan oppresses his brother, events occur that prepare the way for their fraternal strife. Blake traces the trouble back to the jealousy of Satan's emanation, Leutha:

> She spake: I am the Author of this Sin! by my sugges-
> tion
> My Parent power Satan has committed this transgres-
> sion.
>
> (11:35-36)

The actions of Leutha, who descends from Beulah to stop the bickering with her claim of responsibility for Satan's behavior, are usually taken to reflect Blake's attitude toward Milton's genealogy of Sin in *Paradise Lost*.[13] Leutha plays the part of Milton's Sin and Savior both as she emerges willfully from the breast of Satan and later descends to atone for that very act, illustrating Blake's conviction that atonement thrives on the sin it alleviates. But Leutha's actions amount to more than just intertextual commentary. They enact a critique of all theories of experience that favor the individual over the world he or she inhabits. Leutha's original sin is jealousy, and jealousy as psychologist Erwin Straus reminds us "has its roots in the unresolved ambiguity of the Allon," by which he means the otherness of the world at large.[14] What Leutha envies is not so much her rival, Elynittria, as the irreducible otherness of that rival:

> For her light is terrible to me. I fade before her im-
> mortal beauty.
> O wherefore doth a Dragon-form forth issue from my
> limbs
> To seize her new born son? Ah me! the wretched
> Leutha!
>
> (12:1-3)

Jealousy prompts Leutha to destroy what she cannot possess, an impulse she circumvents by communicating it to Satan, who hides envy under admiration.

> This to prevent, entering the doors of Satans brain
> night after night
> Like sweet perfumes I stupified the masculine percep-
> tions
> And kept only the feminine awake. hence rose his soft
> Delusory love to Palamabron: admiration join'd with
> envy
> Cupidity unconquerable!
>
> (12:4-8)

Satan's mistreatment of Palamabron begins in his Emanation's envy of another.

But notice the form that Leutha's Delilah-like seduction of Satan takes. As a Daughter of Beulah, she like Ololon is one of the Muses to whom Blake appeals in his invocation ("Daughters of Beulah! Muses who inspire

the Poets Song!" [2:1]). Her relations with Satan in the passage above amount to a parody of the call for inspiration that opens the poem. Blake is careful to construct the scenes in parallel terms. "The doors of Satans brain" resembles the phrase that Blake uses to describe his own entrances to Beulah, "The portals of my Brain" (2:3). The crucial difference between these scenes, the circumstance that makes one productive and the other destructive, is that Satan's source of inspiration is *his own* emanation Leutha, whereas Blake receives illumination from without. Satan's actions are all self-inspired, guided by an internal economy of drives that has gone neurotic. Under Leutha's ministrations Satan becomes a Freudian case study, venting repressed fantasies in dreams and acting out of unknown motives. The stage is set for a devious hermeneutics that can see through surfaces to baser meanings. The only problem is that Blake implicitly rejects such therapies as solipsistic and self-validating. Satan's whole internal economy (his repression of jealousy and the substitution of a benign motive for a hostile one) is the product of Leutha's influence, which originates within Satan himself. By submitting to Leutha Satan has shut down his dialogue with the world. His "masculine perceptions" are stupified; he remains uninfluenced by something other than himself. His situation may appear to be susceptible to Freudian analysis, but Blake's real point is that all such analyses construct the internal economy they seek to examine by severing the creative relation between individual and world. What Blake needs and works to construct in **Milton** is a hermeneutics that reinforces rather than violates this relation.

I raise this whole issue to suggest that Freudian readings of Blake's myth, which often offer themselves as criticism's cutting edge, fail to accommodate the whole story of the struggle against madness. Blake makes clear, as we have seen, that madness for a time at least was a real possibility, but for reasons that in his view were as much external as internal. Freudian readings of his poetry, especially **Milton,** resist taking these circumstances into account. Cooper's generally astute analysis of Blake's progressive self-mastery assumes that Blake's myth is the brainchild of a purely internal economy of drives. That mythology is thus "an unregenerate disguising of the human" that allows a "concealment of anxieties" and which "the poet must annihilate in order to become fully himself."[15] Without describing those anxieties, Cooper insists that Blake produced his myth to conceal them. Mythology in this view is a neurotic symptom, and **Milton** becomes a symbolic self-analysis, a "struggle toward self-integration" that shows Blake "repossessing his mythology as personal vision."[16] Aside from the last ambiguous claim (how does this process work—is repossessing a mythology like reviving repressed memories?), Cooper's Freudian approach fails to substantiate at least one fundamental assumption: that Blake's myth, the whole

sprawling symbolism of fall and apocalypse, is a projection of the internal dynamics of his mind. Nor does he examine the origins of so sublime a projection, the pathogenesis that engenders it. Without such attempts to authenticate the claims of his Freudian hermeneutics, Cooper's bold assertions are self-validating and his compelling interpretations dead at the roots. The project of self-integration that Cooper claims drives the composition of **Milton** turns dubious, perhaps more Freud's desideratum than Blake's own. After all, "self annihilation" is Blake's term for the process Cooper calls self-mastery, and for Blake it involves the clarification of identity by rejecting false accretions rather than by reintegrating projected complexes.[17]

I suspect that Cooper is trading on certain arguments advanced twenty years ago by Harold Bloom. In an influential article entitled "The Internalization of the Quest-Romance," Bloom invokes Freud's theory of romance to prepare the way for his own theory of Romantic poetry. As Freud would have it, romance is a literary wish fulfillment that originates in the conjunction between an actual experience and a repressed memory of an earlier event. Bloom accepts the internal economy of drives that this theory assumes, but weakens its empirical validity by interpreting repressed memory "to mean also the recall of an earlier insight, or yearning, that may not have been experiential."[18] By thus attenuating Freud's empirical foundations, Bloom is free to invent a theory of romance that presumes an internal mental economy without relation to the world of experience. Romantic poetry thus enacts an internalization of the quest Romance in which the world of the quester is a purely mental landscape: "The hero of internalized quest is the poet himself, the antagonists of quest are everything in the self that blocks imaginative work, and the fulfillment is never the poem itself, but the poem beyond that is made possible by the apocalypse of imagination."[19] At least one recent critic would find fault with this position for too readily assenting to the pet ideas of Romantic poetry, naively recapitulating its ideology.[20] I believe further that the theory collapses because Bloom cuts through the branch he sits on. Take the "experiential" away from Freud and you are left with nothing solid beneath you. The presumed internal economy that drives creativity functions with no clear external, observable impetus.

Bloom ingeniously repairs this crucial lapse in his later theory by introducing the literary precursor as the precipitating cause of creative activity.[21] Poetry then is reduced to the product of an Oedipal struggle between poet and precursor. Clever as this adjustment is, it acquiesces uncritically to the implied causality at the heart of Freud's method: that repression (as of the precursor) breeds neurosis (in this case poetry). This assumption has recently come under robust attack, and it behooves us as literary critics to admit the weakness of Freud's

arguments, especially when they become the basis for critical theories of such grand designs as Bloom's. Adolph Grünbaum has shown, to my mind persuasively, that the whole edifice of psychoanalytic theory rests squarely upon empirical foundations.[22] Precisely on these grounds, however, Freud's argument that repression causes neurosis crumbles. For Freud fails to corroborate his argument with compelling therapeutic results.[23] His theory retreats from the world of experience exactly where it makes its greatest diagnostic claims upon that world. Grünbaum's conclusion, that the repression etiology "should now be regarded as *generically* devoid of clinical evidential support," renders suspect the integrity of critical theories that take repression as their *sine qua non*.[24]

For such theories necessarily detach themselves from the sole context that could validate them. When Bloom insists that "the enigma of poetic authority can be resolved only in the context of repression," he advocates a theory, like Freud's, whose explanatory power is ultimately ontogenetic.[25] As a source of authority, "repression" is no less fictive than the poetry it aims to explain, which is fine if we are content with a criticism that authenticates its own claims. Should we desire a more credible kind of validity, however, I believe we must seek it in the world of experience. Without the "experiential" a Freudian hermeneutic leads only to self-validating assertions; even with it, such a method remains hobbled by the limitations of Freud's own assumptions. No wonder criticism has failed to come to terms with the problem of madness in Blake's **Milton**. It cannot be approached as simple internalization since, as Blake depicts it in the **"Bard's Song,"** madness arises in a specific "experiential" situation. Criticism will have to admit the pertinence of such a context before it can reach a full appreciation of Blake's **Milton**.

And this means giving ear to Jerome J. McGann when he exhorts allegiance to "the concrete, human particulars" that comprise poetic works.[26] McGann has freed critics of Romantic poetry from an uncritical absorption in its central beliefs, and he has done so precisely by testing such beliefs against "the originary context of the author and his world."[27] An adequate criticism of Blake's **Milton** might therefore take as its premise McGann's "First Thesis on the Philosophy of Criticism": "Poetry is, from the individual's point of view, a particular type of human *experience*; from a social point of view, however, it is an *event*. Criticism studies these experiences and events in their successive and interrelated apparitions."[28] McGann's own historical criticism tends to emphasize the latter of the two vectors of inquiry he identifies here. He thus approaches Blake's poem as itself an event in social history, a prophetic reassessment of John Milton—in the midst of the Napoleonic Wars—that enacts "a denunciation of those wars, and especially a denunciation of England for its hypocritical

righteousness."[29] If, as McGann insists, this social import is fundamental to an adequate criticism of Blake's poem, then so too is its "experiential" context. Criticism must pursue the individual as well as the social agenda of McGann's "First Thesis," for human experience, personal and public, provides the only credible hedge against a self-validating hermeneutic.

The **"Bard's Song"** shows Blake laboring under significant psychological distress at Felpham. The conventional biographical reading of *Milton* at least takes this lived context seriously enough to apply it to the symbolic drama of the poem. What has not been understood, however, is the extent to which pathological experience enters into this drama. Most clinical (as opposed to Freudian) theories of psychopathology maintain that stress can foster discontent and extreme stress can induce pathology. Blake proves himself a keen clinician in the **"Bard's Song"** when he attributes the possibility of madness in part to an oppressive situation. The two illuminations around which the poem is organized, those two dire confrontations with something wholly other, attest to the pathological character of a certain element of his experience during these stressful years. If more contemporary psychological researches than Freud's take into account the facts of lived experience without reducing them to repressed antecedents, then it is to such researches that we must turn to vindicate the relevance—to poetry and criticism—of the "experiential."

One empirically credible clinical text, for instance, teaches that personality deviations often "occur under psychological stress of an exceptional kind," and the description it gives of such stress is particularly germane to the lived context of Blake's *Milton*: "these stresses may be of the kind to demand adaptations to a change of circumstance, a relaxation of established habits, an increase in responsibility, or a situation which puts demand on flexibility of attitude or confident self-reliance."[30] Whatever else can be said about the Felpham years, no one doubts that they put extreme demand on Blake's flexibility of attitude and confident self-reliance. Blake's letters bear stirring witness to the menacing effects of such stress. Early in 1803, the great year of crisis, Blake confides to his friend Thomas Butts that he is "under the direction of Messengers from Heaven, Daily & Nightly," a congenial enough situation for a poet, except that for Blake it involves a distressing anxiety:

> if we fear to do the dictates of our Angels, & tremble at the Tasks set before us, . . . Who can describe the dismal torments of such a state!—I too well remember the Threats I heard!—If you, who are organised by Divine Providence for Spiritual communion, Refuse, & bury your Talent in the Earth, even tho' you should want Natural Bread, Sorrow & Desperation pursues you thro' life, & after death Shame & confusion of face to eternity.[31]

What is strange here is that Blake attests to having *heard* such withering diatribes, which resemble nothing so much as the auditory hallucinations typical of today's schizophrenics.[32] It is as good a gloss on the **"Bard's Song"** as any we possess—and yet is spoken not by Blake but by some authoritative other. A passage like this one indicates that at Felpham Blake experienced pathological distortions of consciousness, which he presents in his letters and in *Milton* as visions.[33]

Such hallucinatory experience is quite in keeping with personality deviations that originate at least partly in stress. At their worst they can acquire an awesome magnitude and complexity:

> Emotional experiences of a highly complex kind may occur, e.g. of a religious kind including massive and complicated visual and auditory hallucinations, internally coherent, and the receipt of "messages" supposedly from God or His angels . . . [that] are not chaotic or disorganized, but bear the stamp of the personality of the recipient, and may contain elements of genuine and exalted mysticism.[34]

Such a description uncannily comprehends a large component of Blake's poetry, as for instance the panoramic theophany with which Blake brings the visionary drama of *Milton* to a close:

> And I beheld the Twenty-four Cities of Albion
> Arise upon their Thrones to Judge the Nations of the Earth
> And the Immortal Form in whom the Twenty-four appear Four-fold
> Arose around Albions body: Jesus wept & walked forth
> From Felphams Vale clothed in Clouds of blood, to enter into
> Albions Bosom, the bosom of death & the Four surrounded him
> In the Column of Fire in Felphams Vale; then to their mouths the Four
> Applied their Four Trumpets & them sounded to the Four winds.
>
> (42:16-23)

Taken metaphorically, this passage arouses primarily intertextual interest as an inversion of St. John's apocalypse. But taken literally—as vision—it betrays an aberration of Blake's relation to the world, a pathological distortion of consciousness. The two illuminations at the heart of *Milton,* the descents of Milton and Ololon, are similar hallucinatory distortions that originate at least in part in the stressful circumstances of the Felpham years.

But having said this we have not said much. The real significance of Blake's visions rests not in their mere occurrence, but in the use to which Blake puts them. If pathology is to blame for certain of Blake's psychological and literary idiosyncrasies, poetry is their therapist,

a source and means of treatment. For it is in writing about his experience that Blake comes to terms with it, masters it. Situated in the context of mythology, his visions acquire a meaning. A star descending is no mere illusion but Milton, returned to fulfill his own and his heir's prophetic vocation. A virgin in the garden is no trick of optics but Ololon, alienated totality of the prophet's creative labors. Hallucinatory experience takes on legitimacy and significance through myth, which in *Milton* possesses a specific personal function, for it becomes Blake's means of interpreting that radical otherness he confronts in vision.

As McGann reminds us, "every poem is an action, and its text is its residual form."[35] We must not allow the formal complexity of Blake's mythology to distract us from its personal, therapeutic activity. Blake writes in part to live; his mythology enacts a purposeful interpretation of pathological experience—hence his confidence that such experience is in fact proof of poetic empowerment. Blake discovers through his myth the purpose of his suffering: "that in three years I might write all these Visions" (36:24). Writing visions is not quite the same thing as seeing visions; the difference is a mythology that subsumes them, a poetry that gives them a local habitation and a name, and by doing so becomes an act of healing in the life of its author. Vision thus becomes something more than mere hallucination by being situated in a context that legitimates and interprets it. Without his myth to interpret pathological experience, Blake may well have ended a madman whose hallucinations assert priority over the living world. But in his dogged effort to master this experience he created a poetry that functions partly as its therapy. Mythology acts for Blake as a hermeneutics of hallucination, a means of interpreting pathological experience and integrating it meaningfully into the common round of life. As such myth enforces contact with the world and participates in the ongoing human effort of rendering it meaningful. It is in this sense that we can conclude that Blake's works and the mythology they elaborate "are not static 'things' [but] dynamic events in the field of human experience."[36]

Far from being something to escape from, then, myth enacts a vital therapeutic function for Blake personally. When Cooper argues that Blake's progressive self-mastery during the course of *Milton* ends in an escape from mythology, he misses the drama of Blake's effort to master, not himself, but pathological experience. Because myth is the means of this mastery, it remains important to Blake throughout his poetic career. It is hard to believe that the author of *Jerusalem,* that epic peroration on Albion's quarrel with his emanation, has altogether fled mythology. But Cooper reaches this conclusion primarily because he views Blake's myth as a projection, to use Freud's phrase, of "the structural relations of his own psyche to the outer world," a symptom

in other words of anxieties whose removal would breed self-integration. If we jettison this dated machinery and approach Blake's *Milton* with an eye for the "experiential" we discover the real function of mythology as an interpretation of and therapy for pathological experience.

For there stands Ololon, in Blake's garden. Her appearance elicits from Blake less wonder than self-effacing hospitality:

> Virgin of Providence fear not to enter into my Cottage
> What is thy message to thy friend: What am I now to do
> Is it again to plunge into deeper affliction? behold me
> Ready to obey, but pity thou my Shadow of Delight
> Enter my Cottage, comfort her, for she is sick with fatigue.
>
> (36:28-32)

Not simply a "mythologically projected portion of himself,"[37] Ololon confronts Blake as something *other,* a being *in* the world not normally *of* it. She holds the same status as those messengers in Blake's letter to Butts who direct him "Daily & Nightly," the nature of whose influence is not "without trouble or care."[38] Viewed as hallucinatory experience, this encounter shows Blake trying to understand his prophetic role *vis à vis* his vision. Remaining faithful to it means risking affliction. Blake stands between Ololon and Catherine, vision and world, and he must create a meaningful relation between them.

And it is the function of *myth* to create this relation. For the encounter between Ololon and Blake, literal enough as vision, acquires an aesthetic significance in the context of myth by becoming a re-vision of the earlier encounter between Leutha and Satan at the end of the **"Bard's Song."** The two scenes are isomorphic. Leutha and Ololon are both Daughters of Beulah and both appear to fulfill the call for inspiration that opens the poem. But where Leutha's descent ends ultimately in her separation from Satan, consolidating his isolation, Ololon's ends in her reunion, through Blake's illumination, with her counterpart, Milton. Blake's vision of the virgin now becomes a significant re-enactment of an aesthetic precedent. Myth transforms vision into a meaningful event, in this case the descent of an emanation in pursuit of her original. Through his myth Blake interprets pathological experience as a significant moment in that visionary drama whose outcome has supreme relevance for all men and women. A pathology of consciousness gives way to a poetry of conscience as Blake puts vision to prophetic use. Myth in *Milton* thus enacts a healing as through it Blake masters the distortion of human experience that is vision and re-establishes a living relationship with the world:

> Terror struck in the Vale I stood at that immortal sound
> My bones trembled. I fell outstretchd upon the path

A moment, & my Soul returnd into its mortal state
To Resurrection & Judgment in the Vegetable Body
And my sweet Shadow of Delight stood trembling by
 my side.

 (42:24-28)

It is Blake's myth, and not self-mastery, that allows him to stand at the end of **Milton** unmolested by his own pathological experience, eagerly awaiting apocalypse.

First and last, **Milton** depicts the trials and traumas of vision, the ordeal of experiencing and mastering a pathological distortion of consciousness. A criticism adequate to the poem's rigors must interrogate such experience, not as a psychological curiosity, but as a pained occasion for understanding the truth about the human world. Blake once confessed his belief that "Understanding or thought is not natural to Man [;] it is acquired by means of Suffering & Distress i.e [.] Experience" (p. 555). Vision was just such an experience. It posed a threat—severest at Felpham—to Blake's mental health and happiness. But by interpreting hallucinatory experience through the hermeneutics of his mythology, Blake overcame that threat and acquired a deepened understanding of the world. Perhaps this explains Blake's fierce devotion to the powers of his prophecy, devotion he voices through his Bard: "Mark well my words; they are of your eternal salvation."[39] In this refrain from the **"Bard's Song," Milton** reaches beyond Blake and toward ourselves, becoming an activity in *our* world, a part of *our* experience. An adequate criticism of this activity must begin with Blake, but it cannot stop there. It must continually come to terms with what was and is the experience of **Milton.**

Notes

1. Harold Bloom, *Blake's Apocalypse* (1963; rpt. Ithaca: Cornell Univ. Press, 1970), p. 363.

2. These are the respective approaches of the following studies: Northrop Frye, *Fearful Symmetry* (Princeton: Princeton Univ. Press, 1947) and W. J. T. Mitchell, "Blake's Radical Comedy," in Stuart Curran and Joseph Anthony Wittreich, Jr., eds., *Blake's Sublime Allegory* (Madison: Univ. of Wisconsin Press, 1973); Susan Fox, *Poetic Form in Blake's* Milton (Princeton: Princeton Univ. Press, 1976); Mark Bracher, *Being Formed: Thinking Through Blake's* Milton (Barrytown: Station Hill Press, 1985).

3. See especially Thomas A. Vogler, "Blake: Mental Fight," in *Preludes to Vision* (Berkeley: Univ. of California Press, 1971), and John Howard, *Blake's* Milton (Rutherford: Associated Univ. Presses, 1976).

4. Vogler, p. 44.

5. *The Complete Poetry and Prose of William Blake,* ed. David V. Erdman, newly rev. edn. (Berkeley:

Univ. of California Press, 1982), 15:47-48, 36:26-27. All references are to this edition, cited by plate and line numbers, unless otherwise noted.

6. Frye, p. 327.

7. Andrew M. Cooper, "Blake's Escape from Mythology: Self-Mastery in *Milton,*" in *Doubt and Identity in Romantic Poetry* (New Haven: Yale Univ. Press, 1988), p. 64.

8. Ibid., p. 72.

9. Ibid.

10. Hallucinatory experience as I understand it is not simply sensation in the absence of stimuli. It is a distortion in the relation that usually holds between consciousness and the world. The psychologist Erwin Straus puts the matter succinctly: "hallucinations are not a mere addition [to consciousness], a kind of foreign body in a normal modality. They originate in distorted modalities. As caricatures of normal structures, the distortions signify pathological modes of being-in-the-world." See Erwin Walter Maximilian Straus, *Phenomenological Psychology,* trans. Erling Eng (New York: Basic Books, 1969), p. 288.

11. Bloom, *Blake's Apocalypse,* p. 315.

12. For a thorough discussion of this action, see James Rieger, "'The Hem of Their Garments': The "Bard's Song" in *Milton,*" in *Blake's Sublime Allegory,* pp. 259-80.

13. Bloom, *Blake's Apocalypse,* p. 321.

14. Straus, p. 76.

15. Cooper, pp. 68, 71, 71.

16. Ibid., pp. 71, 61.

17. Just so John Howard understands the process: "Self-annihilation . . . is the individual's mental act of removing the dominance of his selfhood, which is only part of his psyche, the servant who has made himself into a God," *Blake's* Milton, p. 177.

18. Harold Bloom, "The Internalization of the Quest-Romance," in *Romanticism and Consciousness,* ed. Harold Bloom (New York: Norton, 1970), pp. 3-23, p. 4.

19. Ibid., p. 8.

20. See Jerome J. McGann, *The Romantic Ideology* (Chicago: Univ. of Chicago Press, 1983).

21. Harold Bloom's full argument appears at its polemical best in *The Anxiety of Influence* (Oxford: Oxford Univ. Press, 1973).

22. Adolph Grünbaum, *The Foundations of Psycho-analysis* (Berkeley: Univ. of California Press, 1984). Frederick Crews discusses some of the implications of Grünbaum's work for literary criticism in *Skeptical Engagements* (Oxford: Oxford Univ. Press, 1986).

23. For purposes of exposition I am somewhat simplifying Grünbaum's critique. Grünbaum faults Freud's repression etiology on two counts: first, Freud never cogently showed that the removal of a particular repression results in the cure of its collateral neurosis; second, Freud never guarded against the possibility that other influences, as for instance a placebo-effect, were responsible for lifting a neurosis. For the full argument, see Grünbaum, pp. 177-89.

24. Ibid., p. 185.

25. Harold Bloom, *Poetry and Repression* (New Haven: Yale Univ. Press, 1976), p. 26. Jerome J. McGann criticizes Bloom's hermeneutics along similar lines: "no structure of falsification ever enters Bloom's critical discourse, which is authoritative and definitive throughout." Bloom thus denies the pertinence for poetry of history and human experience and instead "represents as critical fact what is patently narrative mythology." See *Social Values and Poetic Acts* (Cambridge, MA: Harvard Univ. Press, 1988), pp. 142, 143.

26. McGann, *The Romantic Ideology,* p. 11.

27. Jerome J. McGann, *The Beauty of Inflections* (Oxford: Clarendon Press, 1985), p. 3.

28. Ibid., p. 343.

29. McGann, *Social Values and Poetic Acts,* p. 47.

30. Eliot Slater and Martin Roth, *Clinical Psychiatry,* 3rd edn. (Baltimore: Williams and Wilkins, 1969), p. 131.

31. *The Letters of William Blake,* ed. Geoffrey Keynes, 3rd edn. (London: Clarendon Press, 1980), p. 48.

32. Compare, for instance, the many descriptions of such hallucinatory experience in Eugen Bleuler, *Dementia Praecox, or the Group of Schizophrenias,* trans. Joseph Zinkin (New York: International Univ. Press, 1950), or Julian Jaynes, "Schizophrenia," in *The Origin of Consciousness in the Breakdown of the Bicameral Mind* (Boston: Houghton Mifflin, 1977), pp. 404-32.

33. For further evidence of Blake's hallucinatory experience at Felpham, see his letters of 21 September 1800, 2 October 1800, 22 November 1800, 10 January 1803, 25 April 1803.

34. Slater and Roth, p. 115.

35. McGann, *Social Values and Poetic Acts,* p. 55.

36. Ibid., p. 243.

37. Cooper, p. 72.

38. *Letters,* p. 48.

39. Jerome J. McGann attends closely to the ambiguity of this line's textual deployment. See his instructive discussion of *Milton* in *Towards a Literature of Knowledge* (Chicago: Univ. of Chicago Press, 1989), pp. 21-30, where he reaches conclusions similar to mine: "Blake's poetry rather looks 'towards,' calls out 'to,' reciprocal forms of activity—acts which are 'unexampled' in the previous experience of the authors of those acts, 'Blake's audience,'" (p. 31).

Sheila A. Spector (essay date spring 1993)

SOURCE: Spector, Sheila A. "Blake's *Milton* as Kabbalistic Vision." *Religion and Literature* 25, no. 1 (spring 1993): 19-33.

[*In the following essay, Spector discusses aspects of religious mysticism in* Milton.]

In *Milton,* Blake confronts a problem most Christian mystics avoid: how to describe life in this world. The majority of Western esoterica focuses on the non-material plane, describing spatially what is above and below, and temporally that which occurred before time and that which will exist after time. Thus, it leaves the material cosmos to the exoterically inclined, who prefer, instead, to delineate our state of existence in the phenomenological here and now. What is missing from much mystical literature, therefore, is the bridge spanning the distance between what is below and above, the gap between past and future. While most forms of mysticism posit the ethical life as the means of getting from "here" to "there," ethics generally is defined in terms of a moral code, a system of dos and don't's, which Blake pointedly denigrates as a Tree of Moral Virtue. Consequently, most mystical systems lack the kind of mythic representation of a theological system which would appeal to the iconoclastic Blake.

Hence Blake's problem in *Milton.* While, as is generally recognized, the other epic prophecies concentrate on the "two eternities"—*The Four Zoas* dealing with Creation and the Fall and *Jerusalem* focusing on the Apocalypse—*Milton,* coming between the other two both chronologically and thematically, must delineate the means of getting from the one to the other.[1] In other words, in *Milton,* Blake must flesh out what happens

during this period of time which, from the cosmic perspective, is merely "a Moment: a Pulsation of the Artery."[2] The dilemma is both mythic and thematic. Mythically, Blake must explain *how* Albion, the representative of mankind, gets up from the couch on which he falls in *The Four Zoas,* and from which he does not rise again until the climactic apocalypse of *Jerusalem.* Even more difficult, though, is Blake's thematic problem, for he must develop a theology of right action which will, ultimately, explain *why* Albion is able to rise again. Blake's solution is a narrative sequence which resembles the approaches found in a number of kabbalistic texts. Specifically, *Milton* seems to reflect the conflation of two historically distinct forms of Jewish mysticism: Lurianic Kabbalah and Merkavah Mysticism.

Technically, Kabbalah signifies the movement of Jewish mysticism which crystallized in medieval Provence; however, the word is commonly generalized to refer to the entire history of Jewish mysticism, from its antecedents in the Bible through the modern period. While scholars have always recognized kabbalistic elements in Blake's work, early criticism has been hampered by incomplete or inaccurate sources of information regarding mysticism in general, and Kabbalism in particular. Scholars like William James and Evelyn Underhill, though historically important for their ground-breaking studies in the field of mysticism, are both philosophically and culturally limited. In the past few decades, their work has been superseded by that of W. T. Stace, R. C. Zehner, and the contributors to Stephen T. Katz's three anthologies: *Mysticism and Philosophical Analysis, Mysticism and Religious Traditions,* and most recently, *Mysticism and Language.* Consequently, studies like Helen C. White's *The Mysticism of William Blake* and Jacomina Korteling's *Mysticism in Blake and Wordsworth* are not only outdated but are methodologically flawed as well. The same kinds of limitations are also found in earlier scholarship on Blake's use of Kabbalism. Bernhard Fehr and Denis Saurat relied on flawed sources which predated the historically accurate scholarship begun only after World War I, and compendia of Blake's use of the occult, like those of Milton O. Percival, Laura De Witt James, and Desiree Hirst, fail to distinguish adequately among the various strands of the occult to which Blake had access. Asloob Ahmad Ansari's "Blake and the Kabbalah" represents an early application of modern kabbalistic scholarship to the work of Blake.

Even though these early studies may be inadequate, they still attest to Blake's participation in the long historical tradition—dating back to the intertestamental period—of interaction between Jewish and Christian mystics. The modern strand of Christian Kabbalism was chronologically preceded by the literature of Jewish converts from the end of the thirteenth through the fifteenth century. More significantly, however, sources to which Blake might have had access probably evolved from the Platonic Academy associated with the Medicis in Florence, for the work of these Italian Neo-Platonists led not only to the more popularized incorporation of kabbalistic elements into the occult but also to the two-volume *Kabbala Denudata* (1677-84), a Latin anthology of kabbalistic texts. The editor, Christian Knorr von Rosenroth, and the primary contributors, Henry More and Franciscus Mercurius van Helmont, hoped ultimately that the *Denudata* would lead to a form of Kabbalism capable of uniting all Catholics, Protestants, and Jews. Although we may lack direct evidence for Blake's specific kabbalistic sources, we can reasonably infer that he did derive most of his information—whether formally or informally—from these Christianized strands.[3]

Lurianic Kabbalah, historically the most significant form of Jewish mysticism, was developed in response to the Jewish expulsion from Spain in the late fifteenth century. Motivated by the search for an explanation of why God would destroy such a vibrant and thriving Jewish community, contemporary mystics concluded that somehow the Iberian Jews had failed to live appropriately and had failed to bridge the gap between "now" and "then." In his attempt to discern the proper way of life, Isaac Luria (1534-72) developed a myth which not only accounted for Creation and the Fall and projected an Apocalypse but also detailed the kind of behavior in this world that would enable us to get to the next, that is, to overcome the effects of the Fall and thereby bring about cosmic regeneration.

Luria's myth of regeneration involves activities on both the macrocosmic and the microcosmic planes. Because the Fall is said to have tainted the cosmos as a whole, causing what had originally been intended as a purely spiritual realm to descend into materiality, regeneration on the macrocosmic level is essential. For that purpose, *Adam Kadmon,* Primordial Man, is charged with the task of separating out the "shards of dross" from the original "lights of purity" so that the shards will fall down of their own weight, thus enabling the lights to rise again to their source. The result will be the restoration of a purely spiritual cosmos. Correspondingly, on the microcosmic level, man has the obligation of purifying all souls so that humanity can be regenerated along with the rest of the cosmos. According to Luria, *Adam Rishon,* Created Man, who was intended to be purely spiritual, originally contained within himself all souls. However, as a result of the Fall, some souls became separated and were subsequently tainted by the shards of dross. Therefore, man's obligation in the fallen world is to effect regeneration of the microcosm by fulfilling all 613 commandments of the Bible, but because no soul can complete these obligations in a single lifetime, all must undergo a series of revolutions, complet-

ing in each successive incarnation those commandments omitted in previous lifetimes, until the total complement has been fulfilled. Finally, when the lights of the macrocosm and the souls of the microcosm have all been purified, the cosmos will be reunited and the cycle of existence will have been completed.

In contrast to Lurianic Kabbalah, which occurs relatively late in the history of Jewish mysticism, Merkavah or Chariot Mysticism is the earliest form, ultimately deriving from the visions of Isaiah, Ezekiel, and Daniel. Reflecting mystical interpretations of the biblical accounts, the body of Merkavah literature employs Chariot visions as the means of both theosophical speculation and mystical contemplation. Throughout this literature, a detailed cosmogony is developed based on a series of seven heavens through which the Chariot ascends, and the *Nahar Di'nur,* the fiery river of purification, runs through them. Theosophically, the literature contains various speculations about specific characteristics of the Divine Presence seated on the Heavenly Throne, ultimately focusing on what became known as *Shi'ur Komah,* the "measure of the body." In addition, the Chariot vision was used as the basis of mystical contemplation involving the paradoxical belief that concentration on details of the Chariot as it *descended* through the heavens would enable the soul to ascend to the level of the Throne.

In *Milton,* Blake develops his theme of vision by conflating these two forms of mysticism into a single poetic structure. The poetic is articulated best at the Apocalypse of *Jerusalem,* when Los exclaims:

> I care not whether a Man is Good or Evil; all that I care
> Is whether he is a Wise Man or a Fool. Go! put off Holiness
> And put on Intellect.

(91.54-56, E [*The Complete Poetry and Prose of William Blake,* edited by David V. Erdman] 252)

This theme, which controls the development of *Milton,* actually corresponds relatively closely to Luria's explanation of the Fall. According to the most prevalent form of the myth, the Fall was caused by *Din,* the Divine hypostasis signifying judgment. Believing itself omnipotent, *Din* attempted to draw all of the lights of Creation into its own vessel which, unfortunately, proved too weak and broke, thereby releasing all of the shards of dross into the cosmos. Morally, the breaking of the vessels is interpreted as signifying the loss of balance which had originally been obtained between *Din* (Blake's Wrath) and its contrary *Hesed* (Blake's Pity). The result is an overabundance of *Rigor* (Blake's Holiness) in our cosmos. Intellectually, this initial fault is interpreted as the attempt by the Rational Soul (Urizen, in Blake's myth) to usurp the position of the Imaginative Soul (Luvah). Originally, Reason was intended to provide a conduit to higher levels of mental activity, but as a result of the Fall, it considered itself the height of all things, becoming instead a barrier between humankind and its higher functions. Therefore, in both Blake and Luria, the purpose of existence in the fallen world is defined in terms of the attempt to develop Intellect, or as Blake says in the Preface to *Milton*: "Would to God that all the Lords people were Prophets."

The overall plot structure of *Milton* corresponds to a Lurianic-type myth of existence: the **"Bard's Song"** depicting Creation and the Fall, and the poem itself the separation of the shards in preparation for "the Great Harvest & Vintage of the Nations" (43.1, E 144).[4] In the **"Bard's Song,"** Blake revises Milton's interpretation of the Fall by displacing the original fault away from "man's first disobedience" and towards, instead, an initial loss of judgment which, like *Din*'s attempt to draw all of the lights into its own vessel, resulted in cosmic chaos. Thus, when Satan sought and finally was given Palamabron's station at the Harrow of the Almighty, he lost control over the horses. And conversely, upon returning to his Mills, where Palamabron had served, Satan "found all confusion" (8.5, E 101). Thus, the lights of purity, Palamabron, had been contaminated by the vessels of dross, Satan, who had from creation been assigned to the Mills where his work was to be, as Los thundered, "Eternal Death . . . / . . . thou canst not have Eternal Life" (4.17-18, E 98). After this initial loss of order, all of creation became polarized around the good Palamabron and the evil Satan: Theotormon and Bromion for Satan, Michael and Thulloh against Satan's deeds.

Similar to Lurianic Kabbalah, the **"Bard's Song"** depicts a pre-Adamic Creation and Fall, the action chronologically preceding the biblical narrative which begins with the organization of the corporeal cosmos. In this account, though, the slaying of Thulloh (on Plate 8) signals the introduction of materiality, i.e., death, into the cosmos. After the burial, Milton's own poem, *Paradise Lost,* is brought in through Palamabron's invocation of the Great Solemn Assembly conflating Milton's Councils in Hell and Heaven. At this point, what is now Milton's Satan rages, though his sin is not disobedience but loss of vision for "his bosom grew / Opake against the Divine Vision" (9.29-30, E 103). The effect of his sin is not damnation, but the polarization of good and evil into the kabbalistic *Rigor* (Blake's Holiness):

> He created Seven deadly Sins drawing out his infernal scroll,
> Of Moral laws and cruel punishments upon the clouds of Jehovah
> To pervert the Divine voice in its entrance to the earth.

(9.21-23, E 103)

Like Luria's *Din* (judgment), Satan intends to prevent man from perceiving anything higher than base rationality.

Thus, the Fall precedes creation of the material cosmos and the original sin is the loss of vision. Moral Virtue is actually the loss of Divine order and, therefore, a product of the satanic imposture. The historical Milton, like Los, has misjudged the situation. Just as the latter had mistakenly believed that Satan was capable of driving the Harrow of the Almighty, so too the former had erroneously assumed that Moral Virtue was Divine, rather than demonic. Therefore, Milton's entire theology is the obverse of truth, his allegory of Satan, Sin, and Death not being, as he had intended, a description of Original Sin but, from Blake's perspective, the means of regenerating the cosmos in order to overcome the effects of the Fall. When Satan is judged guilty, his daughter Leutha, a demonic parody of the Son in *Paradise Lost,* "Offer[s] herself a Ransom for Satan, taking on her, his Sin" (11.30, E 105) and then unites with Palamabron to produce the material cosmos: "In dreams she bore the shadowy Spectre of Sleep, & namd him Death. / . . . Intricate labyrinths of Times and Spaces unknown" (13.40-43, E 107). As a result, by the end of the **"Bard's Song,"** the character Milton has two tasks to perform. First, in terms of the kabbalistic myth, he must separate out the shards of dross from the lights of purity. But also, he must correct his own vision, which has been dimmed by the satanic imposture of Moral Virtue. Ultimately, however, the two are one and the same, the separation of the shards being tantamount to the restoration of his visionary faculty.

In the poem proper, the actions taken on both the macrocosmic and the microcosmic planes reflect Blake's attempt to replace the concept of Moral Virtue, which he had discredited in the **"Bard's Song,"** with Intellect as the primary force of the cosmos. In Lurianic Kabbalah, *Adam Kadmon,* Primordial Man, had originally been created to exist as a passive model for *Adam Rishon,* Created Man, to emulate. However, because of the cosmic repercussions of the Fall, *Adam Kadmon* was forced to assume an active role in restoration. Though he is said not to comprehend fully the actions he takes, still he labors constantly to separate out the shards from the lights in preparation for the final reunification of the cosmos, depicted sexually as his reunion with his female counterpart.

As Blake's version of *Adam Kadmon,* Los is essentially different from his kabbalistic prototype, his original fault is his own lapse of judgment—after imposing a form on Urizen, "he became what he beheld" (3.29, E 97). Consequently, not only has he contributed to the Fall, but his own intellect must itself be restored before he can complete cosmic regeneration. Therefore, the Los sections of Book the First focus on the restoration

of Los's own intellectual powers. At first, he obstructs what he believes to be erroneous interference by Milton, but then, after Milton re-forms reason: "Thus Milton stood forming bright Urizen" (20.10, E 114), Los regains his own intellectual powers, "recollect[ing] an old Prophecy in Eden recorded" (20.57, E 115). Finally, Los is able to assume his proper role in restoration. Now part of the cosmic effort, "he also stoop'd down / And bound [Blake's] sandals on in Udan-Adan" (22.8-9, E 117), thus becoming identified with *Adam Kadmon,* "that Shadowy Prophet who Six Thousand Years ago / Fell from [his] station in the Eternal bosom" (22.15-16, E 117).

From here on, Los's behavior conforms fairly closely to that of his kabbalistic prototype. He accepts his obligation to strive for regeneration, "that the Seven Eyes of God may have space for Redemption" (23.52, E 119), though he does not really comprehend the purpose of his specific actions: "But how this is as yet we know not, and we cannot know" (23.53, E 119). Still, as "The Watchman of Eternity" (24.9, E 119), he strives to restore Intellect (25.18-21, E 121) by separating the shards from the lights of purity:

> Therefore you must bind the Sheaves not by Nations or Families
> You shall bind them in Three Classes; according to their Classes
> So shall you bind them. Separating What has been Mixed.
>
> (25.26-28, E 122)

Finally, at the "Great Harvest & Vintage of the Nations" (43.1, E 144), he will be reunited with his female counterpart: "And Los & Enitharmon rose over the Hills of Surrey" (42.31, E 144).

Interlaced with Los's actions as *Adam Kadmon* are Milton's as *Adam Rishon.* According to Luria, the behavior of Created Man is related to that of Primordial Man in much the same way that the microcosm reflects the macrocosm. Therefore, just as *Adam Kadmon* strives to separate the shards, so does *Adam Rishon* attempt to purify the soul, undergoing a series of revolutions until all of the commandments have been fulfilled. Simultaneously, man is expected to unite with his wife, each sexual act being said to assist in the reunification of *Adam Kadmon* and his female counterpart. The macrocosmic union symbolizes the cosmic reunification, ultimately to be achieved through the sexual union of the Godhead and His Female Counterpart, the *Shekhinah* (Blake's Jerusalem).

Blake's treatment of *Adam Rishon*/Milton is consistent with the way in which he characterizes *Adam Kadmon*/Los, identifying Milton's wrong reason, specifically his erroneous theology of Moral Virtue, as the cause of the

Fall. Because Milton has completely misidentified man's function in the universe, he, like Human Reason in Luria's myth and Urizen in Blake's, has not only usurped the position of higher mental faculties, but has at the same time prevented man from seeing beyond the limitations of base rationality. Therefore, as he realizes at the end of the **"Bard's Song,"** "I in my Selfhood am that Satan: I am that Evil One! / He is my Spectre!" So like *Adam Rishon*, Milton realizes that he must undergo at least one more revolution in order to correct the fault of his previous incarnation: "in my obedience to loose him from my Hells / To claim the Hells, my Furnaces, I go to Eternal Death" (14.30-32, E 108). Leaving his heavenly body behind, Milton unites with his Shadow, the vehicle for his descent, and travels back to earth where he assumes the physical body, entering Blake's left foot.[5] Then, after reforming Urizen, that is, after correcting the fault of his previous incarnation, Milton waits for his female counterpart to descend so that they can reunite, thereby enabling Los and Enitharmon to reunite in preparation for "the Great Harvest & Vintage of the Nations."

As a universal myth of fall and redemption, the Lurianic strand provides the archetypal structure for *Milton,* a prophecy about the loss of vision in the corporeal cosmos. But in order to develop the thematic content, the minute particulars of the vision itself, Blake superimposes Merkavah Mysticism on the Lurianic base. Developed as a form of speculation, as well as contemplation, Merkavah mysticism is distinct from more familiar forms of mysticism in that it does not advocate a process of emptying out so that the mind can subsequently be filled by the Divine *pleroma.* Instead, Jewish mystics focus on the details of Divine visions, thus filling their minds with images of the Divinity through which they hope to achieve their own visions.[6] This kind of contemplation on the biblical Chariot visions led to fairly well-developed descriptions not only of the Chariot itself, but often, of the situation under which the prophet received his vision, the descent of the Chariot through the heavens, the transport to the Heavenly Throne, and finally the Divine Presence seated on the Throne.

Ololon, Milton's emanation and hence his vision, is the means by which these two forms of mysticism are united. In terms of the plot structure, Milton's descent is caused by his recognition that through his erroneous theology, he has caused the intellectual distortions which permitted the satanic imposture. Thematically, those distortions are identified as the loss of vision and, symbolically, that spiritual blindness is depicted by the loss of his emanation. Hence he makes a decision "To go into the deep her to redeem & himself perish?" (2.20, E 96). But as Milton learns from descending through the vortices (the heavens of Merkavah mysticism), perspectives vary:

> The nature of infinity is this: That every thing has its
> Own Vortex; and when once a traveller thro Eternity.
> Has passd that Vortex, he percieves it roll backward behind
> His path, into a globe itself infolding; like a sun.

> (15.21-24, E 109)

Thus, when viewed from the perspective of Los as *Adam Kadmon* (Primordial Man), the entire poem from the **"Bard's Song"** through the Last Vintage depicts the means by which the macrocosm will be renovated, and from the perspective of Milton as *Adam Rishon* (Created Man), the action constitutes the means by which the microcosm will be regenerated. However, from the perspective of Blake, here depicted as the prophet in the wilderness: "the earth / A vortex not yet pass'd by the traveller thro' Eternity" (15.34-35, E 109), all is an incomprehensible mystical vision: "for man cannot know / What passes in his members till periods of Space & Time / Reveal the secrets of Eternity" (21.8-10, E 115). And Ololon is the vehicle of Blake's vision.[7]

Ololon's introduction on Plate 21 contains the initial description of Milton's Chariot vision. First characterized as "a sweet River, of mild & liquid pearl" (21.15, E 115), Ololon is linked with the River Chebar, at whose banks Ezekiel experienced his vision of the Chariot, but the description also foreshadows her incarnation as the *Nahar Di'nur,* the fiery river of purification said to connect all seven heavens of the cosmos. Referring to "those who Milton drove / Down into Ulro" (21.16-17, E 115), Blake exploits the kind of language found in Merkavah mysticism, the *descent* of the Chariot being said to facilitate the *ascent* through the heavens. This concept is made literal by the end of the plate. Soon after the introduction of Ololon, the Divine Family determines to form the Chariot:

> In the Four Points of heaven East, West & North & South
> Enlarging and enlarging till their Disks approachd each other;
> And when they touch'd closed together Southward in One Sun
> Over Ololon: and as One Man, who weeps over his brother,
> In a dark tomb, so all the Family Divine. wept over Ololon.

> (21.36-42, E 116)

Ololon decides to descend "to death in Ulro among the Transgressors" (21.46, E 116), and the Divine Presence on the Throne is identified "as One Man even Jesus / Uniting in One with Ololon" (21.58-59, E 116).

Book the Second is devoted to Ololon's descent. Opening with the reversed inscription: "How wide the Gulf & Unpassable! between Simplicity & Insipidity / A Negation is not a Contrary," the title page possibly associ-

ates this section of Blake's vision with the mirror imagery characteristic of Merkavah mysticism, for Ezekiel is said to have perceived his vision by gazing into the River Chebar. Like others of its genre, this Chariot vision begins with the descent through the heavens, starting in Beulah, which "is evermore Created around Eternity" (30.8, E 129). Beneath Beulah are the three states of Ulro: Alla, Al-Ulro, and finally Or-Ulro, whose "fiery Gates" are sought by Ololon (34.19, E 134). Like the *Nahar Di'nur*, Ololon becomes the path through which the heavens are linked, for "a wide road was open to Eternity, / By Ololons descent thro Beulah to Los & Enitharmon" (35.35-36, E 135). The Divine Presence comes with her, "for they saw the Lord in the Clouds of Ololon" (35.41, E 136).

Finally, in her last appearance, when "as a Moony Ark Ololon descended to Felphams Vale" (42.7, E 143), she literally becomes the incarnation of Blake's Chariot vision:

> And I beheld the Twenty-four Cities of Albion
> Arise upon their Thrones to Judge the Nations of the
> Earth
> And the Immortal Four in whom the Twenty-four ap-
> pear Four-fold
> Arose around Albions body: Jesus wept & walked
> forth
> From Felphams Vale clothed in Clouds of blood, to
> enter into
> Albions Bosom, the bosom of death & the Four sur-
> rounded him
> In the Column of Fire in Felphams Vale; then to their
> mouths the Four
> Applied their Four Trumpets & them sounded to the
> Four winds.
>
> (42.16-23, E 143)

Like Ezekiel, Blake is overcome by his vision: "My bones trembled. I fell outstretchd upon the path" (42.25, E 143).

In spite of all of these obvious similarities between *Milton* and Merkavah Mysticism, there is one fundamental difference. The characteristic paradox embodied by visions of the Chariot results from the fact that while this literature is referred to as "the *descent* of the Chariot," in fact, it describes the *ascent* of the visionary himself who is transported up through the succession of heavens until he ultimately reaches the level of the Divine Throne where he perceives the Divine Presence. In Blake's version, however, the *descent* is a *descent*. This difference between *Milton* and its mystical prototypes results from Blake's belief in an incarnate Christ. While the ancient Jewish visionaries projected a transcendent God with whom they could achieve only a spiritual union, Blake asserts an internal Savior, defined as the visionary faculty which enables humankind to develop its own divinity. Therefore, from her first appearance,

Ololon is pictured with "Jesus the Saviour . . . in the Clouds of Ololon" (21.60, E 116), their coupling projects the series of sexual unions which will yield cosmic restoration. From this perspective, Ololon's renunciation of her virginity is the equivalent of Christ's self-sacrifice:

> Then as a Moony Ark Ololon descended to Felphams
> Vale
> In clouds of blood, in streams of gore, with dreadful
> thunderings
> In the Fires of Intellect that rejoic'd in Felphams Vale
> Around the Starry Eight: with one accord the Starry
> Eight became
> One Man Jesus the Saviour. wonderful! round his
> limbs
> The Clouds of Ololon folded as a Garment dipped in
> blood.
>
> (42.7-12, E 143)

Their acts of self-annihilation, in turn, reflect back on the initial act of self-sacrifice performed by Milton after he hears the Bard's Song.

Ultimately, the controlling motif of the poem as a whole is the concept of incarnation, defined here as the visionary faculty, which enables the individual to develop the Christ within.[8] If not the physical center, certainly the heart of *Milton* is still the **"Bard's Song,"** that mysterious prelude which instructs Milton as to where he erred in his lifetime. At the end of the **"Song,"** "The loud voic'd Bard terrify'd took refuge in Miltons bosom" (14.9, E 108), the Prophet of Eternity becomes incarnate in the prophet of the seventeenth century. Then, after descending through the vortices, Milton becomes incarnate in Blake, as does Los. Finally, like the Charioteers of Merkavah literature, Los transports Blake: "For when Los joind with me he took me in his firy whirlwind" (36.21, E 137), to the cottage where Blake actually experiences his vision of the Merkavah:

> Descending down into my Garden, a Human Wonder
> of God
> Reaching from heaven to earth a Cloud & Human
> Form
> I beheld Milton with astonishment.
>
> (37.13-15, E 137)

Peeling off the layers of incarnation, we find that Los, as *Adam Kadmon* (Christ to Christian Kabbalists), provides Blake with the authentic Chariot vision. However, Blake is incapable of perceiving that vision until after he has internalized both Milton and the Bard, that is, until after he has re-visioned *Paradise Lost* in its corrected form. Then, he can be transported to his cottage, i.e., experience the true vision, which he records in his prophecy *Milton.* Thus, his fainting at the climax of the poem corresponds to the visionary's loss of consciousness at perceiving the Divine Presence on the Throne.

When viewed from the perspective of the kabbalistic prototypes, *Milton* emerges as a mystical interpretation of Blake's own life. As has been amply demonstrated by others, the poem incorporates biographical incidents, biblical figures and historical events, not to mention contemporary philosophy, psychology, and science. All elements combine to produce an encyclopedic panorama of the present corporeal world, that realm which is mystically defined as the distance between what is below and what is above, what was before time and what will be after time. But the amalgamation only coheres when we remember that "the Writing / Is the Divine Revelation in the Litteral expression" (42.13-14, E 143). In mystical literature, the literal level of time and space is viewed only as the vehicle for ascending to the level of vision.[9] In fact, mystics believe that ultimately, there is no literal level, only the visionary realm in which "all the Lords people [are] Prophets." *Milton,* therefore, is neither a biographical record of Blake's life, nor an examination of the scientific dimensions of eyesight. Rather, these material facts provide the basis for our own Chariot vision as together we, Blake's readers, "go forth to the Great Harvest & Vintage of the Nations."

Notes

1. W. J. T. Mitchell notes that "*Milton,* in other words, is Blake's attempt to bridge the gap between the ironic, critical view of the world that had permeated his earlier prophetic books, and a comic, redemptive view of a new order" (284).

2. *Milton,* 29.3, in *The Complete Poetry and Prose,* 127. All Blake citations are from the Erdman edition. For a discursive bibliography of modern scholarship on *Milton,* see Mary Lynn Johnson's "William Blake," especially pp. 224-31.

3. For good introductions to Jewish mysticism in general, see Gershom G. Scholem's *Major Trends in Jewish Mysticism* and *Kabbalah.* We have no complete Lurianic texts in English, though Knorr von Rosenroth's *Kabbala Denudata* contains a Latin version of Luria's treatise on the revolution of souls (later translated into French in 1905 by Edgard Jegut). The second edition of the *Denudata* contains van Helmont's *Adumbratio Kabbalae Christianae,* a detailed explanation of how the Lurianic myth can be used to justify Christianity, once one recognizes that *Adam Kadmon,* Primordial Man, is really Christ. The *Adumbratio* also contains a section on "The Modern Constitution," life in the phenomenological world. While the *Adumbratio* is not available in English, it was translated into French in 1899.

A comprehensive analysis of Merkavah Mysticism can be found in Ithamar Gruenwald's *Apocalyptic and Merkavah Mysticism.* This first period of Jewish mysticism is closely intertwined with the early history of Christianity as well as with Gnosticism, in both its Greek and Jewish forms (see Scholem's *Jewish Gnosticism, Merkabah Mysticism,* and *Talmudic Tradition*). Therefore, many of the elements which I cite in relation to Jewish Merkavah mysticism can be found in contemporaneous, non-Jewish sources and certainly in the mysticism of St. Paul as well as the Apocalyptic vision of *Revelation.* Presumably, the fact that these elements were shared by both Jewish and Christian mystics made them even more attractive to Blake's syncretic mind. My own *Jewish Mysticism: An Annotated Bibliography on the Kabbalah in English* contains virtually all English-language materials through the early 1980s, and in "Kabbalistic Sources—Blake's and His Critics," I analyze the sources to which Blake might have had access.

4. Mary Lynn Johnson's thesis in "'Separating What Has Been Mixed': A Suggestion for a Perspective on *Milton*" that "the major principle of unity in *Milton,* and a major element in the neo-Christian provision Blake worked out for man's salvation, is the conversion of sets of twos (apparent opposites) into threes (genuine contraries separated from an unreal negation)" is quite close to the kabbalistic belief that the polarized "left" and "right" will ultimately be merged into the ameliorating "central column" of reunification (11). While acknowledging the complexity of *Milton,* scholars have consistently recognized a unifying principle. Susan Fox asserts that the epic has "a comprehensible poetic structure" (3), one which David Fuller attributes to "the one human-divine imagination in which the experience has its being . . . a moment in and yet out of time" (46-47), a moment which Peter Otto believes "is traced against, the fracture of our time and space" (208).

5. The belief in two bodies goes back to St. Paul: "It is sown a natural body; it is raised a spiritual body" (1 Cor xv.44). Blake incorporates the concept in his characterization of Tirzah as the natural body (see my "Sources and Etymologies of Blake's 'Tirzah'"). The "shadow," *zel,* is a kabbalistic concept. Defined as an outer covering for the soul, a necessary intermediary for preventing the fierce heat of the soul from burning up the body, the term is close enough to the Hebrew *zelem,* "shadow," to enable Kabbalists to associate the "shadow" with the principle of individuality (Scholem, *Kabbalah,* 158-59).

6. Although scholars used to assume that all mystical experiences were fundamentally identical, Stephen T. Katz asserts in "Language, Epistemology, and Mysticism," that the content of mystical visions is culturally determined, so that Buddhist, Christian,

and Jewish mystics, for example, will all have substantially different and culturally distinct visions.

7. To Paul Youngquist, this is not vision but pathology: "First and last, *Milton* depicts the trials and traumas of vision, the ordeal of experiencing and mastering a pathological distortion of consciousness. . . . [Vision] posed a threat—severest at Felpham—to Blake's mental health and happiness. But by interpreting hallucinatory experience through the hermeneutics of his mythology, Blake overcame that threat and acquired a deepened understanding of the world" (569).

8. Dennis M. Welch applies Thomas J. J. Altizer's general discussion of "Incarnation and *Kenosis*" (*The New Apocalypse*, 63-75) to *Milton* in particular and shows "that Milton and his emanation's actions are kenotic, based on biblical and Miltonic sources and used to portray an aesthetic vision in which the immanent and the transcendent, the generate and regenerate, the temporal and eternal are identified. By emptying themselves and descending fully into the world and the flesh, Milton and Ololon form a new incarnation, take on the state of self-annihilation, and exalt all things in their eternal identities" (2). As a result, according to James Rieger, "Despite the surface complexity, *Milton* demands simply and relentlessly that the incarnation, passion, and resurrection of Christ be repeated in every man" (270).

9. The primary distinction between conventional and mystical language is that while the former is used "informatively," that is, to communicate information, the latter is used "transformatively," to transform the reader's consciousness so that s/he, in turn, can experience the vision for her/himself. On the mystical use of language, see Frederick J. Streng's "Language and Mystical Awareness," and Lawrence J. Hatab's "Mysticism and Language," as well as the essays in Katz's *Mysticism and Language*.

Works Cited

Ansari, Asloob Ahmad. "Blake and the Kabbalah." *William Blake: Essays for S. Foster Damon*. Ed. Alvin H. Rosenfeld. Providence: Brown UP, 1969. 199-220.

Altizer, Thomas J. J. *The New Apocalypse: The Radical Christian Vision of William Blake*. East Lansing: Michigan State UP, 1967.

Blake, William. *The Complete Poetry and Prose*. Ed. David V. Erdman. New York: Doubleday, 1982.

Fehr, Bernhard. "William Blake und die Kabbala." *Englische Studien* 54 (1920): 139-48.

Fox, Susan. *Poetic Form in Blake's* Milton. Princeton: Princeton UP, 1976.

Fuller, David. "*Milton*, and the Development of Blake's Thought." *An Infinite Complexity: Essays in Romanticism*. Ed. J. R. Watson. Edinburgh: Durham UP, 1983. 46-94.

Gruenwald, Ithamar. *Apocalyptic and Merkavah Mysticism*. Leiden: E. J. Brill, 1980.

Hatab, Lawrence J. "Mysticism and Language." *International Philosophical Quarterly* 22 (1982): 51-64.

Hirst, Desiree. *Hidden Riches: Traditional Symbolism from the Renaissance to Blake*. New York: Barnes & Noble, 1964.

James, Laura De Witt. *William Blake: The Finger on the Furnace*. New York: Vantage, 1956.

Johnson, Mary Lynn. "'Separating What Has Been Mixed': A Suggestion for a Perspective on *Milton*." *Blake Studies* 6 (1973): 11.

———. "William Blake." *The English Romantic Poets: A Review of Research and Criticism*. Ed. Frank Jordan. New York: MLA, 1985. 113-253.

Katz, Stephen T. "Language, Epistemology, and Mysticism." *Mysticism and Philosophical Analysis*. New York: Oxford UP, 1978. 22-74.

———, ed. *Mysticism and Language*. New York: Oxford UP, 1992.

———, ed. *Mysticism and Philosophical Analysis*. New York: Oxford UP, 1978.

———. *Mysticism and Religious Traditions*. New York: Oxford UP, 1983.

Korteling, Jacomina. *Mysticism in Blake and Wordsworth*. 1928. New York: Haskell House, 1966.

Mitchell, W. J. T. "Blake's Radical Comedy: Dramatic Structure as Meaning in *Milton*." *Blake's Sublime Allegory: Essays on* The Four Zoas, Milton, Jerusalem. Eds. Stuart Curran and Joseph Anthony Wittreich, Jr. Madison: U of Wisconsin P, 1973. 281-307.

Otto, Peter. "Visionary Deconstruction: The "Bard's Song" in Blake's *Milton*." *Philological Quarterly* 66, no. 2 (Spring 1987): 207-30.

Percival, Milton O. *William Blake's Circle of Destiny*. New York: Columbia UP, 1938.

Rieger, James. "'The Hem of Their Garments': The "Bard's Song" in *Milton*." *Blake's Sublime Allegory: Essays on* The Four Zoas, Milton, Jerusalem. 259-80.

Rosenroth, Christian Knorr von, ed. *Kabbala Denudata*. 2 vols. 1677-84. New York: Georg Olms Verlag, 1974.

Saurat, Denis. *Blake and Modern Thought*. 1929. London: Russell & Russell, 1964.

Scholem, Gershom G. *Jewish Gnosticism, Merkabah Mysticism, and Talmudic Tradition.* New York: Jewish Theological Seminary, 1965.

———. *Kabbalah.* New York: Quadrangle, 1974.

———. *Major Trends in Jewish Mysticism.* New York: Schocken, 1941.

Spector, Sheila A. *Jewish Mysticism: An Annotated Bibliography on the Kabbalah in English.* New York: Garland, 1984.

———. "Kabbalistic Sources—Blake's and His Critics'." *Blake* 17, no. 3 (Winter 1983-84): 84-99.

———. "Sources and Etymologies of Blake's 'Tirzah.'" *Blake* 23, no. 4 (Spring 1990): 176-83.

Streng, Frederick J. "Language and Mystical Awareness." *Mysticism and Philosophical Analysis.* Ed. Stephen T. Katz. New York: Oxford UP, 1978. 141-69.

Welch, Dennis M. "'Cloth'd with Human Beauty': *Milton* and Blake's Incarnational Aesthetic." *Religion and Literature* 18, no. 2 (Summer 1986): 1-15.

White, Helen C. *The Mysticism of William Blake.* 1927. New York: Russell & Russell, 1964.

Youngquist, Paul. "Criticism and the Experience of Blake's *Milton.*" *Studies in English Literature* 30, no. 4 (Autumn 1990): 555-71.

Marc Kaplan (essay date 1995)

SOURCE: Kaplan, Marc. "Blake's *Milton*: The Metaphysics of Gender." *Nineteenth-Century Contexts* 19, no. 2 (1995): 151-78.

[*In the following essay, Kaplan analyzes the symbolic functions of male and female identities in* Milton. *Kaplan asserts that Blake's vision of the universe is essentially hierarchical in character and is dominated by a distinctly masculine sensibility.*]

I

"But Time & Space are Real Beings a Male & a Female Time is a Man Space is a Woman," William Blake says in his 1810 description of the lost painting **"A Vision of the Last Judgment"** (563).[1] Blake's entire artistic effort is dedicated to the revelation (and revelation for Blake is synonymous with creation) of a humanized cosmos, a world experienced in every detail as a projection of ourselves. As the statement above indicates, however, Blake's anthropomorphic vision produces a gendered universe. I believe it can be further demonstrated in the analysis of Blake's **Milton** that the poet's mythic cosmos is not only gendered, but hierarchical and masculinist in character.

Since Susan Fox's groundbreaking essay in 1977, an apparent sexist element in Blake's poetry has come to be acknowledged by most, if not all, commentators on the author. Fox suggested that the doctrine of contrariety with which Blake organizes his visionary universe "crystallized around the central metaphor of male and female" ("The Female as Metaphor in William Blake's Poetry" (510)), but that this ostensible principle of mutuality is undermined by "stereotypic metaphors of femaleness" (507), to wit, that Blake's females are either "weak or power-hungry" (507), and that they in fact become symbols of the very qualities of weakness or power-hunger in themselves. Subsequently, in *Romanticism and Gender,* Anne K. Mellor has observed that in Blake's mythology, the female is always "secondary to the male" because "males (or the masculine dimension of the psyche) create ideas, forms, designs; females (or feminine states of mind) can desire (and thus inspire) these forms but not create them" (22). Brenda Webster, proceeding from a Freudian perspective, makes similar claims in her study of the poet, and Margaret Storch has likened Blake's male supremacism to that of D. H. Lawrence.

The poet has not been without his champions. Diana Hume George, though like Storch and Webster both Freudian and feminist, is perhaps Blake's most eloquent defender against the charge of sexism. In terms of *Milton* specifically, she argues that Blake "does make an implicit decision to retain the conventional connotations of femininity and masculinity, in order to disclose their contents and redeem their values," and she justifies Blake's method:

> If gender is clothing, or ancillary to humanity in its essence, then the characterization of eternity and Beulah as active—masculine and passive—feminine is not contradictory. It is perhaps the only way the relationships of eternity can be expressed in the fallen world, since humanity is divided into sexes in the fallen world, and there are no words for people without gender.
>
> (171)

George herself, however, offers an alternative strategy that Blake might have pursued when, a few pages earlier, she describes Blake's use of the Bible:

> The mature Blake never shied from a challenge to approach the Bible as an adversary, but he worked from within scripture rather than without it . . . [I]t became his lifelong effort to read the Bible perversely, that is, to disclose its symbolic truths.
>
> (169)

Such perversity or subversiveness, I shall argue, is precisely what is missing from Blake's use of traditional male-female symbology in *Milton.*

Most recent defenses of Blake's sexual politics have not come from Freudians like George, however, but from critics employing poststructuralist methodologies.

Rather than directly refuting claims such as those of Fox and Mellor, these writers tend to begin by accepting a problematic depiction of gender as part of the manifest level of Blake's poetry. Then they proceed to use textual strategies to vindicate the poet (or at least the poem—the writer's intentionality is a non-issue in these analyses). Elizabeth Langland's study of **"The Sick Rose"** is representative of this method: she first offers a reading in which the poem presents apparent antifeminine biases; then she demonstrates how Blake's language undermines and subverts those biases. A similar case is made by Nelson Hilton for *Visions of the Daughters of Albion.* He uses a thorough knowledge of background materials on Mary Wollstonecraft (about whom more below) to show that Blake's eye (his text) saw more than his heart knew.

These and other poststructuralist reconsiderations of Blake are valuable and provocative, but it is the intention of this essay to elaborate upon those problems in the manifest level of the poetry pointed out by Fox and Mellor. Before Blake's text can be "saved" from its problematic representation of gender, we must first know from precisely what it is to be saved. Blake's sexism is as personalized as any of the other features of his myth. Further, gender hierarchy is not an incidental element but a fundamental component of that mythology. To say, as Fox does in the quotation above, that male/female relationship is the central metaphor in Blake's poetry, is to acknowledge that it is all-in-all, because no poet was ever more committed to the trope than Blake, who saw it as the basis not just of literature but of all mental liberation. Fox's argument (that the doctrine of contrariety with which Blake organizes his myth is really a doctrine of masculine hierarchy) implies that it is now necessary to reconsider carefully all of Blake's major poetry in terms of his portrayal of gender. It is relevant that Fox, who initially approached Blake without a feminist agenda, arrived at her conclusions about Blake in the course of a study of *Milton,* because *Milton* is the poem in which Blake most fully elaborates a metaphysics of gender. Through an examination of *Milton,* I hope to extend Fox's argument into a demonstration that a masculinist model of gender is the foundation stone, the ground upon which Blake seeks to moor his visionary cosmos.

Insofar as *Milton* portrays Milton's journey through that visionary universe, it is one of a number of "quest" poems by male Romantic writers. Harold Bloom, in his famous essay "The Internalization of Quest-Romance," pointed out that the key Romantic strategy was to turn the quest into a psychological rather than an external odyssey. As Marlon Ross has noted, that essay serves as the basis for Bloom's theory of influence in which the poet is seen to be on a quest for power that will free him from the influence of a literary "father" (22-23). Ross, however, goes on to identify the masculinist na-

ture of this quest (and of Bloom's theory as a result). The male Romantic poets, according to Ross, describe the internal quest in what he calls "masculine metaphors of power" (23). The quest itself is, in his account, an attempt to reclaim for the poet a traditionally and exclusively male power in the world.

As Ross describes the situation, the male Romantic poets were responding to a two-edged historical phenomenon at the beginning of the nineteenth century (22-28). First, advances in science, commerce, and democratic governance had usurped the poet's traditional functions of providing a coherent vision of the world and of spurring social progress. Poetry was becoming marginalized, as it was depicted in Thomas Love Peacock's celebrated satire, which inspired Shelley's *Defense of Poetry* as a response. Secondly, the era saw what Ross calls "the rise of women as nurturers of literary discourse" (22), manifested in the increasing participation of women in literary life, both as readers and as authors. Poetry was further diminished in apparent significance by its association with a marginalized group, and denigrated as "unmanly." The male Romantic quest, in Ross's view, was an effort to reclaim both the poet's former power and the masculine forms in which it had previously been expressed. Indeed, as Ross implies, these poets attempted to conflate poetic power and masculinity. Wordsworth's Alpine journey in *The Prelude* then becomes in Mellor's words (after Ross), not a quest for "the 'higher'—and potentially universal—self he dreamed of, but rather a specifically masculine self" (*Romanticism and Gender* 147).

Milton offers perhaps even better evidence in support of Ross's argument than *The Prelude*. Blake does not look to nature for the source of poetic power. "Nature" to Blake's radical subjectivity is only a mental category, and a fallen (and traditionally female) one at that. Instead, Blake looks to culture, the accumulated great works of the mind, for the source of that power, and finds it in Milton, to him the greatest of cultural heroes. That Blake considers poetic power to be crucially masculine is immediately evident in the title page illustration that shows the naked, powerfully muscled eternal form of Milton on the verge of his return to earth (the preponderance of muscular male forms in Milton's visual art will be dealt with at length below). Blake images Milton as the quintessence not just of poetic power but of true maleness in his tradition.

Unlike Wordsworth, who climbs a literal mountain to attain power, Blake, in an ingenious reversal of the usual quest structure, has the power come to him: Milton descends from heaven to join Blake in Felpham. As with Wordsworth, however, the goal is the reconstitution of male hegemony. Milton descends in order to correct his Puritan errors in repressing his masculine sexual desire, and as we shall see presently, to purge

the masculine true self of its contamination by female qualities, a corruption described in the **"Bard's Song"** that begins the poem.

These feminine qualities, I will demonstrate, all have their root in the traditional linkage that Blake in his mythic cosmos makes between the feminine and the spatial/immanent/immediate, as opposed to the masculine transcendent/temporal. To attempt to modify this absolute binarism is for Blake a crucial error (Mellor has identified the establishment of binarisms as in itself a key tenet of masculine Romanticism [*Romanticism and Gender* 3]). The statement by the poet which I presented at the beginning of this essay was not completely rendered: the words "Time is a Man Space is a Woman" are in fact followed by "& her Masculine Portion is Death." Blake's construction of gender in *Milton* is fundamentally hierarchical. Proper order in the universe cannot be restored until woman entirely puts off her "Masculine Portion" and submits, sexually and spiritually, to the inspired male.

Blake did not have to append those final six words to imply a hierarchy in the relationship of masculine time to feminine space. Simone de Beauvoir observed in *The Second Sex* that males in our culture have always been granted the capacity for transcendence while woman is condemned to immanence (63-65). Transcendent (male) time is valorized over the (female) immanence of space. When Blake in *Milton* tells us that "Los is by mortals nam'd Time Enitharmon is named Space" (121; 24:68), he reveals a great deal indirectly about the relationship of his most important male-female couple. In the earlier prophecies, Los, though he has moments of weakness, is the most positive of Blake's mythical characters, the one who does the most to bring about the redemption of the universe. Enitharmon, his consort, does have moments of redemptive power, but far more often she is depicted as at best misguided and often pernicious and destructive, if not, as in *Europe,* an outright demiurge. Blake's allegory of Los and Enitharmon is an attempt to materialize and humanize the abstractions of Time and Space, but the allegory cannot disguise the fact that Blake's metaphysic is founded upon the hierarchical division protested by de Beauvoir.

Of recent studies of *Milton,* Mark Bracher's *Being Form'd* most concentrates on Blake's metaphysics. Bracher construes *Milton* as a pre-Derridean attack on "the metaphysics of presence" (xiv), maintaining that Blake in *Milton* anticipates the contemporary poststructuralist argument against "immediate presence," the basic experience of the self as a totally present individual that constitutes ordinary human consciousness, the immanent reality of our everyday lives. This "immediate presence," according to Bracher, is the Spectre or Selfhood that in *Milton* must be continually annihilated, both by Milton and by his Emanation, Ololon. Self-

Annihilation makes possible what Bracher calls "mediated presence" (xiv), a more complex relational presence that is not linked to any conscious perception of self and exists in the minds of others, through memory and through the medium of art.

Bracher is not concerned with the difference that gender makes to Blake's metaphysic. When he defines mediated presence as "occurring only by virtue of temporal displacement or the intervention or assistance of another individual or event" (xiv), he implies that Blake valorizes (male) time over (female) space. The valorization of male over female can be seen more clearly if we use Bracher's identification of Los-time as the "actualizing power" of the mind, the ability to bring the imagination into material reality, and Enitharmon-space as the "total immediate actuality of each moment": Los is the creator, Enitharmon the created (46). Presence itself is secondary to the ability to bring things into presence. Bracher's analysis in fact precisely confirms Mellor's observation, cited above, that in Blake's poetry males create forms while the female can only desire and inspire them. Woman is linked to the immanent, but she crucially cannot experience this immanence herself. Rather, she has the presence of a nonself-conscious *object* to the eye of a (male) subject. However, she can lure the male "actualizing power" into a fruitless attempt to seize total immanence—this is the female's ostensible power to inspire, which taken too far produces an idolatry.

Many contemporary theorists, including the influential French feminists Cixous, Irigaray, and Kristeva, use a critique of presence much like the one that Bracher finds in Blake as a ground from which to launch a feminist argument—basically, to make a claim similar to that of de Beauvoir, that woman has been imprisoned in immanence.[2] Blake, like the deconstructive feminists, sees how this male pursuit of woman has at its heart the quest for total self-immanence, and he, like the feminist authors, rejects that quest as false and idolatrous. The question then remains: does Blake see the problem as immanence or as the female? If the problem is the female, in the sense that she is essentially and irrevocably linked to the immanent and nontranscendent, then the argument against presence becomes an argument against the feminine.

Blake never says outright that the link between the female and the immanent is final, but much of his imagery suggests this. Susan Fox has observed that in *Milton,* "Blake does not say that all females are weak, but he does imply that all weakness is female" (*Poetic Form in Blake's* Milton 215). In terms of a critique of presence, immanence/space in the poem is always feminized and always seen as limiting or lacking, while the temporal capacity for transcendence and freedom is masculinized. Blake at the climax of *Milton* finally in-

dicates a mode of transcendence for woman, but it is an unsatisfactory alternative previously presented in the earlier prophecies: total submission, both personal and sexual, to the already transcendent male, by which she presumably borrows some of his innate power. Woman escapes the trap of presence only by putting aside as secondary and deficient everything in her that is female, everything that makes her recognizable as woman.

Attacks on the notion of an innate link between the female and the immanent were already being made in Blake's own time. (Robert Essick and Joseph Viscomi, attempting to fix a date on the production of **Milton,** conclude that Blake started etching the plates "no earlier than 1804" [17] and that the first printing "may not have taken place until late 1810 or early 1811" [38].) When Blake's contemporary Mary Wollstonecraft in *A Vindication of the Rights of Woman* complains of the consignment of women in her society to the realm of "sensation" or "the senses" and the "sensibility" derived from them, she is protesting against precisely that condition that de Beauvoir calls imprisonment in immanence—that is, the realm of immediate sense experience. "Many are the causes that, in the present corrupt state of society, contribute to enslave women by cramping their understandings and sharpening their senses" (22), Wollstonecraft declares, implying here what she elsewhere states directly: a faulty education has produced the current debased state of womanhood, and a rational education is the remedy; women are not in some elemental way destined to be the creatures of sensation.

Wollstonecraft is talking about real women in history, but she is aware that the real problems of real women are generated by metaphysical notions about femaleness such as those that underlie the cosmology of **Milton.** She sees how easily culturally inculcated gender biases can come to be regarded as essential principles of female existence: "Women subjected by ignorance to their sensations, and only taught to look for happiness in love, refine on sensual feelings, and adopt metaphysical notions respecting that passion, which leads them shamefully to neglect the duties of life" (183).

Mention of Wollstonecraft again raises the question of Blake's association with the most important feminist thinker of his time and place. "Though circumstantial, the evidence that Blake was personally acquainted with Wollstonecraft is compelling," maintains Nelson Hilton in a recent and very thorough summary of that evidence (69-78). However, even if Blake did not know Wollstonecraft well, and even if he chose to ignore *A Vindication of the Rights of Woman,* he would necessarily have had contact with her ideas by virtue of the fact that he prepared, at their mutual friend Joseph Johnson's behest, a series of illustrations for a new edition of her children's book, *Original Stories from Real Life,* pub-

lished in 1791. Though there is no overt polemic in *Original Stories,* Wollstonecraft's feminist perspective is everywhere present in that the book depicts two young girls being taught lessons of rationality, morality, and industriousness—rather than charm, etiquette, and sensibility—by a wise governess.

Wollstonecraft was not idiosyncratic relative to her era, but representative and influential. She was a key part of an unofficial movement among women writers toward the development of what Mellor calls "the rational woman" (*Romanticism and Gender* 40-41), rational not only in the sense of receiving the same mental training as men, but also in terms of possessing a moral code and common sense with which to deal with all the ambiguities of experience. The rational woman is the goal of numerous polemics of the time, not only by avowed admirers of Wollstonecraft like Mary Hays (*An Appeal to the Men Of Great Britain* [1799]) and Mary Anne Radcliffe (*The Female Advocate* [1799]), but also of the later and much more conservative Priscilla Wakefield (*Reflections on the Present Condition of the Female Sex* [1817]). Though Wakefield begins with a quote from Adam Smith and advocates the maintenance of a rigid system of social classes, her main demands are identical with those of the radical Radcliffe: educate women and open to them some of the professions reserved to men.

The new rational woman was not simply an ideal proposed by polemicists, however. She appears as a realistically drawn character in novels by female writers attempting to represent the actual experience of women in their time. Since women did not yet receive an intellectual education, these female characters tend to demonstrate their rationality in the second of the two ways described by Mellor, that of developing sound judgment and moral acuity, while avoiding the traps of excessive sensibility. This new woman of good sense appears in such novels as *Belinda* by Maria Edgeworth, *Marriage* by Susan Ferrier, and *The Memoirs of Emma Courtney* by Wollstonecraft's admirer (and occasional critic) Mary Hays. The most celebrated portraits of this moral rational woman are, of course, in the novels of Jane Austen, who repeatedly finds sensibility wanting when compared to sense.

The valorization of the rational woman is necessarily a repudiation of the notion that women's consciousness is bounded by the limits of immanent sensation. And to the argument that woman as object-presence creates by inspiring men to create, Wollstonecraft responded eloquently, "I do not wish (women) to have power over men, but over themselves" (62). Within the mythic universe of **Milton,** Blake would have his female characters yield up their sexual power over males, but he does not satisfy Wollstonecraft's demand for genuine power in recompense.

II

One of the most imaginative features of Blake's subjective universe is the ingenuity with which he elaborates the notion that psychology equals geography: the projection of our mental state constitutes our location. The Blakean cosmos, with its four realms of Ulro, Generation, Beulah, and Eden, has been well charted by earlier interpreters. What these prior readings have ignored or failed to emphasize sufficiently is the degree to which Blake's four worlds present an image of the universe based on a hierarchy of gender. Ulro, the hell-realm of depression, is the world of hermaphroditism, Blake's trope for solipsism. The realm of Generation, the ordinary state of human existence, is the realm of Contraries, of male and female sexual difference. Beulah is the realm "where Contrarieties are equally True" (129; 30:1). This world is the Innocence world of childhood, or of Innocence recaptured in adulthood through sexual love. Blake identifies Beulah as a specifically female realm, and he depicts this femaleness in terms of the two characteristics that he has invariably identified throughout his earlier poems as female: maternal nurturance and sexual submissiveness. Eden, Blake's paradise, is masculinized into a realm of fiery ejaculation and mental warfare.

These genderings of mythic space do not simply provide structural form to Blake's imaginative universe; they also regularly enact subordinations of the feminine, which are particularly complex in the realm of Beulah. Blake describes the creation of Beulah and its relation to Eden at the outset of Book II of **Milton**:

> Beulah is evermore Created around Eternity; appearing
> To the Inhabitants of Eden, around them on all sides.
> But Beulah to its Inhabitants appears within each district
> As the beloved infant in his mothers bosom round encircled
> With arms of love & pity & sweet compassion. But to
> The Sons of Eden the moony habitations of Beulah,
> Are from Great Eternity a mild & pleasant Rest.
>
> (129; 30:8-14)

Beulah is designed as a respite from the grueling activity of Eden, Blake's highest realm. Its inhabitants experience themselves as male subjects surrounded by a nurturant female world ("in his mothers bosom"). Eden/Eternity is a world of violent but creative energy: "As the breath of the Almighty, such are the words of man to man / In the great Wars of Eternity, in fury of Poetic Inspiration" (129; 30:18-19). Eden is the realm of process rather than presence; it is dynamic and kinetic. Process was valorized by other of Blake's Romantic contemporaries, but Blake masculinizes process and sets it against the feminine of presence.

Beulah, the heaven of orthodox religion, is the realm of the female and, as such, the realm of total presence, the immanence discussed earlier. Yet it is also described as dreamlike and insubstantial: "It is a pleasant lovely Shadow / Where no dispute can come. Because of those who Sleep" (129; 30:2-3). Woman is identified with the immanent precisely because she ostensibly lacks consciousness ("those who Sleep"). Beulah is both immanent and insubstantial because self-conscious presence is never totally attainable. It is a dream-goal pursued but never reached. As Bracher notes, "Beulah is a state not of actual existence, but of latent, incipient or dormant existence—an ideal realm" (185-186). This accounts for the "shadowy" character of Beulah. It might be more correct to say that, rather than a realm of presence, Beulah is the world of the contemporary Derridean concept of "nostalgia for presence," a presence that never has existed nor can exist. In identifying the female with a presence that can never be fully attained, Blake places her in a classic double-bind. She is consigned to the realm of the immanent, then immanence is declared to be an illusion. Beulah/the female is at once oppressively present and yet unreal, derivative and "shadowy."

Milton has been seen as Blake's definitive criticism of Beulah as the traditional heaven or ideal of spiritual existence. As Harold Bloom argues, "The ambiguities of Beulah were first explored by Blake in **Songs of Innocence** and **The Book of Thel**; in **Milton** they are totally exposed" (*Blake's Apocalypse* 348). Also totally exposed, however, is the gender problem noted by Susan Fox above. While woman can ostensibly enter Eden, each and every characteristic that might be considered womanly or female is identified with Beulah, and identified as well with the limitations of that state. In contrast, the true paradise of Eden is portrayed almost entirely in masculine imagery. What then, becomes of woman in Eden? Blake employs an unsatisfactory strategy that he will use again, more explicitly, in **Jerusalem**. As Fox has remarked, "Questions about the relationship between the sexes are referred to a better life where there are no sexes" (*Poetic Form in Blake's* Milton 217). However, whenever Blake describes this better life, one ostensibly beyond sex and gender, he depicts it in masculine images.

Blake opens both books of **Milton** with an invocation of Beulah and its inhabitants. The very first lines of the poem begin:

> Daughters of Beulah! Muses who inspire the Poets Song
> Record the journey of immortal Milton thro' your Realms
> Of terror & mild moony lustre, in soft sexual delusions
> Of varied beauty, to delight the wanderer and repose
> His burning thirst & freezing hunger! Come into my hand
>
> (96; 2:1-5)

The ambiguous nature of Beulah, its connection with the sexual, of the sexual with delusion, and of all these with the feminine, are made clear immediately. In their earthly form, the Daughters of Beulah are the Daughters of Albion:

> And this is the manner of the Daughters of Albion in their beauty
> Every one is threefold in Head & Heart & Reins, & every one
> Has three Gates into the Three Heavens of Beulah which shine
> Translucent in their Foreheads & their Bosoms and their Loins
> Surrounded with fires unapproachable: but whom they please
> They take up into their Heavens in intoxicating delight
>
> (98; 5:5-10)

These Daughters are sexual temptresses, and their sinister nature is indicated by their threefold being. Threes in Blake's symbolism are almost always ominous: "Here the Three Classes of Men take their Sexual texture Woven / The Sexual is Threefold: the Human is Fourfold" (97; 4:4-5). The sexual, the Beulaic and the feminine, is deficient, less than fully human. Blake's females are frequently temptresses leading the male on by willful manipulation of the false dream that a total self-presence can be achieved through sex.

A similar sinister linkage of the sexual, the spatial, the threefold, and the female is made with great clarity and economy in Blake's notebook poem, **"The Crystal Cabinet,"** believed to have been composed around the same time as the beginning of *Milton* (1803-04). The sexual paradise is a confined space that is actually a prison, a prison over which woman presides:

> The Maiden caught me in the Wild
> Where I was dancing merrily
> She put me into her Cabinet
> And Lockd me up with a golden Key
>
> (488; lines 1-4)

The male prisoner has submitted voluntarily to this vaginal incarceration, indeed his own phallic desire ("a golden Key") has become the instrument of woman. Within the cabinet, he finds the spaces of Beulah: "And within it opens into a World / And a little lovely Moony Night" (488; lines 7-8). The moon and all things "moony" are in Blake's work always connected with Beulah. Blake accepts rather than subverts the traditional link between woman and the "lunar" (dreams, delusions, and reflected rather than self-generated light). Within the sexual space of Beulah, all is threefold: the Maiden, her smile, and her kiss. The sexual is delusive, however. When the protagonist tries to seize the "inmost Form" (488; line 21) of the woman, the cabinet

bursts and leaves him a helpless baby, now dependent upon a "Weeping Woman pale" (489; line 26). Sexual love alone cannot provide final satisfaction. If the ultimate is pursued through sex, the result is despair. Though the problem is ostensibly universal to all humanity, Blake depicts it through a male protagonist, a female villain, and masculine sexual metaphors of excitation, tumescence, and climactic burst, followed by a postcoital depression that arouses painful memories of childhood helplessness and reliance on the mother. For Blake, the situation is compounded by the fact that the male becomes sexually and emotionally dependent on the female. Though the Maiden who began the poem as a temptress and jailer has been transformed into a benign mother, she still threatens male power. In the postorgasmic moments when elemental feelings are resurgent, woman feels the same despondence as man, but she is more capable of controlling those feelings and thereby controlling the male because of her (in Blake's mind) linkage to the world of fallen nature that again surrounds them both.

"The Crystal Cabinet" demonstrates how the female-spatial paradise of Beulah is vulnerable to the passage of time, which is only transcended in the masculine-temporal paradise of Eden-Eternity. As a result of this deficiency, Beulah is a precarious paradise that if dwelt in too long, will burst and leave the traveler in the hell of Ulro, just as sexual orgasm builds and bursts. Milton sees this close link between the two states when in his descent he discovers that the two realms actually border one another:

> Then on the verge of Beulah he beheld his own Shadow;
> A mournful form double; hermaphroditic: male & female
> In one wonderful body. and he enterd into it
> In direful pain for the dread shadow, twenty-seven-fold
> Reachd to depths of direst Hell, & thence to Albions land:
> Which is this earth of vegetation on which now I write.
>
> (108-109; 14:36-41)

At the edge of Beulah, one can pass directly into the hell of Ulro even before the "higher" realm of Generation, "this earth of vegetation." "Up" and "down" are relative terms in *Milton*; at times, Eden is described as surrounded by Beulah. But at other times, Milton's journey is described as a descent and, as in Wordsworth, the heights are portrayed as the source of masculine power. Milton's descent is a progressive *feminization* of the soul. Where Eden is the masculine paradise of mental warfare, Beulah is the "female" paradise in which the masculine subject is surrounded by a feminine universe as mother/lover. In Generation, male and female are potentially productive Contraries, but Milton goes

directly into the "hermaphroditic" hell of Ulro where the female has been internalized by the (presumably masculine) self. The implication is that the female comforts of Beulah can contaminate, weaken, and "womanize" the soul.

If the female-spatial can be a prison in the paradise of Beulah, it is even more a confinement in the world of Generation, where Blake calls it Canaan:

> An aged Woman raving along the Streets (the Space is named
> Canaan) then she returnd to Los weary frighted as from dreams
> The nature of a Female Space is this: it shrinks the Organs
> Of Life till they become Finite & Itself seems Infinite.
>
> (104; 10:3-6)

The enclosing female spaces of Beulah can become a trap, a crystal cabinet; in Generation, space traps us in an opposite fashion by making distances appear to extend infinitely, causing human beings to "shrink" by comparison. Though the masculine Satan/Urizen is the architect of this fallen space, the female is again linked with containment and restriction. As so often occurs in Blake's cosmology, woman herself suffers from these "female" characteristics of the universe: Enitharmon raves and weeps through the endless streets of the city of Generation.

At the start of the poem, Milton is residing in a heaven which is the false Beulaic paradise of presence. Milton descends into the fallen world to bring about its redemption, and at the celebrated moment where he enters Blake's left foot Milton experiences an epiphany:

> Then Milton knew that the Three Heavens of Beulah were beheld
> By him on earth in his bright pilgrimage of sixty years
> In those three females whom his Wives, & those three whom his Daughters
> Had represented and containd.
>
> (110; 15:51-17:2)

Milton realizes that the orthodox heaven he had envisioned while on earth was only the false "threefold" heaven of Beulah. Further, he realizes that this heaven was a projection of the traditionally female virtues of pity and love (including woman's sexual love, but repressed and projected into an otherworldly paradise) as he saw them manifested in his wives and daughters, who together constitute his Emanation, Ololon. Though Ololon is portrayed as a completely positive figure in *Milton,* her femaleness makes her suspect, and it is this femaleness that she must ultimately cast off in order to be redeemed. Blake hints at this by identifying her as the sixfold sum of Milton's three wives and three daughters. As noted earlier, "threefold"-ness in Blake's system is almost invariably sinister.

Shortly after Milton enters Blake's foot, Los, the prophetic spirit who is "by mortals nam'd Time" (121; 24:68), enters the poet as well. Though his revelation in his aspect as time is an important element in *Milton,* Los retains his identity from Blake's earlier poetry where he was depicted as the spirit of "Vision" or the imagination, the capacity to organize perception meaningfully. For Blake, this capacity is identical with the principle of masculinity, and Los's authoritative tone conveys Blake's sense of masculine re-empowerment:

> I am that Shadowy Prophet who Six Thousand Years ago
> Fell from my station in the Eternal bosom. Six Thousand Years
> Are finishd. I return! both Time & Space obey my will.
>
> (117; 22:15-17)

This speech makes it clear that in Blake's cosmos, time subsumes space, Los subsumes Enitharmon, the masculine subsumes the feminine. This strategy was observed in Blake's visual art by Mellor ("Blake's Portrayal of Women" 151), and it is a device that Blake employs repeatedly in the text of *Milton* in a manner that Alan Richardson has described as the "colonization of the feminine" in male Romantic poetry. Richardson points out that male poets of the era often dealt with their ambivalence toward the growing empowerment of women by first acknowledging feminine power and then trying to incorporate feminine characteristics in a "higher" male self (13-20). In *Milton,* masculine time is the redeemer; he is "the mercy of Eternity; without Times swiftness / Which is the swiftest of all things: all were eternal torment:" (121; 24:72-73). Woman's place is vital but subordinate: "And between every two Moments stands a Daughter of Beulah / To feed the Sleepers on their Couches with maternal care" (126; 28:48-49). The redeeming quality of female space comes into being only as a consequence of the creation of Moments of Time by Los.

This hierarchical gendering of redeemed space is particularly evident at the end of Book I:

> The Sky is an immortal Tent built by the Sons of Los
> And every Space that a Man views around his dwelling-place:
> Standing on his own roof, or in his garden on a mount
> Of twenty-five cubits in height, such space is his Universe;
>
> (127; 29:4-7)

Such redeemed space in the material world is clearly *masculinized,* a "Tent built by the Sons of Los" in the act of "colonizing" the role of the Daughters of Beulah, who create space everywhere else in the poem. The descent of Ololon, Milton's Emanation, brings about the final redemption of the "delusive" paradise of Beulah.

The acceptance of (masculine) process, with death and change as some of its necessary manifestations, makes possible a vision of material nature as a redeemed paradise, the childhood realm of Innocence reclaimed. Yet even this materialized Beulah is too close to the orthodox heaven of presence. Milton, in conversation with the Seven Angels of the Presence who preside over the illusion of immanence in the world, rejects the quest for total presence, which is identical with the quest for the elusive female of **"The Crystal Cabinet"**: "I have turned my back upon these Heavens builded on cruelty / My Spectre still wandering thro' them follows my Emanation" (131; 32:3-4).

This rejection makes possible the revelation by the angels to Milton of the doctrine of States. This doctrine of States constitutes Blake's effort to remake the universe into a metaphysical structure of levels of redemption: "Distinguish therefore States from Individuals in those States. / States Change: but Individual Identities never change nor cease:" (132; 32:22-23). Memory, Reason, and most of our other faculties are States that in fallen life determine our behavior as we pass through them. The only escape from the determinism of States is through the dynamic faculty of the Imagination: "The Imagination is not a State: it is the Human Existence itself" (132; 32:32). Gender is ostensibly a State, one partially determined by our locus in one of Blake's four meta-States. In Generation we are either male or female. In Beulah we are a male subject surrounded by a female universe, unless we linger there too long and become "contaminated" by its femininity, internalize the feminine, and tumble into the hermaphroditism of Ulro. In Eden, we are all masculine, engaging in the Wars of Eternity.

The Imagination, ostensibly not a State, is identified with Eden, which is depicted entirely in images of cosmic masculinity. Blake's metaphysics means to free us from all States, including gender, but in fact it presents a conundrum: a system that would deliver us from the tyranny of States is itself fundamentally and hierarchically gendered. The problem is made clear immediately after the presentation of the doctrine of States, when "the Divine Voice" is heard in the **"Songs of Beulah"**:

> When I first Married you, I gave you all my whole
> Soul
> I thought that you would love my loves & joy in my
> delights
> Seeking for pleasures in my pleasures O Daughter of
> Babylon
> Then thou wast lovely, mild & gentle. now thou art
> terrible
> In jealousy & unlovely in my sight, because thou hast
> cruelly
> Cut off my loves in fury till I have no love left for
> thee
>
> (132; 33:2-7)

Blake, as he frequently does in the earlier prophecies, presents female tolerance of male promiscuity as the image of paradise. This key moment in the poem is meant to portray the redemption of Beulah, whose Daughters now sing a song of male sexual license, the words of which are dictated by the masculine Divine Voice breaking through from Eden in the wake of Milton's descent. Jealousy is always for Blake an intrinsically female quality that woman must learn to put aside in the interest of redemption. "Elynittria! whence is this Jealousy running along the mountains / British women were not Jealous when Greek & Roman were Jealous" (104; 10:14-15), Los protests to Elynittria, the Emanation of Palamabron, early in the poem. Presently we shall see that Blake equates jealousy in a male with effeminacy. Jealousy can be the result of lingering too long in the "female" realm of Beulah. The world of Beulah is redeemed, in fact, by renouncing this "female" jealousy, the jealousy that turns the sexual cabinet of **"The Crystal Cabinet"** into a prison. Jealousy is a fallen concomitant of the desire for absolute presence, which is the dream of Beulah. One perceives oneself to be deficient in presence and mistakenly endows the possessions of another with the power to confer total presence. Jealousy for Blake might be said to be the inverse of that masculinization or "colonization of the feminine" practiced elsewhere in the poem. Here the feminine has wrongfully (in Blake's view) colonized the male.

With the redemption of the flawed "feminine" paradise of Beulah by the abandonment of the "female" vices of jealousy and possessiveness, Blake's gendered metaphysics has been fully delineated. The metaphysical structure described in **Milton** is thus the poem's most important contribution to Blake's hierarchically ranked mythology of gender. We may now turn our attention to the specific representation of gender in the characters whose actions are the subject of **Milton**'s illustrations and poetry.

III

Milton's illustrations are unique relative to other Blake works in that they depict males almost exclusively, particularly in the full-page plates. Further, as W. J. T. Mitchell has noted, these male characters are usually nude, muscular figures, isolated in heroic postures, often with sexual overtones (48). Not just Los and Milton, but William Blake himself and his deceased brother Robert are represented by these muscular titans. There are none of the female nudes of the Lambeth books or the marginal sketches in the manuscript of **The Four Zoas.** The one partial exception is the image of the exhausted lovers on Plate 42D,[3] but even there the woman's body is obscured by the prostrate form of the male beside her. The book's principal female character, Ololon, is not represented in any of the large images unless

she is the central figure on the book's climactic plate (50A). Enitharmon, much less significant in **Milton** than in **The Four Zoas,** is represented in a large design only on 10D, where she is shown as a madwoman running through the streets, her spread arms describing the limiting span of the arch that frames her, an image of Urizenic restriction.

Mitchell explains the predominance of male figures in **Milton** as a result of the poem's thematic preoccupation with "a brotherhood of male prophets who exist both in and out of time and space" (64). Margaret Storch describes the situation more critically, contending that **Milton** represents the triumph of "an elevated ideal of masculinity and brotherhood" over "the oppressive presence of women" (131). Storch means "presence" to be taken literally and physically, but on the basis of the argument I have advanced about Blake's metaphysics, "oppressive presence" can also be taken to be that spatial immanence that Blake and his tradition associate with women.

The predominance of male figures in **Milton**'s art is complemented by a similar inequality within the poem. Both Milton and his Emanation, Ololon, make the courageous move to face "Self-Annihilation" or "Eternal Death" (in Bracher's terms, the absolute abdication of self-conscious presence), but their paths to this goal are different, and the difference is determined by gender. As the key male and female couple of the poem, Milton and Ololon are frequently conflated with the other characters of their sex/gender. In portraying the relatedness of his male figures, Blake employs an imaginative paradox worthy of **The Marriage of Heaven and Hell.** The more conjoined his male characters become, the more they perceive themselves as "One Man," confident, individualized, and thoroughly masculine. The first such union is that of Milton and Blake. Blake describes Milton's entry into his foot:

> Then first I saw him in the Zenith as a falling star,
> Descending perpendicular, swift as the swallow or swift;
> And on my left foot falling on the tarsus, enterd there;
> But from my left foot a black cloud redounding spread over Europe.

(110;15:47-50)

We are presented here with the metonymic detail that characterizes **Milton** alone among Blake's longer poems. Milton enters the "actual" left foot of the "actual" William Blake. Later, Blake will witness the union of Milton and Ololon in the garden of his cottage in Felpham. He will be joined there by his wife, Catherine, in a passage that ostensibly recapitulates an actual incident. This "real" William Blake enters the poem in the moment described above, at the precise instant that Milton enters Blake. The "literal" William Blake is not

only particularized as the person writing the poem, he becomes even further individuated as no less than the center (or at least a center) of Western history. From Blake's foot the cloud of impending apocalypse spreads out over a continent.

Soon thereafter, Milton/Blake is joined by a third male figure, Los:

> Los descended
> to me:
> And Los behind me stood; a terrible flaming Sun: just close
> Behind my back; I turned round in terror, and behold.
> Los stood in that fierce glowing fire; & he also stoop'd down
> And bound my sandals on in Udan-Adan; trembling I stood
> Exceedingly with fear & terror, standing in the Vale
> Of Lambeth: but he kissed me and wished me health.
> And I became One Man with him arising in my strength:
> Twas too late now to recede. Los had enterd into my soul:
> His terrors now posses'd me whole! I arose in fury & strength.

(116-117; 22:5-14)

Los possesses Blake because Blake has realized that Los—and Milton—were a part of him all along. Whereas the entry of Milton gave Blake the sense both of himself as an individual and a center of history, the addition of Los, yet a third entity, makes him even more unique. From his own personal position in the world, in the seemingly inconsequential act of binding on a sandal, Blake becomes a center not just of history but of the prophetic vision that is to redeem history. This entry of Los has paradoxically made Blake even more individual, even more "One Man," than he was before. The poet's quest for masculine power creates individuation or, to use Marlon Ross's term, the self-possession that male Romantics conflate with masculinity (23).

The suggestion of homosexual fellatio in the design showing the descent of Los (47A) as well as in the image depicting the struggle of Milton and Urizen (45A) has been noted by Storch (148-149), Mitchell (67), and others. . . . In the picture of Los, the fellatio is only implied; Los wears a loincloth and appears to be some distance behind Blake (who portrays himself as a muscular titan, just like his "brethren"). In the picture of Milton and Urizen, however, Milton is totally naked and Urizen's head is pressed against his loins.

I believe that the suggestion of fellatio in these pictures is conscious and intentional. Locating Blake's work within the context of an early-nineteenth-century discourse on male homosexuality, however, becomes immediately problematic. David I. Halperin has pointed

out that the term "homosexuality" is but a century old, and the concept to which it refers—classification of the personality of a subject on the basis of the biological sex of the chosen partner—scarcely older than that (15-40). Louis Crompton, searching for an analogous term that would have been comprehensible in Blake's time, settles with some reservations on "Greek love" (9-11). Moreover, the temper of the era in England—Crompton maintains, "This age was . . . the most homophobic in English history" (261)—made open discussion of the subject rare. Crompton refers frequently to a 1785 pamphlet by Jeremy Bentham as virtually the only important treatise on the issue in English letters of the time. More ominously, sodomy was an offense punishable by death in England, and Crompton notes that executions were carried out at a rate of two a year in the early years of the nineteenth century, a period when capital punishment for the same offense was becoming quite rare on the Continent (16).

Though it was certainly taboo in Blake's England, Halperin has remarked that homosexuality *per se* was not equated with femininity in Blake's time; the latter quality was rather associated with submissiveness (being the partner penetrated) as opposed to dominance (being the penetrator) in the sexual act. Blake would have been typical of males of his time if he viewed sexual acts between males as much less disturbing (assuming always that one identified with the dominant/penetrator) than a perceived femininity "invading" the male personality. Marlon Ross has described how Byron, who according to Crompton was actively bisexual for much of his life, nevertheless needed to "feminize" the work of poets whom he disliked while guarding against any "softness" or vulnerability in his own work: "Any display of emotional effusion in his poetry must therefore be framed with a feminine cause or undercut with masculine derision or both" (31). Sonia Hofkosh notes that Byron, in a letter to Walter Scott, subtly transforms Scott into a woman to be seduced, thereby establishing his (Byron's) own dominance (99-104). I will suggest presently that Blake uses homosexuality as trope in much the same manner as Byron, and to the same end: to assert his own masculine superiority. The fact that sodomy was a hanging offense might have appealed to the seditious streak in Blake, whose means (the portrayal of fellatio) is here more subversive than his goal: the celebration of a conventional masculine triumph.

I would contend further that the imagery in the two designs is "homosexual" without being "homoerotic," by which I mean that the pictures are not calculated primarily to arouse sexual feeling (though the flames around Los do suggest orgasm) but rather to portray relationship between the characters (for a truly erotic depiction of fellatio, see Blake's illustration for *Paradise Lost, The Temptation and Fall of Eve*).[4] The two Milton plates depict inverse situations. The picture of Los's descent

configures the phallic metaphor that is only implied in the poetry. Blake's head, positioned before the loins of Los, is infused with the orgasmic energies of the imagination; Blake "becomes" the phallus of Los. The concentration of the male self into the phallus becomes the concentration of perception that produces individuation. The "I" of the erect phallus is for Blake the metaphor for the concentration of Blake, Los, and Milton in "One Man," one "I"-dentity. The descent of masculine power into the poet William Blake is now complete. Though Blake is nominally the submissive partner in this act of fellatio, he and Los in fact become equals. They are depicted as physically identical in every feature.

The picture of Milton and Urizen, in contrast, portrays fellatio as a hierarchical relationship. While Blake takes on Los's vitality and "becomes" an erect phallus, Urizen hangs limp and flaccid from Milton's loins. Despite the fact that he receives Milton's semen, he does not become inspired. Instead, his fellatio appears as a symbol of surrender. Though Milton is literally passing a part of himself into Urizen, it is Milton who becomes stronger. Rays of energy shoot out from his head, in part because he is being brought to orgasm but also because he is being placed in the exalted position of dominance as the recipient of fellatio. The direct, physical act of fellatio between Urizen and the not-yet-redeemed Milton is contrasted with the indirect spiritual union of Blake and Los, in which both partners are exalted. Indeed, the union of Los and Blake takes place amid the flames of Eden, whereas Milton and Urizen meet on a darkened shore beneath the night sky of a fallen world.

To use terms currently fashionable, Blake in these designs denigrates the phallocentric in favor of the phal*l*ogocentric; the latter being a case where the phallic is completely removed from biology and made into a masculine principle of the spirit or consciousness. The difference between these two terms is precisely the difference implied in the contrast between the two plates just discussed, with the masculine phallic depicted as either an Edenic form of brotherhood in the union of Los and Blake (47A) or a fallen form of brotherhood that has degenerated into a master and a servant (45A).

The union of Los and Milton with Blake produces a composite who is paradoxically one being, a true "Individual" and not a "State." The "threefold" nature of this union, ordinarily a negative for Blake (and particularly so in **Milton**), is modified by the climactic reunion with Ololon that brings about a "fourfold" state, the state Blake associates with Vision. The initial bonding of Milton, Los, and Blake does restore unity, however, repairing the three-way rift of the brothers Rintrah, Palamabron, and Satan that is the subject of the **"Bard's Song,"** the poem's opening section. Satan is responsible for the corruption of "Pity and Love" (107; 13:48). He puts on the appearance of Pity, rightfully the quality

associated with his brother, Palamabron. The appropriation of Pity by Satan (whose quality is Reason, by virtue of his link to Urizen, revealed later in the poem) is made by Blake to reinforce subtly an underlying system of gender. Los, the father of the three brothers, hints of this when he says, "I should have remember'd that pity divides the soul / And man, unmans:" (102; 8:19-20). But a fuller revelation comes when Leutha, Satan's Emanation and the first important female character in the poem, comes forward to accuse herself of responsibility for Satan's sin:

> entering the doors of Satans brain night after night
> Like sweet perfumes I stupified the masculine perceptions
> And kept only the feminine awake. hence rose his soft
> Delusory love to Palamabron: admiration join'd with envy
> Cupidity unconquerable!
>
> (105; 12:4-8)

Satan has become feminized; he has internalized rather than projected his Emanation into the object-world where it belongs. This is identical to the situation described earlier in terms of Blake's doctrine of States. If one lingers too long in the realm of Beulah, one can become "contaminated" by its femaleness and sink into hermaphroditic Ulro. The result in the case of Satan is cupidity, a "female" envy of the works of others that replaces (masculine) creativity.

When Milton realizes that "I in my Selfhood am that Satan" (108; 14:30), he voluntarily undergoes the same process of feminization as did Satan, and he sees at the edge of Beulah "his own Shadow" as "A mournful form double; hermaphroditic: male & female" (108; 14:37). In Milton's descent, he attempts to differentiate himself from the female, but finds himself "In conflict with those Female forms, which in blood & jealousy / Surrounded him, dividing & uniting without end or number" (110; 17:7-8). The female in the poem has become a trope for chaos and the breakdown of form. Milton in his journey realizes that his earthly response to the threat of formlessness had been the repressiveness of orthodox Christian morality:

> He saw the Cruelties of Ulro, and he wrote them down
> In iron tablets: and his Wives & Daughters names were these
> Rahab and Tirzah, Milcah & Malah & Noah & Hoglah.
> They sat rangd round him as the rocks of Horeb round the land
> Of Canaan: and they wrote in thunder smoke and fire
> His dictate; and his body was the Rock Sinai;
>
> (110; 17:9-14)

Blake here argues that Milton adopted the cruelties of Mosaic law and imposed them on his three wives and three daughters, his sixfold Emanation, who then became both victims and vessels of the law's cruelty. But the allusion imbedded in the women's names is perhaps Blake's single most problematic use of a Biblical source. The names are those of the five Daughters of Zelophehad, plus Rahab.

In order to convey the true import of the reversal Blake is attempting here, we must examine the crux of the episode of Zelophehad's daughters in *Numbers*. The daughters of Zelophehad plead for their right to the inheritance of their father, who died sonless:

> Why should the name of our father be done away from among his family, because he hath no son? Give unto us therefore a possession among the brethren of our father. And Moses brought their cause before the Lord. And the Lord spake unto Moses, saying, The daughters of Zelophehad speak right: thou shalt surely give them a possession of an inheritance among their father's brethren; and thou shalt cause the inheritance of their father to pass unto them. And thou shalt speak unto the children of Israel saying, If a man die and he have no son, then ye shall cause his inheritance to pass unto his daughter.
>
> (27.4-8)

The episode is hardly a polemic on behalf of women's rights—the daughters are allowed their inheritance only in the absence of a male—but it is an incremental step toward a concept of gender equality. Yet Blake has chosen to apply it as a metaphor for the corruption of the female by orthodox legalism. Granted that the male, in this case Milton, is for Blake the author of this corruption, there are nonetheless many Biblical stories that Blake might have invoked that present far more obvious instances of women who are corrupted by appropriating the power of the oppressor—Jezebel, for instance. Blake's peculiar choice of this story to serve as a metaphor for woman corrupted betrays an underlying discomfort with women's equality.

Two of these Daughters, Rahab and Tirzah, join to constitute another "multiple" female. Just as the properly masculine inner self has been tainted by internalizing the feminine, the rightfully female and emanative external world has become (in Blake's eyes) improperly masculine and willful. Rahab and Tirzah (who represent respectively the temptation toward religion as power and the temptation toward religion as repressive morality) try to entice Milton to come across the river Arnon, and Blake characterizes them as "The Twofold form Hermaphroditic: and the Double-sexed / The Female-male & the Male-female, self-dividing stood" (113; 19:32-33). The blurring of the delineations of gender contributes to the blending of Rahab and Tirzah into a single entity. The female is associated with the destabilization of the self. The frequency with which these sphinxlike hermaphrodites appear in the later poetry, always as figures of dread, suggests an anxiety in-

spired by the loss of binary distinctions of gender. The mocking tone of Rahab/Tirzah's speech is clear as she tries to "tease" Milton across the river. Her call to "bring with thee Jerusalem" (113; 19:46) is important, because Jerusalem is the type of the "good" submissive woman represented in this poem by Ololon. The invitation of Rahab-Tirzah is an invitation to put off the well-defined, hierarchical division of gender roles, the female aspect of which is symbolized by Ololon.

Milton's descent, as I have indicated, involves a certain "feminization" of the masculine self, heroically undertaken as a prelude to Self-Annihilation, which is a rejection of the power of (female) immanence. The temptation of Milton by Rahab-Tirzah is a temptation to even greater "feminization," which Milton rejects by this Self-Annihilation. His courage prompts the similar descent of Ololon, but she does not become similarly "masculinized," even as a transitional state. Blake seems incapable of conceiving of a female with any traditionally "masculine" attributes as a positive figure.

Blake even states categorically that the female can endure no "corruption" by the masculine when Ololon finally descends into Generation. First, her descent into Beulah causes a burst of female lamentation and makes possible the vision of the fallen world of nature as a Beulaic paradise. From there she enters the world of Generation, passing the "Polypus" of sexual incarnation, and at that point becomes an individual, rather than a collective being:

> For Ololon step'd into the Polypus within the Mundane Shell
> They could not step into Vegetable Worlds without becoming
> The enemies of Humanity except in a Female Form
> And as One Female, Ololon and all its mighty Hosts
> Appear'd: a Virgin of twelve years
>
> (136-137; 36:13-17)

Any incarnation of Ololon in other than a clearly recognizable "Female Form" will make her become "The enemies of Humanity." The Emanation must not attempt to usurp the prerogatives of the masculine self; this would amount to the same kind of "contamination" that can take place in Beulah, where the masculine self is in constant danger of becoming "feminized." When Blake speaks of Ololon taking the "Female Form," he is not referring to biological sex alone. He means that Emanations must willingly embrace their secondary status. He makes this clear by the example of the particular "Female Form" that Ololon assumes: a twelve-year-old virgin, at once woman and child, and the object of one of the most historically persistent of all male sexual-power fantasies.

All of Blake's metaphysical pyrotechnics in the poem's finale cannot obscure the disturbing quality of this revelation of the ideal female as a willing victim. Blake

knows that the sacrificial nature religions that he condemns a few lines later—"The Wicker Man of Scandinavia in whom / Jerusalem's children consume in flames among the Stars" (137; 37:11-12)—favored just such victims for their rituals. In one of his cleverest reversals, Blake makes Ololon take on the guilt of promulgating Natural Religion:

> Are those who contemn Religion & seek to annihilate it
> Become in their Femin[in]e portions the causes & promoters
> Of these Religions, how is this thing? this Newtonian Phantasm
> This Voltaire & Rousseau: this Hume & Gibbon & Bolingbroke
> This Natural Religion! this impossible absurdity
> Is Ololon the cause of this?
>
> (141; 40:9-14)

Ololon is not the cause of Natural Religion, either in its ancient or modern Deist form, yet as Emanation she is the object of a pursuit that produces Natural Religion, the quest for absolute presence. Because of her womanhood she is implicated in the pernicious actions of Rahab and Tirzah, so she offers herself up as a willing sacrifice, though her sacrifice comes in the form of sexual submission. Through this submission, she will escape the "female" trap of immanence. Blake believes that since he sacrifices the virgin on the altar of sex rather than that of blood, he is superior to the Scandinavians. So he is, but only in degree, not in kind.

Blake's account of the submission of Ololon in fact retains the blood-sacrifice metaphor:

> So saying, the Virgin divided Six-fold & with a shriek
> Dolorous that ran through Creation a Double Six-fold Wonder!
>
> Then as a Moony Ark Ololon descended to Felphams Vale
> In clouds of blood, in streams of gore, with dreadful thunderings
>
> (143; 42:3-4, 7-8)

The piercing of the virgin's maidenhead replaces the thrust of the sacrificial knife. In choosing the metaphor of blood sacrifice, the supreme ritual of Natural Religion, Blake again depicts female heroism as the willing embrace of the image of an ancient victimization, in contrast to the many images of male heroism throughout the poem.

There is one moment, however, just before Ololon's metaphorical defloration, that when taken out of context sounds like a feminist epiphany:

> Is this our Femin[in]e Portion the Six-fold Miltonic Female

Terribly this Portion trembles before thee O awful
 Man
Altho' our Human Power can sustain the severe con-
 tentions
Of Friendship, our Sexual cannot: but flies into the
 Ulro.
Hence arose all our terrors in Eternity! & now re-
 membrance
Returns upon us! are we Contraries O Milton, Thou &
 I

(143; 41:30-35)

The exaltation of friendship over sexuality is very simi-
lar to that in *A Vindication of the Rights of Woman.* The
terms are those that Wollstonecraft uses and Blake may
have indeed taken Ololon's declaration directly from
her.[5] Is this a moment of self-realization for Ololon (and
Blake as well)? Does she now stand before Milton as
his fully equal Contrary?

An examination of the context of the speech makes it
clear that precisely the opposite is true. First, Ololon
does not come to this epiphany on her own. She is in
fact guided to it by Milton, whose long speech immedi-
ately precedes hers. As he descends to meet her in the
Felpham garden, he wastes no time in asserting his ab-
solute authority: "But turning toward Ololon in terrible
majesty Milton / Replied. Obey thou the Words of the
Inspired Man" (142; 40:28-29). Blake, who is after all
one with both Milton and Los, implicitly endorses ev-
ery word of Milton's long lecture. It is Milton who
shows Ololon the difference between the Sexual and the
Human:

These are the Sexual Garments, the Abomination of
 Desolation
Hiding the Human Lineaments as with an Ark & Cur-
 tains
Which Jesus rent: & now shall wholly purge away
 with Fire
Till Generation is swallowd up in Regeneration

(142-43; 41:25-28)

Hence, when the shaken Ololon says, "Terribly this por-
tion trembles before thee O awful Man," she trembles
not in fear or anger but in what (for Blake) is entirely
appropriate awe at Milton's male authority.

This may sound much more like a putting *on* of Sexual
Garments than a casting off, but we must understand
what the casting off of Sexual Garments means to Blake.
The Sexual Garments were put on when Milton and
Ololon descended through the Polypus of physical in-
carnation. They can be put off only through the *sexual
act,* which for Blake means the complete submission of
woman to man. Blake's ideal woman casts off the false
modesty and the teasing allure that energize the frus-
trating game of sexual pursuit, but the male is not re-
quired to make a similar sacrifice. Blake wants to end
the game of hunter and hunted by having the prey will-

ingly submit to the hunter. This would indeed end the
game, but not the problem that underlies it. This total
submission of one person to another does not sound
much like the dynamic opposition of Contraries intro-
duced in *The Marriage of Heaven and Hell.* There,
Blake asserts that "Opposition is true Friendship" (42),
which is surely the sort of friendship Wollstonecraft had
in mind when she declared friendship more powerful
than sex. Susan Fox has maintained, "Contraries are by
definition equal, but the females in the poem, however
crucial and powerful Blake intended them to be, are not
convincingly equal to their male contraries" (*Poetic
Form in Blake's* Milton 214).

This pattern of gender subordination culminates in
Blake's rendition of his "actual" experience beholding
the vision at the end of *Milton.* The "literal" is always a
vexed issue in Blake's work, but it is generally held
that Blake in his garden at Felpham did in fact experi-
ence an inner illumination that left him momentarily
stunned and lying on the ground, where he was found
by his worried spouse. This is the moment described
when Blake finds himself returned to his "mortal state /
To Resurrection & Judgment in the Vegetable Body"
(143;42:26-27). However intricately symbolic, Blake's
tropes carry inevitable implications about a hierarchy of
gender in our mundane "Vegetable" world. These impli-
cations can be conclusively demonstrated by looking at
Blake's characterization of his wife Catherine here:
"And my sweet Shadow of Delight stood trembling by
my side" (143;42:28). Earlier, when Ololon first de-
scended into the garden, Blake implored her to "pity
thou my Shadow of Delight" (137; 36:31) and to enter
the cottage to comfort the worried Catherine. Blake's
declaration of affection for his wife is moving and genu-
ine, but the terms with which he describes her strik-
ingly encapsulate the gender hierarchies that condition
the structure of *Milton.* "Sweet Shadow of Delight" is a
capsule description of all the positive females of Blake's
myth: "Sweet" (submissive, maternal and/or sexually
forthcoming); "Shadow" (emanative, secondary, unreal);
"of Delight" (intensely and essentially sexual). Further,
Catherine's trembling evokes the reverential trembling
of Ololon before Milton earlier. Both shudder in awe of
the visionary power of "the Inspired Man." Diana Hume
George again defends Blake: "Blake's intention is not
to equate emanations with female humanities, but obvi-
ously that is the effect" (169). Passages like the descrip-
tion of Catherine above, however, suggest that the equa-
tion of actual women and Emanations *is* Blake's
intention. "Distinguish therefore States from Individuals
in those States," declares the Divine Voice in *Milton,*
but Blake's own words demonstrate that a belief in a
hierarchical system of gender, however metaphysical
and fabulous, will inevitably shape and color one's per-
ception of individuals in this world.

Milton's final scene, read in the light of Marlon Ross's argument, is so startling as to approach the comic. Ross, we recall, contends that the male Romantic poet, in response to a growing feeling of powerlessness and marginality in society, initiates an internal quest for the wellsprings of masculine power in a transcendent realm outside the bounds of ordinary (as defined by society) experience. The climax of *Milton* finds Blake having achieved his goal. He has, in the eternal world of the mind, linked himself with Milton, his culture's greatest male hero, and likewise joined himself to Los, the principle of the imagination, which for Blake is also the principle of masculinity. In the mortal world, however, the literal world of "the Vegetable Body," the poet lies prone on the ground in front of his cottage, paralyzed, helpless as a child, with a pitying woman standing alone above him (a scene that recalls the climax of **"The Crystal Cabinet"**). The image is intended as one of triumph, but it in fact portrays an overwhelming ambivalence: the poet is simultaneously totally powerless in one world, while being totally empowered in a second. This second world is entirely internal and mental. The former world, the world of nature *and* society, of politics, history, and growing female empowerment, has been conceded by the poet to, among others, women.

A similar ambivalence characterizes the movement of the poem as a whole. The Selfhood or Spectre that Blake/Los/Milton rejects through Self-Annihilation, the self of what Bracher calls immediate presence, is a subjectivity always completely present to and conscious of itself. This self is in fact the autonomous, unified, immortal self that Mellor has identified as a characteristic goal of masculine Romanticism. In embracing mediated presence, a relational presence that exists *only* in the minds of others, Blake has moved in the direction of what Mellor has defined as the feminine counter-principle to the autonomous masculine Romantic self: a self constituted by and within the interrelation of a community (*Romanticism and Gender* 3-4). Despite this nod toward feminine Romanticism, Blake cannot be what Mellor has called an "ideological cross-dresser" (*Romanticism and Gender* 171), a writer who has adopted the perspectives of the opposite gender, because his tropes constantly identify the female with the false immediate presence of the Spectre-Self. In this manner, Blake subverts his own potential subversiveness, and *Milton* as a poem remains divided and ambivalent, an ambivalence so powerfully dramatized in the conundrum presented by its final image.

Notes

1. All citations of Blake's writing are from David V. Erdman's *The Complete Poetry and Prose of William Blake*. Citations are noted parenthetically in the text and refer to the page in Erdman's edition, followed, when appropriate, by plate and line number.

2. In one form or another, Helene Cixous, Luce Irigaray, and Julia Kristeva all employ Derrida's criticism of the metaphysic of presence as an argument against masculine hierarchy. The presence valorized by this metaphysics is the conscious *self-presence* attributed to the male, as opposed to the ostensibly unconscious immanence of the female. Cixous, in "Sorties," offers a list of gendered binarisms (for Cixous all our cultural binarisms are rooted in gender) that includes the group "Form, convex, step, advance, seed, progress" attributed to the male and the group "Matter, concave, ground—which supports the step, receptacle" attributed to the female (91). In other words, woman provides the inert immanence, the subsumption of which is the goal of the self-conscious male. Cixous also postulates a female value system called the Realm of the Gift which contrasts with the masculine Realm of the Proper, the source of propriety-property-appropriation. Toril Moi, in *Sexual/Textual Politics*, calls this Realm of the Proper "a textbook illustration of Derrida's 'metaphysics of presence'" (112). The very title of Luce Irigaray's *This Sex Which is Not One* implies a critique of presence. Within the text, Irigaray refuses to answer the question "What is a woman" contending that "the question 'what is . . . ?' is the question—the metaphysical question—to which the feminine does not allow itself to submit" (122). Moi remarks (referring to Cixous, and implicitly to Irigaray as well), "Even the question 'What is it?' is denounced as a sign of the masculine impulse to imprison reality in rigid hierarchical structures" (111). Most apposite to Blake and *Milton*, Julia Kristeva, in "Women's Time," questions the conventional assignation of time to the male as opposed to "the problematic of space, which innumerable religions of matriarchal (re)appearance attribute to 'woman'" (191). Blake shares these authors' critique of the (masculine) cult of self-presence, but not their criticism of the designation of the female as essentially immanent and unconscious.

3. All pictorial references are to the compendium of copies A and D in Erdman's *The Illuminated Blake*.

4. The 1808 picture is reproduced in black-and-white in Bindman (151). The design is one of Blake's most startling sexual images. Eve sucks a fruit held in the mouth of serpent while standing beneath a huge tree, its hanging fruit evoking a shower of drops of semen. (Blake probably has in mind the upas tree, a favorite Romantic symbol and the subject of his own "A Poison Tree.") The snake is coiled sensuously around Eve's body and the fruit in his mouth can be seen as the end of a penis. Blake appears to be condemning phallocen-

trism as the first idolatry, and the source of the breach between man and woman: Adam faces away from Eve on the other side of the tree, with an expression of dismay. If this is so, Blake has managed to criticize the phallocentric while at the same time criticizing woman by making her the initiator of phallic idolatry through her sexual fascination with the penis.

5. Wollstonecraft's exact phrasing is as follows: "This passion, naturally increases by suspense and difficulties, draws the mind out of its accustomed state, and exalts the affections; but the security of marriage, allowing the fever of love to subside, a healthy temperature is thought insipid, only by those who have not sufficient intellect to substitute the calm tenderness of friendship, the confidence of respect, instead of blind admiration, and the sensual emotions of fondness.

This is, must be, the course of nature.—Friendship or indifference inevitably succeeds love" (30).

Works Cited

Beauvoir, Simone de. *The Second Sex.* Ed. and Trans. M. H. Parshley. New York: Vintage Books, 1989.

Bindman, David. *William Blake: His Art and Times.* London: Thames and Hudson, 1982.

Blake, William. *The Complete Poetry and Prose of William Blake.* Ed. David V. Erdman. New York: Doubleday, 1988.

Bloom, Harold. *Blake's Apocalypse.* Ithaca: Cornell UP, 1963.

———. "The Internalization of Quest Romance." *Romanticism and Consciousness.* Ed. Harold Bloom. New York: Norton, 1970. 3-24.

Bracher, Mark. *Being Form'd.* Barrytown, N.Y.: Station Hill P, 1985.

Cixous, Helene. "Sorties." *New French Feminisms.* Ed. Elaine Marks and Isabelle de Courtivron. New York: Schocken Books, 1981.

Crompton, Louis. *Byron and Greek Love: Homophobia in Nineteenth-Century England.* Berkeley: U of California P, 1985.

Erdman, David V., ed. *The Illuminated Blake.* Garden City, N.Y.: Doubleday, 1974.

Essick, Robert N., and Joseph Viscomi. Introduction. *William Blake*: Milton, a Poem. Princeton: William Blake Trust/Princeton UP, 1993.

Fox, Susan. "The Female as Metaphor in William Blake's Poetry." *Critical Inquiry* 3.3 (1977): 507-514.

———. *Poetic Form in Blake's* Milton. Princeton: Princeton UP, 1976.

George, Diana Hume. *Blake and Freud.* Ithaca: Cornell UP, 1980.

Halperin, David I. *One Hundred Years of Homosexuality.* New York: Routledge, 1990.

Hilton, Nelson. "An Original Story." *Unnam'd Forms: Blake and Textuality.* Ed. Nelson Hilton and Thomas A. Vogler. Berkeley: U of California P, 1986. 69-104.

Hofkosh, Sonia. "The Writer's Ravishment: Woman and the Romantic Author—the Example of Byron." Mellor, *Romanticism and Feminism* 93-115.

Irigaray, Luce. *This Sex Which is Not One.* Trans. Catherine Parker and Caroline Burke. Ithaca: Cornell UP, 1985.

Kristeva, Julia. "Women's Time." *The Kristeva Reader.* New York: Columbia UP, 1986. 187-213.

Langland, Elizabeth. "Blake's Feminist Revision of Literary Tradition in 'The Sick Rose.'" *Critical Paths: Blake and the Argument of Method.* Ed. Donald Ault, Mark Bracher, and Dan Miller. Durham: Duke UP, 1987. 225-244.

Moi, Toril. *Sexual/Textual Politics.* New York: Methuen, 1985.

Mitchell, W. J. T. "Style and Iconography in Blake's Milton." *Blake Studies* 6.1 (1973): 47-72.

Mellor, Anne K. "Blake's Portrayal of Women." *Blake: An Illustrated Quarterly* 16.3 (1983): 148-150.

———, ed. *Romanticism and Feminism.* Bloomington: Indiana UP, 1988.

———. *Romanticism and Gender.* New York: Routledge, 1993.

Numbers. The Holy Bible. King James version. New York: American Bible Society, 1991.

Richardson, Alan. "Romanticism and the Colonization of The Feminine." Mellor, *Romanticism and Feminism* 13-26.

Ross, Marlon B. *The Contours Of Masculine Desire. Romanticism and the Rise of Women's Poetry.* New York: Oxford UP, 1989.

Storch, Margaret. *Sons and Adversaries.* Knoxville: U of Tennessee P, 1990.

Webster, Brenda. *Blake's Prophetic Psychology.* Athens: U of Georgia P, 1983.

Wollstonecraft, Mary. *A Vindication of the Rights of Woman.* New York: Norton, 1988.

Betsy Bolton (essay date spring 1997)

SOURCE: Bolton, Betsy. "'A Garment Dipped in Blood': Ololon and Problems of Gender in Blake's *Milton*." *Studies in Romanticism* 36, no. 1 (spring 1997): 61-101.

[*In the following essay, Bolton examines themes of sexuality and feminine identity in Blake's depiction of Ololon.*]

Would to God that all the Lords people were Prophets.

On a first reading, Milton's psychedelic plot baffles and bemuses. Multiple, contradictory and overlapping accounts of the same actions are frequently given; events often occur on four different levels simultaneously.[1] Reading *Milton* for its plot can be an exercise in frustration. At times, the confusion of reading contributes to the power of the prophecy, for *Milton* is structured around a progressive commission of dramatic mistakes. The poem presents its visions as inspired errors; yet some errors seem more inspired—or at least more visibly thematized—than others. In the pages that follow, I will argue that gender and sexuality in particular run through the fabric of this prophecy as a frayed and contradictory strand. *Milton* claims that "The Sexual is Threefold: the Human is Fourfold";[2] the prophecy suggests with some consistency that to confuse humanity with the sexually differentiated state in which we find ourselves is to lose an entire dimension of perception, to find our senses contracted, limited to the realms of Beulah and Generation and shut out of Eden. Yet the poem offers a confused and confusing definition of "The Sexual," one which moves uneasily among biological sexes, gender roles and erotic attraction.[3] While *Milton* explicitly thematizes (and thus begins to correct) the limits of certain gendered stereotypes, other assumptions about gender or sexuality remain invisible, part of the poem's mechanics, its material base. Focusing on what remains opaque in relation to gender and sexuality should bring into stronger relief some of the political issues attendant on poetry structured as prophecy.

I

Let me begin with the most striking and perhaps least recognized error in the poem: Blake's address to Ololon in his garden at Felpham. First, a little history: Ololon as a name refers both to a river in Eden, and to a group of Eternals living on the banks of that river; misunderstanding Milton's mission, they drive his darkened image out of Eden. Realizing what they have done, they repent and descend in turn, taking on a variety of forms in the process: in Beulah, they appear as clouds (in which the Lord is visible); in Blake's garden (the world of Generation) they become a twelve-year-old virgin. That virginal figure, answering Milton's call to self-

annihilation, splits six-fold, and Ololon becomes in rapid sequence a dove, an ark, clouds of blood, streams of gore and finally a "Garment dipped in blood / Written within & without in woven letters"; she becomes, in fact, "the Divine Revelation in the Litteral Expression." What exactly the reader is to make of this remains an open question.

In the midst of the kaleidoscopic transformations which structure Blake's prophecy, certain moments stand out as more accessible than others: Ololon's appearance in the garden at Felpham seems easier to grasp than most. The community of immortals takes on the form of a twelve-year-old virgin in a deliberate attempt at reassurance and alliance:

> They could not step into Vegetable Worlds without becoming
> The enemies of Humanity except in a Female Form
> And as One Female, Ololon and all its mighty Hosts
> Appear'd: a Virgin of twelve years nor time nor space was
> To the perception of the Virgin Ololon but as the
> Flash of lightning but more quick the Virgin in my Garden
> Before my Cottage stood for the Satanic Space is delusion
> Walking in my Cottage Garden, sudden I beheld
> The Virgin Ololon & address'd her as a Daughter of Beulah [:]
> .
> Virgin of Providence fear not to enter into my Cottage
> What is thy message to thy friend: What am I now to do
> Is it again to plunge into deeper affliction? behold me
> Ready to obey, but pity thou my Shadow of Delight
> Enter my Cottage, comfort her, for she is sick with fatigue
>
> (36/40:13-32)

While Ololon could potentially appear as "the enemies of Humanity," they choose to avoid such a threatening form. Blake's illustration of this passage emphasizes its simplicity and accessibility: while most of the other designs in the poem feature close-ups of straining human bodies, this sketch presents a more distant child-like picture of a house, a garden, a man and descending angel. . . . After struggling throughout the poem to comprehend Blake's shifting models of overlapping worlds, the reader may find it a relief to return to the domestic space of a cottage garden—and a simpler mode of representation. Yet such relief may lead in turn to an error in judgment. The second book of *Milton* begins with the warning (engraved in mirror-writing about the title): "How wide the Gulf & Unpassable! between Simplicity & Insipidity." Is the design of Blake's garden to be judged simple or insipid? And what difference might this judgment make to a reading of the poem?

At first glance, the words addressed to Ololon by Blake's persona are as comforting as the design: he promises to do whatever is needed, asking only that this

"Virgin of Providence" comfort his wife Catherine, his "Shadow of Delight." Blake specifically addresses Ololon as a Daughter of Beulah, a figure associated with encircling arms "of love & pity & sweet compassion" (30:12) but one incapable of withstanding the "exceeding unbounded" life (and mental strife) of Man [sic] in Eternity. Blake's mistake here seems to me quite astounding—so outrageous as to be almost self-parodic. Blake as poet and character alike is a prophet, a seer of visions; the poet concludes *A Vision of the Last Judgment* with the following account of his powers:

> What it will be Questioned When the Sun rises do you not see a round Disk of fire somewhat like a Guinea O no no I see an Innumerable company of the Heavenly host crying Holy Holy Holy is the Lord God Almighty I question not my Corporeal or Vegetative Eye any more than I would Question a Window concerning a Sight I look thro it & not with it.
>
> (565-66)

Yet the character Blake mistakes Ololon (an Innumerable company of the Heavenly host) for a Virgin and a Daughter of Beulah. While the second book of *Milton* is generally careful to mark the perceptual limitations of the vegetable world—the Lark and Wild Thyme of Felpham Vale are, for instance, carefully translated back into mighty angels, the messengers of Los—Blake's persona apparently finds the female figure of Ololon so familiar, so transparently human, as to be unrecognizable in practice.

Blake's error is of course perfectly "natural": he mistakes himself for the hero of the poem (What am I now to do / Is it again to plunge into deeper affliction? behold me / Ready to obey"). On a rush of self-aggrandizement, he condescends to Ololon, sending her off to do the women's work of comforting the sick. Ololon does not accuse Blake of error, though 'she' does remind him of "[their] Act / In great Eternity which thou knowest!" Though Ololon describes 'herself' as "terrified," this terror does not seem to inhibit her action.[4] "Mild was the voice, but more distinct than any earthly / That Miltons Shadow heard" (37:5): Ololon's response to Blake ("Knowest thou of Milton . . . him I seek!") functions as a call to which Milton responds by condensing all of his Fibres, appearing in Blake's Garden as a Cloud, a Human form, a Covering Cherub—a giant form uniting the many layers of Eden, Beulah, Generation and Ulro. Both in summoning Milton and in obeying his call to self-annihilation, Ololon seems the clearest hero of this last act of the prophecy. But this heroism, like Ololon her (their) self, can be difficult to recognize.

Blake's mistake makes visible the limits of his perceptions in this section of the poem: his partial blindness encompasses both Ololon and Milton. Milton too appears in a variety of forms on the various levels of the poem: in Eden, he is an "Image Divine tho' darken'd"; on the edge of Beulah, he enters into his Shadow, "a mournful form double; hermaphroditic." In Beulah, he appears as a wintry globe; in Generation (the vegetable world where Blake and his readers exist) he becomes a falling star, a part of Blake's foot (!) and a black cloud. Seeking his six-fold Emanation (a figure composed of his three wives and three daughters) Milton descends still further to Ulro, where his body appears as "the Rock Sinai"; yet his Human Shadow continues to travel in the Mundane Shell, a void outside of existence, until he actively confronts the demonized Urizen in the streams of Arnon. Trying to "place" Milton at any given moment in the poem is an extraordinarily complicated project, and the character Blake sees only the level of Generation clearly.

Following Milton's appearance, the poet-persona catalogues the mythical and historical figures included within the Miltonic Shadow. While this catalogue appears to encompass all of human history, its scope is notably limited to the forms of Generation and the figure of Satan: Blake sees each of the 27 Churches; he stands in Satan's bosom and views its desolations at length—but Milton, as distinct from Satan, remains largely invisible in the terms of this catalogue. Ololon's vision seems more perceptive than Blake's: her description of Milton comes after the poet's challenge to Satan,[5] and focuses on his divine aspect, his mission and his actions in other regions:

> *I see* thee strive upon the Brooks of Arnon. there a dread
> And awful Man *I see,* oercovered with the mantle of years.
> *I behold* Los & Urizen. *I behold* Orc & Tharmas;
> The Four Zoa's of Albion & thy Spirit with them striving
> In Self annihilation giving thy life to thy enemies.
>
> (40:4-8; my emphases)

The Blake-persona's description of Milton's Shadow extends for 79 lines of verse and contains five references to vision; Ololon's description of Milton is condensed into five lines, and contains four of the same references to vision. The poet's vision ranges widely yet lacks depth: Ololon's account goes straight to the heart of Milton's Self, yet remains so concise as to be incomprehensible to strictly mortal eyes and ears. Blake's (limited) observation of Milton's Shadow and Satan's bosom leaves him passive; Ololon's more comprehensive sight builds steadily toward an act of self-annihilation that brings Jesus himself into being and presages the harvest of the apocalypse. The figure Blake mistook for a Daughter of Beulah frightened of mental strife becomes "A Garment of War"; meanwhile, the would-be hero Blake trembles and faints, and then finds comfort at his side in the form of his "sweet Shadow of

Delight." The two women discounted by Blake appear as strong or, in the case of Ololon, far stronger than the poet himself.

What are the consequences of Blake's "misreading" of Ololon? The action of the poem seems to continue unchecked, which would suggest the mistake is minor. Yet it throws serious doubt on the effectiveness of the prophecy, the quality of its reception. The poet-persona can visualize the entire vegetable world as a sandal to strap on and walk through eternity: if even he is so drastically limited in his vision and his understanding of the actors in this drama, what hope is there for less privileged readers? Indeed, some critics celebrate what I am calling the crowning error of the poem: in the process, they underestimate Ololon and overestimate the character Blake. According to Harold Bloom, for instance, "Blake now enters into the dignity of his final role in the poem, which is to be the seer of the Miltonic Great Marriage. . . . The dialogue between Ololon and Blake is worthy of the occasion."[6] Along the same lines, G. E. Bentley described Plate 41 of *Milton* in the following terms: "The whole plate is a very dark design of a naked man whose head gives off light supporting a kneeling, dropping, White-haired figure in a long robe. The naked man seems to be standing in a river or small lake." . . .[7] He then goes on to suggest that this plate may represent the line "Before Ololon Milton stood" (42:1). Bentley's suggestion ignores several of his own observations: the white hair of the figure and the river in which the naked man stands. It seems to me far more plausible that the plate represents a scene just preceding the plate: "Urizen faints in terror striving among the Brooks of Arnon / With Miltons Spirit" (40:53). Only an assumption of female passivity and weakness supports Bentley's preferred reading. Unfortunately, the poem provides plenty of material to support such an assumption.

2

Milton's confusion over gender and eroticism intersects in complicated ways with Blake's attempt to replace or redeem Greek and Roman models of epic poetry. A large part of Blake's dislike for such models derives from the physical violence, or "corporeal war," these earlier epics detail and encouraged. The Preface to *Milton,* for instance, describes Greeks and Romans as "silly . . . slaves of the Sword"; Milton himself in announcing his descent is brought to complain that "the Nations still / Follow after the detestable gods of Priam; in pomp / Of warlike selfhood, contradicting and blaspheming" (14-16). Again in the Preface to *Milton,* Blake claims, "We do not want either Greek or Roman Models if we are but just & true to our own Imaginations, those Worlds of Eternity in which we shall live for ever; in Jesus our Lord." "Want" here should perhaps be read as a lack: "there will be no *lack* of Greek and

Roman models if we are but just & true to our own Imaginations." *Milton* contains elements of various Greek (if less clearly Roman) models, appropriated with varying degrees of success. But the central model for the poem is of course *Paradise Lost,* itself "infected by the general malady" of warlike selfhood. Blake eventually modifies his attack on Greek if not Roman models; in *A Vision of the Last Judgment* he announces: "Let it here be Noted that the Greek Fables originated in Spiritual Mystery & Real Vision . . . The Nature of my Work is Visionary or Imaginative it is an Endeavour to Restore 'what the Ancients called' the Golden Age" (555). Blake's later prophecies work to redeem the warlike models of Greece (and *Paradise Lost*) by translating corporeal war into an epic of intra-psychic transformation.

Redemption, however, seems far from secure. Blake's exploration of intrapersonal conflict or strife tends to take shape around questions of gender roles, biological sex and erotic connections. These three categories are interwoven throughout *Milton* in odd and anxious but fairly consistent ways, producing 1) a radical constriction and devaluation of feminine gender roles, 2) the doubled figure of the hermaphrodite and 3) repeated suggestions of homoeroticism at key moments in the text. Why should an attempt to unravel warlike Selfhood and the slavery of the sword produce the sexual miscellany of homoeroticism, hermaphrodites and misogyny? Blake's engagement with determinate biology in the figure of the hermaphrodite seems in context an attempt to free erotic energy for radical political purposes, but because that biology continues to rely on and defend fixed gender definitions, the politics of the poem become distinctly skewed. Not surprisingly, the torque of *Milton*'s sexual politics seems to gravitate around the elements of *Paradise Lost* at play within Blake's later epic. Thus in order to trace the transformation of corporeal war into an oddly syncopated war among the sexes, I want to focus first on two moments in which *Milton* invokes *Paradise Lost*: the first episode uses elements of *Paradise Lost* to rewrite an earlier creation myth; the second episode offers its own revision of Satan's expulsion from heaven.

Milton begins with a Bard's song which presents three different stories of creation: the first describes a world "Indefinite and Opake" taking shape as Urizen's ghastly body. The second tale tells of strife among the Eternals as Los's sons squabble over who has the better job: Satan the Miller and Palamabron the Harvester switch places for a day through Satan's urging, and both create chaos out of the other's job. This leads to accusations, to mourning, to battle (in which an apparently innocent party, Thulloh, is killed) and finally to judgment by an Assembly of the Eternals. Rintrah, the only son not involved in the original dispute is mysteriously held to blame; Satan nonetheless becomes furious and disowns

his family, becoming opaque—in this moment, Los and Enitharmon recognize Satan as Urizen, marking the way both stories of creation reach the same conclusion.

Leutha, Satan's Emanation, comes forward to redeem him by offering a third version of this creation myth. Lusting after Palamabron but frightened off by his emanation Elynittria, Leutha persuades Satan to take over Palamabron's Harrow, so that she herself may play the role of Elynittria. Unfortunately, neither Leutha nor Satan is up to the challenge of the Harrow, and chaos ensues—at which point, Satan disowns his Emanation and becomes opaque. Enitharmon creates a space to protect Satan; Elynittria, having been scolded by Los for jealousy, brings Leutha to Palamabron's tent, where the former gives birth to Death and to Rahab, the female figure known elsewhere in **Milton** as Virgin Babylon Mother of Whoredoms. This conclusion to the Bard's Song gives the third creation story more weight, for it extends history beyond the point reached by the earlier two myths: Death and Church history take shape only in this final story. The **"Bard's Song"** ends and the Bard's audience, an Assembly of Eternals, question his truth and his sources. Claiming the truth of Inspiration, the Bard takes refuge in Milton's bosom—and Milton promptly announces his descent.

These three creation myths might be read, respectively, as perverse renditions of central Blakean texts: *Genesis,* Hesiod's *Theogony*[8] and Milton's *Paradise Lost*. In *Genesis* 2, verses 6 and 7, "there went up a mist from the earth, and watered the whole face of the ground. And the Lord God formed man of the dust of the ground, and breathed into his nostrils the breath of life; and man became a living soul." Milton's opening offers a grotesque parody: "Hanging upon the wind, Two Nostrils bent down into the Deep / And a fifth Age passed over & a State of dismal woe" (3:20-21). Hesiod's *Theogony* presents the struggles of the gods: Blake presents the squabbles of the divine family. Not surprisingly, however, it is the third account which seems to have the strongest impact on the listening Milton. Leutha's tale, introduced with the claim, "I am the Author of this Sin!" (11:35), rewrites the physical battles of the Divine Family as a story of frustrated sexual desire—and in that rewriting quotes directly from *Paradise Lost*.

At first glance, the conflict among brothers appears to have been translated into a story of heterosexual desire: a tale in which female jealousy is the culprit. Yet the terms of that translation produce, at least metaphorically, the uncanny figure of the hermaphrodite, reintegrating female jealousy back into a male psyche:

> She spake: I am the Author of this Sin! by my suggestion
> My Parent power Satan has committed this transgression.

> I loved Palamabron & I sought to approach his Tent,
> But beautiful Elynittria with her silver arrows repelld me.
> For her light is terrible to me. I fade before her immortal beauty.
> O wherefore doth a Dragon-form issue from my limbs
> To sieze her new born son? Ah me! the wretched Leutha!

> (11:35-12:3)

"She spake" marks the public formality of this speech before the assembly: the near rhyme between suggestion and transgression make the lines seem perhaps a bit too pat, a bit too carefully constructed. And indeed the heterosexual frame of this story rapidly begins to seem an artificial construct. Leutha's greatest sin appears to be her meddling with Satan's gender:

> entering the doors of Satans brain night after night
> Like sweet perfumes I stupefied the masculine perceptions
> And kept only the feminine awake; hence rose his soft
> Delusory love to Palamabron: admiration join'd with envy
> Cupidity unconquerable! my fault, when at noon of day
> The Horses of Palamabron call'd for rest and pleasant death:
> I sprang out of the Breast of Satan, over the Harrow beaming
> In all my beauty! that I might unloose the flaming steeds
> As Elynittria use'd to do; but too well those living creatures
> Knew that I was not Elynittria, and they brake the traces
> But me, the servants of the Harrow saw not: but as a bow
> Of varying colours on the hills; terribly rag'd the horses

> (12:4-15)

Leutha seduces Satan into femininity, in part to keep herself from murdering Elynittria's first-born son: an act, perhaps, of masculine aggression. What first appeared as Satan's (suspect) homoerotic attraction to Palamabron is presented more essentially as female heterosexual desire. Yet this revision of homoeroticism toward heterosexual desire produces as its by-product the figure of Satan as a hermaphrodite: female and male in one body, its masculinity overwhelmed by femininity gone out of control. This hermaphrodite is a contradiction in terms: delusion bound to love, admiration to envy. The desire to drive the Harrow appears in this context to have been Leutha's rather than Satan's: still, all goes well until Leutha tries to play Elynittria's part. The emphasis on Elynittria's power and glory, both in this passage and the previous one, suggests that Leutha desires Palamabron less than she desires the place held by the "Shadow of his Delight": Elynittria herself. As

she fails to take Elynittria's place, Leutha appears on the scene not in propria persona, but as a rainbow over the hills—the symbol of an old covenant which fails to hold. *Milton* may begin with a call to move beyond the models of corporeal war presented by Greek and Roman literature, yet at this moment in the poem, interpersonal antagonism and unacknowledged aggression and desire seem to infect even the Judeo-Christian image of a truce between God and humans.

Precisely at this moment, when aggression revises what might be called the Christian epic of history, Blake presents his most explicit allusion to *Paradise Lost*. The horses having run out of control, Leutha forms the Serpent in an attempt to regain command:

> To do unkind things in kindness! with power armd, to say
> The most irritating things in the midst of tears and love
> These are the stings of the Serpent! thus did we by them; till thus
> They in return retaliated, and the Living Creatures maddend.
> The Gnomes labourd. I weeping hid in Satans inmost brain;
> But when the Gnomes refus'd to labour more, with blandishments
> I came forth from the head of Satan! back the Gnomes recoil'd.
> And call'd me Sin, and for a sign portentous held me.
>
> (12:38-39)

Compare Sin, addressing Satan in *Paradise Lost*:

> Then shining heav'nly fair, a goddess armed
> Out of thy head I sprung: amazement seized
> All th'host of heav'n; back they recoiled afraid
> At first, and called me Sin, and for a sign
> Portentous held me; but familiar grown,
> I pleased, and with attractive graces won
> The most averse, thee chiefly.[9]

Where *Paradise Lost* presents Sin as an Athena-figure, a "goddess armed," Leutha seems little more than an incompetent. Yet she too is armed, and her weapons are the more vicious for being less visible: "to say / The most irritating things in the midst of tears and love" is enough to madden any living creature. The gnomes also enter into battle with these new weapons: what Leutha has produced is a full-flown war of words, which leads in the end to Satan's descent to Eternal Death. One wonders how much of an advance on Greek, Roman and Miltonic models this really is.

In Milton's epic, Satan spawns Death by incestuously coupling with his daughter Sin; Leutha (Sin) breeds Death not with Satan, but rather in dallying with Palamabron, thus fulfilling one part of Blake's *Vision of the Last Judgment*:

> In Hell all is Self Righteousness there is no such thing there as Forgiveness of Sin . . . Forgiveness of Sin is only at the Judgment Seat of Jesus the Saviour where the Accuser is cast out. not because he Sins but because he torments the Just & makes them do what he condemns as Sin & what he knows is opposite to their own Identity
>
> (*VLJ* [*Vision of the Last Judgment*] 565)

Satan torments Palamabron (the Just) & makes him do what he (Satan) condemns as Sin & what he knows is opposite to Palamabron's own Identity. In this version of the story, Palamabron takes on Satan's Sin (as a lover), becoming complicit in the creation of Death, though this is opposite to his own identity. Milton, having heard this revised story of "impious war in heaven," exclaims,

> What do I here before the Judgment? without my Emanation?
> With the daughters of memory, & not the daughters of inspiration?
> I in my Selfhood am that Satan: I am that Evil One!
>
> (14:28-30)

The second line could be taken as a comment on the story he's just heard: this is a mangled tale, he might protest—badly constructed from bits and pieces of his own writing, and clearly uninspired. W. J. T. Mitchell has argued persuasively that Leutha's attempt to ransom Satan models for Milton the necessity of his descent.[10] Yet while Leutha does in some ways show Milton what he must do, that demonstration may be less a matter of modelling for Milton the act of Ransom and more a matter of showing Milton the horror he (in the figure of the hermaphroditic Satan) has become. Leutha claims authorship of Sin even as she quotes lines authored by Milton; the poet may be forced to descend simply in order to rewrite and reclaim his text.

In this episode of the prophecy, rewriting war as sexual conflict and delusion produces not one but two hermaphrodites. Satan's apparent homoeroticism is rewritten as female (heterosexual) desire which is also the Blakean female will: Satan, controlled by his Emanation Leutha, is the first hermaphrodite. But Leutha is also powerfully focused on Elynittria, whose beauty makes her fade: one might read this as an instance of female homoeroticism. When Leutha, failing in her attempt to "be" Elynittria, springs out of Satan's head, she becomes a figure like Athena, a masculine goddess—in certain versions of classical mythology, another hermaphrodite.

Condemnation of female characters accompanies the figure of the hermaphrodite. While Leutha's confession and attempt to ransom Satan evoke sympathy, nonetheless her actions are shown to have been at the root of the battle between Satan and Palamabron and among

their various followers. Even after she has confessed and been forgiven, her actions (which seem limited to the sexual) serve only to produce the figure of Death on the one hand and Rahab and Tirzah (also associated with hermaphrodites) on the other. Leutha is the figure of the stereotypical "bad woman" in the Bard's Song, but even the "good woman" Elynittria is shown to be responsible for the evil events recounted: protecting Palamabron from Leutha is indirectly responsible for the war in heaven; giving Leutha to Palamabron leads to natural religion, cruelty and death for those within Satanic space. Elynittria is damned if she does and damned if she doesn't: whatever action she takes leads to death and destruction.

The tale Leutha authors revises the creation story of the *Theogony* in the direction of *Paradise Lost,* but this first move away from Greek and Roman models merely blames conflict and strife on the women involved in the story. The fact that 'good' and 'bad' women seem equally culpable underlines the functional role of their responsibility as it echoes the feminization of error (through the figures of Sin and Eve) in Milton's story of the fall. Blake's first metaphoric invocation of the hermaphrodite disrupts this straightforward assigning of blame as it disrupts a one-to-one equation of body and (sexual) identity. Leutha's desire seems remarkably freefloating, capable of invading and overwhelming Satan's perceptions—even her body moves in and out of his without reference to physical constraint. Yet her authorship of sin seems as open to dispute as Satan's authority for action and self-justification. Where two are one, responsibility and authority appear confused and partial concepts.

This first, largely metaphoric invocation of the hermaphrodite gives way later in the poem to far more concrete references—but the figure of the hermaphrodite continues to appear in relation to the fall of man, as refigured by Satan's expulsion from heaven and Milton's descent.[11] Milton's descent to Eternal Death begins with an entry into hermaphrodite form:

> Then on the verge of Beulah he beheld his own Shadow;
> A mournful form double; hermaphroditic: male & female
> In one wonderful body. and he entered into it
> In direful pain for the dread shadow, twenty-seven-fold
> Reached to the depths of direst Hell, & thence to Albions land:
> Which is this earth of vegetation on which now I write.

(14:36-41)

The twenty-seven "folds" of this double-sexed Shadow are enumerated in the character Blake's vision of the twenty-seven Heavens and their Churches:

> Adam, Seth, Enos, Cainan, Mahaleleel, Jared, Enoch, Methuselah, Lamech: these are Giants mighty Hermaphroditic
> Noah, Shem, Arphaxad, Cainan the second, Salah, Heber,
> Peleg, Reu, Serug, Nahor, Terah, these are the Female-Males
> A Male within a Female hid as in an Ark & Curtains,
> Abraham, Moses, Solomon, Paul, Constantine, Charlemaine
> Luther, these seven are the Male-Females, the Dragon Forms
> Religion hid in War, a Dragon red & hidden Harlot
>
> All these are seen in Miltons Shadow who is the Covering Cherub.

(37:35-44)

Within Milton's Shadow or Satan's opacity, the Churches have been subdivided into three groups of hermaphroditic forms. First, figures from before the Flood appear as "Giants mighty Hermaphroditic." Figures associated with Biblical history, the period of Blake's second patriarchs, are represented as "the Female-Males / A Male within a Female hid as in an Ark & Curtains." The third group of figures, associated with the often military spread of organized religion, appear by contrast as "the Male-Females, the Dragon Forms / Religion hid in War, a Dragon red & hidden Harlot." These three kinds of hemaphrodites are oddly central to the events occurring in Felpham Vale: Milton descending into Blake's garden is indeed a giant form hermaphroditic, "Reaching from heaven to earth a Cloud & Human form" (37:14). Rahab, also known as Mystery Babylon or religion hid in war, dwells in the striking desolation of Satan's bosom, constituting both in herself and in conjunction with Satan a male-female hermaphrodite. Finally, Ololon (a mirror image of Rahab Babylon) literalizes the second, female-male version of hermaphroditism: she (re)descends to Felpham's Vale "as a moony Ark" (42:7), thereby replacing the simile, "A Male within a Female hid *as in* an Ark & Curtains" with the (poetic) actuality of a moony Ark which becomes the covering (curtain) of a garment dipped in blood.

Milton's *Paradise Lost* complicated Greek-style myths of war in heaven with the sexual politics of a fall from grace, intensifying the familiar association of sex and war already present in Greek and Roman models. But Blake's epic chronology insists that sexual reconfiguration of war in heaven has been complemented in historical terms by religious war on earth. Within this chronology, the hermaphrodite becomes an epic image for the confusion of religion and war—and its alienating effects. Where erotic energy joins separate bodies together in sexual consummation, the hermaphrodite displays two sexes at odds in a single body. Blake's use of

the hermaphrodite seems more than purely metaphoric or coincidental: in the eighteenth century more generally, this biologically coded figure marked a point of slippage between political disruption and physical identity. According to Randolph Trumbach, for instance, the eighteenth century marked a gradual transition from a system centered around two genders (male and female) and three sexes (men, women and hermaphrodites) to a system including four genders (heterosexual men and women and homosexual men and women) and two sexes (male and female). At the beginning of the century,

> sodomitical acts contravened the gender system only when they violated the patriarchal code, that is when adult men allowed themselves to be penetrated and when women penetrated women. Because there was no third gender to which to assign individuals who inverted the patriarchal order in their sexual acts by penetrating or being penetrated in violation of their gender status, such persons were likely to be classified as hermaphrodites, that is as biologically deviant. In men, this classification was sometimes understood to be symbolic, but in the case of women, they were likely to be examined by doctors for signs of actual clitoral enlargement.[12]

The hermaphrodite thus provided an image for deviance at once sexual and political—a deviance for which biological grounding seemed more essential for women than for men. Over the course of the century, sexual behavior comes to be discussed more in terms of two sexes, (male and female), two "normal" genders (heterosexual men and women) and two deviant genders (the molly and the tommy, or in upper-class terms, the sodomite and the sapphist). Yet the development of a deviant female gender (the sapphist) lagged behind that of the male: sapphism was slower to be named, described, recognized. The metaphorical use of "hermaphrodite" for men shifted relatively quickly towards the use of the term sodomite or molly; while "hermaphrodite" was sometimes applied to women in a metaphorical sense at the beginning of the century, "its purpose was usually to stigmatize female clothing that seemed to impinge on the male domain" [Trumbach 116-17]. The turn to biology in explaining female sexual deviance led to a strong association of hermaphroditism with female biology: not that all women were hermaphrodites, but for writers such as James Parsons, all hermaphrodites were likely to be women.[13] Other writers warned that mutual masturbation in young girls "would result in the enlargement of the clitoris and that this might eventually cause them to be classified as hermaphrodites" [Trumbach 118]. The figure of the hermaphrodite could thus be used to stigmatize women's use of "masculine" clothing and female homoeroticism, even when the latter did not include penetration.

The asymmetry between male and female hermaphroditism and the link between charges of female hermaphroditism and masculine dress are both central to Blake's deployment of the figure. He privileges hermaphroditism imagined as a male-within-a-female (forerunner of the tommy or sapphist), and devalues that of a female-within-a-male (forerunner of the molly or sodomite). At the same time, however, Blake also privileges male homoeroticism, and presents the transformative potential of the hermaphrodite as depending upon the (politically conservative) relations established between its male and female parts. Within *Milton,* militarized religion and warlike Selfhood can be superseded only through the transformation of Milton's relation to his female Emanation. Such a transformation depends both on Milton's willingness to seek out and redeem his Emanation—and on Ololon's willingness to accept a subordinate role in relation to Milton, 'her' willingness to take on the eccentric and external role of the garment.

The end of the prophecy rewrites Ololon's expulsion of Milton from Eden into an (apparently) less threatening confrontation between man and woman. Both Ololon and Milton can be seen as hermaphroditic forms (Milton a "giant form hermaphroditic," Ololon a neuter virgin composed of male multitudes in Eden), yet their confrontation is staged not only as a struggle for self-recognition and understanding, but also as a battle between the sexes. The prophecy claims that Ololon "could not step into Vegetable Worlds without becoming / The enemies of Humanity except in a Female Form"—though the logic behind this claim is never elucidated. Ololon (first a plural then once again a female figure) gradually "recognize/s" the form they themselves have unwittingly taken on and the space in which they find themselves. Specifically, Ololon describe themselves as a female form, and as a contrary to Milton's masculinity: "Is this our Femin[in]e Portion the Six-fold Miltonic Female / . . . are we Contraries O Milton, Thou & I?" [41:30-35]. As male and female figures, Milton and Ololon can more clearly be seen as contraries: this recognition of sexual opposition undoes the necessity of war, which now can be presented as a mistake, almost as an accident. "O Immortal! how were we led to War the Wars of Death"? [41:36] This recognition also transforms the "Void Outside of Existence" into "a Womb"—but the womb is also the (masculine) "Death Couch of Albion" (41:37-42:1).

To move beyond these deathly forms, Ololon is asked to recognize and acknowledge her/their contribution to the figure of the Covering Cherub—a recognition which will lead in turn to a demand for self-annihilation. In dialogue with Milton, Ololon defines herself as the paradoxical cause of violence, having produced in multiple human forms the "absurdity" of Natural Religion and the cruelty associated with moral virtue. This self-

definition remains inseparable from the figure of the hermaphroditic female-within-the-male:

> Are those who contemn Religion & seek to annihilate it
> Become in their Femin[in]e portions the cause and promoters
> Of these Religions, how is this thing? This Newtonian Phantasm
> This Voltaire & Rousseau: this Hume & Gibbon & Bolingbroke
> This Natural Religion! this impossible absurdity
> Is Ololon the cause of this? O where shall I hide my face?
> These tears fall for the little-ones: the Children of Jerusalem
> Lest they be annihilated in thy annihilation.
>
> No sooner had she spoke but Rahab Babylon appeard
> Eastward upon the Paved work across Europe & Asia
> Glorious as the midday Sun in Satans bosom glowing:
> A Female hidden in a Male, Religion hidden in War
> Namd Moral Virtue; cruel two-fold Monster shining bright
> A Dragon red & hidden Harlot which John in Patmos saw.
>
> (40:9-22)

The first of these stanzas implicitly presents a series of hermaphrodites: Newton, Voltaire, Rousseau, Hume, Gibbon and Bolingbroke are men considered in their "feminine portions": this combination of masculinity and femininity comprises Natural Religion as an impossible absurdity. The second stanza frames that impossible absurdity as a female character Rahab (herself a hermaphrodite: the feminine portion of the preceding list of names) within a male: Satan. The figure of the hermaphrodite is inwardly doubled: a "two-fold Monster" seen by a male prophet, John in Patmos. Ololon's self-indictment exposes the symbolic contradiction of sceptical philosophy and moral virtue. The desire to hide 'her' face is spoken rather than acted out: Ololon's articulation of shame and responsibility means Rahab can no longer remain hidden in Satan. Yet Ololon's rejection of this contradiction reinscribes her as female as she weeps over the Children of Jerusalem.

Ololon's articulation of her/their faults presents a self-indictment parallel to (though more extended than) Milton's earlier acknowledgment "I in my Selfhood am that Satan!" The act of self-annihilation appears at first an equally symmetrical endeavor. Milton commands Ololon with "terrible majesty" to follow his example:

> Obey thou the Words of the Inspired Man
> All that can be annihilated must be annihilated
> That the Children of Jerusalem may be saved from slavery
> There is a Negation, & there is a Contrary
> The Negation must be destroyd to redeem the Contraries

> The Negation is the Spectre; the Reasoning Power in Man
> This is a false Body: an Incrustation over my Immortal
> Spirit; a Selfhood, which must be put off & annihilated alway
> To cleanse the Face of my Spirit by Self-examination.
>
> To bathe in the Waters of Life; to wash off the Not Human
> I come in Self-annihilation & the grandeur of Inspiration.
>
> (40:29-41:2)

It's not entirely clear from this speech which of Milton's words are to be obeyed, for rather than giving instructions to Ololon, he describes the actions he himself should take. Satan has been described as Milton's Spectre: this then is the Negation, the false Body, the Incrustation which must be put off. Milton shows Ololon what to do by his own example. Yet Satan, last seen thundering on the stormy sea, is never clearly put off, never clearly annihilated: he simply remains unmentioned through the remainder of the poem. And the prophecy represents Ololon's and Milton's separate experiences of self-annihilation in strikingly asymmetrical terms.

Ololon's self-annihilation seems by far the more explicit: the figure of the virgin divides into six parts "with a shriek / Dolorous that ran thro all Creation" and disappears into the depths of Milton's shadow. What remains of Ololon then takes on a series of non-human forms: an ark, clouds of blood, streams of gore and finally a "Garment dipped in blood" which is itself a "litteral expression" of divine revelation. Self-annihilation figured as loss of virginity seems at best an experience of violence, a loss of autonomy and agency. Milton's self-annihilation, by contrast, seems far more gradual, peaceful and creative. His image of self-annihilation as "bath[ing] in the Waters of Life" both recalls and revises Urizen's attempt to baptize Milton in the icy waters of the Jordan. Milton's response is that of the sculptor-artist: he humanizes the demon Urizen by reshaping his figure with warm clay.

> Silent they met, and silent strove among the streams, of Arnon
> Even to Mahanaim, when with cold hand Urizen stoop'd down
> And took up water from the river Jordan: pouring on
> To Miltons brain the icy fluid from his broad cold palm.
> But Milton took of the red clay of Succoth, moulding it with care
> Between his palms: and filling up the furrows of many years
> Beginning at the feet of Ruizen, and on the bones

Creating new flesh on the Demon cold, and building him,
As with new clay a Human form in the Valley of Beth Peor.

(18:51-19:14)

> Silent Milton stood
> before
> The darkend Urizen; as the sculptor silent stands before
> His forming image; he walks round it patient labouring.

(20:7-9)

These passages undo the not-Human by a process of addition and accretion, rather than the casting off described to Ololon, or even the washing off described in 41:2. Milton's silence marks the absence of Ololon's "shriek / Dolorous"—but whether this suggests his greater self-control or her greater suffering is difficult to determine. The moment of self-annihilation in this struggle between men ("one giving life, the other death / To his adversary" [19:29-30]) seems to come when "Urizen faints in terror striving among the Brooks of Arnon / With Miltons Spirit" (39:53-54). Blake draws attention to this moment with the image (already discussed) of plate 41; the fact that Bentley reads this image as a figure of the female Ololon highlights the potentially erotic connection between the two men. The "great Miltonic marriage" Bloom envisions occurring between Milton and Ololon is not much of a marriage—the two figures never touch as man and woman—they come together only as Jesus and the garment of God. Yet Milton and the fainting Urizen do in fact touch: in this moment of surrender, Milton supports the humanized Urizen, whose icy, stony façade is finally undone. If a marriage occurs in **Milton,** it is not the heterosexual union of contraries, but rather an intensification of similarities: Milton announces that he himself is Satan, whom Los and Enitharmon have already recognized as Urizen. Milton striving with Urizen reshapes himself in Human form. At the same time, however, this re-union of the self is framed as a homoerotic attraction of opposite types: the redeemed and the elect who meet on Albion's hills. And after Ololon's transformation into the non-human forms of ark and bloody garment, Milton joins with the Starry Eight to become "One Man," the figure of Jesus. The act of self-annihilation is thus profoundly asymmetrical: Ololon, a female (and a) hermaphrodite, vanishes, sublimated into symbols surrounding the masculine figure of Jesus—a figure produced by the intensification, the homoerotic doubling of the male (and hermaphroditic) subject.[14]

The asymmetry between Ololon and Milton turns on a rough equation of femininity with forms of clothing—covering and revelation at once—and of masculinity with humanity. Milton's call to self-annihilation returns repeatedly to degraded examples of the garment imagery that resounds throughout the poem:

> To cast off Rational Demonstration by Faith in the Saviour
> To cast off the rotten rags of Memory by Inspiration
> To cast off Bacon, Locke & Newton from Albions covering
> To take off his filthy garments, & clothe him with Imagination

(41:3-6)

The clothing motif vanishes into talk of Poetry, State Government and moral hypocrisy, only to return in the closing lines of this address:

> These are the Sexual Garments, the Abomination of Desolation
> Hiding the Human Lineaments as with an Ark & Curtains
> Which Jesus rent: & now shall wholly purge away with Fire
> Till Generation is swallowed up in Regeneration.

(41:25-28)

Ololon's response suggests that these sexual garments are specifically associated with *female* sexuality.[15] They progress (in 'her' voice) from a recognition of "our Femin[in]e Portion the Six-fold Miltonic Female" to an acceptance of partial responsibility for gendered violence ("O Immortal! how were we led to War the Wars of Death"?) to a self-purging of (virgin) femininity:

> So saying, the Virgin divided Six-fold & with a shriek
> Dolorous that ran thro all Creation a Double Six-fold Wonder!
> Away from Ololon she divided & fled into the depths
> Of Miltons Shadow as a Dove upon the stormy Sea.

(42:3-6)

Ololon's subsequent forms suggest how difficult Blake found it to purge "Sexual Garments" from "Human Lineaments." Once the figure of the virgin has been annihilated, rather than taking on other human forms, becoming capable of experiencing and "authoring" revelation, Ololon is all the more firmly equated with the role of (bloody) garment, upon which revelation is "literally" written. Thus while Blake's first, largely metaphoric invocation of hermaphroditism serves to unsettle assumptions of female responsibility for humanity's fall from grace, his more concrete or literal deployment of the figure seems to limit women's role in revelation to the first stages of transformation: subordination and self-annihilation.

As "Common opinion" in the eighteenth century shifted from a focus on three bodies to a focus on two bodies ("male and female created he them"), Blake invoked the already outdated concept of the hermaphrodite to shift from two bodies (male and female) to one body

alone. In his work, the hermaphrodite comes to be a figure for sexual division—for the mistaken belief in differentiated male and female bodies when (outside the limits of Generation) the poet will admit the existence of only one "Human" body. Yet that one body remains male. Blake's denial of two biological sexes can be read as both profoundly radical and profoundly conservative, as more recent debates around the claim "Woman does not exist" may demonstrate. On the one hand, a single Human body solves the kinds of problems Mary Wollstonecraft encountered in her attempt to claim for women "male" virtues and education. If Humanity lies beyond sexual division, all members of that single humanity have an equal claim to virtue and education. On the other hand, Blake rather notably does *not* succeed in writing beyond the sexes: the female remains within the structure of his prophecies as a degraded or an invisible term.

As Milton's "terrible majesty" in addressing Ololon-as-virgin may suggest, this prophetic structure reinscribes and supports patriarchal, even monarchical, systems of power. Yet Blake's more explicit political project remains the radically democratic attempt to create prophets. Within the world of the prophecy, the category of sex remains both a constraint (when sex is understood as biological fixity) and as a source of power and energy (when sex is understood as erotic desire). "The Sexual is Threefold: the Human is Fourfold"—but *Milton* repeatedly demonstrates the difficulty (one might say impossibility) of thinking beyond the boundaries of the sexual.

3

The Preface to *Milton* calls upon contemporary artists to transcend the constraints of social support and critique—and to move beyond Greek and Roman models for painting and literature. As a whole, the prophecy works to purge the Christian epic *Paradise Lost* of an over-reliance on the warlike conventions of the classical epic. Yet *Paradise Lost* itself brought the conventions of warlike selfhood home to seventeenth-century England. This Christian epic links war in heaven to strife on earth as it denounces the inversion of traditional sexual politics: strife appears as daughters seduce fathers (Sin and Satan) and wives persuade their husbands to sin (Eve and Adam). Blake's *Milton* seems to accept the premise that relations between men and women ideally require the willing subordination of women. It complicates this premise by trying to present men and women as two halves of a single (married) identity—but as Blackstone would remind us, that single identity remains that of the man. The only role remaining for women seems to be that of the garment. I want to argue that Blake's association of female identity with garment imagery is another ambivalent bequest from the Greek and Roman models he was attempting to re-

vise or supersede: it appears perhaps most clearly in the painter James Barry's contemporary epic, *The Birth of Pandora*. . . .

Since there is no direct evidence that Blake was influenced by Barry's *Birth of Pandora,* I will try to limit myself to pointing out what seem to me a remarkable set of parallels. Both artists clearly knew of and respected each other's work[16]—and both demonstrated a visual and conceptual fascination with *Paradise Lost.* During the 1790's, Barry engaged in two large-scale projects: one vast canvas depicting the Olympian gods at the birth of Pandora and a series of illustrations from *Paradise Lost.* As a result of various career problems (including his expulsion from the Royal Academy), Barry never completed the *Paradise Lost* series. Still, extant paintings show intersections between Barry's work and Blake's painting: "Fire" from *Tiriel* may have influenced or been influenced by Barry's "Satan calling the Legions,"[17] and the frontispiece to *Milton* . . . is loosely reminiscent of Barry's *Satan, Sin and Death.* . . . In this latter example, Blake replaces the armed struggle between Satan and Death with Milton's raised arm, which seems to call a halt to that earlier struggle, even as it marks the splitting of the self, the name "MIL/TON."[18]

Between 1790 and 1809, Barry produced three markedly varied descriptions of his Pandora project. John Barrell suggests that in each account,

> whatever else the proposed picture is required to do, it has one task which never changes: to define and to preserve the difference between male and female, as if for Barry that difference is felt to be confused and blurred. . . . Barry's seemingly endless involvement with the Pandora project reveals how the question of sexual differentiation is inseparable from that other, no less intractable question, of the origins and the political function of art.[19]

Barry's first extended description of the piece presents Pandora as the joint creation of the Olympians: the product which unifies a community visibly differentiated by gender and occupation. The female (and highly sexualized) figure of Pandora becomes a visual key for social unity. This first framing of the Pandora project is likely to have held little appeal for Blake: one suspects that a society unified by—and thus in part subordinated to—a figure of female sexuality and passivity would have seemed to him more of a perversion than an ideal.

In his second description of the painting, his 1798 *Letter to the Dilettanti Society,* Barry presents Minerva, goddess of painting (in tapestry), as the figure linking the Birth to Pandora to the origins of painting.[20] Minerva, the most masculine (and hermaphroditic) of Olympian goddesses, at first appears to sustain the "Master art" of painting in its public, cognitive function: the

kind of painting she is said to represent advances well beyond the lower art of "merely copying . . . actual, casual, ordinary nature" to produce a "new moulding and imitation" of nature. The Greeks "reserved this Master Art, this Art par excellence, to employ the . . . exertions and skill of the mistress of all, of Minerva, or Wisdom itself" (2: 586). Yet as Barry focuses on the scene of Minerva teaching Pandora to paint (in tapestry), the lessons of "this Art par excellence" are rapidly subordinated to the lessons of femininity:

> an art which was capable of being made subservient to all the social duties, and where it was impossible to excel in it, without the acquisition of such information, respecting all the concerns and dearest interests of humanity, as could not fail, when joined with the superior sentiment and graces of feminine softness, to become the solace and anodyne against the numberless and unavoidable miseries of life: and as wives, mothers, daughters, sisters, citizens, and above all, as friends, these endearing accomplishments . . . could not fail of rendering them the graceful ornaments of all stations.
>
> (2: 595)

Barry's "Master art" of public representations and cognition begins to seem indistinguishable from the arts of the mistress of the house—an affair for the Dilettanti Society after all. The tension at work in this description of the painting is also visually encoded at its center, as Pandora's upswept hair recalls Barry's earlier *Venus*. . . . Thus while the goddess of Love appears *in propria persona* on the left of the painting, she is also visually present in the reclining figure Minerva attempts to instruct. Painting becomes a hermaphroditic art, mingling elements of masculine skill and wisdom with those of feminine consolation.

Barry's *Birth of Pandora* places two female figures at the center of society: the goddess of wisdom, visibly associated with a figure of female sexuality through a garment which records one Greek myth of "war in heaven." The garment Minerva displays to Pandora is described in 1798 as "a tapestry robe . . . in which is represented . . . the story of Jove fulminating the Titans, or the punishment of that pride and arrogance which was likely soon to become apparent in the descendants of poor Pandora" (2: 595). As Minerva exhorts Pandora "to the performance of . . . respectable matrimonial duties," she also holds up before her student a picture of what happens to those who rebel. In Barry's "Fragment on Pandora" (written c. 1805, published posthumously 1809), the fabric becomes a more ceremonial covering:

> While Pandora is thus dressing by the Graces, her head is attentively turned towards Minerva, who with one hand is shewing her a shuttle, and earnestly exhorting her to the performance of those respectable matrimonial duties, the essence of which depends on the acquisition of that intimate knowledge of manners and

things, which will enable her to design and fabricate such tapestry (truly feminine work) as the famous Peplon, or covering, which Minerva is holding up in the other hand.

> (2: 153)

The "famous Peplon" was, according to Barry and his sources, "the principle ornament" of the Panathenea, which was in turn a festival celebrating the political unity of Athens. The Peplus was embroidered by the virgins of the city; on it was represented "the battle of the gods and giants. Amongst the gods was Jupiter hurling his thunder-bolts against that rebellious crew, and Minerva seated in her chariot, appearing the vanquisher of Typhon, or Encalladus" (2: 158). Thus the design of the robe held by Minerva remains roughly constant between 1798 and 1809, though in Barry's later description, local politics mingled with divine mythology: "The names of those Athenians who had been eminent for military virtue, were also embroidered on it; Potter says, had their effigies on it, whence men of true courage and bravery were said to be Axiou tou peplou, i.e., worthy of the Peplus" (2: 158). Barry's final account of the scene of Pandora's instruction thus attempts to reconcile strikingly different approaches to art—so that the public celebration of military virtue can be paradoxically described as "truly feminine work." Yet as John Barrell notes, "the solution thus proposed to the problem of gender can equally be read as a new version of the problem itself. What had been a function of the body in history painting has simply been displaced onto an item of clothing, and an item of female clothing at that" (186).

Blake's *Milton* reenacts Barry's gesture of displacement as a structural conflation or condensation of divergent terms. Garments in *Milton* appear not as a solution to the problem of gender, but as a peculiarly female embodiment of suffering. Indeed, Barry's description of the Peplus as woven by virgins and celebrating Athenian military valor through embroidered effigies of military heroes seems almost a perfect prototype for the garments of the Shadowy Female:

> My Garments shall be woven of sighs & heart broken
> lamentations.
> The misery of unhappy Families shall be drawn out
> into its border
> Wrought with the needle with dire sufferings, poverty,
> pain and woe
> Along the rocky Island & thence throughout the whole
> Earth
> There shall be the sick Father & his starving Family:
> there
> The Prisoner in the stone Dungeon & the Slave at the
> Mill
> I will have writings written all over it in Human Words
> That every Infant that is born upon the Earth shall
> read
> And get by rote as a hard task of a life of sixty years.

I will have Kings inwoven upon it & Councellors &
 Mighty Men.
The Famine shall clasp it together with buckles &
 Clasps
And the Pestilence shall be its fringe & the War its
 girdle
To divide into Rahab & Tirzah that Milton may come
 to our tents
For I will put on the Human Form & take the Image
 of God,
Even Pity & Humanity, but my Clothing shall be Cru-
 elty
And I will put on Holiness as a breastplate & as a hel-
 met
And all my ornaments shall be of the gold of broken
 hearts
And the precious stones of anxiety & care & despera-
 tion & death
And repentance for sin & sorrow & punishment &
 fear
To defend me from thy terrors O Orc! my only be-
 loved!

(18:5-25)

In place of Minerva instructing Pandora in the "acquisi-
tion of an intimate knowledge of manners and things,"
the lessons of the Shadowy Female are to be learned by
every human being "as a hard task of sixty years."
These are the lessons of misery: "dire sufferings, pov-
erty, pain and woe." As military heroes were embroi-
dered on the peplon, so kings, counsellors and mighty
men are inwoven on these garments—once again, Greek
and Roman models lead to pomp of warlike selfhood.
The Shadowy Female warns, "I will put on the Human
Form & take the Image of God, / Even Pity & Human-
ity, but my Clothing shall be Cruelty / And I will put on
Holiness as a breastplate & as a helmet." In Barry's
painting, Minerva appears dressed in a helmet and a
somewhat softened breastplate; her face is stern, per-
haps even cruel.

Orc's rebuke to the Shadowy Female re-presents her
garments as a Satan and a Covering Cherub; he also
tries to return his mate to her properly Female Form:

Orc answered. Take not the Human Form O loveliest.
 Take not
Terror upon thee! Behold how I am & tremble lest
 thou also
Consume in my Consummation; but thou maist take a
 Form
Female & lovely, that cannot consume in Mans con-
 summation
Wherefore dost thou Create & Weave this Satan for a
 Covering [?]
When thou attemptest to put on the Human Form, my
 wrath
Burns to the top of heaven against thee in Jealousy &
 Fear.
Then I rend thee asunder, then I howl over thy clay &
 ashes
When wilt thou put on the Female Form as in times
 of old

With a Garment of Pity & Compassion like the Gar-
 ment of God
His garments are long sufferings for the Children of
 Men
Jerusalem is his Garment & not thy Covering Cherub
 O lovely
Shadow of my delight who wanderest seeking for the
 prey.

(18:4-38)

In many ways, this is an artist's critique: the Shadowy
Female and Barry alike have no business equating an
eternal with a merely mortal form—for such an equa-
tion results in the human form becoming Satan, the
Covering Cherub. Yet there exists a proper "Female
Form" to which the Shadowy Female should return:
Orc's speech suggests that Jerusalem, the garment of
God, may offer a redeemed version of this Satanic cov-
ering. Both garments—that of the Shadowy Female and
Jerusalem alike—represent suffering, but while the
former actually creates suffering, the latter (Jerusalem
as the Garment of God) becomes the means by which
the Divine Saviour takes on himself the sufferings of
humanity. At the end of the prophecy, Jerusalem ap-
pears as the figure of Ololon redeemed: the garment of
God, represented in brief succession as a multitude, a
virgin, a dove, an ark, clouds of blood and streams of
gore and finally a garment dipped in blood:

Then as a Moony Ark Ololon descended to Felphams
 Vale
In clouds of blood, in streams of gore, with dreadful
 thunderings
Into the Fires of Intellect that rejoic'd in Felphams
 Vale
Around the Starry Eight: with one accord the Starry
 Eight became
One Man Jesus the Saviour. wonderful! round his
 limbs
The Clouds of Ololon folded as a Garment dipped in
 blood
Written within & without in woven letters: & the Writ-
 ing
Is the Divine Revelation in the Litteral expression:
A Garment of War, I heard it namd the Woof of Six
 Thousand Years.

(42:7-15)

This garment dipped in blood is uncannily close to the
garments of the Shadowy Female: both fabrics bear
writing, both are named as garments of war. The Shad-
owy Female adorns her garment with "writings written
all over it in Human Words;" the garment which Ololon
becomes is likewise "Written within & without in wo-
ven letters"—but in the place of Human Words, this
writing becomes "the Divine Revelation in the Litteral
expression." Every human being, "every Infant that is
born upon the Earth shall read / And get by rote as a
hard task of a life of sixty years" the writing contained
within the garment of the Shadowy Female; the gar-
ment which is Ololon must be learned not by rote but

by heart over the course of Six Thousand Years—that space of time in which the Poet's Work is done.

Blake's insistence on the centrality of the Poet's Work, and the excentricity of female figures and garment imagery parallels Barry's final conceptual revision of *The Birth of Pandora.* The painter's extended "Fragment on Pandora" maintains the scene of Minerva instructing Pandora as the center of the project, but the terms of creation have been extensively reframed. In his description of the painting, Barry promotes Vulcan to the position of artist-in-chief: "Calliope (the most advanced figure of the muses, who attentively surround Apollo) has her hand on the shoulder of Vulcan, as it were (agreeably to her office) pointing him out as the ingenious, sublime artificer of that Pandora, whose education and interests occupy the attention of the whole assembly" (2: 154). Barry likewise shifts the reader's attention away from the kind of painting Pandora is being taught, towards the kinds of creation ascribed to the limping god:

> whilst the fascinating manners and mental qualities of Pandora are made to be the gift of other gods, yet the substratum or material fabrication, organization, and vitality, are obtained from the complicated energies and skill of Vulcan, whose character (instead of the mere blacksmith) is by this ingenious and most apposite fable, exalted into the more sublime symbol of the active principle, the busy element of fire, the great operator even of the other elementary energies which counteract the torpor and inertness of mere material things
>
> (2: 154)

As Barry emphasized Vulcan's role in the creation of Pandora, Blake makes a sculptor-blacksmith the hero of his narrative and the center of his prophecy. Milton and Los are both shapers of inanimate matter, and midway through the poem Los joins with Blake, the poem's hero-in-waiting. Like Vulcan, Los (the Spirit of Prophecy) is an "ingenious sublime artificer," albeit one who continues to labor at his forge: his Sons are sculptors and artists. Yet the real art of prophecy appears only when the descending poet Milton himself becomes a sculptor: "Silent Milton stood before / The darkened Urizen; as the sculptor silent stands before / His forming image; he walks round it patient labouring." In Hesiod's *Theogony* and *Works and Days,* Hephaistos, the limping god, is one of the gods largely responsible for crafting Pandora as a *kalon kakon,* a "beautiful evil." In Barry's account of the "Birth of Pandora," Vulcan provides the material "fabrication, organization and vitality" which supports the gifts of all the other gods; meanwhile Barry separates the "evil" of Pandora from her body into the contents of "that fatal vase" (2: 154). In Blake's *Milton,* by contrast, the emblematic labor of the prophetic artist is neither the creation of a beautiful evil nor the mere fabrication and organization of raw materials; rather, the prophet's arduous task is to transform the icy intellect, to humanize the demons of Ab-

stract Horror and perceptual limitation (Urizen as the boundary of the *horizon*).

As we have seen, Barry's description of the *Birth of Pandora* tends to present the scene of instruction as the center of the painting; yet in seeking the center, the viewer's eye is also drawn to the figure of the third Grace who is in the process of tying a sandal on Pandora's extended foot. In the right foreground as well, "Mercury putting on his talaria [winged sandals] is preparing to carry down Pandora to her destined husband" (2: 154). This doubled donning of sandals recurs, oddly rearranged, in **Milton.** After Milton has fallen into Blake's left foot,

> all this Vegetable World appeard on my left Foot,
> As a bright sandal formd immortal of precious stones & gold:
> I stooped down & bound it on to walk forward thro' Eternity
>
> (21:12-14)

Where Barry's Vulcan organizes bits and pieces of inanimate matter into a female form, Blake shows the entire Vegetable World, still unified, suddenly transformed into a humble article of prophetic apparel. (It would hardly do, in Blake's terms, for a figure of the Eternal Great Humanity Divine to be composed out of some primal soup of dismembered parts.) While Barry's Pandora is to be *carried* to her destined husband, Blake's sandal is designed explicitly for *walking* through Eternity; in these terms, the character Blake seems closer to the figure of Mercury than to that of Pandora. Blake does indeed appear to move forward through (or into) Eternity, for the next stanza brings the poem's first mention of Ololon, and of the lamentations that will lead to Ololon's descent. And even as Ololon begins to be shaped as a composite figure, made up of multitudes, so the character Blake is refigured in composite terms, combined with Los:

> While Los heard indistinct in fear, what time I bound my sandals
> On; to walk forward thro' Eternity, Los descended to me:
> And Los behind me stood; a terrible flaming Sun: just close
> Behind my back; I turned round in terror, and behold.
> Los stood in that fierce glowing fire; & he also stoop'd down
> And bound my sandals on in Udan-Adan; trembling I stood
> Exceedingly with fear & terror, standing in the Vale
> Of Lambeth: but he kissed me and wishd me health.
> And I became One Man with him arising in my strength:
> Twas too late now to recede. Los had enterd into my soul:
> His terrors now posses'd me whole! I arose in fury & strength.
>
> (22:4-14)

While the Graces, Mercury and Pandora all remained distinct, Blake and Los become a single, composite form. The energies of this passage seem (fiercely, flamingly) erotic as well as creative: the design . . . positions Blake's kneeling figure in between the legs of the sun-god; Blake's head, turned backwards to face Los, is just slightly lower than the juncture of those legs. The two men kiss; Los "enters" Blake's soul and in emotional terms "possess[es] him whole"—and Blake is strengthened by the experience of possession.

At the same time, Los stooping down to bind on Blake's sandals establishes Blake in the position of Barry's Pandora, being dressed by an immortal. (The erotic charge of Pandora's upswept hair may also have been channeled into this moment of union between the two prophets.) Joseph Wittreich points out that within the conventions of prophecy "to strap on the sandal is a sign that the prophet, no longer impoverished, has achieved an integrated personality, is about to throw 'his whole self into his prophecy', making 'not his lips alone, but his whole personality,' the vehicle for the divine word" (Wittreich 250). The reshuffling (so to speak) of sandals replaces Pandora, the created female, with the combined figure of Blake and Los, the integrated prophet and creative male artist. What cannot be integrated is the figure of Pandora. Blake and Los remain unified through an item of clothing, the sandal, which points back toward that unrecuperable supplement.

By the conclusion of the poem, not only the sandal but also the garment imagery identified with the Covering Cherub has become a figure for poet and prophecy combined. But here again it is Ololon rather than Blake who has thrown their/her/its whole self into the prophecy, and as a result, ceased to appear in human form (at least for the duration of this poem). The twelve-year-old virgin and the Eternal Host alike sacrifice themselves to the prophecy: rather than giving voice to the prophecy, they give their lives. In Barry, the peplus depicts male figures and connects two female figures. In Blake, the garment dipped in blood is still a female figure (Jerusalem) connecting two men: Jesus/Milton and Blake, the man who bears witness to this prophecy. Like the sandal on which Blake walks forward through eternity, this garment, once female and now a literal expression of the divine revelation, ties vision back to earth. Blake says of his union with Los: "I became One Man with him arising in my strength." So too the Starry Eight become "One Man Jesus the Saviour. wonderful!" In each case, however, this One Man seems to be grounded in a vanished female figure whose return to inanimate matter lends sacrificial strength to the prophet. Blake's "One Man," his rejection of sexual duality depends upon an ever-present, ever-vanishing and devalued female term. Perhaps for this reason, within the six thousand years of the Poet's Work in the realm of Generation, Ololon continues to appear as a "Garment of war."

4

The comparison of Blake's prophecy with Barry's life project indicates the extent to which the politics of art are inseparable from the politics of gender (more specifically, perhaps, the politics of masculinity) during the early romantic period. I have tried to argue for the importance of considering such gender politics within a slightly larger historical context. The eighteenth century, shifting from three sexes to two, produced two (asymmetrically) stigmatized genders: the sodomite and the sapphist. Blake, in moving from two sexes to one, seems to produce two stigmatized sexes—women and hermaphrodites—as he privileges men and creates a space for an unstigmatized homoeroticism. Yet this is perhaps too unified and coherent a reading of the poem: Satan's delusive love for Palamabron is condemned (if only for its delusion) and hermaphrodites are often described as both beautiful and cruel in a poem which emphasizes the cruelty of almost all created forms.

One might do better to note the prevalence of sexual deviance in a poem delivering a call to action in an age which equated sexual and political deviance quite directly. Blake's One Man, challenging the heterosexual base of patriarchy, can be read as a profoundly political figure—though its politics carry dangerous consequences for women. Barry gradually dethrones the female figures at the center of his epic painting; Blake unravels the female (Ololon) at the turning point of his prophetic narrative. Blake's construction of the One Man produces a proliferation of whores, hermaphrodites and homoeroticism in *Milton*—a violent irony in view of the poem's title character—but the treatment of women and hermaphrodites within the prophecy might be said to comprise Blake's own Covering Cherub as well as that of his predecessor.

Still, there is a Self within that (masculine) Hood, for Blake as for Milton—and Blake's Self becomes visible in part through the dramatic limits of his ability to see Ololon and Milton at the close of the poem. In *A Vision of the Last Judgment,* Blake says that in relation to Chronos or Time, "I have 'however' somewhat accomodated my Figure of Time to 'the' Common opinion as I myself am also infected with it & my Visions also infected & I see Time Aged alas too much so." In the very next paragraph, he goes on to assert, "Allegories are things that Relate to Moral Virtues Moral Virtues do not Exist they are Allegories & dissimulations 'But Time & Space are Real Beings a Male & a Female Time is a Man Space is a Woman & her Masculine Portion is Death'" (563). The assertion "But Time & Space

are Real Beings a Male & a Female" sounds especially odd, following as it does this tautology of allegorical non-existence, and Blake's earlier acknowledgement of infected vision. The positioning of the gendered formula, "Time is a Man Space is a Woman & her Masculine Portion is Death," invites us to read it also as an infection of vision, as an allegory and a dissimulation.

The formula "Time is a Man Space is a Woman" places gender and division at the heart of the poet's work, for time and space are the raw material of poetic creation. But error is also raw material for poetry. In *A Vision of the Last Judgment,* Blake conflates error and creation:

> Error is Created Truth is Eternal Error or Creation will be Burned Up & then & not till then Truth or Eternity will appear It is Burnt up the Moment Men cease to behold it I assert for My self that I do not behold the Outward Creation & that to me it is hindrance & not Action it is as the Dirt upon my feet No part of Me.
>
> (565)

The syntax here conflates error and creation: both exist only to be burnt up, unbeheld, to define what is "No part of Me." Yet if creation and error are synonymous, how is the poet to justify his own acts of creation (error)? This passage suggests that creation and prophecy are not necessarily equivalent (or even assimilable) terms: prophecy presents a call to annihilation, to the conflagration that ushers in Eternity; poetry and art create mistaken yet consoling forms. Blake becomes One Man not with Milton, annihilating himself to become the Divine Saviour, but rather with the Shadowy Prophet Los(s), whose sons devote themselves to adorning (and thus perpetuating) Satanic space.

Still those ornaments provide a source of sustenance. The most famous and most frequently excerpted passages of Book One transform time and space alike into imagination; they do so in part by envisioning time in spatial terms and space as a figure of Eternity:

> But others of the Sons of Los build Moments & Minutes & Hours
> And Days & Months & Years & Ages & Periods; wondrous buildings
> And every Moment has a Couch of gold for soft repose,
> (A Moment equals a pulsation of the artery)
> And between every two Moments stands a Daughter of Beulah
> To feed the Sleepers on their Couches with maternal care.
> And every Minute has an azure Tent with silken Veils.
> And every Hour has a bright golden Gate carved with skill.
> And every Day & Night, has Walls of brass & Gates of adamant,
> Shining like precious stones & ornamented with appropriate signs:
> And every Month, a silver paved Terrace builded high:

> And every Year, invulnerable Barriers with high Towers.
> And every Age is Moated deep with Bridges of silver & gold.
> And every Seven Ages is Incircled with a Flaming Fire.
> Now Seven Ages is amounting to Two Hundred Years
> Each has its Guard. each Moment Minute Hour Day Month & Year.
> All are the work of Fairy hands of the Four Elements
> The Guard are Angels of Providence on duty evermore . . .

While the material splendor of this passage entices and soothes, its terraces and precious stones also recall Satan's fall into opacity: "his bosom grew / Opake against the Divine Vision: the paved terraces of / His bosom inwards shone with fires, but the stones becoming opake!" (9:30-33). More generally, the emphasis on enclosure ("Walls of brass & Gates of adamant," "invulnerable Barriers," "Moated deep," "Incircled with a Flaming Fire") ought perhaps to raise suspicions. This passage produces a highly ornamented fortress mentality in relation to time; the close of the passage—its most famous lines—promptly renounces these elaborate enclosures:

> Every time less than a pulsation of the artery
> Is equal in its period & value to Six Thousand Years.
>
> For in this Period the Poets Work is Done: and all the Great
> Events of Time start forth & are concievd in such a Period
> Within a Moment: a Pulsation of the Artery.
>
> (28:44-29:3)

The "Pulsation of the Artery" places time quite specifically in the channels of the body even as it disrupts the elaborate and minute boundaries of "Moments & Minutes & Hours / And Days & Months & Years & Ages & Periods." Blake closes the circle of eternity by inserting "such a Period / Within a Moment": the largest unit fits back within the smallest. Here the Satanic translation of time into space is redeemed by being quite literally humanized—at once embodied in the pulsation of the artery and transformed into "Poets Work," the labors of the imagination.

Yet that pulsation of the artery also marks the limits of creation: limits that include the poet's own particular blindnesses and limitations. I began this essay at the end of the prophecy, and in many ways have been reading backwards all along. Let me end with the poem's beginning:

> Daughters of Beulah! Muses who inspire the Poets Song
> Record the journey of immortal Milton thro' your Realms
> Of terror & mild moony lustre, in soft sexual delusions

Of varied beauty, to delight the wanderer and repose
His burning thirst & freezing hunger!

 (2:1-5)

The Muses are to record Milton's journey in "soft sexual delusions of varied beauty": the record will be deluded, unevenly beautiful, and limited to what can be understood within the three-fold realm of sex. The journey can be recorded in no other way: if creation itself is error, poetic creation is soft sexual delusion. For Blake to speak four-fold, fully Human truth would be to watch his words burn up before his eyes. The prophecy as a whole is thus framed as error—but an error which produces varied beauty, capable of granting delight as it satisfies burning thirst and freezing hunger.

"Come down into my hand," Blake continues,

> By your mild power; descending down the Nerves of
> my right arm
> From out the Portals of my Brain, where by your min-
> istry
> The Eternal Great Humanity Divine. planted his Para-
> dise,
> And in it caus'd the Spectres of the Dead to take sweet
> forms
> In likeness of himself.
>
> (2:6-10)

The Eternity of mental strife Blake describes has of course been this world of his own imagination all along—an imagination set in the land of Albion—and the spectres that appear (Milton, Urizen, Satan) are likenesses of himself. If the spectral Milton must descend to retrieve and make peace with his Feminine Portion, his likeness to Blake suggests at least some prophetic awareness of the gender trouble distorting the prophecy. The prophecy itself is admittedly sexual delusion: Blake's Muses descending from his brain to offer him consolation, repose, delight. The One Man is in fact, one man. In his annotations to the Bishop of Llandaff's *Apology for the Bible,* Blake wrote:

> Prophets, in the modern sense of the word, have never existed Jonah was no prophet in the modern sense for his prophecy of Ninevah failed Every honest man is a Prophet he utters his opinion both of private and of public matters / Thus / If you go on So / the result is So / He never says such a thing shall happen let you do what you will. a Prophet is a Seer not an Arbitrary Dictator.
>
> (617)

As a prophet in the classical sense, Blake is perhaps most remarkable for his unflinching honesty. It remains possible to wonder, nonetheless, what prophetic songs Ololon and the Daughters of Enitharmon might have sung to Catherine Blake—and what an eighteenth-century prophet, an honest woman speaking her opinion of both private and public matters, might have made of Blake's *Milton.*

Notes

1. As most readers willing to tackle *Milton* will know, these levels consist of: 1) Eden, the realm of Eternity or human perfection; 2) Beulah, "evermore Created around Eternity" as a resting place for "all the weak & weary / Like Women and Children" (31:1-2); 3) Generation, the "vegetable world" in which we live; and 4) Ulro, a realm of materialist thought (like that of Bacon, Locke, Newton) and lifeless matter.

2. William Blake, *Milton, a poem in 12 Books,* plate 4:5. In *The Complete Poetry and Prose of William Blake,* eds. David Erdman and Harold Bloom (Berkeley: U of California P, 1982). Future references to this edition will be noted parenthetically in the body of the text. References to *Milton* will be by plate and line number; references to other works such as *A Vision of the Last Judgment (VLJ)* will be by page number.

3. I take these terms from Valerie Traub, "Desire and the Differences it Makes" in *The Matter of Difference: Materialist Criticism of Shakespeare,* ed. Valerie Wayne (Ithaca: Cornell UP, 1991). Abbe Blum drew my attention to Traub's piece; through her careful reading of an earlier draft she also helped pull this essay into sharper focus.

4. By contrast, "Seeing Miltons Shadow, some Daughters of Beulah trembling / Returnd, but Ololon remain before the Gates of the Dead" (34:47-48).

5. In sequence and presumably in time, though one is hesitant to make claims about chronology in this poem.

6. Harold Bloom, *Blake's Apocalypse* (New York: Doubleday, 1963) 352-53.

7. G. E. Bentley, Jr., ed., *William Blake's Writings* (Oxford: Clarendon, 1978) 1: 407-8.

8. "Hesiod's *Theogony* [was a] work Blake admired and one that provides the best introduction to the large design of Blake's own mythology" (Joseph Anthony Wittreich, Jr. "Opening the Seals: Blake's Epics and the Milton Tradition" in *Blake's Sublime Allegory,* eds. Stuart Curran and Joseph Anthony Wittreich, Jr. [Madison: U of Wisconsin P, 1973] 246); this is a claim to which I shall return.

9. John Milton, *Paradise Lost,* ed. Scott Elledge (New York: Norton, 1975) 2.757-63. Future references to *Paradise Lost* will be to this edition and will be noted parenthetically in the text.

10. W. J. T. Mitchell, "Blake's Radical Comedy: Dramatic Structure as Meaning in Milton" in *Blake's Sublime Allegory* 293.

11. If the "Bard's Song" rewrites the struggles of the theogony into the sexual fall of *Paradise Lost,* the body of the prophecy (and this prophecy has more of a "body" than most texts) rewrites Milton's version of the expulsion of Satan from heaven. In *Paradise Lost,* Lucifer is said to have been cast out of heaven by his own pride (1.36-37):

> He trusted to have equaled the Most High,
> If he opposed; and with ambitious aim
> Against the throne and monarchy of God
> Raised impious war in heav'n and battle proud
> With vain attempt. Him the Almighty Power
> Hurled headlong flaming from th'ethereal sky
> With hideous ruin and combustion down
> To bottomless perdition, there to dwell
> In adamantine chains and penal fire,
> Who durst defy th'Omnipotent to arms.
>
> (40-49)

In *Milton,* of course, it is Milton himself who is driven out of Eden by the Eternals living on the banks of the river Ololon. Blame rests with the Eternals rather than with Milton: they are "Drunk with the Spirit, burning round the Couch of death"; "wrathful, fill'd with rage!", they create needless destruction, rending "the heavens round the Watchers in a fiery circle" (20:44-46). Yet these spiritual drunkards are quick to see their error and repent, though the source of their enlightenment remains obscure to the reader. Indeed, Ololon laments for "seven days of Eternity" before the cause of lamentation is finally specified: "they lamented that they had in wrath & fury & fire / Driven Milton into the Ulro; for now they knew too late / That it was Milton the Awakener" (21:31-33). One wonders what they thought Milton was to begin with: the poem specifies that "they stood / Looking down into Beulah" before rending the heavens. The masculine multitudes of Ololon may have experienced Leutha's sexual jealousy—but this is merely implied rather than clearly stated.

12. Randolph Trumbach, "London's Sapphists: From Three Sexes to Four Genders in the Making of Modern Culture" in *Body Guards: The Cultural Politics of Gender Ambiguity,* eds. Julia Epstein and Kristina Straub (New York: Routledge, 1991) 114.

13. James Parsons, *A Mechanical and Critical Inquiry into the Nature of Hermaphrodites* (London, 1741).

14. Yet while Milton is presented as a male hermaphrodite within the realm of Generation, this feature of his generated body seems to be ignored at the crucial moment of self-annihilation.

15. Various critics have noted the prevalence of garment imagery in the poem, but usually in gender neutral terms. Harold Bloom remarks, for instance, that "[i]f there is a single central image in Milton, it is the garment, from the weavings of Enitharmon's looms that cover the three classes of men through Milton's taking off the robe of the promise on to the appearance of Jesus in the apocalyptic 'Garment dipped in blood' that emerges from the dispelled clouds of Ololon on the forty-second plate" (*Blake's Apocalypse* 396), and James Rieger adds to this list "the cruelty in which the Shadowy Female clothes the image of God, Jerusalem's long sufferings as the garment of God, and the vegetable world that Blake binds on as a bright sandal to walk forward through eternity" (James Rieger, "'The Hem of their Garments': The "Bard's Song" in *Milton*" in *Blake's Sublime Allegory* 278). Elsewhere in his essay, Rieger also draws attention to the garments of creation: the "gorgeous clothed Flies" and the prophetic trees which are "the Sons of Los! These the Visions of Eternity / But we see only as it were the hem of their garments" (26:10-11). In many cases, garments associated with male figures are seen in a positive light, while those associated with women are viewed as abomination.

16. Barry, for instance, appears repeatedly in Blake's annotations to *The Works of Sir Joshua Reynolds* (1798) in contexts that suggest Blake identified with the older artist:

> Having spent the Vigour of my Youth & Genius under the Opression of Sr Joshua & his Gang of Cunning Hired Knaves Without Employment & as much as could possibly be Without Bread, The Reader must Expect to Read in all my Remarks on these Books Nothing but Indignation & Resentment While Sr Joshua was rolling in Riches Barry was Poor & [Independent] 'Unemployed except by his own Energy'.
>
> (636)

> Who will Dare to Say that [Fine] 'Polite' Art is Encouraged, or Either Wished or Tolerated in a Nation where The Society for the Encouragement of Art. Sufferd Barry to Give them, his Labour for Nothing A Society Composed of the Flower of the English Nobility & Gentry—[A Society] Suffering an Artist to Starve while he Supported Really what They under pretence of Encouraging were Endeavouring to Depress.— Barry told me that while he did that Work—he Lived on Bread & Apples.
>
> (636)

These notes echo (or resound in) the warning of *Milton*'s Preface: "Suffer not the fash[i]onable Fools to depress your powers by the prices they pretend to give for contemptible works or the expensive advertizing boasts that they make of such works; believe Christ & his Apostles that there is a Class of Men whose whole delight is in Destroying." Though he is no longer a young man, Barry may be one of the Painters called on quite directly by the Preface: a consideration of Barry's work may help illuminate some of the difficulties in Blake's.

17. See William Pressly, *The Life and Art of James Barry* (New Haven: Yale UP, 1981).

18. In relation to this splitting, see Thomas Vogler, "Re:Naming *Mil/ton*" in *Unnam'd Forms: Blake and Textuality,* eds. Nelson Hilton and Thomas Vogler (Berkeley: U of California P, 1986).

19. John Barrell, "The Birth of Pandora and the Origin of Painting" in *The Birth of Pandora and the Division of Knowledge* (Philadelphia: U of Pennsylvania P, 1992) 149-50. Barrell's essay offers a useful guide through Barry's various descriptions of his Pandora project.

20. According to Barry, "[t]he employment for which Minerva is peculiarly distinguished from all the celestial personages, is her skill in the labours of the loom. . . . [S]he was sovereignly skilful in the art of painting in tapestry. . . . By the skilful labours of the loom the ancients always understood the art of making pictures in tapestry" (James Barry, *The Works of James Barry,* ed. Edward Fryer [London: Cadell and Davies, 1809] 2: 585).

Kevin D. Hutchings (essay date summer 1997)

SOURCE: Hutchings, Kevin D. "Locating the Satanic: Blake's *Milton* and the Poetics of 'Self-Examination.'" *European Romantic Review* 8, no. 3 (summer 1997): 274-97.

[In the following essay, Hutchings examines Milton's relationship to Satan in Milton.*]*

During an interview in 1984, Alessandro Fontana asked Michel Foucault the following question: "In that descent into hell that a long meditation, a long search represents—a descent in which one sets off in a sense in search of a truth—what type of reader would you like to meet and tell this truth to?" In answer, Foucault remarked that he would like to meet with a reader who doesn't "know" him as an author, a reader who will read him in "disorder and confusion" according to a

"law . . . of all possible readings" ("Aesthetics," 52). One can't help but notice striking parallels between this exchange and the central action of Blake's *Milton* (1804-10). Certainly, John Milton's journey in this epic poem represents a "long search" for "truth," a search which involves a "descent into [a] hell" that Milton calls "Eternal Death" (14:14; E [*The Complete Poetry and Prose of William Blake,* edited by David V. Erdman] 108).[1] Moreover, during the course of his journey, Milton encounters Blake, a kind of prototype of the Foucauldian reader, who is aware of the need to read Milton's prophetic texts anew. Indeed, in an advertisement for his 1809 Exhibition of Paintings, Blake employs as his motto a famous passage from *Paradise Lost*: "'*Fit Audience find tho' few*'" (E 527; cf. Milton 7.31); and, in his own epic poem, Blake sets himself up as the quintessentially "fit" representative of such an audience—a reader who dares to read Milton in "disorder and confusion" rather than, to borrow another phrase from Foucault, "reading [him] out of others' readings" ("Aesthetics," 52). But Blake is not content merely to question the contexts in which Milton's oeuvre has been read—he must also question those assumptions which had informed Milton's own interpretive practices, for as Blake argues, it was Milton's acceptance of conventional discourses of subjectivity and morality which contributed to the failure of his revolutionary practice.

In order that critical analysis and revolutionary practice may be informed by the more rigorous understanding of the relationship between subjectivity and language which Foucault advocates, it is necessary to analyze the authorial subject not as a sovereign agent, but as a "complex and variable function of discourse" ("Nietzsche, Genealogy, History," 138).[2] Foucault's paradigm of subjectivity enables an understanding that discursive regimes regulate the status of texts and the manner of their reception (123). Such an insight is clearly important to Blake's *Milton*: the text embodies a profound awareness that Milton's name and works had been assimilated by the English status quo during the course of the eighteenth century. As Joseph Wittreich argues, part of Blake's project in *Milton* is to address "the disfigurations of [Milton's] vision caused by obfuscating commentaries of the eighteenth century—commentaries committed, for the most part, to deradicalizing Milton's vision by harnessing it to orthodoxy" ("Blake's Milton," 62). Indeed, the importance of reading Milton anew or "against" the cultural grain has implications which reach beyond the realm of poetic discourse, for, as Peter Otto points out, the works of a "great poet," in becoming part of our cultural heritage, "bequeath to language certain possibilities of thought and expression" (75). Blake's *Milton* demonstrates a strong sense of dissatisfaction with the "possibilities of thought and expression" that established practices of reading John Milton and his "works" had lent to the

language of English culture, for cultural regulation of discourse tends to naturalize and thus perpetuate the dominant discursive regime. As a necessary alternative to reading general cultural texts and the poetry of John Milton passively (that is, in accordance with dominant interpretations and the reading practices that presuppose and generate such interpretations), *Milton* proposes the adoption of a reading practice based on what its opening lyric refers to as "Mental Fight" (1:13; E 95).

The very title page of *Milton* thematizes the poem's critique of, or mental fight against, the cultural *function* of Milton the author, for it depicts Milton actively resisting the petrific orthodoxy that has become associated with his own name. In the body of the text, the reader learns that John Milton's words have become "dictate" and that his body—what might be read as his textual body—has become so hardened that it is "the Rock Sinai" (17:14; E 110). This reference to "the Rock Sinai" associates Milton's name with the restraints of Mosaic law, for Mount Sinai is, of course, the place where Moses received the ten commandments. Although Wittreich argues that Milton redeemed himself during his lifetime by turning away from the "terrifying theology" of *Paradise Lost* and returning to a "Christocentric theology" in *Paradise Regained* ("Blake's Milton," 68), Blake's text emphasizes the fact that *Paradise Lost* remained the chief text associated with Milton during the eighteenth century. Indeed, *Paradise Lost* was so central to Milton's institutionalized cultural legacy that "Milton" himself had literally become, as a version of Blake's title page for *Milton* suggests, "a Poem in 12 Books." However, the title page also prefigures the poem's critique of the cultural petrification and commodification of "Milton," for, as a number of critics have pointed out, it presents an image of a naked and dynamic Milton involved in the act of breaking his own name with his outstretched right hand (the hand that the historical Milton explicitly associated with the writing of poetry)[3] and stepping forward into the gap or space produced by this breakage.

In Blake's poem, Milton revises his Selfhood and his revolutionary politics by actively engaging in a Blakean mode of "Self-examination" (40: 37; E 108). Milton must examine and revise his political vision, for, as an apologist for Cromwell's government, he participated in a regicidal politics which resulted not in the ushering in of freedom but in the establishment of a new and rigid orthodoxy—and it is perhaps ultimately for this reason that "Charles calls on Milton for Atonement" in Blake's epic (5:39; E 99). At the theoretical level, the Puritan revolution failed in part because, by focusing on the monarchy as the ultimate particular symbol of oppression, Milton and the radical Puritans effaced what Gayatri Spivak calls "the tremendous, unmotivated monitory force of the general" (32); that is, they wrote themselves out of their own complicitous role in the or-

ganization or polarization of the "moving base of differential force field" (32) which always underpins the established power relationship within which a revolutionary politics may be deployed. Resistance, in other words, plays a crucial role in the organization of hegemonic power and its circulation of knowledge, causing an interimplication of orthodoxy and revolution.[4] The regicidal apologist, however, does not sufficiently recognize this. In a sense, he rejects the monarch while generally accepting the subjective "sovereignty" of this supreme subject; for regicide can only be justified by pointing to the intentionality of the sovereign as the ultimate locus and cause of oppression, an act which effaces the discursive "field of force" and the complicity of the revolutionary in the polarization of this field in a particular way.

This aspect of Miltonic revolution can be clarified by a brief examination of some of the autobiographical commentary that comprises Milton's *Second Defence of the English People*.[5] In one sense, the political aims that Milton articulates here can be seen as truly revolutionary, despite the fact that he historically allied himself with a Puritan oligarchy which was, as Leopold Damrosch has put it, "at all times conservative in its social intentions."[6] Milton's stated concern as a pamphleteer, for example, is to advance nothing less than "the liberation of all human life from slavery" (*Second Defence* 323). Articulated and carried out in the context of a highly stratified society, such a project is courageously radical, placing Milton in the Blakean category of the "Reprobate," that revolutionary "Class" of poet-prophets which attacks the established order to prepare the way for the Apocalypse.[7]

As he proceeds in the *Second Defence,* however, Milton reveals the difficulty and danger of his position as a prose writer. He repeatedly asserts, for example, that he did not write about "the rights of kings" until Charles had already "been declared an enemy by Parliament," emphasizing that he never wrote in defence of regicide until after Charles had been executed (325). In a climate of dangerous political uncertainty, Milton's reticence to speak out is understandable: he could not allow the prose writings of his "left hand" to put in jeopardy the radical message he planned to disseminate in the poetic prophecies that his right hand would bequeath "to aftertimes" (*The Reason of Church Government* 168-169). And yet, from a Blakean perspective, Milton takes his political caution too far. Milton explains, for example, that he wrote *The Tenure of Kings and Magistrates* "after the death of the king . . . to reconcile men's minds, rather than to determine anything about Charles (which was not my affair, but that of the magistrates . . .)" (*Second Defence* 325).[8] Blake, who repeatedly contrasts the passive and conservative faculty of Memory with the active, transformative faculty of Inspiration,[9] would have found this admission irritat-

ing, to say the least; for writing to reconcile "men" with their history (in this case, the memory of regicide) is a highly conservative act, one that is clearly at odds with the Reprobate spirit of prophecy. At this point, at least from a Blakean perspective, Milton places himself squarely in the orthodox Class of the "Elect": forsaking a truly radical "liberation of all human life," he becomes, as it were, a card-carrying member of the conservative Puritan orthodoxy.

But it would be misleading to identify Milton unproblematically as a traitor to the cause of liberty. It is necessary to bear in mind, for example, that Milton exhibits as much scorn for mercenaries of the pen as Blake does for unscrupulous artisans in his Preface to **Milton.** While Blake speaks out against "ignorant Hirelings" who allow "fash[i]onable Fools to depress [their] powers by the prices they pretend to give for contemptible works" (Plate 1; E 95), Milton articulates a similar degree of contempt for men who cling "with suppliant expression to the doors of Parliament," and for those self-seekers who loiter "in the hallways of the lower assemblies" (*Second Defence* 325). Clearly, as Hayley so fervently argued, Milton was no mere "Hireling."[10] Certainly Blake would not have revered him—as he so plainly did—if he had thought otherwise. As Wittreich has put it, Milton worked intentionally "to undermine rather than to uphold the reigning orthodoxies" ("Opening the Seals," 26). And yet, intentionality and action are often irreconcilable; and the two distinct and conflicting aspects of Milton's political writing that I have delineated above—the radical and conservative aspects—constitute what Blake likely saw as a profoundly *divided* Milton, a Milton whose own revolutionary impulses are strangely co-opted by the exigencies of his historical situation.

Perhaps the problem of a self-divided Milton can be clarified in light of some of the rhetoric Milton uses in his discussion of regicide. He declares in the *Second Defence* that he wrote *The Tenure of Kings and Magistrates* to demonstrate "what was in general permissible against tyrants" (325). Such a project resembles an act of Foucauldian "parrhesia"—the "free speech" of "the governed, who can and must question those who govern them, in the name of the knowledge, [and] the experience they have" ("Aesthetics," 51-2). Certainly, from a Blakean standpoint, Milton is correct to question authority; however, by identifying tyranny directly with the king (by the simple act of *naming* him "tyrant") Milton effaces the wider tyranny of the *discursive* regime and thus runs the danger of helping to perpetuate this tyranny. Such an insight is indeed Blakean: Blake sees tyranny largely as *systemic,* not as the mere product of an individual sovereign will. Hence, the naming and slaying of tyrants in **Milton** belongs to the "Covering Cherub" (37:8, 37:44; E 137, 138), as Blake's character Milton makes clear in his ultimate confrontation

with Satan (and as I shall demonstrate in the pages ahead). All of this boils down to a problem articulated in **Milton** by Palamabron (who is, of course, Blake himself in the biographical allegory); although he actively takes steps to defeat Satan's tyranny (even naming it as such), Palamabron adds a careful and crucial qualifier: "But we must not be tyrants also!" (7:25; E 101). For Palamabron/Blake, tyranny is by no means a stable term in a purely oppositional equation; hence, tyranny cannot be comfortably objectified and demarcated by the revolutionary who would resist its oppression.

In short, then, I would argue that Blake conceptualizes the error of Milton's revolutionary politics chiefly in terms of its narrowness of focus. By being a spokesman for a revolutionary movement which identified power directly with the monarchy, Milton subscribed to what Foucault calls "the system of Law-and-Sovereign." Such a paradigm fails to see that power relationships are "strictly relational [in] character" and that their very existence "depends on a multiplicity of points of resistance" in "the strategic field of power relations." As Foucault summarizes this insight, "there is no single locus of great Refusal, no soul of revolt, source of all rebellions, or pure law of the revolutionary" (*The History of Sexuality,* 95-96). An effective alternative to Milton's "system of Law-and-Sovereign," on the other hand, would involve looking for "the most immediate, the most local power relations at work" in order to identify how these local relations may be complicitous with the discursive structures which constitute relations of power on a larger scale (97). Arguably, the protagonists in Blake's epic accomplish this critical task largely by engaging in Blakean "Self-Examination," a critical process which analyzes and questions the relationship between individual subjectivity and discursive authority.

Blake's critique of popularized conceptions of subjectivity and poetic authority is most strikingly apparent in his reconceptualization of poetic inspiration, one of the standard motifs which has organized traditional views of unified authorial subjectivity. In a letter written to Thomas Butts in 1803, Blake described his experience of writing **The Four Zoas** and **Milton**[11] in what at first appear to be patently Miltonic terms: "I have written this Poem from immediate Dictation twelve or sometimes twenty or thirty lines at a time," Blake declared, adding that he had done so "without Premeditation & even against my Will" (E 728-29). As David Riede points out, Blake's description of the process of writing his poem clearly echoes a passage from *Paradise Lost,* wherein Milton refers to his

> celestial patroness, who deigns
> Her nightly visitation unimplored,
> And dictates to me slumbering, or inspires
> Easy my unpremeditated verse.

(9.21-24)

In these passages each poet refers to some form of external dictation as the source of the poetic text, and each discusses his own lack of premeditation in the act of writing. The crucial difference between these discussions is, arguably, one of subjective control: whereas Milton describes the inspiration he receives as "Easy," Blake declares that his own inspiration occurs "even against my Will." Unlike Milton's, Blake's assertion problematizes his own poetic authority, for, rather than underscoring the ease with which he is able to manipulate language and its sources, Blake's remark emphasizes the irresistible power that an *external* discourse exercises *over him.*

Riede argues that Blake's admission that he writes "even against my Will" suggests that the poet "lacks control over his own imagination, [and] is unable to combat successfully the imposition of an authoritarian will beyond his own" (260-261). While this observation is not entirely incorrect, it does not adequately characterize the problem of authority in **Milton.** For what Blake wishes to show in **Milton** is that sovereign self-control is an *illusion,* indeed a fiction that paradoxically generates passivity on the part of its adherents.[12] When he declares that he writes against his will, Blake does not articulate an unfortunate lack of control on his part—something that *might* be successfully combatted—but rather the impossibility of such control, an awareness that his selfhood or subjectivity is in fact *constituted* by external forces. Unlike Milton, in short, Blake acknowledges that the act of writing involves a radical obliteration of the sovereign self.

The different invocations in **Milton** and *Paradise Lost* exhibit similarly opposed views of poetic authority and subjectivity. *Paradise Lost* opens, of course, with the famous invocation to a singular and external "heavenly muse," an invocation in which Milton asks the muse for aid, instruction, and purification, in order, as he puts it, that "*I* may assert eternal providence, / And justify the ways of God to men" (1.25-26; my emphasis). Blake, on the other hand, asks the plural "Daughters of Beulah" to "Come into my hand / . . . descending down the Nerves of my right arm / From out the Portals of my Brain" (2.5-7; E 96). In sharp contrast to his precursor, in other words, Blake begins his epic by invoking a plurality of Muses who, by inhabiting his brain, are internal rather than external to the self,[13] and, in so doing, he demonstrates that his subjectivity is, as it were, multiplicitous and *self*-different. Unlike his predecessor, Blake does *not* present himself as the unified source and authoritative guarantor of meaning in the text he produces.

Blake's invocation contains other elements which stress its importance to an analysis of subjectivity in the text. For example, in writing of the "*mild* power" (1:6; E 96, my emphasis) of his Muses, Blake acknowledges a cer-

tain danger implicit in this power—and hence in his own inspired poetic discourse—for he later characterizes the Satanic adversary as imbued with "*incomparable mildness*" (7:4; E 100, my emphasis). Satan embodies quintessentially, that is, the very quality—"mildness"—that Blake uses to define the power of his own muses. Blake may speak with prophetic authority, then, but his text demonstrates an awareness of the ways in which revolutionary poetic resistance, by being constituted in the context of a given power relationship, shares a certain continuity with that which it sets out to oppose, and this continuous relationship between revolutionary and hegemonic terms in the social order raises the perilous possibility that resistance will reinscribe rather than transform existent power structures.

At this point the objection may arise that Satan's mildness, unlike that of Blake's muses, is the product of willful deception and is, therefore, quite simply a false attribute. The text, however, repeatedly complicates such a notion by suggesting that the intending self can in fact engage in something like *honest* deception. Palamabron certainly suggests as much: "You know Satan's mildness and his self-imposition, / Seeming a brother, being a tyrant, *even thinking himself a brother* / While he is murdering the just" (7:21-23; E 100; my emphasis). Palamabron declares a few lines later, moreover, that "*Satan's self, believ'd* / That he had not oppres'd the horses of the Harrow, nor the servants" (7:39-40; E 101; my emphasis). Finally, as if to underscore the importance of this insight, the narrator confirms yet again on the following plate that Satan "himself believ'd / That he had not opress'd nor injur'd the refractory servants" (8:1-3; E 101). Clearly, when it comes to dealing with the "incomparably mild" Satanic adversary (who, as we later discover, is the Selfhood itself), intention is not to be trusted. Satan's example emphasizes the importance of questioning "mild power" in *all* of its manifestations.

One cannot help but think at this point of Blake's patron, William Hayley, whom Blake allies with Satan in **Milton**'s biographical allegory. Hayley would likely have been honestly baffled and appalled if he had known the extent to which Blake considered his intended benevolent patronage an instance of Satanic "self-imposition." But "Corporeal Friends" are, as Blake puts it, "Spiritual Enemies" (see 4:26; E 98); for Corporeal Friendship distracts the poet-prophet from the work that belongs to "his own station" (7:41; E 101). The Satan/Hayley nexus demonstrates once again the danger of assuming that the Satanic can be comfortably located in the intentionality of the subject. Because the Satanic "Refuse[s] Form" (3:41; E 97), those who would unselfcritically invoke intention to objectify its tyranny—those who naively consider themselves "mild" opponents of a purely "external" Satanic impulse—run the danger of becoming, like Los, that which they behold

(3:29; E 97). This is why, as Peter Otto has demonstrated in his analysis of the **"Bard's Song,"** every effort in Eternity to oppose Satanic power merely functions further to increase and consolidate that power (56-62).

Blake's curious description in Book I of Leutha's manipulations of Satan suggests the existence of further continuities or parallels between the Satanic regime and its poetic-prophetic opposition. Leutha, we are told, has exercised manipulative control over Satan by "entering the *doors* of [his] brain" (12:4; E 105, my emphasis). This passage recalls Blake's invocation of the muses, whom Blake asks to come into his hand "From out the *Portals* of my Brain" (2:7; E 96, my emphasis). The two passages are similar insofar as the brains of key characters are figured poetically as having doorways through which different entities may enter and exit (the *OED* defines "portal" as "a poetical or rhetorical synonym for 'door'"). The poetic similarity here suggests that it would be productive to read Leutha as a type (or anti-type) of the muse. However, it is significant that, while the muses in Blake's invocation come *out* of the poet's brain upon conscious demand, Leutha *enters* Satan's brain by stealth. The difference between Blake and Satan might be conceptualized, then, in terms of their respective capacities for self-critical awareness. Satan is at first unaware that he is *not* a unified, self-sufficient subject, while Blake articulates from the beginning of the poem an awareness of his own subjective multiplicity.

Later, when Satan discovers Leutha's presence within himself, he drives her "from his inmost Brain," at which time we are told that "the doors clos'd with thunders sound" (12:48; E 106). When he realizes that he is inhabited by an Other, that is, Satan attempts to recoup his cherished sense of unified subjectivity by means of violence and denial. However, Satan's earlier presentation in the text as a powerful agent—one who consciously strategizes to usurp authority—has already been undermined, for Leutha's confession demonstrates that Satan has *all along* been subject to a form of "external" control. In other words, even Satan's driving away of Leutha in the wake of the flattering tribute paid to him by Elynittria and her singing women (12:42-48; E 106) cannot function convincingly to reestablish his status as a self-sufficient agent; Leutha's former interventions have already highlighted the fact that Satan's acts of eviction and self-enclosure represent attempts to reclaim what amounts merely to a *fiction* of sovereign agency. In sharp contrast to Satan's treatment of Leutha, Blake retains the muses which inhabit him—and hence retains his acknowledged sense of self-difference—by invoking their aid to work cooperatively with him in the production of his poetic prophecy.

Blake's epic also highlights the disunified status of the self in its presentation of the character of Milton. Milton is depicted in the poem not as a human person with whom the reader may comfortably identify, but as a *figure* representing and very much caught up in certain discursive phenomena. Milton's discursive character is especially apparent in the passage where Blake describes his descent into the garden at Felpham. At this point, Blake beholds in Milton "The Monstrous Churches of Beulah, the Gods of Ulro dark" and "Twelve monstrous dishumanizd terrors Synagogues of Satan" (37:16-17; E 137). In the long passage that follows Blake expands on this description of a discursively-constituted Milton, identifying in Milton's "Shadow" or selfhood "all the historical periods . . . of false doctrine and all the heathen gods Milton had himself identified as Satan's fallen angels" (Essick 198). Elsewhere, moreover, the poem represents Milton as a figure of corrupted Puritanism, repressed and oppressive sexuality, and, most importantly, ineffectual revolution. These representations suggest that Milton is not an authoritative "source" of textual meaning but is implicated, both as a human subject and as an "author" in a given cultural milieu, in a complex network of discursive relations. In Blake's poem, Milton's realization that he must return to earth to correct the errors of his lifetime involves an understanding that he must engage in acts of "Self-examination" in which he will "re-read" his conception of his selfhood and its relationship to the world.

At this point it is necessary to distinguish Blakean "Self-examination" from orthodox modes of this practice; for Blake's notion of this analytical activity is characteristically iconoclastic. Once again, it can be helpful to invoke Foucault. In a discussion of "pastoral technology," Foucault argues that Christianity appropriated self-examination from the Hellenistic world, altering it profoundly in the process. Whereas in the earlier context self-examination helped one to attain "self-mastery and the domination of one's passions," it becomes, in the Christian context, a mode of the surveillance of power. As Foucault puts it, its new "aim was not to close self-awareness in upon itself, but to enable it to open up entirely to its director—to unveil to him the depths of the soul." The ultimate goal of this Christianized self-examination is the attainment of the virtue of "total obedience," a subjective docility which "is not, as for the Greeks, a provisional means to an end, but rather an end in itself" ("Politics and Reason," 69-70). This process of pastoral technology aims at the "government of individuals by their own verity" (71), involving what Blake would undoubtedly have seen as an insidious internalization of the Moral Law.

Blake's conviction that Milton's revolutionary politics had been frustrated by orthodox modes of Self-examination is evident from the beginning of *Milton.* Most significantly, Blake introduces his precursor by situating him in a Pauline universe resembling that

which Milton himself depicted in *Paradise Lost*: a universe wherein unquestioning obedience to ineffable transcendental principles is the essential prerequisite to spiritual salvation. The appalling consequences of Milton's situation become apparent when, in a parodic response to the opening invocation of *Paradise Lost*—where Milton asks his muse to "say first what cause / Moved our grandparents in that happy state, / . . . to fall off / From their creator, and transgress his will" (1.28-31)—Blake asks his own Muses to "Say first! what moved Milton, who walkd about in Eternity / One hundred years, pondring the intricate mazes of Providence / Unhappy tho in heav'n . . . To go into the deep [his emanation] to redeem & himself perish" (2.16-20; E 96). By depicting Milton as unhappy in, of all places, a Pauline/Miltonic heaven of his "own" construction, Blake develops a reading scenario that contains what he sees as previous errors (Rajan 205), a reading scenario which emphasizes the danger of Milton's passive and obedient internalization of an inherited Pauline discourse. As a docile subject before the law, Milton has allowed his prophetic voice to be effectively stifled.

The consequences of Milton's behaviour are emphatically clear in Blake's epic. Milton, who impotently ponders "the intricate mazes of Providence," resembles the devils of his own *Paradise Lost,* who, in their hellish arguments concerning the nature of good and evil, find themselves "in wandering mazes lost" (2.561). The allusion implicit in Blake's use of the word "mazes," which aligns the heaven of *Milton* with the hell of *Paradise Lost,* functions as an aspect of Blake's critique of Milton's doctrine (articulated by Raphael) of noncritical obedience to the authority of a distant sky-god. The irony of Milton's situation in Blake's poem is striking. The poet-prophet who had devoted his earthly existence to "the liberation of all human life from slavery" is not only powerless to ease the "torment" of his enslaved "Sixfold Emanation"; in this heaven of his own making—which represents the culmination of his earthly desire—he cannot even begin to liberate himself. It is only when he takes off "the robe of the promise, & ungird[s] himself from the oath of God" (14:13; E 108)—when he frees himself from his destructively passive obedience to authority—that Milton can begin to correct the errors of his own revolutionary politics and engage in a new, distinctively Blakean mode of Self-examination.

It is interesting to note that Milton's transformation in heaven begins at the moment in which the "loud voic'd Bard" takes "refuge in Miltons bosom" (14:9; E 108), for at this juncture Milton becomes explicitly multiple and self-different. Moreover, in internalizing the Bard, Milton internalizes that which is "Inspired" (13:51; E 107), and this process ultimately helps him to cast off "the daughters of memory"—who "get their inspiration from traditions, books, and other secondary sources"

(Damon 43)—in favor of "the daughters of inspiration" (14:29; E 108) who help Milton to engage in the rigorous practices of "Self-examination" which he subsequently adopts. The following plate emphasizes the transformation of Milton's self-reflexive or critical faculty: invested with "the Spirits of the Seven Angels of the Presence," Milton can engage in "perceptions of his Sleeping Body" (15:3-4; E 109)—perceptions which symbolize his newfound ability to analyze critically, as it were, the errors of his former passive or "Sleeping" self, errors which had disabled his earthly revolutionary politics.

In order productively to revise his politics, Milton must reconsider his reading of Pauline doctrine, for, as Thomas Vogler has put it, "Paul's function for Blake's *MILTON* is comparable to that of those authors Michel Foucault calls 'founders of discursivity,' because they produce in addition to their own works 'the possibilities and the rules for the formation of other texts'" (151).[14] For Foucault Christianity marks a break with Antiquity insofar as it is a "religion of the text" wherein "morality [takes] on increasingly the form of a code of rules" ("Aesthetics," 49). In *Milton,* Blake questions the rules of Milton's orthodox Christianity by focusing on their major codifier, St. Paul, and, conversely, he intervenes in Pauline discourse in part by transforming one of its major productions—the "author" Milton.

Milton thematizes poetically something resembling a Foucauldian interventionist "return" to the discursive origin[15] when Blake announces Milton's arrival on earth: "Then first I saw him in the Zenith as a falling star, / Descending perpendicular, swift as the swallow or swift; / And on my left foot falling on the tarsus, enterd there" (15:47-49; E 110). This passage enacts a poetic "return" in two important ways. Most obviously, Blake's pun on "tarsus" equates the Blake-Milton convergence with St. Paul, for prior to his conversion Paul was known, of course, as Saul of Tarsus. Blake reinforces this textual allusion, moreover, with a pictorial one; for as Erdman points out in his analysis of the illumination on Plate 17, the posture in which Blake depicts himself as Milton enters his foot is a variant of the posture in which Blake depicts Saul in his watercolour painting of Saul's encounter with Christ on the road to Damascus just prior to his Christian conversion (233).[16] Blake's visual and poetic allusions to St. Paul can be read as suggesting that Milton, in his own writing, failed himself to enact an effective return to the discursive "origin" and, because of this failure, uncritically subscribed to the established doctrines of the Pauline Church. Blake's intertextual gestures also imply that Milton, because he has already left his worldly life, can only return to the writings of St. Paul by way of Blake, a living "author" and reader who is aware of the need for a revisionary "return."

But Blake emphasizes the fact that this revisionary "return" is fraught with danger, for when Milton enters Blake's tarsus Blake ominously adds: "But from my left foot a black cloud redounding spread over Europe" (15:50; E 110). Although it is possible to read this passage in a positive light,[17] the image of the black cloud is nonetheless foreboding; for as Vogler points out (150-51), it alludes to the "False Tongue" that speaks of the "fibrous left foot black (22:35; E 117)" rather than the productive vision of the "Vegetable World" that appears on Blake's "left Foot, / As a bright sandal formd immortal of precious stones & gold" (21:12-13; E 115). The revisionary encounter with St. Paul that Blake figures in the scene of his convergence with Milton is dangerous because Paul himself has, to a great extent, established the terms that the revolutionary prophet must adopt in order to engage Paul in debate. In short, Blake-Milton must adopt a Pauline vocabulary to contest Pauline discourse. But the danger of this circumstance, as Blake demonstrates when he fastens on his "bright sandal" to "walk forward thro' Eternity" (21:13-14; E 115), need not be crippling. For when Blake rereads Pauline doctrine, he deploys a tactic analogous to what Foucault calls "'reverse' discourse" (*The History of Sexuality,* 101), a discourse of resistance that is critically *aware* of its situation "within" the power relations which constitute the established discursive framework. Blake's discourse is one of "reversal" in the Foucauldian sense, for it attacks Pauline dualism by using the same vocabulary and the same categories that orthodoxy uses to support it.

Arguably, the difference between Blake's reading of Pauline texts in *Milton* and Milton's reading of them in *Paradise Lost* is one of critical strategy (or lack thereof); whereas Blake considers Pauline doctrine actively, in the spirit of "Mental Warfare," Milton reads it passively, "in the letter"—that is, in terms of its orthodox reception.[18] Most importantly, Milton seeks the "heavenly father . . . beyond the skies" (20:32; E 114), thus subscribing to Paul's literal separation of the proximate and the distant, Flesh and Spirit (263). We witness this subscription, for example, in the opening lines of *Paradise Lost,* where Milton invokes the muse "that on the *secret* top / of Oreb, or of Sinai, didst inspire / [Moses]" (1.6-8; my emphasis). Milton's references in this passage to secrecy and to Moses privilege, respectively, "mystery" and the moral law, two aspects of "Milton's Religion" (22:39) that profoundly offended Blake, who chose rather to direct his critical gaze "inward" towards the proximate self rather than "outward" towards the distant and mysterious theological abstraction that is Milton's God.

Blake's critique of Milton's reading of Pauline doctrine concerns Milton's particular conceptualization, then, of the grand object—or Supreme Subject—of his poetic theodicy. In their modes of conceptualizing God and the Creation, the differences between *Paradise Lost* and *Milton* are striking. Whereas *Paradise Lost* purports to be enacted in an external cosmos, with much of the crucial action occurring at a "distance" in the abstract realms of heaven, hell, chaos, or a primordial Eden, *Milton* is, as Christine Gallant puts it, "quite intentionally enacted in Blake's own 'Human Brain'" (116). Moreover, for Blake, the metaphysical origin is not a *secret* moment hidden in an inaccessible past; rather, it is latent in *every* moment and may be made manifest in every pulsation of the artery. Blake's distaste for abstract spirituality is apparent in his highlighting of virtually all aspects of human physiology. Hence, the centrality in *Milton* of Albion (the human form divine), the occurrence of many of the poem's key events within Albion's body, the presentation of Allamanda and Bowlahoola (the nervous system and motile organs respectively), the extended poetic discussions of human Energy, and the poetic figuration of all time and space as existing within a single globule of human blood. Blake's foregrounding of the human body and his willingness to question the discursive representation of metaphysical origins suggest that his historical revisions of Christian discourse have more in common with those of the "genealogist" who constructs what Foucault calls a "counter-memory" than those of the traditional historian who constructs a "monumental history."[19] Like the metaphysicians and traditional historians whom Foucault critiques by way of reference to Nietzsche, Milton examines things *furthest* from himself in the hope of attaining the ultimate reward of a final *separation* from the self in a distant heaven. The triumph of the Spirit or *Logos* as it is represented in *Paradise Lost* entails the mortification and *defeat* of the human body.[20] For Blake, who sees the body as a kind of machine of redemption, such a "triumph" results rather in physiological and spiritual pathology, the major symptom of which is the character Milton's divided self—his separation from Ololon, his Six-fold Emanation.

As I mentioned earlier, the central problem with Milton's politics involved his objective identification of tyranny; and Milton's encounter with Ololon both highlights this problem and suggests a way to surmount it. To name a king "tyrant" is to take a firm stand within a discursive order that itself constitutes the will to power. But the act of naming, like all speech acts, is not simply an exercise of the speaker's will to power; it is, more importantly, an act of submission *to* power. For when "a man" speaks, as Foucault notes, "he has been caused to behave in a certain way. His freedom has been subjected to power. He has been submitted to government" ("Politics and Reason," 84). Certainly Milton had little choice but to speak on behalf of Cromwell's government during the Interregnum. But from Blake's standpoint, Milton speaks as it were too soon—that is, without sufficient engagement in the Mental Warfare that would enable him to consider the "law of all pos-

sible readings." Unlike Milton, whose adherence to various orthodoxies associates him with the "Rock Sinai," Ololon is characterized in terms of fluidity, as "a sweet River" (21:15; E 115). Indeed, her very name signifies ambiguously an entity of uncertain number (Ololon is both singular and plural) and unstable identity (she/it/they are associated with the "nameless Shadowy Mother").[21] Hence, Milton's reunion with Ololon suggests, if not the possibility of *escaping* the fixed order of petrific orthodoxy, certainly an introduction into this order of something excessive, perplexing, and not entirely containable.[22] At the very least, Milton's separation from Ololon in Book One signifies the reductive nature of Satanic sovereign self-enclosure, that harmful fiction which Milton must learn to overcome if he is to escape the violent "Orc cycle" in which his earthly revolutionary practice has entrapped him.

And yet, despite the profundity of Blake's critique of Miltonic revolution, Blake himself undoubtedly requires the help of his poetic precursor in order effectively to resist the dominant discursive regime which is his own inheritance. As Wittreich puts it, "Blake's willingness to subject himself to Milton's influence [is] in full sympathy with the prophetic dictum that the precursor, even if sometimes mistaken, is not an oppressor but a liberator" ("Blake's Milton," 71). Blake's pairing of himself with Milton in his poetic prophecy echoes the story of the "two Witnesses" in Revelation, thus recalling "all the famous pairs of prophets in the Old Testament: Moses and Aaron, Elijah and Elisha, Zerubbabel and Joshua" (74). Hence, the Milton/Blake dyad emphasizes the *dialogical* rather than self-contained character of true prophetic vision. The union of living poet and influential precursor functions further to problematize the notion of unified subjective authority by emphasizing what David Clark has called, in a related discussion, "the contextualizing presence [in the self] of other selves" (186). In Blake's vision, the apocalypse does not signify the eradication of difference but rather its ultimate embracement in a spirit of "Mental Warfare" which continually displaces authoritarian positions.

And yet, if the primary impulse of *Milton* is to question authority, how do we reconcile Blake's appeals in the text to his own visionary authority, appeals embodied in such imperatives as those which the Bard repeatedly articulates when he says: "Mark well my words! they are of your eternal salvation"? Do these imperatives not seek to establish a new authoritative hegemony—a hegemony of the "inspired" prophet? A brief consideration of Blake's conceptualization of the relationship between artistic creativity and human prophecy can be helpful to the formulation of an answer to this difficult question.

In *A Descriptive Catalogue,* Blake writes that "To suppose that Art can go beyond the finest specimens of Art that are now in the world, is not knowing what Art is; it

is being blind to the gifts of the spirit" (E 544). Although Blake privileges here "the finest specimens of Art" and "the gifts of the spirit," he does so with an understanding that the spirit of prophecy and hence of artistic creation is available not only to a select few of "Genius" but to all members of humanity. As Blake told Crabb Robinson, "all men partake of [the faculty of Vision]—but it is lost by not being cultivated" (cited in Ackroyd 342). Or, as he so succinctly puts it in *Milton,* "*Every one* is a fallen Son of the Spirit of Prophecy" (24:75; E 121; my emphasis). In terms of human artistic output, then, competition between separate human subjects (for example, between living artists and their deceased precursors) to produce "the finest specimens of Art" is emphatically not the issue at stake; what is important for Blake, rather, is the realization through art of the prophetic potential which gives rise to all human creativity.

A brief consideration of the intertextual character of Blakean prophecy will help to clarify this point. Wittreich has argued that "prophecy involves a way of relating"; however, Wittreich includes in this intertextual relationship only the interconnected and interdependent network of relations which he sees as existing between explicitly prophetic texts ("Blake's Milton," 77-78). But Blake in fact takes the idea much further: because all humans are potential prophets in Blake's eyes, prophecy logically implies an ideal form of human relations *in general.* And in order to actualize this ultimate scenario, it is necessary in the meantime rigorously to engage in the critical process of "Self-examination" and its concomitant questioning of authorized readings of received texts—as Blake so emphatically instructs us to do, and as Blake does himself so relentlessly, in *Milton.* This reading of Blake's apocalyptic vision brings us back to the question of Blake's prophetic authority: given Blake's opposition to authoritative positions, is his own prophetic authority an irreconcilable contradiction? In light of his many prescriptive and authoritative declarations, one may be tempted to answer this question in the affirmative. However, it is necessary to bear in mind the crucial paradox that informs Blake's position: he speaks authoritatively of the need relentlessly to *question* authority—and hence his own position—for such questioning he regards as the crucial prerequisite to human apocalyptic transformation.

This questioning of authority as it is manifested in the discursive continuum linking subjective and institutional realities is perhaps the key to understanding and overcoming the "Orc cycle," in which unexamined revolutionary activity continually reinscribes the oppressive regimes that it strives to overthrow. It is exceedingly difficult to escape the Orc cycle, for, as Blake remarks, "every Man born is joined / Within into One mighty Polypus, and this Polypus is Orc" (29:30-31; E 127). Orc is a Polypus, for he lacks the capacity to engage in

mental warfare: he is a center of affective impulse "without Thought or Vision" (24:38; E 120). In other words, Orc's revolutionary activity derives from blind impulse unreflexively constituted by the field of discursive force relations in which he functions. Blake's assertion that "Every man born is joined" to Orc emphasizes how easily revolutionary activity can be co-opted by the structures it would oppose. Significantly, Milton descends to earth to "set free / Orc from his Chain of Jealousy" (20:60-61; E 115), that is, to put an end to the vicious cycle of vengeance and conquest that accompanies an uncritical naming of tyrants and objectification of tyranny.

Milton's final encounter with Satan—who symbolizes the authoritative "will" that Milton's mission ultimately opposes—proves that he has in fact gained a new understanding of the complexities of political intervention. When he meets the adversary face to face, Milton utters his famous speech:

> Satan! my Spectre! I know my power thee to annihilate
> And be a greater in thy place, & be thy Tabernacle
> A covering for thee to do thy will, till one greater comes
> And smites me as I smote thee & becomes my covering.
> Such are the Laws of thy false Heavns! but Laws of Eternity
> Are not such: know thou: I come to Self Annihilation
> Such are the Laws of Eternity that each shall mutually
> Annihilate himself for others good, as I for thee[.]
>
> (38:29-36; E 139)

In this passage Milton articulates his understanding that annihilating Satan—the mere symbol of evil—would not *transform* established relations of power, but would merely perpetuate the cycles of vengeance characterizing the existing order. As Robert Essick and Joseph Viscomi put it, Milton realizes that "Satan is a part of [his] own selfhood" (202); hence, Milton rejects the opportunity of setting himself up as "a greater in [Satan's] place" in favour of the alternative of "Self Annihilation." Milton's newly-formulated argument against vengeance demonstrates his newfound realization that revolutionary activity, constituted as it is in contexts where discursive fields of force are polarized, can merely invert the relationship of the terms that organize the poles, and hence can replicate the discursive structures which it seeks to subvert and transform. For Milton, "Self Annihilation" by way of "Self-examination" is an alternative revolutionary tactic, an "unexampled deed" (2:21; E 96) providing a way to address "the most immediate" and "local" manifestations of power (*The History of Sexuality,* 97)—those that exist *within* the self but which nonetheless are continuous with the so-called "external" world, "an outside" which, as it turns out, "is fallacious" (37:9; E 137). Such a critical task is both frightening and disturbing, for in order to begin to understand and deal with one's complicity with established systems of power it is necessary, as Milton learns, to submit the comforting fiction of self-sovereignty to "Eternal Death." But, as Blake insists in **Milton,** it is only by way of such a "descent into hell" that individuals can hope ultimately to reap the multiplicitous "Great Harvest" of apocalyptic truth.

Notes

1. All references to Blake's writing in this essay are from David V. Erdman's edition of *The Complete Poetry and Prose of William Blake.* In my parenthetical citations I refer first to plate and line numbers (for example, 14:14) and secondly, for ease of reference, to the page number where the citation occurs in the Erdman edition (for example, E 108).

2. Discourse, in the Foucauldian sense of the term, does not refer to mere verbal exchange between subjects; it is, rather, a widespread and pervasive human activity "articulated on the basis of social relationships" (137). Such a view of discourse insists on an understanding that language, like the social relationships and institutions in which it circulates and functions, is always inextricably involved in systems of power. Foucault deploys, moreover, a rigorous definition of "power": it is "not an institution, and not a structure; neither is it a certain strength we are endowed with; it is the name that one attributes to a complex strategical situation in a particular society" (*History of Sexuality,* 93).

3. See *The Reason of Church Government* (Milton 168).

4. It is for this reason that one must question E. P. Thompson's otherwise touching conclusion in *Witness Against the Beast* that there is "Never, on any page of Blake, . . . the least complicity with the kingdom of the Beast" (229).

5. It is well-known that Blake was familiar with Milton's prose. Wittreich ("Opening the Seals," 34) and Frye (159) have argued, respectively, for example, that *The Reason of Church Government* and the *Areopagitica* significantly influenced Blake's thought. I would like to add here the suggestion that the autobiographical utterances of the *Second Defence* did not go unnoticed by Blake, but offered him a peculiar vantage point from which to consider the political activity of his predecessor. If Blake did not know the *Second Defence* first hand (and he likely did, having taught himself to read Latin), he would certainly have known it through William Hayley. In his *Life of Milton,* Hayley acknowledges the importance of

the *Second Defence,* calling it Milton's "own vindication" (123) and "summary account of his own writings" (94). I should point out that Hayley analyzes all of the passages in the *Second Defence* that I consider below, summarizing their content and/or quoting them extensively in both the original Latin and in his own English translation (94, 96).

6. Private correspondence, 26 October, 1996.

7. For Blake's discussions of the "Three Classes" in *Milton* see 11:21-26 (E 105) and 25:31-41 (E 122).

8. Hayley paraphrases this passage as follows: "He [Milton] declares, that without any personal malevolence against the deceased monarch . . . it [*The Second Defence*] was written to compose the minds of the people" (94).

9. See, for example, the opening paragraph to the Preface to *Milton,* where Blake contrasts the "Daughters of Memory" with the "Daughters of Inspiration" (Plate 1; E 95).

10. One of Hayley's stated intentions in *The Life of Milton* is to "refut[e], in the course of this narrative, the charge of servile flattery, which he [Milton] is falsely accused of having lavished upon Cromwell" (98; see also 126ff.).

11. According to David Riede, Blake was working on these poems simultaneously, and had not yet differentiated them at the time of his letter to Butts (260).

12. Foucault points out that "*self*-control is integrated into the practice of controlling others" ("Concern for Truth," 258, my emphasis). The danger implicit in the cultivation of the idea of subjective agency, then, is that it can blind the subject to the fact that it has already inescapably *interiorized* modes of control.

13. Blake's employment of the preposition "out" in this passage causes a certain amount of syntactical ambiguity: it is not entirely clear whether the muses *already* inhabit his brain and subsequently come "out" of this site and into his hand, or if the muses have previously been *out*side of the poet and are internalized in the act of invocation. The crucial point in either case is that Blake conceptualizes the muses as internal to the self *during* the act of writing.

14. Vogler's remark that St. Paul functions in Blake as a founder of discursivity is interesting in light of Foucault's assertion that it is only in the nineteenth century that we witness the historical arrival of writers who can be considered as "initiators of discursive practice." For Foucault, writers like Marx and Freud occupy this kind of position;

the Church Fathers, he argues, occupy a "'transdiscursive' position" ("What is an Author?" 131)—a position which spans discourses rather than inaugurates them. Foucault's argument would seem to be supported by the fact that St. Paul himself practised reading the Old Testament typologically, reading it, that is, for its pre-figurations of the inevitable arrival of Jesus Christ and the Christian Church. Despite the inconsistency between Vogler and Foucault in this regard, however, I am convinced that Vogler does not misread St. Paul's *function* for the Blakean text. His remark coincides with my own view, which I delineate below, that the Blakean text figures poetically and philosophically the necessity of a "return" to the textual origins of the Christian church. For Blake, I would suggest, Paul's major problem involved the fact that his doctrines—and subsequent orthodox readings of them—were too *consistent* with the framework of the already-established moral Law from which Christ came to *free* humanity. Blake's criticism of Paul might be conceptualized as follows: whereas Paul *should* have made the kind of break with tradition that would have established him as an "initiator of discursive practice," he merely occupied a "'transdiscursive' position."

15. In order to question and revise inherited discourses, it is necessary and inevitable, as Foucault argues, to "return to the origin" ("What is an Author?" 134), for we define the validity of a statement made within a given discursive practice "with respect to the work of the initiator" (134). Foucault insists that we return to the texts of initiators of discourse not to correct them but to probe their omissions, to question "those things registered in the interstices of the text, its gaps and absences. We return to those empty spaces that have been masked by omission or concealed in a false and misleading plenitude" (135).

16. See print 154 in: Geoffrey Keynes, comp. *William Blake's Illustrations to the Bible: A Catalogue.* London and New York: 1957.

17. In his complex reading of this passage, for example, David Riede sees the black cloud as figuring poetically the scales that are said to have fallen from St. Paul's eyes at the time of his conversion (261-62). One could also read the black cloud according to Hermetic doctrine (with which Blake was familiar). For Hermes, the creation of something new is always accompanied by unpleasant by-products: "Evil and foulness are accidents which follow on the making of things, just as rust forms on metal or dirt collects on a man's body; but the metalworker did not make the rust, nor did

the father who begot the body make the dirt" (cited in Tuveson 14).

18. See David Riede's comparative analysis of Blake's and Milton's readings of Galatians 4:21-28, wherein Riede offers an example of Blake's refusal to read the New Testament "in the letter" (263). See also Thomas Vogler's explication of the significance of the same biblical passage (149-50).

19. Rather than contemplating heights and distances (the "noblest," "purest," most secret and abstract phenomena), "effective" history, Foucault argues, "shortens its vision to those things nearest to it—the body, the nervous system, nutrition, digestion, and energies" ("Nietzsche, Genealogy, History," 155). *Milton*'s disruptive reading of the texts of Blake's predecessors, with its carnivalesque focus on the body and its physiological processes, would suggest that *Milton* is in agreement with Foucault's contention that "Historical sense has more in common with medicine than philosophy." And, with its diagnoses of the body's pathologies, the poem accords with the Foucauldian assertion that the task of an "effective history" "is to become a curative science" (156).

20. Blake's emphasis on the body demonstrates another crucial difference between Blakean and orthodox Christian modes of Self-examination. As Foucault points out, "Christian techniques of [self-]examination, confession, guidance, obedience, have an aim: to get individuals to work at their own 'mortification' in this world. Mortification is not death, of course, but it is a renunciation of this world and of oneself: a kind of everyday death. A death which is supposed to provide life in another world" ("Politics and Reason," 70). In his relentless critique of Pauline dualism, Blake vociferously opposes the notion that Christian self-mortification can be productive of spiritual life.

21. I am indebted here to Thomas Vogler's ground-breaking psychoanalytic study of Ololon's character. (See especially pages 143-47).

22. And yet, the fact that Ololon, like Satan, is repeatedly characterized in terms of "mildness" (see, for example, 21:15-16 and 37:5-7) suggests that there can be no easy solution to the revolutionary's dilemma: even the radical otherness that Ololon represents can not entirely escape discursive inscription. Thus, Blake's characterization of Ololon, and the role she/it/they play in relation to Milton, emphasizes the need for an incessantly vigilant and open-ended process of revolutionary Self-examination.

Works Cited

Ackroyd, Peter. *Blake*. London: Sinclair-Stevenson, 1995.

Blake, William. *The Complete Poetry and Prose of William Blake*. Rev. ed. Ed. David V. Erdman. New York and London: Doubleday, 1982.

———. *Milton a Poem. The Illuminated Blake: William Blake's Complete Illuminated Works with a Plate-by-Plate Commentary*. 1804. Ed. David V. Erdman. New York: Dover, 1974.

Clark, David L. "Against Theological Technology: Blake's 'Equivocal Worlds.'" *New Romanticisms: Theory and Critical Practice*. Ed. David L. Clark and Donald C. Goellnicht. Toronto: U of Toronto P, 1994. 164-222.

Cooper, Andrew M. "Blake's Escape From Mythology: Self-mastery in *Milton*." *Studies in Romanticism* 20 (1981): 85-110.

Damon, S. Foster. *A Blake Dictionary: The Ideas and Symbols of William Blake*. 3rd ed. Providence, Rhode Island: Brown UP, 1973.

Essick, Robert N., and Joseph Viscomi. Introduction. *Milton a Poem*. William Blake. Ed. Robert N. Essick and Joseph Viscomi. Princeton: Princeton UP, 1993.

Foucault, Michel. "Nietzsche, Genealogy, History." *Language, Counter-Memory, Practice*. Trans. Donald F. Bouchard and Sherry Simon. Ithaca, NY: Cornell UP, 1977. 139-64.

———. "What Is an Author?" *Language, Counter-Memory, Practice*. Trans. Donald F. Bouchard and Sherry Simon. Ithaca, NY: Cornell UP, 1977. 113-38.

———. *The History of Sexuality*. Trans. Robert Hurley. New York: Vintage, 1978.

———. "An Aesthetics of Existence." Trans. Alan Sheridan. *Michel Foucault: Politics, Philosophy, Culture: Interviews and Other Writings*. New York and London: Routledge, 1988. 47-53.

———. "The Concern for Truth." Trans. Alan Sheridan. *Michel Foucault: Politics, Philosophy, Culture: Interviews and Other Writings*. New York and London: Routledge, 1988. 255-67.

———. "Politics and Reason." *Michel Foucault: Politics, Philosophy, Culture: Interviews and Other Writings*. Trans. Alan Sheridan. New York and London: Routledge, 1988. 57-85.

———. "Politics and the Study of Discourse." Trans. Colin Gordon. *The Foucault Effect: Studies in Governmentality*. Ed. Graham Burchell et al. Chicago: U of Chicago P, 1991. 53-72.

Frye, Northrop. *Fearful Symmetry: A Study of William Blake*. Rev. ed. Princeton: Princeton UP, 1970.

Gallant, Christine. *Blake and the Assimilation of Chaos.* Princeton: Princeton UP, 1970.

Hayley, William. *The Life of Milton.* New York: Garland, 1971.

Keynes, Geoffrey. *William Blake's Illustrations to the Bible: A Catalogue.* London and New York: n.p., 1957.

Milton, John. *John Milton.* Ed. Stephen Orgel and Jonathan Goldberg. New York: Oxford UP, 1992.

Otto, Peter. *Constructive Vision and Visionary Deconstruction: Los, Eternity, and the Productions of Time in the Later Poetry of William Blake.* Oxford: Clarendon P, 1991.

Rajan, Tilottama. *The Supplement of Reading: Figures of Understanding in Romantic Theory and Practice.* Ithaca: Cornell UP, 1991.

Riede, David. "Blake's *Milton*: on Membership in the Church Paul." *Re-membering Milton: Essays on the Texts and Traditions.* Ed. Mary Nyquist and Margaret W. Ferguson. New York and London: Methuen, 1987. 257-77.

Simpson, David. "Reading Blake and Derrida—Our Caesars Neither Dead nor Buried." *Unnam'd Forms: Blake and Textuality.* Eds. Nelson Hilton and Thomas A. Vogler. Berkeley: U of California P, 1986. 11-25.

Spivak, Gayatri Chakravorty. *Outside in the Teaching Machine.* New York and London: Routledge, 1993.

Thompson, E. P. *Witness Against the Beast: William Blake and the Moral Law.* New York: New Press, 1993.

Tuveson, Ernest Lee. *The Avatars of Thrice Great Hermes: An Approach to Romanticism.* Lewisburg: Bucknell UP, 1982.

Vogler, Thomas A. "Re: Naming *MIL/TON.*" *Unnam'd Forms: Blake and Textuality.* Ed. Nelson Hilton, et al. Berkeley: U of California P, 1986. 140-76.

Wittreich, Joseph Anthony, Jr. "Opening the Seals: Blake's Epics and the Milton Tradition." *Blake's Sublime Allegory: Essays on* The Four Zoas, Milton, Jerusalem. Ed. Stuart Curran and Joseph Anthony Wittreich, Jr. Madison: U of Wisconsin P, 1973. 23-58.

———. "Blake's Milton: 'To Immortals, . . . A Mighty Angel.'" *Milton Studies* 11 (1978): 51-82.

Julia M. Wright (essay date 2004)

SOURCE: Wright, Julia M. "'A State About to be Created': Modeling the Nation in *Milton.*" In *Blake, Nationalism, and the Politics of Alienation,* pp. 111-34. Athens: Ohio University Press, 2004.

[*In the following essay, Wright examines* Milton's *underlying political meaning, interpreting the figure of Milton as a type of nationalist hero, a martyr to Blake's conception of English identity.*]

Self is the medium least refined of all
Through which opinion's searching beam can fall;
And, passing there, the clearest, steadiest ray
Will tinge its light and turn its line astray. . . .
But 'tis not only individual minds
That habit tinctures, or that interest blinds;
Whole nations, fooled by falsehood, fear, or pride,
Their ostrich-heads in self-illusion hide.

Thomas Moore, *The Sceptic* (1809)

Blake's first published epic, *Milton,* is usually read as a formally interesting spiritual autobiography, representing Blake's relationship with his bardic and mystic precursor, Milton,[1] as well as his vision of spiritual, if not apocalyptic, renovation or apotheosis,[2] in a fragmented, multiperspectival text.[3] Blake's personal identification with the poem is such that it is common in Blake criticism to find one of the poem's narrators referred to as Blake himself.[4] Such readings provide valuable insights into the main plot—or, rather, the central incident—of the poem, but they necessarily marginalize the political context of Milton's quest for self-annihilation and reunion with his emanation, a context energized by Milton's recent recuperation as a national bard. In *Milton,* Blake not only subverts the prevailing national narrative formally, as discussed in chapters 1 and 2, but explicitly critiques the cultural roots that inform it. These cultural origins are, like the bookish tyrants of *Europe,* propagated textually through the printing press. But it is not books generally, or the *Book of Urizen* symbolically, that Blake condemns in *Milton.* Instead, Blake singles out, in the preface, "The Stolen and Perverted Writings of Homer & Ovid: of Plato & Cicero" (*M* [*Milton*], 1)—classical texts.[5] Blake contends that classical texts infect English culture with classical paradigms and values, particularly false gods, imperialist militarism, and sacrifice: "Shakspeare & Milton were both curbd by the general malady & infection from the silly Greek & Latin slaves of the Sword" (*M,* 1). By doing so, Blake shows a sensitivity to hegemony's dependence on classical models in the promotion of duty and self-sacrificing heroism during the domestic and military conflicts of the Romantic period. In *Milton,* the protagonist thus not only functions as a representation of a poet, but as a symbol for the neoclassical national culture to which Milton was iconically related. Milton's purification at the climax of the poem is thus the cultural purification of England anticipated by the preface:

This is a false Body: an Incrustation over my Immortal
 Spirit; a Selfhood, which must be put off & annihilated alway
To cleanse the Face of my Spirit by Self-examination.
To bathe in the Waters of Life; to wash off the Not
 Human
I come in Self-annihilation & the grandeur of Inspiration
To cast off Rational Demonstration by Faith in the
 Saviour

To cast off the rotten rags of Memory by Inspiration
To cast off Bacon, Locke & Newton from Albions
 covering
To take off his filthy garments, & clothe him with
 Imagination
To cast aside from Poetry, all that is not Inspiration
That it no longer shall dare to mock with the asper-
 sion of Madness
Cast on the Inspired.

(*M,* 40.35-41.9)

when the New Age is at leisure to Pronounce; all will
 be set
right: & those Grand Works of the more ancient &
 consciously
& professedly Inspired Men, will hold their proper
 rank, & the
Daughters of Memory shall become the Daughters of
Inspiration. Shakspeare & Milton were both curbd by
 the general
malady & infection from the silly Greek & Latin
 slaves of the
Sword. . . . We do not want either Greek or Roman
 Models if we
are but just & true to our own Imaginations.

(*M,* 1)

Milton, the new national martyr and the author of the
quintessential national epic, is an ideal figure to enact
Blake's own nationalist solution: to cast off that which
is not, in Blake's view, English.

MILTON AND NATIONALIST MARTYRDOM

While there are many references to British geography,
Albion, British historical figures, commerce, and politi-
cal issues in the poem, they have often been marginal-
ized or elided in Blake criticism as the scale of the
poem is limited to the poet and extended to a mytho-
logical metareality. But, as Wittreich argues,

> Milton . . . provides Blake with a precedent for cel-
> ebrating the English as the second chosen people and
> the poet as their deliverer. He began *Paradise Lost* by
> equating England with Israel and himself with Moses.
> Blake, therefore, introduces **Milton** with a lyric that
> makes similar claims. England, he promises, will be
> the great agent in the apocalypse and the poet—a new
> and more successful Moses—will be the nation's awak-
> ener and guide.[6]

While Bloom suggests that "[t]he poem **Milton** is not
written to correct *Paradise Lost* so much as to invoke
Milton as a savior for Blake and for England, and there-
fore for mankind,"[7] this final step—"therefore for man-
kind"—is not so clear and is very much at odds with
contemporary representations of Milton.

Milton was often figured as a savior for England in the
limited national sense. In Wordsworth's sonnet "Lon-
don, 1802" Milton appears as a Christlike national sav-
ior who, like Arthur, Merlin, and other British heroes,
should rise in the nation's hour of need:

Milton! thou should'st be living at this hour:
England hath need of thee: she is a fen
Of stagnant waters: altar, sword, and pen,
Fireside, the heroic wealth of hall and bower
Have forfeited their ancient English dower
Of inward happiness. We are selfish men;
Oh! raise us up, return to us again;
And give us manners, virtue, freedom, power.
Thy soul was like a Star and dwelt apart:
Thou hadst a voice whose sound was like the sea;
Pure as the naked heavens, majestic, free,
So didst thou travel on life's common way,
In cheerful godliness; and yet thy heart
The lowliest duties on itself did lay.[8]

This view of Milton as an important player in a specifi-
cally national epic was developed in the latter years of
the eighteenth century. Milton was "more or less anath-
ematised" in Johnson's *Lives of the Poets,*[9] as well as
characterized as a regicide apologist; his authorship of
Paradise Lost was omitted in Bayle's *A General Dic-
tionary* (1697)[10]; and he makes no appearance in War-
ton's copious *History of English Poetry* (1774). Mil-
ton's work remained in print and retained an audience
throughout the century, of course, but Milton's literary
star rose primarily with his representation as the hero of
Protestantism and English liberty in the wake of the
conflict that damaged England's sense of itself as the
Protestant center of liberty—the American Revolution.

It is the additional cultural resonance offered by the
American Revolution that arguably helps to explain not
only Milton's rapid recuperation, but also the perva-
siveness of references to the poet in political contexts,
as various writers sought to contest or use Milton's cul-
tural weight in support of their own arguments. The ex-
tent of such appropriations was pronounced enough to
warrant comment in Hazlitt's essay on Shakespeare and
Milton. Referring to a passage in *Paradise Lost,* Hazlitt
claims that

> when any interest of a practical kind takes a shape that
> can be at all turned into this, (and there is little doubt
> that Milton had some such in his eye in writing it),
> each party converts it to its own purposes, feels the ab-
> solute identity of these abstracted and high specula-
> tions; and that, in fact, a noted political writer of the
> present day has exhausted nearly the whole account of
> Satan in the *Paradise Lost,* by applying it to a charac-
> ter whom he considered as after the devil (though I do
> not know whether he would make even that exception)
> the greatest enemy of the human race.[11]

This engagement with Milton's texts led to the poet's
canonization, completely in the literary sense and very
nearly in the sacred sense. Thus, Francis Jeffrey refers
to passages on Milton in a critical essay by Thomas
Campbell as "offerings not unworthy of the shrine."[12]

Milton, however, is not a generic national savior. A fig-
ure of rebellion for some and the hero of a more impe-
rial nationalism for others, Milton was exploited by

various competing definitions of nationalism. Milton's function as Blake's savior is particularly entangled with the nationalism that perhaps did the most to lift Milton from the literary and ideological margins that he inhabited in the decades that followed his death, the nationalism that restores England's status as the seat of Protestant liberty and values sacrifice for the national good. At the end of the eighteenth century, Milton was appropriated to serve an English, Protestant iconography that was disseminated and promoted to support a nationalist agenda that included militarist expansion and commercial exploitation. This agenda was validated by the belief, supported through reference to Milton's writings, that England had a divinely sanctioned mission. In *Milton*, however, Blake separates the prophetic Milton from the Milton amenable to such a political agenda without denying that those elements are present. While Frye argues that "though [Blake] symbolizes humanity by the name of his own nation, his 'Albion' has nothing to do with the frantic jingoism which a confused idea of the same symbolism might easily develop, and has developed in our day,"[13] the poem, I would argue, has everything to do with "frantic jingoism"—or rather, in more moderate language, everything to do with discarding one brand of patriotism in favor of another.

In the eighteenth century, Milton, as a figure for English national identity, was caught between two irreconcilable views of the nation. First, there was "royal national government" that "taught English people to look to the central government rather than to lord and priest."[14] In this system, most prominent during the Renaissance, the monarch was the focus of nationalist sentiment and political power. The royal system was later subverted, however, most dramatically in the execution of Charles I, by a view that defined the nation as a relationship between its populace and its institutions, arguably in recognition of the shift of power (both economic and intellectual) toward a broader demographic base. This revised view of the subject's fealty facilitated the generation of a nationalism that transcends class differences—or at least appears to do so—through the unifying ideologies of Protestantism, cultural supremacy, and commercialism. In a sense, the Protestant dimension of English national identity was extended to the secular: rather than defining the monarch as the bodily representative of the nation and the mediator through whom each subject expresses nationalism, each subject of the state could have a personal, unmediated relationship to the nation by embodying on a personal level a commitment to nationalist ideologies and a national identity that were ostensibly equally available to all. As Colley argues convincingly in *Britons,* the promotion of a Protestant national identity facilitated a kind of "mass patriotism" and a renovation of the monarchy's position as ideological rather than divinely granted to the person of the king.[15] The elite still set the agenda, but they did so under the guise of an allegiance

to institutions—the Anglican church, Parliament, and the commercial infrastructure—that they revered as much as those outside of the aristocratic oligarchy. It is this brand of nationalism that became more powerful during Blake's lifetime, particularly after the French Revolution and during the wars that ensued.[16] And it is a brand of nationalism that was particularly amenable to nonaristocratic heroes who displayed great devotion to fundamental institutions. Thus, instead of being rejected as a regicide apologist, Milton could be rehabilitated as a national martyr, described by Behrendt as "the preeminent exemplar of the visionary bard who sacrificed comfort, health (and eyesight), and contemporary fame in service to his country."[17] A self-sacrificing, decidedly Protestant parliamentarian such as Milton could be a powerful figure in popular nationalist discourse—just as a sacrificed, decidedly aristocratic, Protestant king had been a powerful figure in the elitist nationalist discourse in which Milton had been represented very differently.

This view of Milton as a self-sacrificing patriot is particularly important to emergent nationalism because of the emphasis on national martyrs in its iconography, an iconography that was communicated through a medium important to both Blake and *Milton*—painting. Behrendt identifies Blake's *Milton* not as a spiritual (auto)biography, but as a form of history painting within the "apotheosis tradition" "that fuses topical and biblical allusion [in] an apocalyptic view of war."[18] Such paintings were not, however, just produced to generate transcendence, but were used to generate political consensus through visual propaganda.[19] This propaganda was effective because it employed compelling iconography and could be reproduced for the masses in cheap engravings. It promoted duty, sacrifice for the national good, and other qualities that served particular political aims, such as facilitating the elite's self-representation as dutifully laboring to support key national institutions. Colley argues that Benjamin West's *Death of Wolfe* "caused a sensation" because it "took classical and Biblical poses of sacrifice and brought them into the British here and now," "start[ing] a vogue for paintings of members of the British officer class defying the world, or directing it, or dying in battle at the moment of victory."[20] Blake resists the assimilation of the individual into the self-sacrificing posture of the national subject, complaining in his **"Annotations to Reynolds's *Discourses*,"** "A History Painter Paints The Hero, & not Man in General" (**"Anno. Reynolds,"** 652).[21] Colley, moreover, demonstrates that the notion of the dutiful British subject who sacrifices all for the good of the nation was developed at the same time that Protestantism became a crucial divine validation for Britain's commercial and military power. Classicism became the conduit for such lessons: "patriotism of a kind was embedded in the classical curriculum. The emphasis on Greek and Roman authors and ancient history meant a con-

stant diet of stories of war, empire, bravery and sacrifice for the state."[22] It was the classical model of self-sacrificing aristocrats that informed the "paintings of members of the British officer class . . . dying at the moment of victory."[23]

The elite in Britain thus, at least in part, justified its existence in an age of radicalism and revolution through this nation-producing cult of self-sacrifice.[24] The view of the ruling classes as dutiful servants of the nation was so well-established in this period that it became a powerful rubric in the Victorian era, giving rise to Rudyard Kipling's notorious phrase "the White Man's burden" in the poem of that name. In *Tom Brown's Schooldays,* Thomas Hughes articulates it concisely in Arthur's description of his near-death epiphany: "I was beginning to see my way to many things, and to feel that I might be a man and do a man's work. To die without having fought, and worked, and given one's life away, was too hard to bear."[25] As early as 1784, however, the paradigm was being parodied. In John Boyne's *General Blackbeard Wounded at the Battle of Leadenhall* (3 January 1784), a clear parody of West's painting of Wolfe, the artist "lampoon[s] the very concept of a heroic death scene" and the model of duty which it underwrites.[26] Even Keats's "Ode on a Grecian Urn" echoes this reaction against classically inspired representations of sacrifice: the figures are "coming to the sacrifice" in a "Cold Pastoral" of unfulfilled desire ("never canst thou kiss, / Though winning near the goal"), trapped in the "slow time" of the "Sylvan historian," suggesting the stultification of a society that cannot escape the models of the distant, classical past it too readily valorizes aesthetically.[27] Blake's *Milton* participates in this subversion of the contemporary mythologizing of the aristocracy and martial elite through the rhetoric of the classics.

But Blake goes further, interrogating the operation of sacrifice within that mythologizing dynamic.[28] Sacrifice, including self-sacrifice, is not an isolatable construct within the poem: it is intimately linked, through the neoclassical ideology in which it is an important mechanism, to a violent economy in which, in the most general terms, destruction empowers the destroyer's clique, not least by establishing a network of sacrificial debt that traps all of the nation's subjects. Self-sacrifice raises the stakes, uniting the population behind its martyrs and the ideology in whose service they are enlisted. A few decades after Blake composed *Milton,* Ernest Renan remarked on the importance of shared sacrifice in the production of nationalist conviction:

> More valuable by far than common customs posts and frontiers conforming to strategic ideas is the fact of sharing, in the past, a glorious heritage and regrets, and of having, in the future, [a shared] programme to put into effect, or the fact of having suffered, enjoyed, and hoped together. . . . [S]uffering in common unifies

more than joy does. Where national memories are concerned, griefs are of more value than triumphs, for they impose duties, and require a common effort. A nation is therefore a large-scale solidarity, constituted by the feeling of the sacrifices that one has made in the past and of those that one is prepared to make in the future.[29]

But self-annihilation removes individual destruction from a public economy, and ends the communal suffering that validates that suffering in the name of the national agenda. Milton's own *Paradise Regain'd* can shed some light on this economy. In that poem, the Son delivers a condemnation of imperialism that is also a condemnation of earthly glory and the sacrifice it demands:

> They err who count it glorious to subdue
> By Conquest far and wide . . . what do these Worthies,
> But rob and spoil, burn, slaughter, and enslave
> Peaceable Nations, neighbouring, or remote,
> Made Captive, yet deserving freedom more
> Then those thir Conquerours, who leave behind
> Nothing but ruin wheresoe're they rove,
> And all the flourishing works of peace destroy,
> Then swell with pride, and must be titl'd Gods,
> Great Benefactors of mankind, Deliverers,
> Worship't with Temple, Priest and Sacrifice;
> One is the Son of *Jove,* of *Mars* the other.[30]

In his rejection of secular glory, Milton links imperial conquest with the pursuit of that glory, destruction, self-aggrandizement, sacrifice, and Roman gods. In other words, he maps the same economy in which destruction empowers the destroying social group under a classical rubric, and so links it intimately to nationalism and imperialism.[31] This is crucial to Blake's *Milton*—and Blake's Milton.

SELF-SACRIFICE AND THE ANNIHILATION OF NATIONALIST SELFHOOD

As Milton moves toward self-annihilation in *Milton,* Blake describes a nation—in geographic, economic, historical, mythological, and political detail—that is being undermined and oppressed by particular constructs, especially classical gods, "Moral Law," "Milton's Religion," commerce, Satanic tyranny, and the glorification of war. In *Milton,* all of these oppressive constructs are related to, but not contained by, the selfhood that Milton seeks to overcome. In this context, "Selfhood" functions as a sign for nationalism, as it does in Moore's poem *The Sceptic.*[32] It is the nexus of ideological constructs that inhabit and distort identity, generating a British landscape of "Satanic mills" and sacrifice rather than a pastoral Jerusalem. Milton's rejection of selfhood in Blake's poem is thus, on one level, the national bard's repudiation of the nationalist ideology in which he was implicated. By producing an alternative narrative of Milton that critiques this version of nationalism

in favor of the precapitalist pastoral ideal, Blake defamiliarizes a central nationalist icon and renders the prevailing nationalist narrative alien and alienating in terms of content as well as form.

Shortly after the conclusion of the **"Bard's Song,"** "Milton rose up from the heavens of Albion," "And Milton said, I go to Eternal Death! The Nations still / Follow after the detestable Gods of Priam; in pomp / Of warlike selfhood, contradicting and blaspheming" (*M,* 14.10, 14.14-16). Blake's Milton, however, is himself implicated in this "warlike selfhood":

> I will go down to self annihilation and eternal death,
> Lest the Last Judgment come & find me unannihilate
> And I be siez'd & giv'n into the hands of my own
> Selfhood. . . .
> I in my Selfhood am that Satan.
>
> (*M,* 14.22-24, 14.30)

Satan, earlier, is linked to the cult of sacrifice and self-sacrifice:

> Satans Druid Sons
> Offer the Human Victims throughout all the Earth, and
> Albions
> Dread Tomb immortal on his Rock, overshadowd the
> whole Earth:
> Where Satan making to himself Laws from his own
> identity.
> Compell'd others to serve him in moral gratitude &
> submission
> Being call'd God. . . .
> And it was enquir'd: Why in a Great Solemn Assembly
> The Innocent should be condemn'd for the Guilty?
> Then an Eternal rose
> Saying. If the Guilty should be condemn'd, he must
> be an Eternal Death
> And *one must die for another* throughout all Eternity.
> Satan is fall'n from his station & never can be
> redeem'd
> But must be new Created continually moment by mo-
> ment
> And therefore the Class of Satan shall be calld the
> Elect.
>
> (*M,* 11.7-12, 11.15-21; my emphasis)

With Druidic and Nordic associations,[33] as well as classical ones, Satan is aligned with various repressive and imperialist regimes as well as the "pomp / Of warlike selfhood" (*M,* 14.15-16), the Elect, the repressive portion of Milton, and the charge of "making to himself Laws from his own identity / Compell[ing] others to serve him in moral gratitude & submission" (*M,* 11.10-11). The Satanic position that Christ articulates in *Paradise Regain'd* is thus extended and ascribed to Milton's "Selfhood," a selfhood that he must annihilate.

Blake draws a clear distinction between self-annihilation and self-sacrifice. Self-annihilation is entirely personal; it is the individual's destruction of selfhood for the good of that individual. Conversely, self-sacrifice posits a social system of exchange in which "one must die for another," demanding the destruction of the self for a good that the sacrificed individual cannot realize but someone who has not abnegated selfhood can realize through a national economy. Crucially, self-annihilation operates in a limited, closed system, while self-sacrifice functions in an open, social one—hence Blake's references to a never-ending chain of sacrifices, "throughout all Eternity," so that Satan can "be new Created continually" (*M,* 11.18, 11.20).[34] Self-sacrifice, in other words, binds individuals into an aggregate, linking them, as Renan's remarks suggest, through bonds of duty and obligation rather than affection. Self-sacrifice, moreover, posits a power structure in which self-abnegation draws benefits from a higher authority and, as crucially, operates in propagandist discourse as an example to be followed by others for the greater good, implicating the members of the group in a rigid hierarchy as well as a duty-bound unit. It is the classical "cult of heroism" of the period, populated by men of rank "who had been indoctrinated . . . with Greek and Roman classics in which heroes sternly sacrificed their lives for the sake of honour and country,"[35] that Blake critiques at length in **Milton.** Daniel J. O'Neil also implicates such modes of self-sacrifice in Romantic organicism, arguing that it offers "a rejection of Lockean individualism. . . . They appealed back to an older Greco-Medieval tradition that perceived man as a link in a chain or a cell in a body. Accordingly, such thinking emphasized the common good and man's duties in contrast to natural and individual rights."[36] As O'Neil notes, "The implication of organismic thinking is that the sacrifice of an individual or one generation for the collective well-being is not an unreasonable request; the organism survives"[37]—a model with clear investments in the kinds of national narratives discussed in chapters 1 and 2. In **Milton,** however, the individual's well-being supersedes the collective, as Milton's self-annihilation corrects, at least for the poet, the self-sacrificing model in which "one must die for another throughout all Eternity" (*M,* 11.18), a "Human Harvest" (*M,* 42.33).

The broader social implications of everlasting Satanic sacrifice are elucidated further in related passages. The outline of the sacrificial system immediately precedes Leutha's self-sacrifice, and that offering is emphasized by the Bard's refrain:

> when Leutha . . . beheld Satans condemna-
> tion
> She down descended into the midst of the Great Sol-
> emn Assembly
> Offering herself a Ransom for Satan, taking on her,
> his Sin.
> Mark well my words. they are of your eternal salva-
> tion!
>
> (*M,* 11.28-31)

Repetitions of key phrases and images—"created continually," the Bard's refrain, and the three classes—link these passages, nonlinearly, to an earlier discussion of sacrifice:

> So Los spoke! Satan trembling obeyd weeping along the way.
> Mark well my words, they are of your eternal Salvation
> Between South Molton Street & Stratford Place: Calvarys foot
> Where the Victims were preparing for Sacrifice . . .
> Christ took on Sin in the Virgins Womb, & put it off on the Cross
> All pitied the piteous & was wrath with the wrathful & Los heard it.
>
> (*M,* 4.19-22, 5.3-4)

> For the Elect cannot be Redeemd, but Created continually
> By Offering & Atonement in the crue[l]ties of Moral Law
> Hence the three Classes of Men take their fix'd destinations
> They are the Two Contraries & the Reasoning Negative.
> While the Females prepare the Victims. the Males at Furnaces
> And Anvils dance the dance of tears & pain.
>
> (*M,* 5.11-16)

"Offering & Atonement in the crue[l]ties of Moral Law": in this chain of affiliated references to sacrifice, and particularly self-sacrifice, Satan is "Created continually" through the sacrifice of innocents and the circulation of sin—as if it were a transferable debt, like the obligation of Wordsworth's Michael, which forces the sacrifice of Luke—and that sacrifice of innocents is linked to British imperialism.

This interpenetration of capitalism, imperialism, and self-sacrifice in Blake's characterization of nationalism can be further comprehended through Colley's analysis of the constitution of British national identity via industrial and commercial power as well as military and imperial strength. Colley argues that commercial interests, and more generally individuals' concerns for their own prosperity, often determined political loyalties; "there was a real sense in which this commercial bonanza was dependent on government investment in naval power and imperialism. . . . [W]ar and empire indisputably played a vital part in breaking into and securing markets."[38] The arts were also encouraged through the market for engravings. Eaves notes the pattern in the promotion of engraving: "Since the commercial spirit . . . is also the national spirit, the English merchant helps English art clarify its own identity. In the new Rome the improved Maecenas is commercial. . . . Boydell realized that engraving was more than another depart-

ment of the arts. It was the missing link with commerce: engraving, as it reproduces painting, makes painting commercial."[39] These three values—imperial success, military power, and a strong commercial sector, particularly in the international domain—are inseparably intertwined in the constitution of British identity at the turn of the century. The many references in *Milton* to the commercial sector, especially its industrial component, can usefully be viewed in this context.

CONSTITUTING THE NEOCLASSICAL NATION

In *Milton,* moreover, Satan is identified as a state: "We are not Individuals but States: Combinations of Individuals. . . . Distinguish therefore States from Individuals in those States. . . . Satan & Adam are States Created" (*M,* 32.10, 32.22, 32.25). It is fairly common, in discussions of this passage and others on the same subject, to limit the significance of "state" to the nonpolitical. States are thus identified as "states of existence" or "states of mind," often in an evolutionary context, so that one passes from one state to the other as one moves toward Eden.[40] While Blake does associate states with embodiment (*M,* 32.10-29) and identifies four states—Beulah, Alla, Al-Ulro, and Or-Ulro—that are located in different regions of the body, the so-called doctrine of states is complicated by Blake's use of the term in political contexts. As Esterhammer notes, "Throughout Blake's work, the term 'state' seems more strongly influenced than has been realized by the notion of a state as a political entity and, secondly, the state(ment) as a linguistic entity. An expanded sociopolitical context can reveal profound connections among Blake's states, political states, and the speech acts on which both depend."[41] Blake is using clearly polysemic language here and generating a complex framework that is both ontologically and politically implicated. Damrosch writes of the doctrine, "[T]he invention of states represents a decisive change in Blake's myth, and I think an unfortunate one. Instead of showing that all parts of the self must be rehabilitated and harmonized, he now defines the qualities that he dislikes . . . as illusory and external to the self."[42] But this is precisely what interests me about it: Blake represents characters under the sway of external, cultural forces throughout his work, from the female characters in *Visions* [*of the Daughters of Albion*], *America,* and *Europe* to the pestilential errors of *Jerusalem,* but the doctrine of the states attempts to define and organize those forces into an intracultural topography. They are not simply "external to the self," but map systems that the self inhabits, including political systems (sometimes embodied in the constitutions about which Esterhammer writes) or states. Thus the Seven Angels not only declare that they are "not Individuals but States: Combinations of Individuals" (*M,* 32.10), but also claim that they "were combind in Freedom & holy Brotherhood" (*M,* 32.15) while defining themselves against "those combind by Satans Tyranny"

(*M,* 32.16), opposing the radicalism associated with the French and American revolutions, as well as the Irish uprising, to the British nationalism that was used against all three.

The conditions under which these "Individuals" were combined also determine the definition of their lineaments: the Seven Angels have "Human Form / Because [they] were combind in Freedom & holy Brotherhood / While those combind by Satans Tyranny . . . are Shapeless Rocks" (*M,* 32.14-17). In his analysis of Blake's valorization of visual line, Eaves makes an observation that is particularly relevant to this passage in *Milton*: "The distinguishing mark of these mental copies is clear and determinate outline, which the whole force of training, experience, and imagination teaches artists to separate from the blurry cultural ghosts and demons that haunt their minds. Demons (in their New Testament form) are external forces that take up internal residence—a kind of mental parasite that causes the host to be unlike itself."[43] Not only does the latter remark strongly suggest the various mergings of *Milton*—such as "Los had enterd into my soul" (*M,* 22.13), "He hath enterd into the Covering Cherub" (*M,* 23.14), and the infamous "Milton entering my Foot" (*M,* 21.4)—but the former suggests the "Shapeless Rocks" of tyranny that must be superseded by Milton and his "State."[44] Plate 32 of *Milton* defines two States: one, the Angels', is constituted under the ideals of radical politics, has members who therefore have definite form, and gives Milton "vision & dream beatific" (*M,* 32.2); the other, Satan's, is constituted under the tyranny of one who "destroyed the Human Form Divine" (*M,* 32.13), has members who are "Shapeless," and causes both "Sacrifice" and "Chains of imprisonment" (*M,* 32.17). Satan, who is identified at length with the classical, restrictive model, creates a political state of self-sacrifice and bondage—similar to that which the elite promoted by valorizing classical heroism and restraint. This breaks down the human form, just like the diseases that infect Albion in *Jerusalem* and the alienated baggage that is "Cast off" at the end of *Milton* (see chapter 6).

In *A Vision of The Last Judgment,* roughly contemporary with *Milton,* Blake makes a related argument: "Nations Flourish under Wise Rulers & are depressd under foolish Rulers it is the same with Individuals as Nations works of Art can only be produced in Perfection where the Man is either in Affluence or is Above the Care of it . . . this is A Last Judgment when Men of Real Art Govern & Pretenders Fall. . . . [R]eflect on the State of Nations under Poverty & their incapability of Art" (*VLJ* [*A Vision of The Last Judgment*], 561). While P. B. Shelley argues that the architects of what is good in society are poets—not only artists of all kinds, but "the institutors of laws, and the founders of civil society and the inventors of the arts of life"—and that a decay in social life is coincident with a decay in drama,[45] Blake

is more apocalyptic and binary: there is not an evolutionary cycle of rise and fall, but there are "Wise Rulers" creating vital societies and "Real Art," while "foolish Rulers" achieve the converse. Nevertheless, both poets claim that sociopolitical culture and artistic culture are mutually determining. Satan, in this context, is not just the rational selfhood that interferes with vision, as Blake describes it in *A Vision of The Last Judgment*: "I have . . . represented those who are in Eternity by some in a Cloud. . . . [T]hey merely appear as in a Cloud when any thing of Creation Redemption or Judgment are the Subjects of Contemplation, tho their Whole Contemplation is Concerning these things the Reason they so appear is The Humiliation of 'the Reasoning & Doubting' Selfhood" (*VLJ,* 563). Satan is also the tyrannical and "foolish Ruler," and his rule has particular features and origins, embedded in culture and the origin of the state. As the "Selfhood" of the national bard, which must be annihilated, the Satanic tyrant is at once the model that infects Albion and the political state that results from that infection.

This perceived conflict between true artistic creation and destructive militarism resonates with contemporary nationalist discourse. In his essay "On the Edge of Europe: Ireland in Search of Oriental Roots, 1650-1850," Joseph Th. Leerssen outlines a pattern that is useful to the present discussion:

> The Canaanites driven from Israel; the Phoenicians, supplanted by the Greek expansion; the Carthaginians, dispossessed by the Romans; and the Gaels, subdued and belittled by the English; in each case, the Phoenicio-Gaelic tradition is "runner-up," unlike victors who have their day and then decline, they are perennial, and form a tradition which links all these phases of Western civilization . . . an orientalist tradition of civility, starting with Solomon's temple . . . a tradition which elevates their cultivation over the military efficiency of their oppressors. An anti-classicist attempt is thus made to impugn the Graeco-Roman tradition as an intolerant, imperialist one, and to link its victims, from Phoenecia to Ireland, into a great tradition in its own right.[46]

In **"The Laocoön,"** it should be recalled, Blake describes the classical statue as "[Jehovah] & his two Sons Satan & Adam as they were copied from the Cherubim / of Solomons Temple by three Rhodians & applied to Natural Fact. or. History of Ilium" (**"L"** [**"The Laocoön"**], C-D). Blake's anticlassical position is not, of course, fully coincident with the Phoenicianism described by Leerssen; Blake is concerned with the Gothic, not the Gaelic. But as a politicized construct in which the Greco-Roman tradition is aligned with British imperialism and militarism, while an orientalized tradition is aligned with culture and civility, it has useful parallels to the political vision of *Milton.* As discussed in chapter 2, this anticlassicism also had historical support in the rise of gothic nationalism. In his study *National Identity,* Smith notes that neoclassical

movements "swept through Europe" in the late eighteenth century, characterizing "classical antiquity as a plateau of civilization that was being realized again in modern Europe but on an even higher plane"—and it is that neoclassical imperialism to which Blake objects so strenuously in *Milton*.[47]

Blake explicitly identifies militarism with imperial classical roots, particularly those of Rome, Greece, and Troy. The Trojans are not only identified with the founding of Rome and, through Virgil's *Aeneid,* aligned with Rome's conflict with Carthage in ways that resonate with Leerssen's observations. The Trojans also played an important role in the nationalist establishment of England's imperial genealogy through Geoffrey of Monmouth's claim that Brutus, the great grandson of Aeneas, was the first king of England.[48] After listing a series of powerful, imperial nations, beginning with "Italy Greece & Egypt" (*M*, 14.6), Blake's Milton complains, "The Nations still / Follow after the detestable Gods of Priam; in pomp / Of warlike selfhood" (*M*, 14.14-16). The Trojan deities are consistently aligned with egotism. Milton concludes his condemnation of the nations with the assertion "I in my Selfhood am that Satan" (*M*, 14.30), while the narrator sees within Milton's "Selfhood deadly" (*M*, 37.10) "the Gods of Ulro dark" (*M*, 37.16), who number twelve (*M*, 37.17, 37.34) and include "Saturn Jove & Rhea" (*M*, 37.33)—and "the Twelve Gods are Satan" (*M*, 37.60). In the poem, selfhood—specifically Milton's selfhood—Satan, and the Trojan gods are linked. Rintrah and Palamabron also condemn the Trojan deities by associating them with self-centeredness: "Asserting the Self-righteousness against the Universal Saviour, / Mocking the Confessors & Martyrs, claiming Self-righteousness . . . With Laws from Plato & his Greeks to renew the Trojan Gods, / In Albion" (*M*, 22.42-43, 22.53-54). Even Greek music is condemned: it is identified with Natural Religion in Rahab and Tirzah's temptation of Milton (*M*, 19.46-47). In Los's vision of oppression and apocalypse, the Trojan gods again appear. In this context, however, their historical alignment is clarified. Los laments,

> Lambeth ruin'd
> and given
> To the detestable gods of Priam, to Apollo: and at the Asylum
> Given to Hercules, who labour in Tirzahs Looms for bread
> Who set Pleasure against Duty: who Create Olympic crowns
> To make Learning a burden & the Work of the Holy Spirit: Strife.
> T[o] Thor & cruel Odin who first reard the Polar Caves

> Lambeth mourns calling Jerusalem. she weeps & looks abroad
> For the Lords coming, that Jerusalem may overspread all Nations.

(*M*, 25.48-55)

The Lord is Albion, "our friend and ancient companion" (*M*, 25.62). In this context, the Trojan deities are not identified just with militarism and egotism, but also with cultural formations from capitalism to the valorization of restraint, classical education, and nationalism. The subsequent reference to Odin further ties the classical gods to imperialism. As I have noted elsewhere, contemporary scholarship on northern mythology and antiquities claimed that Odin was not a god but an exile from Asia who participated in a Scythian revolt against the Roman empire and escaped to northern Europe after it failed.[49] Moreover, Odin is vilified in Mallet's *Northern Antiquities* for being a conqueror of northern Europe despite his anti-imperialist activities against Rome.[50]

In *Milton,* Blake narrates the self-annihilation of a sacrificial selfhood, ending the sacrificial chain of Protestant martyrdom that Milton began. ("They weave a new Religion from new Jealousy of Theotormon! / Miltons Religion is the cause: there is no end to destruction!" [*M*, 22.38-39].) He also narrates the annihilation of neoclassical, pro-imperialist, nationalism:

> making War upon the Lambs Redeemed
> To perpetuate War & Glory. to perpetuate the Laws of Sin . . .
> Shewing the Transgresors in Hell, the proud Warriors in Heaven:
> Heaven as a Punisher & Hell as One under Punishment:
> With Laws from Plato & his Greeks to renew the Trojan Gods,
> In Albion.

(*M*, 22.44-45, 22.51-54)

This emphasis on the infection of "Albion" by classical thought is a recurring one and it is tied to Blake's critique of sacrifice. Blake is condemning not only classicism and militarism, but also the political iconography prevalent at the time and used to promote sacrifice to the state—particularly, as in West's painting, on the battlefield—propagating a view of the elite as nationalist martyrs, giving their lives to save their country. In *Milton,* Blake repeatedly attacks the influence of classical models on British nationalism and culture and offers in its place his own construction of proper national identity: "We do not want either Greek or Roman Models if we are but just & true to our own Imaginations," and so contest "the detestable Gods of Priam," including Apollo, "Who set Pleasure against Duty" (*M*, 1,

25.49, 25.51). In other words, Milton's self-sacrifice was a terribly classical thing to do—and thus not, for Blake, very English. Satan is constructed as the nexus of these negative features and is the embodiment of the propaganda being distributed during the Romantic period to promote duty among the populace. He is a tyrant who follows the classical gods and selfhood, the destroyer of definite form, an Urizenic dictator from the elite, and a promoter of self-sacrifice. Satan, in other words, figures classically inspired hegemony, marking the interpenetration of culture and politics in the pursuit of glorious empire. Satan is not simply Milton's "Selfhood," but national egotism, the cipher that contains the hegemonic ideologies that were dressed up, through neoclassical heroism, as popular nationalism. To rephrase Milton's declaration by way of illustration, and with apologies to Frye, "I in English nationalism am that frantic jingoism." I am suggesting not that easy equivalences should be drawn between selfhood and nationalism or Satan and jingoism, but that Milton, Satan, and the renovation envisioned in *Milton* are implicated in the national renovation represented in the preface's famous lyric in ways specific to a critique of the prevalent contemporary nationalist ideology and iconography.

"No Part of Me": Nationalist Art(ifice)

At issue here are the implications of the art chosen to represent and propagate national ideals in order to forge a shared nationalist sense of self. In *Milton,* Blake invalidates not only the classical origins of those models, but also the "English" productions on which they are based. In examining the British urge to compete with France on cultural terms, Colley refers to a number of contests held to encourage and uncover native artistic talent, which in turn created a vogue for nationalist collections. English art was placed on a line of genealogical descent from Roman art, just as the English nation was rendered a distant cousin of Rome through claims of a shared Trojan descent, and the classical style formed the basis of artistic education in the period; moreover, when collectors abandoned national works they turned to classical artifacts. It is in this context that Blake declares, in the preface to *Milton,* "Painters! on you I call! Sculptors! Architects! Suffer not the fash-[i]onable Fools to depress your powers by the prices they pretend to give for contemptible works or the expensive advertizing boasts that they make of such works. . . . We do not want either Greek or Roman Models" (*M,* 1). Blake counters not just classicism, but also the promotion of classicism as a model for guiding nationalist aspirations. The "fashionable Fools" are "Hirelings in the Camp, the Court, & the University: who would if they could, for ever depress Mental & prolong Corporeal War" (*M,* 1). Such an assertion goes beyond a reference to the elite's support of the Napole-onic Wars, to the promotion of a national identity that was bound up in militarism, self-sacrifice, a sense of national mission, and a broad asceticism in which Milton was specifically implicated—an asceticism that served the interests of those seeking to maintain popular support for the financial and human costs of Britain's excessive military aspirations during the period.

Blake does not limit his critique to the content of the propaganda but also condemns its forms, particularly the epic. As Behrendt shows in "'The Consequence of High Powers': Blake, Shelley, and Prophecy's Public Dimension," biblical prophecy was written from the margins and classical epic from the center, the former seeking to transform society by returning it to lost values and the latter celebrating society's fulfillment of its values and auspicious origins. As discussed earlier, the relationship between the current society and its defining origin—or, rather, the perceived governing paradigm of the current society and the perceived governing paradigm of the origin—is fundamental to this opposition. The historical timeline is reduced to a comparison of the endpoints, and complicated by the different constructions of those endpoints that can be distilled from the "facts." Geoffrey Hill, for instance, suggests that the myth of the "Norman Yoke" places the Magna Carta in a list of concessions that the oppressed Saxons "extorted from their rulers,"[51] so that English history becomes defined by the struggle for liberty. Milton's epic vision was no different, functioning as a construction of national origin that some of Blake's contemporaries found unsettling. In *The Tremulous Private Body,* Francis Barker contends that Milton's essay *Areopagitica,* by arguing that texts should be evaluated and censored after they are published, inaugurates a new model of the relationship between state and subject: "in the Miltonic 'state'—that set of relations marked out in *Areopagitica*—it is already possible to detect the outline of that modern settlement which founds itself on a separation of realms between the public arena of the state apparatus and another domain of civil life. . . . The subject . . . may do as he pleases up to the point of transgression where its activity will be arrested by the agents of the apparatus who patrol the frontier between the two spaces."[52] These are the seeds of the surveillance that Foucault describes in *Discipline and Punish.* Barker argues that transferring the censorship of the text from before to after publication places on the publisher the onus of self-discipline—he should police himself or suffer the consequences, rather than be warned in advance that a work is unacceptable. Barker goes on to suggest that Milton identified self-discipline as an English characteristic, that "all of Milton's descriptions of social life emphasize the stability, maturity and sobriety of the English nation"; thus, by writing laws with certain expectations of the subject, "The state succeeds in . . . pre-constituting that subject as one which is already internally disciplined, censored, and thus an ef-

fective support of domination."[53] Blake anticipates this Foucauldian observation in his parenthetical remark, "Temperance, Prudence, Justice, Fortitude, the four pillars of tyranny" (*M,* 29.49). Milton, in other words, arguably helped to construct a national identity that was founded on a dutiful people following, almost inexorably, a religious epic narrative that he himself, with his self-sacrifice and "epic 'true virtue and valour,'" embodied.[54] But Blake associated duty and similar restraints with bondage and slavery. Just as Milton constitutes in his writings a national identity that is innately dutiful, Blake outlines a national identity that has been corrupted by fundamentally foreign writings that promote dutiful behavior—including Milton's.

But it is clear that Blake also posits a national identity that precedes this corruption. Classical "Models" have infected English literature, even the work of its most exemplary poets, and so deflected that tradition from individuals' imaginative visions; but that tradition can be purged: "Shakespeare & Milton were both *curbd* by the general malady & infection from the silly Greek & Latin slaves of the Sword. . . . We do not want either Greek or Roman Models if we are but *just and true to our own Imaginations,* those Worlds of Eternity in which we shall live for ever: in Jesus our Lord" (*M,* 1; my emphasis). This deflection, according to *Milton*'s preface, affects the governing classes of national society, including the military, the aristocracy, and the broader artistic community. Blake's preface argues for England's return to a pastoral ideal purged of classical corruption, specifically rejecting the militaristic and artistic paradigms, and institutions, that he identifies with that alien influence. Hence, in *Milton,* Blake's first published epic, the poet begins with a condemnation of the cultures that produced the models, both poetic and ideological, on which English literature's notions of epic are founded. "The Stolen and Perverted Writings of Homer & Ovid: of Plato & Cicero. which all Men ought to contemn," declares Blake in the preface, "are set up by artifice against the Sublime of the Bible" (*M,* 1). Milton, along with Shakespeare, is accused of being infected by such artifice. In the opening address of *Jerusalem,* "To the Public," Blake returns to the same poets and again condemns a verse form, this time blank verse:

> When this Verse was first dictated to me I consider'd a Monotonous Cadence like that used by Milton & Shakspeare & all writers of English Blank Verse, derived from the modern bondage of Rhyming, to be a necessary and indispensible part of Verse. But I soon found that in the mouth of a true Orator such monotony was not only awkward, but as much a bondage as rhyme itself. . . . Poetry Fetter'd, Fetters the Human Race! Nations are Destroy'd, or Flourish, in proportion as Their Poetry Painting and Music, are Destroy'd or Flourish![55]
>
> (3)

In his address, Blake thus makes an equation between Milton and Shakespeare, a nationally specific form of verse, and bondage, linking free verse form to national vitality. As in *Milton,* artistic forms are linked to destructive and restricting national cultures: "For we have Hirelings in the Camp, the Court, & the University: who would if they could, for ever depress Mental & prolong Corporeal War. . . . [B]elieve Christ & his Apostles that there is a Class of Men whose whole delight is in Destroying" (*M,* 1). In one of the poem's final plates, Blake associates the impoverished versifier with destructive power on a national level:

> To cast aside from Poetry, all that is not Inspiration
> That it no longer shall dare to mock with the aspersion of Madness
> Cast on the Inspired, by the tame high finisher of paltry Blots,
> Indefinite, or paltry Rhymes; or paltry Harmonies.
> Who creeps into State Government like a caterpillar to destroy![56]
>
> (*M,* 41.7-11)

This oppression of the human imagination is tied not only to the promotion of war but also to the creation of neoclassical nationalism. The poem is traversed by references to nations, especially references to the division of the population and the globe into such political organizations. In the same passage that describes the action of the press on human consciousness, that action is linked to both the existence and production of nations:

> The Wine-press on the Rhine groans loud, but all its central beams
> Act more terrific in the central Cities of the Nations
> Where Human Thought is crushed beneath the iron hand of Power.
> There Los puts all into the Press, the Opressor & the Opressed
> Together, ripe for the Harvest & Vintage & *ready for the Loom.*[57]
>
> (*M,* 25.3-7; my emphasis)

> you must bind the Sheaves not by Nations or Families
> You shall bind them in Three Classes; according to their Classes
> So shall you bind them. Separating What has been Mixed
> Since Men began to be *Wove into Nations* by Rahab & Tirzah . . .
> When under pretence to benevolence the Elect Subdud All.
>
> (*M,* 25.26-31; my emphasis)

> They became Nations in our sight [Los's] beneath the hands of Tirzah.
>
> (*M,* 24.16)

This use of weaving to figure the combination of individuals into families and nations is not simply another

iteration of the connection between form and state. Inscribed weaving (*textere*) is also used to figure the social structure of the combined state:

> My Garments shall be woven of sighs & heart broken
> lamentations
> The misery of unhappy Families shall be drawn out
> into its border. . . .
> I will have Writings written all over it in Human
> Words
> That every Infant that is born upon the Earth shall
> read
> And get by rote as a hard task of a life of sixty years
> I will have Kings inwoven upon it, & Councellors &
> Mighty Men.
>
> (*M*, 18.6-7,12-15)

There is a complex of related figures here, making up an iconography in which a nation is produced when the populace is oppressed or "Subdud" and then woven into a hierarchical structure governed by kings and "Mighty Men." In broad terms, then, Blake's view of the nation is similar to Gellner's:

> The basic deception and self-deception practised by nationalism is this: nationalism is, essentially, the general imposition of a high culture on society, where previously low cultures had taken up the lives of the majority, and in some cases of the totality, of the population. It means that generalized diffusion of a school-mediated, academy-supervised idiom, codified for the requirements of reasonably precise bureaucratic and technological communication. It is the establishment of an anonymous, impersonal society, with mutually substitutable atomized individuals, held together above all by a shared culture of this kind, in place of a previous complex structure of local groups, sustained by folk cultures reproduced locally and idiosyncratically by the micro-groups themselves.[58]

The garment is a constitution, establishing the national order that contains and restrains the population, and it is such a garment that Milton, in Blake's rewriting of his life, must cast off.[59]

At issue here is not just the relation between form and content, or propaganda and political consensus, but the modeling of the perceptual domain through cultural artifacts. Recognizing the division of societies into technologically or artistically competent cultures only begins to allow us to grasp this. Blake's *Milton* not only condemns classical and commercial paradigms, but also offers new models that redefine the culture of the national state. In the context of a critique of the infection of the national body by Greek and Roman texts and models, Blake's re-visioning of space, time, mythology, the relationship between the individual and the state, and the formation of nations cannot be purely aesthetic in function. As an exercise in modeling, *Milton* ranges from physics to commerce, from geography to history, and from wine making to war. In Blake's later writings,

the emphasis on national affiliations in *America* and *Europe* is extended and transformed. Rather than Americans and Daughters of Albion, the engravings "Laocoön" and "On Homers Poetry"/"On Virgil," as well as *Milton* and *Jerusalem,* posit national ideologies that are communicated through cultural artifacts that are historically specific. In *America* and *Europe,* Albion's Guardian oppresses the British and American peoples via the metanational Urizenic book, but in these later texts, "Greek or Roman Models" constrain "our own Imaginations" (*M,* 1) and "Desolate Europe with Wars" ("On Homers Poetry") through a variety of works that are named: in "On Virgil," the culprits are "Homer Virgil & Ovid"; in *Milton,* the list is extended to include "The Stolen and Perverted Writings of Homer & Ovid: of Plato & Cicero," as well as the classically influenced "Shakspeare & Milton" (*M,* 1). Blake thus historicizes the development of paradigms to which he objects, returning to the model of infection that appears in "Gwin, King of Norway" and locating the responsibility for human actions in cultural forces rather than abstracted or supernatural ones. In *Milton,* Blake describes this process explicitly, or at least with relative explicitness, writing, "This . . . is the Printing-Press / Of Los; and here he lays his words in order above the mortal brain / As cogs are formd in a wheel to turn the cogs of the adverse wheel" (*M,* 27.8-10). In *Milton,* however, Blake does not simply engage the issue of cultural hybridity and the political force of culture. He is specifically concerned with the political iconography that supported a particular brand of British nationalism—militarist, dutiful, self-sacrificing, imperial, and hungry for glory. Through Albion, Blake separates national identity from that brand of nationalism: that nationalism, or "jingoism," does not serve Albion but Satan, and it is not derived from British traditions but from classical ones. The nationalism that government propaganda, and the rehabilitation of Milton, circulated to interpellate the population into a sense of community that valorized a willingness to sacrifice for that community's defining political agenda is thus defamiliarized in the sense of being framed as a nonfamilial strain infecting the proper national familiar and family. In *Milton,* Blake's resistance to interpellation into governing communal paradigms—the linearity of writing in the artistic community; national narratives, in the pseudoantiquarian texts; models of social relations, in *Europe, America,* and *Visions of the Daughters of Albion;* codes of gender and authority, in the preludiums; and prevailing models of political health—is reflected in the putative origin and exemplar of certain nationalist paradigms escaping his own error, and casting off that which is "Not Human."

Notes

References to all of Blake's writings, except "The Laocoön," will be to the *Complete Poetry and Prose of*

William Blake, rev. ed., ed. David V. Erdman (New York: Doubleday, 1988), and all references to the Bible will be to the King James version. Blake's texts will be cited by line, plate, and chapter numbers where applicable, and by Erdman's page number where not. All references to Blake's engravings will be to *The Illuminated Books of William Blake,* 6 vols., gen. ed. David Bindman (Princeton: Princeton University Press, 1998), cited by the plate number in the Erdman edition, unless otherwise specified. Because of editorial issues discussed in chapter 1, all references to the texts of "The Laocoön," except where editions are specified, are my own transcriptions from reproductions of the design (with reference also to various editions of the texts), with the quadrant in which the quotation is located being indicated by A (upper left-hand), B (upper right-hand), C (lower left-hand), and D (lower right-hand).

1. [Northrop] Frye goes as far as to suggest that "[f]or Blake, . . . to imitate Milton is to imitate Jesus, just as, for Virgil, to imitate Homer was to imitate 'nature'" (*Fearful Symmetry* [1947; reprint, Princeton: Princeton University Press, 1969], 322). The power of this reading of *Milton* is such that the poem is central to [Harold] Bloom's formulation of the dynamics of poetic influence. As early as 1970, Bloom wrote that it is the "anxiety of influence" that Blake "had labored heroically to overcome in *Milton*" ("Blake's *Jerusalem*: The Bard of Sensibility and the Form of Prophecy" [1970], reprinted in *The Ringers in the Tower* [Chicago: University of Chicago Press, 1971], 75). In *Anxiety of Influence,* Bloom depends on Blake's poem for a language to discuss that anxiety, from applying the States to the stages of "Poetic Influence" to identifying the Covering Cherub with "creative anxiety" (*The Anxiety of Influence: A Theory of Poetry* [New York: Oxford University Press, 1973], 30, 36). William Dennis Horn argues, "For Bloom this story [*Milton*] stands as a type for the dynamics of influence in which the newcomer can overcome his belatedness only by assimilating and then correcting his precursor" ("Blake's Revisionism: Gnostic Interpretation and Critical Methodology," in *Critical Paths,* [edited by Dan Miller, Mark Bracher, and Donald Ault, 72-98. Durham, N.C.: Duke University Press, 1987,] 73). This issue is too fundamental to Blake criticism to enumerate fully the more interesting examinations of it, but Joseph Wittreich's study warrants special mention: Joseph Anthony Wittreich Jr., *Angel of Apocalypse: Blake's Idea of Milton* (Madison: University of Wisconsin Press, 1975). Jackie DiSalvo pays scant attention to *Milton,* but generatively traces Milton's influence through the rest of Blake's corpus in *War of Titans: Blake's Critique of Milton and the Politics*

of Religion (Pittsburgh: University of Pittsburgh Press, 1983).

2. Critics vary in their assessments of the degree of secularity of this individual renovation. Frye, for instance, suggests, "*Milton* is an individual prologue to the omen of something universal coming on. The Last Judgment lies on the distant horizon, and is prophesied in the final line of the poem" (*Fearful Symmetry,* 323); and calls it "the great poem of individual awakening" (*A Study of English Romanticism* [Chicago: University of Chicago Press, 1968], 38). Bloom maintains that "*Milton* . . . is shown casting off his own selfhood and moving toward a visionary emancipation that Blake desires as his own," but, "What belonged to religious convention or 'moral virtue' in the historical Milton is of no help to Blake, nor was it to Milton himself, in Blake's view" ("Commentary," [in *The Complete Poetry and Prose of William Blake,* rev. ed., edited by David V. Erdman, 894-970. New York: Doubleday, 1988,] 909). Erdman argues for a more secular version of apocalyptic renovation, a "*mental* liberation" after which "Blake" is "mentally ready for the Great Harvest," which has apocalyptic overtones (*Prophet against Empire,* [Rev. ed. Garden City, N.Y.: Doubleday, 1969,] 423). See also Florence Sandler, "The Iconoclastic Enterprise: Blake's Critique of 'Milton's Religion,'" *Blake Studies* 5 (1972): 13-57; Thomas R. Frosch argues, "In *Milton,* Blake expands his analysis of the obstructions within the imagination" (*The Awakening of Albion: The Renovation of the Body in the Poetry of William Blake* [Ithaca: Cornell University Press, 1974], 41).

3. [S. Foster] Damon argues, "The act of the poem is one, but the causes are so complex that Blake had to invent an original structure, to suggest the simultaneousness of all the material. He introduced material without any preparation, abruptly changing the subject over and over" (*A Blake Dictionary,* [rev. ed. London: Brown University Press, 1988,] 280). More recently, critics have noted that this narrative fragmentation is also a fragmentation of narrative perspective, whether "antiperspectivism" (Frosch, *Awakening of Albion,* 116) or "the shifting of visionary perspectives" (Bloom, *Blake's Apocalypse,* [Garden City, N.Y.: Doubleday, 1963,] 310). See also, for instance, [Susan] Fox, *Poetic Form* [*Poetic Form in Blake's* Milton, Princeton: Princeton University Press, 1976,] 6; Wittreich, *Angel of Apocalypse*; and Mark Bracher, *Being Form'd: Thinking Through Blake's* Milton (Barrytown, N.Y.: Station Hill, 1985).

4. Bloom, for instance, writes, "Blake goes with Los to the gate of the city of Golgonooza. . . . One

point of this incident is to show us that Blake is now distinct from Palamabron" (*Blake's Apocalypse,* 334). While contesting the theoretical premises behind the "readiness of even sympathetic readers to confuse a poet's life and his imagination," Frye maintains that "[t]here are . . . borderline cases where it is impossible wholly to separate art and biography, and Blake's *Milton* is one of them" (*Fearful Symmetry,* 326, 327). It is my position that the "I" of the poem is always distinct from Blake; while the poem contains some references that suggest a correspondence between a figure in the poem and the historical Blake, their signification is transformed by their poetic context.

5. It is worth noting that Blake did not include the preface in two of the copies of *Milton,* C and D, though Essick and Viscomi suggest that it was provisionally included in copy C (*Milton, A Poem,* 39 n). There are various theories regarding why the preface was excluded in the later copies of the poem, but no textual or extratextual evidence has yet emerged to give us clear direction on the subject.

6. Wittreich, *Angel of Apocalypse,* 239.

7. Bloom, *Blake's Apocalypse,* 308.

8. Wordsworth, "London, 1802," in *William Wordsworth,* [edited by Stephen Gill. New York: Oxford University Press, 1989,] 286. Paul Keen uses Wordsworth's sonnet to begin his discussion of the poet's ideological transition from radicalism to a more Burkean position, indicating the utility of Milton in a more conservative nationalism than one might expect, given his earlier status as a regicide apologist; see Paul Keen, "Critical Leapfrog: Wordsworth's Canonical Ambivalence," *Critical Mass* 3 (1992): 21-29.

9. [John] Lucas, *England and Englishness,* [London: Hogarth, 1990,] 12.

10. Wittreich, *Angel of Apocalypse,* 271 n. Regarding the reception of Milton's support of regicide during the eighteenth century, see, for example, James King, "Cowper, Hayley, and Samuel Johnson's 'Republican' Milton," in *Studies in Eighteenth-Century Culture,* vol. 17, ed. John Yolton and Leslie Ellen Brown (East Lansing, Mich.: Colleagues Press, 1987), 229-38; Lucas, *England and Englishness,* 45-46; and Wittreich, *Angel of Apocalypse,* 272 n. Pre-Romantic discomfort with Milton's politics extended to his works. John Dennis thus stressed its "formal achievement," and, in an illustrated edition of *Paradise Lost,* "the radical intention of Milton's work is . . . deliberately subverted, or undercut" (Lucas, *England and Englishness,* 17, 16).

11. William Hazlitt, *Lectures on the English Poets* (1818; reprint, Toronto: Oxford University Press, 1952), 100.

12. Francis Jeffrey, "Review of *Specimens of the British Poets; with Biographical and Critical Notices, and an Essay on English Poetry,*" by Thomas Campbell, *Edinburgh Review* 31 (March 1819): 478.

13. Frye, *Fearful Symmetry,* 340.

14. Boyd C. Shafer, *Faces of Nationalism: New Realities and Old Myths* (New York: Harcourt Brace Jovanovich, 1972), 35.

15. [Linda] Colley, *Britons,* [New Haven: Yale University Press, 1992,] 28.

16. Besides Colley, see, for example, Shafer, *Faces of Nationalism,* esp. 121-22. The Schofield incident is relevant in this context, not because Blake's swift dismissal of the soldier from his Felpham garden and his anxiety over the ensuing trial for sedition gives us a deeper sense of Blake's anti-militarist feeling during the years that he wrote *Milton,* but because of the larger dynamic at work. As G. E. Bentley Jr. points out, "the journal of John Marsh, among other documents, indicates that popular support for the military in Sussex in 1803 and 1804 was very muted" ("*Rex v. Blake*: Sussex Attitudes toward the Military and Blake's Trial for Sedition in 1804," *Huntington Library Quarterly* 56 [1993]: 88). Such evidence lends further support to Colley's argument, in *Britons,* that many regions of Britain were less than enthusiastic when it came to supporting the national military. The Schofield incident was arguably, as Bentley proposes in "*Rex v. Blake,*" "not so much *Rex v. Blake* as *Rex v. Vox Populi* or *The Military v. the People*" (88), complicating attempts to arouse nationalist support for military efforts.

17. [Stephen C.] Behrendt, *Reading William Blake,* [New York: St. Martin's, 1992,] 154.

18. Ibid., 154, 155.

19. See Colley, *Britons,* 178-82.

20. Ibid., 179.

21. To quote a passage from [Ernest] Gellner already cited in the introduction, "Far from revelling in the defiant individual will, nationalists delight in feelings of submission or incorporation in a continuous entity greater, more persistent and more legitimate than the isolated self" (*Nations and Nationalism,* [Oxford: Blackwell, 1983,] 133).

22. Colley, *Britons,* 167-68.

23. Ibid., 179.

24. I take the term "cult of self-sacrifice" from Daniel J. O'Neil, "The Cult of Self-Sacrifice: The Irish Experience," *Éire-Ireland* 24 (1989): 89-105. O'Neil's comments on Italian nationalism during World War I are also applicable here: "the nation-building effort seems intimately intertwined with the cult of sacrifice. Even a peaceful, revolutionary transition to nationhood often must be elevated to heroic status with its pantheon of martyrs. The nation cannot be born without blood and suffering" (93).

25. Thomas Hughes, *Tom Brown's Schooldays* (1857) (Markham, Ontario: Puffin, 1971), 243.

26. Cindy McCreery, "Satiric Images of Fox, Pitt, and George III: The East India Bill Crisis, 1783-1784," *Word & Image* 9 (1993): 177-78.

27. John Keats, "Ode on a Grecian Urn," in *The Poems of John Keats,* ed. Jack Stillinger (Cambridge: Harvard University Press, 1978), lines 31, 45, 17-18, 2-3.

28. Michael Ferber tentatively points to such a reading, suggesting that Blake's critique of self-sacrifice or atonement contends that the "elect" "create themselves (their Selves) by their belief in the atonement" (*The Social Vision of William Blake* [Princeton: Princeton University Press, 1985], 77). My aim here is to historicize that contention, and suggest that Blake was identifying an influential cultural construct rather than simply engaging a theological point.

29. Ernest Renan, "What Is a Nation?" trans. Martin Thom, in *Nation and Narration,* [edited by Homi K. Bhabha, 8-22. New York: Routledge, 1990,] 19.

30. John Milton, *Paradise Regain'd,* in *The Complete Poetry of John Milton,* ed. John T. Shawcross, rev. ed. (Garden City, N.Y.: Doubleday, 1971), 3.71-72, 3.74-84.

31. My concern here is with nationalism and anticlassicism in *Milton,* particularly in connection to the rhetoric of sacrifice invoked by neoclassical nationalist ideology. I have dealt with other issues related to this line of enquiry—Blake's representation of Cromwell's Latin secretary, Milton, apocalyptic critiques of imperialism, and imperial genealogies (Greece, Rome, Egypt, Britain)—elsewhere, in my essay "'Greek & Latin Slaves of the Sword': Rejecting the Imperial Nation in Blake's *Milton,*" in *Milton and the Imperial Vision,* ed. Elizabeth Sauer and Balachandra Rajan (Pittsburgh: Duquesne University Press, 1999), 255-72.

32. Moore's satire was published in 1809 and therefore appeared in the first part of the period in which Blake's *Milton* may have been composed.

33. See, for example, the identification of Satan's false exterior with "the Wicker Man of Scandinavia" (*M,* 37.11) and the reference to "Satans Druid sons" who "Offer the Human Victims throughout all the Earth" (*M,* 11.7, 11.8).

34. This distinction has certain continuities with the formal distinction discussed in chapter 2: self-sacrifice operates, in a sense, like a linear narrative, combining individuals into a coherent aggregate through bonds of causation; self-annihilation, however, is closed off from the whole, and so its iterations are not contained within a governing narrative or causal relationship.

35. Colley, *Britons,* 180.

36. O'Neil, "The Cult of Self-Sacrifice," 91-92. O'Neil suggests that Burke, the Romantic period's great defender of the status quo, exemplified this type of thinking.

37. Ibid., 92.

38. Colley, *Britons,* 69-70.

39. [Morris] Eaves, *Counter-Arts* [*The Counter-Arts Conspiracy,* Ithaca: Cornell University Press, 1992,] 68. Eaves here refers to engraver and print seller John Boydell (for a short biographical sketch of Boydell, see Eaves, *Counter-Arts,* xxiv).

40. Damon, for example, defines "States" as "stages of error" (*A Blake Dictionary,* 386); Fox argues, "Each of these units [states] shelters a collection of fallen individuals, who pass successively from unit to unit, 'state' to 'state,' until they may pass beyond states altogether" (*Poetic Form,* 141); Frosch suggests that it is "Blake's literal contention that worlds, total fabrics of internal and external being, are as fluid and changeable as psychic states. The state of mind is instead the new way in which we are to see ourselves in relation to our condition," *Awakening of Albion,* 94; and Bloom contends, "The State of Milton . . . is a state of self-annihilation" (*Blake's Apocalypse,* 348-49). For one of the more nuanced and comprehensive examinations of Blakean states and individual conditions, see Jeanne Moskal, *Blake, Ethics, and Forgiveness* (Tuscaloosa: University of Alabama Press, 1994), chap. 3. See also, for example, Edward J. Rose, "Blake's Metaphorical States," *Blake Studies* 4 (1971): 9-31.

41. [Angela] Esterhammer, *Creating States,* [Toronto: University of Toronto Press, 1994,] 203-4. As Esterhammer added in a conference version of some of this material, "In a historical period when Blake heard of political states being created and abolished all around him, in revolutionary France, in all parts of Europe, and throughout the British

Empire, political connotations are close at hand" ("Blake's *Jerusalem* and the Language of Constitutions" [paper presented at the inaugural conference of the North American Society for the Study of Romanticism, London, Canada, 29 August 1993]). For some examples of Blake's clear use of the term "state" in its political sense, see the "Annotations to Bacon's *Essays Moral, Economical and Political,*" in which, for instance, Blake writes, "Is Nobility a portion of a State i.e Republic" (624).

42. [Leopold] Damrosch, *Symbol and Truth* [*Symbol and Truth in Blake's Myth,* Princeton: Princeton University Press, 1980,] 154.

43. Eaves, [*William Blake's*] *Theory of Art,* [Princeton: Princeton University Press, 1982,] 29.

44. See also Eaves's remark, "The picture of emotion as shapeless is embedded in a number of familiar ideas about art: in the usual eighteenth-century definition of sublimity, for instance, where strong, impetuous emotion is associated with vagueness" (*Theory of Art,* 59).

45. Percy Bysshe Shelley, "A Defence of Poetry," [in *Shelley's Poetry and Prose,* edited by Donald H. Reiman and Sharon B. Powers. New York: Norton, 1977,] 482, 492.

46. Joseph Th. Leerssen, "On the Edge of Europe: Ireland in Search of Oriental Roots, 1650-1850," *Comparative Criticism* 8 (1986): 100, 101.

47. [Anthony D.] Smith, *National Identity,* [reprint, Reno: University of Nevada Press, 1991,] 87, 88.

48. The story of Brutus appears in Geoffrey of Monmouth's twelfth-century text *Historia Regum Britanniae,* and was regularly cited by English writers over the next five hundred years, from Layamon, who penned a poem titled *Brut* (c. 1200), to William Warner's *Albion's England or Historical Map of the Same Island* (1586) and Milton's *History of Britain.* Brutus is represented as the conqueror of the indigenous population, but the founder of the writer's people, so that the English are not the descendants of brutes, so to speak, but the imperial Brutus.

49. Thomas Warton, "Of the Origin of Romantic Fiction in Europe" (1774), *The History of English Poetry,* 3 vols., additional notes by Ritson, Ashby, et al. (London: Tegg, 1840), 1:xx; John Bell, *Bell's New Pantheon,* 2 vols. (1790; reprint, New York: Garland, 1979), 2:233; [Paul Henri] Mallet, *Northern Antiquities,* [translated by Bishop [Thomas] Percy. 2 vols. 1770. Reprint, New York: Garland, 1979,] 1:59-62.

50. See [Julia M.] Wright, "'Empire Is No More,'" [in *Blake: An Illustrated Quarterly* 26 (1992): 26-29,] 28.

51. Geoffrey Hill, "The Norman Yoke," *Puritanism and Revolution: Studies in Interpretation of the English Revolution of the Seventeenth Century* (London: Secker and Warburg, 1958), 57.

52. Francis Barker, *The Tremulous Private Body: Essays in Subjection* (New York: Methuen, 1984), 46.

53. Ibid., 46, 47.

54. Lucas, *England and Englishness,* 45. Arguably, this elision of Milton with his "strong words" informs what S. H. Clark identifies as a "contest" in *Milton* "between prophetic voice and the play of writing" ("Blake's *Milton* as Empiricist Epic: 'Weaving the Woof of Locke,'" *Studies in Romanticism* 36 [1997]: 463).

55. Erdman suggests that the composition of *Milton* and *Jerusalem* overlapped and that the preface to *Milton* in particular might be of later date ("Textual Notes," [in *The Complete Poetry and Prose of William Blake,* rev. ed., edited by David V. Erdman, 786-893. New York: Doubleday, 1988,] 809), so linking that preface to an early plate in *Jerusalem* is not necessarily anachronistic. However, I would suggest that similarities between the genre and concerns of the two plates are sufficient grounds for placing them in conjunction; if they are not contemporary, the later plate is arguably an allusion to the earlier, though we may never know which was which.

56. It is tempting to suggest that Blake's description of the uninspired was influenced by Robert Southey's appointment to the position of poet laureate in 1813. Our inability to fix a date for the poem makes this suggestion at once possible to speculate and difficult to assert: the first three copies of the poem are printed on 1808 paper, and Erdman suggests that the plates were engraved in 1809-1810, but the fourth copy was printed on 1815 paper; plate 41 is common to all four versions, and Erdman's dating of the plates is contingent on the assumption that *Milton* was nearly complete when Blake wrote *Public Address* (see "Textual Notes," 806).

57. By linking the printing press to the "Wine-press on the Rhine," Blake may be alluding to the story that Johann Gutenberg's first press was a modified wine press.

58. Gellner, *Nations and Nationalism,* 57.

59. Compare [Thomas] Paine's discussion of the language of the English and French constitutions and of the significance of other writings when discussing the French state (esp. 111-16). Paine asserts, for instance, "As Mr Burke has not written on

constitutions, so neither has he written on the French revolution" (*Rights of Man,* [1791-1792. Edited by Henry Collins. Markham, Ont.: Penguin, 1983,] 115).

FURTHER READING

Criticism

Barfoot, C. C. "'Milton Silent Came Down My Path': The Epiphany of Blake's Left Foot." In *Moments of Moment: Aspects of the Literary Epiphany,* edited by Wim Tigges, pp. 61-84. Amsterdam: Rodopi, 1999.

Discusses the symbolic importance of epiphany in *Milton.*

Behrisch, Erika. "'The Great Map of Mankind': Corporeal Cartography and the Route to Discovery in William Blake's *Milton.*" *English Studies in Canada* 27, no. 4 (December 2001): 435-58.

Examines the relationship between Blake's depictions of the human body and his conception of the self in *Milton.*

Clark, S. H. "*Milton* as Empiricist Epic: 'Weaving the Woof of Locke.'" *Studies in Romanticism* 36, no. 3 (fall 1997): 457-82.

Compares Blake's attitude toward empiricism in *Milton* with the philosophy of John Locke.

Curran, Stuart. *Sublime Allegory: Essays on* The Four Zoas, Milton, Jerusalem. Madison: University of Wisconsin Press, 1973, 384 p.

Offers a range of critical reactions to Blake's prophetic poems.

DiSalvo, Jackie. *War of Titans: Blake's Critique of Milton and the Politics of Religion.* Pittsburgh: University of Pittsburgh Press, 1983, 391 p.

Discusses the influence of Milton's religious ideas on Blake's poem.

Fuller, David. "*Milton,* and the Development of Blake's Thought." In *An Infinite Complexity: Essays in Romanticism,* edited by J. R. Watson, pp. 46-94. Edinburgh: Edinburgh University Press for the University of Durham, 1983.

Discusses Blake's treatment of imagination, reason, and Christianity in *Milton.*

Goslee, Nancy M. "'In Englands green & pleasant Land': The Building of Vision in Blake's Stanzas from *Milton.*" *Studies in Romanticism* 13 (1974): 105-25.

Offers a close reading of Blake's *Milton.*

Herzing, Thomas W. "Book I of Blake's *Milton*: Natural Religion as an Optical Fallacy." *Blake Studies* 6, no. 1 (1973): 19-34.

Examines themes of poetic genius and redemption in *Milton.*

Howard, John. *Blake's* Milton: *A Study in Selfhood.* Rutherford: N.J.: Farleigh Dickinson University Press, 1976, 300 p.

Discusses representations of spirituality and selfhood in *Milton.*

Hutchings, Kevin. "'The Nature of Infinity': *Milton*'s Environmental Poetics." In *Imagining Nature: Blake's Environmental Poetics,* pp. 114-52. Montreal & Kingston: McGill-Queens University Press, 2002.

Examines the relationship between nature, time, and Newtonian physics in *Milton.*

Lawson, Mildred. "Creative and Sexual Energy in Blake's *Milton.*" *American Notes and Queries* 15 (1977): 68-70.

Analyzes Blake's conception of the link between artistic genius and human sexuality.

Lussier, Mark. "Blake's Vortex: The Quantum Tunnel in *Milton.*" *Nineteenth Century Contexts* 18, no. 3 (1994): 263-91.

Discusses Blake's attitude toward science in *Milton.*

Mathews, Lawrence. "'The Value of the Saviours Blood': The Idea of Atonement in Blake's *Milton.*" *Wascana Review* 15, no. 1 (spring 1980): 72-86.

Discusses Blake's attitudes toward New Testament ideals of atonement and redemption.

McConnell, Will. "Blake, Bataille, and the Accidental Processes of Material History in *Milton.*" *CLIO* 26, no. 4 (summer 1997): 449-72.

Compares Blake's representations of the human body with those of Georges Bataille.

Mitchell, W. J. T. "Style and Iconography in the Illustrations of Blake's *Milton.*" *Blake Studies* 6, no. 1 (1973): 47-71.

Offers an in-depth analysis of illustrations in *Milton.*

Otto, Peter. "Visionary Deconstruction: The 'Bard's Song' in Blake's *Milton.*" *Philological Quarterly* 66, no. 2 (spring 1987): 207-230.

Examines the episodic nature of *Milton.*

Pierce, Frederick E. "Genesis and General Meaning of Blake's *Milton.*" *Modern Philology* 25, no. 2 (November 1927): 165-78.

Examines the influence of William Hayley's 1796 literary biography *The Life of Milton* on Blake's *Milton*.

Pierce, John B. "Rewriting Milton: Orality and Writing in Blake's *Milton*." *Studies in Romanticism* 39, no. 3 (fall 2000): 449-70.

Discusses the influence of oral poetic traditions on Blake's *Milton*.

Wright, Julia M. "'Greek and Latin Slaves of the Sword': Rejecting the Imperial Nation in Blake's *Milton*." In *Milton and the Imperial Vision*, edited by Balachandra Rajan and Elizabeth Sauer, pp. 255-72. Pittsburgh: Duquesne University Press, 1999.

Examines Blake's attitudes toward nationalism and imperialism in *Milton*.

Additional coverage of Blake's life and career is contained in the following sources published by Thomson Gale: *Authors and Artists for Young Adults,* **Vol. 47;** *British Writers,* **Vol. 3;** *British Writers Retrospective Supplement,* **Vol. 1;** *Children's Literature Review,* **Vol. 52;** *Concise Dictionary of British Literary Biography, 1789-1832; Dictionary of Literary Biography,* **Vols. 93, 163;** *DISCovering Authors; DISCovering Authors 3.0; DISCovering Authors: British Edition; DISCovering Authors: Canadian Edition; DISCovering Authors Modules: Most-studied Authors* **and** *Poets; Exploring Poetry; Literary Movements for Students,* **Vol. 1;** *Literature and Its Times Supplement,* **Vol. 1:1;** *Literature Resource Center; Major Authors and Illustrators for Children and Young Adults,* **Eds. 1, 2;** *Nineteenth-Century Literature Criticism,* **Vols. 13, 37, 57, 127;** *Poetry Criticism,* **Vols. 12, 63;** *Poetry for Students,* **Vols. 2, 12;** *Poets: American and British; Something About the Author,* **Vol. 30;** *Twayne's English Authors; World Literature and Its Times,* **Vol. 3;** *World Literature Criticism; World Poets;* **and** *Writers for Children.*

Francis James Child
1825-1896

American editor, critic, and librettist.

INTRODUCTION

Child was a prominent American literary scholar, philologist, and author. At the time of its original publication in 1857-58, his landmark *English and Scottish Ballads* represented the most comprehensive compilation of traditional ballads ever collected and included some of the first substantial commentary on the ballad form, raising it to the level of serious literary scholarship. Over the last 30 years of his life, Child devoted his energies to revising and expanding his ballad collection, and the definitive edition of his life's work, *The English and Scottish Popular Ballads,* appeared in ten volumes between 1882 and 1898. Child's choice of ballads for his compilation is noteworthy, in that it reflects his rigorous principles concerning the essential characteristics of what he regarded as the traditional "popular" ballad. While other scholars and writers, notably Sir Walter Scott, had published important ballad collections in the past, Child's work was the first to assert the primacy of ballads whose origins could be traced directly to oral traditions, as opposed to those found in broadsides and other texts, which he regarded as adulterated. One of Harvard College's best-liked professors during an academic career spanning 50 years, Child was as esteemed for his warm personality, his generosity with his students, and his passion for learning as he was for his scholarship. His death in 1896 inspired tributes from numerous colleagues and friends. In addition to his contributions to the field of ballad studies, Child achieved renown for his critical essays "Observations on the Language of Chaucer," and "Observations on the Language of Gower's *Confessio Amantis,*" treatises which remain valuable to scholars today. Child is also recognized as the founder of folklore studies in the United States, and in his later years he played a vital role in the creation of the American Folklore Society and the American Dialect Society.

BIOGRAPHICAL INFORMATION

Child was born in Boston, Massachusetts, on February 1, 1825, the third of eight children. His father, Joseph Child, was a sail manufacturer. Child demonstrated extraordinary academic ability at a young age and, although raised in a humble household, his intellectual talents eventually earned him acceptance to a prestigious college preparatory school, the Boston Latin School. In 1842 Child was admitted on a scholarship to Harvard College, where he excelled in classics, literature, and writing. After graduating first in his class in 1846, Child remained at Harvard as a tutor, first in mathematics and later in political science and economics. During his early teaching career, Child dedicated much of his energy to studying literature, and he published his first book, *Four Old Plays. Three Interludes*: Thersytes, Jack Jugler, *and Heywood's* Pardoner and Frere*: and* Jocaste, a Tragedy *by Gascoigne and Kinwelmarsh,* in 1848.

A year later Child took a leave of absence from Harvard to travel to Germany, where he pursued doctoral studies in philology at the Universities of Göttingen and Berlin, returning to the United States in 1851 without completing his degree. Upon his return to Harvard, Child was named the Boylston Professor of Rhetoric and Oratory. In 1852 he accepted an invitation to serve as general editor of the *British Poets* series, an exhaustive attempt to compile updated editions of classics of English literature. Child's most significant individual contribution to the series was *The Poetical Works of Edmund Spenser* (1855), a comprehensive collection of the poet's verse that included valuable notes and commentary by Child. During these years Child also made his first foray into the study of traditional English ballads, and his preliminary effort, the collection titled *English and Scottish Ballads,* appeared in eight volumes in 1857-58. In 1860 Child married Elizabeth Ellery Sedgwick, with whom he had four children.

In the 1860s and 1870s, as Child began to research ballad manuscripts more exhaustively, his theories concerning questions of authenticity and the true ballad form began to evolve. He developed a network of contacts in Europe, among them the Danish scholar Svend Hersleb Grundtvig, whose *Danmarks gamle Folkeviser* had an important influence on Child's own work. With the help of Grundtvig, Scottish scholars William Macmath and William Walker, and others, Child was able to track down original manuscripts of popular ballads in churches and monasteries throughout northern Europe. During these years Child also produced important scholarly works on other subjects. His more notable works included the long essay "Observations on the Language of Chaucer," published in the *Memoirs of the American*

Academy of Arts and Sciences in 1862, which represented a vital contribution to the study of Chaucer's meter and diction; and "Observations on the Language of Gower's *Confessio Amantis*," a supplement to the Chaucer essay, published in 1868. An outspoken supporter of the Union cause, Child edited two collections of writings related to the Civil War: *War-songs for Freemen* (1862), a compilation of songs sung by infantrymen, to which Child contributed several of his own original ballads; and *Poems of Religious Sorrow, Comfort, Counsel and Aspiration* (1863). In 1862 he also authored *Il pesceballo, opera seria in un atto; musica del maestro Rossibelli-Donimozarti,* a libretto that parodied traditional opera motifs.

In 1876 Child earned the distinction of being named the first Professor of English at Harvard University. A year later he published "Ballad Poetry," a brief essay outlining his central ideas concerning ballad authenticity, in the 1877 edition of *Johnson's New Universal Cyclopaedia.* In 1882 Child published the first volume of his massive *English and Scottish Popular Ballads,* an expansion of his earlier collection of ballads. Nine more volumes followed over the course of the next 16 years, securing Child's reputation as the world's foremost authority on English ballads. Although he originally intended to include a long essay to accompany the work, he never completed it. Child died in Cambridge on September 11, 1896, following a brief illness. The final volume of *The English and Scottish Popular Ballads* appeared in 1898.

MAJOR WORKS

Child's magnum opus, *English and Scottish Popular Ballads,* represents the culmination of his life's work and remains the most substantial and comprehensive collection of popular ballads in the English language. A revised and enlarged edition of Child's earlier collection, *English and Scottish Ballads, The English and Scottish Popular Ballads* is the product of Child's extensive research over a 30-year period and offers the finest elucidation of his theories concerning the ballad form. Throughout the work, Child established clear distinctions between what he considered true "popular" ballads and the commercial, typically adulterated ballads printed on broadsides. *The English and Scottish Popular Ballads* also contains Child's copious annotations and notes on the ballads, which examine such issues as place and date of origin, circulation throughout the European continent, and the existence of corresponding ballads in other languages. The work also includes multiple versions of many of the ballads, demonstrating a range of variations in meter and phrasing. Most scholars regard Child's *English and Scottish Popular Ballads* as the foundation of modern ballad study, and his work is widely considered the benchmark for other ballad collections in English.

In addition to his ballad scholarship, Child also achieved renown for his studies of English literature. His "Observations on the Language of Chaucer" and "Observations on the Language of Gower's *Confessio Amantis*" remain valuable inquiries into the innovative approach to language and meter of these two authors.

CRITICAL RECEPTION

During his lifetime, Child enjoyed a reputation as a meticulous and diligent scholar, a prodigious intellect, and an accomplished prose stylist. His commentaries on the works of Edmund Spenser, Geoffrey Chaucer, and John Gower earned the esteem of the most prominent scholars and writers of his day, and his observations were widely acknowledged as groundbreaking in their insight and approach. Although Child's ballad research attracted widespread attention in his lifetime, it wasn't until after his death that writings devoted to his work began to emerge. Enthusiastic early commentators included the scholars Francis Barton Gummere, Walter Morris Hart, and George Lyman Kittredge, all of whom based much of their own research on Child's findings. While most readers accepted *The English and Scottish Popular Ballads* as the definitive work in the field, there were some notable detractors, among them T. F. Henderson and Louise Pound, both of whom objected to Child's strict definitions concerning ballad authenticity and quality. In 1930, one of the first in-depth analyses of Child's work, offering a comprehensive overview of Child's scholarly methods, appeared in Sigurd Bernhard Hustvedt's *Ballad Books and Ballad Men.* While scholarly attention to Child's career waned in the middle of the twentieth century, the early 1980s saw a resurgence of interest in his contributions to the study of folklore in the United States. Most modern critics, among them Jo McMurtry, Michael J. Bell, and Roy Palmer, have offered positive assessments of Child's body of work, although there have been some exceptions. In a 1981 essay in *Folk Music Journal,* Dave Harker objected to what he perceived as the veneration of Child's ideas in academic circles, arguing that unquestioning acceptance of Child's findings had exerted a negative impact on further advances in the field of ballad studies. In 1994 Sigrid Rieuwerts published a valuable study examining Child's categorizations of ballad genres. Rieuwerts also edited, with Tom Cheesman, *Ballads into Books,* a 1999 collection of critical essays concerning Child's legacy.

PRINCIPAL WORKS

Four Old Plays. Three Interludes: Thersytes, Jack Jugler, *and Heywood's* Pardoner and Frere: *and Jocaste, a Tragedy by Gascoigne and Kinwelmarsh* [editor] (plays) 1848

The Poetical Works of Edmund Spenser [editor] (poetry) 1855

English and Scottish Ballads. 8 vols. [editor] (poetry) 1857-58; revised and enlarged as *The English and Scottish Popular Ballads,* 1882-98

Il pesceballo, opera seria in un atto; musica del maestro Rossibelli-Donimozarti (libretto) 1862

"Observations on the Language of Chaucer" (criticism) 1862; published in journal *Memoirs of the American Academy of Arts and Sciences*

War-songs for Freemen [editor] (poetry) 1862

Poems of Religious Sorrow, Comfort, Counsel and Aspiration [editor] (poetry) 1863; revised, 1866

Observations on the Language of Gower's Confessio Amantis (criticism) 1868

The Childe of Bristowe, a Legend of the Fourteenth Century [editor] (poetry) 1886

A Scholar's Letters to a Young Lady: Passages from the Later Correspondence of Francis James Child (letters) 1920

Letters on Scottish Ballads, from Professor Francis J. Child to W. W., Aberdeen (letters) 1930

The Scholar Friends: Letters of Francis James Child and James Russell Lowell (letters) 1952

CRITICISM

Francis James Child (letter date 25 August 1872)

SOURCE: Child, Francis James. "To Professor Svend Grundtvig, Copenhagen." In *Ballad Books and Ballad Men: Raids and Rescues in Britain, America, and the Scandinavian North since 1800,* by Sigurd Bernhard Hustvedt, pp. 252-55. Cambridge: Harvard University Press, 1930.

[*In the following excerpt from a letter originally written on August 25, 1872, Child describes the guiding principles behind his search for English and Scottish ballads.*]

I wish you were here just now, that I might have your opinion on two points which give me a great deal of trouble. One is the compass and the other the arrangement of the collection. The English and Scotch Ballads will not compare with the Danish in point of age. I cannot say exactly what limit you fix to *Gamle*[1] *Folkeviser.* We cannot of course exclude all ballads which have not been taken from the mouths of the people—nor perhaps include all such. The oldest Robin Hood ballads are derived from MS., and very many others of the best and oldest, and on the other hand some ballads written in comparatively recent times, especially historical ones, are found in the mouths of the people. The immense collections of Broadside ballads, the Roxburghe and Pepys, of which but a small part has been printed, doubtless contain some ballads which we should at once declare to possess the popular character, and yet one the whole they are veritable dung-hills, in which, only after a great deal of sickening grubbing, one finds a very moderate jewel. Some of the later Robin Hood ballads I have scarcely patience or stomach to read: but the declension is so gradual from the freshest and raciest to the thoroughly *vulgar,* (by which I mean always the *essentially* vulgar, the absolutely mean and stupid) that it will be very hard, and to me at this moment looks impossible, to draw a line. It is not easy always to distinguish a ballad and what we should call a short romance. Is 'Arthur and the King of Cornwall' a ballad? 'The Horn of King Arthur' I incline to exclude, and yet I fear that my reasons are vague. Of all the chivalrous ballads I should, as now minded, retain only 'The Boy and the Mantle', 'The Marriage of Gawain', and perhaps 'Arthur and the King of Cornwall'. Is same to be said in behalf of 'King Arthur's Death'?[2] What should I do about the 'Suffolk Miracle'? (all these in vol. 1 [of *English and Scottish Ballads*]). 'The Outlaw Murray' and 'Auld Maitland',[3] in vol. vi., try me sorely. I wish I could rid myself of them. It is a pity one can't consistently insist on the lyrical, or singable, character as a criterion. That makes order in the Appendix to vol. vii [of *English and Scottish Ballads*],[4] Historical Ballads, very sensibly. They are the very ones, the historical ballads, that I shall have most trouble with.—As to arrangement a very good German review spoke in terms of strong disapprobation of the one I made. I never pretended that the arrangement was founded on a deeper principle than convenience. Some sort of classification everybody expects. Outlaw ballads separate themselves pretty well—but shall I put 'Johnie of Breadislee' and 'Johnie Cock' with Robin Hood—or with the later Scotch outlaws, Johnie Armstrong and the rest? *Tragica,*[5] from the use of the title in Danish and Romaic, shows, as the least consideration makes obvious of itself, how natural such a division is. Many of the oldest ballads would in any language come under that head. I cannot imitate *your* division, the matter being so different. My *Trylleviser*[6] will make a natural class, and I have no doubt that this class should come first. But what to put second I wot not—for even if I retain the division I have made, I think that the earliest ballads under several heads are practically *coeval.* I do not quite see where you mean to put, say, the *Tragica* that have no *Trylleri*[7] in them, and no history, or Humorous ballads like *King John and the Abbot.*—I am in no haste to settle this question for a year, but as I find the same difficulty now that troubled me twelve years ago, I don't expect to come to an altogether happy solution.—I shall have no appendixes. They seem adapted merely to disarm the objections of people who might complain that the mass was too great for anybody to pick out the re-

ally good. That first collection it was important to make tolerably saleable. I shall make no concession to such a consideration in the one which I hope to make.

I shall esteem it an act of true friendship if you will speak with the utmost plainness concerning any matter in which you think I am wrong or likely to go wrong.

As it is very uncertain when, if ever, we shall secure Herd's, Jamieson's, and Mrs. Brown's manuscripts,⁸ and as it is most desirable to get at them, I shall occupy myself at present with reading up the ballads of other nations, and I will begin with the South, where to be sure I shall not find very much. First I will run through the Spanish and Portuguese. Your help will save me a great deal of labor with the Scandinavians. I shall not esteem it necessary to search in any place where *you* have passed and shall probably not read more than you point out to me. I have indeed a desire to survey the whole field minutely with my own eye, but I have not confidence enough in my health lasting long enough to finish the work if I do.—I don't read Finnish. Perhaps you do. I might write to Prof. Ahlquist⁹ of Helsingfors, to ask for such hints as he might be able to give. I wish Felix Liebrecht¹⁰ would give me a note or two, and still more that some man who knows the Slavic¹¹ field well might be got to help us.

I mean to try to see if anything can be done in Scotland towards retrieving such ballads as may be left with the people. But we must not wait for such things, nor for the missing manuscripts. Set down, when you feel like it, all that you think important of all kinds, about our ballads and we will bring things into order by and by. Criticise my proceedings *like an enemy*.

Notes

1. Child underlines the word *Gamle* (*old*) to indicate his special interest here in the age of the Danish popular ballads.

2. In the notes accompanying his letter of January 29, 1880, Grundtvig proposed that Child place 'King Arthur's Death' and 'Auld Maitland' among the imitations in the suggested Fourth Class. See the notes to that letter, p. 285. For Child's disposition of the other ballads mentioned in this letter, see the various indexes to the *E. S. P. B.* [*English and Scottish Popular Ballads*].

3. [Ibid.]

4. Vol. VII of Child's *English and Scottish Ballads*.

5. Child refers here to a collection of Danish ballads published in 1657 under the designation *Tragica*.

6. Ballads of magic and marvel; Grundtvig had a division of *trylleviser* in his *DgF* [*Danmarks gamle Folkeviser* (1853-)].

7. Magic, enchantment.

8. On these manuscripts, see Child's letters of July 1 and October 3, 1873, and May 8, 1874.

9. August Ahlquist (1826-89), author of various works on the Finnish language and related subjects.

10. Felix Liebrecht later was one of Child's correspondents. For a review by him of Pts. I-IV of *E. S. P. B.*, see *Englische Studien,* IX, 445-448.

11. Among those who subsequently assisted Child in the Slavic field were Theodor Vetter and Professor Leo Wiener.

Nation (essay date 17 September 1896)

SOURCE: "Professor Child." *Nation* 63, no. 1629 (17 September 1896): 209-10.

[*In the following excerpt, the critic offers a brief overview of Child's contribution to the field of ballad scholarship.*]

Francis James Child, who died on Friday, was one of the last of the remarkable men who, in the latter half of the century, have done so much to make the name of their university illustrious. . . .

The great work of his life has been his ***English and Scotch Ballads,*** a monument of research and scholarship which can never be superseded, his industry and the thoroughness of his investigations having made it complete. His aim was to trace to its sources and preserve in an authentic form this whole body of popular literature, and at the close of his life he was able to say that he believed not a single ballad had eluded his search. An introduction remained to be written, but the work itself was done. The labor and linguistic knowledge involved in it no one who had not some acquaintance with the daily course of his studies would be likely to understand. Not merely constant correspondence with scholars all over the world, with reference to forms of ballads existing in foreign countries, but also endless collation of texts and manuscripts, was required, and all this in addition to his regular duties. The shelves of the university library are enriched by a precious collection of volumes gathered together in the course of these labors. His other contributions to literature and scholarship have been mainly as an editor. The general editorship of the American edition of the ***British Poets,*** in which was included an edition of Spenser [***The Poetical Works of Edmund Spenser***] under his charge, was among them, as were also ***Four Old Plays*** (1848), a collection of ***Poems of Sorrow and Comfort*** (1865), and two invaluable papers published in the

Transactions of the American Academy of Arts and Sciences, **'Observations on the Language of Chaucer and Gower,'** which conclusively settled long-disputed questions with regard to the forms of Chaucer's language and versification. A number of lectures before the Lowell Institute have never been published. Had his time for twenty-five years not been so taken up with the almost mechanical labor of hearing recitations and correcting examination-books, he would no doubt have accomplished more. To those who are aware how his time was further limited by self-imposed tasks of all sorts, public and private, it is surprising that he should have accomplished so much.

A. Lang (essay date December 1896)

SOURCE: Lang, A. "Obituary: Professor Child." *Folk-Lore* 7, no. 4 (December 1896): 416-17.

[*In the following excerpt, Lang discusses the far-reaching impact of Child's body of work, describing his voluminous collection of English and Scottish ballads as "one of the chief glories of American scholarship."*]

In 1861 Mr. Child published eight volumes of English ballads [***English and Scottish Ballads***], omitting "The Bonny Hynd," "The Baffled Knight," "The Jolly Beggar," "The Keach in the Creel," and "The Earl of Errol." Scott had published the first of these, Charles Kirkpatrick Sharpe had printed the last. Probably American modesty stood in Mr. Child's way. Of variants, only "the more important" were given. They were arranged in accordance with "the probable antiquity of the story, not the age of the actual form or language," which has necessarily been modernised in oral recitation. "The most authentic copies" of the texts were selected; but Mr. Child had not then access to many manuscript collections. References to parallel ballads and stories in other than Teutonic languages were comparatively meagre.

In 1882 (so the dedication to Mr. Furnivall is dated) Mr. Child began to publish his new and, as far as possible, exhaustive edition of ballads (Houghton, Mifflin, and Co., Boston). He had been engaged for ten years in stimulating collectors in Scotland, Canada, and the United States. He had obtained the use of MSS., such as Motherwell's, Kinloch's, Jamieson's transcript of Mrs. Brown's, Islay's, and the MSS. at Abbotsford. Looking over those, one day, I was beset by an importunate temptation to "fake" a ballad or two, have them copied in bad ink on old paper, and thrust them into the mass for the purpose of deceiving Mr. Child. The temptation was resisted. It is superfluous to praise the method, industry, and learning of the great new edition. As the work went on, the editor was enabled to add corrections and fresh variants. Thus I was fortunate enough to be able to rectify the topography of "Jamie Telfer" from notes on a first edition of the "Border Minstrelsy" at Branxholme Park; for Sir Walter, oddly enough, had gone wrong, deceived by the distribution of the same place-names on Ettrick and Teviot. I think, too, that I nearly, or quite, converted Mr. Child from the Kirkpatrick Sharpe heresy about the late date (1719) of "The Queen's Marie." His mind was uncommonly open to facts and argument. In the same way amateurs of ballads everywhere found him a courteous and prompt correspondent. His new edition transcended the old, for his knowledge at least of European ballads and *Märchen,* for comparative purposes, was vastly extended. Perhaps he had still a good deal to learn about the popular tales and poems of the uncivilised races, which are often valuable for purposes of comparison. There was no other defect in his equipment, except that he might have been better seen in Scottish history. The mystery of "The Maid of Norway," and the strange affair of "The False Maid," are unnoticed in Mr. Child's preface to "Sir Patrick Spens." Other examples might be given.

It is understood that Mr. Child had finished his edition before his regretted death; but it does not appear that he had completed an Essay on Popular Ballads in general, their origin and diffusion, a topic full of difficult problems. In England the questions of this branch of folk-lore have been much neglected; with Mr. Child's completed work before him some scholar should attempt to do what is necessary. Probably Mr. Child may at least have left notes indicating his general conclusions, and one of his pupils may be able to finish his work. It is, indeed, a *magnum opus,* and one of the chief glories of American scholarship, though produced under great difficulties, caused by the distance from European libraries, and the daily task-work of a teacher. English balladists will of course be anxious to assist, in any way within their power, the labours of the American editor, who may complete "the unfinished window in Aladdin's tower."

C. E. Norton (essay date December 1897)

SOURCE: Norton, C. E. "Francis James Child." *Harvard Graduates Magazine* 6, no. 22 (December 1897): 161-69.

[*In the following excerpt, Norton provides an overview of Child's career as a scholar.*]

In 1851, on the resignation of Professor Channing as Boylston Professor of Rhetoric, Child was appointed his successor, with leave of absence for study in Europe before assuming the duties of the position. The opportu-

nities which Europe then afforded to the young American scholar were diligently made use of. He obtained the degree of Doctor of Philosophy at Göttingen in 1854, and in the autumn of the same year he returned to his work at Harvard. A great part of his time was employed in the teaching of English composition, and in the drudgery of correcting students' exercises, but he had an indefatigable industry and a steady ardor of learning, and he found time to carry on his own special studies. He undertook the general superintendence of a series of the works of the chief British poets [*British Poets*], and himself prepared for it the edition of Spenser [*The Poetical Works of Edmund Spenser*] (1855) in five volumes, which for the use of the general reader still remains the best. For the same series he compiled a Collection of Ballads [*English and Scottish Ballads*] in eight volumes, published in 1857-58, which in extent of range, in judgment in selection, and in amount of literary and historical illustration, was far superior to any preceding similar work. But a more important piece of work, one of original investigation and displaying "wonderful industry, acuteness, and accuracy,"[1] was the treatise issued in the *Memoirs* of the American Academy of Arts and Sciences, in 1862, under the modest title of **"Observations on the Language of Chaucer,"**[2] which was followed in 1868 by a Supplement, entitled **"Observations on the Language of Gower's *Confessio Amantis.*"**[3] "It is difficult at the present day," says Professor Kittredge, speaking of the first of these treatises, "to imagine the state of Chaucer philology at the moment when this paper appeared. Scarcely anything, we may say, was known of Chaucer's grammar and metre in a sure and scientific way. Indeed, the difficulties to be solved had not even been clearly formulated. . . . Mr. Child not only defined the problems, but provided for most of them a solution which the researches of younger scholars have only served to substantiate. He also gave a perfect model of the method proper to such investigations,—a method simple, laborious, and exact."[4]

For many years after this Mr. Child published little, but with steady purpose devoted such leisure as his incessant professional task allowed to the increase of his already vast stores of learning, and to the accumulation of the material for the main work of his life, a complete critical edition of *The English and Scottish Ballads.* At length in 1882 appeared the first part of his work. The character of the undertaking was set forth in a prospectus: The popular ballads existing in the English language had never been collected into one body; a large portion of the remains of the ballads was unprinted; the text of much that was in print was vitiated by editorial changes: it was now proposed to publish all in their entirety and their purity; to include every independent version of every ballad, and to record all important variations of different copies, both printed and manuscript; each ballad was to have a proper preface, and, in the case of those ballads which the English have in common with other nations, an account was to be given of related traditions. The work was to be completed by a general introduction, a glossary, and indexes.

The vast scale of this matured design became obvious on the publication of the first part. The wide range of the themes of the ballads, the immense variety of local, historical, and romantic tradition exhibited by them, the broad diffusion among mankind of the legends which many of them embodied, opened a field of investigation of enormous extent, requiring acquaintance alike with many languages and many literatures. The task was one which only a scholar possessed of exceptional acquisitions could hope to accomplish satisfactorily, and from which even the most industrious might have shrunk. It had hardly a parallel in the variety of learning which it exacted for its due performance, and this was not all: it demanded in no less measure fine critical acumen and poetic appreciation,—the gifts of taste and culture as well as of scholarship. Mr. Child possessed them all.

"It was my wish," he said in the advertisement prefixed to the first part, "not to begin to print *The English and Scottish Popular Ballads* until this unrestricted title should be justified by my having at command every valuable copy of every known ballad. . . . What is still lacking is believed to bear no great proportion to what is in hand. . . . Meanwhile the uncertainties of the world forbid a longer delay to publish so much as has been got together."

From year to year the parts followed in rapid succession,—rapid in view of the character of the work,—and in the advertisement to part ix, which appeared in the spring of 1894, Mr. Child had the satisfaction of saying that, to the extent of his knowledge of sources, the collection was complete, with the exception of a single ballad, "which is probably a variety of one or another here given in several forms." Such had been the extraordinary success of his research, in which he had been aided by many English and foreign scholars glad to assist in the perfecting of a work which was of interest to them in itself, and which roused their admiration by the manner in which it was executed. . . .

It is impossible not to regret that Mr. Child should not have done more independent literary work. The several introductions to the Ballads in his great collection, excellent as they are in their kind, and astonishing in the extent and thoroughness of the learning which they exhibit, very seldom afford him free space for the display of his own genius; but here and there the page is lighted up with a gleam of fancy or of humor, and more rarely with a flash of poetic imagination that reveal the restraint which the editor had imposed upon himself. His style when at freedom was of the best, for it was the simple expression of the man.

Notes

1. These are the terms used by Mr. A. J. Ellis, the learned author of the *History of English Pronunciation* [(1869)].

2. *Memoirs* of the American Academy, New Series, vol. viii, pp. 445-502.

3. Ibid., vol. ix, pp. 265-315.

4. From the admirable appreciation of Professor Child's character and works in the *Atlantic Monthly* for December, 1896.

Quarterly Review (review date July 1898)

SOURCE: Review of *The English and Scottish Popular Ballads,* edited by Francis James Child. *Quarterly Review* 188, no. 375 (July 1898): 66-89.

[*In the following excerpt, the critic examines the lasting impact of Child's ballad scholarship.*]

In the late Professor Child's **English and Scottish Ballads** we have a piece of work to which the indefatigable labour of half a lifetime was devoted, but for the completion of which even half a lifetime was not sufficient. During the years 1857 and 1858 appeared, under his editorship and bearing the same title, a collection of ballads in eight small volumes, which proved, however, but the forerunner of an undertaking of much wider scope and intention, a work designed to include 'every obtainable version of every extant English or Scottish ballad, with the fullest possible discussion of related songs or stories in the popular literature of all nations.' The first part of this great work appeared in 1882, and at the time of his death in 1896 Professor Child was engaged upon the tenth and final part, which, besides a glossary and bibliography, was planned to include a general introduction to the subject. Save in one respect the book as we have it is complete; but the introduction, to write which Professor Child was qualified as no living man is qualified, was barely commenced, and by his too early death the world of scholarship has sustained a loss that cannot be repaired.

> 'A few pages of manuscript,' Professor Kittredge, who writes the memoir for this book, tells us, 'the last thing written by his pen, almost illegible, were found among his papers, to show that he had actually begun the composition of this essay, and many sheets of excerpts testified to the time he had spent in refreshing his memory as to the opinions of his predecessors, but he had left no collectanea that could be utilized in supplying the Introduction itself. He was accustomed to carry much of his material in his memory till the moment of composition arrived, and this habit accounts for the fact that there are no jottings of opinions and no sketch of precisely what line of argument he intended to take.'

Of the absolute completeness of the work, however, as far as it had been carried, there can be no doubt. Profound learning, the most minute and careful study of details, and a fine literary instinct meet in it, and Professor Child's **English and Scottish Ballads** must take rank as the final and definitive collection. Dealing as it does with versions and readings in ballads and groups of ballads treated separately, little criticism of a general character can be offered of the work as a whole in the present paper, but the completion of such a work ought not to pass unnoticed, and the occasion is a fitting one to sum up the main results of a study of the ballad poetry of this country, one of the most important and interesting fields in the domain of its literature.

W. W. Newell (review date July-September 1898)

SOURCE: Newell, W. W. Review of *The English and Scottish Popular Ballads,* edited by Francis James Child. *Journal of American Folk-Lore* 11, no. 42 (July-September 1898): 240-41.

[*In the following excerpt, Newell evaluates the significance of Child's work.*]

The task which Professor Child had set himself consisted in a complete edition of English ballads, including every valuable copy of every known ballad. As the material can never be increased, this edition [**The English and Scottish Popular Ballads**] must forever remain a monument of the industry, sagacity, and learning of its author. As necessary to the elucidation and comprehension of the songs, all other ballad literature has been drawn on for illustration, the brief prefaces to the ballads constituting models of comparative research.

It had been the intention of Professor Child to introduce into this concluding part a brief general introduction, treating important questions of theory, relating to the periods, sources, and manner of composition of the ballads; but this study remained unexecuted and he left no notes sufficient to indicate his opinions. This theoretical examination, which in his mind occupied a secondary place, therefore remains for others to complete. This work, however, has established important principles.

First, in regard to diffusion. The pride which Scotland has taken in its popular songs has led to a very general but altogether erroneous view of their origin. Almost all writers who have undertaken to treat of Scottish or Border ballads have regarded these as of local development, the expression of the nature, society and character of North Britain, a treasure quite distinct from any belonging to England proper. On the contrary, it may be said that there is no such thing as a distinctively Scottish popular song, unless a few later historical ballads

are to be so called. In general, Scottish ballads are only surviving dialectic forms of old English. Again, English ballads, for the most part, appear to be only branches of a West European tree.

Next, as to date. The great majority of the songs are of modern record. But the manuscript of one piece, No. 23, is attributed to the thirteenth century. It may be presumed that a considerable portion of the ballads recently taken down have been sung from a time as remote; and there is no unlikelihood that some of them might, in substance, have been heard two or three centuries earlier. In 1883 the writer of this notice affirmed (*Games and Songs of American Children* [(1884)], p. 11): "The English ballad was already born when Canute the Dane coasted the shore of Britain; its golden age was already over when Dante summed up mediæval thought in the 'Divina Commedia;' its reproductive period was at an end when Columbus enlarged the horizon of Europe to admit a New World; it was a memory of the past when the American colonies were founded." These views were at the time unreservedly approved by Professor Child, and in spite of all the admitted difficulties of the subject, we believe his opinion, as respects the outlines of the doctrine, had undergone no alteration. His comparative notes (such as those contained in prefaces to Nos. 7 and 59) indicate a very ancient origin for certain ballads.

George Lyman Kittredge (essay date 1898)

SOURCE: Kittredge, George Lyman. "Francis James Child." In *The English and Scottish Popular Ballads,* edited by Francis James Child, pp. xxiii-xxxi. Boston: Houghton, Mifflin and Company, 1898.

[*In the following excerpt, Kittredge offers an overview of Child's career, examining his work both as an author and as a professor.*]

Throughout his service as professor of rhetoric, Mr Child, hampered though he was by the requirements of his laborious office, had pursued with unquenchable ardor the study of the English language and literature, particularly in their older forms, and in these subjects he had become an authority of the first rank long before the establishment of the English chair enabled him to arrange his university teaching in accordance with his tastes. Soon after he returned from Germany he undertook the general editorial supervision of a series of the *British Poets,* published at Boston in 1853 and several following years, and extending to some hundred and fifty volumes. Out of this grew, in one way or another, his three most important contributions to learning: his edition of Spenser, his **'Observations on the Language of Chaucer and Gower,'** and his *English and Scottish Popular Ballads.*

Mr Child's Spenser [*The Poetical Works of Edmund Spenser*] appeared in 1855.[1] Originally intended, as he says in the preface, as little more than a reprint of the edition published in 1839 under the superintendence of Mr George Hillard, the book grew upon his hands until it had become something quite different from its predecessor. Securing access to old copies of most of Spenser's poems, Mr Child subjected the text to a careful revision, which left little to be done in this regard. His Life of Spenser was far better than any previous biography, and his notes, though brief, were marked by a philological exactness to which former editions could not pretend. Altogether, though meant for the general reader and therefore sparingly annotated, Mr Child's volumes remain, after forty years, the best edition of Spenser in existence.

The plan of the *British Poets* originally contemplated an edition of Chaucer, which Mr Child was to prepare. Becoming convinced, however, that the time was not ripe for such a work, he abandoned this project, and to the end of his life he never found time to resume it. Thomas Wright's print of the *Canterbury Tales* from the Harleian MS. 7334 had, however, put into his hands a reasonably faithful reproduction of an old text, and he turned his attention to a minute study of Chaucer's language.[2] The outcome was the publication, in the *Memoirs* of the American Academy of Arts and Sciences for 1863, of the great treatise to which Mr Child gave the modest title of **'Observations on the Language of Chaucer's *Canterbury Tales.'*** It is difficult, at the present day, to imagine the state of Chaucer philology at the moment when this paper appeared. Scarcely anything, we may say, was known of Chaucer's grammar and metre in a sure and scientific way. Indeed, the difficulties to be solved had not even been clearly formulated. Further, the accessible mass of evidence on Anglo-Saxon and Middle English was, in comparison with the stores now at the easy command of every tyro, almost insignificant. Yet, in this brief treatise, Mr Child not only defined the problems, but provided for most of them a solution which the researches of younger scholars have only served to substantiate. He also gave a perfect model of the method proper to such inquiries—a method simple, laborious, and exact. The **'Observations'** were subsequently rearranged and condensed, with Professor Child's permission, by Mr A. J. Ellis for his work *On Early English Pronunciation*; but only those who have studied them in their original form can appreciate their merit fully. "It ought never to be forgotten," writes Professor Skeat, "that the only full and almost complete solution of the question of the right scansion of Chaucer's *Canterbury Tales* is due to what Mr Ellis rightly terms 'the wonderful industry, acuteness, and accuracy of Professor Child.'" Had he produced nothing else, this work, with its pendant, the

'Observations on Gower,'[3] would have assured him a high place among those very few scholars who have permanently settled important problems of linguistic science.

Mr Child's crowning work, however, was the edition of *The English and Scottish Popular Ballads,* which the reader now has before him. The history of this is the history of more than half a lifetime.

The idea of the present work grew out of Mr Child's editorial labors on the series of the *British Poets,* already referred to. For this he prepared a collection in eight small volumes (1857-58) called *English and Scottish Ballads.*[4] This was marked by the beginnings of that method of comparative study which is carried out to its ultimate issues in the volumes of the present collection. The book circulated widely, and was at once admitted to supersede all previous attempts in the same field. To Mr Child, however, it was but the starting-point for further researches. He soon formed the plan of a much more extensive collection on an altogether different model. This was to include every obtainable version of every extant English or Scottish ballad, with the fullest possible discussion of related songs or stories in the "popular" literature of all nations. To this enterprise he resolved, if need were, to devote the rest of his life. His first care was to secure trustworthy texts. In his earlier collection he had been forced to depend almost entirely on printed books. No progress, he was convinced, could be made till recourse could be had to manuscripts, and in particular to the Percy MS. Accordingly he directed his most earnest efforts to securing the publication of the entire contents of the famous folio. The Percy MS. was at Ecton Hall, in the possession of the Bishop's descendants, who would permit no one even to examine it. Two attempts were made by Dr Furnivall, at Mr Child's instance, to induce the owners to allow the manuscript to be printed,—one as early as 1860 or 1861, the other in 1864,—but without avail. A third attempt was more successful, and in 1867-68 the long-secluded folio was made the common property of scholars in an edition prepared by Professor Hales and Dr Furnivall.[5]

The publication of the Percy MS. not only put a large amount of trustworthy material at the disposal of Mr Child; it exposed the full enormity of Bishop Percy's sins against popular tradition. Some shadow of suspicion inevitably fell on all other ballad collections. It was more than ever clear to Mr Child that he could not safely take anything at second hand, and he determined not to print a line of his projected work till he had exhausted every effort to get hold of whatever manuscript material might be in existence. His efforts in this direction continued through many years. A number of manuscripts were in private hands; of some the whereabouts was not known; of others the existence was not sus-

pected. But Mr Child was untiring. He was cordially assisted by various scholars, antiquaries, and private gentlemen, to whose coöperation ample testimony is borne in the Advertisements prefixed to the volumes in the present work. Some manuscripts were secured for the Library of Harvard University—notably Bishop Percy's Papers, the Kinloch MSS, and the Harris MS.,[6]—and of others careful copies were made, which became the property of the same library. In all these operations the indispensable good offices of Mr William Macmath, of Edinburgh, deserve particular mention. For a long series of years his services were always at Mr Child's disposal. His self-sacrifice and generosity appear to have been equalled only by his perseverance and wonderful accuracy. But for him the manuscript basis of *The English and Scottish Popular Ballads* would have been far less strong than it is.

Gradually, then, the manuscript materials came in, until at last, in 1882, Mr Child felt justified in beginning to print. Other important documents were, however, discovered or made accessible as time went on. Especially noteworthy was the great find at Abbotsford (see the Advertisement to Part VIII). In 1877 Dr David Laing procured, "not without difficulty," leave to prepare for Mr Child a copy of the single manuscript of ballads then known to remain in the library at Abbotsford. This MS., entitled "Scottish Songs," was so inconsiderable, in proportion to the accumulations which Sir Walter Scott had made in preparing his Border Minstrelsy, that further search seemed to be imperatively necessary. In 1890 permission to make such a search, and to use the results, was given by the Honorable Mrs Maxwell-Scott. The investigation, made by Mr Macmath, yielded a rich harvest of ballads, which were utilized in Parts VII-IX. To dwell upon the details would be endless. The reader may see a list of the manuscript sources at pp. 397ff. of the fifth volume; and, if he will observe how scattered they were, he will have no difficulty in believing that it required years, labor, and much delicate negotiation to bring them all together. One manuscript remained undiscoverable, William Tytler's Brown MS., but there is no reason to believe that this contained anything of consequence that is not otherwise known.[7]

Meanwhile, concurrently with the toil of amassing, collating, and arranging texts, went on the far more arduous labor of comparative study of the ballads of all nations; for, in accordance with Mr Child's plan it was requisite to determine, in the fullest manner, the history and foreign relations of every piece included in his collection. To this end he devoted much time and unwearied diligence to forming, in the Library of the University, a special collection of "Folk-lore," particularly of ballads, romances, and *Märchen.* This priceless collection, the formation of which must be looked on as one of Mr Child's most striking services to the university, numbers some 7000 volumes. But these figures by no

means represent the richness of the Library in the departments concerned, or the services of Mr Child in this particular. Mediæval literature in all its phases was his province, and thousands of volumes classified in other departments of the University Library bear testimony to his vigilance in ordering books, and his astonishing bibliographical knowledge. Very few books are cited in the present collection which are not to be found on the shelves of this Library.

In addition, Mr Child made an effort to stimulate the collection of such remains of the traditional ballad as still live on the lips of the people in this country and in the British Islands. The harvest was, in his opinion, rather scanty; yet, if all the versions thus recovered from tradition were enumerated, the number would not be found inconsiderable. Enough was done, at all events, to make it clear that little or nothing of value remains to be recovered in this way.

To readers familiar with such studies, no comment is necessary, and to those who are unfamiliar with them, no form of statement can convey even a faint impression of the industry, the learning, the acumen, and the literary skill which these processes required. In writing the history of a single ballad, Mr Child was sometimes forced to examine hundreds of books in perhaps a dozen different languages. But his industry was unflagging, his sagacity was scarcely ever at fault, and his linguistic and literary knowledge seemed to have no bounds. He spared no pains to perfect his work in every detail, and his success was commensurate with his efforts. In the Advertisement to the Ninth Part (1894), he was able to report that the three hundred and five numbers of his collection comprised the whole extant mass of this traditional material, with the possible exception of a single ballad.[8]

In June, 1896, Mr Child concluded his fiftieth year of service as a teacher in Harvard College. He was at this time hard at work on the Tenth and final Part, which was to contain a glossary, various indexes, a bibliography, and an elaborate introduction on the general subject. For years he had allowed himself scarcely any respite from work, and, in spite of the uncertain condition of his health,—or perhaps in consequence of it,—he continued to work at high pressure throughout the summer. At the end of August he discovered that he was seriously ill. He died at Boston on the 11th day of September. He had finished his great work except for the introduction and the general bibliography. The bibliography was in preparation by another hand and has since been completed. The introduction, however, no other scholar had the hardihood to undertake. A few pages of manuscript,—the last thing written by his pen,—almost illegible, were found among his papers to show that he had actually begun the composition of this essay, and many sheets of excerpts testified to the time he had spent in refreshing his memory as to the opinions of his predecessors, but he had left no collectanea that could be utilized in supplying the Introduction itself. He was accustomed to carry much of his material in his memory till the moment of composition arrived, and this habit accounts for the fact that there are no jottings of opinions and no sketch of precisely what line of argument he intended to take.

Mr Child's sudden death was felt as a bitter personal loss, not only by an unusually large circle of attached friends in both hemispheres, but by very many scholars who knew him through his works alone. He was one of the few learned men to whom the old title of "Master" was justly due and freely accorded. With astonishing erudition, which nothing seemed to have escaped, he united an infectious enthusiasm and a power of lucid and fruitful exposition that made him one of the greatest of teachers, and a warmth and openness of heart that won the affection of all who knew him. In most men, however complex their characters, one can distinguish the qualities of the heart, in some degree, from the qualities of the head. In Professor Child no such distinction was possible, for all the elements of his many-sided nature were fused in his marked and powerful individuality. In his case, the scholar and the man cannot be separated. His life and his learning were one; his work was the expression of himself.

As an investigator Professor Child was at once the inspiration and the despair of his disciples. Nothing could surpass the scientific exactness of his methods and the unwearied diligence with which he conducted his researches. No possible source of information could elude him; no book or manuscript was too voluminous or too unpromising for him to examine on the chance of its containing some fact that might correct or supplement his material, even in the minutest point. Yet these qualities of enthusiastic accuracy and thoroughness, admirable as they undoubtedly were, by no means dominated him. They were always at the command of the higher qualities of his genius,—sagacity, acumen, and a kind of sympathetic and imaginative power in which he stood almost alone among recent scholars. No detail of language or tradition or archæology was to him a mere lifeless fact; it was transmuted into something vital, and became a part of that universal humanity which always moved him wherever he found it, whether in the pages of a mediæval chronicle, or in the stammering accents of a late and vulgarly distorted ballad, or in the faces of the street boys who begged roses from his garden. No man ever felt a keener interest in his kind, and no scholar ever brought this interest into more vivifying contact with the technicalities of his special studies. The exuberance of this large humanity pervades his edition of the ***English and Scottish Ballads.*** Even in his last years, when the languor of uncertain health sometimes got the better, for a season, of the spirit with

which he commonly worked, some fresh bit of genuine poetry in a ballad, some fine trait of pure nature in a stray folk-tale, would, in an instant, bring back the full flush of that enthusiasm which he must have felt when the possibilities of his achievement first presented themselves to his mind in early manhood. For such a nature there was no old age.

From this ready sympathy came that rare faculty—seldom possessed by scholars—which made Professor Child peculiarly fit for his greatest task. Few persons understand the difficulties of ballad investigation. In no field of literature have the forger and the manipulator worked with greater vigor and success. From Percy's day to our own it has been thought an innocent device to publish a bit of one's own versifying, now and then, as an "old ballad" or an "ancient song." Often, too, a late stall-copy of a ballad, getting into oral circulation, has been innocently furnished to collectors as traditional matter. Mere learning will not guide an editor through these perplexities. What is needed is, in addition, a complete understanding of the "popular" genius, a sympathetic recognition of the traits that characterize oral literature wherever and in whatever degree they exist. This faculty, which even the folk has not retained, and which collectors living in ballad-singing and tale-telling times have often failed to acquire, was vouchsafed by nature herself to this sedentary scholar. In reality a kind of instinct, it had been so cultivated by long and loving study of the traditional literature of all nations that it had become wonderfully swift in its operations and almost infallible. A forged or retouched piece could not deceive him for a moment; he detected the slightest jar in the genuine ballad tone. He speaks in one place of certain writers "who would have been all the better historians for a little reading of romances." He was himself the better interpreter of the poetry of art for this keen sympathy with the poetry of nature.

Constant association with the spirit of the folk did its part in maintaining, under the stress of unremitting study and research, that freshness and buoyancy of mind which was the wonder of all who met Professor Child for the first time, and the perpetual delight of his friends and associates. It is impossible to describe the charm of his familiar conversation. There was endless variety without effort. His peculiar humor, taking shape in a thousand felicities of thought and phrase that fell casually and as it were inevitably from his lips, exhilarated without reaction or fatigue. His lightest words were full of fruitful suggestion. Sudden strains of melancholy or high seriousness were followed, in a moment, by flashes of gaiety almost boyish. And pervading it all one felt the attraction of his personality and the goodness of his heart.

Professor Child's humor was not only one of his most striking characteristics as a man; it was of constant service to his scholarly researches. Keenly alive to any incongruity in thought or fact, and the least self-conscious of men, he scrutinized his own nascent theories with the same humorous shrewdness with which he looked at the ideas of others. It is impossible to think of him as the sponsor of some hypotheses which men of equal eminence have advanced and defended with passion; and, even if his goodness of nature had not prevented it, his sense of the ridiculous would not have suffered him to engage in the absurdities of philological polemics. In the interpretation of literature, his humor stood him in good stead, keeping his native sensibility under due control, so that it never degenerated into sentimentalism. It made him a marvelous interpreter of Chaucer, whose spirit he had caught to a degree attained by no other scholar or critic.

To younger scholars Professor Child was an influence at once stimulating and benignant. To confer with him was always to be stirred to greater effort, but, at the same time, the serenity of his devotion to learning chastened the petulance of immature ambition in others. The talk might be quite concrete, even definitely practical,—it might deal with indifferent matters; but, in some way, there was an irradiation of the master's nature that dispelled all unworthy feelings. In the presence of his noble modesty the bustle of self-assertion was quieted and the petty spirit of pedantic wrangling could not assert itself. However severe his criticism, there were no personalities in it. He could not be other than outspoken,—concealment and shuffling were abhorrent to him,—yet such was his kindliness that his frankest judgments never wounded; even his reproofs left no sting. With his large charity was associated, as its necessary complement in a strong character, a capacity for righteous indignation. "He is almost the only man I know," said one in his lifetime, "who *thinks no evil*." There could be no truer word. Yet when he was confronted with injury or oppression, none could stand against the anger of this just man. His unselfishness did not suffer him to see offences against himself, but wrong done to another roused him in an instant to protesting action.

Professor Child's publications, despite their magnitude and importance, are no adequate measure either of his acquirements or of his influence. He printed nothing about Shakspere, for example, yet he was the peer of any Shaksperian, past or present, in knowledge and interpretative power. As a Chaucer scholar he had no superior, in this country or in Europe: his published work was confined, as we have seen, to questions of language, but no one had a wider or closer acquaintance with the whole subject. An edition of Chaucer from his hand would have been priceless. His acquaintance with letters was not confined to special authors or centuries. He was at home in modern European literature and profoundly versed in that of the Middle Ages. In his immediate territory,—English,—his knowledge, linguistic and literary, covered all periods, and was alike exact

and thorough. His taste and judgment were exquisite, and he enlightened every subject which he touched. As a writer, he was master of a singularly felicitous style, full of individuality and charm. Had his time not been occupied in other ways, he would have made the most delightful of essayists.

Fortunately, Professor Child's courses of instruction in the university—particularly those on Chaucer and Shakspere—gave him an opportunity to impart to a constantly increasing circle of pupils the choicest fruits of his life of thought and study. In his later years he had the satisfaction to see grow up about him a school of young specialists who can have no higher ambition than to be worthy of their master. But his teaching was not limited to these,—it included all sorts and conditions of college students; and none, not even the idle and incompetent, could fail to catch something of his spirit. One thing may be safely asserted: no university teacher was ever more beloved.

And with this may fitly close too slight a tribute to the memory of a great scholar and a good man. Many things remain unsaid. His gracious family life, his civic virtues, his patriotism, his bounty to the poor,—all must be passed by with a bare mention, which yet will signify much to those who knew him. In all ways he lived worthily, and he died having attained worthy ends.

Notes

1. *The Poetical Works of Edmund Spenser.* The text carefully revised, and illustrated with notes, original and selected, by Francis J. Child. Boston: Little, Brown, and Company. 1855. 5 vols.

2. *The Canterbury Tales* of Geoffrey Chaucer. A new text, with illustrative notes. Edited by Thomas Wright. London, printed for the Percy Society, 1847-51. 3 vols.

3. The paper entitled 'Observations on the Language of Chaucer' was laid before the American Academy of Arts and Sciences on June 3, 1862, and was published in the *Memoirs* of the Academy, Vol. VIII, pt. ii, 445-502 (Boston, 1863). The second paper, entitled 'Observations on the Language of Gower's *Confessio Amantis*', was laid before the Academy on January 9, 1866, and appeared in *Memoirs*, IX, ii, 265-315 (Boston, 1873). A few copies of each paper were struck off separately, but these are now very hard to find. Mr Ellis's rearrangement and amalgamation of the two papers, which is by no means a good substitute for the papers themselves, may be found in Part I of his *Early English Pronunciation*, London, 1869, pp. 343-97.

4. *English and Scottish Ballads.* Selected and edited by Francis James Child. Boston, 1857-58.

5. How inseparable were the services of Dr Furnivall and those of Professor Child in securing this devoutly wished consummation may be seen by comparing Dr Furnivall's Forewords (I, ix, x), in which he gives much of the credit to Mr Child, with Mr Child's Dedication (in vol. I of the present collection), in which he gives the credit to Dr Furnivall.

6. Since Mr Child's death the important "Buchan original MS" has been secured for the Child Memorial Library of the University,—a collection endowed by friends and pupils of the dead master.

7. See V, 397 b.

8. This is 'Young Betrice,' No 5 in William Tytler's lost Brown MS. (V, 397), which "may possibly be a version of 'Hugh Spencer's Feats in France'" (see II, 377; III, 275).

Francis B. Gummere (essay date January 1904)

SOURCE: Gummere, Francis B. "Primitive Poetry and the Ballad, Part 3." *Modern Philology* 1, no. 3 (January 1904): 373-90.

[*In the following excerpt, Gummere analyzes Child's criteria for including ballads in his collection.*]

It seems that no test is left, that I can discover, by which one may pass upon the claims of a ballad to its place in any collection. Spirit, purpose, and meaning disappear, for such criticism, from the great work of Professor Child. "This Ninth Part [of *The English and Scottish Popular Ballads*]," he wrote in 1894, "completes the collection of English and Scottish ballads to the extent of my knowledge of sources"—with the exception of one uncopied piece in a lost manuscript. But how "complete"? It is clear that the notion of a traditional ballad existed in very exact shape for Professor Child, when one thinks of the host which he rejected. In *Johnson's Cyclopædia* [(1877)] he made a provisional statement of this notion; but it was not final, and he wished it to be neither quoted nor regarded as final. The statement is both negative and positive. With his sturdy commonsense, Mr. Child balked at the idea of folk-made poetry as set forth by Wilhelm Grimm; with sturdy particular sense, however, gained from long commerce with his subject, he goes on to say that, although men and not communities make the ballad, it comes from a period when people are not divided into markedly distinct classes, when "there is such community of ideas and feelings that the whole people form an individual." It must be traditional, then, and sprung from that homogeneous, unlettered community which all the great writers on balladry, including Ferdinand Wolf, himself a resolute skeptic about communal authorship, have demanded as a necessary condition of the original ballad.

Frank Preston Stearns (essay date 1905)

SOURCE: Stearns, Frank Preston. "Francis J. Child." In *Cambridge Sketches*, pp. 40-54. Philadelphia: J. B. Lippincott Company, 1905.

[*In the following excerpt, Stearns discusses the expertise, and passion, with which Child pursued his ballad scholarship.*]

Besides his regular college duties, Professor Child had three distinct interests to which he devoted himself in leisure hours with all the energy of an ardent nature. The first of these, editing a complete edition of the old English ballads [*The English and Scottish Popular Ballads*], was the labor of his life, and with it his name will always be associated, for it is a work that can neither be superseded nor excelled. He was the first to arouse English scholars to the importance of this, as may be read in the dedication of a partial edition taken from the Percy manuscripts and published in London in 1861. He recognized in them the true foundation of the finest literature of the modern world, and he considered them so much the better from the fact that they were not composed to be printed, but to be recited or sung. Matthew Arnold wrote in a letter from America: "After lecturing at Taunton, I came to Boston with Professor Child of Harvard, a very pleasant man, who is a great authority on ballad poetry," very warm praise, considering the source whence it came. Late in life Professor Child edited separate versions in modern English of some curious old ballads, and sent them as Christmas presents to his friends.

It is not surprising that he should have been interested as well in the rude songs of the British sailors, which he heard on crossing the ocean. He was mightily amused at their simple refrain:

> Haul in the bowlin', long-tailed bowlin',
> Haul in the bowlin' Kitty, O, my darlin'.

"That rude couplet," he said, "contains all the original elements of poetry. Firstly, the anthropomorphic element; the sailor imagines his bowline as if it had life. Secondly, the humorous element, for the bowline is all *tail*. Thirdly, the reflective element; the monotonous motion makes him think of home,—of his wife or sweetheart,—and he ends the second line with 'Kitty, O, my darlin'.' I like such primitive verses much better than the 'Pike County Ballads,' a mixture of sentiment and profanity."

Walter Morris Hart (essay date 1906)

SOURCE: Hart, Walter Morris. "Professor Child and the Ballad." *Publications of the Modern Language Association of America* n.s. 14, no. 4 (1906): 755-807.

[*In the following excerpt, Hart discusses Child's definition of the popular ballad. Hart examines the unique qualities of a number of ballads, while evaluating Child's commentaries on them.*]

I.

In that article ["**Ballad Poetry**"] in the *Universal Cyclopædia* which Professor Child "wished to be neither quoted nor regarded as final,"[1] but which must here be combined with other tentative or fragmentary statements, he defined the *popular ballad* as "a distinct and very important species of poetry. Its historical and natural place," he said, "is anterior to the appearance of the poetry of art, to which it has formed a step, and by which it has been regularly displaced, and, in some cases, all but extinguished. Whenever a people in the course of its development reaches a certain intellectual and moral stage, it will feel an impulse to express itself, and the form of expression to which it is first impelled is, as is well known, not prose, but verse, and in fact narrative verse. The condition of society in which a truly national or popular poetry appears explains the character of such poetry. It is a condition in which the people are not divided by political organization and book-culture into markedly distinct classes, in which consequently there is such community of ideas and feelings that the whole people form an individual. Such poetry, accordingly, while it is in its essence an expression of our common human nature, and so of universal and indestructible interest, will in each case be differenced by circumstances and idiosyncrasy. On the other hand, it will always be an expression of the mind and heart of the people as an individual, and never of the personality of individual men. The fundamental characteristic of popular ballads is therefore the absence of subjectivity and of self-consciousness. Though they do not 'write themselves,' as William Grimm has said, though a man and not a people has composed them, still the author counts for nothing, and it is not by mere accident, but with the best reason, that they have come down to us anonymous. Hence, too, they are extremely difficult to imitate by the highly civilized modern man, and most of the attempts to reproduce this kind of poetry have been ridiculous failures.

"The primitive ballad, then, is popular, not in the sense of something arising from and suited to the lower orders of a people. As yet, no sharp distinction of high and low exists, in respect to knowledge, desires, and tastes. An increased civilization, and especially the introduction of book-culture, gradually gives rise to such a division; the poetry of art appears; the popular poetry is no longer relished by a portion of the people, and is abandoned to an uncultivated or not over-cultivated class—a constantly diminishing number."

But "the popular ballad is not originally the product or the property of the lower orders of the people. Nothing, in fact, is more obvious than that many of the ballads

of the now most refined nations had their origin in that class whose acts and fortunes they depict—the upper class—though the growth of civilization has driven them from the memory of the highly polished and instructed, and has left them as an exclusive possession to the uneducated. The genuine popular ballad had its rise in a time when the distinctions since brought about by education and other circumstances had practically no existence. The vulgar ballads of our day, the 'broadsides' which were printed in such large numbers in England and elsewhere in the sixteenth century or later, belong to a different genus; they are products of a low kind of *art,* and most of them are, from a literary point of view, thoroughly despicable and worthless.

"Next it must be observed that ballads which have been handed down by long-repeated tradition have always departed considerably from their original form. If the transmission has been purely through the mouths of unlearned people, there is less probability of willful change, but once in the hands of professional singers there is no amount of change which they may not undergo. Last of all comes the modern editor, whose so-called improvements are more to be feared than the mischances of a thousand years. A very old ballad will often be found to have resolved itself in the course of what may be called its propagation into several distinct shapes, and each of these again to have received distinct modifications. When the fashion of verse has altered, we shall find a change of form as great as that in the *Hildebrandslied,* from alliteration without stanza to stanza with rhyme. In all cases the language drifts insensibly from ancient forms, though not at the same rate with the language of every-day life. The professional ballad-singer or minstrel, whose sole object is to please the audience before him, will alter, omit, or add, without scruple, and nothing is more common than to find different ballads blended together.

"There remains the very curious question of the origin of the resemblances which are found in the ballads of different nations, the recurrence of the same incidents or even of the same story, among races distinct in blood and history, and geographically far separated." It is not necessary to go back to a common ancestry to explain these resemblances. "The incidents of many ballads are such as might occur anywhere and at any time; and with regard to agreements that can not be explained in this way we have only to remember that tales and songs were the chief social amusement of all classes of people in all the nations of Europe during the Middle Ages, and that new stories would be eagerly sought for by those whose business it was to furnish this amusement, and be rapidly spread among the fraternity. A great effect was undoubtedly produced by the crusades, which both brought the chief European nations into closer intercourse and made them acquainted with the East, thus facilitating the interchange of stories and greatly enlarging the stock."

This account of authorship and transmission may be illustrated and supplemented by *obiter dicta* from ***The English and Scottish Popular Ballads.*** "The author counts for nothing;" the ballad is essentially anonymous: that Expliceth quod Rychard Sheale means merely that "The Hunting of the Cheviot" (162) "was of course part of his stock as minstrel; the supposition that he was the author is preposterous in the extreme."[2]. . . .

In transmission, then, and even in the best of it, the ballad ordinarily fares but ill, "departs from the original form," becomes less typically ballad; and, generally speaking, the older it is, the earlier it is caught and fixed in print, the better. Professor Child has thus special praise for those Robin Hood ballads which "have come down to us in comparatively ancient form."[3] "Robin Hood's Death" (120, B) is "in the fine old strain."[4] "Robin Hood and the Beggar" (134, II), "by far the best of the Robin Hood ballads of the secondary, so to speak cyclic, period," is "a composition of some antiquity,"[5] "Thomas Rymer" (37) "is an entirely popular ballad as to style, and must be of considerable age."[6] One is not to expect in a late or modern ballad the excellence found in an early or ancient one. "Robin Hood's Chase" (146) "is a well-conceived ballad, and only needs to be older."[7] "Walter Lesly" (296) is "a late, but life-like and spirited ballad."[8] "The Hunting of the Cheviot" (162, B) "is a striking . . . example of the impairment which an old ballad would suffer when written over for the broadside press."[9] Version M of "Young Beichan" (53) "was probably a broadside or stall copy, and is certainly of that quality, but preserves a very ancient traditional feature."[10] The "ridiculous ballad" of "John Thomson and the Turk" (266) finds a place in the collection because it is "a seedling from an ancient and very notable story."[11] "The Knight's Ghost" (265) "has not a perceptible globule of old blood in it, yet it has had the distinction of being more than once translated as a specimen of Scottish popular ballads."[12] Scott's later edition of "Tam Lin" (39) "was corrupted with eleven new stanzas, which are not simply somewhat of a modern cast as to diction, as Scott remarks, but of a grossly modern invention, and as unlike popular verse as anything can be."[13] Scott's version of "Jellon Grame" (90) has four stanzas of its own, "which are evidently not simply modernized, but modern."[14] Certain stanzas in version Bb of "Archie o Cawfield" (188) "are indifferent modern stuff."[15] The "modern ballad" on the subject of "The Heir of Linne" (267) is "an inexpressibly pitiable ditty."[16]

Certain counterfeits, imitations, or "spurious" ballads, wholly or almost wholly the work of editors or modern writers, are included in Professor Child's collection.

"Robin Hood and the Tinker" (127) is a "contemptible imitation of imitations."[17] Buchan's version of "Young Waters" (94) is, for the most part, "a counterfeit of the lowest description. Nevertheless it is given in an appendix; for much the same reason that thieves are photographed."[18] "Young Ronald" (304) is an example of the "spurious" ballad, and the reasons for its inclusion are given at some length. "If any lover of ballads should feel his understanding insulted by the presentation of such a piece as this, I can have no quarrel with him. There is certainly much in it that is exasperating. . . . In this and not a very few other cases, I have suppressed disgust, and admitted an actually worthless and manifestly—at least in part—spurious ballad, because of a remote possibility that it might contain relics, or be a debased representative, of something genuine and better. Such was the advice of my lamented friend, Grundtvig, in more instances than those in which I have brought myself to defer to his judgment."[19] For the same reason is included "The Laidley Worm of Spindleston Heughs": "This composition of Mr. Lamb's—for nearly every line of it is his[20]—is not only based on popular tradition, but evidently preserves some small fragments of a popular ballad, and for this reason is given in an Appendix."[21]. . . .

III.

It is clear that to Professor Child's mind it was necessary that the ballad should tell a story. "The word *ballad* in English signifies a narrative song, a short tale in lyric verse."[22] Thus the English versions of "Geordie" (209) are said to be mere 'goodnights,' whereas "the Scottish ballads have a proper story, with a beginning, middle, and end, and (save one late copy), a good end, and they are most certainly . . . independent of the English."[23] "Dugall Quin" (294) is a "little ballad, which has barely story enough to be so called."[24] To the "English 'ditty' (not a traditional ballad) . . . there is very little story."[25]

Necessary as the story is, however, it is seldom completely told in the ballad; something is left to the hearers' imagination. Sometimes the close of the story is omitted: "it is not said (except in the spurious portions of E) that the lady was carried back by her husband, but this may perhaps be inferred from his hanging the gypsies. In D and K we are left uncertain as to her disposition."[26] Transitions are usually abrupt,—"abrupt even for a ballad" in "Willie's Lady" (6) from stanza 33 to stanza 34.[27] Jamieson, in printing "The Bonny Birdy" (82), introduced several stanzas 'to fill up chasms.' "But the chasms, such as they are, are easily leapt by the imagination, and Jamieson's interpolations are mere bridges of carpenter's work."[28] Of "Sir Patrick Spens" (58), "Percy's version [A] remains, poetically, the best. It may be a fragment, but the imagination easily supplies all that may be wanting; and if more of the

story, or the whole, be told in H, the half is better[29] than the whole."[30] These abrupt transitions do not, then, result in incoherence, which accompanies corruption and is a sign of degeneracy. Thus "The Carnal and the Crane" (55) "had obviously been transmitted from mouth to mouth before it was fixed in its present incoherent and corrupted form by print."[31] "Young Bearwell" (302) is "one of not a few flimsy and unjointed ballads found in Buchan's volumes, the like of which is hardly to be found elsewhere."[32] After an attempt to make the story of "The White Fisher" (264) hang together, Professor Child concludes: "But we need not trouble ourselves much to make these counterfeits reasonable. Those who utter them rely confidently upon our taking folly and jargon as the marks of genuineness."[33] Coherence, on the contrary, is a characteristic of the true ballad, an important phase of ballad excellence. "I am persuaded that there was an older and better copy of this ballad ["Bewick and Graham" (211)] than those which are extant. The story is so well composed, proportion is so well kept, on the whole, that it is reasonable to suppose that certain passages (as stanzas 3, 4, 50) may have suffered some injury."[34] Introductions, not closely connected with the ballad story, are not characteristic. "The narrator in the Ever Green poem reports at second hand: as he is walking, he meets a man who, upon request, tells him the beginning and the end. Both pieces have nearly the same first line. The borrowing was more probably on the part of the ballad, for a popular ballad would be likely to tell its tale without preliminaries."[35]. . . .

IV.

The English and Scottish Popular Ballads of 1882-1898 has naturally superseded the ***English and Scottish Ballads*** of 1857-1859, and Professor Child himself shared the general tendency to underestimate the real value of the earlier collection. It was of course made on a different plan; its limits were not so clearly defined, and it did not attempt to give every version of every known ballad. Many of the sources, moreover, were not yet open. One is, then, surprised to find that, of the three hundred and five ballads printed in the later collection, only ninety are new; and these are, for the most part, unimportant additions to the body of ballad literature. They are distributed as follows: 15 in volume I, 16 in II, 11 in III, 25 in IV, 23 in V. Thus 59 of the 90 occur in the last three volumes; of these there is not one of first importance. Of the remaining 31 not more than 10 can be regarded as really valuable additions, though such an estimate must of necessity be based more or less upon personal impression. Some of these were already accessible, in Buchan's versions, or elsewhere: "Willie's Lyke-Wake" (25), "Lizie Wan" (51), "The King's Dochter Lady Jean" (52), "Brown Robyn's Confession" (57), "Fair Mary of Waltington" (91). These, doubtless, were omitted because of the nature of their

subject-matter; it was only in the later collection that Professor Child "had no discretion."[36] Other important ballads were not yet accessible, or not yet discovered: "St. Stephen and Herod" (22), "The Laily Worm and the Machrel of the Sea" (36), "The Queen of Elfan's Nourice" (40), "The Unquiet Grave" (78), "The Great Silkie of Sule Skerry" (113). Of the ten, only four are included in Professor Gummere's collection. The main addition of the later collection is thus rather in the way of new versions of important ballads, or of more authentic versions based directly upon the manuscripts; in the citation of a larger number of foreign parallels; and, generally, in the matter contained in the introductions.

The *Ballads* [*English and Scottish Ballads*] contained 115 pieces which do not appear in the later collection. The nature of such material, since it is excluded from the "complete" *English and Scottish Popular Ballads,* is significant as throwing some additional light upon Professor Child's conception. In many cases the reason for exclusion is made clear by Professor Child himself, in comments in the earlier or in the later collection. Of the whole group of lays and romances contained in Book I of the *Ballads,* he says: "Some of the longer pieces in this book are not of the nature of ballads, and require an apology. They were admitted before the limits of the work had been determined with exactness."[37] If such pieces as these do not fulfil the lyrical requirement of the true ballad, others cannot fulfil the requirement of plot, and the songs of the *Ballads,* like "A Lyke Wake Dirge," "Fair Helen of Kirconnel," or "The Lowlands of Holland"[38] find no place in the later collection. The *Ballads* contains also translations from the Danish, and the original and translation of a modern Greek parallel of the Lenore story; these are naturally not included in *The English and Scottish Popular Ballads.*

The later collection is much more chary of the admission of broadsides or sheet-ballads: in many cases they are relegated to introductions or appendices; in many more, omitted. *William Guiseman* is cited merely, under "Brown Robin's Confession" (57), as "a copy, improved by tradition, of the 'lament' in 'William Grismond's Downfal,' a broadside of 1650."[39] "The Lament of the Border Widow," which occurs in Book VI of the *Ballads,* "shows broader traces of the sheet-ballad," and is quoted in the introduction to No 106 for "those who are interested in such random inventions (as, under pardon, they must be called)."[40] Of "The Lady Isabella's Tragedy" Professor Child says in the later collection: "Though perhaps absolutely the silliest ballad that ever was made, and very far from silly sooth, the broadside was traditionally propagated in Scotland without so much change as is usual in such cases."[41] Even in the *Ballads* one finds this comment: "The three following pieces ["The Spanish Virgin," "Lady Isabella's Tragedy," "The Cruel Black"] are here inserted merely as

specimens of a class of tales, horrible in their incidents but feeble in their execution, of which whole dreary volumes were printed and read about two centuries ago. They were all of them, probably, founded on Italian novels."[42] Although the *Ballads* includes "Macpherson's Rant," it is declared "worthy of a hangman's pen."[43] A number of tales which employ a highly artificial stanza, such as "The Fray of Suport," "The Raid of the Reidswire," or "The Flemish Insurrection," do not find their way into the later collection.

Traces of the modern editor or author become less common in the later collection. Versions "modernized and completed by Percy" (Book I, Nos. 1b and 5b) are excluded. The cynical "Twa Corbies" appears only in the introduction to "The Three Ravens"; and Motherwell's edition, declared already in the *Ballads* to be a "modernized version,"[44] does not appear at all. Motherwell's "Bonnie George Campbell" suffers a like fate, and this, we infer, because "Motherwell made up his 'Bonnie George Campbell' from B, C, D."[45] As, no doubt, not merely modernized but modern, "Sir Roland" is excluded. "This fragment, Motherwell tells us, was communicated to him by an ingenious friend, who remembered having heard it sung in his youth. He does not vouch for its antiquity, and we have little or no hesitation in pronouncing it a modern composition."[46] Similarly, "Lady Anne" "is on the face of it a modern composition, with extensive variations, on the theme of the popular ballad."[47] It is printed in the appendix to No 20. "Earl Richard" is "an entirely modern composition, excepting only the twenty lines of Herd's fragment."[48] Of "Auld Maitland" Professor Child says: "Notwithstanding the authority of Scott and Leyden, I am inclined to agree with Mr Aytoun, that this ballad is a modern imitation, or if not that, a comparatively recent composition. It is with reluctance that I make for it the room it requires."[49] The essential anonymity of the ballad, in Professor Child's final conception, naturally excludes pieces like Henryson's "Robene and Makyne" and "The Bludy Serk," which had found their way into the *Ballads.*[50]

There are but few instances of definite praise, as ballads, of pieces included in the earlier collection and excluded from the later. "The Children in the Wood" is said to be "perhaps the most popular of all English ballads. Its merit is attested by the favor it has enjoyed with so many generations, and was vindicated to a cold and artificial age by the kindly pen of Addison."[51] We must not forget, however, that Professor Child was fifty years nearer the kindly pen of Addison. The cold and artificial age, moreover, was also sentimental and moral; and why, with it, this ballad was so popular, a single stanza will show:

> You that executors be made,
> And overseers eke

Of children that be fatherless,
 And infants mild and meek;
Take you example by this thing,
 And yield to each his right,
Lest God with such like miserye
 Your wicked minds requite.

(vv. 153 ff.)

"The Blind Beggar's Daughter of Bednall's Green" is said to be printed from a modern broadside, yet it is characterized as "this favorite popular ballad."[52] "The Nutbrowne Maid" is "this matchless poem," "this beautiful old ballad."[53] Yet, clearly, it is not a popular ballad at all.

On the whole, it is not difficult to see why the 115 ballads are excluded from the later collection; and one gets the impression that, had Professor Child chosen to enforce the conception of the ballad which he already had in mind, most of them would have been excluded from the earlier collection as well. This impression is deepened by an examination of the comments scattered through the **Ballads.**

He already regarded the ballad as inimitable:[54] "The exclusion of the 'Imitations' . . . may possibly excite the regret of a few. . . . Whatever may be the merit of the productions in question, they are never less likely to obtain credit for it, than when they are brought into comparison with their professed models."[55] Again, "Sir Patrick Spens," "if not ancient, has been always accepted as such by the most skilful judges, and is a solitary instance of a successful imitation, in manner and spirit, of the best specimens of authentic minstrelsy."[56]

Professor Child had already fallen foul of the editors, and their alterations and interpolations.[57] It is interesting to see how, in many cases, he anticipated the corrections and comments made possible, for the later collection, by access to the manuscripts. Of "The Child of Elle" he says: "So extensive are Percy's alterations and additions, that the reader will have no slight difficulty in detecting the few traces that are left of the genuine composition."[58] Compare: "So much of Percy's 'Child of Elle' as was genuine, which, upon the printing of his manuscript, turned out to be one fifth."[59] Again, Percy acknowledges interpolations, which "might with some confidence be pointed out. Among them are certainly most, if not all, of the last twelve stanzas of the Second Part, which include the catastrophe to the story."[60] In Percy, he says in the later collection, "Sir Cawline" "is extended to nearly twice the amount of what is found in the manuscript, and a tragical turn is forced upon the story."[61] Again: "We have given 'Gil Morrice' as it stands in the *Reliques* (iii. 132,) degrading to the margin those stanzas which are undoubtedly spurious."[62] The stanzas thus degraded turned out to be actually spurious.[63] Condemnation of Buchan is scattered

throughout the **Ballads.** Thus: "Some resolution has been exercised, and much disgust suppressed, in retaining certain pieces from Buchan's collections, so strong is the suspicion that, after having been procured from very inferior sources, they were tampered with by the editor."[64] Again: "One uncommonly tasteless stanza [41, A, 53], the interpolation of some nursery-maid,[65] is here omitted. Too many of Buchan's ballads have suffered in this way, and have become both prolix and vulgar."[66] Even in the **Ballads** Professor Child placed "no confidence in any of Allan Cunningham's *souvenirs* of Scottish song,"[67] and his early suspicions[68] of the character of Cunningham's version of Gil Brenton are confirmed in the later collection.[69] "King Henry," printed in the earlier collection "without the editor's [Jamieson's] interpolations,"[70] appears in the same form in the later, except that stanza 14 is printed in small type, as not being in the Jamieson-Brown MS. Again, in "The Bonny Birdy," "the lines supplied by Jamieson have been omitted."[71] There is an interesting comment on these lines in the later collection.[72]

Professor Child was already aware that change of nationality was accompanied by change of the scene of action.[73] He quoted Scott's account of the locality of "The Douglas Tragedy" [= "Earl Brand" (7, B)], and added: "After so circumstantial a description of the scene, . . . the reader may be amused to see the same story told in various Scandinavian ballads, with a no less plausible resemblance to actual history. This, as has already been pointed out under "Guy of Warwick" and "Kempion,"[74] is an ordinary occurrence in the transmission of legends."[75]

He noted, too, the tendency of ballads to combine: "The natural desire of men to hear more of characters in whom they have become strongly interested, has frequently stimulated the attempt to continue successful fictions."[76] "Sweet William's Ghost" is often made the sequel to other ballads.[77]

So far as subject-matter is concerned, we find in the **Ballads** the same conception of the relation of ballad and fact. "Jane Shore" "adheres to matter of fact with a fidelity very uncommon,"[78] and this is, perhaps, one reason why it does not find a place in the later collection.[79] We may contrast, on the other hand, the two statements in regard to the relation of "Hind Horn" and the romance: "Metrical romances . . . are known in many cases to have been adapted for the entertainment of humbler hearers, by abridgment in the form of ballads." He regards "Hind Horn" as a case of this sort.[80]

Style and plot, finally, are a test of genuineness: "I cannot assent to the praise bestowed by Scott on "The Outlaw Murray." The story lacks point and the style is affected—not that of the unconscious poet of the real *traditional* ballad."[81] Though there without comment, it is placed at the very end of the later collection.

From a comment like this it is obvious that Professor Child already had in mind the conception of "a real *traditional* ballad," a "specimen of authentic minstrelsy."[82] Although he admitted to the earlier collection lays, romances, songs, broadsides and sheet-ballads, as well as modern or modernized compositions, yet he was aware that all these differed from the true ballad. This true ballad, he conceived, was inimitable, in matter and manner. In transmission it might suffer, from the invention of a nursery-maid, from Buchan's beggar, from a "hangman's pen," from the modern editors. It drew its subject-matter from fact (to which it was not loyal), from romances, from other ballads. In quality the subject-matter was not "horrible." In style the true ballad was not feeble in execution, not prolix and vulgar, and not affected. The earlier conception was not as complete as the later, and it was by no means so rigorously enforced. In regard to specific compositions, there was, as is to be expected, some change of opinion. But the significant fact is that for at least forty years Professor Child retained without essential change his conception of the traditional ballad as a distinct literary type. . . .

VI.

We are now in position to attempt a summary of Professor Child's conception of the popular ballad. He regarded it as a distinct species of poetry, which precedes the poetry of art, as the product of a homogeneous people, the expression of our common human nature, of the mind and heart of the people, never of the personality of an individual man, devoid, therefore, of all subjectivity and self-consciousness. Hence the author counts for nothing; hence, too, the ballad is difficult to imitate and most attempts in this way are ridiculous failures. In transmission the ballad regularly departs from the original form, least in the mouths of unlearned people, more in the hands of professional singers or editors. It is at its best when it has come down by a purely domestic tradition, yet even so it is sometimes influenced by printed literature; and much depends on the experience and selection of the reciters, and on their varying memory, which is, however, ordinarily remarkable for its tenacity. Less fortunate is the ballad when it passes through low mouths or hands, suffering corruption of various kinds,—in the style of the attorney's clerk, or the housemaid or the serving-man, or ostler, or blind beggar. In the hands of the *bänkelsänger* or of the minstrel, the ballad departs still further from its original form. Or, rewritten for the broadside press, it is seriously enfeebled, or retrenched and marred, though it may retain some original features, and there are thus degrees of departure from the original matter and manner. The broadside may, in turn, become tradition. It is, so far as it appears in Professor Child's later collection, always founded on tradition, and this tradition lives after the composition of the broadside, and may influence the later versions of the printed form. Last comes the modern editor, and by him the ballad is sometimes lengthened,—by combination of different versions, by interpolation of new stanzas, always more or less unlike the popular style; or it is sometimes "improved," or retouched, or emended, or altered,—changed to something in glaring contrast to the groundwork. Some results of the vicissitudes of transmission are, the change of the hero's nationality, of his name, of his rôle; change of the scene of action; corruption of diction resulting in perversion of sense or in nonsense; introduction of learned words. The ballad thus suffers in transmission, and is at its best when it is early caught and fixed in print. It is sometimes counterfeited or imitated, and counterfeits are included in the later collection for contrast, for much the same reason that thieves are photographed, or because they may contain relics of something genuine or better.

Of the Subject-Matter of the ballad, the sources may be, and in the best instances are, purely popular, consisting of material which appears only in popular literature. Professor Child mentions no instance where a prose tale is the source of a ballad, but the ballad, he says, may sometimes be resolved into a prose tale. Popular origin is attested by foreign parallels in folk-literature. Of such literature certain features or themes are characteristic, such as the quibbling oath, the miraculous harvest, the childbirth in the wood, the testament, the riddle, heroic sentiment, etc. The source may, again, be an actual occurrence, in which case the ballad, while not deliberate fiction, is yet not loyal to the fact. Or the source may be a romance, or the source of a romance, in which case oral tradition may be older than written, the ballad older than the romance. Or the source may be earlier ballads, mechanically and deliberately put together in later ones, made over and assimilated in the "Gest of Robin Hood." In the course of transmission certain features appear which are not characteristic of popular literature; the subject-matter of the true ballad does not deal in extravagance, or exaggeration, or platitude; it is not prosaic, over-refined, cynical, sophisticated, sentimental, unnatural, trite, or moral, though the "pungent buckishness" of the broadside, and the gay cynicism of the minstrel, are foreign to it.

So far as Technique is concerned, the ballad must have plot. The story may not be completely told; conclusion, transitions, and preliminaries may be omitted; but the result is not nonsense, the ballad is not incoherent. At its best it is, however, brief. It is careless of geography, and, except in some,—and some of the best,—of the Robin Hood ballads, it touches Setting lightly. In dealing with the Supernatural it does not attempt to explain the action or to describe supernatural figures; ghosts, however, do not walk without reason.

In Style the ballad is artless and homely, and in it the conceit, and literary or learned words and phrases, are

out of place. Yet it has certain conventions of its own, such as the "commonplace," the repetition of a message by a messenger, the verbally similar treatment of similar incidents as they occur in different ballads. Emotionally, the ghost ballad is impressive and affecting; and, in general, the ballad may be infectious, or spirited and life-like, or pathetic, or tender, or humorous, or vigorous and not lacking in color or flavor. It is essentially lyrical, and its lyrical quality is not less essential than plot. Often it absolutely requires the support of a melody and the comment of a burden. This burden sometimes foreshadows the calamity, sometimes enhances by contrast the gloom of the conclusion. It is usually less than the stanza with which it was sung; and, unlike the refrain, it was sung, not after the stanza, but with it. It is sometimes of different metre, sometimes not. The absence of the burden is in no case proof that it never existed.

Notes

1. Professor Gummere in *Modern Philology,* I, [no. 3 (January 1904):] 378.

2. [*The English and Scottish Popular Ballads* (1882-98),] III, 303. [Subsequent references to this work will list volume and page.]

3. [ibid.] III, 42.

4. III, 103.

5. III, 159.

6. I, 320.

7. III, 206.

8. V, 168.

9. III, 305.

10. I, 455.

11. V, 1.

12. IV, 437.

13. I, 335.

14. II, 302.

15. III, 486.

16. V, 12. Cf. also I, 35, IV, 10, 142, 401, for passages condemned as "modern."

17. III, 140.

18. II, 342.

19. V, 182.

20. Communicated by the Rev. Mr Lamb to Hutchinson "with this harmless preamble: 'a song 500 years old, made by the old Mountain Bard, Duncan Frasier, living on Cheviot, A. D. 1270.'"

21. I, 308.

22. *Universal Cyclopædia* [(1874)], "Ballad Poetry." The lyrical element is of equal importance; see p. 790, below.

23. [*The English and Scottish Popular Ballads,*] IV, 126.

24. V, 165.

25. IV, 192. ["The Broom of Cowdenknows" (217)].

26. IV, 63. ["The Gypsie Laddie" (200)].

27. I, 82.

28. II, 260.

29. Surely better *as ballad.* Cf. p. 796, below.

30. II, 18.

31. II, 7.

32. V, 178.

33. IV, 435.

34. IV, 145.

35. III, 317.

36. "Sheath and Knife" (16), also, was accessible but omitted.

37. *Ballads,* I, xi, n. "Certain short romances which formerly stood in the First Book, have been dropped from this second Edition [1860], in order to give the collection a homogeneous character." *Ballads* [1860], I, xii.

38. "A song," II, 317. (Where merely volume and page are given the reference is still to the later collection; references to the earlier are preceded by the word *Ballads.*)

39. II, 16.

40. II, 429.

41. V, 34, n.

42. *Ballads,* III, 360.

43. *Ballads,* VI, 263.

44. *Ballads,* III, 61.

45. IV, 142.

46. *Ballads,* I, 341.

47. I, 218, n.

48. *Ballads,* III, 293.

49. *Ballads,* VI, 220. Cf. Mr Andrew Lang's plea for "Auld Maitland," *Folk-Lore,* XIII, 191 ff.

50. See also the comments on the Rev. Mr Lamb's "Laidley Worm of Spindleston Heugh," *Ballads*, I, 386, and cf. p. 772, above.

51. *Ballads*, III, 128.

52. *Ballads*, IV, 161.

53. *Ballads*, IV, 143 f.

54. Cf. p. 757, above.

55. *Ballads*, V, iv.

56. *Ballads*, III, 148-149.

57. Cf. p. 767, above.

58. *Ballads*, III, 225.

59. I, 88.

60. *Ballads*, III, 173.

61. II, 56.

62. *Ballads*, II, 30.

63. II, 275.

64. *Ballads*, I, ix, n.

65. Cf. p. 762, above.

66. *Ballads*, I, 306 n.

67. *Ballads*, II, 220.

68. *Ballads*, I, 270.

69. See I, 62, and, for the omitted couplets, I, 80-81.

70. *Ballads*, I, 265.

71. *Ballads*, II, 22.

72. II, 260. See, also, the comments on Jamieson's "Child Rowland and Burd Ellen," *Ballads*, I, 416, and *English and Scottish Popular Ballads*, V, 201, n.

73. Cf. p. 769, above.

74. *Ballads*, I, 256.

75. *Ballads*, II, 115.

76. *Ballads*, II, 64.

77. *Ballads*, II, 45.

78. *Ballads*, VII, 194.

79. Cf. the comment on "The Hunting of the Cheviot," *Ballads*, VII, 25.

80. *Ballads*, IV, 17. For the later comment, see p. 777, above.

81. *Ballads*, VI, 22.

82. *Ballads*, III, 148-149.

T. F. Henderson (essay date 1912)

SOURCE: Henderson, T. F. "The Origin and Authorship of Ballads." In *The Ballad in Literature*, pp. 57-96. Cambridge: Cambridge University Press, 1912.

[*In the following excerpt, Henderson critiques Child's conception of the popular ballad. Henderson takes particular issue with Child's method of scholarship, arguing that many of his fundamental assertions are unsupported by evidence or even logic.*]

In an article ["**Ballad Poetry**"] on the ballad in *Johnson's Encyclopedia* [(1877)]—which, however, he did not desire to be "regarded as final"—Professor Child . . . describes "the historical and natural place" of the ballad as "anterior to the appearance of the poetry of art, to which it has formed a step, and by which it has been regularly displaced, and in some cases all but extinguished." "The condition of society," he also says, "in which a truly national or popular poetry appears, explains the character of such poetry. It is a condition in which the people are not divided by political organization and book culture into markedly distinct classes, in which, consequently, there is such community of ideas and feelings that the whole people form one individual. Such poetry, accordingly, while it is in its essence an expression of our common human nature, and so of universal and indestructible interest, will in each case be differentiated by circumstances and idiosyncrasy. On the other hand, it will always be an expression of the mind and heart of the people as an individual and never of the personality of individual men. The fundamental characteristic of popular ballads is, therefore, the absence of subjectivity and of self-consciousness. Though they do not write themselves, as William Grimm has said, though a man and not a people has composed them, still the author counts for nothing, and it is not by mere accident, but with the best reasons that they have come down to us anonymous." Further, he expresses the opinion that "the incidents of many ballads are such as might occur anywhere, and at any time, and with regard to agreements that cannot be expressed in this way, we have only to remember that tales and songs were the chief social amusement of all classes of people in all the nations of Europe during the Middle Ages, and that new stories would be eagerly sought for by those whose business it was to furnish this amusement, and be rapidly spread among the fraternity. A great effect was undoubtedly produced by the crusades, which both brought the chief European nations into closer intercourse and made them acquainted with the East."

Combining the statements of Child in his *Cyclopedia* article with various dicta in the prefaces to different ballads [in his **English and Scottish Ballads**], Mr W. M. Hart, in the *Publications of the Modern Language*

Association of America for 1906, after recording them, thus sums up Child's "conception of the popular ballad." "He regarded it as a distinct species of poetry which precedes the poetry of art, as the product of a homogeneous people, the expression of our common human nature, of the mind and heart of the people, never of the personality of an individual man, devoid, therefore, of all subjectivity and self-consciousness. Hence the author counts for nothing." Child's explanation of similarity in the plots of ballads of different nations and his assignment of the authorship of ballads to individuals are passed by. A summary cannot include everything, but these are important, even cardinal, omissions; for the statements of Child imply (1) that ballads generally, or at least the ballads known to us, are not earlier than the crusades; (2) that though popular, and usually drawing their material from popular sources, they are not of popular, in the sense of being of communal, origin, but have all an individual authorship; (3) that they were the work, many of them at least, of a fraternity whose "tales and songs were the chief social amusement of all classes of people." From the perusal merely of Mr Hart's summary, we could not even infer that Child definitely attributed individual authorship to the ballad. On the contrary, we would be apt to conclude that he deemed it the mysterious creation of the "popular imagination," the combined achievement of "a homogeneous people," which, by means of it, found expression for "its mind and heart."

But while Mr Hart seems, therefore, to have, unconsciously, rendered the views of Child a little more akin than Child intended to the "popular imagination" theory, the character of Child's statements may partly excuse this. We are told, for example, that "the author counts for nothing." He made the ballad—this Child affirms, though the summary of Mr Hart may leave it an open question—and yet he counts for nothing! Why? Apparently because the ballad is "an expression of our common human nature," of "the mind and heart of the people as an individual, and never of the personality of individual men." But what do these pronouncements exactly signify? Do they mean merely that the ballad belongs to that class of verse, which, to use the words of M. Jeanroy, "instead of expressing the author's own sentiments, paints character, recounts an adventure, creates personages; so that it is unnecessary that he should manifest himself in his work, except as actor or author of the scene he describes, it being enough that his work is objective?" Child may have meant partly this, but he evidently meant something more. While, if he assumes, he does not distinctly state that the ballad is objective, he lays special stress on the fact that it is "an expression of the mind and heart of the people as an individual." In his view, the reason why the personality of the author does not manifest itself in the ballad, is because the sentiments it expresses are those of "our common human nature," and this for the reason that the ballad belongs to an age when there were no definite class distinctions, and therefore such "a community of ideas and feelings that the whole people form one individual." But to find such a society would it not be necessary to go almost to the cradle of mankind? Whereas, have we not been told that ballads are the work of a special fraternity in the Middle Ages and intended for the amusement of all classes? Nay, if Child's words be interpreted literally, how in a society with no idiosyncratic peculiarities would it be possible to find ballad themes, for do not ballads derive their special interest largely from the fact that they narrate exceptional deeds or events? True, they appeal mainly to the common emotions of human nature, to the sense of wonder, pity, horror, awe; but many other forms of verse appeal to man's common emotions. As already stated, ballads are not, as a rule, burdened with any moral lesson, they are destitute of didactic intent, they are not reflective in tone, or expressive of special individual moods, or a record of individual experience, or a manifestation of idiosyncrasies of thought or sentiment peculiar to the author. But various other forms of verse are in this sense impersonal. This was the tendency of nearly all the older verse; and most of the old surviving songs, and many of the new ones, are, in essence, "an expression of our common human nature"; they appeal to every one without distinction of class. So do the greater dramas, the dramas of Greece and Shakespeare, if not of Shaw and Ibsen. Also, much of the higher emotional literature tends to do so; for it emanates from the permanent realities, not from the passing fashions and conventions, of life. This is its title to exemption from earthly oblivion; and even the ballad, as we know it, with all its traditional excrescences, defects and malformations, possesses, by virtue of the character of its aim and appeal, its peculiar method and its emotional sincerity, a certain permanent interest. The romance, from which it often borrowed its themes, has now become archaic: the life has gone out of it; but the ballad has laid hold of its essence, and in a condensed form recreated it. Though often concerned with a past strangely different from our present, with semi-savage conditions of society, and superstitions well-nigh extinct, it yet often appeals with curious dramatic intensity to the primary passions and emotions. In this sense the ballad is certainly impersonal; but while doubtless holding it to be impersonal in this sense, Child also clearly held it to be impersonal in another. He held it to be so in the sense that "the author counts for nothing," counts so absolutely for nothing that it is "with the best reasons" it "has come down to us anonymous." Of course, in addition to the ballad, much old verse "has come down to us anonymous": some of the best of the old lyrics are so; but it would seem that the ballad is anonymous by a special providence of its own, and a providence entirely in accordance with the fitness of things.

Why, then, are we to accept, not merely without regret, but with special satisfaction, this decree of providence about the ballad? How is it that here alone in literature the author "counts for nothing?" The author of anything must count—if we may put it so—for everything, so far as that thing is concerned, though the merely mechanical maker of anything can hardly be termed the author of it: he is only an imitator, not a creator. Therefore the mere fact that any form of literature is impersonal, does not justify the statement that the author of it counts for nothing. "God save the King" is impersonal, so is "The Marseillaise," and so are "Scots wha hae" and "Auld Lang Syne": even though not epical or dramatic, though subjective rather than objective, they express common and not individual sentiments. And yet does the author of them count for nothing?

What, then, is the specific difference between them and the ballad that prompted Child's unique pronouncement about the ballad? It would appear to be not merely that the ballad is the expression of "our common human nature," but a common, undistinguished expression of it, an expression of it wholly lacking in individual art. We are, in fact, told that the ballad is anterior to the poetry of art. But what, again, does this mean? Can there, in the strictest sense, be a poetry anterior to the poetry of art? Is poetry not like painting or music, essentially an art? Is the ballad wholly artless? Is there no art in its metrical arrangement, in its rhyme, in its diction, in its construction as a complete whole, in its dramatic form, in its method of evolving the situation, in its use—in many ballads—of a peculiarly effective refrain. And was there no poetry of art anterior to the crusades? Some hold, as we shall see, that this is largely, mainly or wholly, communal art; but not so Child. While affirming that it is "with the best reasons" the ballad has come down to us anonymous, he yet attributes to it an individual authorship. What, then, are "the best reasons" for its providential anonymity? They would appear to be mainly one: that so essentially popular is it in its theme and the character of its appeal, that it matters nothing who its original author may have been, or how it was originally composed. So completely common must it be (so it would seem), both in style and matter, that no curiosity need be felt as to who wrote it. The proper destiny of its author is inglorious obscurity, and its appropriate place is enshrinement in the heart and memory of the people.

But while such a theory seems to lack consistency and coherence, it also takes a great deal for granted. It implies that we have a pretty definite knowledge of the style, expression and construction of each ballad as it came from the brain of its author, whereas our knowledge of most ballads is a knowledge of them only as preserved in tradition, and often in the tradition of many generations. The reasoning of Child on this point seems,

therefore, to move mainly in a vicious circle, for it is not only conceivable but actually certain, that many ballads owe much of the "impersonality" that now characterizes them, much of the similarity in phraseology and manner, many of their peculiar lapses in rhyme, much of what is described as "truly popular" in their style, much of their jejuneness and commonness, to the influence of their long enshrinement in the people's memory and their long contact with its mind and heart.

And the strange thing is that Child himself has practically said so. "At every stage of oral transmission," so has he incidentally remarked, "we must suppose that some accidental variations from what was delivered would be introduced and occasionally some wilful variations. Memory will fail at times; at times the listener will hear amiss or will not understand, and a perversion of sense will ensue or absolute nonsense—nonsense which will be servilely repeated, and which repetition may make more gross." He affirms that in tradition, even in the best of it, the ballad "departs from the original form," and he has special praise for those of the Robin Hood ballads, which, having been early preserved in MS., "have come down to us in comparatively ancient form." Of "Robin Hood and the Monk" (119) he wrote: "Too much could not be said in praise of this ballad, but nothing need be said. It is very perfect of its kind; and yet we have others equally good, and beyond doubt should have had more, if they had been written down early, as this was, and had not been left to the chances of tradition. Even writing would not have saved all, but writing has saved this (in large part), and in excellent form." But if this be so, what a different, how much more correct and evidently how much higher an estimate we might have formed of the achievements of the old balladists, had they, themselves, got their verses written down, so that they might possibly, many of them, have come down to us unimproved by amenders and unimpaired by tradition! And had the authors' names been attached to them, surely so much the better, so much the more in accordance with the fitness of things! And yet we are told of this fine ballad, with its consummate introductory stanzas, already quoted (p. 11); of "Sir Patrick Spens" (58), regarding which Child affirmed it would be hard to find in ballad poetry or elsewhere "happier or more refined touches" than those in two of its stanzas; of "Edward" (13), the language of which is, we are told, apart from the word "brand," "entirely fit," entirely fit in the ballad sense; of the "Lochmaben Harper" (192), pronounced to have "the genuine ring of the best days of minstrelsy," and many others, "fine old ballads," spoiled though they are more or less by tradition: we are told of them all that "the author counts for nothing!"

We may, however, be reminded of another statement of Professor Child, that ballads are at their best when "the

transmission has been purely through the mouths of un-learned people." But even if this be true, it is so only in a limited, a mnemonic, sense: also, only of the ballad of tradition can it be true; and that it is so is by no means certain. Many of the ballads of Denmark have been pre-served in the tradition of ladies; and so have a few of the old songs and some of the old ballads of Scotland; and while, in this tradition, they are certainly superior as literature, they probably accord more with the origi-nal than when they have passed through the mouths of unlearned people. True, unlearned people have limited powers of invention; unlearned tradition is also some-times tenacious of the general gist of the story, for it is the story that specially appeals to it; and there are some remarkable instances of stanzas being apparently pre-served, during many generations, in one tradition—whether wholly unlearned or not—which have been lost in another. But unlearned tradition evidently indulges in inventions of a sort. Generally, also, it is very careless as to expression and rhyme, or rather it tends to make the ballad "popular," in the sense of being mean and common and rude in style, and "impersonal," destitute of the traces of individual authorship, for the simple reason that it has been gradually remoulded by the pro-cesses of instinctively stupid interference with the origi-nal text, by the ignorant touches of those by whom it has during many generations been preserved, by their inevitable preference for their own colloquial and, in a literary sense, obtuse method of expression, and the generally prosy and jejune, and often confused charac-ter of their notions and sentiments.

Thus to say of a ballad that it is "truly popular in style" is a somewhat ambiguous eulogy. While it is to a bal-lad's advantage not to have been sophisticated by the deliberate improvements of the learned or the poetic editor, it is also to its detriment to have passed through the crucible of unlearned generations; and the "truly popular in style" of tradition, may sometimes be very unlike the "truly popular in style" of the original ballad. Moreover, we have been told by Child, in the words of Mr Hart, that "a whole ballad may even be completely derived from print, and yet, in the course of time, revert to the popular form." But the popular form here re-ferred to is not the form of the original ballad before it passed through the hands of the poetaster and became a broadside: it is merely the popular traditional form. And, further, if tradition possesses the power of causing printed verse to assume a "popular form," it must be very difficult to tell what has been the original character of any lyric-epic or any piece of narrative verse, which has happened in the course of time to have assumed the form of a ballad "truly popular in style."

Gamaliel Bradford (essay date 1929)

SOURCE: Bradford, Gamaliel. "Portrait of a Scholar: Francis James Child." In *As God Made Them: Portraits of Some Nineteenth-Century Americans,* pp. 205-36. Boston: Houghton Mifflin Company, 1929.

[*In the following excerpt, Bradford provides an over-view of Child's academic career. Bradford asserts that Child's talents as a scholar lay not only in his vast eru-dition, but also in the strength of his moral character.*]

Professor Child will be chiefly remembered for his thor-ough, profound, and probably final work on the old En-glish ballads [*The English and Scottish Popular Bal-lads*]. To be sure, he himself would have been the first to insist that no scholarly work could be really final; yet there are few to whom his own admirable saying, 'Do it so it shall never have to be done again,'[1] would be more perfectly applicable. The immense research, not only into all possible English and Scottish sources, both oral and manuscript, but into the comparative folklore and legend of the Continental languages, was no more remarkable than the tact and unerring instinct which distinguished the true from the false and separated what was enduringly human from what was pretentiously lit-erary. Professor Kittredge—and no man living is more competent to judge—declares that 'as an investigator Professor Child was at once the inspiration and the de-spair of his disciples. Nothing could surpass the scien-tific exactness of his methods and the unwearied dili-gence with which he conducted his researches.'[2] Yet at the same time what mainly touched and interested him in all the mass of archæological fact was the human heart, 'that universal humanity which always moved him, wherever he found it, whether in the pages of a mediæval chronicle, or in the stammering accents of a late and vulgarly distorted ballad, or in the faces of the street boys who begged roses from his garden.'[3]

And this vast effort of research was pursued side by side with a round of college duties which many men would have deemed sufficient occupation for an ordi-nary life. Correspondence was carried on with scholars all over the world. Time had to be made, had to be snatched, had to be stolen. 'He was reminded . . . of the paucity of materials, and particularly of the slender margin of leisure which had been at his disposal for original work. "Yes," he assented, as he stood by the fireplace, "I hadn't much time for it; but I kept the books and papers ready on my desk, and sat down to them, even if there were only twenty minutes or so free."'[4] In his light and casual way he could make fun of all the labor, 'procrastination, a vice, which I find by practice to be as bad as it is said to be in the copybooks,'[5] but few men have overcome procrastina-

tion by sterner habit of routine. Above all, he understood the distinction, so difficult to make in his line of work, between a distracted over-conscientiousness, which vainly torments itself, and a frivolous disregard of exactitude. How many scholars might profit by his maxim, so simply expressed to Lowell, 'I must not be careless, but must still less be fussy.'[6] For fussiness has ruined some of the best work of the world.

It must not be supposed that great results were achieved in this case, any more than in others, without difficulties and rebuffs and failures and discouragements. There were times when things went well and times when they did not. 'I work now every day on this material, and sometimes am in good spirits about it and sometimes very low.'[7] There were the endless interruptions, interruptions of necessary duty, attended to with cheerfulness, but taking time and strength, interruptions of unnecessary bores, who wasted a day with tedious chat and dissipated precious hours when what at least seemed worthy things might have been accomplished. There was the inevitable doom, always treading on the heels of accomplishment and threatening to snatch it away: 'I have had another panic about not living to see the end of the thing, and have been like the hermit in the desert who is running from death. The only way to get on is to work doggedly through dull and pleasant alike, and just now the work is dull.'[8]

Also, there were the external discouragements, the flaunt of false scholarship, the blare of insincere publicity. There was the apparent trend of education away from the things of the spirit to the material, the expedient, the so-called practical, which took more account of body than of soul. To all these annoyances Child was in a sense indifferent, nobly indifferent. 'The most grotesque distortions, spread abroad as fresh conquests of truth, by the great army [of notoriety seekers], drew from him no more than his favorite comment, "Let the children play."'[9] Yet there were moments when such things fretted and depressed.

But, on the whole, the work was full of delight, as varied as it was absorbing; and the worker asked nothing better than to give his life to it. 'His life and his learning were one; his work was the expression of himself,' says Professor Kittredge, admirably.[10] There was the delight of discovery, the long, dull grind for days of slow turning over of dusty folios, and then the sudden surprise of coming across some bit of grace and freshness, some revelation of music or color, such pleasure as gleams through the comment on a Scandinavian folk-song, 'It is a jewel that any clime might envy.'[11] There was always that keen, quick sense of humanity, the manifold sympathy with human nature, which is so often lacking to great scholarship, but which was ever

present in Child and never failing, ready at any moment to detect the natural touch under archaic disguises and the quaint stiffness of the traditional phrase.

It was this intense human instinct which made his public lectures and readings so delightful and popular. He took the old texts and put life into them as the author might have done himself. Hear what Lowell says of his reading of Chaucer: 'He wound into the meaning of it (as Doctor Johnson says of Burke) like a serpent, or perhaps I should come nearer to it if I said that he injected the veins of the poem with his own sympathetic humor, till it seemed to live again. I could see his hearers take the fun before it came, the faces lighting with the reflection of his.'[12]

The same fresh and natural human grace touches and colors the introductions and notes of the great edition of the ***Ballads*** and makes them alive. Songs that might seem quaint and stiff in their dialectic garb, might fail to stir and move us merely from their secular remoteness, somehow acquire vigor and vitality under his touch, seem to be dealing with scenes and persons, at any rate with passions, such as are flowing and fighting about us daily. The vast erudition involved in the scholar's researches shows itself without a shade of pedantry, because it is not taken too seriously, is served up to us in a delicate, playful vein, which proves at once that the caterer understood the fragility as well as the profound human truth of the eternal trifles he was dealing with. A few illustrations here and there will hardly suffice to convey the charming tone of the whole. But how tender is the reference to 'the beautiful fancy of plants springing from the graves of star-crossed lovers, and signifying by the intertwining of stems or leaves, or in other analogous ways, that an earthly passion has not been extinguished by death.'[13] How dainty is the play of whimsical humor in the comment: 'They cast lots, and the lot falls on Annie—a result which strikes us as having more semblance of the "corrupted currents of this world" than of a pure judgment of God';[14] or in this other, 'The phrase looks more malicious than *naif* . . . and implies, I fear, an ex-sufflicate and blown surmise about female virtue.'[15] While there is an enchanting hint of fun in the remark as to the legendary danger of kissing one's love in hell: 'How the lover escaped in this instance is not explained. Such things happen sometimes, but not often enough to encourage one to take the risk.'[16]

When one appreciates this gift of apt and delicate expression, one is tempted to regret that Child did not do more original writing. The grace and wit of his letters alone would suffice to prove that he might have done far more for the world in this way than he actually did. But any desire for general literary fame was restrained

by the charming innate modesty which was so conspicuous in him always and which shows in the earnest request to Lowell: 'I wish you would *alter the note* [of compliment] and strike out on page 160 "who has done more," etc. I am content to have "fittingly" remain, if you think it should, but that is quite flattery enough for me.'[17]. . . .

. . . [W]ith what we have seen of Child's temperament it will be understood that his love for the old songs was far more than the mere scholar's absorption in his erudite specialty. He entered fully into their romantic, riotous atmosphere, as Scott did. He reveled in their color, their naïve, swift, simple tempests of passion and laughter. Their rude music always awoke an answering echo in his spirit. He was condemned to live in the academic, somewhat formal conventions of a New England college town, and he accepted those conventions outwardly with all due observance, no man more so. But inwardly he felt the restraint of them, felt himself cabined, cribbed, confined, rebelled with humorous vigor and indignation. 'I am too much impromptu,' he sighs; 'I ought to live with more prevision and art.'[18] With what mischievous enjoyment he quotes the comment of a French friend upon the Cambridge ladies: '*Bonnes mères de famille probes,* as Mlle. Le Clerc said of the women of Cambridge (she added *mais pas un attrait*).'[19] How whimsically pathetic is his illustration of the conflict between song and work: 'I drop my work any half an hour to go out and see if another adonis is springing or a meadow rue showing its claret-colored head. So false are fables: *la cigale ayant chanté tout l'été,* etc. One should work all winter to be ready to sing all summer, and sing all summer to be able to work the winter through. One or the other one must do, sing or work. I find that I cannot work if I go out under the pretence of just looking at this or that, and I hoped for a rain yesterday (not very earnestly) to keep me indoors.'[20]

Into these staid, decorous surroundings of prosaic propriety the great, loud, sweet old songs swept like a burst of wind and sunshine, and stirred the childish professorial heart to laughter and tears. How winning is Gummere's picture of Child humorously enlarging on the idle, trivial, mirthful matter that enchanted him: '"Preposterous!" he said, "to have to work in such stuff when you could have Young's *Night Thoughts* or Cowper's *Task* for the asking. The impudence of the thing!" And he suddenly broke into a kind of chant, reciting the last stanza of the rollicking ballad, and ended in a burst of laughter. He was fairly "going" now, and went on, in a kind of prose parody of that highly moral strain with which Chaucer concludes the *Troilus,* to bewail his task of dealing with so many bandits, outlaws, roisterers, silly girls, Lord Lovels, and other chuckle-heads of tradition, setting withal a harmless little trap of quotation, as characteristic as might be. "You remember the line,

'Of Jove, Apollo, of Mars, of swich canaille?'

he asked, with a sly emphasis on the last word."[21]

In short, the release from the tameness and monotony of daily life that some of us find in the mystery story, he found more romantically and poetically in the primitive passions and elementary tragedy and comedy of popular song.

Notes

1. [F. B.] Gummere, [Article on Child, in *Atlantic Monthly,* March, 1909, vol. 103,] p. 422.

2. *Life,* in *Ballads* [*The English and Scottish Popular Ballads,* 1857-59,] vol. I, p. xxix.

3. *Ibid.*

4. Gummere, p. 423.

5. To Lowell, MS [Harvard College Library].

6. To Lowell, MS.

7. To Lowell, MS.

8. *Letters* [*A Scholar's Letters to a Young Lady,* edited by M. A. DeWolfe Howe, 1920,] p. 47.

9. Gummere, p. 421.

10. *Life,* in *Ballads,* vol. I, p. xxix.

11. *Ballads,* vol. I, p. 88.

12. Lowell to Norton, Feb. 18, 1877, *Letters of James Russell Lowell* [(1894)], vol. II, p. 192.

13. *Ballads,* vol. I, p. 96.

14. *Ballads,* vol. I, p. 244.

15. *Ballads,* vol. I, p. 270.

16. *Ballads,* vol. I, p. 322.

17. To Lowell, MS.

18. *Letters,* p. 54.

19. *Letters,* p. 4.

20. *Letters,* p. 53.

21. Gummere, p. 424.

Sigurd Bernhard Hustvedt (essay date 1930)

SOURCE: Hustvedt, Sigurd Bernhard. "Francis James Child and Other Americans." In *Ballad Books and Ballad Men: Raids and Rescues in Britain, America, and the Scandinavian North since 1800,* pp. 205-29. Cambridge: Harvard University Press, 1930.

[*In the following excerpt, Hustvedt analyzes Child's process in collecting English and Scottish ballads, examining the evolution of his scholarship through a discussion of the various editions of the work.*]

In justice it must be said that disinterested zeal has been a powerful factor in the careers of the ballad men.

Of this disinterestedness, Francis James Child had an unusually large share. There is nothing to show that he had any axes to grind, unless it were the edged tool of the honest workman. He had nothing to hope for from the Earl of Northumberland. He had no expectation of enhancing the prestige of his ancestry through connecting his line with the heroes of Border story. He was not moved by the negative incentive of proving that some bishop or other either did not possess at all a famous manuscript or, if he did possess it, had made felonious use of it. He was not nerved to action by the inferior type of patriotism that plumes itself on demonstrating that Scotchmen have erred or that Englishmen have blundered. He could not even have been actuated in any measurable degree by that positive patriotism which, in Scott and in Grundtvig, made literary work a service of piety for their native heath and their forbears. Child's scholarship was devoted to the literature of a country which was his own only through the bonds of tradition and speech. In so far it was fitting that his special studies were directed toward the language and the poetical traditions of Great Britain. If there remained at the back of his mind, as there must have remained, a feeling that through his exertions he might bring some credit to his own country and some recognition to his university and to himself, so much might well be allowed even to the most unselfish of men. His governing motive, in the edition of Spenser [*The Poetical Works of Edmund Spenser*] and in the enquiries into the language of Chaucer and Gower ["**Observations on the Language of Chaucer**" and "**Observations on the Language of Gower's *Confessio Amantis*"**] and, finally, in the edition of the ballads [*The English and Scottish Popular Ballads*], seems to have been that of doing a work that he liked in a fashion that competent judges might be expected to approve.

It would be instructive if we were able to follow in detail the development of Child's interest in popular traditions, as we follow Walter Scott from his infantile admiration of *Hardyknute* to his publication of the *Minstrelsy*. The means of such a tracing of footsteps in the case of Child are wanting to me. His biographers have told us of his varied tastes and his unusual acquirements in school and in college. On being graduated from Harvard College in 1846, he was appointed a tutor in mathematics and later in other subjects, including English; and he continued to serve Harvard College and Harvard University throughout his life. From 1849 to 1851 he carried on his studies in Europe, particularly in the universities of Göttingen and Berlin, where he devoted his attention in great part to branches of philology. There can be no doubt that his stay in Germany had a determining influence on his later career. There he found the linguistic disciplines, not least in the Germanic field, in a state of forwardness which may be defined by the mere mention of the name of Jakob Grimm. He found folklore, just becoming known in Europe under that title, in a place of honor won through decades of searching investigation, in which again the Grimm brothers had taken a signal part. He found medieval studies contesting for preëminence with the older humanities. German scholars, critics, and men of letters had for a long time been, and still were, occupied with the collection and the poetical use of their native tales, ballads, and songs. What Child already knew of English traditional lore must have taken on a new meaning in this environment.

When Child came to undertake his first edition of popular poetry, the *English and Scottish Ballads,* of 1857-59, he had undoubtedly had no small opportunity to familiarize himself with the general contents, the various systems of arrangement, and the noticeable differences in the principles and practices of editing as illustrated in a large number of collections covering a considerable lapse of years not only in Great Britain but in Germany and other foreign countries. He knew what was involved in the acrimonious charges of Ritson against Percy. He had studied the procedure of editors like Herd and Scott, Motherwell and Kinloch, Buchan and many more. He was acquainted with the chief Scandinavian collections, not however including Grundtvig's first volumes, which did not come to his attention until later. He had of course learned to know while in Germany, if not before, Wilhelm Grimm's book of translations from the Danish and the volumes of Arnim and Brentano, and of Uhland. He could not have been unaffected by the stimulating German critical debates of the past decades as to the proper modes of dealing with older literature and particularly the way to edit folk-poetry as exemplified by such a poet and scholar as Uhland: The bibliographical lists placed conspicuously in the first volume of his *English and Scottish Ballads* show that he had already at his command resources most respectable in compass. He was in a position to survey almost all of the available printed ballad texts, to come to a decision as to the inclusion or exclusion of given poems, and to arrive at a critical standpoint with reference to the mode of editing them.

Child wrote to Grundtvig, fifteen years afterward, that his first collection had been somewhat precipitated by the desire of the publishers to hasten the issuance of the voluminous series of the *British Poets* of which the ballads made a part.[1] To this circumstance he meant to lay some of the imperfections of the work. The spirit of the apology may be readily understood in the case of an editor who continued to advance in knowledge of his subject. To us these imperfections are less positive than they are comparative, when the first collection is examined side by side with the later, immensely superior collection.

One of the possible defects of the ***English and Scottish Ballads,*** of which the editor was conscious at the time,[2] has to do with the admission of poems that are hardly to be described as ballads at all but rather as shorter romances, and of poems that are indeed ballads but not of the type that are now commonly thought of as *ancient.* On this score it must be noticed that Child himself does not stress the *popular* character of his ballads here as he does in the later collection; and, further, that his own subsequent studies had a great deal to do with the more exact definition of what *popularity* really implies. Another thing that counts relatively against the merits of the earlier work is that at this period he had no such means of controlling the authenticity of individual texts as he had afterward. It will be recalled that at this time the *Percy Folio Manuscript* was still sequestered, and so remained for another twenty years; that the very existence of many of the other capital manuscripts was practically unknown; and that under the prevailing conditions Child had no access to those that were known to exist. He was therefore under the necessity in most cases of choosing among the available printed texts. In some instances he exercised this selective judgment under rather lively scruples. For *Auld Maitland* he makes room "with reluctance."[3] His suspicions of Buchan were even at this early date so much aroused that he was impelled to announce that "some resolution has been exercised, and much disgust suppressed, in retaining certain pieces from Buchan's collections";[4] doubts and qualms over the same editor were to trouble his deliberations more than once in determining upon the canon for the later definitive work. It is historically important to notice these early critical perturbations in Child's mind, since they were no doubt chiefly instrumental in leading him to undertake the laborious task of digging out those manuscripts and rare printed books that were to form the substantial foundation for his second edifice. The value he placed upon individual texts clearly underwent modification in the course of his further studies. In consideration of the limitations of textual supply and means of control, the choice of readings in the ***English and Scottish Ballads*** will appear little open to cavil.

On one point, in particular, there is no hesitation, no temporizing. As a statement in the Preface runs, "The Editor, after selecting the most authentic copies, has carefully adhered to the originals as they stand in the printed collections, sometimes restoring a reading which has been changed without reason, and in all cases indicating deviations, whether his own or those of others, in the margin."[5] This cardinal principle, arrived at without knowledge of Grundtvig's fiery baptism into the same faith, is to be remarked not only for its assurance of honest dealing at this period but for its potential force in relation to the exhaustive enquiries that were to supervene. Child had surely been influenced by the repeated assertions of this principle by his predecessors among the English and Scottish editors. In the course of illuminating experience with ballad books he had been taught to regard skeptically even the more solemn asseverations of fidelity to text. In his own case, growing familiarity with earlier discrepancies between tenet and practical tendency must have formed a strong inducement to hold fast to the good tenet and to search out the means of uncovering and correcting the bad tendency. That persuasion once formed, no ballad editor's word could be considered quite as good as his bond; so Child was confirmed in his purpose of seeing the bonds themselves, the original sources, and of governing himself only by what he found therein nominated.

Having made up his mind to include in the ***English and Scottish Ballads*** almost all of the ancient ballads and to print them unaltered according to the best readings obtainable, Child had to face, almost unavoidably in so large a collection, the problem of classification. It is clear from what he says and what he does, that this matter gave him pause. He announces a scheme of arrangement and declares in the same breath that the grouping is not to be regarded as a consideration of much importance. He cut the knot by adopting a system of books divided according to subject; within the books the plan is chronological, the sequence being decided by the probable antiquity of the story. In this way he arrives at a division into nine books, which may be briefly described as follows: ballads of romance and chivalry; ballads involving superstitions; tragic love-ballads; other tragic ballads; love-ballads not tragic; Robin Hood ballads; Border ballads; historical ballads; and miscellaneous ballads. While this grouping in its main features is not unlike that which Grundtvig, unknown to Child, had chosen for the Danish ballads, it is more complicated and less manifestly suitable than Grundtvig's arrangement into the four classes of mythical ballads, ballads of marvel and magic, historical ballads, and ballads of chivalry and romance. Child remained unsatisfied with his own scheme, as his change of policy in the second edition and his later correspondence with Grundtvig over the question testifies. In Child's final edition there is little trace of the original classification.

Of the critical apparatus in the first edition, the longish introduction to the book of Robin Hood may be singled out for its surgical excision of the large mass of fanciful theory and legend that had become incrusted about the outlaw's fame. Most of the shorter prefaces to individual numbers throughout the collection are confined to apt quotation from the comments of previous editors, to brief information as to the sources and earlier appearances of the texts, and to the noting of parallels to the stories. Here we discover in tentative form the comparative method that was to mark the mature scholarship of the editor. In the nature of a forecast, too, we may regard the printing of distinct versions of a number

of the pieces. Again it must be said, however, that the collection was no mere prophecy, but a definite accomplishment.

The second edition of the *English and Scottish Ballads* (1860) exhibits no very vital changes. A few ballads have been added. A good number of the poems from the former Book First have disappeared, the editor having come to the conclusion that they were rather romances than ballads. As a result of this reduction, the whole number of books falls to eight: of the earlier nine, one is gone and the other eight remain substantially as before. The internal principle of chronological order is retained. The individual prefaces have been elaborated in many instances through the increase of references to parallels and the like. The bibliography has undergone some changes; recent English and Scottish titles have been added, and among the foreign titles appears the significant addition of two or three volumes of Grundtvig.

The rewritten preface shows some changes of opinion. The word *popular* has taken on increased importance as a defining term; it is made to imply "the spontaneous products of nature" as against the works of the professional ballad-maker. In this connection occurs the remark, dictated by no small reverence for the chosen poetry of the people, "No words could express the dulness and inutility of a collection which should embrace all the Roxburghe and Pepys broadsides—a scope with which this publication was most undeservedly credited by an English journal." Child might have been surprised could he have foreseen the appearance of the bulky tomes of the Ballad Society and the volumes with which men of Child's own school, like Professor Percival and Professor Rollins, were to illuminate the non-popular ballads. Child had taken the Grundtvig fever, as his resounding praise of the Danish editor in this Preface bears witness. That this fever is likely to prove both quotidian and tertian may be gathered from Child's intimation that if no more qualified editor should arise, he meant himself in due time to wrestle seriously with the problems of balladry still awaiting solution.

No more qualified editor arose.

As the resolution ripened in Child's mind to set about the preparation of a comprehensive and definitive edition of the ballads, four principal fields of exploration presented themselves: He must get behind all of the printed texts to the sources. He must circumscribe the ground so as to exclude ballads not popular and to include ballads and versions of ballads which had not yet come to his knowledge. He must arrive at a satisfactory theoretical view of the material and so determine the general arrangement of the collection and the larger questions of interpretation of the texts. He must study the whole available mass of popular literature, espe-

cially as recorded in all of the European tongues, in order to set forth the numerous foreign parallels and relationships in a broad comparative survey. Some of these problems we have seen to have been with him from the beginning of his interest in the whole subject. They became more imperative after he had brought out his first two editions and had made up his mind to essay the still greater project. There is no attempt here to assert a chronological sequence in the case of the four major requirements. During the years that he was actively engaged in shaping the new work for publication, no one of the needful considerations can have been far from his thoughts.

The long and fascinating story of the search for manuscripts and the securing of them in the original or in exact copies could be pieced together only by the recovery of Child's letters to numerous persons in Great Britain over a period of considerably more than a quarter of a century. The main progress of the quest, nevertheless, can be followed through his printed acknowledgments of assistance and through extant letters addressed to him by many people who aided him in tracking down elusive sources and in recovering manuscripts long hidden or believed to have been permanently lost. Among the more important of these desired helps may be enumerated the Abbotsford MSS, the MSS of Mrs. Brown, of Buchan, of Motherwell, of Kinloch, the Glenriddell MSS, and the Sharpe and Skene MSS; there were others besides, the brief record of which will be found in Child's published list of sources. What the published record cannot reveal is the tangle of difficulties in which the prospective editor found himself involved in trying to gain possession or use of these indispensable means. Some of the manuscripts, in the control of the original owners or of their heirs, were being held under vague prospects of publication in another form. Some had got into the hands of collectors who were quick to sense the possibility of revenue and who were quite justified in protecting financial investments often representing considerable sums. In certain cases Child was able to gain the purposed end through bargaining and purchase. In other instances, extensive negotiation had to be resorted to in order to secure even the right to copy what he needed, negotiations which frequently took on the dignity of diplomacy. In still other cases, an inconvenient and laborious rummaging among family papers had to be undertaken even to ascertain the existence of a manuscript. Obviously, Child could never have accomplished all of this business alone, especially separated as he was by an Atlantic from the field of operations. His position for a number of years became that of managing director of a complicated inquisition.

A great stone was lifted when in 1867-68 Furnivall and Hales, largely through the active participation of Child himself, succeeded in editing the *Percy Folio Manu-*

script. For a time, as we learn from a letter of Child's to Grundtvig,[6] Child endeavored to induce the Ballad Society, through Furnivall, to undertake the publication of the popular ballads. This attempt failing by reason of the unavoidable engagements of the Ballad Society with the Roxburghe and the Pepys collections, Child temporarily abandoned the hope of seeing the work done, until an offer of assistance from Grundtvig in 1872 gave him courage to take up the burden anew. Among his first steps was the launching of the campaign to secure access to the manuscripts. Furnivall became one of his principal helpers. A number of others came to his assistance, of whom may be mentioned David Laing, J. B. Murdoch, and Miss Mary Fraser Tytler. Child has named many more in his public acknowledgments. Among them was William Macmath, of Edinburgh; and no single person appears to have a better right to be distinguished as Child has distinguished him. His letters to Child begin in 1873 and continue almost without interruption until the last volume came from the press. Macmath's services were of many sorts. In the course of the years he contributed a number of individual texts and many shrewd bits of practical counsel. He was particularly insistent that Child should not be hurried into print before he had done what was humanly possible to arrive at the original sources of all of the ballads. He acted as Child's agent in negotiations leading to the purchase or the use of several of the most necessary documents. With his own hand he copied thousands of lines of text. Of the capital manuscript sources which he helped to unearth, to copy, or to secure for Child by purchase, particular mention should be made of the Glenriddell MSS, the Kinloch MSS, and the Abbotsford MSS. Macmath's fidelity brought in the Abbotsford MSS for use almost at the eleventh hour, as will appear by reference to the appropriate sections of Child's volumes.

Through the manuscripts Child not only was enabled to govern the texts that had been printed; he secured at the same time many texts and versions that had not been printed at all. Meanwhile he was engaged by other means in adding to his growing tally, notably by an attempt, never wholly given over, at rescuing what might still survive in oral tradition. In January, 1873, apparently upon taking a fresh lease of determination and hope, he inserted in *Notes and Queries* an appeal for aid in securing manuscripts of older date and more especially for individual collaboration in recovering anything in the way of traditional ballads or fragments that yet remained in the memories of the people. Whatever should be thus rescued was to be sent to Furnivall, who had offered to act for Child. Twenty-five hundred copies of this appeal were printed as leaflets to be circulated in Scotland, Furnivall adding a footnote of commendation. Furnivall took it upon himself, too, to see to the distribution of the circulars. A pleasant glimpse of the procedure is afforded through a letter from Charles

Eliot Norton to Child,[7] in which he tells of having secured from Carlyle a list of Scottish schoolmasters, to some of whom Norton and members of his family were engaged at London in addressing the leaflets. Though Child later deplored the almost total want of fruits from this appeal, because of the drying up of the springs of oral tradition, yet he gained the indirect advantage of making his undertaking more widely known and in the course of years no doubt direct contributions sufficient to reward his hopes in part. During the 'seventies he continued from time to time to insert notices in *Notes and Queries* asking after the whereabouts of manuscripts, calling for possible waifs and strays that might still be lurking in print, or begging for copies of specific texts from some broadside or other. In October, 1880, he published in the same periodical a second more general request for assistance in recovering ballads that might still be discovered floating down the thinning current of oral transmission. He explains that a pretty thorough search has demonstrated that little of the sort is to be expected from Scotland, but that remnants of Anglo-Irish balladry might with reasonable expectation be looked for in Ireland, where as yet no systematic attempt has been made to form a collection of that kind. He therefore asks if interested persons would not make an effort to explore Ireland for non-Celtic popular poetry.

To lend point to his request he adds the information that a friend in New York has recovered there a version of "Sir Hugh," ultimately from an Irish source. In further pursuit of this clue, Child issued in January, 1881, a circular of four pages addressed especially to students in colleges, noting his disappointing experiences with reference to Scotland, expressing anew his belief that Ireland is a more hopeful field, and asking particularly that those who should see his circular endeavor to find immigrant Anglo-Irish ballads in the various regions of the United States. In this case he is able to refer to the discovery by himself of two ballads of this class in his own immediate neighborhood. What is needed now is an extensive search throughout the country not only for Irish, but for English and Scottish poetical traditions that may have been carried into America by immigrants of older and newer date. The circular gives instructions for the proper recording of what may be found and presents two ballad texts in full to show the sort of thing that is wanted.

The immediate results of the sending out of the circular were not the most encouraging. Some texts, nevertheless, came to Child in this way; among the more active collaborators may be mentioned Miss Margaret Reburn, whose communications, not always of the highest value, occupy a separate volume among the Child Manuscripts. In the more than forty years that have passed since that time, a respectable number of the true popular texts have come to light in America, some of which found

their way into Child's collection, some of which have been individually or collectively published elsewhere, and others of which remain as an unpublished aftermath in the hands of private collectors or in folklore archives here and there throughout the country. In the circular Child mentions that he has secured the usufruct of all the known manuscript collections but two or three. Other manuscript sources, it is true, turned up afterward; but the public appeals for oral survivals here sketched show how thoroughly Child employed all the possible means of making his work literally comprehensive. Throughout his life he continued unremitting in the pursuit of that aim.

It will be remembered that in the first edition of the ***English and Scottish Ballads,*** Child made a rather complicated arrangement of the texts and that in the Preface he expressed the opinion that the arrangement was rather a matter of convenience than of vital necessity.[8] It will be understood as well that questions of order are necessarily bound up with questions of the character of a number of the individual pieces, such as, for example, whether the Robin Hood ballads are to be considered as historical or as romantic, or whether "Sir Patrick Spens" is to be placed in one or in the other of these two groups. For Child, therefore, these considerations were certain to obtrude themselves anew as he faced the task of deciding upon a sequence for the texts to be inserted in the definitive edition. His dubieties on this score occasionally came to the surface in correspondence with various European scholars. The problem was most fully discussed, however, and eventually solved through an exchange of letters with Svend Grundtvig.

Grundtvig made the first advance in a letter dated February 17, 1872, in which he refers to his pleasure in having learned to know, some ten years before, Child's earlier ballad edition and in finding there a proper scholarly approach to the subject. He has now heard that Child intends to publish a new and improved edition and therefore offers to give any aid that might be acceptable. Child answers that he has long been wanting to establish a connection with the Danish editor; he gives some information as to the state of his preparations and closes gratefully with Grundtvig's proffer of assistance, but for the timely coming of which, he says, he might have been tempted to abandon his ambitions. In this way began a correspondence between the two which continued till Grundtvig's death in 1883. In the extended series of communications Child, as was natural under the circumstances, takes in the main the part of the querist and Grundtvig the part of the informant; yet in not a few cases Child is able to give a *quid pro quo.* Although various detailed items come to be dealt with in the course of the years, the correspondence has not proceeded far before it is clear that the principle of arrangement has become the uppermost difficulty in Child's mind, so that he repeatedly asks Grundtvig's opinion on this point. At one period Child has come to the conclusion that the knot may be cut by the adoption of no more than two main classes, the romantic and the historical; in other respects he explicitly adopts Grundtvig's methods, but the arrangement of the Danish ballads, into four classes, appears to be unsuited to the English and Scottish. In this judgment Grundtvig concurs, and therefore, in a letter of August 25, 1877, proposes that a division of the English and Scottish ballads should be made, not according to subject-matter as in the Danish, but according to form; a metrical classification which would place first the ballads in the two-line stanza, next those in the four-line stanza of eight and six, and last those in the four-line stanza of eight and eight would, he contends, be natural and historical. This principle, with some modifications, Child eventually adopted. Meanwhile Grundtvig supplied him with a detailed exemplification of this arrangement,[9] with critical observations of various kinds, with notes on Scandinavian parallels, and with unprinted Scandinavian texts. Grundtvig was no doubt Child's most valuable correspondent so far as these larger problems of interpretation and editing were concerned, just as Macmath was the most valuable in the matter of tracing and securing manuscripts and individual texts. While Macmath was continually urging Child not to be rushed into publication before he had exhausted all possible sources of texts, Grundtvig kept prodding him to begin to publish without anxious waiting for the attainment of an impossible ideal. These two complementary counsels of perfection served Child's constitutional and scholarly requirements most admirably; to them we owe in great measure the practical completion of Child's work as the most perfect illustration of the motto of *Festina lente* which his allotted years permitted to him.

Many of Child's queries to Grundtvig were concerned with items of information that might be of service in illustrating the individual ballads through references to foreign parallels, to the occurrence of a ballad theme in other literary forms, to anything in popular lore that would be useful by way of commentary. On similar subjects he maintained an extensive correspondence with a large number of European scholars, such as W. W. Skeat and Andrew Lang in Great Britain, Felix Liebrecht and Reinhold Köhler in Germany, Kaarle Krohn in Finland, Pitrè in Italy, and many others. Through these means he was able to build up gradually a vast fund of miscellaneous note materials the value of which soon became apparent once actual printing was under way. Meanwhile Child was not content merely to reap a harvest from the industry of other men. From the time of his earliest occupation with the ballads, his attention was directed toward the proper illustration of the texts. This interest continued, with some abatement in favor of other studies, throughout his life. To that end it was necessary to form a huge collection of books of ballads in print and a multitude of works covering the wider

field of general folklore and outlying domains in the sciences and the humanities. As Professor Kittredge has pointed out in his sketch of the life of Child, one of Child's great services was the bringing together, in the course of many years, of a very valuable special collection of folklore in the Harvard College Library, toward the formation of which the library authorities and private persons collaborated generously. As these indispensable aids were gathered for his needs, Child was placed in a favorable position to prosecute the special studies necessary to the right selection of his texts, their proper disposition, and their interpretation. All this meant the laborious acquiring of familiarity with all of the earlier printed books of English and Scottish ballads and of the more important at least of the foreign collections. It meant a detailed study of hundreds of versions and the painful collation of a large number of them. It involved a careful study of the critical comments of preceding editors. It entailed an acquaintance with practically everything of pertinence that had appeared in print in some form or other, often in the remoter corners of little-known books and periodicals. It required exploration of the constantly broadening reaches of general folklore, of history, of ancient and modern literatures in many tongues. Child gave himself without stint, though not without groanings over various unavoidable distractions, to the severe regimen. So his activities went on year after year until, part by part, the work was done.

The English and Scottish Popular Ballads began to appear in 1882. The work was published in ten parts, intervals of a year or two between the successive instalments being occupied in preparing the next section for publication, a preparation which involved not merely the putting in order of a sheaf of copy but the never-ending search for new texts or versions from manuscripts or from other sources, and the constant supplementing of the fund of critical information. This serial mode of publication, in which again Child patterned after Grundtvig, if it was not absolutely necessary because of the volume of the material, was in many ways decidedly advantageous; it made possible the inclusion, to name one capital instance, of many texts from the Abbotsford MSS, which became available only after the larger part of the work was already in print. The chief disadvantage came to be that the editor did not live to see the publication of Part Ten. He had, however, prepared that part too for the press, with the exception of the final touches upon the indexes and the bibliography and the actual writing of the General Preface, of which he left only a few pages of manuscript. The editorial supervision of Part Ten thus fell to Professor G. L. Kittredge, who for more than a dozen years had been closely associated with Professor Child as a colleague and as a collaborator in the ballad work, and whose independent studies had further equipped him for the task. From Professor Kittredge came also the memorial essay on Professor Child's life included in Part Ten of his book. In the capacity of Child's literary executor, Professor Kittredge has arranged and indexed the Child MSS, in which the story of the ballad collection may be read in detail. These MSS and the Child Memorial Library of which they form a part remain as a permanent monument at home; and *The English and Scottish Popular Ballads* carry abroad the remembrance of the *Sapienza e Amore e Virtute* of the editor.

Much as we have cause to regret that Child's pen fell from his hand just as he had begun, in the last month of his life, to set down in order those persuasions about the nature and qualities of the ballads which had grown up in his mind through decades of absorption in the one purpose, the loss of the General Preface is less deplorable than it might at first thought appear. More than once in his letters to various correspondents he expressed the conviction that it was his principal duty to rescue all of the texts that were still to be recaptured. Notwithstanding what he did manage to write down of formal and occasional deliverances of a theoretical or critical kind, his best essay on the ballads will perhaps be held to lie in solution in the selected number of versions that crowd his volumes. He was a modest man, remarkably free from scholarly arrogance and yet firm as need be in a once secured footing. The definite article in his title was put there deliberately. His first Advertisement makes it clear that he intended to gather under one roof all of the truly popular ballads; and there is nothing in the later volumes to indicate material doubt of the fulfilment of his aim. He does admit some numbers, like "The Suffolk Miracle," "John Thompson and the Turk," and "Young Ronald," for which he entertained no high admiration; in the case of the last named, he explains in the preface that he includes this ballad "because of a remote possibility that it might contain relics, or be a debased representative, of something genuine and better." Such was the advice in cases of this sort, he says, of Grundtvig—and he might have added, of Macmath. He preferred to err through inclusion rather than through exclusion. So he arrives at a certain number of ballads and at a given number of versions, not as one who is delivering a ballad Koran to the world, but as one who has come to the thoughtful conclusion that this is the canon of popular balladry.[10] Critics may shake their heads over the admittance of this version or the rejection of that or may reach the opinion that there should have been two hundred and seventy-five or three hundred and fifty popular ballads rather than exactly three hundred and five. Child's roster of the elect, aside from later discoveries, may have no more prospect of remaining unshaken in a world of changing values than, for example, a system of philosophy. *The English and Scottish Popular Ballads,* nevertheless, is now and bids fair to remain something of a criterion. The collection will always be a record of the mature judgment of a patient and intelligent scholar

who knew his way about in the subject and whose nominations of the ballads entitled to be classified as *popular* will have an authoritativeness that could not attach to a pretended infallibility.

While it is true that the collection itself may be taken as a definition of the character and the distinctive features of the popular ballad, it cannot be denied on the other hand that the choice of texts was dictated by opinions based on a long-continued study of a great body of traditional verse, native and foreign, and on a mass of critical views garnered from many seasons and many lands. In a very real sense Child's theories determined the choice of texts and the texts again influenced the theory. For this reason an examination of the editor's critical tenets will help to explain the genesis and the limits of the collection. The few pages of the General Preface left in manuscript contain not much more than a beginning of a statement of the reasons for undertaking the collection, the great reason being that earlier editors, Percy and Scott, and even Kinloch and Motherwell, had altered and combined their texts.[11] Beyond this point Child's strength did not carry him. In the prefaces and notes of the *English and Scottish Ballads* and of the later collection are to be found a multitude of comments which, pieced together, make up a considerable tissue of criticism. In the article on **"Ballad Poetry"** in the *Universal Cyclopædia* we have the one connected, though not fully conclusive, presentation of the editor's views.[12] As he sees it, the *popular* ballad, or "narrative song," is a "distinct and very important species of poetry," historically anterior to the poetry of art. "Though these ballads do not 'write themselves,' as William Grimm has said, though a man and not a people has composed them, still the author counts for nothing, and it is not by mere accident, but with the best reason, that they have come down to us anonymous." They become popular through being accepted and traditionally transmitted by a people in which "there is such community of ideas and feelings that the whole people form an individual." They are not to be identified, therefore, with merely the lower classes. "Many of the ballads of the now most refined nations had their origin in . . . the upper class," though in the course of time they have sunk down to be the cherished possession of the commonalty. In the course of tradition they take on technical peculiarities which make them almost impossible to imitate. Such popular narrative poems have at various times thriven among the Spaniards, the Germans, the Scandinavians, the people of Great Britain, and the various Slavic races, and to a less degree among other nations of Europe. As we know them they date from the Middle Ages. The often striking correspondences between the ballads of different nations need not be explained by the hypothesis of prehistoric common origin; similar stories may arise independently in different regions, and in many cases the likeness may be accounted for through borrowing, in which the Crusades may have

had a powerful influence. "Ballads are best preserved by oral tradition in Norway and the Faroe Isles." As for Britain, "the English have preserved but a moderate number of very early ballads.[13] . . . A large part of our whole stock has been recovered within the last 130 years from the oral tradition of Scotland."[14]

These are some of the outstanding features of Child's view of the ballads. His chief work, as he conceived it, consisted in the collection and the incidental definition of the popular ballads of England and Scotland. For an ultimate purpose, if one were required, we may look to these words from his cyclopædia article: [Popular poetry] "can not lose its value. Being founded on what is permanent and universal in the heart of man, and now by printing put beyond the danger of perishing, it will survive the fluctuations of taste, and may from time to time serve, as it notoriously did in England and Germany a hundred years ago, to recall a literature from false and artificial courses to nature and truth."

Notes

1. See Child's letter to Grundtvig, March 26, 1872, [in Appendix A].

2. See the Preface to the *English and Scottish Ballads* (*E. S. B.*), I, xi, n.; cf. 2d ed. (1860), I, xii.

3. *E. S. B.,* VI, 220.

4. *E. S. B.,* I, ix.

5. *E. S. B.,* I, xi.

6. March 26, 1872, [Appendix A].

7. Unpublished letter from Charles Eliot Norton to Child, December 30, 1872, in Child MSS, XI, 13.

8. Years afterward William Macmath wrote to Child, *à propos* of the placing of a recently discovered text of "The Great Silkie" out of its natural order in the collection: "I am quite with you in what you say as to the difficulties of arrangement. It is a thing I have thought about. But, after all, I am not sure that you were wrong when you said on a former occasion (you said many good things then, some of which you are not *always* ready to stick to!), 'Strictness is offensive as well as useless. Perhaps it is impossible. Ballads are not like plants or insects, to be classified to a hair's breadth.'" Child MSS, XXIV, 468 f.; letter of March 10, 1886.

9. See Appendix B for Grundtvig's proposed order of the English and Scottish ballads; cf. his letters of August 25, 1877, and of January 29, 1880.

10. According to Professor Walter Morris Hart's analysis of the differences in contents between the *English and Scottish Ballads* and *The English and*

Scottish Popular Ballads, Child in his final edition excluded 115 of the pieces admitted into the earlier collection and added only ninety new titles; the definitive edition increased immensely, of course, the number of new versions under the individual titles. Among the excluded items were romances, lyrics, broadsides, and dishonest ballads of various kinds; see Professor Hart's article on "Professor Child and the Ballad," in the *Publications of the Modern Language Association of America,* XXI, No. 4 (December, 1906), 792 ff.

11. A fragment of Professor Child's General Preface, almost the last specimen of his writing, has been preserved among the Child MSS, XVI, 132-137. In the same volume will be found various note materials, excerpts from the works of such scholars as Steenstrup, Gaston Paris, Ferdinand Wolf, and others, which apparently were to be employed in the composition of the Preface.

12. Professor Walter Morris Hart has provided a most useful conspectus of Professor Child's critical views, drawn from the article in the *Universal Cyclopædia* [(1877)] and from *obiter dicta* in his various ballad editions; in "Professor Child and the Ballad," as cited above.

13. See Professor Ewald Flügel's "Zur Chronologie der englischen Balladen," in *Anglia,* XXI (N. S. XI) (1899), 312 ff., for an index of Child's ballads according to the date of their first appearance in manuscript or in print.

14. The direct quotations are all drawn from the article in the *Universal Cyclopædia,* 1877 ff.

D. K. Wilgus (essay date 1959)

SOURCE: Wilgus, D. K. "The Ballad War I: The Morphology of Dry Bones." In *Anglo-American Folksong Scholarship since 1898,* pp. 3-52. New Brunswick, N.J.: Rutgers University Press, 1959.

[*In the following excerpt, Wilgus discusses Child's theories concerning the authorship of popular ballads. Wilgus argues that Child's ideas differ significantly from those of the later communal school of ballad scholarship.*]

THE CAUTION OF FRANCIS JAMES CHILD

Before plunging into the arena of the battle, it is well to consider briefly the limited pronouncements of Francis James Child. Later critics have almost uniformly regretted that the admitted paragon of ballad editors did not live to write the critical introduction to his collection; for his subsequent reputation, it may be as well that he

wrote no more. His very silence tended to remove him from the conflict. His students—whom Louise Pound later termed "the Harvard School of communalists"— were, like other literary evolutionists, able to take shelter freely in his authoritative collection. Even the most violent opponents of the communalists revered Child's work and refused (or did not dare) to associate the "great scholar and a sane one" with the extravagances of "the school of Child."

What was Child's view of ballad origins? Though communalists believed that "he held in essentials the views Gummere developed at length," Walter Morris Hart, in his 1906 synthesis of Child's scattered remarks,[1] failed to prove the case. In addition to the "mere *obiter dicta*" of his ballad introductions, Child left only a résumé of **"Ballad Poetry"** in *Johnson's Universal Cyclopaedia* (1874), which Gummere reported Child wished "to be neither quoted nor regarded as final." Because the article is the one extended statement made by Child, and because Hart drew upon it for the comments most favorable to the communal position and found that "for at least forty years Professor Child retained without essential change his conception of the traditional ballad as a distinct literary type," it is necessary to consider the résumé.

Child explicitly denied three fundamental tenets of the communalists: that ballads were dance songs, that they were of group authorship, and that they originated among the peasantry or in a classless society. *Ballad* "means by derivation, a dance song, but . . . the application of the word in English is quite accidental"; ballads were made by "a man and not a people"; ballads are "popular, not in the sense of something arising from and suited to the lower orders of the people," for many of them "had their origin in that class whose acts and fortunes they depict—the upper class." But these statements are set in a context favorable to the views of the literary evolutionists, and consequently they have been accidentally or deliberately overlooked.

Child, for whom the ballad held a place "anterior to the appearance of the poetry of art," believed that this "truly national or popular poetry" developed in a stage of society in which "there is such a community of ideas and feelings that the whole people form one individual." His statement is undoubtedly metaphorical and cannot be understood by those who try to translate metaphor into scientific fact, or by those who refuse to understand metaphor at all. This community of thought and feeling (not the homogeneous society of his followers) explains why the composition of one man "will always be an expression of the mind and heart of a people as an individual and never the personality of individual men." Thus Child accounts for the objectivity of the popular ballads, for he grants nothing to transmission but change. In an oblique reference to the alleged uni-

formity of ballad style, Child writes that though ballad poetry is always "in its essence an expression of our common human nature [it] will in each case be differenced by circumstances and idiosyncrasy." Specific characteristics of ballad style may derive, then, not from universal poetic origins, but from the unique cultural situation. Child's comments on the age of ballads are reasonably clear. Although he considers as ballads the Germanic songs referred to by Tacitus, his avoidance of a formal definition places him outside the camp of those communalists who argued for the existence of ancient Germanic songs with the characteristics of extant ballads. Child's position is that popular narrative songs existed before the introduction of the rhymed stanza and "seem to have been in use from the earliest recorded time"; but he mentions no formal elements connecting the English and Scottish ballads with earlier popular narratives.

Child's conception of ballad authors is by no means precise. In a passage denying the necessity to go back to the "cradle of mankind" to explain resemblances among ballads of various nations, he refers to the transmission of at least ballad plots among professional entertainers of the Middle Ages. Yet he does not specifically connect these minstrels with ballad authorship. His recognition of individual authorship is, however, worth quoting:

> Though they do not "write themselves," as William Grimm has said, though a man and not a people has composed them, still the author counts for nothing, and it is not by mere accident, but with the best reason, that they have come down to us anonymous.

Although quoting correctly in *Old English Ballads,* Gummere later paraphrased this as "although men and not communities make the ballad,"[2] a rendering that distorts Child's statement. Critics such as T. F. Henderson have made merry with the statement that the author counts for nothing, but more revealing is the fact that Gummere by inference did so, too, writing, in *Old English Ballads* [(1894)], in reference to Ludwig Uhland's remarks on *Volkslied:*

> . . . what does Uhland really teach us? Certainly no distinctive notion about the making of a ballad. He rests too much in a phrase. He avoids the mystery in which the Grimms took refuge; but instead he flies to image and allegory. He concedes the individual act in authorship, and then denies its significance.
>
> (p. lvi)

To this strategy Gummere applies Hosea Biglow's phrase, "frontin' south by north." Is there reason to wonder that Gummere did not wish Child's article quoted or regarded as final?

Child's statements are rather like those of John Geddie, who, in *The Balladists* (1896), could write of a "Ballad Age," when such poetry sprung up naturally and sponta-neously" and of a "voice . . . not of an individual poet, but of an age and of a people" while still believing in "original ballad-writers." Geddie, however, was an early "Darwinian" critic in seeing the Scottish ballads as, "in their present form, the outcome of a long and strenuous process of selection. . . . As a rule, what was fittest . . . survived and was perpetuated in this evolution of the ballad" (pp. 11-13). Child had apparently no conception of transmission as evolution or progress.

If anywhere Child approaches the communal position, it is in his placing of national poetry "anterior to the appearance of the poetry of art, to which it formed a step." In classifying the "vulgar ballads of our day, the broadsides," as "a different genus . . . products of a low kind of *art,*" he may have meant merely that the broadsides were conscious appeals to the lower classes as contrasted with the unconscious appeal made by the popular ballad in an era when knowledge, desires, and tastes were relatively uniform. But Child's remarks were certainly understood differently, and, using the opposed categories of art and nature, his pupil, Gummere, began a defense of popular poetry.

Notes

1. "Professor Child and the Ballad," *PMLA,* XXI (1806), 755*ff.*

2. "Primitive Poetry and the Ballad," *MP* [*Modern Philology*], I (1903), 478.

Dave Harker (essay date 1981)

SOURCE: Harker, Dave. "Francis James Child and the 'Ballad Consensus.'" *Folk Music Journal* 4, no. 2 (1981): 146-64.

[*In the following essay, Harker argues that while* The English and Scottish Popular Ballads *remains a valuable contribution to contemporary folklore studies, Child's selection of the ballads is based on arbitrary criteria, and his assertions regarding their original composition are unscientific. According to Harker, the reverence with which modern scholars have regarded Child's work has in fact proven to be a significant obstacle to further advances in the field.*]

To many people, Child's **The English and Scottish Popular Ballads** has the immobility of a monument. Its sheer bulk, wealth of detail, and apparently exhaustive critical apparatus do, indeed, present a formidable appearance; yet a closer inspection of the theoretical foundations of Child's edifice will reveal not only a circularity of argument, but also, ironically, a distinct lack of self-confidence.[1] Bert Lloyd was one of the first to challenge the notion of an 'unquestioned aristocracy' of so-called 'Child ballads', which

can only refer to a limited selection of ballads, if at all. And whatever the literature dons might think, not all these nobles are in Francis J. Child's *English and Scottish Popular Ballads,* nor can all the items in that great compilation be numbered among the peers of the folk song realm. The majority of Child's selection represents but one stage of the ballad, a middle stage lying between the old form of epic song and the newer form of domestic ballad, journalistic ballad, street song and the like.[2]

So, when Walter Hart noted in 1906 that 'the significant fact is that for at least forty years Professor Child retained without essential change his conception of the traditional ballad as a distinct literary type' ('PCB' ['Professor Child and the Ballad'], p. 800), he pointed to the basis of the theoretically incestuous process which underpins the formation of what I propose to call the 'ballad consensus'.

* * *

We still do not have a full-length critical or biographical study of Child. There are sketches available,[3] but the US folklore industry has yet to grasp the nettle of coming to terms with its founding father. Only a brief outline is possible here. Child was born in Boston in 1825, the third child of eight in a sailmaker's family. He went to state schools, but was 'discovered' by the headmaster of the town's Latin School, and encouraged to prepare himself for Harvard. He entered the college when he was seventeen, his fees being paid for him, and he quickly excelled in classics, English, and mathematics. He graduated in 1846, and was appointed college tutor in mathematics, then in history and political economy ('FJC' ['Francis James Child'], pp. xxiii-xxiv). Between 1849 and 1851, he travelled in Europe, returning to become Professor of Rhetoric and Oratory. He was 'at home in the best methods and traditions of German universities', and was later awarded an honorary doctorate from Göttingen ('FJC', pp. xxiv-xxv). Above all, he was influenced by the ideals of Germanic philology:

> The ideals of erudition and of a large humanity were not even suspected of incompatibility. The imagination was still invoked as the guide and illuminator of learning. The bond between antiquity and mediaevalism and between the Middle Ages and our own century was never lost from sight.
>
> ('FJC', p. xxv)

Kittredge felt that Child's 'greatest contribution to learning'

> may even, in a very real sense, be regarded as the fruit of these years in Germany. Throughout his life he kept a picture of William and James Grimm on the mantel over his study fire-place.
>
> ('FJC', p. xxv)

For twenty-five years, Child's interests in literary and linguistic study had to be subordinated to the demands of teaching, administration, and examinations. His pub-

lications, from *Four Old Plays,* through the general editorship of a series of one hundred and fifty volumes of *British Poets,* to his own compilation, *English and Scottish Ballads* of 1857-59, were essentially by-products, almost a leisure-time pursuit, for it was not until 1876 that he was appointed to the more congenial chair of English at Harvard ('FJC', pp. xxiv-xxv). In later years, Child down-graded his first ballad collection, above all to the great Danish ballad scholar, Svend Grundtvig, to whom he wrote that

> The collection was made as a sort of *job*—forming part of one of those senseless huge collections of *British Poets.*
>
> (*BBBM* [*Ballad Books and Ballad Men*], p. 246)

And because it was important to make the book 'tolerably saleable' (*BBBM,* p. 255), the necessary comparative ballad study was sacrificed to 'the progress of the series' (*ESB* [*English and Scottish Ballads*] (1861), I, x). Only in 1872 did the two scholars begin to correspond, and it was Grundtvig who wrote first (*BBBM,* p. 242). Their early letters underline the marginality of ballad study both to their academic careers and to their material concerns (*BBBM,* pp. 242 and 245). We also learn that Child's basic ideas and assumptions about balladry were well-established twenty-five years before the appearance of his magnum opus.

Child knew what he meant by the term 'true popular ballads' (*ESB* (1861), I, vii), by 1861, though he claimed not to have decided finally until a few years later:

> These volumes have been compiled from the numerous collections of Ballads printed since the beginning of the last century. They contain all but two or three of the *ancient* ballads of England and Scotland, and nearly all those ballads which, in either country, have been gathered from oral tradition,—whether ancient or not.
>
> (*ESB* (1861), I, vii)

Yet when we probe this apparently unimpeachable criterion, we find that Child is quick to qualify, especially with regard to the broadside ballad:

> No words could express the dulness and inutility of a collection which should embrace all the Roxburghe and Pepys broadsides.
>
> (*ESB* (1861), I, viii)

If such slurring fails to convince us, we must trust Child's subjective value-judgments:

> Widely different from the true popular ballads, the spontaneous products of nature, are the works of the professional ballad-maker, which make up the bulk of Garlands and Broadsides. These, though sometimes not without grace, more frequently not lacking in humour, belong to artificial literature—of course to an humble department.
>
> (*ESB* (1861), I, vii)

Such couplets—popular/professional, spontaneous/ artificial, nature/art—beg the key questions. Did broadside-makers really try to make 'art', but fail; or were theirs different criteria? Was there only one literary tradition—the current custodians of which included Harvard professors—or were there several? But instead of historical evidence about the nature of majority culture in medieval Britain, Child offers his own opinion, backed up by that of other litterateurs and literature scholars; and in the end, he fudges his previous confident assertions with two catch-all riders:

> This distinction is not absolute, for several of the ancient ballads have a sort of literary character, and many broadsides were printed from oral tradition.
>
> (***ESB*** (1861), I, vii, note)

Later, to Grundtvig, he confessed that he had

> felt obliged to include everything the English [*sic*] had been accustomed to call a *Ballad*, at least in specimens. It is true that I might have separated the proper *Volksballade* from the others: and I wish that I had done so.
>
> (*BBBM*, p. 262)

The 'English', of course, were still the literary mediators, not the people at large.

What focused Child's theory and practice was the appearance of Grundtvig's *Danske Folkeviser.* Though he saw it 'quite late' (*BBBM,* p. 262), he spent the rest of his life adapting himself to Grundtvig's ideas, and apologizing for his own earlier efforts, such as the inclusion of longer pieces in his first ballad collection, because they were 'not of the nature of ballads' (***ESB*** (1857), I, xi note). In his second edition, Child set about a radical restructuring:

> Certain short romances which formerly stood in the First Book, have been dropped . . . in order to give the collection a homogeneous character.
>
> (***ESB*** (1860), I, xii)

And in the 1861 edition, he wrote of the 'popular ballads' that

> Many of the older ones are mutilated, many more are miserably corrupted, but as long as any traces of their originals are left, they are worthy of attention and have received it. When a ballad is extant in a variety of forms, all the most important versions are given.
>
> (***ESB*** (1861), I, viii)

Deference apart, Child knew what an 'original' ballad looked like, and so understood when it had been 'corrupted'. More, he already had a hierarchy of what was to be esteemed 'important', and felt no qualms in relegating 'all those pieces which are wanting in general interest' to an appendix, for the benefit of 'readers

for pleasure' (***ESB*** (1861), I, viii). Already, a self-produced aura of scientificity surrounded his work, supported by his undoubtedly high editorial standards:

> For the Texts, the rule has been to select the most authentic copies, and to reprint them as they stand in the collections, restoring readings that had been changed without grounds, and noting all deviations from the originals, whether those of previous editors or of this edition, in the margin. Interpolations acknowledged by the editors have generally been dropped. In two instances only have previous texts been superceded or greatly improved.
>
> (***ESB*** (1861), I, x)

Yet by relying on his own untheorized assessment of the 'best' previous editors and mediators, in what he terms 'The Principal Collections', Child was simply underwriting his own methods and assumptions, and ignoring other, differing criteria completely, writing off some collections arbitrarily as 'of slight or no importance' (***ESB*** (1861), I, xiii).

Child evidently despaired of matching Grundtvig's edition, for 'the material is not to be had', though 'schoolmaster and clergyman'

> in those retired nooks where tradition longest lingers, have been very active in taking down ballads from the mouths of the people.
>
> (***ESB*** (1861), I, xi)

A large number of manuscripts had been placed at his disposal (***ESB*** (1861), I, xi); but, apart from the publication of the Percy Manuscript, there was little to be done, for

> Civilization has made too great strides in the island of Great Britain for us to expect much more from tradition.
>
> (***ESB*** (1861), I, xi-xii)

'Civilization', in other words, is *defined* as being antagonistic to 'tradition'. And for all his avowed reverence for that abstraction, 'the people', Child had but little respect for real workers in country or in town. In 1857 he wrote:

> One uncommonly tasteless stanza, the interpolation of some nursery-maid, is here omitted. Too many of Buchan's ballads have suffered in this way, and have become both prolix and vulgar.
>
> (***ESB*** (1857), I, 306 note)

In such asides we discover the hidden criteria, most of them *negative,* which were used to 'define' the 'true popular ballads'. Unsurprisingly, such criteria were those of contemporary bourgeois[4] taste, which sometimes required the suppression even of 'true' pieces, because of the objectionable nature of their subjects

(*BBBM*, p. 264). The interested reader was referred to the general index for the sources of pieces like 'The Bonny Hynd' and 'The Baffled Knight', which threatened to offend ears polite (***ESB*** (1861), I, vii, note); yet, as Gershon Legman remarks, when we consider that Child's chosen ballads silently condone sadism, butchery, murder, and any amount of physical violence, it is curious that sexual relations had either to be apologized for or silently omitted.[5]

The whole process of the 'refining definition' was, of course, circular. Exceptions were shanghaied to 'prove' rules. If the ballad was fundamentally inimitable, then 'Sir Patrick Spens',

> if not ancient, has been always accepted as such by the most skilful judges, and is a solitary instance of a successful imitation, in manner and spirit, of the best specimens of authentic minstrelsy.
>
> ('PCB', pp. 796-97)

However, his appeal to authority was by no means a blanket one:

> I cannot assent to the praise bestowed by Scott on 'The Outlaw Murray'. The story lacks point and the style is affected—not that of the unconscious poet of the real *traditional* ballad.
>
> (***ESB*** (1857), VI, 22)

By implication, of course, we are being asked to accept that 'traditional' balladry consists of stories *with* a point, in an *unaffected* style, and not written by a poet conscious of his or her role. And, in general, it never seems to have struck Child as crucial that, while challenging the dubieties of some previous ballad mediators, he was effectively underwriting the mediating practices of the remainder, though they were as innocent of theorizing as could well be. Underpinning Child's apparently objective empirical scholarship, and making it possible, is the prior *assumption* that there are such 'permanent forms' as 'ballad' and 'folksong', just as in literature it is assumed that 'epic' and 'romance' exist, and then

> all our active study is of variations within them, variations that may be admitted to have proximate causes, even a social history, but that in their essential features are taken in practice as autonomous, with internal laws.[6]

So, as in normative literary criticism, *tradition*

> is seen not as it is, an active and continuous selection and re-selection, which even at its latest point in time is always a specific choice, but now more conveniently as an object, a projected reality, with which we have to come to terms on its terms, even though those terms are always and must be the valuations, the selections and omissions, of other men.
>
> ('FLG' ['From Leavis to Goldman'], p. 7)[7]

In the production of ***The English and Scottish Popular Ballads,*** the chief of the 'other men' was Grundtvig, to whom Child all but disowned his previous edition: 'I never pretended that the arrangement was founded on a deeper principle than convenience' (*BBBM*, p. 254); and though 'In general, I suspected everything that was not vouched for by some other [*sic*] collector of credit', he admitted that 'I certainly ought to have proceeded upon a clearer principle' (*BBBM*, p. 270). However, his misgivings did not prevent him from defining 'ballad' for *Johnson's Universal Cyclopaedia,* but he soon wished the article 'to be neither quoted nor regarded as final' ('PCB', p. 756). There, too, what is most noticeable is the almost complete absence of *positive* statements, after the standard dictionary definition of a 'ballad' as 'a narrative song, a short tale in lyric verse' ('PCB', p. 781). Other than that, he adds a Social Darwinist dimension to the place of the 'popular' ballad in cultural history. This 'distinct and very important species of poetry' has a 'historical and natural place',

> anterior to the appearance of the poetry of art, to which it has formed a step, and by which it has been regularly displaced, and, in some cases, all but extinguished.
>
> ('PCB', p. 756)

Hence, in part, the attempt at chronological arrangement in the first compilation: hence, also, the need to dissociate the largely literate culture of nineteenth-century British workers from that of their own ancestors.

Necessarily, Child does violence to any rational (or even empirical) conception of history, resorting instead to the authority of the brothers Grimm, or to the unmitigated romanticism of his favourite editor, William Motherwell:[8]

> Whenever a people in the course of its development reaches a certain intellectual and moral stage, it will feel an impulse to express itself . . . The condition of society in which a truly national or popular poetry appears explains the character of such poetry. It is a condition in which the people are not divided by political organization and book-culture into markedly distinct classes, in which consequently there is such community of ideas and feelings that the whole people form an individual. Such poetry . . . will always be an expression of the mind and heart of the people as an individual, and never of the personality of individual men. The fundamental characteristic of popular ballads is therefore the absence of subjectivity and of self-consciousness. Though they do not 'write themselves', as William Grimm has said, though a man and not a people has composed them, still the author counts for nothing, and it is not by mere accident, but with the best reason, that they have come down to us anonymous.
>
> ('PCB', pp. 756-57)

This alleged cultural homogeneity, before the cultural watershed of the appearance of 'art' (as reinforced by literacy and print), is implicitly contrasted with the cul-

tural variety and individualism of Child's own society, against which he and other liberal intellectuals strove gamely, while forgetting the underlying divisive nature of the capitalist mode of production. Working people's role in even the transmission of balladry is systematically minimized:

> The primitive ballad, then, is popular not in the sense of something arising from and suited to the lower orders of a people. As yet, no sharp distinction of high and low exists, in respect to knowledge, desires, and tastes. An increased civilization, and especially the introduction of book-culture, gradually gives rise to such a division; the poetry of art appears; the popular poetry is no longer relished by a portion of the people, and is abandoned to an uncultivated or not over-cultivated class—a constantly diminishing number . . . The popular ballad is not originally the product or the property of the lower orders of the people. Nothing, in fact, is more obvious than that many of the ballads of the now most refined nations had their origin in that class whose acts and fortunes they depict—the upper class.
>
> ('PCB', p. 757)

The role of 'the lower orders' is merely instrumental.

By contrast, what 'the lower orders' preserved is seen as a positive acquisition for Child's own class culture, in one of its romantic, populist modes; while the products of the broadside publishers, from the sixteenth century to the later nineteenth century, are stigmatized as

> a different genus; they are products of a low kind of *art,* and most of them are, from a literary point of view, thoroughly despicable and worthless.
>
> ('PCB', p. 757)

So, manuscript sources get precedence over printed ones; and the whole range of *alternative,* often commercially-oriented institutions, made and used by the majority British population, are condemned out of hand. In this way does Child seek to impose his own, essentially *static,* conception of cultural development. After each literary 'species' has reached its Darwinian apogee, its status is that of a delicate fossil:

> ballads which have been handed down by long-repeated tradition have always departed considerably from their original form. If the transmission has been purely through the mouths of unlearned people, there is less probability of wilful change, but once in the hands of professional singers there is no amount of change which they may not undergo.
>
> ('PCB', pp. 757-58)

Change *equals* corruption: professionalisation of a social role *equals* individualism; the absence of formal education is all but a *precondition* of accurate transmission, and the only effect of 'unlearned people' on balladry is a deleterious one. Having read the minds of the makers of the 'original form' of the ballad, Child has

no need of any further understanding of the complexities of medieval culture. Instead, he is content to underwrite the cultural expropriation of the majority, historically, and in his own day ('PCB', p. 758).

* * *

The relationship between Child and Grundtvig was fundamentally a commercial one. The Danish scholar had to ask for money, 'painful and disgusting' though it was (*BBBM,* p. 245), in order to help with *The English and Scottish Popular Ballads*:

> Though my assistance is not to be bought, yet it must be paid for, or else, I am sorry to say, it cannot be given. The fact is, that as a professor of the university I have only a small salary, and all my spare hours therefore must be turned to profit, not only in an ideal, but also in a material point of view. . . . To speak plainly, I must value the time it would take me to give you all the information I could wish, to the sum of 500 American dollars.
>
> (*BBBM,* p. 245)

Child's response was matter-of-fact, unsurprised, and even grateful:

> Your cooperation I regard, I need not say, as beyond any money value, and the very small sum you mention it would not be out of my power to advance, in expectation of receiving it back finally from the profits of the work. Unfortunately professors all the world over are for the most part far from independent in their circumstances, and I belong to the great majority, though I fancy I am much better paid than much superior men at Copenhagen.
>
> (*BBBM,* p. 247)

In the event, Grundtvig's cash didn't reach him until almost five years later (*BBBM,* p. 272); though Child's weather-eye for the chance to 'drop the Ballad Society' and to 'seek for a publisher' with a view to getting royalties, indicates that he was well aware of the commercial possibilities of exploiting Grundtvig's reputation and scholarship (*BBBM,* p. 247).

Grundtvig's advice and example was crucial, not only to the contents of Child's magnum opus, but even to its structure. Every problem Child had encountered was gone over thoroughly in their correspondence, with the American placing himself explicitly in the posture of a willing disciple: 'With your help I feel sure that I could do the work somewhat as it ought to be done' (*BBBM,* p. 247). Thus, when the Dane praised Child's first edition, and criticized Hales and Furnivall as 'dilletantes, not scholars', because of their inclusion of 'many insignificant or utterly worthless late transcripts of old metrical tales and romances', compounded by an ignorance of 'corresponding foreign literature' (*BBBM,* p. 243), Child humbly agreed, even though he had been respon-

sible for pushing Furnivall and the Ballad Society into producing the edition of the Percy Manuscript in question (*BBBM*, p. 246). In response to his master's invocation of 'genuine popular ballad lore' (*BBBM*, p. 243), Child claims to have pressed Furnivall for the inclusion of 'the genuine national ballad', which the latter had 'half consented' to do (*BBBM*, p. 247):

> I told him that not even the stolid patience of a book-collector, a most useful though often well nigh imbecile creature, would suffice for twenty years of Roxburghe Ballads.
>
> (*BBBM*, p. 247)

And so as to reassure his mentor, Child reiterated his position on broadsides:

> The immense collections of Broadside ballads, the Roxburghe and Pepys, of which but a small part has been printed, doubtless contain some ballads which we should at once declare to possess the popular character, and yet on the whole they are veritable dung-hills, in which, only after a great deal of sickening grubbing, one finds a very moderate jewel. Some of the later Robin Hood ballads I have scarcely patience or stomach to read: but the declension is so gradual from the freshest and raciest to the thoroughly *vulgar* (by which I mean always the *essentially* vulgar, the absolutely mean and stupid) that it will be very hard, and to me at this moment looks impossible, to draw a line.
>
> (*BBBM*, p. 254)

His solution was to draw on Grundtvig's advice for the problems of 'compass' and 'arrangement' which still gave a 'great deal of trouble', even in 1872 (*BBBM*, p. 253):

> We cannot of course exclude all ballads which have not been taken from the mouths of the people—nor perhaps include all such. The oldest Robin Hood ballads are derived from MS., and very many others of the best and oldest, and on the other hand some ballads written in comparatively recent times, especially historical ones, are found in the mouths of the people . . . It is not easy always to distinguish a ballad and what we should call a short romance . . . 'The Horn of King Arthur' I incline to exclude, and yet I fear that my reasons are vague . . . It is a pity one can't consistently insist on the lyrical, or singable, character as a criterion.
>
> (*BBBM*, pp. 253-54)

He was still puzzled, two years later, and asked Grundtvig's view on the

> *criterion* of a popular ballad, the distinction between ballad and tale, *fabliau,* and between genuine national or people's ballads and all varieties of base kind . . . I should like to have you try to express the more subtle characteristics of an old popular ballad in words.
>
> (*BBBM*, p. 268)

Both men shared a form of romantic, populist nationalism; and Grundtvig not only believed firmly in what he termed 'the Angloscotic department of the common Gothic Middleage Ballad Poetry' (*BBBM*, p. 249), but even suggested that Child should call his new work *The Popular Ballads of the English Race* (*BBBM*, p. 252), allowing some autonomy to the developing culture of each European nation-state:

> there is no doubt that the ballad poetry of the Gothic nations is upon the whole contemporary and of a homogeneous character both with regard to its contents, treatment, style of poetry and form of verse, but nevertheless each department has its own peculiarities.
>
> (*BBBM*, p. 276)

Child seems to have accepted this view without demur, given that he had taken *Danske Folkeviser* 'for a model from the beginning', determining, 'if I ever saw the way to another edition, to make your work my pattern' (*BBBM*, p. 262). In fact, so implicit was Child's faith that he told Grundtvig he did not 'esteem it necessary to search in any place where *you* have passed' (*BBBM*, p. 255), because 'Every time you edit a ballad which occurs in English you do a large part of my work for me' (*BBBM*, p. 282). Only on the mediations of Peter Buchan does Child have qualms. Grundtvig responded:

> what you [namely Child] term the 'vulgarity' of the Buchan texts is to me the best proof of their material authenticity. For it must be remembered—and is well known to the ballad collectors of the old world, where the tradition of bygone days still lingers on,—that in the recent traditions of the common country people (peasantry) the old ballad cannot always appear in a stately and knightly form and apparel, but must in many instances exhibit the traces of a long dwelling in humble company.
>
> (*BBBM*, p. 249)

All Child could do was to try to rationalize his remaining doubts:

> They exhibit an *artificial* vulgarity, it seems to me, and as I have said, there is no variety to this, which makes me fear that it comes from a man and not from a class of people . . . The vulgarity that I mean consists in a tame, mean, unreal style of *expression,* far from *volksmassig* [popular].
>
> (*BBBM*, p. 264)

Implicitly, then, Child claims to understand the nuances of both medieval and contemporary British workers' speech and syntax, on the basis (so far as we can judge) of an extremely limited and predominantly literary knowledge of medieval courtly culture. An apparent humility barely hides a breathtaking pretentiousness.

The problem of arrangement dragged on for years:

> Outlaw ballads separate themselves pretty well . . . My *Trylleviser* will make a natural class, and I have no doubt that this class should come first. But what to put second I wot not.
>
> (*BBBM*, p. 254)

Because he did not wish to do *all* Child's work for him, Grundtvig stressed

> beforehand *you* must have formed your plan and fixed upon the order of contents, which I think ought to be something more systematic than in your former editions, and I should say—without any appendices.
>
> (*BBBM*, p. 249)

When his employer persisted in picking his brains, Grundtvig back-tracked:

> In fact I do not think that the question of arrangement is of any great weight or consequence. The chief point is that the edition contains every bit of genuine ballad lore, and consequently all that *may be* genuine, and I might say, all that *has been so.*
>
> (*BBBM*, p. 260)

Instead of bothering about niceties of form, Grundtvig urged his pupil to start publishing—this was in 1874 (*BBBM*, p. 266). Yet Child demurred (*BBBM*, p. 269):

> I shall be reluctant to begin until I have got most of the matter ready. The question of arrangement puzzles me exceedingly. There is not a sufficient criterion for me to make an unexceptionable division. I might make three divisions of the earliest—later—and recent; but of course they would be called arbitrary, and would be so in some degree. I should have to separate a great mass of the Robin Hood ballads from the few really early ones. This is what I shall probably do, however. I shall be very glad to have your opinion.
>
> (*BBBM*, p. 257)

Of course, a chronological order would have been more problematical than he admits: indeed, he later asked Grundtvig if he had 'formed any view as to the time when the English ballads were produced' (*BBBM*, p. 278). In any event, by 1875 he

> decided to make only two divisions, 'Romantic', stretching the name, and Historical. I have not made up my mind precisely as to the order of individual pieces, but shall put the 'Wonder Ballads' first.
>
> (*BBBM*, p. 269)

The cash nexus (he had yet to be paid) obliged Grundtvig to produce what was to be the rationale for the arrangement, though he had misgivings too:

> Upon the whole I think the subject, the theme, the contents is [*sic*] no rational or natural principle of classification for the English Ballads, and ought not to be the ruling principle here, if another more suitable and scientifically warrantable may be found.
>
> This is what I have tried to find, and which I now flatter myself to have found, in making not the subject, but *the form,* the meter of the ballad the ruling principle of division . . . the subject of the ballad should be made only a secondary help in the arrangement.
>
> (*BBBM*, p. 277)

Child immediately appropriated the formula, forgetting to acknowledge its source until Grundtvig remarked on his apparent discourtesy (*BBBM*, pp. 290 and 292). Indeed, he asked the Dane to 'go on with the arrangement, with a *reason* now and then in difficult cases' (*BBBM*, p. 278), as though Grundtvig were the equivalent of a present-day research assistant. In fact, there may have been more than a touch of irony in Grundtvig's apparent pleasure in having his ideas adopted wholesale by 'the very best men of the present day' (*BBBM*, p. 284)!

Even in the 1870s, Child worried about what he termed 'the chemistry of the English and Scottish ballad', which seemed to him to be '*mostly,* as indeterminable as that of Greek myths' (*BBBM*, p. 272). This difficulty did not prevent him from asserting that 'The sources . . . may be regarded as sealed or dried up forever', or from trying to collect 'such ballads as may be left with the people' in Scotland (*BBBM*, pp. 248 and 255).

> I have endeavored by a considerable amount of correspondence—and by the circulation throughout Scotland of an 'Appeal', two thousand copies of which were dispersed, so that every clergyman and schoolmaster in the country was reached, both to ascertain how much is left of traditional ballads in the memory of the people, and to get, whatever there is, collected. Several gentlemen have taken a warm interest in the matter, and some have pushed their enquiries very zealously. The fruits, however, are small. I have not received *one* ballad that has not before been printed, and the copies taken down from recitation are in general much inferior to those that have already been printed.
>
> (*BBBM*, p. 256)

This was in 1873: four years later, he felt that he had 'got all the manuscripts that are to be had', and had 'no reason to wait longer' for what might arise from his friends' collecting in Aberdeenshire (*BBBM*, p. 271), given that most collected texts were 'recollections of *modern print,* a most undesirable aftergrowth of oral tradition' (*BBBM*, p. 263).

Apart from the general problems arising from using people from one class to collect cultural products from another, in 1880 Child came across other material blockages in a postal blitz amongst the 'gentlemen' of Shetland:

> I had supposed that, as the Scotch had been 300 years in possession of the islands, enough of them might have gone there to plant Scottish ballads. But that seems doubtful; at any rate, an intelligent correspondent says that the Scotch clergy as *a class* have done their best to destroy any relic of antiquity in the shape of tradition or ballad. Some Norse traditions of value may remain, and the Norse population are said to be much more amenable to appeals in behalf of traditional remains.
>
> (*BBBM*, p. 283)

Still he persisted with his 'gentlemen' amateurs, though by 1881 he had evidently abandoned Great Britain in favour of his own country.

> I have issued circulars (there are to be 1000) inviting students throughout the country to unite in gathering ballads from the Irish American population.
>
> (*BBBM*, p. 288)

And, disclaimers apart, that circular *specifies* what Child meant by a ballad

> he gives instructions for the proper recording of ballads, burdens, and airs, and prints copies of 'The Cruel Sister' and of 'Sir Hugh' by way of specimens of the sort of thing desired.
>
> (*BBBM*, p. 288 note)

In just this way were Child's followers to harden up his collection of ballads into the effective definition of 'popular balladry' in general.

* * *

The English and Scottish Popular Ballads began appearing in 1882. Child justified the 'unrestricted title' by 'having at command every valuable copy of every known ballad' (***ESPB*** [***The English and Scottish Popular Ballads***], I, vii). In fact, he had 'not found one unknown ballad since the *Percy MS* was printed' in 1867-68 (*BBBM*, p. 274): and, compared with his first collection, of the three hundred and five ballads in the new edition,

> only ninety are new; and these are, for the most part, unimportant additions to the body of ballad literature . . . The main addition of the later collection is thus rather in the way of new versions of important ballads, or of more authentic versions based directly upon the manuscripts; in the citation of a larger number of foreign parallels; and, generally, in the matter contained in the introductions.
>
> ('PCB', pp. 792-93)

One hundred and fifteen ballads had been excised from the first collection ('PCB', p. 793), most of which would not have appeared there, had Child been clearer as to his criteria ('PCB', p. 796). Even in the later work, those criteria (though present) are never systematically argued through in the promised (and perpetually delayed) 'elaborate introduction'. Instead, we have scribbled notes, a set of extracts from other scholars, and the *obiter dicta* sprinkled through his works ('PCB', p. 755, and 'FJC', p. xxix).

The debt to Grundtvig is acknowledged, but only sparingly (***ESPB***, I, ix); yet Hustvedt believed that not only the plan but even the *contents* of the work published by Child were attributable to Grundtvig, especially to his *Index* of English and Scottish ballads, which itself changed over the years. For example, the second *Index* seems to have been pruned according to specific criteria:

> the following have been excluded, out of different reasons, partly because they were of too local a character, as the Border ballads, partly as decidedly political pieces, some also while they seemed to be of too recent a date or were of a doubtful antiquity.
>
> (*BBBM*, p. 301)

Child asked Grundtvig for a recommended list for the new edition, in the later 1870s, and several items were then restored to favour (*BBBM*, p. 302). This third *Index,* Hustvedt is sure, 'exercised a considerable influence on the formation of the canon of English balladry' (*BBBM*, p. 303);[9] though Child rejected the book-based chronology offered to him, in favour of a chronology of his manuscript sources (*BBBM*, pp. 303-04).[10] The hierarchy of those sources is made explicit:

> Of hitherto unused materials, much the most important is a large collection of ballads made by Motherwell.
>
> (***ESPB***, I, vii)

Next came items from Kinloch's collection, followed by the ballads sung by the professor's daughter, Mrs Brown of Falkland, to which 'No Scottish ballads are superior in kind' (***ESPB***, I, vii).[11] But Child also relied on the collecting work of other English amateurs, like Frank Kidson and the Rev. Sabine Baring-Gould (***ESPB***, II, v, and IV, v), whose reliability has lately been questioned.[12] Robert White, the Newcastle antiquarian who had purchased John Bell's collection of manuscript songs, allowed Child to look through his collections in 1873, and subsequently made 'a copy of such things as I needed' (***ESPB***, I, viii). In this case, the 'copy' which appeared in the American's edition is not the same as the version which appears in the manuscript collection.[13]

Because Child was for the most part mediating the mediations of other collectors, it was all but inevitable that he believed that

> The gathering from tradition has been, as ought perhaps to have been foreseen at this late day, meagre, and generally of indifferent quality.
>
> (***ESPB***, I, vii)[14]

None the less, *tradition* remained the keystone of the new collection, supplemented by the notion of 'oral transmission', at every stage of which

> we must suppose that some accidental variations from what was delivered would be introduced, and occasionally some wilful variations. Memory will fail at times; at times the listener will hear amiss, or will not under-

stand, and a perversion of sense will ensue, or absolute nonsense,—nonsense which will be servilely repeated, and which repetition may make more gross.

(***ESPB***, v, 309)

Ironically, Child elsewhere claimed that the wilful, servile, forgetful and generally unintelligent people who sustained this process often transmitted accurately. Indeed, he believed that the ballad was 'at its best'

> when it has come down by a purely domestic tradition, yet even so it is sometimes influenced by printed literature; and much depends on the experience and selection of the reciters, and on their varying memory, which is, however, ordinarily remarkable for its tenacity.

('PCB', p. 805)

Thus, his earlier statements notwithstanding, the broadside ballad 'may . . . become tradition' ('PCB', p. 805), and it is certain that 'old tradition does not come to a stop when a ballad gets into print' ('PCB', p. 760). One of his versions of 'Queen Eleanor's Confession' was probably one of the 'traditional variations of printed copies':

> The ballad seems first to have got into print in the latter part of the seventeenth century, but was no doubt circulating orally sometime before that, for it is in the truly popular tone.

(***ESPB***, III, 255)

Child seems to have been coming to believe that, because the ballad 'suffers in transmission', it will be 'at its best when it is early caught and fixed in print' ('PCB', pp. 805-06). Yet Hart found that Child's later collection

> is much more chary of the admission of broadsides or sheet-ballads: in many cases they are relegated to introductions or appendices; in many more, omitted.

('PCB', p. 793)[15]

The advantage to Child of the broadside was its minimization of the human element in the process of transmission; and, if anything, his contempt for those agents seems to have increased. 'Hind Etin', in one version, 'has been not simply damaged by passing through low mouths, but has been worked over by low hands' (***ESPB***, I, 360); while the very idea that Richard Sheale, the Tamworth minstrel, could have written a version of 'The Hunting of the Cheviot' 'is preposterous in the extreme' (***ESPB***, III, 303). No evidence is adduced: the piece is at most 'part of his stock as minstrel' (***ESPB***, III, 303). Child knows better than the very agents in the culture what is and is not *traditional* (***ESPB***, I, 317).

Other acts of faith are required of Child's disciples. Apparently, the 'lyrical quality' of a piece 'is to be regarded as no less significant than plot as the trait of a true ballad' (***ESPB***, II, 204 note):

A simple but life-like story, supported by the burden and the air, these are the means by which such old romances seek to produce an impression.

(***ESPB***, II, 204 note)

Either we agree, with Child, that 'Johnie Cock' really is a 'precious specimen of the unspoiled traditional ballad', or we don't: he does not deign to argue (***ESPB***, III, 1). And, in general, we must subscribe to a long list of criteria, almost all of them negatives, which effectively constitute Child's ballad 'idea'. Hart summarized these 'litmus tests' thus:

> Necessary as the story is . . . it is seldom completely told in the ballad . . . Transitions are usually abrupt . . . These abrupt transitions do not, then, result . . . in incoherence, which accompanies corruption and is a sign of degeneracy . . . Coherence, on the contrary, is a characteristic of the true ballad, an important phase of ballad excellence.

('PCB', pp. 782-83)

Brevity, apparently *is* a ballad characteristic; but then come more negatives:

> Introductions, not closely connected with the ballad story, are not characteristic . . . The action is seldom carefully localized . . . In dealing with the supernatural the way of the true ballad is to omit description or explanation . . . Ghosts, though not thought sufficiently strange to demand special treatment, should, nevertheless, 'have fair reason for walking'.

('PCB', pp. 783-85)

Chipping and peeling away at the whole body of song, so as to get at (or at least near) the kernel of the 'true ballad', Child is able to make that imaginative leap ahead of the evidence, operating on the principle that, as Hart put it, there are 'degrees of departure from the popular style', and 'degrees of departure from the popular matter' ('PCB', p. 766). Intuitively, Child feels himself possessed of the essence, the 'idea', and he builds up a kind of negative photo-fit picture, with only an occasional positive detail on the 'face'. The 'English ballad', apparently, is characterized by 'innocuous humour' (***ESPB***, III, 258). A change of nationality is 'accompanied by change of the scene of action'; and ballads have a tendency to 'combine' ('PCB', p. 798). Ballad style is 'artless and homely' ('PCB', p. 785); and ballads have their own conventions, the most striking of which is the use of 'commonplaces' ('PCB', p. 788). But then we return to the shadows around the face, to the things which the ballad is *not*. 'Learned words do not occur in ballads' (***ESPB***, v, 309). Extravagance, exaggeration, cynicism, sophistication, overrefinement, moralizing, and triteness of plot, are 'not characteristic' ('PCB', pp. 779-81). Ballad subjectmatter is not 'horrible', and ballad style is 'not feeble in execution, not prolix and vulgar, and not affected'

('PCB', p. 800). Neither was a ballad historically accurate: 'A strict accordance with history . . . would be almost a ground of suspicion' (*ESPB,* II, 19).

Such a web of arbitrary assertion should give pause to those people inclined to fetishize Child's *The English and Scottish Popular Ballads,* and is the reason why he was not only unwilling but *unable* to theorize his assumptions. Having disowned his article in the *Universal Cyclopaedia* ('PCB', p. 755), and with no contemporary scholar having what Kittredge termed the 'hardihood' to do his job for him ('FJC', p. xxix), later generations have been left to struggle as best they can with the whole mass of information. We have to try to tease out underlying principles from insufficient data; but we can fairly conclude that Child's magnum opus is simply its own definition—a product of a particular stage of academic scholarship. And so long as we are careful not to confuse its underpinning ideology with science, or to take at face value its comments on the cultures from which the ballads came, and through which they passed, we may continue to use the texts as highly mediated examples of the kinds of songs described by late nineteenth century English-speaking literary scholars as 'ballads'. About the lives, interests and general culture of the people who made, remade and used these songs, however, a compilation such as Child's can tell us almost nothing.[16]

Notes

N.B. In order to minimize repetition, each source will be given in full when first mentioned, but will then be referred to in the text in parentheses by the initials of the title (which are given after the first full reference to that title), and the edition, where necessary.

1. The chief sources are Sigurd Bernhard Hustvedt's *Ballad Criticism in Scandinavia and Great Britain during the Eighteenth Century* (*BCSGB*) (New York: American-Scandinavian Foundation, 1916), and especially his *Ballad Books and Ballad Men* (*BBBM*) (Cambridge Mass.: Harvard University Press, 1930), which contains the Child-Grundtvig correspondence during the years 1872-83, and the *Index* compiled during the preparation of *The English and Scottish Popular Ballads* (*ESPB*) (Cambridge Mass.: Houghton, Mifflin and Company, 1882-98) which has been reprinted (New York: Dover, 1965). Additionally, there is Walter Morris Hart's 'Professor Child and the Ballad' ('PCB'), which contains Child's *obiter dicta* from the article in the *Universal Cyclopaedia* and from the editions of *English and Scottish Ballads* (*ESB*) (for example Boston Mass.: Little, Brown and Company, 1857-59, and London: Sampson Low, Son and Company, 1861). Hart's article may be found in the Dover reprint of Child *ESPB* (1965),

v, and in the *Publications of the Modern Languages Association of America,* 21 (1906), 755-807.

2. A. L. Lloyd, *Folk Song in England* (*FSE*) (London: Lawrence and Wishart, 1967), p. 135.

3. For example G. L. Kittredge, 'Francis James Child' ('FJC'), in Child *ESPB* (1965), I, xxiii-xxxi.

4. This term, and all other terms associated with marxist analysis, will be used here strictly in their scientific meanings.

5. See, for example, G. Legman, *The Horn Book* (New York: University Books, 1964), pp. 343-52.

6. Raymond Williams, 'From Leavis to Goldman' ('FLG'), *New Left Review,* 67 (1971), 7.

7. Compare David Ian Harker, 'Popular Song and Working-Class Consciousness in North-East England' (unpublished Ph.D. thesis, University of Cambridge, 1976), pp. 5-14.

8. Compare William Motherwell, *Minstrelsy Ancient and Modern* (Glasgow: J. Wylie, 1827), Introduction *passim.*

9. Compare Child, *ESPB,* v, 182.

10. Interestingly, almost 51% of Child's main texts came from printed sources (including broadsides), while the remaining 49% came from either manuscript or oral sources.

11. A preliminary survey reveals that of the 1700 and more texts used by Child in *ESPB* (excluding appendices, but including major additions, and using the first-given source for each variant), Motherwell's MSS, note-book, and published texts account for almost 12%, Buchan's for almost 9%, and Kinloch's and Scott's for 7% apiece. Together with Herd and Percy, the work of six individuals accounted for approximately 43% of the texts used.

12. See, for example, A. E. Green's 'Foreword' to Frank Kidson, *Traditional Tunes* (Wakefield: E. P. Publishing, 1970), pp. v-xviii.

13. *The Bell/White Manuscript Song Collection,* edited by David Ian Harker and Frank Rutherford (Durham: The Surtees Society, forthcoming).

14. Only about 5% of Child's texts seem to have come from such sources, directly.

15. Some 15% of Child's main texts seem to have come from broadsides and garlands, and especially those which have to do with Robin Hood.

16. See, for example, David Buchan, *The Ballad and the Folk* (London: Routledge and Kegan Paul,

1972), and the critiques of that work which are now appearing—for example, Bob Munro, 'The Bothy Ballads', *History Workshop Journal,* 3 (Spring 1977), 184-93.

For an analysis of the mediating work of Cecil Sharp, see the early article by the present writer, 'Cecil Sharp in Somerset: Some Conclusions', *Folk Music Journal,* 2 (1972), 220-40, and the development of that work, which will include a brief analysis of the connections between Sharp's work and that of A. L. Lloyd, 'May Cecil Sharp be praised?', *History Workshop Journal* (forthcoming).

Jo McMurtry (essay date 1985)

SOURCE: McMurtry, Jo. "Francis James Child (1825-1896), Harvard, and *The English and Scottish Popular Ballads.*" In *English Language, English Literature: The Creation of an Academic Discipline,* pp. 65-110. London: Mansell Publishing Limited, 1985.

[*In the following excerpt, McMurtry examines the evolution of Child's intellectual development, from his early years as a Harvard instructor through the publication of* The English and Scottish Popular Ballads.]

On completing his undergraduate career with distinction, having been chosen class orator, and having won a Bowdoin Prize for an essay on **"The Moral Views of Plato as Unfolded in the Gorgias,"** Child was immediately offered an instructorship at Harvard. In view of his literary interests, which had taken precedence over his other subjects although he continued to receive excellent marks in everything, it may seem odd that the instructorship was in mathematics. A narrow concept of specialization was not typical of the times, however. College instructors were versatile beings.

Harvard clearly wanted to do its best to match Child's preferences to the work they could give him, for the catalogues' faculty lists for the period show a continual edging over into greener pastures. By 1849, mathematics left behind, Child appears as "Tutor in History and Political Economy, and Instructor in Elocution." (The word "tutor" did not carry the connotation it did in the older British universities, that of someone who supervised all the studies of a specific group of students. Like "instructor," the word simply meant a fairly low-ranking member of an academic department.) Elocution, as we have noticed, was closely linked to the study of rhetoric and thus to the ancestral form of the English Department as it evolved at Harvard and in many other places.

An effective way of indicating to one's university the direction in which one's scholarly interest lies is to publish something in that area, and this Child rather quickly did, becoming an editor of English drama. In 1848 his *Four Old Plays* was published by George Nichols and Company of Cambridge and was well received as a competent scholarly production. These plays dated from the sixteenth century and consisted of the anonymous "Thersytes" and "Jack Juggler," John Heywood's "The Pardoner and the Friar," all short pieces in the interlude tradition, and a longer tragedy, *Jocasta,* adapted from Euripides by Francis Kinwelmarsh and George Gascoigne. Child edited the texts from a printed source of considerable rarity—one of thirty-five copies printed in 1820 for the Roxburghe Club, one of the most elite of the British "printing societies." By choosing this collection of plays, Child did more than make the texts more easily available. Through his editorial and critical apparatus, he put the plays into a useful context from the standpoint both of literary history and of philology.

This early work is overshadowed by Child's later achievements with the popular ballads and is seldom mentioned in accounts of his career, but it gives some interesting indications of Child's way of going about things. Introduction, notes, and glossary are thorough and sound. Each of the plays is related to its antecedents in Greek or Roman literature and is also discussed in terms of its themes as treated in other English works; Child comments, for example, on Dryden's later treatment of the Alcmena story in Plautus's *Amphitryon,* the source of the anonymous "Jack Juggler." The sense of literature as embracing many countries, languages, and historical periods is everywhere in Child's commentaries, foreshadowing the sensibility he was later to bring to his studies of the ballads. Another of Child's basic attitudes, later to reappear frequently, had to do with the nineteenth-century public's scruples as to less than refined language. Here Child announced his determination to adhere to the originals in their complete and accurate forms. "The indelicacies of language, which are somewhat frequent in these interludes, never amounting to immoralities, though sufficiently gross, have not been considered of such a nature as to justify a mutilation of the text,"[1] he states firmly. Finally, since the edition retains the sixteenth-century spelling and punctuation, both notes and glossary demonstrate Child's extensive knowledge of the earlier forms of the English language, a knowledge he had acquired on his own in what spare time he could find.

Whether or not in direct response to the appearance of *Four Old Plays,* Harvard in 1849 provided Child with a leave of absence enabling him to go abroad for further studies. For a scholar with philological leanings in the mid-nineteenth century, there was only one destination. . . .

The University of Berlin differed from Harvard in ways which Child must have found exhilarating. Academic life was on a much larger scale. There was more of ev-

erything—more scholars, more lectures, more books old and new, more awareness of the latest advances of knowledge in a wide variety of fields. And into all of this foreign visitors were welcome to plunge. (The ability to speak and read German was, of course, fairly essential to full enjoyment; but this prerequisite seemed to give Child no trouble, as languages came easily to him.) One could attend lectures without having matriculated for a specific degree, and the state of Prussia, which maintained and supervised the universities, had taken several steps to ensure the depth and variety of lectures available. Full professors, for example, were required to give a certain number of free lectures in their subject—as many, in some cases, as two a week. Thus any student who felt a sudden impulse toward a subject had no difficulty in following it up. Further enrichment of the lecture scene came from the institution of the *privatdocent,* a peculiarly German arrangement in which a sort of assistant professor, approved by the university to which he was attached but not salaried, might give lectures and charge fees for them. Matthew Arnold, whose endorsement of the German system was enthusiastic, describes this state of things from the perspective of the 1880s:

> In general, as I have said, the professors and *Privatdocenten* arrange together to parcel out the field of instruction between them, and one supplements the other's teaching; still a *Privatdocent* may, if he likes, lecture on just the same subject that a professor is lecturing on; there is absolute liberty in this respect. The one precaution taken against undue competition is, that a *Privatdocent* lecturing on a professor's subject is not allowed to charge lower fees than the professor. It does honor to the disinterested spirit in which science is pursued in Germany, that with these temptations to competition the relations between the professors and the *Privatdocenten* are in general excellent. . . . But it is evident how the neighborhood of a rising young *Privatdocent* must tend to keep a professor up to the mark, and hinder him from getting sleepy and lazy. If he gets sleepy and lazy, his lecture room is deserted. The *Privatdocent,* again, has the standard of eminent men under his eyes, and everything stimulates him to come up to it.[2]

This example of a free and constructive sharing between old and young scholars in a common academic pursuit may have served as a model for Child's later generous relationships with his own students. In Germany, too, professors were encouraged to teach subjects simply because they thought them worth doing, even if the general public or the student body had never heard of them; and such an atmosphere may have helped Child to develop his own initiative in this regard. For some years thereafter, the lectures in English which Child gave at Harvard were more his idea than the authorities', and Child had to invest a great deal of his own energy in the project before results were apparent.

At Berlin, Child came under the influence of the great Jacob Grimm, whose linguistic theories had begun startling the world only a few decades previously, and of Grimm's various followers (including, we might surmise, a few intense young *privatdocenten*). While Grimm's theories of language were of special interest to Child in their bearings on Anglo-Saxon and early English, the view held by Grimm of world literature as an interconnected pattern was also to form the basis of Child's work in the ballads. Several ballads of which only puzzling fragments can be found in English are illuminated by Child's knowledge of their counterparts in German or Danish. . . .

The direction of Child's endeavors was set by his interests within the field of English philology, which interests tended to go back in time, toward the earlier phases both of the linguistic forms and of the patterns of literature, e.g., dramatic, narrative, which had developed in the more recent centuries. He was also drawn to an appreciation of the individual talent, or individual genius perhaps, as seen in his love for Shakespeare and Chaucer. His equally strong passion for the anonymous folk ballad might seem to fit in rather strangely here, but in fact Child often treated the ballad as though it were the product of some single creative urge, almost as though the anonymous ballad-maker had a definable personality. This sensitivity enabled him to navigate with a clear inner certainty of what was and what was not by his own standards a folk ballad, a matter to be dealt with a bit later.

These preferences were modified by the circumstances in which Child worked. First, the need of the times was for editions, for simply getting the body of English literature into print in accurate form. This is the need which publishers sensed and with which scholars, including Child, would concur. Second, the texts needed for the kind of study Child preferred were not easily accessible to an American. The texts were across the ocean. This last problem was one which Child approached in two ways—either to work from a dependable printed edition to which he did have access, or to enlist the aid of colleagues more fortunately located.

In using the first of these methods, Child generally chose as good a text as he could find and then added to its usefulness by placing the work in its historical context and supplying as much assistance with the language problems as space would permit. Child's first scholarly publication, *Four Old Plays,* described above, reflects his principles here. In the 1850s Child continued this type of contribution by supervising the preparation of several titles in the *British Poets* series carried on by Houghton Mifflin. His own major contribution here was a five-volume edition (later reprinted in other formats) of the poetry of Spenser [*The Poetical Works of Edmund Spenser*].

a cycle, but neither of these attributes is required. The supernatural was often an important element. It could not, however, be introduced gratuitously. Ghosts, as Child explains, should

> have a fair reason for walking . . . In popular fictions [i.e., the traditional ballad] the motive for their leaving the grave is to ask back plighted troth, to be relieved from the inconveniences caused by the excessive grief of the living, to put a stop to the abuse of children by stepmothers, to repair an injustice done in the flesh, to fulfill a promise; at the least, to announce the visitant's death.[4]

The process of assembling all this material is exhausting even to contemplate. Child was based thousands of miles from the texts he wanted to examine. Frequent trips to the British Isles were financially infeasible; Harvard did what it could to assist its faculty's research, but the budget was a slim one. Child made the most of this type of opportunity when he got it, in 1873 managing not only to examine manuscript collections in the British Museum but to make personal contact with Furnivall in London and William Macmath in Edinburgh, each of whom was to become a close collaborator as the work progressed. For the most part, however, Child depended on an increasingly complex network of helpers, working by remote control, so to speak.

A useful aid in this enterprise, as Child got it under way in the 1870s, was the existence of his 1857 *English and Scottish Ballads.* People could see at once what sort of thing was wanted. In fact, many of the actual ballads in the two collections are the same, although the earlier work made no attempt to include every version and was based upon less authentic printed sources. Of the 305 titles included in *The English and Scottish Popular Ballads,* only 90 had not also appeared in *English and Scottish Ballads.* A substantial number of titles from *English and Scottish Ballads,* 115, had in the meantime been dropped; Child felt on further investigation that these were later inventions, not true popular ballads from the oral tradition, or that they belonged in some literary category other than that of the narrative.

Child's helpers, ranging from eminent foreign scholars to simpler folk willing to check a reference or locate a manuscript fragment far from the compiler's study on Kirkland Street, numbered in the scores and sent to Child, as the years went on, enough correspondence to fill thirty-one volumes in the Harvard archives.[5] As the successive parts of the collection appeared, Child's lists of those to whom he owed thanks grew longer and longer. Some of these acknowledgees appear elsewhere in the present study, indicating once again the small and interdependent world of nineteenth-century scholarship. In an 1882 volume Child mentioned, among many others, Walter William Skeat and Henry Bradshaw of Cam-

bridge (both of whom reappear in chapter five, the latter assisting the former); John Payne Collier, who has figured more dubiously in chapter one; and Edward Arber, the former student of Henry Morley, in 1882 at the University of Birmingham. A further category of helpers was made up of Child's American friends, in particular friends able to travel abroad with some frequency; Child gives special thanks to "Mr. James Russell Lowell, Minister of the United States at London."

Of Child's long-distance colleagues the top two, Furnivall and Macmath, gave of their time and energy in ways typical of their quite different personalities. Furnivall's general exuberance and his many literary connections made him a natural contact point. Near the beginning of his quest, for example, Child put an announcement in the British journal *Notes and Queries* asking that scholars willing to share ballad lore get in touch with him through Furnivall. Furnivall also assisted Child in sending out a circular to the clergymen and schoolmasters of Scotland—two occupations which Furnivall and Child apparently thought sufficiently literate and also sufficiently close to the lives of the people—in search of any ballads or fragments of ballads which might have remained alive in the folk tradition. This last attempt was disappointing; virtually nothing turned up; but this lack of success confirmed Child's impression that the kind of material he wanted could best be found in the older manuscripts.

It was with regard to manuscripts that Furnivall performed his most dramatic service to Child's efforts. As something of an astonishing victory, since the attempt had been made before, Furnivall in the 1860s acquired permission to publish the Percy Manuscript, a mid-seventeenth-century collection of early ballads. This treasure had already led a life crowded with incident. It had been found by Thomas Percy, later Bishop of Dromore, in the parlor of his friend Humphrey Pitt in Shropshire; here the manuscript, far from occupying a place of honor, was being used by the maids to light the fire. Pages from both the front and the back had already been torn away. Percy asked for and was given the remainder, took it away, and sent it to a bookbinder who in trimming the edges cut off some of the top and bottom lines of writing. As if these deprivations were not enough, the manuscript then underwent alteration at the hands of Percy himself, who, having become genuinely fond of the songs, undertook to improve them, and in bringing out an edition in 1765 (*Reliques of Ancient English Poetry*) he added, deleted, and polished with considerable disregard for the integrity of the pieces. By the nineteenth century, scholars had become both curious and suspicious about the original. The heirs of Bishop Percy denied access to it, and Furnivall's circumventing this obstacle was a complex procedure involving repeated attempts, fortunate timing, the assis-

tance of mutual friends, and a bit of bribery. The story is told, from Furnivall's standpoint entirely, in the introduction to the edition of the manuscript which Furnivall and John Wesley Hales (a Shakespeare and Milton scholar and an early proponent of the teaching of English) published in 1867-68. This work, in four volumes, was dedicated to Child—a compliment which Child returned by dedicating *The English and Scottish Popular Ballads* to Furnivall because, as Child then said, his collection could not have been made had he not had the Percy ballads in their original form at his disposal.

Child's other major colleague, Macmath, differed from Furnivall in that he had virtually no other literary projects in hand except the collecting of ballads. Macmath held a full-time job as a law scrivener which did not allow him a great deal of leisure time, while Furnivall, though originally trained in the law and for a few years a practicing barrister, had devoted his life to scholarly labors and subsisted on a minimal salary as a teacher of evening classes at the Working Men's College, London. Macmath, however, in his bits of spare time managed to accomplish some remarkable things. He found and transcribed manuscripts in private collections, in archives, in it would seem any depository in which a scrap of old paper could hide itself. (Macmath's earliest communication with Child concerned a ballad fragment discovered in a collection of law papers dating from 1590.) One pictures Macmath methodically ransacking the garrets of Edinburgh. At one point, when the library assembled by Walter Scott at Abbotsford proved to contain a rich vein of manuscript ballads, Macmath devoted his summer holidays—three weeks a year, for three years running—to searching and copying this material. His training as a scrivener meant that his accuracy could be depended upon, and he wrote, of course, a clear and beautiful hand.

Macmath's relationship to Child is a curious one, as Reppert has pointed out in his Harvard dissertation of 1953. Macmath was neither a coeditor nor an employee—simply a volunteer helper, like many others in the project, but on a very large scale. Child did reimburse Macmath for costs incurred in finding or transcribing the texts he supplied, a procedure which brought about their only quarrel when one job ran much higher than estimated,[6] but Macmath's basic motive seems to have been simply a longing to see the old ballads accurately in print. His love of the genre sprang from direct exposure to them, for ballads were known and sung by the older members of his own family. Macmath's aunt, in fact, Miss Jane Webster, supplied Child's collection with sixteen variant versions and thus makes a rare direct connection between *The English and Scottish Popular Ballads* and the elusive folk memory.

Notes

1. Francis James Child, ed., *Four Old Plays* (Cambridge, Mass.: George Nichols, 1848), p. xvii.

2. Matthew Arnold, *Higher Schools and Universities in Germany* (London: Macmillan, 1868. 2d ed., 1882), pp. 143-44.

3. Sigurd Bernhard Hustvedt, *Ballad Books and Ballad Men* (Cambridge, Mass.: Harvard University Press, 1930), p. 223.

4. *The English and Scottish Popular Ballads,* vol. 5, p. 59; commentary on ballad 272, "The Suffolk Miracle."

5. A more accessible sample of this type of correspondence, demonstrating Child's thoroughness and that of his helpers, appears in "The Gruntvig-Child Correspondence," Appendix A (pp. 241-300) of Hustvedt's *Ballad Books and Ballad Men.* The letters cover the period from 1872 to 1883. In 1883 Svendt Gruntvig died, having become world famous as a collector and editor of Danish ballads. Both sides of the correspondence were written in English.

6. [James Donald] Reppert, *F. J. Child and the Ballad* [(PhD. diss., Harvard University, 1953)], p. 31.

Michael J. Bell (essay date October 1988)

SOURCE: Bell, Michael J. "'No Borders to the Ballad Maker's Art': Francis James Child and the Politics of the People." *Western Folklore* 47, no. 4 (October 1988): 285-307.

[In the following essay, Bell offers an in-depth analysis of Child's 1874 essay, "Ballad Poetry." According to Bell, Child's essay not only provides a basic description of the ballad form, but also presents a seminal work of folklore theory.]

Child, for whom the ballad held a place "anterior to the appearance of the poetry of art," believed that this "truly national or popular poetry" developed in a stage of society in which "there is such a community of ideas and feelings that the whole people form one individual." His statement is undoubtedly metaphorical and cannot be understood by those who try to translate metaphor into scientific fact, or by those who refuse to understand metaphor at all.

D. K. Wilgus[1]

Professor Child wished his essay on **"Ballad Poetry"** to be neither quoted nor regarded as final.

Francis B. Gummere[2]

I

Imagine that D. K. Wilgus was wrong. Imagine that Child meant what he wrote to be taken quite literally. Imagine further that Gummere was also wrong. Imagine that Child considered what he wrote in *Johnson's Universal Cyclopedia* to be an accurate, reasonable, if abbreviated, résumé of his views on the ballad. Imagine, then, how folklorists would have to revise what they know about Francis James Child. For one, we would have to acknowledge that Child had a formal ballad theory. We might decide not to accept the theory he held. We might even decide that he was not the paragon of ballad scholarship he is often presented to be. But we would have to admit that his ideas on the ballad were serious scholarship and not the oblique, half-hearted utterances they are said to be. We also would have to face the possibility, given the clearly "communalist" language in even the short extract quoted by Wilgus, that Gummere was, as he always claimed, merely a student of Child's who had adumbrated and refined what his teacher had first proposed. Francis James Child may have been the true father of Louise Pound's infamous "Harvard school of communalists," neither as "great" nor as "sane" nor as free from responsibility for the excesses of "the school of Child" as she and others have wished.[3]

The simplest way of testing these conceits, of course, would be to read what Child published in 1874 and see if it confirms either Wilgus's or Gummere's interpretation of his work. If Child wished his language to be interpreted as metaphoric, then we should have little trouble seeing the poetic in what he wrote. If what he wrote is merely an incomplete résumé of his ideas, then this too should be easy to recognize. If our project is to read Child accurately, however, we must begin by reading him literally. We cannot assume to recognize Child's words for what they are simply because those words appear to be transparent. Neither can we assume we understand his intentions simply because those intentions have been taken for granted so long. The Francis James Child of American folk studies' history, the known Child, must, for the moment, disappear from view to be replaced by a stranger making demands on our attention: our encounter is with a novel, even enigmatic, discourse of uncertain purpose and obscure rhetoric. And we, for a while, will have to imagine ourselves as extremely naive readers asking of each sentence in turn not "What did our Child mean?" but "What did this other Child say?"

II

To begin with, he said more than might be expected. Most American folklorists know Child's ideas second-hand, through D. K. Wilgus's explication in *Anglo-American Folksong Scholarship*, Morris Hart's essay in *PMLA*, Sigurd Hustvedt's review in *Ballad Books and Ballad Men*, or Dave Harker's assault in *The Folk Music Journal*.[4] The original document is not readily accessible, and, besides, what would be the point? We know that it cannot be very important, for if it were, the theoretical debates over the nature of the ballad would have made much more of it, and it would certainly have been required reading along with all the other early seminal works of folklore scholarship, including Child's own great collection. So, Child's contribution on **"Ballad Poetry"** must be a slight thing, a few paragraphs at best in an unimportant, and now forgotten, encyclopedia.

The truth is quite different. *Johnson's Universal Cyclopedia* was a major accomplishment of nineteenth-century American intellectual culture. It was the first American encyclopedia to draw its contributors exclusively from the greatest intellects in the United States, representing one of the first attempts by an American publisher to demonstrate that American scholars were of sufficient national and international stature to serve as the final arbitrators of knowledge. Moreover, the entry on **"Ballad Poetry"** extends over five pages of double column printing, and includes both an extended definition (approximately 4000 words) and an extensive bibliography.[5]

Child begins by declaring that the word ballad signifies "a narrative song, a short tale in lyric verse." The word originally meant, he notes, a dance-song, but its application to its present use is "quite accidental." He continues: "The popular ballad, for which our language has no unequivocal name, is a distinct and very important species of poetry. Its historical and natural place is anterior to the appearance of the poetry of art, to which it has formed a step, and by which it has been regularly displaced, and, in some cases, all but extinguished." A provocative opening for a document supposedly without serious content. Literature, Child tells us, is not just a catalogue of dead genres, of formalized contrasts between prose and poetry or between the poetry of the people and the poetry of art. Literature is alive, and, more importantly, it is evolving: an organic process in which literary forms are born, live because conditions allow them to, and die when they can no longer survive the environment. Thus, the popular ballad is not only a form of poetic expression, but also a distinct species, a first link, in the great chain of poetry. And, like all first links, it is condemned by its nature to oblivion.

The characterization of literature as organic, and specifically as biological, is by no means unique to Child or to his era; both are among the more prominent characteristics by which we recognize nineteenth-century thinking. Still, while nineteenth-century middle-class thinkers may have been generally in the business of turning culture into nature, it is important to remember

that there were several distinct and competing natures in 1874, and it was possible for a scholar to steep his or her writing in organic imagery and never intend it to be read as strict social evolution. As if to illustrate this fact, Child follows his initial claims with an explanation of the relationship of literature to culture that owes far more to Wordsworth than to Spencer. "Whenever a people in the course of their development reaches a certain intellectual and moral stage," he argues, "it will feel an impulse to express itself, and the form of that expression to which it is first impelled is, as is well-known, not prose but verse, and, in fact, narrative verse." More specifically, this ability to create narrative verse is the direct product of social evolution: "The conditions of society in which a truly national or popular poetry appears explain the character of such poetry. It is a condition in which the people are not divided by political organizations and book-culture into markedly distinct classes, in which consequently there is such a community of ideas and feelings that the whole people form an individual." Popular poetry appears, and by extension can only survive, in a society marked by a freedom from gross distinction. Child's age of popular poetry is one in which the people all have access to the same knowledge in the same ways and are all governed by the same beliefs and values. As a result, there is such a uniformity of desire and expectation that, despite their differences of rank, or power, or prestige, the whole community can be said to think and feel as one.

Clearly, though they are not modern men and women, the makers of Child's narrative poetry are not primeval either; they are differentiated from their fellowmen and women, past and present, merely by the external circumstances of their lives. Popular culture produced popular poetry because popular poets could not read or write and did not live in defined nation states: neither the poets nor the ordinary people possessed the means to segregate themselves. And their poetry, Child continues, "while it is in its essence an expression of our common human nature, and so of universal and indestructible interest, will in each case be differentiated by circumstance and idiosyncrasy. On the other hand, it will always be an expression of the mind and heart of the people as an individual, and never of the personality of individual men." Other than language, there could be no borders to the ballad-makers' art because they possessed no way to exclude the mass of the people from participation. Prior to writing, all things that needed to be said must be said aloud and heard to be recorded, and without nations no spoken idea could be stopped at the frontier for lack of a passport.

In Child's opinion, then, the salient characteristic of popular culture was the inability of its members to articulate and identify their own individuality. Child did not believe in mass minds. His psychology was more direct. He had no question that the human biology produced one and only one kind of human being. What distinguished one human from another was the nature of the artifacts they produced in different ages. "The fundamental characteristic of popular ballads," Child wrote, "is, therefore, the absence of subjectivity and self-consciousness. Though they do not write themselves as William Grimm has said, though a man and not a people has composed them, still the author counts for nothing, and it is not by mere accident, but with the best reason, that they come down to us anonymous." People in popular culture were still exactly as people are today, in Child's view; all that was different was the times of popular poets. Popular poetry was anonymous because its authors lacked the capacity to distance themselves from the acts of creation and call attention to the process of their creativity. Likewise, modern poets such as Wordsworth and Coleridge could not imitate the popular ballad because they had no way of escaping the reflexive consciousness of their roles as poets; their attempts at popular poetry always reeked of the self-consciousness of the imitator.

After in this first paragraph laying out the broad strokes of his definition, Child (one might think) would fill in his picture with some historical or textual information about ballad poetry. Encyclopedia readers would expect to learn more about where ballads came from and what they were like. Instead, Child pauses momentarily and uses the next paragraph to refine exactly what he means by the term, "popular." "The primitive ballad," he writes, "then, is popular not in the sense of something arising from and suited to the lower orders of a people. As yet, no sharp distinction of high and low exists in respect to knowledge, desires, and tastes. An increased civilization, and especially the introduction of book-culture, gradually gives rise to such a division; the poetry of art appears; the popular poetry is no longer relished by a portion of the people, and is abandoned to an uncultivated or not over-cultivated class—a constantly diminishing number." Obviously, Child wishes to insure that his readers do not confuse the common meaning of the word "popular" with its scientific use. His "popular" defines a specific cultural constellation in which a whole community knows, wants, and values the same things in the same ways, and he needs to make sure that his readers do not mistake his usage for one that would imply the ordinary usage that popular culture was either the product or exclusive possession of the poor. Ballads might now be found only among the uncultured and unlettered; that, however, was not their natural home but merely a fact of their history, and more particularly, of the literary history that first made them possible and then rendered them obsolete. It had nothing at all to do with their value. "Being founded on what is permanent and universal in the heart of man, and now by printing put beyond the danger of perishing, [the ballad] will survive the fluctuations of taste, and may from time to time serve, as it notoriously did

in England and Germany a hundred years ago, to recall a literature from false and artificial courses to nature and truth."

Child may have intended his pause to merely clarify a sticky point of definition, but it also points to another, larger, historical problem in need of its own explication. Child uses "popular" to characterize the narrative and ballad poetry he was describing because that had been the term used in the eighteenth century, when the materials first began to attract critical attention. Then, in accord with the Enlightenment's use, "popular" represented one of the most positive indices of community (as in the American Constitution's "We the People"). In the aftermath of the American and French Revolutions, and particularly after the Napoleonic era, however, the term was used increasingly in conservative political discourse to characterize all unacceptable movements, and those who participated in them as low and unruly mobs. This was particularly the case in England, where revulsion at the French overthrow of monarchy was deep and extensive, but it was also the case in the United States where Jacksonian democracy and the first waves of immigration were challenging the political status quo. By 1874, the transformation of the term's meaning was complete, hence Child's need to differentiate his use from his audience's expectations.[6]

It is interesting to note, however, that Child did not solve his problem by substituting the term "folk" for "popular," as he could have easily done. He certainly knew the term. W. J. Thomas's "good Saxon compound" had been in use for nearly thirty years and nothing was more final that its claim of equivalence: "Folklore, *the lore of the people.*"[7] Moreover, Child had studied in Germany where he could not have avoided encountering first hand the original "Volk" in use as a scientific classification. It could be the case that he felt "folk" to be just as problematic as "popular" and simply felt more comfortable explaining the scientific meaning of the latter term rather than the former. But I think it is more likely that Child found "folk" even more problematic; there were no folklore societies in 1874 to sanction its substitution for "popular" or to guarantee that it would mean exactly what the now discredited "popular" meant.

Worse, in most usages of the times, "folk" defined a far more encompassing historical community and a far more intense idea of social ties than did the older "popular." In 1874, "folk" still carried its attachments to the German Romantic and philological tradition, a fact Thomas himself was at pains to indicate in his definition of "folk" as that great primeval, pan-Aryan, host tied together by language and blood and whose descendents in modern Europe still participated in the race and culture of their ancestors despite the diversity of their political allegiances. Thoms's very invention of the term "folk-lore" had been intended to call attention to the fundamental differences between the systematic nature of folklife as defined by the German Aryan theory and the disorganization of the random study of popular antiquities. Child's usage of "popular" does not carry any of this baggage. His "people" are the social communities of the recent past, and even though they may reach back to the tribal cultures of Europe during the ages of Greece and Rome, he avoids any claim that they stretch back to the dawn of human time. Child's "people" are a discernible feature of the recent past and derive their unity from the bonds of faith and feudal law of the world in which they find themselves.

His clarification completed, Child then proceeds to provide his readers with an extended description of the ballad poetry of various European nations, beginning with the Scandinavian-Germans who, he asserts, have best preserved their early ballads, through the Germans (whose mythological and historical "ballads" Tacitus described) and on to Charlemagne, who, we learn, had the "old traditional songs of his people collected and committed to writing, and even made them one of the subjects of school instruction." Christianity and its clergy worked systematically to eliminate this "heathen poetry" so that by the fourteenth century nearly all the older heroic popular poetry had disappeared. In the fifteenth and sixteenth centuries, however, "a second growth of popular song appears, some of it springing, doubtless, out of shoots from the old stock which had lived through the long interval, some of it fresh product of the age." Child continues: "These ballads were popular in the large and strict sense; that is, they were the creation and manifestation of the whole people, great and humble, who were still one in all essentials, having the same beliefs, the same ignorance, and the same tastes, and living in much closer relations than now. The diffusion of knowledge and the stimulation of thought through the art of printing, the religious and intellectual consequences of the Reformation, the intrusion of cold reflection into a world of sense and fancy, broke up the national unity. The educated classes took a direction of their own, and left what had been a common treasure to the people in the lower sense, the ignorant and unschooled mass."

Once more Child reiterates his original claims: ballads are popular in the strict use of the word; they are the products of a people who deeply share the same world-view until it is broken by print, Protestantism, and science. What had been the property of all was left to those peasants untouched by the moral and intellectual revolutions that ended the high Middle Ages and the Renaissance and brought on the modern era. What is interesting is that Child wants to guarantee that his audience will acknowledge only certain texts as legitimate and only certain experiences as productive of popular poetry. Child directly identifies the who and the what of

his ballad ages, and more importantly, the specifics of their demise. Scandinavian-German popular culture has sway, at least, from the time of Tacitus in the first century until the Reformation in the sixteenth. Of its first age and its first poems, we know very little; we know a great deal more of the second ballad age: that despite the influence of Catholic Christianity, it remained essentially a popular culture governed by the social and mental conditions required to produce genuine ballads. And like its predecessor, the ballad age of the fifteenth and sixteenth centuries remained an age of "sense and fancy." But unlike that earlier, heroic age it could not withstand the attacks upon its walls. It succumbed to its reformers and gave way to modern thought and self-conscious artistry.

There is something wryly delightful in Child's image of European history from the early Middle Ages to the Renaissance as a world of immediacy and unity untouched by sour national destinies or sober intellect. And the delight increases as that image is refined in the course of his survey. Remarking on the late arrival of Christianity to Germany, England, and the whole of Scandinavia, he notes of those countries: ". . . the peasantry long maintained a higher position. They were not an oppressed and ignorant class, but free men, who shared fully in the indigenous culture, and so were well fitted to keep and transmit their poetical heritage." A few sentences later, while discussing ballad preservation, he notes: "Sweden has a few manuscripts, and Denmark a great number, written mostly by noble ladies living on their estates, and giving the ballads as they were sung three or four hundred years ago, in the lord's castle as well as in the peasant's hut;" and still later:

> The Spanish alone of the Latin nations can boast a ballad poetry of great compass and antiquity. Following the law of analogy where documents are wanting, the origin of these ballads would be put between the years 1000 and 1200, the period when the Spanish nationality and language had been developed to that degree which invariably incites and leads to epic song. . . . During the century that follows we find occasional mention of ballad-singers, but no ballads. As in Germany, the popular poetry, after that first bloom of the national genius, was supplanted by art poetry, among the higher classes, and it passed out of notice for two or three hundred years. A reaction set in the sixteenth century. This was the glorious period of Spanish history, and the return to national poetry was a natural consequence of the powerful stirring of the national mind.

It is when he shifts his attention from Western to Slavic Europe and from cultures in which the ballad is memory to ones in which it lives, however, that Child fully realizes the history he has been trying to create. He writes of the Servians, "a race that has not outlived the ballad era," that:

> Vuk has collected many hundreds of their songs, one-third of them epic, and every one of them from the mouths of the people. . . . So far the Servians are like the German nations: the distinction is that the fountain of popular poetry still flows, and that heroic poems produced among the Servians in this century are essentially similar to the older ones, and not at all inferior. We find the national poetry there in a condition closely resembling that in which it was among the races of Northern and Eastern Europe many hundred years ago. New songs appear with new occasions, but do not supersede the older ones. The heroic ballads are chanted at taverns, in the public squares, in the halls of the chiefs, to the accompaniment of a simple instrument. Sometimes they are only recited, and in this way are taught by the old to the young. All classes know them: the peasant, the merchant, the hayduk (the klept of the modern Greek, a sort of Robin Hood), as well as the professional bard. No class scorns to sing them—not even the clergy or the chiefs.

Child concludes his essay with "one or two general remarks" (in fact three), intended "to prevent misconceptions and to supply omissions." He once more addresses the problem inherent in his use of the term "popular." His concern is still that some in his audience might believe the popular ballad an inferior form because it is now the property of the lower classes. "Nothing, in fact, is more obvious," he writes," than that many of the ballads of the now most refined nations had their origin in that class whose acts and fortunes they depict—the upper classes—though the growth of civilization has driven them from the memory of the highly polished and instructed, and has left them as an exclusive possession to the uneducated. The genuine popular ballad had its rise in a time when the distinctions since brought about by education and other circumstances had practically no existence." Given that this is the third time that Child has made this point in almost exactly the same language, we might safely say that his claim is not "obvious" at all and is made no more obvious by its repetition. What *is* obvious is that he advocated a position as much ideological as factual.[8] Encyclopedias justify their existence with a promise to contain the whole truth. They are the one place where a reader can encounter the most up-to-date version of the structures of thought that define a culture. In reality, of course, encyclopedia articles are written by someone with not only "all" the facts but also a point of view, as Child's next comment makes clear: "The vulgar ballads of our day, the 'broadsides' which were printed in such huge numbers in England and elsewhere in the sixteenth century or later, belong to a different genus; they are products of a low kind of art, and most of them are, from a literary point of view, thoroughly despicable and worthless."

Such words are hardly a kindly critic's judgment, but they do serve to remind us that Child is committed to insuring that his audience understands that popular poetry is qualitatively different from any poetry they have experienced. It is not the poetry of art, or of artful, re-

fined imitators, or of the broadside makers. Neither is it, merely because it might be found there, the poetry of the poor and working-class. Popular poetry is above class, or, more accurately, both before and beyond class. The popular ballad is the poetry of a people untouched by modern civilization's need to create and acknowledge distinction. For Child, it is truly a selfless poetry, a genuine *high* art, possessed of none of the self-display of modern creations, the product of that portion of the community whose lives and fortunes it details rather than of those whom circumstance has made its final owners.

Child's intentions are even more apparent in his second comment on ballad transmission. All ballads, he notes, change with time, but not always for the same reasons. In the mouths of the people, the change is seldom "willful," but in the hands of a professional singer "there is no amount of change they may not undergo" and in the hands of a modern editor "improvements are more to be feared than the mischances of a thousand years." Regardless of the particular cause, however, the nature of ballad transmission produces variety. Passed from one singer to another, ballads took on distinct, local shapes and these in their turn could create their own particular modifications; they slid naturally away from the older forms, from alliteration without stanzas to stanza with rhyme, from heroic epic to historical ballad, from one original text to multiple versions, from narration to lyric. "In all cases, the language drifts insensibly from ancient forms, though not at the same rate as with the language of everyday life. The professional ballad-singer or minstrel, whose sole object is to please the audience before him, will alter, omit, or add, without scruple, and nothing is more common than to find different ballads blended together."

By Child's final point on the question of ballad origins, his intentions are unmistakable. "There remains," he writes, "the very curious question of the origin of the resemblances which are found in the ballads of different nations, the recurrence of the same incidents or even of the same story, among races distinct in blood and history, and geographically far separated." Curious indeed, inasmuch as the problem of independent invention would be the crucial question of ethnology throughout the late nineteenth and early twentieth centuries, but Child's concern is with the older philological version of the debate. Following on Grimm's proof that in the case of linguistic materials the presence of common cultural elements between diverse and distant populations for whom no recent historical connection could be found indicated that at some point in the distant past those groups must have shared a single ancestry, for years philologists had argued that a similar law must function for the whole of the rest of culture. To Child, this claim of a primeval connection stretched the bounds of credibility. ". . . [S]o stupendous an hypothesis is

scarcely necessary. The incidents of many ballads are such as might occur anywhere and at any time; and with regard to agreements that can not be explained in this way we have only to remember that tales and songs were the chief social amusement of all classes of people in all the nations of Europe during the Middle Ages, and that new stories would be eagerly sought for by those whose business it was to furnish this amusement, and be rapidly spread among the fraternity." No magical equation, no gaze back to the beginnings of mankind, was needed to explain ballad correspondence. Ballads were alike because they were full of events and feelings that were common to everyone and possible everywhere. And Europe, for all its principalities, was still bound by a common law, a common faith, and a common taste. "A great effect," he concluded, "was undoubtedly produced by the crusades, which both brought the chief European nations into closer intercourse and made them acquainted with the East, thus facilitating the interchange of stories and thus enlarging the stock."

III

What are we to make of all this? If nothing else, it must be acknowledged that Francis James Child was not talking in metaphors and he was not talking casually. Those thoughts may not be as complete, final, or fully refined as they might have been if his audience had been professionals instead of the general public, but Child is sincere and committed in his efforts to make ballad poetry intelligible. Moreover, Child's language and style are clearly those of a man who is dealing with a scientific question in a scientific manner. His essay on ballad poetry is sober and serious, written in a fashion designed to explain his subject, to establish precise boundaries for reasonable discussion, and also to bring it into repute.

The irony, of course, is that any folklorist need be told that a scholar of Child's stature was serious. Unfortunately, what little we know of Child, the man, comes either in anecdote or in memoriam: first, there is Boston's own, the boy of the dock wanderings who rose to become a great professor of English at Harvard; this Child is usually a grandfatherly, twinkly sort of man who was everyone's friend and favorite teacher. The second Child, and the one familiar to most folklorists, is the great collector—forever seated in his library in correspondence with the other great rescuers of European ballad heritage or pouring over the texts of ancient ballads to cast out the spurious from the genuine. These images, however fail to note that Child was engaged in an intellectual business every bit as serious as that practiced by any folklorist or literary critic today. Francis James Child may have loved the ballads for their "sense and fancy," but he spent his academic life viewing them with "cold reflection."

Why, then, should Child's words have been so threatening that Gummere would turn them into idle musings

and Wilgus into metaphor? The answer lies in misreading and fear. In Gummere's case, his own theory of the ballad reached directly and consciously into the great traditions of continental philology and German Romanticism that Child was rejecting in his essay. Gummere's communalism is, in fact, the critical and scientific accomplishment of that school of folk studies. Even as Gummere wrote, however, the mantle of Child lay so completely over the whole of ballad studies in America that any scholar who stood in opposition to the master's interpretation would have been simply ignored, no matter how brilliant his or her analyses were. Gummere's vested interests, as D. K. Wilgus has pointed out, lay in convincing others that what Child said in 1874 was not relevant to the great ballad wars.[9] As long as Child himself did not want his opinions to be quoted or treated as final, they could not be used as an arsenal against the Communalist Theory. And Gummere was safe to go his own way and still claim Child as his mentor.

In Wilgus's own case, the history of ballad studies was the culprit. By the time he wrote, folklorists were so used to thinking that Child did not have a ballad theory (or worse, secretly thought that his ballad theory might be what Gummere and his followers always claimed it was) that it was better to discount anything he said rather than discover that it might contain the dreaded seeds of communalism, and to leave Child alone on his pedestal as the great collector and editor rather than discover that he might have been an equally great, but hopelessly outdated, theorist. Wilgus's own reaction is the best evidence of this desire. Confronted with all the right communalist words in all the right communalist places, he would call Child's sentiments metaphor and Gummere's, only pages later, wrong. Of course, Wilgus was absolutely correct to separate Child out from Gummere's horde. Child was not a communalist. He was simply a scholar using a standard critical language of his times to express a basic theory of ballad poetry. Gummere, for that matter, was doing exactly the same with exactly the same critical language. The difference is that, though they used the same words, they did not mean the same things. Gummere's approach to popular poetry was a radical revision of the standard practice of nineteenth-century ballad scholarship. His concern with writing an anthropology of that moment of "intellectual and moral development" where even Child's people burst forth in song, required a restructuring of the terms in which ballad scholarship expressed itself. The truth, therefore, is not that Child used a communalist language, but that Gummere appropriated, modified, and, in some cases, radicalized a conventional discourse to suit his own needs.

It is not enough, however, that we merely credit Child with knowing his own mind and speaking it clearly. It is also important to acknowledge that Child is writing folklore theory. The world of scholarship judges the greatness of its members on the basis of their contributions to theory, and, in this respect folk studies are no different. We respect our great collectors and compilers, acknowledging their long hours in the library or the field, but we honor only those few whose work made possible the way we look at or think about the most fundamental issues that make us folklorists and our work scientific. One hundred years of criticism have made Francis James Child a hollow man without theory and without place in the great chain of ideas that forms the modern discipline of Folk Studies. Neither is true. The essay on **"Ballad Poetry"** contains a theory of popular culture both important in its own right and central to the development of American folklore scholarship in the twentieth century.

Child's theory of the popular is important because it departs decisively from the assumptions of its age. The Herderian tradition invented and valorized the folk because it needed a way of rewriting a history that was not in its favor. Herder and his followers desired to achieve political independence for the diverse ethnic communities of Western Europe. Unfortunately, two thousand years of recorded history demonstrated that desire alone could not overcome the social and political ties that modern European states and principalities cited to justify the status quo. The folk were the nationalists' way of positing an original, organically whole, unsullied community who, because they existed prior to recorded history, were free of the claims of political sovereignty that history produced. In place of this nationalistic, idealistic view of folk culture, Child brought the folk into history. His "people" were real and recognizable. They existed because of the particular culture of the Middle Ages and their poetry was unselfconscious and impersonal because that culture, balanced as it was between the ancient and the modern, had not yet discovered the means by which to transform the "mind and heart of the people" into the knowing glances of the powerful and the powerless.

Moreover, Child's point of departure was crucial to the development of a scientific American folklore scholarship. American history simply could not produce a "Herderian" folk. The times of America's history—the Renaissance to the nineteenth century—were too new, and, even if one allowed that America's relative isolation from European culture might give rise to the kind of community needed to create a folk, the time of that isolation was too short to make such a development possible. Child's history of the people provided a way out of the trap of time. His "people" still existed at the time of America's settlement, and, while their culture was atrophying, it was still possible that a part of it might be imported to the new world to survive momentarily. Theoretically, his "people," though they were in history, were not defined by history alone. History created the "people" by creating the conditions wherein a

genuinely popular psychology might flourish. If one ignored history and concentrated on that psychology, or, better, if one reversed the relationship and asserted that psychology created history, then thought and action and not times and circumstances became the determining criteria of what was popular or folk and what was not.[10]

IV

Still, if Child's theory is not communalist, then what is it? To use his own characterizations, Child's approach to the ballad is Romantic in the large and strict sense of the term. Child's voice speaking in the essay on Ballad Poetry could as easily be that of Coleridge in the *Biographia Literaria* or Wordsworth in the *Preface* to the Edition of 1815, or Emerson or Lowell.[11] Francis James Child is an American Romantic scholar/critic, an inheritor of the great traditions of German Idealism, English Romanticism, and American Transcendentalism. His romanticism expresses itself most formally, however, in the ways in which he deals with the nature of the imagination, the dilemma of self-consciousness, and the question of origins. Child divides the mind into two basic configurations: the popular mind, again, is moved by "sense and fancy" while the modern mind is controlled by "cold reflection." These terms may appear merely to convey the quality of the contrast Child was trying to create, but, they are, in fact, the classic romantic triad for differentiating between the mind's ability to perceive and man's ability to think. Coleridge, to cite one of the clearest examples, in Chapter XII of the *Biographia* divides the imagination thus:

> The IMAGINATION then, I consider either as primary, or secondary. The primary IMAGINATION I hold to be the living Power and prime Agent of all human Perception, and as a repetition in the finite mind of the eternal act of creation in the infinite I AM. The secondary Imagination I consider as an echo of the former co-existing with the conscious will, yet still as identical with the primary in the kind of its agency, and differing only in degree, and in the mode of its operation. It dissolves, diffuses, dissipates, in order to recreate; or where the process is rendered impossible, yet still at all events it struggles to idealize and to unify. It is essentially *vital,* even as all objects (as objects) are essentially fixed and dead. FANCY, on the contrary, has no other counters to play with, but fixities and definites. The Fancy is indeed no other than a mode of Memory emancipated from the order of time and space; while it is blended with, and modified by that empirical phenomenon of the will, which we express by the word CHOICE. But equally with the ordinary memory the Fancy must receive all its materials ready made from the law of association.[12]

For Coleridge, the primary imagination is responsible for human perception, tying mankind to nature and presenting a continuous flow of original contacts with the world. Secondary imagination interrupts our continuous awareness of the world. It breaks the flow of perception

and destroys the sameness that results from the primary imagination's transformation of the world into an unconscious, changeless, undifferentiated place; it creates difference. Fancy operates distinctly from both forms of imagination, though like the secondary imagination it operates upon primary sensations. Fancy, however, works only with what is known and given "ready made." It may blend and modify its contents, "choose," and arrange, but it cannot fuse.

Moreover, it is clear that Coleridge saw the two forms of the imagination as the end poles of a process of growth in which fancy was the middle term. Thus, mankind began its collective life flooded with sensation and able only to experience the world as a continuous given over which it had no control and which it could not shut out. From this stage, eventually, fancy emerged to bring order to experience through arrangement. It saw correspondences between the various patterns of experience and, operating as a "mode of Memory," it was able to group feelings and events so that those that seemed like others through the haze of remembering would be called alike. From the interplay of primary imagination and fancy, and yet not as fancy at all, secondary imagination emerged: a synthetic and analytic faculty, capable of discovering the hidden orders of things, and where such order was not present nor possible, capable of inventing that order. Secondary imagination was a finite echo of the original "I AM," and though it could not bring forth something from nothing, it could recreate by unifying what could not be joined together.[13]

Child is not Coleridge, but notice how closely the criteria of "sense," "fancy," and "reflection" Child introduces to distinguish the popular poet's imagination from that of the modern artist correspond to Coleridge's triad. Child's popular poet operates in a world of unity of knowledge and desire, a world of primary imagination, a world without difference. It is such a world of unity that the whole community, for all their differences as persons, live and respond as what the modern world would call a single person. Likewise, it is a world in which sensation is molded by fancy alone. Child's ballad poets do not reflect and they cannot display a point of view. Their expression—of the ideas and feelings of the whole people—springs forth unfettered by personality's canny eye, not "dissolved" or "diffused" through the filter of secondary imagination but merely remembered and arranged with no stamp of authorship.

Child's poetics also articulated the dilemma of self-consciousness in Romantic terms. For the Romantics, self-consciousness was both a blessing and a burden. The source of true originality and the chief way to overcome the deadening sameness of ordinary perceptions, secondary imagination altered sense and gave the power to shape experience into art. But it also put its own dis-

tance between people and the primary experience of the world. The power of secondary imagination to create novelty contained always the possibility that its disruptions might slip into cliché or nonsense. Inevitably, unless it was renewed, its echo canceled out difference just as effectively as sensation's stream. Thus, the Romantic poets were ever in quest of ways to recreate the original freshness of primary imagination, of ways to touch nature with truly childlike awe.[14]

Child, too, saw the value and terror of reflection, though this is one of the points where his poetics diverged from standard Romantic intentions. Though Child, too, was interested in the effects of consciousness on the poetic impulse, he was engaged in telling its history and not in overcoming its impact. His task in his essay on ballad poetry was to describe the historical conditions under which popular poetry emerged into the world, and, particularly, to set forth the conditions by which it evolved from its first tentative impulses, to narrative verse, and through to its shift to prose. Despite the restrictions of space and a lay audience, he made very clear the broad outlines of his intentions. Reflection produced the modern world, modern science and modern poetry, and that was a good. But it also drew a boundary between modern self-consciousness and the simpler consciousness of popular culture. Across this Romantic equivalent of the Fall, modern poets and critics could see only dimly the beauty of ballad poetry, and nothing could bring it under their power. All its forms were ". . . extremely difficult to imitate by highly civilized modern man, and most of the attempts to reproduce this kind of poetry have been ridiculous failures." Coleridge, Wordsworth, Longfellow, Emerson, even James Russell Lowell, Child's closest friend, might write ballads, epics, and songs that gave them access to the original freshness of sensation, but they were not poets in the original sense that the ballad makers were. Ballad poetry was impossible in the modern world, and where it was possible the world was not modern.

Child also worked hard to distance his theory of ballad poetry's origins from the German Romantic folklore theory of the racial inheritance of culture. He does not believe in mystical pasts, or collective (un)con- sciousnesses, or "singing and dancing throngs," or in any of the other rhetoric of racial or collective memories. But this strong dose of scientific realism does not make his position on origins any less Romantic. Child's ballad makers were real people, but his beliefs about those people were just as visionary, just as total and organic as any paean or lament by a nineteenth-century Romantic for his culture's Golden Age. His "people" have not lost their original identity. Theirs is still a natural society in which individuals are not separated from themselves by self-consciousness or from nature by the subjectivity that self-consciousness breeds. Child's people,

quite literally, are not estranged from their work, not severed from the material world, and not split off from their fellow man. They are, as only a Victorian Romantic might imagine them, unalienated.[15]

Given the social and political realities of the United States in 1874, it is not surprising that a middle-class Harvard professor might desire the "people" to be undifferentiated. From the end of the Civil War until the turn of the century, American cultural life was in an almost perpetual state of upheaval. The war itself was a devastating assault on the bourgeois' belief in an organic native tradition, and the facts of modern life only served to further undermine the Gilded Age's belief in order and stability. The sudden explosion of the cities, mass immigration, the migration of former slaves to the city, the brutal expansion of industry, the rise of an American working-class, the creation of professional classes, all endlessly combined to guarantee that no individual felt wholly secure and no locale felt free from instability.[16]

Child's "people" offered a classic ideological stance from which to confront this loss of the center and to claim a social advantage in a disguised form. His theory of the popular accounted for the instability of modern life by demonstrating that it was the outcome of the inevitable progress of human consciousness away from community and toward individualism. But it also provided a catalogue of worthy alternative values. The culture of the popular was produced by a singleness of faith, feeling and social class that was no longer possible. But if democratic political traditions could create a new faith, if the democratization of education could engineer a sincere nationality, if technology and material progress could overcome social distinctions, then the flux of American life might be transformed into an orderly modernity. More importantly, since democracy, education and technology were already the cornerstones of Child's own New England middle-class life, then that life could become the norm against which the progress of American culture might be measured and the success or failure of others to achieve Americanness might be judged.

Child, of course, wrote no such progressive future for America in his essay. In the same way that he was no Coleridge, he was also no Whitman demanding the creation of an authentically democratic culture.[17] Nonetheless, for all its dry scholarship, the hidden agenda of the essay on **"Ballad Poetry"** remains the thoroughly modern crisis of self and community. Implicit in Child's argument is the realization that modern life is premised on a paradox: the more modern one is—that is, the more self-conscious and refined—the more that refinement will lead to a flight from the masses bound by ancestral convention. How, then, is a modern society to involve its best individuals in the ongoing work of com-

munal life? The immediate answer is that modern life can only retain its sense of community by identifying the forces which make genuine social life possible and by insuring that modern institutions promote rather than inhibit their development. Child's rigorous description of traditional poetry was potentially more effective than any polemic simply because it displayed the social form of science. He was reporting the "objective facts" of social history in as clear and concise a manner as he could, with no axe to grind, no special interest to promote, and surely nothing to gain.

V

In his preface to the *Discourse on Inequality,* Rousseau writes: "It is no light undertaking to separate what is original from what is artificial in the present nature of man, and to know correctly a state which no longer exists, which perhaps never existed, which probably never will exist, and about which it is nevertheless necessary to have precise notions in order to judge our present state accurately." His remarks speak both to the magnitude of what Francis James Child accomplished and to what we, his heirs, owe him. Child gave his readers the first published statement by an American scholar that systematized who the folk were, what folklore was and what value folklore served beyond the gratification of antiquarian desires. He told them that the folk were the whole people, high and low, acting as one with themselves and living in a world of shared values. He told them that the folk were not some mystical ancestor, but a people of the recent past before the invention of printing and the rise of nation states drove a wedge between the classes and fragmented knowledge and values. He told them that these "people" were folk not because of their biological inheritance but because they lived in times and circumstances that made them folk. He told them that folklore was the art of the "people" who lived in such times, and that it made itself known by the absence of any subjectivity or self-consciousness in its text or texture. He told them that folklore did not speak to the personal and private but to the universal and public, that unlike the art of their world it did not need special languages or acquired tastes to enjoy its meaning or understand its intent. He told them that folklore belonged to all the "people" because, despite the fact that only one voice spoke in creation, all voices could be heard. He told them, finally, that folklore opened up the past and made it possible for modern generations to look into the actual, historical conditions that made their lives what they were. He told them that folklore was the other side of modernity, that it was the ground against which their own understandings, beliefs and desires figured, where they could understand their growth and evolution as a community.

That he did so without mentioning either "folk" or "folklore" is irrelevant. Francis James Child could not use those terms in 1874 without loading himself down with an unwelcome intellectual baggage. So, he wrote "people" and "popular" and made sure that his audience understood exactly what those two terms meant. His students required no such artifice; less than twenty years later, they would found the American Folklore Society with Child as the first president, call themselves folklorists, and write a new definition of folklore that would say categorically what Child would not. In the 1892 edition of the same *Johnson's Universal Cyclopedia,* William Wells Newell, the chief of their number, would write an homage to Child. Defining folklore as the formerly universal customs and beliefs of the whole community now preserved by the conservative and less educated classes, Newell goes on to assert that folklore is marked best by its "external characteristic," its *orality,* and then continues with an almost exact gloss of Child's major ideas. Folklore persists until the introduction of writing creates a "reading class" who begin to think and act as individuals and ultimately form an "intellectual aristocracy." This aristocracy eventually brings the community "under the influence of superior minds and exact observations" and the formerly universal folk culture is reduced to a mere shadow. Accordingly, Newell concludes: "folklore, or oral tradition, is the supplement of literature; folklore and literature may be represented as two provinces, which taken together include the whole field of human thought."[18] I have no space to demonstrate here the full extent of Child's influence, but this little is enough to make the point that Francis James Child was no metaphor maker speaking off the record when he wrote his essay on **"Ballad Poetry,"** but an active, vital scholar whose ideas would become the foundation for an American theory of folklore. We do him and ourselves a disservice by honoring him in any other way.[19]

Notes

1. D. K. Wilgus, *Anglo-American Folksong Scholarship since 1898* (New Brunswick, N.J., 1959), 7.

2. Among the many places Gummere's comment can be found is in the notes to his article, "The Ballad and Communal Poetry," *Harvard Studies and Notes in Philology,* 5 (1897): 40-56, reprinted in *The Critics and the Ballad,* ed. MacEdward Leach and Tristram P. Coffin (Carbondale, Ill., 1961), 20-21, n. 261. See also, F. B. Gummere, "Primitive Poetry and the Ballad," *Modern Poetry* 1 (1903-04): 378.

3. Louise Pound, as quoted in Wilgus, 6.

4. Morris Hart, "Professor Child and the Ballad," *PMLA,* 21 (1906): 755-807; Sigurd B. Hustvedt, *Ballad Books and Ballad Men* (Cambridge, Mass., 1930); and Dave Harker, "Francis James Child and the 'Ballad Consensus'," *The Folk Music Journal* 4 (1981): 146-164. Of these three, plus Wilgus, Harker's analysis is the most interesting.

It goes beyond merely reading Child and provides a scathing analysis of Child's politics, especially as they effect his definitions of the "people." Unfortunately, in his quest to point out the immensely negative effects of Child's New England conservatism (though he does not identify it as such) on later ballad scholarship, he neglects the equally positive and liberating aspects of Child's transformation of ballad studies away from philological and evolutionary anthropology.

5. Francis James Child, "Ballad Poetry," *Johnson's Universal Cyclopedia* (New York, 1874), 464-68. All quotes from Child unless otherwise indicated are drawn from this article. For two different contemporary responses to Child's definition of the ballad, see, again Hart, "Professor Child and the Ballad," and also Thomas F. Henderson, *The Ballad in Literature* (Cambridge, 1912), esp. 57-72. A not wholly complementary review of Child's work as a ballad editor can be found in Thomas Davidson's "Prof. Child's Ballad Book," *American Journal of Philology* 5 (1884): 466-78.

6. For a history of the rise and fall of the term "popular," see Harry C. Payne, "Elite versus Popular Mentality in the Eighteenth Century," *Historical Reflections/Réflections Historiques* 2 (1975-76): 183-208, and Daniel Cottom, *The Civilized Imagination* (Cambridge, 1985), esp. the chapter "On Taste."

7. William Thoms, "Folklore," *The Athenaeum* No. 982 (August 22, 1846): 862-3, reprinted in *The Study of Folklore,* ed. Alan Dundes (Englewood Cliffs, N.J., 1959), 4-6.

8. My use of the concept "ideology" here derives from Raymond Williams, *Marxism and Literature* (New York, 1977), 55-71. For the purposes of this essay, ideology will be defined as the attempt by one class to represent its interests as if they were the universally valid and common interests of the entire community. In this sense, ideology is both the beliefs common to a single class and an attempt by that class to create a false consciousness about the world at large.

9. Wilgus, 8.

10. An excellent place to see this transformation in action is in William Wells Newell's introduction to his *Games and Songs of American Children* (New York, 1884).

11. Emerson's essay on experience can be found in *The Collected Works of Ralph Waldo Emerson* (Boston, 1903-04). Lowell's lectures mark the one of the institutional beginnings of literary/aesthetic criticism in the United States and provide a valuable context for interpreting many of Child's arguments. Lowell's original lectures remain unpublished, but a newspaper summary of them, including the three of most interest to folklorists, "The Ballad," "The Poet," and "The Imagination," can be found in James Russell Lowell, *Lectures on the English Poets* (Cleveland, 1897).

12. Samuel Taylor Coleridge, *Biographia Literaria,* I, ed. J. Shawcross (Oxford, 1907), 202. Coleridge's contrast of imagination and fancy is by no means his invention. The relation between the two was a consistent topic of literary criticism as early as the end of the seventeenth century and was one of the dominant themes of critical inquiry throughout the eighteenth century. For a survey of this critical literature, see Walter Jackson, *The Probable and the Marvelous: Blake, Wordsworth, and the Eighteenth-Century Critical Tradition* (Athens, Ga., 1978), esp. 11-38.

13. Arden Reed, personal communication, 1985. My reading of Coleridge and its application to Child is heavily indebted to Reed's *Romantic Weather: The Climates of Coleridge and Baudelaire* (Hanover and London, 1983), esp. his Chapter 5, "Imagination(s) and Fancy," 182-205.

14. See in particular Geoffrey Hartman, "Romanticism and Antiself-Consciousness," *Centennial Review* 6 (1962): 553-565, as well as Mark A. Schneider, "Goethe and the Structuralist Tradition," *Studies in Romanticism* 18 (1979): 457-478. For general background on the aesthetic and political contexts of these ideas in the Romantic movement, see M. H. Abrams, *The Mirror and the Lamp: Romantic Theory and the Critical Tradition* (London and New York, 1946); M. H. Abrams, *Natural Supernaturalism: Tradition and Revolution in Romantic Literature* (London and New York, 1971); Leslie Brisman, *Romantic Origins* (Ithaca and London, 1978); Geoffrey Hartman, *Wordsworth's Poetry, 1787-1814* (New Haven, 1964); and Wallace Jackson, *The Probable and the Marvelous* (Athens, Ga., 1978).

15. For a stinging review of this entire rhetoric, see Raymond Williams, *The Country and the City* (New York, 1973). For a discussion of another Romantic's views on alienation, see Bertell Ollman, *Alienation: Marx's Conception of Man in Capitalist Society* (London and New York, 1971).

16. Two excellent interpretations of the effects of the upheavals of the Gilded Age on American culture are Robert H. Wiebe. *The Search for Order, 1877-1920* (New York, 1967) and Alan Trachtenberg, *The Incorporation of America: Culture and Society in the Gilded Age* (New York, 1982). Two other useful works that trace the effects of these changes on intellectual life are T. J. Jackson Lears, *No*

Place of Grace: The Quest for Alternatives to Modern American Culture 1880-1920 (New York, 1981), and Cecilia Tichi, *Shifting Gears: Technology, Literature, Culture in Modernist America* (Chapel Hill, N.C., 1987).

17. Whitman's argument for a genuine popular culture can be found in his *Democratic Vistas* (1871). A shorter version of the argument can be found in his "Democracy," *The Galaxy* IV (1867): 919-933, reprinted in *Democratic Vistas 1860-1880,* ed. Alan Trachtenberg (New York, 1970), 350-366.

18. William Wells Newell, "Folklore," *Johnson's Universal Cyclopedia,* 2nd Edition, (New York, 1892), 452, 453.

19. I would like to thank Charles Baxter, David Hereshoff, Jerry Herron, Arden Reed, Michael Scrivener, and especially Sandra Dolby Stahl and Jay Mechling for their criticism of this essay.

Sigrid Rieuwerts (essay date January-December 1994)

SOURCE: Rieuwerts, Sigrid. "'The Genuine Ballads of the People': F. J. Child and the Ballad Cause." *Journal of Folklore Research* 31, nos. 1-3 (January-December 1994): 1-34.

[*In the following excerpt, Rieuwerts examines Child's evolving conception of the ballad genre.*]

THE MISSING BALLAD CONCEPT

On April 26, 1896, F. J. Child wrote to William Walker in Aberdeen: "I have promised to print in the Autumn, and I want very much to be done with the business" ([in Walker] 1930:33). The "business" Child was referring to was the publication of his monumental collection of the English and Scottish popular ballads. But before the autumn of that year, on the 11th of September 1896, Child died and it was left to George Lyman Kittredge, Child's nominated successor, to see the last part of *The English and Scottish Popular Ballads* through the press. Kittredge found the manuscript "substantially complete, with the exception of the Bibliography, and nearly ready for the press" (in Child 1882-98, 5:vi), yet even so the final part was not published before January 1898.

Since the ninth part, published in April 1894 by Child himself, completed the collection of ballads, the tenth part contained no ballad texts with the exception of additions and corrections to already published ballads. The last part was intended rather as the key to the whole collection, giving "a list of sources, a full and careful glossary, an index of titles and matters and other in-

dexes, and a general preface" (Child 1882-98, 5:v), as Child's advertisement read in April 1894 for the concluding part ten. The general preface by Child, which might have explicated his intentions, never saw the light of day: "Among the Child MSS preserved in Harvard College Library there is a piece of yellow notepaper with a single paragraph at the top and several abbreviated notes, mostly references to books, at the bottom. This little scrap Child scribbled out in August 1896 in an effort to begin at last his long-awaited essay on ballad literature. He died almost in the very act of writing it" (Reppert 1974:197).

D. K. Wilgus has argued that for Child's subsequent reputation, "it may be as well that he wrote no more" (1959:6), since in the absence of an authoritative and definitive article on ballad theory, everyone could lay claim to his work without being faced with a contradictory statement made by the most famous ballad scholar himself. As a result, Child has been perceived as having no ballad concept at all: "One hundred years of criticism," observed Michael Bell recently, "have made Francis James Child a hollow man without theory and without place in the great chain of ideas that forms the modern discipline of Folk Studies" (1988:298).

Such a dismissal is all the more surprising since to folklorists, *The English and Scottish Popular Ballads* has long been *the* standard collection and reference book in ballad studies. Thelma James's famous dictum of 1933 that a "Child-ballad"—as the English and Scottish popular ballad is often referred to—"means little more than one collected and approved by Professor Child" (1933:59) has been repeated time and again and regrettably, it is still widely accepted today that we have no record of Child's "criteria of selection" (see McCarthy 1990:2).

Given the fact that subsequent scholars have found defining the genre difficult, if not impossible, it is neither "our good fortune" (Andersen 1991:39) nor a matter for regret that Child has left us no clear-cut and easy-to-apply definition of the English and Scottish ballads. Albert Friedman, for example, has argued that it is impossible to define the traditional ballad by anything but example (1961:6-7).[1] It seems that many scholars have not gone far enough into the materials to realize that Child had specific selection criteria and knew exactly what he wanted to publish: the genuine ballads of the people. Thus, one might say Child ultimately defined the popular ballad not so much in word as in deed, not so much by theorizing as by editing. And although the collector and editor of *The English and Scottish Popular Ballads* would probably be the first to acknowledge that he may not always have abided by his own distinctions and principles, he offered the popular ballads to the extent of his knowledge of sources. Our discussions of the inclusion of one ballad and the omission of an-

other fall short if they fail to take into account both Child's ballad concept and the availability of the material.

James's highly critical article of 1933, which has since then been basic to most discussions of the ballad, therefore needs to be challenged: the content changes she rightly notes between Child's earlier and later ballad collections, and indeed even between the different editions of one and the same collection, are not indicative of a missing ballad concept, but of a changing one. In the following essay, Child's changing perception of the ballad as a genre will be described in some detail.

The Changing Ballad Concept

Child edited ballads for more than forty years, and it can hardly come as a surprise that his ideas about ballads changed over that period of time. And yet, many ballad scholars today would not even say that Child had a ballad concept, let alone a changing perception of the genre. It has been argued that all of the information about his concept of the genre are "scattered, often contradictory, observations" (Andersen 1991: 39) mainly to be found in his correspondence, his students' lecture notes, and his headnotes to individual ballads. To make matters worse, only a fraction of the materials is available in printed form: Harvard College Library still houses huge stores of unprinted ballad material relating to Child, such as the Child Manuscripts in thirty-three folio volumes. There is definitely no scarcity of material on Child's ballad concept, but only an urgent need to make his correspondence and notes available.

And yet, even the little in print of Child's thinking on the subject of English and Scottish popular ballads, namely his article **"Ballad Poetry,"** is known only secondhand to most American folklorists (Bell 1988:286): the original article appeared in a now forgotten encyclopedia and is not readily available. Indeed, if **"Ballad Poetry"** had not been the source for W. M. Hart's study on "Professor Child and the Ballad," it probably would not have been known at all. Bell argues that Child's article deserves much greater attention because "the essay on Ballad Poetry contains a theory of popular culture important in its own right and central to the development of American folklore scholarship in the twentieth century" (1988:298). In his admirable discussion of the article, Bell not only stresses that Child had a formal ballad theory, but also that his essay **"Ballad Poetry"** is "an accurate, reasonable, if abbreviated, résumé of his views on the ballad" (1988:285).

Still, Bell fails to realize—as have many before him— that this is only *one* of a chain of articles the editor of **The English and Scottish Popular Ballads** wrote on ballad poetry. Child's hitherto unknown contributions to ballad theory—two articles reprinted here for the first time in order to ensure that not another generation of ballad scholars will be accused of knowing Child's ballad concept only secondhand—are not only important in their own right but also mark a crucial stage in Child's thinking on the popular ballads. Both are concerned with the publication of *Bishop Percy's Folio Manuscript* (1867-68). When we take a closer look at Child's ballad concept and the particular steps leading to **The English and Scottish Popular Ballads,** it is evident that the publication of the Percy Folio Manuscript was the most important step of all. Child's changing ballad concept will be at the center of our attention and we will be particularly concerned with establishing how and why this American professor came to edit the folk ballads of the English-speaking world in the first place, while considering what motivated him and why he did it in the way he did.

Two Articles in The Nation: Questions of Authorship

It is not difficult to see why in one hundred years of criticism it has almost completely gone unnoticed that Child wrote more than one article on ballad poetry: Child published his views on the popular ballads in *The Nation,* whose general practice was to print articles anonymously.[2]

The two articles reprinted here are both reviews of *Bishop Percy's Folio Manuscript,* edited by Frederick J. Furnivall and John W. Hales (1867-68). The first review, entitled **"Bishop Percy's Folio Manuscript,"** was published August 29, 1867; the second article, which includes a discussion of James Maidment's *Scotish Ballads and Songs* (1868), was entitled **"Ballad Books"** and appeared on September 3, 1868. Child is not listed in the index to *The Nation* as author of either article, but this was to be expected. As the editor explains in his preface, authors' names were not published and "only the longer articles . . . , and in many volumes only a small percentage of these" have the contributors' names penciled against their respective contributions in a partially annotated and incomplete file held in the office of *The Nation* (Haskell 1951, 1:iv). In the case of the articles on *Bishop Percy's Folio Manuscript,* the author's name is absent even from the files. Child is, however, attributed with the authorship of **"Ballad Books"** in Poole and Fletcher's *Index to Periodical Literature* (1882:88). In addition, the article corresponds closely with information we have from other sources. For example, the author of **"Ballad Books"** suggests that the Ballad Society should reverse its decision and publish the manuscript ballads first and the broadside collections later, and we know from Child's letter of March 26, 1872 to Grundtvig (see Hustvedt 1970:246-47), and also from Furnivall's *First Report of the Ballad Society,* that this suggestion had been made by Professor Child (1869:3).

Although Child has never been credited with the earlier review of the first volume of *Bishop Percy's Folio Manuscript,* the evidence is equally compelling. In the first place, the two reviews are very similar in style and content. And in the second, the review includes detailed information on the Percy Manuscript that only very few people, among them Child, could have had at that time. It is well documented that ever since Ritson's attacks on Percy's integrity and his questioning of the very existence of the folio manuscript (see Furnivall and Hales 1867-68, 1:xvii-xxiv), the public had not been allowed even a glimpse of it, let alone access to a list of its contents (Percy 1765, 1:lxxxi-lxxxv; Furnivall and Hales 1867-68, 1:ix). Given that the manuscript was shrouded with secrecy until it went on loan to Frederick James Furnivall, his letter to the editor of *The Nation* in response to the first review is of particular importance:

> Sir: In the name of my fellow-editor of the Percy Folio, Mr. Hales, and for myself, I thank you heartily for the friendly notice of our work that appeared in your number of August 29. It is the most appreciative and the best review we have had, evidently written by a man who knows his subject better than any one who has noticed in print our work here; and coming as it does from your side of the water, from a writer who evidently knows our old literature so well, it has been a double pleasure to us to read it.

(Furnivall 1867b:279)

Since Furnivall was in charge of the Percy Folio Manuscript, he could not possibly have entertained any doubts as to the author of the first Percy Folio Manuscript review in *The Nation.* And when Furnivall describes the reviewer as an American who is thoroughly familiar with ballad poetry and old literature, he is clearly pointing in Francis James Child's direction. Of all his friends and helpers, the Harvard professor is the only one who matches Furnivall's description.

Indeed, Child is even mentioned by name in connection with Chaucer. The reviewer urges the Early English Text Society "to do something, and do a great deal, for Chaucer, of whom we have still but one text, and who is, critically speaking, unreadable, and will be, until his language has been thoroughly studied in several *printed* versions" (Child 1867:167). Furnivall responds to this plea by setting up the Chaucer Society and he specifically says that it was for "Professor Child of Harvard" that this society for the printing of Chaucer texts was established in 1868 (Furnivall 1869:3).[3]

CHILD'S EDITORIAL PROJECTS

BRITISH POETS

When we put Child's two articles from *The Nation* into the context of his thinking on the subject of ballad poetry, it is important also to realize that Child first came to publish ballads in his role as general editor of a huge series of reprints of British poetry. In the mid-nineteenth century, English literature was very popular in America, but it proved difficult to obtain copies of the original editions, especially of the older English literature. Thus, the market for reprints flourished, and Child's list of publications indicates that he seems to have taken a particular interest in meeting this demand: *The text carefully revised, and illustrated with notes, original and selected, by Francis J. Child* is the subtitle of ***The Poetical Works of Edmund Spenser,*** issued by Child in 1855, but it is applicable to almost all his works.

The first book Child published, at the age of just twenty-three, was a new edition of ***Four Old Plays*** (1848). According to Kittredge, "This was a remarkably competent performance. The texts are edited with judgment and accuracy; the introduction shows literary discrimination as well as sound scholarship, and the glossary and brief notes are thoroughly good. There are no signs of immaturity in the book, and it is still valued by students of our early drama" (in Child 1882-98, 1:xxiv). Kittredge's praise of the young Child's sound scholarship, however, contrasts sharply with a contemporary review of ***Four Old Plays.*** Child presented a copy of the book to J. Payne Collier, the first chairman of the Percy Society, who welcomed it as "a most creditable and well-edited republication" (1850:209), but thanked him at the same time by pointing out important errors and inaccuracies. He uses Child's book "to impress upon editors in this country the necessity of accuracy, not only for the sake of readers and critics here, but for the sake of those abroad, because Mr Child's work illustrates especially the disadvantage of the want of that accuracy" (Collier 1850:209). Collier acknowledged that Child was "in no way responsible" for the poor republication, since he used a defective reprint in England for his own reprint in America (1850:210). However, his scathing review leaves the reader in no doubt that Child's book is no piece of sound scholarship:

> Unfortunately, Mr. Child reprinted in America from this defective reprint in England; but his sagacity prevented him from falling into some of the blunders, although it could not supply him with the wanting line; and his notes are extremely clear and pertinent. I shall not go over the thirty-nine other errors.

(Collier 1850:209)

Child set particular store by the accuracy of the text and to be found guilty of reprinting from a defective copy could not have boosted the young editor's confidence. Nevertheless, two years later, in 1852, Child accepted the general editorship of the reprints of ***British Poets*** in 130 volumes. Although the reprints were advertised as "a complete collection . . . from Chaucer to Wordsworth," they were neither complete nor did they include a volume on Chaucer. The missing Chaucer volume is all the more remarkable since Child made his

name as a Chaucer expert only a few year later in 1862 with his influential article, humbly entitled **"Observations on the Language of Chaucer."** Child must have felt that he could do no real justice to Chaucer. Here we see an interesting parallel to his later ballad collection *The English and Scottish Popular Ballads*: without a preceding publication of the Percy Folio Manuscript, no proper ballad collection is possible, nor a Chaucer edition without more Chaucer texts in print.

ENGLISH AND SCOTTISH BALLADS

Child's 130-volume edition of **British Poets** was based on an earlier collection (*The Aldine Edition of the British Poets* [1830-53]) and thus consisted mainly of reprints he saw through the press with alterations and additions. This involved Child sometimes correcting the text, sometimes collecting and editing the poetry from existing work, and sometimes even leaving volumes for others to edit (for example, his friends James Russell Lowell and Charles Eliot Norton). However, Child himself "selected and edited" the narrative poetry of unknown British poets and published them as **English and Scottish Ballads** in eight volumes (1857-59). In his preface to the first volume of 1857, the editor proclaims:

> The compilation now offered to the public will be found more comprehensive in its plan than any of its kind which has hitherto appeared. It includes nearly all that is known to be left to us of the *ancient* ballads of England and Scotland, with a liberal selection of those which are of later date. Of traditional ballads preserved in a variety of forms, all the important versions are given, and no genuine relic of olden minstrelsy, however mutilated or debased in its descent to our times, has on that account been excluded, if it was thought to be of value to the student of popular fiction.
>
> (Child 1857-59, 1:ix)

English and Scottish Ballads was intended to give the "genuine relics of olden minstrelsy," a plan reminiscent of Percy's *Reliques of Ancient English Poetry,* which offered "select remains of our ancient English bards and minstrels" (Percy 1765, 1:7). Child also follows Percy in his arrangement of ballads into "Books" and their further subdivision "chiefly according to the order of time" (Percy 1765, 1:8): "In the several books, the ballads are grouped with some attention to chronological order, the probable antiquity of the story, and not the actual age of the form or language, regulating the succession," Child explains in his preface (1857-59, 1:x). Furthermore, in his choice of material, Child is heavily influenced by *Reliques,* even taking many of his texts directly from Percy's collection.

Romances, ballads of non-popular origin or transmission, broadsides, and lyrical pieces are to be found juxtaposed to the genuine traditional ballad in both collections, and the only difference between them consists in Child's exclusion of ballad imitations. Although he raises some questions as to their value, he nevertheless excludes the ballad imitations on practical rather than aesthetic grounds: "The addition of another volume to a compilation already so bulky, seemed highly objectionable. Besides, whatever may be the merit of the productions in question, they are never less likely to obtain credit for it, than when they are brought into comparison with their professed models" (1857-59, 5:iv).

Given so much agreement in scope and arrangement, there can be no doubt that Child's **English and Scottish Ballads** was modelled after Percy's *Reliques of Ancient English Poetry.* It should be borne in mind that Child was no ballad expert at that time. The role he saw for himself was that of a faithful editor whose duty it was to select and edit a comprehensive collection of early English poetry for his series that could serve to illustrate "the gradual improvements of the English language and poetry from the earliest ages down to the present" (Percy 1765, 1:8). And was there any better way to accomplish this than to make a widely respected ballad edition like Percy's his model? Thus, there was no need for Child to concern himself with questions regarding the nature of the popular ballads, their origin and transmission. He could fully concentrate on his role as editor. Indeed, he wants it to be known that he has not only taken great pains in selecting the most authentic copies, but has also "carefully adhered to the originals as they stand in the printed collection" (1857-59, 1:xi). He would have liked to edit his texts from the manuscripts themselves, but with none available he has to resign himself to printed collections. In addition, since many of the texts in **English and Scottish Ballads** stem from the *Reliques,* Child is especially interested in the Percy Folio Manuscript in order "to be able to cancel or register the numerous alterations which Bishop Percy made in the ballads taken from his famous manuscript, but that invaluable document has fallen into hands which refuse an inspection of it even to the most eminent of English scholars" (1857-59, 1:xi).

This particular reference to the Percy Folio Manuscript and its whereabouts has undergone remarkable changes in subsequent editions of **English and Scottish Ballads.** In the rewritten preface of May 1860, Child complains, "We have not even the Percy Manuscript at our command, and must be content to take the ballads as they are printed in the *Reliques,* with all the editor's changes. This manuscript is understood to be in the hands of a dealer who is keeping it from the public, in order to enhance its value" (1860, 1:xi). And again in August 1866, the information regarding the location of the manuscript is updated. It is "still in the hands of the grandchildren of Bishop Percy, but unfortunately they are not disposed to give it to the world" (1866, 1:xi). Eventually, in a Postscript to the text, we are informed, "The Percy

Manuscript is soon to be printed by the Early English Text Society" (1866, 1:xi). The rewritten prefaces clearly exemplify the importance the Percy Manuscript was taking on for Child: not having the manuscript at one's command has at first been only a regrettable inconvenience, but it then became an absolute prerequisite for further ballad collections. And yet, Child's *English and Scottish Ballads* was the most comprehensive ballad collection of its time: there should not have been a need for a further collection in any case. So why was Child so desperate to have the Percy Manuscript made available?

THE SECOND EDITION OF ENGLISH AND SCOTTISH BALLADS

A comparison of the various editions of *English and Scottish Ballads,* and especially of the prefaces of 1857 and 1860, surprisingly shows that these changes were prompted by Svend Grundtvig's *Danmarks gamle Folkeviser,* a ballad collection that would have been available in 1857, for it had been published in parts from 1852 onwards. Child, however, was at that time only marginally interested in the subject of ballad poetry, and he does not seem to have taken any notice of the Danish ballad collection until after he finished *English and Scottish Ballads* in 1859. "I wish I could leave you Svend Grundtvig for your leisure moments. I will try to get through with the two first vols in the course of the vacation," Child writes to Lowell, in a letter thought to date from January 1860. He adds, "I mean now sooner or later to make a clean sweep of the whole field, of *Northern* ballads at least" (in Howe and Cottrell 1970:12).

Child was indeed to make a "clean sweep" of the whole field with his later collection, entitled *The English and Scottish Popular Ballads* (1882-98). "Ever since I attempted an edition of the English and Scotch ballads," he writes in his first letter to Svend Grundtvig on March 26, 1872, "I have had the intention of making some day a different and less hasty work. I had at the time neither leisure nor materials, and as you, better than anybody, could perceive, but a very insufficient knowledge of the subject. The collection was made as a sort of *job*— forming part of one of those senseless huge collections of *British Poets*" (in Hustvedt 1970:246).

Insufficient knowledge and lack of material were singled out as the two main reasons for the dissatisfaction Child felt about his own work. He praised *Danmarks gamle Folkeviser* as "a work which has no equal in its line, and which may in every way serve as a model for collections of National Ballads" (1860, 1:xi). But although Grundtvig's ballad collection served him as a starting point and model for a different and less hasty work, Child soon realized that the role of the editor of Danish ballads was remarkably different from that of the editor of English ballads: "Such a work as Grundtvig's can

only be imitated by an English editor, never equalled, for the material is not at hand" (1860, 1:xi). Not having a firm grasp of the subject nor having the material at hand were the two major obstacles to a new and definitive ballad collection. And indeed, it was to take Child more than twenty years to secure manuscripts and material from oral tradition and to gain sufficient knowledge of the subject to feel confident enough to commence editing and printing the standard work on English ballads, *The English and Scottish Popular Ballads.*

PERCY'S AND GRUNDTVIG'S COLLECTIONS AS ROLE-MODELS

An early glimpse of what his later standard work on ballads was supposed to look like can be caught by examining Child's reworking of the *English and Scottish Ballads* in 1860 and 1866. In the knowledge of Grundtvig's ballad collection, Child attempted to give the second edition of *English and Scottish Ballads* a new direction, but the scope for introducing changes without altering the character of the book altogether was necessarily very limited. Although only a few changes could be made to the material itself (Child drops some short romances and adds one or two ballads), the material was now presented in a different light by enlarging some of the prefaces considerably or even apologizing for some original notes and commentaries. "The Introductory Notices prefixed to the several ballads may seem dry and somewhat meagre," he confesses, and apologizes also for the very imperfect references to ballads in other languages: "These prefaces are intended to give an account of all the printed forms of each ballad, and references to the books in which they were first published. In many cases also, the corresponding ballads in other languages, especially Danish, Swedish, and German, are briefly pointed out. But these last notices are very imperfect" (1860, 1:x).

The differing prefaces provide ample illustrations for Child's change of heart and mind. While he offers his first compilation of *English and Scottish Ballads* in 1857 to the student of popular fiction as being "more comprehensive in its plan than any of its kind which has hitherto appeared" (1857, 1:ix), in the rewritten preface of the second edition of *English and Scottish Ballads* in 1860, Child merely states that "these volumes have been compiled from the numerous collections of Ballads printed since the beginning of the last century" (1860, 1:vii). The shift of emphasis is even more apparent when it comes to the role of oral tradition. In 1857, following in Percy's footsteps, Child firmly places the ballad in the past and speaks of it as a "genuine relic of olden minstrelsy, (however mutilated or debased in its descent to our times)." In 1860, under the influence of Grundtvig's collection, Child not only offers "the *ancient* ballads of England and Scotland," but also "nearly all those ballads which, in either country, have been gathered from oral tradition,—whether ancient or not" (1860, 1:vii).

In the light of *Danmarks gamle Folkeviser,* Child makes these changes to **English and Scottish Ballads** in May 1860 "in order to give the collection a homogeneous character" (1860, 1:xii). This homogeneity, of course, could only be achieved by applying a clear ballad concept—something which was conspicuously lacking from the first edition. In the second edition, the important distinction between the true popular ballad and artificial literature which was later to form the basis of **The English and Scottish Popular Ballads** is made for the first time:

> Widely different from the true popular ballads, the spontaneous products of nature, are the works of the professional ballad-maker, which make up the bulk of Garlands and Broadsides. These, though sometimes not without grace, more frequently not lacking in humor, belong to artificial literature,—of course to an humble department.
>
> (1860, 1:vii)

And although this distinction comes close to being retracted by a footnote, which states, "This distinction is not absolute, for several of the ancient ballads have a sort of literary character, and many broadsides were printed from oral tradition" (1860, 1:vii), from this point on it is nevertheless the guiding light in Child's search for material.

The reshaping of **English and Scottish Ballads** in 1860 is a significant step towards **The English and Scottish Popular Ballads** of 1882-98, which to a certain degree can be called Child's third attempt to produce the standard work of ballad poetry. While the first edition of **English and Scottish Ballads** (1857-59) was modelled on Percy's *Reliques of Ancient English Poetry* and the second edition of 1860 was inspired by Grundtvig's *Danmarks gamle Folkeviser,* both forces can still be seen at work in his crowning ballad collection.

The second edition does exhibit "very vital changes" (cf. Hustvedt 1970:212) and should not simply be classed as a reprint of **English and Scottish Ballads,** because only this edition contains a clear ballad concept and lends support to the need for a thorough investigation into the available material from oral tradition and manuscript sources.

Child's Developing Concept of the Popular Ballad

Insufficient Material

It was pointed out earlier that according to Child, Grundtvig's Danish ballad collection could in no way be equalled by an English editor for lack of support by the people: "All Denmark seems to have combined to help on his labors; schoolmasters and clergymen, in those retired nooks where tradition longest lingers, have been very active in taking down ballads from the mouth of the people, and a large number of old manuscripts have been placed at his disposal" (Child 1860, 1:xi).

In contrast to the Danish situation, Child could not fall back on a large number of old manuscripts nor rely on the assistance of schoolmasters and clergymen. Almost all the texts in **English and Scottish Ballads** had to be given from printed collections, but since Child valued a particular ballad primarily for its antiquity and poetic quality, the source of the material did not really matter. However, if his new collection **The English and Scottish "Popular" Ballads** (emphasis mine) was to include only "ballads from the mouth of the people," then he needed to concentrate on material from oral tradition and manuscripts. By shifting his emphasis from the poetic to the "popular" quality of the ballad, the Percy Folio Manuscript assumed an even greater importance. Its non-availability became a great burden to him and he passionately believed that the "greatest service that can now be done to English Ballad-literature is to publish this precious document" (1860, 1:xi).

The announcement he could make at the end of his 1866 edition of **English and Scottish Ballads**—that the Percy Manuscript was about to be published—must have given him enormous pleasure, since he had tried for many years to secure the valuable manuscript. The founder of the Early English Text Society, Frederick James Furnivall, who as an Englishman felt it "a disgrace that an American should take more interest in an English MS. than oneself, and the more a disgrace that in this case the genuineness or falsity of the text of a score of our best ballads was involved" (Furnivall and Hales 1867-68, 1:x), made several attempts to secure the precious manuscript. Despite Furnivall's failure, Child "pegged away" and eventually, after he added fifty pounds to Furnivall's offer of a hundred pounds to Bishop Percy's grandchildren, the right was obtained to hold the manuscript for six months (later extended to thirteen months) to make and print one copy of it. Thus, "the cause of the printing of Percy's MS.," as Furnivall testifies in his preface, was

> the insistence, time after time, by Professor Child, that it was the duty of English antiquarian men of letters to print this foundation document of English balladry, the basis of that structure which Percy raised, so fair to the eyes of all English speaking men throughout the world. Above a hundred years had gone since first the *Reliques* met men's view, a Percy Society had been born and died, but still the Percy Manuscript lay hid in Ecton Hall, and no one was allowed to know how the owner who made his fame by it had dealt with it, whether his treatment was foul or fair.
>
> (Furnivall and Hales 1867-68, 1:ix)[4]

The Percy Society mentioned by Furnivall was specifically established in 1840 for the "Publication of Ancient Ballads, Poetry, and Popular Literature." Among

the fifteen members of the council of that society, we find many names associated with songs and ballads, including William Chappel, John Payne Collier, Thomas Crofton Croker, J. O. Halliwell, Edward Rimbault, and Thomas Wright. Also James Maidment, the local secretary for Edinburgh, and his fellow citizen David Laing distinguished themselves as members. No membership list is attached to the First Annual Report of the Percy Society, but we are told that the number of members, limited by the laws of the Percy Society to 500, was "rapidly filling." Though no record has yet come to light, it would be surprising, given Child's interest in poetry and ancient ballads, if he had not also been a member of the Percy Society. In any case, it is apparent from his **"Bishop Percy's Manuscript"** review and from his list of ballad collections in **English and Scottish Ballads** that he was familiar with the society's printing proposals and its actual publications (The Percy Society 1841:13-16).

CHILD'S FIRST ARTICLE IN THE NATION

In his first Percy Manuscript review, Child criticizes the Percy Society for its poor management and its "excessive antiquarianism" (1867:167). In particular, "a little more good sense, including a stricter plan and a dash of financial shrewdness" were wanting. Among its publications are found, he said, "some reprints of Garlands, and two *poor* volumes of ballads, but with these a large amount of miscellaneous trash which it makes one yawn to think of" (167, emphasis mine). The Percy Society would not have failed to gain sufficient support and to ensure for itself a lasting good name, Child argues, if it had proposed to print "all the Romances of Chivalry and the National Ballads, properly so called" or indeed had attempted to give to the world in full the Percy manuscript, which is "the one thing which a society bearing the name of Percy might have expected to undertake before any other" (167). But the dissolution of the Percy Society was determined in March 1852 (see "Percy Society" 1852:238), and it was left to the Early English Text Society, or more accurately to its founder, Frederick James Furnivall, to step aside from its regular course and to edit and issue the Percy Manuscript as a special publication.

Not unexpectedly, Child is full of praise for the Early English Text Society in his first review. He lifts the Society high above other printing clubs established in England and commends it warmly to "the patronage of Americans." In fact, Child devotes more space to the discussion of the Percy Society and the Early English Text Society than to the book he was supposed to review and to which he himself had contributed so much. When it is mentioned, for example, that "each piece is prefaced by an excellent introduction, all, except one or two, by Mr. Hales," Child could have acknowledged the "one or two" prefaces he himself wrote (167; see

also Furnivall and Hales 1867-68, 1:xxv). Therefore, when Child—an insider—states, "We do not know when an important literary task has been undertaken with more spirit or executed with more fidelity," he clearly means every word of it. While Child says little about the actual publication of *Bishop Percy's Folio Manuscript* by Furnivall and Hales, he deals with the manuscript itself in more detail, mainly by answering three questions: what we were to expect of the manuscript, what it really looked like, and what its publication meant for our understanding of Percy's *Reliques of Ancient English Poetry.*

Regarding the first question, the manuscript was expected to contain "more than thirty of the best and most ancient of the English ballads; in fact, about one-fifth of all that now remains of a precious species of literature in which Great Britain, with (or without) the single exception of Denmark, holds a pre-eminence" (167). Since at least some of the ballads were known to have been "improved" by Percy prior to their publication, and since some of the best of these are exclusive to the Percy Manuscript, there was no way of knowing what to expect in terms of individual texts. Regarding the famous manuscript itself, no nicely written and illuminated manuscript was to be expected, but, as Child put it, "a dirty, scrubby, ill-written, mutilated old book" (167). Only those, however, who worked with the actual manuscript could have known that "it is a folio of 521 pages, imperfect by reason of the loss of the first and last pages and of one half of fifty-four pages at the beginning" (167).

As to its contents: "nearly two hundred pieces of all sorts, mostly ballads and romances, with fortunately only the smallest admixture of moral and didactic dulness" (167). Some of the pieces, however, are grouped together "for good reasons" and published separately in "an appendix" entitled *Loose and Humorous Songs*. These pieces are, as Child says, "the opposite of moral and didactic, not the harmless *coprolites* of a remote age, but rank and noxious specimens of comparatively modern dirt" (167). *Loose and Humorous Songs* is the only volume for which Child's assistance is not acknowledged. He even warns his friend Lowell about these unacceptable, dirty pieces from the Folio Manuscript: "There is an appendix of 'Loose Songs,'" he writes, "of which the editors have made a very ostentatious concealment, which if it ever comes in your way I advise you to put up the chimney (where it will be in its element) or into the fire—where the authors no doubt are!! They are just as dirty as they can be, and I am glad that I am not particularly responsible for their coming out" (in Howe and Cottrell 1970:18).[5]

In the same letter of June 23, 1867, to Lowell, Child privately shows his disappointment about the first volume of the Percy Manuscript: "Poor stuff most of it and

in the main not new—but it's all genuine, bad or good, and answers my purpose" (in Howe and Cottrell 1970:18). Overall, the aesthetic value of the Percy manuscript material was disappointing. And yet, with the genuineness of the ballads being Child's main concern, the publication of the Percy Folio Manuscript answered his purpose: he had the satisfaction of working with the authentic texts from the manuscript and was now able to go beyond the printed versions in Percy's *Reliques.*

With the publication of the folio manuscript, Percy's editorial practice of refurbishing and restoring texts was fully exposed for the first time. However disappointed Child might have been, he does not join in the chorus of those who think "scorn of polish and elegance, and declare the bishop a greater botch than the scribe" (167). Although he equally does not approve of Percy's puffing out, pomatuming, stuffing and powdering of texts,[6] he shows remarkable sympathy for the bishop:

> Nothing shall induce us to speak with disrespect of Bishop Percy. Any one can see from his prefaces that he loved a ballad—not wisely, but well. He was no prig and no pedant, and through all his apologies it is plainly perceptible that in his heart he much preferred the "artless productions of the old rhapsodists" to the compositions of some "who had all the advantages of learning." We also incline to think that he knew the people of his time, and that that "polished age" would not have tolerated the uncouth ballads of the manuscript had they not been first trimmed and doctored by the bishop.
>
> (167)

CHILD'S SECOND ARTICLE IN THE NATION

How Percy trimmed and doctored his folio manuscript material is explained more fully in Child's second review, written after the publication of the manuscript was completed in three volumes in 1868. In it, Child accuses Percy of destroying "the affecting simplicity and artless beauties of the originals," the very reason ballads are admired, by correcting and completing for a polished age "a story which was already complete." Child's verdict in his first review that the taste shown in the choice of pieces was excellent is reiterated in his second with an important modification: "Percy did, it is true, give us the best ballads; but he gave only one, we believe, as it stands in the manuscript, and that only in an appendix" (1868:192). Only one "genuine" ballad in Percy's *Reliques*—a startling revelation. Considering also that less than a quarter of its contents was actually printed by Percy, the enthusiasm over the manuscript and its publication must surely have dwindled. Nevertheless, to Child and those who set "a true estimation on popular poetry" (1868:192), it was a relief to the mind to have this "invaluable and strictly unique collection of poetry" rescued from "the chances of destruc-

tion and the niggardliness of its owners" and to have placed it "within the reach and under the guardianship of thousands" (1867:167).

Thinking about countless other ballads that "perished like the generations of the leaves," Child made himself melancholic, and yet, he knows it is an irreversible process. Ballad times are gone, or, as Child put it more graphically, "A supercivilized man of the eighteenth or nineteenth century can no more think, or *un*think, himself into the mental condition of a ballad-maker than he can put off his flesh and sit in his bones" (1867:167). Child clearly believed that the time for ballad-making is long gone. And unless we want to return to a primitive and uncivilized state of society, "all we can do now, is to put beyond danger what we happen to retain, and to seek out and save what is just ready to perish" (Child 1868:192-93). Therefore, having secured the Percy Folio Manuscript was regarded as only the first step. The next step has to be to try to rescue what was about to be lost.

And indeed, Child was not alone in his endeavors. In his "Foreword," written at the completion of the publication of the Percy Folio Manuscript on March 12, 1868, Furnivall offered to continue with the publication of ballads:

> As we have made a fair start at Ballads with this Percy book, it seems a pity to stop till we have reprinted the whole of the rest of the collections. We are bound to go through with them. I have therefore made arrangements for a *Ballad Society,* which will begin to publish next year, and work steadily through the whole of our Ballad collections. One *can not* be content with selections and scraps.
>
> (Furnivall and Hales 1867-68, 1:xxv-xxvi)

More specifically, Furnivall proposes to print

> the whole of Pepys's Collection in the library of Magdalene College, Cambridge, the Roxburghe and Bagford Collections in the British Museum, the Ashmole, Rawlinson, and Douce in the Bodleian, Mr. Ewing's Collection (if he will allow it), and such MS. Ballads as can be found,—as they stand, without selection or castration.
>
> (Furnivall and Hales 1867-68, 1:xxv)

PUBLICATIONS OF THE BALLAD SOCIETY

The Ballad Society was thus the direct outcome of Furnivall's work on the Percy Folio Manuscript. In fact, we learn from a letter to Grundtvig that Child himself had suggested "the forming of a Ballad Society for the collecting and printing of all such remains of popular ballads as could be found in the memory of the people or in manuscripts" (in Hustvedt 1970:262). Although the proposed society attracted about 200 members before publication commenced, it did not arouse only un-

bounded enthusiasm. To have "all our Ballads" in print is clearly too much for the editor of *Notes and Queries*: "Great as is Mr. Furnivall's energy, we doubt if it will suffice to carry this scheme into effect. What moderate library will be ably [sic] to devote room for the volumes which these ballads alone will occupy?" ("Ballad Society" 1868:428). Sensing that some subscribers might be frightened away by the prospect of being swamped with an enormous number of ballad volumes, Furnivall restates the purpose of the Ballad Society in his reply to *Notes and Queries*: "We do not mean to print *all* the English ballads, new as well as old, but only the comparatively old ones in the known collections" ("Ballad Society" 1868:480). Altogether he envisages thirty volumes, with, he hoped, three volumes to be issued annually, requiring not more than ten years to complete the Ballad Society's work.

Furnivall, however, turned out to be overly optimistic. Right from the beginning, the Ballad Society was beset with problems and not even Child could lend his wholehearted support. In the *First Report of the Ballad Society,* Furnivall gives an account of Child's reaction to the proposed scheme of the society: "Professor Child of Harvard, for whom the print of the Percy Folio had been undertaken, for whom the Chaucer Society had been established, at once said that printed Ballads first, and Manuscript ones afterwards, would not do for him; he wanted his horse before his cart, not after it" (1869:3).

Child voices his criticism of the proposed proceedings of the Ballad Society not only privately to Furnivall, but also publicly in his second review of *Bishop Percy's Folio Manuscript*. The Harvard scholar makes it very clear that although he is generally pleased with the scheme of the Ballad Society, he is "not favorably struck by the order of proceedings": why should they publish the great collections of broadsides or flying leaves first, and the manuscript ballads only "when Mr. Furnivall, or whoever their editor may be, has had time to collect them," he asks (1868:193). Child leaves no doubt that he despises ballads of the Roxburghe and Pepys quality. To him the broadside collections are just dark heaps that needed to be turned in case there is a true jewel, a genuine ballad of the people, hidden among them. He therefore tries to convince Furnivall, who was after all the founder and director of the Ballad Society, to change its scheme and attend to the manuscript ballads first, because these, he argues, are not only "more in danger of destruction," but their value is also "immeasurably greater" (1868:193). By having the ballads from manuscripts published first—and indeed, he feared it might never come to that if all the broadside collections had to be published first—Child hopes to discover "a few fine ballads" and obtain "the genuine texts of corrupted and highly 'edited' ones already known" (1868:193).

Again, the emphasis is on the genuineness of the ballads and their poetic quality. The texts themselves, their language and style, was Child's overriding concern. But not so for Furnivall: he judged ballads, even those from manuscripts, to be "poor in verse." To him, they were only "valuable as illustrations of the social state and life of their time" (Furnivall and Morfill 1868-72, 1:v). As long as the texts were genuine and not highly edited, the ballads answered Furnivall's purpose, and it did not really matter whether they were taken from a manuscript or a broadside collection. To him, there was no particular need to go beyond the printed collections, and indeed, he doubted that there were still "old Ballads of high imagination, deep pathos or sweet fancy" in manuscript form that had not already been printed over and over again (Furnivall and Morfill 1868-72, 1:v). Child, on the other hand, thought it probable that much might still be gathered of the genuine popular ballads by ransacking public libraries and hunting up private manuscripts as well as tracing the singers themselves, along with the nurses who taught them: "From these sources, public libraries, parish scrap-books, and the memory of living persons, it is probable that much might be gathered" (1868:193).

Thus, even before the Ballad Society had issued a single volume, it became clear that Child's and Furnivall's views on the ballad, and especially their reasons for offering them to the public, were very different. If the genuine ballads were indeed "showing the first efforts of ancient genius, *and* exhibiting the customs and opinions of remote ages" (Percy 1765, 1:1-2; emphasis mine), then Child was primarily interested in the former and Furnivall in the latter. But for whatever reasons, they were united in their attempts to recover the forgotten literary traditions of the English-speaking world.

BALLADS FROM MANUSCRIPTS

Furnivall only "very reluctantly" gave way to Child's request and set about "to get together a small volume of manuscript ballads" (Furnivall 1869:3). It was not intended to be the first year's issue of the newly formed society, but as it happened, neither the Roxburghe nor the Civil War collections could be produced in time. Furnivall felt it would be disastrous to postpone the commencement of the Ballad Society's publications, and therefore, he hastily put together *Ballads from Manuscripts,* or as the subtitle more aptly describes the first part of the collection: "Ballads of the Condition of England in Henry VIII.'s and Edward VI.'s Reigns." Furnivall only succeeded in producing the first of the two volumes envisaged. The cause of this failure, he said, was "the newness and difficulty of the subject to me" (Furnivall 1869:4).

By printing the ballads from manuscripts first, as Child had suggested, the Ballad Society not only failed to attract new subscribers, but almost certainly lost some.

Furnivall's *Ballads from Manuscripts* was far from favorably received. As one greatly disappointed reviewer complained in *Notes and Queries,* "Our national ballads may be counted by hundreds, we might say thousands; and in the two Parts now issued, containing some three hundred and fifty pages, we have some dozen ballads (?)" ("Notes on Books" 1869:255). Moreover, he entreats the Ballad Society to steer clear of the two rocks ahead of them to avoid suffering shipwreck:

> In the first place, they must be careful to print ballads and ballads only: not *poems,* like the *Image of Ypocresie* (which numbers 2,576 lines, fills eighty-six pages, and has already been printed . . .) . . . In the second, not to overload the ballads with such a mass of illustration and dissertation as is here hung on to the ballad "Nowe a dayes"—the ballad occupies eight pages, the comment nearly a hundred.
>
> ("Notes on Books" 1869:255)

Furnivall rejected this well-intentioned and well-justified criticism out of hand, making it known that he believed he understood his own business better than any of his critics. He was especially adamant when it came to his illustrations and introductions: "It is not for the jingle that historical Ballads are to be sought, but for the light they throw on the sufferings, the sympathies, the hopes, the fears, the life, of Englishmen in former days; and these must be illustrated from contemporary documents" (Furnivall and Morfill 1868-72, 1:ix-x).

Subsequent parts of *Ballads from Manuscripts,* however, containing ballads chiefly from the Reign of Queen Elizabeth, were no longer selected and edited by Furnivall, but by W. R. Morfill. Although the new editor heeded the advice of the reviewer and filled his pages with more texts than notes and commentaries, *Ballads from Manuscripts* was nevertheless a disaster for the Ballad Society. Apart from failing to ensure a favorable public response and to attract subscribers, it discredited the study of ballad poetry. The items in *Ballads from Manuscripts* were in the main neither ballads nor material taken from manuscripts, and were therefore nothing like the genuine ballads of the people Child had in mind when he proposed the publication, or indeed the Ballad Society.

The truth is that Child himself had wished to be editor of the manuscript ballads, and the collection he offered to the Ballad Society was nothing less than what was later to be *The English and Scottish Popular Ballads.* It was, as Child recalled in his letter to Grundtvig, "the fear of dying with nothing done" which prompted him to action (in Hustvedt 1970:246). His proposal to undertake "a proper edition of the English and Scotch ballads," however, was turned down by his enthusiastic friend. Furnivall argued that Child's project could not even be contemplated for lack of material; and besides,

the Ballad Society had already committed itself to print the Roxburghe and Pepys collections and that that work would take twenty years to complete. Child did not accept Furnivall's rejection, and after much persuasion, "Furnivall half consented to introduce the genuine national ballad into his scheme" (Child, in Hustvedt 1970:247). Ever since working on his second edition of *English and Scottish Ballads,* Child had wanted to make a proper ballad collection, and in a way it seemed appropriate to make it part of the Ballad Society's publications. Given the society's poor financial situation and its long-term commitment, it is, however, difficult to imagine that Child, by using the society instead of a publisher, could really have escaped all control "both as to the extent of the work and the rate of publication" (Child, in Hustvedt 1970:246). Since Child's collection was meant to be the standard work on ballads, he was in no doubt that it would occupy him for a number of years.

FINAL PREPARATIONS FOR THE ENGLISH AND SCOTTISH POPULAR BALLADS

On February 17, 1872, barely four years after the Ballad Society was set up, Svend Grundtvig wrote to Child for the first time, thanking him for "the very flattering mention" he had been given in *English and Scottish Ballads* and offering his help and cooperation for a new and revised edition (in Hustvedt 1970:243). Grundtvig saw in Child, "a fellow-scholar, who knew beforehand the literature in question, and knew how to distinguish the very different kinds of poetical productions, older and later, popular and artificial, which by English editors, ever since the time of Bishop Percy, have been mixed up indiscriminately under the general head of 'Old Ballads'" (in Hustvedt 1970:243). Child was, of course, delighted with Grundtvig's letter. He knew only too well that without *Danmarks gamle Folkeviser,* he would not have distinguished older popular from later artificial poetical productions. The prospective editor of the genuine English ballads was very pleased indeed to accept Grundtvig's assistance, especially since Furnivall only half-consented to Child's proposal and even this "only lately." "Your letter at once puts matters into a different position," Child replied to Grundtvig on March 26, 1872, and added, "I feel sure that I could do the work somewhat as it ought to be done. . . . In the second place, I should at once drop the Ballad Society and seek for a publisher" (in Hustvedt 1970:247).

As we have noted before, Child saw lack of material and insufficient knowledge of ballad lore as the two main obstacles he faced in preparing the standard ballad collection. With the publication of the Percy Folio Manuscript, at least "the foundation document of English balladry" (Furnivall and Hales 1867-68, 1: ix) was at his disposal. And with Grundtvig offering his advice and criticism, the second obstacle was also removed.

Confident that the work could now be done properly, Child launched an appeal for "Old Ballads" ["**Professor Child's Appeal"**] in *Notes and Queries* on January 4, 1873. It is interesting to read on what kind of material *The Popular Ballads of the English Race by Professor F. J. Child,* as Grundtvig called the collection (in Hustvedt 1970:252), were to be based:

> I am engaged in preparing an edition of the English and Scottish Ballads, which is intended to embrace all the truly "popular" ballads in our language, in all their forms. I purpose [sic] to get in every case as near as possible to genuine texts, collating manuscripts, and early printed books and broadsides, and discarding editorial changes not critically justifiable. To do this to the full extent, it is essential that I should have the use of the original transcripts of ballads derived from recitation in recent times.
>
> (1873:12)

Child voiced his interest in even the smallest fragment of a ballad whether printed or unprinted, including ballads from oral tradition:

> Something also must still be left in the memory of men, or better, of *women,* who have been the chief preservers of ballad-poetry. May I entreat the aid of gentlewomen in Scotland, or elsewhere, who remember ballads that they have heard repeated by their grandmothers or nurses? May I ask clergymen and schoolmasters, living in sequestered places, to exert themselves to collect what is left among the people?
>
> (1873:12)

Any material was to be sent to Furnivall. Among those who responded was William Macmath, who was later to become Child's chief correspondent on ballads (see Reppert 1956:512, *pass.*).

Only a few months later, in the summer of 1873, Child suddenly found himself sent to England for health reasons. The eight weeks he spent in England and Scotland enabled him to meet some of his correspondents and to trace various ballad manuscripts, among them those of Herd, Buchan, Motherwell, and Jamieson. "I . . . did all I could to forward my ballad-work," he remarked to Grundtvig (in Hustvedt 1970:258), and with the feeling of having accomplished something, he set about his ballad work with new vigor on his return to Harvard.

"Ballad Poetry"

One of the results of his tour abroad was an article published in *Johnson's Cyclopaedia* in 1874. In this article, called **"Ballad Poetry,"** he elaborated on the distinction, adopted from Grundtvig for his second edition of *English and Scottish Ballads,* between the popular ballads, as spontaneous products of nature, and the broadsides, as an artificial literature. The true popular ballad,

or "the genuine ballad of the people," as he preferred to say, was to Child what "effusions of nature" were to Percy or *Volkspoesie* to Herder. The English language, he complained, has "no unequivocal name" for it and Child sometimes even used the German term *Volksballade* (see Child in Hustvedt 1970:262).

Child viewed the popular ballad as "a distinct and very important species of poetry" (1874, 1:464; see also Rieuwerts, forthcoming). The conditions for its creation and survival no longer exist, he argued, and consequently the popular ballad is no longer a living genre. "Its historical and natural place is anterior to the appearance of the poetry of art, to which it has formed a step, and by which it has been regularly displaced, and, in some cases, all but extinguished" (Child 1874, 1:464). Child particularly emphasized the artlessness of the true popular ballads, "the absence of subjectivity and of self-consciousness" (Child 1874, 1:464). Consequently, broadsides, described as "products of a low kind of art," along with ballads from the mouths of "professional singers" or the hands of "modern editors" have no place in the ballad collection of the people (Child 1874, 1:466).

Since Child saw the popular ballad as "founded on what is permanent and universal in the heart of man," he considered it to be truly international in character (Child 1874, 1:464). Clearly, Child viewed his role as "editor of English ballads" within the wider context of collecting and preserving the genuine poetry of all peoples (Child, in Dal 1978:189). When he speaks of English ballads, he does not, as Harker erroneously assumes (1985:105), refer to the ballads of the English nation, thereby excluding, for example, the Irish and Scottish; rather, he uses that expression to denote all the popular ballads in the English language. And it is interesting to observe that Child's article focuses mainly on ballad poetry not in the English language. "I have been accumulating in our College Library ballad-books in all languages," Child told Grundtvig in 1872 (in Hustvedt 1970:246). As a member (and for almost thirty years secretary) of the Library Council of Harvard University, he was well positioned to do so.

In seeking this distinct type of poetry, Child hoped to recover the earliest literary records of man. All traces of the popular ballad, however small, were welcome, and in this respect, questions of definition did not even arise. For Grundtvig, Child's adviser on scope and arrangement, the matter is quite simple: "The chief point is that the edition contains every bit of genuine ballad lore, and consequently all that *may be* genuine, and I might say, also all that *has been so*" (in Hustvedt 1970:260). It is better to include a ballad no more than ten percent genuine than to lose a ballad one hundred percent. Following his Danish friend's advice, Child included ballads of popular origin, "attested by foreign parallels in

folk-literature," and also ballads of popular transmission, attested by several genuine versions, i.e., versions "not prosaic, over-refined, cynical, sophisticated, sentimental, unnatural, trite, or moral" (Hart 1906:806,866).

In sum, the year 1874 was an important landmark for the subsequent publication of *The English and Scottish Popular Ballads.* Not only could Child report that, with one exception, "I shall have all the materials which I am to look for" (in Hustvedt 1970:265), but he had also formed a definite idea of the ballads he meant to insert. While for *English and Scottish Ballads* he had felt "obliged to include everything that the English had been accustomed to call *Ballad*" (in Hustvedt 1970:262), in the new edition he was finally determined to include only the genuine popular ballads.

PUBLICATION OF THE "GENUINE POPULAR BALLADS"

Although the preliminary work seemed to have been completed by 1874, the first part of *The English and Scottish Popular Ballads* did not come out before December 1882. On receiving the first volume of Child's collection, Grundtvig admitted to "some feeling of paternal pride, and perhaps a bit of national vanity, seeing the plan and the principles of editing and illustrating popular ballads, fostered by me 35 years ago, now universally acknowledged and even carried into execution on the other side of the ocean" (in Hustvedt 1970:296-97). And Child gratefully repaid his debt by saying that he had "closely followed" the plan of Grundtvig's *Old Popular Ballads of Denmark* and had furthermore "enjoyed the advantage of Professor Grundtvig's criticism and advice" (1882-98, 1:ix). It is important to realize, however, that Child also owed a great deal to another man, and consequently *The English and Scottish Popular Ballads* was not dedicated to Svend Grundtvig, but to Frederick J. Furnivall, which he, according to a common friend, in "all ways so truly deserved" (Lowell, in Howe and Cottrell 1970:52):

> My Dear Furnivall: Without the Percy MS. no one would pretend to make a collection of the English Ballads, and but for you that manuscript would still, I think, be beyond reach of man, yet exposed to destructive chances. Through your exertions and personal sacrifices, directly, the famous and precious folio has been printed; and, indirectly, in consequence of the same, it has been transferred to a place where it is safe, and open to inspection. This is only one of a hundred reasons which I have for asking you to accept the dedication of this book from
>
> Your grateful friend and fellow-student, F. J. Child.
>
> Cambridge, Mass., December, 1882.

(Child 1882-98, 1:[5])

Furnivall and Grundtvig were both instrumental in bringing about the publication of *The English and Scottish Popular Ballads,* the one by publishing the foundation document of English balladry, and in a way, also by his failure to discern and edit the popular ballads, and the other by setting the standard and advising on scope and arrangement.

By the time the second part of Child's ballad collection appeared in June 1884, Grundtvig had already died. The deep personal grief Child felt at the loss of his friend and mentor was matched by his own determination to see *The English and Scottish Popular Ballads* completed. For this reason, he took the precaution of arranging his material into some sort of order to ensure continued publication of the work should the necessity arise, and he also nominated George Lyman Kittredge as his successor. Relieved and encouraged that the publication of *Danmarks Gamle Folkeviser* continued after Grundtvig's death on July 14, 1883, Child wrote to Axel Olrik:

> That Grundtvig's magnificent and absolutely incomparable work should not be finished has seemed to me almost a tragic circumstance, both for the glory of Denmark and for the world of letters. . . . Now you will complete it: his chief wish will be gratified, his reputation will be secured, for ever, and yours also.

(in Dal 1978:189)

In this revealing letter Child speaks of the unfinished ballad collection as a tragic circumstance. Only a *finished* work would be for the glory of Denmark and the world of letters, and would spread Grundtvig's fame. There can be no doubt that Child himself would have wanted to finish *The English and Scottish Popular Ballads* for the glory of the English-speaking world and for the world of letters as well as for his own fame, since these three considerations had initially motivated him. With *The English and Scottish Popular Ballads,* Child sought to present all the truly popular ballads in all their forms in the English language, thereby documenting an early stage of literature as well as accomplishing something for which he would be remembered. And Child certainly completed what he set out to do by giving all the known ballads to the extent of his knowledge of sources. The notes to the individual ballads, the indices and glossaries, and even the general preface were to him only of secondary importance.

Although much has been made of the fact that Child did not live to write the general preface to *The English and Scottish Popular Ballads,* I would argue that his work is nevertheless complete. For even if Child had lived to see the publication of the last part of the collection through the press himself, he almost certainly would not have included the long awaited general preface. It is well known that Child found it very difficult to start on the preface, postponing it time and again. In the last two years of his life, Child was in no "favourable condition" for writing a carefully elaborated intro-

duction. He had in mind "a general preface on the characteristics and history of popular ballads," for which he was disposed—quite literally—to "review all the ballad poetry of the world" (in Walker 1930:18). This is a very important point often missed by those who attempt to reconstruct Child's unwritten introduction. Like **"Ballad Poetry,"** the general preface to *The English and Scottish Popular Ballads* on the characteristics and history of popular ballads was never meant to be confined to ballads in the English-speaking world, let alone to selection criteria. There are more reasons why I regard *The English and Scottish Popular Ballads* as complete without the general essay on ballad poetry. In his 1856 introduction to *English and Scottish Ballads,* he had announced an "Essay on the History of Ballad Poetry" for the last volume (Child 1857-59, 1:xii). This essay, however, never saw the light of day, not even in a second enlarged and revised edition, yet nobody to my knowledge has complained about its incompleteness. This explanatory note, written in September 1858, appeared in the "Advertisement to Volume V":

> It was the Editor's wish and intention to insert in the concluding volume an essay on the History of Ballad Poetry. Owing to a press of occupations, and other circumstances, partly unforeseen, this purpose could not be carried out, in a manner at all satisfactory, without causing an unwarrantable delay in the completion of the work, and the execution of the original design has been therefore postponed for the present. What has been written by Percy, Ritson, Scott, Motherwell, Dauney, Chappell, and others, might afford valuable assistance in such an inquiry, but a wide and thorough examination of the topic is yet to be made.
>
> (Child 1857-59, 5:iv)

Furthermore, Child has been allotted only 250 pages for the concluding part. As he stresses in a letter to William Walker: "It would be undesirable to make Part X much bigger than the others, and Part X must absolutely be the last" (in Walker 1930:26). Even if Child had lived to write his long-awaited essay, he would not have had space for it in his monumental collection: the posthumously published part already contains 260 pages without the essay! In short, given the tight printing schedule ("I must begin to print in October," he writes on August 6, 1896 [in Walker 1930:36]), and his persistent ill-health, chances are that Child would have slighted the preface in any case.

For Child, ballad collecting and editing became a never ending process, almost a way of life. It speaks volumes that in 1877, years before any part of *The English and Scottish Popular Ballads* was printed, he thought of "making a second and final edition" (in Hustvedt 1970:274). The one thing that kept him going to the very end was the burning desire that he, Francis James Child, would give to the world in completeness and correctness all that was left, or all that could be found, of the genuine ballads of the English-speaking people.

Notes

1. See also Shields 1991, p. 40: "The body of song which Child called the 'true popular ballads' (*ESPB* [*The English and Scottish Popular Ballads*] I, p. vii) and never really defined except by editing is not easy to define by other means."

2. Daniel Haskell explains that "The New York *Nation,* established in 1865, was for many years, . . . one of the leading journals of opinion and literary criticism in the United States. . . . [T]he articles and reviews were generally unsigned, although many of the leading writers and moulders of opinion in this country and abroad were among its contributors" (1951, 1:iii).

3. It is also interesting to note that Child used exactly the same words, namely that he wanted "to do something" for Chaucer when he wrote his "Observations on the Language of Chaucer" (1862:445).

4. Furnivall and Hales actually dedicated *Bishop Percy's Folio Manuscript: Ballads and Romances* to "Professor Francis James Child of Harvard University, Massachusetts, U.S. at whose instigation, and to relieve English antiquarians from whose reproaches (too well deserved,) THIS WORK was first undertaken" (1867-68, 1:xi).

5. Child's view that the "dirty" matter should not have been printed is echoed in an exchange of letters between a certain Fitzhopkins and Dixon, the editor of the two poor ballad collections for the Percy Society, in *Notes and Queries* ("Fastidiousness" 1868).

6. Furnivall used these expressions in describing the "fashionable requirements" Percy supplied in order to have his ballads accepted by the polite society: "He puffed out the 39 lines of the "Child of Ell" to 200; he pomatumed the "Heir of Lin" till it shone again; he stuffed bits of wool into "Sir Cawline, Sir Aldingar"; he powdered everything" (Furnivall and Hales 1867-68, 1:xvii).

References Cited

The Aldine Edition of the British Poets

1830-53. 58 vols. London: William Pickering.

Andersen, Flemming G.

1991 "Technique, Text, and Context: Formulaic Narrative Mode and the Question of Genre." In *The Ballad and Oral Literature,* ed. Joseph Harris, 18-39. Harvard English Studies No. 17. Cambridge, Mass.: Harvard University Press.

"Ballad Society"

1868 *Notes and Queries.* Series 4, vol. 1:428,480.

Bell, Michael J.

1988 "'No Borders to the Ballad Maker's Art': Francis James Child and the Politics of the People." *Western Folklore* 47:285-307.

Child, Francis James

1862 "Observations on the Language of Chaucer." *Memoirs of the American Academy. New Series* 8:445-502.

[1874] 1902 "Ballad Poetry." In *Universal Cyclopaedia and Atlas,* ed. Rossiter Johnson. Rev. and enl. by Charles K. Adams, 1:464-68. 12 vols. New York: Appleton.

[Child, Francis James]

1867 "Bishop Percy's Folio Manuscript." *The Nation* 5:166-67.

1868 "Ballad Books." *The Nation* 7:192-93.

1873 "Old Ballads. Prof. Child's Appeal." *Notes and Queries,* Series 4, Vol. 11:12.

Child, Francis James, ed.

1848 *Four Old Plays. Three Interludes: Thersytes, Jack Jugler, and Heywood's Pardoner and Frere; and Jocasta, a tragedy by Gascoigne and Kinwelmarsh.* With an introduction and notes. Cambridge: Nichols.

1853-66 *British Poets.* Boston: Little, Brown and Company.

1855 *The Poetical Works of Edmund Spenser: The text carefully revised and illustrated with notes, original and selected.* Boston: Little, Brown and Company.

1857-59 *English and Scottish Ballads.* 8 vols. Boston: Little, Brown and Company.

1860 *English and Scottish Ballads.* 2nd series. 8 vols. Boston: Little, Brown and Company.

1866 *English and Scottish Ballads.* 2nd series. 2nd edition. 8 vols. Boston: Little, Brown and Company.

1882-98 *The English and Scottish Popular Ballads.* 5 vols. Boston: Houghton, Mifflin and Co.

Collier, J. Payne

1850 "English and American Reprints of Old Books." *Notes and Queries,* Series 1, Vol. 1:209-10.

Dal, Erik

1978 "Francis James Child and Denmark after the Death of Svend Grundtvig 1883." *Norveg: Folkelivsgransking* 21:183-96.

"Fastidiousness"

1868 *Notes and Queries,* Series 4, Vol. 2:381, 475, 522.

Friedman, Albert B.

1961 *The Ballad Revival: Studies in the Influence of Popular on Sophisticated Poetry.* Chicago: University of Chicago Press.

Furnivall, Frederick J.

1867a "Bishop Percy's Folio MS." *The Nation* 4:176-77.

1867b "Bishop Percy's Folio, and the Early English Text Society." *The Nation* 5:279.

1869 *First Report of the Ballad Society, January 1869.* London: Taylor.

Furnivall, Frederick J., and John W. Hales, eds.

1867 *Bishop Percy's Folio Manuscript: Loose and Humorous Songs.* London: Trübner.

1867-68 *Bishop Percy's Folio Manuscript: Ballads and Romances.* 3 vols. London: Trübner.

Furnivall, Frederick J., and W. R. Morfill, eds.

1868-72 *Ballads from Manuscripts.* 2 vols. Hereford: Austin.

Grundtvig, Svend, ed.

1853-90 *Danmarks gamle Folkeviser.* 5 vols. Copenhagen: Forlagt af Samfundet til den Danske Litteaturs Fremme.

Harker, Dave

1985 *Fakesong: The Manufacture of British "Folksong" 1700 to the Present Day.* Milton Keynes: Open University Press.

Hart, Walter Morris

1906 "Professor Child and the Ballad." *Publications of the Modern Language Association* 21:755-807.

Haskell, Daniel C., comp.

1951 *The Nation: Volumes 1-105, New York, 1865-1917: Index of Titles and Contributors.* 2 vols. New York: New York Public Library.

Howe, M. A. DeWolfe, and G. W. Cottrell

1970 *The Scholar-Friends: Letters of Francis James Child and James Russell Lowell.* Westport, Conn.: Greenwood.

Hustvedt, Sigurd B.

1970 [1930] *Ballad Books and Ballad Men.* Cambridge, Mass.: Harvard University Press, 1930; New York: Johnson Reprint.

James, Thelma

1933 "The English and Scottish Popular Ballads of Francis J. Child." *Journal of American Folklore* 46:51-68.

McCarthy, William Bernard

1990 *The Ballad Matrix: Personality, Milieu, and the Oral Tradition.* Bloomington: Indiana University Press.

"Notes on Books, etc: Ballads from MSS"

1869 *Notes and Queries,* Series 4, Vol. 3:255.

The Percy Society for the Publication of Ancient Ballads, Songs, Plays, Minor Pieces of Poetry, and Popular Literature

1841 Annual Report—Report of the Auditors—Council, 1841-42—Laws of the Percy Society—Members' Names. London: Richards.

1852 *Notes and Queries,* Series 1, Vol. 5:238.

Percy, Thomas

1891 [1765] *Reliques of Ancient English Poetry, Consisting of Old Heroic Ballads, Songs, and Other Pieces of Our Earlier Poets Together with Some Few of Later Date.* Ed. Henry B. Wheatley. 3 vols. London: Swan Sonnenschein.

Poole, William Frederick, and William I. Fletcher

1882 *An Index to Periodical Literature.* Boston: Osgood.

Reppert, James D.

1956 "William Macmath and F. J. Child." *Publications of the Modern Language Association* 71:510-20.

1974 "F. J. Child and the Ballad." In *The Learned and the Lewed: Studies in Chaucer and Medieval Literature,* ed. Larry D. Benson, 197-212. Harvard English Studies No. 5. Cambridge, Mass.: Harvard University Press.

Rieuwerts, Sigrid

n.d. "From Percy to Child: The Popular Ballad as 'A Distinct and Very Important Species of Poetry.'" In *Ballads and Boundaries: Proceedings of the 23rd International Conference of the Kommission für Volksdichtung, Los Angeles, June 21-24, 1993,* ed. James Porter. Los Angeles: University of California Press. Forthcoming.

Shields, Hugh

1991 "Popular Modes of Narration and the Popular Ballad. In *The Ballad and Oral Literature,* ed. Joseph Harris, 40-59. Harvard English Studies No. 17. Cambridge, Mass.: Harvard University Press.

[Walker, William]

1930 *Letters on Scottish Ballads from Professor Francis J. Child to W. W[alker].* Aberdeen: Bon-Accord Press.

Wilgus, D. K.

1959 *Anglo-American Folksong Scholarship since 1898.* New Brunswick: Rutgers University Press.

Roy Palmer (essay date 1996)

SOURCE: Palmer, Roy. "'Veritable Dunghills': Professor Child and the Broadside." *Folk Music Journal* 7, no. 2 (1996): 155-66.

[*In the following essay, Palmer discusses Child's attitude toward broadside ballads, examining the subtle distinctions between commercial and popular ballads that emerge in Child's writings.*]

The contempt for ballad singers and their wares which frequently surfaces in print can also be found in pictures. Hogarth's famous engraving of a hanging day at Tyburn shows a marginal woman, ragged, raddled and obese, mouth agape, baby on one arm and hand of the other to her ear, who proffers copies of 'The Last Dying Speech and Confession of the Idle [Apprentice]'.[1] Half a century later, in about 1810, an even more slatternly woman, this time sans infant but with hand still cupped to ear—news, no doubt, to those who thought this was a mannerism invented by Ewan MacColl—appears with ballads for sale on the fringe of another execution crowd, this time at Newgate Gaol, in the drawing by Rowlandson.[2]

Singing and selling seem to be synonymous in such contexts, and this is confirmed by another Rowlandson drawing, 'Street Scene', which depicts a ballad singer. . . .[3] The subject, this time male, has his mouth open, shouting if not singing, and he holds a bundle of ballads. The social level at which he operates is clearly indicated by the people who have assembled to hear him: they include housemaids, a boy chimney-sweep and a brick-dust seller.

Such images are amply paralleled in literature, with Shakespeare's Autolycus and Jonson's Nightingale providing perhaps the most famous examples.[4] The very expression, 'ballad singer', eventually became a term of disparagement. Nicholas Worsdale, mate of the *William,* was held to be grossly insubordinate in 1729 when he declared that he valued his captain no more than a ballad singer.[5] Rather more than a century later, Mrs Transome in George Eliot's novel, *Felix Holt,* complains of her son, Harold, that 'he will not listen to me any more than if I were an old ballad-singer'.[6]

Even relatively sympathetic observers made disparaging comments. John Freeth of Birmingham—himself a balladeer, albeit in books at three shillings and sixpence rather than sheets at a penny—wrote in 1765:

> Paupers and Ballad-singers too,
> With all the rag-tag tattered crew,

That often at a glass-house swarm,
To keep their wretched bodies warm.[7]

The radical journalist, W. E. Adams, described in slighting terms those who sold the ballads printed in the 1830s and '40s by the equally radical Thomas Willey of Cheltenham:

> The passage leading to Willey's printing office was crowded on the morning of an execution with an astonishing collection of ragamuffins and tatterdemalions, greasy, grimy and verminous. Soon they were bawling their doleful wares all over the town.[8]

Such wares, doleful and otherwise, were often given short shrift by those literary commentators who deigned to consider them at all. The celebrated 'Q'—Sir Arthur Quiller-Couch—peered with distaste from his lofty vantage point at the 'crab-apple stage of Broadsides' through which he saw 'the Ballad' passing as it declined 'into Sterility'.[9] 'Q' gives no sources in his collection, *The Oxford Book of Ballads,* though he nods in the preface to Child, Furnivall and Hales (his three dedicatees), together with Scott, Allingham, Ritson, Herd, Jamieson, Sidgwick and Baring-Gould. His enormous condescension goes well beyond the broadside. He announces that 'the Ballad has been dead, or as good as dead, for two hundred years', and concludes that to compare it with the work of recognized poets would be unfair, 'much as any contrast between children and grown folk would be unfair'.[10] Even so, knowingly or otherwise, Quiller-Couch admitted to his anthology many items of broadside provenance or influence.

Someone of whom one might have entertained better hopes joined 'Q' in his dislike of crab-apple balladry. Baring-Gould wrote that 'a few—but only a few, unspoiled folk songs have found their way into print on broadsides', and again: 'The ballad-vendor, who vended his broadsheets, did much to corrupt the taste of the peasant.'[11] Cecil Sharp followed suit, once more pursuing the peasant, last seen in England some centuries earlier: 'It was only very rarely that a genuine ballad found its way on to a broadside without suffering corruption. A broadside version of a ballad is usually, therefore, a very indifferent one, and vastly inferior to the genuine peasant song.'[12] Yet, Sharp was interested enough to amass and then draw on a large collection of street ballads, as did Baring-Gould. So, too, did Frank Kidson, who at least was lukewarm on the subject rather than hostile: 'The folk-song collector cannot ignore the ballad sheet, for upon it are the words of many folksongs of which he may obtain only fragmentary versions from the singer.'[13]

The American ballad scholar, Francis James Child (1825-1896), also gathered an extensive collection of street ballads, garlands and chapbooks which is now in the Houghton Library at Harvard University. However, throughout his career he carefully distinguished between what he believed to be 'ancient ballads' and the rest—between 'true popular ballads' and 'the works of the professional ballad-maker, which make up the bulk of Garlands and Broadsides'. The former are 'the spontaneous products of nature', the latter, 'though sometimes not without grace, more frequently not lacking in humour, belong to artificial literature—of course to an humble department'. Child admits that 'this distinction is not absolute, for several of the ancient ballads have a sort of literary character, and many broadsides were printed from oral tradition'. This justifies his 'gleaning' broadside ballads, but he nevertheless asserts that 'the popular ballads demand much more liberal treatment'.[14]

So far I have been quoting from the 1860 Preface to Child's anthology, *English and Scottish Ballads,* which preceded his definitive and better-known *English and Scottish Popular Ballads.*[15] He expresses himself even more strongly in a letter of 1872 to the Danish scholar, Svend Grundtvig:

> The English and Scotch Ballads will not compare with the Danish in point of age. . . . We cannot of course exclude all ballads which have not been taken from the mouths of the people—nor perhaps include all such. The oldest Robin Hood ballads are derived from MS., and very many others of the best and oldest, and on the other hand some ballads written in comparatively recent times, especially historical ones, are found in the mouths of the people. The immense collections of Broadside ballads, the Roxburghe and Pepys, of which but a small part has been printed, doubtless contain some ballads which we should at once declare to possess the popular character, and yet on the whole they were veritable dung-hills, in which, only after a great deal of sickening grubbing, one finds a very moderate jewel.[16]

The use of the word 'dunghills' clearly reveals Child's revulsion from bawdy material. This is explicit in his comment on the 'rank and noxious specimens of comparatively modern dirt, such as would suit the age of Charles II' in Bishop Percy's folio manuscript.[17] Child is even more vehement in a letter advising a friend, should the Percy *Loose and Humorous Songs* volume ever come his way, 'to put [it] up the chimney (where it will be in its element) or into the fire—where the authors no doubt are!!'[18] This is not the place in which to mount a defence of the volume but I venture to suggest in passing that it contains at least one item, 'The Sea Crabb', which ought to have found a place in the Child canon.[19]

In contrast with the 'very moderate jewels' that might be obtained from street balladry, Child believed that there existed old—and old was a key word in his vocabulary—'genuine national or people's ballads'.[20] These were at once impersonal, classless and universal,

produced at a point in social evolution 'anterior to the appearance of the poetry of art', and popular, though 'not in the sense of something arising from and suited to the lower orders of a people'.[21] On the other hand,

> the vulgar ballads of our day, the 'broadsides' which were printed in such large numbers in England and elsewhere in the sixteenth century or later, belong to a different genus; they are products of a low kind of *art,* and most of them are, from a literary point of view, thoroughly despicable and worthless.[22]

For almost half a century, latterly much under the influence of Professor Grundtvig, Child agonized over classification. Making war, not love, seems to have been one of his guiding principles, for he much prefers violence to sex. He is preoccupied with aesthetics and antiquity, though his view of a classless golden age 'anterior to the appearance of the poetry of art' does not stand up to serious scrutiny, or history. His earliest ballad, 'Judas' (Child 23), is from a manuscript of the thirteenth century (some considerable time after the emergence of 'the poetry of art'). Copies of only nine others predate the sixteenth century and over two hundred come from the eighteenth and nineteenth centuries.[23]

If in theory Child held to a particular view of what might be admitted to his grand florilegium, in practice he acted differently.[24] One scholar contends that 'a "Child ballad" means little more than one collected and approved by Professor Child'.[25] Another argues that Child's canon contains only 135 genuinely oral ballads, or about forty-four percent of the whole.[26]

A close examination of Child's work reveals the extent to which he relied on the despised garlands and broadsides. Not only does he cite these as sources for at least one version of a third (106 or thirty-four percent) of the 305 ballads in his canon, but in sixty-two cases (twenty percent of the whole) these provide the prime or sole version. At least two of these are the work of professional ballad-makers—Martin Parker and Laurence Price in these cases—of whom Child so strongly disapproved.[27]

In addition, broadsides account for B versions of seventeen more of the ballads, not counting these in cases where the A version is also a broadside.[28] In three more instances Child refers to broadside texts without giving them,[29] and he prefers to ignore broadside versions in at least seven others.[30]

The biggest single group of Child's prime versions drawn from street ballads includes many of those concerning Robin Hood, with twenty-eight examples.[31] Other items, more or less surprisingly, are 'Riddles Wisely Expounded' (Child 1), 'The Elfin Knight' (Child 2), 'The Twa Sisters' (Child 10, entitled 'The Miller and the King's Daughter'), 'The Carnal and the Crane' (Child 55), 'Dives and Lazarus' (Child 56), 'Fair Margaret and Sweet William' (Child 74), 'Fair Mary of Wallington' (Child 91), 'The Bailiff's Daughter of Islington' (Child 105), 'The Famous Flower of Servingmen' (Child 106), 'The Knight and Shepherd's Daughter' (Child 110), 'Adam Bell' (Child 116), 'Gude Wallace' (Child 157), 'King Henry V's Conquest of France' (Child 164), 'Johnie Armstrong' (Child 169), 'Hughie Grame' (Child 191, entitled 'The Life and Death of Sir Hugh the Grime'), 'Bewick and Graham' (Child 211), 'Sir James the Rose' (Child 213), 'Bonny Lizie Baillie' (Child 227), 'The Duke of Gordon's Daughter' (Child 237), 'James Harris (The Daemon Lover)' (Child 243), 'The Suffolk Miracle' (Child 272), 'King Edward the Fourth and a Tanner of Tamworth' (Child 273), 'The Friar in the Well' (Child 276), 'The Crafty Farmer' (Child 278), 'The George Aloe and the Sweepstake' (Child 285), 'The Sweet Trinity (The Golden Vanity)' (Child 286), 'Captain Ward and the Rainbow' (Child 287), 'The Young Earl of Essex's Victory' (Child 288), 'The Mermaid' (Child 289), 'The West-country Damosel's Complaint' (Child 292) and 'The Brown Girl' (Child 295). In all, this is not only a substantial amount but a wide-ranging cross section of Child's material.

There seems to be no discernible pattern, except that perhaps a smaller proportion of Scottish than English material falls into the broadside category, probably because the trade did not develop in Scotland until the second half of the eighteenth century—a factor, observes David Buchan, 'which contributes greatly to the difference in Scottish and English ballad traditions'.[32] However, I am not looking for a pattern but for evidence that Child's practice is at variance with his remarks about finding jewels in dunghills or 'a dark heap' (as he put it less graphically elsewhere).[33]

One of his (self-imposed) problems was that some broadside texts provided older and fuller versions than those available from oral tradition. In some cases, as we have seen, he silently adopted them. In others he just as quietly ignored them. His A version of 'The Unquiet Grave' (Child 78), originally published in 1868, was 'written down from the lips of a girl in Sussex'. It ends with what some may feel to be mawkish piety:

> The stalk is withered dry, my love,
> So will our hearts decay;
> So make yourself content, my love,
> Till God calls you away.

Instead of this, a version issued several decades earlier by two Birmingham printers has three concluding verses, two with the motif of impossible tasks and the third with a stoic resolution:

> Go fetch me a nut from a dungeon deep
> Or water from a stone,

Or milk white from a maiden's breast,
For maidens they have none.

How can I get a nut from a dungeon deep,
Or water from a stone,
Or milk white from a maiden's breast,
If maidens have got none?

Weep not for me my own true love,
Weep not for me I pray,
For I must leave you in this wide world,
And return back to my grave.[34]

These verses have no equivalent in any of the four versions canonized by Child, and one wonders whether to ascribe the omission of so markedly superior a text to oversight or to prejudice. Certainly, Child's attitude to street literature seems to have hardened in the interval between the publication of his two anthologies. 'The later collection', Walter Morris Hart comments, 'is much more chary of the admission of broadsides or street-ballads: in many cases they are relegated to introductions or appendices; in many more, omitted.'[35]

In passing, Child makes a number of adverse comments on broadsides. He instances his B version of 'The Hunting of the Cheviot' (Child 162) as 'a striking but by no means solitary example of the impairment which an old ballad would suffer when written over for the broadside press'.[36] He does not say 'could', but 'would'. Again, he suggests that 'a collation'—by which I take it he means a comparison—between his A version of 'Sir Andrew Barton' (Child 167), from Percy's manuscript, and his B version, from seven broadsides, 'will show how ballads were retrenched and marred in the process of preparing them for the vulgar press'.[37]

Yet Child did make concessions—in words, that is, as well as tacitly—to broadsides. His M version of 'Young Beichan' (Child 53) is retained, despite being 'probably a broadside or stall copy', on the grounds that it 'preserves a very ancient traditional feature'.[38] He concedes that 'tradition does not stop when a ballad gets into print',[39] and that it may exert an influence on subsequent printings. On 'Prince Heathen' (Child 104) he comments: 'the fragment A . . . is partly explained by B, which is no doubt some stall-copy, reshaped from tradition.'[40] In the case of 'The Baffled Knight' (Child 112), 'E is, in all probability, a broadside copy modified by tradition.'[41] Conversely, he allows that even his paragon, Mrs Brown of Falkland, Fife, might have been influenced by print, while contending that 'no Scottish ballads are superior in kind' to those she recited.[42]

Child did not set out merely to accumulate as many versions as possible of his chosen ballads, or if he did it was only to select those which came closest to the criteria he had established. Had he been so minded, he could have studied the extent to which the 'vulgar press'

disseminated items from his canon during a particular period, in a particular place, or in the work of a particular printer. For example, 'Lady Isabel and the Elf-Knight' (Child 4) has as its E version 'the common English stall copy' entitled 'The Outlandish Knight'.[43] H. O. Nygard has suggested with reference to this ballad that 'the entire tradition in England and Scotland is influenced by the broadside press, which seems to have given the song its currency'.[44] As early as 1827 J. H. Dixon wrote:

> A friend of mine, who resided for some years on the borders, used to amuse himself by collecting old ballads, printed on halfpenny sheets, and hawked up and down by itinerant minstrels. In his common-place book I found one, entitled 'The Outlandish Knight', evidently, from the style, of considerable antiquity, which appears to have escaped the notice of Percy and other collectors. Since then I have met with a printed one, from the popular press of Mr Pitts, the six-yards-for-a-penny song-publisher, who informs me that he has printed it 'ever since he was a printer [1802], and that Mr Marshall, his predecessor, printed it before him'.[45]

In offering the text, Dixon felt that he had to 'expunge', as he put it, certain 'expressions *contra bonos mores*' (the vulgar press again) which seem to have boiled down to the scandalous expressions 'silken stays' and 'naked woman'. In further reticence he left the letter unsigned but felt it desirable to add 'a few stanzas, wherein I have endeavoured to preserve the simplicity of the original', this being the putative better-quality article which existed before Marshall and Pitts got their inky hands on it. One verse will suffice as an example. It comes after the 'damoselle', as Dixon styles her, has pushed the knight into the sea:

> That ocean wave was the false one's grave,
> For he sunk right hastily;
> Though with dying voice faint, he pray'd to his saint,
> And utter'd an Ave Marie.[46]

Dixon had the good sense to drop his own verses in 1846 when he published the 'common English stall copy' of 'The Outlandish Knight',[47] presumably from Pitts.[48] Later still, in 1868, he acknowledged his 'juvenile' letter of 1827, adding this information:

> My visit to Mr Pitts led to an intimacy between us. He was at that time quite blind. I was somewhat surprised to find in the ballad-printer of Seven Dials a gentlemanly, well-educated man, with a wonderful store of information on ballad and chapbook literature.[49]

The ballad was also issued in London by Birt, Catnach, Disley, Fortey, and Such, as well as by Pitts, which gives an indication of its popularity.[50] Further afield, editions appeared in Birmingham (printed respectively by J. Russell and W. Wright), Brighton (Hook), Edinburgh (Charles Sanderson), Manchester (Pearson), Portsea [Portsmouth] (Williams), Worcester (Sefton), and

probably elsewhere.[51] It would thus be possible to plot the spread of the ballad in space and also in time, given the dating of the printers, and the Sanderson firm in Edinburgh was in existence as late as the 1940s.

Similar studies of how other Child ballads fared in this way might be instructive, especially if the results were compared and contrasted with records deriving from oral tradition. One might also ask, hoping not to fall to the level of a parlour game, which ballads of broadside origin Child might have additionally canonized. 'The Boatswain of Dover', 'Box on her Head', 'Fanny Blair', 'The Golden Glove', 'The Green Bed', 'The Sheffield Apprentice', 'Thorney Moor Woods', 'Van Dieman's Land' and 'The Week before Easter' would be among my candidates. Most of these Child would have dismissed out of hand as belonging to 'an humble department' of 'artificial literature'. Yet they would satisfy many of his criteria: 'a short tale in lyric verse', 'an expression of the mind and heart of the people', 'the absence of subjectivity and self-consciousness', 'the author counts for nothing', 'handed down by long-repeated tradition'.[52]

Among them I have taken a particular interest in 'Van Dieman's Land', in which three poachers (one of them from Nottingham) are transported for fourteen years, their only consolation provided by a female convict from Birmingham. It is possible to speculate that the ballad, inspired by events in Warwickshire, was first published in the Midlands in about 1830 before being reprinted at least a dozen times elsewhere.[53] In editions produced as far apart as Portsmouth and Glasgow the topographical detail remains constant, though a version printed in Preston removes the scene to Dublin and Galway.[54]

Success spawned a sequel, 'Young Henry the Poacher', in which the Warwickshire narrator and his five comrades are again transported to Van Diemen's Land, though Sydney is mentioned as their place of confinement. Solace this time comes from a woman who hails from Wolverhampton. Again, there are frequent printings, with topography constant in some but varied to Hertfordshire or Lancashire in others.[55]

Both street ballads entered oral tradition, sometimes hybridizing as they did so. They changed and developed. 'Van Dieman's Land', as printed in Glasgow in the 1850s by James Lindsay, retained the Nottingham-Birmingham terminology but added this coda:

> Now if I had a thousand pounds laid down all in my
> hand,
> I'd give it all for liberty, if that I could command;
> Again to England I'd return, and be a happy man,
> And bid adieu to poaching and to Van Dieman's
> Land.[56]

However, some eighty years later, when the song reached John Ord through oral transmission, its protagonists hailed from Glasgow and Dundee, and their grief mingled with defiance:

> Although the poor of Scotland do labour and do toil.
> They're robbed of every blessing and produce of the
> soil;
> Your proud, imperious landlords, if we break their
> command,
> They'll send you to the British hulks, or to Van Di-
> eman's Land.[57]

The same verse occurs in the version sung by Jimmy McBeath (see Appendix).

With a heavy charge of emotion and of history, 'Van Dieman's Land' and 'Young Henry the Poacher' (a version of the latter from Walter Pardon is also included in the Appendix) were sung through much of the English-speaking world for well over a century. Indeed, they remain in oral circulation to this day, or did so until very recently. One wonders whether Professor Child might not have plucked them from the dunghill.

Child was well acquainted with the work of the eighteenth-century philosopher, Herder, and he followed him in adhering to 'the true, genuine, characteristic song of a people' which came from the putatively unsullied wellsprings of tradition. When these 'dried up', only 'muck and weeds' remained.[58] For Herder this had happened by the 1770s; a century later Child asserted: 'The fountain of oral tradition, though still flowing copiously in some Scandinavian countries, is now nearly dry in England and Scotland.'[59] He could not know that the living water would continue to well up for another hundred years, though one might reproach him for his lack of faith in the process. Child saw plenty of 'muck and weeds', often in the shape of street ballads, but despite their theoretical excommunication he quietly admitted a good many, as we have seen, to the ranks of the 305 which he canonized.

Notes

1. This has been widely reproduced, including in Christopher Hibbert, *The Road to Tybum: The Story of Jack Sheppard and the Eighteenth Century Underworld* (London: Longmans, Green, 1957), facing p. 129.

2. Reproduced in David D. Cooper, *The Lesson of the Scaffold* (London: Allen Lane, 1974), between pp. 84 and 85. A kind of close-up of the same or a similar figure is shown in Rowlandson's 'Last Dying Speech and Confession' (Cooper, facing p. 84).

3. Reproduced in John Hayes, *Rowlandson Watercolours and Drawings* (London: Phaidon Press,

1972), plate 127, and in Roy Palmer, *The Sound of History: Songs and Social Comment* (Oxford: Oxford University Press, 1988), p. 10.

4. Respectively in *A Winter's Tale* and *Bartholomew Fair.*

5. Marcus Rediker, *Between the Devil and the Deep Blue Sea: Merchant Seamen, Pirates and the Anglo-American Maritime World, 1700-1750* (Cambridge: Cambridge University Press, 1987), p. 166.

6. George Eliot, *Felix Holt, the Radical,* 3 vols (Edinburgh and London: W. Blackwood, 1866), III, 133 (Chapter 42).

7. John Freeth, 'Hospitality', in *Poems of Warwickshire: An Anthology,* ed. by Roger Pringle (Kineton: Roundwood Press, 1980), p. 51.

8. William Edwin Adams, *Memoirs of a Social Atom,* 2 vols (London: Hutchinson, 1903; repr. New York: Kelley, 1968), I, 143.

9. *The Oxford Book of Ballads,* ed. by A. T. Quiller-Couch (Oxford: Clarendon Press, 1910; repr. 1927), p. vii.

10. Quiller-Couch, p. xvi.

11. Sabine Baring-Gould, *Strange Survivals: Some Chapters in the History of Man* (London: Methuen, 1892), pp. 199 and 213.

12. Cecil J. Sharp, *English Folk Song: Some Conclusions,* 4th edn, rev. by Maud Karpeles (London: Mercury Books, 1965), p. 125.

13. Frank Kidson, 'English Folk-Song', in Frank Kidson and Mary Neal, *English Folk-Song and Dance* (Cambridge: Cambridge University Press, 1915), pp. 1-94 (p. 85).

14. *English and Scottish Ballads,* ed. by F. J. Child, 8 vols (Boston, MA: Little, Brown, 1875), pp. vii-viii (Preface to the 1860 edn). Originally published: Boston, MA: Shepard, Clark & Brown, 1857-59.

15. *The English and Scottish Popular Ballads,* ed. by F. J. Child, 5 vols (Boston and New York: Houghton, Mifflin, 1882-98; repr. New York: Dover, 1965).

16. F. J. Child, letter of 25 August 1872, in *Ballad Books and Ballad Men: Raids and Rescues in Britain, America and the Scandinavian North since 1800,* by S. B. Hustvedt (Cambridge, MA: Harvard University Press, 1930), p. 253. I am indebted to Leslie Shepard for this reference.

17. [F. J. Child], 'Bishop Percy's Folio Manuscript' [anonymously published review], *The Nation* (29 August 1867), p. 167; repr. in Sigrid Rieuwerts, '"The Genuine Ballads of the People": F. J. Child and the Ballad Cause', *Journal of Folklore Research,* 31 (1994), 1-34 (pp. 27-29; quotation from p. 29). I am grateful to Sigrid Rieuwerts for communicating a copy of her paper.

18. Letter to James Russell Lowell, 23 June 1867, in M. A. DeWolfe Flowe and G. W. Cottrell, *The Scholar-Friends: Letters of Francis James Child and James Russell Lowell* (Westport, CN: Greenwood, 1970), p. 18.

19. *Bishop Percy's Folio Manuscript: Loose and Humorous Songs,* ed. by Frederick J. Furnivall and John W. Hales (London: Trübner, 1867), pp. 99-100.

20. See note 16.

21. F. J. Child, 'Ballad Poetry', in *Universal Cyclopaedia and Atlas,* ed. by Rossiter Johnson, rev. and enl. by Charles K. Adams, 12 vols (New York: Appleton, 1908), I, 464-68, (p. 464). I am indebted to Leslie Shepard for a copy of this article. The suggestion by D. K. Wilgus that Child's comments are 'metaphorical' is rejected by Michael J. Bell in his article, '"No Borders to the Ballad Maker's Art": Francis James Child and the Politics of the People', *Western Folklore,* 47 (1988), 285-307.

22. Child, 'Ballad Poetry', p. 466.

23. See E. Flügel, 'Zur Chronologie der Englischen Balladen', *Anglia,* 21, n.s. 51 (1899), 312-58.

24. See Dave Harker, 'Francis James Child and the "Ballad Consensus"', *Folk Music Journal,* 4.2 (1981), 146-64.

25. Thelma G. James, 'The English and Scottish Popular Ballads of Francis J. Child', *Journal of American Folklore,* 46 (1933), 51-68 (p. 59).

26. J. Barre Toelken, 'An Oral Canon for the Child Ballads: Construction and Application', *Journal of the Folklore Institute,* 4 (1967), 75-101 (p. 92). I have reservations about some of the Child ballads which Toelken excludes; David Buchan takes the view that 'Child possessed a remarkable capacity for distinguishing the stylistic traits of oral—or as he would call it, popular—balladry' (*The Ballad and the Folk,* London: Routledge and Kegan Paul, 1972, p. 277).

27. Parker, 'A True Tale of Robin Hood' (Child 154), and Price, 'Robin Hood's Golden Prize' (Child 147a).

28. Child 45, 46, 54, 84, 109, 120, 122, 123, 142, 145, 162, 167, 207, 233, 271, 274, 279.

29. Child 228, 248 and 278 (Addendum).

30. Child 78, entitled 'The Weeping Lover' (see below); 170, entitled 'Death of the Royal Queen Jane', printed by Collard of Bristol (British Library, 'A Collection of Ballads Printed at Various Places in the Provinces', 1876 e.3, fol. 441); 188, entitled 'The Bold Prisoner', printed by Bloomer of Birmingham (Vaughan Williams Memorial Library); 221, entitled 'The Squire of Edinburgh', printed by Harkness of Preston, stock no. 396 (Cambridge University Library, Madden Collection); 275, 'Get Up and Bar the Door', printed by Williams of Portsea (British Library, 'A Collection'; this is one of nine references in Rainer Wehse, *Schwanklied und Flugblatt in Grossbritannien* (Frankfurt am Main: Lang, 1979), no. 253); 281, 'The Keach in the Creel' (two examples in Wehse, no. 142), and 293, entitled 'Jock of Hazledean', printed by Harkness of Preston, stock no. 344 (Cambridge University Library, Madden Collection).

31. Child 117, 124, 126-131, 133-136, 137 (manuscript copied from broadside?), 138, 139, 141, 143, 144, 146-154, and 156.

32. Buchan, p. 215. See also E. B. Lyle, 'Child's Scottish Harvest', *Harvard Library Bulletin,* 25 (1977), 125-54.

33. F. J. Child, 'Ballad Books' [anonymously published review], *The Nation,* 3 September 1868, pp. 192-93; repr. in Rieuwerts, pp. 30-34 (p. 32).

34. 'The Weeping Lovers', printed by W. Wright of Birmingham between 1827 and 1829, and by R. Heppel of Birmingham between 1827 and 1831 (Bodleian Library, 2806 c.17 (460, 461)). W. Jackson and W. Pratt, both of Birmingham, issued versions under the title of 'Cold Blows the Wind' (see Roy Palmer, 'Street Ballads of Birmingham' (1990), unpublished typescript deposited in Vaughan Williams Memorial Library, London. See also David Atkinson, 'The Wit Combat Episode in "The Unquiet Grave"', *Lore and Language,* 12 (1994), 11-30).

35. W. M. Hart, 'Professor Child and the Ballad', *Publications of the Modern Language Association of America,* 21, n.s. 14 (1906), 755-807 (p. 793).

36. *The English and Scottish Popular Ballads,* iii, 305.

37. *The English and Scottish Popular Ballads,* iii, 334.

38. *The English and Scottish Popular Ballads,* i, 455.

39. *The English and Scottish Popular Ballads,* ii, 464, note.

40. *The English and Scottish Popular Ballads,* ii, 424.

41. *The English and Scottish Popular Ballads,* ii, 480.

42. *The English and Scottish Popular Ballads,* ii, 296, and i, vii. See also 'The Oral Ballads of Mrs Brown', in Buchan, pp. 62-73.

43. Another 'stall copy', entitled 'The Historical Ballad of May Culzean', features as version Dd in Child's Addendum.

44. Holger Olof Nygard, *The Ballad of 'Heer Halewijn', its Forms and Variations in Western Europe: A Study of the History and Nature of a Ballad Tradition,* Folklore Fellows Communications, 169 (Helsinki: Suomalainen Tiedeakatemia; Knoxville: University of Tennessee Press, 1958), p. 260.

45. William Hone, *The Every-day Book, or, Everlasting Calendar of Popular Amusements,* 3 vols (London: Tegg, 1827), iii, col. 129; reprinted in *John Pitts: Ballad Printer of Seven Dials, London, 1765-1844,* by Leslie Shepard (London: Private Libraries Association, 1969), p. 36. Of Pitts's predecessor, Shepard writes: 'As Richard Marshall died in 1779, this is more likely his son John Marshall for whom Pitts worked in Aldermary Church Yard. However, Pitts actually first set up in business on his own account in 1802, twenty-one years before the death of John Marshall in 1823' (p. 37).

46. Hone, col. 131.

47. *Ancient Poems, Ballads, and Songs of the Peasantry of England,* coll. and ed. by J. H. Dixon, Early English Poetry, 17 (London: Percy Society, 1846), pp. 74-77.

48. The Pitts sheet is reproduced in facsimile in Shepard, p. 38.

49. *Notes and Queries,* 4th series, 1 (April 1868), 344-45.

50. Steve Roud, *Folksong Index,* version 2, Electronic Indexes, 1 (Enfield Lock: Hisarlik Press, forthcoming), no. 21. I am indebted to Steve Roud for sending me (a computer illiterate) a print-out of his information on 'The Outlandish Knight'.

51. See note 50.

52. Child, 'Ballad Poetry', pp. 465-66.

53. See my note, which no one, to my knowledge, has so far contested: 'The Origin of "Van Dieman's Land" and "Young Henry the Poacher": A Hypothesis', *Folk Music Journal,* 3.2 (1976), 161-64.

54. Harkness sheet, stock no. 662 (Cambridge University Library, Madden Collection, vol. 18, fol. 1199). See also Roud, no. 519.

55. See Roud, no. 221.

56. Sheet in the possession of Adam McNaughtan, who kindly gave me a copy.

57. 'The Poachers', in *The Bothy Songs and Ballads of Aberdeen, Banff & Moray, Angus and the Mearns,* coll. and ed. by J. Ord (Paisley: Gardner, 1930), p. 384. Cf. 'Van Dieman's Land' in *The Grieg-Duncan Folk Song Collection,* Volume 2, ed. by Patrick Shuldham-Shaw and Emily B. Lyle (Aberdeen: Aberdeen University Press in association with the School of Scottish Studies, University of Edinburgh, 1983), no. 252.

58. *Volkslieder,* ed. by J. G. von Herder (Leipzig, 1778-79), Preface to vol. 2. The original remarks contrast 'die treuen, wahrhaften, charakteristischen Gesänge eines Volkes' with the kind mentioned in this remark: 'eigentlicher Gesang ist entweder verhallet oder, wenn man nicht Kot und Unkraut zusammen auftragen will, ist's schlimm und arm, ein deutscher Percy zu werden' ('genuine songs have either died away or, if one does not want to offer excrement and weeds at the same time, to become a German Percy is [a] vile and barely profitable [labour]'). I am grateful to Sigrid Rieuwerts for drawing my attention to Herder's comments, and to Hamish Henderson for construing them.

59. Child, speaking in a lecture of 1878; quoted in Lyle, 'Child's Scottish Harvest', p. 142.

Jill Terry Rudy (essay date May 2004)

SOURCE: Rudy, Jill Terry. "Transforming Audiences for Oral Tradition: Child, Kittredge, Thompson, and Connections of Folklore and English Studies." *College English* 66, no. 5 (May 2004): 524-44.

[*In the following excerpt, Rudy examines Child's role in establishing the study of English as an academic discipline.*]

Child holds a notable and conflicted place in the historiography of English studies. In recent histories, his ballad research has been reduced to a metaphor of an intradisciplinary battle among literature, rhetoric, and composition. Graff draws the lines by stating, "It is symptomatic, for example, that [. . .] Child [. . .] was not able to concentrate on teaching literature courses until 1876—and then only after an offer from the new Johns Hopkins University 'led to his being wholly relieved at last of the burden of correcting undergraduate compositions'" (40-41). Susan Miller reasserts Child's role in the dominance of literature over rhetoric, although she sees his position as lamentable rather than as victorious: "We also have heard so much and so of-

ten about the 'victory' of Francis Child at Harvard in giving over rhetoric for literature when he threatened to leave for Johns Hopkins in 1875" (125). While Child preferred teaching advanced students and writing for colleagues, his preference for a somewhat elite audience did not mean he valued literature over rhetoric. Contrary to the split constructed by Graff and Miller, David Bynum suggests that Child's ballad research actually united his training in rhetoric and literature: "Concerned as he thus so greatly was with rhetoric, oratory, and the motives of those mental disciplines, Child was inevitably drawn into pondering the essential differences between speech and writing, and to searching for the origins of thoughtful expression in English" (4). Child's ballad research connects folklore, rhetoric, and literary study and establishes disciplinary hierarchies and an audience of specialists.

The shift in audience for Child's ballad work can be recognized in the two collections he edited. From 1857 to 1859, Child published an eight-volume collection, *English and Scottish Ballads.* This work was part of the *British Poets* series; Child compiled ballads from collections published by Percy, Scott, and others. Danish ballad scholar Svend Grundtvig wrote Child in 1872 to compliment him on the "scholarlike and rational manner" with which he treated ballads (Hustvedt 243). Writing in return, Child mentioned the inadequacies of the collection. He explained, "I have had the intention of making some day a different and less hasty work [. . .]. The collection was made as a sort of *job*—forming part of one of those senseless huge collections of *British Poets*" (Hustvedt 246). Grundtvig, Child, and members of the Early English Text Society recognized that a revised, scholarly collection should publish more texts from manuscript sources and should include comparisons with other oral genre traditions. This new purpose shifted the collection toward a specialized audience and away from the general public.[1] Scholars of literary history saw getting unpublished manuscripts into print as significant work, although Grundtvig also printed versions collected from "oral recitation" (Hustvedt 245). Child distanced ballads from contemporary oral circulation, stating that "the sources of the English and Scottish ballads may be regarded as sealed or dried up for ever" (Hustvedt 248). Assuming that oral sources were sealed made printing a definitive collection seem attainable; a work with accurate texts and comparative notes would be worthy of the title, *The English and Scottish Popular Ballads.* Grundtvig wrote, "I deem this to be of no small consequence to the literary world, as your book no doubt will be a standard work" (Hustvedt 244). While Child wrote broadly in terms of "put[ting] the world in possession of all the English ballads" (Hustvedt 283), his main audience was literary specialists.

The concluding portion of Bynum's statement gives clues to the intellectual milieu that influenced Child's sense of audience. In the eighteenth and nineteenth centuries, scholars in the midst of professionalizing were intent on discovering "origins of thoughtful expression" not only in English but in a variety of vernacular languages as well (Bynum 4). The collection, publication, and scholarship on ballads and other oral traditions emerged along with ideas and practices of disciplinarity and scholarly professionalism. Culture, according to Clifford Siskin, emerged as a useful category to describe all the knowledge that had been dismissed as not very useful by the Royal Society and scientists in general (75). If knowledge needed to be narrowed to create depth, Siskin posits that the idea of culture validated the selection and study of the "cultured part of culture" as the best forms of expression and knowledge (76). Scholars aware of evolutionary theories in science recognized that some genres of oral composition displayed cultural, historical, and linguistic merit in a sort of developmental relationship with written literature. Child explained his view of the ballad as "anterior to the appearance of the poetry of art, to which it has formed a step among every people that has produced an original literature" (qtd. in Dugaw 58). Thus converging ideas about culture, literary origins, and professionalism informed Child's career, his research on popular ballads, and his publications for general and specialized audiences. As English departments emerged, these ideas helped place textual and genre issues at the research forefront and connected the study of literature and language with cultural and national history; this focus invited oral genres to be studied along with written. But scholars increasingly expected to publish their work to communicate to an audience of peers. The focus on literary history and published research was not uniformly supported by English professors, but Child's position at Harvard helped make philological research a force in English studies.

Philology combined the rigor and systematization of a linguistic and literary research method with the values and goals of unearthing cultural history and even influencing national status. Similar to Child's intending to give the "world" the English and Scottish ballads, philological scholarship assumed a wide audience while printing publications most directly for philologically trained specialists. Philological methods involved the diachronic study of linguistic and literary change along with a textual component that supported and extended the linguistic component: "Philology is not just a grand etymological or lexicographic enterprise. It also involves restoring to words as much of their original life and nuances as we can manage [. . .]. Philology also encompasses the forms in which texts express their messages" (Ziolkowski 7). The drive toward textual accuracy and genre study suggested by Child's second ballad collection is related to philological methods. Phi-

lologists compared manuscripts to detect errors and establish, and then print and publish, an authentic original text (Pedersen 82). While Graff has posited philology as merely a mechanism of professionalism, a way to make literary study rigorous and systematic (67-72), the standards set were meant to substantiate statements on the relationship of language, literature, cultural history, and the spirit of a nation. Hans Robert Jauss explains the lofty goal: "to represent in the history of literary works [Dichtwerke] the idea of national individuality on its way to itself" (3). By seeking to use accurate texts to show the literary and cultural history of a nation, philologists often worked from strong nationalist sentiments. These sentiments encouraged scholars to envision presenting their work to the common people to encourage national pride and comparison with oral and written expressions of other nations. In practice, the ability to print accurate texts and to initiate comparative studies of linguistic traditions often delayed or derailed scholarly plans to make generalizations for the public.

Child's ballad project was geared toward a specialized audience though grounded in the hope of an egalitarian past. The collection could be best appreciated, used, and validated by specialists who recognized Child's particular training and skills. For example, he rejected most printed broadside ballads and other "vulgar" forms that he found in manuscripts; his desire to be definitive about the ballad collection did not mean that he would be all-inclusive. His ballad corpus can be seen as an attempt to extract the "cultured part of culture" (Siskin 76) in the genre to show that ballads and other oral genres could be legitimate study objects. Child followed rigorous standards of scholarship; he worked for years on obtaining accurate manuscripts, compiling only "true" ballads, and printing all possible versions with extensive notes. However, he died before writing the general introductory treatise that would explain his selection and editing criteria, his definition of *ballad,* and his view of how the genre fit into cultural and national history (Bendix 84-88). Without this introduction, it is difficult to understand what Child's ideas about ballads may suggest about cultural history or about the relationship of speech and literacy. Child did state his egalitarian assumptions about the genre in an entry for *Johnson's New Universal Cyclopedia* published in 1875. Using the increasingly popular language of developmental stages, Child explained that the ballad would develop at a stage when a group still is unified, when "[t]he people are not divided by political organization and book-culture into markedly distinct classes [. . .]. As of yet, no sharp distinction of high and low exists, in respect to knowledge, desires, and tastes" (qtd. in Dugaw 59). Ironically, Child sees "increased civilization, and especially the introduction of book-culture," as the cause of social hierarchy and the demise of bal-

lads (qtd. in Dugaw 59). His collections, influenced by print and professional culture, demonstrate the social divisions Child sought to predate with the ballads themselves.

Child's collections turned the popular ballads into a contained element of culture that, paradoxically, distanced them from the natural expression of a people that he and others assumed the oral genre to represent. The definitive collection provided a canon of written texts for ballad scholars to collect or analyze. Child used established philological methods to select and print the ballads, and the act of selection and publication appealed to an exclusively trained, literate audience. Because so much of his research focused on textual accuracy, Child's attempt to be definitive minimized opportunities to explore how ballads could influence social life in particular groups and across national boundaries. The potential gain of studying ballads as a poetic and musical component of a group's social life was not realized because the format of assigning numbers to ballad texts did not invite discussion about performance or use. The ballads look like written poems, rather than appearing on the page as songs performed in specific social situations by individuals or groups. Ethnomusicologist and folklorist Harris Berger has called this process of entextualizing oral genres "textual empiricism." Berger defines the term: "Most [folklorists] took the text as a thing-in-itself rather than as a problematic record of past practices and experiences. Here I shall use 'textual empiricism' to refer to any scholarly approach that treats the text alone as its object of study" (3). As English studies emerged and professionalized, the positivistic assumptions that equated written literature with cultural development also supported the philological goal of printing accurate texts from original manuscript versions. Child's research both validated and problematized the place of oral genres in English studies. His canon of published ballads, written for specialists more than the public, reinforced the status of book-culture itself.

Note

1. Richard Bauman and Charles Briggs explain the nineteenth-century assumptions of the mediating role of specialists in vernacular textuality: "Only scholars [. . .] could identify the fundamental characteristics of this collective knowledge and re-entextualize it properly on the printed page" (216). They also discuss why publishing traditional texts became connected with the emerging nation-state (217-25).

Works Cited

Bauman, Richard, and Charles L. Briggs. *Voices of Modernity: Language Ideologies and the Politics of Inequality.* Cambridge: Cambridge UP, 2003.

Bendix, Regina. *In Search of Authenticity: The Formation of Folklore Studies.* Madison: U of Wisconsin P, 1997.

Berger, Harris M. *Metal, Rock, and Jazz: Perception and the Phenomenology of Musical Experience.* Hanover, NH: Wesleyan UP, 1999.

Bynum, David. *Four Generations of Oral Literary Studies at Harvard University.* Cambridge, MA: Center for the Study of Oral Literature, Harvard U, 1974.

Dugaw, Dianne, ed. *The Anglo-American Ballad: A Folklore Casebook.* New York: Garland, 1995.

Graff, Gerald. *Professing Literature: An Institutional History.* Chicago: U of Chicago P, 1987.

Hustvedt, Sigurd B. *Ballad Books and Ballad Men: Raids and Rescues in Britain, America, and the Scandinavian North since 1800.* Cambridge: Harvard UP, 1930.

Jauss, Hans Robert. *Toward an Aesthetic of Reception.* Trans. Timothy Bahti. Minneapolis: U of Minnesota P, 1982.

Miller, Susan. *Textual Carnivals: The Politics of Composition.* Carbondale: Southern Illinois UP, 1991.

Pedersen, Holger. *Linguistic Science in the Nineteenth Century: Methods and Results.* Trans. John Webster Spargo. Cambridge: Harvard UP, 1931.

Siskin, Clifford. *The Work of Writing: Literature and Social Change in Britain, 1700-1830.* Baltimore: Johns Hopkins UP, 1998.

Ziolkowski, Jan M. Introduction. *On Philology.* Ed. Jan M. Ziolkowski. University Park: Penn State UP, 1990. 1-15.

FURTHER READING

Biographies

Gummere, Francis Barton. "A Day with Professor Child." *Atlantic Monthly* 103 (March 1909): 421-25.
 Offers personal reminiscences of Child, as both a colleague and a friend.

Varnum, Robin. "Harvard's Francis James Child: The Years of the Rose." *Harvard Library Bulletin* 36, no. 6 (summer 1998): 291-319.
 Provides an overview of Child's life and career.

Criticism

Atkinson, David. "The English Revival Canon: Child Ballads and the Invention of Tradition." *Journal of American Folklore* 114, no. 453 (summer 2001): 370-80.

Reviews two 1997 audio recordings of Child's ballads.

Bronson, Bertrand Harris. *The Ballad as Song.* Berkeley: University of California Press, 1969, 324 p.
Discusses Child's approach to questions of authenticity in his ballad research.

Cheesman, Tom, and Sigrid Rieuwerts, eds. *Ballads into Books: The Legacies of Francis James Child.* Bern: Peter Lang, 1999, 283 p.
Includes a range of critical evaluations of Child's contributions to ballad scholarship.

Gerould, Gordon Hall. *The Ballad of Tradition.* Oxford: Clarendon Press, 1932, 311 p.
Examines Child's unique approach to ballad scholarship.

Gummere, Francis Barton. *The Popular Ballad.* Boston: Houghton, Mifflin and Company, 1907, 360 p.
Includes a discussion of Child's theories of ballad scholarship.

Howe, M. A. Dewolfe, and G. W. Cottrell Jr., eds. *The Scholar-Friends: Letters of Francis James Child and James Russell Lowell.* Westport, Conn.: Greenwood Press, 1970, 84 p.
Provides annotated selections from the correspondence between the two scholars.

Pound, Louise. *Poetic Origins and the Ballad.* New York: Macmillan Company, 1921, 247 p.
Questions a number of Child's assertions concerning the defining qualities of popular ballads.

Reppert, James. "F. J. Child and the Ballad." In *The Learned and the Lewd: Studies in Chaucer and Medieval Literature,* edited by Larry D. Benson, pp. 197-212. Cambridge: Harvard University Press, 1974.
Examines Child's ballad scholarship within the context of British folk literature from the Middle English period.

Rieuwerts, Sigrid. "From Percy to Child: The 'Popular Ballad' as a Distinct and Very Important Species of Poetry." In *Ballads and Boundaries: Narrative Singing in an Intercultural Context: Proceedings of the 23rd International Ballad Conference of the Commission for Folk Poetry (Société Internationale d'Ethnologie et de Folklore),* edited by James Porter, pp. 13-20. Los Angeles: UCLA, Department of Ethnomusicology & Systematic Musicology, 1995.
Discusses Child's ideas concerning the poetic qualities of the popular ballad.

———. "The Folk-Ballad: The Illegitimate Child of the Popular Ballad." *Journal of Folklore Research* 33, no. 3 (September-December 1996): 221-26.
Examines Child's role in the foundation of folklore scholarship in the United States.

Additional coverage of Child's life and career is contained in the following sources published by Thomson Gale: *Dictionary of Literary Biography,* **Vols. 1, 64, 235; and** *Literature Resource Center.*

Nikolai Mikhailovich Karamzin
1766-1826

(Also transliterated as Nikolay; also Mikhaylovich; also Karamsin) Russian historian, short story writer, poet, essayist, editor, and translator.

The following entry provides an overview of Karamzin's life and works. For additional information on his career, see *NCLC*, Volume 3.

INTRODUCTION

Karamzin, a historian, author, and linguist, was a pre-eminent figure in early nineteenth-century Russian letters. In his early career, Karamzin achieved fame with his sentimental fiction and nonfiction, and he is regarded by scholars as the writer primarily responsible for introducing the sentimental genre to Russian literature. His best-known works from his youth include the short stories "Bednaya Liza" ("Poor Liza") and "Ostrov Borngol'm" ("The Island of Bornholm"), both originally published in *Moskovsky zhurnal,* as well as the nonfiction *Pis'ma Russkogo puteshestvennika* (1797-1801; *Travels from Moscow through Prussia, Germany, Switzerland, France, and England*), which chronicles the author's travels through Western Europe in 1789-90.

By the early 1800s, Karamzin had become more reactionary in his views, and he devoted his mature work to addressing questions of Russian national identity and the merits of autocratic rule. Karamzin's conservatism brought him into close contact with the young Tsar Alexander I, who elevated the author to the rank of Imperial Historiographer. In this capacity Karamzin dedicated the remainder of his life to writing his 12-volume *Istoriya gosudarstva Rossiiskogo* (1818-29). Considered Karamzin's magnum opus, *Istoriya gosudarstva Rossiiskogo* was a landmark work in Russian historical scholarship and cast its shadow across Russian literature throughout the nineteenth century, inspiring such diverse authors as Aleksandr Pushkin, Nikolai Gogol, and Fyodor Dostoevsky. Karamzin was also the first Russian author to achieve widespread recognition outside of his native country, and during his lifetime his writings were translated into German, Italian, French, English, and Polish.

Many scholars credit Karamzin with modernizing Russian literary prose. He introduced numerous western European phrases and grammatical constructions into the Russian lexicon, effectively supplanting the outmoded Slavonic language of the Orthodox Church with a more cosmopolitan and accessible writing style. At the same time, Karamzin's own elegant, sophisticated, and erudite prose served as a model for many of his contemporaries. His influence became so pervasive that the prime of his career is often called the "Karamzin era" of Russian literature. Karamzin is also regarded as his nation's first literary critic, and his editorship of the journals *Moskovsky zhurnal* and *Vestnik Evropy* set the standard for subsequent Russian periodical publications. While Karamzin fell into relative obscurity in the early twentieth century, scholars in the Soviet Union and abroad began to rediscover his work in the 1960s, leading to a substantial new body of criticism devoted to his writings. Although most modern historians fault Karamzin's history for its lack of scholarly rigor, as well as for its obvious political biases, few dispute its importance in awakening the Russian national consciousness on the eve of the modern age.

BIOGRAPHICAL INFORMATION

Karamzin was born on December 1, 1766, on his family's estate on the Volga River, near the city of Simbirsk. He was the son of Mikhail Egorovich Karamzin, a retired army officer, and Ekaterina Petrovna Pasukhina. Karamzin's mother died when he was only two; his father remarried a year later. Surrounded by educated, well-read adults throughout his childhood, Karamzin became an avid reader at a young age, receiving guidance from his family physician, who introduced him to the classics of Western literature. At the age of ten, Karamzin left home to attend boarding school in Simbirsk. He later attended school in Moscow, where he studied under the tutelage of the philosophy professor Johann Matthias Schaden. During these years Karamzin's education was dominated by the influence of western European literature and culture, and he quickly gained a reading knowledge of French, German, and English.

After completing secondary school in 1781, Karamzin joined the Preobrazhensky Guards regiment in St. Petersburg. Military life proved uninteresting to the aspiring author, however, and he devoted much of his free time to writing poetry and becoming acquainted with the city's vibrant literary scene. He published his first book, a translation of Salomon Gessner's *Das hölzerne*

Bein titled *Dereviannaia noga,* in 1783. Karamzin's military career ended abruptly a year later, following the death of his father. Karamzin resigned from his regiment and returned to Simbirsk to supervise the settlement of his father's estate. While in Simbirsk he was briefly associated with the local freemason society, *Zlatoi venets* ("The Golden Crown"). After returning to Moscow later that year, Karamzin joined the Druzheskoe uchenoe obshchestvo ("Friendly Learned Society"), an altruistic brotherhood dedicated to enlightenment ideals, where he became acquainted with a number of young writers, among them Aleksei Kutuzov and Aleksandr Petrov, who would influence the development of Karamzin's literary style. During this period Karamzin published translations of several German and English works, including Shakespeare's *Julius Caesar* (published as *Iulii Tsezar,* 1787), in addition to contributing essays, short stories, and poems to journalist Nikolai Novikov's *Detskoe chtenie dlia serdtsa i razuma,* a journal for children. Karamzin also served as editor of the journal from 1787 to 1789.

In 1789 Karamzin embarked on an extended journey through western Europe, writing numerous letters chronicling his experiences. Returning to Russia eighteen months later, Karamzin founded the *Moskovsky zhurnal,* in which he published his travel writings, as well as short stories, essays, literary criticism, and poetry. The journal proved extremely popular with the public and helped introduce the sentimental style to Russian literary circles. The ensuing years witnessed an increase in government repression of publishing activities in Russia, largely in reaction to the aftermath of the French Revolution, and in 1793 Karamzin retreated from literary fame in order to live at a friend's estate outside of the city. In spite of the more stringent censorship laws, Karamzin continued to publish his writings throughout the 1790s, even after a number of his associates were imprisoned or exiled. During these years Karamzin's political views also underwent a transformation, as he became sympathetic to the autocratic policies of Empress Catherine the Great, considering them vital in preserving an alternative to the political unrest that had embroiled much of western Europe.

In 1801 Karamzin married Elizaveta Ivanovna Protasova. The marriage proved short-lived, however, as Protasova died a year later while giving birth to their daughter, Sofia. In 1802 Karamzin founded a new journal, *Vestnik Evropy,* dedicated to promoting his new political ideology. Karamzin's support for the centralized authority of the Tsar—and for Russia's rigid class structure in general—brought him to the attention of Tsar Alexander I, who in 1803 appointed Karamzin to the position of Imperial Historiographer, a title he would hold until his death. That year he married Ekaterina Andreevna Kolyvanova and settled into a country estate outside of Moscow. After receiving his royal appointment, Karamzin abandoned his publishing activities in order to devote himself exclusively to writing historical works. In 1811 he wrote *O drevnei i novoi Rossii v ee politicheskom i grazhdanskom otnosheniiakh* (1861; *Karamzin's Memoir on Ancient and Modern Russia*), a political tract criticizing liberal reforms in western Europe. The work's condemnatory tone rankled the Tsar, however, particularly as many of his closest advisors espoused liberal ideals. Karamzin fell out of favor in court for the next several years, and his *Memoir on Ancient and Modern Russia* was not published until well after his death. Karamzin nevertheless maintained his privileged access to state libraries and archives, allowing him to continue research on his ambitious historical work, *Istoriya gosudarstva Rossiiskogo,* the first eight volumes of which appeared in 1818. The work proved an immediate success, and Karamzin's reputation as Russia's premier author was secured. Karamzin produced four more volumes of *Istoriya gosudarstva Rossiiskogo* over the remaining eight years of his life. He died after a long illness on May 22, 1826.

MAJOR WORKS

Karamzin first earned critical and popular acclaim with the publication of his short story "Poor Liza" in the *Moskovsky zhurnal* in 1792. The story recounts the tragic life of a naïve flower seller, Liza, who falls in love with a sophisticated gentleman named Erast. Erast quickly seduces the young peasant girl, only to abandon her to marry a wealthy widow, driving the distraught Liza to drown herself in a pond. The story met with widespread praise upon its original publication, earning comparisons with Johann von Goethe's 1774 novel *Die Leiden des jungen Werthers* (*The Sorrows of Young Werther*), and single-handedly launched the Russian sentimental movement. Karamzin caused a similar sensation a year later with the publication of "The Island of Bornholm," a Gothic tale concerning a young adventurer who travels to an obscure Danish island to rescue a young woman from captivity.

Karamzin's account of his travels through Europe, *Travels from Moscow through Prussia, Germany, Switzerland, France, and England,* also serves as an important example of Russian sentimental writing from the period. Modeled after Laurence Sterne's *A Sentimental Journey through France and Italy,* published in 1768, Karamzin's travel writings are noteworthy for their highly subjective point of view and reflect the author's moods and personal philosophy as much as they chronicle his observations of life in Europe. The work is also significant as a reflection of the author's burgeoning cosmopolitanism during this stage of his career; Karamzin's early encounters with European culture would exert a powerful impact on both his aesthetic

and his political sensibility, as well as on his prose style. *Travels from Moscow through Prussia, Germany, Switzerland, France, and England* originally appeared in serial form in the *Moskovsky zhurnal* and was later republished in six volumes between 1797 and 1801.

Karamzin devoted the last two decades of his life to composing his epic *Istoriya gosudarstva Rossiiskogo,* a 12-volume history of Russia. The publication of the first eight volumes of the work in 1818 was a watershed moment in the field of Russian history. The work immediately impressed readers with the scope of its ambition, as well as with its literary style. Karamzin was the first historian to attempt to chronicle the complete history of the Russian nation from its obscure origins to the era of the Romanov dynasty. Also among the first works in any genre to describe, in detail, the Russian national character, the *Istoriya gosudarstva Rossiiskogo* was a vital expression of patriotism at a time when Russia was just beginning to gain recognition as a major world power. Equally important, the work differed from more traditional Russian history texts in its prose style, eschewing the less elegant and formal approach of earlier works for a more evocative, almost novelistic narrative voice. Indeed, the work's straightforward, descriptive, and accessible style contributed to its widespread popularity and earned it comparisons to the writings of Sir Walter Scott and other prominent European authors of the period.

CRITICAL RECEPTION

Most scholars agree that it would be difficult to overestimate the significance of Karamzin's impact on Russian literature in the first half of the nineteenth century. His innovative and eloquent style left an indelible mark on Russian prose writing and set the standard for other works of literature during his lifetime. His *Istoriya gosudarstva Rossiiskogo* was especially revered among Russian authors and inspired Aleksandr Pushkin to refer to Karamzin as the "Columbus of Russian history." Even members of the younger generation of writers from the 1820s, whose liberal politics clashed with Karamzin's conservative views, could not help but admire their elder's mastery of Russian prose. The *Istoriya gosudarstva Rossiiskogo* became the standard historical text in Russian schools for nearly a hundred years, and new translations of Karamzin's works appeared throughout the nineteenth century.

With the Bolshevik revolution of 1917, Karamzin's espousal of autocratic government made his works an obvious target for Soviet censors, and his work fell into virtual obscurity for the next several decades. Commentary on Karamzin's career began to appear outside of the Soviet Union in the 1930s, notably Anatole Ma-

zour's brief assessment of Karamzin's historical writings in *Outline of Modern Russian Historiography,* published in 1939. Mazour was among the first to voice the complaint that Karamzin's view of history put undue focus on the importance of the Tsar and other powerful leaders in shaping history, while essentially ignoring the role of the masses. Karamzin's reputation in the Soviet Union underwent a radical reformation in the 1960s, as scholars began to recognize the importance of his work both for its influential prose style and for its indisputable role in shaping conservative political theory in Russia in the nineteenth century. During the same period, the work of such scholars as Richard Pipes, Anthony Cross, and Henry Nebel proved instrumental in establishing a field of Karamzin scholarship in English. In recent decades scholars have also begun to explore Karamzin's experimentation with new literary forms, his role in shaping political ideology during the reign of Alexander I, and the influence of the European Enlightenment on Karamzin's literary sensibility.

PRINCIPAL WORKS

Dereviannaia noga: Shveitsarskaia idiliia [translator; from *Das hölzerne Bein,* by Salomon Gessner] (prose) 1783

Iulii Tsezar [translator; from *Julius Caesar,* by William Shakespeare] (play) 1787

"Bednaya Liza" ["Poor Liza"] (short story) 1792; published in the journal *Moskovsky zhurnal.*

Pis'ma Russkogo puteshestvennika. 6 vols. [*Travels from Moscow through Prussia, Germany, Switzerland, France, and England*; also published as *Letters of a Russian Traveler: 1789-1790*] (sketches) 1797-1801

Sochineniia Karamzina. 8 vols. (short stories, poetry, and essays) 1803-04

**Istoriya gosudarstva Rossiiskogo.* 12 vols. (history) 1818-29

O drevnei i novoi Rossii v ee politicheskom i grazhdanskom otnosheniiakh [*Karamzin's Memoir on Ancient and Modern Russia: A Translation and Analysis*] (history) 1861; also published as *Zapiska o drevnei i novoi Rossii,* 1914

Pis'ma N. M. Karamzina k I. I. Dmitrievu (letters) 1866

Izbrannye sochineniia. 2 vols. (short stories, poetry, and essays) 1964

Polnoe sobranie stikhotvorenii (poetry) 1966

Selected Prose of N. M. Karamzin (short stories and essays) 1969

**These volumes are collectively referred to in English as *History of the Russian State.*

CRITICISM

Henry Brougham (review date January 1804)

SOURCE: Brougham, Henry. Review of *Travels from Moscow through Prussia, Germany, Switzerland, France, and England,* by Nikolai Karamzin. *Edinburgh Review* 3, no. 6 (January 1804): 321-28.

[*In the following excerpt, Brougham offers an in-depth critique of Karamzin's book of travel writings.*]

A Book of travels by a native of Moscow [*Travels from Moscow Through Prussia, Germany, Switzerland, France, and England*], excites the same sort of interest with any uncommon natural phenomenon—a horse in Venice, for instance—or a tree in Scotland. Such a work, too, claims somewhat more indulgence than we may always be disposed to extend to the productions of more fruitful soils. We are apt to be satisfied, if we here and there meet with a slight resemblance of those excellencies which elsewhere abound in an unlimited number and degree. Nor should we be at all inclined to murmur at being forced to lower our standard of excellence, if the object, after all, could only be made to correspond with it. . . .

M. Karamsin left Moscow, his native city, and the seat of every thing that is dear to his heart, with the intention of performing, in the most comfortable vehicles, the easier and safer parts of the tour of Europe, in a year and a half. Accordingly, the first letter which he addresses to his friends, is occupied with describing the poignancy of his grief at the commencement of so dreadful an undertaking, and so long a separation. It contains a long address to *his own heart* upon this matter; and concludes with advising his friends to console themselves, if possible, during his absence. His wailing continues with scarcely any intermission till he arrives at Riga; but at some parts of his piteous journey, particularly at Narva, his perplexities thickened, and he seems to have reached the utmost depth of human woe.

> 'God only knows the state of my mind at that moment; certainly all pleasing ideas of travelling were banished from it. Oh! had it then been possible, my friends, to have transported myself to you! I silently execrated those restless wishes of the human breast, which hurry us away continually from one object to another, from true enjoyments to those which are illusive, as soon as the former cease to be new to us. Our imaginations are attracted by deceitful appearances, and we are instigated to seek for pleasure in the uncertainty of future events.

> 'Every thing has its limits. When the huge wave dashes against the shore, it returns and precipitates itself into the deep abyss, though but just before it appeared to touch the skies.—Just in the moment when my heart was full of affliction,' & c.

And truly all this is not without reason; for his travelling-carriage had broken down, and he had actually got wet into the skin. Nor is it possible to imagine how far his distress might have proceeded, had not a young man of prepossessing countenance invited him to take shelter in a house, where an old man, whose goodness of heart was marked in his face, questioned him about his travels with 'manifest sincerity,' while his wife gave him excellent bread and coffee. It is needless to add, that this adventure is followed by an animated apostrophe to hospitality and benevolence.

In travelling through Courland, M. Karamsin generally feeds heartily, and tells us upon what, and for how much. But at one inn, the evening was so fine, the rivulet so clear, and the foliage so shady, that he declined supping, and walked out alone. He beheld the setting sun. This brought to his recollection that he once saw it before at Moscow with great pleasure. 'Could I,' he exclaims, 'then imagine, that just a twelvemonth afterwards I should enjoy the beauty of the closing day near an inn in Courland? I took out my pocket-book, together with my pen and ink, and wrote what you have now read.' About a month after his separation from his friends, he finds his heart more composed, and grows so plump, that he facetiously compares himself to the 'knight of the jolly figure.'

One of our knight's common exploits is the visiting of famous authors; but this he always performs without any ceremony—he carries no introductions. 'Boldness,' he observes, 'which takes towns, opens the doors of philosophers.' His manœuvre on all these occasions is the same. He tells the unhappy sage whom he is determined to converse with, that he is travelling for the purpose of seeing the greatest living authors. Some are taken in; but others seem to have received his assaults rather coolly. Wieland, in particular, positively refused to harbour him, though he professed to have come to Weimar for the sole purpose of seeing the author of *Oberon.* However, by the most persevering importunity, he at last forced even this pass; and though the poet told him that the reason of his shyness was his fear lest an utter stranger might publish, according to the German fashion, the conversations which passed; and though our author removed his apprehensions, by saying he was not a German, and could not write for the German public; yet he does publish, in German, a full account of all the interviews which he had with Wieland, containing the very words used by him in talking upon a great variety of topics; among others, upon the subject of his own peculiarities of feeling and habits. Such is the conduct of those who have their heads stuffed so full of sentiment as to leave no room for either prudence or propriety.

None of the authors upon whom M. Karamsin intruded, in his own easy manner, appears to have delighted him more than M. Weisse of Leipsig, the great writer of

children's books. 'He is a little man, about 60 years of age, whose excellence of heart beams in each feature. In his garden, he walks with a red night-gown and white hat; but when he comes home, he puts on a bag-wig, retaining the night-gown.' He treated our traveller with lemonade.

At Frankfort, M. Karamsin observed, that, 'during bad weather, it appeared destitute of inhabitants, for then every body staid at home excepting those obliged to go abroad; but in good weather it seemed very populous, for then they are allured by the sunshine, like ants from their holes.' Vol. I. p. 205. After several other remarks, equally judicious and profound, he is drawn aside from his general view of the town, by a very 'attractive solitary house,' with a 'small garden,' a most 'inviting old chesnut tree,' and, still more irresistible, 'race of children.' So many charms, concentrated in one spot, prove almost too much for the sensibilities of this gentle Moscovite; and we are agreeably surprised when he escapes with a description of the race, and a farewell address to the house and the tree.

From Germany our traveller hastens to Switzerland,— 'the country of innocence and bliss—where the inhabitants serve none but God, lead a life that is only a pleasing dream, and therefore scarcely feel the pain of dying;—where sprightly lads and lasses play on the banks of the impetuous Rhine, pull handfuls of flowers, and throw them at each other;—the contented rustic whistles a merry tune, and gives the passengers a friendly nod.' In such a paradise M. Karamsin is altogether overcome with his emotions; he cannot keep his seat amidst so many exquisite objects of fine phrenzy. 'What a country! What scenery!' he cries, when two wersts beyond Basle—and 'jumps out of the carriage,' throws himself on the 'blooming shores of the Rhine,' and 'kisses the earth in a transport.' In a note, he adds, what our readers may probably have some difficulty of believing, that he was then *only* twenty-four years old. He sometimes, however, asks leave to kiss the inhabitants, as well as the ground, and meets with rather an uncourteous return from these children of nature. At a peasant's marriage, he is overcome with the happiness of the parties, and resolves to leave them a token of remembrance. He gives the bride a small copper coin— she stares, by turns, at the bridegroom, the gift, and the donor; who rejoices at their new happiness, and quotes something from Haller's poems. His love and bounty towards the all-interesting Swiss was not unrepaid; for though the engaging rustics did frequently laugh at him, they were often kind. Thus, a young shepherd, in a valley, with a limpid streamlet, foliage, cottage, and other ingredients of sentimental situation, complied with M. Karamsin's request to give him a drink of water—saying with a smile, 'drink, my friend, a glass of our water.' Nor was so wondrous an act of natural benevolence thrown away. 'I was about,' says our traveller, 'to press

the good natured obliging man to my heart as my brother. Oh, my friends, why were we not born in those times when all men were shepherds and brethren?' Nay, such is the effect of a cup of Swiss water, that M. Karamsin declares, he would willingly renounce his superior knowledge and illumination, to regain the original state of nature. It also enabled him to read very clearly in the shepherd's eyes, at his departure, a fervent wish for his happiness. (II. 5. 6. & 7). But the grand enjoyment of this country was Lavater; whose vanity M. Karamsin fed, while he ate his dinners, and was permitted to purchase his MSS; that is, his printed, but unpublished works, which the physiognomist would upon no account give to the world in the common way, but sold to as many as would take them from him privately. He discovers Lavater not only to be the best of men, but a truly great man; because he never reads the works in which he is either praised or censured; and is very angry with our brethren of the *General German Review,* for not comprehending Lavater's definition of the purpose of existence, viz. 'that the constant, most solid, and most suitable existence, is the purpose of existence.' All this, our traveller thinks, is not only correct, but perfectly familiar. This truly great man, we are told, is a 'friend to ahs! and ohs!;' and is captivated with two Danes, one of whom strikes his forehead, and stamps with his feet, while the other holds his hands, and fixes his eyes on heaven, whenever Lavater speaks with warmth, (II. 27).

After enjoying, in such delectable society, all the luxuries of laughing, kissing, weeping, and sighing—with a thunder storm, a water party, and weddings and funerals in abundance, M. Karamsin set out for France. In his way towards the frontiers, he remarked some odd inscriptions on old houses. One of these contains a specimen of *non sequitur,* scarcely surpassed by any of our author's own reasonings. '*Build thy hope on God, for this house is called the Black Sow.*' At Ferney, M. Karamsin meets with two young Englishmen on their travels. It would have been difficult for such a triple compound to have been formed, without some singular explosion—'They drank some excellent wine, with the most devout wishes for the eternal felicity of Voltaire!' (II. 101).

At Lyons, M. Karamsin finds ample allowance of sentimental food. He sees Vestris dance, 'with his soul in his feet;' is quizzed by two young Frenchmen, and, mistaking it for French politeness, is thrown into 'a kind of rapture;'—recollects that he is upon ground over which Yorick wandered in search of the tombs of *Amandus* and *Amanda,* and expresses no small astonishment, that the bustle of the Revolution should be so interesting as to make the Lyonese 'care very little about the monuments of love and tenderness,' (II. 206).

In a receptacle for madmen, M. Karamsin meets with a sufferer, who excites in him a very natural sort of sympathy.

> One of these unhappy beings was sitting on the gallery, at a small table, and had paper, pen, and ink. Immersed in profound thoughts, he leaned his elbow on the table.—"That is a philosopher," said our conductor, smiling; "paper and ink are dearer to him than bread." 'But what does he write?'—"God knows! probably nonsense; but why should he be deprived of so harmless a pleasure?"—'You are right,' answered I, sighing.

(II. 191)

In Paris, our traveller fares, if possible, still better. Here his soul is in a constant flow. He makes a pilgrimage to Ermenonville, and finds, that after a man has seen the sun set on Rosseau's grave, he may say, 'I have had one happy moment in my life.' (III. 184). In the Church of St Dennis, he feasts, among other things, on the portrait of the Maid of Orleans, who was, he tells us, the heroine of *Voltaire's Pucelle,* (III. 164). In the *rue de la Ferronerie,* where Henry IV. was assassinated, he would not live for the whole world; he is even enraged at his coachman for stopping on that ground, because it did not open to swallow up the detestable Ravillac, (III. 77). The wretchedness of an old beggar woman in the *Bois de Boullogne* affords him an excellent treat, and upon very cheap terms; for, after drawing from her a full account of her miseries, and making her submit to a variety of sympathetic exclamations, he only presses her hand, and departs, (III. 31.-2. & 3). The following passage contains a curious anecdote, if indeed we can at all rely on M. Karamsin's information.

> Here poverty often teaches people the most singular means of getting a livelihood: How many are there here who have not a single sous of certain income, and yet daily appear well dressed at the Palais-Royal, in the theatres and public walks; and who, were we to judge from their looks, live as free from care as the fowls of heaven?—But how is this done? In many different ways—they have methods without number of gaining something, which are not known in any place but Paris.

> Thus for example: a well-dressed man, of a noble appearance, who, over his dish of *bavaroise,* talks fluently, tells all kinds of pleasant anecdotes, and jokes with great ease and freedom, may be seen every day in the *Caffé de Chartres;* and how does he live? By the sale of bills pasted up, which every night, when all others are asleep, he tears down from the corners of the streets, and carries to the pastry-cooks, who give him a few sous for his trouble. He then lays himself down quietly on his bundle of straw, in some *grenier,* and sleeps sounder than many a Crœsus.

> Another, who is seen every day at the Thuilleries, and the Palais-Royal, and who, by his dress, might be taken for an ecclesiastic, is a farmer; and what kind of a one do you think? He farms the hair pins which are lose in

the Italian theatre. When the curtain drops, and the company are leaving the house, he makes his first appearance in it; and while the lights are extinguishing, he goes from box to box, in order to search for the lost pins; not one of them escapes his Lynxean eye, let it lie where it may; and when the last candle is extinguished, our farmer picks up his last pin, and, with the hope of not dying next morning of hunger, hastens to the broker to sell him his treasure.

(III. 112, 113)

It is fair, however, to warn our readers against implicit confidence in this traveller, whose ignorance and imagination are perpetually misleading him. Lavoisier, he says, has made all the Parisian ladies so fond of chemistry, that they analyse the sensibilities of the heart by chemical rules, (III. 69). At a meeting of the Royal Society of London, he saw what, we believe, has seldom been observed by others, the President 'passing his judgment upon various works, but with great candour and moderation.' (III. 243). In Newgate he learnt, that convicts often preferred being hanged in their native country, rather than being transported with bad company, (III. 232); and in a trading vessel, he heard a drunk steersman request the captain rather to throw him overboard than strike him, because that to an Englishman is worse than death, (III. 322).

In England, the last object of M. Karamsin's tour, he is apparently so much exhausted with his previous delights, that he can scarcely enjoy himself at all. Besides, 'the English in general do not much care about sallad and garden herbs; roast-beef and beef-steaks are their usual food, and hence their blood becomes thick, and themselves phlegmatic, melancholy, and not unfrequently self-murderers,' (III. 200). Their hairdressers, too, are dull and clumsy. 'Alas, I am no longer in Paris,' he exclaims, 'where the powder-puff of the ingenious lively Rulet played like a gentle zephyr round my head, and strewed it with a resplendent white aromatic rime!' (213). Moreover, the climate begins to affect even M. Karamsin. He surprises himself philosophising; but this, he says, must be excused, as 'merely the effect of the air, for here lived Newton, Locke, and Hobbes,' (215). He meets, however, with some things to console him in his distresses, particularly a number of beautiful children, 'all little *Emilius's* and *Sophias*;'—a blind beggar and his dog, which understood physiognomy—some ballad-singers, who gave him an opportunity of shedding tears: and then M. Karamsin is much more independent of external resources than most travellers; for he is happy if, after all the fatigues of the day, he can once more behold at night his '*dear portmanteau,*' (III. 218). He returns to Russia by the Baltic, and on his approach to its happy shores, is overwhelmed with unruly joy.

Anatole G. Mazour (essay date 1958)

SOURCE: Mazour, Anatole G. "The Nineteenth Century and After: Karamzin (1766-1826)." In *Modern Russian Historiography,* pp. 62-74. Princeton, N.J.: D. Van Nostrand Co., 1958.

[*In the following essay, Mazour offers an in-depth analysis of Karamzin's historical writings. Mazour asserts that the significance of Karamzin's* History of the Russian State *lies in its literary qualities, rather than in the strength of its scholarship.*]

The true heir of the eighteenth-century historians was Nikolay Mikhailovich Karamzin. Son of a Simbirsk squire, he was sent to Moscow to receive his education at a private school and then at the university in the same city. In his younger days he associated himself with the distinguished publisher, N. I. Novikov, was on friendly terms with the leading Freemasons, I. P. Turgenev, A. M. Kutuzov, and I. V. Lopukhin, favored Masonic liberal ideas, and for a while even toyed with the ideas of Rousseau. From May, 1789, to September, 1790, Karamzin toured western Europe, including England, and recorded his impressions in his widely read *Letters of a Russian Traveler.*[1] While abroad, he observed closely the life of western Europe, chiefly from the point of view of a philosopher and *literatus.* His first impressions inclined him to a great admiration for Western civilization. England failed to arouse the enthusiasm of the "Russian traveler," and except for a warm appreciation of the Anglo-Saxon judicial genius he left the British Isles "as cold as the English themselves"; but Paris made an overwhelming impression upon him and nearly converted him to cosmopolitanism.[2] This city, the pulse of European political and social life, made him believe that nationalism must eventually yield to universalism. One must be a man first and a Slav after. What is good for mankind is good for Russians.[3]

While in Paris, Karamzin already bemoaned the absence of an adequate interpretative history of Russia written in the style of a Tacitus or a Gibbon. He resented any suggestion that Russia had no past. On the contrary, he argued, Russia had a glorious history which she could proudly present before western Europe; all she needed was a Russian Tacitus and Michelangelo to demonstrate her greatness. Russia, wrote Karamzin in one of his letters from Paris, "had her own Charles the Great—Vladimir; her own Louis XI—Tsar Ivan III; her own Cromwell—Godunov, and such an emperor as Peter I western Europe had never seen."[4] In later years Karamzin seems to have reserved the role of Tacitus for himself.

Karamzin's spontaneous outburst of poetic enthusiasm about the West proved of short duration. Even while journeying in western Europe, Karamzin cautioned against rash adoption in Russia of outside ideas for fear that it might do violence to entrenched traditions and ancient customs. Such a policy, he warned, must in the end lead to nothing but ruin. Later he began to discard other vestiges of the cosmopolitan idea he cherished in his earlier years, exchanging it for conservative nationalism. The violent nature of the French Revolution, climaxed by Bonapartism and the devastating wars, forced him to recoil. He began to revise his earlier views; by 1811 Karamzin vacillated no longer for he knew precisely where he stood. In his famous **Memorandum on Old and New Russia,** presented during that year to Alexander I, he proved himself *plus royaliste que le roi.* His former enthusiasm for Peter's reforms now came in for a more "rational" re-examination; he came to regard the changes as an unhappily forced breakdown of old institutions, valuable customs, and manners. He blamed his former idol for interfering with the natural course of national history and for undermining the spirituality of the Russian church. He criticized Peter for curbing the privileges of the nobility, without which class the monarchy itself was inconceivable. He warned that the nobility and the institution of serfdom were two pillars on which autocracy rested.

Casting off his former cosmopolitanism, Karamzin based his new views upon historical precedents as he saw them. If Peter I, he said, had made Russians citizens of the world, he also contributed to their neglecting to be citizens of their own country. His relentless drive, continued Karamzin, forced Peter to employ tyrannical methods. He uprooted the traditional old capital of Moscow and exchanged it for the swampy northern city of St. Petersburg. He tampered with the hereditary privileges of the gentry and thereby endangered the social structure; he modified the status of the church and thereby stripped the faith of spirituality. After Peter's death, he said, political pygmies replaced the giant and proved instrumental in further weakening Russian autocracy.

Catherine II saved the monarchy from an oncoming catastrophe: though her reign was not entirely free of blemishes, her brilliant rule restored the prestige of autocracy. Here, incidentally, Karamzin and Shcherbatov were in complete agreement, though reaching it by somewhat devious paths. Their common link was the tender subject of the place of nobility in Russian society, a subject upon which both writers could see eye to eye. Karamzin reprimanded the enlightened Empress for the notorious favoritism at court, which in the end was bound to have a demoralizing effect upon the prestige of the Russian nobility. In the reign of Catherine II he detected "more glitter than validity," and, though appreciating the accomplishments of the period, concluded that there was another side to the picture which Russia must blushingly admit, a deterioration of morals. The ghost of Shcherbatov must have smilingly nodded when

Karamzin recorded his views. And after the brief and sorrowful rule of Paul I, came Alexander I, whom Karamzin urged to learn his lessons from history and under no circumstances to consent to any form of limited monarchical government. "Autocracy founded and resurrected Russia; any change of the established political order was bound to lead to complete ruin."[5] Such is briefly the political physiognomy of Karamzin. We must now return to the subject that concerns us most, Karamzin the historian.

On his return from abroad, Karamzin continued to lead an easygoing life, occupying himself chiefly with literary writing—poetry and prose. As he grew older, his interest in history increased. What made him popular at court were his panegyrics to Catherine II and the famous ode dedicated to Alexander I on the occasion of his accession to the throne, as well as the frequent articles in the *Messenger of Europe,* which Karamzin published and edited. He had already demonstrated his reverence for monarchy and his firm belief that all virtue radiated from the purple robe.[6] In 1803 Karamzin petitioned Alexander I to grant him an allowance so that he would be able to devote himself entirely to the writing of history. By imperial decree on October 31, 1803, the state granted Karamzin the title of "Historiographer" and allowed him an annual pension of two thousand rubles on condition that he write a complete history of Russia. The following year he retired as editor of the *Messenger of Europe* and began to write his ***History of the Russian State,*** a work which gave him wide publicity and initiated the legend of his being the "first Russian historian."[7] The work appeared in 1816 in eight volumes; it was followed in 1821 by the ninth and in 1824 by the tenth and eleventh volumes. In 1826 he died without completing the twelfth volume, which leads up to the seventeenth century.[8]

The title of Karamzin's history is in itself revealing: it is a history of the Russian state, not of the Russian people. It is not even that: it is a rhetorical, panegyrical narrative which endeavors to prove that autocracy alone has bestowed all the blessings that the Russian Empire ever enjoyed; it is an album of sovereigns accompanied by descriptions of the most florid style. The approach of the author to his subject encompassed, no doubt, a gigantic sweep, but he was badly handicapped by his "monarchical blinders." Besides, Karamzin began his history without proper training for such work; critical history was totally alien to him. His contemporaries, Schlözer or Niebuhr, had no influence whatever upon him. Being more a representative of sentimental romanticism in fiction than of scholarly historical writing, he was naturally inclined to consider history to be in large part a beautiful narrative, in which the characters were either heroes to be worshiped or villains to be deplored. The masses did not count, everything emanated from a single source—strong government, and justice "radiated

from the purple robe." Such an outlook was not unexpected since already during his journey abroad Karamzin had been inspired with the idea of the seemingly empty past of Russia made into a beautiful dramatic narrative. All one must possess, Karamzin thought, was "mind, taste, and talent"; then he could "select, inspirit, and illuminate, and the reader would be amazed to see how, for instance, a Nestor Chronicle could be transformed into something attractive, powerful, worthy of the attention not only of Russians but also of foreigners."[9] With such aims and a generous pension from the state, Karamzin could give free rein to his artistic pen, his poetic vision, and his political bias.

Naturally, Karamzin could not avoid discussing the question that had already been debated since the times of Lomonosov: the origins of the Russian state. He went back to the early Greek writers, chiefly Herodotus, glided hastily over the confusing morass of ancient references to a legion of tribes in the north and the south, and—for fear of bogging down—conveniently accepted the Scythians as the most logical precursors of Russian history. Karamzin thus brushed aside the Norman theory; the legend of the "invitation" extended to the Varangians "to come to rule and reign" over the Slavs he dismissed as of no importance by giving the general impression of a Varangian admixture in the early Kievan state and nothing more.

According to Karamzin, early Kievan Russia reached a high degree of development because of its strong monarchical government. The downfall of old Russia he explained by the established political custom of dividing the state among the royal heirs and by the bitter rivalry among the princes, which in the end contributed to the triumph of the Mongols. As for the princes, in Basil III, Karamzin saw an extremely colorful figure; without him history would have looked like a "peacock without a tail." But of all the Muscovite grand princes who built the future state of Russia, Ivan III was considered by Karamzin as the greatest of them all; he looked upon this ruler not only as the true founder of the national state but also as the father of Russian autocracy. This was the traditional "Great Russian" interpretation, the theory that the entire historical process was centrifugal rather than centripetal, a theory later to be vigorously opposed by members of the Ukrainian school, notably M. Hrushevsky.

In fairness to Karamzin, it must be stated that his ***History of the Russian State*** is not without its merits, in spite of its pontifical presentation and obvious bias. Throughout all the volumes there was a novel unity in his narrative that made the course of Russian history seem meaningful. The fact that Karamzin was primarily a literary artist with no pretense to scholarship had one positive effect: his manner of writing. His florid literary style tended to liberate Russian writing from the anti-

quated church-Slavonic terminology that was greatly admired by members of the old school and to introduce a style more elegant, vigorous, and flowing—even though rhetorical—a style that appealed to the literary aesthetes of his time.[10] Many people compare Karamzin's writings with those of Sir Walter Scott, while some detect a definite influence of the latter upon him. Undoubtedly, as the volumes began to make their appearance, they awakened an unprecedented interest in national history.[11] To Pushkin, Karamzin was the "Columbus of Russian History."

Finally, and most significantly, Karamzin's *Notes,* or appendices, that accompanied the volumes included an extraordinary number of references to various rare sources formerly unknown or previously not utilized. Here, it can be said most assuredly, the author accomplished a prodigious feat. The value of these *Notes* became even greater when during the Moscow fire of 1812 many of the cited sources, including Karamzin's private library and the state archival depositories, completely and irretrievably perished. The nature of the lost documents is known to us only through Karamzin's voluminous references.[12] Altogether, Karamzin's **History of the Russian State** contains 6,538 references, veritably a history in itself!

Karamzin enjoyed the rare privilege of access to many private and state archives. He utilized the private collection of manuscripts of Musin-Pushkin and the equally valuable library of the Synod. He familiarized himself with numerous chronicles: the Hypatian, the Laurentian, the Troitsky (which, incidentally, perished during the Moscow fire), and others. He consulted the various Codes of Laws of the fourteenth and fifteenth centuries, and the medieval literary writings, such as *The Lay of the Host of Igor*; he read the early accounts of foreign travelers in eastern Europe. No preceding writer could claim more extensive consultation of sources than Karamzin; to date he crowned all efforts whether in literary style or in historical synthesis.

Despite these merits, his work is now a mere curiosity rather than acceptable study and reading material. It totally lacks historical perspective, since Karamzin could not conceive of an historical process; like the eighteenth-century rationalist, he saw in history only evil or benevolent sovereigns who led the country either to disaster or to glory. It is very doubtful that Karamzin could have examined sufficiently the sources to which he refers in his footnotes, though the archives were at his disposal and he was generously aided by high officials and friends, among them M. Muravyev, the Assistant Minister of Education; Count N. Rumyantsev; A. Malinovsky, Head of the Archives; and his close friend, A. I. Turgenev, who gathered and copied documents for him abroad, particularly at the papal archives. It was a physical impossibility within the comparatively short period of his time, interrupted by frequent illnesses, for him to go over the voluminous amount of material referred to; and though he never mentions them, Karamzin relied in great part upon references cited in secondary authorities, thereby creating an impression of extraordinary erudition.[13]

Of the secondary authorities which greatly aided Karamzin, Schlözer's edition of the Nestor Chronicle must be mentioned for the earlier period of Russian history, and Shcherbatov's for the later. The history of Shcherbatov was not only a ready pattern for the literary embroidery of Karamzin but also the best guide to the sources. Professor Milyukov, by comparing page after page, has shown quite convincingly how closely Karamzin followed the general outline of Shcherbatov.[14] To Shcherbatov's bulky work all Karamzin had to add was stylistic refinement and poetic imagination, precisely the qualities Prince Shcherbatov had lacked, and history was indeed bound to become well "selected, inspirited, and illuminated." A single citation from Karamzin, describing the eve of the historic battle of Kulikovo of September 8, 1380, will prove better than any lengthy discourse the accuracy of this statement:[15]

> The noise of arms had not quieted down in the town, and the people looked with emotion at the brave warriors ready to die for the Fatherland and the Faith. It seemed as if the Russian people had awakened after a deep sleep: the long terror of the Tartars had vanished from their hearts as if removed by some supernatural power. They reminded one another of the glorious Vozhsk battle; they enumerated all the evils they had suffered from the barbarians during the hundred and fifty years and wondered at the shameful patience of their forefathers. Princes, boyars, townsmen, peasants, all were fired with equal enthusiasm, for the tyranny of the Khans oppressed all equally, from the throne to the hut. What was more just than the sword at such a noble and unanimous call?

Patriotic? To this skeptical query Karamzin's disarming reply was that where there is no love, there is no soul. He never shrank before such accusations. "I know that I need the impartiality of an historian; forgive me, but I was not always able to conceal my love for the Fatherland."[16] It was this very "soul" that made his history so popular; the first edition of three thousand sets at the prohibitive price of fifty-five rubles a set was sold out within twenty-five days.[17] But the very qualities which made Karamzin's history popular undermined its value in the eyes of the critical scholar.

Even in Karamzin's lifetime his work drew fire because of its patriotic bias and its obsolete interpretation of the past.[18] As a precursor of Slavophilism, the criticism came naturally from the Westerners, or "skeptics" as they were called in Russian historiography, who were under the influence chiefly of Schlözer and Niebuhr. Polevoy considered Karamzin's **History** an outdated

piece of work before it was produced; Pogodin thought even the title of the twelve-volume work a mistake and the author as far from Gibbon as intellectual England was from Russia.[19] In 1818 M. Kachenovsky, editor of the *Messenger of Europe*, wrote a review in which he described it as "a chronicle masterfully recorded by an artist of superb talent, but not a history." The poet Vyazemsky called Karamzin the Field Marshal Kutuzov of History for he saved his country from the "invasion of oblivion"; in the field of history he demonstrated to the world that the Russians had a fatherland much as did Kutuzov on the field of battle in 1812.

Most of the Decembrists condemned Karamzin for his panegyric presentation of autocracy. Nikita Muravyev disapproved of it on the grounds that "history belongs to the people and not to tsars"; M. Fonvizin thought Karamzin concealed the political freedom which the Russian people had enjoyed in their earlier period of history, and instead forced Russian autocracy to the footlights of the national scene. N. Bestuzhev lamented that thus far all people wrote about was tsars and heroes, but few mentioned the sufferings and needs of the people. M. Lunin declared that autocracy was immoral and that God alone was entitled to the power claimed by autocracy. N. I. Turgenev recorded in his diary of 1818, after he read Karamzin's history, that the record of the past was the possession of the people and not the tsars and that despotism was concealed from the eye of the reader of this account. A. Pushkin, though considering the history a "creative work of a great writer" and referring to Karamzin as the "Columbus of Russian history," nonetheless discerned the weakness when he dedicated the biting four-line epigram which reads:

> In his history, beauty and simplicity
> Prove without bias
> The necessity of autocracy
> And the charm of the knout.

Among Karamzin's critics may be mentioned the later historian N. G. Ustryalov (1805-1870). He expressed his views in an historical essay in which he credited Karamzin with much that was due him, yet cautiously adding a few subtly formulated notes to his praises. History, he stated, is not a gallery of princes and tsars, but a chain of interlocking events. The purpose of the historian is to show pragmatically the gradual changes that the state has undergone and to explain how the state came to be what it is. Karamzin's *History of the Russian State,* declared Ustryalov, failed completely to come near such an accomplishment; he crowded his pages with accounts of royal members and failed in the end to reveal the genuine moving forces in Russian history.

But these were only isolated voices drowned by the general hosannas to the author; "Old Russia" extolled

Karamzin as the first national historian, and his twelve-volume work remained for a long time the official history of Russia.

Notes

1. N. M. Karamzin, *Pisma russkogo puteshestvennika* [*Letters of a Russian Traveler*], 2nd edition, 2 vols., Moscow, 1846; *Briefe eines reisenden Russen,* 6 vols. in 3, Leipzig, 1801-03; *Travels from Moscow, through Prussia, Germany, Switzerland, France and England,* tr. from the German, 3 vols., London, 1803; *Lettres d'un voyageur russe en France, en Allemagne et en Suisse (1789-1790),* Paris, 1867. See the latest edition of Karamzin's *Letters* published by Columbia University Press, 1957.

2. M. Pogodin, *N. M. Karamzin, po ego sochineniyam, pismam i otzyvan sovremennikov* [*N. M. Karamzin, as Revealed in His Work and Letters and in the Opinions of His Contemporaries*], Moscow, 1866, Vol. I, 139-44.

3. V. V. Sipovsky, *N. M. Karamzin, avtor* Pisem russkogo puteshestvennika [N. M. Karamzin, Author of *Letters of a Russian Traveler*], St. Petersburg, 1900, 416-17; *Russkaya Mysl',* VII, 1891, 22-23. See also *Starina i Novizna,* I, 60; *Pisma Karamzina k I. I. Dmitriyevu* [*Letters of Karamzin to I. I. Dmitriev*], St. Petersburg, 1866, 248-49.

4. [A. N.] Pypin, *Istoriya russkoy literatury* [*History of Russian Literature*], St. Petersburg, 1913, IV, 222-23; [M. I.] Koyalovich, [*Istoriya russkogo samosoznaniya* (*History of Russian Self-Realization*). St. Petersburg, 1893,] 143; Pogodin, *op. cit.,* II, 1-2.

5. N. M. Karamzin, *Zapiska o drevney i novoy Rossii* [*Memorandum on Old and New Russia*], St. Petersburg, 1914.

6. N. M. Karamzin, *Istoricheskoye pokhvalnoye slovo Ekaterine Vtoroy* [*A Historical Word of Praise for Catherine II*], Moscow, 1802.

7. Pogodin, *op. cit.,* I, 396-97.

8. N. M. Karamzin, *Istoriya gosudarstva rossiyskogo* [*History of the Russian State*], 12 vols., St. Petersburg, 1816-29; another edition, Moscow, 1903; French tr. by St. Thomas and Jauffret, 11 vols., Paris, 1819-26; German tr., 11 vols., Riga, 1820-33.

9. Pogodin, *op. cit.,* II, 2.

10. *Zhurnal Ministerstva Narodnogo Prosveshcheniya,* CXXXIV, 1867, 20 ff.

11. *Chteniya v Imperatorskom obshchestve istorii i drevnostey rossiyskikh pri Moskovskom universitete,* III, 1862, 23.

12. *Zhurnal Ministerstva Narodnogo Prosveshcheniya,* CXXXIII, 1867, 17-18.

13. Compare the different views of M. I. Koyalovich, *Istoriya russkogo samosoznaniya,* 143 ff., and P. N. Milyukov, *Glavniye techeniya russkoy istoricheskoy mysli* [(*Main Currents in Russian Historical Thought*), Moscow, 1898], 152 ff.

14. Milyukov, *op. cit.,* 161-63; also 187-190.

15. Karamzin, *Istoriya gosudarstva rossiyskogo,* St. Petersburg, 1819, V, 64.

16. Pypin, *Istoriya russkoy literatury,* IV, 224.

17. *Russky istorichesky zhurnal,* I, 1917, 14.

18. *Zhurnal Ministerstva Narodnogo Prosveshcheniya,* XVVVIII, 1867, 47.

19. N. Barsukov, *Zhizn i trudy M. P. Pogodina* [*The Life and Works of M. P. Pogodin*], St. Petersburg, 1889, II, 333. See also E. Kovalevsky, *Graf Bludov i ego vremya* [*Count Bludov and his Time*], St. Petersburg, 1866, 232; *Dekabrist N. I. Turgenev. Pis'ma k bratu S. I. Turgenevu* [*The Decembrist N. I. Turgenev. Letters to his Brother S. I. Turgenev*], Moscow, 1936, 349; [K. N.] Bestuzhev-Ryumin, [*Biografii i Kharakteristiki* (*Biographical Essays*), St. Petersburg, 1882,] 205-30; [N. L.] Rubinstein, [*Russkaya istoriografia* (*Russian Historiography*), Moscow, 1941,] 166-188; [M. N.] Tikhomirov, [*Ocherki istorii istoricheskoy nauki v SSSR* (*Studies of the History of Historical Science in the USSR*), Moscow, 1995, Vol. I,] 277-88.

R. E. McGrew (essay date February 1959)

SOURCE: McGrew, R. E. "Notes on the Princely Role in Karamzin's *Istorija gosudarstva Rossijskago*." *American Slavic and East European Review* 18, no. 1 (February 1959): 12-24.

[*In the following essay, McGrew examines the historical significance of Karamzin's* History of the Russian State. *According to McGrew, Karamzin's belief in the importance of autocratic rule exerted a profound influence on Russian politics throughout the nineteenth century.*]

While the intrinsic worth of Nikolaj Mikailovich Karamzin's work still may be debated, his importance in Russian history has become clear. Karamzin popularized Russian history for his own day and through history gave form and content to Russian conservatism. Even his sharpest critics recognized these contributions, and Alexandre Koyré referred in a cutting note to Karamzin's arguments which appeared with monotonous regularity throughout the nineteenth century. A. N. Pypin pointed out that Karamzin's ideas had an immediate practical effect, for he was able to influence the new Tsar, Nicholas I, in the moment of crisis which began his reign, and Karamzin's views formed the substructure for Nicholaevan conservatism.[1]

The *History of the Russian State* was Karamzin's best known historical work and achieved an immense popularity. The first edition of 3,000 copies was sold out in twenty-five days, it became the fashion to read Russian history, à la Karamzin, and no boudoir was complete without a copy. This popularization had more far-reaching effects, for Karamzin was responsible for creating a demand for ancient Russian history in the school curricula.[2] All this points to wide currency for Karamzin's ideas within the educated class and goes far toward explaining the "monotonous regularity" with which his ideas appeared in the nineteenth century.

The *Zapiska o drevnej i novoj rossii* is rightly regarded as Karamzin's political testament, but this work, presented to Alexander I in March, 1811, never had the currency that the *History* enjoyed. It was treated as a state document and went unpublished until 1837 when fragments appeared in *Sovremennik*. The first complete edition was published in *Russky arkhiv* in 1870. The *Zapiska* has a strong appeal for the historian, for in it Karamzin speaks specifically not only of the ancient past, but of Peter, Catherine, Paul, and most especially, Alexander. This work, however, remained in the archives, and while it was known to some, it was by no means widely known. The *History* was well known and popular and it contained the basic elements of Karamzin's ideology. It is, therefore, of major importance in defining Karamzin's immediate influence on a broad reading public.[3]

The *History of the Russian State* divided Russian development into three distinct stages: the pre-political, the monarchic, and the autocratic. Each stage defined or re-defined the Prince's role in society, and taken together, they indicated progressive growth. Within these stages a rhythmic pattern emerged, beginning in the pre-political, building to a climax with Vladimir the Holy and Yaroslav the Wise, then receding as the Kievan monarchy broke apart to reach the nadir in the Tartar invasions. The ascending line began again in the Mongol period and reached a new climax with Ivan III and Vasily Ivanovich, only to begin a precipitous descent through Ivan IV and Boris Godunov to another low point in the Time of Troubles. Karamzin died before he could complete the pattern, and the re-ascending line, prefigured in the later chapters of Volume XII, broke off abruptly. Its continuation, however, may be noted in the *Zapiska*.[4]

The distinguishing feature of this pattern was fluctuation between anarchy and authority. Anarchy existed in inverse proportion to the extent of the Prince's power and his regard for the general welfare in exerting that power. Absolute anarchy existed when there was no Prince who could control the Russian lands. Moral anarchy appeared within a framework of political perversion when the Prince retained the artifacts of power but used them against the public interest, or when an illegitimate sovereign, either collective or individual, usurped the princely role. The high points in the rhythm of Russian development were the reigns of those sovereigns strong and wise enough to maintain Russia's internal unity and external security, while the low points marked the most intense periods of moral and political dislocation.

These generalized patterns were focused on the Prince, and it was this that led Kizevetter to conclude that Karamzin wrote a history of rulers rather than a history of the state.[5] This conclusion is only partially true. The Prince played a dual role in the *History of the Russian State.* On one side the Prince was part of a developing institutional structure, and the existence of a Prince marked the line between anarchy and the state. Karamzin noted, for example, that before the Varangians came, the lands of the East Slavs lacked any political coherence, and only local centers of authority existed. These lived in a state of nature characterized by constant and bitter strife until finally they escaped by appealing to the Varangians who then laid the foundations of the Russian monarchy.[6] The prince's other role was as an actor. Here Karamzin seemed to follow a mechanistic theory of historical causation which explained complicated results in terms of simple causes and laid Russia's glory or degradation squarely on the shoulders of her rulers. This appearance is misleading, however, and the interaction of the institutional and personal roles of the Prince saved Karamzin's *History* from being just a history of rulers and made it a history of the state, or better, a history of sovereignty.

Karamzin believed that Russia's greatness stemmed from wise autocracy, and the *History* showed how autocracy developed and how it was best maintained.[7] The Kievan monarchy was the first Russian state, and under Kiev's great rulers, Oleg, Vladimir, and Yaroslav, Russia rose to heights of culture and power which made her more than Europe's peer. The great Kievan Princes controlled their lands, repressed dissident and divisive forces and maintained the unity and the security of their state. Even the wise may err, however, and though Svjatoslav began the practice of dividing his estate, he was followed in that practice by both Vladimir and Yaroslav. This policy undermined the monarchy, opened Russia to civil war and anarchy and left her drained and helpless to face the Mongol conquerors.[8]

Karamzin's discussion of Kievan Rus' emphasized the Prince as actor. Oleg consolidated the Russian lands, Vladimir introduced Christianity and maintained the state, Yaroslav ratified the laws, while Svjatoslav undermined the monarchy, Svjatopolk overextended it, Ysjaslav deserted it and Mstislav tyrannized it. Each ruler committed particular acts which affected the state directly, and each played a role in determining the state's final destiny. Karamzin centered on the Prince as actor, and stressed the personal responsibility he carried.[9]

The Prince was also part of a governmental system, and as such, could go only as far as conditions allowed him. The Kievan monarchy was by no means absolute, and the Kievan Prince was hedged about and challenged. This was true from the very beginning. Karamzin noted the Slavic libertarian tradition and pointed to the Slav's public assemblies and their fierce individualism. The Varangians came by sufferance, and the independence of the Russian people was, for the most part, untouched. That spirit of independence, untouched and uncrushed, was a source of trouble which had constantly to be guarded against by the Prince.[10]

There were other elements as well which checked princely action and presented positive dangers to state unity. The Varangians held to the tradition that the Great Prince was a companion in arms, and that the Prince's guard, together with the supreme council, shared his power. The soldiers limited the Prince by taking the lion's share of plunder, and when the Prince collected tribute, the soldiers received a portion. The appanage princes were a latent threat, and the system of succession made anarchic feudalism a constant danger.[11]

Karamzin characterized the Kievan system as one which joined the advantages and abuses of despotism and of liberty. When Kiev's great rulers were in control, the people were tranquil and obeyed without murmuring. When the great rulers passed, however, and Russia came to have several rulers, then the people asserted themselves and dreamed of ruling. A Prince of genius and strength could hold the Kievan state together. But a Prince lacking those characteristics soon found himself a prisoner of the system. The Kievan state was only a monarchy, and there were elements in it which were disruptive of absolute authority and therefore dangerous to progress.[12]

Svjatoslav's tragic error bred civil war, and by the time the Tartars appeared, Kiev's glory was already dimmed. The Tartars extinguished it. A somber pall cloaked Russia's life. Beneath that pall, however, a progressive principle was stirring. The foundations of autocracy were being laid. Karamzin's description of the Tartar conquest is immensely important. In it he completed his criticism of the Kievan system and the Kievan Princes. Furthermore, he was able to indicate the necessary pre-

conditions for autocracy and weave their formation into the fabric of his work.

Under Tartar rule, Russia became a jungle, and the law of survival was the only moral imperative. The Tartars governed Russia from afar, but their representatives treated the Russians as slaves, and the Russians, their national pride debased, kissed the fist that struck them. The people became untrustworthy as the need to fool the Tartars accustomed them to deceit. Security could be purchased, and the Russians became avid hoarders willing to endure any shame to gather money. But real security could not be bought, and moral barbarism produced total anarchy. Force replaced law. Russians and Tartars pillaged with impunity. Neither life nor property was safe upon the roads, and the only real protection within doors was a stout lock and a strong arm. Banditry was epidemic, and the very rudiments of civilized society were known only from the past. When law was finally restored, it appeared in a form hitherto unknown among the Russians. The death penalty was widely used, and corporal punishment became an essential element. Russia had been brutalized, and stringent measures were necessary to restrain primitive instincts.[13]

Society's degradation marked a change in social and political forms. The libertarian tradition was repressed and disappeared. Ambitious rulers went to Sarai, effaced themselves before the Khans and returned to exercise the tyrannic powers granted by their conquerors. Only at Novgorod and Pskov did the *vech* bell ring assembling the people, and in the new cities which rose to power, the tradition of popular assemblies failed to appear at all.[14] The cities lost their privilege of electing their military chiefs, and even the boyars, who had been independent aristocrats, saw their rights abrogated as they became dependents of the Prince. In sum, the checks on monarchical authority were destroyed, and no voice remained that could legitimately be raised against the sovereign.[15]

Anarchy and brutalization were Karamzin's final arguments against checks on monarchy. The praise he lavished on the great Kievan Princes was based on their effective control of dissident and destructive tendencies, but the weakness of the Kievan system appeared even in the work of Kiev's greatest rulers. Only a Prince of genius, a St. Vladimir or a Yaroslav the Wise, could contain the inner forces of destruction and maintain the state. Too many challenges existed, and too few rulers possessed both genius and strength. It was necessary to complete princely power before political and social progress could be constant.[16] Vladimir and Yaroslav themselves had debased monarchical authority by sanctioning the roto system. The only recourse possible was to purge Russia's system of liberty's poisons and create a Prince who not only would be the Great Prince, but who would be the Autocrat. Karamzin viewed the Slav's

tradition of independence as a positive evil, and though he spoke nostalgically of the great *vech* bell which was silenced, he thought the silencing a marked improvement. The Tartar yoke was onerous, but under it authority made great strides, and while the change in status of the people and the boyars was undoubtedly obnoxious, Karamzin called it Providence's richest gift to Russia.[17]

In an ingenuous passage, Karamzin justified this stand and completed his rationalization of autocracy. He pointed out that Rome required a dictator in her hour of greatest danger, and that Russia, helpless and dismembered, could hardly accept less. Only a single hand could restore authority, and neither the populace nor the aristocracy was sufficient to the challenge. He then remarked that optimism has no place in history, and that the historian should never scrutinize events for proof that everything is for the best. Batu's invasion was one of the greatest calamities in history. It crushed the nation, strewed Russia with cinders and corpses, and imposed a state of slavery as long in duration as it was cruel in effect. Yet the optimism which Karamzin denied came bubbling out when he wrote that even so this calamity was advantageous. It would have been far better had one of Yaroslav's descendants avoided the disaster, re-established monarchical unity and assured the state's integrity and internal tranquility. But no such leader appeared, and the logic of Karamzin's exposition militated against such an appearance. The internal structure of the Kievan monarchy had basic flaws, and a cataclysm was necessary to destroy them. The Tartars provided that upheaval and accomplished what no Prince could have done in his own right. Further, as the Tartars weakened or destroyed the checks on monarchy, so they raised up the Moscow dynasty which, from the time of Ivan Kalita, built an autocratic state on new foundations.[18]

The Mongols changed basic Russian institutions, and thereby changed the Prince's role. As the autocrat emerged, the nobility appeared in an altered guise as mere advisers dependent on the Prince, while the populace, having lost its traditional rights, was expected simply to obey. The autocrat became both the sum of Russia's institutions and the primary focus of her history. As sovereignty incarnate, the Prince's actions took on new meaning, affecting all phases of Russian life directly. The Prince's dual role became one, and the causal patterns of Karamzin's *History* now centered on a single point.[19]

The essence of Karamzin's conservatism appeared in his depiction of the princely role in the period from 1462-1612. Tendencies which he noted in the opening volumes became realities, and the basic issues of princely morality and the proper goals for princely authority were given their fullest definition. Karamzin had established that for Russia there was only the choice

between absolute authority and anarchy. The remainder of the work explained the autocracy and completed the autocratic theme.

The Russian autocracy under Ivan III astonished foreign observers. The monarch exercised complete power and maintained that power simply and directly. Ivan III and his successor, Vasily, fixed forever the nature of Russian government, and autocracy became the sole constitution and the unique base for Russian progress and prosperity. This, Karamzin insisted, was not tyranny, for the autocrat fostered the rule of law. The autocrat's primary duty was to serve his subjects' welfare, and the public welfare was the essence of the rule of law.[20]

Ivan III above all served Russia's welfare. He recognized Russia's backwardness and through his contacts with Venice and the Papacy brought Western artisans and architects to aid in re-developing the arts and commerce.[21] He reduced the power of the appanage princes, brought Novgorod within the circle of Muscovite control, threw off for good and all the Tartar yoke, and raised Russia to the status of a great power, respected by other European states.[22] In achieving these ends, he exercised moderation and followed the rules of prudence faithfully. He avoided infringing solemn treaties, avoided arbitrary acts, and eschewed acts of violence which were always dangerous to the throne.[23] And when his policies were successful, and Russia was firmly set on the road to greatness, he again showed prudence by refusing to become immersed in foreign affairs at the expense of his estates. The alliances he accepted were useful to Russia, and Ivan never served as the instrument for another nation's polity. His sole concern was the welfare of his people, and the result of so much care was that Russia, an independent power, enjoyed a calm exterior and had nothing to fear from foreign enemies.[24]

Karamzin compared Ivan III to Peter the Great, and in the comparison, the qualities of the good Prince emerged even more clearly. Both, he pointed out, were great, but Ivan showed the greater perspicacity. Although he recognized European superiority and introduced European artisans, he never dreamed of either introducing new customs or of changing the national character of his subjects. Ivan imported expert craftsmen or military men only to embellish the capital or improve the army. He did not forbid the empire to foreigners, but he received only those whose talents he could use, and if he chose to honor them, he did so as a great monarch without humiliating his nation. Although Karamzin deferred his detailed discussion of Peter to its proper place in the chronological framework, the implication was clear that Peter failed in those areas where Ivan succeeded, and that thanks to his prudence and care, Ivan ruled in greater conformity with the true interests of the state.[25]

The monarch contrasting most sharply with Ivan III was Ivan IV. His excesses and illegal actions pointed up the virtues of Ivan III, and the melancholy consequences of his reign of terror underscored the necessity for wise and virtuous governance. Vasily Ivanovich, the father of Ivan IV, had maintained the tradition established by Ivan III, and his reign was an extension of his predecessor's. He was moderate in his acts, made his decisions in council, and enlightened his opinions by listening to the experienced servants who surrounded him. Even so, he knew how to be a master and pressed his prerogatives with firmness and dispatch. He loved peace without fearing war, and never neglected an opportunity to increase his power. He was in all respects worthy to take up the scepter.[26] That scepter was tarnished, however, when it finally reached the hands of Ivan IV. The interregnum from Vasily's death in 1533 to Ivan's coronation in 1547 saw Russia subjected to oligarchic rule.[27] The people suffered, and the young Prince was prevented by his advisers from knowing of their suffering. Russia's only hope was that years and reason would mature his judgment and prepare him to rule for the welfare of his subjects.[28]

This hope was faint, and Karamzin asserted that Ivan lacked the qualities of a good Prince even in the early days. Capricious and mercurial, he abandoned himself to violent rages and unworthy amusements. When he exercised his sovereignty, he did so to please his whim. He was falsely persuaded that arbitrary actions proved his independence, never seeing that by neglecting the state he submitted to the nobles. Karamzin accused Ivan of never learning the first axiom of monarchy: the sovereign is only independent to the extent that he is virtuous. Never, Karamzin asserted, was Russia worse governed, as the nobility aggrandized themselves in the name of the Tsar.[29]

The inevitable result of so much evil was civil strife, and when Moscow burned in 1547, the people rose against the Glinskys, massacred their servitors, and murdered the Tsar's uncle. Ivan could only tremble, and Anastasia prayed. The fault lay with Ivan, and Sylvester of Novgorod appeared like a prophet of Israel to warn the Tsar of God's wrath and the destruction which must follow it. Sylvester blamed the young ruler for Russia's misfortunes, and then instructed Ivan in the way of God's mercy and in the divine precepts which the Prince must follow. Karamzin quoted Kurbsky to the effect that Sylvester awakened the desire for good in Ivan's heart, and the historian himself noted that from this encounter dated Ivan IV's glory.[30]

Sylvester worked a miracle, for the very atmosphere of the Russian court changed, and the sovereign power was established on principles of wisdom, moderation, sweetness, and peace. Karamzin pointed the moral with great satisfaction. Only in an autocratic state could such

a rapid change take place, for in an autocracy every-thing depends on the will of the sovereign who can lead his millions either to ruin or to happiness.[31] So long as virtue ruled Ivan, Russia would be happy, but when the old passions reasserted themselves, her future would be dark. Those passions rose again when Anastasia's death destroyed Ivan's balance, and from 1560 until his death in 1584, Ivan tyrannized over Russia.[32]

Although he had tried to emulate Ivan the Great and become known as a monarch who ruled according to the law, Ivan IV became best known for his utter denial of legality and morality. Karamzin's description of the terrors and accomplishments of Ivan IV takes up all of Volume IX of the *History* and need not concern us here. Karamzin did point out that each act of brutality created fear among the boyars, and that Ivan read fear as hatred and struck again and again. But Karamzin refused to accept any excuse for Ivan, and pointed out that the only plots which existed were in the Tsar's troubled mind.[33] Indeed, Karamzin wondered which was the more astonishing, the Tsar who destroyed without thought of reason, or the people who allowed themselves to be destroyed and then mourned the tyrant's death.[34]

Although Karamzin granted that Ivan IV sometimes acted as a great monarch should,[35] he emphasized his disregard of law and his ignoring the common weal. Ivan's reign, however, was instructive. The life of a tyrant, Karamzin declaimed, is a calamity for humanity, but his history offers useful lessons to sovereigns and to nations. To the extent that that history inspires a horror of evil, it fosters virtue, and as history illuminates the evil ways of tyrants, it shows sovereigns what pitfalls to avoid. The people may have pardoned Ivan, for whatever reason, but history cannot pardon as easily as the people. Ivan the Terrible was a tyrant who abrogated moral law and neglected the welfare of his nation. That tyranny and that neglect not only tortured Ivan's Russia, but opened the way to weakness and decay under Ivan's successors.[36]

The effects of tyranny live on after the tyrant has passed away, and Karamzin opened his tenth volume by quoting Tacitus that the first days following the death of a tyrant are the happiest for the people. But a cruel reign often prepares the way for a weak one, for the new sovereign fears that he will resemble his odious predecessor, and will, therefore, allow a relaxation of authority which can be disastrous. Russia had not only seen a tyrant pass, but now saw a man better fitted for the monastery than the throne prepare to succeed him. Feodor Ivanovich was weak, and his weakness worsened the after-effects of tyranny.[37]

When the sovereign is weak, others seek power, and the great nobles vied among themselves. The man who achieved the pinnacle was Boris Godunov. Karamzin

described Godunov as a man of superlative abilities but marked by a tragic flaw. Glory and power were his obsessions, and he saw virtue as only a means to an end. Godunov, who was born only to be a subject, coveted the Tsar's position, and in reaching for it, brought down himself and Russia.[38] Godunov became indispensable to Feodor, and the Tsar, who feared responsibility, allowed his adviser to rule in his name. Russia appeared to enjoy prosperity in those days, but underneath the surface burned the fires of unrest. It was known that Godunov was the first power in the state, and it was known that Feodor bore only the Tsar's title. These facts bred hatred. Godunov tried to win the nobles to him, to gain the support of the townspeople, but each new move only intensified the feelings against him. Boris Godunov had no legitimate claim on the autocracy, and absolute power in the hands of even the most worthy subjects displeases the nation.[39]

Godunov went even farther. The murder of Dmitri Ivanovich left Russia without an heir, and when Feodor died, Godunov was selected to wear the crown. Karamzin pointed out that this appeared the logical choice, for Godunov, in spite of opposition, had ruled strongly and well during Feodor's lifetime. But this was only the appearance, for the new sovereign, a man endowed with great human wisdom, had gained his crown by crime, and Heaven's rage menaced the criminal sovereign and the unhappy nation.[40]

Sylvester might threaten Ivan IV with Heaven's wrath and mean it, but to Karamzin the phrase was only figurative. Following Boris' coronation, the contentious boyars and the dissatisfied populace grew more restive, and when the first False Dmitri appeared at the head of a Polish force, no one rallied the resistance. The reason was Boris. He commanded respect neither as man nor ruler, and this lack of attachment to the sovereign bred indifference for the honor of the country.[41]

The death of Boris Godunov and the victory of the False Dmitri opened another period of anarchy in Russian history. This time the autocrats had failed, and the nation again sprawled supine before its enemies. Karamzin noted history's judgment on Godunov, and remarked that although he was among the wisest rulers in history, his name, even centuries after, was pronounced with horror. The historian applauded that judgment, for Boris bathed Russia with the blood of his victims, and practiced persiflage where only truth and honesty could succeed. This unhappy Tsar wore the mask of virtue, but the benefits he brought Russia through wise judgments and considered acts were more than obscured by his willingness to betray basic principles of governance whenever ambition demanded it. Boris committed the sin of ambivalence, for he was sullied with a tyrant's crimes yet lacked the tyrant's character. He seemed incapable of distinguishing right and

wrong, and viewed his worst actions as strokes of state. He lacked Ivan's blind fury, yet he was capable of acts as cruel. He opened the abyss before Russia, profaned the throne and prepared the way for cutthroats, imposters, and avengers who practised their awful acts on a helpless state.[42]

Boris Godunov provided Karamzin with an example of the Prince who allowed ambition to rule him and thus defied both absolute moral law and the rule that Princes exist only for the state's welfare. Godunov was a wise ruler and capable of statesmanship, but his wisdom and his statecraft could not overcome his tragic flaw. Like Macbeth he could cry, "I have no spur / To prick the sides of my intent. but only Vaulting ambition. . . . ," and like Macbeth his ambition brought ruin in its train.[43] Godunov aspired to a position which should never have been his, and opened the way to that position by murder. This led to Karamzin's second point. Legitimacy and a defined line of succession are essential to the welfare of the state. Godunov lacked that legitimacy, and thus debased and ultimately destroyed the ruling house.

Russia's collapse in the Time of Troubles contrasted with the breakdown of the Kievan state. Kiev suffered structural weaknesses which, combined with errors by her rulers, destroyed her power. Muscovite Russia fell as a consequence of Ivan IV's tyranny and Feodor's weakness combined with the illegal and immoral ambitions of Boris Godunov. The structure was sound, but the men who controlled it were not. Consequently, Karamzin could view the failures of Kiev as proof of institutional inadequacies, while the failure of Muscovite Russia was a human failure. Autocracy itself was not questioned, but the uses to which autocracy was put were.

Karamzin was not overtly teleological in his approach, but as he attempted to explain tradition's sanction for the autocrat, a teleological element crept in. Since history was the holy book of nations whose lessons guided the statesman and inspired the citizen, the present was always before the historian's eyes as he looked at the past. The lessons which Karamzin presented were to be read by the men of his own time, and the reflection of his time was mirrored in the past. The patterns of Russian history proved conclusively that autocracy was necessary, for Russia was most splendid when she was most strongly ruled. But Russia's rulers had also to be virtuous and guide themselves by the general welfare, for otherwise tyranny and moral anarchy followed. The *History of the Russian State* portrayed the Prince as an historical necessity and then demanded that he be both strong and good, for he was also the prime mover in Russia's destiny.[44]

Notes

1. A. Koyré, *La philosophie et le problème national en Russia au début du XIXe siecle* (Paris, 1929), p. 26; A. N. Pypin, *Die Geistigen Bewegungen in Russland in der ersten Hälfte des XIX Jahrhunderts, uebertragen von Dr. Boris Menzies* (Berlin, 1894), pp. 374-76. See also M. Pogodin, *N. M. Karamzin,* (Moscow, 1866), II, 460; "Imperator Nikolaj Pavlovich i Karamzin v poslednie ego dni," *Russky arkhiv* (Moscow, 1906), pp. 122-27.

2. A. A. Kizevetter, "N. M. Karamzin," *Russkij istoricheskij zhurnal* (Moscow, 1917), Book I, p. 14. The first eight volumes of the *History* were published at St. Petersburg in 1816, and successive volumes appeared through 1826. A French translation, *L'histoire de l'empire de la Russie* was published at the same time at Paris, at first under Karamzin's supervision. The edition cited in this paper, unless otherwise indicated, is *Istorija gosudarstva rossijskago,* 12 volumes (St. Petersburg, 1892). Cited hereafter as *Ist. gos. ross.*

3. Pypin gives a summary and critical analysis of the *Zapiska, op. cit.,* 306ff. N. Tourgueneff [Turgenev] published a French translation of selections from the *Zapiska* in *La Russie et les russes,* 3 volumes, (Paris, 1848), I, 496ff. For the memorandum itself, see: *Zapiska o drevnej i novoj rossii, Russkij arkhiv,* 1870, 2229-2350.

4. The high points of the recent period were Alexej Mikhailovich, Peter the Great (qualified), and Catherine the Great. The burden of Karamzin's argument to Alexander was that he should follow the wise principles of Catherine while avoiding her excesses, and recognize that the autocracy in its historic form was essential to Russia's welfare. See: *Zapiska, op. cit.,* 2245 ff. On Alexander, see 2271 ff.

5. Kizevetter, *op. cit.,* 19.

6. *Ist. gos. ross.,* I, 13-20; 37 ff; 75. Karamzin pointed out that both great men and great nations go through infancy and ought not to be ashamed of it. The pre-political, or pre-Varangian, period was Russia's infancy, and the path to political maturity opened only with the coming of a Prince. The state of nature resumed when monarchy was destroyed by the practice of dividing the Great Prince's estates. See: *Ist. gos. ross.,* I, 119-20; 131; II, 19. III, *passim* describes the struggle for power during Kiev's decline.

7. In the introduction, Karamzin expressed both his belief in autocracy and his faith that history guides the statesman, and inspires and comforts the citizen. The *History* can be read as an extended "statesman's handbook." See: *Ist. gos. ross.,* (St. Petersburg, 1816), I, ix, xxviii.

8. On Russia's glory and her equality with Europe, *Ibid.*, V, 226ff. On dividing the estates and undermining the monarchy, I, 119-120; 131. Karamzin saw this breakup of authority as feudalism, a word which he used as the antonym of monarchy. II, 19. See also: II, 45-46; III, 128.

9. The organization of the work furthers the sense of emphasis on the Prince. After the opening chapters, the *History* settles down to a reign by reign pattern. Social and economic conditions are handled in separate chapters, and only occasionally form part of the integrated account. Within each chapter, Karamzin keeps the focus of his interest on the Prince, and he digresses only to return. Even during the civil wars in later Kievan history, he attempts to use this organization and carefully follows the fortunes of the contending princes. *Ibid.*, III, *passim*. Some of the more interesting judgments in the *History* are in the "cultural" chapters. See: I, chapter 10; V, chapter 4.

10. On the spirit of independence and individualism, see *Ibid.*, I, 37ff. Karamzin criticized Nestor's chronology, but he accepted the story of voluntary submission to the Varangians. I, 34-36. As further proof that the Slavs were not conquered, Karamzin cited Yaroslav's code which made no distinction between Slavs and Varangians. II, 44. The populace was fickle and untrustworthy, and the assemblies in which the people exposed their trust were unstable. See: II, 88; III, 18 (for popular reactions on the death of Andrej of Suzdal); III, 95-96 (On popular rising in Novgorod, 1215); IV, 174.

11. *Ibid.*, I, 158-60. In this passage Karamzin pointed out that the appanage grants were theoretically in the power of the Great Prince, but that their holders came to regard them as patrimonies.

12. *Ibid.*, III, 128.

13. *Ibid.*, V, 227-29.

14. Karamzin noted that only a single council was held at Moscow and that was treated by the annalists as an extraordinary event. *Ibid.*, V, 230.

15. *Ibid.*, V, 230-31.

16. During the Kievan civil war, some of the men who gained control were men of virtue, as Mikhail II or Yaroslav of Galich, but few were able to attain more than momentary success, and no one of them was able to establish a solid line of succession. See: III, 27; 45-46; and for summation, 128.

17. *Ibid.*, V, 231.

18. *Ibid.*, V, 231-35. Karamzin assigned autocracy a "progressive role," and it is hard to escape the conclusion that, in spite of its horrors, he regarded the Tartar conquest positively since it advanced autocracy. Karamzin singled out for special mention the very elements which had challenged the Kievan rulers as the elements which were seriously weakened or destroyed by the Tartars, thus clearing the way for autocracy and progress.

19. Karamzin noted these changes when he introduced Ivan III's reign. He pointed out that Russia's history entered a new phase and that Ivan III realized the promise of autocracy. The *History* itself, he went on, reflects that promise, for it no longer catalogues the senseless quarrels of princes, but rather describes a nation dedicated to conquering its glory and independence. *Ibid.*, VI, 3-4. The intimate relationship between princely acts and societal responses may be seen in the discussion of Ivan Kalita's crime, which Karamzin severely criticized, and in the miraculous change in Russian life following Sylvester's warning to Ivan IV. See below for discussion. See: IV, 152-153; VIII, 66-67.

20. *Ibid.*, VII, 123-24. Karamzin asserted earlier that the principal end of organized society was the security of the individual and the maintenance of property. II, 31. This idea remained basic, but he expanded it as he discussed the reign of Ivan III. See below.

21. *Ibid.*, VI, 46-50; 110.

22. *Ibid.*, VI, 62ff; 218.

23. *Ibid.*, VI, 62-63.

24. *Ibid.*, VI, 222. This was one of the more striking lessons that Karamzin thought history taught. He praised the foreign policy of Catherine II for it secured the external security of the state. Furthermore, he asserted, Catherine never involved herself in useless foreign wars. Karamzin sharply criticized Alexander I for failing to follow Catherine's lead and for become needlessly embroiled in Europe after 1804. He suggested that the European powers were using Russia, and that Alexander acted against the best interests of the state. See: *Zapiska, op. cit.*, 2274-82.

25. *Ibid.*, VI, 222-223. See: *Zapiska, op. cit.* 2249ff. for detailed statement concerning Peter's reforms and the errors involved in them.

26. *Ibid.*, VII, 4.

27. Karamzin criticized the regency of Helen Glinsky for she was unable to control her council, and he thought a council without a sovereign was like a body without a head. The oligarchy which resulted was worse than tyranny. Karamzin compared an irascible monarch to an angry deity. The people could accommodate themselves to his whims and

recognize his rights to those whims. An oligarchy lacked legitimacy, and men only saw other men tyrannizing over them. This raised a spirit of detestation and ultimately rebellion. *Ibid.,* VIII, 3-6. This point of view did not however, soften Karamzin's criticism of Ivan IV's tyranny. See: IX, 273-275.

28. *Ibid.,* VIII, 54.

29. *Ibid.,* VIII, 59-60.

30. *Ibid.,* VIII, 62-64. The Church played a culture-bearing role in Karamzin's analysis, and at crucial moments, as in the case of Sylvester, would intervene to show the Tsar the way, or as in the case of the Suzdal rioters, to calm the population. The Churchmen were to aid the Prince and were a prop for the state. See: *Ibid.,* I, 155; III, 18; V, 229-30. Karamzin criticized the Metropolitan Cyprion for fleeing Moscow as the Tartars approached. He betrayed his duty to the Church and the people by seeking personal safety. V, 50.

31. *Ibid.,* VIII, 66-67.

32. *Ibid.,* IX, 3-4

33. *Ibid.,* IX, 12; 273-75.

34. *Ibid.,* IX, 106; 273-75.

35. *Ibid.,* IX, 275ff.

36. *Ibid.,* IX, 294; X, 3.

37. *Ibid.,* X, 3-6.

38. *Ibid.,* X, 7.

39. *Ibid.,* X, 43ff.

40. *Ibid.,* X, 141.

41. *Ibid.,* XI, 95.

42. *Ibid.,* XI, 109.

43. Shakespeare impressed Karamzin at an early age, and on occasion his handling of the princely role has Shakespearean overtones. Pogodin was enthusiastic about Karamzin's capacities as a Shakespeare scholar, but Pypin qualified that enthusiasm. See: Pogodin, *op. cit.,* I, 29; 38-39. Pypin, *op. cit.,* 267-268.

44. States, Karamzin pointed out, are not mineral-like aggregations but are the product of their rulers' genius. *Ist. gos. ross.,* VI, 222.

Henry M. Nebel, Jr. (essay date 1967)

SOURCE: Nebel, Henry M., Jr. "Moscow and St. Petersburg." In *N. M. Karamzin: A Russian Sentimentalist,* pp. 36-49. The Hague: Mouton & Co., 1967.

[*In the following essay, Nebel examines Karamzin's early career as a writer and editor.*]

A. Moscow: The Journals

The masonic period of Karamzin's literary apprenticeship coincided with a period of sharp hostility between St. Petersburg and Moscow, when the passive cultural competition threatened to break into open political conflict. These events are closely tied to the foreign liaisons, putative and real, of the Moscow Rosicrucians. In 1786, Frederick William II succeeded to the Prussian throne. He was a Rosicrucian as were several members of his entourage. Earlier, Schwartz had contacted some of these people.[1] Now, the Moscow Rosicrucians found themselves in a sort of "secret" alliance with a powerful faction of the Prussian government. In 1787, Russia's relations with Prussia had deteriorated. Together with Sweden, the Prussians were considering attacking Catherine while she was busy with the Turks in the south. Aware of this, Catherine was suspicious of any group which maintained relations, however tenuous, with the government of Frederick William II.[2] She had long since been distrustful of the masons[3] and now began harassing the order, increasing censorship of their publications, and persecuting the masons themselves.[4] Finally, in 1791 she forced Novikov to close his publishing house and, in the spring of 1792, had him arrested.[5] He was imprisoned and several of his associates exiled.

In this dangerous atmosphere of government suspicion and distrust, Karamzin's masonic period came to an end. In the spring of 1789 he stated that he could not "participate further in the meetings [of the masons] because of personal convictions. I had to bid them farewell."[6] And he concludes, "We parted amicably." How "amicable" the parting was is open to some doubt. The masons never did forgive his defection and always remained cold to him.[7] Anastasia Pleščeeva, whom Karamzin had met in 1786 through Kutuzov, in a letter to the latter berates the "scoundrel" and "Tartuffe" who was responsible for Karamzin's leaving Moscow.[8] The "scoundrel" and "Tartuffe" remains unknown but Pleščeeva's comment suggests some personal difficulty and casts doubt on the amicability of the farewell.

While some unknown difficulty may have played a part in Karamzin's immediate break with the masons, a more significant explanation seems to lie in his own statement that "personal convictions" led him to part company with the brethren. The masons contributed a great deal to Karamzin's intellectual maturation but he never accepted their narrow religious-mystical orientation wholeheartedly. In addition to rejecting the mystical tendencies of the circle, he also rejected the masonic view that only literature of an extreme moral tendentiousness could exorcise the devils of skepticism, atheism and materialism abroad in the Russian land. Karamzin was a writer rather than a preacher and such tendencies served only to interfere with the pursuit of

his own aesthetic interests. These "convictions" were reason enough during these years for him to follow his own bent more and the masonic ends less, and, eventually, to sever his connection with the circle.

Upon his return from Europe and England in September 1790, Karamzin began a new phase of his literary career. In the November issue of the *Moskovskie vedomosti* [*Moscow News*], Karamzin announced his intention "to publish a journal" of poetry and prose.[9] It was further announced that the journal would be "published in Moscow, whence the title, *Moscow Journal*"; and that it would contain works translated from "German, English, and French journals, information on significant recently-published books and theatrical performances, and miscellany". In conclusion, the editor solicited from his readers any material except "theological, mystical, excessively scholarly, pedantic, dry pieces".

While Karamzin was later to complain that the 300 subscribers barely paid the printing cost, the number far exceeded the circulation of all but two other journals in the last half of the century.[10] This success was a personal triumph of the young editor and publisher. He correctly evaluated and was able to satisfy the cultural needs of his readers. Aware of the oppressive political climate, except for his ode **"K milosti"** [**"To Mercy"**], Karamzin carefully avoided articles or commentaries dealing with political problems.[11] And in obvious reference to the masonic interests, he also avoided "theological, mystical . . . pieces."

In general, the various sections of the *Moscow Journal* illustrate the young editor's interest in the aesthetic aspect of literature and his concept of what Russian culture needed at this stage of its development. Karamzin popularized the short tale[12] (*povest'*) in his journals, and it remained the dominant prose genre until well into the twenties of the nineteenth century. Simple stories of virtuous people with no momentous or difficult problem left unresolved, these tales appealed to the unsophisticated young and old alike and, undoubtedly, helped develop a "reading habit" among the Russian public.[13]

The interest in European sentimental literature, which had so marked Karamzin's early years, continued to be evident in this journal. In 1791, he published his own translations of Macpherson's "Songs of Selma" and "Carthon", the first to be made directly from the English (see below, Chapter III). Karamzin also published two pieces from Sterne: "Maria", 1791, and "The Story of Le Fever", 1792.[14] He also introduced a new genre, the ballad, to his readers in the *Moscow Journal*. Karamzin had become familiar with German adaptations of Spanish *romanceros* while in Weimar and he proceeded to develop this genre in Russian literature. He began by translating a rather unsentimental Spanish ballad, "Graf Gvarinos" ("Count Guarinos"), 1791, then created an original romantic ballad, **"Raisa"**, 1791, in the style of G. A. Bürger's poems, and ended by developing a type of sentimental tale in verse, **"Alina"**, 1797-1800. In these narrative poems, Karamzin moved steadily in the direction of greater complexity of characterization and greater verisimilitude of setting and action.

The *Moscow Journal* lasted two years, 1791-1792, and the reasons for its termination are not clear.[15] In the December issue of 1792, he announced his intention to cease publication and thanked his public for undertaking "the task of reading the *Moscow Journal*".[16]

The last years of Catherine's reign were gloomy and difficult for Karamzin. Petrov, his intellectual guide and friend, died in the beginning of 1793, and Karamzin's "eternal grief" took long to pass. Many of his masonic friends had suffered grievously at Catherine's hands: Novikov was imprisoned, Lopuxin, an intimate, was exiled, and Kutuzov languished abroad in self-imposed exile. In the spring of 1793, Karamzin moved to the country and, for the next several years, lived either on his estate near Simbirsk or in Znamenskoe, Anastasia Pleščeeva's country seat near Moscow.

It was a period of persecution, whether real or imagined. Karamzin's withdrawal from Moscow gave rise to rumors that he had been banished or that he was dead or exiled.[17] Perhaps government suspicion of the masons, which still lingered, prompted these rumors. Perhaps the conduct of Catherine toward him set tongues wagging. She was not openly hostile but, rather, cold and aloof toward him, one of the foremost men-of-letters of that time.

In the isolation of the country, Karamzin found ample time for literary pursuits. In his farewell message in the *Moscow Journal,* he wrote that he would devote his "free hours" to the composition of "some trifle; perhaps my friends will write something too":

> These fragments or complete pieces I intend to publish in a magazine entitled *Aglaja,* one of the beloved Graces Thus, *Aglaja* will replace the *Moscow Journal.* It will be distinguished from the latter by the most precise choice of words, in general, the purest, i.e., a better style because I will not have to publish it on schedule.[18]

The first book of *Aglaja* appeared in 1794 and the second in 1795. His friends, Dmitriev and Xeraskov, had contributed three poems and Karamzin, the remainder of the material.[19]

The obscurantist repression that had followed in Russia after the French Revolution, had endangered the gains of the Russian Enlightenment. Karamzin, in several essays published in *Aglaja,*[20] comes to the defense of

learning, science, and art. Those who decry human knowledge and intellectual progress are labelled "misosophists", and Karamzin belittles their claims that all the world's calamities are the fault of the Enlightenment. It is quite the contrary, Karamzin maintains, for science and art are essentially moral in nature, acting to improve and perfect the individual and society. The Enlightenment creates a love for harmony, or the "good", within man, and an abhorrence of disharmony, or "vice".[21]

At the end of 1795, Karamzin outlined another scheme to Dmitriev. "I am thinking of publishing an *Almanac des Muses* next year", he writes and adds that he hopes Xeraskov, Neledinskij-Meleckij, Deržavin, (see below, Chapter III), and others will contribute. Karamzin evidently pursued the project zealously for already in August 1796 the first volume was published, its Gallic title changed into *Aonidy* [*Aonides*], an echo of the Grecian *Aglaja* and the famous French *Almanac des Muses*.

Catherine II died in November 1796 and Paul ascended the throne. Karamzin, perhaps remembering Paul's partiality toward the masonic movement, looked to the release of his imprisoned friends and an improvement in the political climate. He wrote to his brother in December 1796:

> The Sovereign wants to reign with truth and mercy and to show his subjects his beneficence. The Trubeckojs, I. V. Lopuxin, Novikov are to be rewarded for their sufferings. The first are to be made senators, Lopuxin, a secretary in the Emperor's retinue, and Novikov, it is said, will be the director of the University.[22]

Although one of the Trubeckojs and Lopuxin became senators and Novikov was freed, the events of Paul's regime quickly dispelled Karamzin's hopes. Only a month after he wrote the letter to his brother, Karamzin's close friend, Dmitriev, was placed under house arrest on charges of treason. He was quickly found innocent, but this event disturbed Karamzin deeply and he wrote to Dmitriev on January 5, 1797:

> I embrace you in tears, my dear friend. The thunder which roared over you resounded in my heart. What an occurrence! I was beside myself with amazement. Your innocence cannot be long in doubt; but what a situation.[23]

Karamzin did not undertake any new or bold ventures during Paul's regime. He confined himself to a republication of material printed earlier. The **Letters of a Russian Traveler,** which had been published serially in the *Moscow Journal* and *Aglaja,* appeared in four volumes in 1797; because of difficulties with the censor, the fifth and final volume did not appear until 1801, after Paul's death.

In August 1797, Karamzin published the second book of *Aonides* in a larger format and with more varied selections and, some three months later, he published an article in the *Spectateur de Nord,* a journal published in Hamburg in the French language. This article, **"Un mot sur la littérature russe",** a general survey of Russian literature, was made more significant by the announcement of the discovery of a Russian epic poem, *Slovo o polku Igoreve,* [*Lay of the Host of Igor*], which dates back to the twelfth century.

In 1798 Karamzin was busy with a translation project, to be called *Panteon* [*Pantheon*]. He was translating Cicero, Buffon, Rousseau for this work which was to consist of "all types of creations, important and unimportant. Consequently it will include tales, excerpts, and Arabian anecdotes . . .".[24] He submitted this material to the censor in July 1798, and when it was returned, it had been severely expurgated. The entire plan of the book was destroyed; the works of Demosthenes and Cicero were rejected because the authors were republicans. In a letter to Dmitriev, Karamzin berates a society where "we have an Academy, a University . . . and literature is under the counter!"[25] He made the changes called for and *Pantheon* was published in December, despite the censor who stood "as a black bear in my path".[26]

Alexander I ascended the throne on March 12, 1801, and there was a promise of a more liberal era. Karamzin, as well as his contemporaries, believed they had already glimpsed this. Vigel', an interesting memoirist of the period, describes the mood somewhat rapturously: "I am not able to describe what took place at that time. Everyone experienced a sort of moral release. Everyone's looks became more gracious; their steps, more brisk; and their breathing, freer".[27]

Karamzin now began a very happy period, which was not unmixed with sorrow. A month after the young Tsar ascended the throne of "All the Russias", Karamzin married Elizaveta Ivanovna Protasova, the youngest sister of Anastasia Ivanovna. An idyllic year of happiness followed but it soon became evident that his wife was suffering from a serious illness, perhaps tuberculosis, and a premonition of tragedy possessed Karamzin. Elizaveta Ivanovna soon became pregnant and, in March 1802, gave birth to a daughter, Sophia. The strain of childbirth was too much for her delicate constitution and, on April 4, 1802, she died, and her husband and small child were "deprived of the sweet angel . . .".[28]

The liberal promise of Alexander took positive form. Soon after his ascension, more tolerant instructions were issued to the censor: "Reasonable and modest research for truth, not only must not be subject to any censorship, however moderate, but must enjoy complete freedom of publication . . .".[29] Contacts with foreigners, which had been prohibited during Paul's reign, were once more allowed. Foreign books could be mailed to Russia. Printing houses, closed by Paul, were re-

opened. In this promising liberal atmosphere Karamzin began a new journal with a significant title, *Vestnik Evropy* [*European Herald*], whose aim—Karamzin wrote in one of the later issues—will be to "conform to its title, to contain all the major European news in literature and politics . . .".[30]

Thus, the *European Herald* differed from Karamzin's other publishing ventures. In the politically repressive atmosphere of Catherine's years, Karamzin confined his interests to literature, art, and drama. In the liberal climate of Alexander's early years, he introduced social and political problems in his journal.

In a series of articles, Karamzin again took up his defense of the Russian Enlightenment.[31] He praises Novikov for expanding the book trade, requests the support of the nobility in helping needy students become teachers, waxes enthusiastic about Alexander's establishment of schools for the lower classes, and, finally, praises a series of science lectures in the University of Moscow for the edification of the general public. Karamzin's moral views are clearly illustrated in these articles. Education is a moral force and, for Russia to become a great power, education of the broad masses is necessary.[32] At this time, he does not venerate the peasants as "children of nature". In the **"Pis'mo sel'skago žitelja"**[33] [**"Letter of a Country Dweller"**], he frankly states peasants are "lazy by nature, habit, and by an ignorance of the advantages of industriousness"; only a strict, paternalistic control will help the peasant live a good life.

This suspicious attitude toward the natural goodness of primitive man, reflects a decided moderation in Karamzin's sentimental views, which seem to have been affected by the frustrations and harassment of the nineties. In a series of anecdotal essays published in the *European Herald,* Karamzin derides the sentimental apotheosis of love, the blessing of solitude, and extreme emotional or rational characters.

"Moja ispoved"[34] [**"My Confession"**], 1802, an amusing lampoon upon the "confession" literature that followed Rousseau's great success, satirizes the sentimental idealization of love. The writer, Count N. N., a thoroughgoing materialist and skeptic, recounts his amatory adventures, chief of which is the amusingly cruel seduction of his ex-wife. He had moved into her household, been accepted "as a brother" by the Prince, her husband, and courted her by rationally playing upon her sentimental weaknesses. His ex-wife attempts to justify her own unfaithfulness by asserting the primacy of the emotions and, consequently, the nobility of her ignoble act.

Another essay, **"Anekdot",**[35] [**"Anecdote"**] 1803, demonstrates that solitude may lead not to self-perfection but to a Hydra of debauchery. Liodor, the chief charac-

ter, decides to retire to the country after the deaths, first, of his beloved, and, then, of his best friend. However, isolated from society he grows bored and commits an unspecified immoral act, for which he is exiled. Karamzin concludes with a warning against man's isolating himself from others, for it is "against the plan of Nature, one must not be dead to the world before death". The last essay, **"Čuvstvitel'nyj i xolodnyj, dva xaraktera"**[36] [**"The Emotional and the Cold, Two Characters"**] ridicules personality extremes and points out that the sentimental character can destroy himself through an excess of emotions while the overly judicious individual, alien to sensitivity, can find no deep meaning to life.

These various essays are a critique of sentimentalism—as presented in Karamzin's early stories—as well as a tentative exploration of the moral weakness within the materialist's outlook. A moral code, promising happiness, can not be predicated entirely on emotional responses; it has to be guided by reason. And, conversely, reason alone can not lead to a satisfaction of emotional needs, since it leads, more often than not, into an alley of evanescent desires, where pleasure depends on novelty and novelty is soon exhausted.

The success of the *European Herald*—"one of the most interesting and widely circulated of all Russian journals of the period"[37]—was due entirely to Karamzin's indefatigable efforts. For two years he wrote or translated almost every article. In simple and lucid prose, Karamzin discussed Bonaparte and Pitt, the Austrian coalition and French relations, elucidating, as well as commenting upon, the political scene and, thus, fulfilled the aims set down in his initial letter.

Toward the end of 1803 and at the very height of the journal's success, he relinquished the editorship to P. A. Sumarokov, the son of the famous classicist, and began a new career as official historiographer of the Russian state.

B. St. Petersburg: The History

In September 1803, Karamzin wrote to Murav'ëv, his close friend and former tutor to the Tsar, requesting a government stipend "to write a History, neither vulgar nor shameful. . . ."[38] Murav'ëv evidently pleaded successfully, for in about a month an *Ukaz* was published in Alexander's name granting Karamzin an annual stipend of 2,000 rubles to write a "complete history of our Fatherland".[39] The last issue of the *European Herald* was published under Karamzin's aegis in February 1804, and he wrote to Murav'ëv: "I am now studying only that which pertains to History."[40]

In a letter to Murav'ëv, Karamzin calculated the course of his historical writing: "In five or six years I hope to reach the Romanovs and, until I do, I do not intend to

print anything. . . ."[41] Karamzin erred magnificently in his calculation. He worked assiduously for the next twenty-two years on his history and still had not reached the first Romanov, who ascended the throne of Moscow in 1613.

The effect of the conservative political spirit of Moscow was clearly reflected in Karamzin's actions and writing of these years. In 1809, Count F. V. Rostopčin, the leader of the Moscow nobility, introduced Karamzin to the Emperor's sister, Grand Duchess Catherine Pavlovna. She was a woman of strong character, who had some influence on Emperor Alexander. He admired her greatly and listened to her opinions. Evidently Karamzin's views, as expressed in his conversations with the Grand Duchess, conformed to those of her aristocratic entourage, which for personal and political reasons, was hostile to M. M. Speranskij, Alexander's State Secretary and close advisor.[42] The policies of Speranskij, a poor priest's son and a "parvenu" in the words of Karamzin's biographer,[43] were considered potentially dangerous to the Russian aristocracy, who feared a diminution of their power if Speranskij's projected constitutional reforms were carried out.

The Grand Duchess had encouraged Karamzin to write a paper summarizing the views he had expressed before her circle. This paper, *Zapiska o drevnej i novoj Rossii* [*Memoir on Ancient and Modern Russia*] was delivered personally to the Grand Duchess in February 1811, and proved to be a polemic not only directed against Speranskij but also against the Emperor himself, who had contributed many of the ideas found in the State Secretary's project.[44] Karamzin saw in Speranskij's projected reforms an attempt to eradicate the Russian nobility, the bulwark and defender of the Russian state.

Karamzin's entrance into court society was not completely voluntary. In his letters to his brother and Dmitriev in 1811, he rails against the "worldly vanity" of the court in Tver', where the Grand Duchess maintained an official residence, and the destruction of his peace and quiet as a result of his frequent trips there.[45] Other, more tumultuous events soon further discomforted Karamzin. In June 1812, Napoleon crossed the Nieman and began the invasion which was to end in the devastation of Karamzin's beloved Moscow. For the next several years, Karamzin's life was insecure. In the spring of 1813, he moved his family to his wife's estate,[46] and in the fall to Moscow. He continued to work on his history, completing the first eight volumes, up to the middle of the reign of Ivan IV (the Terrible), by the end of 1815. Early in 1816 he moved to St. Petersburg to arrange for the publication of these volumes.

The Emperor greeted him warmly when he was presented on March 15, 1816 and agreed to print the first eight volumes in the military printing house in St. Petersburg. Karamzin transported his family to St. Petersburg in the spring, hoping to remain about two years guiding his volumes through the press and, then, to return to Moscow. But he was possessed by a strange premonition in the summer of 1816 that he would die in Petersburg, without ever returning to his "quiet Moscow".[47] This premonition proved true. He stayed on in St. Petersburg, a reluctant celebrity invited to court functions and an eager editor working incessantly on his history but he never again returned to Moscow.

Karamzin's social contacts in Petersburg were conditioned by the circumstances of his last years in Moscow. He was a controversial figure who continually eschewed controversy. In the first decade of the nineteenth century a linguistic dispute arose over the path of development of the Russian literary language. This dispute was not new but centered on one of the major cultural problems of the eighteenth century, the need to create a literary language of greater flexibility in style and expression. In general, there were two possible solutions to this problem: the resultant language could be oriented toward the Old Slavonic language and find its vocabulary for the more modern concepts in the Church texts, or it could reject the past entirely, raise the conversational language to a literary level, and borrow from modern foreign languages. Lomonosov, the odist, grammarian, and scientist, suggested a compromise around the middle of the century, favoring a circumspect use of the vocabulary of Church Slavonic and opposing indescriminate borrowings from foreign sources. Karamzin favored bringing the written language closer to the spoken language, avoiding archaic Slavonic expressions, and borrowing words and syntactical patterns from the French.

In the beginning of the nineteenth century, Admiral A. S. Šiškov, a linguist and future Minister of Education, decided that Karamzin's innovations were undermining Russia. They were anti-national and anti-religious, and it was all due to the French. "If Europe is now drinking a cup of bitterness, it is because, before she was vanquished by the arms of France, she had been conquered by the language", he indignantly exclaimed.[48] He suggested a return to the older Slavonic, which had been used "from Nestor to Lomonosov, from the Igor Tale to Deržavin" to create unforgettable monuments of Russian literature.[49] In 1803, he published an anonymous pamphlet, **"Rassuždenie o starom i novom sloge rossijskogo jazyka"** [**"Dissertation on Old and New Styles of the Russian Language"**] in which he expounded these ideas and, in 1810, he helped form a literary society, "Beseda ljubitelej russkogo slova" [A Company of Lovers of the Russian Word], dedicated to a defense of the Russian tongue.

A group of Karamzin's adherents defended his ideas as set forth in his poetry and prose of the nineties. On October 14, 1815, at the home of S. S. Uvarov, the "un-

known literary men from Arzamas"⁵⁰ (i.e. "from the sticks") organized a literary circle and the first meeting of the group was held on October 22.⁵¹ The Arzamas society opposed the solemnity and formal pomp of the Beseda group. Their symbol was a goose, the chief product of the town of Arzamas; it was inscribed on their coat of arms and was the chief course of their weekly dinners. They had foolish nicknames for each other, and their ceremonies were a burlesque of the masonic rituals. Karamzin and his friend, Dmitriev, were honorary members from the very beginning.

While in Petersburg, Karamzin took great pleasure in the society of this circle, even reading portions of his unpublished history to them, and he seemed to be attempting to recreate his Moscow environment in St. Petersburg. The young adherents, who now made their pilgrimages to his home and sought his advice, had for the most part formed his social circle during his last years in Moscow. However similar the society, it was still St. Petersburg that he saw on his daily walks, it was still far from Moscow. No circle of friends could replace the memories that tied him to the past. Ostaf'evo, the Vjazemskij estate became a sacred shrine: "It is remembered by my heart. There we enjoyed all the delights of life and not a little of its sadness"⁵² He railed against St. Petersburg and swore that "I shall never leave my bones here".⁵³ This oath was not fulfilled while his earlier premonition was. He died in St. Petersburg on May 22, 1826, and was buried in the Nevskoe Cemetery where a marble slab decorated with a laurel wreath bears the simple inscription, "Karamzin".

Notes

1. For example, Wolner, who became a high state functionary.

2. To complicate matters further, in 1787 the Moscow masons blundered magnificently when they approached Catherine's son, Grand Duke Paul, and sought to convert him to their order. Catherine suspected that he had designs on her throne. When the Empress was apprised of this overture to her son, she interpreted it as vindication of a political conspiracy against her, [V.] Bogoljubov, [*N. I. Novikov i ego vremja* (Moscow, M. and S. Sabašnikov, 1916),] p. 199.

3. In the play of 1789, *Tajna protivonelepago obščestva* [*Secret of a Society Opposing Absurdity*], she ridiculed them. In 1782, she published a decree attempting to abolish "societies, associations, brotherhoods, and such similar gatherings . . . harmful to the general welfare." See [George] Vernadskij, [*Russkoe masonstvo v carstvovanie Ekateriny II* (*Zapiski istoriko-filologičeskogo fakul'teta,* Vol. CXXXII) (Petrograd, Akcionernoe obščestvo, 1917),] p. 227. Her later play *Obman-*

ščik [*The Deceiver*], 1785, and *Šaman sibirskoj* [*Siberian Shaman*], 1786, continued this hostility toward the masons.

4. Several books, published by Novikov, were proscribed and Novikov was subjected to a loyalty test, Bogoljubov, pp. 388 ff.

5. In the investigation that followed, papers were discovered attesting to some contact with the Berlin Rosicrucians. In the examination of Novikov, every effort was made to prove the existence of some conspiracy but without success. See Bogoljubov, *op. cit.,* pp. 420 ff.

6. [M.] Pogodin, [*Nikolaj Mixajlovič Karamzin,* 2 vols., (Moscow, A. I. Mamontov, 1866),] I, pp. 68-9. . . .

7. V. V. Sipovskij, *N. M. Karamzin, Avtor* Pisem russkago putešestvennika [*N. M. Karamzin, Author of the* Letters of a Russian Traveler] (= *Zapiski istoriko-filogičeskago fakul'teta Imperatorskago s. petersburgskago universiteta* [*Notes of the Historical-Philological Faculty of the Imperial St. Petersburg University*], Part XLIX (St. Petersburg, n.p., 1899), p. 142.

8. As quoted, *ibid.,* p. 144.

9. [P. N.] Berkov, [*Istorija russkoj žurnalistiki XVIII veka* (Moscow-Leningrad, Akademija nauk, 1952),] pp. 497-8.

10. *Truten'* and *Živopisec* which date back to 1769 and 1772, respectively.

11. The early nineties were marked by political oppression. A. N. Radiščev's book, *Putešestvie iz Peterburga v Moskvu* [*Journey from Petersburg to Moscow*], 1790, a radical attack on serfdom, was ordered burned as "a work . . . infected with the French error" and its author was exiled. Novikov was imprisoned and sentenced to fifteen years in prison. "K milosti", [M.] *Karamzin*-[I.] *Dmitriev,* [*izbrannye stixotvorenija,* edited by A. Ja. Kučerov (= *Biblioteka poèta osnovana M. Gor'Kim,* Bol'šaja serija) (Leningrad, Sovetskij Pisatel', 1953),] pp. 98-99, written soon after the arrest of Novikov, requested that Catherine show mercy to the downfallen.

12. "Frol Silin", 1791, "Bednaja Liza", 1791, "Natal'ja, bojarskaja doč'" ["Natalie, the Boyar's Daughter"], 1792, were all published in the *Moskovskij žurnal.*

13. V. G. Belinsky, "Literary Reveries", *Selected Philosophical Works,* translator unknown (Moscow, Foreign Languages Publishing House, 1948), p. 45.

14. Karamzin saw Sterne as an expert in analyzing the heart and man's subjective experiences. He

was not aware that Sterne was, perhaps, a Rabelaisian humorist, spoofing the entire sentimental style. For a presentation of this aspect of Sterne, see Ernest Nevin Dilworth, *The Unsentimental Journey of Laurence Sterne* (Morningside Heights, New York, King's Crown Press, 1948).

15. In a letter to his readers published in November 1791 (quoted by Pogodin, *op. cit.,* I, pp. 188-90) Karamzin complained that the income from his subscribers barely covered his printing costs. Consequently, financial difficulties may have forced him to cease publication. Another reason might have been certain difficulties with the authorities. Novikov was arrested in April 1792 and Karamzin's ode "K milosti" seems to have been censored before it could be published (see Petrov's letter of July 19, 1792 in *Sočinenija Karamzina* [*Works of Karamzin*], ed. V. V. Sipovskij (Petrograd, Akademija nauk, 1917), p. 417. Karamzin's name came up in the governmental inquiry into the masonic affair with the harsh implication that he had been sent abroad for subversive reasons (see, Pogodin, *op. cit.,* I, p. 213 for a description of this investigation and its relation to Karamzin).

16. As quoted, *ibid.*

17. N. M. Karamzin, *Pis'ma N. M. Karamzina k I. I. Dmitrievu* [*Letters of N. M. Karamzin to I. I. Dmitriev*], eds. Ja. Grot and P. Pekarskij (St. Petersburg, Akademija nauk, 1866), pp. 59, 62.

18. As quoted, Pogodin, *op. cit.,* I, pp. 215-16.

19. In addition to several poems, the first book contained several essays and a small piece celebrating the virtues of the lowly "Čto nužno avtoru" ["What is Necessary to an Author"], "Nečto a naukax, iskusstvax i prosveščenii" ["Something on the Sciences, Arts, and Enlightenment"]; the essay on virtue among the lowly: "Nežnost' druzby v nizkom sostojanii" ["Tenderness of Friendship in Poor Circumstances"], an excerpt from the *Letters of a Russian Traveler*; a short story reflecting Ossianic influences, "Ostrov Borngol'm" ["The Island of Bornholm"], and one reflecting the influence of Marmontel, "Julija" ["Julia"]. The second book included his romantic tale, "Sierra Morena", a continuation of the *Letters of a Russian Traveler,* and several essays and dialogues: an essay "Afinskaja žizn'" ["Athenian Life"] and two dialogues, "Melodor k Filaletu" ["Melodorus to Philaletus"], and "Filalet k Melodoru" ["Philaletus to Melodorus"].

20. The two dialogues referred to in footnote 19 are in *Soč. Karamzina,* III, pp. 436-45, 446-57. Also the important essay, "Nečto o naukax, iskusstvax i prosveščenii", *ibid.,* pp. 373-403.

21. "Nečto o naukax . . . ," *ibid.,* p. 398.

22. As quoted, Pogodin, *op. cit.,* I, p. 262.

23. *Pis'ma Karamzina k Dmitrievu,* p. 72.

24. *Ibid.,* p. 93.

25. *Ibid.,* p. 97.

26. *Ibid.,* p. 99.

27. F. F. Vigel', *Zapiski* [*Memoirs*] (Moscow, n.p., 1891), I, p. 180.

28. From a letter to his brother as quoted by Pogodin, *op. cit.,* I, p. 180.

29. A. K. Borozdin, *Literaturnye xarakteristiki XIX veka* [*Literary Characteristics of the XIX Century*] (St. Petersburg, n.p., 1903), I, p. 19.

30. Quoted by Pogodin, *op. cit.,* I, p. 339.

31. "O Knižnoj torgovle . . .", *Soč. Karamzina,* III, pp. 545-50; "O vernom sposobe imet' v Rossii dovol'no učitelej" ["A Real Method for Having Sufficient Teachers in Russia"], *ibid.,* pp. 340-7; "O novom obrazovanii narodnago prosveščenija v Rossii" ["On the New Form of Popular Enlightenment in Russia"], *ibid.,* pp. 348-58; "O publičnom prepodavanii nauk v Moskovskom universitete" ["On the Public Teaching of Sciences in Moscow University"], *ibid.,* pp. 611-17.

32. The glory of Switzerland and England lies in the education of the peasants, "O novom obrazovanii. . . .", *ibid.,* pp. 349-51. Cf. this idea with that of Schaden, Chapter I.

33. *Ibid.,* pp. 567-80.

34. *Ibid.,* pp. 504-21.

35. *Ibid.,* pp. 538-55.

36. *Ibid.,* pp. 618-40.

37. Marcelle Ehrhard, *V. A. Joukovski et la préromantisme russe* (Paris, Librairie Ancienne Honore Champion, 1938), p. 67.

38. As quoted by Pogodin, *op. cit.,* II, p. 18.

39. *Ibid.,* I, p. 397.

40. As quoted, *ibid.,* II, p. 20.

41. As quoted by Pogodin, *ibid.,* p. 24.

42. The Grand Duchess' request for special favors had been turned down several times by Speranskij. The upper aristocracy also viewed Speranskij's measures as a veiled attempt to destroy it as a class. This group formed a sort of noble opposition in Moscow to the policies of Alexander I. For a discussion of Speranskij's reforms and projects,

see: Marc Raeff, *Michael Speransky* (The Hague, Martinus Nijhoff, 1957), Chapter V "Plans of Reform", pp. 119-68.

43. Pogodin, *op. cit.,* II, p. 60.

44. V. Ključevskij, *Kurs russkoj istorii* [*Course in Russian History*] (Moscow, Gosudarstvennoe social'no-èkonomičeskoe izdatel'stvo, 1937), V, p. 277. Speranskij drew up his reforms on the basis of materials which Alexander I gave him. This was in 1808. By the fall of that year, Speranskij submitted the reworked material to the Sovereign, who proceeded to revise it to conform to his own ideas.

45. See his letter of April 9, *Pis'ma Karamzina k Dmitrievu,* p. 143; and his letter to his brother of April 12, 1811 as quoted in Pogodin, *op. cit.,* II, p. 85.

46. In 1804, Karamzin married Catherine Andreevna Vjazemskaja, the daughter of an old friend, Prince Andrej Ivanovič Vjazemskij.

47. *Pis'ma Karamzina k Dmitrievu,* p. 193.

48. Quoted from [Marcelle] Ehrhard, [*V. A. Joukovski et le préromantisme russe* (Paris, Librairie Ancienne Honoré Champion, 1938),] p. 68.

49. *Ibid.,* p. 69.

50. From Bludov's poem, "Videnie v kakoj-to ograde" ["Vision within Some Sort of Enclosure"], where a gathering of "obscure people" discuss literature while dancing. M. Dmitriev in *Meloči iz zapasa moej pamjati* [*Trifles from the Storehouse of my Memory*] (Moscow, 1869) pp. 81-3 opines that the Arzamas circle was formed in imitation of a school of young sculptors grouped in Arzamas about the painter, Stupin.

51. D. Tomaševskij, *Puškin* (Moscow-Leningrad, Akademija nauk S.S.S.R., 1955) I, p. 110, lists some of the members: Batjuškov, a poet and nephew of Karamzin's early protector, Murav'ëv; Vjazemskij, Karamzin's brother-in-law; Žukovskij, the poet and former editor of the *Vestnik Evropy,* among others.

52. Letter of July 1819, to N. I. Krivcov, quoted by Pogodin, *op. cit.,* II, pp. 333-5.

53. *Ibid.,* p. 396. Quoted from a letter to Malinovskij, December 11, 1822.

L. G. Kisljagina (essay date 1968)

SOURCE: Kisljagina, L. G. "The Question of the Development of N. M. Karamzin's Social Political Views in the Nineties of the Eighteenth Century: N. M.
Karamzin and the Great French Bourgeois Revolution." In *Essays on Karamzin: Russian Man-of-Letters, Political Thinker, Historian, 1766-1826,* edited by J. L. Black, pp. 91-104. The Hague: Mouton, 1975.

[*In the following essay, originally published in Russian in 1968, Kisljagina examines the evolution of Karamzin's attitudes toward the French Revolution.*]

The Great French Bourgeois Revolution of 1789 was such a momentous event of world history that no contemporary could remain indifferent to it. For some, the Revolution meant the approach of a new epoch—the "Age of Reason", the idyllic "Golden Age". For them it aroused hopes and expectations. For others, the Revolution evoked hostility, passion, and a feeling of uncertainty about the future.

The French Revolution played a determining role in the formation of the social-political views of N. M. Karamzin, then still a young aspiring writer absorbing the influences of the leading ideas of the time. However, Karamzin's attitude toward this great event of the eighteenth century underwent a definite evolution.

While the problem of his attitude to the French Revolution has often been examined in literature, no unified view on the question has been formulated. No monograph exists which examines all the stages of Karamzin's changing attitude to the revolution.

The historian of Russian literature A. D. Galaxov claimed that Karamzin expressed his opinion of the revolution in the *Letters of a Russian Traveller*: "he spoke favourably about it and remained true to that until the end of his life".[1] Galaxov recognized that the text of the *Letters of a Russian Traveller* were revised by Karamzin and that the parts about the French Revolution were different in the manuscript than in the printed version. But he attributed the alterations to censorship considerations, rather than a change in the views of Karamzin himself.

In the opinion of V. V. Sipovskij,[2] Karamzin was an "enthusiast of the Revolution" only at its outset, and his sympathies towards it gradually evaporated as it progressed. Another reason for Karamzin's changing attitude to the Revolution was "a cooling of his youthful dreams". Sipovskij considerably exaggerated Karamzin's sympathy for the Revolution. This can be explained by the erroneous view Sipovskij had of eighteenth century social movements. He saw in Karamzin a student of the French philosophers and freemasons, whose ideological positions he felt were similar. This led him to overestimate the degree of influence the French Enlightenment had on Karamzin.

Many Soviet investigators of Karamzin's writings have noticed his constant preoccupation with the Revolution. Interesting ideas on this question came from S. A.

Makašin. Makašin saw Karamzin as the writer who "most deeply experienced and reflected in his art impressions of the revolutionary cataclysm which destroyed the very foundations of the aristocratic-monarchical culture in Europe". Most characteristic of Karamzin, according to Makašin, was his interpretation of the Revolution, "not as an accidental and transient event, but as a vast historical process . . .".[3] Besides this, Soviet historical literature often lays emphasis on the negative attitude of Karamzin towards the French Revolution.

A new approach to the question of Karamzin's outlook on the French Revolution is that of Ju. M. Lotman. He said, rightly, that in characterizing Karamzin's attitude to the Revolution "we must reject the attempt to construe it from relevant passages in *Letters of a Russian Traveller*". For this purpose, all the material from the *Moscow Journal*[4] should be cited. In my view, this is not enough. In order to determine the relationship of Karamzin to the French Revolution one must study everything he wrote during the last decade of the eighteenth century. Only then can one understand and follow the evolution of Karamzin's feelings towards the Revolution.

In the circumstances of the last years of Catherine II's reign and during Paul's reign, the very topic of the French Revolution was too offensive to be dealt with objectively.[5] For this reason, Karamzin's relation to the Revolution in its first years is a complicated matter and is not easily explained. The basic source of information on the question is the *Letters of a Russian Traveller.* But one must keep in sight the fact that the full text of the *Letters* came out only in 1801, and that it was substantially different than the original manuscript (the manuscript for the *Letters of a Russian Traveller* has not been preserved). Karamzin made changes concerning England and France[6] in the text of the 1801 edition. He omitted the lines which characterized his attitude to the Revolution in 1789-90, and he substituted for them a text which mirrored his outlook to the revolution as it took shape at the beginning of the nineteenth century. The views and attitudes of Karamzin at the start of the Revolution can be seen in those parts of the *Letters* which were published in *Moscow Journal*. An article about Russian literature which Karamzin wrote for the Hamburg émigré journal *Spectateur du Nord* in 1797 is also very helpful in explaining his views on the French Revolution. Makašin maintains that in this article Karamzin included sections of *Letters of a Russian Traveller,* which had been removed by Karamzin himself and published only in French.[7] We do not have the information on which he based this conclusion, but it is certainly possible. Undoubtedly the article in the *Spectateur du Nord* reflected Karamzin's position during the first years of the revolution, more accurately than the text of the *Letters* published in 1801. The article was closer to the manuscript of the *Letters* than the published text.

Let us now turn to the text of the *Letters of the Russian Traveller.* The first mention of events in France is found in a letter from Frankfurt-am-Main dated July 29, that is, fifteen days after the storming of the Bastille. In the article for the *Spectateur du Nord,* Karamzin wrote that he learned of the French Revolution in Frankfurt and that he hurried into Alsace, i.e. into France. At that time throughout France a broad movement was developing among the working masses. Peasants, not waiting for the establishment of a National Assembly, refused to pay the hated feudal extortions. With weapons in their hands, they burst into the nobles' castles and burned the old feudal agreements. Karamzin arrived in Strasbourg, the capital of Alsace, on August 6, 1789. This is how he described the situation in Alsace: "there are signs of agitation everywhere in Alsace. Entire villages are arming and the villagers are sewing cockades on their hats. Postmasters, postilions, and old women talk of revolution. And in Strasbourg a new revolt is in the making. The whole garrison is aroused. Soldiers do not listen to their officers . . . meanwhile in the outskirts of Strasbourg crowds of brigands are plundering the monasteries."[8]

Karamzin hurriedly left unsettled Strasbourg and went to Switzerland, "in order to breathe peaceful freedom . . .".[9] In spite of the fact that Karamzin spent the entire winter in Switzerland, he constantly expected news from France and willy-nilly became a witness of revolutionary events. Only on the first of March did Karamzin leave Geneva and, "pinning on the tricoloured cockade", he travelled through Lyons to Paris. He arrived in Paris on March 27, 1790, and stayed there until the end of May. On June 4, he wrote to I. I. Dmitriev that he had already started from London (according to the *Letters,* Karamzin stayed in Paris during April, May and June; July and August in England).

What did Karamzin see in France? And how did he describe it to his readers?

In England and Switzerland, Karamzin noted the simple circumstances of citizens and peasants, and the absence of luxuries and wealth, but France was represented in the pages of the *Letters* as a country full of contrasts. In spite of the fact that the fields were well worked, he said, through the countryside there wandered a large number of beggars, "with pale faces" and "ragged clothes".[10] Paris was also revealed as a city of contrasts. As Sipovskij ascertained, Karamzin took his description of Paris from *Contrasts of Paris*[11] a book written by Mercier, an author who held progressive views on the revolution during the Girondin period.

"Paris", wrote Karamzin, "seems to be a splendid city when you travel into it from the Versailles road", but if one travels through the Saint-Antoine district, then he will be startled by the "narrow, filthy, muddy streets, dilapidated houses and people in ragged clothing".[12] In Paris, stressed Karamzin, you see "an outrageous confusion of wealth and poverty". He emphasized the contrasts in Paris and in the places where Parisians could stroll. In the Champs-Elysées, "the poor people, exhausted from their week's labour, rest, and in the Tuileries garden stroll the so-called best people, cavaliers and ladies, dropping powder and rouge on the ground".[13]

Karamzin regarded the excesses of the people and the "disorder" unfavourably. This was reflected, for example, in the irony with which Karamzin spoke about the "postmasters, postilions and old women" who talked of the Revolution, and in the comical description of the episode involving the drunken landlord of an inn, Andrew, who aroused the whole village against him, "declaring in his drunkenness before the entire world, that he spat on the nation".[14] With a smile, he described a street scene of a quarrel between some old women and a sexton, which was accompanied by cries from the mob of "à la lanterne!" Karamzin's hostility to the French people who started out on the path to revolution was strengthened over the years. The editorial corrections in the *Letters* that Karamzin subsequently made demonstrate this. Here is an example:

1792 edition

. . . The local people rebelled but in French . . . to muffle the street noise which . . .

1797 edition

. . . the local rabble rebelled, but in French . . . to muffle the noise of drunken rebels . . .

In France, Karamzin saw a people discussing revolution, the nation, and patriotism; a people making short work of its enemies. The people, in his opinion, had become "a most terrible despot", causing uproar, and inciting everyone to revolution, "the poor and the lazy, those who were work-shy since the era of so-called French liberty".[15]

He saw how they burned the castles and how the nobility fled from their homesteads. He concluded, in horror, that the "courteous Frenchmen", who quite recently had been singing from Calais to Marseilles "pour un peuple aimable et sensible, le premier bien est un bon Roi",[16] had now fearlessly burst into the Royal Court and were persecuting those who had escaped into the chambers of the King and Queen. This kind of revolution he feared and despised. The thought of a people aroused made him worry about the fate of France, and the danger that "this most beautiful kingdom in the world . . . sooner or later would resemble contemporary Egypt".[17]

This anxiety was evoked by his observation that the most distinguished nobility and clergy had lost their moral right to the leading positions in the state, and were wallowing in luxury, vice, and idleness. In this he followed Montesquieu, according to whom the King found his support among the nobility and the clergy. Montesquieu also reproached the secular and spiritual feudal lords for their parasitism and luxury. Evidently it was Montesquieu's *Esprit des Lois* which prompted Karamzin's ideas about the danger which threatened the French throne, for in his opinion "up to this time, the French nobility and clergy seem to be poor defenders of the throne".[18] He came to this conclusion as a result of observing the upper society of Paris—"the most distinguished nobility and the wealthiest inhabitants". For a description of this society on the eve of the revolution, Karamzin used a literary device, telling it through the lips of Abbé N. The reader is presented with the image of an idle society, which gave itself up to "horrible games", and whose members flung themselves into one fad after another. "Everyone philosophized, took on airs, and intrigued . . . and I do not know to what we would have finally resorted from boredom if the thunder of revolution had not crashed over us", said Abbé N. in the *Letters of a Russian Traveller.*[19]

But there is another side to Karamzin's attitude towards the Revolution. He platonically admired republics of the type described in Montesquieu's *Esprit des Lois,* and in the songs and idylls of Swiss poets. Hence his delight upon entering Switzerland, and also his disappointment as he became more acquainted with life in the Swiss cantons, were understandable. But, though disappointed in the Swiss Republic, Karamzin did not cease to cherish the kind of republic he had created in his imagination, but which was unrealizable in real life. This ideal republic was founded on the abstract principles of virtue, freedom, and brotherhood. Although he dreamed about an idyllic republic in those years, Karamzin followed the apologists of the French Enlightenment, Montesquieu, and Voltaire. He thereby acknowledged that the most acceptable form of government was a constitutional monarchy, like the English one. In English history, he said in the *Letters,* there was not a single "French Revolution", and as a result England had the Magna Carta, in which "the King vowed to preserve the rights of the English".[20]

In its initial stages, the French Revolution did not go beyond the bounds of constitutional monarchy. Therefore Karamzin, worrying that the popular movement would wipe the French State from the face of the earth, bided his time and waited to see which way the Revolution would turn. He preferred to withhold judgment. The authority of the King of France was still great. Even among the most radically-disposed members of the National Assembly, there was a strong monarchical tendency. Stressing this tendency, Karamzin wrote "the

people still love the Royal Family",[21] in the *Letters,* after telling how the Royal Family was greeted in the courtyard of a church.

After the major crisis, which broke out during the October days in Paris, several days of calm followed. "The Revolution", according to the definition of Jaurés, a historian of the French Revolution, "developed profoundly, though superficially there seemed only minor disturbances".[22] The King had made his peace, it seemed, with the Revolution, and had signed the "Declaration of the Rights of Man and the Citizen". A speech made by the King on the 4th of December gave the impression that he had finally come to terms with the Revolution.

It is well known that the German and Swiss intelligentsia greeted the news of the Revolution with sympathy. Kant impatiently awaited news from revolutionary France. Goethe noted the Battle of Valmy as the beginning of a new era; Schiller and Klopstock received the rank of French citizen from the French Legislative Assembly.[23] Even Lavater, known for his conservative views, welcomed the French Revolution.

The Revolution had just begun when Karamzin was travelling through Switzerland. Thus he constantly found himself in an atmosphere of social and political enthusiasm, which enveloped the progressive ranks of the Swiss intelligentsia. One must not forget the fact that this sense of exhilaration, connected with the start of the Revolution, gripped a man who was then under the influence of the French *philosophes*. It is possible to argue about the degree of influence the dominant social-political ideas of the time had on Karamzin's opinions, but one cannot deny it completely. All this taken together explains why neither in the *Moscow Journal* nor in the following years, including 1797, did Karamzin anywhere express hostility towards the Revolution.

It was characteristic of Karamzin that during his sojourn in Paris he attended a meeting of the National Assembly and followed the debates with interest. In his article about Russian literature he praised Mirabeau for his ability and did justice to his eloquence, while at the same time giving credit to Mirabeau's opponent, Abbé Maury, "seeing them as if they were Achilles and Hector".[24] One should not regard Karamzin's willingness to discuss both orators, who belonged to different political camps, as a sign that he was apolitical. Rather this should be explained by Karamzin's tolerance, and his attempt to explain what was going on without denying everything new introduced by the Revolution or anything new introduced by the revolutionaries. Even here Karamzin did not express any dislike of Mirabeau, the tribune of the Revolution.

Thus in the *Letters* which were published in the *Moscow Journal* Karamzin wrote very little about the Revolution. As long as there was no political section in the *Moscow Journal,* Karamzin could circumvent questions raised by the Revolution. Meanwhile the Revolution continued to occupy his attention. Already in the first book of the journal he had inserted brief notes on the plays which were being shown in Paris. There he promised readers that information about Parisian drama, translated from the *Mercure de France* "will be reported, if not in every book, then at least in some numbers". Parisian plays which in one way or another mirrored revolutionary events were reported in subsequent issues. Among the plays reviewed were *Les Rigeurs du Cloitre* by Fievee, *Le Convalascent de qualité, ou l'Aristocrate,* a comedy by Fabre d'Eglantine, and others. The theme of the first piece was connected with the destruction of the monastic orders, and the intervention of the State in Church matters, the National Guard playing the role of liberators. The significance of the second piece was the recognition by the French nobility of the new order and the new laws established by the Revolution. In the September 1791 book of the journal Karamzin inserted a short review of Harney's play *Conquest of Freedom.* "It depicts the national disarray", reported the editor of *Moscow Journal,* "the taking of the Bastille and so on, which can be of interest only to the Parisian public".[25] In the *Letters,* Karamzin gave a full account of Chenier's tragedy *Charles IX,* which was presented in Lyons. Karamzin was not pleased with the play (he did not admire Melpomene), but he related the impetuous reaction of the audience to it, noticing that "the author had recent events in mind, and every word referring to conditions in contemporary France met with applause from the audience".[26]

In order to clarify exactly what tragedy Karamzin was recounting to the Russian readers, let us turn to K. Deržavin, the historian of the French theatre during the epoch of revolution. "This tragedy", wrote Deržavin, "dealt with and distinctively interpreted a series of disturbing contemporary questions. . . . All the elements of the tragedy, which revealed the despotism, the tyranny of wicked ministers, and of royal power, insofar as it placed itself above the interests of its subjects, evoked a lively response from bourgeois society of the first period of the Revolution, and alarmed the reactionary camp."[27]

"A monster, destroying his native land, to whom Pluto himself dictated, and whose ink-well was held by Satan" the author was called by one of the reactionary Feuillants. But Camille Desmoulins announced that "this play promotes our cause better than the days of October".[28]

In this way Karamzin informed readers not about the harmless plays which were on in Paris, but about plays inspired by revolutionary Paris, and which aroused hatred among the enemies of the Revolution. Besides this, Karamzin reported on new French literature in the *Mos-*

cow *Journal*, for example, Volney's book *Les Ruines, ou Méditations sur les Révolutions des Empires* and Mercier's book on Rousseau. This information was accompanied by the comment, "these two books can be called the most important productions of French literature during the past year".[29] There was no need to say more about the books. Both authors were revolutionaries of the pre-Jacobin period.

Although the political ideals of Mercier did not go much beyond the separation of executive power (the King) from the legislative, and the subordination of the first to the second, his book was inspired by revolutionary pathos. The author proved that by his writings Rousseau anticipated and prepared the growth of revolution in France. Volney in *Les Ruines* set himself the task of depicting "revolutionary Empires", to show what factors promoted the growth of great states, and their internal collapse and destruction. Volney's scheme included the emancipation of man from the remnants of the Middle Ages, from national oppression, from religion, and from the power of the clergy.

Karamzin did not express any opinion on these books in the journal. However, the very fact that their existence was reported to Russian readers must have provoked interest among those who were curious about the Revolution and the books must have been available in bookshops. Evidently, Karamzin himself maintained his interest in the Revolution and it induced in him, if not sympathy, then at least not hostility.

Everything said above justifies the thesis of Karamzin's lack of animosity towards the Revolution in its first three years. His attitude to it can be defined rather as a guarded, watchful one. It is noteworthy that even in his 1797 article about Russian literature for the *Spectateur du Nord*, Karamzin did not express one word against the Revolution. On the contrary, he included in it lines from the manuscript of the ***Letters,*** which he did not dare publish in the *Moscow Journal*. In the article, the Revolution is regarded as the beginning of a new epoch. "The French Revolution", wrote Karamzin, "is one of these movements which determine the fate of people for centuries to come. It is the beginning of a new epoch; I see it, and Rousseau foresaw it."[30]

It is evident from this how seriously Karamzin approached an evaluation of the historical role of the Revolution. But this does not mean that Karamzin accepted the Revolution.

From 1789 to 1792, right up to the execution of Louis XVI, Karamzin seemed benevolently inclined towards the Revolution since he associated it with the struggle against despotism and tyranny, the establishment of constitutional monarchy, and the further progress of the Enlightenment. He hoped to see a revolution like the English one. He hoped that a compromise could be arranged between the National Assembly and the King, and that as a result progressive laws would be passed and France would move further along the road of enlightenment. The development of the Revolution in the first few years did not contradict these expectations. Only the popular excesses caused him anxiety. His alarm diminished somewhat after the events of the 5th and 6th of October, 1789. These resulted in a clearer demarcation of class lines. The bourgeois majority in the Constituent Assembly, motivated by fears of revolutionary action by the masses, gradually moved away from the other elements of the Third Estate and began to have recourse to repression against the people and their leaders. The gunfire on the Champ de Mars demonstrated that the *haute bourgeoisie* was attempting by force of arms to crush their recent ally, the people, and had come to a compromise with the royal power. In September 1791 the Constituent Assembly practically restored the power of Louis XVI in full, and gave him a constitution to sign. On September 30, 1791, the Assembly finished its work and dissolved itself. The King in a manifesto on the dissolution of the Constituent Assembly decided to proclaim that "the end of the Revolution has set in".[31]

Yet in the middle of 1792, the situation in France changed abruptly. A popular rising in Paris on August 10th robbed Louis XVI of his throne. Then began the struggle between the Montagne and the Gironde. The armed forces of the European monarchs penetrated French territory. On January 21, 1793, came the execution of the King, and the establishment of the Jacobin dictatorship.

These developments proved unacceptable to Karamzin, for it was quite unlike the ideal world which he had drawn in his imagination. He was seized with despair. The edifice of his philosophy crumbled before his very eyes "like the castles in the air of his youth".[32] The eighteenth century, the century of Enlightenment, sentiment and reason stood in "blood and flames . . . among murder and destruction". "Would you believe", he wrote to I. I. Dmitriev on June 26th, 1793, how "the terrible events in Europe agitate my entire soul? I run in a dense forest of gloom, but the thought of the destruction of cities and the immolation of people rends my heart. Call me Don Quixote, but that great prince could not have loved his Dulcinea as passionately as I love mankind."[33]

Only recently, Karamzin had seen evidence that the worst of the human misery would be over by the end of the century, that by that time "a union of theory with practice would occur". In other words, people "will believe in the sacred laws of pure reason", they will begin to practise them and there will set in the reign of the general weal, good will triumph. But what he saw was

something else: "Ferocious wars lay Europe waste, the centre of art and science, the depository of all the most precious treasures of the human mind", and the "unfortunate philanthropist measures out his grave in two steps, so that he can lie down in it with a heart torn by deceit. . . ."[34]

Thus, in his opinion, evil had triumphed in the world, and Karamzin came to the pessimistic conclusion that "evil will always be with us and people will always be people".[35] Worse than that was the spectre that revolution gave rise to cruelty. In times of revolution, people became accustomed to the "phenomenon of villainy", and lost their "sensibility". Karamzin now saw that the Revolution was not a triumph of virtue and tender morality, but of rebellion, villainy and reprisals, which drew ever-increasing numbers of people into their orbit.

At the heart of Karamzin's sociology lay a faith in the growth of reason, acquired from a study of the French Enlightenment. Karamzin understood the growth of human society as a process leading from ignorance to enlightenment and moral perfection. Not long before, in his words, he had found proof that "the human race is raising itself".

Then the Revolution, which at first he was prepared to understand as a natural stage in the growth of mankind, brought the country in which enlightenment had achieved its highest stage of development to the edge of the abyss. France, it now seemed, stood on the brink of the grave.

Again and again, he turned to the events in France. Now he felt an urgent need to interpret all that was going on, to find an explanation for all the events. In 1793 he wrote an original tract in the form of two letters, **"Melodor to Filalet"** and **"Filalet to Melodor"**, in which he examined the problem of the fate of the world and the role of man in that world. This production has immense significance for an understanding of Karamzin's social views. For us, the letters are still interesting, as Karamzin draws new conclusions about the Revolution in them. Here he aligns his "consoling" philosophy, as he now calls it, with reality and tries to find an explanation for the happenings in the world.

Melodor, who is Karamzin until 1793, until the collapse of his earlier views, is a man forced to recognize the disintegration of his "consoling philosophy". "Is it possible", asks Melodor in his letter, "that the human species has advanced in our time, to the pinnacle of enlightenment, only by the agency of some kind of strange and mysterious sign, to be compelled to fall back from the heights into the depths of barbarism, and again, little by little, to emerge once more, like Sisyphus' stone?"[36] Can it be, he said conjecturing further, that the

moral life of people is "an eternally cyclical movement, forever repeated . . . , always interchanging truth and error, virtue and vices?"[37]

Filalet-Karamzin analyzed Melodor's conclusions and gave his estimate of the world situation, interpreting events in a new fashion. The philosophy of Filalet-Karamzin found peace in faith in a beneficent Providence, in His good plan: "I really believe", he said, "that this world is a cave of brigands and villains, the virtuous are alien plants on the terrestrial globe, enlightenment is a sharp dagger in the hands of murderers! No, my friend! Let them show me henceforth that God does not exist."[38]

Now Karamzin was armed with a theory of "pre-established harmony" according to which all events in the world are explained by some higher expediency. "Perhaps", said Filalet, "what seems like some great disorder to mortals, is a marvellous harmony to angels; perhaps what seems destructive to us, is for celestial beings, some new and perfect event."[39] It is not given to man to penetrate into the secrets of the heavenly plan, since that stands outside the realm of human understanding. Armed with such a philosophy, Karamzin found an explanation for all the ruin of the moral order; for every evil (and revolution he now regarded as a moral evil) is explained not by the wickedness of human nature, but by a higher scheme of things. Just as in the physical world there are staggering events, for example the Lisbon and Messina earthquakes, so in the moral world are such happenings possible. And since the world continues to exist after earthquakes, then we "can be comforted by the thought that the destiny of the human species is not eternal delusion and that people will sometime cease to torment themselves and each other".[40]

But if the Revolution can be explained by a higher order of things, then what caused the spiritual confusion of people like Karamzin-Melodor? Filalet gave an answer to this too. The cause lay in the "unwarranted worship of the eighteenth century and, consequently, in expecting too much from it".[41] Life had not shown just how far the world was from being perfect, or how subject the minds of our contemporaries were to terrible delusion.[42] But, further, Filalet expressed the hope that ahead "better times await us, that human nature will become more perfect . . . and present evil will serve future good". He rejected Melodor's notion about the cyclical development of man. "Your idea about the constant rise and fall of human reason seems to me to be a castle in the air; I see no basis for it . . . why not believe that the centuries serve as a kind of staircase to rationality, on which reason gradually reaches perfection, sometimes quickly, sometimes slowly?"[43]

Thus after the events of 1793 Karamzin came to the conclusion that revolution was evil. Its cause was man's

moral imperfection. But Karamzin retained his belief in the moral progress of man, attainable only as a result of slow, evolutionary growth. He included this conviction in the first full edition of the **Letters**:

> Every civil society which has existed for centuries is sacred to good citizens and, even in the least perfect, one must be astonished at the wonderful harmony, concord and order. Utopia will always be the dream of a good heart, or it may be brought about by the gradual working of time, through the slow but true and safe achievements of the mind, enlightenment, education and good morals.[44]

Thus it seems to us that one cannot simply talk about the hostile attitude of Karamzin to the French Revolution. His attitude to it passed through a definite evolution. During the first stage of the revolution he took the position of a neutral observer. Until the execution of the King and the accession of the Jacobins to power, there was a time in which he was prepared to come to terms with the Revolution. But after 1793 N. M. Karamzin passed through a difficult spiritual crisis and adopted a hostile attitude to the Revolution. Recognizing revolution as a regular phenomenon in the development of mankind, he nevertheless stuck to his preference for the evolutionary path of development.

Notes

1. A. D. Galaxov, "Biografičeskie i literaturnye zametki o Karamzine", *Žurnal Ministerstva narodnogo prosveščenija,* Pt. 135 (January 1867), 26.

2. See V. V. Sipovskij, *N. M. Karamzin, avtor 'Pisem russkogo putešestvennika'* (St. Petersburg, 1899).

3. *Literaturnoe nasledstvo* 29/30 (Moscow, 1937), XXII.

4. Ju. M. Lotman, "A. N. Radiščev v bor'be s obščestvenno-političeskimi vozzrenijami i dvorjanskoj èstetikoj N. M. Karamzina", Dissertation (Leningrad, 1951), 297.

5. About the relation of Russian society to the French Revolution see the book by M. M. Štrange, *Russkoe obščestvo i francuzskaja revoljucija 1789-1794 gg.* (Moscow, 1956), and the articles: P. K. Alfirenko, "Rossija i francuzskaja buržuaznaja revoljucija", in *Očerki istorii SSSR, XVIII vek, vtoraja polovina* (Moscow, 1956); A. Kaganova, "Francuzskaja buržuaznaja revoljucija konca XVIII veka i sovremennaja ej russkaja pressa", *Voprosy istorii* 7 (1947); A. Ja. Kučerov, "Francuzskaja revoljucija i russkaja literatura XVIII v.," *XVIII vek* (Moscow-Leningrad, 1935); S. Makašin, "Literaturnye vzaimootnošenija Rossii i Francii XVIII-XIX vv.", *Literaturnoe nasledstvo* 29/30 (Moscow, 1937).

6. See V. V. Sipovskij, 160ff.

7. *Literaturnoe nasledstvo* 29/30, XXII.

8. *Moskovskij žurnal* (October, 1791) 52-53.

9. Ibid., 72.

10. N. M. Karamzin, *Sočinenija,* II, published by A. Smerdin [sic] (1848), 436. [Smerdin should read Smirdin, editor.]

11. [Kisljagin's words, *Kontrasty Pariža,* can only be translated as *Contrasts of Paris.* The actual title of L. S. Mercier's book was *Tableau de Paris* (1782), editor.]

12. Karamzin, *Sočinenija,* II, 446.

13. Ibid., 447.

14. Ibid., 493.

15. Ibid., 428.

16. Ibid., 460.

17. Ibid., 433.

18. Ibid., 461.

19. Ibid., 457-458.

20. Ibid., 706, 738.

21. Ibid., 460.

22. Žan Žores [Jean Jaurès], *Istorija Velikoj francuzskoj revoljucii,* I (Moscow, 1922), 274.

23. See A. Presnov, op. cit., 67.

24. *Pis'ma N. M. Karamzina k I. I. Dmitrievu* (St. Petersburg, 1866), 179. [Kisljagina, or her publisher, made an error here. For the correct citation, see N. M. Karamzin, *Izbrannye sočinenija,* I (Moscow-Leningrad, 1964), 504, editor.]

25. *Moskovskij žurnal* (September, 1791), 327.

26. Ibid. (October/November, 1792), 86.

27. K. Deržavin, *Teatr Francuzskoi revoljucii 1789-1799* (Moscow, 1937), 67.

28. Ibid., 69.

29. *Moskovskij žurnal* (January, 1792), 151. [Both books were published in 1791, editor.]

30. *Pis'ma N. M. Karamzina k I. I. Dmitrievu,* 478.

31. A. Z. Manfred, *Velikaja francuzskaja buržuaznaja revoljucija* (Moscow, 1956), 122.

32. Karamzin, *Sočinenija,* I, 38.

33. *Pis'ma N. M. Karamzina k I. I. Dmitrievu,* 42.

34. Karamzin, *Sočinenija,* III, 439.

35. Ibid., I, 39.

36. Ibid., III, 442.

37. Ibid., 444.

38. Ibid., 449. [In Kisljagina's version, the words "Providence", "God", and "His", were, of course, not capitalized, editor.]

39. Ibid.

40. Ibid., 452.

41. Ibid.

42. Ibid., 453.

43. Ibid., 454-455.

44. Ibid., 462. [Kisljagina made another error here. This particular reference must be to volume II of Karamzin's works. For a more recent copy of the same paragraph see N. M. Karamzin, *Izbrannye sočinenija*, I (Moscow-Leningrad, 1964), 382, editor.]

A. G. Cross (essay date January 1969)

SOURCE: Cross, A. G. "N. M. Karamzin's *Messenger of Europe* (*Vestnik Yevropy*), 1802-3." *Forum for Modern Language Studies* 5, no. 1 (January 1969): 1-25.

[*In the following essay, Cross examines the impact of* Vestnik Yevropy, *a journal edited by Karamzin, on Russian literature and politics in the early nineteenth century. Cross analyzes the evolution of Karamzin's ideas during this critical phase of his career, evaluating in particular the influence of European Enlightenment ideals on his subsequent historical writings.*]

In the summer of 1790 the twenty-three-year-old Nikolay Karamzin returned to Russia after extensive travels through Germany, Switzerland, France and England. Eager to make his name as a writer and to pass on the fruits of his European education, Karamzin resolved to publish the *Moscow Journal* (*Moskovskiy zhurnal*, 1791-2) which became the broadsheet of Russian sentimentalism and initiated what was to be known as the "Karamzin period of Russian literature". In his memoirs F. F. Vigel' saw the journal as the rallying-point for "all noble-minded youths and all truly sensitive women",[1] and P. A. Vyazemsky considered that "Karamzin in the *Moscow Journal* destroyed the Gothic towers of a decaying literature and on its ruins lay the foundations of a new European publication, which awaited for its ultimate completion skilled, industrious hands".[2]

Karamzin's versatility and talent were revealed from the first number of the *Moscow Journal*. As a journalist he showed his ability to produce a journal comparable in presentation and content with the European models he so admired; he introduced as a basic feature informed criticism of Russian and foreign books and plays; he published carefully chosen and written translations from Western originals on a wide range of subjects; he mustered contributions from the leading poets of the day and provided in his own ***Letters of a Russian Traveller*** (***Pis'ma russkogo puteshestvennika***) and in sentimental stories such as **'Poor Liza' ('Bednaya Liza')** and **'Nathalie, the Boyar's Daughter' ('Natal'ya, boyarskaya doch'')** examples of accomplished Russian prose writing, which caught the imagination of the reading public and ensured the success of sentimentalism as a literary vogue in Russia. Not least, the *Moscow Journal* heralded a stylistic revolution: without the carefully wrought embroidery of what became known as the "new style" (*novyy slog*) the emotional finesse and nuance on which sentimentalism relied could not have been realized. The implications of sentimentalism as something more than a literary style are equally evident in the journal: the spirit of Karamzin's work is independent, enlightened, humane.

Although Karamzin's activity as a writer extends over a period of more than forty years (from the publication of his first translation in 1783 until his death in 1826, when he was working on the twelfth volume of his monumental history of Russia) his major literary output is concentrated in a period of thirteen years. It is a period bounded by two important journals, the *Moscow Journal* and the *Messenger of Europe*. In the 1790's Karamzin's desire to encourage the development of Russian literature and bring Russia in line culturally with the West inspired his stream of publications. He strove to provide examples of entertaining and accomplished writing and to fashion a literary language able to compete with French or English in its range and richness.

Nevertheless, in this period his work and philosophy of life were affected by political, non-literary events in Europe and Russia. Repressive measures under Catherine and Paul threatened not only his friends but his own very existence as a writer. After the unrelieved gloom of Paul's reign it is not surprising that Karamzin shared in the wave of optimism which swept through Russia on Alexander's accession. Vigel' described how "everyone felt a kind of moral expansion, looks became kinder, the walk bolder, the breathing freer";[3] Nikolay Grech sought to characterize the change by specific reference to Karamzin's own sentiments:

> It is impossible to describe the astonishment, joy, enthusiasm, aroused by what was in fact an unfortunate, loathsome event [Paul's murder]. Russia breathed freely. Nobody thought of pretending any more. Karamzin remarked justly in his memoir on the state of Russia: "Who was more unfortunate than Paul! Tears at his death were shed only within his family". Not only in words but in writing, in print, particularly in poems,

people expressed their joyful feelings of release from his tyranny. Karamzin in his ode on Alexander's accession said: "Hearts are ready to breathe in You: / Our spirit is revived by hope. / Thus does the appearance of sweet spring / Bring with it oblivion / Of all the dark horrors of winter."[4]

Yet this did not, and could not, signal a complete return by Karamzin to the beliefs and enthusiasms of his youth. He continued to speak as a Philalet, advocating a philosophy of moderation and caution.[5] Karamzin's experiences and new interests in the decade between the *Moscow Journal* and the *Messenger of Europe* modified his approach to journalism: in the earlier journal he had been pre-eminently a man of letters; to this role he now added those of an historian and a political publicist. His erstwhile propaganda for Russian enlightenment took on a new nationalistic colouring. The *Messenger of Europe* is the focal point of Karamzin's thought and work at the beginning of Alexander's reign; it is the culmination of his years of work for Russian literature and his swan song before his entry into "the temple of History".[6] Although his reputation and influence were considerable throughout Alexander's reign it was not until the publication of the first eight volumes of his ***History of the Russian State*** (***Istoriya gosudarstva rossiyskogo***) in 1818 that Karamzin again occupied the literary limelight.

Karamzin was both the editor and chief contributor of the *Messenger of Europe*; he left his stamp on every aspect of its contents and presentation as indelibly as he had done on his earlier journal. Karamzin himself was perhaps not fully aware to what degree he assumed his new role as public tribune; in the foreword to the first issue (as well as in an article at the end of 1802) he emphasized his concern for literature and enlightenment and expressed the hope that the political section for "the sake of Europe will not be very rich and interesting".[7] The journal is divided into two parts: 'Literature and Miscellany' and 'Politics', but politics dominate the journal not only in the form of European news but also as open discussion of Russia's internal reforms. 'Literature and Miscellany' brings to a close Karamzin's work as a poet, translator, story writer and reformer of the Russian literary language, whereas 'Politics' concentrates his earlier scattered ideas and remarks on historical, political and social questions into a comprehensive system and points to the future development of his career.

I

In certain respects the literary section of the *Messenger of Europe* continues the traditions of the *Moscow Journal*. Of the original five features Karamzin planned for his earlier journal, three—Russian works in verse and prose, translations, and interesting anecdotes—remained; a fourth—critical reviews of Russian books—

was continued with severe limitations in its scope and, consequently, in its interest, and the fifth—drama criticism—was completely rejected.

There is little that was new or interesting in the literary works Karamzin chose to translate. He turned once more to Mme de Genlis, whose religiosity, cloying moralizing and attacks on 'false' philosophers pervaded a series of stories appearing from part II of the journal. Characteristic of the prevailing tastes of the day was the translation of a tale by August Lafontaine,[8] who rivalled Genlis, Marmontel and Kotzebue in popularity with the Russian reading public. English, French and German journals provided Karamzin with a wealth of Eastern allegories, moral fables and news snippets of a literary nature.

Despite the orientation on foreign literature, which Karamzin had himself indicated in an editorial at the end of 1802,[9] original contributions from Karamzin and his friends provided the main literary interest in the journal. Ivan Dmitriyev, now living in retirement in Moscow and collaborating closely with Karamzin, regularly contributed poems; there were also poems by G. R. Derzhavin, M. M. Kheraskov and Yu. A. Neledinsky-Meletsky, but the one poem of particular note was Vasily Zhukovsky's version of Gray's *Elegy*.[10] Karamzin's own verse in the *Messenger of Europe*, which included the **'Hymn to Fools'** (**'Gimm gluptsam'**), **'Melancholy'** (**'Melankholiya'**) and **'To Virtue'** (**'K dobrodeteli'**), formed a distinctive and important coda to his work as a poet, but it is his prose rather than his verse which marks the final stage of his role as a literary innovator. **'A Knight of Our Time'** (**'Rytsar' nashego vremeni'**), **'Martha'** (**'Marfa-posadnitsa'**), **'My Confession'** (**'Moya ispoved'**) and **'The Man of Feeling and the Cold-Blooded Man'** (**'Chuvstvitel'nyy i kholodnyy'**) reveal his search for new themes and narrative techniques.[11]

Karamzin's unwillingness to continue his drama and book reviews was rooted in his changed attitude towards literary criticism. In the opening 'Letter to the Editor', which he wrote himself, Karamzin formulated his new position:

> But does criticism really teach one how to write? Do not models and examples act more strongly? And have not talents everywhere preceded learned and stern judgement? La critique est aisée, et l'art est difficile! Write whoever is able to write well: that is the best criticism of bad books![12]

At the end of 1802 he was insisting:

> As far as the criticism of new Russian books is concerned, we do not consider it a true requirement of our literature (not to mention the unpleasantness of dealing with the easily injured vanity of people). It is more

useful for an author to be judged than to judge. Good criticism is the luxury of literature; it is born of great riches, and as yet we are not Croesuses. It is better to add to the general *estate* than to be concerned with its evaluation.[13]

Karamzin was now in direct opposition to the standpoint he had adopted in the *Moscow Journal* in the dispute between V. S. Podshivalov and F. O. Tumansky over the value of criticism.[14] He had learnt from bitter experience how resentful such writers as Tumansky and N. P. Nikolev were of criticism; he knew also that his critical reviews had been considered an impertinence by the Moscow freemasons and parodied by Ivan Krylov and A. I. Klushin in their *Spectator* (*Zritel'*).[15] Clear evidence of his *volte-face* was the exclusion of the exchanges between Tumansky and Podshivalov from the second edition of the *Moscow Journal,* which was published at this time (1802-3). But Karamzin's change of heart came equally from his new patriotic fervour and his conviction that young Russian authors were to be encouraged rather than condemned: "We are not aristocrats in literature: we do not look at names but at works, and we are sincerely glad to help the emergence of young authors."[16]

The change in emphasis in Karamzin's attitude did not bring an absolute renunciation of criticism: although, as the Soviet critic G. P. Makogonenko has demonstrated,[17] Karamzin tended to substitute for the review the leading article, in which he propounded criticism of a general rather than specific nature. He stated: ". . . we make no promise that sometimes we will not discuss old and new Russian books, it is merely that we do not accept a definite obligation to be critics."[18] The criticism in the *Messenger of Europe,* unlike that in the *Moscow Journal,* is indeed occasional and unsystematic, but nonetheless of considerable extent and importance. Karamzin exercised restraint when reviewing Russian works, but was outspoken with foreign literature.

Karamzin reviewed recent foreign, predominantly French, works, which were not yet available in Moscow, such as J. J. Barthélemy's *Voyage en Italie,* Mme de Staël's *Delphine* and Chateaubriand's *Génie du Christianisme.*[19] Karamzin's attack on Chateaubriand's work is heavily ironical—and both the technique and tone are reminiscent of his review of Nikolev's *Spoilt Darling* (*Baloven'*), in the *Moscow Journal*:

> we cannot imagine anything more foolish than this nonsense. Such is the way some of the new French authors write. I assure readers that my new translation is as faithful as any in the world.[20]

Foreign works in Russian translation were also reviewed. Karamzin was particularly enthusiastic about N. I. Strakhov's translation of Barthélemy's *Voyage du jeune Anacharsis,* which he considered one of the outstanding works of the eighteenth century,[21] and he praised the "zealous patriotism" of A. Storkh, whose historical survey of Russian trade was being translated from German.[22] The third of such reviews—of a translation of E. F. Lantier's *Voyages d'Antenor* (*Antenorovy puteshestviya po Gretsii i Azii,* Moscow 1802), is particularly interesting for its similarity to Karamzin's reviews of translated works in the *Moscow Journal*; it is even introduced under the heading 'Criticism' and reveals his old techniques at every turn. An examination of the book's contents is followed by close attention to the quality of the translation. Nevertheless, aware that a review of this nature contradicted his new position, Karamzin was at pains to minimize the effect of his criticism:

> But isn't such criticism carping? We are not to blame if we find here no very important mistakes; and thus discovering from our unsuccessful attempt at criticism that the translator has taken measures to ensure against criticism, we close the Russian Antenor.[23]

These reviews apart, the main criticism in the *Messenger* is contained in two major articles, one by Dmitriyev and the other by Karamzin. Dmitriyev's 'On Russian Comedies' ('O russkikh komediyakh') is the only dramatic criticism in the journal: it advances a concept of genteel comedy in opposition to coarse naturalism and attacks the vogue for vulgar farce and comedy.[24] Karamzin's article is devoted to the life and work of Ippolit Bogdanovich, whose death in 1802 occasioned a flood of inept epitaphs in the *Messenger.*[25] **'On Bogdanovich and his Works' ('O Bogdanoviche i yego sochineniyakh')** is a notable milestone in the history of Russian literary criticism. Karamzin attempted to trace Bogdanovich's development as an author, to analyse his main work *Dushen'ka,* and to compare it with La Fontaine's *Les Amours de Psyché et de Cupidon,* which was its model. Uniting an exposition of certain systematic theories on the nature and obligations of art, a wide knowledge of his subject, and an ability to write in a lucid and engaging style, Karamzin was obviously at the same time serving his basic thesis in the *Messenger*—applaud, rather than condemn, things Russian—and thereby modifying his true assessment of Bogdanovich's worth. As late as 1800 G. P. Kamenev heard Karamzin criticising Bogdanovich's work, particularly certain lines from his translation of Voltaire's poem on the Lisbon earthquake,[26] although by 1803 he could write: "Bogdanovich translated [the poem] so successfully that many lines match the beauty and strength of the French."[27] In addition, Karamzin tended to re-create Bogdanovich in his own sentimentalist image and basic facts from Bogdanovich's biography serve as a starting point for an exposition of Karamzin's views on the joys of artistic creation, on the requirements for a peaceful life, or even on the undesirability of stern criticism.[28] On the other hand, Karamzin's comparison of the relative values of prose and verse on the basis of

concrete examples and his assessment of Bogdanovich's contribution to Russian literature are objective and valuable.

II

Karamzin's desire to review Russian literature more indulgently than he had done in the 1790's and to relate its development to post-Petrine Russia's advance towards enlightenment was already evident in the *Pantheon of Russian Authors* (*Panteon rossiyskikh avtorov,* 1801-2) which, although conceived in Paul's reign, is pre-eminently in the spirit of Alexander's. Karamzin in fact reviewed his *Pantheon* in the *Messenger* and printed in full his notes on Prokopovich, Trediakovsky and Lomonosov. These are prefaced by his attempt at a periodization of 18th-century Russian literature:

> Feofan and Kantemir comprise this first epoch: this is followed by Lomonosov and Sumarokov; the third must be termed the reign of Catherine the Great, already rich in the number of authors; and we are still awaiting the fourth.[29]

Karamzin was engaged not only in formulating an apology for earlier Russian literature but in directing Russia's immediate literary development. The fourth period was to be the reign of Alexander, which he had described in his programme for the *Messenger* as a time

> when the sciences and arts by their rapid progress promise even greater successes; when talents, in free peace and ease, can devote themselves to all subjects which are useful and dear to the soul; when in the present intellectual climate, literature should have a greater influence than ever before on morality and happiness.[30]

Despite the fact that there was still a lack of talent and taste in Russian authors, he believed that "in Russia literature can be even more useful than in other lands: feeling is newer and fresher in us; the beautiful therefore acts more strongly on the heart and bears greater fruit."[31]

Karamzin had clearly rejected his view of literature as private consolation for the poet and his friends, to which he had been driven by adverse conditions in Russia and Europe. His path to a utilitarian and patriotic view of art was both logical and predictable. The disillusionment he had suffered from events in France bolstered his patriotic feeling and suggested the important role that Russia might play in European affairs. The task of literature was therefore not only to consolidate Russia's eminence in the eyes of Europe but also to inspire pride in Russians:

> It is nearer and dearer for Russian talent to praise what is Russian in this happy time, when the Monarch and Providence itself call us to true glory. Russians must be taught to respect what is their own; they must be shown

how it can become the subject for an artist's inspiration and for the strong effects of art on the heart. Not only the historian and the poet, but also the painter and the sculptor are organs of patriotism.[32]

Pursuing this aim in another essay, **'On Love of One's Country and National Pride'** (**'O lyubvi k otechestvu i narodnoy gordosti'**), he exaggerated the importance of certain (unspecified) works of Russian literature:

> The successes of our literature [. . .] show the great ability of Russians. Have we not long known what style in verse and prose is?—and we can in certain respects already compare ourselves with foreigners. Already in the 16th century in France Montaigne was philosophising and writing—is it any wonder that in general they write better than we do? On the other hand, isn't it a wonder that some of our works can be placed alongside the best of theirs both for the painting of ideas as well as for nuances of style? Let us at least be just, dear compatriots, and feel the value of our own. . . .[33]

He follows this with an eulogy of the Russian language:

> Our language is expressive not only for lofty rhetoric, for loud, colourful poetry but also for tender simplicity, for the sounds of the heart and sensibility. It is richer in harmony than French and more able to render tones in the outpouring of the soul; it offers more *analogous* words, i.e. in accord with the action being expressed—an advantage enjoyed only by root languages. Our misfortune is that we all wish to speak French and do not think of perfecting our own language: is it surprising that we are thus unable to express in it certain subtleties in conversation?[34]

Karamzin reiterated these views in an important essay directly concerned with the problems of Russian literature and language, **'Why Are There Few Writers of Talent in Russia?'** (**'Ot chego v Rossii malo avtorskikh talantov?'**). In his analysis of literary backwardness in Russia, Karamzin sought the causes "not in the climate, but in the circumstances of Russian civic life".[35] He demanded application and study from the aspiring writer and an ability to understand and use language. In contrast to the previous essay, Karamzin was now concerned with realities rather than possibilities. Thus the comparative immaturity of the Russian language was acknowledged as well as the lack of inspiring models in most literary genres. He saw the normal solution to the problem of the development of a language in the spoken word, but stressed that society women, the usual source for attractive language, spoke only French. He did not consider, however, going beyond polite society to the Russian-speaking classes, for this would be to bypass the gentry whose enlightenment and advancement were his political concerns. Consequently his solution was intellectual and artificial. It relied on the example of fully developed European languages and the potentialities within the Russian language that a man of talent or genius might reveal:

What is there left for an author to do? Invent and devise expressions, sense the best choice of words, give to the old a certain new sense, present them in a new combination, but so skilfully as to deceive readers and conceal from them the unusualness of the expression.[36]

These were the principles Karamzin followed consistently, founded on his view that "the French write as they speak, and Russians still have to speak on many subjects in the way a talented man will write."[37]

Karamzin's concern with national needs and virtues in matters of language and literature did not necessarily bring him into conflict with the basic tenets of his earlier cosmopolitanism. The *Messenger* reveals his tendency to point out the failings and inadequacies of other literatures, particularly of contemporary English literature,[38] but Karamzin was far from renouncing his love of great writers and thinkers, essential to his understanding of enlightenment. His theoretical admiration for the true cosmopolitan mind is upheld in a translation he made of Herder's *Gespräch über eine unsichtbar-sichtbare Gesellschaft* (1793) (*Razgovor o nevidimo-vidimom obshchestve*). The desired society, unlike Freemasonry, was one "which is not secret, not hidden from the light, but working openly, not with ceremonies and symbols, but with lucid words and deeds, not confined to two or three nations, but everywhere where there is true enlightenment."[39] Above national prejudices and petty strife, the society would draw its inspiration from the world of books and a love of humanity.

> In conversation with Homer, Plato, Xenophon, Tacitus, Bacon, Fénelon, I do not think of what state they belonged to, what class they were from, and what temples they prayed in.[40]

Retaining his love of such ideals, Karamzin stressed the nobility of patriotism. Truly great writers, for instance, are shown to be great patriots; Klopstock "attempted to shame his pitiful fellow citizens and ceaselessly praised love for one's country in a land where for several decades the nation had respected only what was foreign".[41] Karamzin was sensitive to the negative connotations of the word "cosmopolitan" and contrasted sham cosmopolitan with the inspiring example of Peter the Great:

> He was a Russian in his soul and a patriot; and those gentlemen anglomaniacs or gallomaniacs wish to call themselves cosmopolitans. Only we ordinary people cannot soar with our minds above *base* patriotism; we stand on the earth, Russian earth; we look at the world not through the spectacles of systematic philosophers but with our own natural eyesight.[42]

Peter was central to Karamzin's concept of Russian enlightenment; his reforms marked the beginning of Russia's accelerated advance towards equality with the West and his example, according to Karamzin's thesis, inspired Catherine and Alexander. Reviewing a poem by André Chénier on enlightenment, Karamzin pointedly added the footnote: "And Peter the Great?" to Chénier's tribute to Frederick the Great as the supreme national enlightener.[43] At the same time Karamzin's interest in pre-Petrine Russia increased and he attempted to show how deep went the roots of Russian culture and history. As yet he chose to see no conflict between Peter's revolutionary methods and Russian traditions, for Russian history provided a further boost to Russian national pride and self-awareness:

> I do not trust that love for country which despises its chronicles or is not interested in them: we must know the present; we should be informed about the past.[44]

III

Karamzin's interest in history was becoming his major preoccupation; already in 1801, he saw clearly his future career as an historian, as his first ode to Alexander shows. During his editorship of the *Messenger* he took the opportunity to share the fruits of his study with his readers, hereby serving both his personal interests and the wider aims of the journal.

'Nathalie, the Boyar's Daughter', **'The Bird of Paradise'**, (**'Rayskaya ptichka'**, 1791), the opening pages of **'Poor Liza'**, as well as the unfinished poem **'Il'ya Muromets'** (1794), showed Karamzin's willingness to use (or abuse) Russian history and legend; but **'Martha'** was his first true historical tale. In December 1802, the month before he published **'Martha'**, he gave what might be regarded as the theoretical as well as the patriotic justification for such attempts. His essay **'On the Incidents and Characters in Russian History, Which May Provide Subjects for the Arts'** (**'O sluchayakh i kharakterakh v rossiyskoy istorii, kotoryye mogut byt' predmetom khudozhestv'**) is primarily concerned with possible subjects for painting, but Karamzin's suggestions were directed at all creative artists. Closely linked with this article and with the fictional re-creation of Martha is another essay by Karamzin, entitled **'Information on Martha the Burgomistress from the Life of St Zosima'** (**'Izvestiye o Marfe Posadnitse, vzyatoye iz zhitiya Zosimy'**, June 1803). Apart from the new information it gives on Martha's character, the essay is a call to "a skilled pen" to "represent for us a gallery of Russian women, famed in history or deserving of this honour".[45] His list of such women essentially continues the earlier one containing suggestions for suitable subjects for painting. Karamzin was possibly prompted once more by foreign example; Mme de Genlis, in an article translated by Karamzin, had written: "Most of all I would like to represent with my brush the most famous women in history, their main traits and virtues, their lives."[46]

As a result of his historical studies Karamzin came to acknowledge the importance of preserving folk songs

and proverbs. He said with approval of Bogdanovich that "he published Russian proverbs in which were preserved the valuable remains of our forefathers' thought, their true conceptions about good and their wise rules for life."[47] Karamzin himself printed a Yakut folk song which "depicts with simplicity and life the attachment of this good-natured people to animals, which are indeed worthy of man's gratitude."[48] Karamzin saw the need to collect all manner of historical anecdotes and legends; indeed, this was a patriotic duty:

> How good it would be to collect all Russian legends which are related either to history or old customs! I would praise the Russian who would undertake to travel round some of the regions of our fatherland with such an intention. . . .[49]

He regretted that the oral accounts of old people who remembered Peter the Great, Anne and Elizabeth had not been copied down and religiously preserved.[50] He himself recorded an alleged meeting with an old couple, who had been married more than eighty years; his old peasant is made to utter a string of proverbs and near-proverbs—obviously indicative of antique wisdom—in a typically stylized sentimental manner:

> Ya khotel znat' lyubyat li oni drug druga?—"kak ne lyubit'! muzh da zhena bol'she, chem brat da sestra". "Boites' li vy smerti?" "Chego boyat'sya? My, slava Bogu, pozhili. Smert' ne beda." "Tebe ne zhal' budet starushki?"—"Chego zhalet'! Komu nibud' nadobno umeret' prezhde."—"A yesli ona perezhivyot tebya?"—"Nu chto zhe? v svete ne bez dobrykh lyudey; dadut yey ugolok."[51]

Karamzin was anxious not only to preserve information about the past but also to have recorded in print all the glorious deeds of the present for the edification of posterity:

> We are to blame for having as yet no collection of true anecdotes about Russian national virtue which would disarm all misanthropes. I would not include in such a collection anything fictional or untrue—nor anything exaggerated: truth by itself is attractive.[52]

There was a tendency to find Russian equivalents for anything the West could offer and English example in all things *pro bono patriæ* seemed to present a particular challenge to Russian patriotism. The third article in the opening number of the *Messenger* told of an English scheme to erect a monument to the country's past glories and victories,[53] and a footnote to a later translation recorded the dedication of a monument in Westminster Abbey by a "grateful King and Country" to a fallen soldier.[54] Karamzin formulated the need for such information about Russia to be recorded in the first story of Russian **'Good Deeds'** (**'Blagodeyaniye'**) to be printed in the *Messenger*:

> Acts of philanthropy are an adornment of their age and country. Whenever and wherever men act virtuously, every sensitive heart rejoices; but the nearer the philanthropist is to us the greater our pleasure. If a Russian touches me with his magnanimity, then I rejoice as a man and still more as a son of Russia. A patriot who loves virtue in all lands worships it in his own country; it is the greatest service to the state, and its example is not only consoling but useful in civil relations, since it has a salutary influence on general morals.[55]

He ended by inviting "all patriots, all friends of mankind, to send him information about events that are consoling for the feeling heart".[56] Soon stories of unsung Russian virtues were being printed in increasing numbers in the *Messenger*. The honesty of the Russian peasant was extolled together with the generosity of the gentry.[57]

If Karamzin collected proverbs, folk-songs, anecdotes of the past and present out of a belief in their patriotic and historical value, he also contributed historical articles which were the fruit of careful research and documentation. He brought to his essays a high degree of literary art, attempting to make Russian history living and real for his readers. In a sense, he was the first accomplished popularizer of Russian history. He presented examples from earlier Russian history for a recent Moscow earthquake ['**On the Moscow Earthquake of 1802**'],[58] informed his readers of the historical associations of places and buildings in and around Moscow ['**A Journey around Moscow**'],[59] explained the origin and function of the Secret Chancellery ['**On the Secret Chancellery**'],[60] and analysed the causes of the Moscow revolt of 1648 ['**On the Moscow Revolt in the Reign of Aleksey Mikhaylovich**'],[61] Karamzin was seemingly intent on shaming his fellow Russians for their ignorance of Russia's past and at the same time preparing the way for his future career as an historian. His historical essays refer to the rudimentary state of Russian historiography, the limitations of the chronicles and the prejudices of foreign travellers;[62] he corrected mistakes made by his immediate predecessors V. N. Tatishchev and M. M. Shcherbatov,[63] attacked foreigners like P.-C. Levesque for writing ill-informed works on the history of Russia,[64] and regretted that the Professor of Russian History in the Russian Academy had been a foreigner.[65] He believed that "because we have no respectable history, the great and wondrous deeds of our forefathers are little known to us; but there is sufficient for an eloquent pen":[66] Karamzin saw, and rightly, that pen as his.[67] His comments on the tasks facing the historian anticipate features of his yet unwritten history: on the one hand, there is his strong interest in character and on the other, the yardstick of virtue and morality. He translated the views of other historians on the writing of history and in the early volumes of his own work he was obviously aware of Antoine Thomas' belief that "an historian should not describe in detail those events which cannot be described dramatically; i.e. divided into *statement, development* and *conclusion*. Otherwise such descriptions will be tedious and can only interest

contemporaries, who have sympathy for them because of their involvement.”[68] Making a distinction between historians and chroniclers, Karamzin declared that “our chroniclers are not Tacituses: they did not judge tsars; they related not all their deeds, only the most brilliant—military successes, evidence of religious devotion, etc.”:[69] it was precisely because he detected elements of both types of writer in him that Pushkin was to term Karamzin “our first historian and last chronicler”.[70]

IV

Combining the moral and emotional aspects of enlightenment and patriotism with a specific interest in social and political institutions was Karamzin’s concern for Russian advances in education. He regarded education as an internal, patriotic matter and was heavily sarcastic of foreign attempts to criticize or influence Russian methods. In **‘An Aberration’** (**‘Strannost’’**) he ridiculed a Frenchman’s scheme to set up a school near Paris, where among other subjects young Russians would be taught their native language; Karamzin insisted on the need for Russians to be brought up and educated in Russia:

> We know that everyone should grow up in his homeland and early become accustomed to its climate, habits, character of its people, way of life and government; we know that in Russia alone it is possible to become a good Russian—and for our national happiness neither the French nor the English are necessary to us.[71]

In **‘My Confession’** he criticized the sort of gentry education that could lead to contempt for one’s country.[72] He was therefore very ready to praise all measures to improve educational facilities within Russia. Karamzin had praised Catherine for her national schools, the importance of which he emphasized again in his **‘Historical Panegyric to Catherine II’** (**‘Istoricheskoye pokhval’noye slovo Yekaterine II’**, 1802),[73] and when Alexander introduced a number of educational reforms Karamzin heralded them with a series of essays in the *Messenger.*[74]

In his role as an enlightened patriot Karamzin agitated for the replacing of foreign tutors by Russians for “there will never be perfect moral education until we have good Russian teachers, who alone are able to instil the feelings and principles of a good Russian into a young heart.”[75] His fervour for the cause of enlightenment made him condemn ignorance as “antipatriotic, even a sign of opposition to the Tsar” for

> it hinders every enactment of the ruler’s benevolent intentions at every step, stops it, removes the strength from great and wise laws, encourages abuses, injustices and in a word, does not allow the state to enjoy its general internal prosperity which alone deserves to be the aim of a truly great, that is to say virtuous, monarch.[76]

Although Karamzin saw enlightenment as a progressive force, destroying prejudice, ignorance and reaction, he believed that it would lead not to revolution but to a strengthening of the social *status quo*; his views recall strongly the prevalent masonic attitude towards enlightenment as manifest in *Children’s Reading for the Heart and Mind* (*Detskoye chteniye dlya serdtsa i razuma*, 1785-9), where encouragement of learning went hand-in-hand with a defence of the class system.

Karamzin in the *Messenger* assumed the role of apologist of the Russian gentry—a role which allowed him to criticize, indulgently, existing abuses within that class in the name of its ideal function and character. He believed that

> the gentry is the soul and noble image of the whole nation. I love to imagine the Russian gentry not only with a sword in its hands, not only with the scales of Themis, but also with the laurels of Apollo as well as with the symbols of the goddess of agriculture.[77]

Although he recognized that a learned member of the gentry was a rarity in any country and that teachers would have to be found from among the lower classes,[78] he was soon proudly publishing details about the first “gentleman-professor” in Russia—Grigory Glinka of Derpt University.[79] Such events gave force to his thesis that “excellent knowledge is necessary to affirm the illustrious rights of the gentry”.[80]

Turning to the central critical question of the relationship between master and serf, Karamzin saw enlightenment leading to a decrease in arbitrary power:

> Those loathsome tyrants, comfortingly for the good heart few in number, who forget that, for a true member of the gentry, to be a good master is to be the father of one’s subjects, could no longer act in darkness.[81]

He expanded this view in what is perhaps the most optimistic and idyllic essay he wrote for the *Messenger*—**‘Pleasing Prospects, Hopes and Desires of the Present Time’** (**‘Priyatnyye vidy, nadezhdy i zhelaniya nyneshego vremeni’**):

> Enlightenment destroys the abuse of a master’s power, which even according to our existing laws is not tyrannical and unlimited. A member of the Russian gentry gives necessary land to his peasants; he is their protector in civil affairs and their helper in accidental or natural disasters: these are his duties! For this he demands from them half the working days in a week: this is his right![82]

Given just masters and such an understanding of his position, the peasant was to be content with his lot and serve his country as his station in life allowed. Enlightenment, Karamzin argued, allowed the peasant to see the justice of his position; educated European peasants

who "bless their modest lot in civil society, consider themselves not its victims but beneficiaries like other classes, all of which must work, if in different ways, for their own and their country's benefit."[83]

In his defence of the Russian social system Karamzin was consciously reacting against what he considered were ill-informed attacks and criticism from foreigners;[84] his most open defence of serfdom, **'The Letter of a Country Dweller'** ('Pis'mo sel'skogo zhitelya'), rejects foreign travellers' explanation of the laziness of the Russian peasant as a consequence of the evils of slavery. Karamzin saw the serfs as "lazy by nature, habit and ignorance of the advantages of industry."[85] In addition, they had an incorrigible weakness for drinking, the *bête noire* to which Karamzin pointed in any discussion of emancipation without enlightenment.[86] Karamzin was heavily critical of the study-bound scholar's pipe-dreams, the systematic philosopher's theories, which ignored realities;[87] faithful to his gospel of the middle way, Karamzin saw change coming gradually, unhurriedly:

> Time moves forward the reason of nations, but quietly and slowly; woe to the lawgiver who flies ahead! The wise man goes step by step, looking around him. God sees whether I love mankind and the Russian people; whether I am prejudiced, whether I worship the loathsome idol of self-interest—but for the true prosperity of our peasants I wish only that they have good masters and the means to enlightenment, which alone will make possible all that is good.[88]

Karamzin was firmly opposed to immediate emancipation. He was unable to envisage freeing the peasants without land—and this he considered at that time impracticable; equally he believed that without some degree of education and awareness of the many problems facing them, the peasants would abuse their liberty with idleness and drink. His caution was apt to be interpreted as reactionary by a generation of eager young reformers, his defence of serfdom as a preference for slavery over freedom.[89]

V

Karamzin's defence of gentry supremacy and serfdom was one aspect of a comprehensive statement on the type of government and society he envisaged for Russia. It was based on certain beliefs fundamental even to his early writings, but modified by his experiences, both public and private, during the reigns of Catherine and Paul. Karamzin's writings in the first years of Alexander's reign reveal him to be a consummate political publicist.

He greeted Alexander's accession as he had Paul's—with an ode. Encouraged by the gift of a signet ring from the tsar, he wrote a further ode for Alexander's coronation and by the end of 1801 he had completed for publication his **'Historical Panegyric to Catherine II'**. These three works outline Karamzin's demands on the young tsar and anticipate the main arguments of the *Messenger of Europe*. The burden of his odes is the need for a code of civil laws which would ensure the freedom of the individual and define the responsibilities of the citizen.[90] There is no suggestion that the law was *above* the monarch, for he was supreme and answerable only to God; nevertheless, fear of history's judgement was an incentive for a monarch to be virtuous:

> To tyrants my scroll is frightening;
> To good monarchs it is kind.[91]

Karamzin's panegyric to Catherine was an attempt to veil his demands on the new reign under praise for certain aspects of Catherine's; Karamzin was prompted to this stratagem by promises contained in Alexander's first manifesto:

> Accepting the throne, We accept the responsibility of governing the nation entrusted to Us by God according to the laws and heart of Our most august grandmother, the Empress Catherine the Great.[92]

Karamzin's allegedly historical survey of Catherine's achievements is a fantasy of what might have been; he elected to forget the reasons for his limited praise during her reign and portray Catherine in an ideal light. She became an indispensable part of his scheme of Russian development, which linked her name with those of Peter the Great and Alexander. For his new tasks of civic oratory Karamzin used all the devices and pathos of his sentimental style, as a contemporary satirist clearly recognized.[93]

Following a short introduction, in which he drew attention to the "immortal pages" of Montesquieu's *Esprit des lois,* a work of immense importance for both Catherine's and his own political concepts,[94] Karamzin reviewed Catherine's achievements under the three heads of victories, lawgiving and institutions. The result, however, is essentially an outline of Karamzin's own political and social views, to be illustrated not only from the pages of the *Messenger* but from such later writings as the *Memoir on Ancient and Modern Russia* (*Zapiski o drevney i novoy Rossii,* 1811), the **'Opinion of a Russian Citizen'** (**'Mneniye russkogo grazhdanina'**, 1819) and **'Thoughts on True Freedom'** (**'Mysli ob istinnoy svobode'**, 1826). Karamzin justified Catherine's wars as necessary for Russia's security, attacked "impudent and malicious Poland",[95] and when praising Catherine's wise choice of military leaders carefully omitted to mention Potyomkin—possibly a survival of the old masonic antipathy towards him.[96] The third section, where Karamzin extolled such institutions as the Academy of Arts, the National Schools, the Orphans' Home and even the wise censorship,[97] was the Russian

response to the social institutions which Karamzin considered to be one of England's glories.[98] It is, however, the discussion of Catherine the lawgiver that is the most revealing source of Karamzin's views on systems of government and the relationship of individual and state. Karamzin portrayed Catherine as favouring comprehensive laws and opposed to all arbitrary power,

> since She knew that personal security is the first blessing of a man and that without it our life is an eternal torturing worry amidst all the other forms of happiness and enjoyment. This mild spirit in government, proof of Her love and respect for mankind, was to be the main characteristic of Her decrees.[99]

Karamzin dwelt at length on Catherine's arguments in favour of autocracy contained in her *Nakaz* and attempted to illustrate their justice by examples: he pointed to the sorry failure of contemporary France to rule itself and its need of a "Corsican soldier" to save itself from utter collapse.[100] Simultaneously with his support for autocracy Karamzin reaffirmed his love of the great Republicans of history. Although he had himself rejected the possibility of realizing the ideal republic in the modern world,[101] he admired the republican virtues. Nevertheless, the demands on the individual in a republic were too high; and loss of civic virtue brought the downfall of a republic:

> Either people have to be angels or every complex form of government based on the action of different wills becomes eternal dissension and the people become the unhappy instrument of a few ambitious men, who sacrifice their country for their own personal benefit.[102]

The idea of autocracy as the time-hallowed and only fitting form of government for Russia was propounded by Karamzin throughout the *Messenger*. Whenever possible, Karamzin praised Alexander as the wise autocrat and connected Russia's imminent glory with his personal rule and example.[103] He was particularly anxious that false courtiers or advisers should not blind Alexander to his true obligations to his country or attempt to impinge upon his power. In his first ode Karamzin spoke of these "sly flatterers";[104] in his essay on the Moscow revolt of 1648 he painted the picture of a good tsar, a "little father" to his people but prevented from helping them by the machinations of his favourites.[105] As distinct from their position Karamzin's was that of a loyal well-intentioned patriot, one of the "unhypocritical friends of good / Able to speak the truth."[106] The picture emerges of a Russia ruled by a wise autocrat, beneath whom the gentry, the ever-increasing bourgeoisie and the peasantry performed their duties loyally and virtuously, respecting the contribution of every member of society to the general prosperity and content with their position: for the rejected western models of republics and constitutional monarchies Karamzin substituted his own autocratic Arcadia.

VI

Behind Karamzin's persuasive and insistent arguments in favour of what Pushkin was to call the "necessity of autocracy / And the charms of the knout"[107] stood a fear of upheaval, of tyranny by one man or many, or more specifically, the spectre of the French Revolution which had haunted and influenced his thought for more than a decade:

> The Revolution has elucidated ideas: we have seen that the civil order is holy even in its most local or chance defects, that authority is not tyranny for nations but protection from tyranny, that when it shatters the beneficent aegis, a people becomes the victim of terrible disasters which are incomparably more evil than all the usual abuses of authority, that even Turkish rule is better than anarchy, which is always the consequence of state conflict, that all the bold theories of the mind, which from the study wishes to prescribe new laws for the moral and political world, must remain in books, together with other more or less curious products of wit, that the institutions of antiquity have a magical force, which cannot be replaced by any force of intellect, that only time and the good will of legal government should correct the imperfections in civil societies, and that with this trust in the action of time and the wisdom of the authorities, we private citizens must live peacefully, obey willingly and perform all possible good around us.[108]

He admitted that all the outstanding minds of the day had desired "great changes and novelties in the constitution of societies", but they had learnt that "revolution was the abuse of freedom".[109] To provide an example of a great European mind, seduced by the French Revolution and eventually rejecting it, Karamzin chose to translate an article on Klopstock by Archenholz. Not only is the central passage an apology for Karamzin's own attitude to the Revolution, but the article as a whole echoes many of Karamzin's ideas on both patriotism and literary works:

> Klopstock, like all true philanthropists and all people of unusual intelligence, who are not egoists but friends of the general good, was a friend of the French Revolution, when it seemed a beneficial change in human destiny in France. Together with others he hoped that a strong and enlightened nation could be its own wise lawgiver: at that time much appeared captivating, especially from afar. Above all, his humane heart was enraptured by the famous decree of the National Assembly that France would forever reject wars of aggression—a decree made in the dawn of this great event but soon mocked and forgotten by the new rulers of France. But this passionate love for the new freedom of the French gradually died as a result of subsequent events and finally disappeared completely during the terrors of the Convention,[110]

Karamzin's desire to exorcise the French influence is apparent from the very first number of the *Messenger*. In addition to a translation entitled 'A History of the

French Revolution, Selected from Latin Authors' ('Istoriya frantsuzskoy revolyutsii, izbrannaya iz latinskikh pisateley'), in which the horrors and excesses of each stage of the Revolution were illustrated by quotations from Tacitus, Sallust and others,[111] the piece 'Alcibiades to Pericles' ('Al'tsibiad k Periklu') was full of obvious allusions to the pseudo-wisdom of the revolutionary leaders.[112] A third article 'Ladies' Wigs' ('Zhenskiye pariki') linked the fashion for wigs with the "unfortunate victims" of the Revolution; Karamzin in an original essay **On the Light Dress of Fashionable Beauties' ('O lyogkoy odezhde modnykh krasavits XIX veka'**), published three months later in April 1802, attacked Russian women for imitating the shameless French women, "who danced contredanses on the graves of their parents, husbands and lovers!"[113]

Karamzin sighed for the civilization of pre-revolutionary days; he was anxious to record all that suggested the return of gentle morals and amiability. Translated articles such as 'On Habit' ('O privychke') and 'On Politeness and Bon Ton' ('Ob uchtivosti i khoroshem tone'),[114] together with remarks about the "bad taste of *the nouveaux riches*" and the wish to see "social subtleties" reintroduced,[115] recall Karamzin's aphorism from 1793 that "politeness, affability, is the flower of society"[116] and stress his constant desire to encourage such qualities among the Russian gentry.

VII

Articles about French personalities and life in Paris, as well as more general works from French sources, fill a considerable part of the 'Literature and Miscellany' section of the *Messenger*. Not unexpectedly, the political fortunes of France occupy a prominent place in the journal's 'Politics' section. It is this section which truly justifies the journal's title by informing the Russian public of the internal affairs of European countries.

It was not, however, merely a process of translating interesting articles from the foreign press; Karamzin was involved in European events but was equally intent on using foreign material to comment on Russia's internal problems. To this aim Karamzin often re-edited or freely translated foreign originals, so that external authority seemingly supported opinions he had expressed elsewhere or felt unable to voice openly. This technique has been convincingly demonstrated by Yu. M. Lotman with reference to translated articles on widely differing topics,[117] but Lotman's article apart, little attention has been paid to Karamzin's political translations and especially his original political surveys.

Karamzin began his political commentaries with a detailed survey of a decade of upheaval in Europe, in which he stressed the desire of all countries for prolonged peace and stable government. His attention was directed above all to France, and particularly to Napoleon. It is Napoleon who dominated the *Messenger* both as a personality and as the key to European peace. In this opening essay Karamzin characterized him as a "new Caesar, a new Clovis"[118] and observed that:

> the dangerous and foolish Jacobin principles, which brought the rest of Europe to arms against the Republic, have disappeared in their own homeland, and France, despite the name and a few republican forms of government, is now in fact nothing other than a true monarchy.[119]

It was, among other things, the realization of Napoleon's autocratic designs that led to a change in Paul's attitude to France; Alexander, although carefully wooed by the English government, was also well disposed towards Napoleon. Karamzin was therefore reflecting the official line, and indeed Karamzin's attitudes to Napoleon reflect the numerous changes in Russian opinion towards him in the years 1800-12. Nevertheless, Napoleon's restitution of the monarchy in all but name seemed to support Karamzin's thesis of the one, and one only, historically justified form of government for a country. Every issue of the *Messenger* contained references to Napoleon and during the two years of Karamzin's editorship over thirty articles dealt directly with him and his actions. Napoleon met Karamzin's demands on a Great Man, such as he had set out in his **'Historical Panegyric to Catherine II'**:

> they decide the fate of mankind, determine its path; with inexplicable force they draw millions of people to some aim designed by Providence; they create and destroy kingdoms; they form epochs, of which all others are but the consequence; in a sense, they form a chain in the immensity of centuries, stretching their hands one to another, and their life is the history of peoples.[120]

Napoleon possessed what Montaigne had called "un peu de folie",[121] without which nothing great was achieved in life, for "fundamental rationalism was never a merit in heroes of ambition".[122] Although Karamzin saw Napoleon as a great general and leader of men, he also detected certain human weaknesses in him which denied him the accolade of great *and* virtuous:

> By killing the monster of the Revolution, he has earned the eternal gratitude of France and even of Europe. In this respect we shall always thank him willingly as a great doctor, who has cured heads of a dangerous giddiness. We shall regret that he has not the legislative wisdom of Solon and the pure virtue of Licurgus, who having formed Sparta, banished himself forever from his homeland! That is an heroic action before which all the Lodis and Marengos of the world disappear! After two thousand seven hundred years it still fires the mind and a good youth reading the life of Licurgus weeps in rapture. . . . Evidently it is far easier to be a skilful general and a cunning politician than to be a great, that is to say, heroically virtuous man.[123]

Despite the blemishes, Karamzin was ready to acclaim Napoleon, especially when he re-established the authority of the church or helped the advancement of enlightenment.[124]

Karamzin followed closely French legislative decrees as well as France's sponsoring of the constitution mania which affected in particular Switzerland and Italy. In 1802 he expressed the wish that independence be restored to the Swiss for "republican freedom and independence belong to Switzerland as much as her granite and snow-covered mountains: man does not destroy the works of nature."[125] Therefore, when the Landammann Alois Reding organized a secessionist movement among the small Swiss cantons, Karamzin was enraged by this rejection of history:

> It is a pity that such cruel and ambitious men influence the fate of that good but simple people, who lived for so many centuries in happy union with the large cantons, and who now, following the promptings of one malicious egoist, demand partition.[126]

The strife that followed in Switzerland caused him to reiterate his view that without national virtue a Republic was doomed:

> That is why a monarchy is far more happy and reliable; it does not put excessive demands on its citizens and can raise itself from a degree of morality at which republics would fall.[127]

Karamzin's hostility towards Reding continued from issue to issue,[128] but in March 1803 he translated a German article, in which Reding was praised as a selfless and dedicated patriot.[129] This is essentially an illustration of Karamzin's desire to present an objective picture of European events, although his own point of view was clearly stated in his 'News and Comment' ('Izvestiya i zamechaniya') column. Karamzin also made use of German material for 'external' criticism of both France and Germany. Certain German journalists were strongly pro-English and delighted in revealing the "hypocrisies" of French policy;[130] Karamzin himself found satisfaction in playing off the French press against its English counterpart, pointing out their readiness to abuse and libel their opponents.[131]

Karamzin's interest in English affairs is the counterbalance to his absorption with Napoleon; he himself made the revealing opposition that "in the one we are curious to know about national affairs and in the other, the actions of Consul Bonaparte".[132] His interest was primarily in English patriotism, in social institutions rather than political forms.[133] He tended to point out that the much vaunted English political system, especially Parliament and democratic elections, were not so ideal or worthy of imitation. In an amusing account of an English election Karamzin quoted Rousseau's remark that this was the only time Englishmen enjoyed true freedom, but warned that "these elections may be called merely a ceremony: the ministers control them unseen, in agreement with the best people in each district."[134]

Karamzin's political commentary in the *Messenger* coincided with a brief period of peace in Europe. The first number announced the imminent meeting at Amiens, but the last issues were filled with apprehension lest hostilities resumed. As Napoleon prepared to invade England, Karamzin was led to wonder whether victory for France or England would be the better outcome for Europe; admiration for Napoleon conflicted with his love of England:

> England abuses its dominance at sea, but who would wish the French to conquer this most fortunate country in the world, where wise laws reign and the citizens prosper.[135]

Yet it is important to note that the prospects of a new European conflict did not plunge Karamzin into despair and anguish—as the events of the Terror and the Revolutionary Wars had done. The reason behind his comparative equanimity was his patriotic faith in Russia and his new independence of Europe. His confidence was founded not only on Russia's internal strength and identity, given to it by the accession of Alexander, but also on its European mission and influence:

> It can despise the usual tricks of diplomacy and, elected by Fate, can, it seems, be a true intermediary between nations.[136]

He proudly recorded that Russia's intervention into German affairs made it "an object of universal respect, universal trust", that the Corfu islanders had welcomed Russian help and that even England acknowledged Russia's might.[137]

VIII

The *Messenger of Europe* offered the Russian public a rich variety of reading matter, but it was a journal dominated by the personality and interests of one man, given unity both by his style and by the persistence of certain themes and ideas. Compared with the *Moscow Journal,* the *Messenger* is pre-eminently a political rather than a literary journal; Karamzin's desire for cultural enlightenment is linked with his propaganda for a particular social and political system, within which his ideals could be realized. The journal was the messenger of European affairs to the degree that European experience could demonstrate, negatively or positively, a course for Russian development; it is essentially the testament of a man who had learnt and taken much from Western culture but who now felt the tide to be turning and wished to encourage Russians to an awareness of their greatness and potential.

Karamzin had himself lived happily under the influence of Western literature and thought since his schooldays and had freely acknowledged in his story **'Liodor'** (1792) that Russians were still apprentices of the West in all things, even in literature.[138] Now he felt assured of his standing as a writer in Russia and abroad; he was the one contemporary Russian author widely known in the West and in the period 1797-1803 translations of the 'Letters', stories and articles appeared in Danish, English, French, German, Greek and Polish.[139] Karamzin drew attention to English, French and German versions of his work in the pages of the *Messenger*,[140] and it was from the *Messenger* that Johannes-Gottfried Richter, already the translator of the 'Letters' translated articles and stories for publication in his *Russische Miszellen* (1803-4).[141]

The *Messenger of Europe* occupies a distinguished place in the history of Russian journalism as the first of the *tolstyye zhurnaly* and its importance was immediately recognized by Karamzin's contemporaries. It was initially published in 600 copies, but was so successful that the first number was republished and the monthly printing doubled to 1200 copies. Of the tributes to Karamzin's achievement perhaps the most impressive, because it was unexpected, came from an opponent, the Shishkovite and Decembrist Wilhelm Kyukhel'beker, who read in exile the works Karamzin had written in the 19th century. Although he was fundamentally opposed to Karamzin's views,[142] he felt obliged to acknowledge the merits of the *Messenger*:

> It must be admitted that for its time this journal is extremely good; and even today it would not occupy the last place among our publications for the attractiveness of its articles, and almost the first place for its language.[143]

A month later, in June 1832, he admitted:

> They have brought me two volumes of Karamzin's *Messenger* and two of his successors'. What a difference! One must be just to Karamzin that as a journalist he was a master of his craft.[144]

Notes

1. F. F. Vigel', *Zapiski*, 2 vols., Moscow, 1928, I, p. 131.

2. *Arzamas i arzamasskiye protokoly*, Leningrad, 1933, p. 240.

3. Op. cit., p. 125.

4. N. I. Grech, *Zapiski o moyey zhizni*, Moscow-Leningrad, 1930, p. 190.

5. In the second volume of his literary almanac *Aglaya* (1795) Karamzin published an exchange of letters between Melodor and Philalet, illustrating the philosophical crisis he underwent as a result of the Reign of Terror in France. Melodor represented Karamzin the disillusioned idealist and Philalet the worldly-wise guarded optimist. The debate was continued in the 'Dialogue on Happiness' ('Razgovor o shchastii', 1797).

6. *Sochineniya Karamzina*, 3 vols., St Petersburg, 1848, I, p. 210. (*Note*: Whenever possible, subsequent references are made to this edition, which includes Karamzin's major articles from the *Messenger of Europe*: Karamzin, followed by volume and page.)

7. *Vestnik Yevropy*, I, 1802, January, No. 1, p. 8.

8. Ibid., VIII, 1803, April, No. 7, pp. 173-92.

9. Ibid., VI, 1802, December, No. 23, p. 227.

10. Ibid., No. 24, pp. 319-25.

11. An analysis of Karamzin's prose fiction in the journal lies outside the scope of the present article. Its importance, however, has been recognized in a number of recent studies, e.g. V. I. Fyodorov, "Istoricheskaya povest' N. M. Karamzina 'Marfa Posadnitsa'" (*Uchonyye zapiski Moskovskogo gorodskogo ped. instituta*, LXII, No. 6, Moscow, 1957, pp. 109-20); Yu. M. Lotman, "Puti razvitiya russkoy prozy 1800-1810-kh godov" (*Uchonyye zapiski Tartuskogo gos. universiteta*, vypusk 104, Tartu, 1961, pp. 3-57); *Istoriya russkogo romana*, I, Moscow-Leningrad, 1962, pp. 71-83; F. Z. Kanunova, "K evolyutsii sentimentalizma N. M. Karamzina ('Marfa Posadnitsa')" (*Uchonyye zapiski Tomskogo gos. universiteta*, No. 50, 1965, pp. 3-13); F. Z. Kanunova, "Evolyutsiya sentimentalizma Karamzina ('Moya ispoved'')" (*Rol' i znacheniye literatury XVIII veka v istorii russkoy kul'tury. XVIII vek*, sbornik 7, Moscow-Leningrad, 1966, pp. 286-290).

12. *Vestnik Yevropy*, I, 1802, January, No. 1, p. 7.

13. Ibid., VI, December, No. 23, pp. 228-9. (Karamzin's new views on criticism were embraced by Zhukovsky, who began editing the *Messenger* in 1808: "Criticism and luxury are the daughters of wealth; but we are not yet Croesuses in literature!": ibid., 1808, January, No. 1, p. 9.)

14. *Moskovskiy zhurnal*, V, 1792, February, pp. 277-90.

15. Ya. L. Barskov, *Perepiska moskovskikh masonov XVIII-go veka, 1780-1792*, Petrograd, 1915, p. 90; *Zritel'*, II, St Petersburg, 1792, June, pp. 158-9.

16. *Vestnik Yevropy*, VI, p. 228.

17. G. P. Makogonenko, "Literaturnaya positsiya Karamzina v XIX veke" (*Russkaya literatura*, Leningrad, 1962, No. 1, p. 90).

18. *Vestnik Yevropy,* VI, p. 229.

19. Ibid., III, 1802, May, No. 10, pp. 103-19; VII, 1803, January, No. 2, pp. 136-40; III, 1802, June, No. 11, pp. 242-4.

20. Ibid., p. 244.

21. Ibid., X, 1803, July, No. 13, pp. 57-8. (Cf. A. G. Cross, "N. M. Karamzin and Barthélemy's *Voyage du jeune Anacharsis*" in *Modern Language Review,* LXI, 1966, July, No. 3, pp. 467-72.)

22. Ibid., V, 1802, September, No. 17, p. 56.

23. Ibid., III, 1802, May, No. 10, p. 146.

24. Ibid., II, 1802, April, No. 7, pp. 232-236. (Cf. Karamzin's remarks to Dmitriyev on Klushin's *Laughter and Grief [Smekh i gore]* in 1793: *Pis'ma N. M. Karamzina k I. I. Dmitriyevu,* St Petersburg, 1866, pp. 36-7.)

25. The response was so great that Dmitriyev wrote 'An Epitaph on Epitaphs' ('Epitafiya Epitafiyam, sochinyonnaya odnim iz avtorov epitafiy'): *Vestnik Yevropy,* IX, 1803, May, No. 9, p. 46. The standard may be judged from the fact that Karamzin was obliged to make two grammatical corrections in an epitaph of two lines!: ibid., VIII, 1803, March, No. 6, p. 140.

26. N. Vtorov, "Gavrila Petrovich Kamenev" (*Vchera i segodnya,* I, St Petersburg, 1845, p. 50).

27. Karamzin, I, p. 610.

28. Ibid., pp. 615, 643-4, 647. (Cf. Karamzin's conversation with Wieland in the 'Letters' when all three topics were discussed: ibid., II, p. 149.)

29. *Vestnik Yevropy,* V, 1802, October, No. 20, p. 285. (In his notes on Kantemir in the *Pantheon* Karamzin had divided the 18th century into *four* periods.)

30. Ibid., I, 1802, January, No. 1, pp. 3-4.

31. Ibid., p. 5.

32. Karamzin, III, pp. 551-2.

33. Ibid., p. 473.

34. Ibid., pp. 474-5.

35. Ibid., p. 527.

36. Ibid., p. 528.

37. Ibid., p. 529. The idea of "writing as one speaks" was taken up by adherents of Karamzin, such as Batyushkov, but had been expressed as early as 1778 by F. G. Karin, a follower of Sumarokov: V. I. Saitov, "Fyodor Grigor'yevich Karin. Odin iz maloizvestnykh pisateley vtoroy poloviny XVIII veka" (*Bibliograf,* St Petersburg, 1893, No. 1, p. 16).

38. *Vestnik Yevropy,* II, 1802, March, No. 5, p. 56. (Cf. Karamzin, II, p. 749.)

39. Ibid., VI, 1802, November, No. 22, p. 124.

40. Ibid., p. 126.

41. Ibid., IX, 1803, June, No. 11, p. 172.

42. Ibid., pp. 167-8. (Cf. Karamzin, III, p. 609.)

43. Ibid., I, 1802, January, No. 1, p. 44.

44. Karamzin, III, p. 552.

45. Ibid., I, p. 384.

46. *Vestnik Yevropy,* IX, 1803, June, No. 11, p. 201.

47. Karamzin, I, p. 641.

48. *Vestnik Yevropy,* VI, 1802, November, No. 22, p. 133 (A detailed analysis of Karamzin's changing attitude to folk literature is given by N. N. Trubitsyn, *O narodnoy poezii v obshchestvennom i literaturnom obikhode pervoy treti XIX veka,* St Petersburg, 1912, pp. 328-32.)

49. Ibid., X, 1803, July, No. 13, pp. 60-1.

50. Karamzin, I, pp. 424-5.

51. Ibid., p. 470.

52. *Vestnik Yevropy,* III, 1802, May, No. 10, p. 140.

53. Ibid., I, 1802, January, No. 1, pp. 17-9.

54. Ibid., p. 48.

55. Ibid., II, 1802, March, No. 5, p. 52.

56. Ibid., p. 55.

57. Ibid., VIII, 1803, March, No. 5, pp. 39-42; April, No. 7, pp. 227-9; No. 8, pp. 298-301; IX, May, No. 10, pp. 124-6; June, No. 11, p. 235; No. 12, pp. 291-4; XII, November, Nos. 23-4, pp. 268-75.

58. 'On the Moscow Earthquake of 1802' ('O moskovskom zemletryasenii 1802 goda'): Karamzin, III, pp. 581-4.

59. 'A Journey around Moscow' ('Puteshestviye vokrug Moskvy'): Karamzin, I, pp. 448-57; 'Historical Reminiscences and Observations on the Way to the Holy Trinity Monastery' ('Istoricheskiye vospominaniya i zamechaniya na puti k Troitse'): ibid., pp. 458-501.

60. 'On the Secret Chancellery' ('O taynoy kantselarii'): ibid., pp. 419-26.

61. 'On the Moscow Revolt in the Reign of Aleksey Mikhaylovich' ('O moskovskom myatezhe v tsarstvovaniye Alekseya Mikhaylovicha'): ibid., pp. 398-418.

62. Ibid., pp. 420-1, 487.

63. Ibid., pp. 422-3, 485.

64. Ibid., p. 419.

65. Ibid. (Karamzin was referring to A. L. Schlözer [1735-1809].)

66. Ibid., p. 479.

67. Karamzin had himself in mind at the end of his essay on Martha: "a *gallery of famous women* could be a highly attractive work if an author of talent and taste would present these characters with the lively colours of love for the fair sex and the homeland. Is it necessary to say who should be entrusted with such a work in our time?": ibid., p. 387.

68. *Vestnik Yevropy,* II, 1802, March, No. 6, p. 134.

69. Karamzin, I, p. 424.

70. A. S. Pushkin, *Polnoye sobraniye sochineniy,* XI, Moscow-Leningrad, 1949, p. 120.

71. Karamzin, III, p. 607. (Cf. Karamzin's letter to Alexander Turgenev on the same subject in September 1816: ibid., p. 740.)

72. Ibid., pp. 505-7.

73. Ibid., I, p. 361.

74. 'On the New Schools for the Nobility, Established in Russia' ('O novykh blagorodnykh uchilishchakh, zavodimykh v Rossii'): *Vestnik Yevropy,* II, 1802, April, No. 8, pp. 358-66; 'On the New Organization of National Enlightenment in Russia' ('O novom obrazovanii narodnogo prosveshcheniya v Rossii'): Karamzin, III, pp. 348-359; 'On a Reliable Method of Acquiring Sufficient Teachers in Russia' ('O vernom sposobe imet' v Rossii dovol'no uchiteley'): Karamzin, III, pp. 340-347; 'On the Public Teaching of the Sciences at Moscow University' ('O publichnom prepodavanii nauk v Moskovskom universitete'): ibid., III, pp. 611-7.

75. *Vestnik Yevropy,* II, 1802, April, No. 8, p. 363.

76. Karamzin, III, p. 349.

77. Ibid., p. 597.

78. Ibid., pp. 343-4.

79. *Vestnik Yevropy,* IX, 1803, June, No. 11, pp. 197-9. (Karamzin later printed part of Glinka's first work, *The Temple of Svetovid* (*Khram Svetovida*), a laboured investigation into the gods of Slavic mythology: ibid., X, August, No. 15, pp. 173-86.)

80. Karamzin, III, p. 616.

81. Ibid., I, p. 339.

82. Ibid., III, p. 591. (Cf. ibid., p. 580.)

83. Ibid., p. 351.

84. Ibid., pp. 573-4, 350.

85. Ibid., p. 573.

86. Ibid., p. 570; I, p. 406.

87. In his 'Historical Panegyric to Catherine II' Karamzin revealed clearly the distinction he made between philosophical theorizing and political expediency: ". . . even good in a philosophical sense may be harmful in politics, as soon as it is out of step with the civil state of a nation. A sad truth, but demonstrated by experience!": ibid., I, p. 370.

88. Ibid., III, p. 575.

89. Cf. Pushkin's account of a conversation he had with Karamzin on this subject and Karamzin's violent rejection of the accusation: A. S. Pushkin, *Polnoye sobraniye sochineniy,* XII, 1949, p. 306.

90. In a later essay Karamzin said "a full methodical collection of civil laws, clearly and wisely written" was Russia's most pressing need: Karamzin, III, p. 592.

91. Ibid., I, p. 209.

92. A. M. Skabichevsky, *Ocherki istorii russkoy tsenzury* (1700-1863), St Petersburg, 1892, p. 86.

93. "Odin s ulybkoyu umil'noy / Zhelal dela tvoi vospet' / I slov pustya potok obil'nyy / Mnil slavu Tomasa imet'. / K romanam, k pastoral'nu slogu / Imeya strast'—skroil eklogu / I slovo milaya vkleil / Tvoi i lavry i trofei / I khramy vse, i mavzoley / Slezoyu nezhnoy okropil.": *Russkaya starina,* XCII, St Petersburg, 1897, November, p. 306.

94. Karamzin, I, p. 280.

95. Karamzin, I, p. 289. (Karamzin's antipathy towards Poland also informs his 'Opinion of a Russian Citizen.')

96. G. V. Vernadsky, *Russkoye masonstvo v tsarstvovaniye Yekateriny II,* Petrograd, 1917, pp. 236-8.

97. He stressed the need for censorship because reason might stray from truth; he had been quick to forget the excesses of censors under Catherine and Paul.

98. Karamzin, II, p. 723.

99. Ibid., I, pp. 303-4.

100. Ibid., p. 312.

101. Nevertheless, true to the theories of Montesquieu and Rousseau on the suitability of a republic for a

small country, Karamzin defended Switzerland's system: ibid., I, pp. 313, 320.

102. Ibid., I, pp. 312-3.

103. Ibid., III, pp. 345, 349, 357.

104. Ibid., I, p. 202.

105. Ibid., pp. 402-3. (Cf. Karamzin's translation of an article giving a similar view of Louis XVI: *Vestnik Yevropy,* I, 1802, January, No. 1, pp. 18-28.)

106. Ibid., p. 203. (Cf. his epigraph to the *Memoir on Ancient and Modern Russia*: "There is no flattery on my tongue.")

107. This epigram on Karamzin's *History* is not included in the Academy edition of Pushkin's work, but Pushkin's authorship of it is well argued by B. V. Tomashevsky, *Pushkin. Issledovaniya i materialy,* I, Moscow-Leningrad, 1956, pp. 208-15.

108. Karamzin, III, pp. 585-6. (Cf. ibid., II, pp. 462-3.)

109. Ibid., pp. 586, 587.

110. *Vestnik Yevropy,* IX, 1803, June, No. 11, pp. 175-6.

111. Ibid., I, 1802, January, No. 1, pp. 20-37.

112. Ibid., pp. 9-16.

113. Karamzin, III, p. 522.

114. *Vestnik Yevropy,* VII, 1803, January, No. 2, pp. 85-91; XI, 1803, May, No. 9, pp. 24-30.

115. Ibid., I, 1802, January, No. 1, p. 33.

116. Karamzin, III, p. 387.

117. Yu M. Lotman, "Evolyutsiya mirovozzreniya Karamzina (1789-1803)", *Uchonyye zapiski Tartuskogo gos. universiteta,* vypusk 51, Tartu, 1957, pp. 150-5.

118. Karamzin, I, p. 527.

119. Ibid., p. 530. (Karamzin also translated a speech by Baron Nekker favouring monarchy over a republic: *Vestnik Yevropy,* V, 1802, October, No. 20, pp. 301-19.)

120. Ibid., I, pp. 276-7. (Cf. "Not the French people but Providence placed this astonishing man at such a degree of greatness": *Vestnik Yevropy,* III, 1802, June, No. 11, p. 270.)

121. Quoted by Karamzin in his 'Man of Feeling and the Cold-Blooded Man': ibid., III, p. 620.

122. Karamzin was here referring to Napoleon's plans to invade England: *Vestnik Yevropy,* X, 1803, August, No. 15, p. 230.

123. Karamzin, I, p. 552.

124. *Vestnik Yevropy,* III, 1802, May, No. 9, pp. 77-94; II, April, No. 7, pp. 276-7.

125. Karamzin, I, p. 536.

126. *Vestnik Yevropy,* V, 1802, September, No. 18, p. 157.

127. Ibid., October, No. 20, pp. 319-20.

128. Ibid., VI, 1802, November, No. 21, p. 74; No. 22, p. 156; December, No. 24, pp. 330-1.

129. Ibid., VIII, 1803, March, No. 6, pp. 146-54.

130. Particularly Archenholz, whom Karamzin called in the 'Letters' "this well-known anglomaniac": Karamzin, II, p. 691.

131. *Vestnik Yevropy,* II, 1802, April, No. 8, p. 386; IV, August, No. 15, p. 247; VI, November, No. 22, p. 165.

132. Ibid., IV, 1802, August, No. 16, p. 329.

133. See A. G. Cross, "Karamzin and England" (*Slavonic and East European Review,* XLIII, 1964, No. 100, December, pp. 101-6).

134. *Vestnik Yevropy,* IV, 1802, July, No. 13, p. 73.

135. Ibid., XI, 1803, September, No. 18, p. 160.

136. Karamzin, III, p. 590.

137. *Vestnik Yevropy,* V, 1802, October, No. 19, p. 232; X, 1803, August, No. 15, pp. 213-5, 232.

138. *Moskovskiy zhurnal,* V, 1792, March, p. 315.

139. S. Ponomaryov, *Materialy dlya bibliografii literatury o N. M. Karamzine,* St Petersburg, 1883, pp. 46-51.

140. *Vestnik Yevropy,* VII, 1803, February, No. 3, p. 229; X, August, No. 15, pp. 195-8; XI, October, No. 20, p. 291; XII, November, Nos. 21-2, p. 50.

141. V. I. Kuleshov, "Iz istorii russko-nemetskikh literaturnykh svyazey ('Vestnik Yevropy' N. M. Karamzina i 'Russische Miszellen' I. G. Rikhtera)" (*Slavyanskaya filologiya,* V, Moscow, 1963, pp. 436-51).

142. "It is impossible to agree with all Karamzin's historical, literary and philosophical opinions": V. K. Kyukhel'beker, *Dnevnik,* Leningrad, 1929, p. 88.

143. Ibid., pp. 60-1.

144. Ibid., pp. 64-5. (Karamzin's immediate successors on the *Messenger* were P. Sumarokov, M. T. Kachenovsky and Zhukovsky.)

Roger B. Anderson (essay date winter 1971)

SOURCE: Anderson, Roger B. "Karamzin's Concept of Linguistic 'Cosmopolitanism' in Russian Literature." *South Central Bulletin* 31, no. 4 (winter 1971): 168-70.

[*In the following essay, Anderson discusses Karamzin's unique innovations in the art of Russian prose writing.*]

One of the most important contributions Karamzin made during his vigorous life was to establish a workable, consistent model for the Russian literary language. Before his appearance late in the eighteenth century, prose writers united virtually all possible lexical levels including Old Slavonic, chancery terms, vernacular language of the street, folk expressions, a multitude of technical jargon, and an almost unbridled use of foreign words or barbarisms. The result was a hodge-podge. Karamzin's avowed aim was to streamline the written language so as to approximate the oral speech of well-bred society. In order to accomplish his task he suggested the exclusion of numerous lexical funds including Slavonic forms no longer used in educated speech, all chancery items, scholasticisms and other professional jargon, and vulgar expressions of the street or of folk dialects.[1]

Since the educated salon was caught up in the new world-view of western sentimentalism, Karamzin naturally included a large number of foreign words and phrases in his language reforms. Whole foreign words like *nervy* or *melanxolija* appear, conveying concepts and feelings for which Russian had no equivalents. Other words and phrases are carefully translated into Russian lexeme by lexeme (e.g., *ja delajus' lišnym* or *ubivat' vremja*). Karamzin also encouraged the use of calques which could carry a new, metaphorical meaning. With these he could approximate ideas found in western languages that also had no equivalent in Russian. Perhaps the most quoted example of this category is *čuvstvovat'*, in which the second meaning of the English "to feel" or the French *sentir* carries directly into Russian. Finally, Karamzin was most adept at making up new words based on existing forms, often the result of adding the suffix *-nost'* (e.g. *vljublënnost'*). The fact that most of them are retained in contemporary Russian testifies to Karamzin's aptness in such made-up words.

In his choice of syntax Karamzin also relies heavily on western models. His sentences are a good deal shorter than those of Lomonosov and are much less prone to inversions than those of any Russian predecessor. Even though Karamzin's typical sentence retains the rhythmical periodicity for which he is famous, it normally breaks down into a series of shorter, much more simple clauses that simulate the cadence of human speech. As Ja. K. Grot points out, Karamzin successfully weeded out earlier hypotactic complexities which interfered with the candid flow of thought.[2] Karamzin's new syntactic models rely on two or three relative clauses rather than on the four or sometimes five dependent clauses common to earlier eighteenth-century prose writers.[3]

Western lexical and phraseological influence has historically been the most controversial aspect of Karamzin's linguistic reforms. It is his attitude toward that influence that I would like to discuss here.

Karamzin came at the end of a century in which Russia was all but engulfed by western culture. The Russian language was especially susceptible to foreign influences because of its limited potential for articulating concepts and feelings long popular in the West. Critics have often faulted Karamzin for aping the West at the expense of Russian's historical ties with Slavonic linguistic roots. Admiral Šiškov's vilification of Karamzin's use of foreign phraseology is infamous. Karamzin's reliance on external sources in structuring the literary language bears the often pejorative name of "cosmopolitanism." His statements "it is good to write for Russians, but it is yet better to write for all people," or "what is good for all people cannot be bad for Russians" make it tempting to label him a *zapadnik* and be done with it.

In point of fact, however, the great majority of the barbarisms and calques Karamzin uses were introduced into Russian much earlier in the century (or, as Kovalëvskaja[4] and Hüttl-Worth[5] point out, even in the seventeenth century). Karamzin himself often criticized Russian writers for using foreign words indiscriminately. He recommended a judicious approach to barbarisms, using them only when Russian had no native equivalent. If anything, Karamzin used fewer loan words than his contemporaries, a fact consistently overlooked by Šiškov.[6]

There is more to Karamzin's "cosmopolitanism" than parroting the latest western fashion. He speaks very clearly about the necessity of each national language, including Russian, to contribute its own special flavor to the communal storehouse of European esthetics. What makes western literature great for Karamzin is the confluence of national identities within the larger framework of western taste. He specifically states that French, British, and German writers were adept at preserving their own national personalities while yet sharing the common literary values of Europe. The main emphasis of Karamzin's language reforms was to attain the same status for Russian writers. His goal of establishing Russia as a contributing member of the western literary establishment is revealed in his remarks to the Imperial Russian Academy in 1818 [**"Reč, proiznesënnaja na toržestvennom sobranii imperatorskoj Rossijskoj akademii"**]. He says:

> Krasoty osobennye, sostavljajuščie xarakter slovesnosti narodnoj ustupajut krasotam obščim; pervye izmenjajutsja, vtorye večny. Xorošo pisat' dlja rossijan: eščë lučše pisat' dlja vsex ljudej. Esli nam oskorbitel'no idti pozadi drugix, to možem idti rjadom s drugimi, k celi vsemirnoj dlja čelovečestva. . . .[7]

Then, in the same speech he can say:

> sxodstvuja s drugimi evropejskimi narodami, my i raznstvuem s nimi v nekotoryx sposobnostjax, obyčajax, navykax, . . . Siju istinu otnesëm i k slovesnosti: bu-

duči zercalom uma i čuvstva narodnogo, ona takže dolžna imet' v sebe nečto osobennoe, nazametnoe v odnom avtore, no javnoe vo mnogix. Imeja vkus francuzov, imeem i svoj sobstvennyj.[8]

B. V. Tomaševskij points out that Karamzin carefully used foreign linguistic forms (usually French) only as models for making Russian more expressive in its own right.[9] The intent was never to make Russian imitative of French or any other language. Karamzin says as much in his statement:

Čto ostaëtsja delat' avtoru? Vydumyvat', sočinjat' vyraženija; ugadyvat' lučšij vybor slov; davat' starym nekotoryji novyj smysl, predlagat' ix v novoj svjazi, no stol' iskusno, čtoby obmanut' čitatelej i skryt' ot nix neobyknovennost' vyraženija![10]

P. I. Makarov, a spokesman for the Karamzin school, recommends the inclusion of only those foreign words that most smoothly complement existing Russian sounds and standards of taste.[11]

Karamzin's goal of integrating Russian into the establishment of western stylistics is apparent once it is sought. A. I. Efimov, in his study of **"Natal'ja bojarskaja doč',"** suggests that Karamzin freely mixes western-inspired phrases with unmistakably Russian ones.[12] The western clichés are rendered in calques and characteristically incorporate a periphrasis (one of the favorite stylistic features of western poetics of the time). For example Karamzin has:

1. cvety ljubvi,

2. predmet ljubvi,

3. predmet nežnyx pobuždenij,

4. vesna žizni,

5. sladkie slëzy nežnosti,

6. trogatel'nyj čelovek.

Efimov then lists a sampling of highly visible Russian phrases from the same story:

1. v Moskve belokammenoj, v prestol'nom grade,

2. velikij xlebosol,

3. krasnye devuški,

4. solnce krasnoe,

5. žil-byl,

6. pyl' v glaza pustit'.

The Russian items break down into three categories:

1. Folk tale clichés (e.g. žil-byl),

2. Ossified folk epic clichés (e.g. the post-positional adjective in "Moskva belokamennaja"),

3. Folk expressions or idioms (e.g. vo ves' dux or ne ljuba ne slušaj, a govorit' ne mešaj).

There are not as many Russian phrases as there are western calques, but the contrastive effect is striking when the lists are compared. Late in the nineteenth century, critics like P. N. Polevoj still openly admired Karamzin's adroit union of Russian phrases with those from western sentimentalism.[13] The subordinate role Polevoj ascribes to the Russian contributions reaffirms Karamzin's basic design of adding Russian flavor to stable stylistic conventions of the west.

A contrapuntal relationship between Russian words or phrases and elegant western calques sometimes occurs within the same sentence. In "Prekrasnaja carevna . . . ," for instance, there is an active conversation between the two. In one sentence the western cliché "krylataja boginja" appears close to the Russian folk *topos* "prekrasnaja carevna." At another point we have the western mythological reference to "zefiry" and "Psiša." Directly after these we find the Russian fairy tale phrase "v nekotorom carstve, v nekotorom gosudarstve žil-byl car' dobryj čelovek." Karamzin then quickly returns to purely western poetic items like "čuvstvitel'noe serdce." On the same page Karamzin mixes the archaic Russian form "vlasy" and the folk simile "kak gorddyj lebed'" to the western image "lazur efirnaja" and the calque "zvezda ljubvi." V. V. Vinogradov refers to the same working arrangement between Russian and standardized western vocabulary when he cites a critic contemporary to Karamzin, D. N. Bludov. Bludov suggests that Russian writers, like Karamzin, search out and use native folk expressions that might be harmonious with western sentimental phrases.[14] Again, the consistent emphasis is on conforming to fundamentally western modes of expression, but with the addition of a purely Russian flavor.

In the same spirit of eclecticism, Karamzin makes such international and Russian phrases stand as actual complementary halves. A periphrasis usually accompanies this union. The recognizable Russian segment ordinarily follows the more "poetic" western expression and almost translates the calque into common Russian. For example, from ***Rycar' našego vremeni***:

Dunul severnyj veter na nežnuju grud' nežnoj roditel'nicy, i genij žizni eë pogasil svoj fakel' . . . Da, ljubeznyj čitatel', ona prostudilas'.

The sudden intervention of a common Russian "translation" of the western calque vividly accentuates the juxtaposition. There is also ample room to consider the tongue-in-cheek effect of such a pairing. The dignity of a phrase like "nežnaja grud' nežnoj roditel'nicy" is

hardly enhanced by its pedestrian translation "ona pros-tudilas." Nevertheless, by introducing the blunt Russian "translation," Karamzin helped legitimize its co-existence with the western phrase. Here is another ex-ample this time from **"Natal'ja bojarskaja doč'"**:

> . . . groznaja carica xlada vossela na ledjanoj prestol svoj i doxnula v'jugami na russkoe carstvo, to est' zima nastupila. . . .

Here again the elegant, western-inspired periphrasis is highly contrastive with the more conversational Russian equivalent "zima nastupila."

As has been mentioned above, many western phrases within the counterpoint are distinctively poetic in origin (usually bound to periphrasis). But, Karamzin does not limit the union of western and Russian phraseology only to such poetic turns of speech. He also selects purely informational phrases, the kind that appear in any western language, and contrasts them to colorful Russian equivalents. For example, in the famous first line of **"Bednaja Liza"** one reads:

> . . . nikto bolee moeo ne brodit peškom, bez plana, bez celi—kuda glaza gljadjat.

"Brodil bez plana, bez celi" and "kuda glaza gljadjat" are similar in that they convey the same general idea, but stylistically they are quite different. "Brodit'" is in-ternational in that the word has close approximations in a number of western languages (e.g. *errer* in French, *spazieren* in German, "to roam" in English). It is neu-tral stylistically. "Kuda glaza gljadjat," on the other hand, carries the obvious stamp of a Russian idiom. Another example is from Karamzin's last story, **"Marfa posadnica"**:

> Previlikaja zala byla zapolnena slušateljami, tak čto nekuda bylo upast' jabloku.

The neutral style of the first expression, "zala byla zapolnena," again contrasts sharply with the Russian idiom "nekuda bylo upast' jabloku." The resultant mix-ture of Russian flavor to a style firmly grounded in western models furthers Karamzin's special vision of "cosmopolitanism."

Karamzin's theoretical approach to Russian literature consistently reflects two goals. One is his desire to ac-celerate Russia's movement toward full inclusion within the pale of western European ideas and esthetics—what he called enlightenment. Second, he diligently worked to stimulate a sense of national identity among Russian writers that would enrich that European community through Russia's presence. Karamzin well understood that Russia had a great deal of catching up to do with the West. For a while, Russia would have to receive the advantages of western stylistic achievements more than

it could offer in return by way of its own literary ac-complishments. But Karamzin was convinced that Rus-sia's *literati* would emerge in the end with an original contribution to the western community. As he optimisti-cally said:

> A kto roždën s izbytkom vnutrennix sil, tot i nyne, na-čav podražaniem, svojstvennym junoj slabosti, budet nakonec *sam soboju*—ostavit' putevoditelej, i svobod-nyj dux ego, kak orël derznovennyj, uedinenno vosparit v gornix prostranstvax.[15]

Karamzin freed the Russian prose language from the clumsiness of old Slavonicisms and the offensive cru-dity of vulgar speech. He concentrated his efforts on developing those possibilities of polite conversational Russian that most easily complemented western taste of the late eighteenth century. Within those limits he fash-ioned an imaginative and remarkably graceful vehicle for the expression of thought and feeling. His concept of "cosmopolitanism," the co-mingling of western and recognizable Russian phrases in a grand communal fund, has historically proven of enormous benefit to the Russian literary language. Vinogradov is convinced that Karamzin's simpler syntax stabilized the Russian sen-tence for future generations of writers.[16] Perhaps the greatest tribute to Karamzin's stylistic innovations comes from D. D. Blagoj when he says that it was that new language which provided the basis for Puškin's great accomplishments with literary Russian.[17] Without Karamzin's sensitive experimentation, could there have been a Puškin?

Notes

1. See G. Vinokur, "Vosemnadcatyj vek," *Istorija russkogo literaturnogo jazyka* (Moscow, 1959), for a detailed discussion of Karamzin's systematic exclusion of various word sources.

2. Ja. K. Grot, *Karamzin v istorii russkago jazyka* (St. Peterburg, 1867), pp. 34-35.

3. See K. Skipina, "O čuvstavitel'noj povesti," in *Russkaja proza,* ed. B. Éixenbaum and Ju. Tyn-janov (Mouton, 1963), esp. p. 18.

4. E. G. Kovalëvskaja, "Inojazyčnaja leksika v proiz-vedenijax N. M. Karamzina," in *Materialy i issle-dovanija po leksike russkoog jazyka XVIII veka* (Ak. Nauk, 1965).

5. Gerta Hüttl-Worth, "Foreign Loan Words in Rus-sian, an Historical Sketch, 1550-1800," *University of California Publications in Linguistics,* XXVIII [(1963)], 8-13.

6. Grot, p. 23.

7. N. M. Karamzin, "Reč', proiznesënnaja na torž-estvennom sobranii imperatorskoj Rossijskoj aka-demii," in *N. M. Karamzin-izbrannye sočinenija,* II (Moscow-Leningrad, 1964), 238.

8. *Ibid.,* p. 239.

9. B. V. Tomaševskij, *Stilistika i stixosloženie* (Leningrad, 1959), p. 45.

10. *N. M. Karamzin-izbrannye sočinenija,* II, 185.

11. P. I. Makarov, *Vestnik Evropy* (1816), Č. 87, 280.

12. A. I. Efimov, "Fraziologičeskij sostav povesti Karamzina 'Natal'ja bojarskaja doč'," *Materialy i issledovanija po istorii russkogo literaturnogo jazyka,* I (Ak. Nauk, 1949), 90.

13. P. N. Polevoj, *Istorija russkoj literatury* (Sankt Peterburg, 1872), p. 455.

14. V. V. Vinogradov, *Problema avtorstva i teorija stilej* (Moscow, 1961), p. 242.

15. *N. M. Karamzin-izbrannye sočinenija,* II, 761.

16. V. V. Vinogradov, *Očerki po istorii russkogo literaturnogo jazyka XVII-XIX vv.* (Leiden, 1949), pp. 180-81.

17. D. Blagoj, "Puškin i russakaja literatura XVIII veka," *Puškin—rodonačal'nik novoj russkoj literatury* (Moscow, 1941), p. 119.

Richard Pipes (essay date 1975)

SOURCE: Pipes, Richard. "Karamzin's Conception of the Monarchy." In *Essays on Karamzin: Russian Man-of-Letters, Political Thinker, Historian, 1766-1826,* edited by J. L. Black, pp. 105-26. The Hague: Mouton, 1975.

[*In the following essay, Pipes discusses the origin of Karamzin's ideas concerning the role of the monarchy in Russian history. According to Pipes, Karamzin's belief that autocratic power is the surest guarantor of individual freedom is firmly rooted in eighteenth-century, rather than nineteenth-century, political philosophy.*]

> I desire neither a constitution nor representatives, but in my heart I remain a republican, and yet a loyal subject of the Russian tsar; here is a contradiction, but not in reality!
>
> Karamzin to Dmitriev (1818)

The natural inclination of the mind in studying history, viewing as it does all events *ex post facto* and aware as it is of their consequences, is to consider past occurrences as part of what followed rather than of what preceded. This is due not only to our propensity to impose upon historical phenomena patterns of cause and effect derived from everyday experience, but also to the greater interest which most of us have in periods nearer and therefore more pertinent to our own time. This tendency, natural as it may be, often leads to a miscon-struction of historical events. For, obviously, people—the subject of historical investigation—are guided by ideas and experiences of their own and preceding times, and not by those which followed. The historian thus may be said to be handicapped by his own knowledge; and nothing is intellectually more difficult, as well as fascinating, for the historian than to subject himself to the laborious process of cleansing his mind of the knowledge of *post facto* occurrences, as he must in order to understand properly the events under investigation.

Karamzin is a case in point. In some ways, for reasons beyond his control, he became the object of a dispute between nineteenth-century Russian conservatives and liberals, a dispute that took place under circumstances quite different from those which prevailed when he had formulated his political ideas. Consequently, he is often appraised in terms of nineteenth-century issues, a century to which he belonged physically (in part at least, since he lived from 1766 to 1826) but in which he never felt at home intellectually. The notion of "autocracy" (*samoderžavie*), which lies at the heart of his entire political philosophy, cannot be interpreted in terms of events and disputes which emerged after his death, when the conflict over the Russian constitution was well on its way. By then the conditions, issues, and even the very terminology of the debate had changed beyond recognition.

Karamzin's political thought is meaningful only when viewed from the vantage point of the preceding century. This entails the use of eighteenth-century terminology, a conception of the state and sovereignty quite different from the one to which the succeeding century has accustomed us, and above all, a feeling for the mood of Europe in Karamzin's lifetime. For the Western world was then in the first throes of a revolution whose long-range import was hidden from the eyes of contemporaries, and when the coming nineteenth century—to us an age of irretrievable serenity—threatened to turn into a graveyard of civilization.

1

To begin with, Karamzin, unlike his intellectual successors, was not a political man. He was born and raised in a society that considered the business of politics unsuitable for a gentleman and best left to scribes drawn from families of burghers and clergymen and known as *ljudi krapivnogo semini* (pettifoggers). In his time politics had not yet acquired the almost religious significance which it was to have for succeeding generations, parting friend from friend and dividing society into hostile camps. Though keenly interested in politics, being a witness of the French Revolution and the great changes which followed it, he always regarded politics as an avocation, second to literature and history, and far less

important than the pursuit of art and of friendship. His principal concern was with culture. He was Russia's first professional man of letters, and even his *History* [*History of the Russian State*], which kept him busy during the second half of his life, was strongly permeated with a belletristic and dramatic spirit. Concern for culture—culture in general and that of Russia in particular—constitutes also the background of his interest in politics.

To understand why this was so one must consider Karamzin's early development. From the very beginning of his literary career, he associated with circles and movements which, though broadly connected with the Enlightenment, were hostile to its extreme rationalist manifestations, and sought a compromise in the eighteenth-century conflicts between faith and reason, tradition and progress. The freemason circle of Novikov, for which Karamzin worked as a writer and translator from 1784 to 1789, as well as the Sentimentalist movement in Russian literature, which he headed after breaking with the freemasons, stressed the moral and emotional, rejecting the extreme anti-traditionalism and rationalism of French encyclopedic thought then dominant at the court in St. Petersburg. Both took a pessimistic view of man's condition, both saw progress as feasible only in terms of the inner self-perfection of man, both rejected legislative manipulation as a means of attaining human happiness. Karamzin early in his life arrived at the conclusion that progress was primarily a cultural phenomenon, in which political and social factors played a secondary role. A better society could be brought about solely by the imperceptible action of time, through the slow but certain safe advance of the human mind, enlightenment, education, and good manners. "When men shall be persuaded that virtue is indispensable to their own happiness, then shall the golden age have arrived, and man shall enjoy the peaceful blessings of life under *every* form of government."[1]

This view of progress, which Karamzin upheld to the end of his life, determined to a large extent his attitude toward politics. Progress, which was to be internal, individual and moral, could not be promoted through the positive action of governments; rather, it called for a government which left its citizens the widest possible scope for the exercise of civil liberties, providing them at the same time with the maximum of external and internal security. A pessimistic appraisal of man's condition, coupled with confidence in the ability of men—given freedom and security—gradually to improve themselves, lies at the base of Karamzin's whole political outlook.

The writings of Karamzin are crowded with paeans in favor of "liberty"; it is the source of all wealth and power, a "golden thing", the loss of which, next to physical suffering, is one of life's two genuine tragedies.[2] Freedom Karamzin understood largely in the sense of the "rule of law": "Freedom exists where there are laws, where the good man lives without fear; where they are absent, slavery prevails."[3] As he grew older, Karamzin tended increasingly to view freedom as something inner, spiritual, as "freedom which comes not from the Sovereign, not from a Parliament, but which every one of us secures for himself with God's help. Freedom [which] we must attain in our hearts through a peaceful conscience and trust in Providence"[4]—much in the manner in which a Gogol or Tolstoj was later to understand it. But, this evolution notwithstanding, Karamzin continued throughout his life to place great emphasis on the establishment of civil liberties on a firm foundation of law.[5] It was this ingredient in his political thought which was so unpalatable to some reactionaries of his time and earned him the reputation of a "Jacobin".[6]

The establishment of civil liberty depends, in turn, upon firm government. Like Hobbes, Karamzin considered law without the sword a worthless parchment: "Law without authority is nothing."[7] Only a government which is strong, respected, even feared can keep in check the natural predatory instincts of man, and forcefulness is the necessary (though not a sufficient) quality of every sound government. Nothing can excuse weakness: "In politics weakness is guilt."[8]

The belief in the interdependence of civil liberty and political power is a central tenet of Karamzin's political theory, and the search for a political system able to reconcile them constitutes the principal purpose of his political inquiries. The existence of such an interdependence seemed to him to be demonstrated by the entire course of Russian history. Whenever Russian governments were weak and incapable of resisting internal or external pressures, the rule of law weakened, and in the ensuing anarchy the desire of men to save their lives and possessions led them to barter their liberties for security. The ancient Russians lost their republican liberties and institutions like the *veče* as a consequence of the weakness of the Kievan state. This weakness led first to internal disintegration and then foreign conquest. The princes of Moscow who undertook to free the Russian nation from the Tatar lords experienced no difficulty in depriving their subjects, eager to be saved from foreign domination, of their civil liberties. "Political slavery [of a state] is incompatible with civil freedom",[9] and civil liberty cannot survive where internal struggles for power sap the strength of the state. Firm authority is therefore the foremost principle of good government; it alone creates the conditions in which other political virtues can flourish.

Such are the premises from which Karamzin approached the problems of government. His analysis was carried out with the help of concepts developed by French

thinkers of the eighteenth century, especially Montesquieu and, to a lesser extent, the Physiocrats. Indeed, with a certain shift of emphasis from economics to civil liberties, the question which Karamzin sought to resolve was not unlike that confronting the Physiocrats, who desired virtually complete freedom of economic activity under a government sufficiently strong and "disinterested" to resist the pressures of divergent social groups endeavoring to use the supreme political authority for their own purposes.[10]

2

In the eighteenth century, at least until Montesquieu, political systems were customarily divided in accordance with the Aristotelian triad into republics, aristocracies, and monarchies. The distinguishing feature of each system was the number of persons in whom the right of sovereignty was legally vested: in republics it was the property of all, in aristocracies of a few, in monarchies of one. Though the occurrence of so-called "mixed" governments was recognized, the tendency of political thought of this period was to operate in terms of such archetypes. This tendency was further strengthened by Montesquieu's reform of current political terminology. In his search for the most practical political system, Karamzin followed closely Montesquieu's categories and historical approach, adapting both to Russian conditions.

In politics Karamzin was a thorough-going pragmatist. In his opinion the value of all institutions was relative, and the ultimate test of every government was its ability to rule effectively, not its conformance to this or that political philosophy:

> For forms of government let fools contest
> Whate'er is best administered is best.
>
> (Pope)

Certainly any system, even the worst, is preferable to anarchy. "Every civil society, confirmed by centuries, is for good citizens a sanctuary, and in the most imperfect one must admire a certain wonderful harmony, order, and arrangement."[11] Karamzin was fond of quoting Solon to the effect that while his laws were not perfect, they were the best which could be devised for the Athenians.[12] Although he always admired English institutions (like many of his Russian contemporaries, he was an ardent Anglophile), he never thought it prudent to transplant English institutions to other countries. English liberties, he observed in the 1790s after his return from London, were not so much a product of the activity of Parliament and other British institutions as of the high degree of public enlightenment; this was the true "Palladium" of English liberty. To copy British laws was unwise: "What is good in England will be bad in another country."[13] It is more important for institutions and laws to conform to the traditions and character of the people to whom they are meant to apply than to abstract formulae of justice or perfectibility. Karamzin, like conservatives in other countries at this time, fully accepted Montesquieu's historical, relativist approach to politics. All his political views bore on concrete situations: his advice was meant to apply only to Russia, and moreover to Russia at the level of cultural development at which he knew it.

Karamzin also accepted Montesquieu's conception of the political *principe,* that is, the specific "human passion which sets [the political system] into motion",[14] and with it the conviction that the decline of great states usually begins with the corruption of their particular *principe.* The *principe* of the two types of what Montesquieu called "republican" governments—democracy and aristocracy—was "virtue", which in the former entailed "love of country" and "equality", in the latter "moderation".[15]

Using these categories, Karamzin disposed of these two types of government as inappropriate for Russia. The main shortcoming of republics was their *principe,* that is, virtue. Karamzin's pessimistic view of human nature, especially his consistent rejection of the idea of equality, precluded the acceptance of a political system erected on such a foundation. If, nevertheless, he persisted to the end of his life in reiterating his "republicanism", it was because, like many other eighteenth-century thinkers, he used this term to mean not so much a concrete system of government (since, aside from the American republic, whose experience was hardly applicable to Europe, and the short-lived and quite unstable French Republic, there were then no large republics in existence) but an ideal, an order attainable only in the remote future when men became truly perfect. Being "a republican" meant to believe in the worth of virtue, justice, progress—objects which, in Karamzin's view least of all could be attained by the republican system. "My heart, no less then the hearts of others", Karamzin wrote in 1802, "is set on fire by the virtue of great republicans—but how durable were its brilliant epochs?"[16] In this sense Catherine II, too, considered herself a "republican".[17]

Karamzin also rejected the aristocratic order. To understand how it was possible for a defender of the rights of the upper classes like Karamzin to be hostile to the political ambitions of his own class—a phenomenon contrary to much of Western experience—one must bear in mind that the Russian nobility consisted of two groups: the old, titled aristocracy, and the service gentry. Though since the time of Peter I no legal distinction had been made between these two groups, their traditions and aspirations were dissimilar. The true aristocracy with its ancient, inherited titles had throughout the sixteenth and seventeenth centuries waged bitter fights with the mon-

archy to assert its rights and compel the Crown to hear and respect its advice. These conflicts ended with an undisputed victory for the monarchy, assisted by the gentry. The gentry were the creation of the Crown, which had bestowed on them certain legal and economic benefits (notably landed estates with bonded peasants); they were dependent on the Crown and loyal to it. The last significant effort by the old aristocracy to circumscribe the power of the Crown and to introduce an aristocratic system of government was made in 1730 and was suppressed by the monarchy at the request and with the active help of the gentry. In Karamzin's time the ambitions of the aristocratic groups were no more than a faint memory, and certainly a *Fronde* was by then quite out of the question. Yet in condemning on principle all those Russians who in the past had wanted to impose limitations on the Crown, Karamzin acted as a true representative of his own class, the gentry. To him Kurbskij was a "traitor", and so too were the boyars who in the reign of Ivan IV and during the Time of Troubles had sought to weaken monarchical power.[18] He similarly condemned the nobility's attempt to impose "conditions" on Anne.[19] All these attempts by the "many-headed hydra of aristocracy", as he called it, had been inspired by selfish motives and inevitably led to internal conflicts. Aristocracy, judged by past experience, was incapable of providing firm authority. To be effective, political authority must be kept intact: "Two political authorities in one state are like two dreadful lions in one cage, ready to tear each other apart."[20] The history of Poland provided ample proof of that truism.

Democracy and aristocracy are thus rejected as unable to satisfy one of the two prerequisites of good government, namely forcefulness; the former because its *principe* rests upon an unrealistic estimate of human nature; the latter because it entails a division of authority and therefore leads to civil strife. Firm government can be assured only by a system which concentrates sovereignty in the hands of a single person, that is, a monarchy. Karamzin is an out-and-out monarchist; but when we attempt to ascertain more precisely what Karamzin means by the term "monarchy", we run at once into semantic difficulties.

Karamzin favored in Russia a type of government called *samoderžavie*. While this Russian term is a literal translation of the Greek *autokrateia* and thus may be correctly rendered as "autocracy", its English equivalent has implications which may be misleading. As Ključevskij has shown, the term *samoderžavie*, which was first used in Russia by Ivan III, originally meant the *independence* of the grand princes of Moscow, their freedom from all external control, in particular from that of the Tatar khans.[21] Later on, beginning with Ivan IV, this concept was broadened to include the notion of the *limitlessness* of the tsar's power; that is, a term originally coined for external application, to define Russia's rela-

tions with foreign powers, was now broadened to apply also to the relationship between the monarch and his subjects. While in the succeeding centuries the definition of the Russian monarchy theoretically included both these ingredients, in practice the situation was by no means clear, and at times the monarchy's independence (external as well as internal) was more heavily stressed than its limitlessness, its freedom of action more than its scope.[22] This emphasis was due to purely practical considerations: what was challenged in the monarchy from the sixteenth to the eighteenth centuries was not so much the extent of its authority (which was in any case limited by the size of the country, the relative inadequacy of the administrative apparatus, and other natural factors) as its monopoly of authority. In effect, therefore, the concept of *samoderžavie* and its derivatives came to mean exactly what the concept "sovereignty" meant in the West, and as one scholar justly observed, these concepts had in Russia parallel histories.[23]

Now according to the political nomenclature current in the eighteenth century, the monarchic system of government was one in which sovereignty was vested in a single person. In the words of Montesquieu, "In monarchies the prince is the source of all power, political and civil."[24] For this reason, in the eighteenth century, up to and including the time of Karamzin, in Russian political literature as well as legal documents, the French terms *monarchie, monarchique, souverain,* and so forth, were rendered as *samoderžavie* or *samoderžavstvo,* and *samoderžavnyj.* Feofan Prokopovič in his *Pravda voli monaršej* (1722), the best known absolutist tract of the reign of Peter I, used the terms *samoderžavie* and *monarxija* interchangeably, as when he wrote that the political system "in which . . . all authority is vested in the hands of a single person . . . is called monarchy (*monarxija*), that is, autocracy (*samoderžavstvo*)".[25] Catherine II, in the French version of her *Instruction,* written forty years later, translated the terms *samoderžavie* and *samoderžavnyj* as *souverain* and *monarchique* rather than *autocratique.*[26] This usage must still have been prevalent as late as the 1820s, for the Dictionary of the Russian Academy of Sciences published at that time defined the adjective *samoderžavnyj* as *samovlastnyj,* "comprising legislative functions", and the noun *samoderžec* as "the sovereign, supreme authority, ruling *samovlastno* without depending on anyone".[27]

An analysis of Karamzin's use of the term *samoderžavie* reveals that he understood it in this sense, that is, as a system in which full sovereignty was vested in one person. He concluded the analysis of early Russian history which opens his **Memoir on Ancient and Modern Russia** with the statement that "Russia perished from the division of authority, and was saved by wise *samoderžavie*—the contrast between "division of authority" and "*samoderžavie*" implying that he considered the in-

divisibility of supreme power, i.e. of sovereignty, the distinguishing feature of the latter. Elsewhere in the same work he remarked that following the accession of the Romanov dynasty in 1613, when true autocracy was established in Russia, "no one besides the monarch could either judge or invest; all authority derived from that of the monarch". And further, "In Russia the sovereign is the living law. . . . In the Russian monarch concentrate all the powers; our government is fatherly, patriarchal."[28]

Thus it seems clear that Karamzin used the term *samoderžavie* in much the same sense in which contemporary Western thinkers used the term "sovereignty", and *samoderžec* meant to him the "sovereign" or "monarch". What he had in mind was not so much *unlimited* authority—for, as we shall see, he wanted it limited in several ways—as *undivided* authority. He certainly did not wish this concept to imply the right of the monarch to rule at will, without regard for the wishes of his subjects or the law. This is evident from the clear-cut distinction that, again following Montesquieu, he drew between the two subspecies of royal government.

One of the many contributions which Montesquieu made to European political thought was to revise the traditional Aristotelian scheme of political systems. This he did by first dividing them into two main categories; those which entrust sovereignty to the many and those which entrust it only to one, and then further dividing each of these categories; into two subgroups; on the one hand, democracies and aristocracies, and on the other monarchies and despotisms (Aristotle's pure and concept variants of rule by one man). The distinction between democracies and aristocracies lay in the extent to which sovereign power was fragmented: in democracies it was the property of all, in aristocracies of the few; the distinction between monarchies and despotisms was not in the number of those who possessed sovereignty, but in the manner in which sovereignty was exercised. According to Montesquieu's nomenclature, the power of monarchs and despots was the same, that is, both had exclusive possession of sovereignty; but in every other respect the two systems differed. The monarchical system is one in which "a single person governs by fundamental laws", by "fixed and established laws" with the assistance and through the agency of various intermediary and dependent orders, the most important of which is the nobility ("no monarchy, no nobility; no nobility, no monarchy"), and a repository of laws. In despotisms, on the other hand, the only law is the whim of the ruler; the subjects, including the "well-born", lack rights; and the prince rules the whole country directly, that is, he dispenses with the services of the intermediate orders. The *principe* of monarchy is "honor", that of despotism "fear". A monarchy turns into a despotism when the ruler "wants to govern everything by himself", when he changes more in the constitution of the state than is necessary, when he deprives "some of his subjects of their hereditary employments to bestow them arbitrarily upon others".[29]

This distinction is vital for an understanding of Karamzin's concept of monarchy. His desire to have the Russian Crown endowed with all the attributes of sovereignty did not in the least mean that he wanted it to acquire the prerogatives of limitless power in the sense in which they have been claimed by the modern totalitarian state. Political authority which recognized no law was to him a tyranny or a despotism and not a monarchy, since the very definition of monarchy entailed the concept of government by law. Indeed, the principal difference between monarchies and despotisms in this interpretation lay in their opposite attitudes to law. In Karamzin's works, therefore, a sharp distinction was always drawn between *samoderžavie* on the one hand and despotism (*despotija*) or tyranny (*tiranija*) on the other. While both these systems were firm and forceful, and as such to Karamzin always preferable to unstable, ineffective republics, only one of them—true monarchy, or *samoderžavie,* could provide what Karamzin required of all good government, namely a mixture of liberty and firmness.

The fatal defect of despotism is that it produces an atmosphere of fear and uncertainty in a country and in this way undermines the foundations of culture. On this ground Karamzin condemned despotism, whether in France as during the Revolution and under Napoleon, or in Russia. Russia, in Karamzin's analysis, has only had two despots in her history: Ivan IV (in the latter part of his reign) and Paul I. His unprecedented censure of these two tsars, and especially the frank criticism of Ivan IV in the ninth volume of the ***History*** (the criticism of Paul was contained in the ***Memoir*** and was not published in Russia until the beginning of the twentieth century although it was known from widely circulating manuscript copies) were to cause Karamzin trouble with reactionary groups at Court and the bureaucracy who regarded him with suspicion for his praise of civil freedoms and his defense of Novikov.[30]

By adhering to this distinction and differentiating between Russian monarchs who ruled without regard to law and those who respected it, Karamzin made it quite clear that he considered *samoderžavie* not so much rule without legitimate limits as rule without external constraints; a system which allowed the subjects no political rights, but did leave them the full measure of civil rights. He evolved this conception in the first decade of the nineteenth century in reaction to the designs of Alexander I and his advisors to provide Russia with a written constitution and representative institutions which, if carried out, would have inevitably impinged upon the authority of the tsar and divested him of a share of sovereign power.

3

Karamzin based his advocacy of such a system of absolute monarchy largely on pragmatic arguments. First of all, its *principe*, "honor", seemed to him best suited to the natural impulses of man: love of distinction, ambition, vanity. Unlike Voltaire who had criticized Montesquieu for allegedly wishing to found monarchy upon "vices", Karamzin found Montesquieu's formulation acceptable precisely for that reason: "A republic cannot survive without a high degree of national virtue. This is the reason why monarchical government is far happier and more promising: it does not demand of citizens extraordinary things, and may progress while at a level of moral development at which republics collapse."[31]

Furthermore, *samoderžavie* was well adapted to Russia's geographic and historical conditions. Like many of his contemporaries Karamzin believed in a correlation between the size of a state and its system of government: the larger the country, the more concentrated should be its political power. An excessively rapid change in the dimensions of the state was thought inevitably to react on its political institutions. The belief that Russia, as the largest European power, needed a highly centralized system of government was virtually axiomatic in Russian public opinion of the time. "Il n'y avoit qu'une Puissance ainsi concentrée dans la seule personne du Souverain [*samoderžec* in the Russian version] capable de produire un degré d'impulsion proportionné a l'étendue d'un aussi vaste Empire", Catherine II wrote at the beginning of her *Instruction*.[32] With this Karamzin agreed—Russia consists of very many and very diverse parts, each of which has its special civic needs: "what save unlimited monarchy can produce in such a machine the requisite unity of action?"[33] With an admirable consistency he cautioned against further expansion of the Russian state, mindful of the warnings of Montesquieu that overextended monarchies turn either into despotisms or into aristocracies, and in some instances—the prime example being ancient Rome—disintegrate altogether.[34] He approved therefore neither of the third partition of Poland nor of the acquisition of Finland, though for some reason he had no objection to Russian expansion in the Black Sea area.[35]

The soundness of this argument, if it required further proof, could be conclusively shown by the entire course of Russian history. In Karamzin's interpretation Russia's historical experience taught that whenever the power of the sovereign was emasculated, Russia fell apart and her subjects turned into slaves; only absolute monarchy was capable of restoring to her independence and greatness. The survival of civil rights in Russia was, historically speaking, entirely dependent upon the preservation of strong, centralized authority. As a consequence of her evolution, autocracy had in fact become "an indispensable property of Russia, her only

political constitution, the sole basis of her unity, strength, welfare".[36] It "has founded and resuscitated Russia. Any change in her political constitution has led in the past and must lead in the future to perdition . . ."[37] In so arguing, Karamzin was not proposing a new interpretation of Russian history, but merely enlarging upon a view widely accepted by Russian historians in the eighteenth century. Tatiščev, Müller, Schlözer, Ščerbatov, and Boltin—all the pioneers of Russian historiography—agreed that Russia's traditional system of government, the one best adapted to her conditions and national character, was a system in which all political power was concentrated in the hands of the monarch.[38] The inspiration that moved Karamzin to write his audacious **Memoir on Ancient and Modern Russia** and the reason for the extreme urgency of its tone ("I see danger, but not as yet destruction!") was the conviction that the constitutional and administrative designs of Alexander I and his advisors would alter a traditional system of government and thereby bring about the country's internal collapse.

Having little regard for legalistic or philosophical considerations in politics, Karamzin rested his case for absolutist government in Russia largely on such practical arguments: in the final analysis, what mattered to him was that the system worked, not that it was "right", "just", or "lawful". Yet at least on one occasion he argued that insofar as Russia had a constitutional, legal commitment to a specific political system, that commitment was to autocracy. In 1613, when the nation had elected the Romanov dynasty, it gave the new tsar and his successors the right to rule autocratically:

> The sorrows caused by the rebellious aristocracy [of the Time of Troubles] had enlightened the citizens as well as the aristocrats themselves. Both unanimously proclaimed Michael an autocrat, an unlimited monarch; both, fired with love for the fatherland, exclaimed merely: *God and the Sovereign!* . . . They inscribed a charter which they laid at the throne. This document, inspired by the wisdom of experience, and confirmed by the will of the boyars and the people, is the holiest of all the state charters. The princes of Moscow had instituted autocracy—the fatherland conferred it on the Romanovs.[39]

The charter to which Karamzin refers has not survived, and modern scholars doubt whether it had ever existed at all.[40] For the purpose of the present inquiry, however, the question of its existence is irrelevant. In Karamzin's time it was widely believed that at the accession of the Romanovs the deputies to the Land Assembly which had elected them prepared a state charter legally establishing the dynasty and entrusting it with autocratic power. Schlözer, the German historian of Russia active in the second half of the eighteenth century, also considered it the juridical foundation of Russia's statehood, her "constitution".[41] This charter made it possible for

Karamzin to strengthen his cases for absolute monarchy: he could assert not only that it was the most suitable for Russia geographically, historically, and otherwise, but that it also had constitutional force. If the subjects had the sacred duty to obey their sovereign, then the tsar, in turn, was obligated to preserve *samoderžavie* and resist all attempts to restrict his power; he might rule badly, but rule he must. "You may do everything", Karamzin admonished Alexander I, "but you may not limit your authority by law."[42] The only legal limitation of sovereignty was its duty to admit of no legal limitations.

Sovereignty must be intact, concentrated in the hands of the monarch; legislative, executive, and judicial powers must be combined. But this is not to say that the proper exercise of the royal prerogative entails no circumscriptions, since—according to definition—only despotism is truly unlimited in its use of power. The true monarchy is confined in several ways, by moral and historical considerations, as well as by its obligation to respect laws of its own making.

> [The] unlimited authority of the [Russian] monarchs impressed foreigners as *tyranny*; in their ill-considered judgment they forgot that *tyranny* is merely abuse of autocracy, which occurs in republics as well, when powerful citizens or dignitaries oppress society. Autocracy means not the absence of laws: for where there is *obligation* there also is *law*; at no time and no place did anyone ever doubt the obligation of the monarch to attend to the happiness of the nation.[43]

> The Sovereign, no less than the people, must fulfill his sacred obligation, the violation of which breaks the ancient covenant between authority and obedience and tumbles the nation from the level of civic existence into the chaos of private natural law.[44]

Public happiness and welfare are best promoted through the maintenance of peace and order, that is, by protecting the subjects from external and internal enemies. Karamzin views the function of the state very much as did the Physiocrats, to whom it entailed principally the preservation of *liberté, propriété,* and *sûreté*.[45] His emphasis on firm government must not mislead us into believing that he wanted an all-powerful state. On the contrary, he wanted sovereignty unified not in order to enlarge its scope but in order to keep it out of the hands of "selfish" groups; his position in this respect was at least as consistent as that of the Physiocrats, who in seeking the political system most likely to ensure economic freedom settled on what they called *despotisme légal*. Karamzin too desired a state which would not be too active, or at any rate, no more so than the requirements of security dictated. He consequently rejected Enlightened Absolutism. Although he sympathized wholeheartedly with its aims, he considered it an illegitimate use of royal authority. He preferred Henry IV to Louis XIV, Frederick William I to Frederick the

Great—kindly, passive, frugal kings to dynamic reformers.[46] Joseph II appeared to him an "unfortunate victim" of an excessive reformatory zeal.[47] Of Russian monarchs he probably liked best Alexej Mixajlovič, the second Romanov, whose reign was later in the nineteenth century much idealized by the Slavophiles. Peter I, Russia's great transformer, on the other hand, he censured for his unwarranted interference in the lives of his subjects:

> Manners may change naturally . . . to proscribe statutes for them is an act of violence, which is illegal also for an autocratic monarch. The people, in their original covenant with the kings, had told them: "Guard our safety abroad and at home, punish criminals, sacrifice a part to save the whole." They had not said: "Fight the innocent inclinations and tastes of our domestic life." In this realm the sovereign may equitably act only by example, not by decree.[48]

The function of the monarchy is thus conceived in essentially negative terms. It has the moral obligation to limit the sphere of its action, confining it to matters which may truly be said to come within the purview of *raison d'état*.

A second restrictive factor is the monarchy's obligation to rule by law. Karamzin does not make use of arguments based on natural law, since he considers positive law to take precedence over natural law. But the monarch's authority to issue laws does not exempt him from the obligation of obeying them: he cannot, without good cause, change legislation and revoke rights which he had once promulgated. The importance of law and freedom within law as preconditions of progress in Karamzin's thought has been indicated above; to him power without law was as odious as law without power was impotent.

One of the most important laws binding the Russian Crown was the estate legislation of Catherine II. Technically speaking, until 1785 no Russian subject had any civil rights, and from the legal point of view, regardless of origin or status, they were entirely at the emperor's mercy. The control which a strong monarch like Peter I exercised over the nobles was every bit as great as that which these nobles exercised over their serfs; in fact, one Russian historian goes so far as to consider the Russian nobility in the first half of the eighteenth century to have been "in bondage" to the Crown.[49] Of course, between theory and practice there was a gulf vast enough to make all the difference, especially during the reigns of Peter's successors. But while the nobility gained *de facto* rights and rid itself of its duties, its privileged position became first normalized in legal terms only in the reign of Catherine II with the charter of 1785, known as the *Žalovannaja Gramota Dvorjanstvu*. This charter not only confirmed all the privileges acquired by the upper class in the course of the eigh-

teenth century, but also gave it a body of civil rights which stipulated that no nobleman would be deprived of his honor, life, property, or title without a trial by his peers, that noblemen were free to travel abroad, to dispose of their property and to hold assemblies, that they were exempt from corporal punishment, and so forth. In effect it made the nobility the first social group in Russia to be endowed with civil rights on a Western model.

To Karamzin this charter constituted the other pillar of the Russian constitution: it not only accorded with the country's monarchic government, but was essential to it. In his words, Catherine "transformed slaves of the tsar into human beings" and thus helped cleanse the Russian monarchy of elements of despotism.[50]

Somewhat inconsistently, Karamzin regarded these rights as legally binding upon the very monarchy which he had elsewhere stated was empowered to do anything except legally limit its own authority. Violations of the nobles' rights, such as those perpetrated by Paul I, corrupt the *principe* of the monarchic system and transform it into a tyranny. "The rights of the well-born", Karamzin wrote in connection with Alexander's attempted reforms, "are not something apart from monarchial authority, they are its principal, indispensable instrumentality. . . ."[51] Karamzin felt so strongly on this subject that in 1819 he interceded personally with Alexander I on behalf of a gentlewoman who, without a trial, had been sentenced by the Senate to penal servitude. Such action was a clear violation of the Charter of 1785 which, among other things, had guaranteed that no noble person would be sentenced to any penalty except by trial, and sentenced to forced labor only by imperial decree. "Does the Senate, in order to safeguard the interest of the treasury, have the right to destroy the Charter of the Nobility, the law of the realm?" he asked a friend in this connection.[52] His concern for the destiny of the monarchic system, which he considered indissolubly bound up with the noble estate, and for the rule of law, also inspired Karamzin's criticism of the administrative-bureaucratic reforms of Speranskij. He wanted the process, begun by Catherine, of granting the Russian estates legal (if unequal) rights to be continued by her successors, and he evidently wished Russia to receive something in the nature of her own Bill of Rights: "Protect with the sacredness of the law", he urged Alexander, "the inviolability of the Church, the Sovereign, the officials, and the personal safety of all Russians; strengthen our civic bonds, attend to the inalienability of property, to inheritance, purchase, testaments, mortgages, and so forth."[53]

Although in matters of religion Karamzin never progressed beyond a tepid deism (even in his youthful masonic days he had been much more attracted by Novikov's cultural activities than by his mysticism), he wanted the clergy and the Church to enjoy a secure position within the state structure, and he questioned Peter's use of the Church establishment for political ends. The Church must not be subordinate to the monarchy, for this causes it to lose its moral force, and prevents it from fulfilling its main function, which is to serve as the public conscience: "Spiritual authority ought to have a separate sphere of action, apart from secular authority, but it should function in close union with it."[54] Its rights, too, must be respected.

Russia must also possess what Karamzin, following Montesquieu, called a "repository of laws" (*xranilišče zakonov*), represented by the Senate and Synod.[55] They serve as the legal "memory" of the country and help keep the monarchy within the bounds of law. The importance which Karamzin attached to law induced him to call repeatedly for its codification. In fact, the methods of codifying Russian law which he outlined in his *Memoir* were remarkably similar to the ones which Speranskij was actually to adopt in the reign of Nicholas I.[56]

Finally, the autocratic monarch is confined by historical tradition. He must not do anything which may upset the state's constitution, nor must he issue decrees for which the subjects are unprepared. In general, he should endeavor to steer the ship of state along its traditional course, changing it, if at all, only by the smallest of degrees, and always eschewing novelty because "all novelty in the political order is an evil to which recourse is to be had only of necessity; for time alone gives statutes their requisite firmness, since we respect more that which we have respected for a long time, and do everything better from habit".[57]

4

An analysis of Karamzin's writings reveals that his conception of the monarchy was in all essentials identical to that evolved by Montesquieu in the *Spirit of Laws*. Like Montesquieu, Karamzin regarded the monarchic system as one characterized by the consignment of indivisible sovereignty to one person, by the rule of fixed laws, by the execution of administrative functions with the assistance of "intermediate, subordinate, and dependent" orders, the most important of which is the nobility, and by the possession of repositories of law. Like Montesquieu, Karamzin distinguished this system in its structure and in its spirit from despotism, which signifies arbitrary rule, contempt for law and for the civil rights of subjects, and failure to make use of the "intermediate orders".

Where Karamzin did depart from Montesquieu was in his views of the political measures best calculated to preserve civil liberties. For whereas the Frenchman, in the celebrated eleventh book of the *Spirit of Laws*, argued that individual liberty could best be assured in a

monarchy where the executive, legislative, and judicial functions of sovereignty were distributed, Karamzin was equally convinced that, in Russia at any rate, the very opposite principle held true. There the preservation of civil liberty depended on strong government, and strong government could be assured only if the monarchy held all the legitimate political powers firmly in its own hands. If this view should seem incongruous today, we must not forget two vital differences between Karamzin's time and our own. First of all, when Karamzin spoke of the state, he had in mind not the modern egalitarian, democratic state where political and civil rights are to a large extent interdependent, but one where the body politic was made up of a number of well-defined, corporate estates which by their very existence confined political authority to a relatively narrow field of action. If, in point of fact, Russian reality never came close to this ideal of a corporate class state, in the time of Karamzin it was still reasonable to believe that by an extension of the policies of Catherine II such a state could actually be established. All of Karamzin's political proposals were based on the assumption that this would be the case and that consequently a balance of power would be created between the Crown and the estates, each independent within its sphere and confined to it. In the second place, the time in which he lived was one of great social and political unrest. The memory of the Pugačev Rebellion, which had raged near his native region when Karamzin was a child; the disorder and terror of Revolutionary France, as well as the incessant bloodshed of the Napoleonic era; the disintegration of the great Polish-Lithuanian Commonwealth—all these events seemed to indicate the paramount need for political stability and firmness.

The glaring weakness of Karamzin's solution lay, of course, in his failure to indicate *how* political authority could be made to stay within its proper limits without being subjected to some kind of external control. This was the problem to which Speranskij was to address himself and try to solve with his project of constitutional reforms. Karamzin, when faced with it, could do no more than voice the belief that public opinion generally made it difficult for a tyrant to follow a good monarch, and to seek consolation in the thought that despots were altogether rare—Russia, in her whole long history, having had only two.[58]

Was he unaware of this weakness? It is difficult to say. He seemed to feel that Russia had a choice of two alternatives, neither quite satisfactory, each a gamble: monarchy or democracy. With his view of life and human nature, he preferred to take a chance on excessive power, legally unlimited though exercised with the utmost circumspection. It was better to run the risk of the monarchy turning occasionally into "despotism" than to deprive the Crown of a share of sovereignty and thus, by weakening its force, risk anarchy and all the evils which flow in its wake. In his time, it must be borne in mind, the threat to freedom seemed to come not from too strong but from too weak government.

Notes

1. N. M. Karamzin, *Pis'ma russkogo putešestvennika* (letter dated "April 1790", but probably written several years later), in *Russkaja proza XVIII veka* (Moscow-Leningrad, 1950), II, 446; emphasis added.

2. *Vestnik Evropy* 7 (1802), 262; "Marfa Posadnica", *Vestnik Evropy* 1 (1803), 25; "Razgovor o ščasti", *Sočinenija Karamzina* (St. Petersburg, 1848), III, 494-495.

3. [N. M. Karamzin], *Sočinenija Karamzina* (Petrograd, 1917), I, 271.

4. "Mysli ob istinnoj svobode", *Neizdannye sočinenija i perepiska Nikolaja Mixajloviča Karamzina* (St. Petersburg, 1862), Part I, 195.

5. It may be noted here that for the purpose of this essay no difference will be drawn between the political ideas of the young and the mature Karamzin. Such differences exist, but they do not affect the essential features of his political philosophy. On this subject the reader is referred to an illuminating essay by Wolfgang Mitter, "Die Entwicklung der politischen Anschauungen Karamzins", *Forschungen zur Osteuropäischen Geschichte* 2 (Berlin, 1955), 165-285, especially p. 279.

6. In 1810 Goleniščev-Kutuzov, a mediocre poet connected with Šiškov and his linguistic school, sent the police a denunciation against Karamzin, in which he repeated the current charge of "Jacobinism": "Take his 'Marfa Posadnica'. What a republican spirit! . . . He made a drunken and stupid hag deliver speeches in favor of the liberties of the Novgorodians and orate like Demosthenes." A. M. Skabičevskij, *Očerki istorii russkoj cenzury* (St. Petersburg, 1892), 161-162. Grand Duke Constantine likewise considered Karamzin a Jacobin and expressed amazement that the censors had permitted his *History* to appear in print. *Russkaja Starina*, LXXIX, 202-203.

7. Richard Pipes, *Karamzin's Memoir on Ancient and Modern Russia: A translation and analysis* (Cambridge, Mass., 1959), 139; henceforth referred to as *Memoir.*

8. *Sočinenija* (1848), I, 531.

9. *Memoir,* 109.

10. On the general subject of the influence of Montesquieu in Russia, cf. A. Pypin, "Ekaterina II i Montesk'ë," *Vestnik Evropy* CCXXI (May 1903),

272-300; and a superficial article by F. A. Kogan-Bernštejn, "Vlijanie idej Montesk'ë v Rossii v XVIII veke", *Voprosy Istorii* 5, (1955), 99-110; the entire subject of Montesquieu's impact on Russian politics and thought in the second half of the eighteenth century awaits adequate treatment. On the Physiocrats in Russia, see V. Svjatlovskij, *Istorija èkonomičeskix idej v Rossii,* I (Petrograd, 1923).

11. *Pis'ma russkogo putešestvennika,* 446.

12. Ibid., 568; *Memoir,* 133.

13. *Sočinenija* (1848), II, 778-779.

14. Montesquieu, *Spirit of Laws,* Book III, Section 1.

15. Montesquieu, *Spirit of Laws,* Book V, Sections 3 and 8.

16. "Istoričeskoe poxval'noe slovo Imperatrice Ekaterine II", *Sočinenija* (1848), I, 312.

17. In her epitaph Catherine II had, among other things, this to say of herself: "She was good-natured and easy-going; she had a cheerful temperament, republican sentiments, and a kind heart." *Memoirs of Catherine the Great,* K. Anthony, trans. (New York, 1935), 326.

18. *Istorija gosudarstva Rossijskogo,* IX, ch. 2; "O moskovskom mjateže v carstvovanie Alekseja Mixajloviča", *Sočinenija* (1848), I, 418.

19. *Memoir,* 127.

20. *Memoir,* 139.

21. V. I. Ključevskij, *Bojarskaja duma drevnej Rusi* (Moscow, 1883), 258-260.

22. The confusion prevailing in Russian legal terminology concerning this term is reflected in Russia's Fundamental Laws. Article 1 of the *Svod Zakonov* (ed. 1892) read: "Imperator Rossijskij est' monarx samoderžavnyj i neograničennyj." In the Fundamental Laws of 1906, in which the powers of the tsar were clearly curtailed, Article 4 reads: "Imperatoru Vserossijskomu prinadležit verxovnaja samoderžavnaja vlast'." The omission of the word "neograničennyj" (unlimited) and the retention of the term "samoderžavnyj" in 1906 seem to indicate that (1) the two were not synonymous, and (2) the concept of *samoderžavie* did not necessarily entail the concept of unlimited authority. Cf. N. M. Korkunov, *Russkoe gosudarstvennoe pravo* (St. Petersburg, 1909), I, 210-215, and N. I. Lazarevskij, *Lekcii po russkomu gosudarstvennomu pravu* (St. Petersburg, 1908), I, 123-129, for a discussion of this problem. It may be noted here that three centuries before these events Tsar Šujskij, a limited monarch like Nicholas II after 1906, was also called *samoderžec* in official state documents.

23. G. Gurvič, *"Pravda voli monaršej" Feofana Prokopoviča i ee zapadnoevropejskie istočniki* (Juriev, 1915), 46.

24. *Spirit of Laws,* Book II, Section 4.

25. Gurvič, 47.

26. N. D. Čečulin, ed., *Nakaz Imperatricy Ekateriny II,* in Imperatorskaja Akademija Nauk, *Pamjatniki russkogo zakonodatel'stva 1649-1832,* No. 2 (St. Petersburg, 1907), Articles 9, 10, 13, and so forth.

27. Imperatorskaja Rossijskaja Akademija, *Slovar'Akademii Rossijskoj,* VI (St. Petersburg, 1822), 18-19. In contrast, a twentieth-century Russian dictionary defines the term *samoderžavie* as "a system of government with *unlimited* authority of the monarch", and *samoderžavnyj* as "possessing full authority, disposing of *unlimited* authority and power" (emphasis added). D. N. Ušakov, ed., *Tolkovyj slovar' russkogo jazyka* (Moscow, 1940), IV, 32-33.

28. *Memoir,* 110, 112, 197.

29. *Spirit of Laws,* Book VIII, Section 6.

30. Karamzin wrote in 1815 to A. I. Turgenev of Ivan IV: "In comparison with Ivan [IV], Caligula and Nero were mere children." *Russkaja Starina* 2 (1899), 468. Karamzin is the only person known to have publicly defended Novikov at the time of the latter's arrest in 1792. He did so in a poem entitled "K milosti" ("To Mercy"), in which, in language of great boldness, considering the panic which had seized Russian society after Novikov's arrest, he urged Catherine to safeguard the freedoms of her subjects. *Sočinenija Karamzina* (1917), I, 61-63.

31. *Sočinenija* (1848), I, 543.

32. *Nakaz,* Article 9.

33. *Memoir,* 139.

34. Cf. Montesquieu's *Considerations sur les causes de la grandeur des Romains et de leur decadence* [(1734)]; Roger B. Oake, "Montesquieu's Analysis of Roman History", *Journal of the History of Ideas* (January, 1955), 44-59.

35. *Pis'ma N. M. Karamzina k I. I. Dmitrievu* (St. Petersburg, 1866), 50,031 (letter dated September 6, 1794); later Karamzin did approve of the partitions of Poland as returning to Russia her rightful patrimony. Of Finland, Karamzin wrote: "We did conquer Finland; let the *Moniteur* praise this acquisition! We know what it had cost us apart from men and money. A state requires for its security not only physical but also moral might. Whenever we sacrifice honor and justice, we impair the lat-

political philosophy. Black argues that Karamzin's faith in Enlightenment ideals were starkly at odds with the social customs of the Russian aristocracy.]

As a man of letters, Nicholas Karamzin (1766-1825) has been described as the leading representative of Russian sentimentalism and of modern Russian prosewriting. He has also been singled out as his nation's first literary critic and a founding father of its periodical press. He served as a key spokesman for a blossoming Russian national consciousness in the 1790's and, in 1818, printed the first parts of a *History of the Russian State* (*Istoriia gosudarstva Rossiiskago*), which left a greater impression on Russia's reading public than any other historical work written before the Revolution of 1917[1].

As a young man in the late 1770's, Karamzin studied at a *pension* in Moscow directed by J. M. Schaden, who inculcated in his young pupils the didactic and moralistic philosophy of Ch. F. Gellert, whose book *Moralische Vorlesungen* was the school's main text[2]. A sense of morality, a love for virtue, and an abhorrence of evil were brought together in the school with an assault on the secularism, cynicism, and skepticism which Muscovites associated with the 'Voltairianism' of the court at St. Petersburg. A few years after leaving Schaden's school, Karamzin began a long time association with N. I. Novikov (1744-1818), the famous Freemason-publisher who was bitterly opposed to the foppishness, immorality, atheism and Francophilism which he had found in the capital city[3]. The young Karamzin became a translator in 1785 for the Friendly Learned Society (*Druzheskoe uchenoe obshchestvo*), which had been founded by Novikov and J. G. Schwartz in 1781. Here he was indoctrinated with Freemason idealism, their concept of service to mankind, and their idea that enlightenment without a moral base is a potentially dangerous phenomenon[4].

While working with Novikov and other Moscow Freemasons, Karamzin undertook the translation of several important European works. Among them was Albrecht von Haller's, *Vom Ursprung des Ubels,* in which Karamzin's own comments anticipated his belief in man's basic goodness, and his idealisation of the arcadianlike existence of Swiss shepherds. He also helped Novikov edit the first Russian journal for children, *Readings for Children* (*Detskoe chtenie*), which had a nationalist, moralising tone and even an in-resident hero appropriately named Goodheart (*Dobroserdom*)[5]. But Karamzin was never attuned to the mysticism which also was characteristic of Moscow's Freemasons, and in 1790 he parted company with them to undertake a 'Grand Tour' of Europe. He hoped to meet Europe's great writers and to fashion a career in letters for himself. It was there that he took on a realistic view of the world, and came to recognise the dangers inherent in the sharp cleavages of Russian society.

While in Europe, Karamzin observed the effects of the French Revolution at first hand, but showed a surprising lack of hostility towards it until the onset of terror conducted by the Jacobin dictatorship, and regicide in 1793. Before that time, he looked upon events in France with a far from jaundiced eye, wore a cockade, sat in the French Assembly, and claimed to be somewhat distantly amused at the entire affair. On his return to Moscow, he published the *Moscow Journal* (*Moskovskii zhurnal,* 1791-1792), which soon became one of the most popular magazines in Russia. In it, Karamzin printed reviews of French books and drama, and did not criticise the revolution as long as it remained within the bounds of reason and enlightenment[6].

In his famous *Letters of a Russian Traveller* (*Pis'ma russkago puteshestvennika*), the initial parts of which appeared in the journal[7], Karamzin indicated that he blamed the course of revolution on the decline of morals in France, the excesses of the French nobility, and their liking for luxury. Karamzin's first reproaches, then, were not directed so much at the ideals of the revolutionaries as they were at the weaknesses in French society which had provoked them.

Letters from Switzerland, and later from England, demonstrate Karamzin's high regard for the simple and honest life-style which he observed in those lands. He noted with satisfaction that there was little evidence of luxury or of ostentatious wealth in either, and that the people were content and happy in their close family circles. Zurich had the most 'unspoilt morals and piety' of any town in Europe, he said, because its legislators knew that 'luxury [*roskosh'*] is the grave of freedom and good morals'. But Paris was a city filled with contrasts. 'At first sight', he wrote in a letter which he claimed to have written in April, 1790, 'Paris appears to be a most magnificent city'. He went on to describe its beautiful buildings and parks, but then writes: 'Stop here if you do not wish to change your opinion, for if you go further you will see crowded streets, an outrageous confusion of wealth and poverty'. And he contrasts the myriad of 'poor people exhausted from their week's toil' who rest on the grass in the Champs-Elysées, with the 'cavaliers and ladies, dripping powder and paint' who stroll through the Tuileries[8].

The reason for his concern for the wide dichotomy between rich and poor is soon made apparent in the same series of letters. A long conversation with an abbé N, an apparently mythical person whom Karamzin uses to present his own views, portrays a French aristocracy which has become idle, and which wallows in current fads, luxury, and vices. Gambling and apathy had overtaken them, and only revolution jolted them out of total boredom. Nothing could have worried Karamzin more than a vision of an inert aristocracy, France's 'best people', simply allowing revolution to

ter. For our seizure of Finland we are hated by the Swedes and reproached by all the other nations; and I am not certain which did greater harm to Alexander's honor: to have been defeated by the French, or to have been compelled to follow their predatory system." (*Memoir,* 146)

36. *Istorija gosudarstva Rossijskogo,* VII, ch. 4.

37. *Memoir,* 139.

38. N. L. Rubinštejn, *Russkaja istoriografija* ([Moscow], 1941), *passim.*

39. *Memoir,* 117-118.

40. S. Platonov, "Moskovskoe pravitel'stvo pri pervyx Romanovyx", *Žurnal Ministerstva Narodnogo Prosveščenija* (December, 1906), 298-351; M. A. Djakonov, in his *Očerki obščestvennogo i gosudarstvennogo stroja drevnej Rusi* (St. Petersburg, 1910), 449-453, on the other hand, subscribes to another theory, popularized in the eighteenth century by such foreign writers on Russia as Fokkerodt and Strahlenberg, that Michael might have been a *limited* monarch. It is quite clear from the context in which Karamzin refers to the "charter" that he has in mind something quite different, namely, a document making the Romanovs absolute.

41. A. L. Schlözer, *Historische Untersuchung über Russlands Reichsgrundgesetze* (Gotha, 1777), 11-12.

42. *Memoir,* 139.

43. *Istorija gosudarstva Rossijskogo,* VII, ch. 4.

44. *Memoir,* 135.

45. Benedikt Güntzberg, *Die Gesellschafts- und Staatslehre der Physiokraten* (Leipzig, 1907), 75.

46. N. Karamzin, *Travels from Moscow* (London, 1803), I, 62-63.

47. *Sočinenija* (1848), I, 370-371.

48. *Memoir,* 122. Cf. Montesquieu, *Spirit of Laws,* Book XIX, Section 14: When "manners and customs are to be changed, it ought not to be done by laws; this would have too much the air of tyranny: it would be better to change them by introducing other manners and other customs".

49. A. Romanovič-Slavatinskij, *Dvorjanstvo v Rossii* (Kiev, 1912), xvii.

50. *Sočinenija* (1848), I, 336-346, 451; *Memoir,* 131.

51. *Memoir,* 200. Puškin had similar ideas on this subject: "L'hérédité de haute-noblesse est une garantie de son indèpendance—le contraire est nécessairement moyen de tyrannie, ou plutôt d'un despotisme lâche et mou." A. Puškin, "O dvorjanstve", *Polnoe sobranie sočinenij,* XII (Ak. Nauk, Moscow, 1949), 205.

52. *Pis'ma N. M. Karamzina k I. I. Dmitrievu,* 262; *Neizdannye sočinenija* [(1862)], 230-235.

53. *Memoir,* 188-189.

54. *Memoir,* 125.

55. *Memoir,* 204.

56. *Memoir,* 182-190. Cf. N. V. Kalačov, "O značenii Karamzina v istorii russkogo zakonodatel'stva", *Besedy v obščestve ljubitelej rossijskoj slovestnosti pri Imperatorskom Moskovskom Universitete,* Vypusk 1 (Moscow, 1867), Priloženie 1, 1-23. The need of a code of laws for Russia was the subject of Karamzin's last private talk with Alexander I in August 1825; at this meeting Karamzin obtained from Alexander a pledge to provide the country with "fundamental laws"; *Neizdannye sočinenija,* 12.

57. *Memoir,* 147-148.

58. The problem of the relationship between autocracy and rule by law troubled Russian jurists until the Revolution of 1905. An interesting discussion of this question can be found in Korkunov's *Russkoe gosudarstvennoe pravo,* I, 215-222. Writing at the end of the nineteenth century, Korkunov drew a distinction between what he called "subjective" and "objective" law: the former, developed in the West, entailed *rights* of subjects, and hence a limitation of sovereignty; the latter, prevailing in Russia, was the product of sovereign will, and had as its purpose the maintenance of *order.* "In our political system", wrote Korkunov, "legality is not a limitation imposed on authority from without; it is its own creation" (p. 219). This distinction, according to Korkunov, was due to Russia's historical and geographical situation. He too, however, failed to indicate effective guarantees which would assure that the government operated within law, for he dismissed the idea (common in eighteenth-century Russia) of restricting the autocratic government to the legislative sphere alone as impracticable. This is in many respects the fundamental problem of Russian politics.

J. L. Black (essay date 1976)

SOURCE: Black, J. L. "Nicholas Karamzin and the Dilemma of Luxury in 18th Century Russia." *Studies on Voltaire and the Eighteenth Century* 151 (1976): 313-22.

[*In the following essay, Black examines the influence of Karamzin's European travels on the development of his*

destroy the centre of European civilisation. 'Up to this moment', he mused, 'the French nobility and clergy seem to be poor defenders of the throne'[9].

In the sea of praise which surrounded Catherine II in the 1790's, Karamzin stood out as one of the few leading writers who were not happy with her ruling practices. Dedicated to enlightenment, he could find little fault with her efforts in that regard before 1792, when he made a courageous public appeal for her mercy in the case of Novikov. Nor was he disturbed by her foreign policy, for his country remained strong and secure, and he praised her efforts on behalf of education. But in all of his writing before her death, there was no word of eulogy for Catherine. He even wrote in 1793 a **'Reply to my Friend, who Wanted Me to Write an Ode to Catherine the Great'** (not printed until 1796), in which he asked to be excused from doing so[10]. Why such reticence? Although he did not say so specifically, there was one dimension of her public demeanour which clashed with Karamzin's sense of what was right—the favouritism, ostentation and apparent debauchery at court. He could not attack Catherine directly, and he was not so alienated that he wished to write a secret treatise like prince M. M. Shcherbatov's sweeping, *On the Corruption of Morals in Russia*[11]. Instead, he used his pen to portray an ideal society, and to ponder the moral dilemma posed to all European intellectuals by the French Revolution.

A prevailing theme in Karamzin's work of the 1790's was an idealisation of the character and circumstance of the Russian peasantry. He romanticised the relationship between peasant and landowner in **'A Village Holiday and Wedding'** (**'Sel'skii prazdnik i svad'ba'**, 1791), praised the simple farmer in **'Frol Silin'** (1791), and portrayed a hardworking, contented peasant woman in **'Poor Liza'** (1792), his most famous tale of the 'nineties. The same motif appeared in **'Tender Friendship in the Lower Estate'** (**'Nezhnost' druzhby v nizkom sostoianii'**, 1793) where Karamzin had a peasant reply affirmatively when her mistress asked whether she was 'completely happy in her circumstances . . .'. It was this image that he expanded upon in an anti-Rousseau essay, **'Something about the Sciences, Arts and Enlightenment'** (**'Nechto o naukakh, isskustvakh i prosveshchenii'**, 1793), and which became the writer's basic contention after the turn of the century. Furthermore, in **'Conversation about Happiness'** (**'Razgover o shchastii'**, 1797) he intimated that equality was merely an emotional matter and that one need not have political freedom, or riches, to be happy. The opportunity to be happy, which was possible only in a well-ordered, benevolent society, was the only necessary ambition for men of any class.

In 1795, Karamzin published a discussion over the advantages and disadvantages of the European enlightenment. Written in late 1793, it reflected the anguish of his confusion and, undoubtedly, that of many of his contemporaries. Presented in the form of two letters, **'Melodor to Philalet'**, and **'Philalet to Melodor'**, the discussion posed the essential intellectual query of the time: 'Is it possible', said Melodor, 'that the human species has advanced . . . to the pinnacle of enlightenment . . . only to be compelled to fall back . . . into the depths of barbarism . . . like Sisyphus' stone'. Must man in his moral growth follow a cyclical path, 'always interchanging truth and error, virtue and vices?' Karamzin answered his own questions in the words of Philalet: 'Perhaps what seems like some great disorder to mortals is a wonderful harmony to angels . . . the destiny of mankind is not eternal delusion . . . people will sometime cease to torment themselves and each other'. Falling back on the notion of a higher order of things, outside human comprehension, was perhaps an easy solution to his intellectual quandary, but the alternative was too frightening. Without some reason to be optimistic about the future, there could hardly be any reason for man to live at all. Karamzin thus began to reason that a 'Golden Age' lay in the future and not in the past, and blamed his recent confusion on an 'unwarranted worship of the eighteenth century'. As he put it, 'the present evil will serve future good'[12].

Deciding that all was not lost because 'virtue was still a characteristic of mankind', Karamzin added that some kind of leadership was necessary if human virtue was to be successfully reaffirmed. In **'Athenian Life'** (**'Afinskaia zhizn','** 1795), he praised the instructive role of rhetoricians and poets in ancient Greece, implying that moral leadership had to emanate from men of letters like himself[13]. But his definitive answer came in **'Conversation about Happiness'** where, as we have seen, he wrote that men must be satisfied with their lot in life.

Writing throughout the 'nineties on the merits of the simple life, namely patriotism, love of family, honest labour, and belief in God, Karamzin saw at the court in St. Petersburg those very circumstances which he felt had undermined the *ancien régime,* and which endangered the very ideals of the Enlightenment. During the last years of the 18th century, while Paul was attempting to legislate western ideas from Russia and ruling, in Karamzin's horrified opinion, in the manner of Ivan IV (the Terrible), the writer urged Russians to respect religion, morality, friendship and enlightenment[14]. The freer atmosphere of Alexander's reign enabled Karamzin to put on paper those ideas which he had tried to express less directly during Catherine's regime. In 1802 he came back to the notion of 'contrast' as a debilitating force in society. He warned in this case that the American Republic was falling victim already to the moral disease which had struck down France. 'The *spirit of trade* is the main characteristic of America, where everyone strives for acquisitions. Wealth appears in sharp *con-*

trast with poverty and slavery', he wrote in his new journal, *Messenger of Europe* (*Vestnik evropy*). The next year Karamzin complained that the French Republic had fallen prey to the same temptations. The government of France was more interested in the success of the Lyons fabric business than in the welfare of its people. If 'sacrifice is justly called a virtue', he continued, 'then luxury is truly a vice'[15].

He reiterated these feelings again and much more precisely in a **Memorandum on Ancient and Modern Russia** (**Zapiska o drevnei i novoi Rossii**), which he wrote at the request of Catherine Pavlovna, Alexander's sister, in 1811. Intended only for the eyes of Catherine and the Emperor, the memorandum demonstrated Karamzin's previously unexpressed objections to Catherine the Great in no uncertain terms:

> But we must admit that the most brilliant reign of Catherine was not without its dark side. Morals continued to deteriorate ever more in the palaces as well as in the cottages—in the former from the example set by the dissolute court, in the latter from the spread of taverns . . . Do the examples set by Anne and Elizabeth absolve Catherine? Do the riches of the state belong to a man whose only distinction is a handsome face? A hidden weakness is only a weakness; an overt one is a vice, because it seduces others. The violation of canons of morality diminishes the very dignity of the sovereign's office, for . . . people cannot inwardly respect those who are depraved . . . we unwillingly recall her foibles, and blush for mankind . . .
>
> . . . the gentry sunk into debt from the excessive emulation of European luxury . . . we lacked decent upbringing, firm principles, and social morality. The favourite of a great lord, even though of low birth, was not ashamed to live in splendour . . .[16].

Karamzin went on to say that Catherine and others blissfully ignored this development because all other aspects of her reign were so successful. The warning to Alexander here was clear enough. Russia was threatened by Napoleonic France, and Karamzin insisted that autocracy be strengthened so that his nation could withstand the onslaught of Napoleon's armies, and the political idealism of French propaganda. He saw in an indolent, obsequious and extravagant gentry and nobility the seeds of the destruction of his beloved fatherland. Karamzin was to return to this idea again in his **History of the Russian State,** in which he claimed that ambition and self-interest had caused the demise of the Swiss republic. So his feeling that vices and luxury would inevitably weaken the state was tied closely to his predilection for autocracy, firm but enlightened, as a far better socio-political system for Russia than any other. In this, he fit into a Russian tradition which went back to V. N. Tatishchev, the secular technocrat of Peter's reign who gave his son a deathbed admonition in 1750 to live a simple life and to avoid luxuries. 'Wealth is the origin of idleness, and idleness is the beginning of all evils', Tatishchev said with much the same end in mind that Karamzin was to have a half century later. Tatishchev was the ultimate bureaucrat, and wished only for the strengthening of his state. Like Karamzin's, his dislike for luxury was not so much a religious or ideological sentiment as it was a practical one[17].

In the final year of his life, Karamzin was still pleading for an end to the extravagance and selfishness which had become a characteristic of his nation's aristocracy. His disgust with their behaviour was not based on any economic theory, nor on a desire for more democracy, rather he anticipated social and political disaster unless some change for the better set in. Karamzin recognised that there would always be 'freedom and servitude, wealth and poverty, pleasure and suffering', but he hoped to ease the extremes of each. 'Aristocrats!', he wrote in his diary, 'you argue that you have to be powerful and wealthy for the comfort of the weak and the poor, but please make their weakness and poverty a pleasure for them! Nothing can defy feeling; it is impossible to convince the hungry in the utility of hunger. Give us feeling, not theory. The words and books of Aristocrats convince only Aristocrats; and others, looking at their splendour, grind their teeth and keep quiet, or do nothing as long as they are restrained by law or power'[18].

Karamzin was a profound theoretician of autocracy, but throughout his long career he cautioned against extremes of all kinds. He abhorred revolution and all that it stood for. But his warnings against the excesses of luxury and abuse of power, even to the year of the Decembrist Revolt (1825), can be counted with the writings of the 'repentant nobleman', Alexander Radishchev, as a portent of things to come.

Notes

1. Rather than document each instance of Karamzin's early life, which is presented here in the simplest possible form, I suggest the following recent books as the best sources of general information: A. G. Cross, *N. M. Karamzin: A Study of His Literary Career* (*1783-1803*), (Carbondale, Illinois 1971); Hans Rothe, *N. M. Karamzins europäische Reise: Der Beginn des russischen Romans,* (Berlin 1968); Henry M. Nebel, Jr., *N. M. Karamzin: A Russian Sentimentalist,* (The Hague 1967), and *Selected Prose of N. M. Karamzin,* (Evanston, Illinois 1969); Richard Pipes, *Karamzin's Memoir on Ancient and Modern Russia,* (Cambridge, Mass. 1959); F. Kanunova, *Iz istorii russkoi povesti* (*Istoriko-literaturnoe znachenie povestei N. M. Karamzina*), (Tomsk 1967); J. L. Black (ed.), *Essays on Karamzin: Russian Man-of-Letters, Political Thinker, Historian,* (The Hague 1974). The University of Toronto Press is now preparing for

publication my *Nicholas Karamzin and Russian Society in the 19th-Century,* and the University of Moscow is printing for L. G. Kisliagina, *Formirovanie obshchestvenno-politicheskikh vzgliadov N. M. Karamzina (1785-1803 gg.)* [(1976)]. Almost all of Karamzin's works have now been published in the Soviet Union. See also Rudolf Neuhäuser, *Towards the Romantic Age: Essays on Sentimental and Preromantic Literature in Russia,* (The Hague 1974).

2. Karamzin wrote some years later that Gellert's fables were almost his sole reading during his school years, and that Schaden had 'instructed us, his little pupils, in ethics according to *Moralische Vorlesungen*'; see Karamzin, *Izbrannye sochineniia,* i, (Moscow-Leningrad 1964), 159-160.

3. See V. Bogoliubov, *N. I. Novikov i ego vremia* (Moscow 1916), 258, and G. Makogonenko, *N. Novikov i russkoe prosveshchenie XVIII v.,* (Moscow-Leningrad 1952), 106-109.

4. There are a number of good studies of Russian Freemasonry; for a succinct overview in English, see Marc Raeff, *Origins of the Russian Intelligentsia: The Eighteenth-Century Nobility,* (New York 1966), 159-167, and Neuhäuser, *op. cit.,* 17-26.

5. For Novikov's description of his character, Goodheart, who was to be a model for Russian youth, see *Detskoe chtenie dlia serdtsa i razuma,* i, pt. 1 (1785), 7-8.

6. Besides the standard reading noted above, see Iu. Lotman, 'Evoliutsiia mirovozzreniia Karamzina (1789-1803)', *Uchenie zapiski Tartuskogo gos. universiteta,* 51 (1957), 122-166.

7. On the *Letters of a Russian Traveller,* see especially Rothe and Cross, and Roger B. Anderson, 'Karamzin's *Letters of a Russian Traveller*: An Education in Western Sentimentalism', in J. L. Black (ed.), *Essays on Karamzin* [(1975)], 22-41.

8. Karamzin, *Izbrannye sochineniia,* i, 238-239 (on Luxury), and 372-373 (on Paris).

9. *ibid.,* 379-381.

10. See Cross, 156.

11. See M. M. Shcherbatov, *On the Corruption of Morals in Russia,* A. Lentin (ed.), (Cambridge 1969).

12. Karamzin, *Izbrannye sochineniia,* ii, 245-259; Neuhäuser, 'Karamzin's Spiritual Crisis of 1793 and 1794', in *Essays on Karamzin,* 68-70.

13. *Sochineniia Karamzina,* (ed.) A. Smirdin (St. Petersburg 1848), iii, 435.

14. Cross, 154-155. See especially Karamzin's *Pantheon of Foreign Literature (Panteon inostrannoi slovestnosti),* 3 pts. (Moscow 1798).

15. *Vestnik evropy,* xiv (1802), 155-156; xxi (1803), 98. The italics were Karamzin's.

16. Pipes, *Karamzin's Memoir on Ancient and Modern Russia,* 133-134.

17. See Rudolph Daniels *V. N. Tatishchev: Guardian of the Petrine Revolution,* (Philadelphia 1973), 96.

18. Karamzin, 'Thoughts on True Freedom' ('Mysli ob istinnoi svobode'), in *Neizdannyia sochineniia i perepiska Nikolai Mikhailovicha Karamzina,* pt. i (St. Petersburg 1862), 194-195.

Gitta Hammarberg (essay date 1981)

SOURCE: Hammarberg, Gitta. "Metafiction in Russian 18th-Century Prose: Karamzin's *Rycar' našego vremeni* or *Novyj Akteon, vnuk Kadma i Garmonii.*" *Scando-Slavica* 27 (1981): 27-46.

[*In the following essay, Hammarberg examines elements of parody and literary experimentation in Karamzin's* Rycar' našego vremeni.]

> Sej roman voobšče osnovan na vospominanijach molodosti, kotorymi avtor zanimalsja vo vremja duševnoj i telesnoj bolezni: tak po krajnej mere on nam skazyval, otdav ego, s nizkim poklonom, dlja napečatanija v Žurnale.[1]

The novel in question is **Rycar' našego vremeni,** the humble author, N. M. Karamzin. The journal is *Vestnik Evropy,* 1803, 14, and the note is written by its editor, N. M. Karamzin, to introduce what turned out to be the last installment of the novel. The two preceding installments, chapters I-V (dated 1799) and VI-VIII, had appeared in the same journal the previous year in issues 13 and 18, respectively. No further installments appeared.

The playful tone of the introductory note is indicative of the novel itself. The novel is based on the author's personal childhood reminiscences which preoccupied him during a period of spiritual and physical illness—or so the author (Karamzin) told the editor (Karamzin). While Karamzin as author states that his novel consists of reminiscences, Karamzin as editor chooses to remain noncommittal as to the veracity of the sources. This is, of course, a typical literary "editorial" device, and the note by itself can obviously not be taken as absolute proof of the novel's autobiographical nature. There are, however, other indications that corroborate the note on this score, and most scholars view it as a fictional autobiography.[2]

The novel contains "youthful reminiscences" in another sense, as well. Karamzin, as it were, re-evaluates the latter part of the 18th century—both ideas of Rationalist

Enlightenment philosophy (on human nature, politics, education, etc.) and the literature of the preceding era. By the time *Rycar'* appeared Karamzin was already well recognized as what amounts to the leader of the Sentimentalist movement, and the work generally considered his major prose fiction had already been published and continued to be widely imitated.[3] Around the turn of the century, shortly before the appearance of *Rycar'*, Karamzin experienced a "crisis" and his *Weltanschauung* underwent profound changes.[4] The author's "bolezn'" can be seen as a metaphor for this crisis. Perhaps it is also stressed in the introductory note to mitigate the somewhat frivolous focus of the work and the irreverent attitude towards the prevailing literary tradition on the part of its author. I shall return to this point later. At any rate, the larger literary context against which *Rycar'* must be viewed is the dominant Sentimentalist movement to which Karamzin himself had made a major contribution.

The more immediate literary context is Karamzin's own post-crisis prose fiction, which consists mainly of three other rather curious works (chronologically listed according to date of publication): **"Moja ispoved'"**, a "letter to the editor" (1802), **"Marfa-posadnica, ili pokorenie Novagoroda"**; a historical tale (1803, between the second and third installments of *Rycar'*), and, later the same year, a "character sketch", **"Čuvstvitel'nyj i cholodnyj."** All these works appeared in Karamzin's new journal, *Vestnik Evropy,* and together they constitute his last prose fiction before his *magnum opus,* the **Istorija gosudarstva rossijskogo,** which was to preoccupy him for the remaining 23 years of his life.

The *Vestnik Evropy* period can artistically speaking be seen as a transitional, experimental period. Karamzin is no longer completely satisfied with the reigning Sentimentalist style as it had developed in Russia. In all the works of the period he tends to expose the solipsistic and emotive excesses of Sentimentalist writing (including his own earlier work) through parody and satire, both in terms of literary structure, theme, genre, and style. Only now does he fully exploit Sternian humor and play on literary form.[5]

Although Karamzin did not, properly speaking, move beyond the framework of the Sentimentalist system, the *Vestnik Evropy* works indicate, on the one hand, that the system itself was dynamic and allowed for a certain amount of flexibility and, on the other hand, that Karamzin as a writer did not cease to develop, but rather exploited the system to the utmost.[6]

The four *Vestnik Evropy* works mentioned have in general received much less scholarly attention than Karamzin's other prose works. *Rycar'* until recently was not afforded more than the most summary mention in more general contexts of either 18th century literature or "Karamzin", and often was not mentioned at all even where Karamzin's other prose works were discussed.[7] Recently *Rycar'* has fared somewhat better in more specialized works on Karamzin's prose. The works of Lotman, Kanunova, Anderson, and Cross include particularly valuable sections on *Rycar'*.[8] Most critics tend to stress the thematic aspects of the novel (Karamzin's new philosophy, his views of Rousseau's or Locke's works on education, etc.) and usually *Rycar'* is seen as an important stage in Karamzin's development toward a more "objective" historical fiction. His new emphasis on psychological characterization is generally also stressed by the critics, and *Rycar'* has been hailed as the first psychological depiction of a child in Russian literature as well as the first attempt in Russian literature to create a "razvernutyj psichologičeskij portret russkogo dvorjanskogo inteligenta togo vremeni".[9] No major work has so far been devoted exclusively to this novel or even exclusively to the four *Vestnik Evropy* works as a group.[10]

* * *

The events in *Rycar'* can be summarized as the psychological biography of a child, Leon, from birth to age eleven. The following main stages are depicted: his birth and infancy under the loving care of his mother, his mother's untimely death, his early education by the village priest and his first exposure to literature, his early religious experiences through his mother and in his encounter with a ferocious bear, the influence of his father and the provincial male gentry, his acquaintance with countess Émilija Mirova and her subsequent influence on Leon as his "second mother" and teacher, and, finally, his growing sexual awareness as he watches Émilija bathe.

The focus of the narrated event is on Leon's personality as seen against the different external stimuli. Various scholars have interpreted the novel *in toto* precisely as a more or less objective rendering of a child's psychological development, and as a stage in Karamzin's evolution towards "objective" historical fiction. Thus Lotman views the novel as a depiction of the inherent contradictions and complexities of one individual. He sees the image of Leon as fully objective as compared to Karamzin's previous heroes, although Karamzin's subjective method is, in his opinion, still to be felt. This subjectivism, Lotman correctly argues, is transformed—it is no longer of the lyrical, emotionally intensive kind, nor does it, in his opinion, lie in the Sternian digressions, but rather in the fact that "charakter central'-nogo geroja po-prešnemu suščestvuet vne vozdejstvija vnešnych obstojatel'stv". Lotman goes on to state that Karamzin at the time was deeply interested in the politics of the day, but that the task of describing one single individual was not conducive to the (greater?) task of creating a prose style by which he could illus-

trate his growing political concerns, and which could replace the Classicist "political novels", which he scornfully responds to in his **Rycar'**.[11] Kanunova places a similar stress on Karamzin's growing objectivity and also stresses his increased interest in social and environmental motivations for the psychological character development. There is in her work traces of a typically Soviet tendency to spot predecessors to Realism, this time in Karamzin. She hails Karamzin's growing objectivity and considers the subjective elements a fault, an inability to cope with objective description: "s drugoj storony, v črezmernoj legkosti avtorskogo tona, bukval'no podavljaiuščego soboju 'povestvovanie', skazalas' ešče bol'šaja dan' sub''ektivizmu, *neumenie ovladet' ob''ektivnoj maneroj pis'ma*". As for the second part, she correctly points out that the narrative manner is more objective, and that the role of authorial intrusions (i.e., the subjective part) is changed: "propadaet takže *neopravdannaja* 'legkost'' avtorskogo stilja, ton ego stanovitsja strože, a emocional'nost' opravdannee".[12] While her statement is partly correct, I would object to the fact that she imputes the aim of greater objectivity to Karamzin himself, and considers the "unwarranted" remnants of subjectivism a flaw that he was unable to overcome, although he, presumably, tried. Anderson similarly stresses the objectivity of the narrated event (what he calls neutral omniscience): "Neutral omniscience, on the other hand, assumes a prominence which it never had in Karamzin's earlier tales. By that mode he establishes the empirical base on which the *central principle of social influence is erected.*" Like Kanunova, he concludes that the subjective elements (what he calls editorial omniscience—intruding author and commenting author) are "subordinated to a larger and more serious compositional design", i.e., they serve "to organize and make clear the *more objective question* of how social milieu influences a new member in a variety of ways".[13]

Other scholars similarly see **Rycar'** as Karamzin's "attempt to write a *Bildungsroman,* to portray the youthful development of his hero Leon".[14] Thus, the tendency has been to see the narrated event proper as the main theme, while the sections of speech event (the subjective part) are viewed at best as serving to objectify the narrated event, at worst, as failures on Karamzin's part.

I am not disputing the merits of these scholarly works, all of which do treat, in more or less detail, the various aspects of the subjective elements with many astute observations. I merely wish to disagree with their ranking of the subjective elements as somehow inferior or subordinate to the objective ones. It seems to me that Karamzin used subjectivity fully aware of what he was doing. The subjective pronouncements, rather than being subordinated to the objective ones, on the contrary, subordinate the narrated event to the author's main aim, which is not social or even psychological, but *literary*:

to parody the novels of his time, as well as the extreme forms of the Sentimentalist style, including Karamzin's own earlier works. Thus **Rycar',** in my view, should be seen mainly as a sustained work of metafiction, as a fictional work about fiction. My contention is that the depiction of Leon's psychological development (be it subjective or objective) was *not* the author's main aim, although, to be sure, that was one of his aims. **Rycar'** is a work of much greater complexity than it has been credited with. The "true" story of Leon is but one of its levels, and, furthermore, a level which serves as a mere pretext for the author's airing of what are essentially *literary* questions.

The very "objectivity" of the author's presentation of Leon's psychological development is, indeed, "subjective", the "truth" is extremely tenuous and often consciously ambiguous. The so-called objectivity is most pointedly called into question when we compare the views of two of the scholars mentioned, Lotman and Anderson:

> Ostavajas' ubeždennym v *"temperamental'noj"*, *a ne social'noj prirode charaktera,* Karamzin utverždaet složnost', protivorečivost' čelovečeskoj duši.[15]

> "A Knight" represents a new direction for Karamzin's concept of character as both unidealized and *reliant on environment* for his personality and his system of values.[16]

In the following I shall attempt to show how the "objective" "there and then" of Leon's story is subordinated to the "here and now" of the author, or how the speech event subordinates the narrated event to its own aims.

As the title indicates, the author's main protagonist is his own contemporary. The setting is also the author's own environment—in fact, one might meet the (now grown-up) hero in the street and even recognize him. The main difference between the author's "here and now" and the protagonist's "then" is that the author is the adult chronicler of the hero's childhood. The author's mature point of view is contrasted to the hero's innocent one, and the speech event is distanced from the narrated event, not so much temporally or spatially as "perceptually". This is laid bare in several speech event sections. Thus, for instance, the attentions Leon gets from his "second mother" have quite different potentials for the mature author than for the child: "Ščastlivyj rebenok! Bud' osm'ju godami staree, i—kto ne pozavidoval by tvoemu ščastiju?" (p. 779). Sometimes, however, the author plays with the relative temporal proximity (often for satirical purposes). The countess's "strict morals", for example, are footnoted by a whimsical: "nadobno vspomnit', čto éto bylo v starinu; po krajnej mere očen' davno" (p. 776). Such satire is, however, much more prominent in, for example, **"Natal'ja,**

bojarskaja doč'," where it is motivated by the "real" temporal distance between the author and his tale. The difference between maturity and innocence also to some extent colors the author's relationship to Leon—endearing diminutives and child language (*malen'kie ručonki, malen'kaja krovatka,* etc.) reveal the author's paternalistic attitude to his hero. The description of Leon at birth (done, as it were, jointly by the author and the reader-parent-to-be) is the most extreme case in point: "Belen'kim, polnen'kim, s rozovymi gubkami, s grečeskim nosikom, s černymi glazkami, s kofejnymi voloskami na kruglen'koj golovke [. . .]" (p. 757). Overall, however, the emotional involvement of the author, as pointed out by the critics mentioned, is significantly toned down as compared with his earlier works. The author image materializes mostly in his relationship to the reader and his focus on authorial function, his own manipulation of the narrated event.

Let us first look at the author-reader relationship. The allocutional means are utilized to the utmost: imperatives, vocatives, interrogatives; and the explicit dialogue between the author and the reader is especially prominent. In fact, a large part of the work consists precisely of author-reader dialogue as a kind of on-going discussion of the narrated events. The author constantly plays with the reader's expectations, confirms them, frustrates them, poses riddles for the reader and refuses to give him the solutions, takes the reader into his confidence (meždu nami bud' skazano), etc. He involves the reader in a discussion of Leon's reading matter—after naming Leon's favorites he parenthetically asks whether the reader is familiar with the books. He puts words into the reader's mouth—for example, all of chapter II consists of the reader's description of his ideal baby—which turns out to be the exact description of Leon. The author quite obviously makes the reader aware of his own authorial privileges, and, in turn, has the reader's reactions to his tale in mind. For example, in chapter III the reader is teased: "'Konec glave!'—skažet čitatel'", whereupon the author "spites" him, goes on for another half page, and finally reverses the situation: "Mne ešče mnogoe nadobno opisyvat'; beregu bumagu, vnimanie čitatelja i . . . konec glave!" Chapter IV begins with a similarly capricious "truth"-claim directed to the reader:

> Gosudari moi! Vy čitaete ne roman, a byl': sledstvenno, avtor ne objazan vam davat' otčeta v proisšestvijach. *Tak bylo točno*! . .—i bolee ne skažu ni slova. Kstati li? U mesta li? Ne moe delo. Ja idu tol'ko s perom vsled za sud'boju i opisyvaju, čto tvorit ona po svoemu vsemoguščestvu,—dlja čego? sprosite u nee; no skažu vam napered, čto otveta ne polučite.
>
> (p. 761)

There are numerous other twists to the author's truth-claim. After the description of Leon's miraculous escape from the attacking bear (struck dead by lightning),

the author turns to the reader: "Čitatel'! Ver' ili ne ver': no ètot slučaj ne vydumka." However, in the next lines he reveals that he is not in principle adverse to changing the "truth"—within the limits of verisimilitude, of course: "Ja prevratil by medvedja v blagorodnejšego l'va ili tigra, esli by oni . . . byli u nas v Rossii" (p. 768). This, no doubt, is an allusion to the novels of the time with their exoticism—his own miraculous tale, however, is not entirely free from the same trait! There are many other hints of this nature, and the "objective truth" must always be taken with a grain of salt.

Different types of readers are addressed, depending on the context, as in Karamzin's earlier tales. New types of readers appear: cruel people, phlegmatics, and egoists—all contrasted tongue-in-cheek with the innocent child, who will never be like them.

From the very onset the author makes his aim explicit—he wants to entertain his readers and keep them from yawning, and therefore will tell a "romaničeskaja istorija" about a friend of his. Romance is to be his main means of keeping the reader awake. The author "fills in" the reader's anticipated excitement: already in chapter I he, the reader, is immensely curious about the true identity of the protagonist—whom he might even know. The author refuses, however, to reveal the identity, but promises such a true-to-life depiction that the reader might well recognize him in the street. In chapter III the author reveals his intention to "spice up" an otherwise yawn-inspiring story about the Arcadia of childhood innocence—imputing to his reader a salacious interest in the passions of life. We might note that Karamzin's earlier work frequently dealt seriously with Arcadian topics.[17] Here, on the other hand, he secures his reader's attention with a promise of "čto-nibud' sovsem *protivnoe sej nevinnosti, semu ščastiju*" (p. 758).[18] The balance between the innocent and the risqué is quite skillfully maintained. On the one hand, the author quite explicitly promises the romantically inclined reader something to keep him from yawning, and continues to hint at upcoming topics:

> Ja dolžen teper' rasskazyvat' *strannosti* . . . Ne mudreno bylo poljubit' našego geroja, prekrasnogo ličikom, milovidnogo, čuvstvitel'nogo, umnogo, no privjazat'sja k nemu bez pamjati, so vsemi znakami živejšej strasti, k *nevinnomu* rebenku: vot čto nazyvaju *neiz''jasnimoju strannostiju*!
>
> (pp. 773-774)

On the other hand, when the reader is (presumably) prepared to interpret the events described with the author's promises in mind, the author discourages or overtly frustrates such interpretations by telling the reader something seemingly innocent. Thus, after the above promise about some "neiz''jasnimaja strannost'" and after reinforcing the expectations by referring to

women's stories as "toujours un roman" ("in a sense that is obvious to everyone"), the author goes on to tell Emilia's "touching" story. On the surface it is the story of a beautiful virtuous woman and her loveless marriage to an older man, who cannot fullfil her natural inclinations for a deeper relationship. Rather than taking a lover, she distances herself from the social whirl, and all her pent-up romantic propensities are transformed into maternal feelings for Leon, her "adopted son". Meanwhile, her story is full of innuendoes of not so strict morals, and rumors of "koketstvo ot rassejanija". The introduction of her letter to a friend similarly ostensibly reaffirms her strict morals, but, coupled with the author's remarks, also hints at her amorous disposition.

The education which Leon receives from his "vtoraja mamen'ka" is explicitly called the "ob''jasnenie" for the "neiz''jasnimaja strannost'", promised in the above quote. It consists ostensibly of French (mostly lovers' phrases), the ways of the world (which leads her to dress up Leon *à la mode,* and leads Leon into her boudoir to assist her in her toilette, even helping her on with her shoes!), geography (which leads the two to secluded spots in the environs), etc., etc., all of which has quite erotic overtones, and amounts to nothing but a protracted seduction process by an experienced coquette.[19] This ends with an apostrophe to the countess: "Serdce ljubimca tvoego zreet vmeste s umom ego, i *cvet neporočnosti imeet sud'bu drugich cvetov*" (p. 780). This is followed by the reader's anticipated response:

> Čitatel' podumaet, čto my seju ritoričeskoju figuroju gotovim ego k čemu-nibud' *protivnomu nevinnosti*: net! . . vremja ešče vperedi! Geroju našemu ispolnilos' tol'ko odinnadcat' let ot rodu . . .
>
> (p. 780)

The words in italics point to the identity between the author's promise and the reader's presumed expectations. The author's negation must also be seen in an ironical light: if the hero were not eleven, but older, the whole relationship would certainly be less strange and less contrary to innocence!

The "botany of the text" can serve to illustrate the tight-knit structure of the novel, as well as the intricate relationship between speech event and narrated event. On the one hand, the flora is consistently used as an extended metaphor for the relationship between Leon and the female protagonists, and for Leon himself in his development from innocence to sexual receptiveness.

The first flower image is used with reference to Leon's mother:

> *žestokaja* [italics Karamzin's] položila na nee pečat' svoju—i mat' geroja našego nikogda ne byla by suprugoju otca ego, esli by *žestokij* [italic Karamzin's] *v aprele mesjace sorval pervuju fialku na beregu Svijagi!*
>
> (p. 757)

She did not succumb to seduction (the violet was not picked), and she remained "*neporočnaja dušoju i telom*" until her marriage to Leon's father. The seduction site, as well as the other italicized vocabulary is significant, as we shall see later.

The next flower, connected with her, is picked when she teaches Leon religion: "[ona *sryvala*] dlja nego *vesennij lugovoj cvetok*"; she teaches him that "Bog daet nam *cvety*" (p. 767).

Thus the botanical imagery is used to show her virtuous and deeply religious nature and her good influence on Leon.

Leon's childhood innocence is also described in botanical terms. In his total devotion to his mother he is likened to a *sunflower* always striving towards the *sun,* even when the sun is hidden behind *clouds,* and even when he himself begins to "*wither and dry*", as the author rather ominously adds (pp. 759-760). He spends his days reading *on the shores of the Volga river,* amidst *wildflowers,* and "sam on kazalsja prekrasnejšim, oduševlennym *cvetom*", with his *rosy* cheeks and, significantly: "*šljapka* služila emu stolikom: na nee klal on knigu svoju" (p. 766). The description of his reading ends with the author's ecstatic exclamation: "Rodina, *aprel' žizni, pervye cvety vesny duševnoj!*", using the same vocabulary previously connected with his virtuous mother.

The author uses similar botanical imagery to philosophize over the stages of human life. In doing so, he simultaneously foreshadows events to come. Chapter IV consists of a lengthy philosophical digression on the mysteries of time passing, part of which reads:

> vezde sfinksovy *zagadki*, kotorych i sam *Èdip* ne otgadaet.—*Roza vjanet,* ternie ostaetsja [. . .] Junyj ščastlivec, kotorogo žizn' možno nazyvat' ulybkoju *sud'by* i prirody, *ugasaet* v *minutu,* kak meteor
>
> (p. 761)

Here we should note that the first violet, too, was connected with a riddle. The "minute" is subsequently stressed in connection with passions ("koketstvo *minutnoe*") and "*pylkie strasti* imejut rajskie *minuty*—no *minuty*! [italics Karamzin]" in connection with the countess's wishful thinking (pp. 774 and 775). The reference to Oedipus is also ominous.

In chapter V floral imagery serves as a kind of transition between what has been and what is to come. The author apostrophizes time: "I ty, podobno Morfeju, rassypaeš' *makovye cvety* zabvenija: bros' neskol'ko *cvetočkov* na junogo moego geroja" (p. 763). This is followed by a foreshadowing of more grievous things in store for Leon.

The discussion of Leon's reading matter further extends the botanical metaphor in an ominous direction: the author describes Leon's readings as a "*teplica* dlja junoj duši, kotoraja ot sego čtenija *zreet prežde vremeni*" (p. 772). This ostensibly positive characterization is, in the wider context, an artificial environment (as opposed to the wildflowers and the sunflower, nurtured by the sun), which accelerates our "plant's" path to withering.

This becomes obvious when the same floral imagery is used to describe Leon's relationship to his "second mother". Leon's story turns into an Oedipus myth with a new twist—the "mother" is two different persons. After describing the growing familiarity between Ėmilija and Leon in the erotically loaded section referred to above, the author apostrophizes Ėmilija: "Zarja čuvstvitel'nosti ticha i prekrasna, no buri nedaleko. Serdce ljubimca tvoego *zreet* vmesto s umom ego, i *cvet neporočnosti imeet sud'bu drugich cvetov*!" (p. 780). This is literally what happens. In the last chapter the botanical metaphor is further extended: after Leon has watched Ėmilija bathe, Emilija, significantly, places a *rose* on Leon's *cap*, acknowledging her forgiveness and also her ultimate victory over Leon's innocence—the rose is (to continue the author's metaphor) picked, her seduction a *fait accompli*.

To summarize: the floral euphemism is accompanied by the same imagery in the three main stages of Leon's innocence:

1. His mother's virtue was affirmed on the riverbank, in spring, in April (innocence).

2. His reading (accelerating his fall from innocence) took place on the riverbank, in the spring of life, "April", his cap serving to prop up his books.

3. His transgression (fall from innocence) took place on a riverbank and the picked rose was placed on the same cap which previously held his books.

By this detailed analysis I want to stress the striking structural unity of the novel.

These instances of metaphorical use of the flora are, at the same time accompanied by the author's laying bare his own metaphor as *rhetorical* flowers, i.e., his authorial privilege of manipulating the narrated event. Utilizing the device of praeteritio, he tells his reader: "Ja mog by nabrat' dovol'no *cvetov dlja ukrašenija ėtoj glavy*" (p. 758). This is precisely what he does, as we have seen, and it must be taken *literally*. The sunflower metaphor is directly followed by a playful pun on the "rastitel'noe bytie" and his own "razitel'noe sravnenie", and he hopes that his kind female readers might sigh from the bottom of their hearts (both at Leon's innocence and his own striking techniques!) and that they "veleli by *vyrezat' sej cvetok* na svoich pečatjach" (p.

760)—a light metaphorical hint at what will, in fact, later take on a darker significance with the picked rose image. The reference to the fate of the "*cvet neporočnosti*" is directly followed by an address to the reader: "Čitatel' podumaet, čto my seju *ritoričeskoju figuroju* gotovim ego k čemu-nibud' *protivnomu nevinnosti*", referring, as we have seen, to his own promises. This is exactly what he does, and despite his protestations, he finally must admit that: "ljubov' k istine zastavljaet nas opisat' malen'kij slučaj, kotoryj možet byt' rastolkovan i tak i sjak . . ." (p. 780). Here, too, the author lays bare his techniques, and finally (more or less) sanctions the reader's salacious interpretation of the Actaeon scene which follows. In all these instances of revealing his own literary devices, the author uses the language of a professional critic, i.e., he discusses his own fiction as would a critic, which indicates the metafictional nature of **Rycar'** as a whole. Thus, while giving an "objective" description of Leon's development (the "blank slate" of his soul, which is subjected both to good and bad external stimuli), this description at the same time is subjected to the author's own literary analysis. (I shall return to this subject below).

The same "tampering" with the "objective" educational aspects of Leon's development can be seen in the author's presentation of the other influences in Leon's life.

The profound religious teachings of Leon's mother are juxtaposed to the miraculous escape from the bear and the author's absurd tongue-in-cheek comments about tigers and lions.

The male influence is represented by Leon's father and the provincial male gentry. Their influence, although basically positive, is not exempt from authorial irony and humor. The "neutral" document and the personages' own speech is contrasted to the author's ironical speech event statements. The latter reveal that Bacchus had a hand in drafting and signing the friendship pact, and the "enlightenment" of the men is unmasked as arguments and loud discussions about trivia or matters they know nothing about. Their prosaic old age is incongruously commented on in the author's mock-solemn apostrophes to his "bogatyri" and "matadory provincii", with their weak legs, walking sticks, prosaic dress, etc. Nevertheless, their influence on Leon is positive—or at least not harmful.

These prosaic old men are contrasted to the more glorious "bogatyrs" and "matadors", which fill the pages of Leon's books: *Daira, vostočnaja povest'*, "Selim i Damasina" (an African tale), *Nepostojannaja fortuna, ili Pochoždenija Miramonda* (an adventure novel by Fedor Ėmin, published in 1763), and *Istorija lorda N* (apparently *Priključenie milorda, ili Žizn' mladogo čeloveka, byvšego igrališčem ljubvi*, published in 1771).[20]

In juxtaposition to the prosaic company of his father, Leon's readings must be seen as a harmful influence on the young child. Although initially extolled as a "hothouse" (cf. above) for the receptive youngster, the author, either by indirection or in explicit asides to the reader, lays bare their harmful effects. The author describes how Leon was fascinated by the dangerous adventures and heroic friendships depicted in the novels (p. 772). This stands in sharp contrast to the more down-to-earth "adventures" and more domestic friendships in Leon's real provincial environment. Leon also, according to the author, always saw himself as the "izbavitel'" rather than as the "izbavlennyj" when imagining himself as the protagonist of similar adventures. Ironically, in the only adventure that befalls him in the novel describing his own life, the roles are reversed—he is "izbavlennyj" by the countess from the dogs which threaten him in the conclusion to *Rycar'*.

In an aside to the reader the author ironically remarks that, according to the "filosofičeskie mediki", reading can at most hurt the physical well-being of young readers (p. 772). Later, à propos the "beneficial" education Leon receives from the countess, the author remarks "confidentially" to the reader (whimsically laying bare the separation between speech event and narrated event): "Leon (meždu nami bud' skazano!) do togo vremeni ne znal ničego, krome Ezopovych 'Basen', 'Dairy' i velikich tvorenij Fedora Émina" (p. 778), the latter elsewhere "professionally" referred to as "neskladica" (p. 764).

In addition to adventures and heroic friendship, the topic of all of Leon's books is love, and the Eastern tales in particular were famed for their somewhat risqué content. When Leon's reading is first mentioned, however, a great deal of stress is laid on what the youngster found so interesting in the works—*not* the amorous matters, but the adventures themselves, as the author remarks in a lengthy ironical aside to the reader (p. 764). This is followed by another digression on the natural curiosity of children as the basis for their later knowledge and experiences. This digression ends on an ominous note of warning:

> no tam, gde predmetom našego ljubopytstva stanovitsja uže ne istinnaja nužda, no tol'ko suemudrie, tam polet obraščaetsja v pešechodstvo i šagi delajutsja čas ot času trudnee
>
> (p. 765)

Curiosity is a source of learning unless directed onto useless objects. Leon's curiosity is consistently stressed in *Rycar'*, this quality often being used as an epithet describing Leon, and it is, ostensibly, one of the sources of his learning. The books (including, of course, the amorous parts) coupled with his inherent curiosity is an integral part of the novel—it is this same curiosity that ultimately leads him to the river where Émilija bathes (the same vocabulary that is used in the above quote is repeated in the latter scene). Thus, any ideas about virtuous love that should ideally have been instilled in Leon by his books, left him an ill-prepared victim of the mature seductress, and the author's ominous warning comes true. Such authorial foreshadowings are of extreme importance in *Rycar'*. We have already seen that Leon's reading often took place on the riverbank, where he was later to witness the bathing. From the very beginning water imagery is important. Thus, for example, in chapter III the reference to the impact of "šumnye reki" on a vivid imagination also foreshadows the later event—the imagined is, so to speak, re-enacted in real life. In chapter IV Leon's soul "plavala v knižnom svete, kak Christofor Kolomb na Atlantičeskom more, dlja otkrytija . . . sokrytogo" (p. 765). Here both the water imagery and the "otkrytie sokrytogo" again can be seen as the author's metaphorical foreshadowing of Leon's subsequent "discovery" of the "uncovered" countess.

Thus the seemingly "unwarranted" authorial digressions are intimately tied to the central romantic thread of *Rycar'*, and the Émin-type novels are implicitly and explicitly censured as harmful, i.e., the *utile* aspect is denied them.

Rycar' can also be seen as a parody of the exaggerated Sentimentalist diction of the early Sentimentalist writings, including those of Karamzin. This aspect is most poignantly revealed in the author's laying bare of the style he himself uses in the Leon-tale, i.e., by the explicit attention to his authorial function. The author has total control over the narrated event, an aspect consistently stressed in the speech event sections, and most overtly laid bare in the use of praeteritio, by means of which the description of Leon's childhood sets out. After a lengthy discussion with the reader about how to create an interesting story (the romantic "spicing" discussed above), the author goes on to describe what he *could do*:

> ja *mog by* nabrat' dovol'no cvetov dlja ukrašenija étoj glavy; *mog by,* ne otchodja ot istoričeskoj istiny, opisyvat' [. . .] *mog by* ne narušaja ni Aristotelevych, ni Goracievych pravil, desjat' raz peremenit' slog, bystro parja vverch i plavno opuskajas' vniz—to risuja karandašom, to raspisyvaja kist'ju—mešaja važnye mysli dlja uma s trogatel'nymi čertami dlja serdca; *mog by naprimer* skazat': [. . .]
>
> (p. 758)

He *could,* and does in fact, proceed to do precisely that. Using literary terminology, he talks about his own story, which, in fact, is placed in quotation marks as an *example* of what he *could do*. In his "example" he uses precisely the exaggerated diction he describes in his "professional" assessments of his own work. Thus the

Leon-story is used explicitly as an example of the Sentimentalist style the early Karamzin and his epigones were "guilty" of (*naprimer*: [Leon's story]).

After a page-long section of the Leon-story, the author again intrudes and comments on his own style: "ne pravda li, čto ėto moglo by inomu poljubit'sja? Tut est' živopis', i antitezy, i prijatnaja igra slov" (p. 759). By such ironical, "professionally" worded commentary on his own story in progress, he simultaneously mocks other writers who use the devices mentioned. After this comment on style, the author goes on in the same vein to discuss the already mentioned sunflower image, again resorting to "professional" jargon (Zoilus is mentioned, and he points to his "razitel'noe sravnenie", the botanical metaphor). The praeteritio device is employed to the end of chapter III. Thus the whole narrated event gathers momentum as a story the author *could* write, a story which, from the beginning, is subjected to discussion between author and reader. *Rycar'* as a whole is both the story about Leon and the story about the story about Leon. The use of praeteritio is not sustained to the end; it is *as if* the author forgot that he is merely giving an example, and *as if* the story continued of its own inertia (cf.: "Ja idu tol'ko s perom vsled za sud'boju i opisyvaju, čto tvorit ona po svoemu vsemoguščestvu", p. 761). The author "forgets" to end his example with the quotation mark which should properly be there. The discussions with the reader continue, and the first part (ending with chapter V, marked by the date 1799) ends with another metafictional reference to the Leon-story as a "malen'kaja tetradka", which the author will at some time present to his reader, and which will, hopefully, call forth the reader's proper response—tears ("ili ja . . . ne avtor", p. 763)—another ironical comment on the Sentimental author's main aim: to move his reader.

The second part is also continuously interrupted by the author's commentary on his own story. He introduces his "documentary" evidence—only to use it as another butt for his irony. Thus *Rycar'* is metafictional to the core: a Sentimental tale written in the typical Sentimentalist manner is simultaneously being mockingly, parodically scrutinized by its less sentimental (in the proper sense of the word) author.

Not only is *Rycar'* a parody of Sentimentalist writing, it is metafictional in another sense as well: it is a novel about the historical novel as it was represented in Russia during the latter part of the 18th century. This is, perhaps, the most carefully worked out aspect of *Rycar'*—and the aspect which has been most neglected by the critics. *Rycar'* can, in fact, be seen as a parody of the historical novel, mocking what Karamzin sees as the boring Neo-classicist novels, specifically those by Cheraskov: *Numa, ili Procvetajuščij Rym, Kadm i Garmonija,* and *Polidor, syn Kadma i Garmonii.* Novels

like these were written with the serious aim of educating as well as entertaining the reader (the Classicist *utile* and *dulce*). The author's aim was to propagate the ideas of the Enlightenment by showing ideal heroes, who, although they might err temporarily, were always lead on the path to virtue by various Mentors. The heroes were taken from the distant past, often semi-historical, semi-mythological figures, and were always of the highest social standing, often rulers or knights. The Mentors were often goddesses in disguise. Fénelon's *Télémaque* was the prototype *par excellence,* and Cheraskov was his most ardent Russian follower, with the three above mentioned novels to his name.[21] These novels tended to be of enormous dimensions (several volumes), and the tone was unfailingly one of lofty and didactic advice. This is the image that Karamzin parodies in his *Rycar'*. The title itself is indicative: *rycar'* was a most frequent rank in the historical novels. For example, according to Sipovskij:

> V oboich romanach Cheraskova vlijanie rycarskich romanov skazalos' v upotreblenii slov: "rycar'", "rycarskij"—v primenenii k dejstvujuščim licam, priuročennym k vremenam mifičeskim; tak, v romane "Kadm" vavilonskie junoši imenujutsja "rycarjami"; govoritsja o "rycarskom iskusstve"; v romane "Polidor" tože dejstvujut "rycari", upominajutsja "rycarskie podvigi", "rycarskija odeždy" . . .[22]

By applying it to an eleven year old boy, the author of *Rycar'* makes the whole concept absurd. The term is also as anachronistic as in Cheraskov's works although the events are moved to the present era—another break with the tradition. In the author's introduction his opinion of the traditional novels is made quite explicit: they are far from truthful, and can at best be characterized as "prekrasnye kukol'nye komedii", which make the reader yawn. Instead of Numa's toga, the author in order to create more reader interest, dresses his knight in contemporary garb. Instead of the traditional unrounded, virtuous or evil, personages, he sets out to create a psychologically rounded cast of characters. Instead of writing an "istoričeskij roman", he sets out to write a "romaničeskaja istorija". The author's choice of generic label is interesting, in that it shows his triple aim:

1. To write a *romantic* (in the sense of amorous) "*istorija*" (in the sense the term was often used at the time to signify an "escapade" of a slightly scabruous nature, such as a duel or an amorous adventure).

2. To write a story *about the novel* (i.e., romaničeskaja).

3. To write a work of the *novel genre.*

We have already seen that the author's story is precisely a rococo-like romance about the seduction of Leon—the ultimate result of all his so-called education.[23]

As for the novel-format, **Rycar'** consists of an introduction and thirteen chapters—all in 26 pages! The very brevity can be seen as a device mocking the enormity of the traditional novels. After all, the author points out as one of the things that he *could do*:

> ja mog by ešče mnogoe pridumat' i raskrasit' [followed by a long list of possibilities]

> Slova moi tekli by rekoju, esli by ja tol'ko chotel vojti v podrobnosti; no ne choču, ne choču! Mne ešče mnogoe nadobno opisyvat'; beregu bumagu, vnimanie čitatelja, i . . . konec glave!

<div align="right">(p. 760)</div>

His brevity thus parodies those who were not as thrifty with their paper, nor as concerned with their readers' attention span. The fact that a continuation is promised by the author need not mean that he ever intended the novel to continue.[24] Karamzin lived another 23 years after the publication of chapter XIII of **Rycar'**, and, to my knowledge, there are no indications that he ever returned to his novel. It seems to me very unlikely indeed, that he ever intended a continuation. The very tight-knit structure of the novel as it stands seems to support such an assumption. As I have shown, the first twelve chapters clearly lead up to the culminating chapter XIII (the similarity in imagery, the very development of the imagery, foreshadowings, hints, promises, etc.). Structurally the novel is clearly symmetrical: the initial "good" stimulus from Leon's virtuous mother, the intermediate stimuli from the males in his life ("good") and from the books ("bad"), and the last "bad" stimulus from his "second mother", who is not so virtuous. One can only speculate, of course, but the fact remains that the novel, as it stands, is structured as a unit, complete in itself. Perhaps, by promising a continuation, Karamzin intended to mock the traditional novel with its potentially open structure: any number of events could be added (and was!) within the structure of the historical novels, without essentially changing the hero's unfailing path to virtue—the path merely being made longer.

The chapter headings in **Rycar'** parody those in the traditional novels in a Sternian fashion which requires no comment. The contents of the different chapters fulfill the same objective: chapter II, for example, consists of one 10-line authorial chat with the reader!

As a novel about the novel, we can point to the metafictional nature of the work as analyzed above. This aspect is, however, most blatantly laid bare in the choice of hero and plot. In most of the Neo-classical novels (all of Cheraskov's mentioned above) the knight-hero encounters, or is accompanied by one or more Mentors (virtuous nymphs, wise old hermits, etc.). He is also subjected to various temptations, often in the form of seductive women or nymphs. Thus Numa has his Mentor, the nymph Eger, who teaches him true virtue and initiates him into the secrets of a good ruler. Kadm's Mentors are many, his virtuous and faithful wife, Garmonija, being perhaps the main one. His temptations are also many. The seductive nymph, Taksila, for example, leads to his initial downfall. Despite numerous other "downfalls", Kadm is ultimately lead to true virtue. Polidor encounters both Mentors and seductive nymphs. One of the nymphs on his path, the "false" Teandra, has some affinities to **Rycar'**. Polidor is quite taken by her beauty and, despite her admonitions, tries to lift her veil—with disastrous results: he is severely punished. Soon, however, he realizes his faults, finds the "true" Teandra (who, like Fénelon's Mentor, is the human embodiment of the goddess Minerva), and ends up another paragon of virtue. Thus Cheraskov's heroes develop either within the realm of virtue (Numa), or on a complex path which always ends in the realm of virtue (virtue—vice—virtue . . .—virtue). This tendency they share with most other prose works of the era, including those that Leon read. Karamzin comments ironically:

> vo vsech romanach želtogo škapa geroi i geroini, nesmotrja na mnogočislennye iskušenija roka, ostajutsja dobrodetel'nymi; vse zlodei opisyvajutsja samymi černymi kraskami; pervye nakonec toržestvujut, poslednie nakonec, kak prach, isčezajut.

<div align="right">(p. 765)</div>

His own novel reverses the pattern. The knight, Leon, also has his nymph, Diana-Ėmilija, who quite successfully seduces her non-repentant charge. The Mentors are represented by the various "educational" influences in Leon's life. These representatives of "virtue" are, however, one way or another, treated with irony or even mocked, rather than seriously extolled as in Cheraskov.

Most interestingly, the knightly lineage of Leon is revealed in the last chapter, where the author calls him the New Actaeon. Both parts of the "name" are significant. Actaeon is an Ovidian figure, the grandson of Cadmus! Thus **Rycar'** could, properly speaking, be seen as a sequel to Cheraskov's two novels: *Kadm i Garmonija, Polidor, syn Kadma i Garmonii*, and *Akteon, vnuk Kadma i Garmonii*. Leon is, however, a *new* Actaeon, as his story clearly shows. Ovid's Actaeon, after watching Diana bathe in her stream, is punished (as were his grandfather and uncle in Cheraskov) for his transgression: Diana turns him into a stag. Later on his hunting dogs tear him to pieces, as Diana acts in keeping with her strict chastity. The new Actaeon re-enacts his mythical prototype's transgression. The imagery used by the author is quite in accordance with that of Ovid, replete with references (in a humorous authorial aside) to Diana and nymphs, hunting dogs, the "correct" setting, etc. Interestingly enough, the author made a reference to "horns" already in chapter I, in the old

crone's "accurate" prediction of Leon's future (p. 756). Only in the last chapter does their full significance become apparent: Actaeon's metamorphosis into a stag began with horns sprouting on his forehead. The *new* Actaeon's horns, however, remain solely symbolical: he is not punished for his transgression. Although the hunting dogs threaten him for a while, they are called back by Ėmilija-Diana, and instead of Actaeon-Leon being physically transformed, the innocent boy has been mentally transformed into a sexually receptive eleven year old. Thus Karamzin's new "knight" reverses the fate of both his Ovidian prototype and his Russian ancestors: Leon is lead from virtue and innocence into a less virtuous relationship.

I think that we are quite justified in considering **Rycar'** first and foremost as a parody of the 18th century Russian novel in all its aspects. The prominent author image in the novel is that of a Sternian mocker-parodist who parodies both the preceding Sentimentalist writings, the *utile* of Ėmin-type adventure novels and of Eastern tales, both the *utile* and the *dulce* of the Cheraskovian historical novels, and, finally, the very novel genre itself.

Notes

1. *Vestnik Evropy,* 1803, 14, p. 121, as quoted in the notes to N. M. Karamzin, *Izbrannye sočinenija* 1, Moskva 1964, p. 808. I shall henceforth use the 1964 edition when referring to Karamzin's works, citing page numbers in parentheses within my text.

2. G. A. Gukovskij, *Russkaja literatura XVIII veka,* Moskva 1939, p. 511; E. N. Kuprejanova, "Russkij roman pervoj četverty XIX veka", *Istorija russkogo romana* 1, Moskva 1962, p. 73; P. Berkov & G. Makogonenko, "Žizn' i tvorčestvo N. M. Karamzina", introduction to Karamzin 1964, p. 49; H. M. Nebel, *N. M. Karamzin: A Russian Sentimentalist,* The Hague & Paris 1967 (=Slavistic Printings and Reprintings 60), p. 117; A. G. Cross, *N. M. Karamzin: A Study of His Literary Career 1783-1803,* Carbondale . . . 1971, pp. 1, 125; N. Kochetkova, *Nikolay Karamzin,* Boston 1975 (=Twayne's World Author Series 250), p. 107. All these scholars (and a number of others) view *Rycar'* as autobiographical, some do so solely on the basis of the note, others proceed with more caution and bring in added evidence. In the novel itself Karamzin refers to it as a story about a friend of his.

3. *Pis'ma russkogo putešestvennika* (serially, 1791-95, first complete edition in 1801), "Bednaja Liza" and "Natal'ja, bojarskaja doč'" (1792), "Ostrov Borngol'm" (1794), "Sierra-Morena" (1795), "Julija" (1796), to name just a few of the major works. Karamzin was, furthermore, by then an ac-complished translator, journalist, poet, critic, etc.,—aspects of his career which shall not concern us here.

4. See, for example, Ju. M. Lotman, "Ėvoljucija mirovozzrenija Karamzina (1789-1803)", *Učenye zapiski Tartuskogo gosudarstvennogo universiteta* 51, 1957, pp. 122-62; Ju. M. Lotman, "Puti razvitija russkoj prozy 1800-ch-1810-ch godov", *Učenye zapiski Tartuskogo gosudarstvennogo universiteta* 104, 1961, especially pp. 30-6; L. I. Kulakova, "Ėstetičeskie vzgljady N. M. Karamzina", *Russkaja literatura XVIII veka: Ėpocha klassicizma,* Moskva & Leningrad 1964 (XVIII vek 6), pp. 146-75.

5. See F. Z. Kanunova, "Karamzin i Stern", *Russkaja literatura XVIII veka i ee meždunarodnye svjazi,* Leningrad 1975 (=XVIII vek 10), pp. 258-64, where *Rycar'* is viewed as the peak of Karamzin's Sternian inclinations.

6. Without going into all the intricacies of defining Russian Sentimentalism, I shall use Gukovskij's view as a kind of working hypothesis. This view holds that in the Murav'ev-Karamzin school the main structuring principle in a literary text is a solipsistic focus on the author. All the other elements of narrative structure (plot, personages, etc.) are subordinated to this main principle. This idea is treated in great detail in G. A. Gukovskij, *Očerki po istorii russkoj literatury i obščestvennoj mysli XVIII veka,* Leningrad 1938, mainly in the second part, pp. 235-314. Cf. also Lotman 1961, p. 30. Furthermore I shall assume that this focus is formally implemented by a stress on stylistic features which mark the author's speech event in the Jakobsonian sense. For the terminology used here and for further details see: R. Jakobson, "Shifters, Verbal Categories, and the Russian Verb" (1957), reprinted in his *Selected Writings* 2, The Hague 1971, pp. 131-47; R. Jakobson, "Closing Statement: Linguistics and Poetics", *Style in Language,* ed. by T. A. Sebeok, Cambridge, Mass., 1960, pp. 350-77; L. Doležel, *Narrative Modes in Czech Literature,* Toronto 1973, pp. 10, 20-40; I. R. Titunik, *The Problem of Skaz in Russian Literature,* unpublished Ph.D. dissertation, Berkeley, University of California, 1963, pp. 33-46; I. R. Titunik, "The Problem of *Skaz* (Critique and Theory)", *Papers in Slavic Philology* 1, Ann Arbor 1977, pp. 276-301. Thus in Sentimentalist fiction an image of author (*obraz avtora*) is strongly present and the author himself is an important topic of his own work. In Sentimentalist prose fiction, including Karamzin's earlier works, the image of author was that of a "sensitive" person with the emotive, expressive, and subjective features of style exploited to the utmost. My contention in the present

paper is that even in Karamzin's later fiction, and specifically in *Rycar'*, the image of author remained the central structuring principle, although with a lesser stress on the emotive aspects and a greater stress on those aspects of the author image which highlight the author *as author*, i.e., in his authorial reporting function or in his attitude to the prevailing literary tradition. In this sense *Rycar'* is firmly anchored within the Sentimentalist system, although there is a change in emphasis from the "sensitive" to the "professional".

7. Gukovskij 1939, p. 511; Kuprejanova 1962, pp. 73-4; Berkov and Makogonenko 1964, p. 49; Nebel 1967, p. 117, to name just a few of the brief treatments.

8. Lotman 1961, pp. 30-6; F. Z. Kanunova, *Iz istorii russkoj povesti (Istoriko-literaturnoe značenie povestej N. M. Karamzina)*, Tomsk 1967, particularly pp. 144-56; Cross 1971, pp. 123-6; R. B. Anderson, *N. M. Karamzin's Prose: The Teller in the Tale: A Study in Narrative Technique,* Houston 1974, pp. 170-83; Kanunova 1975, pp. 262-3; Kochetkova 1975, pp. 106-7.

9. Berkov and Makogonenko 1964, p. 49 and Gukovskij 1939, p. 511; Kuprejanova 1962, p. 73.

10. See A. Cross, "Karamzin Studies: For the Bicentenary of the Birth of N. M. Karamzin (1766-1966)", *Slavonic and East European Review* 45, 1967, pp. 8-9, and A. Cross, "N. M. Karamzin's 'Messenger of Europe' (*Vestnik Yevropy*), 1802-3", *Forum for Modern Language Studies* 5, 1969, p. 4. Cross mentions the *Vestnik Evropy* works in question, and although he does not analyze them, he cites several pertinent studies for further reference.

11. Lotman 1961, pp. 34-5.

12. Kanunova 1967, p. 154, italics mine.

13. Anderson 1974, pp. 182-3, italics mine.

14. See, for example, Cross 1971, pp. 124-6.

15. Lotman 1961, p. 35, italics mine.

16. Anderson 1974, p. 182, italics mine.

17. A. Cross, "Karamzin's versions of the idyll", *Essays on Karamzin: Russian Man-of-letters, Political Thinker, Historian, 1766-1826*, ed. by J. L. Black, The Hague 1975 (=Slavistic Printings and Reprints 309), pp. 75-90. Here Cross elucidates Karamzin's conception of the Arcadian Golden Age in connection with the idyll topic.

18. Henceforth the italics in Karamzin's texts, if not otherwise indicated, are mine. I am mainly italicizing repeated vocabulary in order to point out the development of similar topics and style.

19. Cf. Kuprejanova 1962, p. 74, where the author points out the affinities between the Ėmilija-Leon romance and Rousseau's relationship to Mme de Warens described in his *Confessions.* Other scholars, for example, Cross 1971, p. 126, make similar observations. Cross 1971, p. 111, points out a more immediate parallel: Karamzin's own "unfinished" tale "Liodor" (begun in 1792).

20. Karamzin 1964, notes, pp. 808-9. Cf. also Kanunova 1967, pp. 88-91, where Cheraskov's novels and *Selim i Damasina* are discussed.

21. V. V. Sipovskij, *Očerki iz istorii russkogo romana* 1:1, S.-Petersburg 1909, pp. 333-41, refers to this type of novel as "psevdoklassičeskij roman tipa 'Telemak'". Cheraskov's three works mentioned are discussed in the same volume, pp. 508-63.

22. Ibid., 1:2, p. 364.

23. Cross 1971, p. 126, characterizes *Rycar'* in the following terms: "In the elaboration of the relationship between Leon and Countess Mirova Karamzin still pays tribute to the unfortunate tradition of rococo sensualism with his suggestive innuendo and ultimate Acteon-Diana set piece." Mr Cross obviously is not one of the readers that Karamzin intended his novel for, i.e., those with slightly salacious minds. Be that as it may, I would nevertheless maintain that this "unfortunate rococo sensualism" is the central focus on one level of *Rycar'*, fully intended by Karamzin, and crucial for the work as a whole.

24. See Cross 1971, p. 111, for an interesting discussion of "fragments" as symptomatic of Sentimentalism and Pre-romanticism in general, and Karamzin in particular.

Tanya Page (essay date summer 1985)

SOURCE: Page, Tanya. "Karamzin's Immoralist Count NN or Three Hermeneutical Games of 'Chinese Shadows.'" *Slavic and East European Journal* 29, no. 2 (summer 1985): 144-56.

[*In the following essay, Page analyzes the character of Count NN, fictional hero of Karamzin's 1802 essay "Moja ispoved'." Page argues that Count NN belongs to the larger tradition of immoral protagonists that became popular in eighteenth-century Russian and European literature.*]

Imagine mankind as dwelling in an underground cave with a long entrance open to light across the whole width of the cave; in this they have been from childhood, with necks and legs fettered, so they have to stay where they are. They cannot move their heads round

because of the fetters, and they can only look forward, but light comes to them from fire burning behind them higher up at a distance. Between the fire and prisoners is a road above their level, and along it imagine a low wall has been built, as puppet showmen have screens in front of their people over which they work their puppets.

The allegory of the cave. Plato, *The Republic,* Book VII.[1]

In the second half of the eighteenth century, immoral heroes enter West European prose fiction in significant numbers, from Richardson's Lovelace (*Clarissa Harlowe,* 1747-48) to demonic immoralists such as the Vicomte de Valmont and the Marquise de Merteuil in Laclos's chef d'œuvre *Liaisons dangereuses* (1782), Juliette in Sade's *Justine* (1791) or Balmont in his "roman philosophique" *Aline et Valcour* (1788-95). Russian eighteenth-century immoral heroes are less well documented, but they too make their presence felt, particularly in the long prose form of the novel. Plutalov in P. Ju. L'vov's *Russian Pamela* (*Rossijskaja Pamela,* 1789) ridicules church rituals and patriotism, honor and friendship, and believes that he can shape other people's minds at will. Razvratin in *Eugene or the Ruinous Consequences of Evil Education and Companionship* (*Evgenij, ili Pagubnye sledstvija durnogo vospitanija i soobščestva,* 1799-1801) by A. E. Izmajlov, laughs at the worship of God, and ridicules virtue, and filial duty. Bezdel'nikov, another evil character from the same novel, leads maidens into debauchery, and looks upon faith as a "political knot with which to tie weak minds."[2] Karamzin's Count NN, the hero and narrator of the tiny essay entitled **"My Confession"** (**"Moja ispoved'"**), which first appeared in print in 1802, in Karamzin's journal *Messenger of Europe* (*Vestnik Evropy*), belongs to the spate of late eighteenth-century immoral heroes. And yet there is about him a distinctive, zestful flair which turns him into an immoral hero of a different order.[3]

Count NN writes in the opening lines of his autobiography that he never reads the *Messenger of Europe,* and goes on to boast that his confession has no moral purpose; indeed, that he is writing without any purpose at all, "just like that" (*pišu—tak!*).[4] There follows his account of his life, which never rises above the physical world of the senses. Count NN was born, he reports, in the upper classes, was never punished in childhood, and at sixteen was sent abroad with a Genevan tutor by the name of Mendel'[5] under whose tutorage the count is initiated to the pleasures of sex and of social success. The young count and Mendel' spend three years in Leipzig, where they give dinners to famous professors and suppers to "nymphs" (I, 731). Mendel' and the count leave Leipzig to travel through Europe; but, after pushing his tutor down the stairs for making advances to his Jenny, the count and Mendel' part ways, and the count starts life on his own. Back in his native Russia

the count wins fame and followers as a seducer of the fair sex. He marries Èmilija to bring some variety to life, and forces her into infidelity. Meanwhile, his extravagance with money and his loose life hasten the death of his mother. His property, with eight thousand souls, is sold at an auction, but still money-lenders pursue him, and he is threatened with the debtors prison. Abandoned by his wife and friends, the count saves himself by formally divorcing Èmilija: the old prince who marries her in gratitude pays off the count's debts. Then Count NN conceives and executes his "example of debauchery unheard of" (I, 738) for its absurdity: he seduces and elopes with his former wife. Eventually, he hastens her death. The count has further countless adventures until, with the loss of his good looks, he turns into a confidant of unfaithful spouses and a money-lender; the count has learnt from experience that he can profit from rich spendthrifts. At the end of his confession the count declares that he has fulfilled his "predestination" (*predopredelenie,* I, 739), and he joyfully exclaims as he surveys the topography of his life, like a traveler looking down from a height at the places he has been to: "This is how I lived!" (I, 739).

In his brief autobiography, unwittingly, the count paints his own satirical self-portrait. This much is clear, and so is the presence of the author Karamzin, who stands behind the count and controls the work's satirical dimension. But the nature, or "point," of the satire is less clear. Is Karamzin satirizing confessional literature, although it was not very substantial on the Russian literary scene in 1798, when, as shall be seen, he originally conceived and wrote **"My Confession"**? Or is Karamzin satirizing vice and corruption in the Russian upper classes? If so, why was Karamzin repeating, some twenty years later, the experience of the satirist Novikov? I shall argue that the satirical component in **"My Confession"** is distinctive and inseparable from Karamzin's engagement in a "game" of philosophical hermeneutics. The clue to the "game" is given in the expression "Chinese shadows" used, it will be shown, by the count in summing up his outlook on life, and by Karamzin in a later work in referring at once to his own creative imagination and to the count's autobiography.

"Chinese shadows" (*kitajskie teni*) is the name of a game, and is defined as follows in the Ušakov dictionary: "A game consisting in performing scenes with the help of shadows cast on a screen by many figures." How is one to interpret the "shadows" projected on the screen? It is my second contention that Karamzin plays the "game" of "Chinese shadows" mainly from the position of Socratic-Platonic philosophy where "shadow" is an appearance of reality.[6] It will be seen that Karamzin's Socrates is an apologist of reason, a philosopher whose greatness for Karamzin lies in the belief that "only planned, unremitting and consistent thinking leads us from darkness into the light of philosophical

truth."[7] In a more modern formulation, for Karamzin as for Plato's Socrates, a "world of existence," with its "shadows," stands in a dialectical relationship to a "world of essence,"[8] with its realities and light, and arrived at through the pursuit of knowledge.

The Hellenic tradition in Karamzin's prose has been noted,[9] and Lotman cites references to Plato's *Republic* from Karamzin's writing in the 1790s.[10] But Socratic-Platonic philosophy is not generally associated with the name of Karamzin. Indeed, it seems fair to say that very little headway in Karamzin's philosophy (ethics, epistemology, and ontology) has been made since Èjxenbaum in 1916 urged the study in depth of "our first philosopher."[11] In the present essay, an initial discussion of Karamzin's interest in the 1790s in the discipline of philosophy in general, and in Socratic-Platonic philosophy in particular, will serve as an introduction to the study of three hermeneutical games of Chinese shadows in **"My Confession."**

A few months before writing **"My Confession,"** Karamzin inserts a miniature philosophical essay in French in his private correspondence with I. I. Dmitriev, describes himself to his friend as a "peripatetic philosopher," and confides to him: "I hope some time to become a philosopher."[12] Earlier in the same decade Karamzin wrote works with an overt philosophical orientation. Such are his interesting critique of Rousseau under the title **"Something About the Sciences, the Arts and the Enlightenment"** (**"Nečto o naukax, iskusstvax i prosveščenii"**), several philosophical dialogues between Filalet and Melodor (**"Melodor To Filalet"** [**"Melodor k Filaletu"**], **"Filalet To Melodor"** [**"Filalet k Melodoru"**], **"A Dialogue On Happiness"** [**"Razgovor o sčastii"**]), and a philosophical fantasia with the title **"Athenian Life"** (**"Afinskaja žizn'"**), not to mention **"My Confession,"** the work of main interest in the present inquiry. In one form or another all these works are associated with the period of ancient Greece.

Karamzin's interest in the 1790s in Socratic-Platonic philosophy and in contemporary eighteenth-century, particularly French philosophy, may be traced back to his education under the Russian Masons—although he appears never to have shared the views of an extreme mystic faction within Russian Masonry. When he returned in 1790 from his travels to Western Europe, this faction met Karamzin with unseemly vicious attacks.[13] But by now Karamzin was well onto his own independent path. This is not the place to take issue with Karamzin scholars on his relation to Russian Masonry after 1790.[14] Suffice it here to draw attention to the very different position of Karamzin and the Masons toward Plato's Socrates. The *Apology* was very popular with the Masons, who sought to emulate Socrates' example in overcoming the fear of death. The Socratic dictum

"Know thyself" found a responsive chord among the Masons whose motto was: "Enter into thyself"; also, like Socrates, the Masons widely believed that "every man has his place in society."[15] By contrast, Karamzin approached the teaching of Plato's Socrates from the position of Aristotle.

The teaching of Socrates in Aristotle's interpretation has been summarized as follows: "(a) virtue, *moral* excellence, is identical with knowledge, and for that reason, all the commonly discriminated virtues are one thing; (b) vice, bad moral conduct, is therefore in all cases ignorance, intellectual error, and (c) wrong-doing is therefore always involuntary."[16] The premises "Ignorance is Vice" and "Knowledge is Virtue" found in Karamzin a very responsive reader, and he would explore the related imagery of "shadows" (for ignorance and vice) and light (for knowledge and virtue). Among Karamzin's works which elucidate the Socratic-Platonic tenets of his philosophy should be singled out **"Something About the Sciences, the Arts and the Enlightenment."** In **"My Confession,"** moreover, Karamzin opposes Rousseau from the same position he had taken six years earlier in **"Something About . . ."** (1793), where he set forth his philosophical objections to Rousseau's *Discours* I (1750).

In *Discours* I, Rousseau argued that the arts and sciences and the Enlightenment corrupt the mores, and that in the state of ignorance man, in fact, is closer to virtue and good.[17] In **"Something About . . . ,"** Karamzin overcame his personal feelings of awe for Rousseau's passionate eloquence in *La Nouvelle Héloïse* and *Émile*[18] and his sincerity (as Karamzin believed) in *Les Confessions*,[19] and argued against his formidable opponent. In the beginning of his philosophical critique, after noting that what he calls modestly his "commentaries" were not culled from anywhere but are his own, Karamzin attacks the *Discours* as, "so to speak, a chaos of logic," where one sees only a false order, or *shadow* of order" (italics mine). The metaphoric "shadow" in its application to false reasoning, and elsewhere the definition of our sensory perceptions as mere appearances, the "*reflections* of objects in man's soul" (II, 125, italics mine), reveal a Socratic-Platonic frame of reference. Similarly revealing is Karamzin's condemnation of Rousseau for idealizing a life that never transcends the physical senses. Karamzin accuses Rousseau of preaching and glorifying the "bliss of animal life! For what else if not an animal is that person who lives only for the gratification of his physical needs?" (II, 137). The person leading an "animal life," Karamzin continues, is condemned to obey the "laws of necessity" (*ustavy neobxodimosti*). According to these "laws," there is "no choice, there is no good, no evil" (II, 138).

Karamzin, who, like Socrates, constructs no system, like Socrates,[20] believes that man must seek philosophical truth: "But man was given a reasoning mind (*razum*),

which must *seek* truth and good" (II, 138, italics in the original). Far from proposing a rejection of the world of the physical senses, Karamzin would have man gather the impressions produced by his sensory perceptions after which the reasoning mind would act upon them, sorting them out and producing abstract ideas. In Karamzin's epistemology and moral philosophy what may be termed the Lockian paradigm "I feel, therefore I am" is only an initial, preliminary stage, later transcended by the reasoning mind. But for this to happen man must become aware of and cultivate his reasoning mind. "Man from his sense perceptions turns to himself as sense-perceiver, and although he is no Descartes, he says: 'Cogito ergo sum'" (II, 126). At a later stage, at last man can begin his search of Truth and Good, which are his highest and the only real values. Rousseau too refers to Socrates, this already in his *Discours* (later, in the words of one scholar, he was "Socratized" by his contemporaries in France and across the Channel).[21] But Rousseau ascribes to Socrates the wisdom of ignorance, to this end citing from the *Apology* Socrates' admission of his not-knowing.[22]

The conceptual link between **"Something About . . ."** and **"My Confession"** has become apparent. Count NN, who in his reckless pursuit of pleasure is portrayed living the "bliss of animal life," in part embodies Rousseau's idealization of ignorance in the *Discours*. In different words, Rousseau is implicated in Count NN's satirical self-portrait. The complete title of his confession, with its oddly clashing associations, will lead to the same ironic conclusion. The title reads in its entirety: **"My Confession. Letter to the Editor of the Journal."** The first portion of the title evokes Rousseau, the author of *Les Confessions*; the second portion, Novikov, who ushered into Russia the satirical genre of the self-caricature in the form of the "Letter To the Editor." (See also Count NN boasting about his talent for drawing caricatures of contemporary celebrities [*satira na lico*] when all the while he draws a moral caricature of himself [*satira nravov*].) Rousseau and Novikov are, to say the least, odd bedfellows. That is, until we find the author of the *Discours* included in Novikov's *Painter* (*Živopisec*, 1772) among satirical portraits of obscurantists: "Rousseau with Reason and [Russian obscurantists] with ignorance prove that the sciences are useless."[23] Rousseau is implicated in the satirical dimension of **"My Confession,"** as the author of the *Discours* rather than *Les Confessions*.

Rousseau was satirized as the proponent of ignorance first by Novikov in the *Painter* and more than two decades later by Karamzin in **"My Confession,"** but there is a fundamental difference in their approaches. Where Novikov has Rousseau arguing "with reason," Karamzin sees a "chaos of logic" and a "shadow of order." Unlike Novikov, Karamzin situates Rousseau in the perspective of Socratic-Platonic philosophy. Karamzin similarly modifies Novikov's method of describing the degradation of man through his reification.[24] Thus with considerable ingenuity Karamzin conveys the count's life in the physical world of the senses through his use of language, wherein the count reveals his gift of transforming, like Midas, live beings into soulless objects and love into a physical emotion. Women, the count avers, are "my main object"—but not of interest or passion, for the expression is truncated after the word "object." The count similarly transforms an earlier neologism of Karamzin, "being-in-love" (*vljubljennost'*): "being-in-love—forgive me this new word—it expresses a *thing*" (*ono vyražaet vešč'*, I, 733; italics mine). "Thing," like "object," reflects the count's mindless, soulless life. But these passages in **"My Confession"** lead directly to the *libertin*'s pursuits as mere "shadows," more precisely, a "play of Chinese shadows." "The entire world," Count NN continues, "seemed to me a disorderly play of Chinese shadows, all rules a rein for weak minds, all duties an unbearable constraint" (I, 732). He recapitulates later, when his former friends have abandoned him after his bankruptcy: "But I was born a philosopher, I bore everything with indifference, and repeated my favorite expression: 'Chinese shadows! Chinese shadows!'" (I, 736). Count NN's perception of life as a play of Chinese shadows takes us back, first to Karamzin's critique of Rousseau from the position of a Socratic-Platonic philosopher, and, further, to the Socratic allegory of the cave with its projections of the shadows of realities.

One last philosophical essay remains to be considered in its relation to **"My Confession." "A Dialogue On Happiness"** was inserted directly above **"My Confession"** in the seventh volume of Karamzin's **Works**, which appeared under his supervision in 1803.[25] In **"A Dialogue,"** Karamzin's Filalet, like all good philosophers in general and Socrates in particular, begins by stating a paradox which he then proceeds to clarify. Happiness, Filalet declares to his despondent and initially uncomprehending friend Melodor, is and is not an "empty phantom," and man on earth can and cannot know happiness (228-29). When happiness consists in wanting every desire gratified, Filalet continues, this amounts to wanting $2 + 2 = 5$, for man's soul is so constituted that with "every minute of enjoyment his happiness, so to speak, dies" (228, 228-32). This happiness is, in Filalet's words, a "shadow of bliss" (246). Happiness is real when man does not "overstep the line drawn by reason around the natural impulses of the passions" (246). He is not a stoic, Filalet emphasizes, for he believes that the human passions are not harmful provided, however, that we draw a circle around them which we shall not overstep. The work's primarily pedagogical value consisted in Karamzin imparting to the reader, through Filalet, his own cherished Socratic principles and ideals. Karamzin enjoins Melodor (and by extension the readers of **"A Dialogue"**) to act upon the Socratic "law of wisdom," the "law of mind" (246), for

only with this "law" can man become the "creator of his bliss" (*blagopolučija*) and can enjoy true happiness.[26]

Karamzin in his letter of 18 January 1798 to I. I. Dmitriev refers to the close proximity in time of the writing of **"A Dialogue"** and **"My Confession,"** and suggests that both works were conceived as philosophical essays. Humorously, he confides: "At the end of last year [1797] I wrote a dialogue on happiness and at the beginning of this one [1798] I took it into my head to write on boredom! Philosophy can console us at times."[27] That the item "on boredom" was none other than **"My Confession"** is suggested by the fact that Count NN sums up his state of mind with the single word "boredom" (I, 732). Our dating of **"My Confession"** from 1798 situates its initial conception and writing *before* the publication in 1801 of the last installment of *Letters of a Russian Traveler,* where, it will be seen, Karamzin in his own voice employs the metaphor of "Chinese shadows." The new chronological sequence no longer allows one to posit an evolution in Karamzin's thought from *Letters* to **"My Confession,"** for not only could Karamzin *not* evolve *backward* in time, but there is little to suggest any substantial change in his philosophy during the 1790s and until 1801.

The short interval of a few months, perhaps only weeks, between the writing of **"A Dialogue"** and **"My Confession"** explains the similar philosophical configuration of the two works, which place an equal emphasis on exposing in the reckless pursuit of the physical pleasures ephemeral realities, mere shadows. Filalet's "empty phantom" of happiness and Count NN's "Chinese shadows" are metaphors for the realities that lie within the physical world of the senses, and are removed from the "law of the mind." The two works, however, receive very different forms. One is a philosophical dialogue, while the other assumes the original form of a satirical-philosophical essay. Filalet in speaking of his "prescription for the moral ailment of boredom" (261) does allude to a satirical device, the moral "prescription" (*lekarstvo*), which like the "Letter To the Editor," was associated with Novikov's satirical journals. But this is, on the part of Filalet, merely an allusion to the device. This is the point: Filalet preaches and the count does not.

Karamzin elaborated the premises and ideals of his Socratic-Platonic philosophy first in his own voice in **"Something About . . ."** and later in the voice of his mouthpiece Filalet in **"A Dialogue."** The same premises and ideals are developed in **"My Confession"** in the metaphor of "Chinese shadows." The count, imprisoned in the world of the physical senses, with its shadows of bliss, and endowed with an insight directed *toward* the same world, by implication stands with his back turned *away* from the light of the mind, from the pursuit of knowledge, and, finally, from virtue. This polarity must be *inferred*. The metaphor of "Chinese shadows" directs us towards the inference: shadows *imply* light. The count's "Chinese shadows" are implicitly offset by light, the light of the world of the mind idealized by Karamzin, the count's creator. We have, figuratively speaking, turned on the light in **"My Confession"** for two of the three hermeneutical games of "Chinese shadows." Both are replays of the opening section of Socrates' allegory of the cave in the Seventh Book of Plato's *Republic.*

The first game has one main protagonist in **"My Confession"**: Count NN. In Plato's *Republic,* in the words of Socrates as reported by Plato, the cave stands for "ignorance," the "world of sight" and "world of becoming" (312; 315; 317). Shadows are projected onto one wall of the cave, and are viewed by prisoners facing this wall. They are chained to their seats so that they can only see the shadows, but not the shapes being carried past them or the light behind them. Count NN, for whom life is but a "play of Chinese shadows," appears to us in a similar "cave." And, inasmuch as he believes that his life was "predestin[ed]" (cf. in **"Something About . . ."** the "laws of necessity" governing "animal life"), he too, "chained" to his seat, faces the wall on which are projected the shadows. Like the prisoners, he can only see the shadows and cannot turn around toward the realities of the world of mind and toward its light. In particular, the count bears a striking resemblance with one "petty soul" in Socrates' allegorical cave. It has been "carrying from childhood," Socrates explains, the "leaden weights of the world of becoming," and Socrates continues: "I mean, which grow into the soul from gorging and gluttony and such pleasures, and twist the soul's eye downward" (317). Similarly, the count from childhood never had any restraint placed upon him, and never imposed any upon himself, but always gratified his every whim. He too possesses a "keen and sharp sight," as we see in his fine insight into the springs of the human psyche, and into the foolishness and calculation, the petty selfishness and vengefulness of the people around him, who are not very different from himself. Finally, like Socrates' "petty soul," he too applies his keen insight not to the pursuit of knowledge but, in Socrates' words, to the "service of vice" so that "the clearer it sees the more evil it does" (317).

The main components from the allegory of the cave which were found in this first replay may now be summarized briefly. They are: the metaphorical "cave" of ignorance and the "shadows" of realities which the chained "prisoners" in the cave, like Count NN, are doomed to view; and one "petty soul" who stands out obtrusively from their midst. This initial game is confined by the narrator-Count NN's narrow vision. For example, the issues of education and of how the prisoners are to be turned around toward the light of the mind

were left out of **"My Confession."** Nor do we find in this first replay the Philosopher who leaves the cave and later returns to it.

The second game of "Chinese shadows" in **"My Confession"** may best be described as autobiographical and personal in character. It offers another limited replay *in miniature* of Socrates' allegory of the cave reported in Plato's *Republic*. Nevertheless, compared with the first one, it offers a more amplified treatment of the imagery of the allegory, and sets forth Karamzin's variant of Socrates' allegorical Philosopher.

Among the allegorical images expanded upon in the second replay is that of the "prisoners" inside the cave, who are doomed to look at shadows and not the realities themselves. The "prisoners" may now be seen to include, besides Count NN and his associates, two diametrically opposed categories of eighteenth-century thinkers, both alien to Karamzin's Socratic-Platonic philosophy. At one extreme, the positivists and materialists, like Helvétius,[28] d'Holbach and Diderot in the West, their Russian followers, and Radiščev,[29] in their philosophical pursuits ran after the "shadows" of the "world of sight" and "world of becoming." At the other extreme, the "haters of enlightenment" (II, 129), like Rousseau and his followers, or the extreme mystics in Russian Masonry, shunned the light of the mind, preaching instead the wisdom of ignorance, and obscurantism. The two extremes met, and they shared with the immoral Count NN their failure to acknowledge the reasoning mind and to turn *toward* the world of the essences.

Finally, among the "prisoners" in the allegorical cave we discern Karamzin *prior* to his travels abroad in Europe. In **"My Confession,"** an earlier Karamzin is played off with a new one: Count NN with his author. Karamzin *after* his travels parallels the Philosopher in the allegory of the cave. Socrates' Philosopher was dragged out of the cave into the light of the sun, from where he returned to his companions down in the cave. Not only did Karamzin embrace the principles and ideals of Socratic-Platonic philosophy, but in real life, and not allegorically, he left his comparatively backward homeland and the Masons, and went out into the light of Western European countries, cultures and thought. He returned to Russia a very different person than when he left,[30] and *Letters* testifies to the pedagogical value for Karamzin of his travels. Moreover, it was in real life that Karamzin's former companions among the Masons turned against him, just as the "prisoners" who never left the cave were set against the Philosopher when he returned to the cave, and mocked him, saying that he had "spoiled his eyesight by going up there, and it was not worthwhile so much as to go up" (315). Circumstances such as these from Karamzin's personal life justify his identification with Socrates' Philosopher. To

a similar identity Karamzin alludes in the closing lines of *Letters*. Addressing his friends the Pleščeevs (to whom *Letters* is dedicated), Karamzin pictures a little retreat prepared by them, in which he would "enjoy in freedom the *Chinese shadows* of my imagination" (I, 601, italics in the original). It now appears that in these lines (written, to repeat, after **"My Confession"**) Karamzin was referring to the Socratic-Platonic orientation of his creative imagination and to the artistic form he gave this philosophy in **"My Confession."**

After the first replay of the allegory of the cave in **"My Confession,"** now the second one comes to a close. Initially, the main protagonist was Count NN, in whom was discerned a marked resemblance with the "prisoners" in "chains" in Socrates' allegorical cave of ignorance. In his outlook on life as a "play of Chinese shadows" the "shadows" appeared as projections of realities in the world of sight. In the second replay the main protagonist was Karamzin. On the figurative screen where there appeared positivist and materialist philosophers, Rousseau, and mystic thinkers, in their midst Karamzin could be discerned, as he had been prior to his enlightening travels abroad. Meanwhile, Karamzin in the present, as the creator of this expanding throng of "prisoners," assumed the role of Socrates' allegorical Philosopher.

The two replays were discussed as hermeneutical games, with emphasis on the word "games." In Plato's words Socrates termed his allegory of the cave a "puppet show" (312; 320). Analogously, in Karamzin's two zestful replays laughter is in order. At one point in the allegory Socrates, in fact, recommends laughter, not at the soul confused and unable to discern anything in the dark cave, but rather, he explains, at oneself when, in returning to the darkness in the cave, one's soul is "confused in coming out of the bright light above" (131). Similarly, Karamzin's laughter appears to have been directed to a large degree toward himself, for Count NN, we suggested, embodies in part Karamzin before his travels abroad.

With the passage of time, the distance between the author and his reader inevitably increases. The materials from Karamzin's life and works first had to be retrieved, and only afterward was it possible to project the two replays in **"My Confession."** In conclusion we address the question: Can a modern reader play a game of Chinese shadows in **"My Confession"** *without* any prior knowledge of the allegory of the cave reported by Plato in the *Republic* and *independently* from the Socratic-Platonic philosophy underlying **"My Confession"**? I believe he can, for the two concepts, the "worlds" of "existence" and "essence," with which Karamzin plays in **"My Confession,"** have engaged numerous modern writers and philosophers.

This game of hermeneutics, unlike the first and second ones, will not be epistemological so much as ontological in character, less concerned with knowledge than with being. Momentarily the light from the world of mind fades away, and the screen turns dark. The figures which previously were silhouetted on a bright screen are now bright. The brightest one moves to the center of the screen, and in it the former silhouette of Count NN can be discerned. To a far greater degree than the figures around him, he is seen living in the world of existence. Existential philosophers have discerned our "screens" from the "world of existence," and our "leaps of faith" from it into the "world of essence"; but Count NN has no need for either. Because he believes that he is free from "all rules" and "all duties," he places no value on social and moral conventions, or, indeed, on systems of any kind. He writes his confession, he declares, without any purpose, as if the act of writing, like all the actions in his life, were an act of being, in the present, here and now. He is most gleeful when his behavior seems furthest removed from a rational context or a causal connection, as in his account of how at court balls abroad he created a stir by dropping, without reason, his female partners on the floor. In one instance, the count's strange behavior is startlingly reminiscent of that of Dostoevskij's Stavrogin: when Count NN and Stavrogin bite a foot and an ear, respectively. The count, during an audience with the Pope, failing to observe the ritual kissing of the Pontiff's slipper, instead suddenly "bit the Pope's foot and made the poor man scream with all his might" (I, 731). Analogously, at the house of the governor, where he was asked to explain his strange comportment, Stavrogin bit hard this official's ear, and the soft-spoken governor endured excruciating pain. Count NN and Stavrogin appear to have been cast in comparable molds, for both seem equally free from "all rules" and "all duties."

In this last interpretation little attention was given to the *immoral* Count NN, to the harm he inflicts upon himself and others in his reckless pursuit of the pleasures of the senses. Rather, this character, walking through life with a certain existential flair, arouses astonishment. All-important in this shift is the intrusion of the issue of freedom. The count's being seems to be free, much as he boasts, and he seems fearless in his strength. But does he really possess this freedom and strength if, as he declares, he fulfilled in life his "predestination"? Karamzin's answer to this question is in the negative, since his "world of existence" is determined by immutable laws (*ustavy neobxodimosti*). Count NN's feeling of freedom is therefore illusory. It is but one more shadow in Karamzin's Socratic game of "Chinese shadows."

Notes

1. *Great Dialogues of Plato,* tr. W. H. D. Rouse, ed. Eric H. Warrington and Philip G. Rouse (New York: New American Library, 1956), 312. Henceforward, references to this edition will be given in parentheses in the text.

2. V. V. Sipovskij, *Očerki iz istorii russkogo romana,* t. I, vyp. 1-j (Zapiski Istoriko-filologičeskogo Fakul'teta Imperatorskogo S.-Peterburgskogo Universiteta, 97; SPb., 1909), 113. Disappointingly, Sipovskij gives only two examples of the immoral type of hero, or "Vol'-terjanec," both from the same work, and after stating that many may be found in Russian eighteenth-century literature.

3. "My Confession" is generally mentioned in studies and articles on Karamzin, but little if any attention is ever given to the humor (not to say laughter) which permeates the work, with the notable exception of Birgitta Hammarberg: Gunvor Birgitta Hammarberg, "Karamzin's Prose Fiction: The Poetics of Co-Creation" (Ph.D. Dissertation, Univ. of Michigan, 1982), 486-516. The Socratic-Platonic tenets, and more broadly, the philosophical considerations motivating the work have not been heretofore a focus of attention: B. Èjxenbaum, "Karamzin," in *O proze* (L.: Xud. lit., 1969), 203-13 (originally published in *Birževye vedomosti,* 2 December 1916); "Karamzin," in *Istorija russkoj literatury,* ed. P. I. Lebedev-Poljanskij et al., vol. 5, Literatura pervoj poloviny XIX veka: Čast' pervaja (M.-L.: AN SSSR, 1941), 55-105; Ju. D. Lotman, "Èvoljucija mirovozzrenija Karamzina (1789-1803)," in *Trudy istoriko-filologičeskogo fakul'teta* (Učenye zapiski Tartuskogo Gosudarstvennogo Universiteta, 51; Tartu, 1957), 155-58; also his "Puti razvitija russkoj prozy 1800-1810-x godov," in *Trudy po russkoj i slavjanskoj filologii* 4 (Učenye zapiski TGU, 104; Tartu, 1961), 31-34; F. Z. Kanunova, "Èvoljucija sentimentalizma Karamzina ('Moja ispoved'')," in *Rol' i značenie literatury XVIII veka v istorii russkoj kul'tury. K 70-letiju so dnja roždenija člena-korrespondenta AN SSSR P. N. Berkova,* ed. D. S. Lixačev et al. (XVIII vek, 7; M.-L.: Nauka, 1966), 286-90; E. N. Kuprejanova, "Russkij roman pervoj četverti XIX veka. Ot sentimental'noj povesti k romanu," in *Istorija russkogo romana,* vol. 1, ed. G. M. Fridlender (M.: AN SSSR, 1962), 72-73; Ju. D. Lotman, "Russo i russkaja kul'tura XVIII veka," in *Èpoxa prosveščenija: Iz istorii meždunarodnyx svjazej russkoj literatury,* ed. M. P. Alekseev (L.: Nauka, 1967), 275-77; A. G. Cross, *N. M. Karamzin: A Study of His Literary Career (1783-1803)* (Carbondale; Southern Illinois Univ. Press, 1971), 129-31.

4. N. M. Karamzin, *Izbrannye sočinenija* (2 vols.; M.-L.: Xud. Lit., 1962), I, 730. Henceforward, reference to this edition, by volume and page number, will be given in the text.

5. Birgitta Hammarberg ("Karamzin's Prose Fiction," 514) cautiously suggests that the name Mendel' may refer to Bernard Mandeville (1670-1733), author of *The Fable of the Bees* (1714), and with whose works Karamzin was acquainted. Mandeville displays an aphoristic style and brilliant wit, particularly in *Modest Defence of Publick Stews: or, an Essay Upon Whoring* (1724), and these qualities are oddly evocative of Karamzin's style in "My Confession"; moreover, Mandeville's argument in favor of turning human vices into public benefits seems to have inspired the count's discussion of money-lenders. However, the count takes pains to stress that Mendel' was a native of Geneva, whereas Mandeville was not. Mendel' can best be associated with Mandeville *and* Rousseau, the citizen of Geneva, since the moral philosophy of Rousseau comes under attack in "My Confession." See below in text. (Bernard Mandeville, *The Fable of The Bees: or Private Vices, Publick Benefits,* ed. F. B. Kaye [2 vols.; Oxford: The Clarendon Press, 1924], I, xvii-xxxii and xxxviii-lxxvi.)

6. A. E. Taylor, *Socrates* (Edinburgh: Peter Davies, 1933), 142-43.

7. Leonard Nelson, *Socratic Method and Critical Philosophy: Selected Essays,* tr. Thomas K. Brown, III (New Haven: Yale Univ. Press, 1949), 16.

8. Paul Foulquié, *L'Existentialisme,* 2nd ed. (Paris: Presses Universitaires de France, 1947), 14.

9. See, for example, the characterization of "Athenian Life" as an "Hellenist dream"; A. G. Cross, *N. M. Karamzin,* 117.

10. Ju. M. Lotman, "Poèzija Karamzina" in N. M. Karamzin, *Polnoe sobranie stixotvorenij,* ed. Ju. M. Lotman (Biblioteka poèta, "Bol'šaja serija"; L.: Sovetskij pisatel', 1966), 8-10.

11. Èjxenbaum, *O proze,* 120.

12. *Pis'ma N. M. Karamzina k I. I. Dmitrievu,* ed. Ja. Grot and P. Pekarskij (SPb.: Imp. Akademija Nauk, 1866), 78, 79. The philosophical essay in French is found on 85-88.

13. See Ja. L. Barskov, *Perepiska moskovskix masonov XVIII-go veka. 1780-1792* (Pg.: Otdelenie russkogo jazyka i slovesnosti Imp. Akademii Nauk, 1915), 70-100, passim.

14. Lotman, who follows an older school of thought, emphasizes Karamzin's break with Masonry, which he ascribes to the influence of contemporary eighteenth-century Western thinkers. However, Lotman gives interesting but oftentimes highly debatable interpretations of the works and of their alleged influence on Karamzin ("Èvoljucija . . . ," 124-25). Vinogradov persuasively argues that "it is impossible to speak of Karamzin's break with Masonry upon his return from his travels abroad," and that the break was with a small faction within Russian Masonry; see V. V. Vinogradov, *Problema avtorstva i teorija stilej* (M.: GIXL, 1961), 251.

15. Richard Lewis Nettleship, *Lectures on the Republic of Plato* (London: Macmillan, 1937), 226.

16. Taylor, *Socrates,* 141.

17. E.g. ". . . nos âmes se sont corrompues à mesure que nos sciences et nos arts se sont avancés à la perfection. . . . On a vu la vertu s'enfuir à mesure que / la lumière / des / sciences et des arts / s'élevait sur notre horizon. . . ." Or: "Dieu toutpuissant . . . délivre nous des lumières . . . et rend nous l'ignorance. . . ." (Jean-Jacques Rousseau, *Du Contrat Social, Discours sur les Sciences et les Arts,* et al. [Paris: Garnier, 1962], 6, 22.)

18. Rousseau's *Émile* and *La Nouvelle Héloïse* were among Karamzin's favorite works. See the article under discussion, II, 137; also I, 277.

19. Karamzin read the first volume of Rousseau's *Les Confessions* (1782) before his departure abroad, and the second (1789) shortly after its publication, during his stay in Geneva in 1789 (II, 150). He praised the psychological qualities of *Les Confessions* (I, 136).

20. Nelson, *Socratic Method,* 4.

21. Raymond Trousson, *Socrate devant Voltaire, Diderot et Rousseau: La conscience en face du mythe* (Paris: Lettres Modernes Minard, 1967), 67-103.

22. Rousseau, *Du Contrat Social,* 9. See also Trousson, 105-24.

23. N. I. Novikov, *Izbrannye sočinenija,* ed. G. P. Makogonenko (M.-L.: Goslitizdat, 1951), 101.

24. André Monnier, *Un publiciste frondeur sous Catherine II: Nicolas Novikov* (Paris: Institut d'Études Slaves, 1981), 218, 214-27.

25. *Sočinenija,* vol. 7 (M.: Tipografija S. Selivanovskogo, 1803). References to this edition will be given in parentheses in the text.

26. One should also trace back to the Socratic-Platonic features of Karamzin's philosophy, and not to eighteenth-century sensationalist and materialistic systems, Filalet's argument that all human sorrows (*goresti*) are physical and temporal in nature, hence easily overcome by reason (255-59). Karamzin's Socratic-Platonic philosophy is also

very striking when Filalet insists that social evils are not intentional but stem from ignorance, as he puts it, "an insufficiency in enlightenment" (267); cf. the Socratic-Platonic premise that vice is ignorance and therefore unintentional.

27. *Pis'ma N. M. Karamzina k I. I. Dmitrievu,* 90.

28. See in Lotman, "Èvoljucija . . . ," 137.

29. See T. Page, "Utilitarianism and Its Rebuttal in the Thought of A. N. Radishchev," in *Western Philosophical Systems in Russian Literature,* ed. Anthony M. Mlikotin (Univ. of Southern California Series in Slavic Humanities, 3; Los Angeles: Univ. of Southern California Press, 1979), 1-10.

30. See note 13 above.

Caryl Emerson (essay date 1986)

SOURCE: Emerson, Caryl. "Boris in History: Karamzin." In *Boris Godunov: Transpositions of a Russian Theme,* pp. 30-87. Bloomington: Indiana University Press, 1986.

[*In the following excerpt, Emerson examines the influence of Karamzin's* History of the Russian State *on Russian literary culture in the early nineteenth century.*]

> *Thus Russia prepared long and well for the most terrible event of her history: with the vile tyranny of Ivan's twenty-four years, with the infernal game of Boris's ambition, with the calamities brought on by vicious famine and widespread brigandage, with the hardening of hearts and corruption of the people—with everything that must precede the collapse of states condemned by Providence either to perish, or to be painfully reborn.[1]*

The appearance, in 1818, of the first eight volumes of Karamzin's **History of the Russian State** was a major cultural event. No Russian history before or since—with the possible exception of Stalin's "Short Course" during the darkest years of Soviet rule—knew so instantaneous a success, or had so concentrated an impact on a reading public. The entire printing of 3,000 copies, almost three times larger than the printings standard for the times, sold out in less than a month.[2] Literary figures of the day greeted the work enthusiastically. Vasily Zhukovsky, after hearing Karamzin read a description of the taking of Kazan, wrote to Dmitriev in a sort of ecstasy:

> What perfection! And what a new epoch has opened up for Russians with the appearance of this history! What a treasure-house for language, for poetry, not to mention all the activity it will generate in the intellect. This history could be called the resurrector of the past centuries of our people's existence. Previously, these centuries had been no more than mummies for us. . . .[3]

Prince Pyotr Viazemsky called Karamzin "our [General] Kutuzov," the man who "saved Russia from an invasion of forgetfulness, called her to life, showed us that we have a fatherland—as many had discovered in 1812."[4] And Pushkin, several years later, recalled in his reminiscences how he had devoured the first volumes of the **History** as a nineteen-year-old: "It was for us a new discovery. Ancient Russia, it seems, was discovered by Karamzin as America had been by Columbus."[5]

This initial enthusiasm, so resonant with patriotic self-consciousness, was in good part a response to the type of history Karamzin had composed. His foreword to the first eight volumes makes explicit the duties of a historian. "History," Karamzin writes, "is in a certain sense the sacred book of peoples, their main and indispensable book" (I, xvii). Its purpose is organic, to "unify what has been handed down to us by the centuries into a system clear and coherent in the harmonious correlation of its parts" (xxvi). Such correlations could be made only by a mind gifted with historical insight, which is a function of the rational patriotism of the historian: "The feelings of 'we,' 'our' enlivens the narrative; and while crude partiality—the result of weak reasoning or a weak soul—is intolerable in a historian, love of country gives his brush ardor, power, appeal" (xxv-xxvi).

The dividing line between patriotism and partiality is a subjective one. Applying to the art of history the same synthesizing criterion that the Abbé Batteux had applied to aesthetics,[6] Karamzin argues that rationalism and sensibility could be coordinated through taste, which is both a sensible decision and a sentiment. The most perfect among modern historians, Karamzin writes, would have been Hume, had he not "unnecessarily prided himself on his impartiality, and thus chilled down a fine creative work" (xxv). One should *feel*, as well as demonstrate, that history is moving in the right direction.

That "right direction" for history was perhaps clearer for Karamzin than for many of his contemporaries.[7] Successful and aggressive revolution in France had sensitized all of Europe to the idea of sudden change, and had made more urgent the historians' search for cause and effect. But 1789 found Karamzin already well formed in other, earlier traditions. For him the French Revolution was a stain on the eighteenth century, a disaster whose sole beneficial result would be to demonstrate irrefutably the sanctity of civil order—even in the presence of social injustice. Karamzin was committed to a Rousseauism without the revolutionary consequences. He insisted upon the authority of personal sentiment without the accompanying social or political rule of the middle class—that very class, in fact, which had championed the claims of individual pathos against the aristocratic criteria of birth and rank. Thus not only the **History** but its author as well was something of an

anachronism. In the Age of Napoleon, Karamzin combined a very *ancien-régime* understanding of political virtue with both sentimentalism and faith in Divine Providence; two decades into the French Revolution he could still speak of history as a "*sacred* book." This soothing blend of old and new was not lost on his readers. In November 1853, the twenty-five-year-old Leo Tolstoy jotted down in his diary that he had been browsing on and off in Karamzin's history. "The style is very fine," he wrote, "and the Foreword evoked a mass of good feelings in me."[8] That was exactly what Karamzin had intended his *History* to do.

Patriotically inspired narrative was not, however, the whole of the *History,* nor the whole reason for its success. The documentation authenticating the narrative was collected in the back of each volume in a section entitled *Primechaniia (Notes). Primechaniia* are clearly more than footnotes—they almost constitute a second text.[9] Several volumes allot more space to them than to the text itself. Sources are not just cited but verified, compared with one another, ranked for reliability, and extensively quoted; Karamzin noted discrepancies among the source material and offered his own resolutions. His sophistication in working with original texts was, for the time, considerable. Many later historians even ranked Karamzin's bibliographical and critical skills superior to those of the meticulous eighteenth-century German scholars who had worked on Russian documents; the historian Nikolai Polevoi, for one, regretted that this aspect of the *History* could not be easily appreciated or verified abroad and in translation.[10]

The *primechaniia* took on new significance after Napoleon's invasion of Russia. In the burning of Moscow in 1812, Musin-Pushkin's magnificent library, as well as Karamzin's, was reduced to ashes.[11] Many original documents would have disappeared without a trace had they not been cited in, or incorporated into, the early and still unpublished drafts of the *History.* Perhaps in response to this abrupt object lesson in the perishability of sources, Karamzin, starting with volume V, supplemented each chapter with lengthy extracts from unpublished material—even when they did not bear directly on his text.

This last aspect of the notes raises an interesting theoretical question. Not only is some of the documentation not relevant to the main text but it is on occasion in direct opposition to it. Among the more celebrated incompatibilities are Karamzin's suggestion, in the narrative, that the name for the Slavs had its origin in *slava* (glory) (I, 13), a thesis that is then refuted in *prim.* #42; and, in volume II, his claim that Vladimir Monomakh received his crown from a Byzantine emperor (II, 100), a story discredited at length in the accompanying *prim.* #220 and #221. In these instances the superscript, which usually binds authority to the narrative,

actually directs the reader to data that undo the intention of the text. Clearly there was a tension between telling the right story and objectively citing the source.

DOUBLE RESPONSE TO DOUBLE TEXT

Karamzin himself admitted, with disarming lightheartedness, that his huge amount of documentation did not make things easier or clearer for the reader. "I am myself aghast at the number of my footnotes and excerpts," he wrote in the foreword (xxvii). "The ancients were more fortunate. They did not know this trifling work, in which half the time is lost, while the mind is bored and the imagination withers. This painful sacrifice offered to authenticity is, however, unavoidable."

Karamzin hoped that his readers would feel free to dip at their own discretion into that "motley jumble, which at times serves as evidence, at times as explanation and supplement" (xxvii).

Part evidence, part explanation, part supplement: so ambivalent is the status of the *Primechaniia* that they more resemble the marginal gloss than the conventional footnote today.[12] Their very bulk in the *History* inevitably raises the issue of the nature and location of the historian's voice—and makes problematic the authority (or authorship) that voice commands. Which text can be said to authenticate the other? Can a tendentious narrative, provided with extensive documentation, reap the benefits of both objective scholarship and creative storytelling? One scholar of the *Primechaniia* has resolved the issue bluntly: "Karamzin . . . had no intention of allowing the results of his research to interfere with the socially and politically derived premises on which he built the narrative of the *History.*"[13]

The issue, however, is considerably more complex and interesting than such a dismissal suggests. As subsequent theorists have pointed out, since Karamzin's time not much progress has been made toward defining exactly what it is that a "reference to a source" is supposed to document:

> No historian in our time can allow himself the luxury of constructing footnotes in the way Karamzin did—putting into them, in extenso, the text of the source utilized. But even when we find a reference to a concrete source in a [contemporary] historical study, we are not always able to tell what the value of the source is (whether it is contemporaneous with the event or written later, tendentious or objective) and whether the point made in the study is stated directly in the source or is a deduction from the source based on a whole series of collateral references.[14]

The respectable way out of this dilemma—at least as regards Karamzin's *History*—has been simply to separate the narrative from the notes. This separating activity began soon after the *History* appeared. Poets de-

lighted in the wealth of newly available plots. Professional historians quickly repudiated the sentimental story line of the main text, while admiring (and frequently consulting) the apparatus. The bifurcated, ambivalent generic identity of the **History** continued to emit contradictory signals to successive generations of readers, and has thus provoked an especially rich and varied critical response.

The opening moves in that response give us some idea of its range and rhetoric. The first eight volumes of the **History** were praised as literature—at least among the advocates of Karamzin's stylistic reforms—and hailed as a monument to Russian culture. But they were criticized, by and large, as ideology. Karamzin's acquaintances among the Masons accused him of being an unbeliever and a Jacobin; the future Decembrists, not surprisingly, labeled him a reactionary.[15] Pushkin, just graduated from the Lycée and already long on intimate terms with the Karamzin family, wounded the Historiographer with his famous epigram:

> With elegance and simplicity his *History*
> Proves to us, utterly impartially,
> The necessity of despotism
> And the charm of the knout.[16]

But the ninth volume (1821), dealing with Ivan IV's "bad years," was received with excitement for both its literary merits and its political boldness. The first eight volumes had been folklore and heroics; volume 9 was about the abuse of power. Karamzin spared nothing in his exposure of Ivan the Terrible's crimes. Kondraty Ryleev, future Decembrist, wrote to Faddei Bulgarin in July 1821: "So that's the Terrible! So that's Karamzin! I don't know what to marvel at more, the tyranny of our Ioann or the talent of our Tacitus."[17] No doubt it was the spirit of this volume that Pushkin had in mind when he wrote his defense of Karamzin in the mid-1820s:

> Our Jacobins are displeased: a few individual observations on the benefit of autocracy, eloquently refuted by the story of events, seemed to them the height of barbarism and humiliation. They forgot that Karamzin printed his **History** in Russia, that having freed him from censorship the sovereign, by this sign of confidence, placed upon Karamzin the obligation of all possible modesty and moderation. He told his story with all the truthfulness of a historian, he everywhere referred to the sources—what more can be demanded of him? I repeat that the **History of the Russian State** is not only the creation of a great writer but the heroic deed of an honorable man.[18]

Few pursued at the time Pushkin's suggestion that there might be a dialogue, and possibly an ironic one, between Karamzin's ideological generalizations and the hard data of his sources. But most critics, in Pushkin's century and in our own, have noted an overall lack of

organic unity between the two parts of the **History,** each of which possesses a certain autonomy and historiographical style of its own.[19] One clue to this peculiar "separability" might be sought in the pre-history of the text, that is, in the state of history-writing before Karamzin.

HISTORY BEFORE KARAMZIN: TWO CATEGORIES

The great impact of Karamzin's **History** on the Russian public was due to a fortunate confluence of circumstances, some created by Karamzin himself and others the product of the political and cultural climate of early nineteenth-century Russia. The rise of Napoleon, and the sacrifice his invasion exacted, stimulated an appetite for heroic stories from the national past. This popular awareness of history, alongside Russia's emerging sense of herself as a major world power, coincided with and reinforced a change in the professional status of history. Encouraged by the liberal atmosphere of Alexander I's early years, historical societies were organized and journals founded. Count Rumiantsev headed a campaign to get chronicles and government documents into print. But this new quantity and visibility of sources did not yet constitute a history. In fact the very profusion of historical materials made all the more plain their lack of coherence. A vivid, if somewhat rhetorical, picture of the state of historical resources in Russia at the time has been provided by Karamzin's first biographer, Mikhail Pogodin:

> Libraries had no catalogues; no one had gathered together the sources, no one had organized or put them into order; chronicles were not researched, explicated, even published in a scholarly way; *gramoty* lay scattered about the monasteries and archives, no one knew the chronographs; not a single part of history had been worked out, neither of the Church, nor of law, literature, trade, customs; no preparation had been made for an ancient geography, chronology was confused, genealogies not studied. . . . Distant European travelers to Russia were known only by rumor; the works of foreign scholars, containing many scattered judgments on ancient Russia, had not been dealt with at all; not a single question out of thousands had been completely resolved, not a single contradiction reconciled.[20]

Russian histories had of course been written in the eighteenth century. But they had not been designed for a general reading public. Before Karamzin, historians of Russia could be divided into two basic categories—and neither particularly attended to the literary aspects of their enterprise. The "monarchical school" (Tatishchev, Lomonosov, Shcherbatov) wrote ideological tracts that breathed love of country but lacked objectivity and anything like a scientific methodology. The "Germans" (Bayer, Müller, Schlözer) were familiar with scholarly method, with Byzantine history and with Western Europe, but often lacked a thorough knowledge of Russian sources and (as in the case of Bayer) of the Russian

language as well.[21] At the end of the nineteenth century, the liberal historian Paul Miliukov offered a neat formulation for these two trends in Russian historiography of the preceding age. The monarchist school, he maintained, was governed by *pol'za,* benefit or purpose, and the Germans by *istina,* scientific truth—and this meant truth taken in a rather narrow sense.[22]

These terms were Miliukov's shorthand for the larger nineteenth-century debate over the purpose and method of history. At one "utilitarian" pole, history was seen as a didactic art form. Its purpose, like Voltaire's "philosophy teaching by example," was to tell a story or stress a moral. The duty of the historian, therefore, was to make details cohere and transmit a strong, positive national image. At the other, "truthful" pole, history aspired to science, to something distinct from art. Documents were expected to speak for themselves, and when they did not, scholars were to keep a source scrupulously separate from their commentary on it. In the Russian eighteenth century both schools produced texts for specialists, or for special purposes. Yet the need for a general and readable survey of Russia's national experience had been recognized throughout Catherine II's reign. The moral benefit of such a history was a central tenet in Enlightenment philosophy. Thus Karamzin set to writing his **History** at a time when both poles in Russian historiography—the "monarchists" and the "Germans"—appeared increasingly inadequate.

This inadequacy was not due to a lack of talent or energy on the part of the early practitioners. It was due, rather, to a lack of audience, and to a lack of appropriate language. The Russian eighteenth century did not possess in its native tongue a narrative style flexible enough to transmit the emerging secular national consciousness. Just as Karamzin had found no native vehicle for Russian sentimentalism in the 1780s, so at the turn of the century he found no domestic vehicle for popular history; the secularized, yet thoroughly sophisticated, Russian lexicon and diction of the **History** was largely Karamzin's own creation.[23] We may appreciate the enthusiasm of his readers and the significance of his accomplishment when we realize that his history was not only a model for future historical scholarship but also an exemplar for discursive prose.

In his foreword Karamzin noted the historians he most admired. They included the English (Gibbon, Hume) and the ancients; conspicuously absent were the two nationalities that had tried their hand at writing specifically *Russian* histories, the German and the French. In that area the models available to Karamzin were either Le Clerc's scurrilous and ill-informed *Histoire physique, moral, et politique de la Russie ancienne et moderne* (1783-94) or, on a much more respectable level, the works of the German School in and outside Russia.[24] With the latter school Karamzin took special issue.

In a memorable phrase, Schlözer had stated—with Lomonosov in mind—that "a short history of 600 years of truth" was preferable to "a long one of 3,000 years of fables."[25] And Karamzin, as if in response, commented on Schlözer in a letter to Aleksandr Turgenev by noting regretfully that the German seemed to admire those historians who "only recognized dates, and hardly ever reflect." In the same letter Karamzin expressed doubts that Schlözer would ever finish his *Nestor.* "What for?" he asked. "For seven or eight people? That's hardly worth doing. The explanations and translation of the text are very poor and often ridiculous. . . ."[26] Karamzin set himself the task of writing a historical narrative that would not only be more "useful," but also more truthful—with a different sort of truth.

This broader truth would include, first, a great deal more than earlier historians had ever admitted as evidence. In his official capacity as historian of the empire, Karamzin had access to many previously closed state and church archives, and could requisition foreign holdings as well. He drew on forty chronicles (twice as many as the previous record, set by Shcherbatov), and ultimately cited 350 authors and titles.[27] Karamzin enlarged not just the quantity but the very quality of the evidence. He treated ritual, legend, and historical song not as "fables" but as documents, whose admittedly unscientific content did not preclude a scientific investigation—and appreciation—of their role in transmitting history.[28] Second, Karamzin openly endorsed Lomonosov's partisan approach to writing about the national past. He intended his **History** to be in part a response to Lomonosov's complaint that Russian history lacked fame and glory only because it had not yet been properly embodied in art.[29] But Karamzin aimed to realize this artistic embodiment with greater factual accuracy than Lomonosov could muster, and within a much more broadly defined historical field.[30] As Karamzin wrote in an 1802 essay outlining events and characters most appropriate as subjects for the arts, "One must know what one loves, and in order to know the present we must have information about the past. . . . Not only the historian and the poet but also the painter and the sculptor can be organs of patriotism."[31] It was possible, Karamzin believed, to produce a work that was at the same time partisan, artistic, *and* true.

KARAMZIN'S *HISTORY*: "PURPOSEFUL" NARRATIVE, "TRUTHFUL" APPARATUS

According to Miliukov, a "scientific" history did not become possible in Russia until the 1820s, the first time the word *nauka* (science) was linked with history in a printed text.[32] But Miliukov insists that Karamzin was not the cause of this new development. Summing up half a century of praise and criticism for the **History,** Miliukov argues in fact the contrary, that Karamzin merely combined (and rather irresponsibly) the two ear-

lier trends in Russian historiography. "Karamzin in all earnestness strove for truth—in his *Notes*. But this was involuntary tribute to that condition introduced by the Germans into Russian historical scholarship . . ." (143).

Since Miliukov's time, readers of histories have become more sceptical, and more aware of the complexities involved in gathering and representing historical data. As Hayden White has argued in a series of influential essays, the nineteenth-century belief in the radical dissimilarity of art to science no longer holds undisputed sway. Both writers and readers of history are more receptive to the idea that "facts" are not unambiguously given, not simply found, but are in part "constructed by the kinds of questions which the investigator asks of the phenomenon before him."[33] This is not to suggest, of course, that history is just another form of fictive narrative. Whereas historians may choose among facts and among modes of emplotment, *what* they choose is still subject to verification. But it is to suggest that history, understood as the changing conventions of a place and an age, affects historical writing itself—and this principle invites a more serious investigation of different forms of historiography. Thus an emphasis on disparities in "fact," between the two parts of the *History* and between the *History* and other versions of the past, has begun to give way to more productive inquiry into the possible ideology underlying Karamzin's vision of historical integrity.

Turning first to Karamzin himself, we find very little self-reflexive commentary on his own creative method. Except for that whimsical advice to his readers in the foreword—that they should "dip into this motley mass" of documentation at their own discretion—Karamzin left no more precise guidelines for integrating narrative and notes. On this and many other questions the Karamzin archive is sparse.[34] Early drafts of the *History* are few and fragmentary. So we can only conjecture about Karamzin's integrating techniques, or seek indirect evidence from contemporaries. Nikolai Polevoi provides a clue in a critical review written one year after Karamzin's death:

> We have heard that the publication of the twelfth volume, unfinished, is now detained by the compilation of notes (the most indispensable ones). The Historiographer usually carried out that portion of his work simultaneously, and on finishing each chapter would then turn to the supplementary explanations of the text; but in putting together the twelfth volume, as if sensing that his time was precious, he hurried to complete the narrative part and planned to deal with the notes afterwards.[35]

Composing text and notes simultaneously, Karamzin may have envisaged a dialogue between the two that was rather fresh, without privileging either side as more "true." This dialogue is worth considering, for it should

not be forgotten that Karamzin, as an eighteenth-century man of letters, was quite sophisticated in matters of narrative voice and in the creation of divergent narrative perspectives. Karamzin wrote in an age when history was still perceived as part of literature. The flexibility that marked sentimental and romantic genres served to sanction a meshing of national and personal events, of public and private spheres. New generic hybrids—the novel-confession, the travel diary, the personal letter as public document—were all bringing the inner man into maximal view apart from his official roles, and self-consciously revealing the poeticality of everyday life. In the 1790s Karamzin himself had experimented with one such hybrid, the travel diary, in his semifictional *Letters of a Russian Traveler.* And long before his appointment as State Historian in 1803, Karamzin had been experimenting with the literary expression of themes from the Russian past.

These literary experiments have some relevance to the *History*. Two of Karamzin's historical tales—**"Natalia the Boyar's Daughter"** (1792) and **"Marfa Posadnitsa"** (1802)—are based on real historical events. But medieval Russian reality in them is little more than a backdrop, a visual ornament, and both language and psychological motivation belong fully to the genres of pastoral and love idyll.[36] Historiographical subtlety, such as there is, comes in the storyteller.

The teller of these historical tales is an active participant in the story, alternately asserting and then undermining its truthfulness.[37] While writing **"Natalia,"** for instance, Karamzin was in the process of translating "The Story of Le Fever" from *Tristram Shandy,* and his own tale is full of Sternean digressions and parodic footnotes elucidating the "historical sources."[38] The text of **"Marfa"** is so saturated with epic rhetoric and Homeric epithet that the tone borders on irony. [. . .] Quite early Karamzin developed a characteristic "image of the author" in his works—and an image, moreover, that implied a certain sort of reader. Author and reader in Karamzin's narratives are intimates, eager to further the same goals, and fully aware of the tricks literature can play.

The very "trickiness" of literature could well have been one reason behind Karamzin's decision to turn to history.[39] For if narrators can manipulate readers and render stories ironic, then authors—even as they orchestrate these effects—inevitably lose authority. Karamzin's literary activity took shape amid eighteenth-century debates over the effectiveness of fiction versus history as a means of moral instruction. Having chosen history, Karamzin did not part with literary devices. But he did more openly acknowledge their power to corrupt and seduce, and stressed the boundary separating history from fiction. As he wrote in an essay of 1803, "In several years, history will occupy us considerably more

than novels; for the mature mind, truth has a special charm which does not exist in fictions."[40]

The "mature mind," Karamzin implies, can confront the truth of history, honestly told in all its moral ambivalence. Readers of novels, on the other hand, are conditioned to distrust narrators—and to identify with, perhaps even to imitate, the heroes of fictional texts. But both categories of reader insist upon *charm*. In this sense Karamzin perceived his new task as an extension into historiography of the service he had provided for Russian fictional literature a decade earlier. It would become his goal to show that the real life of a nation, just like the real life of an individual, is filled with poetry.[41]

This romantic concept of history as heroic biography, as a story to be told through symbolic personalities like tsars, became Karamzin's dominant mode for telling Russia's story. In the *History,* of course, the characters of romance have a more complex role to play than did their counterparts in the historical tales. They are still engaged in a struggle of virtue over vice. But the characters now have their biographies documented by a massive scholarly apparatus, and are themselves subordinated to a suprapersonal national destiny. The author regains authority, yet the storyteller still enchants. Romantic emplotment thus loses romantic irony and begins to serve serious patriotic purpose.

This artistry and partisanship were not naïve. Karamzin constructed his image of a historian carefully amid various alternatives.[42] Throughout his life he remained convinced that a historian should be predominantly a moral, rather than a scientific or (for that matter) a mystical, force. When the quest for universal history created an enthusiasm for broad periodizations and "laws" of history, Karamzin remained unmoved. The so-called Sceptical School, which arose in the first half of the nineteenth century to challenge Karamzin's historical methodology, prided itself (and perhaps justly) on a more politically independent stance. But as Karamzin would have easily divined, its use of sources was hardly more objective.[43] Its "higher criticism," which subjected data to the so-called laws of history, embodied that very mysticism which Karamzin considered so disrespectful to the stories that the sources themselves told.[44] Karamzin's scholarship, in other words, was subjective, but the subjectivity was forthright, not concealed under cover of "objective" laws that presumed to transcend individual interpretation. As his foreword to the *History* intimated, the admission of subjectivity where it must exist was a part of true objectivity.

Not surprisingly, Karamzin's brand of sentimental-moral history has had its periods of greater and lesser favor. It should be remembered, however, that his work was not so much reevaluated critically as it was subjected to shifting definitions of what constituted proper history.

Karamzin had written in the conviction that history was compatible with, perhaps even a part of, poetry—and therefore could combine in one organic whole the particular (in need of verification) and the universal, which was beyond notions of verification and causation. When history and poetry parted ways, Karamzin's type of history seemed anachronistic and improperly motivated. Nikolai Polevoi reviewed the *History* in *Moskovskii telegraf* (1829),[45] when Karamzin had been dead scarcely three years, yet the bulk of his review is taken up with a case for the historian's outdatedness. "For us, the new generation, Karamzin exists only in the history of literature and in his own literary creations. We can no longer be carried away by a personal passion for him, or by his passions . . ." (470). Among those passions, the most damaging was Karamzin's concept of history as a force residing entirely in the Personality. To Polevoi, the *History of the Russian State* was in effect a history of psychologized personalities, and this was intimately bound up with Karamzin's conception of autocracy as a personalized state.

Not until the Marxist historians, it could be argued, was this issue of personality decisively confronted.[46] And not surprisingly, the Soviet historical establishment has been for the most part unsympathetic to Karamzin.[47] Recently, however, there have been signs of new interest in and appreciation of Karamzin's work. In 1979 A. Gulyga lamented the fact that the *History of the Russian State* had been so long out of print, and that no scholarly Soviet edition had yet been published.[48] History, Gulyga insisted, need not be "documentary." Karamzin performs another service; he reminds us that both art and history routinely violate their own definitions. "History," Gulyga wrote, "is the science which forever exceeds its own limits, literature is the art which always oversteps its own boundaries . . ." (215).

Generic flexibility is but one step away from ideological flexibility, and that step was in fact taken in a recent popular Soviet treatment of Karamzin's career as historian. The study concludes by invoking Collingwood, with this observation:

> Every historian is limited by the facts which come down (or do not come down) to him . . . Karamzin writes less than did later historians on economic questions, on the importance of popular resistance, etc. And why? Because with utter sincerity he believes, in the spirit of his upbringing, position, world outlook, that those questions are not that important; we do not agree with him today, but it is quite possible that we ourselves are relegating to the sidelines as secondary something that the twenty-second or twenty-fourth century will talk about most of all.[49]

Such relativism in history is not, certainly, an approved position in the Soviet historical establishment. But the fact that Karamzin provides an occasional opportunity to raise this issue makes his further fate in Soviet historiography worth following.

One aspect of this increased interest in Karamzin's historical method is of special importance to this study. For it could be argued that the most productive feature of Karamzin's system is not its play with the status of historical fact per se—that ground, however reworked, is the familiar one of hostility between text and notes. More useful for a reading of the Boris Tale is an approach exploring the principles by which Karamzin integrated "fact" into the fabric of his narrative.

Such techniques of integration have recently received considerable attention from the new generation of Soviet Karamzin scholars, most notably L. N. Luzianina.[50] One way of reshaping the inquiry, then, would be to assume that many potential narratives lurk in the *Primechaniia*. Whereas Karamzin fully realized only one, that one narrative was a complex hybrid, with multiple ties to its source material. This complexity was noticed a century ago by Mikhail Pogodin. In the 1860s he wrote (already somewhat defensively) that

> Karamzin presented many events as if they were truly re-created in our imagination: he portrayed a number of figures [under discussion are Boris Godunov, the Pretender, and Ermak] in such a way that they actually come to life before us, if not always in their own life then at least in that life which the artist imparted to them at various moments of their activity.[51]

Pogodin is suggesting here that several different levels of authenticity coexist in any history. A historical event can "come to life" in a number of ways: by appearing real to a current generation of readers, or real to the recorder of the event ("the spirit of the source"), or real to the historical participants themselves.

Karamzin does not attempt to re-create the last authenticity, a version of the event as it might have been experienced in its own time. By our standards, Karamzin is in fact quite ahistoric, even anachronistic. He underestimates change and historical specificity on both the individual and cultural planes. But this is not surprising. The generally accepted timetable for universal history (7000 years since the creation of the world, 5000 years of human history since the Flood) made available much less time for change and encouraged a static conception of human nature. As a matter of course Karamzin assumed an unchanging universal psychology and a stable set of motivations for all people in all situations.[52]

We do, however, get the first two authenticities in the *History*: a spirit true to the source, and a spirit true for the early nineteenth-century reader. In fact, the dialogue between these two realities constitutes the key to Karamzin's style. This dialogue is an uneasy one.

Never does Karamzin work out a stable relationship between his own "historian's" viewpoint and the viewpoints embedded in the sources. The boundaries of his own narrative voice are unstable, at times penetrated by the voices of the documents he cites and at other times impermeable to them. Karamzin's own aesthetic principles were in continual flux during his twenty-five years' work on the *History*; he constructed and amended his methodology as he went along. The twelve volumes as a whole therefore reflect [. . .] a set of shifting chronotopes—that is, a set of different realities transmitted by a narrative voice that changes perspective on the time and space of the telling.

DEFINING KARAMZIN'S CHRONOTOPE

Karamzin's various chronotopes are related to one another in a sequence that reflects the historian's evolving attitude toward his sources—and most particularly, his attitude toward the medieval chronicle. As Luzianina has shown in her investigation into the *History*,[53] Karamzin draws on chronicles in two quite different ways. First, he incorporates and comments upon the past events recounted there from the perspective of the present—that is, he objectifies the event as a historian of his own time. Second, he embeds the chronicle account directly in his narrative, fuses his own authoritative voice with the voice of the chronicler, and thus achieves an integrated picture that breathes "the spirit of the time"—which is to say, the time of the chronicler, and, from the perspective of the chronicler, the time of the event as well.

The first approach dominates the early volumes. There, Karamzin keeps the chronicler's voice and the historian's voice carefully separate. Accounts are clearly marked as authored versions by such closing tactics as "Thus our chroniclers tell us . . ." (I, 110) or such opening phrases as "Writers who have seen this with their own eyes have preserved . . ." (I, 58). Chronicle accounts are set off as such by quotation marks, which are visibly repeated (according to the printing conventions of the time) at the beginning of each line. And they are often prefaced with elaborate disclaimers, as in the case of Nestor's manifestly formulaic account of Olga's Revenge against the Drevlianians (I, 108-10):

> Here the chronicler tells us many details incompatible with both the probabilities of reason and the dignity of history, taken, without a doubt, from a popular *folktale*; but as a true event must lie at their base, and since ancient fables are themselves of interest to the inquiring mind as a portrayal of the customs and spirit of the time, we will repeat Nestor's simple tale.

Because Karamzin distances his own time from the time he describes, in these early volumes he rarely censures the Kievan princes morally. Their sins are accepted as sins of the age—although the chronicles upon which the accounts depend often openly lament the internecine strife. Legend, myth, and folklore freely enter the narrative, bracketed by a neutral and uncritical voice

and justified as *kolorit,* "local color"—or, rather, temporal color. In this technique lies an implicit appreciation of changing moral standards, a sense of anachronism, and perhaps a kind of incipient historical relativism as well.

Starting with volume VII, and specifically with the subjugation of Pskov, there is a change in the way the chronicle material is integrated. Factual data from later sources begin to be woven into the laments of the chroniclers. Thus their special tone is no longer isolated but begins to penetrate the larger narrative, participating as a seamless part of the text and thereby partaking of a portion of the historian's authority. The narrative purpose is no longer to juxtapose various accounts of an event from an outside and later perspective but to recreate in the text a "chronicle view of the world."[54] When in 1806 Karamzin wrote, apropos of the *History,* that he had begun to "freely transmit the spirit,"[55] this shift in chronotope must have been already well under way.

As Luzianina demonstrates, the ninth volume (1821), on the tyrannical years of Ivan IV, achieves a significant new synthesis.[56] Karamzin assumes the perspective of the times, partially impersonating its values, and so allows himself to enter the minds of the people he describes. Opening his description of the Terrible Tsar, Karamzin writes:

> History does not resolve the question of man's moral freedom. But by putting forth its own judgment on actions and characters, it clarifies, first, various inherent qualities of people, and, second, the circumstances or impressions of objects that act on the soul.

> (IX, 5)

This new psychological mode of analysis ("clarifying . . . what acts on the soul") was familiar to readers of sentimental fiction. It permitted Karamzin to expose, even to exaggerate, Ivan the Terrible's crimes, while at the same time motivating those crimes with intense inner soliloquies that serve to "explain" the action—however apparently mad. The reader would feel, perhaps even sympathize with, the *intimacy* of the horror. A suffering soul that had become so spectacularly available would doubtless be censured, but it would also be "understood." Thus Karamzin could reveal and condemn the crimes of an individual monarch while retaining an emotional sympathy for the pain, and burden, inherent in the institution of the monarchy as a whole.

This perspective required, however, some major reworking of chronicle material. Karamzin's medieval sources did not approach the inner world that way. The narrative voice of the *History* had begun, we recall, by bracketing the chronicler, and then gradually had absorbed the chronicler's moral tone and world view into itself. Now the narrator had to transcend that perspective. Somehow a thoroughly romantic emplotment would have to be grafted onto the original "chronicle chronotope," where it had little organic place. Karamzin signals the shift in his introductory remarks to Ivan's first mass tortures and executions:

> His soul, once desirous of good, did not of course turn vicious overnight: the achievements of good and evil are gradual. But the chroniclers could not penetrate into that soul's interior, they could not see in it a conscience struggling with turbulent passions; they saw only terrifying deeds, and called Ioann's tyranny an *alien storm,* sent from the depths of Hell to torment and torture Russia.

> (IX, 13)

Karamzin's narrative voice has now gained indiscriminate access to both external and internal perspective. In effect, he combines the psychological perspective of his own time with the events and perspectives of the chronicles, in order to narrate what a chronicler might have seen if he had asked nineteenth-century questions.

Among these "nineteenth-century questions" the most prominent was the question of moral choice. The story of Boris Godunov is in fact structured around this issue, but traces of the older chronicle perspective persist. Although Boris is presumed free to choose—that freedom alone justifies a psychological narrative—the plot prepared for him by the chroniclers makes no provision for this freedom of choice. Thus chronicle accounts take on yet a further authority: fused with the general narrative, they determine not only the "spirit of the times" but also the details of individual moral character. This new fused narration is most evident during descriptions of the Time of Troubles, and especially whenever Karamzin touches upon the death of Dmitri of Uglich. As Luzianina observes, by this point in his writing of the *History* Karamzin had "erased the boundary between an analytical and an emotional attitude toward the facts of history."[57]

In the early volumes of the *History,* then, chronicle narration is introduced to invoke *its own time.* This is the time of the recorder, which is presumed contemporaneous with the event and kept in check by external commentary. By the final volumes, chronicle interpretation is itself a primary source for the psychologized motivation of heroes and villains, and the exemplary victim of this new methodology is Boris Godunov. The portrait that emerges is not Boris in his own time, not even Boris in the chroniclers' time, but Boris as an eternal psychological type, for *any* time, including the time of the historian's writing and of the reader's present. This shift in the chronotope of chronicle material, from limited and encapsulated to essentially universal, is perhaps the single most significant feature in the evolution of Karamzin's historical style.

THE LAYERING OF A SOURCE

Today it can easily be shown that Karamzin was naïve in his use of the medieval chronicle.[58] Although he knew that chroniclers did not tell everything,[59] he apparently believed that they "did not, at least, make anything up either,"[60] and thus could be used as reliable building blocks to reconstruct a historical event. What made a source truthful for Karamzin was its age. In the words of one modern scholar, Karamzin's internal criticism ceased as soon as he had access to "the indubitably authentic, the most ancient (preferably *kharateinye*, parchment) manuscripts, closest to the times described in them."[61] Apart from the manifestly miraculous or fairy-tale aspect of some early chronicle accounts, Karamzin assumed that "a true event lay at the base" of a chronicle view of the world. Thus the distinctiveness of the chronicle, in Karamzin's view, was not to be found in the degree of its veracity but in its special sense of time, its chronotope. "The historian is not a chronicler," Karamzin wrote in his foreword (xxvi-xxvii). "The latter considers only time, while the former considers the affinity and interconnectedness of events."

This view is, of course, a considerable oversimplification. It is true that the organizing principle of Muscovite chronicles remained simple chronology; the sixteenth-century chronicle compilation was conceptually rather primitive as a history-bearing genre.[62] To this extent Karamzin was correct in his claim that chronicles "considered only time." Events of several years' duration were cut up and distributed so that any internal cohesion or thematic unity was lost. As Edward Keenan has colorfully expressed it, ". . . scraps of *vitae*, accounts of miracles and hailstorms, martial tales and fragments of diplomatic correspondence were hung on the 'years,' like a shapeless pile of clothing on a coat rack. . . ."[63]

But even with their coat-rack organization, these "omnibus chronicles" were quite thoroughly ideological. Aleksei Shakhmatov, pioneering Russian philologist, demonstrated at the turn of this century that the language of the chronicles was a carrier of political passions and worldly interests.[64] Soviet scholarship has followed this line, assigning chronicle compilations to medieval genres of literary—and political—creativity.[65] The greatest Soviet medievalist, Dmitri Likhachev, assures us that the famous literary image of Pushkin's Pimen, casting "an indifferent eye on good and evil," was not an accurate representation of the typical chronicler.[66] Chroniclers recorded their accounts in the heat of the moment. It was the later compiler, "mechanically unifying a series of chronicles," who lent them an air of impartial authority. The appearance of objectivity was bestowed by the very process of becoming old, of being recopied and collated by later hands. In effect, therefore, chronicles can only be understood by presuming a double author for each passage: the one who recorded it, and the one who lent the tone of the whole to each part that he compiled.

Karamzin's *History* thus achieves a wonderful irony. By assuming the nonpartisan legitimacy of his sources and then blurring the line between his own critical voice and the voice of the chronicler, Karamzin in effect returns the chroniclers to their original partisan stance. He becomes a later compiler but in reverse, bestowing authority with the increasingly subjective intervention of a narrative "I." It is an "I," furthermore, that pretends to full access and full historical perspective. This constitutes "pretense" because Karamzin could not really return to the original perspective of each passage. He could only add yet another perspective layer—a sort of negation of the negation—which actually complicated perspective under the guise of apparent simplicity.

* * *

This chronotopic approach to the *History* makes possible a more historically responsive criticism than the work has usually received. Without a doubt, the two-part text of the *History* is internally contradictory and double voiced. But the confusion in it comes not merely because two voices, historian's and chronicler's, coexist in a single work. Confusion comes when the boundaries between voices begin to disappear, when the principle for incorporating source material into the narrative begins to shift or change focus. It was this threshold quality of the text that Pushkin surely had in mind when he called Karamzin "our first historian and our last chronicler."[67]

Notes

1. N. M. Karamzin, *Istoriia Gosudarstva Rossiiskogo,* vol. XI (St. Petersburg: Evdokimov, 1892; reprint ed. Slavistic Printings and Reprintings 189/11, The Hague, Mouton, 1969), 72. All references are made to this twelve-volume edition. Translations are my own.

2. Ya. Eidel'man, *Poslednii letopisets* (Moscow: "Kniga," 1983), 95. The first eight volumes of the *History* were published in 1818 (although vols. I-III are inscribed 1816, and vols. IV-VIII, 1817); volume IX appeared in 1821, volumes X and XI in 1824, and the twelfth volume, left incomplete at the author's death, was published in 1829.

3. Zhukovsky to I. I. Dmitriev, 18 Feb. 1816. In V. A. Zhukovskii, *Sochineniia v trekh tomakh,* vol. 3 (Moscow: Khudozhestvennaia literatura, 1980), 483.

4. P. A. Viazemsky, as cited in N. L. Rubinshtein, *Russkaia istoriografiia* (Moscow: OGIZ/Gospolitizdat, 1941), 186. Efforts to verify this

quotation in Viazemsky's own writings have been unsuccessful. I thank William Mills Todd, however, for referring me to various echoes of this sentiment, especially in Viazemsky's *Staria zapisnaia knizhka* (Leningrad: Izdatel'stvo pisatelei, 1929), 71.

5. A. S. Pushkin, "[Iz avtobiograficheskikh zapisok]," Nov. 1824. *P:Pss* XII, 305.

6. See the discussion in Henry M. Nebel, Jr., *N. M. Karamzin, A Russian Sentimentalist* (The Hague: Mouton, 1967), 88-90.

7. For the discussion that follows, I am indebted to Sidney Monas, whose provocative commentary on a late draft of this chapter is everywhere reflected and especially in this paragraph.

8. L. N. Tolstoi, *Sobranie sochinenii,* vol. 19 (Moscow: Khudozhestvennaia literatura, 1965), 120.

9. For an excellent analysis of the *Primechaniia,* but one that nevertheless does not attempt to resolve their ambivalent authority, see J. L. Black, "The Primečanija: Karamzin as a 'Scientific' Historian of Russia," in *Essays on Karamzin: Russian Man-of-Letters, Political Thinker, Historian, 1766-1826,* ed. J. L. Black (The Hague: Mouton, 1975), 127-47.

10. See N. Polevoi, "Spor v nemetskikh zhurnalakh ob *Istorii gosudarstva Rossiiskogo,*" *Moskovskii telegraf* XVIII (1827): 216-17: "Without a doubt Schlözer, creator of a critical survey of northern history, would have read with lofty envy the first chapters of the *History of the Russian State*; they are written with the help of his far-sighted criticism, but perfected to an extent that Schlözer could not have expected from his own indirect researches."

11. Karamzin to A. I. Turgenev, 21 January 1813: "My library had the honor of turning into ashes together with the Palace of Facets; my manuscripts, however, are safe and sound in Ostafievo. It's great pity about the Pushkin manuscripts: they all burned, except those that were with me. An irretrievable loss for our History! The University also lost everything: the library, the study." "Pis'ma N. M. Karamzina k A. I. Turgenevu," *Russkaia starina* 97 (January-March 1899): 237.

12. For an excellent discussion of the potential of the gloss, see Lawrence Lipking, "The Marginal gloss," *Critical Inquiry* 3, no. 4 (Summer 1977): 609-55. In Lipking's view (612), the gloss serves to reaffirm the relation of part to whole in an environment where parts cohere: the world is a book, and glosses help to understand what is already there, "an unfolding of parallel, equally authoritative meanings into infinity" (622). By the end of the seventeenth century the gloss had lost its authority; authors had become self-conscious. The gloss began to suggest not the fulfillment of One Text but the disintegration of texts into many infinitely valid readings. Facts, so-called, were relegated to footnotes.

See also the opening comments in Shari Benstock, "At the Margin of Discourse: Footnotes in the Fictional Text," *PMLA* (March 1983): 204:

> By definition, footnotes are physically more constrained than the primary text . . . their purpose being to elaborate on the text without engulfing it; at the same time, they are freer to adopt a new line of rhetoric. Again, this split capability invites a shift in perspective and function, and the notations adjust the limits of the textual universe in which they participate. . . . Finally, footnotes appear to be (and often are) afterwords, appended to a text that is not in itself fully accessible to readers. . . . They allow the writer to step outside the critical discourse and comment on it from a perspective that may be different from (and in a voice that may be separate from) that established in the text.

The *Primechaniia* seem to lie somewhere between footnote and gloss. Karamzin awards both parts of his *History* equal but different authority: his *primechanie* is not (as is a footnote) a true gesture of submission to a largely scholarly truth upon which the text is dependent.

13. J. L. Black, "The Primečanija," 137-38.

14. J. Luria (Ya. S. Lur'e), "Problems of Source Criticism (with Reference to Medieval Russian Documents)," trans. Michael Cherniavsky, *Slavic Review* XXVII, 1 (1968): 21.

15. See M. O. Koialovich, *Istoriia russkogo samosoznaniia* (St. Petersburg, 1884), 172-75. Nikita Muraviev devoted an entire lengthy essay to refuting the foreword, insisting that "not peace but eternal battle should exist between evil and good," and that the role of history was not to "reconcile us with imperfection" but to "urge us on to perfection." See "Zapiska Nikity Murav'eva 'Mysli ob Istorii Gosudarstva Rossiiskogo' N. M. Karamzina," in "Dekabristy-kritiki 'Istorii Gosudarstva Rossiiskogo' N. M. Karamzina," *Literaturnoe nasledstvo* I (Dekabristy-literatory) (Moscow: Izd. Akademii nauk SSSR, 1954), 585.

16. *P:Pss* XVII, 16. In Pushkin's defense, however, it should be noted that this epigram—however

cruel—was not wrong. It is precisely the *necessity* of autocracy that Karamzin was defending, in keeping with his understanding of human nature and the lessons of Russian history. I thank Sidney Monas for this observation.

Several anti-Karamzin epigrams of the period were attributed to Pushkin, but he ultimately acknowledged authorship of only one. For an extended discussion of Pushkin's motivations behind this and later statements on Karamzin, which includes good background on the aesthetic and political reception of the *History* in the teens and twenties (the odd alliances it fostered, the parodies it spawned, and the surprise of its "archaicized" sentimental style), see V. Vatsuro, "'Podvig chestnogo cheloveka,'" *Prometei* (Moscow) 5 (1968): 8-51.

17. K. F. Ryleev to F. Bulgarin, 20 July 1821. In *Sochineniia i perepiska Kondratiia Fyodorovicha Ryleeva* (St. Petersburg: tip. Glazunova, 1874), 215.

18. A. S. Pushkin, "[Iz avtobiograficheskikh zapisok]," *P:Pss* XII, 306. Pushkin wrote the passage in 1824-25 and published it in *Severnye Tsvety* in 1828. The poet himself had just been released from institutional censorship into the personal censorship of the tsar; he was not yet fully aware of what that entailed. For an excellent discussion of Pushkin's defense of Karamzin in terms of the institutions of literature in the 1820s (patronage, the salon, and commercial publishing), see William Mills Todd III, "Institutions of Literature in Early-Nineteenth-Century Russia: Boundaries and Transgressions," in *Literature and History: Theoretical Problems and Russian Case Studies,* ed. Gary Saul Morson (Stanford: Stanford University Press, 1986), 79-85.

19. See, for example, Rubinshtein, *Russkaia istoriografiia,* 176-77; V. I. Astakhov, *Kurs lektsii po russkoi istoriografii,* Part One (Kharkov: Izd. Kharkovskogo univ-ta, 1959), 144-45; B. P. Gorodetskii, *Dramaturgiia Pushkina* (Moscow: Akademia nauk, 1953), 142-44.

20. M. Pogodin, *Nikolai Mikhailovich Karamzin po ego sochineniiam, pis'mam i otzyvam sovremennikov,* II (Moscow: tip. Mamontova, 1866), 24-25. It should be pointed out, however, that Pogodin's "picture of pre-Karamzinian chaos" was subjected to severe criticism by Paul Miliukov in the 1890s. See *Glavnyia techeniia,* 129, in note 22 below.

21. Rubinshtein, *Russkaia istoriografiia,* 153.

22. P. Miliukov, *Glavnyia techeniia russkoi istoricheskoi mysli,* 3d. (St. Petersburg: Averianov, 1913), 143. The work, first published in 1897, was quickly recognized as the first radical reconsideration of Karamzin in the context of the nineteenth century.

23. For an excellent brief survey of Karamzin's contributions to language in the context of the eighteenth century, see Hans Rogger, *National Consciousness in Eighteenth-Century Russia* (Cambridge: Harvard University Press, 1960), ch. III ("Towards a National Language"), especially 120-25.

24. For a good discussion of Karamzin's positive (and negative) models, see K. N. Bestuzhev-Riumin, "Karamzin kak istorik," *Zhurnal ministerstva narodnogo proveshcheniia,* pt. 83 (St. Petersburg: Golovin, 1867): 1-20, especially 9-12.

25. Cited in J. L. Black, *Nicholas Karamzin and Russian Society in the Nineteenth Century: A Study in Russian Political and Historical Thought* (Toronto: University of Toronto Press, 1975), 38.

26. Karamzin to A. I. Turgenev, 3 April 1810. "Pis'ma N. M. Karamzina k A. I. Turgenevu, 1806-1826," *Russkaia starina* 97 (February 1899): 231.

27. Eidel'man, *Poslednii letopisets,* 57.

28. In a brief essay on his sources (included in the early printings of the *History* but omitted in later editions), Karamzin listed fourteen categories of historical material he had utilized as evidence. Among the expected chronicles, state papers, and church documents one finds (for example) "rituals," and then an entry on "ancient coins, medals, inscriptions, folktales, songs, proverbs." See "Ob istochnikakh rossiiskoi istorii do XVII veka," in N. M. Karamzin, *Istoriia Gosudarstva Rossiiskogo,* vol. I (St. Petersburg, 1818), xxvii-xxxv.

29. See Lomonosov's introduction to his *Ancient Russian History* (1766): "Anyone who sees in Russian legends deeds and heroes equal and similar to the Greeks and Romans has no reason to denigrate us in the face of them but should lay the blame on the heretofore insufficiency of our art. It was through art that Greek and Latin writers transmitted their heroes to eternal posterity, in full glory." "Vstuplenie" to *Drevniaia rossiiskaia istoriia ot nachala rossiiskogo naroda do konchiny velikogo kniazia Yaroslava pervogo* (St. Petersburg: Akademiia nauk, 1766); reprinted in M. V. Lomonosov, *Polnoe sobranie sochinenii* VI (Moscow-Leningrad: Akademiia nauk, 1952), 170.

Lomonosov's 1764 essay, "Idei dlia zhivopisnykh kartin iz rossiiskoi istorii" ("Ideas for vivid pictures from Russian history") is a forerunner of Karamzin's 1802 essay, "On Events and Characters in Russian History that Can Be the Subject of

the Arts." See also the discussion by T. S. Karlova, "Esteticheskii smysl istorii v tvorcheskom vospriiatii Karamzina," in *XVIII Vek,* sb. 8 (Derzhavin i Karamzin v literaturnom dvizhenii XVIII-nachala XIX veka) (Nauka, Leningrad, 1969), 282-83.

30. Lomonosov himself is subject to numerous "corrections" in Karamzin's notes. For a brief discussion, see J. L. Black, "The Primečanija," 146.

31. N. M. Karamzin, "O sluchaiakh i kharakterakh v rossiiskoi istorii, kotorye mogut byt' predmetom khudozhestv" ("On Events and Characters in Russian History that Can Be the Subject of the Arts"), originally published in *Vestnik Evropy,* 1802, no. 24. Cited here from *Sochineniia Karamzina,* 4th ed., vol. 7 (St. Petersburg: tip. Smirdina, 1834), 223, 222.

32. Miliukov credits this formulation to Srednii-Kamashev, whose article "Istoriia, kak nauka" appeared in *Vestnik Evropy* in 1827 ([Miliukov,] *Glavnye techeniia,* 5).

33. Hayden White, "The Burden of History" (1966), in *Tropics of Discourse* (Baltimore: Johns Hopkins University Press, 1978), 28, 43.

34. For reasons both political and physical (his connection with Novikov and the Masons, the later Moscow Fire), Karamzin either destroyed, or witnessed the destruction of, many of his personal papers. Letters addressed to him have not survived. Since his family was not subject to the official postmortem search (as was, say, Pushkin's widow), personal materials were dispersed in private hands. See Eidel'man, *Poslednii letopisets,* 60, 148.

Even under the best circumstances, however, Karamzin's archive might well have provided no "keys" to his development. As one recent scholar has remarked, "[His] letters are not a very reliable source. The Historiographer never entrusted himself fully to paper. Privy to state service for decades, he was accustomed to being cautious. . . . His favorite form was the hint, his favorite trope, the figure of passing over in silence. In general he was a man of few words." Vatsuro, "'Podvig chestnogo cheloveka,'" 31.

35. N. Polevoi, "Spor v nemetskikh zhurnalakh ob *Istoriia Gosudarstva Rossiiskogo,*" *Moskovskii telegraf* XVIII (1827): 208.

36. See N. Apostolov, "Karamzin, kak romanist-istorik," in *Zhurnal ministerstva narodnogo prosveshcheniia* (Petrograd: Senatskaia), Part 62 (April 1916): 190-98.

37. For a detailed analysis of the various narrative voices developed by Karamzin in his prose, see

Roger B. Anderson, *N. M. Karamzin's Prose: The Teller in the Tale* (Houston: Cordovan Press, 1974), especially 86-100, 190-208, 264-70.

38. "More than one old man has assured me of the truth of this," Karamzin's narrator informs the reader in a footnote to his assertion that Natalia's father, Matvei, was a good host. "Natalia, boiarskaia doch'," in N. M. Karamzin, *Izbrannye sochineniia,* vol. I (Moscow-Leningrad: Khudozhestvennaia literatura, 1964), 624.

39. I am grateful to Judith Vowles of Yale University for sharing with me her thoughts on this topic, which draw on her own research into Karamzin's vexed relationship with eighteenth-century literary models. See also the discussion in Henry M. Nebel, Jr., *N. M. Karamzin, A Russian Sentimentalist* (The Hague: Mouton, 1967), ch. VIII ("Prose: Historical, Moral, and Romantic Tales"), especially 151.

40. "Istoricheskiia vospominaniia i zamechaniia na puti k Troitse," in N. M. Karamzin, *Sochineniia Karamzina,* vol. 8 (Moscow: tip. Selivanskogo, 1804), 377.

41. See G. Makogonenko, "Literaturnaia pozitsiia Karamzina v XIX veke," *Russkaia literatura,* no. 1 (1962): 68-106, especially 103-104.

42. Karamzin criticized, for example, the fragmentation and failure to synthesize events that marked some contemporary historians. Commenting on Fesler's *History of Hungary* in a letter to A. I. Turgenev, he allowed that the man "wrote intelligently and well," but his work was all "copied from others without discrimination, without criticism . . . it is a compilation, but not a creation, there is no unity, no character, no soul." (Karamzin to A. I. Turgenev, 20 October 1815, in "Pis'ma N. M. Karamzina k A. I. Turgenevu, 1806-1826," *Russkaia starina* 97 [February 1899]: 469.) The improper unity was no improvement, however. Karamzin was exasperated with the new "philosophical" schools of history. When he received from S. S. Uvarov one of Schlegel's recent books, he retorted, "Isn't he just chasing after the specter of new ideas? He makes secondary causes primary, it's a sort of historical mysticism. . . ." (Cited in Eidel'man, *Poslednii letopisets,* 74.)

43. "The skeptical school," one recent scholar has noted, "understood the critique of a source basically as a confrontation of its testimony with some general system of historical development established *a priori.*" See J. Luria (Ia. S. Lur'e), "Problems of Source Criticism (with Reference to Medieval Russian Documents)," 2.

44. See Bestuzhev-Riumin, "Karamzin kak istorik," 11: "Everything foggy [*tumannoe*] was repellent

to Karamzin." Also consider Pogodin's comment on Karamzin's naïve methodology: "While telling his tale, Karamzin did not think about system; he presumed, apparently, that system should emerge naturally from the narration; he wanted only the truth, which would itself instruct, and every pre-determined direction of history was harmful to it." M. Pogodin, *Nikolai Mikhailovich Karamzin,* II, 194.

45. N. Polevoi, *"Istoriia Gosudarstva Rossiiskago (Sochinenie N. M. Karamzina),"* *Moskovskii telegraf* (1829, Part 27): 467-500.

46. An instructive, if extreme, example might be found in Mikhail Pokrovsky, whose *History of Russia from Earliest Times* (1910-14) was a work as fraught with controversy as Karamzin's own. Pokrovsky represented a mode of social and mate-rialist historiography wedged, as it were, between the nineteenth-century historians (still organized around the reigns of tsars) and the *re*-glorification of heroes and great national leaders under Stalin. An admirer of Lenin, Pokrovsky was not blind to the force of great men in history. But he opposed portraying Russia's past as a series of tsars, and just as strenuously opposed a past composed of Pugachevs. A history of monarchs, *and* one of revolutionaries, were both histories of individual personality, and equally un-Marxist.

Pokrovsky's chapters on the *Smuta* could not be more different from Karamzin's. Issues of murder and guilt are dismissed as slander, and the empha-sis is on the social classes supporting Boris's can-didacy. See M. N. Pokrovskii, *Izbrannye proiz-vedeniia, Book I: Russkaia istoriia s drevneishikh vremen* (vols. I and II) (Moscow: Mysl', 1966), 335-60; also Roman Szporluk, ed., *Introduction to Russia in World History: Selected Essays by M. N. Pokrovskii* (Ann Arbor: University of Michigan Press, 1970), 12-42.

47. As V. I. Astakhov wrote in his standard textbook on Russian historiography: "Karamzin often ut-terly departs from his sources in the interests of giving logical grace to the pragmatic narrative and a rhetorical beauty to the style. In those places where he must document his monarchical point of view, he simply distorts these sources." V. I. Asta-khov, *Kurs lektsii po russkoi istoriografii,* Pt. I, 145.

48. A. Gulyga, "Podvig Karamzina," *Voprosy liter-atury* 10 (October 1979): 211-30. Vatsuro's "'Pod-vig chestnogo cheloveka'" (1968) discusses the *History* in much the same open-minded spirit (see n. 16), stressing Karamzin's distinction between autocracy and despotism, and the legitimacy of Pushkin's defense of Karamzin against the De-cembrists.

49. Eidel'man, *Poslednii letopisets,* 158-59.

50. See L. N. Luzianina, "Problemy istorii v russkoi literature pervoi chetverti XIX veka (Ot 'Istorii Gosudarstva Rossiiskogo' N. M. Karamzina do tragedii A. S. Pushkina 'Boris Godunov')," Diss. for Candidate of Philological Sciences, Leningrad State University, 1972, chapters 1-3. A concise summary of her approach can be found in her sixteen-page *Avtoreferat,* 9-13. For further discus-sion, see L. N. Luzianina, *"Istoriia gosudarstva rossiiskogo* N. M. Karamzina i tragediia Pushkina *Boris Godunov* (k probleme kharaktera letopistsa)," *Russkaia literatura,* no. 1 (1971): 48-55.

51. Pogodin, *Nikolai Mikhailovich Karamzin,* II, 190.

52. Eidel'man, *Poslednii letopisets,* 61-62; see also Makogonenko, "Literaturnaia pozitsiia Karamzina," 105.

53. The discussion that follows on pp. 43-45 is con-densed and adapted from Luzianina, *"Istoriia go-sudarstva,"* 49-51.

54. See Luzianina, *Avtoreferat,* 11: "Karamzin at-tempts, in his own attitude toward what he de-picts, to achieve that 'moral freedom to judge deeds and characters' which, in the historian's opinion, was characteristic of the chroniclers' po-sition. In the final volumes of the *History* we have a type of narration no longer determined by a two-pronged elucidation of the fact [i.e., both as chronicle and as historian's frame.]"

55. Cited in Eidel'man, *Poslednii letopisets,* 150.

56. See Luzianina, *"Istoriia gosudarstva,"* 51.

57. Luzianina, *Avtoreferat,* 11.

58. See, for example, M. B. Rabinovich, *"Boris Go-dunov* Pushkina, *Istoriia* Karamzina i letopisi," in *Pushkin v shkole: sbornik statei* (Moscow: Izd. Akademii pedagogicheskikh nauk RSFSR, 1951), 311-12.

59. N. M. Karamzin, "O taine kantseliarii" (1803), in *Sochineniia Karamzina,* vol. 8 (St. Petersburg: tip. Smirdina, 1835), 130: "Our chroniclers are not Tacituses, they did not judge monarchs, did not relate all their deeds but only the brilliant ones. . . ."

60. N. M. Karamzin, "Ob istochnikakh rossiskoi is-torii do XVII veka," in *Istoriia Gosudarstva Rossi-iskogo* (1818), vol. 1, xxix-xxx.

61. J. Luria (Ia. S. Lur'e), "Problems of Source Criti-cism (with Reference to Medieval Russian Documents)," 1.

62. For a good summary of the history of internal source criticism and the art of decoding chronicles,

see A. G. Kuz'min, *Nachal'nye etapy drevnerusskogo letopisaniia* (The nature of the chronicles and methods for studying them) (Moscow: Izd. Moskovskogo universiteta, 1977), 25-54.

63. Edward L. Keenan, Jr., "The Trouble with Muscovy: Some Observations upon Problems of the Comparative Study of Form and Genre in Historical Writing," *Medievalia et Humanistica,* n.s. no. 5 (1974): 110.

64. For a brief account in English of Shakhmatov's career and his pathbreaking *Razyskaniia o drevneishikh russkikh letopisnykh svodakh* (Findings regarding the ancient Russian Chronicle compilations, 1908), see George Vernadsky, *Russian Historiography: A History* (Belmont, Mass.: Nordland, 1978), 335-40.

65. "The chronicle was intended first and foremost not for posterity, but for contemporaries, and chronicle compilations were put to use in political struggles," Ia. S. Lur'e writes in *Obshcherusskie letopisi XIV-XV vv.* (Leningrad: Nauka, 1976), 15. See also the Introduction to M. D. Priselkov, *Istoriia russkogo letopisaniia XI-XV vv.* (Leningrad: Leningradskii gos. universitet, 1940), 5-15; and V. A. Rybakov, *Drevniaia Rus': Skazaniia, byliny, letopis* (Moscow: Akademiia nauk, 1963), 158: "The time has passed forever when historians could dip into the wealth of chronicle material and, ignoring the differences [among them], cite without discrimination such individual phrases as 'the chronicle says . . .' or 'the chronicler said. . . .' In fact no such common stock of chronicle information existed. . . ."

66. D. S. Likhachev, *Poetika drevnerusskoi literatury* (Moscow: Nauka, 1979), 262-63.

67. A. S. Pushkin, "*Istoriia Russkogo naroda,* sochinenie Nikolaia Polevogo," originally published in *Literaturnaia gazeta,* 1830, no. 4. *P:pss* XI, 120.

Edward Alan Cole (essay date 1997)

SOURCE: Cole, Edward Alan. "A History for a Romantic Age." *Romantic Russia* 1 (1997): 99-108.

[*In the following essay, Cole examines the underlying tension between Enlightenment and Romantic ideals in Karamzin's historical writings.*]

> When we contemplate a great vastness, does not our vision, bypassing all that is near and distinct, ignore the commonplace and proceed to the far horizon, where shadows gather and darken, and the impenetrable begins?
>
> —N. M. Karamzin, 1815

The inclusion in a journal devoted to Romantic Russia of *The History of the Russian State* (*Istoriia Gosudarstva Rossiiskago*) by Nikolai Mikhailovich Karamzin (1766-1826) would at first glance require no justification, given the immense influence of this work throughout the Romantic period. There is hardly a writer, poet, intellectual or critic of the age whose bibliography fails to mention a great debt to Karamzin,[1] a fact that is telling even in the few and unlikely cases when it may have been *pro forma.* As Belinskii noted on the occasion of the publication of the fifth edition of the *History,* "Karamzin revealed to the whole Russian public . . . that the history of its fatherland had to be of interest, and knowledge of it not only useful, but even necessary. A great achievement!"[2]

The established consensus is that Karamzin has been not only the historian for the Romantic Age, but also a major historian for the age of Realism and beyond, right down to the post-Socialist present. Questions of classification arise immediately, however, when one asks whether Karamzin's work is an example of Romantic history, and whether or not the historian himself was in some sense Romantic.[3] There are certainly temptations enough to see him this way. One has only to recall certain of his stories and essays, for example, **"Bornholm Island"** (**"Ostrov Borngol'm"**), **"Sierra-Morena,"** or the superb **"On the Way to Trinity Monastery"** (**"Na puti k Troitse"**), or to reflect on the fact that many have considered that it was Karamzin's literary language and Karamzin's focus on Russia which made possible the quarter-century of brilliance which Belinskii first defined as "the romantic-national" (*romanticheskii-narodnyi*) period.[4] Indeed, it seems that it was none other than Karamzin who introduced the term "Romantic" into Russian.[5]

Most scholars, however, have resisted temptation, and the general view is that Karamzin was, if not a "child of the Age of Reason," at least an eighteenth-century man, and "a good Enlightenment thinker." The classic statement of this view was made by Nicholas V. Riasanovsky: "Karamzin's shadow loomed long after his death in 1826. Yet in his heart and in his mind Karamzin remained a child of the Age of Reason, whose abstract political ideal was a republic of virtuous citizens and whose writing style reflected the lucidity, simplicity, and rationality of a disciple of Voltaire."[6]

And to be sure, most of Karamzin's thought, from beginning to end, fits into a typology of the Enlightenment, especially if one takes a broad view of the movement. Iurii Lotman, for example, was especially persuasive on the subject of Karamzin's politics, which he saw as those of a utopian whose post-French-Revolution revision nonetheless bore the stamp of the classical vision central to the Enlightenment: in short, Karamzin shifted from the ideal of the republic to that

of the principate.[7] J. L. Black looked behind Karamzin's seemingly Romantic nationalism to find a universalism characteristic of the Enlightenment.[8]

Nevertheless, Karamzin, like so many figures of that "transitional" period, does not fit neatly into the typical matrix, and some of the anomalies of his case, especially those peculiar to his historical vision, seem at least suggestive of Romanticism. Some derive from the religious and moral ideals of Novikov and the Moscow Martinists.[9] And some derive from contact with a parallel tradition which Isaiah Berlin identified as the Counter-Enlightenment, a movement coeval with the Enlightenment proper.[10] Particularly tantalizing are traces of the ideas of Johann Gottfried Herder, the father of modern Romantic nationalism, whom Karamzin visited on his trip to Europe in 1790.[11] Remarkably well-read and eclectic, Karamzin not only conversed with the main figures of the Revolution, but also read the German philosophers who would shape the next chapter of European thought.[12] Although it is often impossible to determine the exact ingredients in Karamzin's work, the net effect, at least up until 1803, when he withdrew from journalism to write history, is one of remarkably rich modernity. And coupled with this potential for Romantic thought was also something else perhaps more germane to his commitment to History: his personal reaction to the crisis of the Enlightenment.

The *perelom,* or turning-point in Karamzin's career may provide the key to understanding his History. Famous as a melancholy sentimental writer and journalist, and insofar as he was regarded for his political views, as a probable sympathizer with the French Revolution, one whose views accorded with Novikov's or even with Radishchev's, in 1801 Karamzin emerged into the light of the reign of Alexander I (1801-1825) a journalist with a surprising new orientation: optimistic, avowedly monarchist, and increasingly historical. On the pages of his new publication, *The Herald of Europe* (*Vestnik Evropy*) he kept the Russian public abreast of cultural and political developments in the new Europe of Napoleon.

Karamzin's surprising change of course, somewhat blurred by repeated assurances of faith in the ideals of republican virtue, was capped by the acceptance of the unique position of Imperial Historiographer and a stipend of 2,000 rubles per year. Until the publication of the first eight volumes of the *History* in 1818, the Russian public, which continued to consume new editions of his fiction and to discuss his linguistic innovations, heard from him hardly at all. Karamzin's few extraneous works of these years, known but to a few, confirm the picture of him as a conservative supporter of autocracy.

Biographers have uniformly seen this *perelom* as the result of the French Revolution, but there have been a few interesting elaborations on the theme. In the mid-nineteenth century the critic Appolon Grigor'ev, who on the one hand "wrote what was almost a panegyric to Karamzin," but on the other anticipated certain postmodern criticisms by bewailing the power of Karamzin's Eurocentric historical "matrices" ("valor, grandeur, honor, and so on"), attempted to explain what had happened to the writer during the reign of Paul I (1796-1801). Karamzin the idealist had been threatened by a collision with Russian reality of the kind that had nearly destroyed Radishchev and Novikov at the end of the previous reign. Karamzin, however, took a different path: ". . . not to submit to it, but to subvert it!

> Yes . . . subvert it! That's the very word.
>
> And Karamzin did this. He subverted the reality of his time.
>
> He became the historian "of the Russian state." Perhaps consciously, perhaps not, for it is a question difficult to resolve because a talented person is capable of deceiving himself, he slipped the demands of the western humanistic ideal in, under the facts of our own history, and he first looked upon this strange history from the European angle of view.[13]

A second unusual interpretation, which also holds that Karamzin's *History* was subversive in nature and which incidentally solves the minor problem of the professions of faith in republican virtue, is that of Iurii Lotman, already alluded to above. In Lotman's view, Karamzin believed that virtue produced freedom, equality, brotherhood, and so on, not vice-versa. A republic was thus the natural and resultant political system for a virtuous people. The collision with reality came on the day when Karamzin learned of the execution of Robespierre. Sadder but wiser, Karamzin adopted a revised view of the possibilities: a principate, in short, a monarchy, was a better form, not only because it better took into account people's incapacity for virtue, but because, unlike the republic, a principate could preserve republican ideals while educating the people for citizenship.

This was not an ignoble view: many a virtuous Roman had embraced it in the hour of crisis. In 1801 Napoleon seemed to be demonstrating its wisdom, whereas, paradoxically, the advisors of the new Russian autocrat, Alexander I (1801-1825) seemed bent on Enlightened reforms tending in exactly the wrong direction. Hence, Karamzin took the field, first with his journal, and then with his *History.* The great task was to educate tsar and people in their new roles under the principate.

> Now there arose before Karamzin a second task—to make the Russian reader into a citizen. But to this end, Karamzin concluded, it was necessary that he should possess a history of his country. It was necessary to make him into a historical person. This is really why Karamzin was "tonsured as a historian."[14]

A third unconventional interpretation of the *perelom* is that of Andrew Baruch Wachtel, who reflects a postmodern view that history is not a branch of literature, as in days of old, but simply a genre open to literary criticism. Such a position leaves little room for subversive ideas and sees the historian's task largely as a marketing problem, but it does provide insights helpful toward the solution of another minor problem best indicated by the fact that after the publication of the first eight volumes, Admiral A. S. Shishkov, Karamzin's opponent in the great language controversy, found, somewhat to his own surprise, little to criticize and much to admire in the *History.*

According to Wachtel, Karamzin, who had already essayed other genres such as poetry and philosophy, thought to try his hand at history. But first he had to adopt a new "writing persona" with the *gravitas* appropriate to "his new method." Once this was done, Karamzin was ready for his "central task," which was "to create a viable Russian version of narrative historical discourse and to differentiate it clearly from competing methods of presenting historical material." Wachtel sees the *perelom* as essentially a shift in genre, at least as far as the main text of the *History* is concerned. He also gives way to the temptation to see the notes as a separate work, and posits a "dialogue" between the two. His interpretation, however, has the virtue of emphasizing an important shift in style, which may have been beyond the sentimentalism for which Karamzin was already famous.[15]

One of the great cliches is that Romanticism was a reaction against the Enlightenment, and certainly, in Karamzin's case, something very like that happened and propelled him into the enormous task of writing an extended and informed reflection on his nation's past. But biography is not history, and it is, after all, *The History of the Russian State* which was so important to the Romantic Age, not its author, admirable as he was.

Karamzin's *History* received a warm reception among the Russian reading public. The first edition, printed in a press run of 3,000 eight-volume sets priced relatively high at 55 silver rubles, sold out in twenty-five days in February 1818. A second printing went on sale in July. From that time on it remained enormously popular during the Romantic Age, when it went through three more editions. Indeed right to the present day the *History* has been a favorite with the Russian reading public.[16] And right from the beginning, it has been controversial. Most critics fall into one of two categories, or sometimes into both: (1) representatives of incipient professionalized history who had much to say about Karamzin's location and use of sources, and so on; and (2) ideological opponents, mainly those who objected to Karamzin's seeming neglect of the Russian people. It was this which led one of Karamzin's own supporters to portray the De-

cembrist Uprising as "an armed criticism of *The History of the Russian State,*"[17] and a modern historian to observe: "No wonder that Karamzin's junior contemporaries not only admired him, but also found some criticisms to make, for instance, to the effect that Karamzin's history dealt at length with the state, but omitted the people—that is ignored the romantic revelation."[18]

In part this criticism is but a nineteenth-century Russian manifestation of the eternal debate between the old and the new histories, but insofar as it maintains that in his *History* Karamzin ignored the insights of Romanticism, it raises the question of Romantic History and the relationship of his work to the category.

It is, of course, quite possible that history, the literature of fact and memory, can not participate directly in Romanticism; it is also likely that if this is the case, philosophy, the literature of reason, is also excluded; in its true form, in which the artist ascends to see the face of God and then, dashed down, plunges into the abyss, Romanticism may belong exclusively to poetry, the literature of imagination. Nevertheless, something sometimes called "Romantic History" was practiced in the early nineteenth century, and it would be interesting to see how well Karamzin's *History* fits in.

As a type, Romantic History developed gradually during the eighteenth century, and can count among its theorists Vico, Herder, and perhaps Burke—all figures of the Counter-Enlightenment. Its golden age roughly coincided with the Romantic period in general. It was very popular with the reading public, but amateur history in the best meaning of the word, it did not survive intense scrutiny by the professional and academic discipline. Many of its practitioners, such as those of the *école narrative,* have passed from public memory. The greatest of the Romantics were French, where Michelet emerged as the ideal Romantic historian, and American, where one thinks of Parkman first, then Bancroft and Prescott. Eighteenth-century Britain gave the world Gibbon, Hume, and Robertson, whom Karamzin considered the three greatest historians since Tacitus, and then a Romantic tradition which peaked with Carlyle and Macaulay. Interestingly, Germany, the home of the Philosophy of History and of the Historical Method, lay outside the realm of full Romantic history. What of Russia?

There Karamzin is almost the only major contender. And, although he was not the last, he was the greatest of Russia's amateur historians, bringing to culmination the tradition represented by the names V. N. Tatishchev (1686-1750), M. M. Shcherbatov (1733-1790) and I. N. Boltin (1735-1792).[19] In his own time, Karamzin's works were severely criticized by an early representative of professional historical scholarship, Nikolai Sergeevich Artsybashev (1773-1841), who, it is thought,

might have scored higher with the reading public had he been able to refer them to most of the sources, alas not yet in published form.[20] It is just another of Russia's historical paradoxes that she may have experienced Romantic history sooner than any other European country, presuming, of course, that Karamzin's *History* fits the definition.

The first and most necessary characteristic of the Romantic historian was that he was learned, a man of letters, and usually someone who had established a name in literature before turning to history.[21] He had a tendency to see the material world, especially its ruins, as evocative of a pre-existing world, and he had a driving sense of mission to re-create that world by means of the imagination. He admired the style of Gibbon and Hume, but rejected them as too philosophical. In particular, the Romantic often sought out precisely those medieval centuries which had been such an embarrassment to the classically-oriented Enlightenment. The Romantic Historian also considered himself to be a painter, and his book a canvas. He excelled at "portraits" of his subjects, and often made the landscape serve as a virtual participant in the historical action. Concentration on significant personalities often meant that lesser figures had to be stylized and presented as characteristic types. Great emphasis was laid upon the experience of the past, and in enabling the reader to share in that experience. To the historian, the experiences of common historical figures, immediate and not artificial, were preferable to the musings of the learned. Romantic History was also not intentionally controversial, and its main criticism of other approaches to the subject was that the others were not vivid recreations.

For all his rejection of the "philosophical historians" of the Enlightenment, the Romantic historian nonetheless subscribed to a world view of his own: a conviction that history makes sense and has a Providential logic which can be perceived by an historian, but only as through a glass, darkly. Progress is the historical law of nature, but progress is not simply linear, but spiral, or even dialectic; there are many setbacks, but in general the movement of humanity is toward moral freedom and perhaps, even toward political freedom. A Providential plan notwithstanding, history proceeds, and the cause of humanity advances, only by the actions of heroic individuals. In judging them, and the Romantic Historian did not shrink from judgment, questions of intent and motive were uppermost; closely following upon these was a concern for consequence. The result was necessarily a narrative rather than an analysis. A final characteristic of Romantic History was its tendency to take on the contemporary values of its reading public, which meant, in the century of its blossoming, a tendency toward nationalism.

Any reader of Karamzin's *History,* or even of its famous Preface, can find most of the characteristic of Ro-

mantic History and of the Romantic Historian amply exemplified. This is a great tribute to the author, that he should be so contemporary in his approach at a time when Europeans were wont to excuse "Turks and Russians" for their literary backwardness. Almost all of it is there: the historian was a learned man of letters with an established reputation. He had exactly the right intellectual credentials. While acknowledging the achievements of his predecessors, he believed that his public nevertheless lacked a good history which would link them to their past. He had the painterly bent and a fascination with evocative ruins. Assisted by the ancient chroniclers themselves, who operated with their own stylizations, he left many figures of history in conventional form, concentrating on portraits of the heroic. Character, motive, and the consequences of acts were of paramount importance.[22] He set classical antiquity aside and wrote primarily about what would be considered medieval Russia, had the Russians experienced an antecedent age of classical antiquity. And, despite what his critics claimed on the basis of the title of his work, Karamzin wrote many lines and several whole sections on the conditions of life in Russia. As for her people, they were a powerful force in the *History*; on occasion they displayed all the civic virtues, ultimately their moral judgments of a given ruler were final, and their fate was the ultimate end of the state.[23] In a sense, then, Karamzin was also affected by emerging modern views of the nation, as befit a Romantic Historian.

On the matter of a historical world-view, a belief in, or recognition of "the historical process," readers have been divided in their opinions. Anatole Mazour, for example, dismissed Karamzin as the "typical successor of the eighteenth-century historians" who wrote not so much a history as "an album of sovereigns accompanied by a description in the most resounding style." It totally lacks historical perspective, since Karamzin could not conceive of a historical process; like the eighteenth-century rationalist, he saw in history only evil or benevolent sovereigns who led the country either to disaster or to glory.[24]

Other informed readers, however, have judged Karamzin differently. J. L. Black, for example, who made a detailed reading of the *History* and found that you have to read it closely to detect the underlying structure, concluded that Karamzin not only had a conception of progress but also that he foreshadowed the state school historians of the later nineteenth century, observing that "the notion of the state as an organism apart from the rulers was an important ingredient of Karamzin's scheme, although not readily discernible in the *History*."[25]

And others have sensed that Karamzin, as historian, was not prepared to go beyond the limits of his discipline, much as his critics and readers may have desired

it. And is it not Romantic to recognize the limits of rationality, and to accept that much is simply not given to us to know?

> Critics of the **History** mistakenly reproached Karamzin because he saw no profound idea in the course of events. Karamzin was imbued with the thought that history makes sense. But this sense—the project of Providence—was concealed from people and could not be the subject of historical description. The historian describes human actions, those deeds of people for which they bear moral responsibility. The true sense of history is noumenal. It might be divined poetically, but it lies beyond disciplined history. . . .[26]

Thus, it would seem, the classification of Karamzin depends to a considerable degree on what readers and critics expect of Romantic History or even of history itself.

There is no doubt, however, that Karamzin profoundly influenced the succeeding generations. In fact, it is difficult to imagine what Russian culture, including not only poetry and prose fiction, but also drama, music, sculpture, painting, and even architecture, would have been like without "the treasure house" of Karamzin's **History.** And it is equally difficult to identify anyone with his peculiar talents who could have taken his place. It has often been noted that the times were favorable to Karamzin's reputation. Appearing immediately after the Napoleonic Wars, the first eight volumes obviously spoke to a great curiosity about national identity and the validity of the great cause which had cost so much. The subsequent volumes fed right into a growing curiosity about the meaning of history inspired by Western philosophies of history. And even though his style and his vocabulary might not have been fully Romantic, Karamzin nonetheless spoke a language intelligible to the rising generations and, Romantic or not, provided Russia with a History worthy of a Romantic Age.

Notes

1. See, for example, the entries in Christine A. Rydel, ed., *Dictionary of Literary Biography: Russian Literature in the Age of Pushkin and Gogol. Vol. I Prose, Vol. II Poetry and Drama* (Detroit, Washington, D.C., and London: Bruccoli Clark Layman, publication date forthcoming).

2. Quoted in S. O. Shmidt, "*Istoriia gosudarstva Rossiiskago* v kulture dorevoliutsionoi Rossii," in N. M. Karamzin, *Istoriia Gosudarstva Rossiiskago* (Moscow: Kniga, 1988), vol. 1, p. 28. This article is another excellent source for testimonies to the lasting influence of Karamzin's *History*.

3. The assumption here is that the analytic exercise of classification is very important and productive of insights into the logic of intellectual history; the author is nonetheless aware of countervailing postmodernist opinions to be found, for example, in Michel de Certeau, *The Writing of History* (New York: Columbia Univ. Press, 1988).

4. For an interesting critique of both of these qualifiers, see Appolon Grigor'ev, "Narodnost' i literatura," in Appolon Grigor'ev, *Estetika i kritika* (Moscow: Isskustvo, 1980), pp. 190-91.

5. In the form *romanicheskii*, in *The Letters of a Russian Traveler* (*Pis'ma russkogo puteshestvennika*) as published in his *Moskovskii zhurnal,* 1791-92. Sigrid McLaughlin, "Russia/ Romantičeskij-Romantizm," in Hans Eichner, ed., *'Romantic' and Its Cognates: The European History of the Word* (Toronto: Univ. of Toronto Press, 1972), pp. 418-74.

6. Nicholas V. Riasanovsky, *A Parting of Ways* (Oxford: Oxford Univ. Press, 1976), p. 150. Karamzin is clearly portrayed as an eighteenth-century man in Natalya Kochetkova, *Nikolay Karamzin* (Boston: Twayne, 1975), esp. pp. 131-32. A somewhat more suppositional assertion is made by Andrew Baruch Wachtel, *An Obsession with History: Russian Writers Confront the Past* (Stanford, CA: Stanford Univ. Press, 1994), p. 62. There are many other examples.

7. Iurii Lotman, "Kolumb russkoi istorii," in Karamzin, *Istoriia,* vol. 4, p. 9.

8. J. L. Black, *Nicholas Karamzin and Russian Society in the Nineteenth Century: A Study in Russian Political and Historical Thought* (Toronto: Univ. of Toronto Press, 1975), p. 102.

9. See Eric Bryner, *N. M. Karamzin, eine kirken- und frömmigheits-geschichtliche Studie* (Erlangen: Universität Erlangens, 1974), esp. p. 241.

10. See Isaiah Berlin, *Against the Current: Essays in the History of Ideas* (New York: Viking Press, 1980), pp. 3-4 and *passim.*

11. See K. Bittner, "Herderische Gedanken in Karamzins Geschichtsschau," *Jahrbücher für Geschichte Osteuropas,* 7, No. 3 (1959), 237-69; and H. M. Nebel, *N. M. Karamzin: A Russian Sentimentalist* (The Hague and Paris: Mouton, 1967), pp. 87-88.

12. This is one of the important themes in Iurii Lotman, *Sotvoreniie Karamzina* (Moscow: Kniga, 1987).

13. Appolon Grigor'ev, "Narodnost' i literatura," p. 186 and *passim.*

14. Lotman, "Kolumb russkoi istorii," p. 10.

15. Wachtel, *Obsession with History,* p. 48. Gitta Hammarberg, however, is also convincing in her

conclusion that the *History,* rich in bivocality and polyphony, was "the ultimate sentimentalist accomplishment, its crowning glory," the equivalent of the great odes of classicism, but far more effective and successful. Her views are summarized in Gitta Hammarberg, "Nikolai Mikhailovich Karamzin," in Marcus C. Levitt, ed., *The Dictionary of Literary Biography,* vol. 150: *Early Russian Writers, Late 17th and 18th Centuries* (Detroit, Washington D. C., and London: Bruccoli/ Clark Layman, 1995), pp. 149 and *passim.*

16. Karamzin's *History* was one of the first works demanded by the public when the socialist system began its meltdown. Between 1989 and 1991 no less than seven reprint editions were published, with a total press run of 887,000 sets.

17. Quoted in Lotman, "Kolumb russkoi istorii," p. 14.

18. Riasanovsky, *A Parting of Ways,* p. 150.

19. Russian history before Karamzin had also been enriched by the works of two Germans, G. F. Müller (1705-1783), himself an amateur, and August Ludwig von Schlözer (1733-1809), true scholar, early professional, and the editor of the complete Nestorian Chronicle published in 1802. A concise account of these predecessors can be found in Anatole G. Mazour, *An Outline of Modern Russian Historiography* (Berkeley: Univ. of California Press, 1939).

20. Available as "Zamechaniia na Istoriiu gosudarstva Rossiiskago, Karamzina," *Vestnik Evropy,* pt. 11, Nos. 19-20 (1828) and pt. 11 Nos. 19-20, pt. 12, No. 21 (1839) part 3.

21. This typology is derived from the best single study of Romantic History: David Levin, *History as Romantic Art* (Stanford, CA: Stanford Univ. Press, 1959).

22. See Rudolf Bächtold, *Karamzins Weg nach Geschichte* (Basel: Helling und Lichtenhahn, 1946), pp. 88-89. Baechtold finds that the concern with individual character derived from reading English literature, and that in including it, Karamzin supplied what the chroniclers themselves ignored. See also Kochetkova, *Karamzin,* p. 131.

23. Kochetkova, *Karamzin,* pp. 123-24.

24. Mazour, *Modern Russian Historiography,* pp. 22, 24, 26.

25. Black, *Karamzin,* pp. 104, 115-16.

26. Lotman, "Kolumb russkoi istorii, p. 16. Lotman also hints that Karamzin may have had some desire to penetrate to the noumenon" because on

several occasions the historian referred to his *History* as "an historical poem."

Derek Offord (essay date 1999)

SOURCE: Offord, Derek. "Karamzin's Gothic Tale: 'The Island of Bornholm.'" In *The Gothic-Fantastic in Nineteenth-Century Russian Literature,* edited by Neil Cornwell, pp. 37-58. Amsterdam: Rodopi, 1999.

[*In the following essay, Offord discusses Gothic motifs in Karamzin's "The Island of Bornholm."*]

The focus of N. M. Karamzin's early writings is not so much the characters, events or places described as the sensibility of the narrator. Given this fact, the narrator's moods assume great importance. These moods waver between, at one extreme, a Rousseauesque[1] optimism about the essential goodness of human nature and, at the other, a pessimism evoked by awareness of the vulnerability of individual happiness to evil, fate or human weakness and by reflection on the impermanence of human achievement. The two moods find expression in corresponding literary manners: on the one hand an idyllic or pastoral manner and on the other an elegiacism in which melancholy may shade into anxiety and even terror.

These moods and manners coexist throughout Karamzin's early writings. In his poem **'Recovery'** (**'Vyzdorovlenie'**), published in 1791, an air of gloom, ennui and sorrow, compounded by fearful dreams, is dispersed by tender Nature and a sense of renewal brought about by the sun, dawn, stars and moon.[2] Again, in the poem **'The Graveyard'** (**'Kladbishche'**), published in 1792, two voices offer opposing views of death: the first presents it as terrifying, associating it with howling winds, shaking coffins, rattling bones, toads nestling in skulls and snakes in nettles; the other presents it in terms of tranquillity and reconciliation through such images as a gentle breeze, birds singing on a grave, a dove on a bough, a rabbit in the grass and fragrant flowers.[3]

In the opening paragraphs of the most celebrated example of Karamzin's prose fiction, **'Poor Liza'** (**'Bednaia Liza'**, 1792), the two moods are juxtaposed through contrasting views of the environs of Moscow. On the one hand the narrator paints an idyllic spring and summer picture of meadows and copses, a shining river rippling to the oars of fishermen's boats and plied by barges laden with grain from the provinces, grazing flocks, young shepherds singing simple songs under the shade of oak-trees and a distant view of Moscow's golden cupolas illuminated by the rays of the evening sun. On the other hand he offers a tableau of a deserted

monastery with gloomy Gothic towers, where on autumn days the wind howls fearfully (*strashno*) among the walls and the graves overgrown with grass and in the dark passages between the empty cells. Here the narrator conjures up in his imagination the sad picture of an aged monk praying for release from his earthly fetters, now that he has lost all feeling, and describes scenes depicted on the gates of the monastery which make disturbing reference to troubled times in Russia's medieval past.[4]

In the voluminous *Letters of a Russian Traveller* (*Pis'ma russkogo puteshestvennika*) too both moods are present. The idyllic mood is much in evidence in Switzerland, a country of natural beauty, abundance, freedom and simplicity of morals which Nature has apparently made inaccessible to the vices.[5] The Alpine folk live a life that is pastoral—both literally and metaphorically. They graze their herds on the mountain slopes, sustaining themselves on the milk and cheese which they produce themselves, and live in that state of primeval innocence in which people, unburdened by the anxieties of modern life, are said to be capable of tender feeling and warm human relationships.[6] How well the Alpine shepherdesses, the narrator exclaims, understand the language of the heart![7] Karamzin pays apt homage to Gessner, the 'Swiss Theocritus', a writer dedicated to 'virtue and innocence'.[8] Karamzin's elegiac mood, on the other hand, finds expression in his travelogue in reference to old castles and ruins;[9] in a passage on a monk who had committed suicide;[10] in periodic reflections on the transience of human life and civilisations;[11] in his view of a tomb as a sanctuary;[12] and in his susceptibility to bouts of melancholy nourished by his reading of the eighteenth-century Scottish poet James Thomson[13] and the apocryphal Gaelic epos of Ossian.[14] This mood is particularly striking in a passage that seems to serve as a preliminary sketch for **'Poor Liza'**: wandering in the Bois de Boulogne on the outskirts of Paris, the traveller comes upon a gloomy, deserted sixteenth-century castle, one of whose chambers is inhabited by an old woman who has lost everything, including her beautiful daughter Luiza, whose sad story contains a number of details reproduced in Karamzin's sentimental tale.[15] Medieval buildings may even induce terror, as well as melancholy, as when the narrator visits a Benedictine monastery in Erfurt and in its lugubrious passages visualises a monster of medieval fanaticism.[16]

It will be seen that the elegiac passages in Karamzin's early writings contain quite numerous traces of elements which we now associate with Gothicism, such as frightening images and fearful dreams, a predilection for ruins and the graveyard, a sense of mortality, and the melancholy and even frissons of terror which such places may excite. However, these elements are difficult to disentangle from the general European Preromanticism which Karamzin imbibes and to which he himself contributes, and which in Russia goes under the name Sentimentalism.[17] Their existence in Karamzin's work predates the appearance of the main landmarks of Gothic fiction at its highpoint in the 1790s, such as Ann Radcliffe's novels *The Mysteries of Udolpho* (1794) and *The Italian* (1797), Matthew Lewis's *The Monk* (1796), and other popular works such as Regina Maria Roche's *The Children of the Abbey* (1794) and *Clermont* (1798). Admittedly, some Gothic romances—William Beckford's *Vathek*,[18] Clara Reeve's *The Old English Baron*[19] and Sophia Lee's *The Recess*[20]—were translated into Russian in the years 1792-4[21] (the translation of Reeve's novel emanated from Moscow Masonic circles to which Karamzin was close[22]). But the early novels of Ann Radcliffe—*The Castles of Athlin and Dunbayne* (1789), *A Sicilian Romance* (1790) and *The Romance of the Forest* (1791)—became known in Russia, through French translations, somewhat later, in the late 1790s, and it was not until the early years of the nineteenth century that *A Sicilian Romance* and *The Romance of the Forest* were translated into Russian.[23]

It is therefore best to approach Karamzin's short tale **'The Island of Bornholm'** ('Ostrov Borngol'm'), published in the first number of Karamzin's almanac *Aglaia* in April 1794, not so much as an experiment in a distinctive new European manner—which was in any case not yet clearly defined or widely known in Russia[24]—but rather as a development of a particular strand of Preromanticism represented by poets such as Thomson. Edward Young,[25] Thomas Gray and Ossian, as well as by novelists such as Clara Reeve and Ann Radcliffe.[26] What distinguishes the tale from Karamzin's other early work is not the use of Gothic motifs in it, but its saturation with them and the fact that these motifs are less obviously counterbalanced by an alternative idyllic vision. We need therefore both to identify the Gothic elements in the tale and to attempt to explain their unusual prevalence.[27]

1

The plot of the tale **'The Island of Bornholm'** revolves around a mystery which obsesses the narrator as he voyages from London back to his native Russia after lengthy travels abroad. No sooner has his boat left London than it has to dock at Gravesend to await favourable weather and the narrator goes ashore. Here he encounters a pale thin young man holding a guitar. Oblivious of the narrator, sighing and staring out to sea, the young man sings a sad prelude in Danish (which fortunately the narrator has learnt from a friend in Switzerland during his travels[28]) about Lila, the love he has left behind on the Baltic island of Bornholm, from which he has been banished for ever. At this point the narrator is led back to the boat by the captain, as the wind has changed. After a week-long voyage the boat

puts in at Bornholm for the night. The narrator, his curiosity aroused by the reference to the island in the song he has heard at Gravesend, persuades the captain to allow him to go ashore with some sailors in a dinghy. Local fishermen agree to put the party up for the night and lead them to a grassy plain, at which point the narrator, accompanied by a thirteen-year-old guide, leaves the sailors in order to savour the sunset. He soon glimpses in the distance an old castle, which he makes for against the advice of his guide and reaches as night is falling. Ignoring his guide's advice to return to the fishermen's huts, the narrator requests hospitality and is led into the castle by a servant, who takes him to a little candle-lit room where he is greeted by a grey-haired old man weighed down by sorrow. The narrator is taken to a bed-chamber for the night but his sleep is troubled. Needing fresh air he goes to the window, notices a little door and goes out into the moonlit garden. A long avenue of oak trees leads him up to a sandy knoll in the side of which he sees a small opening. Following a passage and going down some steps he comes to an unlocked door and there, beyond an iron grille with a large lock, he finds a young woman asleep on a bed of straw. She awakes and it becomes apparent from what she says that she has been imprisoned for some terrible transgression and will remain in the cave until she dies. Emerging from the cave and overwhelmed by his impressions, the narrator falls asleep on the grass. He awakes as the sun is rising, to hear the servant telling the old owner of the castle that their visitor had entered the unlocked cave. The old man now recounts 'a most horrifying story' (*uzhasneishuiu istoriiu*) which explains what the narrator has seen, but which the narrator himself tantalisingly refuses to divulge. The narrator rejoins the sailors with whom he had come ashore and they return to the ship and set sail. The tale ends with the narrator standing on deck deep in sorrowful thought.[29]

Karamzin's tale contains many of the standard props of eighteenth-century Gothic fiction. At its centre stands what has been described as the 'major locus of Gothic plots, the castle',[30] perhaps inspired in this case by the ruined thirteenth-century castle of Hammershus at Bornholm's northern tip, once a stronghold of the Swedish bishops of Lund. Karamzin's narrative lovingly reconstructs the castle with copious architectural and decorative detail and abundant reference to its antiquity and current dilapidation. It is a large 'Gothic' building with pointed towers and is surrounded by a deep moat and a high wall with locked gates and raised drawbridges. The courtyard is overgrown with bushes, nettles and wormwood; a tall peristyle of ancient design leads to an iron porch. In the first hall, surrounded by a 'Gothic' colonnade, a lamp casts a pale light on rows of gilded pillars which have long since begun to crumble. Here and there lie pieces of cornice, chunks of pilaster and whole columns which have collapsed. There are long, narrow passages, down which the servant leads the narrator to a bed-chamber hung with ancient weaponry—swords, spears, armour and spiked helmets—and in which there stands a high bed decorated with carving and ancient bas-reliefs and covered by a golden canopy. Finally there is the secret underground cave, damp and cold, with a lamp hanging from the vault, in which a woman is cruelly imprisoned.[31]

Moreover, Karamzin's castle is pervaded by an atmosphere of superstition, gloom and threat that is typical of Gothic fiction. It is a place which people shun, the narrator's guide informs him, for 'God knows what goes on there!' At the castle gates the narrator is greeted by a disembodied voice asking him who he is. The old man in his first utterance forewarns his visitor that 'eternal grief dwells within the walls of this castle'. The master's servant is sinister and taciturn: he is a tall man in a long black coat who, as he leads the visitor through the castle several times, stares silently at him with his penetrating eyes. Sounds jar the nerves: doors slam shut, the drawbridge creaks when raised, footsteps ring out on the steps of the iron porch and the iron door of the bed-chamber closes with a frightening resonance. The narrator, left alone in the bed-chamber, begins to muse on the adventures which the castle may have witnessed in the past and even takes on the persona of a graveyard poet, comparing himself to a man who amid the tombs looks upon the ashes of the dead and brings them back to life in his imagination. His sleep is disturbed by nightmares populated by characteristically Gothic images, both medieval and monstrous. He dreams that all the armour on the walls has turned into knights who come down and stand over him with bared swords, angrily demanding to know why he has intruded into 'terrible [*strashnoe*] sanctuary of the castle' and threatening to kill him for his impudent curiosity. Awakening from this nightmare, the narrator falls back into another in which a terrible thundering sound rumbles through the castle, the windows shake, the doors clang, the floor trembles and an ineffable winged monster flies towards the narrator's bed, roaring and hissing.[32]

However, neither lugubrious setting nor sinister atmosphere is an end in itself. Rather they provide a fitting backdrop to the revelation of some shocking secret. Like Ann Radcliffe's *A Sicilian Romance,* though less explicitly and with a dissimilar, irredeemable outcome, Karamzin's tale brings to light a terrible event that has ruined a family.

Karamzin leaves us in no doubt that the young man at Gravesend and the young woman in the cave are the lovers to which the young man's song alludes (although he does not explicitly tell us that they are). This inference seems to be confirmed by the narrator's admission that the old man's story does unravel the terrible secret of the unknown young man at Gravesend. Moreover,

the young man and the young woman are paired in the narrative by many literary means. The same epithets are applied to them: 'pale' (*blednyi*); 'languorous' (*tomnyi*); 'unhappy' (*neschastnyi*). They share many traits. Both stare with motionless eyes and utter their thoughts in a quiet voice. Both are near to death or associated with it. The young man is more an apparition than a human being; the narrator sees in his eyes the last ray of a life that is going out; his feelings are dead to external objects and he sees and hears nothing. The young woman, for her part, expects to die; her hand is white and withered; her heart, she says, has wasted away from grief, and a question dies on her pale lips. Both the young man and the young woman actually crave death: the young man ends his song with a vow to cast himself with his lover into the roaring waves; the young woman hopes her life will soon end. Furthermore, both elicit pity from the sensitive narrator and in the descriptions of their encounters with him there is some syntactic symmetry.[33]

We are not told explicitly why the relationship of the young man and the young woman is illicit, or what their relationship is to the old man who is master of the castle. The young woman falls silent one word short of defining her relationship with the old man, when she instructs the narrator to tell the one who uttered the terrible curse on her that she bears her end without complaint and will die his 'affectionate, unhappy . . .'. The missing word could be 'wife' and the transgression adultery. However, it is much more likely that the young woman is the daughter of the old man, that the young man is her brother and that the transgression is therefore incest, which so fascinates Gothic writers, beginning with Horace Walpole in his *Castle of Otranto* (1764). That her relationship with the young man *is* illicit is indicated by allusions to law and its infringement in the young man's song, by the thought of crime that immediately comes to the narrator's mind when he sees the young woman in the cave, and by the young woman's immediate avowal to the narrator that she kisses the hand that punishes her.

The dark secret which the Gothic tale in general unlocks is indicative of fears about the triumph of vice over virtue, and about consequent social disintegration, that were experienced by readers of the period (in the 1790s) when Gothic fiction was reaching the peak of its popularity.[34] In Karamzin's narrative, the transgression of which the narrator slowly becomes aware gives rise within him to a disturbing and seemingly irresolvable conflict between the demands of, on the one hand, mind and reason and, on the other, heart and feeling. This conflict finds expression in the tale in consideration of the competing claims to authority of convention and nature, human law and natural law. It is this tension that the young man's song bemoans:

> The laws condemn
> the object of my love;
> But who, oh heart, can
> resist thee?
> What law is more sacred
> than your innate feelings?
> What power is stronger
> than love and beauty?

For the young man Nature is the highest authority and he does not believe that he has sinned before her in yielding to his passion. Nature thundered, but did not strike the lovers in their embrace. Humans, on the other hand, are cruel and pitiless, as attested by the parental curse which the young man's love has brought down on him and as a result of which he has been banished from Bornholm. The tension between different conceptions of law which runs through the young man's song arises again when the narrator comes upon the young woman asleep in her prison. He cannot believe that she has committed some grave crime, for both her sweet countenance and his own heart assure him that she is innocent. It is significant in this regard that it seems to the narrator that the cave in which Lila is imprisoned is man-made rather than natural. The old man, on the other hand, cleaves to the established authority of convention: he is quite unable to understand why the heavens have unleashed their anger on a weak, grey-haired old man who has loved virtue and respected its holy laws. Thus for all his apparent benignity and civility, he conforms to a certain degree to the Gothic type of the tyrannical master of a feudal castle and the castle itself, seen in this light, takes on its characteristically Gothic role as the seat of medieval barbarism.

2

The tension between reason and feeling, mind and heart, convention and Nature which pervades '**The Island of Bornholm**' mirrors the conflict that was taking place in late eighteenth-century Russia between the broad cultural movements of Classicism and Sentimentalism, or Preromanticism. Karamzin's place in that conflict in the period before he wrote '**The Island of Bornholm**' is clear. His position is reflected in his preface of 1786 to his own translation of *Julius Caesar,* in which he expresses his admiration of Shakespeare for his ability to imitate Nature and to reveal 'all the most secret springs of a man, his innermost motives, the distinguishing characteristic of every passion' and rejects Voltaire's criticism that Shakespeare disregarded rules and propriety.[35] Again, in his short essay '**What does an Author need?**' ('**Chto nuzhno avtoru?**'), written in spring 1793, Karamzin upholds authorial sincerity and sensitivity as prerequisites for successful art. Rousseau, with his passionate love of mankind, is forgiven his failings and is set above other, more learned, writers who tell truths unwarmed by the love of a virtuous heart.[36] Karamzin's early stories '**Poor Liza**' and '**Natal'ia, a**

Boyar's Daughter' ('Natal'ia, boiarskaia doch'', 1792) themselves posed a challenge—psychological, social and moral—to the static, rationally ordered, gentry dominated, refined and symmetrical universe of Russian Classicism. Moreover the concept of virtue, so important to the eighteenth-century Russian mind, was redefined. The cultivation of virtue and nobility of character remained an admirable goal, but these qualities now found expression not so much in restraint of passion and adherence to a golden mean as in indulgence of the emotions and a sensitivity—which to the modern reader appears overblown—to an affecting impression. Thus, whereas for the post-Petrine satirist Kantemir, virtue is conceived in the Stoic sense as a means of protecting one from the vicissitudes of Fortune,[37] in **'Natal'ia, a Boyar's Daughter'** Karamzin's narrator is adamant that 'virtue itself cannot protect us from grief'.[38]

The tale **'The Island of Bornholm'**, for all its Gothicism, fits comfortably into the Sentimentalist framework,[39] for it is informed by the same sensibility as Karamzin's earlier writings. Like the narrator whose soul is famously mirrored in the letters of a Russian traveller, the narrator of **'The Island of Bornholm'** is brimming with emotion and dwells in the realms of heart, spirit and soul (*serdtse, dukh, dusha*) rather than reason (*razum*).[40] He is sensitive to the plight of the young man he sees at Gravesend, immediately recognising his unhappiness and sensing that he has been 'killed by Fate'. Having heard the young man's song, he is prompted 'by an involuntary inner impulse' to throw himself at the singer and press him to his heart, and is prevented from doing so only by the appearance of the captain of the ship, who comes to lead him away so that they may take advantage of the favourable wind that has begun to blow. When he lands on Bornholm, his sensitivity is almost immediately demonstrated by his desire 'to savour for a while yet the pleasures of the evening'.[41] Again, his first words to the young woman in the cave refer to his own sensitivity, which he hopes might help to ease her fate. And, when he leaves the cave, he again reveals his sensitive soul by reflecting on the grief of being excluded from the society of the free and joyful creatures with which Nature abounds, and on the presence of living signs of God's love, such as birdsong, gentle and fragrant breezes and velvety carpets of grass, even among the mossy cliffs of the north.[42]

3

And yet, if the narrator of **'The Island of Bornholm'** is identical in terms of his sensibility with the narrator of Karamzin's earlier sentimental tales and with his 'Russian traveller', nevertheless he does seem also to suffer a broader, more troubling spiritual disturbance than the exquisite melancholy induced by the individual plight of 'poor Liza' in 1792. The cause of this almost existential *Angst* may be sought partly in personal circum-

stances in Karamzin's life and in despondency at developments in Russia. Karamzin's contemporary and close friend A. A. Petrov had died in March 1793, an event which gave rise to the grief expressed in Karamzin's poem **'To a Nightingale'** (**'K solov'iu'**), first published in the same almanac in which **'The Island of Bornholm'** appeared, in which the poet feels as if he has been orphaned and looks ahead to his own death.[43] Moreover, former Masonic friends of Karamzin's had received his *Moscow Journal* (*Moskovskii zhurnal*) coolly. Again, A. N. Radishchev had been arrested and exiled in 1790; the poet and dramatist Ia. B. Kniazhnin had died in prison in 1791; and the publisher, journalist, philanthropist and Mason N. I. Novikov had been arrested in 1792.[44] However, behind Karamzin's crisis of 1793-4, there also lie fears about the extinction of enlightenment and humanist values in the wake of the French Revolution.[45]

The early phase of the French Revolution—the storming of the Bastille, the measures taken against feudalism by the Constituent Assembly and the Declaration of the Rights of Man and Citizen in July and August 1789—do not seem to have troubled Karamzin unduly. It is true that on first arriving in France, in August 1789, he finds that villages in Alsace are in revolt, villagers are sewing cockades to their hats, and a new uprising is beginning in Strasbourg, where soldiers disobey their officers and are unruly in the streets.[46] Occasional disturbing reports of events in France reach him in Switzerland in the autumn of 1789 and the winter of 1789-90: he hears the fear expressed that Swiss who have invested money in France will be bankrupted;[47] and in Basle he witnesses the emotional reunion of a French noble family, separated when the mother and father were forced to flee their burning castle by villagers threatening to kill them.[48] He reports the view that society in Paris, which he reaches in late March 1790, is not what it was before the Revolution, because the wealthiest and most noble families have fled into emigration.[49] He is made indignant during a visit to Versailles at the thought of the Parisian mob attempting, on the night of 5-6 October 1789, to arrest Marie-Antoinette and the king at their palace, and he compares Versailles without the court to the body without the soul.[50] (The degeneration is reflected in the fact that in the best inn the narrator and his companions have to wait two hours to be served a meal![51]) He is moved by the sight of the king and queen in church and evinces sympathy and admiration for them.[52] Reflecting at length on the Revolution in a letter dated April 1790, he presents revolution as an act of folly and warns of the dangers of giving free rein to popular sentiment, showing himself already to be a conservative advocate of a stable political order in general, and an admirer of the French monarchic regime and of the civilisation which flourished under its protection in particular.[53] And yet the disorder which Karamzin witnesses in Strasbourg seems

quite good-natured and does not distract him from his touristic pursuits, such as a visit to the majestic Gothic cathedral, from the top of whose tower, 725 steps high, it was frightening to look down on the town and the people, like insects, below.[54] And at the end of his description of his stay in Paris he reflects that he has lived peacefully and gaily there, a citizen of the world who has looked on the city's agitation with a tranquil soul. Neither the Jacobins nor the aristocrats have done him any harm.[55]

However, a revolution which at the time of Karamzin's sojourn in Paris in the spring of 1790 had had the character of an experiment in constitutional monarchy had, by the time he wrote **'The Island of Bornholm'** in 1793, taken on an altogether different complexion. The tension aroused in Europe by the attempted flight of Louis XVI and the royal family from France, and his arrest at Varennes in June 1791; France's declaration of war on Austria in April 1792 and the subsequent embroilment of the country in war with England, the United Provinces of the Netherlands, Spain and Prussia; the insurrection of August 1792, the involvement of the populace, the *sans-culottes,* in the Revolution and the ensuing ascendancy of the Montagnards and Jacobins over the more moderate Girondins; the trial of Louis XVI and his execution in January 1793; the establishment of the revolutionary government and the institution of the Terror in September 1793 and the execution of Marie-Antoinette in October of that year: all these factors and excesses had filled Karamzin with fear and revulsion by the time he came to prepare the first number of his new almanac in the winter of 1793-4. In these circumstances, it was difficult to sustain the optimistic mood represented by the pastoral manner. Instead, a mood of uncertainty, doubt, foreboding and moral confusion comes to the fore in a fictitious exchange of letters [**"Melodor k Filaletu" ("Melodor and Filalet"**)], which Karamzin wrote in late 1793 and early 1794, between characters to whom he gave the names Melodor and Filalet, or more particularly in the letter of Melodor with which the exchange opens.

Melodor (literally 'giver of music', who may be felt to represent Karamzin's poetic persona) gives voice to the crisis experienced by the optimistic lover of humanity who has imbibed the ideas of the eighteenth-century Enlightenment. Like a traveller sighing over what remains of Troy, he contemplates the ruins of all his hopes and plans (Melodor uses the word *razvaliny,* explicitly relating the favourite Gothic setting to the collapse of his spiritual world). He regards with horror the disintegration of the 'comforting system' devised in an age which, Melodor believes, had witnessed a softening of morals, a refinement of reason and feelings, an increase in the number of life's pleasures, the dissemination of a spirit of sociality and the establishment of milder governments and more amicable relations between peoples.

Together with Filalet, Melodor had reflected on the moral world, the nobility of the human soul and man's greatness of spirit. They had joyfully embraced all mortals as God's creatures and regarded all of Nature as a heavenly garden in which the divinity of mankind was ripening. In short, they had convinced themselves that the human race was climbing towards universal spiritual perfection. And yet the century was ending in blood and flames: Europe, the repository of the arts and sciences, was being devastated by a ferocious war. Surveying the fate of various civilisations, Melodor confronts the possibility that there exists some unknown law according to which humanity suffers a Sisyphean destiny, aspiring to pinnacles of enlightenment only to be cast down, each time a summit is reached, into renewed barbarism. The replacement of a notion of continuous progress by the notion of an eternal alternation of day and night, truth and error, virtue and vice leads Melodor to question the purpose of existence.[56]

The mood expressed by Karamzin through Melodor to a certain extent mirrors that of Gothic fiction at this period, or, to put it another way, Gothic fiction is an apt medium for the expression of a mood such as Melodor's. For Gothic fiction, like Melodor's letter, gropes for a formulation of the anxieties to which the French Revolution—among other factors, such as industrial revolution, urbanisation and attendant economic and social change—had given rise.[57]

The narrator of **'The Island of Bornholm'** shares the uncertainty of the age. He seems to have been confused by what he has witnessed even before he arrives on Bornholm. When the old man, who has long been cut off from the world, asks him whether love reigns on Earth, whether people worship virtue, whether peoples prosper in the countries the narrator has seen, the narrator's answer is ambiguous. The light of the sciences spreads more and more, he says, and yet blood still flows, the unfortunate still shed tears and people, while praising virtue, argue about its substance. On Bornholm the sight of Lila imprisoned in the cave prompts him to reflect on human cruelty and to ask why the Creator has given people the power to make each other and themselves unhappy. He seems though to have no clear answers to the questions that trouble him and the meaning of the tale is therefore perhaps less straightforward than some critics assume. His sympathies may seem to lie with Nature and sensibility.[58] And yet he is not confident enough of the legitimacy of the rights of Rousseau's natural man to protest at the treatment of the young woman according to the laws of convention, or to rail at the old man who has imprisoned her and who is in any case seen to share in the grief at the ruin of the family.[59] On the contrary, the narrator seems to accept what he has seen as *force majeure* and leaves the island without demurral.[60]

4

However, the trauma which Karamzin and his narrator have experienced as a result of the events of the early 1790s, in the case of the author, and the visit to Bornholm, in the case of the narrator, is not an entirely negative phenomenon. For Gothic aesthetics allow such experience a beneficial value: terror, so it is claimed, has an uplifting effect. The most influential eighteenth-century text on the subject is Edmund Burke's treatise *A Philosophical Enquiry into the Origin of our Ideas of the Sublime and the Beautiful* (1757). Burke contrasts beautiful objects, which are characterised by their smallness, delicacy, comprehensibility and perceptibility within the human gaze, with sublime objects, which were vast, magnificent, obscure, awe-inspiring and beyond the grasp of the rational mind. Sublime objects confronted the individual subject with an intimation of its own extinction and excited both delight and horror.[61]

Arguably, the narrator of **'The Island of Bornholm'**, too, gains some profit from his disturbing experience, by means of the access it affords him to a world beyond the mundane. The vocabulary of Gothic aesthetics— *velichestvennyi* ('majestic', 'awful', indeed 'sublime'), *neobozrimyi* ('boundless', 'immense'), *strashnyi* ('fearful', 'frightening', 'terrible'), *uzhas* ('horror')—is ubiquitous in **'The Island of Bornholm'** and sublimity and terror, intensified by a sense of the proximity of death, are ever-present and interlocking forces in the tale. The Thames, down which the narrator's boat speeds at the beginning of his voyage, is 'sublime'. The sweet inertia of the soul into which the narrator slips as he lies on the shore at Gravesend is 'the most striking and the most poetic form of death'. When the ship passes beyond the northern shores of England (or perhaps Karamzin means Britain) the birds which had soared over the vessel return to shore, as if frightened by the 'immensity' of the sea. Now the narrator—who appears to be the sole passenger on board—is confronted by nothing but the roaring sea and misty sky, which present themselves as 'a sublime and terrifying object' and whose infinity (*beskonechnost'*) captivates him. He cites Wieland—though the notion goes back to classical antiquity—to the effect that in the open sea only a slender piece of wood separates the sailor from a watery death. On Bornholm itself, the narrator is titillated by fear. His reception in the castle by the sinister servant creates in him 'an impression of terror, mixed partly with horror, partly with a secret, inexplicable pleasure or, to put it better, with the agreeable expectation of something extraordinary'. Even the gloomy avenue of rustling oak-trees, leading to the cave where Lila is imprisoned, produces a certain reverence (*blagogovenie*) in him. At the end of the tale infinity is again invoked implicitly, as Bornholm is lost to view and the narrator is once more alone between the heavens and the sea.

The sense of horror is provoked above all by mountains, the natural phenomena that most deeply affected Preromantic artists, for it was in mountains that the presence of the Creator was most keenly felt. The taste for mountainous scenery, prefigured in the reverential descriptions of the Bernese Oberland in *The Letters of a Russian Traveller*,[62] is reflected now in repeated references to Bornholm's massive cliffs and crags. It is the 'fearsome cliffs' (*groznye skaly*) of the island that first present themselves to the narrator as he approaches. Thus confronted with the hand of Nature, the horrified narrator, as a trembling mortal, is compelled to acknowledge cold, silent eternity and implacable death. The green plain to which the narrator and accompanying sailors and fishermen ascend from the rocky shore, during what seems in retrospect an idyllic evening interlude before the Gothic nightmare, reminds the narrator of Alpine valleys. Later, as he roams the castle grounds in the middle of the night, he sees in the distance the rocky crags that surround the island like a jagged wall. The mossy cliffs that are terrible to behold, the granite crags and foaming sea, feature again in his reflections upon emergence from the cave as he contemplates the boundless spaces of Nature.[63]

5

There is, finally, one other ray of light in **'The Island of Bornholm'**, besides the possible personal enrichment of the narrator by his terrifying experience.[64] Like Karamzin's fictitious epistoler Filalet, in his reply to Melodor,[65] the narrator seems to preserve intact some hope for the future. This hope he sustains by distancing himself in three ways from the events he has witnessed and by establishing, as a self-conscious Russian, the 'otherness' of Bornholm.[66]

Firstly, the paragraph with which the tale begins establishes emotional distance between the narrator and the events he is to describe, by telling us that the narrator and his listeners are now securely protected in his beloved home from the hostile elements. Winter is setting in: summer and autumn have passed, greenery has faded, the trees have lost their fruit and leaves and snow is beginning to fall. The storyteller and his audience must say goodbye to Nature for the time being. The season of death is, of course, a fitting backdrop to the story which the narrator has to tell, but at the same time the narrator and his listeners may look forward to a joyful tryst with spring and in the meantime they may take shelter before a flaming fire of oak and birch.

Secondly, Bornholm is removed from the narrator's audience by its extreme physical and indeed metaphysical inaccessibility. In order to reach it, one has to cross the huge, empty, fearsome sea. The voyage lasts a week and in the course of it the narrator travels to the edge of human consciousness, passing six days incapacitated by

seasickness with his eyes closed and his heart barely beating, before, on the seventh day, he comes back to life (*ozhil* is the word Karamzin uses). It is out of this journey to the seeming brink of terrestrial life that the narrator arrives at Bornholm. (It is perhaps indicative of the metaphysical dimension of the journey that Karamzin nowhere refers to the narrator in this tale by the matter-of-fact, even somewhat touristic term *puteshestvennik,* which he applies to the narrator of his grand travelogue, but uses instead the more poetic and even quasi-religious word *strannik.*) Even when the narrator reaches Bornholm, he is able to set foot on the island only with difficulty. It is a perilous place for boats, the captain tells him, for there are rocks and shoals concealed on the sea bed and the island has fearsome cliffs on all sides.[67] Once the boat is anchored, the captain at first resists the narrator's entreaty that he be allowed to go ashore in a dinghy. It is only because the narrator, his curiosity aroused by the apparition at Gravesend, is unyielding, that the captain finally agrees to the request, and even then only on condition that his passenger return to the ship early the next morning.

Thirdly, and perhaps most importantly, the narrator establishes ethnic, cultural and religious distance between himself, his listeners and readers, on the one hand, and Bornholm, its history, inhabitants and customs, on the other. We are repeatedly reminded in the tale of the foreignness of the narrator in Bornholm. The narrator strikingly introduces himself at the castle gates as 'foreigner' or more literally 'man from another land' (*chuzhezemets*). The old man and Lila (twice) address him in the same way and the servant, reporting to his master that the narrator has found the cave in which Lila is imprisoned, describes him similarly as '*chuzhestranets*'.[68] Moreover, Russian civilisation is presented by both sides in the story, Danish and Russian, as different from, and superior to, what is termed 'Gothic'. Interested by the news that his visitor is Russian, the old man asserts that the ancient inhabitants of Bornholm, and of the nearby Baltic island of Rügen, were also Slavs, but that the Russians were illuminated by Christianity at an earlier date. The Russians were already building magnificent temples devoted to the one God and glorifying the Creator in their hymns while the Baltic islanders, blinded by error, were still offering bloody pagan sacrifices to their idols. This association of Bornholm with paganism—and implicitly with human sacrifice—is pursued when the thought of druids springs to the narrator's mind, as he roams the castle grounds in the middle of the night and he imagines that he is drawing close 'to the sanctuary where all the secrets and horrors of their worship are preserved'.[69]

Perhaps, then, the Russians should not in the final analysis be too troubled by Karamzin's anxieties about Western Europe and by his narrator's Gothic experience. The relationship between Russia and other nations was

not, in Karamzin's time, being structured exclusively in terms of the antithesis of East and West with which we are familiar from nineteenth-century (and twentieth-century) Russian thought. It was also being conceived in terms of an opposition, inherent in Preromantic literature in general and Gothic literature in particular, between North and South. (It is the 'North' that the traveller in *The Letters of a Russian Traveller* sees himself as representing, even in central European Switzerland.[70]) The Russians, a subtext of **'The Island of Bornholm'** seems to tell us, are one of the northern peoples whose historical moment is approaching and who, even among the northern peoples themselves, enjoy pride of place by virtue of their spiritual heritage, and perhaps by virtue of a native goodness and sensitivity represented in the tale by the narrator. These qualities may help to protect them, in their cosy family hearth, from the cataclysmic events sweeping Europe. Seen in this light, Karamzin's apparently exceptional experiment with the Gothic mode in **'The Island of Bornholm'** is not only an apt expression of his pessimistic mood in 1793-4 but it also chimes both with his early Sentimentalism and with the defence of conservative values with which he was to be concerned during the second half of his career, as political thinker and historian in the age of Alexander I.

Notes

1. In general Karamzin reveres Rousseau as one of the creators of the new sensibility; see, for example, the description of the narrator's pilgrimage to Rousseau's former home at Vevey and to his grave at Ermenonville near Paris, and the reflections to which these visits give rise, in *Pis'ma russkogo puteshestvennika*: N. M. Karamzin, *Izbrannye sochineniia,* 2 vols., Moscow-Leningrad, 1964 (hereafter *Izb. soch.*), vol. 1, pp. 277-81, 490-96. However, see also note 36 below.

2. 'Vyzdorovlenie', *Izb. soch.,* 2, pp. 15-16.

3. 'Kladbishche', ibid., pp. 28-9.

4. 'Bednaia Liza', ibid., 1, pp. 605-06.

5. See, for example, *Pis'ma russkogo puteshestvennika,* in *Izb. soch.,* 1, pp. 207, 225, 238-9.

6. Ibid., pp. 262-3.

7. Ibid., p. 266.

8. Ibid., pp. 242, 245-6.

9. Ibid., pp. 254-5, 274, 351, 401-02.

10. Ibid., pp. 325-8.

11. Ibid., pp. 274, 362-3.

12. Ibid., p. 495.

13. James Thomson (1700-48), author of 'Seasons', is mentioned or quoted in *Pis'ma russkogo puteshestvennika* on pp. 344-5, 572, 587.

14. Ossian, or his poetry, is mentioned in ibid., pp. 172, 363, 598.

15. Ibid., pp. 402-03. The old woman, whose story of course deeply affects and is carefully recorded by the sensitive traveller, had lived quietly and happily in a little hut with her daughter Luiza, in a time when the world was better and people had more goodness. Luiza loved to sing and would go to the woods to gather flowers. Creditors would bother them, but Luiza would talk to them and they would relent. However, Luiza died, leaving the old woman vulnerable. She had been driven from her home by creditors and was now stoically awaiting her death.

16. Ibid., pp. 182-3.

17. The terms 'Sentimentalism' and 'Preromanticism' are much confused in both Russian and Western writing on Russian literature of the second half of the eighteenth century: see G. S. Smith, 'Sentimentalism and Preromanticism as Terms and Concepts', in *Russian Literature in the Age of Catherine the Great,* edited by A. G. Cross, Oxford, Meeuws, 1976, pp. 173-84. In the present essay, the sceptical view towards which Smith tends is accepted: namely that Sentimentalism (which is 'a term found almost exclusively in Russian literary criticism and history') and Preromanticism are 'merely different names for the same literary movement' (pp. 173, 181). For an opposing point of view, according to which Sentimentalism and Preromanticism are different movements, see, for example, Rudolf Neuhäuser, 'Periodization and Classification of Sentimental and Preromantic Trends in Russian Literature between 1750 and 1815', in *Canadian Contributions to the Seventh International Congress of Slavists,* The Hague, Mouton, 1973, pp. 11-39 (especially pp. 31-3).

18. Written in French in 1782 and published in English translation in 1786.

19. The novel first appeared under the title *The Champion of Virtue: a Gothic Story* in 1777; the second edition, entitled *The Old English Baron,* came out in 1778.

20. The novel was first published in 1783-5.

21. See V. E. Vatsuro, 'Literaturno-filosofskaia problematika povesti Karamzina "Ostrov Borngol'm"', in *XVIII vek,* 8, Leningrad, 1969, pp. 190-209 (192): hereafter Vatsuro (1969).

22. Ibid.

23. V. E. Vatsuro, 'A. Radklif, ee pervye russkie chitateli i perevodchiki', *Novoe literaturnoe obozrenie,* 22, 1996, pp. 204-06, 223: hereafter Vatsuro (1996).

24. The point is made explicitly by Vatsuro (1969), pp. 192, 194, who also mentions other writers who are known to Karamzin and who by degrees develop the literary technique of the Gothic novel: J.-P. Florian (1755-94), F. de Baculard d'Arnaud (1718-1805), abbé A. F. Prévost (1697-1763).

25. *Night Thoughts,* the most celebrated work by Edward Young (1683-1765), made a deep impression on Derzhavin as well as on Karamzin.

26. Moscow Sentimentalists following in Karamzin's footsteps, such as P. I. Shalikov and F. V. Sibirskii, tended to see early Gothic works such as the novels of Ann Radcliffe in this light: see Vatsuro (1969), p. 192; and idem (1996), p. 204.

27. The Gothic elements of 'Ostrov Borngol'm' have been most fully explored by Vatsuro (1969). See also Gitta Hammarberg, *From the Idyll to the Novel: Karamzin's Sentimentalist Prose,* Cambridge, Cambridge University Press, 1991, pp. 182-202. For further discussion see Iu. Lotman, 'Evoliutsiia mirovozzreniia Karamzina (1789-1803)', in *Trudy istoriko-filologicheskogo fakul'teta (Uchenye zapiski Tartuskogo gosudarstvennogo universiteta,* 51), Tartu, 1957, pp. 122-62; Henry M. Nebel, *N. M. Karamzin: A Russian Sentimentalist,* The Hague, Mouton, 1967, pp. 145-8, 175; Anthony G. Cross, *N. M. Karamzin: A Study of His Literary Career 1783-1803,* Carbondale, Southern Illinois University Press, 1971, pp. 113-15; Rudolf Neuhäuser, *Towards the Romantic Age: Essays on Sentimental and Preromantic Literature in Russia,* The Hague, Martinus Nijhoff, 1974, pp. 180-82; idem, 'Karamzin's Spiritual Crisis of 1793-1794', in *Essays on Karamzin: Russian Man-of-Letters, Political Thinker, Historian, 1766-1826,* edited by J. L. Black, The Hague, Mouton, 1975, pp. 56-74; Natalya Kochetkova, *Nikolay Karamzin,* Boston, Twayne, 1975, pp. 86-9.

28. The traveller in *Pis'ma russkogo puteshestvennika* befriends a young Danish chemist with whom he travels in Switzerland and France.

29. The tale is reprinted in *Izb. soch.,* 1, pp. 661-73; for an English translation, see *The Selected Prose of N. M. Karamzin,* translated by Henry M. Nebel, Evanston, Northwestern University Press, 1969, pp. 117-31. Since the work is very short, further page references will not be provided.

30. Fred Botting, *Gothic,* London, Routledge, 1996, p. 2.

31. Karamzin's probable sources for the common Gothic motif of a woman's underground prison—passages in French works by Mme de Genlis (1746-1830) and Monvel (J. M. Boutet; 1745-

1812)—are discussed in Vatsuro (1969), pp. 201-2. Other Gothic works in which the motif appears include *A Sicilian Romance* (Ann Radcliffe) and *The Children of the Abbey* (Regina Maria Roche).

32. For further discussion of the narrator's dreams, see Vatsuro (1969), pp. 200-01.

33. When he sees the young man, the narrator observes: 'My gaze could not meet his' (*Vzor moi ne mog vstretit'sia s ego vzorom*); in the cave, on seeing the young woman, he remarks: 'my gaze again met hers' (*vzor moi eshche vstretilsia s ee vzorom*).

34. Botting, p. 5.

35. See *Izb. soch.*, 2, p. 80. A similar defence of Shakespeare against Voltaire is mounted by Horace Walpole in the preface to the second edition of *The Castle of Otranto* (1765): see The World's Classics edition, edited by W. S. Lewis with a new introduction and notes by E. J. Clery, Oxford, Oxford University Press, 1996, pp. 10-14.

36. *Izb. soch.*, 2, pp. 120-22. It should be noted though that in his essay 'Nechto o naukakh, iskusstvakh i prosveshchenii', written in the winter and spring of 1793 and published in the first number of *Aglaia* together with 'Ostrov Borngol'm', Karamzin expresses reservations about Rousseau's belief that enlightenment is a corrupting influence on man. If science and art are an evil, he argues here, then they are a necessary evil, for they are the fruits of man's innate curiosity and desire to improve his life both physically and morally. By showing us the beauties of sublime Nature, they elevate the soul and make it more sensitive and tender and stimulate in us a love of order, harmony and goodness and, conversely, an antipathy to disorder, dissonance and vice. The enlightenment which Rousseau reviles, then, is a 'palladium of good morals': *Izb. soch.*, 2, pp. 122-42 (especially 124-9, 139-40). Even in this essay, though, Karamzin at the outset reiterates his reverence for Rousseau (pp. 122-3).

37. See, for example, Kantemir's notes to line 423 of Satire V and line 121 of Satire VII, in Antiokh Kantemir, *Sobranie stikhotvorenii*, Leningrad, 1956, pp. 142, 167.

38. *Izb. soch.*, 1, p. 652.

39. Support for this assertion seems to be provided by Vatsuro's classification of 'Ostrov Borngol'm' as close to an 'elegiac fragment', a term used by Karamzin himself to describe his work 'Sierra-Morena' (1795): see Vatsuro (1969), p. 195. Vatsuro also notes here the static quality of the tale 'Ostrov Borngol'm', its lack of narrative in the normal sense, representing its main point of difference from the Gothic novel or tale.

40. We might add that in retrospect, with the publication of the complete *Pis'ma russkogo puteshestvennika* in 1801, we also see a clear narratorial connection between 'Ostrov Borngol'm' and the concluding pages of *Pis'ma russkogo puteshestvennika*. Like the narrator of 'Ostrov Borngol'm', the Russian traveller also sails down the Thames and on to the open sea in an English vessel, is racked for days on end by seasickness and marvels at the immensity of the sea, the howling of the storm and man's audacity in the face of Nature. This traveller also reads Ossian and translates Carthon on the voyage and, with his imagination filled with threatening Ossianic images, negotiates the perilous waters past the Norwegian cliffs on a dark and stormy night. Like the visitor to Bornholm, he makes a hackneyed reference to 'Neptune's kingdom' during his voyage (op. cit., pp. 596-600.) It should be noted though that the mood of the concluding pages of the travelogue is quite different from that of the Gothic tale: in the *Pis'ma*, Karamzin is full of wit and exultant as he approaches his native land after a long absence.

41. The narrator has in fact spent the six days prior to his arrival on Bornholm prostrate and virtually unconscious as a result of seasickness. He would therefore appear to be altogether unprepared physically for the exertions of his stay on the island. However, verisimilitude, despite the claims of Karamzin's narrators, is not of great importance in Sentimentalist fiction!

42. This passage is somewhat reminiscent of the reflections prompted in the narrator in *Pis'ma russkogo puteshestvennika* by the story of Luiza's mother in the deserted castle in the Bois de Boulogne (see note 15 above). How much magnificence there is in the physical world, the narrator muses here, and how much calamity there is in the moral world. How can the unfortunate person weighed down by the burden of his being, isolated among the multitude of the cold and the cruel, rejoice at the magnificence of the golden sun, the pure blue sky, the green meadows and woods (op. cit., p. 403.)?

43. 'K solov'iu', *Izb. soch.*, 2, p. 32.

44. See Neuhäuser, 'Karamzin's Spiritual Crisis . . .' (cited note 27 above).

45. As noted, for example, by Vatsuro (1969), p. 190; and Neuhäuser, 'Karamzin's Spiritual Crisis . . .', pp. 67-8.

46. *Pis'ma russkogo puteshestvennika*: in *Izb. soch.*, 1, p. 202.

47. Ibid., p. 291.

48. Ibid., pp. 210-11.

49. On the other hand, another Parisian tells the traveller that Paris had already declined before the outbreak of the Revolution from the heights it had reached under Louis XIV (ibid., pp. 378-80).

50. Ibid., pp. 472-3.

51. Ibid., p. 473.

52. Ibid., pp. 380-1.

53. Ibid., pp. 381-3.

54. Ibid., pp. 202-03.

55. Ibid., p. 507.

56. *Melodor k Filaletu*: in *Izb. soch.*, 2, pp. 245-51. In his reply, Filalet (literally 'lover of truth', who may be felt to represent Karamzin's philosophical persona) writes with resignation and tries to salvage hope amid the prevailing despair. He accepts that the moral order is not so clear to us as the physical order but, seeing God in the natural world, in the movement of the planets and the cycle of the seasons, refuses to believe that God has no function in the moral world and clings to a faith that there is a seed of goodness in the human heart which will again bear fruit when conditions are propitious (ibid., pp. 251-8). This air of resignation and fresh hope is expressed too in an epistle in verse to the poet Dmitriev, which Karamzin wrote in late 1793 in response to a lament by Dmitriev about the rapid passing of the period of happy youth ('Poslanie k Dmitrievu', ibid., pp. 34-8—published in 1794, but not in the almanac *Aglaia*). The renewed faith that individual virtue and goodness may prevail is also reflected in the novella *Iuliia,* published in 1794 (see Neuhäuser, 'Karamzin's Spiritual Crisis . . .', pp. 72-3).

57. It does not seem coincidental that the Gothic novel, if viewed as an appropriate vehicle through which to articulate a sense of moral crisis and social uncertainty, was at its most popular in the decade after the French Revolution (see Botting, p. 5).

58. As argued by Hammarberg (op. cit., p. 199), who believes that the old man's practice of following the divine commandments 'more to the letter than to the spirit' is 'unacceptable to the Sentimental narrator'.

59. That the old man too is crushed by this incestuous or adulterous affair is suggested by the fact that he shares traits with the young man and the young woman. He too speaks in a quiet voice and refers to his dying heart. The narrator likens him to a cold autumn day, one more reminiscent of a sorrowful winter than a joyful summer; the signs of sorrow in his heart do not disappear from his face for a moment, despite his best efforts to be hospitable.

60. This fact does not seem altogether to warrant the conclusion of P. N. Berkov and G. P. Makogonenko, in their introductory article to the collection of Karamzin's works to which reference is made in this essay, that the emotional final paragraph of 'Ostrov Borngol'm' shows that Karamzin sets the 'laws of heaven' and 'virtue' higher than the 'law of innate feelings' (see *Izb. soch.*, 1, p. 39). A similar position (that, in the light of events in France, Karamzin felt 'a need to subordinate one's passions to reason in the name of preservation of virtue') is adopted by P. A. Orlov, in his introductory article in the anthology *Russkaia sentimental'naia povest'*, Moscow, 1979, p. 16. However, the narrator of the 'elegiac fragment' 'Sierra-Morena', published in the second number of *Aglaia* in 1795, still does not accept that the dictates of the heart can be overcome, though one may struggle long and hard against its impulses: see *Izb. soch.*, 1, p. 676.

61. See Botting, p. 39 (and pp. 4, 23-4).

62. *Izb. soch.,* 1, pp. 256-8.

63. Mountains are explicitly associated with horror and sublimity in 'Sierra-Morena': they are among the 'horrors [*uzhasy*] of Nature' which 'exalted, enraptured, nourished [*vozvelichivali, voskhishchali, pitali*]' the soul of the heroine (*Izb. soch.*, 1, p. 675).

64. It should be noted that Gitta Hammarberg interprets the whole tale as an idyll in which the sombre and terrifying features serve to throw the positive features of the work into sharper relief (op. cit., p. 202).

65. See note 56 above.

66. In this respect, as in others, Karamzin behaves in 'Ostrov Borngol'm' like a typical Gothic author, for distancing is a stock device of the northern-European Protestant writers of the late eighteenth century, who in their romances often supposedly observe the history and mores of Catholic southern-European peoples in the late Middle Ages or early modern times.

67. Karamzin is granting himself some fictional licence here: whereas the northern part of the island is composed of granite and does indeed have a rocky cliff coast, the undulating southern part, composed of sandstone, limestone and shale, has a dune coast.

68. The narrator is also addressed twice as '*molodoi chelovek*' ('young man') by the old man; and as '*neschastnoi*' ('wretch') and '*derzkoi*' ('audacious') by the knights in his dream.

69. Germanic pagans and druids also come to the narrator's mind in *Pis'ma russkogo puteshestvennika* (*Izb. soch.*, 1, p. 106), as he travels away from Russia, in the vicinity of Königsberg.

70. Ibid., pp. 266, 291. He also looks forward from the River Elbe, near the beginning of his journey, to his return to his 'distant northern homeland' (p. 151).

FURTHER READING

Biographies

Murav'ev, Vladimir Bronislavovich. *Nikolai Karamzin.* Moscow: Izograf (EKSMO), 2005, 602 p.

Offers a comprehensive overview of Karamzin's life and career.

Shamshurin, Valerii. *Nikolai Karamzin.* Moscow: Novator, 1998, 401 p.

Provides an in-depth portrait of the historian and author.

Criticism

Anderson, Roger B. "The 'Split Personality' of the Narrator in N. M. Karamzin's *Pis'ma Russkogo Puteschestvennika*: A Textual Analysis." *Études Slaves et Est-Européennes* 13 (1968): 20-31.

Examines Karamzin's innovative use of language in *Pis'ma Russkogo Puteschestvennika.*

Bilenkin, Vladimir. "The Sublime Moment: *Velichestvennoe* in N. M. Karamzin's *Letters of a Russian Traveler.*" *Slavic and East European Journal* 42, no. 4 (winter 1998): 605-20.

Examines Karamzin's *Letters of a Russian Traveler* within the context of aesthetic discourse during the Enlightenment. Bilenkin pays particularly close attention to Karamzin's attitudes toward the sublime, arguing that Karamzin's investigations into European notions of individuality and creativity exerted an indelible impact on nineteenth-century Russian literature.

Black, J. L. *Essays on Karamzin: Russian Man-of-Letters, Political Thinker, Historian, 1766-1826.* The Hague: Mouton, 1975, 232 p.

Offers a range of critical perspectives on Karamzin's literary works.

Cross, A. G. "Karamzin Studies: For the Bicentenary of the Birth of N. M. Karamzin (1766-1966)." *Slavonic and East European Review* 45 (1967): 1-11.

Provides a basic overview of Karamzin's life and work.

———. "Problems of Form and Literary Influence in the Poetry of Karamzin." *Slavic Review* 27 (1968): 39-48.

Examines the diverse influences that helped shape Karamzin's unique literary style.

———. "Karamzin's *Moskovskii Zhurnal*: Voice of a Writer, Broadsheet of a Movement." *Cahiers du Monde Russe* 28, no. 2 (April-June 1987): 121-26.

Evaluates Karamzin's work as editor of *Moskovskii Zhurnal.*

Dabars, Zita D. "The Simile in the Poetry of Sumarokov, Karamzin, and Derzhavin." *Russian Literature Triquarterly* 7 (1973): 389-406.

Offers a comparative analysis of the writings of Nikolai Karamzin, Alexsandr Sumarokov, and Gavriil Derzhavin.

Davidson, Dan E. "N. M. Karamzin and the New Critical Vocabulary: Toward a Semantic History of the Term 'Romantic' in Russia." In *Mnemozina: Studia litteraria russica in honorem Vsevolod Setchkarev,* edited by Joachim T. Baer and Norman W. Ingham, pp. 88-94. Munich: Wilhelm Fink Verlag, 1974.

Discusses Karamzin's role in introducing the language of European romanticism into the Russian literary lexicon.

———. "Christoph Martin Wieland in Russia: On the Role of Nikojai Mixajlovic Karamsin (1766-1826)." *Lessing Yearbook* 15 (1983): 213-32.

Examines the influence of Wieland's writings on the work of Nikolai Karamzin.

Emerson, Caryl. "The Boris Plot on Stage: Karamzin, Pushkin, and Musorgsky as Historical Thinkers." In *Intersections and Transportations: Russian Music, Literature, and Society,* pp. 20-32. Evanston, Ill.: Northwestern University Press, 1998.

Discusses the influence of Karamzin's historical writings on later artistic representations of Boris Godunov.

Garrard, J. G. "Karamzin in Recent Soviet Criticism: A Review Article." *Slavic and East European Journal* 11, no. 4 (winter 1967): 464-72.

Evaluates the resurgence of critical interest in Karamzin's work in the 1960s Soviet Union.

Hammarberg, Gitta. "Eighteenth Century Narrative Variations on 'Frol Skobeev.'" *Slavic Review* 46, no. 3-4 (fall-winter 1987): 529-39.

Discusses questions of voice and narrative structure in Karamzin's "Natali'ia, boiarskaia doch'," comparing the story with Ivan Novikov's "Novgorodskikh devushek sviatochnyi vecher" and the anonymous tale "Povest' o Frole Skobeeve."

———."Karamzin's 'Progulka' as Sentimentalist Manifesto." *Russian, Croatian and Serbian, Czech and Slovak, Polish Literature* 26, no. 3 (October 1989): 249-65.

Examines aspects of sentimentalism in Karamzin's early writings.

Herman, David. "Innocents at Home: 'Bednaja Liza' as a Response to *Pis'ma russkogo putesestvennika.*" *Russian, Croatian and Serbian, Czech and Slovak, Polish Literature* 44, no. 2 (August 1998): 159-83.

Examines Karamzin's attitudes toward Russian and European culture in his fiction.

Hixon, Jennifer J. "The Fall of Novgorod in Karamzin's Fiction and History." In *Russian Subjects: Empire, Nation, and the Culture of the Golden Age,* edited by Monika Greenleaf and Stephen Moeller-Sally, pp. 193-210. Evanston, Ill.: Northwestern University Press, 1998.

Examines representations of the fall of Novgorod in Karamzin's body of work. Hixon argues that, while Karamzin clearly admired the republican ideals of Novgorod, he regarded Ivan the Great's conquest of the independent state as a historical necessity, one vital to the future of the Russian nation.

Jensen, Kjeld Bjørnager. "The Fruits of Curiosity: On the Composition of N. M. Karamzin's 'Ос о Бо гол .'" *Svantevit* 4, no. 1 (1978): 51-9.

Examines aspects of sentimentalism in Karamzin's "The Island of Bornholm."

Kleespies, Ingrid. "East West Home Is Best: The Grand Tour in D. I. Fonvizin's *Pis'ma iz Frantsii* and N. M. Karamzin's *Pis'ma russkogo putesestvennika.*" *Russian, Croatian and Serbian, Czech and Slovak, Polish Literature* 52, no. 1-3 (July-October 2002): 251-69.

Compares the influence of European culture on ideas of Russian identity in the two works.

Markov, Vladimir. "Bal'mont and Karamzin: Towards a 'Sociology' of Bal'mont's Poetry." In *Text and Context: Essays to Honor Nils Åke Nilsson,* edited by Peter Alberg Jensen, Barbara Lonnqvist, Fiona Bjorling, Lars Kleberg, and Anders Sjoberg, pp. 71-5. Stockholm: Almqvist & Wiksell, 1987.

Discusses literary approaches to the subject of Russian history in the works of Karamzin and Konstantin Bal'mont.

Uspenskij, Boris A. "The Language Program of N. M. Karamzin and Its Historical Antecedents." In *Aspects of the Slavic Language Question: East Slavic,* edited by Riccardo Picchio, Harvey Goldblatt, and Susanne Fusso. Vol. 2, pp. 237-96. New Haven, Conn.: Yale Concilium on International and Area Studies, 1984.

Analyzes Karamzin's linguistic theories.

Ziolkowski, Margaret. "Hagiography and History: The Saintly Prince in the Poetry of the Decembrists." *Slavic and East European Journal* 30, no. 1 (spring 1986): 29-44.

Examines the influence of Karamzin's historical writings on the poetry of the Decembrists.

Additional coverage of Karamzin's life and career is contained in the following sources published by Thomson Gale: *Dictionary of Literary Biography,* Vol. 150; *Literature Resource Center*; *Nineteenth-Century Literature Criticism,* Vol. 3; and *Reference Guide to Short Fiction,* Ed. 2.

How to Use This Index

The main references

> **Calvino, Italo**
> 1923-1985 CLC 5, 8, 11, 22, 33, 39,
> 73; SSC 3, 48

list all author entries in the following Thomson Gale Literary Criticism series:

AAL = *Asian American Literature*
BG = *The Beat Generation: A Gale Critical Companion*
BLC = *Black Literature Criticism*
BLCS = *Black Literature Criticism Supplement*
CLC = *Contemporary Literary Criticism*
CLR = *Children's Literature Review*
CMLC = *Classical and Medieval Literature Criticism*
DC = *Drama Criticism*
FL = *Feminism in Literature: A Gale Critical Companion*
GL = *Gothic Literature: A Gale Critical Companion*
HLC = *Hispanic Literature Criticism*
HLCS = *Hispanic Literature Criticism Supplement*
HR = *Harlem Renaissance: A Gale Critical Companion*
LC = *Literature Criticism from 1400 to 1800*
NCLC = *Nineteenth-Century Literature Criticism*
NNAL = *Native North American Literature*
PC = *Poetry Criticism*
SSC = *Short Story Criticism*
TCLC = *Twentieth-Century Literary Criticism*
WLC = *World Literature Criticism, 1500 to the Present*
WLCS = *World Literature Criticism Supplement*

The cross-references

> See also CA 85-88, 116; CANR 23, 61;
> DAM NOV; DLB 196; EW 13; MTCW 1, 2;
> RGSF 2; RGWL 2; SFW 4; SSFS 12

list all author entries in the following Thomson Gale biographical and literary sources:

AAYA = *Authors & Artists for Young Adults*
AFAW = *African American Writers*
AFW = *African Writers*
AITN = *Authors in the News*
AMW = *American Writers*
AMWR = *American Writers Retrospective Supplement*
AMWS = *American Writers Supplement*
ANW = *American Nature Writers*
AW = *Ancient Writers*
BEST = *Bestsellers*
BPFB = *Beacham's Encyclopedia of Popular Fiction: Biography and Resources*
BRW = *British Writers*
BRWS = *British Writers Supplement*
BW = *Black Writers*
BYA = *Beacham's Guide to Literature for Young Adults*
CA = *Contemporary Authors*
CAAS = *Contemporary Authors Autobiography Series*
CABS = *Contemporary Authors Bibliographical Series*
CAD = *Contemporary American Dramatists*
CANR = *Contemporary Authors New Revision Series*
CAP = *Contemporary Authors Permanent Series*
CBD = *Contemporary British Dramatists*
CCA = *Contemporary Canadian Authors*
CD = *Contemporary Dramatists*
CDALB = *Concise Dictionary of American Literary Biography*

CDALBS = *Concise Dictionary of American Literary Biography Supplement*
CDBLB = *Concise Dictionary of British Literary Biography*
CMW = *St. James Guide to Crime & Mystery Writers*
CN = *Contemporary Novelists*
CP = *Contemporary Poets*
CPW = *Contemporary Popular Writers*
CSW = *Contemporary Southern Writers*
CWD = *Contemporary Women Dramatists*
CWP = *Contemporary Women Poets*
CWRI = *St. James Guide to Children's Writers*
CWW = *Contemporary World Writers*
DA = *DISCovering Authors*
DA3 = *DISCovering Authors 3.0*
DAB = *DISCovering Authors: British Edition*
DAC = *DISCovering Authors: Canadian Edition*
DAM = *DISCovering Authors: Modules*
 DRAM: *Dramatists Module;* **MST:** *Most-studied Authors Module;*
 MULT: *Multicultural Authors Module;* **NOV:** *Novelists Module;*
 POET: *Poets Module;* **POP:** *Popular Fiction and Genre Authors Module*
DFS = *Drama for Students*
DLB = *Dictionary of Literary Biography*
DLBD = *Dictionary of Literary Biography Documentary Series*
DLBY = *Dictionary of Literary Biography Yearbook*
DNFS = *Literature of Developing Nations for Students*
EFS = *Epics for Students*
EXPN = *Exploring Novels*
EXPP = *Exploring Poetry*
EXPS = *Exploring Short Stories*
EW = *European Writers*
FANT = *St. James Guide to Fantasy Writers*
FW = *Feminist Writers*
GFL = *Guide to French Literature,* Beginnings to 1789, 1798 to the Present
GLL = *Gay and Lesbian Literature*
HGG = *St. James Guide to Horror, Ghost & Gothic Writers*
HW = *Hispanic Writers*
IDFW = *International Dictionary of Films and Filmmakers: Writers and Production Artists*
IDTP = *International Dictionary of Theatre: Playwrights*
LAIT = *Literature and Its Times*
LAW = *Latin American Writers*
JRDA = *Junior DISCovering Authors*
MAICYA = *Major Authors and Illustrators for Children and Young Adults*
MAICYAS = *Major Authors and Illustrators for Children and Young Adults Supplement*
MAWW = *Modern American Women Writers*
MJW = *Modern Japanese Writers*
MTCW = *Major 20th-Century Writers*
NCFS = *Nonfiction Classics for Students*
NFS = *Novels for Students*
PAB = *Poets: American and British*
PFS = *Poetry for Students*
RGAL = *Reference Guide to American Literature*
RGEL = *Reference Guide to English Literature*
RGSF = *Reference Guide to Short Fiction*
RGWL = *Reference Guide to World Literature*
RHW = *Twentieth-Century Romance and Historical Writers*
SAAS = *Something about the Author Autobiography Series*
SATA = *Something about the Author*
SFW = *St. James Guide to Science Fiction Writers*
SSFS = *Short Stories for Students*
TCWW = *Twentieth-Century Western Writers*
WLIT = *World Literature and Its Times*
WP = *World Poets*
YABC = *Yesterday's Authors of Books for Children*
YAW = *St. James Guide to Young Adult Writers*

Literary Criticism Series
Cumulative Author Index

20/1631
See Upward, Allen

A/C Cross
See Lawrence, T(homas) E(dward)

A. M.
See Megged, Aharon

Abasiyanik, Sait Faik 1906-1954
See Sait Faik
See also CA 123; 231

Abbey, Edward 1927-1989 **CLC 36, 59;
TCLC 160**
See also AMWS 13; ANW; CA 45-48; 128;
CANR 2, 41, 131; DA3; DLB 256, 275;
LATS 1:2; MTCW 2; MTFW 2005;
TCWW 1, 2

Abbott, Edwin A. 1838-1926 **TCLC 139**
See also DLB 178

Abbott, Lee K(ittredge) 1947- **CLC 48**
See also CA 124; CANR 51, 101; DLB 130

Abe, Kobo 1924-1993 **CLC 8, 22, 53, 81;
SSC 61; TCLC 131**
See also CA 65-68; 140; CANR 24, 60;
DAM NOV; DFS 14; DLB 182; EWL 3;
MJW; MTCW 1, 2; MTFW 2005; NFS
22; RGWL 3; SFW 4

Abe Kobo
See Abe, Kobo

Abelard, Peter c. 1079-c. 1142 **CMLC 11,
77**
See also DLB 115, 208

Abell, Kjeld 1901-1961 **CLC 15**
See also CA 191; 111; DLB 214; EWL 3

Abercrombie, Lascelles
1881-1938 **TCLC 141**
See also CA 112; DLB 19; RGEL 2

Abish, Walter 1931- **CLC 22; SSC 44**
See also CA 101; CANR 37, 114, 153; CN
3, 4, 5, 6; DLB 130, 227; MAL 5; RGHL

Abrahams, Peter (Henry) 1919- **CLC 4**
See also AFW; BW 1; CA 57-60; CANR
26, 125; CDWLB 3; CN 1, 2, 3, 4, 5, 6;
DLB 117, 225; EWL 3; MTCW 1, 2;
RGEL 2; WLIT 2

Abrams, M(eyer) H(oward) 1912- ... **CLC 24**
See also CA 57-60; CANR 13, 33; DLB 67

Abse, Dannie 1923- **CLC 7, 29; PC 41**
See also CA 53-56; CAAS 1; CANR 4, 46,
74, 124; CBD; CN 1, 2, 3; CP 1, 2, 3, 4,
5, 6, 7; DAB; DAM POET; DLB 27, 245;
MTCW 2

Abutsu 1222(?)-1283 **CMLC 46**
See Abutsu-ni

Abutsu-ni
See Abutsu
See also DLB 203

Achebe, (Albert) Chinua(lumogu)
1930- **BLC 1; CLC 1, 3, 5, 7, 11, 26,
51, 75, 127, 152; WLC 1**
See also AAYA 15; AFW; BPFB 1; BRWC
2; BW 2, 3; CA 1-4R; CANR 6, 26, 47,
124; CDWLB 3; CLR 20; CN 1, 2, 3, 4,
5, 6, 7; CP 2, 3, 4, 5, 6, 7; CWRI 5; DA;
DA3; DAB; DAC; DAM MST, MULT,
NOV; DLB 117; DNFS 1; EWL 3; EXPN;
EXPS; LAIT 2; LATS 1:2; MAICYA 1, 2;
MTCW 1, 2; MTFW 2005; NFS 2; RGEL
2; RGSF 2; SATA 38, 40; SATA-Brief 38;
SSFS 3, 13; TWA; WLIT 2; WWE 1

Acker, Kathy 1948-1997 **CLC 45, 111**
See also AMWS 12; CA 117; 122; 162;
CANR 55; CN 5, 6; MAL 5

Ackroyd, Peter 1949- **CLC 34, 52, 140**
See also BRWS 6; CA 123; 127; CANR 51,
74, 99, 132; CN 4, 5, 6, 7; DLB 155, 231;
HGG; INT CA-127; MTCW 2; MTFW
2005; RHW; SATA 153; SUFW 2

Acorn, Milton 1923-1986 **CLC 15**
See also CA 103; CCA 1; CP 1, 2, 3, 4;
DAC; DLB 53; INT CA-103

Adam de la Halle c. 1250-c.
1285 **CMLC 80**

Adamov, Arthur 1908-1970 **CLC 4, 25**
See also CA 17-18; 25-28R; CAP 2; DAM
DRAM; DLB 321; EWL 3; GFL 1789 to
the Present; MTCW 1; RGWL 2, 3

Adams, Alice (Boyd) 1926-1999 .. **CLC 6, 13,
46; SSC 24**
See also CA 81-84; 179; CANR 26, 53, 75,
88, 136; CN 4, 5, 6; CSW; DLB 234;
DLBY 1986; INT CANR-26; MTCW 1,
2; MTFW 2005; SSFS 14, 21

Adams, Andy 1859-1935 **TCLC 56**
See also TCWW 1, 2; YABC 1

Adams, (Henry) Brooks
1848-1927 **TCLC 80**
See also CA 123; 193; DLB 47

Adams, Douglas (Noel) 1952-2001 .. **CLC 27,
60**
See also AAYA 4, 33; BEST 89:3; BYA 14;
CA 106; 197; CANR 34, 64, 124; CPW;
DA3; DAM POP; DLB 261; DLBY 1983;
JRDA; MTCW 2; MTFW 2005; NFS 7;
SATA 116; SATA-Obit 128; SFW 4

Adams, Francis 1862-1893 **NCLC 33**

Adams, Henry (Brooks)
1838-1918 **TCLC 4, 52**
See also AMW; CA 104; 133; CANR 77;
DA; DAB; DAC; DAM MST; DLB 12,
47, 189, 284; EWL 3; MAL 5; MTCW 2;
NCFS 1; RGAL 4; TUS

Adams, John 1735-1826 **NCLC 106**
See also DLB 31, 183

Adams, Mary
See Phelps, Elizabeth Stuart

Adams, Richard (George) 1920- ... **CLC 4, 5,
18**
See also AAYA 16; AITN 1, 2; BPFB 1;
BYA 5; CA 49-52; CANR 3, 35, 128;
CLR 20; CN 4, 5, 6, 7; DAM NOV; DLB
261; FANT; JRDA; LAIT 5; MAICYA 1,
2; MTCW 1, 2; NFS 11; SATA 7, 69;
YAW

Adamson, Joy(-Friederike Victoria)
1910-1980 **CLC 17**
See also CA 69-72; 93-96; CANR 22;
MTCW 1; SATA 11; SATA-Obit 22

Adcock, Fleur 1934- **CLC 41**
See also CA 25-28R, 182; CAAE 182;
CAAS 23; CANR 11, 34, 69, 101; CP 1,
2, 3, 4, 5, 6, 7; CWP; DLB 40; FW; WWE
1

Addams, Charles 1912-1988 **CLC 30**
See also CA 61-64; 126; CANR 12, 79

Addams, Charles Samuel
See Addams, Charles

Addams, (Laura) Jane 1860-1935 . **TCLC 76**
See also AMWS 1; CA 194; DLB 303; FW

Addison, Joseph 1672-1719 **LC 18**
See also BRW 3; CDBLB 1660-1789; DLB
101; RGEL 2; WLIT 3

Adler, Alfred (F.) 1870-1937 **TCLC 61**
See also CA 119; 159

Adler, C(arole) S(chwerdtfeger)
1932- ... **CLC 35**
See also AAYA 4, 41; CA 89-92; CANR
19, 40, 101; CLR 78; JRDA; MAICYA 1,
2; SAAS 15; SATA 26, 63, 102, 126;
YAW

Adler, Renata 1938- **CLC 8, 31**
See also CA 49-52; CANR 95; CN 4, 5, 6;
MTCW 1

Adorno, Theodor W(iesengrund)
1903-1969 **TCLC 111**
See also CA 89-92; 25-28R; CANR 89;
DLB 242; EWL 3

Ady, Endre 1877-1919 **TCLC 11**
See also CA 107; CDWLB 4; DLB 215;
EW 9; EWL 3

A.E. .. **TCLC 3, 10**
See Russell, George William
See also DLB 19

Aelfric c. 955-c. 1010 **CMLC 46**
See also DLB 146

Aeschines c. 390B.C.-c. 320B.C. **CMLC 47**
See also DLB 176

Aeschylus 525(?)B.C.-456(?)B.C. .. **CMLC 11,
51; DC 8; WLCS**
See also AW 1; CDWLB 1; DA; DAB;
DAC; DAM DRAM, MST; DFS 5, 10;
DLB 176; LMFS 1; RGWL 2, 3; TWA;
WLIT 8

Aesop 620(?)B.C.-560(?)B.C. **CMLC 24**
See also CLR 14; MAICYA 1, 2; SATA 64

Affable Hawk
See MacCarthy, Sir (Charles Otto) Desmond
Africa, Ben
See Bosman, Herman Charles
Afton, Effie
See Harper, Frances Ellen Watkins
Agapida, Fray Antonio
See Irving, Washington
Agee, James (Rufus) 1909-1955 **TCLC 1, 19, 180**
See also AAYA 44; AITN 1; AMW; CA 108; 148; CANR 131; CDALB 1941-1968; DAM NOV; DLB 2, 26, 152; DLBY 1989; EWL 3; LAIT 3; LATS 1:2; MAL 5; MTCW 2; MTFW 2005; NFS 22; RGAL 4; TUS
Aghill, Gordon
See Silverberg, Robert
Agnon, S(hmuel) Y(osef Halevi) 1888-1970 **CLC 4, 8, 14; SSC 30; TCLC 151**
See also CA 17-18; 25-28R; CANR 60, 102; CAP 2; EWL 3; MTCW 1, 2; RGHL; RGSF 2; RGWL 2, 3; WLIT 6
Agrippa von Nettesheim, Henry Cornelius 1486-1535 **LC 27**
Aguilera Malta, Demetrio 1909-1981 **HLCS 1**
See also CA 111; 124; CANR 87; DAM MULT, NOV; DLB 145; EWL 3; HW 1; RGWL 3
Agustini, Delmira 1886-1914 **HLCS 1**
See also CA 166; DLB 290; HW 1, 2; LAW
Aherne, Owen
See Cassill, R(onald) V(erlin)
Ai 1947- **CLC 4, 14, 69; PC 72**
See also CA 85-88; CAAS 13; CANR 70; CP 6, 7; DLB 120; PFS 16
Aickman, Robert (Fordyce) 1914-1981 **CLC 57**
See also CA 5-8R; CANR 3, 72, 100; DLB 261; HGG; SUFW 1, 2
Aidoo, (Christina) Ama Ata 1942- **BLCS; CLC 177**
See also AFW; BW 1; CA 101; CANR 62, 144; CD 5, 6; CDWLB 3; CN 6, 7; CWD; CWP; DLB 117; DNFS 1, 2; EWL 3; FW; WLIT 2
Aiken, Conrad (Potter) 1889-1973 **CLC 1, 3, 5, 10, 52; PC 26; SSC 9**
See also AMW; CA 5-8R; 45-48; CANR 4, 60; CDALB 1929-1941; CN 1; CP 1; DAM NOV, POET; DLB 9, 45, 102; EWL 3; EXPS; HGG; MAL 5; MTCW 1, 2; MTFW 2005; PFS 24; RGAL 4; RGSF 2; SATA 3, 30; SSFS 8; TUS
Aiken, Joan (Delano) 1924-2004 **CLC 35**
See also AAYA 1, 25; CA 9-12R, 182; 223; CAAE 182; CANR 4, 23, 34, 64, 121; CLR 1, 19, 90; DLB 161; FANT; HGG; JRDA; MAICYA 1, 2; MTCW 1; RHW; SAAS 1; SATA 2, 30, 73; SATA-Essay 109; SATA-Obit 152; SUFW 2; WYA; YAW
Ainsworth, William Harrison 1805-1882 **NCLC 13**
See also DLB 21; HGG; RGEL 2; SATA 24; SUFW 1
Aitmatov, Chingiz (Torekulovich) 1928- ... **CLC 71**
See Aytmatov, Chingiz
See also CA 103; CANR 38; CWW 2; DLB 302; MTCW 1; RGSF 2; SATA 56
Akers, Floyd
See Baum, L(yman) Frank
Akhmadulina, Bella Akhatovna 1937- **CLC 53; PC 43**
See also CA 65-68; CWP; CWW 2; DAM POET; EWL 3

Akhmatova, Anna 1888-1966 **CLC 11, 25, 64, 126; PC 2, 55**
See also CA 19-20; 25-28R; CANR 35; CAP 1; DA3; DAM POET; DLB 295; EW 10; EWL 3; FL 1:5; MTCW 1, 2; PFS 18; RGWL 2, 3
Aksakov, Sergei Timofeyvich 1791-1859 **NCLC 2**
See also DLB 198
Aksenov, Vasilii (Pavlovich)
See Aksyonov, Vassily (Pavlovich)
See also CWW 2
Aksenov, Vassily
See Aksyonov, Vassily (Pavlovich)
Akst, Daniel 1956- **CLC 109**
See also CA 161; CANR 110
Aksyonov, Vassily (Pavlovich) 1932- **CLC 22, 37, 101**
See Aksenov, Vasilii (Pavlovich)
See also CA 53-56; CANR 12, 48, 77; DLB 302; EWL 3
Akutagawa Ryunosuke 1892-1927 ... **SSC 44; TCLC 16**
See also CA 117; 154; DLB 180; EWL 3; MJW; RGSF 2; RGWL 2, 3
Alabaster, William 1568-1640 **LC 90**
See also DLB 132; RGEL 2
Alain 1868-1951 **TCLC 41**
See also CA 163; EWL 3; GFL 1789 to the Present
Alain de Lille c. 1116-c. 1203 **CMLC 53**
See also DLB 208
Alain-Fournier **TCLC 6**
See Fournier, Henri-Alban
See also DLB 65; EWL 3; GFL 1789 to the Present; RGWL 2, 3
Al-Amin, Jamil Abdullah 1943- **BLC 1**
See also BW 1, 3; CA 112; 125; CANR 82; DAM MULT
Alanus de Insluis
See Alain de Lille
Alarcon, Pedro Antonio de 1833-1891 **NCLC 1; SSC 64**
Alas (y Urena), Leopoldo (Enrique Garcia) 1852-1901 **TCLC 29**
See also CA 113; 131; HW 1; RGSF 2
Albee, Edward (Franklin) (III) 1928- .. **CLC 1, 2, 3, 5, 9, 11, 13, 25, 53, 86, 113; DC 11; WLC 1**
See also AAYA 51; AITN 1; AMW; CA 5-8R; CABS 3; CAD; CANR 8, 54, 74, 124; CD 5, 6; CDALB 1941-1968; DA; DA3; DAB; DAC; DAM DRAM, MST; DFS 2, 3, 8, 10, 13, 14; DLB 7, 266; EWL 3; INT CANR-8; LAIT 4; LMFS 2; MAL 5; MTCW 1, 2; MTFW 2005; RGAL 4; TUS
Alberti (Merello), Rafael
See Alberti, Rafael
See also CWW 2
Alberti, Rafael 1902-1999 **CLC 7**
See Alberti (Merello), Rafael
See also CA 85-88; 185; CANR 81; DLB 108; EWL 3; HW 2; RGWL 2, 3
Albert the Great 1193(?)-1280 **CMLC 16**
See also DLB 115
Alcaeus c. 620B.C.- **CMLC 65**
See also DLB 176
Alcala-Galiano, Juan Valera y
See Valera y Alcala-Galiano, Juan
Alcayaga, Lucila Godoy
See Godoy Alcayaga, Lucila
Alciato, Andrea 1492-1550 **LC 116**
Alcott, Amos Bronson 1799-1888 ... **NCLC 1, 167**
See also DLB 1, 223

Alcott, Louisa May 1832-1888 . **NCLC 6, 58, 83; SSC 27; WLC 1**
See also AAYA 20; AMWS 1; BPFB 1; BYA 2; CDALB 1865-1917; CLR 1, 38, 109; DA; DA3; DAB; DAC; DAM MST, NOV; DLB 1, 42, 79, 223, 239, 242; DLBD 14; FL 1:2; JRDA; LAIT 2; MAICYA 1, 2; NFS 12; RGAL 4; SATA 100; TUS; WCH; WYA; YABC 1; YAW
Alcuin c. 730-804 **CMLC 69**
See also DLB 148
Aldanov, M. A.
See Aldanov, Mark (Alexandrovich)
Aldanov, Mark (Alexandrovich) 1886-1957 **TCLC 23**
See also CA 118; 181; DLB 317
Aldington, Richard 1892-1962 **CLC 49**
See also CA 85-88; CANR 45; DLB 20, 36, 100, 149; LMFS 2; RGEL 2
Aldiss, Brian W(ilson) 1925- . **CLC 5, 14, 40; SSC 36**
See also AAYA 42; CA 5-8R, 190; CAAE 190; CAAS 2; CANR 5, 28, 64, 121; CN 1, 2, 3, 4, 5, 6, 7; DAM NOV; DLB 14, 261, 271; MTCW 1, 2; MTFW 2005; SATA 34; SCFW 1, 2; SFW 4
Aldrich, Bess Streeter 1881-1954 **TCLC 125**
See also CLR 70; TCWW 2
Alegria, Claribel
See Alegria, Claribel (Joy)
See also CWW 2; DLB 145, 283
Alegria, Claribel (Joy) 1924- **CLC 75; HLCS 1; PC 26**
See Alegria, Claribel
See also CA 131; CAAS 15; CANR 66, 94, 134; DAM MULT; EWL 3; HW 1; MTCW 2; MTFW 2005; PFS 21
Alegria, Fernando 1918-2005 **CLC 57**
See also CA 9-12R; CANR 5, 32, 72; EWL 3; HW 1, 2
Aleichem, Sholom **SSC 33; TCLC 1, 35**
See Rabinovitch, Sholem
See also TWA
Aleixandre, Vicente 1898-1984 **HLCS 1; TCLC 113**
See also CANR 81; DLB 108; EWL 3; HW 2; MTCW 1, 2; RGWL 2, 3
Aleman, Mateo 1547-1615(?) **LC 81**
Alencar, Jose de 1829-1877 **NCLC 157**
See also DLB 307; LAW; WLIT 1
Alencon, Marguerite d'
See de Navarre, Marguerite
Alepoudelis, Odysseus
See Elytis, Odysseus
See also CWW 2
Aleshkovsky, Joseph 1929-
See Aleshkovsky, Yuz
See also CA 121; 128
Aleshkovsky, Yuz **CLC 44**
See Aleshkovsky, Joseph
See also DLB 317
Alexander, Lloyd (Chudley) 1924- ... **CLC 35**
See also AAYA 1, 27; BPFB 1; BYA 5, 6, 7, 9, 10, 11; CA 1-4R; CANR 1, 24, 38, 55, 113; CLR 1, 5, 48; CWRI 5; DLB 52; FANT; JRDA; MAICYA 1, 2; MAICYAS 1; MTCW 1; SAAS 19; SATA 3, 49, 81, 129, 135; SUFW; TUS; WYA; YAW
Alexander, Meena 1951- **CLC 121**
See also CA 115; CANR 38, 70, 146; CP 5, 6, 7; CWP; DLB 323; FW
Alexander, Samuel 1859-1938 **TCLC 77**
Alexeyev, Constantin (Sergeivich)
See Stanislavsky, Konstantin (Sergeivich)

Alexie, Sherman (Joseph, Jr.)
1966- **CLC 96, 154; NNAL; PC 53**
See also AAYA 28; BYA 15; CA 138;
CANR 65, 95, 133; CN 7; DA3; DAM
MULT; DLB 175, 206, 278; LATS 1:2;
MTCW 2; MTFW 2005; NFS 17; SSFS
18
al-Farabi 870(?)-950 **CMLC 58**
See also DLB 115
Alfau, Felipe 1902-1999 **CLC 66**
See also CA 137
Alfieri, Vittorio 1749-1803 **NCLC 101**
See also EW 4; RGWL 2, 3; WLIT 7
Alfonso X 1221-1284 **CMLC 78**
Alfred, Jean Gaston
See Ponge, Francis
Alger, Horatio, Jr. 1832-1899 **NCLC 8, 83**
See also CLR 87; DLB 42; LAIT 2; RGAL
4; SATA 16; TUS
Al-Ghazali, Muhammad ibn Muhammad
1058-1111 **CMLC 50**
See also DLB 115
Algren, Nelson 1909-1981 **CLC 4, 10, 33;**
SSC 33
See also AMWS 9; BPFB 1; CA 13-16R;
103; CANR 20, 61; CDALB 1941-1968;
CN 1, 2; DLB 9; DLBY 1981, 1982,
2000; EWL 3; MAL 5; MTCW 1, 2;
MTFW 2005; RGAL 4; RGSF 2
**al-Hariri, al-Qasim ibn 'Ali Abu
Muhammad al-Basri**
1054-1122 **CMLC 63**
See also RGWL 3
Ali, Ahmed 1908-1998 **CLC 69**
See also CA 25-28R; CANR 15, 34; CN 1,
2, 3, 4, 5; DLB 323; EWL 3
Ali, Tariq 1943- **CLC 173**
See also CA 25-28R; CANR 10, 99
Alighieri, Dante
See Dante
See also WLIT 7
al-Kindi, Abu Yusuf Ya'qub ibn Ishaq c.
801-c. 873 **CMLC 80**
Allan, John B.
See Westlake, Donald E(dwin)
Allan, Sidney
See Hartmann, Sadakichi
Allan, Sydney
See Hartmann, Sadakichi
Allard, Janet **CLC 59**
Allen, Edward 1948- **CLC 59**
Allen, Fred 1894-1956 **TCLC 87**
Allen, Paula Gunn 1939- **CLC 84, 202;**
NNAL
See also AMWS 4; CA 112; 143; CANR
63, 130; CWP; DA3; DAM MULT; DLB
175; FW; MTCW 2; MTFW 2005; RGAL
4; TCWW 2
Allen, Roland
See Ayckbourn, Alan
Allen, Sarah A.
See Hopkins, Pauline Elizabeth
Allen, Sidney H.
See Hartmann, Sadakichi
Allen, Woody 1935- **CLC 16, 52, 195**
See also AAYA 10, 51; AMWS 15; CA 33-
36R; CANR 27, 38, 63, 128; DAM POP;
DLB 44; MTCW 1; SSFS 21
Allende, Isabel 1942- ... **CLC 39, 57, 97, 170;**
HLC 1; SSC 65; WLCS
See also AAYA 18, 70; CA 125; 130; CANR
51, 74, 129; CDWLB 3; CLR 99; CWW
2; DA3; DAM MULT, NOV; DLB 145;
DNFS 1; EWL 3; FL 1:5; FW; HW 1, 2;
INT CA-130; LAIT 5; LAWS 1; LMFS 2;
MTCW 1, 2; MTFW 2005; NCFS 1; NFS
6, 18; RGSF 2; RGWL 3; SATA 163;
SSFS 11, 16; WLIT 1

Alleyn, Ellen
See Rossetti, Christina
Alleyne, Carla D. **CLC 65**
Allingham, Margery (Louise)
1904-1966 **CLC 19**
See also CA 5-8R; 25-28R; CANR 4, 58;
CMW 4; DLB 77; MSW; MTCW 1, 2
Allingham, William 1824-1889 **NCLC 25**
See also DLB 35; RGEL 2
Allison, Dorothy E. 1949- **CLC 78, 153**
See also AAYA 53; CA 140; CANR 66, 107;
CN 7; CSW; DA3; FW; MTCW 2; MTFW
2005; NFS 11; RGAL 4
Alloula, Malek **CLC 65**
Allston, Washington 1779-1843 **NCLC 2**
See also DLB 1, 235
Almedingen, E. M. **CLC 12**
See Almedingen, Martha Edith von
See also SATA 3
Almedingen, Martha Edith von 1898-1971
See Almedingen, E. M.
See also CA 1-4R; CANR 1
Almodovar, Pedro 1949(?)- **CLC 114;**
HLCS 1
See also CA 133; CANR 72, 151; HW 2
Almqvist, Carl Jonas Love
1793-1866 **NCLC 42**
**al-Mutanabbi, Ahmad ibn al-Husayn Abu
al-Tayyib al-Jufi al-Kindi**
915-965 **CMLC 66**
See Mutanabbi, Al-
See also RGWL 3
Alonso, Damaso 1898-1990 **CLC 14**
See also CA 110; 131; 130; CANR 72; DLB
108; EWL 3; HW 1, 2
Alov
See Gogol, Nikolai (Vasilyevich)
al'Sadaawi, Nawal
See El Saadawi, Nawal
See also FW
al-Shaykh, Hanan 1945- **CLC 218**
See Shaykh, al- Hanan
See also CA 135; CANR 111; WLIT 6
Al Siddik
See Rolfe, Frederick (William Serafino Aus-
tin Lewis Mary)
See also GLL 1; RGEL 2
Alta 1942- ... **CLC 19**
See also CA 57-60
Alter, Robert B(ernard) 1935- **CLC 34**
See also CA 49-52; CANR 1, 47, 100
Alther, Lisa 1944- **CLC 7, 41**
See also BPFB 1; CA 65-68; CAAS 30;
CANR 12, 30, 51; CN 4, 5, 6, 7; CSW;
GLL 2; MTCW 1
Althusser, L.
See Althusser, Louis
Althusser, Louis 1918-1990 **CLC 106**
See also CA 131; 132; CANR 102; DLB
242
Altman, Robert 1925- **CLC 16, 116**
See also CA 73-76; CANR 43
Alurista **HLCS 1; PC 34**
See Urista (Heredia), Alberto (Baltazar)
See also CA 45-48R; DLB 82; LLW
Alvarez, A(lfred) 1929- **CLC 5, 13**
See also CA 1-4R; CANR 3, 33, 63, 101,
134; CN 3, 4, 5, 6; CP 1, 2, 3, 4, 5, 6, 7;
DLB 14, 40; MTCW 2005
Alvarez, Alejandro Rodriguez 1903-1965
See Casona, Alejandro
See also CA 131; 93-96; HW 1
Alvarez, Julia 1950- **CLC 93; HLCS 1**
See also AAYA 25; AMWS 7; CA 147;
CANR 69, 101, 133; DA3; DLB 282;
LATS 1:2; LLW; MTCW 2; MTFW 2005;
NFS 5, 9; SATA 129; WLIT 1
Alvaro, Corrado 1896-1956 **TCLC 60**
See also CA 163; DLB 264; EWL 3

Amado, Jorge 1912-2001 ... **CLC 13, 40, 106;**
HLC 1
See also CA 77-80; 201; CANR 35, 74, 135;
CWW 2; DAM MULT, NOV; DLB 113,
307; EWL 3; HW 2; LAW; LAWS 1;
MTCW 1, 2; MTFW 2005; RGWL 2, 3;
TWA; WLIT 1
Ambler, Eric 1909-1998 **CLC 4, 6, 9**
See also BRWS 4; CA 9-12R; 171; CANR
7, 38, 74; CMW 4; CN 1, 2, 3, 4, 5, 6;
DLB 77; MSW; MTCW 1, 2; TEA
Ambrose, Stephen E(dward)
1936-2002 **CLC 145**
See also AAYA 44; CA 1-4R; 209; CANR
3, 43, 57, 83, 105; MTFW 2005; NCFS 2;
SATA 40, 138
Amichai, Yehuda 1924-2000 .. **CLC 9, 22, 57,**
116; PC 38
See also CA 85-88; 189; CANR 46, 60, 99,
132; CWW 2; EWL 3; MTCW 1, 2;
MTFW 2005; PFS 24; RGHL; WLIT 6
Amichai, Yehudah
See Amichai, Yehuda
Amiel, Henri Frederic 1821-1881 **NCLC 4**
See also DLB 217
Amis, Kingsley (William)
1922-1995 **CLC 1, 2, 3, 5, 8, 13, 40,**
44, 129
See also AITN 2; BPFB 1; BRWS 2; CA
9-12R; 150; CANR 8, 28, 54; CDBLB
1945-1960; CN 1, 2, 3, 4, 5, 6; CP 1, 2,
3, 4; DA; DA3; DAB; DAC; DAM MST,
NOV; DLB 15, 27, 100, 139, 326; DLBY
1996; EWL 3; HGG; INT CANR-8;
MTCW 1, 2; MTFW 2005; RGEL 2;
RGSF 2; SFW 4
Amis, Martin (Louis) 1949- **CLC 4, 9, 38,**
62, 101, 213
See also BEST 90:3; BRWS 4; CA 65-68;
CANR 8, 27, 54, 73, 95, 132; CN 5, 6, 7;
DA3; DLB 14, 194; EWL 3; INT CANR-
27; MTCW 2; MTFW 2005
Ammianus Marcellinus c. 330-c.
395 **CMLC 60**
See also AW 2; DLB 211
Ammons, A(rchie) R(andolph)
1926-2001 **CLC 2, 3, 5, 8, 9, 25, 57,**
108; PC 16
See also AITN 1; AMWS 7; CA 9-12R;
193; CANR 6, 36, 51, 73, 107; CP 1, 2,
3, 4, 5, 6, 7; CSW; DAM POET; DLB 5,
165; EWL 3; MAL 5; MTCW 1, 2; PFS
19; RGAL 4; TCLE 1:1
Amo, Tauraatua i
See Adams, Henry (Brooks)
Amory, Thomas 1691(?)-1788 **LC 48**
See also DLB 39
Anand, Mulk Raj 1905-2004 **CLC 23, 93**
See also CA 65-68; 231; CANR 32, 64; CN
1, 2, 3, 4, 5, 6, 7; DAM NOV; DLB 323;
EWL 3; MTCW 1, 2; MTFW 2005; RGSF
2
Anatol
See Schnitzler, Arthur
Anaximander c. 611B.C.-c.
546B.C. **CMLC 22**
Anaya, Rudolfo A(lfonso) 1937- **CLC 23,**
148; HLC 1
See also AAYA 20; BYA 13; CA 45-48;
CAAS 4; CANR 1, 32, 51, 124; CN 4, 5,
6, 7; DAM MULT, NOV; DLB 82, 206,
278; HW 1; LAIT 4; LLW; MAL 5;
MTCW 1, 2; MTFW 2005; NFS 12;
RGAL 4; RGSF 2; TCWW 2; WLIT 1
Andersen, Hans Christian
1805-1875 **NCLC 7, 79; SSC 6, 56;**
WLC 1
See also AAYA 57; CLR 6; DA; DA3;
DAB; DAC; DAM MST, POP; EW 6;
MAICYA 1, 2; RGSF 2; RGWL 2, 3;
SATA 100; TWA; WCH; YABC 1

Anderson, C. Farley
See Mencken, H(enry) L(ouis); Nathan, George Jean
Anderson, Jessica (Margaret) Queale
1916- ... **CLC 37**
See also CA 9-12R; CANR 4, 62; CN 4, 5, 6, 7; DLB 325
Anderson, Jon (Victor) 1940- **CLC 9**
See also CA 25-28R; CANR 20; CP 1, 3, 4, 5; DAM POET
Anderson, Lindsay (Gordon)
1923-1994 **CLC 20**
See also CA 125; 128; 146; CANR 77
Anderson, Maxwell 1888-1959 **TCLC 2, 144**
See also CA 105; 152; DAM DRAM; DFS 16, 20; DLB 7, 228; MAL 5; MTCW 2; MTFW 2005; RGAL 4
Anderson, Poul (William)
1926-2001 **CLC 15**
See also AAYA 5, 34; BPFB 1; BYA 6, 8, 9; CA 1-4R, 181; 199; CAAE 181; CAAS 2; CANR 2, 15, 34, 64, 110; CLR 58; DLB 8; FANT; INT CANR-15; MTCW 1, 2; MTFW 2005; SATA 90; SATA-Brief 39; SATA-Essay 106; SCFW 1, 2; SFW 4; SUFW 1, 2
Anderson, Robert (Woodruff)
1917- ... **CLC 23**
See also AITN 1; CA 21-24R; CANR 32; CD 6; DAM DRAM; DLB 7; LAIT 5
Anderson, Roberta Joan
See Mitchell, Joni
Anderson, Sherwood 1876-1941 ... **SSC 1, 46, 91; TCLC 1, 10, 24, 123; WLC 1**
See also AAYA 30; AMW; AMWC 2; BPFB 1; CA 104; 121; CANR 61; CDALB 1917-1929; DA; DA3; DAB; DAC; DAM MST, NOV; DLB 4, 9, 86; DLBD 1; EWL 3; EXPS; GLL 2; MAL 5; MTCW 1, 2; MTFW 2005; NFS 4; RGAL 4; RGSF 2; SSFS 4, 10, 11; TUS
Andier, Pierre
See Desnos, Robert
Andouard
See Giraudoux, Jean(-Hippolyte)
Andrade, Carlos Drummond de **CLC 18**
See Drummond de Andrade, Carlos
See also EWL 3; RGWL 2, 3
Andrade, Mario de **TCLC 43**
See de Andrade, Mario
See also DLB 307; EWL 3; LAW; RGWL 2, 3; WLIT 1
Andreae, Johann V(alentin)
1586-1654 **LC 32**
See also DLB 164
Andreas Capellanus fl. c. 1185- **CMLC 45**
See also DLB 208
Andreas-Salome, Lou 1861-1937 ... **TCLC 56**
See also CA 178; DLB 66
Andreev, Leonid
See Andreyev, Leonid (Nikolaevich)
See also DLB 295; EWL 3
Andress, Lesley
See Sanders, Lawrence
Andrewes, Lancelot 1555-1626 **LC 5**
See also DLB 151, 172
Andrews, Cicily Fairfield
See West, Rebecca
Andrews, Elton V.
See Pohl, Frederik
Andrews, Peter
See Soderbergh, Steven
Andreyev, Leonid (Nikolaevich)
1871-1919 **TCLC 3**
See Andreev, Leonid
See also CA 104; 185

Andric, Ivo 1892-1975 **CLC 8; SSC 36; TCLC 135**
See also CA 81-84; 57-60; CANR 43, 60; CDWLB 4; DLB 147; EW 11; EWL 3; MTCW 1; RGSF 2; RGWL 2, 3
Androvar
See Prado (Calvo), Pedro
Angela of Foligno 1248(?)-1309 **CMLC 76**
Angelique, Pierre
See Bataille, Georges
Angell, Roger 1920- **CLC 26**
See also CA 57-60; CANR 13, 44, 70, 144; DLB 171, 185
Angelou, Maya 1928- ... **BLC 1; CLC 12, 35, 64, 77, 155; PC 32; WLCS**
See also AAYA 7, 20; AMWS 4; BPFB 1; BW 2, 3; BYA 2; CA 65-68; CANR 19, 42, 65, 111, 133; CDALBS; CLR 53; CP 4, 5, 6, 7; CPW; CSW; CWP; DA; DA3; DAB; DAC; DAM MST, MULT, POET, POP; DLB 38; EWL 3; EXPN; EXPP; FL 1:5; LAIT 4; MAICYA 2; MAICYAS 1; MAL 5; MAWW; MTCW 1, 2; MTFW 2005; NCFS 2; NFS 2; PFS 2, 3; RGAL 4; SATA 49, 136; TCLE 1:1; WYA; YAW
Angouleme, Marguerite d'
See de Navarre, Marguerite
Anna Comnena 1083-1153 **CMLC 25**
Annensky, Innokentii Fedorovich
See Annensky, Innokenty (Fyodorovich)
See also DLB 295
Annensky, Innokenty (Fyodorovich)
1856-1909 **TCLC 14**
See also CA 110; 155; EWL 3
Annunzio, Gabriele d'
See D'Annunzio, Gabriele
Anodos
See Coleridge, Mary E(lizabeth)
Anon, Charles Robert
See Pessoa, Fernando (Antonio Nogueira)
Anouilh, Jean (Marie Lucien Pierre)
1910-1987 . **CLC 1, 3, 8, 13, 40, 50; DC 8, 21**
See also AAYA 67; CA 17-20R; 123; CANR 32; DAM DRAM; DFS 9, 10, 19; DLB 321; EW 13; EWL 3; GFL 1789 to the Present; MTCW 1, 2; MTFW 2005; RGWL 2, 3; TWA
Anselm of Canterbury
1033(?)-1109 **CMLC 67**
See also DLB 115
Anthony, Florence
See Ai
Anthony, John
See Ciardi, John (Anthony)
Anthony, Peter
See Shaffer, Anthony (Joshua); Shaffer, Peter (Levin)
Anthony, Piers 1934- **CLC 35**
See also AAYA 11, 48; BYA 7; CA 200; CAAE 200; CANR 28, 56, 73, 102, 133; CPW; DAM POP; DLB 8; FANT; MAICYA 2; MAICYAS 1; MTCW 1, 2; MTFW 2005; SAAS 22; SATA 84, 129; SATA-Essay 129; SFW 4; SUFW 1, 2; YAW
Anthony, Susan B(rownell)
1820-1906 **TCLC 84**
See also CA 211; FW
Antiphon c. 480B.C.-c. 411B.C. **CMLC 55**
Antoine, Marc
See Proust, (Valentin-Louis-George-Eugene) Marcel
Antoninus, Brother
See Everson, William (Oliver)
See also CP 1
Antonioni, Michelangelo 1912- **CLC 20, 144**
See also CA 73-76; CANR 45, 77

Antschel, Paul 1920-1970
See Celan, Paul
See also CA 85-88; CANR 33, 61; MTCW 1; PFS 21
Anwar, Chairil 1922-1949 **TCLC 22**
See Chairil Anwar
See also CA 121; 219; RGWL 3
Anzaldua, Gloria (Evanjelina)
1942-2004 **CLC 200; HLCS 1**
See also CA 175; 227; CSW; CWP; DLB 122; FW; LLW; RGAL 4; SATA-Obit 154
Apess, William 1798-1839(?) **NCLC 73; NNAL**
See also DAM MULT; DLB 175, 243
Apollinaire, Guillaume 1880-1918 **PC 7; TCLC 3, 8, 51**
See Kostrowitzki, Wilhelm Apollinaris de
See also CA 152; DAM POET; DLB 258, 321; EW 9; EWL 3; GFL 1789 to the Present; MTCW 2; PFS 24; RGWL 2, 3; TWA; WP
Apollonius of Rhodes
See Apollonius Rhodius
See also AW 1; RGWL 2, 3
Apollonius Rhodius c. 300B.C.-c. 220B.C. **CMLC 28**
See Apollonius of Rhodes
See also DLB 176
Appelfeld, Aharon 1932- ... **CLC 23, 47; SSC 42**
See also CA 112; 133; CANR 86; CWW 2; DLB 299; EWL 3; RGHL; RGSF 2; WLIT 6
Apple, Max (Isaac) 1941- **CLC 9, 33; SSC 50**
See also CA 81-84; CANR 19, 54; DLB 130
Appleman, Philip (Dean) 1926- **CLC 51**
See also CA 13-16R; CAAS 18; CANR 6, 29, 56
Appleton, Lawrence
See Lovecraft, H. P.
Apteryx
See Eliot, T(homas) S(tearns)
Apuleius, (Lucius Madaurensis) c. 125-c. 164 ... **CMLC 1, 84**
See also AW 2; CDWLB 1; DLB 211; RGWL 2, 3; SUFW; WLIT 8
Aquin, Hubert 1929-1977 **CLC 15**
See also CA 105; DLB 53; EWL 3
Aquinas, Thomas 1224(?)-1274 **CMLC 33**
See also DLB 115; EW 1; TWA
Aragon, Louis 1897-1982 **CLC 3, 22; TCLC 123**
See also CA 69-72; 108; CANR 28, 71; DAM NOV, POET; DLB 72, 258; EW 11; EWL 3; GFL 1789 to the Present; GLL 2; LMFS 2; MTCW 1, 2; RGWL 2, 3
Arany, Janos 1817-1882 **NCLC 34**
Aranyos, Kakay 1847-1910
See Mikszath, Kalman
Aratus of Soli c. 315B.C.-c. 240B.C. **CMLC 64**
See also DLB 176
Arbuthnot, John 1667-1735 **LC 1**
See also DLB 101
Archer, Herbert Winslow
See Mencken, H(enry) L(ouis)
Archer, Jeffrey 1940- **CLC 28**
See also AAYA 16; BEST 89:3; BPFB 1; CA 77-80; CANR 22, 52, 95, 136; CPW; DA3; DAM POP; INT CANR-22; MTFW 2005
Archer, Jeffrey Howard
See Archer, Jeffrey
Archer, Jules 1915- **CLC 12**
See also CA 9-12R; CANR 6, 69; SAAS 5; SATA 4, 85

Archer, Lee
See Ellison, Harlan (Jay)

Archilochus c. 7th cent. B.C.- **CMLC 44**
See also DLB 176

Arden, John 1930- **CLC 6, 13, 15**
See also BRWS 2; CA 13-16R; CAAS 4; CANR 31, 65, 67, 124; CBD; CD 5, 6; DAM DRAM; DFS 9; DLB 13, 245; EWL 3; MTCW 1

Arenas, Reinaldo 1943-1990 .. **CLC 41; HLC 1**
See also CA 124; 128; 133; CANR 73, 106; DAM MULT; DLB 145; EWL 3; GLL 2; HW 1; LAW; LAWS 1; MTCW 2; MTFW 2005; RGSF 2; RGWL 3; WLIT 1

Arendt, Hannah 1906-1975 **CLC 66, 98**
See also CA 17-20R; 61-64; CANR 26, 60; DLB 242; MTCW 1, 2

Aretino, Pietro 1492-1556 **LC 12**
See also RGWL 2, 3

Arghezi, Tudor **CLC 80**
See Theodorescu, Ion N.
See also CA 167; CDWLB 4; DLB 220; EWL 3

Arguedas, Jose Maria 1911-1969 **CLC 10, 18; HLCS 1; TCLC 147**
See also CA 89-92; CANR 73; DLB 113; EWL 3; HW 1; LAW; RGWL 2, 3; WLIT 1

Argueta, Manlio 1936- **CLC 31**
See also CA 131; CANR 73; CWW 2; DLB 145; EWL 3; HW 1; RGWL 3

Arias, Ron(ald Francis) 1941- **HLC 1**
See also CA 131; CANR 81, 136; DAM MULT; DLB 82; HW 1, 2; MTCW 2; MTFW 2005

Ariosto, Lodovico
See Ariosto, Ludovico
See also WLIT 7

Ariosto, Ludovico 1474-1533 ... **LC 6, 87; PC 42**
See Ariosto, Lodovico
See also EW 2; RGWL 2, 3

Aristides
See Epstein, Joseph

Aristophanes 450B.C.-385B.C. **CMLC 4, 51; DC 2; WLCS**
See also AW 1; CDWLB 1; DA; DA3; DAB; DAC; DAM DRAM, MST; DFS 10; DLB 176; LMFS 1; RGWL 2, 3; TWA; WLIT 8

Aristotle 384B.C.-322B.C. **CMLC 31; WLCS**
See also AW 1; CDWLB 1; DA; DA3; DAB; DAC; DAM MST; DLB 176; RGWL 2, 3; TWA; WLIT 8

Arlt, Roberto (Godofredo Christophersen) 1900-1942 **HLC 1; TCLC 29**
See also CA 123; 131; CANR 67; DAM MULT; DLB 305; EWL 3; HW 1, 2; IDTP; LAW

Armah, Ayi Kwei 1939- . **BLC 1; CLC 5, 33, 136**
See also AFW; BRWS 10; BW 1; CA 61-64; CANR 21, 64; CDWLB 3; CN 1, 2, 3, 4, 5, 6, 7; DAM MULT, POET; DLB 117; EWL 3; MTCW 1; WLIT 2

Armatrading, Joan 1950- **CLC 17**
See also CA 114; 186

Armin, Robert 1568(?)-1615(?) **LC 120**

Armitage, Frank
See Carpenter, John (Howard)

Armstrong, Jeannette (C.) 1948- **NNAL**
See also CA 149; CCA 1; CN 6, 7; DAC; SATA 102

Arnette, Robert
See Silverberg, Robert

Arnim, Achim von (Ludwig Joachim von Arnim) 1781-1831 .. **NCLC 5, 159; SSC 29**
See also DLB 90

Arnim, Bettina von 1785-1859 **NCLC 38, 123**
See also DLB 90; RGWL 2, 3

Arnold, Matthew 1822-1888 **NCLC 6, 29, 89, 126; PC 5; WLC 1**
See also BRW 5; CDBLB 1832-1890; DA; DAB; DAC; DAM MST, POET; DLB 32, 57; EXPP; PAB; PFS 2; TEA; WP

Arnold, Thomas 1795-1842 **NCLC 18**
See also DLB 55

Arnow, Harriette (Louisa) Simpson 1908-1986 **CLC 2, 7, 18**
See also BPFB 1; CA 9-12R; 118; CANR 14; CN 2, 3, 4; DLB 6; FW; MTCW 1, 2; RHW; SATA 42; SATA-Obit 47

Arouet, Francois-Marie
See Voltaire

Arp, Hans
See Arp, Jean

Arp, Jean 1887-1966 **CLC 5; TCLC 115**
See also CA 81-84; 25-28R; CANR 42, 77; EW 10

Arrabal
See Arrabal, Fernando

Arrabal (Teran), Fernando
See Arrabal, Fernando
See also CWW 2

Arrabal, Fernando 1932- ... **CLC 2, 9, 18, 58**
See Arrabal (Teran), Fernando
See also CA 9-12R; CANR 15; DLB 321; EWL 3; LMFS 2

Arreola, Juan Jose 1918-2001 **CLC 147; HLC 1; SSC 38**
See also CA 113; 131; 200; CANR 81; CWW 2; DAM MULT; DLB 113; DNFS 2; EWL 3; HW 1, 2; LAW; RGSF 2

Arrian c. 89(?)-c. 155(?) **CMLC 43**
See also DLB 176

Arrick, Fran **CLC 30**
See Gaberman, Judie Angell
See also BYA 6

Arrley, Richmond
See Delany, Samuel R(ay), Jr.

Artaud, Antonin (Marie Joseph) 1896-1948 **DC 14; TCLC 3, 36**
See also CA 104; 149; DA3; DAM DRAM; DFS 22; DLB 258, 321; EW 11; EWL 3; GFL 1789 to the Present; MTCW 2; MTFW 2005; RGWL 2, 3

Arthur, Ruth M(abel) 1905-1979 **CLC 12**
See also CA 9-12R; 85-88; CANR 4; CWRI 5; SATA 7, 26

Artsybashev, Mikhail (Petrovich) 1878-1927 **TCLC 31**
See also CA 170; DLB 295

Arundel, Honor (Morfydd) 1919-1973 **CLC 17**
See also CA 21-22; 41-44R; CAP 2; CLR 35; CWRI 5; SATA 4; SATA-Obit 24

Arzner, Dorothy 1900-1979 **CLC 98**

Asch, Sholem 1880-1957 **TCLC 3**
See also CA 105; EWL 3; GLL 2; RGHL

Ascham, Roger 1516(?)-1568 **LC 101**
See also DLB 236

Ash, Shalom
See Asch, Sholem

Ashbery, John (Lawrence) 1927- .. **CLC 2, 3, 4, 6, 9, 13, 15, 25, 41, 77, 125, 221; PC 26**
See Berry, Jonas
See also AMWS 3; CA 5-8R; CANR 9, 37, 66, 102, 132; CP 1, 2, 3, 4, 5, 6, 7; DA3; DAM POET; DLB 5, 165; DLBY 1981; EWL 3; INT CANR-9; MAL 5; MTCW 1, 2; MTFW 2005; PAB; PFS 11; RGAL 4; TCLE 1:1; WP

Ashdown, Clifford
See Freeman, R(ichard) Austin

Ashe, Gordon
See Creasey, John

Ashton-Warner, Sylvia (Constance) 1908-1984 **CLC 19**
See also CA 69-72; 112; CANR 29; CN 1, 2, 3; MTCW 1, 2

Asimov, Isaac 1920-1992 **CLC 1, 3, 9, 19, 26, 76, 92**
See also AAYA 13; BEST 90:2; BPFB 1; BYA 4, 6, 7, 9; CA 1-4R; 137; CANR 2, 19, 36, 60, 125; CLR 12, 79; CMW 4; CN 1, 2, 3, 4, 5; CPW; DA3; DAM POP; DLB 8; DLBY 1992; INT CANR-19; JRDA; LAIT 5; LMFS 2; MAICYA 1, 2; MAL 5; MTCW 1, 2; MTFW 2005; RGAL 4; SATA 1, 26, 74; SCFW 1, 2; SFW 4; SSFS 17; TUS; YAW

Askew, Anne 1521(?)-1546 **LC 81**
See also DLB 136

Assis, Joaquim Maria Machado de
See Machado de Assis, Joaquim Maria

Astell, Mary 1666-1731 **LC 68**
See also DLB 252; FW

Astley, Thea (Beatrice May) 1925-2004 **CLC 41**
See also CA 65-68; 229; CANR 11, 43, 78; CN 1, 2, 3, 4, 5, 6, 7; DLB 289; EWL 3

Astley, William 1855-1911
See Warung, Price

Aston, James
See White, T(erence) H(anbury)

Asturias, Miguel Angel 1899-1974 **CLC 3, 8, 13; HLC 1**
See also CA 25-28; 49-52; CANR 32; CAP 2; CDWLB 3; DA3; DAM MULT, NOV; DLB 113, 290; EWL 3; HW 1; LAW; LMFS 2; MTCW 1, 2; RGWL 2, 3; WLIT 1

Atares, Carlos Saura
See Saura (Atares), Carlos

Athanasius c. 295-c. 373 **CMLC 48**

Atheling, William
See Pound, Ezra (Weston Loomis)

Atheling, William, Jr.
See Blish, James (Benjamin)

Atherton, Gertrude (Franklin Horn) 1857-1948 **TCLC 2**
See also CA 104; 155; DLB 9, 78, 186; HGG; RGAL 4; SUFW 1; TCWW 1, 2

Atherton, Lucius
See Masters, Edgar Lee

Atkins, Jack
See Harris, Mark

Atkinson, Kate 1951- **CLC 99**
See also CA 166; CANR 101, 153; DLB 267

Attaway, William (Alexander) 1911-1986 **BLC 1; CLC 92**
See also BW 2, 3; CA 143; CANR 82; DAM MULT; DLB 76; MAL 5

Atticus
See Fleming, Ian (Lancaster); Wilson, (Thomas) Woodrow

Atwood, Margaret 1939- . **CLC 2, 3, 4, 8, 13, 15, 25, 44, 84, 135; PC 8; SSC 2, 46; WLC 1**
See also AAYA 12, 47; AMWS 13; BEST 89:2; BPFB 1; CA 49-52; CANR 3, 24, 33, 59, 95, 133; CN 2, 3, 4, 5, 6, 7; CP 1, 2, 3, 4, 5, 6, 7; CPW; CWP; DA; DA3; DAB; DAC; DAM MST, NOV, POET; DLB 53, 251, 326; EWL 3; EXPN; FL 1:5; FW; GL 2; INT CANR-24; LAIT 5; MTCW 1, 2; MTFW 2005; NFS 4, 12, 13, 14, 19; PFS 7; RGSF 2; SATA 50, 170; SSFS 3, 13; TCLE 1:1; TWA; WWE 1; YAW

Atwood, Margaret Eleanor
See Atwood, Margaret
Aubigny, Pierre d'
See Mencken, H(enry) L(ouis)
Aubin, Penelope 1685-1731(?) **LC 9**
See also DLB 39
Auchincloss, Louis 1917- **CLC 4, 6, 9, 18, 45; SSC 22**
See also AMWS 4; CA 1-4R; CANR 6, 29, 55, 87, 130; CN 1, 2, 3, 4, 5, 6, 7; DAM NOV; DLB 2, 244; DLBY 1980; EWL 3; INT CANR-29; MAL 5; MTCW 1; RGAL 4
Auchincloss, Louis Stanton
See Auchincloss, Louis
Auden, W(ystan) H(ugh) 1907-1973 . **CLC 1, 2, 3, 4, 6, 9, 11, 14, 43, 123; PC 1; WLC 1**
See also AAYA 18; AMWS 2; BRW 7; BRWR 1; CA 9-12R; 45-48; CANR 5, 61, 105; CDBLB 1914-1945; CP 1, 2; DA; DA3; DAB; DAC; DAM DRAM, MST, POET; DLB 10, 20; EWL 3; EXPP; MAL 5; MTCW 1, 2; MTFW 2005; PAB; PFS 1, 3, 4, 10; TUS; WP
Audiberti, Jacques 1899-1965 **CLC 38**
See also CA 25-28R; DAM DRAM; DLB 321; EWL 3
Audubon, John James 1785-1851 . **NCLC 47**
See also ANW; DLB 248
Auel, Jean M(arie) 1936- **CLC 31, 107**
See also AAYA 7, 51; BEST 90:4; BPFB 1; CA 103; CANR 21, 64, 115; CPW; DA3; DAM POP; INT CANR-21; NFS 11; RHW; SATA 91
Auerbach, Berthold 1812-1882 **NCLC 171**
See also DLB 133
Auerbach, Erich 1892-1957 **TCLC 43**
See also CA 118; 155; EWL 3
Augier, Emile 1820-1889 **NCLC 31**
See also DLB 192; GFL 1789 to the Present
August, John
See De Voto, Bernard (Augustine)
Augustine, St. 354-430 **CMLC 6; WLCS**
See also DA; DA3; DAB; DAC; DAM MST; DLB 115; EW 1; RGWL 2, 3; WLIT 8
Aunt Belinda
See Braddon, Mary Elizabeth
Aunt Weedy
See Alcott, Louisa May
Aurelius
See Bourne, Randolph S(illiman)
Aurelius, Marcus 121-180 **CMLC 45**
See Marcus Aurelius
See also RGWL 2, 3
Aurobindo, Sri
See Ghose, Aurabinda
Aurobindo Ghose
See Ghose, Aurabinda
Austen, Jane 1775-1817 **NCLC 1, 13, 19, 33, 51, 81, 95, 119, 150; WLC 1**
See also AAYA 19; BRW 4; BRWC 1; BRWR 2; BYA 3; CDBLB 1789-1832; DA; DA3; DAB; DAC; DAM MST, NOV; DLB 116; EXPN; FL 1:2; GL 2; LAIT 2; LATS 1:1; LMFS 1; NFS 1, 14, 18, 20, 21; TEA; WLIT 3; WYAS 1
Auster, Paul 1947- **CLC 47, 131**
See also AMWS 12; CA 69-72; CANR 23, 52, 75, 129; CMW 4; CN 5, 6, 7; DA3; DLB 227; MAL 5; MTCW 2; MTFW 2005; SUFW 2; TCLE 1:1
Austin, Frank
See Faust, Frederick (Schiller)
Austin, Mary (Hunter) 1868-1934 . **TCLC 25**
See also ANW; CA 109; 178; DLB 9, 78, 206, 221, 275; FW; TCWW 1, 2

Averroes 1126-1198 **CMLC 7**
See also DLB 115
Avicenna 980-1037 **CMLC 16**
See also DLB 115
Avison, Margaret (Kirkland) 1918- .. **CLC 2, 4, 97**
See also CA 17-20R; CANR 134; CP 1, 2, 3, 4, 5, 6, 7; DAC; DAM POET; DLB 53; MTCW 1
Axton, David
See Koontz, Dean R.
Ayckbourn, Alan 1939- **CLC 5, 8, 18, 33, 74; DC 13**
See also BRWS 5; CA 21-24R; CANR 31, 59, 118; CBD; CD 5, 6; DAB; DAM DRAM; DFS 7; DLB 13, 245; EWL 3; MTCW 1, 2; MTFW 2005
Aydy, Catherine
See Tennant, Emma (Christina)
Ayme, Marcel (Andre) 1902-1967 ... **CLC 11; SSC 41**
See also CA 89-92; CANR 67, 137; CLR 25; DLB 72; EW 12; EWL 3; GFL 1789 to the Present; RGSF 2; RGWL 2, 3; SATA 91
Ayrton, Michael 1921-1975 **CLC 7**
See also CA 5-8R; 61-64; CANR 9, 21
Aytmatov, Chingiz
See Aitmatov, Chingiz (Torekulovich)
See also EWL 3
Azorin .. **CLC 11**
See Martinez Ruiz, Jose
See also DLB 322; EW 9; EWL 3
Azuela, Mariano 1873-1952 .. **HLC 1; TCLC 3, 145**
See also CA 104; 131; CANR 81; DAM MULT; EWL 3; HW 1, 2; LAW; MTCW 1, 2; MTFW 2005
Ba, Mariama 1929-1981 **BLCS**
See also AFW; BW 2; CA 141; CANR 87; DNFS 2; WLIT 2
Baastad, Babbis Friis
See Friis-Baastad, Babbis Ellinor
Bab
See Gilbert, W(illiam) S(chwenck)
Babbis, Eleanor
See Friis-Baastad, Babbis Ellinor
Babel, Isaac
See Babel, Isaak (Emmanuilovich)
See also EW 11; SSFS 10
Babel, Isaak (Emmanuilovich) 1894-1941(?) . **SSC 16, 78; TCLC 2, 13, 171**
See Babel, Isaac
See also CA 104; 155; CANR 113; DLB 272; EWL 3; MTCW 2; MTFW 2005; RGSF 2; RGWL 2, 3; TWA
Babits, Mihaly 1883-1941 **TCLC 14**
See also CA 114; CDWLB 4; DLB 215; EWL 3
Babur 1483-1530 **LC 18**
Babylas 1898-1962
See Ghelderode, Michel de
Baca, Jimmy Santiago 1952- . **HLC 1; PC 41**
See also CA 131; CANR 81, 90, 146; CP 6, 7; DAM MULT; DLB 122; HW 1, 2; LLW; MAL 5
Baca, Jose Santiago
See Baca, Jimmy Santiago
Bacchelli, Riccardo 1891-1985 **CLC 19**
See also CA 29-32R; 117; DLB 264; EWL 3
Bach, Richard 1936- **CLC 14**
See also AITN 1; BEST 89:2; BPFB 1; BYA 5; CA 9-12R; CANR 18, 93, 151; CPW; DAM NOV, POP; FANT; MTCW 1; SATA 13
Bach, Richard David
See Bach, Richard

Bache, Benjamin Franklin 1769-1798 **LC 74**
See also DLB 43
Bachelard, Gaston 1884-1962 **TCLC 128**
See also CA 97-100; 89-92; DLB 296; GFL 1789 to the Present
Bachman, Richard
See King, Stephen
Bachmann, Ingeborg 1926-1973 **CLC 69**
See also CA 93-96; 45-48; CANR 69; DLB 85; EWL 3; RGHL; RGWL 2, 3
Bacon, Francis 1561-1626 **LC 18, 32**
See also BRW 1; CDBLB Before 1660; DLB 151, 236, 252; RGEL 2; TEA
Bacon, Roger 1214(?)-1294 **CMLC 14**
See also DLB 115
Bacovia, George 1881-1957 **TCLC 24**
See Vasiliu, Gheorghe
See also CDWLB 4; DLB 220; EWL 3
Badanes, Jerome 1937-1995 **CLC 59**
See also CA 234
Bagehot, Walter 1826-1877 **NCLC 10**
See also DLB 55
Bagnold, Enid 1889-1981 **CLC 25**
See also BYA 2; CA 5-8R; 103; CANR 5, 40; CBD; CN 2; CWD; CWRI 5; DAM DRAM; DLB 13, 160, 191, 245; FW; MAICYA 1, 2; RGEL 2; SATA 1, 25
Bagritsky, Eduard **TCLC 60**
See Dzyubin, Eduard Georgievich
Bagrjana, Elisaveta
See Belcheva, Elisaveta Lyubomirova
Bagryana, Elisaveta **CLC 10**
See Belcheva, Elisaveta Lyubomirova
See also CA 178; CDWLB 4; DLB 147; EWL 3
Bailey, Paul 1937- **CLC 45**
See also CA 21-24R; CANR 16, 62, 124; CN 1, 2, 3, 4, 5, 6, 7; DLB 14, 271; GLL 2
Baillie, Joanna 1762-1851 **NCLC 71, 151**
See also DLB 93; GL 2; RGEL 2
Bainbridge, Beryl (Margaret) 1934- . **CLC 4, 5, 8, 10, 14, 18, 22, 62, 130**
See also BRWS 6; CA 21-24R; CANR 24, 55, 75, 88, 128; CN 2, 3, 4, 5, 6, 7; DAM NOV; DLB 14, 231; EWL 3; MTCW 1, 2; MTFW 2005
Baker, Carlos (Heard) 1909-1987 **TCLC 119**
See also CA 5-8R; 122; CANR 3, 63; DLB 103
Baker, Elliott 1922- **CLC 8**
See also CA 45-48; CANR 2, 63; CN 1, 2, 3, 4, 5, 6, 7
Baker, Jean H. **TCLC 3, 10**
See Russell, George William
Baker, Nicholson 1957- **CLC 61, 165**
See also AMWS 13; CA 135; CANR 63, 120, 138; CN 6; CPW; DA3; DAM POP; DLB 227; MTFW 2005
Baker, Ray Stannard 1870-1946 **TCLC 47**
See also CA 118
Baker, Russell (Wayne) 1925- **CLC 31**
See also BEST 89:4; CA 57-60; CANR 11, 41, 59, 137; MTCW 1, 2; MTFW 2005
Bakhtin, M.
See Bakhtin, Mikhail Mikhailovich
Bakhtin, M. M.
See Bakhtin, Mikhail Mikhailovich
Bakhtin, Mikhail
See Bakhtin, Mikhail Mikhailovich
Bakhtin, Mikhail Mikhailovich 1895-1975 **CLC 83; TCLC 160**
See also CA 128; 113; DLB 242; EWL 3
Bakshi, Ralph 1938(?)- **CLC 26**
See also CA 112; 138; IDFW 3

Bakunin, Mikhail (Alexandrovich)
1814-1876 **NCLC 25, 58**
See also DLB 277

Baldwin, James (Arthur) 1924-1987 . **BLC 1;**
CLC 1, 2, 3, 4, 5, 8, 13, 15, 17, 42, 50,
67, 90, 127; DC 1; SSC 10, 33; WLC 1
See also AAYA 4, 34; AFAW 1, 2; AMWR
2; AMWS 1; BPFB 1; BW 1; CA 1-4R;
124; CABS 1; CAD; CANR 3, 24;
CDALB 1941-1968; CN 1, 2, 3, 4; CPW;
DA; DA3; DAB; DAC; DAM MST,
MULT, NOV, POP; DFS 11, 15; DLB 2,
7, 33, 249, 278; DLBY 1987; EWL 3;
EXPS; LAIT 5; MAL 5; MTCW 1, 2;
MTFW 2005; NCFS 4; NFS 4; RGAL 4;
RGSF 2; SATA 9; SATA-Obit 54; SSFS
2, 18; TUS

Baldwin, William c. 1515-1563 **LC 113**
See also DLB 132

Bale, John 1495-1563 **LC 62**
See also DLB 132; RGEL 2; TEA

Ball, Hugo 1886-1927 **TCLC 104**

Ballard, J(ames) G(raham) 1930- . **CLC 3, 6,**
14, 36, 137; SSC 1, 53
See also AAYA 3, 52; BRWS 5; CA 5-8R;
CANR 15, 39, 65, 107, 133; CN 1, 2, 3,
4, 5, 6, 7; DA3; DAM NOV, POP; DLB
14, 207, 261, 319; EWL 3; HGG; MTCW
1, 2; MTFW 2005; NFS 8; RGEL 2;
RGSF 2; SATA 93; SCFW 1, 2; SFW 4

Balmont, Konstantin (Dmitriyevich)
1867-1943 **TCLC 11**
See also CA 109; 155; DLB 295; EWL 3

Baltausis, Vincas 1847-1910
See Mikszath, Kalman

Balzac, Honore de 1799-1850 ... **NCLC 5, 35,**
53, 153; SSC 5, 59; WLC 1
See also DA; DA3; DAB; DAC; DAM
MST, NOV; DLB 119; EW 5; GFL 1789
to the Present; LMFS 1; RGSF 2; RGWL
2, 3; SSFS 10; SUFW; TWA

Bambara, Toni Cade 1939-1995 **BLC 1;**
CLC 19, 88; SSC 35; TCLC 116;
WLCS
See also AAYA 5, 49; AFAW 2; AMWS 11;
BW 2, 3; CA 29-32R; 150;
CANR 24, 49, 81; CDALBS; DA; DA3;
DAC; DAM MST, MULT; DLB 38, 218;
EXPS; MAL 5; MTCW 1, 2; MTFW
2005; RGAL 4; RGSF 2; SATA 112; SSFS
4, 7, 12, 21

Bamdad, A.
See Shamlu, Ahmad

Bamdad, Alef
See Shamlu, Ahmad

Banat, D. R.
See Bradbury, Ray (Douglas)

Bancroft, Laura
See Baum, L(yman) Frank

Banim, John 1798-1842 **NCLC 13**
See also DLB 116, 158, 159; RGEL 2

Banim, Michael 1796-1874 **NCLC 13**
See also DLB 158, 159

Banjo, The
See Paterson, A(ndrew) B(arton)

Banks, Iain
See Banks, Iain M(enzies)
See also BRWS 11

Banks, Iain M(enzies) 1954- **CLC 34**
See Banks, Iain
See also CA 123; 128; CANR 61, 106; DLB
194, 261; EWL 3; HGG; INT CA-128;
MTFW 2005; SFW 4

Banks, Lynne Reid **CLC 23**
See Reid Banks, Lynne
See also AAYA 6; BYA 7; CLR 86; CN 4,
5, 6

Banks, Russell (Earl) 1940- **CLC 37, 72,**
187; SSC 42
See also AAYA 45; AMWS 5; CA 65-68;
CAAS 15; CANR 19, 52, 73, 118; CN 4,
5, 6, 7; DLB 130, 278; EWL 3; MAL 5;
MTCW 2; MTFW 2005; NFS 13

Banville, John 1945- **CLC 46, 118, 224**
See also CA 117; 128; CANR 104, 150; CN
4, 5, 6, 7; DLB 14, 271, 326; INT CA-
128

Banville, Theodore (Faullain) de
1832-1891 **NCLC 9**
See also DLB 217; GFL 1789 to the Present

Baraka, Amiri 1934- **BLC 1; CLC 1, 2, 3,**
5, 10, 14, 33, 115, 213; DC 6; PC 4;
WLCS
See Jones, LeRoi
See also AAYA 63; AFAW 1, 2; AMWS 2;
BW 2, 3; CA 21-24R; CABS 3; CAD;
CANR 27, 38, 61, 133; CD 3, 5, 6;
CDALB 1941-1968; CP 4, 5, 6, 7; CPW;
DA; DA3; DAC; DAM MST, MULT,
POET, POP; DFS 3, 11, 16; DLB 5, 7,
16, 38; DLBD 8; EWL 3; MAL 5; MTCW
1, 2; MTFW 2005; PFS 9; RGAL 4;
TCLE 1:1; TUS; WP

Baratynsky, Evgenii Abramovich
1800-1844 **NCLC 103**
See also DLB 205

Barbauld, Anna Laetitia
1743-1825 **NCLC 50**
See also DLB 107, 109, 142, 158; RGEL 2

Barbellion, W. N. P. **TCLC 24**
See Cummings, Bruce F(rederick)

Barber, Benjamin R. 1939- **CLC 141**
See also CA 29-32R; CANR 12, 32, 64, 119

Barbera, Jack (Vincent) 1945- **CLC 44**
See also CA 110; CANR 45

Barbey d'Aurevilly, Jules-Amedee
1808-1889 **NCLC 1; SSC 17**
See also DLB 119; GFL 1789 to the Present

Barbour, John c. 1316-1395 **CMLC 33**
See also DLB 146

Barbusse, Henri 1873-1935 **TCLC 5**
See also CA 105; 154; DLB 65; EWL 3;
RGWL 2, 3

Barclay, Alexander c. 1475-1552 **LC 109**
See also DLB 132

Barclay, Bill
See Moorcock, Michael

Barclay, William Ewert
See Moorcock, Michael

Barea, Arturo 1897-1957 **TCLC 14**
See also CA 111; 201

Barfoot, Joan 1946- **CLC 18**
See also CA 105; CANR 141

Barham, Richard Harris
1788-1845 **NCLC 77**
See also DLB 159

Baring, Maurice 1874-1945 **TCLC 8**
See also CA 105; 168; DLB 34; HGG

Baring-Gould, Sabine 1834-1924 ... **TCLC 88**
See also DLB 156, 190

Barker, Clive 1952- **CLC 52, 205; SSC 53**
See also AAYA 10, 54; BEST 90:3; BPFB
1; CA 121; 129; CANR 71, 111, 133;
CPW; DA3; DAM POP; DLB 261; HGG;
INT CA-129; MTCW 1, 2; MTFW 2005;
SUFW 2

Barker, George Granville
1913-1991 **CLC 8, 48**
See also CA 9-12R; 135; CANR 7, 38; CP
1, 2, 3, 4, 5; DAM POET; DLB 20; EWL
3; MTCW 1

Barker, Harley Granville
See Granville-Barker, Harley
See also DLB 10

Barker, Howard 1946- **CLC 37**
See also CA 102; CBD; CD 5, 6; DLB 13,
233

Barker, Jane 1652-1732 **LC 42, 82**
See also DLB 39, 131

Barker, Pat 1943- **CLC 32, 94, 146**
See also BRWS 4; CA 117; 122; CANR 50,
101, 148; CN 6, 7; DLB 271, 326; INT
CA-122

Barker, Patricia
See Barker, Pat

Barlach, Ernst (Heinrich)
1870-1938 **TCLC 84**
See also CA 178; DLB 56, 118; EWL 3

Barlow, Joel 1754-1812 **NCLC 23**
See also AMWS 2; DLB 37; RGAL 4

Barnard, Mary (Ethel) 1909- **CLC 48**
See also CA 21-22; CAP 2; CP 1

Barnes, Djuna 1892-1982 **CLC 3, 4, 8, 11,**
29, 127; SSC 3
See Steptoe, Lydia
See also AMWS 3; CA 9-12R; 107; CAD;
CANR 16, 55; CN 1, 2, 3; CWD; DLB 4,
9, 45; EWL 3; GLL 1; MAL 5; MTCW 1,
2; MTFW 2005; RGAL 4; TCLE 1:1;
TUS

Barnes, Jim 1933- **NNAL**
See also CA 108; 175; CAAE 175; CAAS
28; DLB 175

Barnes, Julian 1946- **CLC 42, 141**
See also BRWS 4; CA 102; CANR 19, 54,
115, 137; CN 4, 5, 6, 7; DAB; DLB 194;
DLBY 1993; EWL 3; MTCW 2; MTFW
2005

Barnes, Julian Patrick
See Barnes, Julian

Barnes, Peter 1931-2004 **CLC 5, 56**
See also CA 65-68; 230; CAAS 12; CANR
33, 34, 64, 113; CBD; CD 5, 6; DFS 6;
DLB 13, 233; MTCW 1

Barnes, William 1801-1886 **NCLC 75**
See also DLB 32

Baroja, Pio 1872-1956 **HLC 1; TCLC 8**
See also CA 104; 247; EW 9

Baroja y Nessi, Pio
See Baroja, Pio

Baron, David
See Pinter, Harold

Baron Corvo
See Rolfe, Frederick (William Serafino Aus-
tin Lewis Mary)

Barondess, Sue K(aufman)
1926-1977 **CLC 8**
See Kaufman, Sue
See also CA 1-4R; 69-72; CANR 1

Baron de Teive
See Pessoa, Fernando (Antonio Nogueira)

Baroness Von S.
See Zangwill, Israel

Barres, (Auguste-)Maurice
1862-1923 **TCLC 47**
See also CA 164; DLB 123; GFL 1789 to
the Present

Barreto, Afonso Henrique de Lima
See Lima Barreto, Afonso Henrique de

Barrett, Andrea 1954- **CLC 150**
See also CA 156; CANR 92; CN 7

Barrett, Michele **CLC 65**

Barrett, (Roger) Syd 1946-2006 **CLC 35**

Barrett, William (Christopher)
1913-1992 **CLC 27**
See also CA 13-16R; 139; CANR 11, 67;
INT CANR-11

Barrett Browning, Elizabeth
1806-1861 **NCLC 1, 16, 61, 66, 170;**
PC 6, 62; WLC 1
See also AAYA 63; BRW 4; CDBLB 1832-
1890; DA; DA3; DAB; DAC; DAM MST,
POET; DLB 32, 199; EXPP; FL 1:2; PAB;
PFS 2, 16, 23; TEA; WLIT 4; WP

Barrie, J(ames) M(atthew)
1860-1937 **TCLC 2, 164**
See also BRWS 3; BYA 4, 5; CA 104; 136;
CANR 77; CDBLB 1890-1914; CLR 16;
CWRI 5; DA3; DAB; DAM DRAM; DFS
7; DLB 10, 141, 156; EWL 3; FANT;
MAICYA 1, 2; MTCW 2; MTFW 2005;
SATA 100; SUFW; WCH; WLIT 4; YABC
1

Barrington, Michael
See Moorcock, Michael

Barrol, Grady
See Bograd, Larry

Barry, Mike
See Malzberg, Barry N(athaniel)

Barry, Philip 1896-1949 **TCLC 11**
See also CA 109; 199; DFS 9; DLB 7, 228;
MAL 5; RGAL 4

Bart, Andre Schwarz
See Schwarz-Bart, Andre

Barth, John (Simmons) 1930- ... **CLC 1, 2, 3,**
5, 7, 9, 10, 14, 27, 51, 89, 214; SSC 10,
89
See also AITN 1, 2; AMW; BPFB 1; CA
1-4R; CABS 1; CANR 5, 23, 49, 64, 113;
CN 1, 2, 3, 4, 5, 6, 7; DAM NOV; DLB
2, 227; EWL 3; FANT; MAL 5; MTCW
1; RGAL 4; RGSF 2; RHW; SSFS 6; TUS

Barthelme, Donald 1931-1989 .. **CLC 1, 2, 3,**
5, 6, 8, 13, 23, 46, 59, 115; SSC 2, 55
See also AMWS 4; BPFB 1; CA 21-24R;
129; CANR 20, 58; CN 1, 2, 3, 4; DA3;
DAM NOV; DLB 2, 234; DLBY 1980,
1989; EWL 3; FANT; LMFS 2; MAL 5;
MTCW 1, 2; MTFW 2005; RGAL 4;
RGSF 2; SATA 7; SATA-Obit 62; SSFS
17

Barthelme, Frederick 1943- **CLC 36, 117**
See also AMWS 11; CA 114; 122; CANR
77; CN 4, 5, 6, 7; CSW; DLB 244; DLBY
1985; EWL 3; INT CA-122

Barthes, Roland (Gerard)
1915-1980 **CLC 24, 83; TCLC 135**
See also CA 130; 97-100; CANR 66; DLB
296; EW 13; EWL 3; GFL 1789 to the
Present; MTCW 1, 2; TWA

Bartram, William 1739-1823 **NCLC 145**
See also ANW; DLB 37

Barzun, Jacques (Martin) 1907- **CLC 51,**
145
See also CA 61-64; CANR 22, 95

Bashevis, Isaac
See Singer, Isaac Bashevis

Bashkirtseff, Marie 1859-1884 **NCLC 27**

Basho, Matsuo
See Matsuo Basho
See also RGWL 2, 3; WP

Basil of Caesaria c. 330-379 **CMLC 35**

Basket, Raney
See Edgerton, Clyde (Carlyle)

Bass, Kingsley B., Jr.
See Bullins, Ed

Bass, Rick 1958- **CLC 79, 143; SSC 60**
See also ANW; CA 126; CANR 53, 93, 145;
CSW; DLB 212, 275

Bassani, Giorgio 1916-2000 **CLC 9**
See also CA 65-68; 190; CANR 33; CWW
2; DLB 128, 177, 299; EWL 3; MTCW 1;
RGHL; RGWL 2, 3

Bastian, Ann **CLC 70**

Bastos, Augusto Roa
See Roa Bastos, Augusto

Bataille, Georges 1897-1962 **CLC 29;**
TCLC 155
See also CA 101; 89-92; EWL 3

Bates, H(erbert) E(rnest)
1905-1974 **CLC 46; SSC 10**
See also CA 93-96; 45-48; CANR 34; CN
1; DA3; DAB; DAM POP; DLB 162, 191;
EWL 3; EXPS; MTCW 1, 2; RGSF 2;
SSFS 7

Bauchart
See Camus, Albert

Baudelaire, Charles 1821-1867 . **NCLC 6, 29,**
55, 155; PC 1; SSC 18; WLC 1
See also DA; DA3; DAB; DAC; DAM
MST, POET; DLB 217; EW 7; GFL 1789
to the Present; LMFS 2; PFS 21; RGWL
2, 3; TWA

Baudouin, Marcel
See Peguy, Charles (Pierre)

Baudouin, Pierre
See Peguy, Charles (Pierre)

Baudrillard, Jean 1929- **CLC 60**
See also DLB 296

Baum, L(yman) Frank 1856-1919 .. **TCLC 7,**
132
See also AAYA 46; BYA 16; CA 108; 133;
CLR 15, 107; CWRI 5; DLB 22; FANT;
JRDA; MAICYA 1, 2; MTCW 1, 2; NFS
13; RGAL 4; SATA 18, 100; WCH

Baum, Louis F.
See Baum, L(yman) Frank

Baumbach, Jonathan 1933- **CLC 6, 23**
See also CA 13-16R; CAAS 5; CANR 12,
66, 140; CN 3, 4, 5, 6, 7; DLBY 1980;
INT CANR-12; MTCW 1

Bausch, Richard (Carl) 1945- **CLC 51**
See also AMWS 7; CA 101; CAAS 14;
CANR 43, 61, 87; CN 7; CSW; DLB 130;
MAL 5

Baxter, Charles (Morley) 1947- . **CLC 45, 78**
See also CA 57-60; CANR 40, 64, 104, 133;
CPW; DAM POP; DLB 130; MAL 5;
MTCW 2; MTFW 2005; TCLE 1:1

Baxter, George Owen
See Faust, Frederick (Schiller)

Baxter, James K(eir) 1926-1972 **CLC 14**
See also CA 77-80; CP 1; EWL 3

Baxter, John
See Hunt, E(verette) Howard, (Jr.)

Bayer, Sylvia
See Glassco, John

Bayle, Pierre 1647-1706 **LC 126**
See also DLB 268, 313; GFL Beginnings to
1789

Baynton, Barbara 1857-1929 **TCLC 57**
See also DLB 230; RGSF 2

Beagle, Peter S(oyer) 1939- **CLC 7, 104**
See also AAYA 47; BPFB 1; BYA 9, 10,
16; CA 9-12R; CANR 4, 51, 73, 110;
DA3; DLBY 1980; FANT; INT CANR-4;
MTCW 2; MTFW 2005; SATA 60, 130;
SUFW 1, 2; YAW

Bean, Normal
See Burroughs, Edgar Rice

Beard, Charles A(ustin)
1874-1948 **TCLC 15**
See also CA 115; 189; DLB 17; SATA 18

Beardsley, Aubrey 1872-1898 **NCLC 6**

Beattie, Ann 1947- **CLC 8, 13, 18, 40, 63,**
146; SSC 11
See also AMWS 5; BEST 90:2; BPFB 1;
CA 81-84; CANR 53, 73, 128; CN 4, 5,
6, 7; CPW; DA3; DAM NOV, POP; DLB
218, 278; DLBY 1982; EWL 3; MAL 5;
MTCW 1, 2; MTFW 2005; RGAL 4;
RGSF 2; SSFS 9; TUS

Beattie, James 1735-1803 **NCLC 25**
See also DLB 109

Beauchamp, Kathleen Mansfield 1888-1923
See Mansfield, Katherine
See also CA 104; 134; DA; DA3; DAC;
DAM MST; MTCW 2; TEA

Beaumarchais, Pierre-Augustin Caron de
1732-1799 **DC 4; LC 61**
See also DAM DRAM; DFS 14, 16; DLB
313; EW 4; GFL Beginnings to 1789;
RGWL 2, 3

Beaumont, Francis 1584(?)-1616 .. **DC 6; LC**
33
See also BRW 2; CDBLB Before 1660;
DLB 58; TEA

Beauvoir, Simone de 1908-1986 **CLC 1, 2,**
4, 8, 14, 31, 44, 50, 71, 124; SSC 35;
WLC 1
See also BPFB 1; CA 9-12R; 118; CANR
28, 61; DA; DA3; DAB; DAC; DAM
MST, NOV; DLB 72; DLBY 1986; EW
12; EWL 3; FL 1:5; FW; GFL 1789 to the
Present; LMFS 2; MTCW 1, 2; MTFW
2005; RGSF 2; RGWL 2, 3; TWA

Beauvoir, Simone Lucie Ernestine Marie
Bertrand de
See Beauvoir, Simone de

Becker, Carl (Lotus) 1873-1945 **TCLC 63**
See also CA 157; DLB 17

Becker, Jurek 1937-1997 **CLC 7, 19**
See also CA 85-88; 157; CANR 60, 117;
CWW 2; DLB 75, 299; EWL 3; RGHL

Becker, Walter 1950- **CLC 26**

Becket, Thomas a 1118(?)-1170 ... **CMLC 83**

Beckett, Samuel (Barclay)
1906-1989 .. **CLC 1, 2, 3, 4, 6, 9, 10, 11,**
14, 18, 29, 57, 59, 83; DC 22; SSC 16,
74; TCLC 145; WLC 1
See also BRWC 2; BRWR 1; BRWS 1; CA
5-8R; 130; CANR 33, 61; CBD; CDBLB
1945-1960; CN 1, 2, 3, 4; CP 1, 2, 3, 4;
DA; DA3; DAB; DAC; DAM DRAM,
MST, NOV; DFS 2, 7, 18; DLB 13, 15,
233, 319, 321; DLBY 1990; EWL 3; GFL
1789 to the Present; LATS 1:2; LMFS 2;
MTCW 1, 2; MTFW 2005; RGSF 2;
RGWL 2, 3; SSFS 15; TEA; WLIT 4

Beckford, William 1760-1844 **NCLC 16**
See also BRW 3; DLB 39, 213; GL 2; HGG;
LMFS 1; SUFW

Beckham, Barry (Earl) 1944- **BLC 1**
See also BW 1; CA 29-32R; CANR 26, 62;
CN 1, 2, 3, 4, 5, 6; DAM MULT; DLB 33

Beckman, Gunnel 1910- **CLC 26**
See also CA 33-36R; CANR 15, 114; CLR
25; MAICYA 1, 2; SAAS 9; SATA 6

Becque, Henri 1837-1899 **DC 21; NCLC 3**
See also DLB 192; GFL 1789 to the Present

Becquer, Gustavo Adolfo
1836-1870 **HLCS 1; NCLC 106**
See also DAM MULT

Beddoes, Thomas Lovell 1803-1849 .. **DC 15;**
NCLC 3, 154
See also BRWS 11; DLB 96

Bede c. 673-735 **CMLC 20**
See also DLB 146; TEA

Bedford, Denton R. 1907-(?) **NNAL**

Bedford, Donald F.
See Fearing, Kenneth (Flexner)

Beecher, Catharine Esther
1800-1878 **NCLC 30**
See also DLB 1, 243

Beecher, John 1904-1980 **CLC 6**
See also AITN 1; CA 5-8R; 105; CANR 8;
CP 1, 2, 3

Beer, Johann 1655-1700 **LC 5**
See also DLB 168

Beer, Patricia 1924- **CLC 58**
See also CA 61-64; 183; CANR 13, 46; CP
1, 2, 3, 4, 5, 6; CWP; DLB 40; FW

Beerbohm, Max
See Beerbohm, (Henry) Max(imilian)

Beerbohm, (Henry) Max(imilian)
1872-1956 **TCLC 1, 24**
See also BRWS 2; CA 104; 154; CANR 79;
DLB 34, 100; FANT; MTCW 2

Beer-Hofmann, Richard
1866-1945 **TCLC 60**
See also CA 160; DLB 81

Beg, Shemus
See Stephens, James

Begiebing, Robert J(ohn) 1946- **CLC 70**
See also CA 122; CANR 40, 88

Begley, Louis 1933- **CLC 197**
See also CA 140; CANR 98; DLB 299;
RGHL; TCLE 1:1

Behan, Brendan (Francis)
1923-1964 **CLC 1, 8, 11, 15, 79**
See also BRWS 2; CA 73-76; CANR 33,
121; CBD; CDBLB 1945-1960; DAM
DRAM; DFS 7; DLB 13, 233; EWL 3;
MTCW 1, 2

Behn, Aphra 1640(?)-1689 .. **DC 4; LC 1, 30,
42; PC 13; WLC 1**
See also BRWS 3; DA; DA3; DAB; DAC;
DAM DRAM, MST, NOV, POET; DFS
16; DLB 39, 80, 131; FW; TEA; WLIT 3

Behrman, S(amuel) N(athaniel)
1893-1973 **CLC 40**
See also CA 13-16; 45-48; CAD; CAP 1;
DLB 7, 44; IDFW 3; MAL 5; RGAL 4

Bekederemo, J. P. Clark
See Clark Bekederemo, J(ohnson) P(epper)
See also CD 6

Belasco, David 1853-1931 **TCLC 3**
See also CA 104; 168; DLB 7; MAL 5;
RGAL 4

Belcheva, Elisaveta Lyubomirova
1893-1991 **CLC 10**
See Bagryana, Elisaveta

Beldone, Phil "Cheech"
See Ellison, Harlan (Jay)

Beleno
See Azuela, Mariano

Belinski, Vissarion Grigoryevich
1811-1848 **NCLC 5**
See also DLB 198

Belitt, Ben 1911- **CLC 22**
See also CA 13-16R; CAAS 4; CANR 7,
77; CP 1, 2, 3, 4, 5, 6; DLB 5

Belknap, Jeremy 1744-1798 **LC 115**
See also DLB 30, 37

Bell, Gertrude (Margaret Lowthian)
1868-1926 **TCLC 67**
See also CA 167; CANR 110; DLB 174

Bell, J. Freeman
See Zangwill, Israel

Bell, James Madison 1826-1902 **BLC 1;
TCLC 43**
See also BW 1; CA 122; 124; DAM MULT;
DLB 50

Bell, Madison Smartt 1957- **CLC 41, 102,
223**
See also AMWS 10; BPFB 1; CA 111, 183;
CAAE 183; CANR 28, 54, 73, 134; CN
5, 6, 7; CSW; DLB 218, 278; MTCW 2;
MTFW 2005

Bell, Marvin (Hartley) 1937- **CLC 8, 31**
See also CA 21-24R; CAAS 14; CANR 59,
102; CP 1, 2, 3, 4, 5, 6, 7; DAM POET;
DLB 5; MAL 5; MTCW 1

Bell, W. L. D.
See Mencken, H(enry) L(ouis)

Bellamy, Atwood C.
See Mencken, H(enry) L(ouis)

Bellamy, Edward 1850-1898 **NCLC 4, 86,
147**
See also DLB 12; NFS 15; RGAL 4; SFW 4

Belli, Gioconda 1948- **HLCS 1**
See also CA 152; CANR 143; CWW 2;
DLB 290; EWL 3; RGWL 3

Bellin, Edward J.
See Kuttner, Henry

Bello, Andres 1781-1865 **NCLC 131**
See also LAW

**Belloc, (Joseph) Hilaire (Pierre Sebastien
Rene Swanton)** 1870-1953 **PC 24;
TCLC 7, 18**
See also CA 106; 152; CLR 102; CWRI 5;
DAM POET; DLB 19, 100, 141, 174;
EWL 3; MTCW 2; MTFW 2005; SATA
112; WCH; YABC 1

Belloc, Joseph Peter Rene Hilaire
See Belloc, (Joseph) Hilaire (Pierre Sebastien Rene Swanton)

Belloc, Joseph Pierre Hilaire
See Belloc, (Joseph) Hilaire (Pierre Sebastien Rene Swanton)

Belloc, M. A.
See Lowndes, Marie Adelaide (Belloc)

Belloc-Lowndes, Mrs.
See Lowndes, Marie Adelaide (Belloc)

Bellow, Saul 1915-2005 **CLC 1, 2, 3, 6, 8,
10, 13, 15, 25, 33, 34, 63, 79, 190, 200;
SSC 14; WLC 1**
See also AITN 2; AMW; AMWC 2; AMWR
2; BEST 89:3; BPFB 1; CA 5-8R; 238;
CABS 1; CANR 29, 53, 95, 132; CDALB
1941-1968; CN 1, 2, 3, 4, 5, 6, 7; DA;
DA3; DAB; DAC; DAM MST, NOV,
POP; DLB 2, 28, 299; DLBD 3; DLBY
1982; EWL 3; MAL 5; MTCW 1, 2;
MTFW 2005; NFS 4, 14; RGAL 4;
RGHL; RGSF 2; SSFS 12; TUS

Belser, Reimond Karel Maria de 1929-
See Ruyslinck, Ward
See also CA 152

Bely, Andrey **PC 11; TCLC 7**
See Bugayev, Boris Nikolayevich
See also DLB 295; EW 9; EWL 3

Belyi, Andrei
See Bugayev, Boris Nikolayevich
See also RGWL 2, 3

Bembo, Pietro 1470-1547 **LC 79**
See also RGWL 2, 3

Benary, Margot
See Benary-Isbert, Margot

Benary-Isbert, Margot 1889-1979 **CLC 12**
See also CA 5-8R; 89-92; CANR 4, 72;
CLR 12; MAICYA 1, 2; SATA 2; SATA-
Obit 21

Benavente (y Martinez), Jacinto
1866-1954 **DC 26; HLCS 1; TCLC 3**
See also CA 106; 131; CANR 81; DAM
DRAM, MULT; EWL 3; GLL 2; HW 1,
2; MTCW 1, 2

Benchley, Peter 1940-2006 **CLC 4, 8**
See also AAYA 14; AITN 2; BPFB 1; CA
17-20R; 248; CANR 12, 35, 66, 115;
CPW; DAM NOV, POP; HGG; MTCW 1,
2; MTFW 2005; SATA 3, 89, 164

Benchley, Peter Bradford
See Benchley, Peter

Benchley, Robert (Charles)
1889-1945 **TCLC 1, 55**
See also CA 105; 153; DLB 11; MAL 5;
RGAL 4

Benda, Julien 1867-1956 **TCLC 60**
See also CA 120; 154; GFL 1789 to the
Present

Benedict, Ruth 1887-1948 **TCLC 60**
See also CA 158; CANR 146; DLB 246

Benedict, Ruth Fulton
See Benedict, Ruth

Benedikt, Michael 1935- **CLC 4, 14**
See also CA 13-16R; CANR 7; CP 1, 2, 3,
4, 5, 6, 7; DLB 5

Benet, Juan 1927-1993 **CLC 28**
See also CA 143; EWL 3

Benet, Stephen Vincent 1898-1943 **PC 64;
SSC 10, 86; TCLC 7**
See also CA 104; 152; DA3; DAM POET;
DLB 4, 48, 102, 249, 284; DLBY 1997;
EWL 3; HGG; MAL 5; MTCW 2; MTFW
2005; RGAL 4; RGSF 2; SUFW; WP;
YABC 1

Benet, William Rose 1886-1950 **TCLC 28**
See also CA 118; 152; DAM POET; DLB
45; RGAL 4

Benford, Gregory (Albert) 1941- **CLC 52**
See also BPFB 1; CA 69-72, 175; CAAE
175; CAAS 27; CANR 12, 24, 49, 95,
134; CN 7; CSW; DLBY 1982; MTFW
2005; SCFW 2; SFW 4

Bengtsson, Frans (Gunnar)
1894-1954 **TCLC 48**
See also CA 170; EWL 3

Benjamin, David
See Slavitt, David R(ytman)

Benjamin, Lois
See Gould, Lois

Benjamin, Walter 1892-1940 **TCLC 39**
See also CA 164; DLB 242; EW 11; EWL
3

Ben Jelloun, Tahar 1944-
See Jelloun, Tahar ben
See also CA 135; CWW 2; EWL 3; RGWL
3; WLIT 2

Benn, Gottfried 1886-1956 .. **PC 35; TCLC 3**
See also CA 106; 153; DLB 56; EWL 3;
RGWL 2, 3

Bennett, Alan 1934- **CLC 45, 77**
See also BRWS 8; CA 103; CANR 35, 55,
106; CBD; CD 5, 6; DAB; DAM MST;
DLB 310; MTCW 1, 2; MTFW 2005

Bennett, (Enoch) Arnold
1867-1931 **TCLC 5, 20**
See also BRW 6; CA 106; 155; CDBLB
1890-1914; DLB 10, 34, 98, 135; EWL 3;
MTCW 2

Bennett, Elizabeth
See Mitchell, Margaret (Munnerlyn)

Bennett, George Harold 1930-
See Bennett, Hal
See also BW 1; CA 97-100; CANR 87

Bennett, Gwendolyn B. 1902-1981 **HR 1:2**
See also BW 1; CA 125; DLB 51; WP

Bennett, Hal **CLC 5**
See Bennett, George Harold
See also DLB 33

Bennett, Jay 1912- **CLC 35**
See also AAYA 10; CA 69-72; CANR 11,
42, 79; JRDA; SAAS 4; SATA 41, 87;
SATA-Brief 27; WYA; YAW

Bennett, Louise (Simone) 1919- **BLC 1;
CLC 28**
See also BW 2, 3; CA 151; CDWLB 3; CP
1, 2, 3, 4, 5, 6, 7; DAM MULT; DLB 117;
EWL 3

Benson, A. C. 1862-1925 **TCLC 123**
See also DLB 98

Benson, E(dward) F(rederic)
1867-1940 **TCLC 27**
See also CA 114; 157; DLB 135, 153;
HGG; SUFW 1

Benson, Jackson J. 1930- **CLC 34**
See also CA 25-28R; DLB 111

Benson, Sally 1900-1972 **CLC 17**
See also CA 19-20; 37-40R; CAP 1; SATA
1, 35; SATA-Obit 27

Benson, Stella 1892-1933 **TCLC 17**
See also CA 117; 154, 155; DLB 36, 162;
FANT; TEA

Bentham, Jeremy 1748-1832 **NCLC 38**
See also DLB 107, 158, 252

Bentley, E(dmund) C(lerihew)
1875-1956 **TCLC 12**
See also CA 108; 232; DLB 70; MSW
Bentley, Eric 1916- **CLC 24**
See also CA 5-8R; CAD; CANR 6, 67;
CBD; CD 5, 6; INT CANR-6
Bentley, Eric Russell
See Bentley, Eric
ben Uzair, Salem
See Horne, Richard Henry Hengist
Beranger, Pierre Jean de
1780-1857 **NCLC 34**
Berdyaev, Nicolas
See Berdyaev, Nikolai (Aleksandrovich)
Berdyaev, Nikolai (Aleksandrovich)
1874-1948 **TCLC 67**
See also CA 120; 157
Berdyayev, Nikolai (Aleksandrovich)
See Berdyaev, Nikolai (Aleksandrovich)
Berendt, John 1939- **CLC 86**
See also CA 146; CANR 75, 83, 151
Berendt, John Lawrence
See Berendt, John
Beresford, J(ohn) D(avys)
1873-1947 **TCLC 81**
See also CA 112; 155; DLB 162, 178, 197;
SFW 4; SUFW 1
Bergelson, David (Rafailovich)
1884-1952 **TCLC 81**
See Bergelson, Dovid
See also CA 220
Bergelson, Dovid
See Bergelson, David (Rafailovich)
See also EWL 3
Berger, Colonel
See Malraux, (Georges-)Andre
Berger, John (Peter) 1926- **CLC 2, 19**
See also BRWS 4; CA 81-84; CANR 51,
78, 117; CN 1, 2, 3, 4, 5, 6, 7; DLB 14,
207, 319, 326
Berger, Melvin H. 1927- **CLC 12**
See also CA 5-8R; CANR 4, 142; CLR 32;
SAAS 2; SATA 5, 88, 158; SATA-Essay
124
Berger, Thomas (Louis) 1924- .. **CLC 3, 5, 8,
11, 18, 38**
See also BPFB 1; CA 1-4R; CANR 5, 28,
51, 128; CN 1, 2, 3, 4, 5, 6, 7; DAM
NOV; DLB 2; DLBY 1980; EWL 3;
FANT; INT CANR-28; MAL 5; MTCW
1, 2; MTFW 2005; RHW; TCLE 1:1;
TCWW 1, 2
Bergman, (Ernst) Ingmar 1918- **CLC 16,
72, 210**
See also AAYA 61; CA 81-84; CANR 33,
70; CWW 2; DLB 257; MTCW 2; MTFW
2005
Bergson, Henri(-Louis) 1859-1941 . **TCLC 32**
See also CA 164; EW 8; EWL 3; GFL 1789
to the Present
Bergstein, Eleanor 1938- **CLC 4**
See also CA 53-56; CANR 5
Berkeley, George 1685-1753 **LC 65**
See also DLB 31, 101, 252
Berkoff, Steven 1937- **CLC 56**
See also CA 104; CANR 72; CBD; CD 5, 6
Berlin, Isaiah 1909-1997 **TCLC 105**
See also CA 85-88; 162
Bermant, Chaim (Icyk) 1929-1998 ... **CLC 40**
See also CA 57-60; CANR 6, 31, 57, 105;
CN 2, 3, 4, 5, 6
Bern, Victoria
See Fisher, M(ary) F(rances) K(ennedy)
Bernanos, (Paul Louis) Georges
1888-1948 **TCLC 3**
See also CA 104; 130; CANR 94; DLB 72;
EWL 3; GFL 1789 to the Present;
RGWL 2, 3

Bernard, April 1956- **CLC 59**
See also CA 131; CANR 144
Bernard, Mary Ann
See Soderbergh, Steven
Bernard of Clairvaux 1090-1153 .. **CMLC 71**
See also DLB 208
Berne, Victoria
See Fisher, M(ary) F(rances) K(ennedy)
Bernhard, Thomas 1931-1989 **CLC 3, 32,
61; DC 14; TCLC 165**
See also CA 85-88; 127; CANR 32, 57; CD-
WLB 2; DLB 85, 124; EWL 3; MTCW 1;
RGHL; RGWL 2, 3
Bernhardt, Sarah (Henriette Rosine)
1844-1923 **TCLC 75**
See also CA 157
Bernstein, Charles 1950- **CLC 142,**
See also CA 129; CAAS 24; CANR 90; CP
4, 5, 6, 7; DLB 169
Bernstein, Ingrid
See Kirsch, Sarah
Beroul fl. c. 12th cent. - **CMLC 75**
Berriault, Gina 1926-1999 **CLC 54, 109;
SSC 30**
See also CA 116; 129; 185; CANR 66; DLB
130; SSFS 7,11
Berrigan, Daniel 1921- **CLC 4**
See also CA 33-36R, 187; CAAE 187;
CAAS 1; CANR 11, 43, 78; CP 1, 2, 3, 4,
5, 6, 7; DLB 5
Berrigan, Edmund Joseph Michael, Jr.
1934-1983
See Berrigan, Ted
See also CA 61-64; 110; CANR 14, 102
Berrigan, Ted **CLC 37**
See Berrigan, Edmund Joseph Michael, Jr.
See also CP 1, 2, 3; DLB 5, 169; WP
Berry, Charles Edward Anderson 1931-
See Berry, Chuck
See also CA 115
Berry, Chuck **CLC 17**
See Berry, Charles Edward Anderson
Berry, Jonas
See Ashbery, John (Lawrence)
See also GLL 1
Berry, Wendell (Erdman) 1934- ... **CLC 4, 6,
8, 27, 46; PC 28**
See also AITN 1; AMWS 10; ANW; CA
73-76; CANR 50, 73, 101, 132; CP 1, 2,
3, 4, 5, 6, 7; CSW; DAM POET; DLB 5,
6, 234, 275; MTCW 2; MTFW 2005;
TCLE 1:1
Berryman, John 1914-1972 ... **CLC 1, 2, 3, 4,
6, 8, 10, 13, 25, 62; PC 64**
See also AMW; CA 13-16; 33-36R; CABS
2; CANR 35; CAP 1; CDALB 1941-1968;
CP 1; DAM POET; DLB 48; EWL 3;
MAL 5; MTCW 1, 2; MTFW 2005; PAB;
RGAL 4; WP
Bertolucci, Bernardo 1940- **CLC 16, 157**
See also CA 106; CANR 125
Berton, Pierre (Francis de Marigny)
1920-2004 **CLC 104**
See also CA 1-4R; 233; CANR 2, 56, 144;
CPW; DLB 68; SATA 99; SATA-Obit 158
Bertrand, Aloysius 1807-1841 **NCLC 31**
See Bertrand, Louis oAloysiusc
Bertrand, Louis oAloysiusc
See Bertrand, Aloysius
See also DLB 217
Bertran de Born c. 1140-1215 **CMLC 5**
Besant, Annie (Wood) 1847-1933 **TCLC 9**
See also CA 105; 185
Bessie, Alvah 1904-1985 **CLC 23**
See also CA 5-8R; 116; CANR 2, 80; DLB
26
Bestuzhev, Aleksandr Aleksandrovich
1797-1837 **NCLC 131**
See also DLB 198

Bethlen, T. D.
See Silverberg, Robert
Beti, Mongo **BLC 1; CLC 27**
See Biyidi, Alexandre
See also AFW; CANR 79; DAM MULT;
EWL 3; WLIT 2
Betjeman, John 1906-1984 **CLC 2, 6, 10,
34, 43**
See also BRW 7; CA 9-12R; 112; CANR
33, 56; CDBLB 1945-1960; CP 1, 2, 3;
DA3; DAB; DAM MST, POET; DLB 20;
DLBY 1984; EWL 3; MTCW 1, 2
Bettelheim, Bruno 1903-1990 **CLC 79;
TCLC 143**
See also CA 81-84; 131; CANR 23, 61;
DA3; MTCW 1, 2; RGHL
Betti, Ugo 1892-1953 **TCLC 5**
See also CA 104; 155; EWL 3; RGWL 2, 3
Betts, Doris (Waugh) 1932- **CLC 3, 6, 28;
SSC 45**
See also CA 13-16R; CANR 9, 66, 77; CN
6, 7; CSW; DLB 218; DLBY 1982; INT
CANR-9; RGAL 4
Bevan, Alistair
See Roberts, Keith (John Kingston)
Bey, Pilaff
See Douglas, (George) Norman
Bialik, Chaim Nachman
1873-1934 **TCLC 25**
See Bialik, Hayyim Nahman
See also CA 170; EWL 3
Bialik, Hayyim Nahman
See Bialik, Chaim Nachman
See also WLIT 6
Bickerstaff, Isaac
See Swift, Jonathan
Bidart, Frank 1939- **CLC 33**
See also AMWS 15; CA 140; CANR 106;
CP 5, 6, 7
Bienek, Horst 1930- **CLC 7, 11**
See also CA 73-76; DLB 75
Bierce, Ambrose (Gwinett)
1842-1914(?) **SSC 9, 72; TCLC 1, 7,
44; WLC 1**
See also AAYA 55; AMW; BYA 11; CA
104; 139; CANR 78; CDALB 1865-1917;
DA; DA3; DAC; DAM MST; DLB 11,
12, 23, 71, 74, 186; EWL 3; EXPS; HGG;
LAIT 2; MAL 5; RGAL 4; RGSF 2; SSFS
9; SUFW 1
Biggers, Earl Derr 1884-1933 **TCLC 65**
See also CA 108; 153; DLB 306
Billiken, Bud
See Motley, Willard (Francis)
Billings, Josh
See Shaw, Henry Wheeler
Billington, (Lady) Rachel (Mary)
1942- .. **CLC 43**
See also AITN 2; CA 33-36R; CANR 44;
CN 4, 5, 6, 7
Binchy, Maeve 1940- **CLC 153**
See also BEST 90:1; BPFB 1; CA 127; 134;
CANR 50, 96, 134; CN 5, 6, 7; CPW;
DA3; DAM POP; DLB 319; INT CA-134;
MTCW 2; MTFW 2005; RHW
Binyon, T(imothy) J(ohn)
1936-2004 **CLC 34**
See also CA 111; 232; CANR 28, 140
Bion 335B.C.-245B.C. **CMLC 39**
Bioy Casares, Adolfo 1914-1999 ... **CLC 4, 8,
13, 88; HLC 1; SSC 17**
See Casares, Adolfo Bioy; Miranda, Javier;
Sacastru, Martin
See also CA 29-32R; 177; CANR 19, 43,
66; CWW 2; DAM MULT; DLB 113;
EWL 3; HW 1, 2; LAW; MTCW 1, 2;
MTFW 2005
Birch, Allison **CLC 65**

Bird, Cordwainer
See Ellison, Harlan (Jay)

Bird, Robert Montgomery
1806-1854 **NCLC 1**
See also DLB 202; RGAL 4

Birkerts, Sven 1951- **CLC 116**
See also CA 128; 133, 176; CAAE 176;
CAAS 29; CANR 151; INT CA-133

Birney, (Alfred) Earle 1904-1995 .. **CLC 1, 4,
6, 11; PC 52**
See also CA 1-4R; CANR 5, 20; CN 1, 2,
3, 4; CP 1, 2, 3, 4, 5, 6; DAC; DAM MST,
POET; DLB 88; MTCW 1; PFS 8; RGEL
2

Biruni, al 973-1048(?) **CMLC 28**

Bishop, Elizabeth 1911-1979 **CLC 1, 4, 9,
13, 15, 32; PC 3, 34; TCLC 121**
See also AMWR 2; AMWS 1; CA 5-8R;
89-92; CABS 2; CANR 26, 61, 108;
CDALB 1968-1988; CP 1, 2, 3; DA;
DA3; DAC; DAM MST, POET; DLB 5,
169; EWL 3; GLL 2; MAL 5; MAWW;
MTCW 1, 2; PAB; PFS 6, 12; RGAL 4;
SATA-Obit 24; TUS; WP

Bishop, John 1935- **CLC 10**
See also CA 105

Bishop, John Peale 1892-1944 **TCLC 103**
See also CA 107; 155; DLB 4, 9, 45; MAL
5; RGAL 4

Bissett, Bill 1939- **CLC 18; PC 14**
See also CA 69-72; CAAS 19; CANR 15;
CCA 1; CP 1, 2, 3, 4, 5, 6, 7; DLB 53;
MTCW 1

Bissoondath, Neil (Devindra)
1955- ... **CLC 120**
See also CA 136; CANR 123; CN 6, 7;
DAC

Bitov, Andrei (Georgievich) 1937- ... **CLC 57**
See also CA 142; DLB 302

Biyidi, Alexandre 1932-
See Beti, Mongo
See also BW 1, 3; CA 114; 124; CANR 81;
DA3; MTCW 1, 2

Bjarme, Brynjolf
See Ibsen, Henrik (Johan)

Bjoernson, Bjoernstjerne (Martinius)
1832-1910 **TCLC 7, 37**
See also CA 104

Black, Benjamin
See Banville, John

Black, Robert
See Holdstock, Robert P.

Blackburn, Paul 1926-1971 **CLC 9, 43**
See also BG 1:2; CA 81-84; 33-36R; CANR
34; CP 1; DLB 16; DLBY 1981

Black Elk 1863-1950 **NNAL; TCLC 33**
See also CA 144; DAM MULT; MTCW 2;
MTFW 2005; WP

Black Hawk 1767-1838 **NNAL**

Black Hobart
See Sanders, (James) Ed(ward)

Blacklin, Malcolm
See Chambers, Aidan

Blackmore, R(ichard) D(oddridge)
1825-1900 **TCLC 27**
See also CA 120; DLB 18; RGEL 2

Blackmur, R(ichard) P(almer)
1904-1965 **CLC 2, 24**
See also AMWS 2; CA 11-12; 25-28R;
CANR 71; CAP 1; DLB 63; EWL 3;
MAL 5

Black Tarantula
See Acker, Kathy

Blackwood, Algernon (Henry)
1869-1951 **TCLC 5**
See also CA 105; 150; DLB 153, 156, 178;
HGG; SUFW 1

Blackwood, Caroline (Maureen)
1931-1996 **CLC 6, 9, 100**
See also BRWS 9; CA 85-88; 151; CANR
32, 61, 65; CN 3, 4, 5, 6; DLB 14, 207;
HGG; MTCW 1

Blade, Alexander
See Hamilton, Edmond; Silverberg, Robert

Blaga, Lucian 1895-1961 **CLC 75**
See also CA 157; DLB 220; EWL 3

Blair, Eric (Arthur) 1903-1950 **TCLC 123**
See Orwell, George
See also CA 104; 132; DA; DA3; DAB;
DAC; DAM MST, NOV; MTCW 1, 2;
MTFW 2005; SATA 29

Blair, Hugh 1718-1800 **NCLC 75**

Blais, Marie-Claire 1939- **CLC 2, 4, 6, 13,
22**
See also CA 21-24R; CAAS 4; CANR 38,
75, 93; CWW 2; DAC; DAM MST; DLB
53; EWL 3; FW; MTCW 1, 2; MTFW
2005; TWA

Blaise, Clark 1940- **CLC 29**
See also AITN 2; CA 53-56, 231; CAAE
231; CAAS 3; CANR 5, 66, 106; CN 4,
5, 6, 7; DLB 53; RGSF 2

Blake, Fairley
See De Voto, Bernard (Augustine)

Blake, Nicholas
See Day Lewis, C(ecil)
See also DLB 77; MSW

Blake, Sterling
See Benford, Gregory (Albert)

Blake, William 1757-1827 . **NCLC 13, 37, 57,
127, 173; PC 12, 63; WLC 1**
See also AAYA 47; BRW 3; BRWR 1; CD-
BLB 1789-1832; CLR 52; DA; DA3;
DAB; DAC; DAM MST, POET; DLB 93,
163; EXPP; LATS 1:1; LMFS 1; MAI-
CYA 1, 2; PAB; PFS 2, 12, 24; SATA 30;
TEA; WCH; WLIT 3; WP

Blanchot, Maurice 1907-2003 **CLC 135**
See also CA 117; 144; 213; CANR 138;
DLB 72, 296; EWL 3

Blasco Ibanez, Vicente 1867-1928 . **TCLC 12**
See Ibanez, Vicente Blasco
See also BPFB 1; CA 110; 131; CANR 81;
DA3; DAM NOV; EW 8; EWL 3; HW 1,
2; MTCW 1

Blatty, William Peter 1928- **CLC 2**
See also CA 5-8R; CANR 9, 124; DAM
POP; HGG

Bleeck, Oliver
See Thomas, Ross (Elmore)

Blessing, Lee (Knowlton) 1949- **CLC 54**
See also CA 236; CAD; CD 5, 6; DFS 23

Blight, Rose
See Greer, Germaine

Blish, James (Benjamin) 1921-1975 . **CLC 14**
See also BPFB 1; CA 1-4R; 57-60; CANR
3; CN 2; DLB 8; MTCW 1; SATA 66;
SCFW 1, 2; SFW 4

Bliss, Frederick
See Card, Orson Scott

Bliss, Reginald
See Wells, H(erbert) G(eorge)

Blixen, Karen (Christentze Dinesen)
1885-1962
See Dinesen, Isak
See also CA 25-28; CANR 22, 50; CAP 2;
DA3; DLB 214; LMFS 1; MTCW 1, 2;
SATA 44; SSFS 20

Bloch, Robert (Albert) 1917-1994 **CLC 33**
See also AAYA 29; CA 5-8R, 179; 146;
CAAE 179; CAAS 20; CANR 5, 78;
DA3; DLB 44; HGG; INT CANR-5;
MTCW 2; SATA 12; SATA-Obit 82; SFW
4; SUFW 1, 2

Blok, Alexander (Alexandrovich)
1880-1921 **PC 21; TCLC 5**
See also CA 104; 183; DLB 295; EW 9;
EWL 3; LMFS 2; RGWL 2, 3

Blom, Jan
See Breytenbach, Breyten

Bloom, Harold 1930- **CLC 24, 103, 221**
See also CA 13-16R; CANR 39, 75, 92,
133; DLB 67; EWL 3; MTCW 2; MTFW
2005; RGAL 4

Bloomfield, Aurelius
See Bourne, Randolph S(illiman)

Bloomfield, Robert 1766-1823 **NCLC 145**
See also DLB 93

Blount, Roy (Alton), Jr. 1941- **CLC 38**
See also CA 53-56; CANR 10, 28, 61, 125;
CSW; INT CANR-28; MTCW 1, 2;
MTFW 2005

Blowsnake, Sam 1875-(?) **NNAL**

Bloy, Leon 1846-1917 **TCLC 22**
See also CA 121; 183; DLB 123; GFL 1789
to the Present

Blue Cloud, Peter (Aroniawenrate)
1933- ... **NNAL**
See also CA 117; CANR 40; DAM MULT

Bluggage, Oranthy
See Alcott, Louisa May

Blume, Judy (Sussman) 1938- **CLC 12, 30**
See also AAYA 3, 26; BYA 1, 8, 12; CA 29-
32R; CANR 13, 37, 66, 124; CLR 2, 15,
69; CPW; DA3; DAM NOV, POP; DLB
52; JRDA; MAICYA 1, 2; MAICYAS 1;
MTCW 1, 2; MTFW 2005; SATA 2, 31,
79, 142; WYA; YAW

Blunden, Edmund (Charles)
1896-1974 **CLC 2, 56; PC 66**
See also BRW 6; BRWS 11; CA 17-18; 45-
48; CANR 54; CAP 2; CP 1, 2; DLB 20,
100, 155; MTCW 1; PAB

Bly, Robert (Elwood) 1926- **CLC 1, 2, 5,
10, 15, 38, 128; PC 39**
See also AMWS 4; CA 5-8R; CANR 41,
73, 125; CP 1, 2, 3, 4, 5, 6, 7; DA3; DAM
POET; DLB 5; EWL 3; MAL 5; MTCW
1, 2; MTFW 2005; PFS 6, 17; RGAL 4

Boas, Franz 1858-1942 **TCLC 56**
See also CA 115; 181

Bobette
See Simenon, Georges (Jacques Christian)

Boccaccio, Giovanni 1313-1375 ... **CMLC 13,
57; SSC 10, 87**
See also EW 2; RGSF 2; RGWL 2, 3; TWA;
WLIT 7

Bochco, Steven 1943- **CLC 35**
See also AAYA 11, 71; CA 124; 138

Bode, Sigmund
See O'Doherty, Brian

Bodel, Jean 1167(?)-1210 **CMLC 28**

Bodenheim, Maxwell 1892-1954 **TCLC 44**
See also CA 110; 187; DLB 9, 45; MAL 5;
RGAL 4

Bodenheimer, Maxwell
See Bodenheim, Maxwell

Bodker, Cecil 1927-
See Bodker, Cecil

Bodker, Cecil 1927- **CLC 21**
See also CA 73-76; CANR 13, 44, 111;
CLR 23; MAICYA 1, 2; SATA 14, 133

Boell, Heinrich (Theodor)
1917-1985 **CLC 2, 3, 6, 9, 11, 15, 27,
32, 72; SSC 23; WLC 1**
See Boll, Heinrich (Theodor)
See also CA 21-24R; 116; CANR 24; DA;
DA3; DAB; DAC; DAM MST, NOV;
DLB 69; DLBY 1985; MTCW 1, 2;
MTFW 2005; SSFS 20; TWA

Boerne, Alfred
See Doeblin, Alfred

Boethius c. 480-c. 524 **CMLC 15**
 See also DLB 115; RGWL 2, 3; WLIT 8
Boff, Leonardo (Genezio Darci)
 1938- **CLC 70; HLC 1**
 See also CA 150; DAM MULT; HW 2
Bogan, Louise 1897-1970 **CLC 4, 39, 46, 93; PC 12**
 See also AMWS 3; CA 73-76; 25-28R; CANR 33, 82; CP 1; DAM POET; DLB 45, 169; EWL 3; MAL 5; MAWW; MTCW 1, 2; PFS 21; RGAL 4
Bogarde, Dirk
 See Van Den Bogarde, Derek Jules Gaspard Ulric Niven
 See also DLB 14
Bogosian, Eric 1953- **CLC 45, 141**
 See also CA 138; CAD; CANR 102, 148; CD 5, 6
Bograd, Larry 1953- **CLC 35**
 See also CA 93-96; CANR 57; SAAS 21; SATA 33, 89; WYA
Boiardo, Matteo Maria 1441-1494 **LC 6**
Boileau-Despreaux, Nicolas 1636-1711 . **LC 3**
 See also DLB 268; EW 3; GFL Beginnings to 1789; RGWL 2, 3
Boissard, Maurice
 See Leautaud, Paul
Bojer, Johan 1872-1959 **TCLC 64**
 See also CA 189; EWL 3
Bok, Edward W(illiam)
 1863-1930 **TCLC 101**
 See also CA 217; DLB 91; DLBD 16
Boker, George Henry 1823-1890 . **NCLC 125**
 See also RGAL 4
Boland, Eavan (Aisling) 1944- .. **CLC 40, 67, 113; PC 58**
 See also BRWS 5; CA 143, 207; CAAE 207; CANR 61; CP 1, 6, 7; CWP; DAM POET; DLB 40; FW; MTCW 2; MTFW 2005; PFS 12, 22
Boll, Heinrich (Theodor)
 See Boell, Heinrich (Theodor)
 See also BPFB 1; CDWLB 2; EW 13; EWL 3; RGHL; RGSF 2; RGWL 2, 3
Bolt, Lee
 See Faust, Frederick (Schiller)
Bolt, Robert (Oxton) 1924-1995 **CLC 14; TCLC 175**
 See also CA 17-20R; 147; CANR 35, 67; CBD; DAM DRAM; DFS 2; DLB 13, 233; EWL 3; LAIT 1; MTCW 1
Bombal, Maria Luisa 1910-1980 **HLCS 1; SSC 37**
 See also CA 127; CANR 72; EWL 3; HW 1; LAW; RGSF 2
Bombet, Louis-Alexandre-Cesar
 See Stendhal
Bomkauf
 See Kaufman, Bob (Garnell)
Bonaventura **NCLC 35**
 See also DLB 90
Bonaventure 1217(?)-1274 **CMLC 79**
 See also DLB 115; LMFS 1
Bond, Edward 1934- **CLC 4, 6, 13, 23**
 See also AAYA 50; BRWS 1; CA 25-28R; CANR 38, 67, 106; CBD; CD 5, 6; DAM DRAM; DFS 3, 8; DLB 13, 310; EWL 3; MTCW 1
Bonham, Frank 1914-1989 **CLC 12**
 See also AAYA 1; 70; BYA 1, 3; CA 9-12R; CANR 4, 36; JRDA; MAICYA 1, 2; SAAS 3; SATA 1, 49; SATA-Obit 62; TCWW 1, 2; YAW
Bonnefoy, Yves 1923- . **CLC 9, 15, 58; PC 58**
 See also CA 85-88; CANR 33, 75, 97, 136; CWW 2; DAM MST, POET; DLB 258; EWL 3; GFL 1789 to the Present; MTCW 1, 2; MTFW 2005

Bonner, Marita . **HR 1:2; PC 72; TCLC 179**
 See Occomy, Marita (Odette) Bonner
Bonnin, Gertrude 1876-1938 **NNAL**
 See Zitkala-Sa
 See also CA 150; DAM MULT
Bontemps, Arna(ud Wendell)
 1902-1973 .. **BLC 1; CLC 1, 18; HR 1:2**
 See also BW 1; CA 1-4R; 41-44R; CANR 4, 35; CLR 6; CP 1; CWRI 5; DA3; DAM MULT, NOV, POET; DLB 48, 51; JRDA; MAICYA 1, 2; MAL 5; MTCW 1, 2; SATA 2, 44; SATA-Obit 24; WCH; WP
Boot, William
 See Stoppard, Tom
Booth, Martin 1944-2004 **CLC 13**
 See also CA 93-96; 188; 223; CAAE 188; CAAS 2; CANR 92; CP 1, 2, 3, 4
Booth, Philip 1925- **CLC 23**
 See also CA 5-8R; CANR 5, 88; CP 1, 2, 3, 4, 5, 6, 7; DLBY 1982
Booth, Wayne C. 1921-2005 **CLC 24**
 See also CA 1-4R; 244; CAAS 5; CANR 3, 43, 117; DLB 67
Booth, Wayne Clayson
 See Booth, Wayne C.
Borchert, Wolfgang 1921-1947 **TCLC 5**
 See also CA 104; 188; DLB 69, 124; EWL 3
Borel, Petrus 1809-1859 **NCLC 41**
 See also DLB 119; GFL 1789 to the Present
Borges, Jorge Luis 1899-1986 ... **CLC 1, 2, 3, 4, 6, 8, 9, 10, 13, 19, 44, 48, 83; HLC 1; PC 22, 32; SSC 4, 41; TCLC 109; WLC 1**
 See also AAYA 26; BPFB 1; CA 21-24R; CANR 19, 33, 75, 105, 133; CDWLB 3; DA; DA3; DAB; DAC; DAM MST, MULT; DLB 113, 283; DLBY 1986; DNFS 1, 2; EWL 3; HW 1, 2; LAW; LMFS 2; MSW; MTCW 1, 2; MTFW 2005; RGHL; RGSF 2; RGWL 2, 3; SFW 4; SSFS 17; TWA; WLIT 1
Borowski, Tadeusz 1922-1951 **SSC 48; TCLC 9**
 See also CA 106; 154; CDWLB 4; DLB 215; EWL 3; RGHL; RGSF 2; RGWL 3; SSFS 13
Borrow, George (Henry)
 1803-1881 **NCLC 9**
 See also DLB 21, 55, 166
Bosch (Gavino), Juan 1909-2001 **HLCS 1**
 See also CA 151; 204; DAM MST, MULT; DLB 145; HW 1, 2
Bosman, Herman Charles
 1905-1951 **TCLC 49**
 See Malan, Herman
 See also CA 160; DLB 225; RGSF 2
Bosschere, Jean de 1878(?)-1953 ... **TCLC 19**
 See also CA 115; 186
Boswell, James 1740-1795 ... **LC 4, 50; WLC 1**
 See also BRW 3; CDBLB 1660-1789; DA; DAB; DAC; DAM MST; DLB 104, 142; TEA; WLIT 3
Bottomley, Gordon 1874-1948 **TCLC 107**
 See also CA 120; 192; DLB 10
Bottoms, David 1949- **CLC 53**
 See also CA 105; CANR 22; CSW; DLB 120; DLBY 1983
Boucicault, Dion 1820-1890 **NCLC 41**
Boucolon, Maryse
 See Conde, Maryse
Bourdieu, Pierre 1930-2002 **CLC 198**
 See also CA 130; 204
Bourget, Paul (Charles Joseph)
 1852-1935 **TCLC 12**
 See also CA 107; 196; DLB 123; GFL 1789 to the Present

Bourjaily, Vance (Nye) 1922- **CLC 8, 62**
 See also CA 1-4R; CAAS 1; CANR 2, 72; CN 1, 2, 3, 4, 5, 6, 7; DLB 2, 143; MAL 5
Bourne, Randolph S(illiman)
 1886-1918 **TCLC 16**
 See also AMW; CA 117; 155; DLB 63; MAL 5
Bova, Ben(jamin William) 1932- **CLC 45**
 See also AAYA 16; CA 5-8R; CAAS 18; CANR 11, 56, 94, 111; CLR 3, 96; DLBY 1981; INT CANR-11; MAICYA 1, 2; MTCW 1; SATA 6, 68, 133; SFW 4
Bowen, Elizabeth (Dorothea Cole)
 1899-1973 . **CLC 1, 3, 6, 11, 15, 22, 118; SSC 3, 28, 66; TCLC 148**
 See also BRWS 2; CA 17-18; 41-44R; CANR 35, 105; CAP 2; CDBLB 1945-1960; CN 1; DA3; DAM NOV; DLB 15, 162; EWL 3; EXPS; FW; HGG; MTCW 1, 2; MTFW 2005; NFS 13; RGSF 2; SSFS 5; SUFW 1; TEA; WLIT 4
Bowering, George 1935- **CLC 15, 47**
 See also CA 21-24R; CAAS 16; CANR 10; CN 7; CP 1, 2, 3, 4, 5, 6, 7; DLB 53
Bowering, Marilyn R(uthe) 1949- **CLC 32**
 See also CA 101; CANR 49; CP 4, 5, 6, 7; CWP
Bowers, Edgar 1924-2000 **CLC 9**
 See also CA 5-8R; 188; CANR 24; CP 1, 2, 3, 4, 5, 6, 7; CSW; DLB 5
Bowers, Mrs. J. Milton 1842-1914
 See Bierce, Ambrose (Gwinett)
Bowie, David **CLC 17**
 See Jones, David Robert
Bowles, Jane (Sydney) 1917-1973 **CLC 3, 68**
 See Bowles, Jane Auer
 See also CA 19-20; 41-44R; CAP 2; CN 1; MAL 5
Bowles, Jane Auer
 See Bowles, Jane (Sydney)
 See also EWL 3
Bowles, Paul (Frederick) 1910-1999 . **CLC 1, 2, 19, 53; SSC 3**
 See also AMWS 4; CA 1-4R; 186; CAAS 1; CANR 1, 19, 50, 75; CN 1, 2, 3, 4, 5, 6; DA3; DLB 5, 6, 218; EWL 3; MAL 5; MTCW 1, 2; MTFW 2005; RGAL 4; SSFS 17
Bowles, William Lisle 1762-1850 . **NCLC 103**
 See also DLB 93
Box, Edgar
 See Vidal, Gore
 See also GLL 1
Boyd, James 1888-1944 **TCLC 115**
 See also CA 186; DLB 9; DLBD 16; RGAL 4; RHW
Boyd, Nancy
 See Millay, Edna St. Vincent
 See also GLL 1
Boyd, Thomas (Alexander)
 1898-1935 **TCLC 111**
 See also CA 111; 183; DLB 9; DLBD 16, 316
Boyd, William (Andrew Murray)
 1952- **CLC 28, 53, 70**
 See also CA 114; 120; CANR 51, 71, 131; CN 4, 5, 6, 7; DLB 231
Boyesen, Hjalmar Hjorth
 1848-1895 **NCLC 135**
 See also DLB 12, 71; DLBD 13; RGAL 4
Boyle, Kay 1902-1992 **CLC 1, 5, 19, 58, 121; SSC 5**
 See also CA 13-16R; 140; CAAS 1; CANR 29, 61, 110; CN 1, 2, 3, 4, 5; CP 1, 2, 3, 4, 5; DLB 4, 9, 48, 86; DLBY 1993; EWL 3; MAL 5; MTCW 1, 2; MTFW 2005; RGAL 4; RGSF 2; SSFS 10, 13, 14

Boyle, Mark
　　See Kienzle, William X(avier)
Boyle, Patrick 1905-1982 **CLC 19**
　　See also CA 127
Boyle, T. C.
　　See Boyle, T(homas) Coraghessan
　　See also AMWS 8
Boyle, T(homas) Coraghessan
　　1948- **CLC 36, 55, 90; SSC 16**
　　See Boyle, T. C.
　　See also AAYA 47; BEST 90:4; BPFB 1;
　　CA 120; CANR 44, 76, 89, 132; CN 6, 7;
　　CPW; DA3; DAM POP; DLB 218, 278;
　　DLBY 1986; EWL 3; MAL 5; MTCW 2;
　　MTFW 2005; SSFS 13, 19
Boz
　　See Dickens, Charles (John Huffam)
Brackenridge, Hugh Henry
　　1748-1816 **NCLC 7**
　　See also DLB 11, 37; RGAL 4
Bradbury, Edward P.
　　See Moorcock, Michael
　　See also MTCW 2
Bradbury, Malcolm (Stanley)
　　1932-2000 **CLC 32, 61**
　　See also CA 1-4R; CANR 1, 33, 91, 98,
　　137; CN 1, 2, 3, 4, 5, 6, 7; CP 1; DA3;
　　DAM NOV; DLB 14, 207; EWL 3;
　　MTCW 1, 2; MTFW 2005
Bradbury, Ray (Douglas) 1920- **CLC 1, 3,**
　　10, 15, 42, 98; SSC 29, 53; WLC 1
　　See also AAYA 15; AITN 1, 2; AMWS 4;
　　BPFB 1; BYA 4, 5, 11; CA 1-4R; CANR
　　2, 30, 75, 125; CDALB 1968-1988; CN
　　1, 2, 3, 4, 5, 6, 7; CPW; DA; DA3; DAB;
　　DAC; DAM MST, NOV, POP; DLB 2, 8;
　　EXPN; EXPS; HGG; LAIT 3, 5; LATS
　　1:2; LMFS 2; MAL 5; MTCW 1, 2;
　　MTFW 2005; NFS 1, 22; RGAL 4; RGSF
　　2; SATA 11, 64, 123; SCFW 1, 2; SFW 4;
　　SSFS 1, 20; SUFW 1, 2; TUS; YAW
Braddon, Mary Elizabeth
　　1837-1915 **TCLC 111**
　　See also BRWS 8; CA 108; 179; CMW 4;
　　DLB 18, 70, 156; HGG
Bradfield, Scott (Michael) 1955- **SSC 65**
　　See also CA 147; CANR 90; HGG; SUFW
　　2
Bradford, Gamaliel 1863-1932 **TCLC 36**
　　See also CA 160; DLB 17
Bradford, William 1590-1657 **LC 64**
　　See also DLB 24, 30; RGAL 4
Bradley, David (Henry), Jr. 1950- **BLC 1;**
　　CLC 23, 118
　　See also BW 1, 3; CA 104; CANR 26, 81;
　　CN 4, 5, 6, 7; DAM MULT; DLB 33
Bradley, John Ed(mund, Jr.) 1958- . **CLC 55**
　　See also CA 139; CANR 99; CN 6, 7; CSW
Bradley, Marion Zimmer
　　1930-1999 **CLC 30**
　　See Chapman, Lee; Dexter, John; Gardner,
　　Miriam; Ives, Morgan; Rivers, Elfrida
　　See also AAYA 40; BPFB 1; CA 57-60; 185;
　　CAAS 10; CANR 7, 31, 51, 75, 107;
　　CPW; DA3; DAM POP; DLB 8; FANT;
　　FW; MTCW 1, 2; MTFW 2005; SATA 90,
　　139; SATA-Obit 116; SFW 4; SUFW 2;
　　YAW
Bradshaw, John 1933- **CLC 70**
　　See also CA 138; CANR 61
Bradstreet, Anne 1612(?)-1672 **LC 4, 30;**
　　PC 10
　　See also AMWS 1; CDALB 1640-1865;
　　DA; DA3; DAC; DAM MST, POET; DLB
　　24; EXPP; FW; PFS 6; RGAL 4; TUS;
　　WP
Brady, Joan 1939- **CLC 86**
　　See also CA 141

Bragg, Melvyn 1939- **CLC 10**
　　See also BEST 89:3; CA 57-60; CANR 10,
　　48, 89; CN 1, 2, 3, 4, 5, 6, 7; DLB 14,
　　271; RHW
Brahe, Tycho 1546-1601 **LC 45**
　　See also DLB 300
Braine, John (Gerard) 1922-1986 . **CLC 1, 3,**
　　41
　　See also CA 1-4R; 120; CANR 1, 33; CD-
　　BLB 1945-1960; CN 1, 2, 3, 4; DLB 15;
　　DLBY 1986; EWL 3; MTCW 1
Braithwaite, William Stanley (Beaumont)
　　1878-1962 **BLC 1; HR 1:2; PC 52**
　　See also BW 1; CA 125; DAM MULT; DLB
　　50, 54; MAL 5
Bramah, Ernest 1868-1942 **TCLC 72**
　　See also CA 156; CMW 4; DLB 70; FANT
Brammer, Billy Lee
　　See Brammer, William
Brammer, William 1929-1978 **CLC 31**
　　See also CA 235; 77-80
Brancati, Vitaliano 1907-1954 **TCLC 12**
　　See also CA 109; DLB 264; EWL 3
Brancato, Robin F(idler) 1936- **CLC 35**
　　See also AAYA 9, 68; BYA 6; CA 69-72;
　　CANR 11, 45; CLR 32; JRDA; MAICYA
　　2; MAICYAS 1; SAAS 9; SATA 97;
　　WYA; YAW
Brand, Dionne 1953- **CLC 192**
　　See also BW 2; CA 143; CANR 143; CWP
Brand, Max
　　See Faust, Frederick (Schiller)
　　See also BPFB 1; TCWW 1, 2
Brand, Millen 1906-1980 **CLC 7**
　　See also CA 21-24R; 97-100; CANR 72
Branden, Barbara **CLC 44**
　　See also CA 148
Brandes, Georg (Morris Cohen)
　　1842-1927 **TCLC 10**
　　See also CA 105; 189; DLB 300
Brandys, Kazimierz 1916-2000 **CLC 62**
　　See also CA 239; EWL 3
Branley, Franklyn M(ansfield)
　　1915-2002 **CLC 21**
　　See also CA 33-36R; 207; CANR 14, 39;
　　CLR 13; MAICYA 1, 2; SAAS 16; SATA
　　4, 68, 136
Brant, Beth (E.) 1941- **NNAL**
　　See also CA 144; FW
Brant, Sebastian 1457-1521 **LC 112**
　　See also DLB 179; RGWL 2, 3
Brathwaite, Edward Kamau
　　1930- **BLCS; CLC 11; PC 56**
　　See also BW 2, 3; CA 25-28R; CANR 11,
　　26, 47, 107; CDWLB 3; CP 1, 2, 3, 4, 5,
　　6, 7; DAM POET; DLB 125; EWL 3
Brathwaite, Kamau
　　See Brathwaite, Edward Kamau
Brautigan, Richard (Gary)
　　1935-1984 **CLC 1, 3, 5, 9, 12, 34, 42;**
　　TCLC 133
　　See also BPFB 1; CA 53-56; 113; CANR
　　34; CN 1, 2, 3; CP 1, 2, 3, 4; DA3; DAM
　　NOV; DLB 2, 5, 206; DLBY 1980, 1984;
　　FANT; MAL 5; MTCW 1; RGAL 4;
　　SATA 56
Brave Bird, Mary **NNAL**
　　See Crow Dog, Mary (Ellen)
Braverman, Kate 1950- **CLC 67**
　　See also CA 89-92; CANR 141
Brecht, (Eugen) Bertolt (Friedrich)
　　1898-1956 **DC 3; TCLC 1, 6, 13, 35,**
　　169; WLC 1
　　See also CA 104; 133; CANR 62; CDWLB
　　2; DA; DA3; DAB; DAC; DAM DRAM,
　　MST; DFS 4, 5, 9; DLB 56, 124; EW 11;
　　EWL 3; IDTP; MTCW 1, 2; MTFW 2005;
　　RGHL; RGWL 2, 3; TWA

Brecht, Eugen Berthold Friedrich
　　See Brecht, (Eugen) Bertolt (Friedrich)
Bremer, Fredrika 1801-1865 **NCLC 11**
　　See also DLB 254
Brennan, Christopher John
　　1870-1932 **TCLC 17**
　　See also CA 117; 188; DLB 230; EWL 3
Brennan, Maeve 1917-1993 ... **CLC 5; TCLC**
　　124
　　See also CA 81-84; CANR 72, 100
Brenner, Jozef 1887-1919
　　See Csath, Geza
　　See also CA 240
Brent, Linda
　　See Jacobs, Harriet A(nn)
Brentano, Clemens (Maria)
　　1778-1842 **NCLC 1**
　　See also DLB 90; RGWL 2, 3
Brent of Bin Bin
　　See Franklin, (Stella Maria Sarah) Miles
　　(Lampe)
Brenton, Howard 1942- **CLC 31**
　　See also CA 69-72; CANR 33, 67; CBD;
　　CD 5, 6; DLB 13; MTCW 1
Breslin, James 1930-
　　See Breslin, Jimmy
　　See also CA 73-76; CANR 31, 75, 139;
　　DAM NOV; MTCW 1, 2; MTFW 2005
Breslin, Jimmy **CLC 4, 43**
　　See Breslin, James
　　See also AITN 1; DLB 185; MTCW 2
Bresson, Robert 1901(?)-1999 **CLC 16**
　　See also CA 110; 187; CANR 49
Breton, Andre 1896-1966 .. **CLC 2, 9, 15, 54;**
　　PC 15
　　See also CA 19-20; 25-28R; CANR 40, 60;
　　CAP 2; DLB 65, 258; EW 11; EWL 3;
　　GFL 1789 to the Present; LMFS 2;
　　MTCW 1, 2; MTFW 2005; RGWL 2, 3;
　　TWA; WP
Breytenbach, Breyten 1939(?)- .. **CLC 23, 37,**
　　126
　　See also CA 113; 129; CANR 61, 122;
　　CWW 2; DAM POET; DLB 225; EWL 3
Bridgers, Sue Ellen 1942- **CLC 26**
　　See also AAYA 8, 49; BYA 7, 8; CA 65-68;
　　CANR 11, 36; CLR 18; DLB 52; JRDA;
　　MAICYA 1, 2; SAAS 1; SATA 22, 90;
　　SATA-Essay 109; WYA; YAW
Bridges, Robert (Seymour)
　　1844-1930 **PC 28; TCLC 1**
　　See also BRW 6; CA 104; 152; CDBLB
　　1890-1914; DAM POET; DLB 19, 98
Bridie, James **TCLC 3**
　　See Mavor, Osborne Henry
　　See also DLB 10; EWL 3
Brin, David 1950- **CLC 34**
　　See also AAYA 21; CA 102; CANR 24, 70,
　　125, 127; INT CANR-24; SATA 65;
　　SCFW 2; SFW 4
Brink, Andre (Philippus) 1935- . **CLC 18, 36,**
　　106
　　See also AFW; BRWS 6; CA 104; CANR
　　39, 62, 109, 133; CN 4, 5, 6, 7; DLB 225;
　　EWL 3; INT CA-103; LATS 1:2; MTCW
　　1, 2; MTFW 2005; WLIT 2
Brinsmead, H. F(ay)
　　See Brinsmead, H(esba) F(ay)
Brinsmead, H. F.
　　See Brinsmead, H(esba) F(ay)
Brinsmead, H(esba) F(ay) 1922- **CLC 21**
　　See also CA 21-24R; CANR 10; CLR 47;
　　CWRI 5; MAICYA 1, 2; SAAS 5; SATA
　　18, 78
Brittain, Vera (Mary) 1893(?)-1970 . **CLC 23**
　　See also BRWS 10; CA 13-16; 25-28R;
　　CANR 58; CAP 1; DLB 191; FW; MTCW
　　1, 2

Broch, Hermann 1886-1951 **TCLC 20**
See also CA 117; 211; CDWLB 2; DLB 85, 124; EW 10; EWL 3; RGWL 2, 3

Brock, Rose
See Hansen, Joseph
See also GLL 1

Brod, Max 1884-1968 **TCLC 115**
See also CA 5-8R; 25-28R; CANR 7; DLB 81; EWL 3

Brodkey, Harold (Roy) 1930-1996 .. **CLC 56; TCLC 123**
See also CA 111; 151; CANR 71; CN 4, 5, 6; DLB 130

Brodsky, Iosif Alexandrovich 1940-1996
See Brodsky, Joseph
See also AAYA 71; AITN 1; CA 41-44R; 151; CANR 37, 106; DA3; DAM POET; MTCW 1, 2; MTFW 2005; RGWL 2, 3

Brodsky, Joseph . **CLC 4, 6, 13, 36, 100; PC 9**
See Brodsky, Iosif Alexandrovich
See also AMWS 8; CWW 2; DLB 285; EWL 3; MTCW 1

Brodsky, Michael 1948- **CLC 19**
See also CA 102; CANR 18, 41, 58, 147; DLB 244

Brodsky, Michael Mark
See Brodsky, Michael

Brodzki, Bella ed. **CLC 65**

Brome, Richard 1590(?)-1652 **LC 61**
See also BRWS 10; DLB 58

Bromell, Henry 1947- **CLC 5**
See also CA 53-56; CANR 9, 115, 116

Bromfield, Louis (Brucker)
1896-1956 **TCLC 11**
See also CA 107; 155; DLB 4, 9, 86; RGAL 4; RHW

Broner, E(sther) M(asserman)
1930- ... **CLC 19**
See also CA 17-20R; CANR 8, 25, 72; CN 4, 5, 6; DLB 28

Bronk, William (M.) 1918-1999 **CLC 10**
See also CA 89-92; 177; CANR 23; CP 3, 4, 5, 6, 7; DLB 165

Bronstein, Lev Davidovich
See Trotsky, Leon

Bronte, Anne
See Bronte, Anne

Bronte, Anne 1820-1849 **NCLC 4, 71, 102**
See also BRW 5; BRWR 1; DA3; DLB 21, 199; TEA

Bronte, (Patrick) Branwell
1817-1848 **NCLC 109**

Bronte, Charlotte
See Bronte, Charlotte

Bronte, Charlotte 1816-1855 **NCLC 3, 8, 33, 58, 105, 155; WLC 1**
See also AAYA 17; BRW 5; BRWC 2; BRWR 1; BYA 2; CDBLB 1832-1890; DA; DA3; DAB; DAC; DAM MST, NOV; DLB 21, 159, 199; EXPN; FL 1:2; GL 2; LAIT 2; NFS 4; TEA; WLIT 4

Bronte, Emily
See Bronte, Emily (Jane)

Bronte, Emily (Jane) 1818-1848 ... **NCLC 16, 35, 165; PC 8; WLC 1**
See also AAYA 17; BPFB 1; BRW 5; BRWC 1; BRWR 1; BYA 3; CDBLB 1832-1890; DA; DA3; DAB; DAC; DAM MST, NOV, POET; DLB 21, 32, 199; EXPN; FL 1:2; GL 2; LAIT 1; TEA; WLIT 3

Brontes
See Bronte, Anne; Bronte, Charlotte; Bronte, Emily (Jane)

Brooke, Frances 1724-1789 **LC 6, 48**
See also DLB 39, 99

Brooke, Henry 1703(?)-1783 **LC 1**
See also DLB 39

Brooke, Rupert (Chawner)
1887-1915 .. **PC 24; TCLC 2, 7; WLC 1**
See also BRWS 3; CA 104; 132; CANR 61; CDBLB 1914-1945; DA; DAB; DAC; DAM MST, POET; DLB 19, 216; EXPP; GLL 2; MTCW 1, 2; MTFW 2005; PFS 7; TEA

Brooke-Haven, P.
See Wodehouse, P(elham) G(renville)

Brooke-Rose, Christine 1926(?)- **CLC 40, 184**
See also BRWS 4; CA 13-16R; CANR 58, 118; CN 1, 2, 3, 4, 5, 6, 7; DLB 14, 231; EWL 3; SFW 4

Brookner, Anita 1928- .. **CLC 32, 34, 51, 136**
See also BRWS 4; CA 114; 120; CANR 37, 56, 87, 130; CN 4, 5, 6, 7; CPW; DA3; DAB; DAM POP; DLB 194, 326; DLBY 1987; EWL 3; MTCW 1, 2; MTFW 2005; NFS 23; TEA

Brooks, Cleanth 1906-1994 . **CLC 24, 86, 110**
See also AMWS 14; CA 17-20R; 145; CANR 33, 35; CSW; DLB 63; DLBY 1994; EWL 3; INT CANR-35; MAL 5; MTCW 1, 2; MTFW 2005

Brooks, George
See Baum, L(yman) Frank

Brooks, Gwendolyn (Elizabeth)
1917-2000 ... **BLC 1; CLC 1, 2, 4, 5, 15, 49, 125; PC 7; WLC 1**
See also AAYA 20; AFAW 1, 2; AITN 1; AMWS 3; BW 2, 3; CA 1-4R; 190; CANR 1, 27, 52, 75, 132; CDALB 1941-1968; CLR 27; CP 1, 2, 3, 4, 5, 6, 7; CWP; DA; DA3; DAC; DAM MST, MULT, POET; DLB 5, 76, 165; EWL 3; EXPP; FL 1:5; MAL 5; MAWW; MTCW 1, 2; MTFW 2005; PFS 1, 2, 4, 6; RGAL 4; SATA 6; SATA-Obit 123; TUS; WP

Brooks, Mel 1926-
See Kaminsky, Melvin
See also CA 65-68; CANR 16; DFS 21

Brooks, Peter (Preston) 1938- **CLC 34**
See also CA 45-48; CANR 1, 107

Brooks, Van Wyck 1886-1963 **CLC 29**
See also AMW; CA 1-4R; CANR 6; DLB 45, 63, 103; MAL 5; TUS

Brophy, Brigid (Antonia)
1929-1995 **CLC 6, 11, 29, 105**
See also CA 5-8R; 149; CAAS 4; CANR 25, 53; CBD; CN 1, 2, 3, 4, 5, 6; CWD; DA3; DLB 14, 271; EWL 3; MTCW 1, 2

Brosman, Catharine Savage 1934- **CLC 9**
See also CA 61-64; CANR 21, 46, 149

Brossard, Nicole 1943- **CLC 115, 169**
See also CA 122; CAAS 16; CANR 140; CCA 1; CWP; CWW 2; DLB 53; EWL 3; FW; GLL 2; RGWL 3

Brother Antoninus
See Everson, William (Oliver)

Brothers Grimm
See Grimm, Jacob Ludwig Karl; Grimm, Wilhelm Karl

The Brothers Quay
See Quay, Stephen; Quay, Timothy

Broughton, T(homas) Alan 1936- **CLC 19**
See also CA 45-48; CANR 2, 23, 48, 111

Broumas, Olga 1949- **CLC 10, 73**
See also CA 85-88; CANR 20, 69, 110; CP 5, 6, 7; CWP; GLL 2

Broun, Heywood 1888-1939 **TCLC 104**
See also DLB 29, 171

Brown, Alan 1950- **CLC 99**
See also CA 156

Brown, Charles Brockden
1771-1810 **NCLC 22, 74, 122**
See also AMWS 1; CDALB 1640-1865; DLB 37, 59, 73; FW; GL 2; HGG; LMFS 1; RGAL 4; TUS

Brown, Christy 1932-1981 **CLC 63**
See also BYA 13; CA 105; 104; CANR 72; DLB 14

Brown, Claude 1937-2002 ... **BLC 1; CLC 30**
See also AAYA 7; BW 1, 3; CA 73-76; 205; CANR 81; DAM MULT

Brown, Dan 1964- **CLC 209**
See also AAYA 55; CA 217; MTFW 2005

Brown, Dee 1908-2002 **CLC 18, 47**
See also AAYA 30; CA 13-16R; 212; CAAS 6; CANR 11, 45, 60, 150; CPW; CSW; DA3; DAM POP; DLBY 1980; LAIT 2; MTCW 1, 2; MTFW 2005; NCFS 5; SATA 5, 110; SATA-Obit 141; TCWW 1, 2

Brown, Dee Alexander
See Brown, Dee

Brown, George
See Wertmueller, Lina

Brown, George Douglas
1869-1902 **TCLC 28**
See Douglas, George
See also CA 162

Brown, George Mackay 1921-1996 ... **CLC 5, 48, 100**
See also BRWS 6; CA 21-24R; 151; CAAS 6; CANR 12, 37, 67; CN 1, 2, 3, 4, 5, 6; CP 1, 2, 3, 4, 5, 6; DLB 14, 27, 139, 271; MTCW 1; RGSF 2; SATA 35

Brown, (William) Larry 1951-2004 . **CLC 73**
See also CA 130; 134; 233; CANR 117, 145; CSW; DLB 234; INT CA-134

Brown, Moses
See Barrett, William (Christopher)

Brown, Rita Mae 1944- **CLC 18, 43, 79**
See also BPFB 1; CA 45-48; CANR 2, 11, 35, 62, 95, 138; CN 5, 6, 7; CPW; CSW; DA3; DAM NOV, POP; FW; INT CANR-11; MAL 5; MTCW 1, 2; MTFW 2005; NFS 9; RGAL 4; TUS

Brown, Roderick (Langmere) Haig-
See Haig-Brown, Roderick (Langmere)

Brown, Rosellen 1939- **CLC 32, 170**
See also CA 77-80; CAAS 10; CANR 14, 44, 98; CN 6, 7

Brown, Sterling Allen 1901-1989 **BLC 1; CLC 1, 23, 59; HR 1:2; PC 55**
See also AFAW 1, 2; BW 1, 3; CA 85-88; 127; CANR 26; CP 3, 4; DA3; DAM MULT, POET; DLB 48, 51, 63; MAL 5; MTCW 1, 2; MTFW 2005; RGAL 4; WP

Brown, Will
See Ainsworth, William Harrison

Brown, William Hill 1765-1793 **LC 93**
See also DLB 37

Brown, William Wells 1815-1884 **BLC 1; DC 1; NCLC 2, 89**
See also DAM MULT; DLB 3, 50, 183, 248; RGAL 4

Browne, (Clyde) Jackson 1948(?)- ... **CLC 21**
See also CA 120

Browne, Sir Thomas 1605-1682 **LC 111**
See also BRW 2; DLB 151

Browning, Robert 1812-1889 . **NCLC 19, 79; PC 2, 61; WLCS**
See also BRW 4; BRWC 2; BRWR 2; CDBLB 1832-1890; CLR 97; DA; DA3; DAB; DAC; DAM MST, POET; DLB 32, 163; EXPP; LATS 1:1; PAB; PFS 1, 15; RGEL 2; TEA; WLIT 4; WP; YABC 1

Browning, Tod 1882-1962 **CLC 16**
See also CA 141; 117

Brownmiller, Susan 1935- **CLC 159**
See also CA 103; CANR 35, 75, 137; DAM NOV; FW; MTCW 1, 2; MTFW 2005

Brownson, Orestes Augustus
1803-1876 **NCLC 50**
See also DLB 1, 59, 73, 243

Bruccoli, Matthew J(oseph) 1931- ... **CLC 34**
See also CA 9-12R; CANR 7, 87; DLB 103

Bruce, Lenny **CLC 21**
See Schneider, Leonard Alfred

Bruchac, Joseph III 1942- **NNAL**
See also AAYA 19; CA 33-36R; CANR 13, 47, 75, 94, 137; CLR 46; CWRI 5; DAM MULT; JRDA; MAICYA 2; MAICYAS 1; MTCW 2; MTFW 2005; SATA 42, 89, 131

Bruin, John
See Brutus, Dennis

Brulard, Henri
See Stendhal

Brulls, Christian
See Simenon, Georges (Jacques Christian)

Brunetto Latini c. 1220-1294 **CMLC 73**

Brunner, John (Kilian Houston)
1934-1995 **CLC 8, 10**
See also CA 1-4R; 149; CAAS 8; CANR 2, 37; CPW; DAM POP; DLB 261; MTCW 1, 2; SCFW 1, 2; SFW 4

Bruno, Giordano 1548-1600 **LC 27**
See also RGWL 2, 3

Brutus, Dennis 1924- ... **BLC 1; CLC 43; PC 24**
See also AFW; BW 2, 3; CA 49-52; CAAS 14; CANR 2, 27, 42, 81; CDWLB 3; CP 1, 2, 3, 4, 5, 6, 7; DAM MULT, POET; DLB 117, 225; EWL 3

Bryan, C(ourtlandt) D(ixon) B(arnes)
1936- **CLC 29**
See also CA 73-76; CANR 13, 68; DLB 185; INT CANR-13

Bryan, Michael
See Moore, Brian
See also CCA 1

Bryan, William Jennings
1860-1925 **TCLC 99**
See also DLB 303

Bryant, William Cullen 1794-1878 . **NCLC 6, 46; PC 20**
See also AMWS 1; CDALB 1640-1865; DA; DAB; DAC; DAM MST, POET; DLB 3, 43, 59, 189, 250; EXPP; PAB; RGAL 4; TUS

Bryusov, Valery Yakovlevich
1873-1924 **TCLC 10**
See also CA 107; 155; EWL 3; SFW 4

Buchan, John 1875-1940 **TCLC 41**
See also CA 108; 145; CMW 4; DAB; DAM POP; DLB 34, 70, 156; HGG; MSW; MTCW 2; RGEL 2; RHW; YABC 2

Buchanan, George 1506-1582 **LC 4**
See also DLB 132

Buchanan, Robert 1841-1901 **TCLC 107**
See also CA 179; DLB 18, 35

Buchheim, Lothar-Guenther 1918- **CLC 6**
See also CA 85-88

Buchner, (Karl) Georg
1813-1837 **NCLC 26, 146**
See also CDWLB 2; DLB 133; EW 6; RGSF 2; RGWL 2, 3; TWA

Buchwald, Art(hur) 1925- **CLC 33**
See also AITN 1; CA 5-8R; CANR 21, 67, 107; MTCW 1, 2; SATA 10

Buck, Pearl S(ydenstricker)
1892-1973 **CLC 7, 11, 18, 127**
See also AAYA 42; AITN 1; AMWS 2; BPFB 1; CA 1-4R; 41-44R; CANR 1, 34; CDALBS; CN 1; DA; DA3; DAB; DAC; DAM MST, NOV; DLB 9, 102; EWL 3; LAIT 3; MAL 5; MTCW 1, 2; MTFW 2005; RGAL 4; RHW; SATA 1, 25; TUS

Buckler, Ernest 1908-1984 **CLC 13**
See also CA 11-12; 114; CAP 1; CCA 1; CN 1, 2, 3; DAC; DAM MST; DLB 68; SATA 47

Buckley, Christopher 1952- **CLC 165**
See also CA 139; CANR 119

Buckley, Christopher Taylor
See Buckley, Christopher

Buckley, Vincent (Thomas)
1925-1988 **CLC 57**
See also CA 101; CP 1, 2, 3, 4; DLB 289

Buckley, William F(rank), Jr. 1925- . **CLC 7, 18, 37**
See also AITN 1; BPFB 1; CA 1-4R; CANR 1, 24, 53, 93, 133; CMW 4; CPW; DA3; DAM POP; DLB 137; DLBY 1980; INT CANR-24; MTCW 1, 2; MTFW 2005; TUS

Buechner, (Carl) Frederick 1926- . **CLC 2, 4, 6, 9**
See also AMWS 12; BPFB 1; CA 13-16R; CANR 11, 39, 64, 114, 138; CN 1, 2, 3, 4, 5, 6, 7; DAM NOV; DLBY 1980; INT CANR-11; MAL 5; MTCW 1, 2; MTFW 2005; TCLE 1:1

Buell, John (Edward) 1927- **CLC 10**
See also CA 1-4R; CANR 71; DLB 53

Buero Vallejo, Antonio 1916-2000 ... **CLC 15, 46, 139, 226; DC 18**
See also CA 106; 189; CANR 24, 49, 75; CWW 2; DFS 11; EWL 3; HW 1; MTCW 1, 2

Bufalino, Gesualdo 1920-1996 **CLC 74**
See also CA 209; CWW 2; DLB 196

Bugayev, Boris Nikolayevich
1880-1934 **PC 11; TCLC 7**
See Bely, Andrey; Belyi, Andrei
See also CA 104; 165; MTCW 2; MTFW 2005

Bukowski, Charles 1920-1994 ... **CLC 2, 5, 9, 41, 82, 108; PC 18; SSC 45**
See also CA 17-20R; 144; CANR 40, 62, 105; CN 4, 5; CP 1, 2, 3, 4, 5; CPW; DA3; DAM NOV, POET; DLB 5, 130, 169; EWL 3; MAL 5; MTCW 1, 2; MTFW 2005

Bulgakov, Mikhail 1891-1940 **SSC 18; TCLC 2, 16, 159**
See also BPFB 1; CA 105; 152; DAM DRAM, NOV; DLB 272; EWL 3; MTCW 2; MTFW 2005; NFS 8; RGSF 2; RGWL 2, 3; SFW 4; TWA

Bulgakov, Mikhail Afanasevich
See Bulgakov, Mikhail

Bulgya, Alexander Alexandrovich
1901-1956 **TCLC 53**
See Fadeev, Aleksandr Aleksandrovich; Fadeev, Alexandr Alexandrovich; Fadeyev, Alexander
See also CA 117; 181

Bullins, Ed 1935- ... **BLC 1; CLC 1, 5, 7; DC 6**
See also BW 2, 3; CA 49-52; CAAS 16; CAD; CANR 24, 46, 73, 134; CD 5, 6; DAM DRAM, MULT; DLB 7, 38, 249; EWL 3; MAL 5; MTCW 1, 2; MTFW 2005; RGAL 4

Bulosan, Carlos 1911-1956 **AAL**
See also CA 216; DLB 312; RGAL 4

Bulwer-Lytton, Edward (George Earle Lytton) 1803-1873 **NCLC 1, 45**
See also DLB 21; RGEL 2; SFW 4; SUFW 1; TEA

Bunin, Ivan Alexeyevich 1870-1953 ... **SSC 5; TCLC 6**
See also CA 104; DLB 317; EWL 3; RGSF 2; RGWL 2, 3; TWA

Bunting, Basil 1900-1985 **CLC 10, 39, 47**
See also BRWS 7; CA 53-56; 115; CANR 7; CP 1, 2, 3, 4; DAM POET; DLB 20; EWL 3; RGEL 2

Bunuel, Luis 1900-1983 ... **CLC 16, 80; HLC 1**
See also CA 101; 110; CANR 32, 77; DAM MULT; HW 1

Bunyan, John 1628-1688 .. **LC 4, 69; WLC 1**
See also BRW 2; BYA 5; CDBLB 1660-1789; DA; DAB; DAC; DAM MST; DLB 39; RGEL 2; TEA; WCH; WLIT 3

Buravsky, Alexandr **CLC 59**

Burckhardt, Jacob (Christoph)
1818-1897 **NCLC 49**
See also EW 6

Burford, Eleanor
See Hibbert, Eleanor Alice Burford

Burgess, Anthony . **CLC 1, 2, 4, 5, 8, 10, 13, 15, 22, 40, 62, 81, 94**
See Wilson, John (Anthony) Burgess
See also AAYA 25; AITN 1; BRWS 1; CDBLB 1960 to Present; CN 1, 2, 3, 4, 5; DAB; DLB 14, 194, 261; DLBY 1998; EWL 3; RGEL 2; RHW; SFW 4; YAW

Burke, Edmund 1729(?)-1797 **LC 7, 36; WLC 1**
See also BRW 3; DA; DA3; DAB; DAC; DAM MST; DLB 104, 252; RGEL 2; TEA

Burke, Kenneth (Duva) 1897-1993 ... **CLC 2, 24**
See also AMW; CA 5-8R; 143; CANR 39, 74, 136; CN 1, 2; CP 1, 2, 3, 4, 5; DLB 45, 63; EWL 3; MAL 5; MTCW 1, 2; MTFW 2005; RGAL 4

Burke, Leda
See Garnett, David

Burke, Ralph
See Silverberg, Robert

Burke, Thomas 1886-1945 **TCLC 63**
See also CA 113; 155; CMW 4; DLB 197

Burney, Fanny 1752-1840 **NCLC 12, 54, 107**
See also BRWS 3; DLB 39; FL 1:2; NFS 16; RGEL 2; TEA

Burney, Frances
See Burney, Fanny

Burns, Robert 1759-1796 ... **LC 3, 29, 40; PC 6; WLC 1**
See also AAYA 51; BRW 3; CDBLB 1789-1832; DA; DA3; DAB; DAC; DAM MST, POET; DLB 109; EXPP; PAB; RGEL 2; TEA; WP

Burns, Tex
See L'Amour, Louis (Dearborn)

Burnshaw, Stanley 1906-2005 **CLC 3, 13, 44**
See also CA 9-12R; 243; CP 1, 2, 3, 4, 5, 6, 7; DLB 48; DLBY 1997

Burr, Anne 1937- **CLC 6**
See also CA 25-28R

Burroughs, Edgar Rice 1875-1950 . **TCLC 2, 32**
See also AAYA 11; BPFB 1; BYA 4, 9; CA 104; 132; CANR 131; DAM NOV; DLB 8; FANT; MTCW 1, 2; MTFW 2005; RGAL 4; SATA 41; SCFW 1, 2; SFW 4; TCWW 1, 2; TUS; YAW

Burroughs, William S. 1914-1997 . **CLC 1, 2, 5, 15, 22, 42, 75, 109; TCLC 121; WLC 1**
See Lee, William; Lee, Willy
See also AAYA 60; AITN 2; AMWS 3; BG 1:2; BPFB 1; CA 9-12R; 160; CANR 20, 52, 104; CN 1, 2, 3, 4, 5, 6; CPW; DA; DA3; DAB; DAC; DAM MST, NOV, POP; DLB 2, 8, 16, 152, 237; DLBY 1981, 1997; EWL 3; HGG; LMFS 2; MAL 5; MTCW 1, 2; MTFW 2005; RGAL 4; SFW 4

Burroughs, William Seward
See Burroughs, William S.

Burton, Sir Richard F(rancis)
1821-1890 **NCLC 42**
See also DLB 55, 166, 184; SSFS 21

Burton, Robert 1577-1640 **LC 74**
See also DLB 151; RGEL 2

Buruma, Ian 1951- **CLC 163**
See also CA 128; CANR 65, 141

Busch, Frederick 1941-2006 .. **CLC 7, 10, 18, 47, 166**
See also CA 33-36R; 248; CAAS 1; CANR 45, 73, 92; CN 1, 2, 3, 4, 5, 6, 7; DLB 6, 218

Busch, Frederick Matthew
See Busch, Frederick

Bush, Barney (Furman) 1946- **NNAL**
See also CA 145

Bush, Ronald 1946- **CLC 34**
See also CA 136

Bustos, F(rancisco)
See Borges, Jorge Luis

Bustos Domecq, H(onorio)
See Bioy Casares, Adolfo; Borges, Jorge Luis

Butler, Octavia E. 1947-2006 **BLCS; CLC 38, 121**
See also AAYA 18, 48; AFAW 2; AMWS 13; BPFB 1; BW 2, 3; CA 73-76; 248; CANR 12, 24, 38, 73, 145; CLR 65; CN 7; CPW; DA3; DAM MULT, POP; DLB 33; LATS 1:2; MTCW 1, 2; MTFW 2005; NFS 8, 21; SATA 84; SCFW 2; SFW 4; SSFS 6; TCLE 1:1; YAW

Butler, Octavia Estelle
See Butler, Octavia E.

Butler, Robert Olen, (Jr.) 1945- **CLC 81, 162**
See also AMWS 12; BPFB 1; CA 112; CANR 66, 138; CN 7; CSW; DAM POP; DLB 173; INT CA-112; MAL 5; MTCW 2; MTFW 2005; SSFS 11

Butler, Samuel 1612-1680 **LC 16, 43**
See also DLB 101, 126; RGEL 2

Butler, Samuel 1835-1902 **TCLC 1, 33; WLC 1**
See also BRWS 2; CA 143; CDBLB 1890-1914; DA; DA3; DAB; DAC; DAM MST, NOV; DLB 18, 57, 174; RGEL 2; SFW 4; TEA

Butler, Walter C.
See Faust, Frederick (Schiller)

Butor, Michel (Marie Francois)
1926- **CLC 1, 3, 8, 11, 15, 161**
See also CA 9-12R; CANR 33, 66; CWW 2; DLB 83; EW 13; EWL 3; GFL 1789 to the Present; MTCW 1, 2; MTFW 2005

Butts, Mary 1890(?)-1937 **TCLC 77**
See also CA 148; DLB 240

Buxton, Ralph
See Silverstein, Alvin; Silverstein, Virginia B(arbara Opshelor)

Buzo, Alex
See Buzo, Alexander (John)
See also DLB 289

Buzo, Alexander (John) 1944- **CLC 61**
See also CA 97-100; CANR 17, 39, 69; CD 5, 6

Buzzati, Dino 1906-1972 **CLC 36**
See also CA 160; 33-36R; DLB 177; RGWL 2, 3; SFW 4

Byars, Betsy 1928- **CLC 35**
See also AAYA 19; BYA 3; CA 33-36R, 183; CAAE 183; CANR 18, 36, 57, 102, 148; CLR 1, 16, 72; DLB 52; INT CANR-18; JRDA; MAICYA 1, 2; MAICYAS 1; MTCW 1; SAAS 1; SATA 4, 46, 80, 163; SATA-Essay 108; WYA; YAW

Byars, Betsy Cromer
See Byars, Betsy

Byatt, Antonia Susan Drabble
See Byatt, A.S.

Byatt, A.S. 1936- **CLC 19, 65, 136, 223; SSC 91**
See also BPFB 1; BRWC 2; BRWS 4; CA 13-16R; CANR 13, 33, 50, 75, 96, 133; CN 1, 2, 3, 4, 5, 6; DA3; DAM NOV, POP; DLB 14, 194, 319, 326; EWL 3; MTCW 1, 2; MTFW 2005; RGSF 2; RHW; TEA

Byrd, William II 1674-1744 **LC 112**
See also DLB 24, 140; RGAL 4

Byrne, David 1952- **CLC 26**
See also CA 127

Byrne, John Keyes 1926-
See Leonard, Hugh
See also CA 102; CANR 78, 140; INT CA-102

Byron, George Gordon (Noel)
1788-1824 **DC 24; NCLC 2, 12, 109, 149; PC 16; WLC 1**
See also AAYA 64; BRW 4; BRWC 2; CD-BLB 1789-1832; DA; DA3; DAB; DAC; DAM MST, POET; DLB 96, 110; EXPP; LMFS 1; PAB; PFS 1, 14; RGEL 2; TEA; WLIT 3; WP

Byron, Robert 1905-1941 **TCLC 67**
See also CA 160; DLB 195

C. 3. 3.
See Wilde, Oscar (Fingal O'Flahertie Wills)

Caballero, Fernan 1796-1877 **NCLC 10**

Cabell, Branch
See Cabell, James Branch

Cabell, James Branch 1879-1958 **TCLC 6**
See also CA 105; 152; DLB 9, 78; FANT; MAL 5; MTCW 2; RGAL 4; SUFW 1

Cabeza de Vaca, Alvar Nunez
1490-1557(?) **LC 61**

Cable, George Washington
1844-1925 **SSC 4; TCLC 4**
See also CA 104; 155; DLB 12, 74; DLBD 13; RGAL 4; TUS

Cabral de Melo Neto, Joao
1920-1999 **CLC 76**
See Melo Neto, Joao Cabral de
See also CA 151; DAM MULT; DLB 307; LAW; LAWS 1

Cabrera Infante, G(uillermo)
1929-2005 **CLC 5, 25, 45, 120; HLC 1; SSC 39**
See also CA 85-88; 236; CANR 29, 65, 110; CDWLB 3; CWW 2; DA3; DAM MULT; DLB 113; EWL 3; HW 1, 2; LAW; LAWS 1; MTCW 1, 2; MTFW 2005; RGSF 2; WLIT 1

Cade, Toni
See Bambara, Toni Cade

Cadmus and Harmonia
See Buchan, John

Caedmon fl. 658-680 **CMLC 7**
See also DLB 146

Caeiro, Alberto
See Pessoa, Fernando (Antonio Nogueira)

Caesar, Julius **CMLC 47**
See Julius Caesar
See also AW 1; RGWL 2, 3; WLIT 8

Cage, John (Milton), (Jr.)
1912-1992 **CLC 41; PC 58**
See also CA 13-16R; 169; CANR 9, 78; DLB 193; INT CANR-9; TCLE 1:1

Cahan, Abraham 1860-1951 **TCLC 71**
See also CA 108; 154; DLB 9, 25, 28; MAL 5; RGAL 4

Cain, G.
See Cabrera Infante, G(uillermo)

Cain, Guillermo
See Cabrera Infante, G(uillermo)

Cain, James M(allahan) 1892-1977 .. **CLC 3, 11, 28**
See also AITN 1; BPFB 1; CA 17-20R; 73-76; CANR 8, 34, 61; CMW 4; CN 1, 2; DLB 226; EWL 3; MAL 5; MSW; MTCW 1; RGAL 4

Caine, Hall 1853-1931 **TCLC 97**
See also RHW

Caine, Mark
See Raphael, Frederic (Michael)

Calasso, Roberto 1941- **CLC 81**
See also CA 143; CANR 89

Calderon de la Barca, Pedro
1600-1681 **DC 3; HLCS 1; LC 23**
See also DFS 23; EW 2; RGWL 2, 3; TWA

Caldwell, Erskine (Preston)
1903-1987 **CLC 1, 8, 14, 50, 60; SSC 19; TCLC 117**
See also AITN 1; AMW; BPFB 1; CA 1-4R; 121; CAAS 1; CANR 2, 33; CN 1, 2, 3, 4; DA3; DAM NOV; DLB 9, 86; EWL 3; MAL 5; MTCW 1, 2; MTFW 2005; RGAL 4; RGSF 2; TUS

Caldwell, (Janet Miriam) Taylor (Holland)
1900-1985 **CLC 2, 28, 39**
See also BPFB 1; CA 5-8R; 116; CANR 5; DA3; DAM NOV, POP; DLBD 17; MTCW 2; RHW

Calhoun, John Caldwell
1782-1850 **NCLC 15**
See also DLB 3, 248

Calisher, Hortense 1911- **CLC 2, 4, 8, 38, 134; SSC 15**
See also CA 1-4R; CANR 1, 22, 117; CN 1, 2, 3, 4, 5, 6, 7; DA3; DAM NOV; DLB 2, 218; INT CANR-22; MAL 5; MTCW 1, 2; MTFW 2005; RGAL 4; RGSF 2

Callaghan, Morley Edward
1903-1990 **CLC 3, 14, 41, 65; TCLC 145**
See also CA 9-12R; 132; CANR 33, 73; CN 1, 2, 3, 4; DAC; DAM MST; DLB 68; EWL 3; MTCW 1, 2; MTFW 2005; RGEL 2; RGSF 2; SSFS 19

Callimachus c. 305B.C.-c.
240B.C. **CMLC 18**
See also AW 1; DLB 176; RGWL 2, 3

Calvin, Jean
See Calvin, John
See also GFL Beginnings to 1789

Calvin, John 1509-1564 **LC 37**
See Calvin, Jean

Calvino, Italo 1923-1985 **CLC 5, 8, 11, 22, 33, 39, 73; SSC 3, 48**
See also AAYA 58; CA 85-88; 116; CANR 23, 61, 132; DAM NOV; DLB 196; EW 13; EWL 3; MTCW 1, 2; MTFW 2005; RGHL; RGSF 2; RGWL 2, 3; SFW 4; SSFS 12; WLIT 7

Camara Laye
See Laye, Camara
See also EWL 3

Camden, William 1551-1623 **LC 77**
See also DLB 172

Cameron, Carey 1952- **CLC 59**
See also CA 135

Cameron, Peter 1959- **CLC 44**
See also AMWS 12; CA 125; CANR 50, 117; DLB 234; GLL 2

Camoens, Luis Vaz de 1524(?)-1580
See Camoes, Luis de
See also EW 2

Camoes, Luis de 1524(?)-1580 . **HLCS 1; LC 62; PC 31**
See Camoens, Luis Vaz de
See also DLB 287; RGWL 2, 3

Campana, Dino 1885-1932 **TCLC 20**
See also CA 117; 246; DLB 114; EWL 3

Campanella, Tommaso 1568-1639 **LC 32**
See also RGWL 2, 3

Campbell, John W(ood, Jr.)
1910-1971 **CLC 32**
See also CA 21-22; 29-32R; CANR 34;
CAP 2; DLB 8; MTCW 1; SCFW 1, 2;
SFW 4

Campbell, Joseph 1904-1987 **CLC 69;
TCLC 140**
See also AAYA 3, 66; BEST 89:2; CA 1-4R;
124; CANR 3, 28, 61, 107; DA3; MTCW
1, 2

Campbell, Maria 1940- **CLC 85; NNAL**
See also CA 102; CANR 54; CCA 1; DAC

Campbell, (John) Ramsey 1946- **CLC 42;
SSC 19**
See also AAYA 51; CA 57-60, 228; CAAE
228; CANR 7, 102; DLB 261; HGG; INT
CANR-7; SUFW 1, 2

Campbell, (Ignatius) Roy (Dunnachie)
1901-1957 **TCLC 5**
See also AFW; CA 104; 155; DLB 20, 225;
EWL 3; MTCW 2; RGEL 2

Campbell, Thomas 1777-1844 **NCLC 19**
See also DLB 93, 144; RGEL 2

Campbell, Wilfred **TCLC 9**
See Campbell, William

Campbell, William 1858(?)-1918
See Campbell, Wilfred
See also CA 106; DLB 92

Campbell, William Edward March
1893-1954
See March, William
See also CA 108

Campion, Jane 1954- **CLC 95**
See also AAYA 33; CA 138; CANR 87

Campion, Thomas 1567-1620 **LC 78**
See also CDBLB Before 1660; DAM POET;
DLB 58, 172; RGEL 2

Camus, Albert 1913-1960 **CLC 1, 2, 4, 9,
11, 14, 32, 63, 69, 124; DC 2; SSC 9,
76; WLC 1**
See also AAYA 36; AFW; BPFB 1; CA 89-
92; CANR 131; DA; DA3; DAB; DAC;
DAM DRAM, MST, NOV; DLB 72, 321;
EW 13; EWL 3; EXPN; EXPS; GFL 1789
to the Present; LATS 1:2; LMFS 2;
MTCW 1, 2; MTFW 2005; NFS 6, 16;
RGHL; RGSF 2; RGWL 2, 3; SSFS 4;
TWA

Canby, Vincent 1924-2000 **CLC 13**
See also CA 81-84; 191

Cancale
See Desnos, Robert

Canetti, Elias 1905-1994 .. **CLC 3, 14, 25, 75,
86; TCLC 157**
See also CA 21-24R; 146; CANR 23, 61,
79; CDWLB 2; CWW 2; DA3; DLB 85,
124; EW 12; EWL 3; MTCW 1, 2; MTFW
2005; RGWL 2, 3; TWA

Canfield, Dorothea F.
See Fisher, Dorothy (Frances) Canfield

Canfield, Dorothea Frances
See Fisher, Dorothy (Frances) Canfield

Canfield, Dorothy
See Fisher, Dorothy (Frances) Canfield

Canin, Ethan 1960- **CLC 55; SSC 70**
See also CA 131; 135; MAL 5

Cankar, Ivan 1876-1918 **TCLC 105**
See also CDWLB 4; DLB 147; EWL 3

Cannon, Curt
See Hunter, Evan

Cao, Lan 1961- **CLC 109**
See also CA 165

Cape, Judith
See Page, P(atricia) K(athleen)
See also CCA 1

Capek, Karel 1890-1938 **DC 1; SSC 36;
TCLC 6, 37; WLC 1**
See also CA 104; 140; CDWLB 4; DA;
DA3; DAB; DAC; DAM DRAM, MST,
NOV; DFS 7, 11; DLB 215; EW 10; EWL
3; MTCW 2; MTFW 2005; RGSF 2;
RGWL 2, 3; SCFW 1, 2; SFW 4

Capella, Martianus fl. 4th cent. - .. **CMLC 84**

Capote, Truman 1924-1984 . **CLC 1, 3, 8, 13,
19, 34, 38, 58; SSC 2, 47, 93; TCLC
164; WLC 1**
See also AAYA 61; AMWS 3; BPFB 1; CA
5-8R; 113; CANR 18, 62; CDALB 1941-
1968; CN 1, 2, 3; CPW; DA; DA3; DAB;
DAC; DAM MST, NOV, POP; DLB 2,
185, 227; DLBY 1980, 1984; EWL 3;
EXPS; GLL 1; LAIT 3; MAL 5; MTCW
1, 2; MTFW 2005; NCFS 2; RGAL 4;
RGSF 2; SATA 91; SSFS 2; TUS

Capra, Frank 1897-1991 **CLC 16**
See also AAYA 52; CA 61-64; 135

Caputo, Philip 1941- **CLC 32**
See also AAYA 60; CA 73-76; CANR 40,
135; YAW

Caragiale, Ion Luca 1852-1912 **TCLC 76**
See also CA 157

Card, Orson Scott 1951- **CLC 44, 47, 50**
See also AAYA 11, 42; BPFB 1; BYA 5, 8;
CA 102; CANR 27, 47, 73, 102, 106, 133;
CPW; DA3; DAM POP; FANT; INT
CANR-27; MTCW 1, 2; MTFW 2005;
NFS 5; SATA 83, 127; SCFW 2; SFW 4;
SUFW 2; YAW

Cardenal, Ernesto 1925- **CLC 31, 161;
HLC 1; PC 22**
See also CA 49-52; CANR 2, 32, 66, 138;
CWW 2; DAM MULT, POET; DLB 290;
EWL 3; HW 1, 2; LAWS 1; MTCW 1, 2;
MTFW 2005; RGWL 2, 3

Cardinal, Marie 1929-2001 **CLC 189**
See also CA 177; CWW 2; DLB 83; FW

Cardozo, Benjamin N(athan)
1870-1938 **TCLC 65**
See also CA 117; 164

Carducci, Giosue (Alessandro Giuseppe)
1835-1907 **PC 46; TCLC 32**
See also CA 163; EW 7; RGWL 2, 3

Carew, Thomas 1595(?)-1640 . **LC 13; PC 29**
See also BRW 2; DLB 126; PAB; RGEL 2

Carey, Ernestine Gilbreth **CLC 17**
See also CA 5-8R; CANR 71; SATA 2

Carey, Peter 1943- **CLC 40, 55, 96, 183**
See also CA 123; 127; CANR 53, 76, 117;
CN 4, 5, 6, 7; DLB 289, 326; EWL 3;
INT CA-127; MTCW 1, 2; MTFW 2005;
RGSF 2; SATA 94

Carleton, William 1794-1869 **NCLC 3**
See also DLB 159; RGEL 2; RGSF 2

Carlisle, Henry (Coffin) 1926- **CLC 33**
See also CA 13-16R; CANR 15, 85

Carlsen, Chris
See Holdstock, Robert P.

Carlson, Ron(ald F.) 1947- **CLC 54**
See also CA 105, 189; CAAE 189; CANR
27; DLB 244

Carlyle, Thomas 1795-1881 **NCLC 22, 70**
See also BRW 4; CDBLB 1789-1832; DA;
DAB; DAC; DAM MST; DLB 55, 144,
254; RGEL 2; TEA

Carman, (William) Bliss 1861-1929 ... **PC 34;
TCLC 7**
See also CA 104; 152; DAC; DLB 92;
RGEL 2

Carnegie, Dale 1888-1955 **TCLC 53**
See also CA 218

Carossa, Hans 1878-1956 **TCLC 48**
See also CA 170; DLB 66; EWL 3

Carpenter, Don(ald Richard)
1931-1995 **CLC 41**
See also CA 45-48; 149; CANR 1, 71

Carpenter, Edward 1844-1929 **TCLC 88**
See also CA 163; GLL 1

Carpenter, John (Howard) 1948- ... **CLC 161**
See also AAYA 2; CA 134; SATA 58

Carpenter, Johnny
See Carpenter, John (Howard)

Carpentier (y Valmont), Alejo
1904-1980 . **CLC 8, 11, 38, 110; HLC 1;
SSC 35**
See also CA 65-68; 97-100; CANR 11, 70;
CDWLB 3; DAM MULT; DLB 113; EWL
3; HW 1, 2; LAW; LMFS 2; RGSF 2;
RGWL 2, 3; WLIT 1

Carr, Caleb 1955- **CLC 86**
See also CA 147; CANR 73, 134; DLB 3

Carr, Emily 1871-1945 **TCLC 32**
See also CA 159; DLB 68; FW; GLL 2

Carr, John Dickson 1906-1977 **CLC 3**
See Fairbairn, Roger
See also CA 49-52; 69-72; CANR 3, 33,
60; CMW 4; DLB 306; MSW; MTCW 1,
2

Carr, Philippa
See Hibbert, Eleanor Alice Burford

Carr, Virginia Spencer 1929- **CLC 34**
See also CA 61-64; DLB 111

Carrere, Emmanuel 1957- **CLC 89**
See also CA 200

Carrier, Roch 1937- **CLC 13, 78**
See also CA 130; CANR 61, 152; CCA 1;
DAC; DAM MST; DLB 53; SATA 105,
166

Carroll, James Dennis
See Carroll, Jim

Carroll, James P. 1943(?)- **CLC 38**
See also CA 81-84; CANR 73, 139; MTCW
2; MTFW 2005

Carroll, Jim 1951- **CLC 35, 143**
See also AAYA 17; CA 45-48; CANR 42,
115; NCFS 5

Carroll, Lewis **NCLC 2, 53, 139; PC 18;
WLC 1**
See Dodgson, Charles L(utwidge)
See also AAYA 39; BRW 5; BYA 5, 13; CD-
BLB 1832-1890; CLR 2, 18, 108; DLB
18, 163, 178; DLBY 1998; EXPN; EXPP;
FANT; JRDA; LAIT 1; NFS 7; PFS 11;
RGEL 2; SUFW 1; TEA; WCH

Carroll, Paul Vincent 1900-1968 **CLC 10**
See also CA 9-12R; 25-28R; DLB 10; EWL
3; RGEL 2

Carruth, Hayden 1921- **CLC 4, 7, 10, 18,
84; PC 10**
See also CA 9-12R; CANR 4, 38, 59, 110;
CP 1, 2, 3, 4, 5, 6, 7; DLB 5, 165; INT
CANR-4; MTCW 1, 2; MTFW 2005;
SATA 47

Carson, Anne 1950- **CLC 185; PC 64**
See also AMWS 12; CA 203; CP 7; DLB
193; PFS 18; TCLE 1:1

Carson, Ciaran 1948- **CLC 201**
See also CA 112; 153; CANR 113; CP 6, 7

Carson, Rachel
See Carson, Rachel Louise
See also AAYA 49; DLB 275

Carson, Rachel Louise 1907-1964 **CLC 71**
See Carson, Rachel
See also AMWS 9; ANW; CA 77-80; CANR
35; DA3; DAM POP; FW; LAIT 4; MAL
5; MTCW 1, 2; MTFW 2005; NCFS 1;
SATA 23

Carter, Angela (Olive) 1940-1992 **CLC 5,
41, 76; SSC 13, 85; TCLC 139**
See also BRWS 3; CA 53-56; 136; CANR
12, 36, 61, 106; CN 3, 4, 5; DA3; DLB
14, 207, 261, 319; EXPS; FANT; FW; GL

2; MTCW 1, 2; MTFW 2005; RGSF 2;
SATA 66; SATA-Obit 70; SFW 4; SSFS
4, 12; SUFW 2; WLIT 4

Carter, Nick
See Smith, Martin Cruz

Carver, Raymond 1938-1988 **CLC 22, 36,
53, 55, 126; PC 54; SSC 8, 51**
See also AAYA 44; AMWS 3; BPFB 1; CA
33-36R; 126; CANR 17, 34, 61, 103; CN
4; CPW; DA3; DAM NOV; DLB 130;
DLBY 1984, 1988; EWL 3; MAL 5;
MTCW 1, 2; MTFW 2005; PFS 17;
RGAL 4; RGSF 2; SSFS 3, 6, 12, 13, 23;
TCLE 1:1; TCWW 2; TUS

Cary, Elizabeth, Lady Falkland
1585-1639 **LC 30**

Cary, (Arthur) Joyce (Lunel)
1888-1957 **TCLC 1, 29**
See also BRW 7; CA 104; 164; CDBLB
1914-1945; DLB 15, 100; EWL 3; MTCW
2; RGEL 2; TEA

Casal, Julian del 1863-1893 **NCLC 131**
See also DLB 283; LAW

Casanova, Giacomo
See Casanova de Seingalt, Giovanni Jacopo
See also WLIT 7

Casanova de Seingalt, Giovanni Jacopo
1725-1798 **LC 13**
See Casanova, Giacomo

Casares, Adolfo Bioy
See Bioy Casares, Adolfo
See also RGSF 2

Casas, Bartolome de las 1474-1566
See Las Casas, Bartolome de
See also WLIT 1

Casely-Hayford, J(oseph) E(phraim)
1866-1903 **BLC 1; TCLC 24**
See also BW 2; CA 123; 152; DAM MULT

Casey, John (Dudley) 1939- **CLC 59**
See also BEST 90:2; CA 69-72; CANR 23,
100

Casey, Michael 1947- **CLC 2**
See also CA 65-68; CANR 109; CP 2, 3;
DLB 5

Casey, Patrick
See Thurman, Wallace (Henry)

Casey, Warren (Peter) 1935-1988 **CLC 12**
See also CA 101; 127; INT CA-101

Casona, Alejandro **CLC 49**
See Alvarez, Alejandro Rodriguez
See also EWL 3

Cassavetes, John 1929-1989 **CLC 20**
See also CA 85-88; 127; CANR 82

Cassian, Nina 1924- **PC 17**
See also CWP; CWW 2

Cassill, R(onald) V(erlin)
1919-2002 **CLC 4, 23**
See also CA 9-12R; 208; CAAS 1; CANR
7, 45; CN 1, 2, 3, 4, 5, 6, 7; DLB 6, 218;
DLBY 2002

Cassiodorus, Flavius Magnus c. 490(?)-c.
583(?) **CMLC 43**

Cassirer, Ernst 1874-1945 **TCLC 61**
See also CA 157

Cassity, (Allen) Turner 1929- **CLC 6, 42**
See also CA 17-20R; 223; CAAE 223;
CAAS 8; CANR 11; CSW; DLB 105

Castaneda, Carlos (Cesar Aranha)
1931(?)-1998 **CLC 12, 119**
See also CA 25-28R; CANR 32, 66, 105;
DNFS 1; HW 1; MTCW 1

Castedo, Elena 1937- **CLC 65**
See also CA 132

Castedo-Ellerman, Elena
See Castedo, Elena

Castellanos, Rosario 1925-1974 **CLC 66;
HLC 1; SSC 39, 68**
See also CA 131; 53-56; CANR 58; CD-
WLB 3; DAM MULT; DLB 113, 290;
EWL 3; FW; HW 1; LAW; MTCW 2;
MTFW 2005; RGSF 2; RGWL 2, 3

Castelvetro, Lodovico 1505-1571 **LC 12**

Castiglione, Baldassare 1478-1529 **LC 12**
See Castiglione, Baldesar
See also LMFS 1; RGWL 2, 3

Castiglione, Baldesar
See Castiglione, Baldassare
See also EW 2; WLIT 7

Castillo, Ana 1953- **CLC 151**
See also AAYA 42; CA 131; CANR 51, 86,
128; CWP; DLB 122, 227; DNFS 2; FW;
HW 1; LLW; PFS 21

Castle, Robert
See Hamilton, Edmond

Castro (Ruz), Fidel 1926(?)- **HLC 1**
See also CA 110; 129; CANR 81; DAM
MULT; HW 2

Castro, Guillen de 1569-1631 **LC 19**

Castro, Rosalia de 1837-1885 ... **NCLC 3, 78;
PC 41**
See also DAM MULT

Cather, Willa (Sibert) 1873-1947 . **SSC 2, 50;
TCLC 1, 11, 31, 99, 132, 152; WLC 1**
See also AAYA 24; AMW; AMWC 1;
AMWR 1; BPFB 1; CA 104; 128; CDALB
1865-1917; CLR 98; DA; DA3; DAB;
DAC; DAM MST, NOV; DLB 9, 54, 78,
256; DLBD 1; EWL 3; EXPN; EXPS; FL
1:5; LAIT 3; LATS 1:1; MAL 5; MAWW;
MTCW 1, 2; MTFW 2005; NFS 2, 19;
RGAL 4; RGSF 2; RHW; SATA 30; SSFS
2, 7, 16; TCWW 1, 2; TUS

Catherine II
See Catherine the Great
See also DLB 150

Catherine the Great 1729-1796 **LC 69**
See Catherine II

Cato, Marcus Porcius
234B.C.-149B.C. **CMLC 21**
See Cato the Elder

Cato, Marcus Porcius, the Elder
See Cato, Marcus Porcius

Cato the Elder
See Cato, Marcus Porcius
See also DLB 211

Catton, (Charles) Bruce 1899-1978 . **CLC 35**
See also AITN 1; CA 5-8R; 81-84; CANR
7, 74; DLB 17; MTCW 2; MTFW 2005;
SATA 2; SATA-Obit 24

Catullus c. 84B.C.-54B.C. **CMLC 18**
See also AW 2; CDWLB 1; DLB 211;
RGWL 2, 3; WLIT 8

Cauldwell, Frank
See King, Francis (Henry)

Caunitz, William J. 1933-1996 **CLC 34**
See also BEST 89:3; CA 125; 130; 152;
CANR 73; INT CA-130

Causley, Charles (Stanley)
1917-2003 **CLC 7**
See also CA 9-12R; 223; CANR 5, 35, 94;
CLR 30; CP 1, 2, 3, 4, 5; CWRI 5; DLB
27; MTCW 1; SATA 3, 66; SATA-Obit
149

Caute, (John) David 1936- **CLC 29**
See also CA 1-4R; CAAS 4; CANR 1, 33,
64, 120; CBD; CD 5, 6; CN 1, 2, 3, 4, 5,
6, 7; DAM NOV; DLB 14, 231

Cavafy, C(onstantine) P(eter) **PC 36;
TCLC 2, 7**
See Kavafis, Konstantinos Petrou
See also CA 148; DA3; DAM POET; EW
8; EWL 3; MTCW 2; PFS 19; RGWL 2,
3; WP

Cavalcanti, Guido c. 1250-c.
1300 ... **CMLC 54**
See also RGWL 2, 3; WLIT 7

Cavallo, Evelyn
See Spark, Muriel (Sarah)

Cavanna, Betty **CLC 12**
See Harrison, Elizabeth (Allen) Cavanna
See also JRDA; MAICYA 1; SAAS 4;
SATA 1, 30

Cavendish, Margaret Lucas
1623-1673 **LC 30**
See also DLB 131, 252, 281; RGEL 2

Caxton, William 1421(?)-1491(?) **LC 17**
See also DLB 170

Cayer, D. M.
See Duffy, Maureen (Patricia)

Cayrol, Jean 1911-2005 **CLC 11**
See also CA 89-92; 236; DLB 83; EWL 3

Cela (y Trulock), Camilo Jose
See Cela, Camilo Jose
See also CWW 2

Cela, Camilo Jose 1916-2002 **CLC 4, 13,
59, 122; HLC 1; SSC 71**
See Cela (y Trulock), Camilo Jose
See also BEST 90:2; CA 21-24R; 206;
CAAS 10; CANR 21, 32, 76, 139; DAM
MULT; DLB 322; DLBY 1989; EW 13;
EWL 3; HW 1; MTCW 1, 2; MTFW
2005; RGSF 2; RGWL 2, 3

Celan, Paul **CLC 10, 19, 53, 82; PC 10**
See Antschel, Paul
See also CDWLB 2; DLB 69; EWL 3;
RGHL; RGWL 2, 3

Celine, Louis-Ferdinand .. **CLC 1, 3, 4, 7, 9,
15, 47, 124**
See Destouches, Louis-Ferdinand
See also DLB 72; EW 11; EWL 3; GFL
1789 to the Present; RGWL 2, 3

Cellini, Benvenuto 1500-1571 **LC 7**
See also WLIT 7

Cendrars, Blaise **CLC 18, 106**
See Sauser-Hall, Frederic
See also DLB 258; EWL 3; GFL 1789 to
the Present; RGWL 2, 3; WP

Centlivre, Susanna 1669(?)-1723 **DC 25;
LC 65**
See also DLB 84; RGEL 2

Cernuda (y Bidon), Luis
1902-1963 **CLC 54; PC 62**
See also CA 131; 89-92; DAM POET; DLB
134; EWL 3; GLL 1; HW 1; RGWL 2, 3

Cervantes, Lorna Dee 1954- **HLCS 1; PC
35**
See also CA 131; CANR 80; CP 7; CWP;
DLB 82; EXPP; HW 1; LLW

Cervantes (Saavedra), Miguel de
1547-1616 **HLCS; LC 6, 23, 93; SSC
12; WLC 1**
See also AAYA 56; BYA 1, 14; DA; DAB;
DAC; DAM MST, NOV; EW 2; LAIT 1;
LATS 1:1; LMFS 1; NFS 8; RGSF 2;
RGWL 2, 3; TWA

Cesaire, Aime (Fernand) 1913- **BLC 1;
CLC 19, 32, 112; DC 22; PC 25**
See also BW 2, 3; CA 65-68; CANR 24,
43, 81; CWW 2; DA3; DAM MULT,
POET; DLB 321; EWL 3; GFL 1789 to
the Present; MTCW 1, 2; MTFW 2005;
WP

Chabon, Michael 1963- ... **CLC 55, 149; SSC
59**
See also AAYA 45; AMWS 11; CA 139;
CANR 57, 96, 127, 138; DLB 278; MAL
5; MTFW 2005; SATA 145

Chabrol, Claude 1930- **CLC 16**
See also CA 110

Chairil Anwar
See Anwar, Chairil
See also EWL 3

Challans, Mary 1905-1983
See Renault, Mary
See also CA 81-84; 111; CANR 74; DA3; MTCW 2; MTFW 2005; SATA 23; SATA-Obit 36; TEA

Challis, George
See Faust, Frederick (Schiller)

Chambers, Aidan 1934- **CLC 35**
See also AAYA 27; CA 25-28R; CANR 12, 31, 58, 116; JRDA; MAICYA 1, 2; SAAS 12; SATA 1, 69, 108, 171; WYA; YAW

Chambers, James 1948-
See Cliff, Jimmy
See also CA 124

Chambers, Jessie
See Lawrence, D(avid) H(erbert Richards)
See also GLL 1

Chambers, Robert W(illiam)
1865-1933 **SSC 92; TCLC 41**
See also CA 165; DLB 202; HGG; SATA 107; SUFW 1

Chambers, (David) Whittaker
1901-1961 **TCLC 129**
See also CA 89-92; DLB 303

Chamisso, Adelbert von
1781-1838 **NCLC 82**
See also DLB 90; RGWL 2, 3; SUFW 1

Chance, James T.
See Carpenter, John (Howard)

Chance, John T.
See Carpenter, John (Howard)

Chandler, Raymond (Thornton)
1888-1959 **SSC 23; TCLC 1, 7, 179**
See also AAYA 25; AMWC 2; AMWS 4; BPFB 1; CA 104; 129; CANR 60, 107; CDALB 1929-1941; CMW 4; DA3; DLB 226, 253; DLBD 6; EWL 3; MAL 5; MSW; MTCW 1, 2; MTFW 2005; NFS 17; RGAL 4; TUS

Chang, Diana 1934- **AAL**
See also CA 228; CWP; DLB 312; EXPP

Chang, Eileen 1921-1995 **AAL; SSC 28**
See Chang Ai-Ling; Zhang Ailing
See also CA 166

Chang, Jung 1952- **CLC 71**
See also CA 142

Chang Ai-Ling
See Chang, Eileen
See also EWL 3

Channing, William Ellery
1780-1842 **NCLC 17**
See also DLB 1, 59, 235; RGAL 4

Chao, Patricia 1955- **CLC 119**
See also CA 163

Chaplin, Charles Spencer
1889-1977 **CLC 16**
See Chaplin, Charlie
See also CA 81-84; 73-76

Chaplin, Charlie
See Chaplin, Charles Spencer
See also AAYA 61; DLB 44

Chapman, George 1559(?)-1634 . **DC 19; LC 22, 116**
See also BRW 1; DAM DRAM; DLB 62, 121; LMFS 1; RGEL 2

Chapman, Graham 1941-1989 **CLC 21**
See Monty Python
See also CA 116; 129; CANR 35, 95

Chapman, John Jay 1862-1933 **TCLC 7**
See also AMWS 14; CA 104; 191

Chapman, Lee
See Bradley, Marion Zimmer
See also GLL 1

Chapman, Walker
See Silverberg, Robert

Chappell, Fred (Davis) 1936- **CLC 40, 78, 162**
See also CA 5-8R, 198; CAAE 198; CAAS 4; CANR 8, 33, 67, 110; CN 6; CP 6, 7; CSW; DLB 6, 105; HGG

Char, Rene(-Emile) 1907-1988 **CLC 9, 11, 14, 55; PC 56**
See also CA 13-16R; 124; CANR 32; DAM POET; DLB 258; EWL 3; GFL 1789 to the Present; MTCW 1, 2; RGWL 2, 3

Charby, Jay
See Ellison, Harlan (Jay)

Chardin, Pierre Teilhard de
See Teilhard de Chardin, (Marie Joseph) Pierre

Chariton fl. 1st cent. (?)- **CMLC 49**

Charlemagne 742-814 **CMLC 37**

Charles I 1600-1649 **LC 13**

Charriere, Isabelle de 1740-1805 .. **NCLC 66**
See also DLB 313

Chartier, Alain c. 1392-1430 **LC 94**
See also DLB 208

Chartier, Emile-Auguste
See Alain

Charyn, Jerome 1937- **CLC 5, 8, 18**
See also CA 5-8R; CAAS 1; CANR 7, 61, 101; CMW 4; CN 1, 2, 3, 4, 5, 6, 7; DLBY 1983; MTCW 1

Chase, Adam
See Marlowe, Stephen

Chase, Mary (Coyle) 1907-1981 **DC 1**
See also CA 77-80; 105; CAD; CWD; DFS 11; DLB 228; SATA 17; SATA-Obit 29

Chase, Mary Ellen 1887-1973 **CLC 2; TCLC 124**
See also CA 13-16; 41-44R; CAP 1; SATA 10

Chase, Nicholas
See Hyde, Anthony
See also CCA 1

Chateaubriand, Francois Rene de
1768-1848 **NCLC 3, 134**
See also DLB 119; EW 5; GFL 1789 to the Present; RGWL 2, 3; TWA

Chatelet, Gabrielle-Emilie Du
See du Chatelet, Emilie
See also DLB 313

Chatterje, Sarat Chandra 1876-1936(?)
See Chatterji, Saratchandra
See also CA 109

Chatterji, Bankim Chandra
1838-1894 **NCLC 19**

Chatterji, Saratchandra **TCLC 13**
See Chatterje, Sarat Chandra
See also CA 186; EWL 3

Chatterton, Thomas 1752-1770 **LC 3, 54**
See also DAM POET; DLB 109; RGEL 2

Chatwin, (Charles) Bruce
1940-1989 **CLC 28, 57, 59**
See also AAYA 4; BEST 90:1; BRWS 4; CA 85-88; 127; CPW; DAM POP; DLB 194, 204; EWL 3; MTFW 2005

Chaucer, Daniel
See Ford, Ford Madox
See also RHW

Chaucer, Geoffrey 1340(?)-1400 .. **LC 17, 56; PC 19, 58; WLCS**
See also BRW 1; BRWC 1; BRWR 2; CD-BLB Before 1660; DA; DA3; DAB; DAC; DAM MST, POET; DLB 146; LAIT 1; PAB; PFS 14; RGEL 2; TEA; WLIT 3; WP

Chavez, Denise (Elia) 1948- **HLC 1**
See also CA 131; CANR 56, 81, 137; DAM MULT; DLB 122; FW; HW 1, 2; LLW; MAL 5; MTCW 2; MTFW 2005

Chaviaras, Strates 1935-
See Haviaras, Stratis
See also CA 105

Chayefsky, Paddy **CLC 23**
See Chayefsky, Sidney
See also CAD; DLB 7, 44; DLBY 1981; RGAL 4

Chayefsky, Sidney 1923-1981
See Chayefsky, Paddy
See also CA 9-12R; 104; CANR 18; DAM DRAM

Chedid, Andree 1920- **CLC 47**
See also CA 145; CANR 95; EWL 3

Cheever, John 1912-1982 **CLC 3, 7, 8, 11, 15, 25, 64; SSC 1, 38, 57; WLC 2**
See also AAYA 65; AMWS 1; BPFB 1; CA 5-8R; 106; CABS 1; CANR 5, 27, 76; CDALB 1941-1968; CN 1, 2, 3; CPW; DA; DA3; DAB; DAC; DAM MST, NOV, POP; DLB 2, 102, 227; DLBY 1980, 1982; EWL 3; EXPS; INT CANR-5; MAL 5; MTCW 1, 2; MTFW 2005; RGAL 4; RGSF 2; SSFS 2, 14; TUS

Cheever, Susan 1943- **CLC 18, 48**
See also CA 103; CANR 27, 51, 92; DLBY 1982; INT CANR-27

Chekhonte, Antosha
See Chekhov, Anton (Pavlovich)

Chekhov, Anton (Pavlovich)
1860-1904 **DC 9; SSC 2, 28, 41, 51, 85; TCLC 3, 10, 31, 55, 96, 163; WLC 2**
See also AAYA 68; BYA 14; CA 104; 124; DA; DA3; DAB; DAC; DAM DRAM, MST; DFS 1, 5, 10, 12; DLB 277; EW 7; EWL 3; EXPS; LAIT 3; LATS 1:1; RGSF 2; RGWL 2, 3; SATA 90; SSFS 5, 13, 14; TWA

Cheney, Lynne V. 1941- **CLC 70**
See also CA 89-92; CANR 58, 117; SATA 152

Chernyshevsky, Nikolai Gavrilovich
See Chernyshevsky, Nikolay Gavrilovich
See also DLB 238

Chernyshevsky, Nikolay Gavrilovich
1828-1889 **NCLC 1**
See Chernyshevsky, Nikolai Gavrilovich

Cherry, Carolyn Janice **CLC 35**
See Cherryh, C. J.
See also AAYA 24; BPFB 1; DLBY 1980; FANT; SATA 93; SCFW 2; SFW 4; YAW

Cherryh, C. J. 1942-
See Cherry, Carolyn Janice
See also CA 65-68; CANR 10, 147

Chesnutt, Charles W(addell)
1858-1932 **BLC 1; SSC 7, 54; TCLC 5, 39**
See also AFAW 1, 2; AMWS 14; BW 1, 3; CA 106; 125; CANR 76; DAM MULT; DLB 12, 50, 78; EWL 3; MAL 5; MTCW 1, 2; MTFW 2005; RGAL 4; RGSF 2; SSFS 11

Chester, Alfred 1929(?)-1971 **CLC 49**
See also CA 196; 33-36R; DLB 130; MAL 5

Chesterton, G(ilbert) K(eith)
1874-1936 . **PC 28; SSC 1, 46; TCLC 1, 6, 64**
See also AAYA 57; BRW 6; CA 104; 132; CANR 73, 131; CDBLB 1914-1945; CMW 4; DAM NOV, POET; DLB 10, 19, 34, 70, 98, 149, 178; EWL 3; FANT; MSW; MTCW 1, 2; MTFW 2005; RGEL 2; RGSF 2; SATA 27; SUFW 1

Chettle, Henry 1560-1607(?) **LC 112**
See also DLB 136; RGEL 2

Chiang, Pin-chin 1904-1986
See Ding Ling
See also CA 118

Chief Joseph 1840-1904 **NNAL**
See also CA 152; DA3; DAM MULT

Chief Seattle 1786(?)-1866 **NNAL**
See also DA3; DAM MULT

Ch'ien, Chung-shu 1910-1998 **CLC 22**
 See Qian Zhongshu
 See also CA 130; CANR 73; MTCW 1, 2

Chikamatsu Monzaemon 1653-1724 ... **LC 66**
 See also RGWL 2, 3

Child, Francis James 1825-1896 . **NCLC 173**
 See also DLB 1, 64, 235

Child, L. Maria
 See Child, Lydia Maria

Child, Lydia Maria 1802-1880 .. **NCLC 6, 73**
 See also DLB 1, 74, 243; RGAL 4; SATA
 67

Child, Mrs.
 See Child, Lydia Maria

Child, Philip 1898-1978 **CLC 19, 68**
 See also CA 13-14; CAP 1; CP 1; DLB 68;
 RHW; SATA 47

Childers, (Robert) Erskine
 1870-1922 **TCLC 65**
 See also CA 113; 153; DLB 70

Childress, Alice 1920-1994 . **BLC 1; CLC 12,**
 15, 86, 96; DC 4; TCLC 116
 See also AAYA 8; BW 2, 3; BYA 2; CA 45-
 48; 146; CAD; CANR 3, 27, 50, 74; CLR
 14; CWD; DA3; DAM DRAM, MULT,
 NOV; DFS 2, 8, 14; DLB 7, 38, 249;
 JRDA; LAIT 5; MAICYA 1, 2; MAIC-
 YAS 1; MAL 5; MTCW 1, 2; MTFW
 2005; RGAL 4; SATA 7, 48, 81; TUS;
 WYA; YAW

Chin, Frank (Chew, Jr.) 1940- **AAL; CLC**
 135; DC 7
 See also CA 33-36R; CAD; CANR 71; CD
 5, 6; DAM MULT; DLB 206, 312; LAIT
 5; RGAL 4

Chin, Marilyn (Mei Ling) 1955- **PC 40**
 See also CA 129; CANR 70, 113; CWP;
 DLB 312

Chislett, (Margaret) Anne 1943- **CLC 34**
 See also CA 151

Chitty, Thomas Willes 1926- **CLC 11**
 See Hinde, Thomas
 See also CA 5-8R; CN 7

Chivers, Thomas Holley
 1809-1858 **NCLC 49**
 See also DLB 3, 248; RGAL 4

Choi, Susan 1969- **CLC 119**
 See also CA 223

Chomette, Rene Lucien 1898-1981
 See Clair, Rene
 See also CA 103

Chomsky, Avram Noam
 See Chomsky, Noam

Chomsky, Noam 1928- **CLC 132**
 See also CA 17-20R; CANR 28, 62, 110,
 132; DA3; DLB 246; MTCW 1, 2; MTFW
 2005

Chona, Maria 1845(?)-1936 **NNAL**
 See also CA 144

Chopin, Kate **SSC 8, 68; TCLC 127;**
 WLCS
 See Chopin, Katherine
 See also AAYA 33; AMWR 2; AMWS 1;
 BYA 11, 15; CDALB 1865-1917; DA;
 DAB; DLB 12, 78; EXPN; EXPS; FL 1:3;
 FW; LAIT 3; MAL 5; MAWW; NFS 3;
 RGAL 4; RGSF 2; SSFS 2, 13, 17; TUS

Chopin, Katherine 1851-1904
 See Chopin, Kate
 See also CA 104; 122; DA3; DAC; DAM
 MST, NOV

Chretien de Troyes c. 12th cent. - . **CMLC 10**
 See also DLB 208; EW 1; RGWL 2, 3;
 TWA

Christie
 See Ichikawa, Kon

Christie, Agatha (Mary Clarissa)
 1890-1976 .. **CLC 1, 6, 8, 12, 39, 48, 110**
 See also AAYA 9; AITN 1, 2; BPFB 1;
 BRWS 2; CA 17-20R; 61-64; CANR 10,
 37, 108; CBD; CDBLB 1914-1945; CMW
 4; CN 1, 2; CPW; CWD; DA3; DAB;
 DAC; DAM NOV; DFS 2; DLB 13, 77,
 245; MSW; MTCW 1, 2; MTFW 2005;
 NFS 8; RGEL 2; RHW; SATA 36; TEA;
 YAW

Christie, Philippa **CLC 21**
 See Pearce, Philippa
 See also BYA 5; CANR 109; CLR 9; DLB
 161; MAICYA 1; SATA 1, 67, 129

Christine de Pizan 1365(?)-1431(?) **LC 9;**
 PC 68
 See also DLB 208; RGWL 2, 3

Chuang Tzu c. 369B.C.-c.
 286B.C. **CMLC 57**

Chubb, Elmer
 See Masters, Edgar Lee

Chulkov, Mikhail Dmitrievich
 1743-1792 **LC 2**
 See also DLB 150

Churchill, Caryl 1938- **CLC 31, 55, 157;**
 DC 5
 See Churchill, Chick
 See also BRWS 4; CA 102; CANR 22, 46,
 108; CBD; CD 6; CWD; DFS 12, 16;
 DLB 13, 310; EWL 3; FW; MTCW 1;
 RGEL 2

Churchill, Charles 1731-1764 **LC 3**
 See also DLB 109; RGEL 2

Churchill, Chick
 See Churchill, Caryl
 See also CD 5

Churchill, Sir Winston (Leonard Spencer)
 1874-1965 **TCLC 113**
 See also BRW 6; CA 97-100; CDBLB
 1890-1914; DA3; DLB 100; DLBD 16;
 LAIT 4; MTCW 1, 2

Chute, Carolyn 1947- **CLC 39**
 See also CA 123; CANR 135; CN 7

Ciardi, John (Anthony) 1916-1986 . **CLC 10,**
 40, 44, 129; PC 69
 See also CA 5-8R; 118; CAAS 2; CANR 5,
 33; CLR 19; CP 1, 2, 3, 4; CWRI 5; DAM
 POET; DLB 5; DLBY 1986; INT
 CANR-5; MAICYA 1, 2; MAL 5; MTCW
 1, 2; MTFW 2005; RGAL 4; SAAS 26;
 SATA 1, 65; SATA-Obit 46

Cibber, Colley 1671-1757 **LC 66**
 See also DLB 84; RGEL 2

Cicero, Marcus Tullius
 106B.C.-43B.C. **CMLC 3, 81**
 See also AW 1; CDWLB 1; DLB 211;
 RGWL 2, 3; WLIT 8

Cimino, Michael 1943- **CLC 16**
 See also CA 105

Cioran, E(mil) M. 1911-1995 **CLC 64**
 See also CA 25-28R; 149; CANR 91; DLB
 220; EWL 3

Cisneros, Sandra 1954- **CLC 69, 118, 193;**
 HLC 1; PC 52; SSC 32, 72
 See also AAYA 9, 53; AMWS 7; CA 131;
 CANR 64, 118; CN 7; CWP; DA3; DAM
 MULT; DLB 122, 152; EWL 3; EXPN;
 FL 1:5; FW; HW 1, 2; LAIT 5; LATS 1:2;
 LLW; MAICYA 2; MAL 5; MTCW 2;
 MTFW 2005; NFS 2; PFS 19; RGAL 4;
 RGSF 2; SSFS 3, 13; WLIT 1; YAW

Cixous, Helene 1937- **CLC 92**
 See also CA 126; CANR 55, 123; CWW 2;
 DLB 83, 242; EWL 3; FL 1:5; FW; GLL
 2; MTCW 1, 2; MTFW 2005; TWA

Clair, Rene .. **CLC 20**
 See Chomette, Rene Lucien

Clampitt, Amy 1920-1994 **CLC 32; PC 19**
 See also AMWS 9; CA 110; 146; CANR
 29, 79; CP 4, 5; DLB 105; MAL 5

Clancy, Thomas L., Jr. 1947-
 See Clancy, Tom
 See also CA 125; 131; CANR 62, 105;
 DA3; INT CA-131; MTCW 1, 2; MTFW
 2005

Clancy, Tom **CLC 45, 112**
 See Clancy, Thomas L., Jr.
 See also AAYA 9, 51; BEST 89:1, 90:1;
 BPFB 1; BYA 10, 11; CANR 132; CMW
 4; CPW; DAM NOV, POP; DLB 227

Clare, John 1793-1864 .. **NCLC 9, 86; PC 23**
 See also BRWS 11; DAB; DAM POET;
 DLB 55, 96; RGEL 2

Clarin
 See Alas (y Urena), Leopoldo (Enrique
 Garcia)

Clark, Al C.
 See Goines, Donald

Clark, Brian (Robert)
 See Clark, (Robert) Brian
 See also CD 6

Clark, (Robert) Brian 1932- **CLC 29**
 See Clark, Brian (Robert)
 See also CA 41-44R; CANR 67; CBD; CD
 5

Clark, Curt
 See Westlake, Donald E(dwin)

Clark, Eleanor 1913-1996 **CLC 5, 19**
 See also CA 9-12R; 151; CANR 41; CN 1,
 2, 3, 4, 5, 6; DLB 6

Clark, J. P.
 See Clark Bekederemo, J(ohnson) P(epper)
 See also CDWLB 3; DLB 117

Clark, John Pepper
 See Clark Bekederemo, J(ohnson) P(epper)
 See also AFW; CD 5; CP 1, 2, 3, 4, 5, 6, 7;
 RGEL 2

Clark, Kenneth (Mackenzie)
 1903-1983 **TCLC 147**
 See also CA 93-96; 109; CANR 36; MTCW
 1, 2; MTFW 2005

Clark, M. R.
 See Clark, Mavis Thorpe

Clark, Mavis Thorpe 1909-1999 **CLC 12**
 See also CA 57-60; CANR 8, 37, 107; CLR
 30; CWRI 5; MAICYA 1, 2; SAAS 5;
 SATA 8, 74

Clark, Walter Van Tilburg
 1909-1971 **CLC 28**
 See also CA 9-12R; 33-36R; CANR 63,
 113; CN 1; DLB 9, 206; LAIT 2; MAL 5;
 RGAL 4; SATA 8; TCWW 1, 2

Clark Bekederemo, J(ohnson) P(epper)
 1935- **BLC 1; CLC 38; DC 5**
 See Bekederemo, J. P. Clark; Clark, J. P.;
 Clark, John Pepper
 See also BW 1; CA 65-68; CANR 16, 72;
 DAM DRAM, MULT; DFS 13; EWL 3;
 MTCW 2; MTFW 2005

Clarke, Arthur C(harles) 1917- **CLC 1, 4,**
 13, 18, 35, 136; SSC 3
 See also AAYA 4, 33; BPFB 1; BYA 13;
 CA 1-4R; CANR 2, 28, 55, 74, 130; CN
 1, 2, 3, 4, 5, 6, 7; CPW; DA3; DAM POP;
 DLB 261; JRDA; LAIT 5; MAICYA 1, 2;
 MTCW 1, 2; MTFW 2005; SATA 13, 70,
 115; SCFW 1, 2; SFW 4; SSFS 4, 18;
 TCLE 1:1; YAW

Clarke, Austin 1896-1974 **CLC 6, 9**
 See also CA 29-32; 49-52; CAP 2; CP 1, 2;
 DAM POET; DLB 10, 20; EWL 3; RGEL
 2

Clarke, Austin C(hesterfield) 1934- .. **BLC 1;**
 CLC 8, 53; SSC 45
 See also BW 1; CA 25-28R; CAAS 16;
 CANR 14, 32, 68, 140; CN 1, 2, 3, 4, 5,
 6, 7; DAC; DAM MULT; DLB 53, 125;
 DNFS 2; MTCW 2; MTFW 2005; RGSF
 2

Clarke, Gillian 1937- **CLC 61**
See also CA 106; CP 3, 4, 5, 6, 7; CWP;
DLB 40

Clarke, Marcus (Andrew Hislop)
1846-1881 **NCLC 19**
See also DLB 230; RGEL 2; RGSF 2

Clarke, Shirley 1925-1997 **CLC 16**
See also CA 189

Clash, The
See Headon, (Nicky) Topper; Jones, Mick;
Simonon, Paul; Strummer, Joe

Claudel, Paul (Louis Charles Marie)
1868-1955 **TCLC 2, 10**
See also CA 104; 165; DLB 192, 258, 321;
EW 8; EWL 3; GFL 1789 to the Present;
RGWL 2, 3; TWA

Claudian 370(?)-404(?) **CMLC 46**
See also RGWL 2, 3

Claudius, Matthias 1740-1815 **NCLC 75**
See also DLB 97

Clavell, James (duMaresq)
1925-1994 **CLC 6, 25, 87**
See also BPFB 1; CA 25-28R; 146; CANR
26, 48; CN 5; CPW; DA3; DAM NOV,
POP; MTCW 1, 2; MTFW 2005; NFS 10;
RHW

Clayman, Gregory **CLC 65**

Cleaver, (Leroy) Eldridge
1935-1998 **BLC 1; CLC 30, 119**
See also BW 1, 3; CA 21-24R; 167; CANR
16, 75; DA3; DAM MULT; MTCW 2;
YAW

Cleese, John (Marwood) 1939- **CLC 21**
See Monty Python
See also CA 112; 116; CANR 35; MTCW 1

Cleishbotham, Jebediah
See Scott, Sir Walter

Cleland, John 1710-1789 **LC 2, 48**
See also DLB 39; RGEL 2

Clemens, Samuel Langhorne 1835-1910
See Twain, Mark
See also CA 104; 135; CDALB 1865-1917;
DA; DA3; DAB; DAC; DAM MST, NOV;
DLB 12, 23, 64, 74, 186, 189; JRDA;
LMFS 1; MAICYA 1, 2; NCFS 4; NFS
20; SATA 100; YABC 2

Clement of Alexandria
150(?)-215(?) **CMLC 41**

Cleophil
See Congreve, William

Clerihew, E.
See Bentley, E(dmund) C(lerihew)

Clerk, N. W.
See Lewis, C.S.

Cleveland, John 1613-1658 **LC 106**
See also DLB 126; RGEL 2

Cliff, Jimmy **CLC 21**
See Chambers, James
See also CA 193

Cliff, Michelle 1946- **BLCS; CLC 120**
See also BW 2; CA 116; CANR 39, 72; CD-
WLB 3; DLB 157; FW; GLL 2

Clifford, Lady Anne 1590-1676 **LC 76**
See also DLB 151

Clifton, (Thelma) Lucille 1936- **BLC 1;
CLC 19, 66, 162; PC 17**
See also AFAW 2; BW 2, 3; CA 49-52;
CANR 2, 24, 42, 76, 97, 138; CLR 5; CP
2, 3, 4, 5, 6, 7; CSW; CWP; CWRI 5;
DA3; DAM MULT, POET; DLB 5, 41;
EXPP; MAICYA 1, 2; MTCW 1, 2;
MTFW 2005; PFS 1, 14; SATA 20, 69,
128; WP

Clinton, Dirk
See Silverberg, Robert

Clough, Arthur Hugh 1819-1861 .. **NCLC 27,
163**
See also BRW 5; DLB 32; RGEL 2

Clutha, Janet Paterson Frame 1924-2004
See Frame, Janet
See also CA 1-4R; 224; CANR 2, 36, 76,
135; MTCW 1, 2; SATA 119

Clyne, Terence
See Blatty, William Peter

Cobalt, Martin
See Mayne, William (James Carter)

Cobb, Irvin S(hrewsbury)
1876-1944 **TCLC 77**
See also CA 175; DLB 11, 25, 86

Cobbett, William 1763-1835 **NCLC 49**
See also DLB 43, 107, 158; RGEL 2

Coburn, D(onald) L(ee) 1938- **CLC 10**
See also CA 89-92; DFS 23

Cocteau, Jean (Maurice Eugene Clement)
1889-1963 **CLC 1, 8, 15, 16, 43; DC
17; TCLC 119; WLC 2**
See also CA 25-28; CANR 40; CAP 2; DA;
DA3; DAB; DAC; DAM DRAM, MST,
NOV; DLB 65, 258, 321; EW 10; EWL
3; GFL 1789 to the Present; MTCW 1, 2;
RGWL 2, 3; TWA

Codrescu, Andrei 1946- **CLC 46, 121**
See also CA 33-36R; CAAS 19; CANR 13,
34, 53, 76, 125; CN 7; DA3; DAM POET;
MAL 5; MTCW 2; MTFW 2005

Coe, Max
See Bourne, Randolph S(illiman)

Coe, Tucker
See Westlake, Donald E(dwin)

Coen, Ethan 1958- **CLC 108**
See also AAYA 54; CA 126; CANR 85

Coen, Joel 1955- **CLC 108**
See also AAYA 54; CA 126; CANR 119

The Coen Brothers
See Coen, Ethan; Coen, Joel

Coetzee, J. M. 1940- **CLC 23, 33, 66, 117,
161, 162**
See also AAYA 37; AFW; BRWS 6; CA 77-
80; CANR 41, 54, 74, 114, 133; CN 4, 5,
6, 7; DA3; DAM NOV; DLB 225, 326;
EWL 3; LMFS 2; MTCW 1, 2; MTFW
2005; NFS 21; WLIT 2; WWE 1

Coetzee, John Maxwell
See Coetzee, J. M.

Coffey, Brian
See Koontz, Dean R.

Coffin, Robert P(eter) Tristram
1892-1955 **TCLC 95**
See also CA 123; 169; DLB 45

Cohan, George M. 1878-1942 **TCLC 60**
See also CA 157; DLB 249; RGAL 4

Cohan, George Michael
See Cohan, George M.

Cohen, Arthur A(llen) 1928-1986 **CLC 7,
31**
See also CA 1-4R; 120; CANR 1, 17, 42;
DLB 28; RGHL

Cohen, Leonard 1934- **CLC 3, 38**
See also CA 21-24R; CANR 14, 69; CN 1,
2, 3, 4, 5, 6; CP 1, 2, 3, 4, 5, 6, 7; DAC;
DAM MST; DLB 53; EWL 3; MTCW 1

Cohen, Leonard Norman
See Cohen, Leonard

Cohen, Matt(hew) 1942-1999 **CLC 19**
See also CA 61-64; 187; CAAS 18; CANR
40; CN 1, 2, 3, 4, 5, 6; DAC; DLB 53

Cohen-Solal, Annie 1948- **CLC 50**
See also CA 239

Colegate, Isabel 1931- **CLC 36**
See also CA 17-20R; CANR 8, 22, 74; CN
4, 5, 6, 7; DLB 14, 231; INT CANR-22;
MTCW 1

Coleman, Emmett
See Reed, Ishmael (Scott)

Coleridge, Hartley 1796-1849 **NCLC 90**
See also DLB 96

Coleridge, M. E.
See Coleridge, Mary E(lizabeth)

Coleridge, Mary E(lizabeth)
1861-1907 **TCLC 73**
See also CA 116; 166; DLB 19, 98

Coleridge, Samuel Taylor
1772-1834 **NCLC 9, 54, 99, 111; PC
11, 39, 67; WLC 2**
See also AAYA 66; BRW 4; BRWR 2; BYA
4; CDBLB 1789-1832; DA; DA3; DAB;
DAC; DAM MST, POET; DLB 93, 107;
EXPP; LATS 1:1; LMFS 1; PAB; PFS 4,
5; RGEL 2; TEA; WLIT 3; WP

Coleridge, Sara 1802-1852 **NCLC 31**
See also DLB 199

Coles, Don 1928- **CLC 46**
See also CA 115; CANR 38; CP 5, 6, 7

Coles, Robert (Martin) 1929- **CLC 108**
See also CA 45-48; CANR 3, 32, 66, 70,
135; INT CANR-32; SATA 23

Colette, (Sidonie-Gabrielle)
1873-1954 .. **SSC 10, 93; TCLC 1, 5, 16**
See Willy, Colette
See also CA 104; 131; DA3; DAM NOV;
DLB 65; EW 9; EWL 3; GFL 1789 to the
Present; MTCW 1, 2; MTFW 2005;
RGWL 2, 3; TWA

Collett, (Jacobine) Camilla (Wergeland)
1813-1895 **NCLC 22**

Collier, Christopher 1930- **CLC 30**
See also AAYA 13; BYA 2; CA 33-36R;
CANR 13, 33, 102; CLR 3; JRDA; MAICYA 1,
2; SATA 16, 70; WYA; YAW 1

Collier, James Lincoln 1928- **CLC 30**
See also AAYA 13; BYA 2; CA 9-12R;
CANR 4, 33, 60, 102; CLR 3; DAM POP;
JRDA; MAICYA 1, 2; SAAS 21; SATA 8,
70, 166; WYA; YAW 1

Collier, Jeremy 1650-1726 **LC 6**

Collier, John 1901-1980 . **SSC 19; TCLC 127**
See also CA 65-68; 97-100; CANR 10; CN
1, 2; DLB 77, 255; FANT; SUFW 1

Collier, Mary 1690-1762 **LC 86**
See also DLB 95

Collingwood, R(obin) G(eorge)
1889(?)-1943 **TCLC 67**
See also CA 117; 155; DLB 262

Collins, Billy 1941- **PC 68**
See also AAYA 64; CA 151; CANR 92; CP
7; MTFW 2005; PFS 18

Collins, Hunt
See Hunter, Evan

Collins, Linda 1931- **CLC 44**
See also CA 125

Collins, Tom
See Furphy, Joseph
See also RGEL 2

Collins, (William) Wilkie
1824-1889 **NCLC 1, 18, 93; SSC 93**
See also BRWS 6; CDBLB 1832-1890;
CMW 4; DLB 18, 70, 159; GL 2; MSW;
RGEL 2; RGSF 2; SUFW 1; WLIT 4

Collins, William 1721-1759 **LC 4, 40; PC
72**
See also BRW 3; DAM POET; DLB 109;
RGEL 2

Collodi, Carlo **NCLC 54**
See Lorenzini, Carlo
See also CLR 5; WCH; WLIT 7

Colman, George
See Glassco, John

Colman, George, the Elder
1732-1794 **LC 98**
See also RGEL 2

Colonna, Vittoria 1492-1547 **LC 71**
See also RGWL 2, 3

Colt, Winchester Remington
See Hubbard, L. Ron

Colter, Cyrus J. 1910-2002 **CLC 58**
See also BW 1; CA 65-68; 205; CANR 10, 66; CN 2, 3, 4, 5, 6; DLB 33

Colton, James
See Hansen, Joseph
See also GLL 1

Colum, Padraic 1881-1972 **CLC 28**
See also BYA 4; CA 73-76; 33-36R; CANR 35; CLR 36; CP 1; CWRI 5; DLB 19; MAICYA 1, 2; MTCW 1; RGEL 2; SATA 15; WCH

Colvin, James
See Moorcock, Michael

Colwin, Laurie (E.) 1944-1992 **CLC 5, 13, 23, 84**
See also CA 89-92; 139; CANR 20, 46; DLB 218; DLBY 1980; MTCW 1

Comfort, Alex(ander) 1920-2000 **CLC 7**
See also CA 1-4R; 190; CANR 1, 45; CN 1, 2, 3, 4; CP 1, 2, 3, 4, 5, 6, 7; DAM POP; MTCW 2

Comfort, Montgomery
See Campbell, (John) Ramsey

Compton-Burnett, I(vy)
1892(?)-1969 **CLC 1, 3, 10, 15, 34; TCLC 180**
See also BRW 7; CA 1-4R; 25-28R; CANR 4; DAM NOV; DLB 36; EWL 3; MTCW 1, 2; RGEL 2

Comstock, Anthony 1844-1915 **TCLC 13**
See also CA 110; 169

Comte, Auguste 1798-1857 **NCLC 54**

Conan Doyle, Arthur
See Doyle, Sir Arthur Conan
See also BPFB 1; BYA 4, 5, 11

Conde (Abellan), Carmen
1901-1996 **HLCS 1**
See also CA 177; CWW 2; DLB 108; EWL 3; HW 2

Conde, Maryse 1937- **BLCS; CLC 52, 92**
See also BW 2, 3; CA 110; 190; CAAE 190; CANR 30, 53, 76; CWW 2; DAM MULT; EWL 3; MTCW 2; MTFW 2005

Condillac, Etienne Bonnot de
1714-1780 **LC 26**
See also DLB 313

Condon, Richard (Thomas)
1915-1996 **CLC 4, 6, 8, 10, 45, 100**
See also BEST 90:3; BPFB 1; CA 1-4R; 151; CAAS 1; CANR 2, 23; CMW 4; CN 1, 2, 3, 4, 5, 6; DAM NOV; INT CANR-23; MAL 5; MTCW 1, 2

Condorcet .. **LC 104**
See Condorcet, marquis de Marie-Jean-Antoine-Nicolas Caritat
See also GFL Beginnings to 1789

Condorcet, marquis de
Marie-Jean-Antoine-Nicolas Caritat
1743-1794
See Condorcet
See also DLB 313

Confucius 551B.C.-479B.C. **CMLC 19, 65; WLCS**
See also DA; DA3; DAB; DAC; DAM MST

Congreve, William 1670-1729 ... **DC 2; LC 5, 21; WLC 2**
See also BRW 2; CDBLB 1660-1789; DA; DAB; DAC; DAM DRAM, MST, POET; DFS 15; DLB 39, 84; RGEL 2; WLIT 3

Conley, Robert J(ackson) 1940- **NNAL**
See also CA 41-44R; CANR 15, 34, 45, 96; DAM MULT; TCWW 2

Connell, Evan S(helby), Jr. 1924- . **CLC 4, 6, 45**
See also AAYA 7; AMWS 14; CA 1-4R; CAAS 2; CANR 2, 39, 76, 97, 140; CN 1, 2, 3, 4, 5, 6; DAM NOV; DLB 2; DLBY 1981; MAL 5; MTCW 1, 2; MTFW 2005

Connelly, Marc(us Cook) 1890-1980 . **CLC 7**
See also CA 85-88; 102; CAD; CANR 30; DFS 12; DLB 7; DLBY 1980; MAL 5; RGAL 4; SATA-Obit 25

Connor, Ralph **TCLC 31**
See Gordon, Charles William
See also DLB 92; TCWW 1, 2

Conrad, Joseph 1857-1924 **SSC 9, 67, 69, 71; TCLC 1, 6, 13, 25, 43, 57; WLC 2**
See also AAYA 26; BPFB 1; BRW 6; BRWC 1; BRWR 2; BYA 2; CA 104; 131; CANR 60; CDBLB 1890-1914; DA; DA3; DAB; DAC; DAM MST, NOV; DLB 10, 34, 98, 156; EWL 3; EXPN; EXPS; LAIT 2; LATS 1:1; LMFS 1; MTCW 1, 2; MTFW 2005; NFS 2, 16; RGEL 2; RGSF 2; SATA 27; SSFS 1, 12; TEA; WLIT 4

Conrad, Robert Arnold
See Hart, Moss

Conroy, (Donald) Pat(rick) 1945- ... **CLC 30, 74**
See also AAYA 8, 52; AITN 1; BPFB 1; CA 85-88; CANR 24, 53, 129; CN 7; CPW; CSW; DA3; DAM NOV, POP; DLB 6; LAIT 5; MAL 5; MTCW 1, 2; MTFW 2005

Constant (de Rebecque), (Henri) Benjamin
1767-1830 **NCLC 6**
See also DLB 119; EW 4; GFL 1789 to the Present

Conway, Jill K(er) 1934- **CLC 152**
See also CA 130; CANR 94

Conybeare, Charles Augustus
See Eliot, T(homas) S(tearns)

Cook, Michael 1933-1994 **CLC 58**
See also CA 93-96; CANR 68; DLB 53

Cook, Robin 1940- **CLC 14**
See also AAYA 32; BEST 90:2; BPFB 1; CA 108; 111; CANR 41, 90, 109; CPW; DA3; DAM POP; HGG; INT CA-111

Cook, Roy
See Silverberg, Robert

Cooke, Elizabeth 1948- **CLC 55**
See also CA 129

Cooke, John Esten 1830-1886 **NCLC 5**
See also DLB 3, 248; RGAL 4

Cooke, John Estes
See Baum, L(yman) Frank

Cooke, M. E.
See Creasey, John

Cooke, Margaret
See Creasey, John

Cooke, Rose Terry 1827-1892 **NCLC 110**
See also DLB 12, 74

Cook-Lynn, Elizabeth 1930- **CLC 93; NNAL**
See also CA 133; DAM MULT; DLB 175

Cooney, Ray **CLC 62**
See also CBD

Cooper, Anthony Ashley 1671-1713 .. **LC 107**
See also DLB 101

Cooper, Dennis 1953- **CLC 203**
See also CA 133; CANR 72, 86; GLL 1; HGG

Cooper, Douglas 1960- **CLC 86**

Cooper, Henry St. John
See Creasey, John

Cooper, J(oan) California (?)- **CLC 56**
See also AAYA 12; BW 1; CA 125; CANR 55; DAM MULT; DLB 212

Cooper, James Fenimore
1789-1851 **NCLC 1, 27, 54**
See also AAYA 22; AMW; BPFB 1; CDALB 1640-1865; CLR 105; DA3; DLB 3, 183, 250, 254; LAIT 1; NFS 9; RGAL 4; SATA 19; TUS; WCH

Cooper, Susan Fenimore
1813-1894 **NCLC 129**
See also ANW; DLB 239, 254

Coover, Robert (Lowell) 1932- **CLC 3, 7, 15, 32, 46, 87, 161; SSC 15**
See also AMWS 5; BPFB 1; CA 45-48; CANR 3, 37, 58, 115; CN 1, 2, 3, 4, 5, 6, 7; DAM NOV; DLB 2, 227; DLBY 1981; EWL 3; MAL 5; MTCW 1, 2; MTFW 2005; RGAL 4; RGSF 2

Copeland, Stewart (Armstrong)
1952- **CLC 26**

Copernicus, Nicolaus 1473-1543 **LC 45**

Coppard, A(lfred) E(dgar)
1878-1957 **SSC 21; TCLC 5**
See also BRWS 8; CA 114; 167; DLB 162; EWL 3; HGG; RGEL 2; RGSF 2; SUFW 1; YABC 1

Coppee, Francois 1842-1908 **TCLC 25**
See also CA 170; DLB 217

Coppola, Francis Ford 1939- ... **CLC 16, 126**
See also AAYA 39; CA 77-80; CANR 40, 78; DLB 44

Copway, George 1818-1869 **NNAL**
See also DAM MULT; DLB 175, 183

Corbiere, Tristan 1845-1875 **NCLC 43**
See also DLB 217; GFL 1789 to the Present

Corcoran, Barbara (Asenath)
1911- **CLC 17**
See also AAYA 14; CA 21-24R; 191; CAAE 191; CAAS 2; CANR 11, 28, 48; CLR 50; DLB 52; JRDA; MAICYA 2; MAIC-YAS 1; RHW; SAAS 20; SATA 3, 77; SATA-Essay 125

Cordelier, Maurice
See Giraudoux, Jean(-Hippolyte)

Corelli, Marie **TCLC 51**
See Mackay, Mary
See also DLB 34, 156; RGEL 2; SUFW 1

Corinna c. 225B.C.-c. 305B.C. **CMLC 72**

Corman, Cid **CLC 9**
See Corman, Sidney
See also CAAS 2; CP 1, 2, 3, 4, 5, 6, 7; DLB 5, 193

Corman, Sidney 1924-2004
See Corman, Cid
See also CA 85-88; 225; CANR 44; DAM POET

Cormier, Robert (Edmund)
1925-2000 **CLC 12, 30**
See also AAYA 3, 19; BYA 1, 2, 6, 8, 9; CA 1-4R; CANR 5, 23, 76, 93; CDALB 1968-1988; CLR 12, 55; DA; DAB; DAC; DAM MST, NOV; DLB 52; EXPN; INT CANR-23; JRDA; LAIT 5; MAICYA 1, 2; MTCW 1, 2; MTFW 2005; NFS 2, 18; SATA 10, 45, 83; SATA-Obit 122; WYA; YAW

Corn, Alfred (DeWitt III) 1943- **CLC 33**
See also CA 179; CAAE 179; CAAS 25; CANR 44; CP 3, 4, 5, 6, 7; CSW; DLB 120, 282; DLBY 1980

Corneille, Pierre 1606-1684 ... **DC 21; LC 28**
See also DAB; DAM MST; DFS 21; DLB 268; EW 3; GFL Beginnings to 1789; RGWL 2, 3; TWA

Cornwell, David (John Moore)
1931- **CLC 9, 15**
See le Carre, John
See also CA 5-8R; CANR 13, 33, 59, 107, 132; DA3; DAM POP; MTCW 1, 2; MTFW 2005

Cornwell, Patricia 1956- **CLC 155**
See also AAYA 16, 56; BPFB 1; CA 134; CANR 53, 131; CMW 4; CPW; CSW; DAM POP; DLB 306; MSW; MTCW 2; MTFW 2005

Cornwell, Patricia Daniels
See Cornwell, Patricia

Corso, (Nunzio) Gregory 1930-2001 . **CLC 1, 11; PC 33**
See also AMWS 12; BG 1:2; CA 5-8R; 193; CANR 41, 76, 132; CP 1, 2, 3, 4, 5, 6, 7; DA3; DLB 5, 16, 237; LMFS 2; MAL 5; MTCW 1, 2; MTFW 2005; WP

Cortazar, Julio 1914-1984 ... **CLC 2, 3, 5, 10, 13, 15, 33, 34, 92; HLC 1; SSC 7, 76**
See also BPFB 1; CA 21-24R; CANR 12, 32, 81; CDWLB 3; DA3; DAM MULT, NOV; DLB 113; EWL 3; EXPS; HW 1, 2; LAW; MTCW 1, 2; MTFW 2005; RGSF 2; RGWL 2, 3; SSFS 3, 20; TWA; WLIT 1

Cortes, Hernan 1485-1547 **LC 31**

Corvinus, Jakob
See Raabe, Wilhelm (Karl)

Corwin, Cecil
See Kornbluth, C(yril) M.

Cosic, Dobrica 1921- **CLC 14**
See also CA 122; 138; CDWLB 4; CWW 2; DLB 181; EWL 3

Costain, Thomas B(ertram)
1885-1965 **CLC 30**
See also BYA 3; CA 5-8R; 25-28R; DLB 9; RHW

Costantini, Humberto 1924(?)-1987 . **CLC 49**
See also CA 131; 122; EWL 3; HW 1

Costello, Elvis 1954- **CLC 21**
See also CA 204

Costenoble, Philostene
See Ghelderode, Michel de

Cotes, Cecil V.
See Duncan, Sara Jeannette

Cotter, Joseph Seamon Sr.
1861-1949 **BLC 1; TCLC 28**
See also BW 1; CA 124; DAM MULT; DLB 50

Couch, Arthur Thomas Quiller
See Quiller-Couch, Sir Arthur (Thomas)

Coulton, James
See Hansen, Joseph

Couperus, Louis (Marie Anne)
1863-1923 **TCLC 15**
See also CA 115; EWL 3; RGWL 2, 3

Coupland, Douglas 1961- **CLC 85, 133**
See also AAYA 34; CA 142; CANR 57, 90, 130; CCA 1; CN 7; CPW; DAC; DAM POP

Court, Wesli
See Turco, Lewis (Putnam)

Courtenay, Bryce 1933- **CLC 59**
See also CA 138; CPW

Courtney, Robert
See Ellison, Harlan (Jay)

Cousteau, Jacques-Yves 1910-1997 .. **CLC 30**
See also CA 65-68; 159; CANR 15, 67; MTCW 1; SATA 38, 98

Coventry, Francis 1725-1754 **LC 46**

Coverdale, Miles c. 1487-1569 **LC 77**
See also DLB 167

Cowan, Peter (Walkinshaw)
1914-2002 **SSC 28**
See also CA 21-24R; CANR 9, 25, 50, 83; CN 1, 2, 3, 4, 5, 6, 7; DLB 260; RGSF 2

Coward, Noel (Peirce) 1899-1973 . **CLC 1, 9, 29, 51**
See also AITN 1; BRWS 2; CA 17-18; 41-44R; CANR 35, 132; CAP 2; CBD; CD-BLB 1914-1945; DA3; DAM DRAM; DFS 3, 6; DLB 10, 245; EWL 3; IDFW 3, 4; LAW; MTCW 1, 2; MTFW 2005; RGEL 2; TEA

Cowley, Abraham 1618-1667 **LC 43**
See also BRW 2; DLB 131, 151; PAB; RGEL 2

Cowley, Malcolm 1898-1989 **CLC 39**
See also AMWS 2; CA 5-8R; 128; CANR 3, 55; CP 1, 2, 3, 4; DLB 4, 48; DLBY 1981, 1989; EWL 3; MAL 5; MTCW 1, 2; MTFW 2005

Cowper, William 1731-1800 **NCLC 8, 94; PC 40**
See also BRW 3; DA3; DAM POET; DLB 104, 109; RGEL 2

Cox, William Trevor 1928-
See Trevor, William
See also CA 9-12R; CANR 4, 37, 55, 76, 102, 139; DAM NOV; INT CANR-37; MTCW 1, 2; MTFW 2005; TEA

Coyne, P. J.
See Masters, Hilary

Cozzens, James Gould 1903-1978 . **CLC 1, 4, 11, 92**
See also AMW; BPFB 1; CA 9-12R; 81-84; CANR 19; CDALB 1941-1968; CN 1, 2; DLB 9, 294; DLBD 2; DLBY 1984, 1997; EWL 3; MAL 5; MTCW 1, 2; MTFW 2005; RGAL 4

Crabbe, George 1754-1832 **NCLC 26, 121**
See also BRW 3; DLB 93; RGEL 2

Crace, Jim 1946- **CLC 157; SSC 61**
See also CA 128; 135; CANR 55, 70, 123; CN 5, 6, 7; DLB 231; INT CA-135

Craddock, Charles Egbert
See Murfree, Mary Noailles

Craig, A. A.
See Anderson, Poul (William)

Craik, Mrs.
See Craik, Dinah Maria (Mulock)
See also RGEL 2

Craik, Dinah Maria (Mulock)
1826-1887 **NCLC 38**
See Craik, Mrs.; Mulock, Dinah Maria
See also DLB 35, 163; MAICYA 1, 2; SATA 34

Cram, Ralph Adams 1863-1942 **TCLC 45**
See also CA 160

Cranch, Christopher Pearse
1813-1892 **NCLC 115**
See also DLB 1, 42, 243

Crane, (Harold) Hart 1899-1932 **PC 3; TCLC 2, 5, 80; WLC 2**
See also AMW; AMWR 2; CA 104; 127; CDALB 1917-1929; DA; DA3; DAB; DAC; DAM MST, POET; DLB 4, 48; EWL 3; MAL 5; MTCW 1, 2; MTFW 2005; RGAL 4; TUS

Crane, R(onald) S(almon)
1886-1967 **CLC 27**
See also CA 85-88; DLB 63

Crane, Stephen (Townley)
1871-1900 **SSC 7, 56, 70; TCLC 11, 17, 32; WLC 2**
See also AAYA 21; AMW; AMWC 1; BPFB 1; BYA 3; CA 109; 140; CANR 84; CDALB 1865-1917; DA; DA3; DAB; DAC; DAM MST, NOV, POET; DLB 12, 54, 78; EXPN; EXPS; LAIT 2; LMFS 2; MAL 5; NFS 4, 20; PFS 9; RGAL 4; RGSF 2; SSFS 4; TUS; WYA; YABC 2

Cranmer, Thomas 1489-1556 **LC 95**
See also DLB 132, 213

Cranshaw, Stanley
See Fisher, Dorothy (Frances) Canfield

Crase, Douglas 1944- **CLC 58**
See also CA 106

Crashaw, Richard 1612(?)-1649 **LC 24**
See also BRW 2; DLB 126; PAB; RGEL 2

Cratinus c. 519B.C.-c. 422B.C. **CMLC 54**
See also LMFS 1

Craven, Margaret 1901-1980 **CLC 17**
See also BYA 2; CA 103; CCA 1; DAC; LAIT 5

Crawford, F(rancis) Marion
1854-1909 **TCLC 10**
See also CA 107; 168; DLB 71; HGG; RGAL 4; SUFW 1

Crawford, Isabella Valancy
1850-1887 **NCLC 12, 127**
See also DLB 92; RGEL 2

Crayon, Geoffrey
See Irving, Washington

Creasey, John 1908-1973 **CLC 11**
See Marric, J. J.
See also CA 5-8R; 41-44R; CANR 8, 59; CMW 4; DLB 77; MTCW 1

Crebillon, Claude Prosper Jolyot de (fils)
1707-1777 **LC 1, 28**
See also DLB 313; GFL Beginnings to 1789

Credo
See Creasey, John

Credo, Alvaro J. de
See Prado (Calvo), Pedro

Creeley, Robert 1926-2005 **CLC 1, 2, 4, 8, 11, 15, 36, 78**
See also AMWS 4; CA 1-4R; 237; CAAS 10; CANR 23, 43, 89, 137; CP 1, 2, 3, 4, 5, 6, 7; DA3; DAM POET; DLB 5, 16, 169; DLBD 17; EWL 3; MAL 5; MTCW 1, 2; MTFW 2005; PFS 21; RGAL 4; WP

Creeley, Robert White
See Creeley, Robert

Crenne, Helisenne de 1510-1560 **LC 113**

Crevecoeur, Hector St. John de
See Crevecoeur, Michel Guillaume Jean de
See also ANW

Crevecoeur, Michel Guillaume Jean de
1735-1813 **NCLC 105**
See Crevecoeur, Hector St. John de
See also AMWS 1; DLB 37

Crevel, Rene 1900-1935 **TCLC 112**
See also GLL 2

Crews, Harry (Eugene) 1935- **CLC 6, 23, 49**
See also AITN 1; AMWS 11; BPFB 1; CA 25-28R; CANR 20, 57; CN 3, 4, 5, 6, 7; CSW; DA3; DLB 6, 143, 185; MTCW 1, 2; MTFW 2005; RGAL 4

Crichton, (John) Michael 1942- **CLC 2, 6, 54, 90**
See also AAYA 10, 49; AITN 2; BPFB 1; CA 25-28R; CANR 13, 40, 54, 76, 127; CMW 4; CN 2, 3, 6, 7; CPW; DA3; DAM NOV, POP; DLB 292; DLBY 1981; INT CANR-13; JRDA; MTCW 1, 2; MTFW 2005; SATA 9, 88; SFW 4; YAW

Crispin, Edmund **CLC 22**
See Montgomery, (Robert) Bruce
See also DLB 87; MSW

Cristina of Sweden 1626-1689 **LC 124**

Cristofer, Michael 1945(?)- **CLC 28**
See also CA 110; 152; CAD; CANR 150; CD 5, 6; DAM DRAM; DFS 15; DLB 7

Cristofer, Michael Ivan
See Cristofer, Michael

Criton
See Alain

Croce, Benedetto 1866-1952 **TCLC 37**
See also CA 120; 155; EW 8; EWL 3; WLIT 7

Crockett, David 1786-1836 **NCLC 8**
See also DLB 3, 11, 183, 248

Crockett, Davy
See Crockett, David

Crofts, Freeman Wills 1879-1957 .. **TCLC 55**
See also CA 115; 195; CMW 4; DLB 77; MSW

Croker, John Wilson 1780-1857 **NCLC 10**
See also DLB 110

Crommelynck, Fernand 1885-1970 .. **CLC 75**
See also CA 189; 89-92; EWL 3

Cromwell, Oliver 1599-1658 **LC 43**

Cronenberg, David 1943- **CLC 143**
See also CA 138; CCA 1

Cronin, A(rchibald) J(oseph)
1896-1981 **CLC 32**
See also BPFB 1; CA 1-4R; 102; CANR 5;
CN 2; DLB 191; SATA 47; SATA-Obit 25

Cross, Amanda
See Heilbrun, Carolyn G(old)
See also BPFB 1; CMW; CPW; DLB 306;
MSW

Crothers, Rachel 1878-1958 **TCLC 19**
See also CA 113; 194; CAD; CWD; DLB
7, 266; RGAL 4

Croves, Hal
See Traven, B.

Crow Dog, Mary (Ellen) (?)- **CLC 93**
See Brave Bird, Mary
See also CA 154

Crowfield, Christopher
See Stowe, Harriet (Elizabeth) Beecher

Crowley, Aleister **TCLC 7**
See Crowley, Edward Alexander
See also GLL 1

Crowley, Edward Alexander 1875-1947
See Crowley, Aleister
See also CA 104; HGG

Crowley, John 1942- **CLC 57**
See also AAYA 57; BPFB 1; CA 61-64;
CANR 43, 98, 138; DLBY 1982; FANT;
MTFW 2005; SATA 65, 140; SFW 4;
SUFW 2

Crowne, John 1641-1712 **LC 104**
See also DLB 80; RGEL 2

Crud
See Crumb, R.

Crumarums
See Crumb, R.

Crumb, R. 1943- **CLC 17**
See also CA 106; CANR 107, 150

Crumb, Robert
See Crumb, R.

Crumbum
See Crumb, R.

Crumski
See Crumb, R.

Crum the Bum
See Crumb, R.

Crunk
See Crumb, R.

Crustt
See Crumb, R.

Crutchfield, Les
See Trumbo, Dalton

Cruz, Victor Hernandez 1949- ... **HLC 1; PC
37**
See also BW 2; CA 65-68; CAAS 17;
CANR 14, 32, 74, 132; CP 1, 2, 3, 4, 5,
6, 7; DAM MULT, POET; DLB 41; DNFS
1; EXPP; HW 1, 2; LLW; MTCW 2;
MTFW 2005; PFS 16; WP

Cryer, Gretchen (Kiger) 1935- **CLC 21**
See also CA 114; 123

Csath, Geza **TCLC 13**
See Brenner, Jozef
See also CA 111

Cudlip, David R(ockwell) 1933- **CLC 34**
See also CA 177

Cullen, Countee 1903-1946 . **BLC 1; HR 1:2;
PC 20; TCLC 4, 37; WLCS**
See also AFAW 2; AMWS 4; BW 1; CA
108; 124; CDALB 1917-1929; DA; DA3;
DAC; DAM MST, MULT, POET; DLB 4,
48, 51; EWL 3; EXPP; LMFS 2; MAL 5;
MTCW 1, 2; MTFW 2005; PFS 3; RGAL
4; SATA 18; WP

Culleton, Beatrice 1949- **NNAL**
See also CA 120; CANR 83; DAC

Cum, R.
See Crumb, R.

Cumberland, Richard
1732-1811 **NCLC 167**
See also DLB 89; RGEL 2

Cummings, Bruce F(rederick) 1889-1919
See Barbellion, W. N. P.
See also CA 123

Cummings, E(dward) E(stlin)
1894-1962 .. **CLC 1, 3, 8, 12, 15, 68; PC
5; TCLC 137; WLC 2**
See also AAYA 41; AMW; CA 73-76;
CANR 31; CDALB 1929-1941; DA;
DA3; DAB; DAC; DAM MST, POET;
DLB 4, 48; EWL 3; EXPP; MAL 5;
MTCW 1, 2; MTFW 2005; PAB; PFS 1,
3, 12, 13, 19; RGAL 4; TUS; WP

Cummins, Maria Susanna
1827-1866 **NCLC 139**
See also DLB 42; YABC 1

Cunha, Euclides (Rodrigues Pimenta) da
1866-1909 **TCLC 24**
See also CA 123; 219; DLB 307; LAW;
WLIT 1

Cunningham, E. V.
See Fast, Howard (Melvin)

Cunningham, J(ames) V(incent)
1911-1985 **CLC 3, 31**
See also CA 1-4R; 115; CANR 1, 72; CP 1,
2, 3, 4; DLB 5

Cunningham, Julia (Woolfolk)
1916- .. **CLC 12**
See also CA 9-12R; CANR 4, 19, 36; CWRI
5; JRDA; MAICYA 1, 2; SAAS 2; SATA
1, 26, 132

Cunningham, Michael 1952- **CLC 34**
See also AMWS 15; CA 136; CANR 96;
CN 7; DLB 292; GLL 2; MTFW 2005;
NFS 23

Cunninghame Graham, R. B.
See Cunninghame Graham, Robert
(Gallnigad) Bontine

**Cunninghame Graham, Robert (Gallnigad)
Bontine** 1852-1936 **TCLC 19**
See Graham, R(obert) B(ontine) Cunning-
hame
See also CA 119; 184

Curnow, (Thomas) Allen (Monro)
1911-2001 **PC 48**
See also CA 69-72; 202; CANR 48, 99; CP
1, 2, 3, 4, 5, 6, 7; EWL 3; RGEL 2

Currie, Ellen 19(?)- **CLC 44**

Curtin, Philip
See Lowndes, Marie Adelaide (Belloc)

Curtin, Phillip
See Lowndes, Marie Adelaide (Belloc)

Curtis, Price
See Ellison, Harlan (Jay)

Cusanus, Nicolaus 1401-1464 **LC 80**
See Nicholas of Cusa

Cutrate, Joe
See Spiegelman, Art

Cynewulf c. 770- **CMLC 23**
See also DLB 146; RGEL 2

Cyrano de Bergerac, Savinien de
1619-1655 **LC 65**
See also DLB 268; GFL Beginnings to
1789; RGWL 2, 3

Cyril of Alexandria c. 375-c. 430 . **CMLC 59**

Czaczkes, Shmuel Yosef Halevi
See Agnon, S(hmuel) Y(osef Halevi)

Dabrowska, Maria (Szumska)
1889-1965 **CLC 15**
See also CA 106; CDWLB 4; DLB 215;
EWL 3

Dabydeen, David 1955- **CLC 34**
See also BW 1; CA 125; CANR 56, 92; CN
6, 7; CP 5, 6, 7

Dacey, Philip 1939- **CLC 51**
See also CA 37-40R, 231; CAAE 231;
CAAS 17; CANR 14, 32, 64; CP 4, 5, 6,
7; DLB 105

Dacre, Charlotte c. 1772-1825(?) . **NCLC 151**

Dafydd ap Gwilym c. 1320-c. 1380 **PC 56**

Dagerman, Stig (Halvard)
1923-1954 **TCLC 17**
See also CA 117; 155; DLB 259; EWL 3

D'Aguiar, Fred 1960- **CLC 145**
See also CA 148; CANR 83, 101; CN 7;
CP 5, 6, 7; DLB 157; EWL 3

Dahl, Roald 1916-1990 **CLC 1, 6, 18, 79;
TCLC 173**
See also AAYA 15; BPFB 1; BRWS 4; BYA
5; CA 1-4R; 133; CANR 6, 32, 37, 62;
CLR 1, 7, 41, 111; CN 1, 2, 3, 4; CPW;
DA3; DAB; DAC; DAM MST, NOV,
POP; DLB 139, 255; HGG; JRDA; MAI-
CYA 1, 2; MTCW 1, 2; MTFW 2005;
RGSF 2; SATA 1, 26, 73; SATA-Obit 65;
SSFS 4; TEA; YAW

Dahlberg, Edward 1900-1977 .. **CLC 1, 7, 14**
See also CA 9-12R; 69-72; CANR 31, 62;
CN 1, 2; DLB 48; MAL 5; MTCW 1;
RGAL 4

Daitch, Susan 1954- **CLC 103**
See also CA 161

Dale, Colin **TCLC 18**
See Lawrence, T(homas) E(dward)

Dale, George E.
See Asimov, Isaac

d'Alembert, Jean Le Rond
1717-1783 **LC 126**

Dalton, Roque 1935-1975(?) **HLCS 1; PC
36**
See also CA 176; DLB 283; HW 2

Daly, Elizabeth 1878-1967 **CLC 52**
See also CA 23-24; 25-28R; CANR 60;
CAP 2; CMW 4

Daly, Mary 1928- **CLC 173**
See also CA 25-28R; CANR 30, 62; FW;
GLL 1; MTCW 1

Daly, Maureen 1921- **CLC 17**
See also AAYA 5, 58; BYA 6; CANR 37,
83, 108; CLR 96; JRDA; MAICYA 1, 2;
SAAS 1; SATA 2, 129; WYA; YAW

Damas, Leon-Gontran 1912-1978 **CLC 84**
See also BW 1; CA 125; 73-76; EWL 3

Dana, Richard Henry Sr.
1787-1879 **NCLC 53**

Daniel, Samuel 1562(?)-1619 **LC 24**
See also DLB 62; RGEL 2

Daniels, Brett
See Adler, Renata

Dannay, Frederic 1905-1982 **CLC 11**
See Queen, Ellery
See also CA 1-4R; 107; CANR 1, 39; CMW
4; DAM POP; DLB 137; MTCW 1

D'Annunzio, Gabriele 1863-1938 ... **TCLC 6,
40**
See also CA 104; 155; EW 8; EWL 3;
RGWL 2, 3; TWA; WLIT 7

Danois, N. le
See Gourmont, Remy(-Marie-Charles) de

Dante 1265-1321 **CMLC 3, 18, 39, 70; PC
21; WLCS**
See Alighieri, Dante
See also DA; DA3; DAB; DAC; DAM
MST, POET; EFS 1; EW 1; LAIT 1;
RGWL 2, 3; TWA; WP

d'Antibes, Germain
See Simenon, Georges (Jacques Christian)

Danticat, Edwidge 1969- **CLC 94, 139**
See also AAYA 29; CA 152, 192; CAAE
192; CANR 73, 129; CN 7; DNFS 1;
EXPS; LATS 1:2; MTCW 2; MTFW
2005; SSFS 1; YAW

Danvers, Dennis 1947- **CLC 70**

Danziger, Paula 1944-2004 **CLC 21**
　　See also AAYA 4, 36; BYA 6, 7, 14; CA
　　112; 115; 229; CANR 37, 132; CLR 20;
　　JRDA; MAICYA 1, 2; MTFW 2005;
　　SATA 36, 63, 102, 149; SATA-Brief 30;
　　SATA-Obit 155; WYA; YAW
Da Ponte, Lorenzo 1749-1838 **NCLC 50**
d'Aragona, Tullia 1510(?)-1556 **LC 121**
Dario, Ruben 1867-1916 **HLC 1; PC 15;**
　　TCLC 4
　　See also CA 131; CANR 81; DAM MULT;
　　DLB 290; EWL 3; HW 1, 2; LAW;
　　MTCW 1, 2; MTFW 2005; RGWL 2, 3
Darley, George 1795-1846 **NCLC 2**
　　See also DLB 96; RGEL 2
Darrow, Clarence (Seward)
　　1857-1938 **TCLC 81**
　　See also CA 164; DLB 303
Darwin, Charles 1809-1882 **NCLC 57**
　　See also BRWS 7; DLB 57, 166; LATS 1:1;
　　RGEL 2; TEA; WLIT 4
Darwin, Erasmus 1731-1802 **NCLC 106**
　　See also DLB 93; RGEL 2
Daryush, Elizabeth 1887-1977 **CLC 6, 19**
　　See also CA 49-52; CANR 3, 81; DLB 20
Das, Kamala 1934- **CLC 191; PC 43**
　　See also CA 101; CANR 27, 59; CP 1, 2, 3,
　　4, 5, 6, 7; CWP; DLB 323; FW
Dasgupta, Surendranath
　　1887-1952 **TCLC 81**
　　See also CA 157
**Dashwood, Edmee Elizabeth Monica de la
　　Pasture** 1890-1943
　　See Delafield, E. M.
　　See also CA 119; 154
da Silva, Antonio Jose
　　1705-1739 **NCLC 114**
Daudet, (Louis Marie) Alphonse
　　1840-1897 **NCLC 1**
　　See also DLB 123; GFL 1789 to the Present;
　　RGSF 2
d'Aulnoy, Marie-Catherine c.
　　1650-1705 **LC 100**
Daumal, Rene 1908-1944 **TCLC 14**
　　See also CA 114; 247; EWL 3
Davenant, William 1606-1668 **LC 13**
　　See also DLB 58, 126; RGEL 2
Davenport, Guy (Mattison, Jr.)
　　1927-2005 **CLC 6, 14, 38; SSC 16**
　　See also CA 33-36R; 235; CANR 23, 73;
　　CN 3, 4, 5, 6; CSW; DLB 130
David, Robert
　　See Nezval, Vitezslav
Davidson, Avram (James) 1923-1993
　　See Queen, Ellery
　　See also CA 101; 171; CANR 26; DLB 8;
　　FANT; SFW 4; SUFW 1, 2
Davidson, Donald (Grady)
　　1893-1968 **CLC 2, 13, 19**
　　See also CA 5-8R; 25-28R; CANR 4, 84;
　　DLB 45
Davidson, Hugh
　　See Hamilton, Edmond
Davidson, John 1857-1909 **TCLC 24**
　　See also CA 118; 217; DLB 19; RGEL 2
Davidson, Sara 1943- **CLC 9**
　　See also CA 81-84; CANR 44, 68; DLB
　　185
Davie, Donald (Alfred) 1922-1995 **CLC 5,
　　8, 10, 31; PC 29**
　　See also BRWS 6; CA 1-4R; 149; CAAS 3;
　　CANR 1, 44; CP 1, 2, 3, 4, 5, 6; DLB 27;
　　MTCW 1; RGEL 2
Davie, Elspeth 1918-1995 **SSC 52**
　　See also CA 120; 126; 150; CANR 141;
　　DLB 139
Davies, Ray(mond Douglas) 1944- ... **CLC 21**
　　See also CA 116; 146; CANR 92

Davies, Rhys 1901-1978 **CLC 23**
　　See also CA 9-12R; 81-84; CANR 4; CN 1,
　　2; DLB 139, 191
Davies, (William) Robertson
　　1913-1995 **CLC 2, 7, 13, 25, 42, 75,
　　91; WLC 2**
　　See Marchbanks, Samuel
　　See also BEST 89:2; BPFB 1; CA 33-36R;
　　150; CANR 17, 42, 103; CN 1, 2, 3, 4, 5,
　　6; CPW; DA; DA3; DAB; DAC; DAM
　　MST, NOV, POP; DLB 68; EWL 3; HGG;
　　INT CANR-17; MTCW 1, 2; MTFW
　　2005; RGEL 2; TWA
Davies, Sir John 1569-1626 **LC 85**
　　See also DLB 172
Davies, Walter C.
　　See Kornbluth, C(yril) M.
Davies, William Henry 1871-1940 ... **TCLC 5**
　　See also BRWS 11; CA 104; 179; DLB 19,
　　174; EWL 3; RGEL 2
Da Vinci, Leonardo 1452-1519 **LC 12, 57,
　　60**
　　See also AAYA 40
Davis, Angela (Yvonne) 1944- **CLC 77**
　　See also BW 2, 3; CA 57-60; CANR 10,
　　81; CSW; DA3; DAM MULT; FW
Davis, B. Lynch
　　See Bioy Casares, Adolfo; Borges, Jorge
　　Luis
Davis, Frank Marshall 1905-1987 **BLC 1**
　　See also BW 2, 3; CA 125; 123; CANR 42,
　　80; DAM MULT; DLB 51
Davis, Gordon
　　See Hunt, E(verette) Howard, (Jr.)
Davis, H(arold) L(enoir) 1896-1960 . **CLC 49**
　　See also ANW; CA 178; 89-92; DLB 9,
　　206; SATA 114; TCWW 1, 2
Davis, Natalie Zemon 1928- **CLC 204**
　　See also CA 53-56; CANR 58, 100
Davis, Rebecca (Blaine) Harding
　　1831-1910 **SSC 38; TCLC 6**
　　See also CA 104; 179; DLB 74, 239; FW;
　　NFS 14; RGAL 4; TUS
Davis, Richard Harding
　　1864-1916 **TCLC 24**
　　See also CA 114; 179; DLB 12, 23, 78, 79,
　　189; DLBD 13; RGAL 4
Davison, Frank Dalby 1893-1970 **CLC 15**
　　See also CA 217; 116; DLB 260
Davison, Lawrence H.
　　See Lawrence, D(avid) H(erbert Richards)
Davison, Peter (Hubert) 1928-2004 . **CLC 28**
　　See also CA 9-12R; 234; CAAS 4; CANR
　　3, 43, 84; CP 1, 2, 3, 4, 5, 6, 7; DLB 5
Davys, Mary 1674-1732 **LC 1, 46**
　　See also DLB 39
Dawson, (Guy) Fielding (Lewis)
　　1930-2002 **CLC 6**
　　See also CA 85-88; 202; CANR 108; DLB
　　130; DLBY 2002
Dawson, Peter
　　See Faust, Frederick (Schiller)
　　See also TCWW 1, 2
Day, Clarence (Shepard, Jr.)
　　1874-1935 **TCLC 25**
　　See also CA 108; 199; DLB 11
Day, John 1574(?)-1640(?) **LC 70**
　　See also DLB 62, 170; RGEL 2
Day, Thomas 1748-1789 **LC 1**
　　See also DLB 39; YABC 1
Day Lewis, C(ecil) 1904-1972 . **CLC 1, 6, 10;
　　PC 11**
　　See Blake, Nicholas; Lewis, C. Day
　　See also BRWS 3; CA 13-16; 33-36R;
　　CANR 34; CAP 1; CP 1; CWRI 5; DAM
　　POET; DLB 15, 20; EWL 3; MTCW 1, 2;
　　RGEL 2

Dazai Osamu **SSC 41; TCLC 11**
　　See Tsushima, Shuji
　　See also CA 164; DLB 182; EWL 3; MJW;
　　RGSF 2; RGWL 2, 3; TWA
de Andrade, Carlos Drummond
　　See Drummond de Andrade, Carlos
de Andrade, Mario 1892(?)-1945
　　See Andrade, Mario de
　　See also CA 178; HW 2
Deane, Norman
　　See Creasey, John
Deane, Seamus (Francis) 1940- **CLC 122**
　　See also CA 118; CANR 42
de Beauvoir, Simone
　　See Beauvoir, Simone de
de Beer, P.
　　See Bosman, Herman Charles
De Botton, Alain 1969- **CLC 203**
　　See also CA 159; CANR 96
de Brissac, Malcolm
　　See Dickinson, Peter (Malcolm de Brissac)
de Campos, Alvaro
　　See Pessoa, Fernando (Antonio Nogueira)
de Chardin, Pierre Teilhard
　　See Teilhard de Chardin, (Marie Joseph)
　　Pierre
de Crenne, Helisenne c. 1510-c.
　　1560 .. **LC 113**
Dee, John 1527-1608 **LC 20**
　　See also DLB 136, 213
Deer, Sandra 1940- **CLC 45**
　　See also CA 186
De Ferrari, Gabriella 1941- **CLC 65**
　　See also CA 146
de Filippo, Eduardo 1900-1984 ... **TCLC 127**
　　See also CA 132; 114; EWL 3; MTCW 1;
　　RGWL 2, 3
Defoe, Daniel 1660(?)-1731 **LC 1, 42, 108;
　　WLC 2**
　　See also AAYA 27; BRW 3; BRWR 1; BYA
　　4; CDBLB 1660-1789; CLR 61; DA;
　　DA3; DAB; DAC; DAM MST, NOV;
　　DLB 39, 95, 101; JRDA; LAIT 1; LMFS
　　1; MAICYA 1, 2; NFS 9, 13; RGEL 2;
　　SATA 22; TEA; WCH; WLIT 3
de Gouges, Olympe
　　See de Gouges, Olympe
de Gouges, Olympe 1748-1793 **LC 127**
　　See also DLB 313
de Gourmont, Remy(-Marie-Charles)
　　See Gourmont, Remy(-Marie-Charles) de
de Gournay, Marie le Jars
　　1566-1645 **LC 98**
　　See also FW
de Hartog, Jan 1914-2002 **CLC 19**
　　See also CA 1-4R; 210; CANR 1; DFS 12
de Hostos, E. M.
　　See Hostos (y Bonilla), Eugenio Maria de
de Hostos, Eugenio M.
　　See Hostos (y Bonilla), Eugenio Maria de
Deighton, Len **CLC 4, 7, 22, 46**
　　See Deighton, Leonard Cyril
　　See also AAYA 6; BEST 89:2; BPFB 1; CD-
　　BLB 1960 to Present; CMW 4; CN 1, 2,
　　3, 4, 5, 6, 7; CPW; DLB 87
Deighton, Leonard Cyril 1929-
　　See Deighton, Len
　　See also AAYA 57; CA 9-12R; CANR 19,
　　33, 68; DA3; DAM NOV, POP; MTCW
　　1, 2; MTFW 2005
Dekker, Thomas 1572(?)-1632 **DC 12; LC
　　22**
　　See also CDBLB Before 1660; DAM
　　DRAM; DLB 62, 172; LMFS 1; RGEL 2
de Laclos, Pierre Ambroise Franois
　　See Laclos, Pierre-Ambroise-Francois
Delacroix, (Ferdinand-Victor-)Eugene
　　1798-1863 **NCLC 133**
　　See also EW 5

Delafield, E. M. **TCLC 61**
See Dashwood, Edmee Elizabeth Monica
de la Pasture
See also DLB 34; RHW

de la Mare, Walter (John)
1873-1956 . **SSC 14; TCLC 4, 53; WLC 2**
See also CA 163; CDBLB 1914-1945; CLR
23; CWRI 5; DA3; DAB; DAC; DAM
MST, POET; DLB 19, 153, 162, 255, 284;
EWL 3; EXPP; HGG; MAICYA 1, 2;
MTCW 2; MTFW 2005; RGEL 2; RGSF
2; SATA 16; SUFW 1; TEA; WCH

de Lamartine, Alphonse (Marie Louis Prat)
See Lamartine, Alphonse (Marie Louis Prat)
de

Delaney, Franey
See O'Hara, John (Henry)

Delaney, Shelagh 1939- **CLC 29**
See also CA 17-20R; CANR 30, 67; CBD;
CD 5, 6; CDBLB 1960 to Present; CWD;
DAM DRAM; DFS 7; DLB 13; MTCW 1

Delany, Martin Robison
1812-1885 **NCLC 93**
See also DLB 50; RGAL 4

Delany, Mary (Granville Pendarves)
1700-1788 **LC 12**

Delany, Samuel R(ay), Jr. 1942- **BLC 1;
CLC 8, 14, 38, 141**
See also AAYA 24; AFAW 2; BPFB 1; BW
2, 3; CA 81-84; CANR 27, 43, 116; CN
2, 3, 4, 5, 6, 7; DAM MULT; DLB 8, 33;
FANT; MAL 5; MTCW 1, 2; RGAL 4;
SATA 92; SCFW 1, 2; SFW 4; SUFW 2

De la Ramee, Marie Louise (Ouida)
1839-1908
See Ouida
See also CA 204; SATA 20

de la Roche, Mazo 1879-1961 **CLC 14**
See also CA 85-88; CANR 30; DLB 68;
RGEL 2; RHW; SATA 64

De La Salle, Innocent
See Hartmann, Sadakichi

de Laureamont, Comte
See Lautreamont

Delbanco, Nicholas 1942- **CLC 6, 13, 167**
See also CA 17-20R, 189; CAAE 189;
CAAS 2; CANR 29, 55, 116, 150; CN 7;
DLB 6, 234

Delbanco, Nicholas Franklin
See Delbanco, Nicholas

del Castillo, Michel 1933- **CLC 38**
See also CA 109; CANR 77

Deledda, Grazia (Cosima)
1875(?)-1936 **TCLC 23**
See also CA 123; 205; DLB 264; EWL 3;
RGWL 2, 3; WLIT 7

Deleuze, Gilles 1925-1995 **TCLC 116**
See also DLB 296

Delgado, Abelardo (Lalo) B(arrientos)
1930-2004 **HLC 1**
See also CA 131; 230; CAAS 15; CANR
90; DAM MST, MULT; DLB 82; HW 1,
2

Delibes, Miguel **CLC 8, 18**
See Delibes Setien, Miguel
See also DLB 322; EWL 3

Delibes Setien, Miguel 1920-
See Delibes, Miguel
See also CA 45-48; CANR 1, 32; CWW 2;
HW 1; MTCW 1

DeLillo, Don 1936- **CLC 8, 10, 13, 27, 39,
54, 76, 143, 210, 213**
See also AMWC 2; AMWS 6; BEST 89:1;
BPFB 1; CA 81-84; CANR 21, 76, 92,
133; CN 3, 4, 5, 6, 7; CPW; DA3; DAM
NOV, POP; DLB 6, 173; EWL 3; MAL 5;
MTCW 1, 2; MTFW 2005; RGAL 4; TUS

de Lisser, H. G.
See De Lisser, H(erbert) G(eorge)
See also DLB 117

De Lisser, H(erbert) G(eorge)
1878-1944 **TCLC 12**
See de Lisser, H. G.
See also BW 2; CA 109; 152

Deloire, Pierre
See Peguy, Charles (Pierre)

Deloney, Thomas 1543(?)-1600 **LC 41**
See also DLB 167; RGEL 2

Deloria, Ella (Cara) 1889-1971(?) **NNAL**
See also CA 152; DAM MULT; DLB 175

Deloria, Vine, Jr. 1933-2005 **CLC 21, 122;
NNAL**
See also CA 53-56; 245; CANR 5, 20, 48,
98; DAM MULT; DLB 175; MTCW 1;
SATA 21; SATA-Obit 171

Deloria, Vine Victor
See Deloria, Vine, Jr.

del Valle-Inclan, Ramon (Maria)
See Valle-Inclan, Ramon (Maria) del
See also DLB 322

Del Vecchio, John M(ichael) 1947- .. **CLC 29**
See also CA 110; DLBD 9

de Man, Paul (Adolph Michel)
1919-1983 **CLC 55**
See also CA 128; 111; CANR 61; DLB 67;
MTCW 1, 2

DeMarinis, Rick 1934- **CLC 54**
See also CA 57-60, 184; CAAE 184; CAAS
24; CANR 9, 25, 50; DLB 218; TCWW 2

de Maupassant, (Henri Rene Albert) Guy
See Maupassant, (Henri Rene Albert) Guy
de

Dembry, R. Emmet
See Murfree, Mary Noailles

Demby, William 1922- **BLC 1; CLC 53**
See also BW 1, 3; CA 81-84; CANR 81;
DAM MULT; DLB 33

de Menton, Francisco
See Chin, Frank (Chew, Jr.)

Demetrius of Phalerum c.
307B.C.- **CMLC 34**

Demijohn, Thom
See Disch, Thomas M(ichael)

De Mille, James 1833-1880 **NCLC 123**
See also DLB 99, 251

Deming, Richard 1915-1983
See Queen, Ellery
See also CA 9-12R; CANR 3, 94; SATA 24

Democritus c. 460B.C.-c. 370B.C. . **CMLC 47**

de Montaigne, Michel (Eyquem)
See Montaigne, Michel (Eyquem) de

de Montherlant, Henry (Milon)
See Montherlant, Henry (Milon) de

Demosthenes 384B.C.-322B.C. **CMLC 13**
See also AW 1; DLB 176; RGWL 2, 3;
WLIT 8

de Musset, (Louis Charles) Alfred
See Musset, Alfred de

de Natale, Francine
See Malzberg, Barry N(athaniel)

de Navarre, Marguerite 1492-1549 ... **LC 61;
SSC 85**
See Marguerite d'Angouleme; Marguerite
de Navarre

Denby, Edwin (Orr) 1903-1983 **CLC 48**
See also CA 138; 110; CP 1

de Nerval, Gerard
See Nerval, Gerard de

Denham, John 1615-1669 **LC 73**
See also DLB 58, 126; RGEL 2

Denis, Julio
See Cortazar, Julio

Denmark, Harrison
See Zelazny, Roger (Joseph)

Dennis, John 1658-1734 **LC 11**
See also DLB 101; RGEL 2

Dennis, Nigel (Forbes) 1912-1989 **CLC 8**
See also CA 25-28R; 129; CN 1, 2, 3, 4;
DLB 13, 15, 233; EWL 3; MTCW 1

Dent, Lester 1904-1959 **TCLC 72**
See also CA 112; 161; CMW 4; DLB 306;
SFW 4

De Palma, Brian 1940- **CLC 20**
See also CA 109

De Palma, Brian Russell
See De Palma, Brian

De Quincey, Thomas 1785-1859 **NCLC 4,
87**
See also BRW 4; CDBLB 1789-1832; DLB
110, 144; RGEL 2

Deren, Eleanora 1908(?)-1961
See Deren, Maya
See also CA 192; 111

Deren, Maya **CLC 16, 102**
See Deren, Eleanora

Derleth, August (William)
1909-1971 **CLC 31**
See also BPFB 1; BYA 9, 10; CA 1-4R; 29-
32R; CANR 4; CMW 4; CN 1; DLB 9;
DLBD 17; HGG; SATA 5; SUFW 1

Der Nister 1884-1950 **TCLC 56**
See Nister, Der

de Routisie, Albert
See Aragon, Louis

Derrida, Jacques 1930-2004 **CLC 24, 87,
225**
See also CA 124; 127; 232; CANR 76, 98,
133; DLB 242; EWL 3; LMFS 2; MTCW
2; TWA

Derry Down Derry
See Lear, Edward

Dersonnes, Jacques
See Simenon, Georges (Jacques Christian)

Der Stricker c. 1190-c. 1250 **CMLC 75**
See also DLB 138

Desai, Anita 1937- **CLC 19, 37, 97, 175**
See also BRWS 5; CA 81-84; CANR 33,
53, 95, 133; CN 1, 2, 3, 4, 5, 6, 7; CWRI
5; DA3; DAB; DAM NOV; DLB 271,
323; DNFS 2; EWL 3; FW; MTCW 1, 2;
MTFW 2005; SATA 63, 126

Desai, Kiran 1971- **CLC 119**
See also BYA 16; CA 171; CANR 127

de Saint-Luc, Jean
See Glassco, John

de Saint Roman, Arnaud
See Aragon, Louis

Desbordes-Valmore, Marceline
1786-1859 **NCLC 97**
See also DLB 217

Descartes, Rene 1596-1650 **LC 20, 35**
See also DLB 268; EW 3; GFL Beginnings
to 1789

Deschamps, Eustache 1340(?)-1404 .. **LC 103**
See also DLB 208

De Sica, Vittorio 1901(?)-1974 **CLC 20**
See also CA 117

Desnos, Robert 1900-1945 **TCLC 22**
See also CA 121; 151; CANR 107; DLB
258; EWL 3; LMFS 2

Destouches, Louis-Ferdinand
1894-1961 **CLC 9, 15**
See Celine, Louis-Ferdinand
See also CA 85-88; CANR 28; MTCW 1

de Tolignac, Gaston
See Griffith, D(avid Lewelyn) W(ark)

Deutsch, Babette 1895-1982 **CLC 18**
See also BYA 3; CA 1-4R; 108; CANR 4,
79; CP 1, 2, 3; DLB 45; SATA 1; SATA-
Obit 33

Devenant, William 1606-1649 **LC 13**

Devkota, Laxmiprasad 1909-1959 . **TCLC 23**
See also CA 123

De Voto, Bernard (Augustine)
 1897-1955 **TCLC 29**
 See also CA 113; 160; DLB 9, 256; MAL
 5; TCWW 1, 2
De Vries, Peter 1910-1993 **CLC 1, 2, 3, 7,
 10, 28, 46**
 See also CA 17-20R; 142; CANR 41; CN
 1, 2, 3, 4, 5; DAM NOV; DLB 6; DLBY
 1982; MAL 5; MTCW 1, 2; MTFW 2005
Dewey, John 1859-1952 **TCLC 95**
 See also CA 114; 170; CANR 144; DLB
 246, 270; RGAL 4
Dexter, John
 See Bradley, Marion Zimmer
 See also GLL 1
Dexter, Martin
 See Faust, Frederick (Schiller)
Dexter, Pete 1943- **CLC 34, 55**
 See also BEST 89:2; CA 127; 131; CANR
 129; CPW; DAM POP; INT CA-131;
 MAL 5; MTCW 1; MTFW 2005
Diamano, Silmang
 See Senghor, Leopold Sedar
Diamond, Neil 1941- **CLC 30**
 See also CA 108
Diaz del Castillo, Bernal c.
 1496-1584 **HLCS 1; LC 31**
 See also DLB 318; LAW
di Bassetto, Corno
 See Shaw, George Bernard
Dick, Philip K. 1928-1982 ... **CLC 10, 30, 72;
 SSC 57**
 See also AAYA 24; BPFB 1; BYA 11; CA
 49-52; 106; CANR 2, 16, 132; CN 2, 3;
 CPW; DA3; DAM NOV, POP; DLB 8;
 MTCW 1, 2; MTFW 2005; NFS 5; SCFW
 1, 2; SFW 4
Dick, Philip Kindred
 See Dick, Philip K.
Dickens, Charles (John Huffam)
 1812-1870 **NCLC 3, 8, 18, 26, 37, 50,
 86, 105, 113, 161; SSC 17, 49, 88; WLC
 2**
 See also AAYA 23; BRW 5; BRWC 1, 2;
 BYA 1, 2, 3, 13, 14; CDBLB 1832-1890;
 CLR 95; CMW 4; DA; DA3; DAB; DAC;
 DAM MST, NOV; DLB 21, 55, 70, 159,
 166; EXPN; GL 2; HGG; LAIT 1, 2;
 LATS 1:1; LMFS 1; MAICYA 1, 2;
 NFS 4, 5, 10, 14, 20; RGEL 2; RGSF 2;
 SATA 15; SUFW 1; TEA; WCH; WLIT
 4; WYA
Dickey, James (Lafayette)
 1923-1997 **CLC 1, 2, 4, 7, 10, 15, 47,
 109; PC 40; TCLC 151**
 See also AAYA 50; AITN 1, 2; AMWS 4;
 BPFB 1; CA 9-12R; 156; CABS 2; CANR
 10, 48, 61, 105; CDALB 1968-1988; CP
 1, 2, 3, 4, 5, 6; CPW; CSW; DA3; DAM
 NOV, POET, POP; DLB 5, 193; DLBD 7;
 DLBY 1982, 1993, 1996, 1997, 1998;
 EWL 3; INT CANR-10; MAL 5; MTCW
 1, 2; NFS 9; PFS 6, 11; RGAL 4; TUS
Dickey, William 1928-1994 **CLC 3, 28**
 See also CA 9-12R; 145; CANR 24, 79; CP
 1, 2, 3, 4; DLB 5
Dickinson, Charles 1951- **CLC 49**
 See also CA 128; CANR 141
Dickinson, Emily (Elizabeth)
 1830-1886 **NCLC 21, 77, 171; PC 1;
 WLC 2**
 See also AAYA 22; AMW; AMWR 1;
 CDALB 1865-1917; DA; DA3; DAB;
 DAC; DAM MST, POET; DLB 1, 243;
 EXPP; FL 1:3; MAWW; PAB; PFS 1, 2,
 3, 4, 5, 6, 8, 10, 11, 13, 16; RGAL 4;
 SATA 29; TUS; WP; WYA
Dickinson, Mrs. Herbert Ward
 See Phelps, Elizabeth Stuart

Dickinson, Peter (Malcolm de Brissac)
 1927- **CLC 12, 35**
 See also AAYA 9, 49; BYA 5; CA 41-44R;
 CANR 31, 58, 88, 134; CLR 29; CMW 4;
 DLB 87, 161, 276; JRDA; MAICYA 1, 2;
 SATA 5, 62, 95, 150; SFW 4; WYA; YAW
Dickson, Carr
 See Carr, John Dickson
Dickson, Carter
 See Carr, John Dickson
Diderot, Denis 1713-1784 **LC 26, 126**
 See also DLB 313; EW 4; GFL Beginnings
 to 1789; LMFS 1; RGWL 2, 3
Didion, Joan 1934- . **CLC 1, 3, 8, 14, 32, 129**
 See also AITN 1; AMWS 4; CA 5-8R;
 CANR 14, 52, 76, 125; CDALB 1968-
 1988; CN 2, 3, 4, 5, 6, 7; DA3; DAM
 NOV; DLB 2, 173, 185; DLBY 1981,
 1986; EWL 3; MAL 5; MAWW; MTCW
 1, 2; MTFW 2005; NFS 3; RGAL 4;
 TCLE 1:1; TCWW 2; TUS
di Donato, Pietro 1911-1992 **TCLC 159**
 See also CA 101; 136; DLB 9
Dietrich, Robert
 See Hunt, E(verette) Howard, (Jr.)
Difusa, Pati
 See Almodovar, Pedro
Dillard, Annie 1945- **CLC 9, 60, 115, 216**
 See also AAYA 6, 43; AMWS 6; ANW; CA
 49-52; CANR 3, 43, 62, 90, 125; DA3;
 DAM NOV; DLB 275, 278; DLBY 1980;
 LAIT 4, 5; MAL 5; MTCW 1, 2; MTFW
 2005; NCFS 1; RGAL 4; SATA 10, 140;
 TCLE 1:1; TUS
Dillard, R(ichard) H(enry) W(ilde)
 1937- .. **CLC 5**
 See also CA 21-24R; CAAS 7; CANR 10;
 CP 2, 3, 4, 5, 6, 7; CSW; DLB 5, 244
Dillon, Eilis 1920-1994 **CLC 17**
 See also CA 9-12R, 182; 147; CAAE 182;
 CAAS 3; CANR 4, 38, 78; CLR 26; MAI-
 CYA 1, 2; MAICYAS 1; SATA 2, 74;
 SATA-Essay 105; SATA-Obit 83; YAW
Dimont, Penelope
 See Mortimer, Penelope (Ruth)
Dinesen, Isak **CLC 10, 29, 95; SSC 7, 75**
 See Blixen, Karen (Christentze Dinesen)
 See also EW 10; EWL 3; EXPS; FW; GL
 2; HGG; LAIT 3; MTCW 1; NCFS 2;
 NFS 9; RGSF 2; RGWL 2, 3; SSFS 3, 6,
 13; WLIT 2
Ding Ling **CLC 68**
 See Chiang, Pin-chin
 See also RGWL 3
Diphusa, Patty
 See Almodovar, Pedro
Disch, Thomas M(ichael) 1940- ... **CLC 7, 36**
 See Disch, Tom
 See also AAYA 17; BPFB 1; CA 21-24R;
 CAAS 4; CANR 17, 36, 54, 89; CLR 18;
 CP 5, 6, 7; DA3; DLB 8; HGG; MAICYA
 1, 2; MTCW 1, 2; MTFW 2005; SAAS
 15; SATA 92; SCFW 1, 2; SFW 4; SUFW
 2
Disch, Tom
 See Disch, Thomas M(ichael)
 See also DLB 282
d'Isly, Georges
 See Simenon, Georges (Jacques Christian)
Disraeli, Benjamin 1804-1881 ... **NCLC 2, 39,
 79**
 See also BRW 4; DLB 21, 55; RGEL 2
Ditcum, Steve
 See Crumb, R.
Dixon, Paige
 See Corcoran, Barbara (Asenath)

Dixon, Stephen 1936- **CLC 52; SSC 16**
 See also AMWS 12; CA 89-92; CANR 17,
 40, 54, 91; CN 4, 5, 6, 7; DLB 130; MAL
 5
Dixon, Thomas, Jr. 1864-1946 **TCLC 163**
 See also RHW
Djebar, Assia 1936- **CLC 182**
 See also CA 188; EWL 3; RGWL 3; WLIT
 2
Doak, Annie
 See Dillard, Annie
Dobell, Sydney Thompson
 1824-1874 **NCLC 43**
 See also DLB 32; RGEL 2
Doblin, Alfred **TCLC 13**
 See Doeblin, Alfred
 See also CDWLB 2; EWL 3; RGWL 2, 3
Dobroliubov, Nikolai Aleksandrovich
 See Dobrolyubov, Nikolai Alexandrovich
 See also DLB 277
Dobrolyubov, Nikolai Alexandrovich
 1836-1861 **NCLC 5**
 See Dobroliubov, Nikolai Aleksandrovich
Dobson, Austin 1840-1921 **TCLC 79**
 See also DLB 35, 144
Dobyns, Stephen 1941- **CLC 37**
 See also AMWS 13; CA 45-48; CANR 2,
 18, 99; CMW 4; CP 4, 5, 6, 7; PFS 23
Doctorow, Edgar Laurence
 See Doctorow, E.L.
Doctorow, E.L. 1931- . **CLC 6, 11, 15, 18, 37,
 44, 65, 113, 214**
 See also AAYA 22; AITN 2; AMWS 4;
 BEST 89:3; BPFB 1; CA 45-48; CANR
 2, 33, 51, 76, 97, 133; CDALB 1968-
 1988; CN 3, 4, 5, 6, 7; CPW; DA3; DAM
 NOV, POP; DLB 2, 28, 173; DLBY 1980;
 EWL 3; LAIT 3; MAL 5; MTCW 1, 2;
 MTFW 2005; NFS 6; RGAL 4; RGHL;
 RHW; TCLE 1:1; TCWW 1, 2; TUS
Dodgson, Charles L(utwidge) 1832-1898
 See Carroll, Lewis
 See also CLR 2; DA; DA3; DAB; DAC;
 DAM MST, NOV, POET; MAICYA 1, 2;
 SATA 100; YABC 2
Dodsley, Robert 1703-1764 **LC 97**
 See also DLB 95; RGEL 2
Dodson, Owen (Vincent) 1914-1983 .. **BLC 1;
 CLC 79**
 See also BW 1; CA 65-68; 110; CANR 24;
 DAM MULT; DLB 76
Doeblin, Alfred 1878-1957 **TCLC 13**
 See Doblin, Alfred
 See also CA 110; 141; DLB 66
Doerr, Harriet 1910-2002 **CLC 34**
 See also CA 117; 122; 213; CANR 47; INT
 CA-122; LATS 1:2
Domecq, H(onorio Bustos)
 See Bioy Casares, Adolfo
Domecq, H(onorio) Bustos
 See Bioy Casares, Adolfo; Borges, Jorge
 Luis
Domini, Rey
 See Lorde, Audre (Geraldine)
 See also GLL 1
Dominique
 See Proust, (Valentin-Louis-George-Eugene)
 Marcel
Don, A
 See Stephen, Sir Leslie
Donaldson, Stephen R(eeder)
 1947- **CLC 46, 138**
 See also AAYA 36; BPFB 1; CA 89-92;
 CANR 13, 55, 99; CPW; DAM POP;
 FANT; INT CANR-13; SATA 121; SFW
 4; SUFW 1, 2

Donleavy, J(ames) P(atrick) 1926- **CLC 1, 4, 6, 10, 45**
See also AITN 2; BPFB 1; CA 9-12R; CANR 24, 49, 62, 80, 124; CBD; CD 5, 6; CN 1, 2, 3, 4, 5, 6, 7; DLB 6, 173; INT CANR-24; MAL 5; MTCW 1, 2; MTFW 2005; RGAL 4

Donnadieu, Marguerite
See Duras, Marguerite

Donne, John 1572-1631 ... **LC 10, 24, 91; PC 1, 43; WLC 2**
See also AAYA 67; BRW 1; BRWC 1; BRWR 2; CDBLB Before 1660; DA; DAB; DAC; DAM MST, POET; DLB 121, 151; EXPP; PAB; PFS 2, 11; RGEL 3; TEA; WLIT 3; WP

Donnell, David 1939(?)- **CLC 34**
See also CA 197

Donoghue, Denis 1928- **CLC 209**
See also CA 17-20R; CANR 16, 102

Donoghue, P. S.
See Hunt, E(verette) Howard, (Jr.)

Donoso (Yanez), Jose 1924-1996 ... **CLC 4, 8, 11, 32, 99; HLC 1; SSC 34; TCLC 133**
See also CA 81-84; 155; CANR 32, 73; CD-WLB 3; CWW 2; DAM MULT; DLB 113; EWL 3; HW 1, 2; LAW; LAWS 1; MTCW 1, 2; MTFW 2005; RGSF 2; WLIT 1

Donovan, John 1928-1992 **CLC 35**
See also AAYA 20; CA 97-100; 137; CLR 3; MAICYA 1, 2; SATA 72; SATA-Brief 29; YAW

Don Roberto
See Cunninghame Graham, Robert (Gallnigad) Bontine

Doolittle, Hilda 1886-1961 . **CLC 3, 8, 14, 31, 34, 73; PC 5; WLC 3**
See H. D.
See also AAYA 66; AMWS 1; CA 97-100; CANR 35, 131; DA; DAC; DAM MST, POET; DLB 4, 45; EWL 3; FW; GLL 1; LMFS 2; MAL 5; MAWW; MTCW 1, 2; MTFW 2005; PFS 6; RGAL 4

Doppo, Kunikida **TCLC 99**
See Kunikida Doppo

Dorfman, Ariel 1942- **CLC 48, 77, 189; HLC 1**
See also CA 124; 130; CANR 67, 70, 135; CWW 2; DAM MULT; DFS 4; EWL 3; HW 1, 2; INT CA-130; WLIT 1

Dorn, Edward (Merton) 1929-1999 **CLC 10, 18**
See also CA 93-96; 187; CANR 42, 79; CP 1, 2, 3, 4, 5, 6, 7; DLB 5; INT CA-93-96; WP

Dor-Ner, Zvi **CLC 70**

Dorris, Michael (Anthony) 1945-1997 **CLC 109; NNAL**
See also AAYA 20; BEST 90:1; BYA 12; CA 102; 157; CANR 19, 46, 75; CLR 58; DA3; DAM MULT, NOV; DLB 175; LAIT 5; MTCW 2; MTFW 2005; NFS 3; RGAL 4; SATA 75; SATA-Obit 94; TCWW 2; YAW

Dorris, Michael A.
See Dorris, Michael (Anthony)

Dorsan, Luc
See Simenon, Georges (Jacques Christian)

Dorsange, Jean
See Simenon, Georges (Jacques Christian)

Dorset
See Sackville, Thomas

Dos Passos, John (Roderigo) 1896-1970 ... **CLC 1, 4, 8, 11, 15, 25, 34, 82; WLC 2**
See also AMW; BPFB 1; CA 1-4R; 29-32R; CANR 3; CDALB 1929-1941; DA; DA3; DAB; DAC; DAM MST, NOV; DLB 4,

9, 274, 316; DLBD 1, 15; DLBY 1996; EWL 3; MAL 5; MTCW 1, 2; MTFW 2005; NFS 14; RGAL 4; TUS

Dossage, Jean
See Simenon, Georges (Jacques Christian)

Dostoevsky, Fedor Mikhailovich 1821-1881 .. **NCLC 2, 7, 21, 33, 43, 119, 167; SSC 2, 33, 44; WLC 2**
See Dostoevsky, Fyodor
See also AAYA 40; DA; DA3; DAB; DAC; DAM MST, NOV; EW 7; EXPN; NFS 3, 8; RGSF 2; RGWL 2, 3; SSFS 8; TWA

Dostoevsky, Fyodor
See Dostoevsky, Fedor Mikhailovich
See also DLB 238; LATS 1:1; LMFS 1, 2

Doty, M. R.
See Doty, Mark (Alan)

Doty, Mark
See Doty, Mark (Alan)

Doty, Mark (Alan) 1953(?)- **CLC 176; PC 53**
See also AMWS 11; CA 161, 183; CAAE 183; CANR 110; CP 7

Doty, Mark A.
See Doty, Mark (Alan)

Doughty, Charles M(ontagu) 1843-1926 **TCLC 27**
See also CA 115; 178; DLB 19, 57, 174

Douglas, Ellen **CLC 73**
See Haxton, Josephine Ayres; Williamson, Ellen Douglas
See also CN 5, 6, 7; CSW; DLB 292

Douglas, Gavin 1475(?)-1522 **LC 20**
See also DLB 132; RGEL 2

Douglas, George
See Brown, George Douglas
See also RGEL 2

Douglas, Keith (Castellain) 1920-1944 **TCLC 40**
See also BRW 7; CA 160; DLB 27; EWL 3; PAB; RGEL 2

Douglas, Leonard
See Bradbury, Ray (Douglas)

Douglas, Michael
See Crichton, (John) Michael

Douglas, (George) Norman 1868-1952 **TCLC 68**
See also BRW 6; CA 119; 157; DLB 34, 195; RGEL 2

Douglas, William
See Brown, George Douglas

Douglass, Frederick 1817(?)-1895 **BLC 1; NCLC 7, 55, 141; WLC 2**
See also AAYA 48; AFAW 1, 2; AMWC 1; AMWS 3; CDALB 1640-1865; DA; DA3; DAC; DAM MST, MULT; DLB 1, 43, 50, 79, 243; FW; LAIT 2; NCFS 2; RGAL 4; SATA 29

Dourado, (Waldomiro Freitas) Autran 1926- **CLC 23, 60**
See also CA 25-28R; 179; CANR 34, 81; DLB 145, 307; HW 2

Dourado, Waldomiro Freitas Autran
See Dourado, (Waldomiro Freitas) Autran

Dove, Rita (Frances) 1952- . **BLCS; CLC 50, 81; PC 6**
See also AAYA 46; AMWS 4; BW 2; CA 109; CAAS 19; CANR 27, 42, 68, 76, 97, 132; CDALBS; CP 5, 6, 7; CSW; CWP; DA3; DAM MULT, POET; DLB 120; EWL 3; EXPP; MAL 5; MTCW 2; MTFW 2005; PFS 1, 15; RGAL 4

Doveglion
See Villa, Jose Garcia

Dowell, Coleman 1925-1985 **CLC 60**
See also CA 25-28R; 117; CANR 10; DLB 130; GLL 2

Dowson, Ernest (Christopher) 1867-1900 **TCLC 4**
See also CA 105; 150; DLB 19, 135; RGEL 2

Doyle, A. Conan
See Doyle, Sir Arthur Conan

Doyle, Sir Arthur Conan 1859-1930 . **SSC 12, 83; TCLC 7; WLC 2**
See Conan Doyle, Arthur
See also AAYA 14; BRWS 2; CA 104; 122; CANR 131; CDBLB 1890-1914; CLR 106; CMW 4; DA; DA3; DAB; DAC; DAM MST, NOV; DLB 18, 70, 156, 178; EXPS; HGG; LAIT 2; MSW; MTCW 1, 2; MTFW 2005; RGEL 2; RGSF 2; RHW; SATA 24; SCFW 1, 2; SFW 4; SSFS 2; TEA; WCH; WLIT 4; WYA; YAW

Doyle, Conan
See Doyle, Sir Arthur Conan

Doyle, John
See Graves, Robert (von Ranke)

Doyle, Roddy 1958- **CLC 81, 178**
See also AAYA 14; BRWS 5; CA 143; CANR 73, 128; CN 6, 7; DA3; DLB 194, 326; MTCW 2; MTFW 2005

Doyle, Sir A. Conan
See Doyle, Sir Arthur Conan

Dr. A
See Asimov, Isaac; Silverstein, Alvin; Silverstein, Virginia B(arbara Opshelor)

Drabble, Margaret 1939- **CLC 2, 3, 5, 8, 10, 22, 53, 129**
See also BRWS 4; CA 13-16R; CANR 18, 35, 63, 112, 131; CDBLB 1960 to Present; CN 1, 2, 3, 4, 5, 6, 7; CPW; DA3; DAB; DAC; DAM MST, NOV, POP; DLB 14, 155, 231; EWL 3; FW; MTCW 1, 2; MTFW 2005; RGEL 2; SATA 48; TEA

Drakulic, Slavenka 1949- **CLC 173**
See also CA 144; CANR 92

Drakulic-Ilic, Slavenka
See Drakulic, Slavenka

Drapier, M. B.
See Swift, Jonathan

Drayham, James
See Mencken, H(enry) L(ouis)

Drayton, Michael 1563-1631 **LC 8**
See also DAM POET; DLB 121; RGEL 2

Dreadstone, Carl
See Campbell, (John) Ramsey

Dreiser, Theodore 1871-1945 **SSC 30; TCLC 10, 18, 35, 83; WLC 2**
See also AMW; AMWC 2; AMWR 2; BYA 15, 16; CA 106; 132; CDALB 1865-1917; DA; DA3; DAC; DAM MST, NOV; DLB 9, 12, 102, 137; DLBD 1; EWL 3; LAIT 2; LMFS 2; MAL 5; MTCW 1, 2; MTFW 2005; NFS 8, 17; RGAL 4; TUS

Dreiser, Theodore Herman Albert
See Dreiser, Theodore

Drexler, Rosalyn 1926- **CLC 2, 6**
See also CA 81-84; CAD; CANR 68, 124; CD 5, 6; CWD; MAL 5

Dreyer, Carl Theodor 1889-1968 **CLC 16**
See also CA 116

Drieu la Rochelle, Pierre(-Eugene) 1893-1945 **TCLC 21**
See also CA 117; DLB 72; EWL 3; GFL 1789 to the Present

Drinkwater, John 1882-1937 **TCLC 57**
See also CA 109; 149; DLB 10, 19, 149; RGEL 2

Drop Shot
See Cable, George Washington

Droste-Hulshoff, Annette Freiin von 1797-1848 **NCLC 3, 133**
See also CDWLB 2; DLB 133; RGSF 2; RGWL 2, 3

Drummond, Walter
See Silverberg, Robert

Drummond, William Henry
1854-1907 **TCLC 25**
See also CA 160; DLB 92

Drummond de Andrade, Carlos
1902-1987 **CLC 18; TCLC 139**
See Andrade, Carlos Drummond de
See also CA 132; 123; DLB 307; LAW

Drummond of Hawthornden, William
1585-1649 **LC 83**
See also DLB 121, 213; RGEL 2

Drury, Allen (Stuart) 1918-1998 **CLC 37**
See also CA 57-60; 170; CANR 18, 52; CN
1, 2, 3, 4, 5, 6; INT CANR-18

Druse, Eleanor
See King, Stephen

Dryden, John 1631-1700 **DC 3; LC 3, 21,
115; PC 25; WLC 2**
See also BRW 2; CDBLB 1660-1789; DA;
DAB; DAC; DAM DRAM, MST, POET;
DLB 80, 101, 131; EXPP; IDTP; LMFS
1; RGEL 2; TEA; WLIT 3

du Bellay, Joachim 1524-1560 **LC 92**
See also GFL Beginnings to 1789; RGWL
2, 3

Duberman, Martin (Bauml) 1930- **CLC 8**
See also CA 1-4R; CAD; CANR 2, 63, 137;
CD 5, 6

Dubie, Norman (Evans) 1945- **CLC 36**
See also CA 69-72; CANR 12, 115; CP 3,
4, 5, 6, 7; DLB 120; PFS 12

Du Bois, W(illiam) E(dward) B(urghardt)
1868-1963 **BLC 1; CLC 1, 2, 13, 64,
96; HR 1:2; TCLC 169; WLC 2**
See also AAYA 40; AFAW 1, 2; AMWC 1;
AMWS 2; BW 1, 3; CA 85-88; CANR
34, 82, 132; CDALB 1865-1917; DA;
DA3; DAC; DAM MST, MULT, NOV;
DLB 47, 50, 91, 246, 284; EWL 3; EXPP;
LAIT 2; LMFS 2; MAL 5; MTCW 1, 2;
MTFW 2005; NCFS 1; PFS 13; RGAL 4;
SATA 42

Dubus, Andre 1936-1999 **CLC 13, 36, 97;
SSC 15**
See also AMWS 7; CA 21-24R; 177; CANR
17; CN 5, 6; CSW; DLB 130; INT CANR-
17; RGAL 4; SSFS 10; TCLE 1:1

Duca Minimo
See D'Annunzio, Gabriele

Ducharme, Rejean 1941- **CLC 74**
See also CA 165; DLB 60

du Chatelet, Emilie 1706-1749 **LC 96**
See Chatelet, Gabrielle-Emilie Du

Duchen, Claire **CLC 65**

Duclos, Charles Pinot- 1704-1772 **LC 1**
See also GFL Beginnings to 1789

Dudek, Louis 1918-2001 **CLC 11, 19**
See also CA 45-48; 215; CAAS 14; CANR
1; CP 1, 2, 3, 4, 5, 6, 7; DLB 88

Duerrenmatt, Friedrich 1921-1990 ... **CLC 1,
4, 8, 11, 15, 43, 102**
See Durrenmatt, Friedrich
See also CA 17-20R; CANR 33; CMW 4;
DAM DRAM; DLB 69, 124; MTCW 1, 2

Duffy, Bruce 1953(?)- **CLC 50**
See also CA 172

Duffy, Maureen (Patricia) 1933- **CLC 37**
See also CA 25-28R; CANR 33, 68; CBD;
CN 1, 2, 3, 4, 5, 6, 7; CP 5, 6, 7; CWD;
CWP; DFS 15; DLB 14, 310; FW; MTCW
1

Du Fu
See Tu Fu
See also RGWL 2, 3

Dugan, Alan 1923-2003 **CLC 2, 6**
See also CA 81-84; 220; CANR 119; CP 1,
2, 3, 4, 5, 6, 7; DLB 5; MAL 5; PFS 10

du Gard, Roger Martin
See Martin du Gard, Roger

Duhamel, Georges 1884-1966 **CLC 8**
See also CA 81-84; 25-28R; CANR 35;
DLB 65; EWL 3; GFL 1789 to the
Present; MTCW 1

Dujardin, Edouard (Emile Louis)
1861-1949 **TCLC 13**
See also CA 109; DLB 123

Duke, Raoul
See Thompson, Hunter S(tockton)

Dulles, John Foster 1888-1959 **TCLC 72**
See also CA 115; 149

Dumas, Alexandre (pere)
1802-1870 **NCLC 11, 71; WLC 2**
See also AAYA 22; BYA 3; DA; DA3;
DAB; DAC; DAM MST, NOV; DLB 119,
192; EW 6; GFL 1789 to the Present;
LAIT 1, 2; NFS 14, 19; RGWL 2, 3;
SATA 18; TWA; WCH

Dumas, Alexandre (fils) 1824-1895 **DC 1;
NCLC 9**
See also DLB 192; GFL 1789 to the Present;
RGWL 2, 3

Dumas, Claudine
See Malzberg, Barry N(athaniel)

Dumas, Henry L. 1934-1968 **CLC 6, 62**
See also BW 1; CA 85-88; DLB 41; RGAL
4

du Maurier, Daphne 1907-1989 .. **CLC 6, 11,
59; SSC 18**
See also AAYA 37; BPFB 1; BRWS 3; CA
5-8R; 128; CANR 6, 55; CMW 4; CN 1,
2, 3, 4; CPW; DA3; DAB; DAC; DAM
MST, POP; DLB 191; GL 2; HGG; LAIT
3; MSW; MTCW 1, 2; NFS 12; RGEL 2;
RGSF 2; RHW; SATA 27; SATA-Obit 60;
SSFS 14, 16; TEA

Du Maurier, George 1834-1896 **NCLC 86**
See also DLB 153, 178; RGEL 2

Dunbar, Paul Laurence 1872-1906 ... **BLC 1;
PC 5; SSC 8; TCLC 2, 12; WLC 2**
See also AFAW 1, 2; AMWS 2; BW 1, 3;
CA 104; 124; CANR 79; CDALB 1865-
1917; DA; DA3; DAC; DAM MST,
MULT, POET; DLB 50, 54, 78; EXPP;
MAL 5; RGAL 4; SATA 34

Dunbar, William 1460(?)-1520(?) **LC 20;
PC 67**
See also BRWS 8; DLB 132, 146; RGEL 2

Dunbar-Nelson, Alice **HR 1:2**
See Nelson, Alice Ruth Moore Dunbar

Duncan, Dora Angela
See Duncan, Isadora

Duncan, Isadora 1877(?)-1927 **TCLC 68**
See also CA 118; 149

Duncan, Lois 1934- **CLC 26**
See also AAYA 4, 34; BYA 6, 8; CA 1-4R;
CANR 2, 23, 36, 111; CLR 29; JRDA;
MAICYA 1, 2; MAICYAS 1; MTFW
2005; SAAS 2; SATA 1, 36, 75, 133, 141;
SATA-Essay 141; WYA; YAW

Duncan, Robert (Edward)
1919-1988 **CLC 1, 2, 4, 7, 15, 41, 55;
PC 2**
See also BG 1:2; CA 9-12R; 124; CANR
28, 62; CP 1, 2, 3, 4; DAM POET; DLB
5, 16, 193; EWL 3; MAL 5; MTCW 1, 2;
MTFW 2005; PFS 13; RGAL 4; WP

Duncan, Sara Jeannette
1861-1922 **TCLC 60**
See also CA 157; DLB 92

Dunlap, William 1766-1839 **NCLC 2**
See also DLB 30, 37, 59; RGAL 4

Dunn, Douglas (Eaglesham) 1942- **CLC 6,
40**
See also BRWS 10; CA 45-48; CANR 2,
33, 126; CP 1, 2, 3, 4, 5, 6, 7; DLB 40;
MTCW 1

Dunn, Katherine (Karen) 1945- **CLC 71**
See also CA 33-36R; CANR 72; HGG;
MTCW 2; MTFW 2005

Dunn, Stephen (Elliott) 1939- .. **CLC 36, 206**
See also AMWS 11; CA 33-36R; CANR
12, 48, 53, 105; CP 3, 4, 5, 6, 7; DLB
105; PFS 21

Dunne, Finley Peter 1867-1936 **TCLC 28**
See also CA 108; 178; DLB 11, 23; RGAL
4

Dunne, John Gregory 1932-2003 **CLC 28**
See also CA 25-28R; 222; CANR 14, 50;
CN 5, 6, 7; DLBY 1980

Dunsany, Lord **TCLC 2, 59**
See Dunsany, Edward John Moreton Drax
Plunkett
See also DLB 77, 153, 156, 255; FANT;
IDTP; RGEL 2; SFW 4; SUFW 1

**Dunsany, Edward John Moreton Drax
Plunkett** 1878-1957
See Dunsany, Lord
See also CA 104; 148; DLB 10; MTCW 2

Duns Scotus, John 1266(?)-1308 ... **CMLC 59**
See also DLB 115

du Perry, Jean
See Simenon, Georges (Jacques Christian)

Durang, Christopher 1949- **CLC 27, 38**
See also CA 105; CAD; CANR 50, 76, 130;
CD 5, 6; MTCW 2; MTFW 2005

Durang, Christopher Ferdinand
See Durang, Christopher

Duras, Claire de 1777-1832 **NCLC 154**

Duras, Marguerite 1914-1996 .. **CLC 3, 6, 11,
20, 34, 40, 68, 100; SSC 40**
See also BPFB 1; CA 25-28R; 151; CANR
50; CWW 2; DFS 21; DLB 83, 321; EWL
3; FL 1:5; GFL 1789 to the Present; IDFW
4; MTCW 1, 2; RGWL 2, 3; TWA

Durban, (Rosa) Pam 1947- **CLC 39**
See also CA 123; CANR 98; CSW

Durcan, Paul 1944- **CLC 43, 70**
See also CA 134; CANR 123; CP 1, 5, 6, 7;
DAM POET; EWL 3

Durfey, Thomas 1653-1723 **LC 94**
See also DLB 80; RGEL 2

Durkheim, Emile 1858-1917 **TCLC 55**

Durrell, Lawrence (George)
1912-1990 **CLC 1, 4, 6, 8, 13, 27, 41**
See also BPFB 1; BRWS 1; CA 9-12R; 132;
CANR 40, 77; CDBLB 1945-1960; CN 1,
2, 3, 4; CP 1, 2, 3, 4, 5; DAM NOV; DLB
15, 27, 204; DLBY 1990; EWL 3; MTCW
1, 2; RGEL 2; SFW 4; TEA

Durrenmatt, Friedrich
See Duerrenmatt, Friedrich
See also CDWLB 2; EW 13; EWL 3;
RGHL; RGWL 2, 3

Dutt, Michael Madhusudan
1824-1873 **NCLC 118**

Dutt, Toru 1856-1877 **NCLC 29**
See also DLB 240

Dwight, Timothy 1752-1817 **NCLC 13**
See also DLB 37; RGAL 4

Dworkin, Andrea 1946-2005 **CLC 43, 123**
See also CA 77-80; 238; CAAS 21; CANR
16, 39, 76, 96; FL 1:5; FW; GLL 1; INT
CANR-16; MTCW 1, 2; MTFW 2005

Dwyer, Deanna
See Koontz, Dean R.

Dwyer, K. R.
See Koontz, Dean R.

Dybek, Stuart 1942- **CLC 114; SSC 55**
See also CA 97-100; CANR 39; DLB 130;
SSFS 23

Dye, Richard
See De Voto, Bernard (Augustine)

Dyer, Geoff 1958- **CLC 149**
See also CA 125; CANR 88

Dyer, George 1755-1841 **NCLC 129**
　　See also DLB 93
Dylan, Bob 1941- **CLC 3, 4, 6, 12, 77; PC 37**
　　See also CA 41-44R; CANR 108; CP 1, 2, 3, 4, 5, 6, 7; DLB 16
Dyson, John 1943- **CLC 70**
　　See also CA 144
Dzyubin, Eduard Georgievich 1895-1934
　　See Bagritsky, Eduard
　　See also CA 170

E. V. L.
　　See Lucas, E(dward) V(errall)
Eagleton, Terence (Francis) 1943- .. **CLC 63, 132**
　　See also CA 57-60; CANR 7, 23, 68, 115; DLB 242; LMFS 2; MTCW 1, 2; MTFW 2005
Eagleton, Terry
　　See Eagleton, Terence (Francis)
Early, Jack
　　See Scoppettone, Sandra
　　See also GLL 1
East, Michael
　　See West, Morris L(anglo)
Eastaway, Edward
　　See Thomas, (Philip) Edward
Eastlake, William (Derry)
　　1917-1997 **CLC 8**
　　See also CA 5-8R; 158; CAAS 1; CANR 5, 63; CN 1, 2, 3, 4, 5, 6; DLB 6, 206; INT CANR-5; MAL 5; TCWW 1, 2
Eastman, Charles A(lexander)
　　1858-1939 **NNAL; TCLC 55**
　　See also CA 179; CANR 91; DAM MULT; DLB 175; YABC 1
Eaton, Edith Maude 1865-1914 **AAL**
　　See Far, Sui Sin
　　See also CA 154; DLB 221, 312; FW
Eaton, (Lillie) Winnifred 1875-1954 **AAL**
　　See also CA 217; DLB 221, 312; RGAL 4
Eberhart, Richard 1904-2005 **CLC 3, 11, 19, 56**
　　See also AMW; CA 1-4R; 240; CANR 2, 125; CDALB 1941-1968; CP 1, 2, 3, 4, 5, 6, 7; DAM POET; DLB 48; MAL 5; MTCW 1; RGAL 4
Eberhart, Richard Ghormley
　　See Eberhart, Richard
Eberstadt, Fernanda 1960- **CLC 39**
　　See also CA 136; CANR 69, 128
Echegaray (y Eizaguirre), Jose (Maria Waldo) 1832-1916 **HLCS 1; TCLC 4**
　　See also CA 104; CANR 32; EWL 3; HW 1; MTCW 1
Echeverria, (Jose) Esteban (Antonino)
　　1805-1851 **NCLC 18**
　　See also LAW
Echo
　　See Proust, (Valentin-Louis-George-Eugene) Marcel
Eckert, Allan W. 1931- **CLC 17**
　　See also AAYA 18; BYA 2; CA 13-16R; CANR 14, 45; INT CANR-14; MAICYA 2; MAICYAS 1; SAAS 21; SATA 29, 91; SATA-Brief 27
Eckhart, Meister 1260(?)-1327(?) .. **CMLC 9, 80**
　　See also DLB 115; LMFS 1
Eckmar, F. R.
　　See de Hartog, Jan
Eco, Umberto 1932- **CLC 28, 60, 142**
　　See also BEST 90:1; BPFB 1; CA 77-80; CANR 12, 33, 55, 110, 131; CPW; CWW 2; DA3; DAM NOV, POP; DLB 196, 242; EWL 3; MSW; MTCW 1, 2; MTFW 2005; NFS 22; RGWL 3; WLIT 7

Eddison, E(ric) R(ucker)
　　1882-1945 **TCLC 15**
　　See also CA 109; 156; DLB 255; FANT; SFW 4; SUFW 1
Eddy, Mary (Ann Morse) Baker
　　1821-1910 **TCLC 71**
　　See also CA 113; 174
Edel, (Joseph) Leon 1907-1997 .. **CLC 29, 34**
　　See also CA 1-4R; 161; CANR 1, 22, 112; DLB 103; INT CANR-22
Eden, Emily 1797-1869 **NCLC 10**
Edgar, David 1948- **CLC 42**
　　See also CA 57-60; CANR 12, 61, 112; CBD; CD 5, 6; DAM DRAM; DFS 15; DLB 13, 233; MTCW 1
Edgerton, Clyde (Carlyle) 1944- **CLC 39**
　　See also AAYA 17; CA 118; 134; CANR 64, 125; CN 7; CSW; DLB 278; INT CA-134; TCLE 1:1; YAW
Edgeworth, Maria 1768-1849 ... **NCLC 1, 51, 158; SSC 86**
　　See also BRWS 3; DLB 116, 159, 163; FL 1:3; FW; RGEL 2; SATA 21; TEA; WLIT 3
Edmonds, Paul
　　See Kuttner, Henry
Edmonds, Walter D(umaux)
　　1903-1998 **CLC 35**
　　See also BYA 2; CA 5-8R; CANR 2; CWRI 5; DLB 9; LAIT 1; MAICYA 1, 2; MAL 5; RHW; SAAS 4; SATA 1, 27; SATA-Obit 99
Edmondson, Wallace
　　See Ellison, Harlan (Jay)
Edson, Margaret 1961- **CLC 199; DC 24**
　　See also CA 190; DFS 13; DLB 266
Edson, Russell 1935- **CLC 13**
　　See also CA 33-36R; CANR 115; CP 2, 3, 4, 5, 6, 7; DLB 244; WP
Edwards, Bronwen Elizabeth
　　See Rose, Wendy
Edwards, G(erald) B(asil)
　　1899-1976 **CLC 25**
　　See also CA 201; 110
Edwards, Gus 1939- **CLC 43**
　　See also CA 108; INT CA-108
Edwards, Jonathan 1703-1758 **LC 7, 54**
　　See also AMW; DA; DAC; DAM MST; DLB 24, 270; RGAL 4; TUS
Edwards, Sarah Pierpont 1710-1758 .. **LC 87**
　　See also DLB 200
Efron, Marina Ivanovna Tsvetaeva
　　See Tsvetaeva (Efron), Marina (Ivanovna)
Egeria fl. 4th cent. - **CMLC 70**
Egoyan, Atom 1960- **CLC 151**
　　See also AAYA 63; CA 157; CANR 151
Ehle, John (Marsden, Jr.) 1925- **CLC 27**
　　See also CA 9-12R; CSW
Ehrenbourg, Ilya (Grigoryevich)
　　See Ehrenburg, Ilya (Grigoryevich)
Ehrenburg, Ilya (Grigoryevich)
　　1891-1967 **CLC 18, 34, 62**
　　See Erenburg, Il'ia Grigor'evich
　　See also CA 102; 25-28R; EWL 3
Ehrenburg, Ilyo (Grigoryevich)
　　See Ehrenburg, Ilya (Grigoryevich)
Ehrenreich, Barbara 1941- **CLC 110**
　　See also BEST 90:4; CA 73-76; CANR 16, 37, 62, 117; DLB 246; FW; MTCW 1, 2; MTFW 2005
Eich, Gunter
　　See Eich, Gunter
　　See also RGWL 2, 3
Eich, Gunter 1907-1972 **CLC 15**
　　See Eich, Gunter
　　See also CA 111; 93-96; DLB 69, 124; EWL 3
Eichendorff, Joseph 1788-1857 **NCLC 8**
　　See also DLB 90; RGWL 2, 3

Eigner, Larry **CLC 9**
　　See Eigner, Laurence (Joel)
　　See also CAAS 23; CP 1, 2, 3, 4, 5, 6; DLB 5; WP
Eigner, Laurence (Joel) 1927-1996
　　See Eigner, Larry
　　See also CA 9-12R; 151; CANR 6, 84; CP 7; DLB 193
Eilhart von Oberge c. 1140-c.
　　1195 .. **CMLC 67**
　　See also DLB 148
Einhard c. 770-840 **CMLC 50**
　　See also DLB 148
Einstein, Albert 1879-1955 **TCLC 65**
　　See also CA 121; 133; MTCW 1, 2
Eiseley, Loren
　　See Eiseley, Loren Corey
　　See also DLB 275
Eiseley, Loren Corey 1907-1977 **CLC 7**
　　See Eiseley, Loren
　　See also AAYA 5; ANW; CA 1-4R; 73-76; CANR 6; DLBD 17
Eisenstadt, Jill 1963- **CLC 50**
　　See also CA 140
Eisenstein, Sergei (Mikhailovich)
　　1898-1948 **TCLC 57**
　　See also CA 114; 149
Eisner, Simon
　　See Kornbluth, C(yril) M.
Ekeloef, (Bengt) Gunnar
　　1907-1968 **CLC 27; PC 23**
　　See Ekelof, (Bengt) Gunnar
　　See also CA 123; 25-28R; DAM POET
Ekelof, (Bengt) Gunnar 1907-1968
　　See Ekeloef, (Bengt) Gunnar
　　See also DLB 259; EW 12; EWL 3
Ekelund, Vilhelm 1880-1949 **TCLC 75**
　　See also CA 189; EWL 3
Ekwensi, C. O. D.
　　See Ekwensi, Cyprian (Odiatu Duaka)
Ekwensi, Cyprian (Odiatu Duaka)
　　1921- **BLC 1; CLC 4**
　　See also AFW; BW 2, 3; CA 29-32R; CANR 18, 42, 74, 125; CDWLB 3; CN 1, 2, 3, 4, 5, 6; CWRI 5; DAM MULT; DLB 117; EWL 3; MTCW 1, 2; RGEL 2; SATA 66; WLIT 2
Elaine ... **TCLC 18**
　　See Leverson, Ada Esther
El Crummo
　　See Crumb, R.
Elder, Lonne III 1931-1996 **BLC 1; DC 8**
　　See also BW 1, 3; CA 81-84; 152; CAD; CANR 25; DAM MULT; DLB 7, 38, 44; MAL 5
Eleanor of Aquitaine 1122-1204 ... **CMLC 39**
Elia
　　See Lamb, Charles
Eliade, Mircea 1907-1986 **CLC 19**
　　See also CA 65-68; 119; CANR 30, 62; CD-WLB 4; DLB 220; EWL 3; MTCW 1; RGWL 3; SFW 4
Eliot, A. D.
　　See Jewett, (Theodora) Sarah Orne
Eliot, Alice
　　See Jewett, (Theodora) Sarah Orne
Eliot, Dan
　　See Silverberg, Robert
Eliot, George 1819-1880 **NCLC 4, 13, 23, 41, 49, 89, 118; PC 20; SSC 72; WLC 2**
　　See Evans, Mary Ann
　　See also BRW 5; BRWC 1, 2; BRWR 2; CDBLB 1832-1890; CN 7; CPW; DA; DA3; DAB; DAC; DAM MST, NOV; DLB 21, 35, 55; FL 1:3; LATS 1:1; LMFS 1; NFS 17, 20; RGEL 2; RGSF 2; SSFS 8; TEA; WLIT 3
Eliot, John 1604-1690 **LC 5**
　　See also DLB 24

Author Index

Eliot, T(homas) S(tearns)
1888-1965 **CLC 1, 2, 3, 6, 9, 10, 13, 15, 24, 34, 41, 55, 57, 113; PC 5, 31; WLC 2**
See also AAYA 28; AMW; AMWC 1; AMWR 1; BRW 7; BRWR 2; CA 5-8R; 25-28R; CANR 41; CBD; CDALB 1929-1941; DA; DA3; DAB; DAC; DAM DRAM, MST, POET; DFS 4, 13; DLB 7, 10, 45, 63, 245; DLBY 1988; EWL 3; EXPP; LAIT 3; LATS 1:1; LMFS 2; MAL 5; MTCW 1, 2; MTFW 2005; NCFS 5; PAB; PFS 1, 7, 20; RGAL 4; RGEL 2; TUS; WLIT 4; WP

Elisabeth of Schonau c.
1129-1165 **CMLC 82**

Elizabeth 1866-1941 **TCLC 41**

Elizabeth I 1533-1603 **LC 118**
See also DLB 136

Elkin, Stanley L(awrence)
1930-1995 .. **CLC 4, 6, 9, 14, 27, 51, 91; SSC 12**
See also AMWS 6; BPFB 1; CA 9-12R; 148; CANR 8, 46; CN 1, 2, 3, 4, 5, 6; CPW; DAM NOV, POP; DLB 2, 28, 218, 278; DLBY 1980; EWL 3; INT CANR-8; MAL 5; MTCW 1, 2; MTFW 2005; RGAL 4; TCLE 1:1

Elledge, Scott **CLC 34**

Eller, Scott
See Shepard, James R.

Elliott, Don
See Silverberg, Robert

Elliott, George P(aul) 1918-1980 **CLC 2**
See also CA 1-4R; 97-100; CANR 2; CN 1, 2; CP 3; DLB 244; MAL 5

Elliott, Janice 1931-1995 **CLC 47**
See also CA 13-16R; CANR 8, 29, 84; CN 5, 6, 7; DLB 14; SATA 119

Elliott, Sumner Locke 1917-1991 **CLC 38**
See also CA 5-8R; 134; CANR 2, 21; DLB 289

Elliott, William
See Bradbury, Ray (Douglas)

Ellis, A. E. .. **CLC 7**

Ellis, Alice Thomas **CLC 40**
See Haycraft, Anna
See also CN 4, 5, 6; DLB 194

Ellis, Bret Easton 1964- **CLC 39, 71, 117**
See also AAYA 2, 43; CA 118; 123; CANR 51, 74, 126; CN 6, 7; CPW; DA3; DAM POP; DLB 292; HGG; INT CA-123; MTCW 2; MTFW 2005; NFS 11

Ellis, (Henry) Havelock
1859-1939 **TCLC 14**
See also CA 109; 169; DLB 190

Ellis, Landon
See Ellison, Harlan (Jay)

Ellis, Trey 1962- **CLC 55**
See also CA 146; CANR 92; CN 7

Ellison, Harlan (Jay) 1934- ... **CLC 1, 13, 42, 139; SSC 14**
See also AAYA 29; BPFB 1; BYA 14; CA 5-8R; CANR 5, 46, 115; CPW; DAM POP; DLB 8; HGG; INT CANR-5; MTCW 1, 2; MTFW 2005; SCFW 2; SFW 4; SSFS 13, 14, 15, 21; SUFW 1, 2

Ellison, Ralph (Waldo) 1914-1994 **BLC 1; CLC 1, 3, 11, 54, 86, 114; SSC 26, 79; WLC 2**
See also AAYA 19; AFAW 1, 2; AMWC 2; AMWR 2; AMWS 2; BPFB 1; BW 1, 3; BYA 2; CA 9-12R; 145; CANR 24, 53; CDALB 1941-1968; CN 1, 2, 3, 4, 5; CSW; DA; DA3; DAB; DAC; DAM MST, MULT, NOV; DLB 2, 76, 227; DLBY 1994; EWL 3; EXPN; EXPS; LAIT 4; MAL 5; MTCW 1, 2; MTFW 2005; NCFS 3; NFS 2, 21; RGAL 4; RGSF 2; SSFS 1, 11; YAW

Ellmann, Lucy 1956- **CLC 61**
See also CA 128; CANR 154

Ellmann, Lucy Elizabeth
See Ellmann, Lucy

Ellmann, Richard (David)
1918-1987 **CLC 50**
See also BEST 89:2; CA 1-4R; 122; CANR 2, 28, 61; DLB 103; DLBY 1987; MTCW 1, 2; MTFW 2005

Elman, Richard (Martin)
1934-1997 **CLC 19**
See also CA 17-20R; 163; CAAS 3; CANR 47; TCLE 1:1

Elron
See Hubbard, L. Ron

El Saadawi, Nawal 1931- **CLC 196**
See al'Sadaawi, Nawal; Sa'adawi, al-Nawal; Saadawi, Nawal El; Sa'dawi, Nawal al-
See also CA 118; CAAS 11; CANR 44, 92

Eluard, Paul **PC 38; TCLC 7, 41**
See Grindel, Eugene
See also EWL 3; GFL 1789 to the Present; RGWL 2, 3

Elyot, Thomas 1490(?)-1546 **LC 11**
See also DLB 136; RGEL 2

Elytis, Odysseus 1911-1996 **CLC 15, 49, 100; PC 21**
See Alepoudelis, Odysseus
See also CA 102; 151; CANR 94; CWW 2; DAM POET; EW 13; EWL 3; MTCW 1, 2; RGWL 2, 3

Emecheta, (Florence Onye) Buchi
1944- **BLC 2; CLC 14, 48, 128, 214**
See also AAYA 67; AFW; BW 2, 3; CA 81-84; CANR 27, 81, 126; CDWLB 3; CN 4, 5, 6, 7; CWRI 5; DA3; DAM MULT; DLB 117; EWL 3; FL 1:5; FW; MTCW 1, 2; MTFW 2005; NFS 12, 14; SATA 66; WLIT 2

Emerson, Mary Moody
1774-1863 **NCLC 66**

Emerson, Ralph Waldo 1803-1882 . **NCLC 1, 38, 98; PC 18; WLC 2**
See also AAYA 60; AMW; ANW; CDALB 1640-1865; DA; DA3; DAB; DAC; DAM MST, POET; DLB 1, 59, 73, 183, 223, 270; EXPP; LAIT 2; LMFS 1; NCFS 3; PFS 4, 17; RGAL 4; TUS; WP

Eminem 1972- **CLC 226**
See also CA 245

Eminescu, Mihail 1850-1889 .. **NCLC 33, 131**

Empedocles 5th cent. B.C.- **CMLC 50**
See also DLB 176

Empson, William 1906-1984 ... **CLC 3, 8, 19, 33, 34**
See also BRWS 2; CA 17-20R; 112; CANR 31, 61; CP 1, 2, 3; DLB 20; EWL 3; MTCW 1, 2; RGEL 2

Enchi, Fumiko (Ueda) 1905-1986 **CLC 31**
See Enchi Fumiko
See also CA 129; 121; FW; MJW

Enchi Fumiko
See Enchi, Fumiko (Ueda)
See also DLB 182; EWL 3

Ende, Michael (Andreas Helmuth)
1929-1995 **CLC 31**
See also BYA 5; CA 118; 124; 149; CANR 36, 110; CLR 14; DLB 75; MAICYA 1, 2; MAICYAS 1; SATA 61, 130; SATA-Brief 42; SATA-Obit 86

Endo, Shusaku 1923-1996 **CLC 7, 14, 19, 54, 99; SSC 48; TCLC 152**
See Endo Shusaku
See also CA 29-32R; 153; CANR 21, 54, 131; DA3; DAM NOV; MTCW 1, 2; MTFW 2005; RGSF 2; RGWL 2, 3

Endo Shusaku
See Endo, Shusaku
See also CWW 2; DLB 182; EWL 3

Engel, Marian 1933-1985 **CLC 36; TCLC 137**
See also CA 25-28R; CANR 12; CN 2, 3; DLB 53; FW; INT CANR-12

Engelhardt, Frederick
See Hubbard, L. Ron

Engels, Friedrich 1820-1895 .. **NCLC 85, 114**
See also DLB 129; LATS 1:1

Enright, D(ennis) J(oseph)
1920-2002 **CLC 4, 8, 31**
See also CA 1-4R; 211; CANR 1, 42, 83; CN 1, 2; CP 1, 2, 3, 4, 5, 6, 7; DLB 27; EWL 3; SATA 25; SATA-Obit 140

Ensler, Eve 1953- **CLC 212**
See also CA 172; CANR 126; DFS 23

Enzensberger, Hans Magnus
1929- **CLC 43; PC 28**
See also CA 116; 119; CANR 103; CWW 2; EWL 3

Ephron, Nora 1941- **CLC 17, 31**
See also AAYA 35; AITN 2; CA 65-68; CANR 12, 39, 83; DFS 22

Epicurus 341B.C.-270B.C. **CMLC 21**
See also DLB 176

Epsilon
See Betjeman, John

Epstein, Daniel Mark 1948- **CLC 7**
See also CA 49-52; CANR 2, 53, 90

Epstein, Jacob 1956- **CLC 19**
See also CA 114

Epstein, Jean 1897-1953 **TCLC 92**

Epstein, Joseph 1937- **CLC 39, 204**
See also AMWS 14; CA 112; 119; CANR 50, 65, 117

Epstein, Leslie 1938- **CLC 27**
See also AMWS 12; CA 73-76, 215; CAAE 215; CAAS 12; CANR 23, 69; DLB 299; RGHL

Equiano, Olaudah 1745(?)-1797 . **BLC 2; LC 16**
See also AFAW 1, 2; CDWLB 3; DAM MULT; DLB 37, 50; WLIT 2

Erasmus, Desiderius 1469(?)-1536 **LC 16, 93**
See also DLB 136; EW 2; LMFS 1; RGWL 2, 3; TWA

Erdman, Paul E(mil) 1932- **CLC 25**
See also AITN 1; CA 61-64; CANR 13, 43, 84

Erdrich, Karen Louise
See Erdrich, Louise

Erdrich, Louise 1954- **CLC 39, 54, 120, 176; NNAL; PC 52**
See also AAYA 10, 47; AMWS 4; BEST 89:1; BPFB 1; CA 114; CANR 41, 62, 118, 138; CDALBS; CN 5, 6, 7; CP 6, 7; CPW; CWP; DA3; DAM MULT, NOV, POP; DLB 152, 175, 206; EWL 3; EXPP; FL 1:5; LAIT 5; LATS 1:2; MAL 5; MTCW 1, 2; MTFW 2005; NFS 5; PFS 14; RGAL 4; SATA 94, 141; SSFS 14; TCWW 2

Erenburg, Ilya (Grigoryevich)
See Ehrenburg, Ilya (Grigoryevich)

Erickson, Stephen Michael 1950-
See Erickson, Steve
See also CA 129; SFW 4

Erickson, Steve **CLC 64**
See Erickson, Stephen Michael
See also CANR 60, 68, 136; MTFW 2005; SUFW 2

Erickson, Walter
See Fast, Howard (Melvin)

Ericson, Walter
See Fast, Howard (Melvin)

Eriksson, Buntel
See Bergman, (Ernst) Ingmar

Eriugena, John Scottus c.
810-877 **CMLC 65**
See also DLB 115

Ernaux, Annie 1940- **CLC 88, 184**
See also CA 147; CANR 93; MTFW 2005;
NCFS 3, 5

Erskine, John 1879-1951 **TCLC 84**
See also CA 112; 159; DLB 9, 102; FANT

Eschenbach, Wolfram von
See Wolfram von Eschenbach
See also RGWL 3

Eseki, Bruno
See Mphahlele, Ezekiel

Esenin, Sergei (Alexandrovich)
1895-1925 **TCLC 4**
See Yesenin, Sergey
See also CA 104; RGWL 2, 3

Eshleman, Clayton 1935- **CLC 7**
See also CA 33-36R, 212; CAAE 212;
CAAS 6; CANR 93; CP 1, 2, 3, 4, 5, 6,
7; DLB 5

Espriella, Don Manuel Alvarez
See Southey, Robert

Espriu, Salvador 1913-1985 **CLC 9**
See also CA 154; 115; DLB 134; EWL 3

Espronceda, Jose de 1808-1842 **NCLC 39**

Esquivel, Laura 1951(?)- ... **CLC 141; HLCS
1**
See also AAYA 29; CA 143; CANR 68, 113;
DA3; DNFS 2; LAIT 3; LMFS 2; MTCW
2; MTFW 2005; NFS 5; WLIT 1

Esse, James
See Stephens, James

Esterbrook, Tom
See Hubbard, L. Ron

Estleman, Loren D. 1952- **CLC 48**
See also AAYA 27; CA 85-88; CANR 27,
74, 139; CMW 4; CPW; DA3; DAM
NOV, POP; DLB 226; INT CANR-27;
MTCW 1, 2; MTFW 2005; TCWW 1, 2

Etherege, Sir George 1636-1692 . **DC 23; LC
78**
See also BRW 2; DAM DRAM; DLB 80;
PAB; RGEL 2

Euclid 306B.C.-283B.C. **CMLC 25**

Eugenides, Jeffrey 1960(?)- **CLC 81, 212**
See also AAYA 51; CA 144; CANR 120;
MTFW 2005

Euripides c. 484B.C.-406B.C. **CMLC 23,
51; DC 4; WLCS**
See also AW 1; CDWLB 1; DA; DA3;
DAB; DAC; DAM DRAM, MST; DFS 1,
4, 6; DLB 176; LAIT 1; LMFS 1; RGWL
2, 3; WLIT 8

Evan, Evin
See Faust, Frederick (Schiller)

Evans, Caradoc 1878-1945 ... **SSC 43; TCLC
85**
See also DLB 162

Evans, Evan
See Faust, Frederick (Schiller)

Evans, Marian
See Eliot, George

Evans, Mary Ann
See Eliot, George
See also NFS 20

Evarts, Esther
See Benson, Sally

Everett, Percival
See Everett, Percival L.
See also CSW

Everett, Percival L. 1956- **CLC 57**
See Everett, Percival
See also BW 2; CA 129; CANR 94, 134;
CN 7; MTFW 2005

Everson, R(onald) G(ilmour)
1903-1992 **CLC 27**
See also CA 17-20R; CP 1, 2, 3, 4; DLB 88

Everson, William (Oliver)
1912-1994 **CLC 1, 5, 14**
See Antoninus, Brother
See also BG 1:2; CA 9-12R; 145; CANR
20; CP 2, 3, 4, 5; DLB 5, 16, 212; MTCW
1

Evtushenko, Evgenii Aleksandrovich
See Yevtushenko, Yevgeny (Alexandrovich)
See also CWW 2; RGWL 2, 3

Ewart, Gavin (Buchanan)
1916-1995 **CLC 13, 46**
See also BRWS 7; CA 89-92; 150; CANR
17, 46; CP 1, 2, 3, 4, 5, 6; DLB 40;
MTCW 1

Ewers, Hanns Heinz 1871-1943 **TCLC 12**
See also CA 109; 149

Ewing, Frederick R.
See Sturgeon, Theodore (Hamilton)

Exley, Frederick (Earl) 1929-1992 **CLC 6,
11**
See also AITN 2; BPFB 1; CA 81-84; 138;
CANR 117; DLB 143; DLBY 1981

Eynhardt, Guillermo
See Quiroga, Horacio (Sylvestre)

Ezekiel, Nissim (Moses) 1924-2004 .. **CLC 61**
See also CA 61-64; 223; CP 1, 2, 3, 4, 5, 6,
7; DLB 323; EWL 3

Ezekiel, Tish O'Dowd 1943- **CLC 34**
See also CA 129

Fadeev, Aleksandr Aleksandrovich
See Bulgya, Alexander Alexandrovich
See also DLB 272

Fadeev, Alexandr Alexandrovich
See Bulgya, Alexander Alexandrovich
See also EWL 3

Fadeyev, A.
See Bulgya, Alexander Alexandrovich

Fadeyev, Alexander **TCLC 53**
See Bulgya, Alexander Alexandrovich

Fagen, Donald 1948- **CLC 26**

Fainzilberg, Ilya Arnoldovich 1897-1937
See Ilf, Ilya
See also CA 120; 165

Fair, Ronald L. 1932- **CLC 18**
See also BW 1; CA 69-72; CANR 25; DLB
33

Fairbairn, Roger
See Carr, John Dickson

Fairbairns, Zoe (Ann) 1948- **CLC 32**
See also CA 103; CANR 21, 85; CN 4, 5,
6, 7

Fairfield, Flora
See Alcott, Louisa May

Fairman, Paul W. 1916-1977
See Queen, Ellery
See also CA 114; SFW 4

Falco, Gian
See Papini, Giovanni

Falconer, James
See Kirkup, James

Falconer, Kenneth
See Kornbluth, C(yril) M.

Falkland, Samuel
See Heijermans, Herman

Fallaci, Oriana 1930- **CLC 11, 110**
See also CA 77-80; CANR 15, 58, 134; FW;
MTCW 1

Faludi, Susan 1959- **CLC 140**
See also CA 138; CANR 126; FW; MTCW
2; MTFW 2005; NCFS 3

Faludy, George 1913- **CLC 42**
See also CA 21-24R

Faludy, Gyoergy
See Faludy, George

Fanon, Frantz 1925-1961 **BLC 2; CLC 74**
See also BW 1; CA 116; 89-92; DAM
MULT; DLB 296; LMFS 2; WLIT 2

Fanshawe, Ann 1625-1680 **LC 11**

Fante, John (Thomas) 1911-1983 **CLC 60;
SSC 65**
See also AMWS 11; CA 69-72; 109; CANR
23, 104; DLB 130; DLBY 1983

Far, Sui Sin ... **SSC 62**
See Eaton, Edith Maude
See also SSFS 4

Farah, Nuruddin 1945- **BLC 2; CLC 53,
137**
See also AFW; BW 2, 3; CA 106; CANR
81, 148; CDWLB 3; CN 4, 5, 6, 7; DAM
MULT; DLB 125; EWL 3; WLIT 2

Fargue, Leon-Paul 1876(?)-1947 **TCLC 11**
See also CA 109; CANR 107; DLB 258;
EWL 3

Farigoule, Louis
See Romains, Jules

Farina, Richard 1936(?)-1966 **CLC 9**
See also CA 81-84; 25-28R

Farley, Walter (Lorimer)
1915-1989 **CLC 17**
See also AAYA 58; BYA 14; CA 17-20R;
CANR 8, 29, 84; DLB 22; JRDA; MAI-
CYA 1, 2; SATA 2, 43, 132; YAW

Farmer, Philip Jose 1918- **CLC 1, 19**
See also AAYA 28; BPFB 1; CA 1-4R;
CANR 4, 35, 111; DLB 8; MTCW 1;
SATA 93; SCFW 1, 2; SFW 4

Farquhar, George 1677-1707 **LC 21**
See also BRW 2; DAM DRAM; DLB 84;
RGEL 2

Farrell, J(ames) G(ordon)
1935-1979 **CLC 6**
See also CA 73-76; 89-92; CANR 36; CN
1, 2; DLB 14, 271, 326; MTCW 1; RGEL
2; RHW; WLIT 4

Farrell, James T(homas) 1904-1979 . **CLC 1,
4, 8, 11, 66; SSC 28**
See also AMW; BPFB 1; CA 5-8R; 89-92;
CANR 9, 61; CN 1, 2; DLB 4, 9, 86;
DLBD 2; EWL 3; MAL 5; MTCW 1, 2;
MTFW 2005; RGAL 4

Farrell, Warren (Thomas) 1943- **CLC 70**
See also CA 146; CANR 120

Farren, Richard J.
See Betjeman, John

Farren, Richard M.
See Betjeman, John

Fassbinder, Rainer Werner
1946-1982 **CLC 20**
See also CA 93-96; 106; CANR 31

Fast, Howard (Melvin) 1914-2003 .. **CLC 23,
131**
See also AAYA 16; BPFB 1; CA 1-4R, 181;
214; CAAE 181; CAAS 18; CANR 1, 33,
54, 75, 98, 140; CMW 4; CN 1, 2, 3, 4, 5,
6, 7; CPW; DAM NOV; DLB 9; INT
CANR-33; LATS 1:1; MAL 5; MTCW 2;
MTFW 2005; RHW; SATA 7; SATA-
Essay 107; TCWW 1, 2; YAW

Faulcon, Robert
See Holdstock, Robert P.

Faulkner, William (Cuthbert)
1897-1962 **CLC 1, 3, 6, 8, 9, 11, 14,
18, 28, 52, 68; SSC 1, 35, 42, 92;
TCLC 141; WLC 2**
See also AAYA 7; AMW; AMWR 1; BPFB
1; BYA 5, 15; CA 81-84; CANR 33;
CDALB 1929-1941; DA; DA3; DAB;
DAC; DAM MST, NOV; DLB 9, 11, 44,
102, 316; DLBD 2; DLBY 1986, 1997;
EWL 3; EXPN; EXPS; GL 2; LAIT 2;
LATS 1:1; LMFS 2; MAL 5; MTCW 1,
2; MTFW 2005; NFS 4, 8, 13; RGAL 4;
RGSF 2; SSFS 2, 5, 6, 12; TUS

Fauset, Jessie Redmon
1882(?)-1961 .. **BLC 2; CLC 19, 54; HR
1:2**
See also AFAW 2; BW 1; CA 109; CANR
83; DAM MULT; DLB 51; FW; LMFS 2;
MAL 5; MAWW

Faust, Frederick (Schiller)
1892-1944 **TCLC 49**
See Brand, Max; Dawson, Peter; Frederick, John
See also CA 108; 152; CANR 143; DAM POP; DLB 256; TUS

Faust, Irvin 1924- **CLC 8**
See also CA 33-36R; CANR 28, 67; CN 1, 2, 3, 4, 5, 6, 7; DLB 2, 28, 218, 278; DLBY 1980

Fawkes, Guy
See Benchley, Robert (Charles)

Fearing, Kenneth (Flexner)
1902-1961 **CLC 51**
See also CA 93-96; CANR 59; CMW 4; DLB 9; MAL 5; RGAL 4

Fecamps, Elise
See Creasey, John

Federman, Raymond 1928- **CLC 6, 47**
See also CA 17-20R, 208; CAAE 208; CAAS 8; CANR 10, 43, 83, 108; CN 3, 4, 5, 6; DLBY 1980

Federspiel, J(uerg) F. 1931- **CLC 42**
See also CA 146

Feiffer, Jules (Ralph) 1929- **CLC 2, 8, 64**
See also AAYA 3, 62; CA 17-20R; CAD; CANR 30, 59, 129; CD 5, 6; DAM DRAM; DLB 7, 44; INT CANR-30; MTCW 1; SATA 8, 61, 111, 157

Feige, Hermann Albert Otto Maximilian
See Traven, B.

Feinberg, David B. 1956-1994 **CLC 59**
See also CA 135; 147

Feinstein, Elaine 1930- **CLC 36**
See also CA 69-72; CAAS 1; CANR 31, 68, 121; CN 3, 4, 5, 6, 7; CP 2, 3, 4, 5, 6, 7; CWP; DLB 14, 40; MTCW 1

Feke, Gilbert David **CLC 65**

Feldman, Irving (Mordecai) 1928- **CLC 7**
See also CA 1-4R; CANR 1; CP 1, 2, 3, 4, 5, 6, 7; DLB 169; TCLE 1:1

Felix-Tchicaya, Gerald
See Tchicaya, Gerald Felix

Fellini, Federico 1920-1993 **CLC 16, 85**
See also CA 65-68; 143; CANR 33

Felltham, Owen 1602(?)-1668 **LC 92**
See also DLB 126, 151

Felsen, Henry Gregor 1916-1995 **CLC 17**
See also CA 1-4R; 180; CANR 1; SAAS 2; SATA 1

Felski, Rita **CLC 65**

Fenno, Jack
See Calisher, Hortense

Fenollosa, Ernest (Francisco)
1853-1908 **TCLC 91**

Fenton, James Martin 1949- **CLC 32, 209**
See also CA 102; CANR 108; CP 2, 3, 4, 5, 6, 7; DLB 40; PFS 11

Ferber, Edna 1887-1968 **CLC 18, 93**
See also AITN 1; CA 5-8R; 25-28R; CANR 68, 105; DLB 9, 28, 86, 266; MAL 5; MTCW 1, 2; MTFW 2005; RGAL 4; RHW; SATA 7; TCWW 1, 2

Ferdowsi, Abu'l Qasem
940-1020(?) **CMLC 43**
See Firdawsi, Abu al-Qasim
See also RGWL 2, 3

Ferguson, Helen
See Kavan, Anna

Ferguson, Niall 1964- **CLC 134**
See also CA 190; CANR 154

Ferguson, Samuel 1810-1886 **NCLC 33**
See also DLB 32; RGEL 2

Fergusson, Robert 1750-1774 **LC 29**
See also DLB 109; RGEL 2

Ferling, Lawrence
See Ferlinghetti, Lawrence

Ferlinghetti, Lawrence 1919(?)- **CLC 2, 6, 10, 27, 111; PC 1**
See also BG 1:2; CA 5-8R; CAD; CANR 3, 41, 73, 125; CDALB 1941-1968; CP 1, 2, 3, 4, 5, 6, 7; DA3; DAM POET; DLB 5, 16; MAL 5; MTCW 1, 2; MTFW 2005; RGAL 4; WP

Ferlinghetti, Lawrence Monsanto
See Ferlinghetti, Lawrence

Fern, Fanny
See Parton, Sara Payson Willis

Fernandez, Vicente Garcia Huidobro
See Huidobro Fernandez, Vicente Garcia

Fernandez-Armesto, Felipe **CLC 70**
See Fernandez-Armesto, Felipe Fermin Ricardo
See also CANR 153

Fernandez-Armesto, Felipe Fermin Ricardo 1950-
See Fernandez-Armesto, Felipe
See also CA 142; CANR 93

Fernandez de Lizardi, Jose Joaquin
See Lizardi, Jose Joaquin Fernandez de

Ferre, Rosario 1938- **CLC 139; HLCS 1; SSC 36**
See also CA 131; CANR 55, 81, 134; CWW 2; DLB 145; EWL 3; HW 1, 2; LAWS 1; MTCW 2; MTFW 2005; WLIT 1

Ferrer, Gabriel (Francisco Victor) Miro
See Miro (Ferrer), Gabriel (Francisco Victor)

Ferrier, Susan (Edmonstone)
1782-1854 **NCLC 8**
See also DLB 116; RGEL 2

Ferrigno, Robert 1948(?)- **CLC 65**
See also CA 140; CANR 125

Ferron, Jacques 1921-1985 **CLC 94**
See also CA 117; 129; CCA 1; DAC; DLB 60; EWL 3

Feuchtwanger, Lion 1884-1958 **TCLC 3**
See also CA 104; 187; DLB 66; EWL 3; RGHL

Feuerbach, Ludwig 1804-1872 **NCLC 139**
See also DLB 133

Feuillet, Octave 1821-1890 **NCLC 45**
See also DLB 192

Feydeau, Georges (Leon Jules Marie)
1862-1921 **TCLC 22**
See also CA 113; 152; CANR 84; DAM DRAM; DLB 192; EWL 3; GFL 1789 to the Present; RGWL 2, 3

Fichte, Johann Gottlieb
1762-1814 **NCLC 62**
See also DLB 90

Ficino, Marsilio 1433-1499 **LC 12**
See also LMFS 1

Fiedeler, Hans
See Doeblin, Alfred

Fiedler, Leslie A(aron) 1917-2003 **CLC 4, 13, 24**
See also AMWS 13; CA 9-12R; 212; CANR 7, 63; CN 1, 2, 3, 4, 5, 6; DLB 28, 67; EWL 3; MAL 5; MTCW 1, 2; RGAL 4; TUS

Field, Andrew 1938- **CLC 44**
See also CA 97-100; CANR 25

Field, Eugene 1850-1895 **NCLC 3**
See also DLB 23, 42, 140; DLBD 13; MAI-CYA 1, 2; RGAL 4; SATA 16

Field, Gans T.
See Wellman, Manly Wade

Field, Michael 1915-1971 **TCLC 43**
See also CA 29-32R

Fielding, Helen 1958- **CLC 146, 217**
See also AAYA 65; CA 172; CANR 127; DLB 231; MTFW 2005

Fielding, Henry 1707-1754 **LC 1, 46, 85; WLC 2**
See also BRW 3; BRWR 1; CDBLB 1660-1789; DA; DA3; DAB; DAC; DAM DRAM, MST, NOV; DLB 39, 84, 101; NFS 18; RGEL 2; TEA; WLIT 3

Fielding, Sarah 1710-1768 **LC 1, 44**
See also DLB 39; RGEL 2; TEA

Fields, W. C. 1880-1946 **TCLC 80**
See also DLB 44

Fierstein, Harvey (Forbes) 1954- **CLC 33**
See also CA 123; 129; CAD; CD 5, 6; CPW; DA3; DAM DRAM, POP; DFS 6; DLB 266; GLL; MAL 5

Figes, Eva 1932- **CLC 31**
See also CA 53-56; CANR 4, 44, 83; CN 2, 3, 4, 5, 6, 7; DLB 14, 271; FW; RGHL

Filippo, Eduardo de
See de Filippo, Eduardo

Finch, Anne 1661-1720 **LC 3; PC 21**
See also BRWS 9; DLB 95

Finch, Robert (Duer Claydon)
1900-1995 **CLC 18**
See also CA 57-60; CANR 9, 24, 49; CP 1, 2, 3, 4, 5, 6; DLB 88

Findley, Timothy (Irving Frederick)
1930-2002 **CLC 27, 102**
See also CA 25-28R; 206; CANR 12, 42, 69, 109; CCA 1; CN 4, 5, 6, 7; DAC; DAM MST; DLB 53; FANT; RHW

Fink, William
See Mencken, H(enry) L(ouis)

Firbank, Louis 1942-
See Reed, Lou
See also CA 117

Firbank, (Arthur Annesley) Ronald
1886-1926 **TCLC 1**
See also BRWS 2; CA 104; 177; DLB 36; EWL 3; RGEL 2

Firdawsi, Abu al-Qasim
See Ferdowsi, Abu'l Qasem
See also WLIT 6

Fish, Stanley
See Fish, Stanley Eugene

Fish, Stanley E.
See Fish, Stanley Eugene

Fish, Stanley Eugene 1938- **CLC 142**
See also CA 112; 132; CANR 90; DLB 67

Fisher, Dorothy (Frances) Canfield
1879-1958 **TCLC 87**
See also CA 114; 136; CANR 80; CLR 71; CWRI 5; DLB 9, 102, 284; MAICYA 1, 2; MAL 5; YABC 1

Fisher, M(ary) F(rances) K(ennedy)
1908-1992 **CLC 76, 87**
See also CA 77-80; 138; CANR 44; MTCW 2

Fisher, Roy 1930- **CLC 25**
See also CA 81-84; CAAS 10; CANR 16; CP 1, 2, 3, 4, 5, 6, 7; DLB 40

Fisher, Rudolph 1897-1934 . **BLC 2; HR 1:2; SSC 25; TCLC 11**
See also BW 1, 3; CA 107; 124; CANR 80; DAM MULT; DLB 51, 102

Fisher, Vardis (Alvero) 1895-1968 **CLC 7; TCLC 140**
See also CA 5-8R; 25-28R; CANR 68; DLB 9, 206; MAL 5; RGAL 4; TCWW 1, 2

Fiske, Tarleton
See Bloch, Robert (Albert)

Fitch, Clarke
See Sinclair, Upton

Fitch, John IV
See Cormier, Robert (Edmund)

Fitzgerald, Captain Hugh
See Baum, L(yman) Frank

FitzGerald, Edward 1809-1883 **NCLC 9, 153**
See also BRW 4; DLB 32; RGEL 2

Fitzgerald, F(rancis) Scott (Key)
1896-1940 ... **SSC 6, 31, 75; TCLC 1, 6, 14, 28, 55, 157; WLC 2**
See also AAYA 24; AITN 1; AMW; AMWC 2; AMWR 1; BPFB 1; CA 110; 123; CDALB 1917-1929; DA; DA3; DAB; DAC; DAM MST, NOV; DLB 4, 9, 86, 219, 273; DLBD 1, 15, 16; DLBY 1981, 1996; EWL 3; EXPN; EXPS; LAIT 3; MAL 5; MTCW 1, 2; MTFW 2005; NFS 2, 19, 20; RGAL 4; RGSF 2; SSFS 4, 15, 21; TUS

Fitzgerald, Penelope 1916-2000 . **CLC 19, 51, 61, 143**
See also BRWS 5; CA 85-88; 190; CAAS 10; CANR 56, 86, 131; CN 3, 4, 5, 6, 7; DLB 14, 194, 326; EWL 3; MTCW 2; MTFW 2005

Fitzgerald, Robert (Stuart)
1910-1985 **CLC 39**
See also CA 1-4R; 114; CANR 1; CP 1, 2, 3, 4; DLBY 1980; MAL 5

FitzGerald, Robert D(avid)
1902-1987 **CLC 19**
See also CA 17-20R; CP 1, 2, 3, 4; DLB 260; RGEL 2

Fitzgerald, Zelda (Sayre)
1900-1948 **TCLC 52**
See also AMWS 9; CA 117; 126; DLBY 1984

Flanagan, Thomas (James Bonner)
1923-2002 **CLC 25, 52**
See also CA 108; 206; CANR 55; CN 3, 4, 5, 6, 7; DLBY 1980; INT CA-108; MTCW 1; RHW; TCLE 1:1

Flaubert, Gustave 1821-1880 **NCLC 2, 10, 19, 62, 66, 135; SSC 11, 60; WLC 2**
See also DA; DA3; DAB; DAC; DAM MST, NOV; DLB 119, 301; EW 7; EXPS; GFL 1789 to the Present; LAIT 2; LMFS 1; NFS 14; RGSF 2; RGWL 2, 3; SSFS 6; TWA

Flavius Josephus
See Josephus, Flavius

Flecker, Herman Elroy
See Flecker, (Herman) James Elroy

Flecker, (Herman) James Elroy
1884-1915 **TCLC 43**
See also CA 109; 150; DLB 10, 19; RGEL 2

Fleming, Ian (Lancaster) 1908-1964 . **CLC 3, 30**
See also AAYA 26; BPFB 1; CA 5-8R; CANR 59; CDBLB 1945-1960; CMW 4; CPW; DA3; DAM POP; DLB 87, 201; MSW; MTCW 1, 2; MTFW 2005; RGEL 2; SATA 9; TEA; YAW

Fleming, Thomas (James) 1927- **CLC 37**
See also CA 5-8R; CANR 10, 102; INT CANR-10; SATA 8

Fletcher, John 1579-1625 **DC 6; LC 33**
See also BRW 2; CDBLB Before 1660; DLB 58; RGEL 2; TEA

Fletcher, John Gould 1886-1950 **TCLC 35**
See also CA 107; 167; DLB 4, 45; LMFS 2; MAL 5; RGAL 4

Fleur, Paul
See Pohl, Frederik

Flieg, Helmut
See Heym, Stefan

Flooglebuckle, Al
See Spiegelman, Art

Flora, Fletcher 1914-1969
See Queen, Ellery
See also CA 1-4R; CANR 3, 85

Flying Officer X
See Bates, H(erbert) E(rnest)

Fo, Dario 1926- **CLC 32, 109; DC 10**
See also CA 116; 128; CANR 68, 114, 134; CWW 2; DA3; DAM DRAM; DFS 23; DLBY 1997; EWL 3; MTCW 1, 2; MTFW 2005; WLIT 7

Fogarty, Jonathan Titulescu Esq.
See Farrell, James T(homas)

Follett, Ken(neth Martin) 1949- **CLC 18**
See also AAYA 6, 50; BEST 89:4; BPFB 1; CA 81-84; CANR 13, 33, 54, 102; CMW 4; CPW; DA3; DAM NOV, POP; DLB 87; DLBY 1981; INT CANR-33; MTCW 1

Fondane, Benjamin 1898-1944 **TCLC 159**

Fontane, Theodor 1819-1898 . **NCLC 26, 163**
See also CDWLB 2; DLB 129; EW 6; RGWL 2, 3; TWA

Fonte, Moderata 1555-1592 **LC 118**

Fontenot, Chester **CLC 65**

Fonvizin, Denis Ivanovich
1744(?)-1792 **LC 81**
See also DLB 150; RGWL 2, 3

Foote, Horton 1916- **CLC 51, 91**
See also CA 73-76; CAD; CANR 34, 51, 110; CD 5, 6; CSW; DA3; DAM DRAM; DFS 20; DLB 26, 266; EWL 3; INT CANR-34; MTFW 2005

Foote, Mary Hallock 1847-1938 .. **TCLC 108**
See also DLB 186, 188, 202, 221; TCWW 2

Foote, Samuel 1721-1777 **LC 106**
See also DLB 89; RGEL 2

Foote, Shelby 1916-2005 **CLC 75, 224**
See also AAYA 40; CA 5-8R; 240; CANR 3, 45, 74, 131; CN 1, 2, 3, 4, 5, 6, 7; CPW; CSW; DA3; DAM NOV, POP; DLB 2, 17; MAL 5; MTCW 2; MTFW 2005; RHW

Forbes, Cosmo
See Lewton, Val

Forbes, Esther 1891-1967 **CLC 12**
See also AAYA 17; BYA 2; CA 13-14; 25-28R; CAP 1; CLR 27; DLB 22; JRDA; MAICYA 1, 2; RHW; SATA 2, 100; YAW

Forche, Carolyn (Louise) 1950- **CLC 25, 83, 86; PC 10**
See also CA 109; 117; CANR 50, 74, 138; CP 4, 5, 6, 7; CWP; DA3; DAM POET; DLB 5, 193; INT CA-117; MAL 5; MTCW 2; MTFW 2005; PFS 18; RGAL 4

Ford, Elbur
See Hibbert, Eleanor Alice Burford

Ford, Ford Madox 1873-1939 ... **TCLC 1, 15, 39, 57, 172**
See Chaucer, Daniel
See also BRW 6; CA 104; 132; CANR 74; CDBLB 1914-1945; DA3; DAM NOV; DLB 34, 98, 162; EWL 3; MTCW 1, 2; RGEL 2; TEA

Ford, Henry 1863-1947 **TCLC 73**
See also CA 115; 148

Ford, Jack
See Ford, John

Ford, John 1586-1639 **DC 8; LC 68**
See also BRW 2; CDBLB Before 1660; DA3; DAM DRAM; DFS 7; DLB 58; IDTP; RGEL 2

Ford, John 1895-1973 **CLC 16**
See also CA 187; 45-48

Ford, Richard 1944- **CLC 46, 99, 205**
See also AMWS 5; CA 69-72; CANR 11, 47, 86, 128; CN 5, 6, 7; CSW; DLB 227; EWL 3; MAL 5; MTCW 2; MTFW 2005; RGAL 4; RGSF 2

Ford, Webster
See Masters, Edgar Lee

Foreman, Richard 1937- **CLC 50**
See also CA 65-68; CAD; CANR 32, 63, 143; CD 5, 6

Forester, C(ecil) S(cott) 1899-1966 . **CLC 35; TCLC 152**
See also CA 73-76; 25-28R; CANR 83; DLB 191; RGEL 2; RHW; SATA 13

Forez
See Mauriac, Francois (Charles)

Forman, James
See Forman, James D(ouglas)

Forman, James D(ouglas) 1932- **CLC 21**
See also AAYA 17; CA 9-12R; CANR 4, 19, 42; JRDA; MAICYA 1, 2; SATA 8, 70; YAW

Forman, Milos 1932- **CLC 164**
See also AAYA 63; CA 109

Fornes, Maria Irene 1930- **CLC 39, 61, 187; DC 10; HLCS 1**
See also CA 25-28R; CAD; CANR 28, 81; CD 5, 6; CWD; DLB 7; HW 1, 2; INT CANR-28; LLW; MAL 5; MTCW 1; RGAL 4

Forrest, Leon (Richard)
1937-1997 **BLCS; CLC 4**
See also AFAW 2; BW 2; CA 89-92; 162; CAAS 7; CANR 25, 52, 87; CN 4, 5, 6; DLB 33

Forster, E(dward) M(organ)
1879-1970 **CLC 1, 2, 3, 4, 9, 10, 13, 15, 22, 45, 77; SSC 27; TCLC 125; WLC 2**
See also AAYA 2, 37; BRW 6; BRWR 2; BYA 12; CA 13-14; 25-28R; CANR 45; CAP 1; CDBLB 1914-1945; DA; DA3; DAB; DAC; DAM MST, NOV; DLB 34, 98, 162, 178, 195; DLBD 10; EWL 3; EXPN; LAIT 3; LMFS 1; MTCW 1, 2; MTFW 2005; NCFS 1; NFS 3, 10, 11; RGEL 2; RGSF 2; SATA 57; SUFW 1; TEA; WLIT 4

Forster, John 1812-1876 **NCLC 11**
See also DLB 144, 184

Forster, Margaret 1938- **CLC 149**
See also CA 133; CANR 62, 115; CN 4, 5, 6, 7; DLB 155, 271

Forsyth, Frederick 1938- **CLC 2, 5, 36**
See also BEST 89:4; CA 85-88; CANR 38, 62, 115, 137; CMW 4; CN 3, 4, 5, 6, 7; CPW; DAM NOV, POP; DLB 87; MTCW 1, 2; MTFW 2005

Forten, Charlotte L. 1837-1914 **BLC 2; TCLC 16**
See Grimke, Charlotte L(ottie) Forten
See also DLB 50, 239

Fortinbras
See Grieg, (Johan) Nordahl (Brun)

Foscolo, Ugo 1778-1827 **NCLC 8, 97**
See also EW 5; WLIT 7

Fosse, Bob .. **CLC 20**
See Fosse, Robert Louis

Fosse, Robert Louis 1927-1987
See Fosse, Bob
See also CA 110; 123

Foster, Hannah Webster
1758-1840 **NCLC 99**
See also DLB 37, 200; RGAL 4

Foster, Stephen Collins
1826-1864 **NCLC 26**
See also RGAL 4

Foucault, Michel 1926-1984 . **CLC 31, 34, 69**
See also CA 105; 113; CANR 34; DLB 242; EW 13; EWL 3; GFL 1789 to the Present; GLL 1; LMFS 2; MTCW 1, 2; TWA

Fouque, Friedrich (Heinrich Karl) de la Motte 1777-1843 **NCLC 2**
See also DLB 90; RGWL 2, 3; SUFW 1

Fourier, Charles 1772-1837 **NCLC 51**

Fournier, Henri-Alban 1886-1914
See Alain-Fournier
See also CA 104; 179

Fournier, Pierre 1916-1997 **CLC 11**
See Gascar, Pierre
See also CA 89-92; CANR 16, 40

Fowles, John 1926-2005 **CLC 1, 2, 3, 4, 6, 9, 10, 15, 33, 87; SSC 33**
See also BPFB 1; BRWS 1; CA 5-8R; 245; CANR 25, 71, 103; CDBLB 1960 to Present; CN 1, 2, 3, 4, 5, 6, 7; DA3; DAB; DAC; DAM MST; DLB 14, 139, 207; EWL 3; HGG; MTCW 1, 2; MTFW 2005; NFS 21; RGEL 2; RHW; SATA 22; SATA-Obit 171; TEA; WLIT 4

Fowles, John Robert
See Fowles, John

Fox, Paula 1923- **CLC 2, 8, 121**
See also AAYA 3, 37; BYA 3, 8; CA 73-76; CANR 20, 36, 62, 105; CLR 1, 44, 96; DLB 52; JRDA; MAICYA 1, 2; MTCW 1; NFS 12; SATA 17, 60, 120, 167; WYA; YAW

Fox, William Price (Jr.) 1926- **CLC 22**
See also CA 17-20R; CAAS 19; CANR 11, 142; CSW; DLB 2; DLBY 1981

Foxe, John 1517(?)-1587 **LC 14**
See also DLB 132

Frame, Janet .. **CLC 2, 3, 6, 22, 66, 96; SSC 29**
See Clutha, Janet Paterson Frame
See also CN 1, 2, 3, 4, 5, 6, 7; CP 2, 3, 4; CWP; EWL 3; RGEL 2; RGSF 2; TWA

France, Anatole **TCLC 9**
See Thibault, Jacques Anatole Francois
See also DLB 123; EWL 3; GFL 1789 to the Present; RGWL 2, 3; SUFW 1

Francis, Claude **CLC 50**
See also CA 192

Francis, Dick
See Francis, Richard Stanley
See also CN 2, 3, 4, 5, 6

Francis, Richard Stanley 1920- ... **CLC 2, 22, 42, 102**
See Francis, Dick
See also AAYA 5, 21; BEST 89:3; BPFB 1; CA 5-8R; CANR 9, 42, 68, 100, 141; CD-BLB 1960 to Present; CMW 4; CN 7; DA3; DAM POP; DLB 87; INT CANR-9; MSW; MTCW 1, 2; MTFW 2005

Francis, Robert (Churchill)
1901-1987 **CLC 15; PC 34**
See also AMWS 9; CA 1-4R; 123; CANR 1; CP 1, 2, 3, 4; EXPP; PFS 12; TCLE 1:1

Francis, Lord Jeffrey
See Jeffrey, Francis
See also DLB 107

Frank, Anne(lies Marie)
1929-1945 **TCLC 17; WLC 2**
See also AAYA 12; BYA 1; CA 113; 133; CANR 68; CLR 101; DA; DA3; DAB; DAC; DAM MST; LAIT 4; MAICYA 2; MAICYAS 1; MTCW 1, 2; MTFW 2005; NCFS 2; RGHL; SATA 87; SATA-Brief 42; WYA; YAW

Frank, Bruno 1887-1945 **TCLC 81**
See also CA 189; DLB 118; EWL 3

Frank, Elizabeth 1945- **CLC 39**
See also CA 121; 126; CANR 78, 150; INT CA-126

Frankl, Viktor E(mil) 1905-1997 **CLC 93**
See also CA 65-68; 161; RGHL

Franklin, Benjamin
See Hasek, Jaroslav (Matej Frantisek)

Franklin, Benjamin 1706-1790 **LC 25; WLCS**
See also AMW; CDALB 1640-1865; DA; DA3; DAB; DAC; DAM MST; DLB 24, 43, 73, 183; LAIT 1; RGAL 4; TUS

Franklin, (Stella Maria Sarah) Miles (Lampe) 1879-1954 **TCLC 7**
See also CA 104; 164; DLB 230; FW; MTCW 2; RGEL 2; TWA

Franzen, Jonathan 1959- **CLC 202**
See also AAYA 65; CA 129; CANR 105

Fraser, Antonia (Pakenham) 1932- . **CLC 32, 107**
See also AAYA 57; CA 85-88; CANR 44, 65, 119; CMW; DLB 276; MTCW 1, 2; MTFW 2005; SATA-Brief 32

Fraser, George MacDonald 1925- **CLC 7**
See also AAYA 48; CA 45-48; 180; CAAE 180; CANR 2, 48, 74; MTCW 2; RHW

Fraser, Sylvia 1935- **CLC 64**
See also CA 45-48; CANR 1, 16, 60; CCA 1

Frayn, Michael 1933- **CLC 3, 7, 31, 47, 176; DC 27**
See also AAYA 69; BRWC 2; BRWS 7; CA 5-8R; CANR 30, 69, 114, 133; CBD; CD 5, 6; CN 1, 2, 3, 4, 5, 6, 7; DAM DRAM, NOV; DFS 22; DLB 13, 14, 194, 245; FANT; MTCW 1, 2; MTFW 2005; SFW 4

Fraze, Candida (Merrill) 1945- **CLC 50**
See also CA 126

Frazer, Andrew
See Marlowe, Stephen

Frazer, J(ames) G(eorge)
1854-1941 **TCLC 32**
See also BRWS 3; CA 118; NCFS 5

Frazer, Robert Caine
See Creasey, John

Frazer, Sir James George
See Frazer, J(ames) G(eorge)

Frazier, Charles 1950- **CLC 109, 224**
See also AAYA 34; CA 161; CANR 126; CSW; DLB 292; MTFW 2005

Frazier, Ian 1951- **CLC 46**
See also CA 130; CANR 54, 93

Frederic, Harold 1856-1898 **NCLC 10**
See also AMW; DLB 12, 23; DLBD 13; MAL 5; NFS 22; RGAL 4

Frederick, John
See Faust, Frederick (Schiller)
See also TCWW 2

Frederick the Great 1712-1786 **LC 14**

Fredro, Aleksander 1793-1876 **NCLC 8**

Freeling, Nicolas 1927-2003 **CLC 38**
See also CA 49-52; 218; CAAS 12; CANR 1, 17, 50, 84; CMW 4; CN 1, 2, 3, 4, 5, 6; DLB 87

Freeman, Douglas Southall
1886-1953 **TCLC 11**
See also CA 109; 195; DLB 17; DLBD 17

Freeman, Judith 1946- **CLC 55**
See also CA 148; CANR 120; DLB 256

Freeman, Mary E(leanor) Wilkins
1852-1930 **SSC 1, 47; TCLC 9**
See also CA 106; 177; DLB 12, 78, 221; EXPS; FW; HGG; MAWW; RGAL 4; RGSF 2; SSFS 4, 8; SUFW 1; TUS

Freeman, R(ichard) Austin
1862-1943 **TCLC 21**
See also CA 113; CANR 84; CMW 4; DLB 70

French, Albert 1943- **CLC 86**
See also BW 3; CA 167

French, Antonia
See Kureishi, Hanif

French, Marilyn 1929- .. **CLC 10, 18, 60, 177**
See also BPFB 1; CA 69-72; CANR 3, 31, 134; CN 5, 6, 7; CPW; DAM DRAM, NOV, POP; FL 1:5; FW; INT CANR-31; MTCW 1, 2; MTFW 2005

French, Paul
See Asimov, Isaac

Freneau, Philip Morin 1752-1832 .. **NCLC 1, 111**
See also AMWS 2; DLB 37, 43; RGAL 4

Freud, Sigmund 1856-1939 **TCLC 52**
See also CA 115; 133; CANR 69; DLB 296; EW 8; EWL 3; LATS 1:1; MTCW 1, 2; MTFW 2005; NCFS 3; TWA

Freytag, Gustav 1816-1895 **NCLC 109**
See also DLB 129

Friedan, Betty 1921-2006 **CLC 74**
See also CA 65-68; 248; CANR 18, 45, 74; DLB 246; FW; MTCW 1, 2; MTFW 2005; NCFS 5

Friedan, Betty Naomi
See Friedan, Betty

Friedlander, Saul 1932- **CLC 90**
See also CA 117; 130; CANR 72; RGHL

Friedman, B(ernard) H(arper)
1926- .. **CLC 7**
See also CA 1-4R; CANR 3, 48

Friedman, Bruce Jay 1930- **CLC 3, 5, 56**
See also CA 9-12R; CAD; CANR 25, 52, 101; CD 5, 6; CN 1, 2, 3, 4, 5, 6, 7; DLB 2, 28, 244; INT CANR-25; MAL 5; SSFS 18

Friel, Brian 1929- **CLC 5, 42, 59, 115; DC 8; SSC 76**
See also BRWS 5; CA 21-24R; CANR 33, 69, 131; CBD; CD 5, 6; DFS 11; DLB 13, 319; EWL 3; MTCW 1; RGEL 2; TEA

Friis-Baastad, Babbis Ellinor
1921-1970 **CLC 12**
See also CA 17-20R; 134; SATA 7

Frisch, Max (Rudolf) 1911-1991 ... **CLC 3, 9, 14, 18, 32, 44; TCLC 121**
See also CA 85-88; 134; CANR 32, 74; CD-WLB 2; DAM DRAM, NOV; DLB 69, 124; EW 13; EWL 3; MTCW 1, 2; MTFW 2005; RGHL; RGWL 2, 3

Fromentin, Eugene (Samuel Auguste)
1820-1876 **NCLC 10, 125**
See also DLB 123; GFL 1789 to the Present

Frost, Frederick
See Faust, Frederick (Schiller)

Frost, Robert (Lee) 1874-1963 .. **CLC 1, 3, 4, 9, 10, 13, 15, 26, 34, 44; PC 1, 39, 71; WLC 2**
See also AAYA 21; AMW; AMWR 1; CA 89-92; CANR 33; CDALB 1917-1929; CLR 67; DA; DA3; DAB; DAC; DAM MST, POET; DLB 54, 284; DLBD 7; EWL 3; EXPP; MAL 5; MTCW 1, 2; MTFW 2005; PAB; PFS 1, 2, 3, 4, 5, 6, 7, 10, 13; RGAL 4; SATA 14; TUS; WP; WYA

Froude, James Anthony
1818-1894 **NCLC 43**
See also DLB 18, 57, 144

Froy, Herald
See Waterhouse, Keith (Spencer)

Fry, Christopher 1907-2005 ... **CLC 2, 10, 14**
See also BRWS 3; CA 17-20R; 240; CAAS 23; CANR 9, 30, 74, 132; CBD; CD 5, 6; CP 1, 2, 3, 4, 5, 6, 7; DAM DRAM; DLB 13; EWL 3; MTCW 1, 2; MTFW 2005; RGEL 2; SATA 66; TEA

Frye, (Herman) Northrop
1912-1991 **CLC 24, 70; TCLC 165**
See also CA 5-8R; 133; CANR 8, 37; DLB 67, 68, 246; EWL 3; MTCW 1, 2; MTFW 2005; RGAL 4; TWA

Fuchs, Daniel 1909-1993 **CLC 8, 22**
See also CA 81-84; 142; CAAS 5; CANR 40; CN 1, 2, 3, 4, 5; DLB 9, 26, 28; DLBY 1993; MAL 5

Fuchs, Daniel 1934- **CLC 34**
See also CA 37-40R; CANR 14, 48

Fuentes, Carlos 1928- .. **CLC 3, 8, 10, 13, 22, 41, 60, 113; HLC 1; SSC 24; WLC 2**
See also AAYA 4, 45; AITN 2; BPFB 1; CA 69-72; CANR 10, 32, 68, 104, 138; CDWLB 3; CWW 2; DA; DA3; DAB; DAC; DAM MST, MULT, NOV; DLB 113; DNFS 2; EWL 3; HW 1, 2; LAIT 3; LATS 1:2; LAW; LAWS 1; LMFS 2; MTCW 1, 2; MTFW 2005; NFS 8; RGSF 2; RGWL 2, 3; TWA; WLIT 1

Fuentes, Gregorio Lopez y
See Lopez y Fuentes, Gregorio

Fuertes, Gloria 1918-1998 **PC 27**
See also CA 178, 180; DLB 108; HW 2; SATA 115

Fugard, (Harold) Athol 1932- . **CLC 5, 9, 14, 25, 40, 80, 211; DC 3**
See also AAYA 17; AFW; CA 85-88; CANR 32, 54, 118; CD 5, 6; DAM DRAM; DFS 3, 6, 10; DLB 225; DNFS 1, 2; EWL 3; LATS 1:2; MTCW 1; MTFW 2005; RGEL 2; WLIT 2

Fugard, Sheila 1932- **CLC 48**
See also CA 125

Fujiwara no Teika 1162-1241 **CMLC 73**
See also DLB 203

Fukuyama, Francis 1952- **CLC 131**
See also CA 140; CANR 72, 125

Fuller, Charles (H.), (Jr.) 1939- **BLC 2; CLC 25; DC 1**
See also BW 2; CA 108; 112; CAD; CANR 87; CD 5, 6; DAM DRAM, MULT; DFS 8; DLB 38, 266; EWL 3; INT CA-112; MAL 5; MTCW 1

Fuller, Henry Blake 1857-1929 **TCLC 103**
See also CA 108; 177; DLB 12; RGAL 4

Fuller, John (Leopold) 1937- **CLC 62**
See also CA 21-24R; CANR 9, 44; CP 1, 2, 3, 4, 5, 6, 7; DLB 40

Fuller, Margaret
See Ossoli, Sarah Margaret (Fuller)
See also AMWS 2; DLB 183, 223, 239; FL 1:3

Fuller, Roy (Broadbent) 1912-1991 ... **CLC 4, 28**
See also BRWS 7; CA 5-8R; 135; CAAS 10; CANR 53, 83; CN 1, 2, 3, 4, 5; CP 1, 2, 3, 4, 5; CWRI 5; DLB 15, 20; EWL 3; RGEL 2; SATA 87

Fuller, Sarah Margaret
See Ossoli, Sarah Margaret (Fuller)

Fuller, Sarah Margaret
See Ossoli, Sarah Margaret (Fuller)
See also DLB 1, 59, 73

Fuller, Thomas 1608-1661 **LC 111**
See also DLB 151

Fulton, Alice 1952- **CLC 52**
See also CA 116; CANR 57, 88; CP 5, 6, 7; CWP; DLB 193

Furphy, Joseph 1843-1912 **TCLC 25**
See Collins, Tom
See also CA 163; DLB 230; EWL 3; RGEL 2

Fuson, Robert H(enderson) 1927- **CLC 70**
See also CA 89-92; CANR 103

Fussell, Paul 1924- **CLC 74**
See also BEST 90:1; CA 17-20R; CANR 8, 21, 35, 69, 135; INT CANR-21; MTCW 1, 2; MTFW 2005

Futabatei, Shimei 1864-1909 **TCLC 44**
See Futabatei Shimei
See also CA 162; MJW

Futabatei Shimei
See Futabatei, Shimei
See also DLB 180; EWL 3

Futrelle, Jacques 1875-1912 **TCLC 19**
See also CA 113; 155; CMW 4

Gaboriau, Emile 1835-1873 **NCLC 14**
See also CMW 4; MSW

Gadda, Carlo Emilio 1893-1973 **CLC 11; TCLC 144**
See also CA 89-92; DLB 177; EWL 3; WLIT 7

Gaddis, William 1922-1998 ... **CLC 1, 3, 6, 8, 10, 19, 43, 86**
See also AMWS 4; BPFB 1; CA 17-20R; 172; CANR 21, 48, 148; CN 1, 2, 3, 4, 5, 6; DLB 2, 278; EWL 3; MAL 5; MTCW 1, 2; MTFW 2005; RGAL 4

Gaelique, Moruen le
See Jacob, (Cyprien-)Max

Gage, Walter
See Inge, William (Motter)

Gaiman, Neil 1960- **CLC 195**
See also AAYA 19, 42; CA 133; CANR 81, 129; CLR 109; DLB 261; HGG; MTFW 2005; SATA 85, 146; SFW 4; SUFW 2

Gaiman, Neil Richard
See Gaiman, Neil

Gaines, Ernest J(ames) 1933- .. **BLC 2; CLC 3, 11, 18, 86, 181; SSC 68**
See also AAYA 18; AFAW 1, 2; AITN 1; BPFB 2; BW 2, 3; BYA 6; CA 9-12R; CANR 6, 24, 42, 75, 126; CDALB 1968-1988; CLR 62; CN 1, 2, 3, 4, 5, 6, 7; CSW; DA3; DAM MULT; DLB 2, 33, 152; DLBY 1980; EWL 3; EXPN; LAIT 5; LATS 1:2; MAL 5; MTCW 1, 2; MTFW 2005; NFS 5, 7, 16; RGAL 4; RGSF 2; RHW; SATA 86; SSFS 5; YAW

Gaitskill, Mary 1954- **CLC 69**
See also CA 128; CANR 61, 152; DLB 244; TCLE 1:1

Gaitskill, Mary Lawrence
See Gaitskill, Mary

Gaius Suetonius Tranquillus
See Suetonius

Galdos, Benito Perez
See Perez Galdos, Benito
See also EW 7

Gale, Zona 1874-1938 **TCLC 7**
See also CA 105; 153; CANR 84; DAM DRAM; DFS 17; DLB 9, 78, 228; RGAL 4

Galeano, Eduardo (Hughes) 1940- . **CLC 72; HLCS 1**
See also CA 29-32R; CANR 13, 32, 100; HW 1

Galiano, Juan Valera y Alcala
See Valera y Alcala-Galiano, Juan

Galilei, Galileo 1564-1642 **LC 45**

Gallagher, Tess 1943- **CLC 18, 63; PC 9**
See also CA 106; CP 3, 4, 5, 6, 7; CWP; DAM POET; DLB 120, 212, 244; PFS 16

Gallant, Mavis 1922- **CLC 7, 18, 38, 172; SSC 5, 78**
See also CA 69-72; CANR 29, 69, 117; CCA 1; CN 1, 2, 3, 4, 5, 6, 7; DAC; DAM MST; DLB 53; EWL 3; MTCW 1, 2; MTFW 2005; RGEL 2; RGSF 2

Gallant, Roy A(rthur) 1924- **CLC 17**
See also CA 5-8R; CANR 4, 29, 54, 117; CLR 30; MAICYA 1, 2; SATA 4, 68, 110

Gallico, Paul (William) 1897-1976 **CLC 2**
See also AITN 1; CA 5-8R; 69-72; CANR 23; CN 1, 2; DLB 9, 171; FANT; MAICYA 1, 2; SATA 13

Gallo, Max Louis 1932- **CLC 95**
See also CA 85-88

Gallois, Lucien
See Desnos, Robert

Gallup, Ralph
See Whitemore, Hugh (John)

Galsworthy, John 1867-1933 **SSC 22; TCLC 1, 45; WLC 2**
See also BRW 6; CA 104; 141; CANR 75; CDBLB 1890-1914; DA; DA3; DAB; DAC; DAM DRAM, MST, NOV; DLB 10, 34, 98, 162; DLBD 16; EWL 3; MTCW 2; RGEL 2; SSFS 3; TEA

Galt, John 1779-1839 **NCLC 1, 110**
See also DLB 99, 116, 159; RGEL 2; RGSF 2

Galvin, James 1951- **CLC 38**
See also CA 108; CANR 26

Gamboa, Federico 1864-1939 **TCLC 36**
See also CA 167; HW 2; LAW

Gandhi, M. K.
See Gandhi, Mohandas Karamchand

Gandhi, Mahatma
See Gandhi, Mohandas Karamchand

Gandhi, Mohandas Karamchand 1869-1948 **TCLC 59**
See also CA 121; 132; DA3; DAM MULT; DLB 323; MTCW 1, 2

Gann, Ernest Kellogg 1910-1991 **CLC 23**
See also AITN 1; BPFB 2; CA 1-4R; 136; CANR 1, 83; RHW

Gao Xingjian 1940- **CLC 167**
See Xingjian, Gao
See also MTFW 2005

Garber, Eric 1943(?)-
See Holleran, Andrew
See also CANR 89

Garcia, Cristina 1958- **CLC 76**
See also AMWS 11; CA 141; CANR 73, 130; CN 7; DLB 292; DNFS 1; EWL 3; HW 1; LLW; MTFW 2005

Garcia Lorca, Federico 1898-1936 **DC 2; HLC 2; PC 3; TCLC 1, 7, 49; WLC 2**
See Lorca, Federico Garcia
See also AAYA 46; CA 104; 131; CANR 81; DA; DA3; DAB; DAC; DAM DRAM, MST, MULT, POET; DFS 4, 10; DLB 108; EWL 3; HW 1, 2; LATS 1:2; MTCW 1, 2; MTFW 2005; TWA

Garcia Marquez, Gabriel 1928- **CLC 2, 3, 8, 10, 15, 27, 47, 55, 68, 170; HLC 1; SSC 8, 83; WLC 3**
See also AAYA 3, 33; BEST 89:1, 90:4; BPFB 2; BYA 12, 16; CA 33-36R; CANR 10, 28, 50, 75, 82, 128; CDWLB 3; CPW; CWW 2; DA; DA3; DAB; DAC; DAM MST, MULT, NOV, POP; DLB 113; DNFS 1, 2; EWL 3; EXPN; EXPS; HW 1, 2; LAIT 2; LATS 1:2; LAW; LAWS 1; LMFS 2; MTCW 1, 2; MTFW 2005; NCFS 3; NFS 1, 5, 10; RGSF 2; RGWL 2, 3; SSFS 1, 6, 16, 21; TWA; WLIT 1

Garcia Marquez, Gabriel Jose
See Garcia Marquez, Gabriel

Garcilaso de la Vega, El Inca 1539-1616 **HLCS 1; LC 127**
See also DLB 318; LAW

Gard, Janice
See Latham, Jean Lee

Gard, Roger Martin du
See Martin du Gard, Roger

Gardam, Jane (Mary) 1928- **CLC 43**
See also CA 49-52; CANR 2, 18, 33, 54, 106; CLR 12; DLB 14, 161, 231; MAICYA 1, 2; MTCW 1; SAAS 9; SATA 39, 76, 130; SATA-Brief 28; YAW

Gardner, Herb(ert George) 1934-2003 **CLC 44**
See also CA 149; 220; CAD; CANR 119; CD 5, 6; DFS 18, 20

Gardner, John (Champlin), Jr. 1933-1982 **CLC 2, 3, 5, 7, 8, 10, 18, 28, 34; SSC 7**
See also AAYA 45; AITN 1; AMWS 6; BPFB 2; CA 65-68; 107; CANR 33, 73; CDALBS; CN 2, 3; CPW; DA3; DAM NOV, POP; DLB 2; DLBY 1982; EWL 3; FANT; LATS 1:2; MAL 5; MTCW 1, 2; MTFW 2005; NFS 3; RGAL 4; RGSF 2; SATA 40; SATA-Obit 31; SSFS 8

Gardner, John (Edmund) 1926- **CLC 30**
See also CA 103; CANR 15, 69, 127; CMW 4; CPW; DAM POP; MTCW 1

Gardner, Miriam
See Bradley, Marion Zimmer
See also GLL 1

Gardner, Noel
See Kuttner, Henry

Gardons, S. S.
See Snodgrass, W(illiam) D(e Witt)

Garfield, Leon 1921-1996 CLC 12
See also AAYA 8, 69; BYA 1, 3; CA 17-
20R; 152; CANR 38, 41, 78; CLR 21;
DLB 161; JRDA; MAICYA 1, 2; MAIC-
YAS 1, SATA 1, 32, 76; SATA-Obit 90;
TEA; WYA; YAW

Garland, (Hannibal) Hamlin
1860-1940 SSC 18; TCLC 3
See also CA 104; DLB 12, 71, 78, 186;
MAL 5; RGAL 4; RGSF 2; TCWW 1, 2

Garneau, (Hector de) Saint-Denys
1912-1943 TCLC 13
See also CA 111; DLB 88

Garner, Alan 1934- CLC 17
See also AAYA 18; BYA 3, 5; CA 73-76,
178; CAAE 178; CANR 15, 64, 134; CLR
20; CPW; DAB; DAM POP; DLB 161,
261; FANT; MAICYA 1, 2; MTCW 1, 2;
MTFW 2005; SATA 18, 69; SATA-Essay
108; SUFW 1, 2; YAW

Garner, Hugh 1913-1979 CLC 13
See Warwick, Jarvis
See also CA 69-72; CANR 31; CCA 1; CN
1, 2; DLB 68

Garnett, David 1892-1981 CLC 3
See also CA 5-8R; 103; CANR 17, 79; CN
1, 2; DLB 34; FANT; MTCW 2; RGEL 2;
SFW 4; SUFW 1

Garnier, Robert c. 1545-1590 LC 119
See also GFL Beginnings to 1789

Garrett, George (Palmer, Jr.) 1929- . CLC 3,
11, 51; SSC 30
See also AMWS 7; BPFB 2; CA 1-4R, 202;
CAAE 202; CAAS 5; CANR 1, 42, 67,
109; CN 1, 2, 3, 4, 5, 6, 7; CP 1, 2, 3, 4,
5, 6, 7; CSW; DLB 2, 5, 130, 152; DLBY
1983

Garrick, David 1717-1779 LC 15
See also DAM DRAM; DLB 84, 213;
RGEL 2

Garrigue, Jean 1914-1972 CLC 2, 8
See also CA 5-8R; 37-40R; CANR 20; CP
1; MAL 5

Garrison, Frederick
See Sinclair, Upton

Garrison, William Lloyd
1805-1879 NCLC 149
See also CDALB 1640-1865; DLB 1, 43,
235

Garro, Elena 1920(?)-1998 .. HLCS 1; TCLC
153
See also CA 131; 169; CWW 2; DLB 145;
EWL 3; HW 1; LAWS 1; WLIT 1

Garth, Will
See Hamilton, Edmond; Kuttner, Henry

Garvey, Marcus (Moziah, Jr.)
1887-1940 ... BLC 2; HR 1:2; TCLC 41
See also BW 1; CA 120; 124; CANR 79;
DAM MULT

Gary, Romain CLC 25
See Kacew, Romain
See also DLB 83, 299; RGHL

Gascar, Pierre CLC 11
See Fournier, Pierre
See also EWL 3; RGHL

Gascoigne, George 1539-1577 LC 108
See also DLB 136; RGEL 2

Gascoyne, David (Emery)
1916-2001 CLC 45
See also CA 65-68; 200; CANR 10, 28, 54;
CP 1, 2, 3, 4, 5, 6, 7; DLB 20; MTCW 1;
RGEL 2

Gaskell, Elizabeth Cleghorn
1810-1865 NCLC 5, 70, 97, 137; SSC
25
See also BRW 5; CDBLB 1832-1890; DAB;
DAM MST; DLB 21, 144, 159; RGEL 2;
RGSF 2; TEA

Gass, William H(oward) 1924- . CLC 1, 2, 8,
11, 15, 39, 132; SSC 12
See also AMWS 6; CA 17-20R; CANR 30,
71, 100; CN 1, 2, 3, 4, 5, 6, 7; DLB 2,
227; EWL 3; MAL 5; MTCW 1, 2;
MTFW 2005; RGAL 4

Gassendi, Pierre 1592-1655 LC 54
See also GFL Beginnings to 1789

Gasset, Jose Ortega y
See Ortega y Gasset, Jose

Gates, Henry Louis, Jr. 1950- ... BLCS; CLC
65
See also BW 2, 3; CA 109; CANR 25, 53,
75, 125; CSW; DA3; DAM MULT; DLB
67; EWL 3; MAL 5; MTCW 2; MTFW
2005; RGAL 4

Gatos, Stephanie
See Katz, Steve

Gautier, Theophile 1811-1872 .. NCLC 1, 59;
PC 18; SSC 20
See also DAM POET; DLB 119; EW 6;
GFL 1789 to the Present; RGWL 2, 3;
SUFW; TWA

Gay, John 1685-1732 LC 49
See also BRW 3; DAM DRAM; DLB 84,
95; RGEL 2; WLIT 3

Gay, Oliver
See Gogarty, Oliver St. John

Gay, Peter 1923- CLC 158
See also CA 13-16R; CANR 18, 41, 77,
147; INT CANR-18; RGHL

Gay, Peter Jack
See Gay, Peter

Gaye, Marvin (Pentz, Jr.)
1939-1984 CLC 26
See also CA 195; 112

Gebler, Carlo (Ernest) 1954- CLC 39
See also CA 119; 133; CANR 96; DLB 271

Gee, Maggie (Mary) 1948- CLC 57
See also CA 130; CANR 125; CN 4, 5, 6,
7; DLB 207; MTFW 2005

Gee, Maurice 1931- CLC 29
See also AAYA 42; CA 97-100; CANR 67,
123; CLR 56; CN 2, 3, 4, 5, 6, 7; CWRI
5; EWL 3; MAICYA 2; RGSF 2; SATA
46, 101

Gee, Maurice Gough
See Gee, Maurice

Geiogamah, Hanay 1945- NNAL
See also CA 153; DAM MULT; DLB 175

Gelbart, Larry
See Gelbart, Larry (Simon)
See also CAD; CD 5, 6

Gelbart, Larry (Simon) 1928- CLC 21, 61
See Gelbart, Larry
See also CA 73-76; CANR 45, 94

Gelber, Jack 1932-2003 CLC 1, 6, 14, 79
See also CA 1-4R; 216; CAD; CANR 2;
DLB 7, 228; MAL 5

Gellhorn, Martha (Ellis)
1908-1998 CLC 14, 60
See also CA 77-80; 164; CANR 44; CN 1,
2, 3, 4, 5, 6 7; DLBY 1982, 1998

Genet, Jean 1910-1986 .. CLC 1, 2, 5, 10, 14,
44, 46; DC 25; TCLC 128
See also CA 13-16R; CANR 18; DA3;
DAM DRAM; DFS 10; DLB 72, 321;
DLBY 1986; EW 13; EWL 3; GFL 1789
to the Present; GLL 1; LMFS 2; MTCW
1, 2; MTFW 2005; RGWL 2, 3; TWA

Genlis, Stephanie-Felicite Ducrest
1746-1830 NCLC 166
See also DLB 313

Gent, Peter 1942- CLC 29
See also AITN 1; CA 89-92; DLBY 1982

Gentile, Giovanni 1875-1944 TCLC 96
See also CA 119

Gentlewoman in New England, A
See Bradstreet, Anne

Gentlewoman in Those Parts, A
See Bradstreet, Anne

Geoffrey of Monmouth c.
1100-1155 CMLC 44
See also DLB 146; TEA

George, Jean
See George, Jean Craighead

George, Jean Craighead 1919- CLC 35
See also AAYA 8, 69; BYA 2, 4; CA 5-8R;
CANR 25; CLR 1; 80; DLB 52; JRDA;
MAICYA 1, 2; SATA 2, 68, 124, 170;
WYA; YAW

George, Stefan (Anton) 1868-1933 . TCLC 2,
14
See also CA 104; 193; EW 8; EWL 3

Georges, Georges Martin
See Simenon, Georges (Jacques Christian)

Gerald of Wales c. 1146-c. 1223 ... CMLC 60

Gerhardi, William Alexander
See Gerhardie, William Alexander

Gerhardie, William Alexander
1895-1977 CLC 5
See also CA 25-28R; 73-76; CANR 18; CN
1, 2; DLB 36; RGEL 2

Gerson, Jean 1363-1429 LC 77
See also DLB 208

Gersonides 1288-1344 CMLC 49
See also DLB 115

Gerstler, Amy 1956- CLC 70
See also CA 146; CANR 99

Gertler, T. .. CLC 34
See also CA 116; 121

Gertsen, Aleksandr Ivanovich
See Herzen, Aleksandr Ivanovich

Ghalib NCLC 39, 78
See Ghalib, Asadullah Khan

Ghalib, Asadullah Khan 1797-1869
See Ghalib
See also DAM POET; RGWL 2, 3

Ghelderode, Michel de 1898-1962 CLC 6,
11; DC 15
See also CA 85-88; CANR 40, 77; DAM
DRAM; DLB 321; EW 11; EWL 3; TWA

Ghiselin, Brewster 1903-2001 CLC 23
See also CA 13-16R; CAAS 10; CANR 13;
CP 1, 2, 3, 4, 5, 6, 7

Ghose, Aurabinda 1872-1950 TCLC 63
See Ghose, Aurobindo
See also CA 163

Ghose, Aurobindo
See Ghose, Aurabinda
See also EWL 3

Ghose, Zulfikar 1935- CLC 42, 200
See also CA 65-68; CANR 67; CN 1, 2, 3,
4, 5, 6, 7; CP 1, 2, 3, 4, 5, 6, 7; DLB 323;
EWL 3

Ghosh, Amitav 1956- CLC 44, 153
See also CA 147; CANR 80; CN 6, 7; DLB
323; WWE 1

Giacosa, Giuseppe 1847-1906 TCLC 7
See also CA 104

Gibb, Lee
See Waterhouse, Keith (Spencer)

Gibbon, Edward 1737-1794 LC 97
See also BRW 3; DLB 104; RGEL 2

Gibbon, Lewis Grassic TCLC 4
See Mitchell, James Leslie
See also RGEL 2

Gibbons, Kaye 1960- **CLC 50, 88, 145**
See also AAYA 34; AMWS 10; CA 151;
CANR 75, 127; CN 7; CSW; DA3; DAM
POP; DLB 292; MTCW 2; MTFW 2005;
NFS 3; RGAL 4; SATA 117

Gibran, Kahlil 1883-1931 . **PC 9; TCLC 1, 9**
See also CA 104; 150; DA3; DAM POET,
POP; EWL 3; MTCW 2; WLIT 6

Gibran, Khalil
See Gibran, Kahlil

Gibson, Mel 1956- **CLC 215**

Gibson, William 1914- **CLC 23**
See also CA 9-12R; CAD; CANR 9, 42, 75,
125; CD 5, 6; DA; DAB; DAC; DAM
DRAM, MST; DFS 2; DLB 7; LAIT 2;
MAL 5; MTCW 2; MTFW 2005; SATA
66; YAW

Gibson, William (Ford) 1948- ... **CLC 39, 63,
186, 192; SSC 52**
See also AAYA 12, 59; BPFB 2; CA 126;
133; CANR 52, 90, 106; CN 6, 7; CPW;
DA3; DAM POP; DLB 251; MTCW 2;
MTFW 2005; SCFW 2; SFW 4

Gide, Andre (Paul Guillaume)
1869-1951 **SSC 13; TCLC 5, 12, 36,
177; WLC 3**
See also CA 104; 124; DA; DA3; DAB;
DAC; DAM MST, NOV; DLB 65, 321;
EW 8; EWL 3; GFL 1789 to the Present;
MTCW 1, 2; MTFW 2005; NFS 21;
RGSF 2; RGWL 2, 3; TWA

Gifford, Barry (Colby) 1946- **CLC 34**
See also CA 65-68; CANR 9, 30, 40, 90

Gilbert, Frank
See De Voto, Bernard (Augustine)

Gilbert, W(illiam) S(chwenck)
1836-1911 **TCLC 3**
See also CA 104; 173; DAM DRAM, POET;
RGEL 2; SATA 36

Gilbert of Poitiers c. 1085-1154 **CMLC 85**

Gilbreth, Frank B(unker), Jr.
1911-2001 **CLC 17**
See also CA 9-12R; SATA 2

Gilchrist, Ellen (Louise) 1935- .. **CLC 34, 48,
143; SSC 14, 63**
See also BPFB 2; CA 113; 116; CANR 41,
61, 104; CN 4, 5, 6, 7; CPW; CSW; DAM
POP; DLB 130; EWL 3; EXPS; MTCW
1, 2; MTFW 2005; RGAL 4; RGSF 2;
SSFS 9

Giles, Molly 1942- **CLC 39**
See also CA 126; CANR 98

Gill, Eric .. **TCLC 85**
See Gill, (Arthur) Eric (Rowton Peter
Joseph)

Gill, (Arthur) Eric (Rowton Peter Joseph)
1882-1940
See Gill, Eric
See also CA 120; DLB 98

Gill, Patrick
See Creasey, John

Gillette, Douglas **CLC 70**

Gilliam, Terry (Vance) 1940- **CLC 21, 141**
See Monty Python
See also AAYA 19, 59; CA 108; 113; CANR
35; INT CA-113

Gillian, Jerry
See Gilliam, Terry (Vance)

Gilliatt, Penelope (Ann Douglass)
1932-1993 **CLC 2, 10, 13, 53**
See also AITN 2; CA 13-16R; 141; CANR
49; CN 1, 2, 3, 4, 5; DLB 14

Gilligan, Carol 1936- **CLC 208**
See also CA 142; CANR 121; FW

Gilman, Charlotte (Anna) Perkins (Stetson)
1860-1935 **SSC 13, 62; TCLC 9, 37,
117**
See also AMWS 11; BYA 11; CA 106; 150;
DLB 221; EXPS; FL 1:5; FW; HGG;

LAIT 2; MAWW; MTCW 2; MTFW
2005; RGAL 4; RGSF 2; SFW 4; SSFS 1,
18

Gilmour, David 1946- **CLC 35**

Gilpin, William 1724-1804 **NCLC 30**

Gilray, J. D.
See Mencken, H(enry) L(ouis)

Gilroy, Frank D(aniel) 1925- **CLC 2**
See also CA 81-84; CAD; CANR 32, 64,
86; CD 5, 6; DFS 17; DLB 7

Gilstrap, John 1957(?)- **CLC 99**
See also AAYA 67; CA 160; CANR 101

Ginsberg, Allen 1926-1997 **CLC 1, 2, 3, 4,
6, 13, 36, 69, 109; PC 4, 47; TCLC
120; WLC 3**
See also AAYA 33; AITN 1; AMWC 1;
AMWS 2; BG 1:2; CA 1-4R; 157; CANR
2, 41, 63, 95; CDALB 1941-1968; CP 1,
2, 3, 4, 5, 6; DA; DA3; DAB; DAC; DAM
MST, POET; DLB 5, 16, 169, 237; EWL
3; GLL 1; LMFS 2; MAL 5; MTCW 1, 2;
MTFW 2005; PAB; PFS 5; RGAL 4;
TUS; WP

Ginzburg, Eugenia **CLC 59**
See Ginzburg, Evgeniia

Ginzburg, Evgeniia 1904-1977
See Ginzburg, Eugenia
See also DLB 302

Ginzburg, Natalia 1916-1991 **CLC 5, 11,
54, 70; SSC 65; TCLC 156**
See also CA 85-88; 135; CANR 33; DFS
14; DLB 177; EW 13; EWL 3; MTCW 1,
2; MTFW 2005; RGHL; RGWL 2, 3

Giono, Jean 1895-1970 **CLC 4, 11; TCLC
124**
See also CA 45-48; 29-32R; CANR 2, 35;
DLB 72, 321; EWL 3; GFL 1789 to the
Present; MTCW 1; RGWL 2, 3

Giovanni, Nikki 1943- **BLC 2; CLC 2, 4,
19, 64, 117; PC 19; WLCS**
See also AAYA 22; AITN 1; BW 2, 3; CA
29-32R; CAAS 6; CANR 18, 41, 60, 91,
130; CDALBS; CLR 6, 73; CP 2, 3, 4, 5,
6, 7; CSW; CWP; CWRI 5; DA; DA3;
DAB; DAC; DAM MST, MULT, POET;
DLB 5, 41; EWL 3; EXPP; INT CANR-
18; MAICYA 1, 2; MAL 5; MTCW 1, 2;
MTFW 2005; PFS 17; RGAL 4; SATA
24, 107; TUS; YAW

Giovene, Andrea 1904-1998 **CLC 7**
See also CA 85-88

Gippius, Zinaida (Nikolaevna) 1869-1945
See Hippius, Zinaida (Nikolaevna)
See also CA 106; 212

Giraudoux, Jean(-Hippolyte)
1882-1944 **TCLC 2, 7**
See also CA 104; 196; DAM DRAM; DLB
65, 321; EW 9; EWL 3; GFL 1789 to the
Present; RGWL 2, 3; TWA

Gironella, Jose Maria (Pous)
1917-2003 **CLC 11**
See also CA 101; 212; EWL 3; RGWL 2, 3

Gissing, George (Robert)
1857-1903 **SSC 37; TCLC 3, 24, 47**
See also BRW 5; CA 105; 167; DLB 18,
135, 184; RGEL 2; TEA

Gitlin, Todd 1943- **CLC 201**
See also CA 29-32R; CANR 25, 50, 88

Giurlani, Aldo
See Palazzeschi, Aldo

Gladkov, Fedor Vasil'evich
See Gladkov, Fyodor (Vasilyevich)
See also DLB 272

Gladkov, Fyodor (Vasilyevich)
1883-1958 **TCLC 27**
See Gladkov, Fedor Vasil'evich
See also CA 170; EWL 3

Glancy, Diane 1941- **CLC 210; NNAL**
See also CA 136, 225; CAAE 225; CAAS
24; CANR 87; DLB 175

Glanville, Brian (Lester) 1931- **CLC 6**
See also CA 5-8R; CAAS 9; CANR 3, 70;
CN 1, 2, 3, 4, 5, 6, 7; DLB 15, 139; SATA
42

Glasgow, Ellen (Anderson Gholson)
1873-1945 **SSC 34; TCLC 2, 7**
See also AMW; CA 104; 164; DLB 9, 12;
MAL 5; MAWW; MTCW 2; MTFW 2005;
RGAL 4; RHW; SSFS 9; TUS

Glaspell, Susan 1882(?)-1948 **DC 10; SSC
41; TCLC 55, 175**
See also AMWS 3; CA 110; 154; DFS 8,
18; DLB 7, 9, 78, 228; MAWW; RGAL
4; SSFS 3; TCWW 2; TUS; YABC 2

Glassco, John 1909-1981 **CLC 9**
See also CA 13-16R; 102; CANR 15; CN
1, 2; CP 1, 2, 3; DLB 68

Glasscock, Amnesia
See Steinbeck, John (Ernst)

Glasser, Ronald J. 1940(?)- **CLC 37**
See also CA 209

Glassman, Joyce
See Johnson, Joyce

Gleick, James (W.) 1954- **CLC 147**
See also CA 131; 137; CANR 97; INT CA-
137

Glendinning, Victoria 1937- **CLC 50**
See also CA 120; 127; CANR 59, 89; DLB
155

Glissant, Edouard (Mathieu)
1928- **CLC 10, 68**
See also CA 153; CANR 111; CWW 2;
DAM MULT; EWL 3; RGWL 3

Gloag, Julian 1930- **CLC 40**
See also AITN 1; CA 65-68; CANR 10, 70;
CN 1, 2, 3, 4, 5, 6

Glowacki, Aleksander
See Prus, Boleslaw

Gluck, Louise (Elisabeth) 1943- .. **CLC 7, 22,
44, 81, 160; PC 16**
See also AMWS 5; CA 33-36R; CANR 40,
69, 108, 133; CP 1, 2, 3, 4, 5, 6, 7; CWP;
DA3; DAM POET; DLB 5; MAL 5;
MTCW 2; MTFW 2005; PFS 5, 15;
RGAL 4; TCLE 1:1

Glyn, Elinor 1864-1943 **TCLC 72**
See also DLB 153; RHW

Gobineau, Joseph-Arthur
1816-1882 **NCLC 17**
See also DLB 123; GFL 1789 to the Present

Godard, Jean-Luc 1930- **CLC 20**
See also CA 93-96

Godden, (Margaret) Rumer
1907-1998 **CLC 53**
See also AAYA 6; BPFB 2; BYA 2, 5; CA
5-8R; 172; CANR 4, 27, 36, 55, 80; CLR
20; CN 1, 2, 3, 4, 5, 6; CWRI 5; DLB
161; MAICYA 1, 2; RHW; SAAS 12;
SATA 3, 36; SATA-Obit 109; TEA

Godoy Alcayaga, Lucila 1899-1957 .. **HLC 2;
PC 32; TCLC 2**
See Mistral, Gabriela
See also BW 2; CA 104; 131; CANR 81;
DAM MULT; DNFS 1; HW 1, 2; MTCW 1,
2; MTFW 2005

Godwin, Gail 1937- **CLC 5, 8, 22, 31, 69,
125**
See also BPFB 2; CA 29-32R; CANR 15,
43, 69, 132; CN 3, 4, 5, 6, 7; CPW; CSW;
DA3; DAM POP; DLB 6, 234; INT
CANR-15; MAL 5; MTCW 1, 2; MTFW
2005

Godwin, Gail Kathleen
See Godwin, Gail

Godwin, William 1756-1836 .. **NCLC 14, 130**
 See also CDBLB 1789-1832; CMW 4; DLB
 39, 104, 142, 158, 163, 262; GL 2; HGG;
 RGEL 2
Goebbels, Josef
 See Goebbels, (Paul) Joseph
Goebbels, (Paul) Joseph
 1897-1945 **TCLC 68**
 See also CA 115; 148
Goebbels, Joseph Paul
 See Goebbels, (Paul) Joseph
Goethe, Johann Wolfgang von
 1749-1832 . **DC 20; NCLC 4, 22, 34, 90,**
 154; PC 5; SSC 38; WLC 3
 See also CDWLB 2; DA; DA3; DAB;
 DAC; DAM DRAM, MST, POET; DLB
 94; EW 5; GL 2; LATS 1; LMFS 1:1;
 RGWL 2, 3; TWA
Gogarty, Oliver St. John
 1878-1957 **TCLC 15**
 See also CA 109; 150; DLB 15, 19; RGEL
 2
Gogol, Nikolai (Vasilyevich)
 1809-1852 **DC 1; NCLC 5, 15, 31,**
 162; SSC 4, 29, 52; WLC 3
 See also DA; DAB; DAC; DAM DRAM,
 MST; DFS 12; DLB 198; EW 6; EXPS;
 RGSF 2; RGWL 2, 3; SSFS 7; TWA
Goines, Donald 1937(?)-1974 ... **BLC 2; CLC**
 80
 See also AITN 1; BW 1, 3; CA 124; 114;
 CANR 82; CMW 4; DA3; DAM MULT,
 POP; DLB 33
Gold, Herbert 1924- ... **CLC 4, 7, 14, 42, 152**
 See also CA 9-12R; CANR 17, 45, 125; CN
 1, 2, 3, 4, 5, 6, 7; DLB 2; DLBY 1981;
 MAL 5
Goldbarth, Albert 1948- **CLC 5, 38**
 See also AMWS 12; CA 53-56; CANR 6,
 40; CP 3, 4, 5, 6, 7; DLB 120
Goldberg, Anatol 1910-1982 **CLC 34**
 See also CA 131; 117
Goldemberg, Isaac 1945- **CLC 52**
 See also CA 69-72; CAAS 12; CANR 11,
 32; EWL 3; HW 1; WLIT 1
Golding, Arthur 1536-1606 **LC 101**
 See also DLB 136
Golding, William (Gerald)
 1911-1993 **CLC 1, 2, 3, 8, 10, 17, 27,**
 58, 81; WLC 3
 See also AAYA 5, 44; BPFB 2; BRWR 1;
 BRWS 1; BYA 2; CA 5-8R; 141; CANR
 13, 33, 54; CD 5; CDBLB 1945-1960;
 CLR 94; CN 1, 2, 3, 4; DA; DA3; DAB;
 DAC; DAM MST, NOV; DLB 15, 100,
 255, 326; EWL 3; EXPN; HGG; LAIT 4;
 MTCW 1, 2; MTFW 2005; NFS 2; RGEL
 2; RHW; SFW 4; TEA; WLIT 4; YAW
Goldman, Emma 1869-1940 **TCLC 13**
 See also CA 110; 150; DLB 221; FW;
 RGAL 4; TUS
Goldman, Francisco 1954- **CLC 76**
 See also CA 162
Goldman, William 1931- **CLC 1, 48**
 See also BPFB 2; CA 9-12R; CANR 29,
 69, 106; CN 1, 2, 3, 4, 5, 6, 7; DLB 44;
 FANT; IDFW 3, 4
Goldman, William W.
 See Goldman, William
Goldmann, Lucien 1913-1970 **CLC 24**
 See also CA 25-28; CAP 2
Goldoni, Carlo 1707-1793 **LC 4**
 See also DAM DRAM; EW 4; RGWL 2, 3;
 WLIT 7
Goldsberry, Steven 1949- **CLC 34**
 See also CA 131

Goldsmith, Oliver 1730-1774 **DC 8; LC 2,**
 48, 122; WLC 3
 See also BRW 3; CDBLB 1660-1789; DA;
 DAB; DAC; DAM DRAM, MST, NOV,
 POET; DFS 1; DLB 39, 89, 104, 109, 142;
 IDTP; RGEL 2; SATA 26; TEA; WLIT 3
Goldsmith, Peter
 See Priestley, J(ohn) B(oynton)
Gombrowicz, Witold 1904-1969 **CLC 4, 7,**
 11, 49
 See also CA 19-20; 25-28R; CANR 105;
 CAP 2; CDWLB 4; DAM DRAM; DLB
 215; EW 12; EWL 3; RGWL 2, 3; TWA
Gomez de Avellaneda, Gertrudis
 1814-1873 **NCLC 111**
 See also LAW
Gomez de la Serna, Ramon
 1888-1963 **CLC 9**
 See also CA 153; 116; CANR 79; EWL 3;
 HW 1, 2
Goncharov, Ivan Alexandrovich
 1812-1891 **NCLC 1, 63**
 See also DLB 238; EW 6; RGWL 2, 3
Goncourt, Edmond (Louis Antoine Huot) de
 1822-1896 **NCLC 7**
 See also DLB 123; EW 7; GFL 1789 to the
 Present; RGWL 2, 3
Goncourt, Jules (Alfred Huot) de
 1830-1870 **NCLC 7**
 See also DLB 123; EW 7; GFL 1789 to the
 Present; RGWL 2, 3
Gongora (y Argote), Luis de
 1561-1627 **LC 72**
 See also RGWL 2, 3
Gontier, Fernande 19(?)- **CLC 50**
Gonzalez Martinez, Enrique
 See Gonzalez Martinez, Enrique
 See also DLB 290
Gonzalez Martinez, Enrique
 1871-1952 **TCLC 72**
 See Gonzalez Martinez, Enrique
 See also CA 166; CANR 81; EWL 3; HW
 1, 2
Goodison, Lorna 1947- **PC 36**
 See also CA 142; CANR 88; CP 5, 6, 7;
 CWP; DLB 157; EWL 3
Goodman, Paul 1911-1972 **CLC 1, 2, 4, 7**
 See also CA 19-20; 37-40R; CAD; CANR
 34; CAP 2; CN 1; DLB 130, 246; MAL
 5; MTCW 1; RGAL 4
GoodWeather, Harley
 See King, Thomas
Googe, Barnabe 1540-1594 **LC 94**
 See also DLB 132; RGEL 2
Gordimer, Nadine 1923- **CLC 3, 5, 7, 10,**
 18, 33, 51, 70, 123, 160, 161; SSC 17,
 80; WLCS
 See also AAYA 39; AFW; BRWS 2; CA
 5-8R; CANR 3, 28, 56, 88, 131; CN 1, 2,
 3, 4, 5, 6, 7; DA; DA3; DAB; DAC; DAM
 MST, NOV; DLB 225, 326; EWL 3;
 EXPS; INT CANR-28; LATS 1:2; MTCW
 1, 2; MTFW 2005; NFS 4; RGEL 2;
 RGSF 2; SSFS 2, 14, 19; TWA; WLIT 2;
 YAW
Gordon, Adam Lindsay
 1833-1870 **NCLC 21**
 See also DLB 230
Gordon, Caroline 1895-1981 . **CLC 6, 13, 29,**
 83; SSC 15
 See also AMW; CA 11-12; 103; CANR 36;
 CAP 1; CN 1, 2; DLB 4, 9, 102; DLBD
 17; DLBY 1981; EWL 3; MAL 5; MTCW
 1, 2; MTFW 2005; RGAL 4; RGSF 2
Gordon, Charles William 1860-1937
 See Connor, Ralph
 See also CA 109

Gordon, Mary 1949- .. **CLC 13, 22, 128, 216;**
 SSC 59
 See also AMWS 4; BPFB 2; CA 102;
 CANR 44, 92, 154; CN 4, 5, 6, 7; DLB 6;
 DLBY 1981; FW; INT CA-102; MAL 5;
 MTCW 1
Gordon, Mary Catherine
 See Gordon, Mary
Gordon, N. J.
 See Bosman, Herman Charles
Gordon, Sol 1923- **CLC 26**
 See also CA 53-56; CANR 4; SATA 11
Gordone, Charles 1925-1995 .. **CLC 1, 4; DC**
 8
 See also BW 1, 3; CA 93-96; 180; 150;
 CAAE 180; CAD; CANR 55; DAM
 DRAM; DLB 7; INT CA-93-96; MTCW
 1
Gore, Catherine 1800-1861 **NCLC 65**
 See also DLB 116; RGEL 2
Gorenko, Anna Andreevna
 See Akhmatova, Anna
Gorky, Maxim **SSC 28; TCLC 8; WLC 3**
 See Peshkov, Alexei Maximovich
 See also DAB; DFS 9; DLB 295; EW 8;
 EWL 3; TWA
Goryan, Sirak
 See Saroyan, William
Gosse, Edmund (William)
 1849-1928 **TCLC 28**
 See also CA 117; DLB 57, 144, 184; RGEL
 2
Gotlieb, Phyllis (Fay Bloom) 1926- .. **CLC 18**
 See also CA 13-16R; CANR 7, 135; CN 7;
 CP 1, 2, 3, 4; DLB 88, 251; SFW 4
Gottesman, S. D.
 See Kornbluth, C(yril) M.; Pohl, Frederik
Gottfried von Strassburg fl. c.
 1170-1215 **CMLC 10**
 See also CDWLB 2; DLB 138; EW 1;
 RGWL 2, 3
Gotthelf, Jeremias 1797-1854 **NCLC 117**
 See also DLB 133; RGWL 2, 3
Gottschalk, Laura Riding
 See Jackson, Laura (Riding)
Gould, Lois 1932(?)-2002 **CLC 4, 10**
 See also CA 77-80; 208; CANR 29; MTCW
 1
Gould, Stephen Jay 1941-2002 **CLC 163**
 See also AAYA 26; BEST 90:2; CA 77-80;
 205; CANR 10, 27, 56, 75, 125; CPW;
 INT CANR-27; MTCW 1, 2; MTFW 2005
Gourmont, Remy(-Marie-Charles) de
 1858-1915 **TCLC 17**
 See also CA 109; 150; GFL 1789 to the
 Present; MTCW 2
Gournay, Marie le Jars de
 See de Gournay, Marie le Jars
Govier, Katherine 1948- **CLC 51**
 See also CA 101; CANR 18, 40, 128; CCA
 1
Gower, John c. 1330-1408 **LC 76; PC 59**
 See also BRW 1; DLB 146; RGEL 2
Goyen, (Charles) William
 1915-1983 **CLC 5, 8, 14, 40**
 See also AITN 2; CA 5-8R; 110; CANR 6,
 71; CN 1, 2, 3; DLB 2, 218; DLBY 1983;
 EWL 3; INT CANR-6; MAL 5
Goytisolo, Juan 1931- **CLC 5, 10, 23, 133;**
 HLC 1
 See also CA 85-88; CANR 32, 61, 131;
 CWW 2; DAM MULT; DLB 322; EWL
 3; GLL 2; HW 1, 2; MTCW 1, 2; MTFW
 2005
Gozzano, Guido 1883-1916 **PC 10**
 See also CA 154; DLB 114; EWL 3
Gozzi, (Conte) Carlo 1720-1806 **NCLC 23**

Grabbe, Christian Dietrich
1801-1836 **NCLC 2**
See also DLB 133; RGWL 2, 3

Grace, Patricia Frances 1937- **CLC 56**
See also CA 176; CANR 118; CN 4, 5, 6, 7; EWL 3; RGSF 2

Gracian y Morales, Baltasar
1601-1658 **LC 15**

Gracq, Julien **CLC 11, 48**
See Poirier, Louis
See also CWW 2; DLB 83; GFL 1789 to the Present

Grade, Chaim 1910-1982 **CLC 10**
See also CA 93-96; 107; EWL 3; RGHL

Graduate of Oxford, A
See Ruskin, John

Grafton, Garth
See Duncan, Sara Jeannette

Grafton, Sue 1940- **CLC 163**
See also AAYA 11, 49; BEST 90:3; CA 108; CANR 31, 55, 111, 134; CMW 4; CPW; CSW; DA3; DAM POP; DLB 226; FW; MSW; MTFW 2005

Graham, John
See Phillips, David Graham

Graham, Jorie 1950- **CLC 48, 118; PC 59**
See also AAYA 67; CA 111; CANR 63, 118; CP 4, 5, 6, 7; CWP; DLB 120; EWL 3; MTFW 2005; PFS 10, 17; TCLE 1:1

Graham, R(obert) B(ontine) Cunninghame
See Cunninghame Graham, Robert (Gallnigad) Bontine
See also DLB 98, 135, 174; RGEL 2; RGSF 2

Graham, Robert
See Haldeman, Joe

Graham, Tom
See Lewis, (Harry) Sinclair

Graham, W(illiam) S(idney)
1918-1986 **CLC 29**
See also BRWS 7; CA 73-76; 118; CP 1, 2, 3, 4; DLB 20; RGEL 2

Graham, Winston (Mawdsley)
1910-2003 **CLC 23**
See also CA 49-52; 218; CANR 2, 22, 45, 66; CMW 4; CN 1, 2, 3, 4, 5, 6, 7; DLB 77; RHW

Grahame, Kenneth 1859-1932 **TCLC 64, 136**
See also BYA 5; CA 108; 136; CANR 80; CLR 5; CWRI 5; DA3; DAB; DLB 34, 141; FANT; MAICYA 1, 2; MTCW 2; NFS 20; RGEL 2; SATA 100; TEA; WCH; YABC 1

Granger, Darius John
See Marlowe, Stephen

Granin, Daniil 1918- **CLC 59**
See also DLB 302

Granovsky, Timofei Nikolaevich
1813-1855 **NCLC 75**
See also DLB 198

Grant, Skeeter
See Spiegelman, Art

Granville-Barker, Harley
1877-1946 **TCLC 2**
See Barker, Harley Granville
See also CA 104; 204; DAM DRAM; RGEL 2

Granzotto, Gianni
See Granzotto, Giovanni Battista

Granzotto, Giovanni Battista
1914-1985 **CLC 70**
See also CA 166

Grass, Guenter (Wilhelm) 1927- ... **CLC 1, 2, 4, 6, 11, 15, 22, 32, 49, 88, 207; WLC 3**
See Grass, Gunter (Wilhelm)
See also BPFB 2; CA 13-16R; CANR 20, 75, 93, 133; CDWLB 2; DA; DA3; DAB; DAC; DAM MST, NOV; DLB 75, 124; EW 13; EWL 3; MTCW 1, 2; MTFW 2005; RGWL 2, 3; TWA

Grass, Gunter (Wilhelm)
See Grass, Guenter (Wilhelm)
See also CWW 2; RGHL

Gratton, Thomas
See Hulme, T(homas) E(rnest)

Grau, Shirley Ann 1929- **CLC 4, 9, 146; SSC 15**
See also CA 89-92; CANR 22, 69; CN 1, 2, 3, 4, 5, 6, 7; CSW; DLB 2, 218; INT CA-89-92; CANR-22; MTCW 1

Gravel, Fern
See Hall, James Norman

Graver, Elizabeth 1964- **CLC 70**
See also CA 135; CANR 71, 129

Graves, Richard Perceval
1895-1985 **CLC 44**
See also CA 65-68; CANR 9, 26, 51

Graves, Robert (von Ranke)
1895-1985 .. **CLC 1, 2, 6, 11, 39, 44, 45; PC 6**
See also BPFB 2; BRW 7; BYA 4; CA 5-8R; 117; CANR 5, 36; CDBLB 1914-1945; CN 1, 2, 3; CP 1, 2, 3, 4; DA3; DAB; DAC; DAM MST, POET; DLB 20, 100, 191; DLBD 18; DLBY 1985; EWL 3; LATS 1:1; MTCW 1, 2; MTFW 2005; NCFS 2; NFS 21; RGEL 2; RHW; SATA 45; TEA

Graves, Valerie
See Bradley, Marion Zimmer

Gray, Alasdair (James) 1934- **CLC 41**
See also BRWS 9; CA 126; CANR 47, 69, 106, 140; CN 4, 5, 6, 7; DLB 194, 261, 319; HGG; INT CA-126; MTCW 1, 2; MTFW 2005; RGSF 2; SUFW 2

Gray, Amlin 1946- **CLC 29**
See also CA 138

Gray, Francine du Plessix 1930- **CLC 22, 153**
See also BEST 90:3; CA 61-64; CAAS 2; CANR 11, 33, 75, 81; DAM NOV; INT CANR-11; MTCW 1, 2; MTFW 2005

Gray, John (Henry) 1866-1934 **TCLC 19**
See also CA 119; 162; RGEL 2

Gray, John Lee
See Jakes, John (William)

Gray, Simon (James Holliday)
1936- **CLC 9, 14, 36**
See also AITN 1; CA 21-24R; CAAS 3; CANR 32, 69; CBD; CD 5, 6; CN 1, 2, 3; DLB 13; EWL 3; MTCW 1; RGEL 2

Gray, Spalding 1941-2004 **CLC 49, 112; DC 7**
See also AAYA 62; CA 128; 225; CAD; CANR 74, 138; CD 5, 6; CPW; DAM POP; MTCW 2; MTFW 2005

Gray, Thomas 1716-1771 **LC 4, 40; PC 2; WLC 3**
See also BRW 3; CDBLB 1660-1789; DA; DA3; DAB; DAC; DAM MST; DLB 109; EXPP; PAB; PFS 9; RGEL 2; TEA; WP

Grayson, David
See Baker, Ray Stannard

Grayson, Richard (A.) 1951- **CLC 38**
See also CA 85-88, 210; CAAE 210; CANR 14, 31, 57; DLB 234

Greeley, Andrew M(oran) 1928- **CLC 28**
See also BPFB 2; CA 5-8R; CAAS 7; CANR 7, 43, 69, 104, 136; CMW 4; CPW; DA3; DAM POP; MTCW 1, 2; MTFW 2005

Green, Anna Katharine
1846-1935 **TCLC 63**
See also CA 112; 159; CMW 4; DLB 202, 221; MSW

Green, Brian
See Card, Orson Scott

Green, Hannah
See Greenberg, Joanne (Goldenberg)

Green, Hannah 1927(?)-1996 **CLC 3**
See also CA 73-76; CANR 59, 93; NFS 10

Green, Henry **CLC 2, 13, 97**
See Yorke, Henry Vincent
See also BRWS 2; CA 175; DLB 15; EWL 3; RGEL 2

Green, Julian **CLC 3, 11, 77**
See Green, Julien (Hartridge)
See also EWL 3; GFL 1789 to the Present; MTCW 2

Green, Julien (Hartridge) 1900-1998
See Green, Julian
See also CA 21-24R; 169; CANR 33, 87; CWW 2; DLB 4, 72; MTCW 1, 2; MTFW 2005

Green, Paul (Eliot) 1894-1981 **CLC 25**
See also AITN 1; CA 5-8R; 103; CAD; CANR 3; DAM DRAM; DLB 7, 9, 249; DLBY 1981; MAL 5; RGAL 4

Greenaway, Peter 1942- **CLC 159**
See also CA 127

Greenberg, Ivan 1908-1973
See Rahv, Philip
See also CA 85-88

Greenberg, Joanne (Goldenberg)
1932- **CLC 7, 30**
See also AAYA 12, 67; CA 5-8R; CANR 14, 32, 69; CN 6, 7; NFS 23; SATA 25; YAW

Greenberg, Richard 1959(?)- **CLC 57**
See also CA 138; CAD; CD 5, 6

Greenblatt, Stephen J(ay) 1943- **CLC 70**
See also CA 49-52; CANR 115

Greene, Bette 1934- **CLC 30**
See also AAYA 7, 69; BYA 3; CA 53-56; CANR 4, 146; CLR 2; CWRI 5; JRDA; LAIT 4; MAICYA 1, 2; NFS 10; SAAS 16; SATA 8, 102, 161; WYA; YAW

Greene, Gael **CLC 8**
See also CA 13-16R; CANR 10

Greene, Graham (Henry)
1904-1991 **CLC 1, 3, 6, 9, 14, 18, 27, 37, 70, 72, 125; SSC 29; WLC 3**
See also AAYA 61; AITN 2; BPFB 2; BRWR 2; BRWS 1; BYA 3; CA 13-16R; 133; CANR 35, 61, 131; CBD; CDBLB 1945-1960; CMW 4; CN 1, 2, 3, 4; DA; DA3; DAB; DAC; DAM MST, NOV; DLB 13, 15, 77, 100, 162, 201, 204; DLBY 1991; EWL 3; MSW; MTCW 1, 2; MTFW 2005; NFS 16; RGEL 2; SATA 20; SSFS 14; TEA; WLIT 4

Greene, Robert 1558-1592 **LC 41**
See also BRWS 8; DLB 62, 167; IDTP; RGEL 2; TEA

Greer, Germaine 1939- **CLC 131**
See also AITN 1; CA 81-84; CANR 33, 70, 115, 133; FW; MTCW 1, 2; MTFW 2005

Greer, Richard
See Silverberg, Robert

Gregor, Arthur 1923- **CLC 9**
See also CA 25-28R; CAAS 10; CANR 11; CP 1, 2, 3, 4, 5, 6, 7; SATA 36

Gregor, Lee
See Pohl, Frederik

Gregory, Lady Isabella Augusta (Persse)
1852-1932 **TCLC 1, 176**
See also BRW 6; CA 104; 184; DLB 10; IDTP; RGEL 2

Gregory, J. Dennis
See Williams, John A(lfred)

Gregory of Nazianzus, St.
329-389 **CMLC 82**

Grekova, I. **CLC 59**
See Ventsel, Elena Sergeevna
See also CWW 2

Grendon, Stephen
See Derleth, August (William)

Grenville, Kate 1950- **CLC 61**
See also CA 118; CANR 53, 93; CN 7; DLB 325

Grenville, Pelham
See Wodehouse, P(elham) G(renville)

Greve, Felix Paul (Berthold Friedrich)
1879-1948
See Grove, Frederick Philip
See also CA 104; 141, 175; CANR 79; DAC; DAM MST

Greville, Fulke 1554-1628 **LC 79**
See also BRWS 11; DLB 62, 172; RGEL 2

Grey, Lady Jane 1537-1554 **LC 93**
See also DLB 132

Grey, Zane 1872-1939 **TCLC 6**
See also BPFB 2; CA 104; 132; DA3; DAM POP; DLB 9, 212; MTCW 1, 2; MTFW 2005; RGAL 4; TCWW 1, 2; TUS

Griboedov, Aleksandr Sergeevich
1795(?)-1829 **NCLC 129**
See also DLB 205; RGWL 2, 3

Grieg, (Johan) Nordahl (Brun)
1902-1943 **TCLC 10**
See also CA 107; 189; EWL 3

Grieve, C(hristopher) M(urray)
1892-1978 **CLC 11, 19**
See MacDiarmid, Hugh; Pteleon
See also CA 5-8R; 85-88; CANR 33, 107; DAM POET; MTCW 1; RGEL 2

Griffin, Gerald 1803-1840 **NCLC 7**
See also DLB 159; RGEL 2

Griffin, John Howard 1920-1980 **CLC 68**
See also AITN 1; CA 1-4R; 101; CANR 2

Griffin, Peter 1942- **CLC 39**
See also CA 136

Griffith, D(avid Lewelyn) W(ark)
1875(?)-1948 **TCLC 68**
See also CA 119; 150; CANR 80

Griffith, Lawrence
See Griffith, D(avid Lewelyn) W(ark)

Griffiths, Trevor 1935- **CLC 13, 52**
See also CA 97-100; CANR 45; CBD; CD 5, 6; DLB 13, 245

Griggs, Sutton (Elbert)
1872-1930 **TCLC 77**
See also CA 123; 186; DLB 50

Grigson, Geoffrey (Edward Harvey)
1905-1985 **CLC 7, 39**
See also CA 25-28R; 118; CANR 20, 33; CP 1, 2, 3, 4; DLB 27; MTCW 1, 2

Grile, Dod
See Bierce, Ambrose (Gwinett)

Grillparzer, Franz 1791-1872 **DC 14; NCLC 1, 102; SSC 37**
See also CDWLB 2; DLB 133; EW 5; RGWL 2, 3; TWA

Grimble, Reverend Charles James
See Eliot, T(homas) S(tearns)

Grimke, Angelina (Emily) Weld
1880-1958 **HR 1:2**
See Weld, Angelina (Emily) Grimke
See also BW 1; CA 124; DAM POET; DLB 50, 54

Grimke, Charlotte L(ottie) Forten
1837(?)-1914
See Forten, Charlotte L.
See also BW 1; CA 117; 124; DAM MULT, POET

Grimm, Jacob Ludwig Karl
1785-1863 **NCLC 3, 77; SSC 36**
See Grimm Brothers
See also CLR 112; DLB 90; MAICYA 1, 2; RGSF 2; RGWL 2, 3; SATA 22; WCH

Grimm, Wilhelm Karl 1786-1859 .. **NCLC 3, 77; SSC 36**
See Grimm Brothers
See also CDWLB 2; CLR 112; DLB 90; MAICYA 1, 2; RGSF 2; RGWL 2, 3; SATA 22; WCH

Grimm and Grim
See Grimm, Jacob Ludwig Karl; Grimm, Wilhelm Karl

Grimm Brothers **SSC 88**
See Grimm, Jacob Ludwig Karl; Grimm, Wilhelm Karl
See also CLR 112

Grimmelshausen, Hans Jakob Christoffel von
See Grimmelshausen, Johann Jakob Christoffel von
See also RGWL 2, 3

Grimmelshausen, Johann Jakob Christoffel von 1621-1676 **LC 6**
See Grimmelshausen, Hans Jakob Christoffel von
See also CDWLB 2; DLB 168

Grindel, Eugene 1895-1952
See Eluard, Paul
See also CA 104; 193; LMFS 2

Grisham, John 1955- **CLC 84**
See also AAYA 14, 47; BPFB 2; CA 138; CANR 47, 69, 114, 133; CMW 4; CN 6, 7; CPW; CSW; DA3; DAM POP; MSW; MTCW 2; MTFW 2005

Grosseteste, Robert 1175(?)-1253 . **CMLC 62**
See also DLB 115

Grossman, David 1954- **CLC 67**
See also CA 138; CANR 114; CWW 2; DLB 299; EWL 3; RGHL; WLIT 6

Grossman, Vasilii Semenovich
See Grossman, Vasily (Semenovich)
See also DLB 272

Grossman, Vasily (Semenovich)
1905-1964 **CLC 41**
See Grossman, Vasilii Semenovich
See also CA 124; 130; MTCW 1; RGHL

Grove, Frederick Philip **TCLC 4**
See Greve, Felix Paul (Berthold Friedrich)
See also DLB 92; RGEL 2; TCWW 1, 2

Grubb
See Crumb, R.

Grumbach, Doris (Isaac) 1918- . **CLC 13, 22, 64**
See also CA 5-8R; CAAS 2; CANR 9, 42, 70, 127; CN 6, 7; INT CANR-9; MTCW 2; MTFW 2005

Grundtvig, Nikolai Frederik Severin
1783-1872 **NCLC 1, 158**
See also DLB 300

Grunge
See Crumb, R.

Grunwald, Lisa 1959- **CLC 44**
See also CA 120; CANR 148

Gryphius, Andreas 1616-1664 **LC 89**
See also CDWLB 2; DLB 164; RGWL 2, 3

Guare, John 1938- **CLC 8, 14, 29, 67; DC 20**
See also CA 73-76; CAD; CANR 21, 69, 118; CD 5, 6; DAM DRAM; DFS 8, 13; DLB 7, 249; EWL 3; MAL 5; MTCW 1, 2; RGAL 4

Guarini, Battista 1537-1612 **LC 102**

Gubar, Susan (David) 1944- **CLC 145**
See also CA 108; CANR 45, 70, 139; FW; MTCW 1; RGAL 4

Gudjonsson, Halldor Kiljan 1902-1998
See Halldor Laxness
See also CA 103; 164

Guenter, Erich
See Eich, Gunter

Guest, Barbara 1920-2006 ... **CLC 34; PC 55**
See also BG 1:2; CA 25-28R; 248; CANR 11, 44, 84; CP 1, 2, 3, 4, 5, 6, 7; CWP; DLB 5, 193

Guest, Edgar A(lbert) 1881-1959 ... **TCLC 95**
See also CA 112; 168

Guest, Judith (Ann) 1936- **CLC 8, 30**
See also AAYA 7, 66; CA 77-80; CANR 15, 75, 138; DA3; DAM NOV, POP; EXPN; INT CANR-15; LAIT 5; MTCW 1, 2; MTFW 2005; NFS 1

Guevara, Che **CLC 87; HLC 1**
See Guevara (Serna), Ernesto

Guevara (Serna), Ernesto
1928-1967 **CLC 87; HLC 1**
See Guevara, Che
See also CA 127; 111; CANR 56; DAM MULT; HW 1

Guicciardini, Francesco 1483-1540 **LC 49**

Guild, Nicholas M. 1944- **CLC 33**
See also CA 93-96

Guillemin, Jacques
See Sartre, Jean-Paul

Guillen, Jorge 1893-1984 . **CLC 11; HLCS 1; PC 35**
See also CA 89-92; 112; DAM MULT, POET; DLB 108; EWL 3; HW 1; RGWL 2, 3

Guillen, Nicolas (Cristobal)
1902-1989 **BLC 2; CLC 48, 79; HLC 1; PC 23**
See also BW 2; CA 116; 125; 129; CANR 84; DAM MST, MULT, POET; DLB 283; EWL 3; HW 1; LAW; RGWL 2, 3; WP

Guillen y Alvarez, Jorge
See Guillen, Jorge

Guillevic, (Eugene) 1907-1997 **CLC 33**
See also CA 93-96; CWW 2

Guillois
See Desnos, Robert

Guillois, Valentin
See Desnos, Robert

Guimaraes Rosa, Joao 1908-1967 **HLCS 2**
See Rosa, Joao Guimaraes
See also CA 175; LAW; RGSF 2; RGWL 2, 3

Guiney, Louise Imogen
1861-1920 **TCLC 41**
See also CA 160; DLB 54; RGAL 4

Guinizelli, Guido c. 1230-1276 **CMLC 49**
See Guinizzelli, Guido

Guinizzelli, Guido
See Guinizelli, Guido
See also WLIT 7

Guiraldes, Ricardo (Guillermo)
1886-1927 **TCLC 39**
See also CA 131; EWL 3; HW 1; LAW; MTCW 1

Gumilev, Nikolai (Stepanovich)
1886-1921 **TCLC 60**
See Gumilyov, Nikolay Stepanovich
See also CA 165; DLB 295

Gumilyov, Nikolay Stepanovich
See Gumilev, Nikolai (Stepanovich)
See also EWL 3

Gump, P. Q.
See Card, Orson Scott

Gunesekera, Romesh 1954- **CLC 91**
See also BRWS 10; CA 159; CANR 140; CN 6, 7; DLB 267, 323

Gunn, Bill .. **CLC 5**
See Gunn, William Harrison
See also DLB 38

Gunn, Thom(son William)
1929-2004 . **CLC 3, 6, 18, 32, 81; PC 26**
See also BRWS 4; CA 17-20R; 227; CANR 9, 33, 116; CDBLB 1960 to Present; CP 1, 2, 3, 4, 5, 6, 7; DAM POET; DLB 27; INT CANR-33; MTCW 1; PFS 9; RGEL 2

Gunn, William Harrison 1934(?)-1989
See Gunn, Bill
See also AITN 1; BW 1, 3; CA 13-16R; 128; CANR 12, 25, 76

Gunn Allen, Paula
See Allen, Paula Gunn
Gunnars, Kristjana 1948- **CLC 69**
See also CA 113; CCA 1; CP 6, 7; CWP;
DLB 60
Gunter, Erich
See Eich, Gunter
Gurdjieff, G(eorgei) I(vanovich)
1877(?)-1949 **TCLC 71**
See also CA 157
Gurganus, Allan 1947- **CLC 70**
See also BEST 90:1; CA 135; CANR 114;
CN 6, 7; CPW; CSW; DAM POP; GLL 1
Gurney, A. R.
See Gurney, A(lbert) R(amsdell), Jr.
See also DLB 266
Gurney, A(lbert) R(amsdell), Jr.
1930- **CLC 32, 50, 54**
See Gurney, A. R.
See also AMWS 5; CA 77-80; CAD; CANR
32, 64, 121; CD 5, 6; DAM DRAM; EWL
3
Gurney, Ivor (Bertie) 1890-1937 ... **TCLC 33**
See also BRW 6; CA 167; DLBY 2002;
PAB; RGEL 2
Gurney, Peter
See Gurney, A(lbert) R(amsdell), Jr.
Guro, Elena (Genrikhovna)
1877-1913 **TCLC 56**
See also DLB 295
Gustafson, James M(oody) 1925- ... **CLC 100**
See also CA 25-28R; CANR 37
Gustafson, Ralph (Barker)
1909-1995 **CLC 36**
See also CA 21-24R; CANR 8, 45, 84; CP
1, 2, 3, 4, 5, 6; DLB 88; RGEL 2
Gut, Gom
See Simenon, Georges (Jacques Christian)
Guterson, David 1956- **CLC 91**
See also CA 132; CANR 73, 126; CN 7;
DLB 292; MTCW 2; MTFW 2005; NFS
13
Guthrie, A(lfred) B(ertram), Jr.
1901-1991 **CLC 23**
See also CA 57-60; 134; CANR 24; CN 1,
2, 3; DLB 6, 212; MAL 5; SATA 62;
SATA-Obit 67; TCWW 1, 2
Guthrie, Isobel
See Grieve, C(hristopher) M(urray)
Guthrie, Woodrow Wilson 1912-1967
See Guthrie, Woody
See also CA 113; 93-96
Guthrie, Woody **CLC 35**
See Guthrie, Woodrow Wilson
See also DLB 303; LAIT 3
Gutierrez Najera, Manuel
1859-1895 **HLCS 2; NCLC 133**
See also DLB 290; LAW
Guy, Rosa (Cuthbert) 1925- **CLC 26**
See also AAYA 4, 37; BW 2; CA 17-20R;
CANR 14, 34, 83; CLR 13; DLB 33;
DNFS 1; JRDA; MAICYA 1, 2; SATA 14,
62, 122; YAW
Gwendolyn
See Bennett, (Enoch) Arnold
H. D. **CLC 3, 8, 14, 31, 34, 73; PC 5**
See Doolittle, Hilda
See also FL 1:5
H. de V.
See Buchan, John
Haavikko, Paavo Juhani 1931- .. **CLC 18, 34**
See also CA 106; CWW 2; EWL 3
Habbema, Koos
See Heijermans, Herman
Habermas, Juergen 1929- **CLC 104**
See also CA 109; CANR 85; DLB 242
Habermas, Jurgen
See Habermas, Juergen

Hacker, Marilyn 1942- **CLC 5, 9, 23, 72,
91; PC 47**
See also CA 77-80; CANR 68, 129; CP 3,
4, 5, 6, 7; CWP; DAM POET; DLB 120,
282; FW; GLL 2; MAL 5; PFS 19
Hadewijch of Antwerp fl. 1250- ... **CMLC 61**
See also RGWL 3
Hadrian 76-138 **CMLC 52**
Haeckel, Ernst Heinrich (Philipp August)
1834-1919 **TCLC 83**
See also CA 157
Hafiz c. 1326-1389(?) **CMLC 34**
See also RGWL 2, 3; WLIT 6
Hagedorn, Jessica T(arahata)
1949- .. **CLC 185**
See also CA 139; CANR 69; CWP; DLB
312; RGAL 4
Haggard, H(enry) Rider
1856-1925 **TCLC 11**
See also BRWS 3; BYA 4, 5; CA 108; 148;
CANR 112; DLB 70, 156, 174, 178;
FANT; LMFS 1; MTCW 2; RGEL 2;
RHW; SATA 16; SCFW 1, 2; SFW 4;
SUFW 1; WLIT 4
Hagiosy, L.
See Larbaud, Valery (Nicolas)
Hagiwara, Sakutaro 1886-1942 **PC 18;
TCLC 60**
See Hagiwara Sakutaro
See also CA 154; RGWL 3
Hagiwara Sakutaro
See Hagiwara, Sakutaro
See also EWL 3
Haig, Fenil
See Ford, Ford Madox
Haig-Brown, Roderick (Langmere)
1908-1976 **CLC 21**
See also CA 5-8R; 69-72; CANR 4, 38, 83;
CLR 31; CWRI 5; DLB 88; MAICYA 1,
2; SATA 12; TCWW 2
Haight, Rip
See Carpenter, John (Howard)
Hailey, Arthur 1920-2004 **CLC 5**
See also AITN 2; BEST 90:3; BPFB 2; CA
1-4R; 233; CANR 2, 36, 75; CCA 1; CN
1, 2, 3, 4, 5, 6, 7; CPW; DAM NOV, POP;
DLB 88; DLBY 1982; MTCW 1, 2;
MTFW 2005
Hailey, Elizabeth Forsythe 1938- **CLC 40**
See also CA 93-96, 188; CAAE 188; CAAS
1; CANR 15, 48; INT CANR-15
Haines, John (Meade) 1924- **CLC 58**
See also AMWS 12; CA 17-20R; CANR
13, 34; CP 1, 2, 3, 4, 5; CSW; DLB 5,
212; TCLE 1:1
Hakluyt, Richard 1552-1616 **LC 31**
See also DLB 136; RGEL 2
Haldeman, Joe 1943- **CLC 61**
See Graham, Robert
See also AAYA 38; CA 53-56, 179; CAAE
179; CAAS 25; CANR 6, 70, 72, 130;
DLB 8; INT CANR-6; SCFW 2; SFW 4
Haldeman, Joe William
See Haldeman, Joe
Hale, Janet Campbell 1947- **NNAL**
See also CA 49-52; CANR 45, 75; DAM
MULT; DLB 175; MTCW 2; MTFW 2005
Hale, Sarah Josepha (Buell)
1788-1879 **NCLC 75**
See also DLB 1, 42, 73, 243
Halevy, Elie 1870-1937 **TCLC 104**
Haley, Alex(ander Murray Palmer)
1921-1992 **BLC 2; CLC 8, 12, 76;
TCLC 147**
See also AAYA 26; BPFB 2; BW 2, 3; CA
77-80; 136; CANR 61; CDALBS; CPW;
CSW; DA; DA3; DAB; DAC; DAM MST,
MULT, POP; DLB 38; LAIT 5; MTCW
1, 2; NFS 9

Haliburton, Thomas Chandler
1796-1865 **NCLC 15, 149**
See also DLB 11, 99; RGEL 2; RGSF 2
Hall, Donald 1928- .. **CLC 1, 13, 37, 59, 151;
PC 70**
See also AAYA 63; CA 5-8R; CAAS 7;
CANR 2, 44, 64, 106, 133; CP 1, 2, 3, 4,
5, 6, 7; DAM POET; DLB 5; MAL 5;
MTCW 2; MTFW 2005; RGAL 4; SATA
23, 97
Hall, Donald Andrew, Jr.
See Hall, Donald
Hall, Frederic Sauser
See Sauser-Hall, Frederic
Hall, James
See Kuttner, Henry
Hall, James Norman 1887-1951 **TCLC 23**
See also CA 123; 173; LAIT 1; RHW 1;
SATA 21
Hall, Joseph 1574-1656 **LC 91**
See also DLB 121, 151; RGEL 2
Hall, (Marguerite) Radclyffe
1880-1943 **TCLC 12**
See also BRWS 6; CA 110; 150; CANR 83;
DLB 191; MTCW 2; MTFW 2005; RGEL
2; RHW
Hall, Rodney 1935- **CLC 51**
See also CA 109; CANR 69; CN 6, 7; CP
1, 2, 3, 4, 5, 6, 7; DLB 289
Hallam, Arthur Henry
1811-1833 **NCLC 110**
See also DLB 32
Halldor Laxness **CLC 25**
See Gudjonsson, Halldor Kiljan
See also DLB 293; EW 12; EWL 3; RGWL
2, 3
Halleck, Fitz-Greene 1790-1867 **NCLC 47**
See also DLB 3, 250; RGAL 4
Halliday, Michael
See Creasey, John
Halpern, Daniel 1945- **CLC 14**
See also CA 33-36R; CANR 93; CP 3, 4, 5,
6, 7
Hamburger, Michael (Peter Leopold)
1924- **CLC 5, 14**
See also CA 5-8R, 196; CAAE 196; CAAS
4; CANR 2, 47; CP 1, 2, 3, 4, 5, 6, 7;
DLB 27
Hamill, Pete 1935- **CLC 10**
See also CA 25-28R; CANR 18, 71, 127
Hamilton, Alexander
1755(?)-1804 **NCLC 49**
See also DLB 37
Hamilton, Clive
See Lewis, C.S.
Hamilton, Edmond 1904-1977 **CLC 1**
See also CA 1-4R; CANR 3, 84; DLB 8;
SATA 118; SFW 4
Hamilton, Elizabeth 1758-1816 ... **NCLC 153**
See also DLB 116, 158
Hamilton, Eugene (Jacob) Lee
See Lee-Hamilton, Eugene (Jacob)
Hamilton, Franklin
See Silverberg, Robert
Hamilton, Gail
See Corcoran, Barbara (Asenath)
Hamilton, (Robert) Ian 1938-2001 . **CLC 191**
See also CA 106; 203; CANR 41, 67; CP 1,
2, 3, 4, 5, 6, 7; DLB 40, 155
Hamilton, Jane 1957- **CLC 179**
See also CA 147; CANR 85, 128; CN 7;
MTFW 2005
Hamilton, Mollie
See Kaye, M(ary) M(argaret)
Hamilton, (Anthony Walter) Patrick
1904-1962 **CLC 51**
See also CA 176; 113; DLB 10, 191

Hamilton, Virginia (Esther)
1936-2002 **CLC 26**
See also AAYA 2, 21; BW 2, 3; BYA 1, 2, 8; CA 25-28R; 206; CANR 20, 37, 73, 126; CLR 1, 11, 40; DAM MULT; DLB 33, 52; DLBY 2001; INT CANR-20; JRDA; LAIT 5; MAICYA 1, 2; MAIC-YAS 1; MTCW 1, 2; MTFW 2005; SATA 4, 56, 79, 123; SATA-Obit 132; WYA; YAW

Hammett, (Samuel) Dashiell
1894-1961 **CLC 3, 5, 10, 19, 47; SSC 17**
See also AAYA 59; AITN 1; AMWS 4; BPFB 2; CA 81-84; CANR 42; CDALB 1929-1941; CMW 4; DA3; DLB 226, 280; DLBD 6; DLBY 1996; EWL 3; LAIT 3; MAL 5; MSW; MTCW 1, 2; MTFW 2005; NFS 21; RGAL 4; RGSF 2; TUS

Hammon, Jupiter 1720(?)-1800(?) **BLC 2; NCLC 5; PC 16**
See also DAM MULT, POET; DLB 31, 50

Hammond, Keith
See Kuttner, Henry

Hamner, Earl (Henry), Jr. 1923- **CLC 12**
See also AITN 2; CA 73-76; DLB 6

Hampton, Christopher 1946- **CLC 4**
See also CA 25-28R; CD 5, 6; DLB 13; MTCW 1

Hampton, Christopher James
See Hampton, Christopher

Hamsun, Knut **TCLC 2, 14, 49, 151**
See Pedersen, Knut
See also DLB 297; EW 8; EWL 3; RGWL 2, 3

Handke, Peter 1942- **CLC 5, 8, 10, 15, 38, 134; DC 17**
See also CA 77-80; CANR 33, 75, 104, 133; CWW 2; DAM DRAM, NOV; DLB 85, 124; EWL 3; MTCW 1, 2; MTFW 2005; TWA

Handy, W(illiam) C(hristopher)
1873-1958 **TCLC 97**
See also BW 3; CA 121; 167

Hanley, James 1901-1985 **CLC 3, 5, 8, 13**
See also CA 73-76; 117; CANR 36; CBD; CN 1, 2, 3; DLB 191; EWL 3; MTCW 1; RGEL 2

Hannah, Barry 1942- **CLC 23, 38, 90**
See also BPFB 2; CA 108; 110; CANR 43, 68, 113; CN 4, 5, 6, 7; CSW; DLB 6, 234; INT CA-110; MTCW 1; RGSF 2

Hannon, Ezra
See Hunter, Evan

Hansberry, Lorraine (Vivian)
1930-1965 ... **BLC 2; CLC 17, 62; DC 2**
See also AAYA 25; AFAW 1, 2; AMWS 4; BW 1, 3; CA 109; 25-28R; CABS 3; CAD; CANR 58; CDALB 1941-1968; CWD; DA; DA3; DAB; DAC; DAM DRAM, MST, MULT; DFS 2; DLB 7, 38; EWL 3; FL 1:6; FW; LAIT 4; MAL 5; MTCW 1, 2; MTFW 2005; RGAL 4; TUS

Hansen, Joseph 1923-2004 **CLC 38**
See Brock, Rose; Colton, James
See also BPFB 2; CA 29-32R; 233; CAAS 17; CANR 16, 44, 66, 125; CMW 4; DLB 226; GLL 1; INT CANR-16

Hansen, Martin A(lfred)
1909-1955 **TCLC 32**
See also CA 167; DLB 214; EWL 3

Hansen and Philipson eds. **CLC 65**

Hanson, Kenneth O(stlin) 1922- **CLC 13**
See also CA 53-56; CANR 7; CP 1, 2, 3, 4, 5

Hardwick, Elizabeth (Bruce) 1916- . **CLC 13**
See also AMWS 3; CA 5-8R; CANR 3, 32, 70, 100, 139; CN 4, 5, 6; CSW; DA3; DAM NOV; DLB 6; MAWW; MTCW 1, 2; MTFW 2005; TCLE 1:1

Hardy, Thomas 1840-1928 **PC 8; SSC 2, 60; TCLC 4, 10, 18, 32, 48, 53, 72, 143, 153; WLC 3**
See also AAYA 69; BRW 6; BRWC 1, 2; BRWR 1; CA 104; 123; CDBLB 1890-1914; DA; DA3; DAB; DAC; DAM MST, NOV, POET; DLB 18, 19, 135, 284; EWL 3; EXPN; EXPP; LAIT 2; MTCW 1, 2; MTFW 2005; NFS 3, 11, 15, 19; PFS 3, 4, 18; RGEL 2; RGSF 2; TEA; WLIT 4

Hare, David 1947- . **CLC 29, 58, 136; DC 26**
See also BRWS 4; CA 97-100; CANR 39, 91; CBD; CD 5, 6; DFS 4, 7, 16; DLB 13, 310; MTCW 1; TEA

Harewood, John
See Van Druten, John (William)

Harford, Henry
See Hudson, W(illiam) H(enry)

Hargrave, Leonie
See Disch, Thomas M(ichael)

Hariri, Al- al-Qasim ibn 'Ali Abu Muhammad al-Basri
See al-Hariri, al-Qasim ibn 'Ali Abu Muhammad al-Basri

Harjo, Joy 1951- **CLC 83; NNAL; PC 27**
See also AMWS 12; CA 114; CANR 35, 67, 91, 129; CP 6, 7; CWP; DAM MULT; DLB 120, 175; EWL 3; MTCW 2; MTFW 2005; PFS 15; RGAL 4

Harlan, Louis R(udolph) 1922- **CLC 34**
See also CA 21-24R; CANR 25, 55, 80

Harling, Robert 1951(?)- **CLC 53**
See also CA 147

Harmon, William (Ruth) 1938- **CLC 38**
See also CA 33-36R; CANR 14, 32, 35; SATA 65

Harper, F. E. W.
See Harper, Frances Ellen Watkins

Harper, Frances E. W.
See Harper, Frances Ellen Watkins

Harper, Frances E. Watkins
See Harper, Frances Ellen Watkins

Harper, Frances Ellen
See Harper, Frances Ellen Watkins

Harper, Frances Ellen Watkins
1825-1911 **BLC 2; PC 21; TCLC 14**
See also AFAW 1, 2; BW 1, 3; CA 111; 125; CANR 79; DAM MULT, POET; DLB 50, 221; MAWW; RGAL 4

Harper, Michael S(teven) 1938- ... **CLC 7, 22**
See also AFAW 2; BW 1; CA 33-36R, 224; CAAE 224; CANR 24, 108; CP 2, 3, 4, 5, 6, 7; DLB 41; RGAL 4; TCLE 1:1

Harper, Mrs. F. E. W.
See Harper, Frances Ellen Watkins

Harpur, Charles 1813-1868 **NCLC 114**
See also DLB 230; RGEL 2

Harris, Christie
See Harris, Christie (Lucy) Irwin

Harris, Christie (Lucy) Irwin
1907-2002 **CLC 12**
See also CA 5-8R; CANR 6, 83; CLR 47; DLB 88; JRDA; MAICYA 1, 2; SAAS 10; SATA 6, 74; SATA-Essay 116

Harris, Frank 1856-1931 **TCLC 24**
See also CA 109; 150; CANR 80; DLB 156, 197; RGEL 2

Harris, George Washington
1814-1869 **NCLC 23, 165**
See also DLB 3, 11, 248; RGAL 4

Harris, Joel Chandler 1848-1908 **SSC 19; TCLC 2**
See also CA 104; 137; CANR 80; CLR 49; DLB 11, 23, 42, 78, 91; LAIT 2; MAI-CYA 1, 2; RGSF 2; SATA 100; WCH; YABC 1

Harris, John (Wyndham Parkes Lucas)
Beynon 1903-1969
See Wyndham, John
See also CA 102; 89-92; CANR 84; SATA 118; SFW 4

Harris, MacDonald **CLC 9**
See Heiney, Donald (William)

Harris, Mark 1922- **CLC 19**
See also CA 5-8R; CAAS 3; CANR 2, 55, 83; CN 1, 2, 3, 4, 5, 6, 7; DLB 2; DLBY 1980

Harris, Norman **CLC 65**

Harris, (Theodore) Wilson 1921- **CLC 25, 159**
See also BRWS 5; BW 2, 3; CA 65-68; CAAS 16; CANR 11, 27, 69, 114; CD-WLB 3; CN 1, 2, 3, 4, 5, 6, 7; CP 1, 2, 3, 4, 5, 6, 7; DLB 117; EWL 3; MTCW 1; RGEL 2

Harrison, Barbara Grizzuti
1934-2002 **CLC 144**
See also CA 77-80; 205; CANR 15, 48; INT CANR-15

Harrison, Elizabeth (Allen) Cavanna
1909-2001
See Cavanna, Betty
See also CA 9-12R; 200; CANR 6, 27, 85, 104, 121; MAICYA 2; SATA 142; YAW

Harrison, Harry (Max) 1925- **CLC 42**
See also CA 1-4R; CANR 5, 21, 84; DLB 8; SATA 4; SCFW 2; SFW 4

Harrison, James (Thomas) 1937- **CLC 6, 14, 33, 66, 143; SSC 19**
See Harrison, Jim
See also CA 13-16R; CANR 8, 51, 79, 142; DLBY 1982; INT CANR-8

Harrison, Jim
See Harrison, James (Thomas)
See also AMWS 8; CN 5, 6; CP 1, 2, 3, 4, 5, 6, 7; RGAL 4; TCWW 2; TUS

Harrison, Kathryn 1961- **CLC 70, 151**
See also CA 144; CANR 68, 122

Harrison, Tony 1937- **CLC 43, 129**
See also BRWS 5; CA 65-68; CANR 44, 98; CBD; CD 5, 6; CP 2, 3, 4, 5, 6, 7; DLB 40, 245; MTCW 1; RGEL 2

Harriss, Will(ard Irvin) 1922- **CLC 34**
See also CA 111

Hart, Ellis
See Ellison, Harlan (Jay)

Hart, Josephine 1942(?)- **CLC 70**
See also CA 138; CANR 70, 149; CPW; DAM POP

Hart, Moss 1904-1961 **CLC 66**
See also CA 109; 89-92; CANR 84; DAM DRAM; DFS 1; DLB 7, 266; RGAL 4

Harte, (Francis) Bret(t)
1836(?)-1902 ... **SSC 8, 59; TCLC 1, 25; WLC 3**
See also AMWS 2; CA 104; 140; CANR 80; CDALB 1865-1917; DA; DA3; DAC; DAM MST; DLB 12, 64, 74, 79, 186; EXPS; LAIT 2; RGAL 4; RGSF 2; SATA 26; SSFS 3; TUS

Hartley, L(eslie) P(oles) 1895-1972 ... **CLC 2, 22**
See also BRWS 7; CA 45-48; 37-40R; CANR 33; CN 1; DLB 15, 139; EWL 3; HGG; MTCW 1, 2; MTFW 2005; RGEL 2; RGSF 2; SUFW 1

Hartman, Geoffrey H. 1929- **CLC 27**
See also CA 117; 125; CANR 79; DLB 67

Hartmann, Sadakichi 1869-1944 ... **TCLC 73**
See also CA 157; DLB 54

Hartmann von Aue c. 1170-c. 1210 .. **CMLC 15**
See also CDWLB 2; DLB 138; RGWL 2, 3

Hartog, Jan de
See de Hartog, Jan

Haruf, Kent 1943- **CLC 34**
See also AAYA 44; CA 149; CANR 91, 131

Harvey, Caroline
See Trollope, Joanna

Harvey, Gabriel 1550(?)-1631 **LC 88**
See also DLB 167, 213, 281

Harwood, Ronald 1934- **CLC 32**
See also CA 1-4R; CANR 4, 55, 150; CBD;
CD 5, 6; DAM DRAM, MST; DLB 13

Hasegawa Tatsunosuke
See Futabatei, Shimei

Hasek, Jaroslav (Matej Frantisek)
1883-1923 **SSC 69; TCLC 4**
See also CA 104; CDWLB 4; DLB
215; EW 9; EWL 3; MTCW 1, 2; RGSF
2; RGWL 2, 3

Hass, Robert 1941- ... **CLC 18, 39, 99; PC 16**
See also AMWS 6; CA 111; CANR 30, 50,
71; CP 3, 4, 5, 6, 7; DLB 105, 206; EWL
3; MAL 5; MTFW 2005; RGAL 4; SATA
94; TCLE 1:1

Hastings, Hudson
See Kuttner, Henry

Hastings, Selina **CLC 44**

Hathorne, John 1641-1717 **LC 38**

Hatteras, Amelia
See Mencken, H(enry) L(ouis)

Hatteras, Owen **TCLC 18**
See Mencken, H(enry) L(ouis); Nathan,
George Jean

Hauptmann, Gerhart (Johann Robert)
1862-1946 **SSC 37; TCLC 4**
See also CA 104; 153; CDWLB 2; DAM
DRAM; DLB 66, 118; EW 8; EWL 3;
RGSF 2; RGWL 2, 3; TWA

Havel, Vaclav 1936- **CLC 25, 58, 65, 123;
DC 6**
See also CA 104; CANR 36, 63, 124; CD-
WLB 4; CWW 2; DA3; DAM DRAM;
DFS 10; DLB 232; EWL 3; LMFS 2;
MTCW 1, 2; MTFW 2005; RGWL 3

Haviaras, Stratis **CLC 33**
See Chaviaras, Strates

Hawes, Stephen 1475(?)-1529(?) **LC 17**
See also DLB 132; RGEL 2

Hawkes, John (Clendennin Burne, Jr.)
1925-1998 .. **CLC 1, 2, 3, 4, 7, 9, 14, 15,
27, 49**
See also BPFB 2; CA 1-4R; 167; CANR 2,
47, 64; CN 1, 2, 3, 4, 5, 6; DLB 2, 7, 227;
DLBY 1980, 1998; EWL 3; MAL 5;
MTCW 1, 2; MTFW 2005; RGAL 4

Hawking, S. W.
See Hawking, Stephen W(illiam)

Hawking, Stephen W(illiam) 1942- . **CLC 63,
105**
See also AAYA 13; BEST 89:1; CA 126;
129; CANR 48, 115; CPW; DA3; MTCW
2; MTFW 2005

Hawkins, Anthony Hope
See Hope, Anthony

Hawthorne, Julian 1846-1934 **TCLC 25**
See also CA 165; HGG

Hawthorne, Nathaniel 1804-1864 ... **NCLC 2,
10, 17, 23, 39, 79, 95, 158, 171; SSC 3,
29, 39, 89; WLC 3**
See also AAYA 18; AMW; AMWC 1;
AMWR 1; BPFB 2; BYA 3; CDALB
1640-1865; CLR 103; DA; DA3; DAB;
DAC; DAM MST, NOV; DLB 1, 74, 183,
223, 269; EXPN; EXPS; GL 2; HGG;
LAIT 1; NFS 1, 20; RGAL 4; RGSF 2;
SSFS 1, 7, 11, 15; SUFW 1; TUS; WCH;
YABC 2

Hawthorne, Sophia Peabody
1809-1871 **NCLC 150**
See also DLB 183, 239

Haxton, Josephine Ayres 1921-
See Douglas, Ellen
See also CA 115; CANR 41, 83

Hayaseca y Eizaguirre, Jorge
See Echegaray (y Eizaguirre), Jose (Maria
Waldo)

Hayashi, Fumiko 1904-1951 **TCLC 27**
See Hayashi Fumiko
See also CA 161

Hayashi Fumiko
See Hayashi, Fumiko
See also DLB 180; EWL 3

Haycraft, Anna 1932-2005
See Ellis, Alice Thomas
See also CA 122; 237; CANR 90, 141;
MTCW 2; MTFW 2005

Hayden, Robert E(arl) 1913-1980 **BLC 2;
CLC 5, 9, 14, 37; PC 6**
See also AFAW 1, 2; AMWS 2; BW 1, 3;
CA 69-72; 97-100; CABS 2; CANR 24,
75, 82; CDALB 1941-1968; CP 1, 2, 3;
DA; DAC; DAM MST, MULT, POET;
DLB 5, 76; EWL 3; EXPP; MAL 5;
MTCW 1, 2; PFS 1; RGAL 4; SATA 19;
SATA-Obit 26; WP

Haydon, Benjamin Robert
1786-1846 **NCLC 146**
See also DLB 110

Hayek, F(riedrich) A(ugust von)
1899-1992 **TCLC 109**
See also CA 93-96; 137; CANR 20; MTCW
1, 2

Hayford, J(oseph) E(phraim) Casely
See Casely-Hayford, J(oseph) E(phraim)

Hayman, Ronald 1932- **CLC 44**
See also CA 25-28R; CANR 18, 50, 88; CD
5, 6; DLB 155

Hayne, Paul Hamilton 1830-1886 . **NCLC 94**
See also DLB 3, 64, 79, 248; RGAL 4

Hays, Mary 1760-1843 **NCLC 114**
See also DLB 142, 158; RGEL 2

Haywood, Eliza (Fowler)
1693(?)-1756 **LC 1, 44**
See also DLB 39; RGEL 2

Hazlitt, William 1778-1830 **NCLC 29, 82**
See also BRW 4; DLB 110, 158; RGEL 2;
TEA

Hazzard, Shirley 1931- **CLC 18, 218**
See also CA 9-12R; CANR 4, 70, 127; CN
1, 2, 3, 4, 5, 6, 7; DLB 289; DLBY 1982;
MTCW 1

Head, Bessie 1937-1986 **BLC 2; CLC 25,
67; SSC 52**
See also AFW; BW 2, 3; CA 29-32R; 119;
CANR 25, 82; CDWLB 3; CN 1, 2, 3, 4;
DA3; DAM MULT; DLB 117, 225; EWL
3; EXPS; FL 1:6; FW; MTCW 1, 2;
MTFW 2005; RGSF 2; SSFS 5, 13; WLIT
2; WWE 1

Headon, (Nicky) Topper 1956(?)- **CLC 30**

Heaney, Seamus (Justin) 1939- **CLC 5, 7,
14, 25, 37, 74, 91, 171, 225; PC 18;
WLCS**
See also AAYA 61; BRWR 1; BRWS 2; CA
85-88; CANR 25, 48, 75, 91, 128; CD-
BLB 1960 to Present; CP 1, 2, 3, 4, 5, 6,
7; DA3; DAB; DAM POET; DLB 40;
DLBY 1995; EWL 3; EXPP; MTCW 1,
2; MTFW 2005; PAB; PFS 2, 5, 8, 17;
RGEL 2; TEA; WLIT 4

Hearn, (Patricio) Lafcadio (Tessima Carlos)
1850-1904 **TCLC 9**
See also CA 105; 166; DLB 12, 78, 189;
HGG; MAL 5; RGAL 4

Hearne, Samuel 1745-1792 **LC 95**
See also DLB 99

Hearne, Vicki 1946-2001 **CLC 56**
See also CA 139; 201

Hearon, Shelby 1931- **CLC 63**
See also AITN 2; AMWS 8; CA 25-28R;
CANR 18, 48, 103, 146; CSW

Heat-Moon, William Least **CLC 29**
See Trogdon, William (Lewis)
See also AAYA 9

Hebbel, Friedrich 1813-1863 . **DC 21; NCLC
43**
See also CDWLB 2; DAM DRAM; DLB
129; EW 6; RGWL 2, 3

Hebert, Anne 1916-2000 **CLC 4, 13, 29**
See also CA 85-88; 187; CANR 69, 126;
CCA 1; CWP; CWW 2; DA3; DAC;
DAM MST, POET; DLB 68; EWL 3; GFL
1789 to the Present; MTCW 1, 2; MTFW
2005; PFS 20

Hecht, Anthony (Evan) 1923-2004 **CLC 8,
13, 19; PC 70**
See also AMWS 10; CA 9-12R; 232; CANR
6, 108; CP 1, 2, 3, 4, 5, 6, 7; DAM POET;
DLB 5, 169; EWL 3; PFS 6; WP

Hecht, Ben 1894-1964 **CLC 8; TCLC 101**
See also CA 85-88; DFS 9; DLB 7, 9, 25,
26, 28, 86; FANT; IDFW 3, 4; RGAL 4

Hedayat, Sadeq 1903-1951 **TCLC 21**
See also CA 120; EWL 3; RGSF 2

Hegel, Georg Wilhelm Friedrich
1770-1831 **NCLC 46, 151**
See also DLB 90; TWA

Heidegger, Martin 1889-1976 **CLC 24**
See also CA 81-84; 65-68; CANR 34; DLB
296; MTCW 1, 2; MTFW 2005

Heidenstam, (Carl Gustaf) Verner von
1859-1940 **TCLC 5**
See also CA 104

Heidi Louise
See Erdrich, Louise

Heifner, Jack 1946- **CLC 11**
See also CA 105; CANR 47

Heijermans, Herman 1864-1924 **TCLC 24**
See also CA 123; EWL 3

Heilbrun, Carolyn G(old)
1926-2003 **CLC 25, 173**
See Cross, Amanda
See also CA 45-48; 220; CANR 1, 28, 58,
94; FW

Hein, Christoph 1944- **CLC 154**
See also CA 158; CANR 108; CDWLB 2;
CWW 2; DLB 124

Heine, Heinrich 1797-1856 **NCLC 4, 54,
147; PC 25**
See also CDWLB 2; DLB 90; EW 5; RGWL
2, 3; TWA

Heinemann, Larry (Curtiss) 1944- .. **CLC 50**
See also CA 110; CAAS 21; CANR 31, 81;
DLBD 9; INT CANR-31

Heiney, Donald (William) 1921-1993
See Harris, MacDonald
See also CA 1-4R; 142; CANR 3, 58; FANT

Heinlein, Robert A(nson) 1907-1988 . **CLC 1,
3, 8, 14, 26, 55; SSC 55**
See also AAYA 17; BPFB 2; BYA 4, 13;
CA 1-4R; 125; CANR 1, 20, 53; CLR 75;
CN 1, 2, 3, 4; CPW; DA3; DAM POP;
DLB 8; EXPS; JRDA; LAIT 5; LMFS 2;
MAICYA 1, 2; MTCW 1, 2; MTFW 2005;
RGAL 4; SATA 9, 69; SATA-Obit 56;
SCFW 1, 2; SFW 4; SSFS 7; YAW

Helforth, John
See Doolittle, Hilda

Heliodorus fl. 3rd cent. - **CMLC 52**
See also WLIT 8

Hellenhofferu, Vojtech Kapristian z
See Hasek, Jaroslav (Matej Frantisek)

Heller, Joseph 1923-1999 . **CLC 1, 3, 5, 8, 11,
36, 63; TCLC 131, 151; WLC 3**
See also AAYA 24; AITN 1; AMWS 4;
BPFB 2; BYA 1; CA 5-8R; 187; CABS 1;
CANR 8, 42, 66, 126; CN 1, 2, 3, 4, 5, 6;

CPW; DA; DA3; DAB; DAC; DAM MST, NOV, POP; DLB 2, 28, 227; DLBY 1980, 2002; EWL 3; EXPN; INT CANR-8; LAIT 4; MAL 5; MTCW 1, 2; MTFW 2005; NFS 1; RGAL 4; TUS; YAW

Hellman, Lillian (Florence)
1906-1984 .. **CLC 2, 4, 8, 14, 18, 34, 44, 52; DC 1; TCLC 119**
See also AAYA 47; AITN 1, 2; AMWS 1; CA 13-16R; 112; CAD; CANR 33; CWD; DA3; DAM DRAM; DFS 1, 3, 14; DLB 7, 228; DLBY 1984; EWL 3; FL 1:6; FW; LAIT 3; MAL 5; MAWW; MTCW 1, 2; MTFW 2005; RGAL 4; TUS

Helprin, Mark 1947- **CLC 7, 10, 22, 32**
See also CA 81-84; CANR 47, 64, 124; CDALBS; CN 7; CPW; DA3; DAM NOV, POP; DLBY 1985; FANT; MAL 5; MTCW 1, 2; MTFW 2005; SUFW 2

Helvetius, Claude-Adrien 1715-1771 .. **LC 26**
See also DLB 313

Helyar, Jane Penelope Josephine 1933-
See Poole, Josephine
See also CA 21-24R; CANR 10, 26; CWRI 5; SATA 82, 138; SATA-Essay 138

Hemans, Felicia 1793-1835 **NCLC 29, 71**
See also DLB 96; RGEL 2

Hemingway, Ernest (Miller)
1899-1961 **CLC 1, 3, 6, 8, 10, 13, 19, 30, 34, 39, 41, 44, 50, 61, 80; SSC 1, 25, 36, 40, 63; TCLC 115; WLC 3**
See also AAYA 19; AMW; AMWC 1; AMWR 1; BPFB 2; BYA 2, 3, 13, 15; CA 77-80; CANR 34; CDALB 1917-1929; DA; DA3; DAB; DAC; DAM MST, NOV; DLB 4, 9, 102, 210, 308, 316; DLBD 1, 15, 16; DLBY 1981, 1987, 1996, 1998; EWL 3; EXPN; EXPS; LAIT 3, 4; LATS 1:1; MAL 5; MTCW 1, 2; MTFW 2005; NFS 1, 5, 6, 14; RGAL 4; RGSF 2; SSFS 17; TUS; WYA

Hempel, Amy 1951- **CLC 39**
See also CA 118; 137; CANR 70; DA3; DLB 218; EXPS; MTCW 2; MTFW 2005; SSFS 2

Henderson, F. C.
See Mencken, H(enry) L(ouis)

Henderson, Sylvia
See Ashton-Warner, Sylvia (Constance)

Henderson, Zenna (Chlarson)
1917-1983 **SSC 29**
See also CA 1-4R; 133; CANR 1, 84; DLB 8; SATA 5; SFW 4

Henkin, Joshua **CLC 119**
See also CA 161

Henley, Beth **CLC 23; DC 6, 14**
See Henley, Elizabeth Becker
See also AAYA 70; CABS 3; CAD; CD 5, 6; CSW; CWD; DFS 2, 21; DLBY 1986; FW

Henley, Elizabeth Becker 1952-
See Henley, Beth
See also CA 107; CANR 32, 73, 140; DA3; DAM DRAM, MST; MTCW 1, 2; MTFW 2005

Henley, William Ernest 1849-1903 .. **TCLC 8**
See also CA 105; 234; DLB 19; RGEL 2

Hennissart, Martha 1929-
See Lathen, Emma
See also CA 85-88; CANR 64

Henry VIII 1491-1547 **LC 10**
See also DLB 132

Henry, O. . **SSC 5, 49; TCLC 1, 19; WLC 3**
See Porter, William Sydney
See also AAYA 41; AMWS 2; EXPS; MAL 5; RGAL 4; RGSF 2; SSFS 2, 18; TCWW 1, 2

Henry, Patrick 1736-1799 **LC 25**
See also LAIT 1

Henryson, Robert 1430(?)-1506(?) **LC 20, 110; PC 65**
See also BRWS 7; DLB 146; RGEL 2

Henschke, Alfred
See Klabund

Henson, Lance 1944- **NNAL**
See also CA 146; DLB 175

Hentoff, Nat(han Irving) 1925- **CLC 26**
See also AAYA 4, 42; BYA 6; CA 1-4R; CAAS 6; CANR 5, 25, 77, 114; CLR 1, 52; INT CANR-25; JRDA; MAICYA 1, 2; SATA 42, 69, 133; SATA-Brief 27; WYA; YAW

Heppenstall, (John) Rayner
1911-1981 **CLC 10**
See also CA 1-4R; 103; CANR 29; CN 1, 2; CP 1, 2, 3; EWL 3

Heraclitus c. 540B.C.-c. 450B.C. ... **CMLC 22**
See also DLB 176

Herbert, Frank (Patrick)
1920-1986 **CLC 12, 23, 35, 44, 85**
See also AAYA 21; BPFB 2; BYA 4, 14; CA 53-56; 118; CANR 5, 43; CDALBS; CPW; DAM POP; DLB 8; INT CANR-5; LAIT 5; MTCW 1, 2; MTFW 2005; NFS 17; SATA 9, 37; SATA-Obit 47; SCFW 1, 2; SFW 4; YAW

Herbert, George 1593-1633 . **LC 24, 121; PC 4**
See also BRW 2; BRWR 2; CDBLB Before 1660; DAB; DAM POET; DLB 126; EXPP; RGEL 2; TEA; WP

Herbert, Zbigniew 1924-1998 **CLC 9, 43; PC 50; TCLC 168**
See also CA 89-92; 169; CANR 36, 74; CD-WLB 4; CWW 2; DAM POET; DLB 232; EWL 3; MTCW 1; PFS 22

Herbst, Josephine (Frey)
1897-1969 **CLC 34**
See also CA 5-8R; 25-28R; DLB 9

Herder, Johann Gottfried von
1744-1803 **NCLC 8**
See also DLB 97; EW 4; TWA

Heredia, Jose Maria 1803-1839 **HLCS 2**
See also LAW

Hergesheimer, Joseph 1880-1954 ... **TCLC 11**
See also CA 109; 194; DLB 102, 9; RGAL 4

Herlihy, James Leo 1927-1993 **CLC 6**
See also CA 1-4R; 143; CAD; CANR 2; CN 1, 2, 3, 4, 5

Herman, William
See Bierce, Ambrose (Gwinett)

Hermogenes fl. c. 175- **CMLC 6**

Hernandez, Jose 1834-1886 **NCLC 17**
See also LAW; RGWL 2, 3; WLIT 1

Herodotus c. 484B.C.-c. 420B.C. ... **CMLC 17**
See also AW 1; CDWLB 1; DLB 176; RGWL 2, 3; TWA; WLIT 8

Herrick, Robert 1591-1674 **LC 13; PC 9**
See also BRW 2; BRWC 2; DA; DAB; DAC; DAM MST, POP; DLB 126; EXPP; PFS 13; RGAL 4; RGEL 2; TEA; WP

Herring, Guilles
See Somerville, Edith Oenone

Herriot, James 1916-1995 **CLC 12**
See Wight, James Alfred
See also AAYA 1, 54; BPFB 2; CA 148; CANR 40; CLR 80; CPW; DAM POP; LAIT 3; MAICYA 2; MAICYAS 1; MTCW 2; SATA 86, 135; TEA; YAW

Herris, Violet
See Hunt, Violet

Herrmann, Dorothy 1941- **CLC 44**
See also CA 107

Herrmann, Taffy
See Herrmann, Dorothy

Hersey, John (Richard) 1914-1993 **CLC 1, 2, 7, 9, 40, 81, 97**
See also AAYA 29; BPFB 2; CA 17-20R; 140; CANR 33; CDALBS; CN 1, 2, 3, 4, 5; CPW; DAM POP; DLB 6, 185, 278, 299; MAL 5; MTCW 1, 2; MTFW 2005; RGHL; SATA 25; SATA-Obit 76; TUS

Herzen, Aleksandr Ivanovich
1812-1870 **NCLC 10, 61**
See Herzen, Alexander

Herzen, Alexander
See Herzen, Aleksandr Ivanovich
See also DLB 277

Herzl, Theodor 1860-1904 **TCLC 36**
See also CA 168

Herzog, Werner 1942- **CLC 16**
See also CA 89-92

Hesiod c. 8th cent. B.C.- **CMLC 5**
See also AW 1; DLB 176; RGWL 2, 3; WLIT 8

Hesse, Hermann 1877-1962 ... **CLC 1, 2, 3, 6, 11, 17, 25, 69; SSC 9, 49; TCLC 148; WLC 3**
See also AAYA 43; BPFB 2; CA 17-18; CAP 2; CDWLB 2; DA; DA3; DAB; DAC; DAM MST, NOV; DLB 66; EW 9; EWL 3; EXPN; LAIT 1; MTCW 1, 2; MTFW 2005; NFS 6, 15; RGWL 2, 3; SATA 50; TWA

Hewes, Cady
See De Voto, Bernard (Augustine)

Heyen, William 1940- **CLC 13, 18**
See also CA 33-36R; 220; CAAE 220; CAAS 9; CANR 98; CP 3, 4, 5, 6, 7; DLB 5; RGHL

Heyerdahl, Thor 1914-2002 **CLC 26**
See also CA 5-8R; 207; CANR 5, 22, 66, 73; LAIT 4; MTCW 1, 2; MTFW 2005; SATA 2, 52

Heym, Georg (Theodor Franz Arthur)
1887-1912 **TCLC 9**
See also CA 106; 181

Heym, Stefan 1913-2001 **CLC 41**
See also CA 9-12R; 203; CANR 4; CWW 2; DLB 69; EWL 3

Heyse, Paul (Johann Ludwig von)
1830-1914 **TCLC 8**
See also CA 104; 209; DLB 129

Heyward, (Edwin) DuBose
1885-1940 **HR 1:2; TCLC 59**
See also CA 108; 157; DLB 7, 9, 45, 249; MAL 5; SATA 21

Heywood, John 1497(?)-1580(?) **LC 65**
See also DLB 136; RGEL 2

Heywood, Thomas 1573(?)-1641 **LC 111**
See also DAM DRAM; DLB 62; LMFS 1; RGEL 2; TEA

Hibbert, Eleanor Alice Burford
1906-1993 **CLC 7**
See Holt, Victoria
See also BEST 90:4; CA 17-20R; 140; CANR 9, 28, 59; CMW 4; CPW; DAM POP; MTCW 2; MTFW 2005; RHW; SATA 2; SATA-Obit 74

Hichens, Robert (Smythe)
1864-1950 **TCLC 64**
See also CA 162; DLB 153; HGG; RHW; SUFW

Higgins, Aidan 1927- **SSC 68**
See also CA 9-12R; CANR 70, 115, 148; CN 1, 2, 3, 4, 5, 6, 7; DLB 14

Higgins, George V(incent)
1939-1999 **CLC 4, 7, 10, 18**
See also BPFB 2; CA 77-80; 186; CAAS 5; CANR 17, 51, 89, 96; CMW 4; CN 2, 3, 4, 5, 6; DLB 2; DLBY 1981, 1998; INT CANR-17; MSW; MTCW 1

Higginson, Thomas Wentworth
1823-1911 **TCLC 36**
See also CA 162; DLB 1, 64, 243

Higgonet, Margaret ed. **CLC 65**
Highet, Helen
 See MacInnes, Helen (Clark)
Highsmith, (Mary) Patricia
 1921-1995 **CLC 2, 4, 14, 42, 102**
 See Morgan, Claire
 See also AAYA 48; BRWS 5; CA 1-4R; 147;
 CANR 1, 20, 48, 62, 108; CMW 4; CN 1,
 2, 3, 4, 5; CPW; DA3; DAM NOV, POP;
 DLB 306; MSW; MTCW 1, 2; MTFW
 2005
Highwater, Jamake (Mamake)
 1942(?)-2001 **CLC 12**
 See also AAYA 7, 69; BPFB 2; BYA 4; CA
 65-68; 199; CAAS 7; CANR 10, 34, 84;
 CLR 17; CWRI 5; DLB 52; DLBY 1985;
 JRDA; MAICYA 1, 2; SATA 32, 69;
 SATA-Brief 30
Highway, Tomson 1951- **CLC 92; NNAL**
 See also CA 151; CANR 75; CCA 1; CD 5,
 6; CN 7; DAC; DAM MULT; DFS 2;
 MTCW 2
Hijuelos, Oscar 1951- **CLC 65; HLC 1**
 See also AAYA 25; AMWS 8; BEST 90:1;
 CA 123; CANR 50, 75, 125; CPW; DA3;
 DAM MULT, POP; DLB 145; HW 1, 2;
 LLW; MAL 5; MTCW 2; MTFW 2005;
 NFS 17; RGAL 4; WLIT 1
Hikmet, Nazim 1902-1963 **CLC 40**
 See Nizami of Ganja
 See also CA 141; 93-96; EWL 3; WLIT 6
Hildegard von Bingen 1098-1179 . **CMLC 20**
 See also DLB 148
Hildesheimer, Wolfgang 1916-1991 .. **CLC 49**
 See also CA 101; 135; DLB 69, 124; EWL
 3; RGHL
Hill, Geoffrey (William) 1932- **CLC 5, 8,**
 18, 45
 See also BRWS 5; CA 81-84; CANR 21,
 89; CDBLB 1960 to Present; CP 1, 2, 3,
 4, 5, 6, 7; DAM POET; DLB 40; EWL 3;
 MTCW 1; RGEL 2; RGHL
Hill, George Roy 1921-2002 **CLC 26**
 See also CA 110; 122; 213
Hill, John
 See Koontz, Dean R.
Hill, Susan (Elizabeth) 1942- **CLC 4, 113**
 See also CA 33-36R; CANR 29, 69, 129;
 CN 2, 3, 4, 5, 6, 7; DAB; DAM MST,
 NOV; DLB 14, 139; HGG; MTCW 1;
 RHW
Hillard, Asa G. III **CLC 70**
Hillerman, Tony 1925- **CLC 62, 170**
 See also AAYA 40; BEST 89:1; BPFB 2;
 CA 29-32R; CANR 21, 42, 65, 97, 134;
 CMW 4; CPW; DA3; DAM POP; DLB
 206, 306; MAL 5; MSW; MTCW 2;
 MTFW 2005; RGAL 4; SATA 6; TCWW
 2; YAW
Hillesum, Etty 1914-1943 **TCLC 49**
 See also CA 137; RGHL
Hilliard, Noel (Harvey) 1929-1996 ... **CLC 15**
 See also CA 9-12R; CANR 7, 69; CN 1, 2,
 3, 4, 5, 6
Hillis, Rick 1956- **CLC 66**
 See also CA 134
Hilton, James 1900-1954 **TCLC 21**
 See also CA 108; 169; DLB 34, 77; FANT;
 SATA 34
Hilton, Walter (?)-1396 **CMLC 58**
 See also DLB 146; RGEL 2
Himes, Chester (Bomar) 1909-1984 .. **BLC 2;**
 CLC 2, 4, 7, 18, 58, 108; TCLC 139
 See also AFAW 2; BPFB 2; BW 2; CA 25-
 28R; 114; CANR 22, 89; CMW 4; CN 1,
 2, 3; DAM MULT; DLB 2, 76, 143, 226;
 EWL 3; MAL 5; MSW; MTCW 1, 2;
 MTFW 2005; RGAL 4

Himmelfarb, Gertrude 1922- **CLC 202**
 See also CA 49-52; CANR 28, 66, 102
Hinde, Thomas **CLC 6, 11**
 See Chitty, Thomas Willes
 See also CN 1, 2, 3, 4, 5, 6; EWL 3
Hine, (William) Daryl 1936- **CLC 15**
 See also CA 1-4R; CAAS 15; CANR 1, 20;
 CP 1, 2, 3, 4, 5, 6, 7; DLB 60
Hinkson, Katharine Tynan
 See Tynan, Katharine
Hinojosa(-Smith), Rolando (R.)
 1929- .. **HLC 1**
 See Hinojosa-Smith, Rolando
 See also CA 131; CAAS 16; CANR 62;
 DAM MULT; DLB 82; HW 1, 2; LLW;
 MTCW 2; MTFW 2005; RGAL 4
Hinton, S(usan) E(loise) 1950- .. **CLC 30, 111**
 See also AAYA 2, 33; BPFB 2; BYA 2, 3;
 CA 81-84; CANR 32, 62, 92, 133;
 CDALBS; CLR 3, 23; CPW; DA; DA3;
 DAB; DAC; DAM MST, NOV; JRDA;
 LAIT 5; MAICYA 1, 2; MTCW 1, 2;
 MTFW 2005 !**; NFS 5, 9, 15, 16; SATA
 19, 58, 115, 160; WYA; YAW
Hippius, Zinaida (Nikolaevna) **TCLC 9**
 See Gippius, Zinaida (Nikolaevna)
 See also DLB 295; EWL 3
Hiraoka, Kimitake 1925-1970
 See Mishima, Yukio
 See also CA 97-100; 29-32R; DA3; DAM
 DRAM; GLL 1; MTCW 1, 2
Hirsch, E.D., Jr. 1928- **CLC 79**
 See also CA 25-28R; CANR 27, 51, 146;
 DLB 67; INT CANR-27; MTCW 1
Hirsch, Edward 1950- **CLC 31, 50**
 See also CA 104; CANR 20, 42, 102; CP 6,
 7; DLB 120; PFS 22
Hirsch, Eric Donald, Jr.
 See Hirsch, E.D., Jr.
Hitchcock, Alfred (Joseph)
 1899-1980 **CLC 16**
 See also AAYA 22; CA 159; 97-100; SATA
 27; SATA-Obit 24
Hitchens, Christopher (Eric)
 1949- ... **CLC 157**
 See also CA 152; CANR 89
Hitler, Adolf 1889-1945 **TCLC 53**
 See also CA 117; 147
Hoagland, Edward (Morley) 1932- .. **CLC 28**
 See also ANW; CA 1-4R; CANR 2, 31, 57,
 107; CN 1, 2, 3, 4, 5, 6, 7; DLB 6; SATA
 51; TCWW 2
Hoban, Russell (Conwell) 1925- ... **CLC 7, 25**
 See also BPFB 2; CA 5-8R; CANR 23, 37,
 66, 114, 138; CLR 3, 69; CN 4, 5, 6, 7;
 CWRI 5; DAM NOV; DLB 52; FANT;
 MAICYA 1, 2; MTCW 1, 2; MTFW 2005;
 SATA 1, 40, 78, 136; SFW 4; SUFW 2;
 TCLE 1:1
Hobbes, Thomas 1588-1679 **LC 36**
 See also DLB 151, 252, 281; RGEL 2
Hobbs, Perry
 See Blackmur, R(ichard) P(almer)
Hobson, Laura Z(ametkin)
 1900-1986 **CLC 7, 25**
 See also BPFB 2; CA 17-20R; 118; CANR
 55; CN 1, 2, 3, 4; DLB 28; SATA 52
Hoccleve, Thomas c. 1368-c. 1437 **LC 75**
 See also DLB 146; RGEL 2
Hoch, Edward D(entinger) 1930-
 See Queen, Ellery
 See also CA 29-32R; CANR 11, 27, 51, 97;
 CMW 4; DLB 306; SFW 4
Hochhuth, Rolf 1931- **CLC 4, 11, 18**
 See also CA 5-8R; CANR 33, 75, 136;
 CWW 2; DAM DRAM; DLB 124; EWL
 3; MTCW 1, 2; MTFW 2005; RGHL
Hochman, Sandra 1936- **CLC 3, 8**
 See also CA 5-8R; CP 1, 2, 3, 4, 5; DLB 5

Hochwaelder, Fritz 1911-1986 **CLC 36**
 See Hochwalder, Fritz
 See also CA 29-32R; 120; CANR 42; DAM
 DRAM; MTCW 1; RGWL 3
Hochwalder, Fritz
 See Hochwaelder, Fritz
 See also EWL 3; RGWL 2
Hocking, Mary (Eunice) 1921- **CLC 13**
 See also CA 101; CANR 18, 40
Hodgins, Jack 1938- **CLC 23**
 See also CA 93-96; CN 4, 5, 6, 7; DLB 60
Hodgson, William Hope
 1877(?)-1918 **TCLC 13**
 See also CA 111; 164; CMW 4; DLB 70,
 153, 156, 178; HGG; MTCW 2; SFW 4;
 SUFW 1
Hoeg, Peter 1957- **CLC 95, 156**
 See also CA 151; CANR 75; CMW 4; DA3;
 DLB 214; EWL 3; MTCW 2; MTFW
 2005; NFS 17; RGWL 3; SSFS 18
Hoffman, Alice 1952- **CLC 51**
 See also AAYA 37; AMWS 10; CA 77-80;
 CANR 34, 66, 100, 138; CN 4, 5, 6, 7;
 CPW; DAM NOV; DLB 292; MAL 5;
 MTCW 1, 2; MTFW 2005; TCLE 1:1
Hoffman, Daniel (Gerard) 1923- . **CLC 6, 13,**
 23
 See also CA 1-4R; CANR 4, 142; CP 1, 2,
 3, 4, 5, 6, 7; DLB 5; TCLE 1:1
Hoffman, Eva 1945- **CLC 182**
 See also CA 132; CANR 146
Hoffman, Stanley 1944- **CLC 5**
 See also CA 77-80
Hoffman, William 1925- **CLC 141**
 See also CA 21-24R; CANR 9, 103; CSW;
 DLB 234; TCLE 1:1
Hoffman, William M.
 See Hoffman, William M(oses)
 See also CAD; CD 5, 6
Hoffman, William M(oses) 1939- **CLC 40**
 See Hoffman, William M.
 See also CA 57-60; CANR 11, 71
Hoffmann, E(rnst) T(heodor) A(madeus)
 1776-1822 **NCLC 2; SSC 13, 92**
 See also CDWLB 2; DLB 90; EW 5; GL 2;
 RGSF 2; RGWL 2, 3; SATA 27; SUFW
 1; WCH
Hofmann, Gert 1931-1993 **CLC 54**
 See also CA 128; CANR 145; EWL 3;
 RGHL
Hofmannsthal, Hugo von 1874-1929 ... **DC 4;**
 TCLC 11
 See also CA 106; 153; CDWLB 2; DAM
 DRAM; DFS 17; DLB 81, 118; EW 9;
 EWL 3; RGWL 2, 3
Hogan, Linda 1947- **CLC 73; NNAL; PC**
 35
 See also AMWS 4; ANW; BYA 12; CA 120,
 226; CAAE 226; CANR 45, 73, 129;
 CWP; DAM MULT; DLB 175; SATA
 132; TCWW 2
Hogarth, Charles
 See Creasey, John
Hogarth, Emmett
 See Polonsky, Abraham (Lincoln)
Hogarth, William 1697-1764 **LC 112**
 See also AAYA 56
Hogg, James 1770-1835 **NCLC 4, 109**
 See also BRWS 10; DLB 93, 116, 159; GL
 2; HGG; RGEL 2; SUFW 1
Holbach, Paul-Henri Thiry
 1723-1789 **LC 14**
 See also DLB 313
Holberg, Ludvig 1684-1754 **LC 6**
 See also DLB 300; RGWL 2, 3
Holcroft, Thomas 1745-1809 **NCLC 85**
 See also DLB 39, 89, 158; RGEL 2
Holden, Ursula 1921- **CLC 18**
 See also CA 101; CAAS 8; CANR 22

Holderlin, (Johann Christian) Friedrich
1770-1843 **NCLC 16; PC 4**
See also CDWLB 2; DLB 90; EW 5; RGWL
2, 3

Holdstock, Robert
See Holdstock, Robert P.

Holdstock, Robert P. 1948- **CLC 39**
See also CA 131; CANR 81; DLB 261;
FANT; HGG; SFW 4; SUFW 2

Holinshed, Raphael fl. 1580- **LC 69**
See also DLB 167; RGEL 2

Holland, Isabelle (Christian)
1920-2002 **CLC 21**
See also AAYA 11, 64; CA 21-24R; 205;
CAAE 181; CANR 10, 25, 47; CLR 57;
CWRI 5; JRDA; LAIT 4; MAICYA 1, 2;
SATA 8, 70; SATA-Essay 103; SATA-Obit
132; WYA

Holland, Marcus
See Caldwell, (Janet Miriam) Taylor
(Holland)

Hollander, John 1929- **CLC 2, 5, 8, 14**
See also CA 1-4R; CANR 1, 52, 136; CP 1,
2, 3, 4, 5, 6, 7; DLB 5; MAL 5; SATA 13

Hollander, Paul
See Silverberg, Robert

Holleran, Andrew **CLC 38**
See Garber, Eric
See also CA 144; GLL 1

Holley, Marietta 1836(?)-1926 **TCLC 99**
See also CA 118; DLB 11; FL 1:3

Hollinghurst, Alan 1954- **CLC 55, 91**
See also BRWS 10; CA 114; CN 5, 6, 7;
DLB 207, 326; GLL 1

Hollis, Jim
See Summers, Hollis (Spurgeon, Jr.)

Holly, Buddy 1936-1959 **TCLC 65**
See also CA 213

Holmes, Gordon
See Shiel, M(atthew) P(hipps)

Holmes, John
See Souster, (Holmes) Raymond

Holmes, John Clellon 1926-1988 **CLC 56**
See also BG 1:2; CA 9-12R; 125; CANR 4;
CN 1, 2, 3, 4; DLB 16, 237

Holmes, Oliver Wendell, Jr.
1841-1935 **TCLC 77**
See also CA 114; 186

Holmes, Oliver Wendell
1809-1894 **NCLC 14, 81; PC 71**
See also AMWS 1; CDALB 1640-1865;
DLB 1, 189, 235; EXPP; PFS 24; RGAL
4; SATA 34

Holmes, Raymond
See Souster, (Holmes) Raymond

Holt, Victoria
See Hibbert, Eleanor Alice Burford
See also BPFB 2

Holub, Miroslav 1923-1998 **CLC 4**
See also CA 21-24R; 169; CANR 10; CD-
WLB 4; CWW 2; DLB 232; EWL 3;
RGWL 3

Holz, Detlev
See Benjamin, Walter

Homer c. 8th cent. B.C.- **CMLC 1, 16, 61;
PC 23; WLCS**
See also AW 1; CDWLB 1; DA; DA3;
DAB; DAC; DAM MST, POET; DLB
176; EFS 1; LAIT 1; LMFS 1; RGWL 2,
3; TWA; WLIT 8; WP

Hongo, Garrett Kaoru 1951- **PC 23**
See also CA 133; CAAS 22; CP 5, 6, 7;
DLB 120, 312; EWL 3; EXPP; RGAL 4

Honig, Edwin 1919- **CLC 33**
See also CA 5-8R; CAAS 8; CANR 4, 45,
144; CP 1, 2, 3, 4, 5, 6, 7; DLB 5

Hood, Hugh (John Blagdon) 1928- . **CLC 15,
28; SSC 42**
See also CA 49-52; CAAS 17; CANR 1,
33, 87; CN 1, 2, 3, 4, 5, 6, 7; DLB 53;
RGSF 2

Hood, Thomas 1799-1845 **NCLC 16**
See also BRW 4; DLB 96; RGEL 2

Hooker, (Peter) Jeremy 1941- **CLC 43**
See also CA 77-80; CANR 22; CP 2, 3, 4,
5, 6, 7; DLB 40

Hooker, Richard 1554-1600 **LC 95**
See also BRW 1; DLB 132; RGEL 2

hooks, bell 1952(?)- **CLC 94**
See also BW 2; CA 143; CANR 87, 126;
DLB 246; MTCW 2; MTFW 2005; SATA
115, 170

Hope, A(lec) D(erwent) 1907-2000 **CLC 3,
51; PC 56**
See also BRWS 7; CA 21-24R; 188; CANR
33, 74; CP 1, 2, 3, 4, 5; DLB 289; EWL
3; MTCW 1, 2; MTFW 2005; PFS 8;
RGEL 2

Hope, Anthony 1863-1933 **TCLC 83**
See also CA 157; DLB 153, 156; RGEL 2;
RHW

Hope, Brian
See Creasey, John

Hope, Christopher (David Tully)
1944- ... **CLC 52**
See also AFW; CA 106; CANR 47, 101;
CN 4, 5, 6, 7; DLB 225; SATA 62

Hopkins, Gerard Manley
1844-1889 **NCLC 17; PC 15; WLC 3**
See also BRW 5; BRWR 2; CDBLB 1890-
1914; DA; DA3; DAB; DAC; DAM MST,
POET; DLB 35, 57; EXPP; PAB; RGEL
2; TEA; WP

Hopkins, John (Richard) 1931-1998 .. **CLC 4**
See also CA 85-88; 169; CBD; CD 5, 6

Hopkins, Pauline Elizabeth
1859-1930 **BLC 2; TCLC 28**
See also AFAW 2; BW 2, 3; CA 141; CANR
82; DAM MULT; DLB 50

Hopkinson, Francis 1737-1791 **LC 25**
See also DLB 31; RGAL 4

Hopley-Woolrich, Cornell George 1903-1968
See Woolrich, Cornell
See also CA 13-14; CANR 58; CAP 1;
CMW 4; DLB 226; MTCW 2

Horace 65B.C.-8B.C. **CMLC 39; PC 46**
See also AW 2; CDWLB 1; DLB 211;
RGWL 2, 3; WLIT 8

Horatio
See Proust, (Valentin-Louis-George-Eugene)
Marcel

**Horgan, Paul (George Vincent
O'Shaughnessy)** 1903-1995 .. **CLC 9, 53**
See also BPFB 2; CA 13-16R; 147; CANR
9, 35; CN 1, 2, 3, 4, 5; DAM NOV; DLB
102, 212; DLBY 1985; INT CANR-9;
MTCW 1, 2; MTFW 2005; SATA 13;
SATA-Obit 84; TCWW 1, 2

Horkheimer, Max 1895-1973 **TCLC 132**
See also CA 216; 41-44R; DLB 296

Horn, Peter
See Kuttner, Henry

Horne, Frank (Smith) 1899-1974 **HR 1:2**
See also BW 1; CA 125; 53-56; DLB 51;
WP

Horne, Richard Henry Hengist
1802(?)-1884 **NCLC 127**
See also DLB 32; SATA 29

Hornem, Horace Esq.
See Byron, George Gordon (Noel)

**Horney, Karen (Clementine Theodore
Danielsen)** 1885-1952 **TCLC 71**
See also CA 114; 165; DLB 246; FW

Hornung, E(rnest) W(illiam)
1866-1921 **TCLC 59**
See also CA 108; 160; CMW 4; DLB 70

Horovitz, Israel (Arthur) 1939- **CLC 56**
See also CA 33-36R; CAD; CANR 46, 59;
CD 5, 6; DAM DRAM; DLB 7; MAL 5

Horton, George Moses
1797(?)-1883(?) **NCLC 87**
See also DLB 50

Horvath, odon von 1901-1938
See von Horvath, Odon
See also EWL 3

Horvath, Oedoen von -1938
See von Horvath, Odon

Horwitz, Julius 1920-1986 **CLC 14**
See also CA 9-12R; 119; CANR 12

Horwitz, Ronald
See Harwood, Ronald

Hospital, Janette Turner 1942- **CLC 42,
145**
See also CA 108; CANR 48; CN 5, 6, 7;
DLB 325; DLBY 2002; RGSF 2

Hostos, E. M. de
See Hostos (y Bonilla), Eugenio Maria de

Hostos, Eugenio M. de
See Hostos (y Bonilla), Eugenio Maria de

Hostos, Eugenio Maria
See Hostos (y Bonilla), Eugenio Maria de

Hostos (y Bonilla), Eugenio Maria de
1839-1903 **TCLC 24**
See also CA 123; 131; HW 1

Houdini
See Lovecraft, H. P.

Houellebecq, Michel 1958- **CLC 179**
See also CA 185; CANR 140; MTFW 2005

Hougan, Carolyn 1943- **CLC 34**
See also CA 139

Household, Geoffrey (Edward West)
1900-1988 **CLC 11**
See also CA 77-80; 126; CANR 58; CMW
4; CN 1, 2, 3, 4; DLB 87; SATA 14;
SATA-Obit 59

Housman, A(lfred) E(dward)
1859-1936 **PC 2, 43; TCLC 1, 10;
WLCS**
See also AAYA 66; BRW 6; CA 104; 125;
DA; DA3; DAB; DAC; DAM MST,
POET; DLB 19, 284; EWL 3; EXPP;
MTCW 1, 2; MTFW 2005; PAB; PFS 4,
7; RGEL 2; TEA; WP

Housman, Laurence 1865-1959 **TCLC 7**
See also CA 106; 155; DLB 10; FANT;
RGEL 2; SATA 25

Houston, Jeanne Wakatsuki 1934- **AAL**
See also AAYA 49; CA 103; 232; CAAE
232; CAAS 16; CANR 29, 123; LAIT 4;
SATA 78, 168; SATA-Essay 168

Howard, Elizabeth Jane 1923- **CLC 7, 29**
See also BRWS 11; CA 5-8R; CANR 8, 62,
146; CN 1, 2, 3, 4, 5, 6, 7

Howard, Maureen 1930- **CLC 5, 14, 46,
151**
See also CA 53-56; CANR 31, 75, 140; CN
4, 5, 6, 7; DLBY 1983; INT CANR-31;
MTCW 1, 2; MTFW 2005

Howard, Richard 1929- **CLC 7, 10, 47**
See also AITN 1; CA 85-88; CANR 25, 80,
154; CP 1, 2, 3, 4, 5, 6, 7; DLB 5; INT
CANR-25; MAL 5

Howard, Robert E(rvin)
1906-1936 **TCLC 8**
See also BPFB 2; BYA 5; CA 105; 157;
FANT; SUFW 1; TCWW 1, 2

Howard, Warren F.
See Pohl, Frederik

Howe, Fanny (Quincy) 1940- **CLC 47**
See also CA 117, 187; CAAE 187; CAAS
27; CANR 70, 116; CP 6, 7; CWP; SATA-
Brief 52

Howe, Irving 1920-1993 **CLC 85**
See also AMWS 6; CA 9-12R; 141; CANR
21, 50; DLB 67; EWL 3; MAL 5; MTCW
1, 2; MTFW 2005

Howe, Julia Ward 1819-1910 **TCLC 21**
See also CA 117; 191; DLB 1, 189, 235;
FW

Howe, Susan 1937- **CLC 72, 152; PC 54**
See also AMWS 4; CA 160; CP 5, 6, 7;
CWP; DLB 120; FW; RGAL 4

Howe, Tina 1937- **CLC 48**
See also CA 109; CAD; CANR 125; CD 5,
6; CWD

Howell, James 1594(?)-1666 **LC 13**
See also DLB 151

Howells, W. D.
See Howells, William Dean

Howells, William D.
See Howells, William Dean

Howells, William Dean 1837-1920 ... **SSC 36;
TCLC 7, 17, 41**
See also AMW; CA 104; 134; CDALB
1865-1917; DLB 12, 64, 74, 79, 189;
LMFS 1; MAL 5; MTCW 2; RGAL 4;
TUS

Howes, Barbara 1914-1996 **CLC 15**
See also CA 9-12R; 151; CAAS 3; CANR
53; CP 1, 2, 3, 4, 5, 6; SATA 5; TCLE 1:1

Hrabal, Bohumil 1914-1997 **CLC 13, 67;
TCLC 155**
See also CA 106; 156; CAAS 12; CANR
57; CWW 2; DLB 232; EWL 3; RGSF 2

Hrabanus Maurus 776(?)-856 **CMLC 78**
See also DLB 148

Hrotsvit of Gandersheim c. 935-c.
1000 .. **CMLC 29**
See also DLB 148

Hsi, Chu 1130-1200 **CMLC 42**

Hsun, Lu
See Lu Hsun

Hubbard, L. Ron 1911-1986 **CLC 43**
See also AAYA 64; CA 77-80; 118; CANR
52; CPW; DA3; DAM POP; FANT;
MTCW 2; MTFW 2005; SFW 4

Hubbard, Lafayette Ronald
See Hubbard, L. Ron

Huch, Ricarda (Octavia)
1864-1947 **TCLC 13**
See also CA 111; 189; DLB 66; EWL 3

Huddle, David 1942- **CLC 49**
See also CA 57-60; CAAS 20; CANR 89;
DLB 130

Hudson, Jeffrey
See Crichton, (John) Michael

Hudson, W(illiam) H(enry)
1841-1922 **TCLC 29**
See also CA 115; 190; DLB 98, 153, 174;
RGEL 2; SATA 35

Hueffer, Ford Madox
See Ford, Ford Madox

Hughart, Barry 1934- **CLC 39**
See also CA 137; FANT; SFW 4; SUFW 2

Hughes, Colin
See Creasey, John

Hughes, David (John) 1930-2005 **CLC 48**
See also CA 116; 129; 238; CN 4, 5, 6, 7;
DLB 14

Hughes, Edward James
See Hughes, Ted
See also DA3; DAM MST, POET

Hughes, (James Mercer) Langston
1902-1967 **BLC 2; CLC 1, 5, 10, 15,
35, 44, 108; DC 3; HR 1:2; PC 1, 53;
SSC 6, 90; WLC 3**
See also AAYA 12; AFAW 1, 2; AMWR 1;
AMWS 1; BW 1, 3; CA 1-4R; 25-28R;
CANR 1, 34, 82; CDALB 1929-1941;
CLR 17; DA; DA3; DAB; DAC; DAM
DRAM, MST, MULT, POET; DFS 6, 18;

DLB 4, 7, 48, 51, 86, 228, 315; EWL 3;
EXPP; EXPS; JRDA; LAIT 3; LMFS 2;
MAICYA 1, 2; MAL 5; MTCW 1, 2;
MTFW 2005; NFS 21; PAB; PFS 1, 3, 6,
10, 15; RGAL 4; RGSF 2; SATA 4, 33;
SSFS 4, 7; TUS; WCH; WP; YAW

Hughes, Richard (Arthur Warren)
1900-1976 **CLC 1, 11**
See also CA 5-8R; 65-68; CANR 4; CN 1,
2; DAM NOV; DLB 15, 161; EWL 3;
MTCW 1; RGEL 2; SATA 8; SATA-Obit
25

Hughes, Ted 1930-1998 . **CLC 2, 4, 9, 14, 37,
119; PC 7**
See Hughes, Edward James
See also BRWC 2; BRWR 2; BRWS 1; CA
1-4R; 171; CANR 1, 33, 66, 108; CLR 3;
CP 1, 2, 3, 4, 5, 6; DAB; DAC; DLB 40,
161; EWL 3; EXPP; MAICYA 1, 2;
MTCW 1, 2; MTFW 2005; PAB; PFS 4,
19; RGEL 2; SATA 49; SATA-Brief 27;
SATA-Obit 107; TEA; YAW

Hugo, Richard
See Huch, Ricarda (Octavia)

Hugo, Richard F(ranklin)
1923-1982 **CLC 6, 18, 32; PC 68**
See also AMWS 6; CA 49-52; 108; CANR
3; CP 1, 2, 3; DAM POET; DLB 5, 206;
EWL 3; MAL 5; PFS 17; RGAL 4

Hugo, Victor (Marie) 1802-1885 **NCLC 3,
10, 21, 161; PC 17; WLC 3**
See also AAYA 28; DA; DA3; DAB; DAC;
DAM DRAM, MST, NOV, POET; DLB
119, 192, 217; EFS 2; EW 6; EXPN; GFL
1789 to the Present; LAIT 1, 2; NFS 5,
20; RGWL 2, 3; SATA 47; TWA

Huidobro, Vicente
See Huidobro Fernandez, Vicente Garcia
See also DLB 283; EWL 3; LAW

Huidobro Fernandez, Vicente Garcia
1893-1948 **TCLC 31**
See Huidobro, Vicente
See also CA 131; HW 1

Hulme, Keri 1947- **CLC 39, 130**
See also CA 125; CANR 69; CN 4, 5, 6, 7;
CP 6, 7; CWP; DLB 326; EWL 3; FW;
INT CA-125

Hulme, T(homas) E(rnest)
1883-1917 **TCLC 21**
See also BRWS 6; CA 117; 203; DLB 19

Humboldt, Alexander von
1769-1859 **NCLC 170**
See also DLB 90

Humboldt, Wilhelm von
1767-1835 **NCLC 134**
See also DLB 90

Hume, David 1711-1776 **LC 7, 56**
See also BRWS 3; DLB 104, 252; LMFS 1;
TEA

Humphrey, William 1924-1997 **CLC 45**
See also AMWS 9; CA 77-80; 160; CANR
68; CN 1, 2, 3, 4, 5, 6; CSW; DLB 6, 212,
234, 278; TCWW 1, 2

Humphreys, Emyr Owen 1919- **CLC 47**
See also CA 5-8R; CANR 3, 24; CN 1, 2,
3, 4, 5, 6, 7; DLB 15

Humphreys, Josephine 1945- **CLC 34, 57**
See also CA 121; 127; CANR 97; CSW;
DLB 292; INT CA-127

Huneker, James Gibbons
1860-1921 **TCLC 65**
See also CA 193; DLB 71; RGAL 4

Hungerford, Hesba Fay
See Brinsmead, H(esba) F(ay)

Hungerford, Pixie
See Brinsmead, H(esba) F(ay)

Hunt, E(verette) Howard, (Jr.)
1918- .. **CLC 3**
See also AITN 1; CA 45-48; CANR 2, 47,
103; CMW 4

Hunt, Francesca
See Holland, Isabelle (Christian)

Hunt, Howard
See Hunt, E(verette) Howard, (Jr.)

Hunt, Kyle
See Creasey, John

Hunt, (James Henry) Leigh
1784-1859 **NCLC 1, 70**
See also DAM POET; DLB 96, 110, 144;
RGEL 2; TEA

Hunt, Marsha 1946- **CLC 70**
See also BW 2, 3; CA 143; CANR 79

Hunt, Violet 1866(?)-1942 **TCLC 53**
See also CA 184; DLB 162, 197

Hunter, E. Waldo
See Sturgeon, Theodore (Hamilton)

Hunter, Evan 1926-2005 **CLC 11, 31**
See McBain, Ed
See also AAYA 39; BPFB 2; CA 5-8R; 241;
CANR 5, 38, 62, 97, 149; CMW 4; CN 1,
2, 3, 4, 5, 6, 7; CPW; DAM POP; DLB
306; DLBY 1982; INT CANR-5; MSW;
MTCW 1; SATA 25; SATA-Obit 167;
SFW 4

Hunter, Kristin
See Lattany, Kristin (Elaine Eggleston)
Hunter
See also CN 1, 2, 3, 4, 5, 6

Hunter, Mary
See Austin, Mary (Hunter)

Hunter, Mollie 1922- **CLC 21**
See McIlwraith, Maureen Mollie Hunter
See also AAYA 13, 71; BYA 6; CANR 37,
78; CLR 25; DLB 161; JRDA; MAICYA
1, 2; SAAS 7; SATA 54, 106, 139; SATA-
Essay 139; WYA; YAW

Hunter, Robert (?)-1734 **LC 7**

Hurston, Zora Neale 1891-1960 **BLC 2;
CLC 7, 30, 61; DC 12; HR 1:2; SSC 4,
80; TCLC 121, 131; WLCS**
See also AAYA 15, 71; AFAW 1, 2; AMWS
6; BW 1, 3; BYA 12; CA 85-88; CANR
61; CDALBS; DA; DA3; DAC; DAM
MST, MULT, NOV; DFS 6; DLB 51, 86;
EWL 3; EXPN; EXPS; FL 1:6; FW; LAIT
3; LATS 1:1; LMFS 2; MAL 5; MAWW;
MTCW 1, 2; MTFW 2005; NFS 3; RGAL
4; RGSF 2; SSFS 1, 6, 11, 19, 21; TUS;
YAW

Husserl, E. G.
See Husserl, Edmund (Gustav Albrecht)

Husserl, Edmund (Gustav Albrecht)
1859-1938 **TCLC 100**
See also CA 116; 133; DLB 296

Huston, John (Marcellus)
1906-1987 **CLC 20**
See also CA 73-76; 123; CANR 34; DLB
26

Hustvedt, Siri 1955- **CLC 76**
See also CA 137; CANR 149

Hutten, Ulrich von 1488-1523 **LC 16**
See also DLB 179

Huxley, Aldous (Leonard)
1894-1963 **CLC 1, 3, 4, 5, 8, 11, 18,
35, 79; SSC 39; WLC 3**
See also AAYA 11; BPFB 2; BRW 7; CA
85-88; CANR 44, 99; CDBLB 1914-1945;
DA; DA3; DAB; DAC; DAM MST, NOV;
DLB 36, 100, 162, 195, 255; EWL 3;
EXPN; LAIT 5; LMFS 2; MTCW 1, 2;
MTFW 2005; NFS 6; RGEL 2; SATA 63;
SCFW 1, 2; SFW 4; TEA; YAW

Huxley, T(homas) H(enry)
1825-1895 **NCLC 67**
See also DLB 57; TEA

Huygens, Constantijn 1596-1687 **LC 114**
See also RGWL 2, 3

Huysmans, Joris-Karl 1848-1907 ... **TCLC 7, 69**
See also CA 104; 165; DLB 123; EW 7; GFL 1789 to the Present; LMFS 2; RGWL 2, 3

Hwang, David Henry 1957- **CLC 55, 196; DC 4, 23**
See also CA 127; 132; CAD; CANR 76, 124; CD 5, 6; DA3; DAM DRAM; DFS 11, 18; DLB 212, 228, 312; INT CA-132; MAL 5; MTCW 2; MTFW 2005; RGAL 4

Hyde, Anthony 1946- **CLC 42**
See Chase, Nicholas
See also CA 136; CCA 1

Hyde, Margaret O(ldroyd) 1917- **CLC 21**
See also CA 1-4R; CANR 1, 36, 137; CLR 23; JRDA; MAICYA 1, 2; SAAS 8; SATA 1, 42, 76, 139

Hynes, James 1956(?)- **CLC 65**
See also CA 164; CANR 105

Hypatia c. 370-415 **CMLC 35**

Ian, Janis 1951- **CLC 21**
See also CA 105; 187

Ibanez, Vicente Blasco
See Blasco Ibanez, Vicente
See also DLB 322

Ibarbourou, Juana de
1895(?)-1979 **HLCS 2**
See also DLB 290; HW 1; LAW

Ibarguengoitia, Jorge 1928-1983 **CLC 37; TCLC 148**
See also CA 124; 113; EWL 3; HW 1

Ibn Battuta, Abu Abdalla
1304-1368(?) **CMLC 57**
See also WLIT 2

Ibn Hazm 994-1064 **CMLC 64**

Ibsen, Henrik (Johan) 1828-1906 **DC 2; TCLC 2, 8, 16, 37, 52; WLC 3**
See also AAYA 46; CA 104; 141; DA; DA3; DAB; DAC; DAM DRAM, MST; DFS 1, 6, 8, 10, 11, 15, 16; EW 7; LAIT 2; LATS 1:1; MTFW 2005; RGWL 2, 3

Ibuse, Masuji 1898-1993 **CLC 22**
See Ibuse Masuji
See also CA 127; 141; MJW; RGWL 3

Ibuse Masuji
See Ibuse, Masuji
See also CWW 2; DLB 180; EWL 3

Ichikawa, Kon 1915- **CLC 20**
See also CA 121

Ichiyo, Higuchi 1872-1896 **NCLC 49**
See also MJW

Idle, Eric 1943- **CLC 21**
See Monty Python
See also CA 116; CANR 35, 91, 148

Idris, Yusuf 1927-1991 **SSC 74**
See also AFW; EWL 3; RGSF 2, 3; RGWL 3; WLIT 2

Ignatow, David 1914-1997 **CLC 4, 7, 14, 40; PC 34**
See also CA 9-12R; 162; CAAS 3; CANR 31, 57, 96; CP 1, 2, 3, 4, 5, 6; DLB 5; EWL 3; MAL 5

Ignotus
See Strachey, (Giles) Lytton

Ihimaera, Witi (Tame) 1944- **CLC 46**
See also CA 77-80; CANR 130; CN 2, 3, 4, 5, 6, 7; RGSF 2; SATA 148

Ilf, Ilya .. **TCLC 21**
See Fainzilberg, Ilya Arnoldovich
See also EWL 3

Illyes, Gyula 1902-1983 **PC 16**
See also CA 114; 109; CDWLB 4; DLB 215; EWL 3; RGWL 2, 3

Imalayen, Fatima-Zohra
See Djebar, Assia

Immermann, Karl (Lebrecht)
1796-1840 **NCLC 4, 49**
See also DLB 133

Ince, Thomas H. 1882-1924 **TCLC 89**
See also IDFW 3, 4

Inchbald, Elizabeth 1753-1821 **NCLC 62**
See also DLB 39, 89; RGEL 2

Inclan, Ramon (Maria) del Valle
See Valle-Inclan, Ramon (Maria) del

Infante, G(uillermo) Cabrera
See Cabrera Infante, G(uillermo)

Ingalls, Rachel 1940- **CLC 42**
See also CA 123; 127; CANR 154

Ingalls, Rachel Holmes
See Ingalls, Rachel

Ingamells, Reginald Charles
See Ingamells, Rex

Ingamells, Rex 1913-1955 **TCLC 35**
See also CA 167; DLB 260

Inge, William (Motter) 1913-1973 **CLC 1, 8, 19**
See also CA 9-12R; CAD; CDALB 1941-1968; DA3; DAM DRAM; DFS 1, 3, 5, 8; DLB 7, 249; EWL 3; MAL 5; MTCW 1, 2; MTFW 2005; RGAL 4; TUS

Ingelow, Jean 1820-1897 **NCLC 39, 107**
See also DLB 35, 163; FANT; SATA 33

Ingram, Willis J.
See Harris, Mark

Innaurato, Albert (F.) 1948(?)- ... **CLC 21, 60**
See also CA 115; 122; CAD; CANR 78; CD 5, 6; INT CA-122

Innes, Michael
See Stewart, J(ohn) I(nnes) M(ackintosh)
See also DLB 276; MSW

Innis, Harold Adams 1894-1952 **TCLC 77**
See also CA 181; DLB 88

Insluis, Alanus de
See Alain de Lille

Iola
See Wells-Barnett, Ida B(ell)

Ionesco, Eugene 1912-1994 ... **CLC 1, 4, 6, 9, 11, 15, 41, 86; DC 12; WLC 3**
See also CA 9-12R; 144; CANR 55, 132; CWW 2; DA; DA3; DAB; DAC; DAM DRAM, MST; DFS 4, 9; DLB 321; EW 13; EWL 3; GFL 1789 to the Present; LMFS 2; MTCW 1, 2; MTFW 2005; RGWL 2, 3; SATA 7; SATA-Obit 79; TWA

Iqbal, Muhammad 1877-1938 **TCLC 28**
See also CA 215; EWL 3

Ireland, Patrick
See O'Doherty, Brian

Irenaeus St. 130- **CMLC 42**

Irigaray, Luce 1930- **CLC 164**
See also CA 154; CANR 121; FW

Iron, Ralph
See Schreiner, Olive (Emilie Albertina)

Irving, John (Winslow) 1942- ... **CLC 13, 23, 38, 112, 175**
See also AAYA 8, 62; AMWS 6; BEST 89:3; BPFB 2; CA 25-28R; CANR 28, 73, 112, 133; CN 3, 4, 5, 6, 7; CPW; DA3; DAM NOV, POP; DLB 6, 278; DLBY 1982; EWL 3; MAL 5; MTCW 1, 2; MTFW 2005; NFS 12, 14; RGAL 4; TUS

Irving, Washington 1783-1859 . **NCLC 2, 19, 95; SSC 2, 37; WLC 3**
See also AAYA 56; AMW; CDALB 1640-1865; CLR 97; DA; DA3; DAB; DAC; DAM MST; DLB 3, 11, 30, 59, 73, 74, 183, 186, 250, 254; EXPS; GL 2; LAIT 1; RGAL 4; RGSF 2; SSFS 1, 8, 16; SUFW 1; TUS; WCH; YABC 2

Irwin, P. K.
See Page, P(atricia) K(athleen)

Isaacs, Jorge Ricardo 1837-1895 ... **NCLC 70**
See also LAW

Isaacs, Susan 1943- **CLC 32**
See also BEST 89:1; BPFB 2; CA 89-92; CANR 20, 41, 65, 112, 134; CPW; DA3; DAM POP; INT CANR-20; MTCW 1, 2; MTFW 2005

Isherwood, Christopher (William Bradshaw)
1904-1986 **CLC 1, 9, 11, 14, 44; SSC 56**
See also AMWS 14; BRW 7; CA 13-16R; 117; CANR 35, 97, 133; CN 1, 2, 3; DA3; DAM DRAM, NOV; DLB 15, 195; DLBY 1986; EWL 3; IDTP; MTCW 1, 2; MTFW 2005; RGAL 4; RGEL 2; TUS; WLIT 4

Ishiguro, Kazuo 1954- . **CLC 27, 56, 59, 110, 119**
See also AAYA 58; BEST 90:2; BPFB 2; BRWS 4; CA 120; CANR 49, 95, 133; CN 5, 6, 7; DA3; DAM NOV; DLB 194, 326; EWL 3; MTCW 1, 2; MTFW 2005; NFS 13; WLIT 4; WWE 1

Ishikawa, Hakuhin
See Ishikawa, Takuboku

Ishikawa, Takuboku 1886(?)-1912 **PC 10; TCLC 15**
See Ishikawa Takuboku
See also CA 113; 153; DAM POET

Iskander, Fazil (Abdulovich) 1929- .. **CLC 47**
See Iskander, Fazil' Abdulevich
See also CA 102; EWL 3

Iskander, Fazil' Abdulevich
See Iskander, Fazil (Abdulovich)
See also DLB 302

Isler, Alan (David) 1934- **CLC 91**
See also CA 156; CANR 105

Ivan IV 1530-1584 **LC 17**

Ivanov, Vyacheslav Ivanovich
1866-1949 **TCLC 33**
See also CA 122; EWL 3

Ivask, Ivar Vidrik 1927-1992 **CLC 14**
See also CA 37-40R; 139; CANR 24

Ives, Morgan
See Bradley, Marion Zimmer
See also GLL 1

Izumi Shikibu c. 973-c. 1034 **CMLC 33**

J. R. S.
See Gogarty, Oliver St. John

Jabran, Kahlil
See Gibran, Kahlil

Jabran, Khalil
See Gibran, Kahlil

Jackson, Daniel
See Wingrove, David (John)

Jackson, Helen Hunt 1830-1885 **NCLC 90**
See also DLB 42, 47, 186, 189; RGAL 4

Jackson, Jesse 1908-1983 **CLC 12**
See also BW 1; CA 25-28R; 109; CANR 27; CLR 28; CWRI 5; MAICYA 1, 2; SATA 2, 29; SATA-Obit 48

Jackson, Laura (Riding) 1901-1991 **PC 44**
See Riding, Laura
See also CA 65-68; 135; CANR 28, 89; DLB 48

Jackson, Sam
See Trumbo, Dalton

Jackson, Sara
See Wingrove, David (John)

Jackson, Shirley 1919-1965 . **CLC 11, 60, 87; SSC 9, 39; WLC 3**
See also AAYA 9; AMWS 9; BPFB 2; CA 1-4R; 25-28R; CANR 4, 52; CDALB 1941-1968; DA; DA3; DAC; DAM MST; DLB 6, 234; EXPS; HGG; LAIT 4; MAL 5; MTCW 2; MTFW 2005; RGAL 4; RGSF 2; SATA 2; SSFS 1; SUFW 1, 2

Jacob, (Cyprien-)Max 1876-1944 **TCLC 6**
See also CA 104; 193; DLB 258; EWL 3; GFL 1789 to the Present; GLL 2; RGWL 2, 3

Jacobs, Harriet A(nn)
1813(?)-1897 **NCLC 67, 162**
See also AFAW 1, 2; DLB 239; FL 1:3; FW;
LAIT 2; RGAL 4
Jacobs, Jim 1942- **CLC 12**
See also CA 97-100; INT CA-97-100
Jacobs, W(illiam) W(ymark)
1863-1943 **SSC 73; TCLC 22**
See also CA 121; 167; DLB 135; EXPS;
HGG; RGEL 2; RGSF 2; SSFS 2; SUFW
1
Jacobsen, Jens Peter 1847-1885 **NCLC 34**
Jacobsen, Josephine (Winder)
1908-2003 **CLC 48, 102; PC 62**
See also CA 33-36R; 218; CAAS 18; CANR
23, 48; CCA 1; CP 2, 3, 4, 5, 6, 7; DLB
244; PFS 23; TCLE 1:1
Jacobson, Dan 1929- **CLC 4, 14; SSC 91**
See also AFW; CA 1-4R; CANR 2, 25, 66;
CN 1, 2, 3, 4, 5, 6, 7; DLB 14, 207, 225,
319; EWL 3; MTCW 1; RGSF 2
Jacqueline
See Carpentier (y Valmont), Alejo
Jacques de Vitry c. 1160-1240 **CMLC 63**
See also DLB 208
Jagger, Michael Philip
See Jagger, Mick
Jagger, Mick 1943- **CLC 17**
See also CA 239
Jahiz, al- c. 780-c. 869 **CMLC 25**
See also DLB 311
Jakes, John (William) 1932- **CLC 29**
See also AAYA 32; BEST 89:4; BPFB 2;
CA 57-60, 214; CAAE 214; CANR 10,
43, 66, 111, 142; CPW; CSW; DA3; DAM
NOV, POP; DLB 278; DLBY 1983;
FANT; INT CANR-10; MTCW 1, 2;
MTFW 2005; RHW; SATA 62; SFW 4;
TCWW 1, 2
James I 1394-1437 **LC 20**
See also RGEL 2
James, Andrew
See Kirkup, James
James, C(yril) L(ionel) R(obert)
1901-1989 **BLCS; CLC 33**
See also BW 2; CA 117; 125; 128; CANR
62; CN 1, 2, 3, 4; DLB 125; MTCW 1
James, Daniel (Lewis) 1911-1988
See Santiago, Danny
See also CA 174; 125
James, Dynely
See Mayne, William (James Carter)
James, Henry Sr. 1811-1882 **NCLC 53**
James, Henry 1843-1916 **SSC 8, 32, 47;**
TCLC 2, 11, 24, 40, 47, 64, 171; WLC
3
See also AMW; AMWC 1; AMWR 1; BPFB
2; BRW 6; CA 104; 132; CDALB 1865-
1917; DA; DA3; DAB; DAC; DAM MST,
NOV; DLB 12, 71, 74, 189; DLBD 13;
EWL 3; EXPS; GL 2; HGG; LAIT 2;
MAL 5; MTCW 1, 2; MTFW 2005; NFS
12, 16, 19; RGAL 4; RGEL 2; RGSF 2;
SSFS 9; SUFW 1; TUS
James, M. R. **SSC 93**
See James, Montague (Rhodes)
See also DLB 156, 201
James, Montague (Rhodes)
1862-1936 **SSC 16; TCLC 6**
See James, M. R.
See also CA 104; 203; HGG; RGEL 2;
RGSF 2; SUFW 1
James, P. D. **CLC 18, 46, 122, 226**
See White, Phyllis Dorothy James
See also BEST 90:2; BPFB 2; BRWS 4;
CDBLB 1960 to Present; CN 4, 5, 6; DLB
87, 276; DLBD 17; MSW
James, Philip
See Moorcock, Michael

James, Samuel
See Stephens, James
James, Seumas
See Stephens, James
James, Stephen
See Stephens, James
James, William 1842-1910 **TCLC 15, 32**
See also AMW; CA 109; 193; DLB 270,
284; MAL 5; NCFS 5; RGAL 4
Jameson, Anna 1794-1860 **NCLC 43**
See also DLB 99, 166
Jameson, Fredric (R.) 1934- **CLC 142**
See also CA 196; DLB 67; LMFS 2
James VI of Scotland 1566-1625 **LC 109**
See also DLB 151, 172
Jami, Nur al-Din 'Abd al-Rahman
1414-1492 .. **LC 9**
Jammes, Francis 1868-1938 **TCLC 75**
See also CA 198; EWL 3; GFL 1789 to the
Present
Jandl, Ernst 1925-2000 **CLC 34**
See also CA 200; EWL 3
Janowitz, Tama 1957- **CLC 43, 145**
See also CA 106; CANR 52, 89, 129; CN
5, 6, 7; CPW; DAM POP; DLB 292;
MTFW 2005
Japrisot, Sebastien 1931- **CLC 90**
See Rossi, Jean-Baptiste
See also CMW 4; NFS 18
Jarrell, Randall 1914-1965 **CLC 1, 2, 6, 9,**
13, 49; PC 41; TCLC 177
See also AMW; BYA 5; CA 5-8R; 25-28R;
CABS 2; CANR 6, 34; CDALB 1941-
1968; CLR 6, 111; CWRI 5; DAM POET;
DLB 48, 52; EWL 3; EXPP; MAICYA 1,
2; MAL 5; MTCW 1, 2; PAB; PFS 2;
RGAL 4; SATA 7
Jarry, Alfred 1873-1907 **SSC 20; TCLC 2,**
14, 147
See also CA 104; 153; DA3; DAM DRAM;
DFS 8; DLB 192, 258; EW 9; EWL 3;
GFL 1789 to the Present; RGWL 2, 3;
TWA
Jarvis, E. K.
See Ellison, Harlan (Jay)
Jawien, Andrzej
See John Paul II, Pope
Jaynes, Roderick
See Coen, Ethan
Jeake, Samuel, Jr.
See Aiken, Conrad (Potter)
Jean Paul 1763-1825 **NCLC 7**
Jefferies, (John) Richard
1848-1887 **NCLC 47**
See also DLB 98, 141; RGEL 2; SATA 16;
SFW 4
Jeffers, (John) Robinson 1887-1962 .. **CLC 2,**
3, 11, 15, 54; PC 17; WLC 3
See also AMWS 2; CA 85-88; CANR 35;
CDALB 1917-1929; DA; DAC; DAM
MST, POET; DLB 45, 212; EWL 3; MAL
5; MTCW 1, 2; MTFW 2005; PAB; PFS
3, 4; RGAL 4
Jefferson, Janet
See Mencken, H(enry) L(ouis)
Jefferson, Thomas 1743-1826 . **NCLC 11, 103**
See also AAYA 54; ANW; CDALB 1640-
1865; DA3; DLB 31, 183; LAIT 1; RGAL
4
Jeffrey, Francis 1773-1850 **NCLC 33**
See Francis, Lord Jeffrey
Jelakowitch, Ivan
See Heijermans, Herman
Jelinek, Elfriede 1946- **CLC 169**
See also AAYA 68; CA 154; DLB 85; FW
Jellicoe, (Patricia) Ann 1927- **CLC 27**
See also CA 85-88; CBD; CD 5, 6; CWD;
CWRI 5; DLB 13, 233; FW

Jelloun, Tahar ben 1944- **CLC 180**
See Ben Jelloun, Tahar
See also CA 162; CANR 100
Jemyma
See Holley, Marietta
Jen, Gish **AAL; CLC 70, 198**
See Jen, Lillian
See also AMWC 2; CN 7; DLB 312
Jen, Lillian 1955-
See Jen, Gish
See also CA 135; CANR 89, 130
Jenkins, (John) Robin 1912- **CLC 52**
See also CA 1-4R; CANR 1, 135; CN 1, 2,
3, 4, 5, 6, 7; DLB 14, 271
Jennings, Elizabeth (Joan)
1926-2001 **CLC 5, 14, 131**
See also BRWS 5; CA 61-64; 200; CAAS
5; CANR 8, 39, 66, 127; CP 1, 2, 3, 4, 5,
6, 7; CWP; DLB 27; EWL 3; MTCW 1;
SATA 66
Jennings, Waylon 1937-2002 **CLC 21**
Jensen, Johannes V(ilhelm)
1873-1950 **TCLC 41**
See also CA 170; DLB 214; EWL 3; RGWL
3
Jensen, Laura (Linnea) 1948- **CLC 37**
See also CA 103
Jerome, Saint 345-420 **CMLC 30**
See also RGWL 3
Jerome, Jerome K(lapka)
1859-1927 **TCLC 23**
See also CA 119; 177; DLB 10, 34, 135;
RGEL 2
Jerrold, Douglas William
1803-1857 **NCLC 2**
See also DLB 158, 159; RGEL 2
Jewett, (Theodora) Sarah Orne
1849-1909 **SSC 6, 44; TCLC 1, 22**
See also AMW; AMWC 2; AMWR 2; CA
108; 127; CANR 71; DLB 12, 74, 221;
EXPS; FL 1:3; FW; MAL 5; MAWW;
NFS 15; RGAL 4; RGSF 2; SATA 15;
SSFS 4
Jewsbury, Geraldine (Endsor)
1812-1880 **NCLC 22**
See also DLB 21
Jhabvala, Ruth Prawer 1927- . **CLC 4, 8, 29,**
94, 138; SSC 91
See also BRWS 5; CA 1-4R; CANR 2, 29,
51, 74, 91, 128; CN 1, 2, 3, 4, 5, 6, 7;
DAB; DAM NOV; DLB 139, 194, 323,
326; EWL 3; IDFW 3, 4; INT CANR-29;
MTCW 1, 2; MTFW 2005; RGSF 2;
RGWL 2; RHW; TEA
Jibran, Kahlil
See Gibran, Kahlil
Jibran, Khalil
See Gibran, Kahlil
Jiles, Paulette 1943- **CLC 13, 58**
See also CA 101; CANR 70, 124; CP 5;
CWP
Jimenez (Mantecon), Juan Ramon
1881-1958 **HLC 1; PC 7; TCLC 4**
See also CA 104; 131; CANR 74; DAM
MULT, POET; DLB 134; EW 9; EWL 3;
HW 1; MTCW 1, 2; MTFW 2005; RGWL
2, 3
Jimenez, Ramon
See Jimenez (Mantecon), Juan Ramon
Jimenez Mantecon, Juan
See Jimenez (Mantecon), Juan Ramon
Jin, Ba 1904-2005
See Pa Chin
See also CA 244; CWW 2
Jin, Ha **CLC 109**
See Jin, Xuefei
See also CA 152; DLB 244, 292; SSFS 17

Jin, Xuefei 1956-
 See Jin, Ha
 See also CANR 91, 130; MTFW 2005;
 SSFS 17
Jodelle, Etienne 1532-1573 **LC 119**
 See also GFL Beginnings to 1789
Joel, Billy .. **CLC 26**
 See Joel, William Martin
Joel, William Martin 1949-
 See Joel, Billy
 See also CA 108
John, Saint 10(?)-100 **CMLC 27, 63**
John of Salisbury c. 1115-1180 **CMLC 63**
John of the Cross, St. 1542-1591 **LC 18**
 See also RGWL 2, 3
John Paul II, Pope 1920-2005 **CLC 128**
 See also CA 106; 133; 238
Johnson, B(ryan) S(tanley William)
 1933-1973 **CLC 6, 9**
 See also CA 9-12R; 53-56; CANR 9; CN 1;
 CP 1, 2; DLB 14, 40; EWL 3; RGEL 2
Johnson, Benjamin F., of Boone
 See Riley, James Whitcomb
Johnson, Charles (Richard) 1948- **BLC 2;**
 CLC 7, 51, 65, 163
 See also AFAW 2; AMWS 6; BW 2, 3; CA
 116; CAAS 18; CANR 42, 66, 82, 129;
 CN 5, 6, 7; DAM MULT; DLB 33, 278;
 MAL 5; MTCW 2; MTFW 2005; RGAL
 4; SSFS 16
Johnson, Charles S(purgeon)
 1893-1956 **HR 1:3**
 See also BW 1, 3; CA 125; CANR 82; DLB
 51, 91
Johnson, Denis 1949- . **CLC 52, 160; SSC 56**
 See also CA 117; 121; CANR 71, 99; CN
 4, 5, 6, 7; DLB 120
Johnson, Diane 1934- **CLC 5, 13, 48**
 See also BPFB 2; CA 41-44R; CANR 17,
 40, 62, 95; CN 4, 5, 6, 7; DLBY 1980;
 INT CANR-17; MTCW 1
Johnson, E(mily) Pauline 1861-1913 . **NNAL**
 See also CA 150; CCA 1; DAC; DAM
 MULT; DLB 92, 175; TCWW 2
Johnson, Eyvind (Olof Verner)
 1900-1976 **CLC 14**
 See also CA 73-76; 69-72; CANR 34, 101;
 DLB 259; EW 12; EWL 3
Johnson, Fenton 1888-1958 **BLC 2**
 See also BW 1; CA 118; 124; DAM MULT;
 DLB 45, 50
Johnson, Georgia Douglas (Camp)
 1880-1966 **HR 1:3**
 See also BW 1; CA 125; DLB 51, 249; WP
Johnson, Helene 1907-1995 **HR 1:3**
 See also CA 181; DLB 51; WP
Johnson, J. R.
 See James, C(yril) L(ionel) R(obert)
Johnson, James Weldon 1871-1938 .. **BLC 2;**
 HR 1:3; PC 24; TCLC 3, 19, 175
 See also AFAW 1, 2; BW 1, 3; CA 104;
 125; CANR 82; CDALB 1917-1929; CLR
 32; DA3; DAM MULT, POET; DLB 51;
 EWL 3; EXPP; LMFS 2; MAL 5; MTCW
 1, 2; MTFW 2005; NFS 22; PFS 1; RGAL
 4; SATA 31; TUS
Johnson, Joyce 1935- **CLC 58**
 See also BG 1:3; CA 125; 129; CANR 102
Johnson, Judith (Emlyn) 1936- **CLC 7, 15**
 See Sherwin, Judith Johnson
 See also CA 25-28R; 153; CANR 34; CP 6,
 7
Johnson, Lionel (Pigot)
 1867-1902 **TCLC 19**
 See also CA 117; 209; DLB 19; RGEL 2
Johnson, Marguerite Annie
 See Angelou, Maya
Johnson, Mel
 See Malzberg, Barry N(athaniel)

Johnson, Pamela Hansford
 1912-1981 **CLC 1, 7, 27**
 See also CA 1-4R; 104; CANR 2, 28; CN
 1, 2, 3; DLB 15; MTCW 1, 2; MTFW
 2005; RGEL 2
Johnson, Paul (Bede) 1928- **CLC 147**
 See also BEST 89:4; CA 17-20R; CANR
 34, 62, 100
Johnson, Robert **CLC 70**
Johnson, Robert 1911(?)-1938 **TCLC 69**
 See also BW 3; CA 174
Johnson, Samuel 1709-1784 . **LC 15, 52, 128;**
 WLC 3
 See also BRW 3; BRWR 1; CDBLB 1660-
 1789; DA; DAB; DAC; DAM MST; DLB
 39, 95, 104, 142, 213; LMFS 1; RGEL 2;
 TEA
Johnson, Uwe 1934-1984 .. **CLC 5, 10, 15, 40**
 See also CA 1-4R; 112; CANR 1, 39; CD-
 WLB 2; DLB 75; EWL 3; MTCW 1;
 RGWL 2, 3
Johnston, Basil H. 1929- **NNAL**
 See also CA 69-72; CANR 11, 28, 66;
 DAC; DAM MULT; DLB 60
Johnston, George (Benson) 1913- **CLC 51**
 See also CA 1-4R; CANR 5, 20; CP 1, 2, 3,
 4, 5, 6, 7; DLB 88
Johnston, Jennifer (Prudence)
 1930- **CLC 7, 150**
 See also CA 85-88; CANR 92; CN 4, 5, 6,
 7; DLB 14
Joinville, Jean de 1224(?)-1317 **CMLC 38**
Jolley, (Monica) Elizabeth 1923- **CLC 46;**
 SSC 19
 See also CA 127; CAAS 13; CANR 59; CN
 4, 5, 6, 7; DLB 325; EWL 3; RGSF 2
Jones, Arthur Llewellyn 1863-1947
 See Machen, Arthur
 See also CA 104; 179; HGG
Jones, D(ouglas) G(ordon) 1929- **CLC 10**
 See also CA 29-32R; CANR 13, 90; CP 1,
 2, 3, 4, 5, 6, 7; DLB 53
Jones, David (Michael) 1895-1974 **CLC 2,**
 4, 7, 13, 42
 See also BRW 6; BRWS 7; CA 9-12R; 53-
 56; CANR 28; CDBLB 1945-1960; CP 1,
 2; DLB 20, 100; EWL 3; MTCW 1; PAB;
 RGEL 2
Jones, David Robert 1947-
 See Bowie, David
 See also CA 103; CANR 104
Jones, Diana Wynne 1934- **CLC 26**
 See also AAYA 12; BYA 6, 7, 9, 11, 13, 16;
 CA 49-52; CANR 4, 26, 56, 120; CLR
 23; DLB 161; FANT; JRDA; MAICYA 1,
 2; MTFW 2005; SAAS 7; SATA 9, 70,
 108, 160; SFW 4; SUFW 2; YAW
Jones, Edward P. 1950- **CLC 76, 223**
 See also AAYA 71; BW 2, 3; CA 142;
 CANR 79, 134; CSW; MTFW 2005
Jones, Gayl 1949- **BLC 2; CLC 6, 9, 131**
 See also AFAW 1, 2; BW 2, 3; CA 77-80;
 CANR 27, 66, 122; CN 4, 5, 6, 7; CSW;
 DA3; DAM MULT; DLB 33, 278; MAL
 5; MTCW 1, 2; MTFW 2005; RGAL 4
Jones, James 1921-1977 **CLC 1, 3, 10, 39**
 See also AITN 1, 2; AMWS 11; BPFB 2;
 CA 1-4R; 69-72; CANR 6; CN 1, 2; DLB
 2, 143; DLBD 17; DLBY 1998; EWL 3;
 MAL 5; MTCW 1; RGAL 4
Jones, John J.
 See Lovecraft, H. P.
Jones, LeRoi **CLC 1, 2, 3, 5, 10, 14**
 See Baraka, Amiri
 See also CN 1, 2; CP 1, 2, 3; MTCW 2
Jones, Louis B. 1953- **CLC 65**
 See also CA 141; CANR 73

Jones, Madison (Percy, Jr.) 1925- **CLC 4**
 See also CA 13-16R; CAAS 11; CANR 7,
 54, 83; CN 1, 2, 3, 4, 5, 6, 7; CSW; DLB
 152
Jones, Mervyn 1922- **CLC 10, 52**
 See also CA 45-48; CAAS 5; CANR 1, 91;
 CN 1, 2, 3, 4, 5, 6, 7; MTCW 1
Jones, Mick 1956(?)- **CLC 30**
Jones, Nettie (Pearl) 1941- **CLC 34**
 See also BW 2; CA 137; CAAS 20; CANR
 88
Jones, Peter 1802-1856 **NNAL**
Jones, Preston 1936-1979 **CLC 10**
 See also CA 73-76; 89-92; DLB 7
Jones, Robert F(rancis) 1934-2003 **CLC 7**
 See also CA 49-52; CANR 2, 61, 118
Jones, Rod 1953- **CLC 50**
 See also CA 128
Jones, Terence Graham Parry
 1942- **CLC 21**
 See Jones, Terry; Monty Python
 See also CA 112; 116; CANR 35, 93; INT
 CA-116; SATA 127
Jones, Terry
 See Jones, Terence Graham Parry
 See also SATA 67; SATA-Brief 51
Jones, Thom (Douglas) 1945(?)- **CLC 81;**
 SSC 56
 See also CA 157; CANR 88; DLB 244;
 SSFS 23
Jong, Erica 1942- **CLC 4, 6, 8, 18, 83**
 See also AITN 1; AMWS 5; BEST 90:2;
 BPFB 2; CA 73-76; CANR 26, 52, 75,
 132; CN 3, 4, 5, 6, 7; CP 2, 3, 4, 5, 6, 7;
 CPW; DA3; DAM NOV, POP; DLB 2, 5,
 28, 152; FW; INT CANR-26; MAL 5;
 MTCW 1, 2; MTFW 2005
Jonson, Ben(jamin) 1572(?)-1637 . **DC 4; LC**
 6, 33, 110; PC 17; WLC 3
 See also BRW 1; BRWC 1; BRWR 1; CD-
 BLB Before 1660; DA; DAB; DAC;
 DAM DRAM, MST, POET; DFS 4, 10;
 DLB 62, 121; LMFS 1; PFS 23; RGEL 2;
 TEA; WLIT 3
Jordan, June 1936-2002 .. **BLCS; CLC 5, 11,**
 23, 114; PC 38
 See also AAYA 2, 66; AFAW 1, 2; BW 2,
 3; CA 33-36R; 206; CANR 25, 70, 114,
 154; CLR 10; CP 3, 4, 5, 6, 7; CWP;
 DAM MULT, POET; DLB 38; GLL 2;
 LAIT 5; MAICYA 1, 2; MTCW 1; SATA
 4, 136; YAW
Jordan, June Meyer
 See Jordan, June
Jordan, Neil 1950- **CLC 110**
 See also CA 124; 130; CANR 54, 154; CN
 4, 5, 6, 7; GLL 2; INT CA-130
Jordan, Neil Patrick
 See Jordan, Neil
Jordan, Pat(rick M.) 1941- **CLC 37**
 See also CA 33-36R; CANR 121
Jorgensen, Ivar
 See Ellison, Harlan (Jay)
Jorgenson, Ivar
 See Silverberg, Robert
Joseph, George Ghevarughese **CLC 70**
Josephson, Mary
 See O'Doherty, Brian
Josephus, Flavius c. 37-100 **CMLC 13**
 See also AW 2; DLB 176; WLIT 8
Josiah Allen's Wife
 See Holley, Marietta
Josipovici, Gabriel (David) 1940- **CLC 6,**
 43, 153
 See also CA 37-40R; 224; CAAE 224;
 CAAS 8; CANR 47, 84; CN 3, 4, 5, 6, 7;
 DLB 14, 319
Joubert, Joseph 1754-1824 **NCLC 9**

Jouve, Pierre Jean 1887-1976 **CLC 47**
See also CA 65-68; DLB 258; EWL 3
Jovine, Francesco 1902-1950 **TCLC 79**
See also DLB 264; EWL 3
Joyce, James (Augustine Aloysius)
1882-1941 **DC 16; PC 22; SSC 3, 26,
44, 64; TCLC 3, 8, 16, 35, 52, 159;
WLC 3**
See also AAYA 42; BRW 7; BRWC 1;
BRWR 1; BYA 11, 13; CA 104; 126; CD-
BLB 1914-1945; DA; DA3; DAB; DAC;
DAM MST, NOV, POET; DLB 10, 19,
36, 162, 247; EWL 3; EXPN; EXPS;
LAIT 3; LMFS 1, 2; MTCW 1, 2; MTFW
2005; NFS 7; RGSF 2; SSFS 1, 19; TEA;
WLIT 4
Jozsef, Attila 1905-1937 **TCLC 22**
See also CA 116; 230; CDWLB 4; DLB
215; EWL 3
Juana Ines de la Cruz, Sor
1651(?)-1695 **HLCS 1; LC 5; PC 24**
See also DLB 305; FW; LAW; RGWL 2, 3;
WLIT 1
Juana Inez de La Cruz, Sor
See Juana Ines de la Cruz, Sor
Judd, Cyril
See Kornbluth, C(yril) M.; Pohl, Frederik
Juenger, Ernst 1895-1998 **CLC 125**
See Junger, Ernst
See also CA 101; 167; CANR 21, 47, 106;
DLB 56
Julian of Norwich 1342(?)-1416(?) . **LC 6, 52**
See also DLB 146; LMFS 1
Julius Caesar 100B.C.-44B.C.
See Caesar, Julius
See also CDWLB 1; DLB 211
Junger, Ernst
See Juenger, Ernst
See also CDWLB 2; EWL 3; RGWL 2, 3
Junger, Sebastian 1962- **CLC 109**
See also AAYA 28; CA 165; CANR 130;
MTFW 2005
Juniper, Alex
See Hospital, Janette Turner
Junius
See Luxemburg, Rosa
Junzaburo, Nishiwaki
See Nishiwaki, Junzaburo
See also EWL 3
Just, Ward (Swift) 1935- **CLC 4, 27**
See also CA 25-28R; CANR 32, 87; CN 6,
7; INT CANR-32
Justice, Donald (Rodney)
1925-2004 **CLC 6, 19, 102; PC 64**
See also AMWS 7; CA 5-8R; 230; CANR
26, 54, 74, 121, 122; CP 1, 2, 3, 4, 5, 6,
7; CSW; DAM POET; DLBY 1983; EWL
3; INT CANR-26; MAL 5; MTCW 2; PFS
14; TCLE 1:1
Juvenal c. 60-c. 130 **CMLC 8**
See also AW 2; CDWLB 1; DLB 211;
RGWL 2, 3; WLIT 8
Juvenis
See Bourne, Randolph S(illiman)
K., Alice
See Knapp, Caroline
Kabakov, Sasha **CLC 59**
Kabir 1398(?)-1448(?) **LC 109; PC 56**
See also RGWL 2, 3
Kacew, Romain 1914-1980
See Gary, Romain
See also CA 108; 102
Kadare, Ismail 1936- **CLC 52, 190**
See also CA 161; EWL 3; RGWL 3
Kadohata, Cynthia (Lynn)
1956(?)- **CLC 59, 122**
See also AAYA 71; CA 140; CANR 124;
SATA 155

Kafka, Franz 1883-1924 ... **SSC 5, 29, 35, 60;
TCLC 2, 6, 13, 29, 47, 53, 112, 179;
WLC 3**
See also AAYA 31; BPFB 2; CA 105; 126;
CDWLB 2; DA; DA3; DAB; DAC; DAM
MST, NOV; DLB 81; EW 9; EWL 3;
EXPS; LATS 1:1; LMFS 2; MTCW 1, 2;
MTFW 2005; NFS 7; RGSF 2; RGWL 2,
3; SFW 4; SSFS 3, 7, 12; TWA
Kahanovitsch, Pinkhes
See Der Nister
Kahn, Roger 1927- **CLC 30**
See also CA 25-28R; CANR 44, 69, 152;
DLB 171; SATA 37
Kain, Saul
See Sassoon, Siegfried (Lorraine)
Kaiser, Georg 1878-1945 **TCLC 9**
See also CA 106; 190; CDWLB 2; DLB
124; EWL 3; LMFS 2; RGWL 2, 3
Kaledin, Sergei **CLC 59**
Kaletski, Alexander 1946- **CLC 39**
See also CA 118; 143
Kalidasa fl. c. 400-455 **CMLC 9; PC 22**
See also RGWL 2, 3
Kallman, Chester (Simon)
1921-1975 **CLC 2**
See also CA 45-48; 53-56; CANR 3; CP 1,
2
Kaminsky, Melvin **CLC 12, 217**
See Brooks, Mel
See also AAYA 13, 48; DLB 26
Kaminsky, Stuart M. 1934- **CLC 59**
See also CA 73-76; CANR 29, 53, 89;
CMW 4
Kaminsky, Stuart Melvin
See Kaminsky, Stuart M.
Kamo no Chomei 1153(?)-1216 **CMLC 66**
See also DLB 203
Kamo no Nagaakira
See Kamo no Chomei
Kandinsky, Wassily 1866-1944 **TCLC 92**
See also AAYA 64; CA 118; 155
Kane, Francis
See Robbins, Harold
Kane, Henry 1918-
See Queen, Ellery
See also CA 156; CMW 4
Kane, Paul
See Simon, Paul
Kanin, Garson 1912-1999 **CLC 22**
See also AITN 1; CA 5-8R; 177; CAD;
CANR 7, 78; DLB 7; IDFW 3, 4
Kaniuk, Yoram 1930- **CLC 19**
See also CA 134; DLB 299; RGHL
Kant, Immanuel 1724-1804 **NCLC 27, 67**
See also DLB 94
Kantor, MacKinlay 1904-1977 **CLC 7**
See also CA 61-64; 73-76; CANR 60, 63;
CN 1, 2; DLB 9, 102; MAL 5; MTCW 2;
RHW; TCWW 1, 2
Kanze Motokiyo
See Zeami
Kaplan, David Michael 1946- **CLC 50**
See also CA 187
Kaplan, James 1951- **CLC 59**
See also CA 135; CANR 121
Karadzic, Vuk Stefanovic
1787-1864 **NCLC 115**
See also CDWLB 4; DLB 147
Karageorge, Michael
See Anderson, Poul (William)
Karamzin, Nikolai Mikhailovich
1766-1826 **NCLC 3, 173**
See also DLB 150; RGSF 2
Karapanou, Margarita 1946- **CLC 13**
See also CA 101
Karinthy, Frigyes 1887-1938 **TCLC 47**
See also CA 170; DLB 215; EWL 3

Karl, Frederick R(obert)
1927-2004 **CLC 34**
See also CA 5-8R; 226; CANR 3, 44, 143
Karr, Mary 1955- **CLC 188**
See also AMWS 11; CA 151; CANR 100;
MTFW 2005; NCFS 5
Kastel, Warren
See Silverberg, Robert
Kataev, Evgeny Petrovich 1903-1942
See Petrov, Evgeny
See also CA 120
Kataphusin
See Ruskin, John
Katz, Steve 1935- **CLC 47**
See also CA 25-28R; CAAS 14, 64; CANR
12; CN 4, 5, 6, 7; DLBY 1983
Kauffman, Janet 1945- **CLC 42**
See also CA 117; CANR 43, 84; DLB 218;
DLBY 1986
Kaufman, Bob (Garnell) 1925-1986 . **CLC 49**
See also BG 1:3; BW 1; CA 41-44R; 118;
CANR 22; CP 1; DLB 16, 41
Kaufman, George S. 1889-1961 **CLC 38;
DC 17**
See also CA 108; 93-96; DAM DRAM;
DFS 1, 10; DLB 7; INT CA-108; MTCW
2; MTFW 2005; RGAL 4; TUS
Kaufman, Moises 1964- **DC 26**
See also CA 211; DFS 22; MTFW 2005
Kaufman, Sue **CLC 3, 8**
See Barondess, Sue K(aufman)
Kavafis, Konstantinos Petrou 1863-1933
See Cavafy, C(onstantine) P(eter)
See also CA 104
Kavan, Anna 1901-1968 **CLC 5, 13, 82**
See also BRWS 7; CA 5-8R; CANR 6, 57;
DLB 255; MTCW 1; RGEL 2; SFW 4
Kavanagh, Dan
See Barnes, Julian
Kavanagh, Julie 1952- **CLC 119**
See also CA 163
Kavanagh, Patrick (Joseph)
1904-1967 **CLC 22; PC 33**
See also BRWS 7; CA 123; 25-28R; DLB
15, 20; EWL 3; MTCW 1; RGEL 2
Kawabata, Yasunari 1899-1972 **CLC 2, 5,
9, 18, 107; SSC 17**
See Kawabata Yasunari
See also CA 93-96; 33-36R; CANR 88;
DAM MULT; MJW; MTCW 2; MTFW
2005; RGSF 2; RGWL 2, 3
Kawabata Yasunari
See Kawabata, Yasunari
See also DLB 180; EWL 3
Kaye, M(ary) M(argaret)
1908-2004 **CLC 28**
See also CA 89-92; 223; CANR 24, 60, 102,
142; MTCW 1, 2; MTFW 2005; RHW;
SATA 62; SATA-Obit 152
Kaye, Mollie
See Kaye, M(ary) M(argaret)
Kaye-Smith, Sheila 1887-1956 **TCLC 20**
See also CA 118; 203; DLB 36
Kaymor, Patrice Maguilene
See Senghor, Leopold Sedar
Kazakov, Iurii Pavlovich
See Kazakov, Yuri Pavlovich
See also DLB 302
Kazakov, Yuri Pavlovich 1927-1982 . **SSC 43**
See Kazakov, Iurii Pavlovich; Kazakov,
Yury
See also CA 5-8R; CANR 36; MTCW 1;
RGSF 2
Kazakov, Yury
See Kazakov, Yuri Pavlovich
See also EWL 3
Kazan, Elia 1909-2003 **CLC 6, 16, 63**
See also CA 21-24R; 220; CANR 32, 78

Kazantzakis, Nikos 1883(?)-1957 **TCLC 2, 5, 33**
See also BPFB 2; CA 105; 132; DA3; EW 9; EWL 3; MTCW 1, 2; MTFW 2005; RGWL 2, 3

Kazin, Alfred 1915-1998 **CLC 34, 38, 119**
See also AMWS 8; CA 1-4R; CAAS 7; CANR 1, 45, 79; DLB 67; EWL 3

Keane, Mary Nesta (Skrine) 1904-1996
See Keane, Molly
See also CA 108; 114; 151; RHW

Keane, Molly **CLC 31**
See Keane, Mary Nesta (Skrine)
See also CN 5, 6; INT CA-114; TCLE 1:1

Keates, Jonathan 1946(?)- **CLC 34**
See also CA 163; CANR 126

Keaton, Buster 1895-1966 **CLC 20**
See also CA 194

Keats, John 1795-1821 **NCLC 8, 73, 121; PC 1; WLC 3**
See also AAYA 58; BRW 4; BRWR 1; CD-BLB 1789-1832; DA; DA3; DAB; DAC; DAM MST, POET; DLB 96, 110; EXPP; LMFS 1; PAB; PFS 1, 2, 3, 9, 17; RGEL 2; TEA; WLIT 3; WP

Keble, John 1792-1866 **NCLC 87**
See also DLB 32, 55; RGEL 2

Keene, Donald 1922- **CLC 34**
See also CA 1-4R; CANR 5, 119

Keillor, Garrison 1942- **CLC 40, 115, 222**
See also AAYA 2, 62; BEST 89:3; BPFB 2; CA 111; 117; CANR 36, 59, 124; CPW; DA3; DAM POP; DLBY 1987; EWL 3; MTCW 1, 2; MTFW 2005; SATA 58; TUS

Keith, Carlos
See Lewton, Val

Keith, Michael
See Hubbard, L. Ron

Keller, Gottfried 1819-1890 **NCLC 2; SSC 26**
See also CDWLB 2; DLB 129; EW; RGSF 2; RGWL 2, 3

Keller, Nora Okja 1965- **CLC 109**
See also CA 187

Kellerman, Jonathan 1949- **CLC 44**
See also AAYA 35; BEST 90:1; CA 106; CANR 29, 51, 150; CMW 4; CPW; DA3; DAM POP; INT CANR-29

Kelley, William Melvin 1937- **CLC 22**
See also BW 1; CA 77-80; CANR 27, 83; CN 1, 2, 3, 4, 5, 6, 7; DLB 33; EWL 3

Kellogg, Marjorie 1922-2005 **CLC 2**
See also CA 81-84; 246

Kellow, Kathleen
See Hibbert, Eleanor Alice Burford

Kelly, Lauren
See Oates, Joyce Carol

Kelly, M(ilton) T(errence) 1947- **CLC 55**
See also CA 97-100; CAAS 22; CANR 19, 43, 84; CN 6

Kelly, Robert 1935- **SSC 50**
See also CA 17-20R; CAAS 19; CANR 47; CP 1, 2, 3, 4, 5, 6, 7; DLB 5, 130, 165

Kelman, James 1946- **CLC 58, 86**
See also BRWS 5; CA 148; CANR 85, 130; CN 5, 6, 7; DLB 194, 319, 326; RGSF 2; WLIT 4

Kemal, Yasar
See Kemal, Yashar
See also CWW 2; EWL 3; WLIT 6

Kemal, Yashar 1923(?)- **CLC 14, 29**
See also CA 89-92; CANR 44

Kemble, Fanny 1809-1893 **NCLC 18**
See also DLB 32

Kemelman, Harry 1908-1996 **CLC 2**
See also AITN 1; BPFB 2; CA 9-12R; 155; CANR 6, 71; CMW 4; DLB 28

Kempe, Margery 1373(?)-1440(?) ... **LC 6, 56**
See also DLB 146; FL 1:1; RGEL 2

Kempis, Thomas a 1380-1471 **LC 11**

Kendall, Henry 1839-1882 **NCLC 12**
See also DLB 230

Keneally, Thomas (Michael) 1935- ... **CLC 5, 8, 10, 14, 19, 27, 43, 117**
See also BRWS 4; CA 85-88; CANR 10, 50, 74, 130; CN 1, 2, 3, 4, 5, 6, 7; CPW; DA3; DAM NOV; DLB 289, 299, 326; EWL 3; MTCW 1, 2; MTFW 2005; NFS 17; RGEL 2; RGHL; RHW

Kennedy, A(lison) L(ouise) 1965- ... **CLC 188**
See also CA 168, 213; CAAE 213; CANR 108; CD 5, 6; CN 6, 7; DLB 271; RGSF 2

Kennedy, Adrienne (Lita) 1931- **BLC 2; CLC 66; DC 5**
See also AFAW 2; BW 2, 3; CA 103; CAAS 20; CABS 3; CAD; CANR 26, 53, 82; CD 5, 6; DAM MULT; DFS 9; DLB 38; FW; MAL 5

Kennedy, John Pendleton
1795-1870 **NCLC 2**
See also DLB 3, 248, 254; RGAL 4

Kennedy, Joseph Charles 1929-
See Kennedy, X. J.
See also CA 1-4R, 201; CAAE 201; CANR 4, 30, 40; CWRI 5; MAICYA 2; MAIC-YAS 1; SATA 14, 86, 130; SATA-Essay 130

Kennedy, William (Joseph) 1928- **CLC 6, 28, 34, 53**
See also AAYA 1; AMWS 7; BPFB 2; CA 85-88; CANR 14, 31, 76, 134; CN 4, 5, 6, 7; DA3; DAM NOV; DLB 143; DLBY 1985; EWL 3; INT CANR-31; MAL 5; MTCW 1, 2; MTFW 2005; SATA 57

Kennedy, X. J. **CLC 8, 42**
See Kennedy, Joseph Charles
See also AMWS 15; CAAS 9; CLR 27; CP 1, 2, 3, 4, 5, 6, 7; DLB 5; SAAS 22

Kenny, Maurice (Francis) 1929- **CLC 87; NNAL**
See also CA 144; CAAS 22; CANR 143; DAM MULT; DLB 175

Kent, Kelvin
See Kuttner, Henry

Kenton, Maxwell
See Southern, Terry

Kenyon, Jane 1947-1995 **PC 57**
See also AAYA 63; AMWS 7; CA 118; 148; CANR 44, 69; CP 6, 7; CWP; DLB 120; PFS 9, 17; RGAL 4

Kenyon, Robert O.
See Kuttner, Henry

Kepler, Johannes 1571-1630 **LC 45**

Ker, Jill
See Conway, Jill K(er)

Kerkow, H. C.
See Lewton, Val

Kerouac, Jack 1922-1969 **CLC 1, 2, 3, 5, 14, 29, 61; TCLC 117; WLC**
See Kerouac, Jean-Louis Lebris de
See also AAYA 25; AMWC 1; AMWS 3; BG 3; BPFB 2; CDALB 1941-1968; CP 1; CPW; DLB 2, 16, 237; DLBD 3; DLBY 1995; EWL 3; GLL 1; LATS 1:2; LMFS 2; MAL 5; NFS 8; RGAL 4; TUS; WP

Kerouac, Jean-Louis Lebris de 1922-1969
See Kerouac, Jack
See also AITN 1; CA 5-8R; 25-28R; CANR 26, 54, 95; DA; DA3; DAB; DAC; DAM MST, NOV, POET, POP; MTCW 1, 2; MTFW 2005

Kerr, (Bridget) Jean (Collins)
1923(?)-2003 **CLC 22**
See also CA 5-8R; 212; CANR 7; INT CANR-7

Kerr, M. E. **CLC 12, 35**
See Meaker, Marijane (Agnes)
See also AAYA 2, 23; BYA 1, 7, 8; CLR 29; SAAS 1; WYA

Kerr, Robert **CLC 55**

Kerrigan, (Thomas) Anthony 1918- .. **CLC 4, 6**
See also CA 49-52; CAAS 11; CANR 4

Kerry, Lois
See Duncan, Lois

Kesey, Ken (Elton) 1935-2001 ... **CLC 1, 3, 6, 11, 46, 64, 184; WLC 3**
See also AAYA 25; BG 1:3; BPFB 2; CA 1-4R; 204; CANR 22, 38, 66, 124; CDALB 1968-1988; CN 1, 2, 3, 4, 5, 6, 7; CPW; DA; DA3; DAB; DAC; DAM MST, NOV, POP; DLB 2, 16, 206; EWL 3; EXPN; LAIT 4; MAL 5; MTCW 1, 2; MTFW 2005; NFS 2; RGAL 4; SATA 66; SATA-Obit 131; TUS; YAW

Kesselring, Joseph (Otto)
1902-1967 **CLC 45**
See also CA 150; DAM DRAM, MST; DFS 20

Kessler, Jascha (Frederick) 1929- **CLC 4**
See also CA 17-20R; CANR 8, 48, 111; CP 1

Kettelkamp, Larry (Dale) 1933- **CLC 12**
See also CA 29-32R; CANR 16; SAAS 3; SATA 2

Key, Ellen (Karolina Sofia)
1849-1926 **TCLC 65**
See also DLB 259

Keyber, Conny
See Fielding, Henry

Keyes, Daniel 1927- **CLC 80**
See also AAYA 23; BYA 11; CA 17-20R, 181; CAAE 181; CANR 10, 26, 54, 74; DA; DA3; DAC; DAM MST, NOV; EXPN; LAIT 4; MTCW 2; MTFW 2005; NFS 2; SATA 37; SFW 4

Keynes, John Maynard
1883-1946 **TCLC 64**
See also CA 114; 162, 163; DLBD 10; MTCW 2; MTFW 2005

Khanshendel, Chiron
See Rose, Wendy

Khayyam, Omar 1048-1131 ... **CMLC 11; PC 8**
See Omar Khayyam
See also DA3; DAM POET; WLIT 6

Kherdian, David 1931- **CLC 6, 9**
See also AAYA 42; CA 21-24R, 192; CAAE 192; CAAS 2; CANR 39, 78; CLR 24; JRDA; LAIT 3; MAICYA 1, 2; SATA 16, 74; SATA-Essay 125

Khlebnikov, Velimir **TCLC 20**
See Khlebnikov, Viktor Vladimirovich
See also DLB 295; EW 10; EWL 3; RGWL 2, 3

Khlebnikov, Viktor Vladimirovich 1885-1922
See Khlebnikov, Velimir
See also CA 117; 217

Khodasevich, Vladislav (Felitsianovich)
1886-1939 **TCLC 15**
See also CA 115; DLB 317; EWL 3

Kielland, Alexander Lange
1849-1906 **TCLC 5**
See also CA 104

Kiely, Benedict 1919- ... **CLC 23, 43; SSC 58**
See also CA 1-4R; CANR 2, 84; CN 1, 2, 3, 4, 5, 6, 7; DLB 15, 319; TCLE 1:1

Kienzle, William X(avier)
1928-2001 **CLC 25**
See also CA 93-96; 203; CAAS 1; CANR 9, 31, 59, 111; CMW 4; DA3; DAM POP; INT CANR-31; MSW; MTCW 1, 2; MTFW 2005

Kierkegaard, Soren 1813-1855 **NCLC 34, 78, 125**
See also DLB 300; EW 6; LMFS 2; RGWL 3; TWA

Kieslowski, Krzysztof 1941-1996 **CLC 120**
See also CA 147; 151

Killens, John Oliver 1916-1987 **CLC 10**
See also BW 2; CA 77-80; 123; CAAS 2; CANR 26; CN 1, 2, 3, 4; DLB 33; EWL 3

Killigrew, Anne 1660-1685 **LC 4, 73**
See also DLB 131

Killigrew, Thomas 1612-1683 **LC 57**
See also DLB 58; RGEL 2

Kim
See Simenon, Georges (Jacques Christian)

Kincaid, Jamaica 1949- **BLC 2; CLC 43, 68, 137; SSC 72**
See also AAYA 13, 56; AFAW 2; AMWS 7; BRWS 7; BW 2, 3; CA 125; CANR 47, 59, 95, 133; CDALBS; CDWLB 3; CLR 63; CN 4, 5, 6, 7; DA3; DAM MULT, NOV; DLB 157, 227; DNFS 1; EWL 3; EXPS; FW; LATS 1:2; LMFS 2; MAL 5; MTCW 2; MTFW 2005; NCFS 1; NFS 3; SSFS 5, 7; TUS; WWE 1; YAW

King, Francis (Henry) 1923- **CLC 8, 53, 145**
See also CA 1-4R; CANR 1, 33, 86; CN 1, 2, 3, 4, 5, 6, 7; DAM NOV; DLB 15, 139; MTCW 1

King, Kennedy
See Brown, George Douglas

King, Martin Luther, Jr. 1929-1968 . **BLC 2; CLC 83; WLCS**
See also BW 2, 3; CA 25-28; CANR 27, 44; CAP 2; DA; DA3; DAB; DAC; DAM MST, MULT; LAIT 5; LATS 1:2; MTCW 1, 2; MTFW 2005; SATA 14

King, Stephen 1947- **CLC 12, 26, 37, 61, 113; SSC 17, 55**
See also AAYA 1, 17; AMWS 5; BEST 90:1; BPFB 2; CA 61-64; CANR 1, 30, 52, 76, 119, 134; CN 7; CPW; DA3; DAM NOV, POP; DLB 143; DLBY 1980; HGG; JRDA; LAIT 5; MTCW 1, 2; MTFW 2005; RGAL 4; SATA 9, 55, 161; SUFW 1, 2; WYAS 1; YAW

King, Stephen Edwin
See King, Stephen

King, Steve
See King, Stephen

King, Thomas 1943- **CLC 89, 171; NNAL**
See also CA 144; CANR 95; CCA 1; CN 6, 7; DAC; DAM MULT; DLB 175; SATA 96

Kingman, Lee **CLC 17**
See Natti, (Mary) Lee
See also CWRI 5; SAAS 3; SATA 1, 67

Kingsley, Charles 1819-1875 **NCLC 35**
See also CLR 77; DLB 21, 32, 163, 178, 190; FANT; MAICYA 2; MAICYAS 1; RGEL 2; WCH; YABC 2

Kingsley, Henry 1830-1876 **NCLC 107**
See also DLB 21, 230; RGEL 2

Kingsley, Sidney 1906-1995 **CLC 44**
See also CA 85-88; 147; CAD; DFS 14, 19; DLB 7; MAL 5; RGAL 4

Kingsolver, Barbara 1955- **CLC 55, 81, 130, 216**
See also AAYA 15; AMWS 7; CA 129; 134; CANR 60, 96, 133; CDALBS; CN 7; CPW; CSW; DA3; DAM POP; DLB 206; INT CA-134; LAIT 5; MTCW 2; MTFW 2005; NFS 5, 10, 12; RGAL 4; TCLE 1:1

Kingston, Maxine (Ting Ting) Hong
1940- **AAL; CLC 12, 19, 58, 121; WLCS**
See also AAYA 8, 55; AMWS 5; BPFB 2; CA 69-72; CANR 13, 38, 74, 87, 128; CDALBS; CN 6, 7; DA3; DAM MULT,

NOV; DLB 173, 212, 312; DLBY 1980; EWL 3; FL 1:6; FW; INT CANR-13; LAIT 5; MAL 5; MAWW; MTCW 1, 2; MTFW 2005; NFS 6; RGAL 4; SATA 53; SSFS 3; TCWW 2

Kinnell, Galway 1927- **CLC 1, 2, 3, 5, 13, 29, 129; PC 26**
See also AMWS 3; CA 9-12R; CANR 10, 34, 66, 116, 138; CP 1, 2, 3, 4, 5, 6, 7; DLB 5; DLBY 1987; EWL 3; INT CANR-34; MAL 5; MTCW 1, 2; MTFW 2005; PAB; PFS 9; RGAL 4; TCLE 1:1; WP

Kinsella, Thomas 1928- **CLC 4, 19, 138; PC 69**
See also BRWS 5; CA 17-20R; CANR 15, 122; CP 1, 2, 3, 4, 5, 6, 7; DLB 27; EWL 3; MTCW 1, 2; MTFW 2005; RGEL 2; TEA

Kinsella, W(illiam) P(atrick) 1935- . **CLC 27, 43, 166**
See also AAYA 7, 60; BPFB 2; CA 97-100, 222; CAAE 222; CAAS 7; CANR 21, 35, 66, 75, 129; CN 4, 5, 6, 7; CPW; DAC; DAM NOV, POP; FANT; INT CANR-21; LAIT 5; MTCW 1, 2; MTFW 2005; NFS 15; RGSF 2

Kinsey, Alfred C(harles)
1894-1956 **TCLC 91**
See also CA 115; 170; MTCW 2

Kipling, (Joseph) Rudyard 1865-1936 . **PC 3; SSC 5, 54; TCLC 8, 17, 167; WLC 3**
See also AAYA 32; BRW 6; BRWC 1, 2; BYA 4; CA 105; 120; CANR 33; CDBLB 1890-1914; CLR 39, 65; CWRI 5; DA; DA3; DAB; DAC; DAM MST, POET; DLB 19, 34, 141, 156; EWL 3; EXPS; FANT; LAIT 3; LMFS 1; MAICYA 1, 2; MTCW 1, 2; MTFW 2005; NFS 21; PFS 22; RGEL 2; RGSF 2; SATA 100; SFW 4; SSFS 8, 21; SUFW 1; TEA; WCH; WLIT 4; YABC 2

Kircher, Athanasius 1602-1680 **LC 121**
See also DLB 164

Kirk, Russell (Amos) 1918-1994 .. **TCLC 119**
See also AITN 1; CA 1-4R; 145; CAAS 9; CANR 1, 20, 60; HGG; INT CANR-20; MTCW 1, 2

Kirkham, Dinah
See Card, Orson Scott

Kirkland, Caroline M. 1801-1864 . **NCLC 85**
See also DLB 3, 73, 74, 250, 254; DLBD 13

Kirkup, James 1918- **CLC 1**
See also CA 1-4R; CAAS 4; CANR 2; CP 1, 2, 3, 4, 5, 6, 7; DLB 27; SATA 12

Kirkwood, James 1930(?)-1989 **CLC 9**
See also AITN 2; CA 1-4R; 128; CANR 6, 40; GLL 2

Kirsch, Sarah 1935- **CLC 176**
See also CA 178; CWW 2; DLB 75; EWL 3

Kirshner, Sidney
See Kingsley, Sidney

Kis, Danilo 1935-1989 **CLC 57**
See also CA 109; 118; 129; CANR 61; CD-WLB 4; DLB 181; EWL 3; MTCW 1; RGSF 2; RGWL 2, 3

Kissinger, Henry A(lfred) 1923- **CLC 137**
See also CA 1-4R; CANR 2, 33, 66, 109; MTCW 1

Kittel, Frederick August
See Wilson, August

Kivi, Aleksis 1834-1872 **NCLC 30**

Kizer, Carolyn (Ashley) 1925- ... **CLC 15, 39, 80; PC 66**
See also CA 65-68; CAAS 5; CANR 24, 70, 134; CP 1, 2, 3, 4, 5, 6, 7; CWP; DAM POET; DLB 5, 169; EWL 3; MAL 5; MTCW 2; MTFW 2005; PFS 18; TCLE 1:1

Klabund 1890-1928 **TCLC 44**
See also CA 162; DLB 66

Klappert, Peter 1942- **CLC 57**
See also CA 33-36R; CSW; DLB 5

Klein, A(braham) M(oses)
1909-1972 **CLC 19**
See also CA 101; 37-40R; CP 1; DAB; DAC; DAM MST; DLB 68; EWL 3; RGEL 2; RGHL

Klein, Joe
See Klein, Joseph

Klein, Joseph 1946- **CLC 154**
See also CA 85-88; CANR 55

Klein, Norma 1938-1989 **CLC 30**
See also AAYA 2, 35; BPFB 2; BYA 6, 7, 8; CA 41-44R; 128; CANR 15, 37; CLR 2, 19; INT CANR-15; JRDA; MAICYA 1, 2; SAAS 1; SATA 7, 57; WYA; YAW

Klein, T(heodore) E(ibon) D(onald)
1947- .. **CLC 34**
See also CA 119; CANR 44, 75; HGG

Kleist, Heinrich von 1777-1811 **NCLC 2, 37; SSC 22**
See also CDWLB 2; DAM DRAM; DLB 90; EW 5; RGSF 2; RGWL 2, 3

Klima, Ivan 1931- **CLC 56, 172**
See also CA 25-28R; CANR 17, 50, 91; CDWLB 4; CWW 2; DAM NOV; DLB 232; EWL 3; RGWL 3

Klimentev, Andrei Platonovich
See Klimentov, Andrei Platonovich

Klimentov, Andrei Platonovich
1899-1951 **SSC 42; TCLC 14**
See Platonov, Andrei Platonovich; Platonov, Andrey Platonovich
See also CA 108; 232

Klinger, Friedrich Maximilian von
1752-1831 **NCLC 1**
See also DLB 94

Klingsor the Magician
See Hartmann, Sadakichi

Klopstock, Friedrich Gottlieb
1724-1803 **NCLC 11**
See also DLB 97; EW 4; RGWL 2, 3

Kluge, Alexander 1932- **SSC 61**
See also CA 81-84; DLB 75

Knapp, Caroline 1959-2002 **CLC 99**
See also CA 154; 207

Knebel, Fletcher 1911-1993 **CLC 14**
See also AITN 1; CA 1-4R; 140; CAAS 3; CANR 1, 36; CN 1, 2, 3, 4, 5; SATA 36; SATA-Obit 75

Knickerbocker, Diedrich
See Irving, Washington

Knight, Etheridge 1931-1991 ... **BLC 2; CLC 40; PC 14**
See also BW 1, 3; CA 21-24R; 133; CANR 23, 82; CP 1, 2, 3, 4, 5; DAM POET; DLB 41; MTCW 2; MTFW 2005; RGAL 4; TCLE 1:1

Knight, Sarah Kemble 1666-1727 **LC 7**
See also DLB 24, 200

Knister, Raymond 1899-1932 **TCLC 56**
See also CA 186; DLB 68; RGEL 2

Knowles, John 1926-2001 ... **CLC 1, 4, 10, 26**
See also AAYA 10; AMWS 12; BPFB 2; BYA 3; CA 17-20R; 203; CANR 40, 74, 76, 132; CDALB 1968-1988; CLR 98; CN 1, 2, 3, 4, 5, 6, 7; DA; DAC; DAM MST, NOV; DLB 6; EXPN; MTCW 1, 2; MTFW 2005; NFS 2; RGAL 4; SATA 8, 89; SATA-Obit 134; YAW

Knox, Calvin M.
See Silverberg, Robert

Knox, John c. 1505-1572 **LC 37**
See also DLB 132

Knye, Cassandra
See Disch, Thomas M(ichael)

Koch, C(hristopher) J(ohn) 1932- **CLC 42**
See also CA 127; CANR 84; CN 3, 4, 5, 6, 7; DLB 289

Koch, Christopher
See Koch, C(hristopher) J(ohn)

Koch, Kenneth (Jay) 1925-2002 **CLC 5, 8, 44**
See also AMWS 15; CA 1-4R; 207; CAD; CANR 6, 36, 57, 97, 131; CD 5, 6; CP 1, 2, 3, 4, 5, 6, 7; DAM POET; DLB 5; INT CANR-36; MAL 5; MTCW 2; MTFW 2005; PFS 20; SATA 65; WP

Kochanowski, Jan 1530-1584 **LC 10**
See also RGWL 2, 3

Kock, Charles Paul de 1794-1871 . **NCLC 16**

Koda Rohan
See Koda Shigeyuki

Koda Rohan
See Koda Shigeyuki
See also DLB 180

Koda Shigeyuki 1867-1947 **TCLC 22**
See Koda Rohan
See also CA 121; 183

Koestler, Arthur 1905-1983 ... **CLC 1, 3, 6, 8, 15, 33**
See also BRWS 1; CA 1-4R; 109; CANR 1, 33; CDBLB 1945-1960; CN 1, 2, 3; DLBY 1983; EWL 3; MTCW 1, 2; MTFW 2005; NFS 19; RGEL 2

Kogawa, Joy Nozomi 1935- **CLC 78, 129**
See also AAYA 47; CA 101; CANR 19, 62, 126; CN 6, 7; CP 1; CWP; DAC; DAM MST, MULT; FW; MTCW 2; MTFW 2005; NFS 3; SATA 99

Kohout, Pavel 1928- **CLC 13**
See also CA 45-48; CANR 3

Koizumi, Yakumo
See Hearn, (Patricio) Lafcadio (Tessima Carlos)

Kolmar, Gertrud 1894-1943 **TCLC 40**
See also CA 167; EWL 3; RGHL

Komunyakaa, Yusef 1947- .. **BLCS; CLC 86, 94, 207; PC 51**
See also AFAW 2; AMWS 13; CA 147; CANR 83; CP 6, 7; CSW; DLB 120; EWL 3; PFS 5, 20; RGAL 4

Konrad, George
See Konrad, Gyorgy

Konrad, Gyorgy 1933- **CLC 4, 10, 73**
See also CA 85-88; CANR 97; CDWLB 4; CWW 2; DLB 232; EWL 3

Konwicki, Tadeusz 1926- **CLC 8, 28, 54, 117**
See also CA 101; CAAS 9; CANR 39, 59; CWW 2; DLB 232; EWL 3; IDFW 3; MTCW 1

Koontz, Dean R. 1945- **CLC 78, 206**
See also AAYA 9, 31; BEST 89:3, 90:2; CA 108; CANR 19, 36, 52, 95, 138; CMW 4; CPW; DA3; DAM NOV, POP; DLB 292; HGG; MTCW 1; MTFW 2005; SATA 92, 165; SFW 4; SUFW 2; YAW

Koontz, Dean Ray
See Koontz, Dean R.

Koontz, Dean Ray
See Koontz, Dean R.

Kopernik, Mikolaj
See Copernicus, Nicolaus

Kopit, Arthur (Lee) 1937- **CLC 1, 18, 33**
See also AITN 1; CA 81-84; CABS 3; CAD; CD 5, 6; DAM DRAM; DFS 7, 14; DLB 7; MAL 5; MTCW 1; RGAL 4

Kopitar, Jernej (Bartholomaus)
1780-1844 **NCLC 117**

Kops, Bernard 1926- **CLC 4**
See also CA 5-8R; CANR 84; CBD; CN 1, 2, 3, 4, 5, 6, 7; CP 1, 2, 3, 4, 5, 6, 7; DLB 13; RGHL

Kornbluth, C(yril) M. 1923-1958 **TCLC 8**
See also CA 105; 160; DLB 8; SCFW 1, 2; SFW 4

Korolenko, V. G.
See Korolenko, Vladimir Galaktionovich

Korolenko, Vladimir
See Korolenko, Vladimir Galaktionovich

Korolenko, Vladimir G.
See Korolenko, Vladimir Galaktionovich

Korolenko, Vladimir Galaktionovich
1853-1921 **TCLC 22**
See also CA 121; DLB 277

Korzybski, Alfred (Habdank Skarbek)
1879-1950 **TCLC 61**
See also CA 123; 160

Kosinski, Jerzy (Nikodem)
1933-1991 **CLC 1, 2, 3, 6, 10, 15, 53, 70**
See also AMWS 7; BPFB 2; CA 17-20R; 134; CANR 9, 46; CN 1, 2, 3, 4; DA3; DAM NOV; DLB 2, 299; DLBY 1982; EWL 3; HGG; MAL 5; MTCW 1, 2; MTFW 2005; NFS 12; RGAL 4; RGHL; TUS

Kostelanetz, Richard (Cory) 1940- .. **CLC 28**
See also CA 13-16R; CAAS 8; CANR 38, 77; CN 4, 5, 6; CP 2, 3, 4, 5, 6, 7

Kostrowitzki, Wilhelm Apollinaris de
1880-1918
See Apollinaire, Guillaume
See also CA 104

Kotlowitz, Robert 1924- **CLC 4**
See also CA 33-36R; CANR 36

Kotzebue, August (Friedrich Ferdinand) von
1761-1819 **NCLC 25**
See also DLB 94

Kotzwinkle, William 1938- **CLC 5, 14, 35**
See also BPFB 2; CA 45-48; CANR 3, 44, 84, 129; CLR 6; CN 7; DLB 173; FANT; MAICYA 1, 2; SATA 24, 70, 146; SFW 4; SUFW 2; YAW

Kowna, Stancy
See Szymborska, Wislawa

Kozol, Jonathan 1936- **CLC 17**
See also AAYA 46; CA 61-64; CANR 16, 45, 96; MTFW 2005

Kozoll, Michael 1940(?)- **CLC 35**

Kramer, Kathryn 19(?)- **CLC 34**

Kramer, Larry 1935- **CLC 42; DC 8**
See also CA 124; 126; CANR 60, 132; DAM POP; DLB 249; GLL 1

Krasicki, Ignacy 1735-1801 **NCLC 8**

Krasinski, Zygmunt 1812-1859 **NCLC 4**
See also RGWL 2, 3

Kraus, Karl 1874-1936 **TCLC 5**
See also CA 104; 216; DLB 118; EWL 3

Kreve (Mickevicius), Vincas
1882-1954 **TCLC 27**
See also CA 170; DLB 220; EWL 3

Kristeva, Julia 1941- **CLC 77, 140**
See also CA 154; CANR 99; DLB 242; EWL 3; FW; LMFS 2

Kristofferson, Kris 1936- **CLC 26**
See also CA 104

Krizanc, John 1956- **CLC 57**
See also CA 187

Krleza, Miroslav 1893-1981 **CLC 8, 114**
See also CA 97-100; 105; CANR 50; CD-WLB 4; DLB 147; EW 11; RGWL 2, 3

Kroetsch, Robert (Paul) 1927- **CLC 5, 23, 57, 132**
See also CA 17-20R; CANR 8, 38; CCA 1; CN 2, 3, 4, 5, 6, 7; CP 6, 7; DAC; DAM POET; DLB 53; MTCW 1

Kroetz, Franz
See Kroetz, Franz Xaver

Kroetz, Franz Xaver 1946- **CLC 41**
See also CA 130; CANR 142; CWW 2; EWL 3

Kroker, Arthur (W.) 1945- **CLC 77**
See also CA 161

Kroniuk, Lisa
See Berton, Pierre (Francis de Marigny)

Kropotkin, Peter (Aleksieevich)
1842-1921 **TCLC 36**
See Kropotkin, Petr Alekseevich
See also CA 119; 219

Kropotkin, Petr Alekseevich
See Kropotkin, Peter (Aleksieevich)
See also DLB 277

Krotkov, Yuri 1917-1981 **CLC 19**
See also CA 102

Krumb
See Crumb, R.

Krumgold, Joseph (Quincy)
1908-1980 **CLC 12**
See also BYA 1, 2; CA 9-12R; 101; CANR 7; MAICYA 1, 2; SATA 1, 48; SATA-Obit 23; YAW

Krumwitz
See Crumb, R.

Krutch, Joseph Wood 1893-1970 **CLC 24**
See also ANW; CA 1-4R; 25-28R; CANR 4; DLB 63, 206, 275

Krutzch, Gus
See Eliot, T(homas) S(tearns)

Krylov, Ivan Andreevich
1768(?)-1844 **NCLC 1**
See also DLB 150

Kubin, Alfred (Leopold Isidor)
1877-1959 **TCLC 23**
See also CA 112; 149; CANR 104; DLB 81

Kubrick, Stanley 1928-1999 **CLC 16; TCLC 112**
See also AAYA 30; CA 81-84; 177; CANR 33; DLB 26

Kumin, Maxine (Winokur) 1925- **CLC 5, 13, 28, 164; PC 15**
See also AITN 2; AMWS 4; ANW; CA 1-4R; CAAS 8; CANR 1, 21, 69, 115, 140; CP 2, 3, 4, 5, 6, 7; CWP; DA3; DAM POET; DLB 5; EWL 3; EXPP; MTCW 1, 2; MTFW 2005; PAB; PFS 18; SATA 12

Kundera, Milan 1929- .. **CLC 4, 9, 19, 32, 68, 115, 135; SSC 24**
See also AAYA 2, 62; BPFB 2; CA 85-88; CANR 19, 52, 74, 144; CDWLB 4; CWW 2; DA3; DAM NOV; DLB 232; EW 13; EWL 3; MTCW 1, 2; MTFW 2005; NFS 18; RGSF 2; RGWL 3; SSFS 10

Kunene, Mazisi (Raymond) 1930- ... **CLC 85**
See also BW 1, 3; CA 125; CANR 81; CP 1, 6, 7; DLB 117

Kung, Hans ... **CLC 130**
See Kung, Hans

Kung, Hans 1928-
See Kung, Hans
See also CA 53-56; CANR 66, 134; MTCW 1, 2; MTFW 2005

Kunikida Doppo 1869(?)-1908
See Doppo, Kunikida
See also DLB 180; EWL 3

Kunitz, Stanley 1905-2006 **CLC 6, 11, 14, 148; PC 19**
See also AMWS 3; CA 41-44R; CANR 26, 57, 98; CP 1, 2, 3, 4, 5, 6, 7; DA3; DLB 48; INT CANR-26; MAL 5; MTCW 1, 2; MTFW 2005; PFS 11; RGAL 4

Kunitz, Stanley Jasspon
See Kunitz, Stanley

Kunze, Reiner 1933- **CLC 10**
See also CA 93-96; CWW 2; DLB 75; EWL 3

Kuprin, Aleksander Ivanovich
1870-1938 **TCLC 5**
See Kuprin, Aleksandr Ivanovich; Kuprin, Alexandr Ivanovich
See also CA 104; 182

Kuprin, Aleksandr Ivanovich
See Kuprin, Aleksander Ivanovich
See also DLB 295
Kuprin, Alexandr Ivanovich
See Kuprin, Aleksander Ivanovich
See also EWL 3
Kureishi, Hanif 1954- .. **CLC 64, 135; DC 26**
See also BRWS 11; CA 139; CANR 113;
CBD; CD 5, 6; CN 6, 7; DLB 194, 245;
GLL 2; IDFW 4; WLIT 4; WWE 1
Kurosawa, Akira 1910-1998 **CLC 16, 119**
See also AAYA 11, 64; CA 101; 170; CANR
46; DAM MULT
Kushner, Tony 1956- **CLC 81, 203; DC 10**
See also AAYA 61; AMWS 9; CA 144;
CAD; CANR 74, 130; CD 5, 6; DA3;
DAM DRAM; DFS 5; DLB 228; EWL 3;
GLL 1; LAIT 5; MAL 5; MTCW 2;
MTFW 2005; RGAL 4; RGHL; SATA 160
Kuttner, Henry 1915-1958 **TCLC 10**
See also CA 107; 157; DLB 8; FANT;
SCFW 1, 2; SFW 4
Kutty, Madhavi
See Das, Kamala
Kuzma, Greg 1944- **CLC 7**
See also CA 33-36R; CANR 70
Kuzmin, Mikhail (Alekseevich)
1872(?)-1936 **TCLC 40**
See also CA 170; DLB 295; EWL 3
Kyd, Thomas 1558-1594 .. **DC 3; LC 22, 125**
See also BRW 1; DAM DRAM; DFS 21;
DLB 62; IDTP; LMFS 1; RGEL 2; TEA;
WLIT 3
Kyprianos, Iossif
See Samarakis, Antonis
L. S.
See Stephen, Sir Leslie
Laȝamon
See Layamon
See also DLB 146
Labe, Louise 1521-1566 **LC 120**
Labrunie, Gerard
See Nerval, Gerard de
La Bruyere, Jean de 1645-1696 **LC 17**
See also DLB 268; EW 3; GFL Beginnings
to 1789
LaBute, Neil 1963- **CLC 225**
See also CA 240
Lacan, Jacques (Marie Emile)
1901-1981 **CLC 75**
See also CA 121; 104; DLB 296; EWL 3;
TWA
Laclos, Pierre-Ambroise Francois
1741-1803 **NCLC 4, 87**
See also DLB 313; EW 4; GFL Beginnings
to 1789; RGWL 2, 3
Lacolere, Francois
See Aragon, Louis
La Colere, Francois
See Aragon, Louis
La Deshabilleuse
See Simenon, Georges (Jacques Christian)
Lady Gregory
See Gregory, Lady Isabella Augusta (Persse)
Lady of Quality, A
See Bagnold, Enid
**La Fayette, Marie-(Madelaine Pioche de la
Vergne)** 1634-1693 **LC 2**
See Lafayette, Marie-Madeleine
See also GFL Beginnings to 1789; RGWL
2, 3
Lafayette, Marie-Madeleine
See La Fayette, Marie-(Madelaine Pioche
de la Vergne)
See also DLB 268
Lafayette, Rene
See Hubbard, L. Ron
La Flesche, Francis 1857(?)-1932 **NNAL**
See also CA 144; CANR 83; DLB 175

La Fontaine, Jean de 1621-1695 **LC 50**
See also DLB 268; EW 3; GFL Beginnings
to 1789; MAICYA 1, 2; RGWL 2, 3;
SATA 18
LaForet, Carmen 1921-2004 **CLC 219**
See also CA 246; CWW 2; DLB 322; EWL
3
LaForet Diaz, Carmen
See LaForet, Carmen
Laforgue, Jules 1860-1887 . **NCLC 5, 53; PC
14; SSC 20**
See also DLB 217; EW 7; GFL 1789 to the
Present; RGWL 2, 3
Lagerkvist, Paer (Fabian)
1891-1974 **CLC 7, 10, 13, 54; TCLC
144**
See Lagerkvist, Par
See also CA 85-88; 49-52; DA3; DAM
DRAM, NOV; MTCW 1, 2; MTFW 2005;
TWA
Lagerkvist, Par **SSC 12**
See Lagerkvist, Paer (Fabian)
See also DLB 259; EW 10; EWL 3; RGSF
2; RGWL 2, 3
Lagerloef, Selma (Ottiliana Lovisa)
.. **TCLC 4, 36**
See Lagerlof, Selma (Ottiliana Lovisa)
See also CA 108; MTCW 2
Lagerlof, Selma (Ottiliana Lovisa)
1858-1940
See Lagerloef, Selma (Ottiliana Lovisa)
See also CA 188; CLR 7; DLB 259; RGWL
2, 3; SATA 15; SSFS 18
La Guma, (Justin) Alex(ander)
1925-1985 . **BLCS; CLC 19; TCLC 140**
See also AFW; BW 1, 3; CA 49-52; 118;
CANR 25, 81; CDWLB 3; CN 1, 2, 3;
CP 1; DAM NOV; DLB 117, 225; EWL
3; MTCW 1, 2; MTFW 2005; WLIT 2;
WWE 1
Laidlaw, A. K.
See Grieve, C(hristopher) M(urray)
Lainez, Manuel Mujica
See Mujica Lainez, Manuel
See also HW 1
Laing, R(onald) D(avid) 1927-1989 . **CLC 95**
See also CA 107; 129; CANR 34; MTCW 1
Laishley, Alex
See Booth, Martin
Lamartine, Alphonse (Marie Louis Prat) de
1790-1869 **NCLC 11; PC 16**
See also DAM POET; DLB 217; GFL 1789
to the Present; RGWL 2, 3
Lamb, Charles 1775-1834 **NCLC 10, 113;
WLC 3**
See also BRW 4; CDBLB 1789-1832; DA;
DAB; DAC; DAM MST; DLB 93, 107,
163; RGEL 2; SATA 17; TEA
Lamb, Lady Caroline 1785-1828 ... **NCLC 38**
See also DLB 116
Lamb, Mary Ann 1764-1847 **NCLC 125**
See also DLB 163; SATA 17
Lame Deer 1903(?)-1976 **NNAL**
See also CA 69-72
Lamming, George (William) 1927- ... **BLC 2;
CLC 2, 4, 66, 144**
See also BW 2, 3; CA 85-88; CANR 26,
76; CDWLB 3; CN 1, 2, 3, 4, 5, 6, 7; CP
1; DAM MULT; DLB 125; EWL 3;
MTCW 1, 2; MTFW 2005; NFS 15;
RGEL 2
L'Amour, Louis (Dearborn)
1908-1988 **CLC 25, 55**
See also AAYA 16; AITN 2; BEST 89:2;
BPFB 2; CA 1-4R; 125; CANR 3, 25, 40;
CPW; DA3; DAM NOV, POP; DLB 206;
DLBY 1980; MTCW 1, 2; MTFW 2005;
RGAL 4; TCWW 1, 2

Lampedusa, Giuseppe (Tomasi) di
.. **TCLC 13**
See Tomasi di Lampedusa, Giuseppe
See also CA 164; EW 11; MTCW 2; MTFW
2005; RGWL 2, 3
Lampman, Archibald 1861-1899 ... **NCLC 25**
See also DLB 92; RGEL 2; TWA
Lancaster, Bruce 1896-1963 **CLC 36**
See also CA 9-10; CANR 70; CAP 1; SATA
9
Lanchester, John 1962- **CLC 99**
See also CA 194; DLB 267
Landau, Mark Alexandrovich
See Aldanov, Mark (Alexandrovich)
Landau-Aldanov, Mark Alexandrovich
See Aldanov, Mark (Alexandrovich)
Landis, Jerry
See Simon, Paul
Landis, John 1950- **CLC 26**
See also CA 112; 122; CANR 128
Landolfi, Tommaso 1908-1979 **CLC 11, 49**
See also CA 127; 117; DLB 177; EWL 3
Landon, Letitia Elizabeth
1802-1838 **NCLC 15**
See also DLB 96
Landor, Walter Savage
1775-1864 **NCLC 14**
See also BRW 4; DLB 93, 107; RGEL 2
Landwirth, Heinz 1927-
See Lind, Jakov
See also CA 9-12R; CANR 7
Lane, Patrick 1939- **CLC 25**
See also CA 97-100; CANR 54; CP 3, 4, 5,
6, 7; DAM POET; DLB 53; INT CA-97-
100
Lane, Rose Wilder 1887-1968 **TCLC 177**
See also CA 102; CANR 63; SATA 29;
SATA-Brief 28; TCWW 2
Lang, Andrew 1844-1912 **TCLC 16**
See also CA 114; 137; CANR 85; CLR 101;
DLB 98, 141, 184; FANT; MAICYA 1, 2;
RGEL 2; SATA 16; WCH
Lang, Fritz 1890-1976 **CLC 20, 103**
See also AAYA 65; CA 77-80; 69-72;
CANR 30
Lange, John
See Crichton, (John) Michael
Langer, Elinor 1939- **CLC 34**
See also CA 121
Langland, William 1332(?)-1400(?) **LC 19,
120**
See also BRW 1; DA; DAB; DAC; DAM
MST, POET; DLB 146; RGEL 2; TEA;
WLIT 3
Langstaff, Launcelot
See Irving, Washington
Lanier, Sidney 1842-1881 . **NCLC 6, 118; PC
50**
See also AMWS 1; DAM POET; DLB 64;
DLBD 13; EXPP; MAICYA 1; PFS 14;
RGAL 4; SATA 18
Lanyer, Aemilia 1569-1645 **LC 10, 30, 83;
PC 60**
See also DLB 121
Lao Tzu c. 6th cent. B.C.-3rd cent.
B.C. ... **CMLC 7**
Lao-Tzu
See Lao Tzu
Lapine, James (Elliot) 1949- **CLC 39**
See also CA 123; 130; CANR 54, 128; INT
CA-130
Larbaud, Valery (Nicolas)
1881-1957 **TCLC 9**
See also CA 106; 152; EWL 3; GFL 1789
to the Present

Lardner, Ring
See Lardner, Ring(gold) W(ilmer)
See also BPFB 2; CDALB 1917-1929; DLB 11, 25, 86, 171; DLBD 16; MAL 5; RGAL 4; RGSF 2

Lardner, Ring W., Jr.
See Lardner, Ring(gold) W(ilmer)

Lardner, Ring(gold) W(ilmer)
1885-1933 **SSC 32; TCLC 2, 14**
See Lardner, Ring
See also AMW; CA 104; 131; MTCW 1, 2; MTFW 2005; TUS

Laredo, Betty
See Codrescu, Andrei

Larkin, Maia
See Wojciechowska, Maia (Teresa)

Larkin, Philip (Arthur) 1922-1985 ... **CLC 3, 5, 8, 9, 13, 18, 33, 39, 64; PC 21**
See also BRWS 1; CA 5-8R; 117; CANR 24, 62; CDBLB 1960 to Present; CP 1, 2, 3, 4; DA3; DAB; DAM MST, POET; DLB 27; EWL 3; MTCW 1, 2; MTFW 2005; PFS 3, 4, 12; RGEL 2

La Roche, Sophie von
1730-1807 **NCLC 121**
See also DLB 94

La Rochefoucauld, Francois
1613-1680 **LC 108**

Larra (y Sanchez de Castro), Mariano Jose de 1809-1837 **NCLC 17, 130**

Larsen, Eric 1941- **CLC 55**
See also CA 132

Larsen, Nella 1893(?)-1963 **BLC 2; CLC 37; HR 1:3**
See also AFAW 1, 2; BW 1; CA 125; CANR 83; DAM MULT; DLB 51; FW; LATS 1:1; LMFS 2

Larson, Charles R(aymond) 1938- ... **CLC 31**
See also CA 53-56; CANR 4, 121

Larson, Jonathan 1960-1996 **CLC 99**
See also AAYA 28; CA 156; DFS 23; MTFW 2005

La Sale, Antoine de c. 1386-1460(?) . **LC 104**
See also DLB 208

Las Casas, Bartolome de
1474-1566 **HLCS; LC 31**
See Casas, Bartolome de las
See also DLB 318; LAW

Lasch, Christopher 1932-1994 **CLC 102**
See also CA 73-76; 144; CANR 25, 118; DLB 246; MTCW 1, 2; MTFW 2005

Lasker-Schueler, Else 1869-1945 ... **TCLC 57**
See Lasker-Schuler, Else
See also CA 183; DLB 66, 124

Lasker-Schuler, Else
See Lasker-Schueler, Else
See also EWL 3

Laski, Harold J(oseph) 1893-1950 . **TCLC 79**
See also CA 188

Latham, Jean Lee 1902-1995 **CLC 12**
See also AITN 1; BYA 1; CA 5-8R; CANR 7, 84; CLR 50; MAICYA 1, 2; SATA 2, 68; YAW

Latham, Mavis
See Clark, Mavis Thorpe

Lathen, Emma **CLC 2**
See Hennissart, Martha; Latsis, Mary J(ane)
See also BPFB 2; CMW 4; DLB 306

Lathrop, Francis
See Leiber, Fritz (Reuter, Jr.)

Latsis, Mary J(ane) 1927-1997
See Lathen, Emma
See also CA 85-88; 162; CMW 4

Lattany, Kristin
See Lattany, Kristin (Elaine Eggleston) Hunter

Lattany, Kristin (Elaine Eggleston) Hunter
1931- **CLC 35**
See Hunter, Kristin
See also AITN 1; BW 1; BYA 3; CA 13-16R; CANR 13, 108; CLR 3; CN 7; DLB 33; INT CANR-13; MAICYA 1, 2; SAAS 10; SATA 12, 132; YAW

Lattimore, Richmond (Alexander)
1906-1984 **CLC 3**
See also CA 1-4R; 112; CANR 1; CP 1, 2, 3; MAL 5

Laughlin, James 1914-1997 **CLC 49**
See also CA 21-24R; 162; CAAS 22; CANR 9, 47; CP 1, 2, 3, 4, 5, 6; DLB 48; DLBY 1996, 1997

Laurence, (Jean) Margaret (Wemyss)
1926-1987 . **CLC 3, 6, 13, 50, 62; SSC 7**
See also BYA 13; CA 5-8R; 121; CANR 33; CN 1, 2, 3, 4; DAC; DAM MST; DLB 53; EWL 3; FW; MTCW 1, 2; MTFW 2005; NFS 11; RGEL 2; RGSF 2; SATA-Obit 50; TCWW 2

Laurent, Antoine 1952- **CLC 50**

Lauscher, Hermann
See Hesse, Hermann

Lautreamont 1846-1870 .. **NCLC 12; SSC 14**
See Lautreamont, Isidore Lucien Ducasse
See also GFL 1789 to the Present; RGWL 2, 3

Lautreamont, Isidore Lucien Ducasse
See Lautreamont
See also DLB 217

Lavater, Johann Kaspar
1741-1801 **NCLC 142**
See also DLB 97

Laverty, Donald
See Blish, James (Benjamin)

Lavin, Mary 1912-1996 . **CLC 4, 18, 99; SSC 4, 67**
See also CA 9-12R; 151; CANR 33; CN 1, 2, 3, 4, 5, 6; DLB 15, 319; FW; MTCW 1; RGEL 2; RGSF 2; SSFS 23

Lavond, Paul Dennis
See Kornbluth, C(yril) M.; Pohl, Frederik

Lawes, Henry 1596-1662 **LC 113**
See also DLB 126

Lawler, Ray
See Lawler, Raymond Evenor
See also DLB 289

Lawler, Raymond Evenor 1922- **CLC 58**
See Lawler, Ray
See also CA 103; CD 5, 6; RGEL 2

Lawrence, D(avid) H(erbert Richards)
1885-1930 **PC 54; SSC 4, 19, 73; TCLC 2, 9, 16, 33, 48, 61, 93; WLC 3**
See Chambers, Jessie
See also BPFB 2; BRW 7; BRWR 2; CA 104; 121; CANR 131; CDBLB 1914-1945; DA; DA3; DAB; DAC; DAM MST, NOV, POET; DLB 10, 19, 36, 98, 162, 195; EWL 3; EXPP; EXPS; LAIT 2, 3; MTCW 1, 2; MTFW 2005; NFS 18; PFS 6; RGEL 2; RGSF 2; SSFS 2, 6; TEA; WLIT 4; WP

Lawrence, T(homas) E(dward)
1888-1935 **TCLC 18**
See Dale, Colin
See also BRWS 2; CA 115; 167; DLB 195

Lawrence of Arabia
See Lawrence, T(homas) E(dward)

Lawson, Henry (Archibald Hertzberg)
1867-1922 **SSC 18; TCLC 27**
See also CA 120; 181; DLB 230; RGEL 2; RGSF 2

Lawton, Dennis
See Faust, Frederick (Schiller)

Layamon fl. c. 1200- **CMLC 10**
See Laȝamon
See also DLB 146; RGEL 2

Laye, Camara 1928-1980 **BLC 2; CLC 4, 38**
See Camara Laye
See also AFW; BW 1; CA 85-88; 97-100; CANR 25; DAM MULT; MTCW 1, 2; WLIT 2

Layton, Irving 1912-2006 **CLC 2, 15, 164**
See also CA 1-4R; 247; CANR 2, 33, 43, 66, 129; CP 1, 2, 3, 4, 5, 6, 7; DAC; DAM MST, POET; DLB 88; EWL 3; MTCW 1, 2; PFS 12; RGEL 2

Layton, Irving Peter
See Layton, Irving

Lazarus, Emma 1849-1887 **NCLC 8, 109**

Lazarus, Felix
See Cable, George Washington

Lazarus, Henry
See Slavitt, David R(ytman)

Lea, Joan
See Neufeld, John (Arthur)

Leacock, Stephen (Butler)
1869-1944 **SSC 39; TCLC 2**
See also CA 104; 141; CANR 80; DAC; DAM MST; DLB 92; EWL 3; MTCW 2; MTFW 2005; RGEL 2; RGSF 2

Lead, Jane Ward 1623-1704 **LC 72**
See also DLB 131

Leapor, Mary 1722-1746 **LC 80**
See also DLB 109

Lear, Edward 1812-1888 **NCLC 3; PC 65**
See also AAYA 48; BRW 5; CLR 1, 75; DLB 32, 163, 166; MAICYA 1, 2; RGEL 2; SATA 18, 100; WCH; WP

Lear, Norman (Milton) 1922- **CLC 12**
See also CA 73-76

Leautaud, Paul 1872-1956 **TCLC 83**
See also CA 203; DLB 65; GFL 1789 to the Present

Leavis, F(rank) R(aymond)
1895-1978 **CLC 24**
See also BRW 7; CA 21-24R; 77-80; CANR 44; DLB 242; EWL 3; MTCW 1, 2; RGEL 2

Leavitt, David 1961- **CLC 34**
See also CA 116; 122; CANR 50, 62, 101, 134; CPW; DA3; DAM POP; DLB 130; GLL 1; INT CA-122; MAL 5; MTCW 2; MTFW 2005

Leblanc, Maurice (Marie Emile)
1864-1941 **TCLC 49**
See also CA 110; CMW 4

Lebowitz, Fran(ces Ann) 1951(?)- ... **CLC 11, 36**
See also CA 81-84; CANR 14, 60, 70; INT CANR-14; MTCW 1

Lebrecht, Peter
See Tieck, (Johann) Ludwig

le Carre, John **CLC 3, 5, 9, 15, 28, 220**
See Cornwell, David (John Moore)
See also AAYA 42; BEST 89:4; BPFB 2; BRWS 2; CDBLB 1960 to Present; CMW 4; CN 1, 2, 3, 4, 5, 6, 7; CPW; DLB 87; EWL 3; MSW; MTCW 2; RGEL 2; TEA

Le Clezio, J. M.G. 1940- **CLC 31, 155**
See also CA 116; 128; CANR 147; CWW 2; DLB 83; EWL 3; GFL 1789 to the Present; RGSF 2

Le Clezio, Jean Marie Gustave
See Le Clezio, J. M.G.

Leconte de Lisle, Charles-Marie-Rene
1818-1894 **NCLC 29**
See also DLB 217; EW 6; GFL 1789 to the Present

Le Coq, Monsieur
See Simenon, Georges (Jacques Christian)

Leduc, Violette 1907-1972 **CLC 22**
See also CA 13-14; 33-36R; CANR 69; CAP 1; EWL 3; GFL 1789 to the Present; GLL 1

Ledwidge, Francis 1887(?)-1917 **TCLC 23**
See also CA 123; 203; DLB 20
Lee, Andrea 1953- **BLC 2; CLC 36**
See also BW 1, 3; CA 125; CANR 82;
DAM MULT
Lee, Andrew
See Auchincloss, Louis
Lee, Chang-rae 1965- **CLC 91**
See also CA 148; CANR 89; CN 7; DLB
312; LATS 1:2
Lee, Don L. .. **CLC 2**
See Madhubuti, Haki R.
See also CP 2, 3, 4, 5
Lee, George W(ashington)
1894-1976 **BLC 2; CLC 52**
See also BW 1; CA 125; CANR 83; DAM
MULT; DLB 51
Lee, (Nelle) Harper 1926- . **CLC 12, 60, 194;
WLC 4**
See also AAYA 13; AMWS 8; BPFB 2;
BYA 3; CA 13-16R; CANR 51, 128;
CDALB 1941-1968; CSW; DA; DA3;
DAB; DAC; DAM MST, NOV; DLB 6;
EXPN; LAIT 3; MAL 5; MTCW 1, 2;
MTFW 2005; NFS 2; SATA 11; WYA;
YAW
Lee, Helen Elaine 1959(?)- **CLC 86**
See also CA 148
Lee, John ... **CLC 70**
Lee, Julian
See Latham, Jean Lee
Lee, Larry
See Lee, Lawrence
Lee, Laurie 1914-1997 **CLC 90**
See also CA 77-80; 158; CANR 33, 73; CP
1, 2, 3, 4, 5, 6; CPW; DAB; DAM POP;
DLB 27; MTCW 1; RGEL 2
Lee, Lawrence 1941-1990 **CLC 34**
See also CA 131; CANR 43
Lee, Li-Young 1957- **CLC 164; PC 24**
See also AMWS 15; CA 153; CANR 118;
CP 6, 7; DLB 165, 312; LMFS 2; PFS 11,
15, 17
Lee, Manfred B. 1905-1971 **CLC 11**
See Queen, Ellery
See also CA 1-4R; 29-32R; CANR 2, 150;
CMW 4; DLB 137
Lee, Manfred Bennington
See Lee, Manfred B.
Lee, Nathaniel 1645(?)-1692 **LC 103**
See also DLB 80; RGEL 2
Lee, Shelton Jackson 1957(?)- .. **BLCS; CLC
105**
See Lee, Spike
See also BW 2, 3; CA 125; CANR 42;
DAM MULT
Lee, Spike
See Lee, Shelton Jackson
See also AAYA 4, 29
Lee, Stan 1922- **CLC 17**
See also AAYA 5, 49; CA 108; 111; CANR
129; INT CA-111; MTFW 2005
Lee, Tanith 1947- **CLC 46**
See also AAYA 15; CA 37-40R; CANR 53,
102, 145; DLB 261; FANT; SATA 8, 88,
134; SFW 4; SUFW 1, 2; YAW
Lee, Vernon **SSC 33; TCLC 5**
See Paget, Violet
See also DLB 57, 153, 156, 174, 178; GLL
1; SUFW 1
Lee, William
See Burroughs, William S.
See also GLL 1
Lee, Willy
See Burroughs, William S.
See also GLL 1
Lee-Hamilton, Eugene (Jacob)
1845-1907 **TCLC 22**
See also CA 117; 234

Leet, Judith 1935- **CLC 11**
See also CA 187
Le Fanu, Joseph Sheridan
1814-1873 **NCLC 9, 58; SSC 14, 84**
See also CMW 4; DA3; DAM POP; DLB
21, 70, 159, 178; GL 3; HGG; RGEL 2;
RGSF 2; SUFW 1
Leffland, Ella 1931- **CLC 19**
See also CA 29-32R; CANR 35, 78, 82;
DLBY 1984; INT CANR-35; SATA 65
Leger, Alexis
See Leger, (Marie-Rene Auguste) Alexis
Saint-Leger
**Leger, (Marie-Rene Auguste) Alexis
Saint-Leger** 1887-1975 .. **CLC 4, 11, 46;
PC 23**
See Perse, Saint-John; Saint-John Perse
See also CA 13-16R; 61-64; CANR 43;
DAM POET; MTCW 1
Leger, Saintleger
See Leger, (Marie-Rene Auguste) Alexis
Saint-Leger
Le Guin, Ursula K(roeber) 1929- **CLC 8,
13, 22, 45, 71, 136; SSC 12, 69**
See also AAYA 9, 27; AITN 1; BPFB 2;
BYA 5, 8, 11, 14; CA 21-24R; CANR 9,
32, 52, 74, 132; CDALB 1968-1988; CLR
3, 28, 91; CN 2, 3, 4, 5, 6, 7; CPW; DA3;
DAB; DAC; DAM MST, POP; DLB 8,
52, 256, 275; EXPS; FANT; FW; INT
CANR-32; JRDA; LAIT 5; MAICYA 1,
2; MAL 5; MTCW 1, 2; MTFW 2005;
NFS 6, 9; SATA 4, 52, 99, 149; SCFW 1,
2; SFW 4; SSFS 2; SUFW 1, 2; WYA;
YAW
Lehmann, Rosamond (Nina)
1901-1990 **CLC 5**
See also CA 77-80; 131; CANR 8, 73; CN
1, 2, 3, 4; DLB 15; MTCW 2; RGEL 2;
RHW
Leiber, Fritz (Reuter, Jr.)
1910-1992 **CLC 25**
See also AAYA 65; BPFB 2; CA 45-48; 139;
CANR 2, 40, 86; CN 2, 3, 4, 5; DLB 8;
FANT; HGG; MTCW 1, 2; MTFW 2005;
SATA 45; SATA-Obit 73; SCFW 1, 2;
SFW 4; SUFW 1, 2
Leibniz, Gottfried Wilhelm von
1646-1716 **LC 35**
See also DLB 168
Leimbach, Martha 1963-
See Leimbach, Marti
See also CA 130
Leimbach, Marti **CLC 65**
See Leimbach, Martha
Leino, Eino **TCLC 24**
See Lonnbohm, Armas Eino Leopold
See also EWL 3
Leiris, Michel (Julien) 1901-1990 **CLC 61**
See also CA 119; 128; 132; EWL 3; GFL
1789 to the Present
Leithauser, Brad 1953- **CLC 27**
See also CA 107; CANR 27, 81; CP 5, 6, 7;
DLB 120, 282
le Jars de Gournay, Marie
See de Gournay, Marie le Jars
Lelchuk, Alan 1938- **CLC 5**
See also CA 45-48; CAAS 20; CANR 1,
70, 152; CN 3, 4, 5, 6, 7
Lem, Stanislaw 1921-2006 **CLC 8, 15, 40,
149**
See also CA 105; CAAS 1; CANR 32;
CWW 2; MTCW 1; SCFW 1, 2; SFW 4
Lemann, Nancy (Elise) 1956- **CLC 39**
See also CA 118; 136; CANR 121
Lemonnier, (Antoine Louis) Camille
1844-1913 **TCLC 22**
See also CA 121
Lenau, Nikolaus 1802-1850 **NCLC 16**

L'Engle, Madeleine (Camp Franklin)
1918- .. **CLC 12**
See also AAYA 28; AITN 2; BPFB 2; BYA
2, 4, 5, 7; CA 1-4R; CANR 3, 21, 39, 66,
107; CLR 1, 14, 57; CPW; CWRI 5; DA3;
DAM POP; DLB 52; JRDA; MAICYA 1,
2; MTCW 1, 2; MTFW 2005; SAAS 15;
SATA 1, 27, 75, 128; SFW 4; WYA; YAW
Lengyel, Jozsef 1896-1975 **CLC 7**
See also CA 85-88; 57-60; CANR 71;
RGSF 2
Lenin 1870-1924
See Lenin, V. I.
See also CA 121; 168
Lenin, V. I. **TCLC 67**
See Lenin
Lennon, John (Ono) 1940-1980 .. **CLC 12, 35**
See also CA 102; SATA 114
Lennox, Charlotte Ramsay
1729(?)-1804 **NCLC 23, 134**
See also DLB 39; RGEL 2
Lentricchia, Frank, Jr.
See Lentricchia, Frank
Lentricchia, Frank 1940- **CLC 34**
See also CA 25-28R; CANR 19, 106, 148;
DLB 246
Lenz, Gunter **CLC 65**
Lenz, Jakob Michael Reinhold
1751-1792 **LC 100**
See also DLB 94; RGWL 2, 3
Lenz, Siegfried 1926- **CLC 27; SSC 33**
See also CA 89-92; CANR 80, 149; CWW
2; DLB 75; EWL 3; RGSF 2; RGWL 2, 3
Leon, David
See Jacob, (Cyprien-)Max
Leonard, Elmore (John, Jr.) 1925- . **CLC 28,
34, 71, 120, 222**
See also AAYA 22, 59; AITN 1; BEST 89:1,
90:4; BPFB 2; CA 81-84; CANR 12, 28,
53, 76, 96, 133; CMW 4; CN 5, 6, 7;
CPW; DA3; DAM POP; DLB 173, 226;
INT CANR-28; MSW; MTCW 1, 2;
MTFW 2005; RGAL 4; SATA 163;
TCWW 1, 2
Leonard, Hugh **CLC 19**
See Byrne, John Keyes
See also CBD; CD 5, 6; DFS 13; DLB 13
Leonov, Leonid (Maximovich)
1899-1994 **CLC 92**
See Leonov, Leonid Maksimovich
See also CA 129; CANR 76; DAM NOV;
EWL 3; MTCW 1, 2; MTFW 2005
Leonov, Leonid Maksimovich
See Leonov, Leonid (Maximovich)
See also DLB 272
Leopardi, (Conte) Giacomo
1798-1837 **NCLC 22, 129; PC 37**
See also EW 5; RGWL 2, 3; WLIT 7; WP
Le Reveler
See Artaud, Antonin (Marie Joseph)
Lerman, Eleanor 1952- **CLC 9**
See also CA 85-88; CANR 69, 124
Lerman, Rhoda 1936- **CLC 56**
See also CA 49-52; CANR 70
Lermontov, Mikhail Iur'evich
See Lermontov, Mikhail Yuryevich
See also DLB 205
Lermontov, Mikhail Yuryevich
1814-1841 **NCLC 5, 47, 126; PC 18**
See Lermontov, Mikhail Iur'evich
See also EW 6; RGWL 2, 3; TWA
Leroux, Gaston 1868-1927 **TCLC 25**
See also CA 108; 136; CANR 69; CMW 4;
MTFW 2005; NFS 20; SATA 65
Lesage, Alain-Rene 1668-1747 **LC 2, 28**
See also DLB 313; EW 3; GFL Beginnings
to 1789; RGWL 2, 3
Leskov, N(ikolai) S(emenovich) 1831-1895
See Leskov, Nikolai (Semyonovich)

Leskov, Nikolai (Semyonovich)
 1831-1895 **NCLC 25; SSC 34**
 See also Leskov, Nikolai Semenovich
Leskov, Nikolai Semenovich
 See Leskov, Nikolai (Semyonovich)
 See also DLB 238
Lesser, Milton
 See Marlowe, Stephen
Lessing, Doris (May) 1919- ... **CLC 1, 2, 3, 6, 10, 15, 22, 40, 94, 170; SSC 6, 61; WLCS**
 See also AAYA 57; AFW; BRWS 1; CA 9-12R; CAAS 14; CANR 33, 54, 76, 122; CBD; CD 5, 6; CDBLB 1960 to Present; CN 1, 2, 3, 4, 5, 6, 7; CWD; DA; DA3; DAB; DAC; DAM MST, NOV; DFS 20; DLB 15, 139; DLBY 1985; EWL 3; EXPS; FL 1:6; FW; LAIT 4; MTCW 1, 2; MTFW 2005; RGEL 2; RGSF 2; SFW 4; SSFS 1, 12, 20; TEA; WLIT 2, 4
Lessing, Gotthold Ephraim
 1729-1781 **DC 26; LC 8, 124**
 See also CDWLB 2; DLB 97; EW 4; RGWL 2, 3
Lester, Richard 1932- **CLC 20**
Levenson, Jay ... **CLC 70**
Lever, Charles (James)
 1806-1872 **NCLC 23**
 See also DLB 21; RGEL 2
Leverson, Ada Esther
 1862(?)-1933(?) **TCLC 18**
 See Elaine
 See also CA 117; 202; DLB 153; RGEL 2
Levertov, Denise 1923-1997 .. **CLC 1, 2, 3, 5, 8, 15, 28, 66; PC 11**
 See also AMWS 3; CA 1-4R; 178; 163; CAAE 178; CAAS 19; CANR 3, 29, 50, 108; CDALBS; CP 1, 2, 3, 4, 5, 6; CWP; DAM POET; DLB 5, 165; EWL 3; EXPP; FW; INT CANR-29; MAL 5; MTCW 1, 2; PAB; PFS 7, 17; RGAL 4; RGHL; TUS; WP
Levi, Carlo 1902-1975 **TCLC 125**
 See also CA 65-68; 53-56; CANR 10; EWL 3; RGWL 2, 3
Levi, Jonathan **CLC 76**
 See also CA 197
Levi, Peter (Chad Tigar)
 1931-2000 **CLC 41**
 See also CA 5-8R; 187; CANR 34, 80; CP 1, 2, 3, 4, 5, 6, 7; DLB 40
Levi, Primo 1919-1987 **CLC 37, 50; SSC 12; TCLC 109**
 See also CA 13-16R; 122; CANR 12, 33, 61, 70, 132; DLB 177, 299; EWL 3; MTCW 1, 2; MTFW 2005; RGHL; RGWL 2, 3; WLIT 7
Levin, Ira 1929- **CLC 3, 6**
 See also CA 21-24R; CANR 17, 44, 74, 139; CMW 4; CN 1, 2, 3, 4, 5, 6, 7; CPW; DA3; DAM POP; HGG; MTCW 1, 2; MTFW 2005; SATA 66; SFW 4
Levin, Meyer 1905-1981 **CLC 7**
 See also AITN 1; CA 9-12R; 104; CANR 15; CN 1, 2, 3; DAM POP; DLB 9, 28; DLBY 1981; MAL 5; RGHL; SATA 21; SATA-Obit 27
Levine, Albert Norman 1923-2005
 See Levine, Norman
 See also CN 7
Levine, Norman 1923-2005 **CLC 54**
 See also CA 73-76; 240; CAAS 23; CANR 14, 70; CN 1, 2, 3, 4, 5, 6; CP 1; DLB 88
Levine, Norman Albert
 See Levine, Norman
Levine, Philip 1928- .. **CLC 2, 4, 5, 9, 14, 33, 118; PC 22**
 See also AMWS 5; CA 9-12R; CANR 9, 37, 52, 116; CP 1, 2, 3, 4, 5, 6, 7; DAM POET; DLB 5; EWL 3; MAL 5; PFS 8

Levinson, Deirdre 1931- **CLC 49**
 See also CA 73-76; CANR 70
Levi-Strauss, Claude 1908- **CLC 38**
 See also CA 1-4R; CANR 6, 32, 57; DLB 242; EWL 3; GFL 1789 to the Present; MTCW 1, 2; TWA
Levitin, Sonia (Wolff) 1934- **CLC 17**
 See also AAYA 13, 48; CA 29-32R; CANR 14, 32, 79; CLR 53; JRDA; MAICYA 1, 2; SAAS 2; SATA 4, 68, 119, 131; SATA-Essay 131; YAW
Levon, O. U.
 See Kesey, Ken (Elton)
Levy, Amy 1861-1889 **NCLC 59**
 See also DLB 156, 240
Lewes, George Henry 1817-1878 ... **NCLC 25**
 See also DLB 55, 144
Lewis, Alun 1915-1944 **SSC 40; TCLC 3**
 See also BRW 7; CA 104; 188; DLB 20, 162; PAB; RGEL 2
Lewis, C. Day
 See Day Lewis, C(ecil)
 See also CN 1
Lewis, Cecil Day
 See Day Lewis, C(ecil)
Lewis, Clive Staples
 See Lewis, C.S.
Lewis, C.S. 1898-1963 ... **CLC 1, 3, 6, 14, 27, 124; WLC 4**
 See also AAYA 3, 39; BPFB 2; BRWS 3; BYA 15, 16; CA 81-84; CANR 33, 71, 132; CDBLB 1945-1960; CLR 3, 27, 109; CWRI 5; DA; DA3; DAB; DAC; DAM MST, NOV, POP; DLB 15, 100, 160, 255; EWL 3; FANT; JRDA; LMFS 2; MAICYA 1, 2; MTCW 1, 2; MTFW 2005; RGEL 2; SATA 13, 100; SCFW 1, 2; SFW 4; SUFW 1; TEA; WCH; WYA; YAW
Lewis, Janet 1899-1998 **CLC 41**
 See Winters, Janet Lewis
 See also CA 9-12R; 172; CANR 29, 63; CAP 1; CN 1, 2, 3, 4, 5, 6; DLBY 1987; RHW; TCWW 2
Lewis, Matthew Gregory
 1775-1818 **NCLC 11, 62**
 See also DLB 39, 158, 178; GL 3; HGG; LMFS 1; RGEL 2; SUFW
Lewis, (Harry) Sinclair 1885-1951 . **TCLC 4, 13, 23, 39; WLC 4**
 See also AMW; AMWC 1; BPFB 2; CA 104; 133; CANR 132; CDALB 1917-1929; DA; DA3; DAB; DAC; DAM MST, NOV; DLB 9, 102, 284; DLBD 1; EWL 3; LAIT 3; MAL 5; MTCW 1, 2; MTFW 2005; NFS 15, 19, 22; RGAL 4; TUS
Lewis, (Percy) Wyndham
 1884(?)-1957 .. **SSC 34; TCLC 2, 9, 104**
 See also BRW 7; CA 104; 157; DLB 15; EWL 3; FANT; MTCW 2; MTFW 2005; RGEL 2
Lewisohn, Ludwig 1883-1955 **TCLC 19**
 See also CA 107; 203; DLB 4, 9, 28, 102; MAL 5
Lewton, Val 1904-1951 **TCLC 76**
 See also CA 199; IDFW 3, 4
Leyner, Mark 1956- **CLC 92**
 See also CA 110; CANR 28, 53; DA3; DLB 292; MTCW 2; MTFW 2005
Lezama Lima, Jose 1910-1976 **CLC 4, 10, 101; HLCS 2**
 See also CA 77-80; CANR 71; DAM MULT; DLB 113, 283; EWL 3; HW 1, 2; LAW; RGWL 2, 3
L'Heureux, John (Clarke) 1934- **CLC 52**
 See also CA 13-16R; CANR 23, 45, 88; CP 1, 2, 3, 4; DLB 244
Li Ch'ing-chao 1081(?)-1141(?) **CMLC 71**
Liddell, C. H.
 See Kuttner, Henry

Lie, Jonas (Lauritz Idemil)
 1833-1908(?) **TCLC 5**
 See also CA 115
Lieber, Joel 1937-1971 **CLC 6**
 See also CA 73-76; 29-32R
Lieber, Stanley Martin
 See Lee, Stan
Lieberman, Laurence (James)
 1935- **CLC 4, 36**
 See also CA 17-20R; CANR 8, 36, 89; CP 1, 2, 3, 4, 5, 6, 7
Lieh Tzu fl. 7th cent. B.C.-5th cent.
 B.C. **CMLC 27**
Lieksman, Anders
 See Haavikko, Paavo Juhani
Lifton, Robert Jay 1926- **CLC 67**
 See also CA 17-20R; CANR 27, 78; INT CANR-27; SATA 66
Lightfoot, Gordon 1938- **CLC 26**
 See also CA 109; 242
Lightfoot, Gordon Meredith
 See Lightfoot, Gordon
Lightman, Alan P(aige) 1948- **CLC 81**
 See also CA 141; CANR 63, 105, 138; MTFW 2005
Ligotti, Thomas (Robert) 1953- **CLC 44; SSC 16**
 See also CA 123; CANR 49, 135; HGG; SUFW 2
Li Ho 791-817 **PC 13**
Li Ju-chen c. 1763-c. 1830 **NCLC 137**
Lilar, Francoise
 See Mallet-Joris, Francoise
Liliencron, (Friedrich Adolf Axel) Detlev von 1844-1909 **TCLC 18**
 See also CA 117
Lille, Alain de
 See Alain de Lille
Lilly, William 1602-1681 **LC 27**
Lima, Jose Lezama
 See Lezama Lima, Jose
Lima Barreto, Afonso Henrique de
 1881-1922 **TCLC 23**
 See Lima Barreto, Afonso Henriques de
 See also CA 117; 181; LAW
Lima Barreto, Afonso Henriques de
 See Lima Barreto, Afonso Henrique de
 See also DLB 307
Limonov, Eduard
 See Limonov, Edward
 See also DLB 317
Limonov, Edward 1944- **CLC 67**
 See Limonov, Eduard
 See also CA 137
Lin, Frank
 See Atherton, Gertrude (Franklin Horn)
Lin, Yutang 1895-1976 **TCLC 149**
 See also CA 45-48; 65-68; CANR 2; RGAL 4
Lincoln, Abraham 1809-1865 **NCLC 18**
 See also LAIT 2
Lind, Jakov **CLC 1, 2, 4, 27, 82**
 See Landwirth, Heinz
 See also CAAS 4; DLB 299; EWL 3; RGHL
Lindbergh, Anne (Spencer) Morrow
 1906-2001 **CLC 82**
 See also BPFB 2; CA 17-20R; 193; CANR 16, 73; DAM NOV; MTCW 1, 2; MTFW 2005; SATA 33; SATA-Obit 125; TUS
Lindsay, David 1878(?)-1945 **TCLC 15**
 See also CA 113; 187; DLB 255; FANT; SFW 4; SUFW 1
Lindsay, (Nicholas) Vachel
 1879-1931 **PC 23; TCLC 17; WLC 4**
 See also AMWS 1; CA 114; 135; CANR 79; CDALB 1865-1917; DA; DA3; DAC; DAM MST, POET; DLB 54; EWL 3; EXPP; MAL 5; RGAL 4; SATA 40; WP

Linke-Poot
See Doeblin, Alfred
Linney, Romulus 1930- **CLC 51**
See also CA 1-4R; CAD; CANR 40, 44, 79; CD 5, 6; CSW; RGAL 4
Linton, Eliza Lynn 1822-1898 **NCLC 41**
See also DLB 18
Li Po 701-763 **CMLC 2; PC 29**
See also PFS 20; WP
Lipsius, Justus 1547-1606 **LC 16**
Lipsyte, Robert 1938- **CLC 21**
See also AAYA 7, 45; CA 17-20R; CANR 8, 57, 146; CLR 23, 76; DA; DAC; DAM MST, NOV; JRDA; LAIT 5; MAICYA 1, 2; SATA 5, 68, 113, 161; WYA; YAW
Lipsyte, Robert Michael
See Lipsyte, Robert
Lish, Gordon 1934- **CLC 45; SSC 18**
See also CA 113; 117; CANR 79, 151; DLB 130; INT CA-117
Lish, Gordon Jay
See Lish, Gordon
Lispector, Clarice 1925(?)-1977 **CLC 43; HLCS 2; SSC 34**
See also CA 139; 116; CANR 71; CDWLB 3; DLB 113, 307; DNFS 1; EWL 3; FW; HW 2; LAW; RGSF 2; RGWL 2, 3; WLIT 1
Littell, Robert 1935(?)- **CLC 42**
See also CA 109; 112; CANR 64, 115; CMW 4
Little, Malcolm 1925-1965
See Malcolm X
See also BW 1, 3; CA 125; 111; CANR 82; DA; DA3; DAB; DAC; DAM MST, MULT; MTCW 1, 2; MTFW 2005
Littlewit, Humphrey Gent.
See Lovecraft, H. P.
Litwos
See Sienkiewicz, Henryk (Adam Alexander Pius)
Liu, E. 1857-1909 **TCLC 15**
See also CA 115; 190
Lively, Penelope 1933- **CLC 32, 50**
See also BPFB 2; CA 41-44R; CANR 29, 67, 79, 131; CLR 7; CN 5, 6, 7; CWRI 5; DAM NOV; DLB 14, 161, 207, 326; FANT; JRDA; MAICYA 1, 2; MTCW 1, 2; MTFW 2005; SATA 7, 60, 101, 164; TEA
Lively, Penelope Margaret
See Lively, Penelope
Livesay, Dorothy (Kathleen)
1909-1996 **CLC 4, 15, 79**
See also AITN 2; CA 25-28R; CAAS 8; CANR 36, 67; CP 1, 2, 3, 4, 5; DAC; DAM MST, POET; DLB 68; FW; MTCW 1; RGEL 2; TWA
Livy c. 59B.C.-c. 12 **CMLC 11**
See also AW 2; CDWLB 1; DLB 211; RGWL 2, 3; WLIT 8
Lizardi, Jose Joaquin Fernandez de
1776-1827 **NCLC 30**
See also LAW
Llewellyn, Richard
See Llewellyn Lloyd, Richard Dafydd Vivian
See also DLB 15
Llewellyn Lloyd, Richard Dafydd Vivian
1906-1983 **CLC 7, 80**
See Llewellyn, Richard
See also CA 53-56; 111; CANR 7, 71; SATA 11; SATA-Obit 37
Llosa, Jorge Mario Pedro Vargas
See Vargas Llosa, Mario
See also RGWL 3
Llosa, Mario Vargas
See Vargas Llosa, Mario

Lloyd, Manda
See Mander, (Mary) Jane
Lloyd Webber, Andrew 1948-
See Webber, Andrew Lloyd
See also AAYA 1, 38; CA 116; 149; DAM DRAM; SATA 56
Llull, Ramon c. 1235-c. 1316 **CMLC 12**
Lobb, Ebenezer
See Upward, Allen
Locke, Alain (Le Roy)
1886-1954 **BLCS; HR 1:3; TCLC 43**
See also AMWS 14; BW 1, 3; CA 106; 124; CANR 79; DLB 51; LMFS 2; MAL 5; RGAL 4
Locke, John 1632-1704 **LC 7, 35**
See also DLB 31, 101, 213, 252; RGEL 2; WLIT 3
Locke-Elliott, Sumner
See Elliott, Sumner Locke
Lockhart, John Gibson 1794-1854 .. **NCLC 6**
See also DLB 110, 116, 144
Lockridge, Ross (Franklin), Jr.
1914-1948 **TCLC 111**
See also CA 108; 145; CANR 79; DLB 143; DLBY 1980; MAL 5; RGAL 4; RHW
Lockwood, Robert
See Johnson, Robert
Lodge, David (John) 1935- **CLC 36, 141**
See also BEST 90:1; BRWS 4; CA 17-20R; CANR 19, 53, 92, 139; CN 1, 2, 3, 4, 5, 6, 7; CPW; DAM POP; DLB 14, 194; EWL 3; INT CANR-19; MTCW 1, 2; MTFW 2005
Lodge, Thomas 1558-1625 **LC 41**
See also DLB 172; RGEL 2
Loewinsohn, Ron(ald William)
1937- .. **CLC 52**
See also CA 25-28R; CANR 71; CP 1, 2, 3, 4
Logan, Jake
See Smith, Martin Cruz
Logan, John (Burton) 1923-1987 **CLC 5**
See also CA 77-80; 124; CANR 45; CP 1, 2, 3, 4; DLB 5
Lo Kuan-chung 1330(?)-1400(?) **LC 12**
Lombard, Nap
See Johnson, Pamela Hansford
Lombard, Peter 1100(?)-1160(?) ... **CMLC 72**
Lombino, Salvatore
See Hunter, Evan
London, Jack 1876-1916 .. **SSC 4, 49; TCLC 9, 15, 39; WLC 4**
See London, John Griffith
See also AAYA 13; AITN 2; AMW; BPFB 2; BYA 4, 13; CDALB 1865-1917; CLR 108; DLB 8, 12, 78, 212; EWL 3; EXPS; LAIT 3; MAL 5; NFS 8; RGAL 4; RGSF 2; SATA 18; SFW 4; SSFS 7; TCWW 1, 2; TUS; WYA; YAW
London, John Griffith 1876-1916
See London, Jack
See also CA 110; 119; CANR 73; DA; DA3; DAB; DAC; DAM MST, NOV; JRDA; MAICYA 1, 2; MTCW 1, 2; MTFW 2005; NFS 19
Long, Emmett
See Leonard, Elmore (John, Jr.)
Longbaugh, Harry
See Goldman, William
Longfellow, Henry Wadsworth
1807-1882 **NCLC 2, 45, 101, 103; PC 30; WLCS**
See also AMW; AMWR 2; CDALB 1640-1865; CLR 99; DA; DA3; DAB; DAC; DAM MST, POET; DLB 1, 59, 235; EXPP; PAB; PFS 2, 7, 17; RGAL 4; SATA 19; TUS; WP
Longinus c. 1st cent. - **CMLC 27**
See also AW 2; DLB 176

Longley, Michael 1939- **CLC 29**
See also BRWS 8; CA 102; CP 1, 2, 3, 4, 5, 6, 7; DLB 40
Longstreet, Augustus Baldwin
1790-1870 **NCLC 159**
See also DLB 3, 11, 74, 248; RGAL 4
Longus fl. c. 2nd cent. - **CMLC 7**
Longway, A. Hugh
See Lang, Andrew
Lonnbohm, Armas Eino Leopold 1878-1926
See Leino, Eino
See also CA 123
Lonnrot, Elias 1802-1884 **NCLC 53**
See also EFS 1
Lonsdale, Roger ed. **CLC 65**
Lopate, Phillip 1943- **CLC 29**
See also CA 97-100; CANR 88; DLBY 1980; INT CA-97-100
Lopez, Barry (Holstun) 1945- **CLC 70**
See also AAYA 9, 63; ANW; CA 65-68; CANR 7, 23, 47, 68, 92; DLB 256, 275; INT CANR-7, -23; MTCW 1; RGAL 4; SATA 67
Lopez de Mendoza, Inigo
See Santillana, Inigo Lopez de Mendoza, Marques de
Lopez Portillo (y Pacheco), Jose
1920-2004 **CLC 46**
See also CA 129; 224; HW 1
Lopez y Fuentes, Gregorio
1897(?)-1966 **CLC 32**
See also CA 131; EWL 3; HW 1
Lorca, Federico Garcia
See Garcia Lorca, Federico
See also DFS 4; EW 11; PFS 20; RGWL 2, 3; WP
Lord, Audre
See Lorde, Audre (Geraldine)
See also EWL 3
Lord, Bette Bao 1938- **AAL; CLC 23**
See also BEST 90:3; BPFB 2; CA 107; CANR 41, 79; INT CA-107; SATA 58
Lord Auch
See Bataille, Georges
Lord Brooke
See Greville, Fulke
Lord Byron
See Byron, George Gordon (Noel)
Lorde, Audre (Geraldine)
1934-1992 **BLC 2; CLC 18, 71; PC 12; TCLC 173**
See Domini, Rey; Lord, Audre
See also AFAW 1, 2; BW 1, 3; CA 25-28R; 142; CANR 16, 26, 46, 82; CP 2, 3, 4, 5; DA3; DAM MULT, POET; DLB 41; FW; MAL 5; MTCW 1, 2; MTFW 2005; PFS 16; RGAL 4
Lord Houghton
See Milnes, Richard Monckton
Lord Jeffrey
See Jeffrey, Francis
Loreaux, Nichol **CLC 65**
Lorenzini, Carlo 1826-1890
See Collodi, Carlo
See also MAICYA 1, 2; SATA 29, 100
Lorenzo, Heberto Padilla
See Padilla (Lorenzo), Heberto
Loris
See Hofmannsthal, Hugo von
Loti, Pierre **TCLC 11**
See Viaud, (Louis Marie) Julien
See also DLB 123; GFL 1789 to the Present
Lou, Henri
See Andreas-Salome, Lou
Louie, David Wong 1954- **CLC 70**
See also CA 139; CANR 120
Louis, Adrian C. **NNAL**
See also CA 223

Louis, Father M.
 See Merton, Thomas (James)
Louise, Heidi
 See Erdrich, Louise
Lovecraft, H. P. 1890-1937 **SSC 3, 52; TCLC 4, 22**
 See also AAYA 14; BPFB 2; CA 104; 133; CANR 106; DA3; DAM POP; HGG; MTCW 1, 2; MTFW 2005; RGAL 4; SCFW 1, 2; SFW 4; SUFW
Lovecraft, Howard Phillips
 See Lovecraft, H. P.
Lovelace, Earl 1935- **CLC 51**
 See also BW 2; CA 77-80; CANR 41, 72, 114; CD 5, 6; CDWLB 3; CN 1, 2, 3, 4, 5, 6, 7; DLB 125; EWL 3; MTCW 1
Lovelace, Richard 1618-1657 . **LC 24; PC 69**
 See also BRW 2; DLB 131; EXPP; PAB; RGEL 2
Lowe, Pardee 1904- **AAL**
Lowell, Amy 1874-1925 ... **PC 13; TCLC 1, 8**
 See also AAYA 57; AMW; CA 104; 151; DAM POET; DLB 54, 140; EWL 3; EXPP; LMFS 2; MAL 5; MAWW; MTCW 2; MTFW 2005; RGAL 4; TUS
Lowell, James Russell 1819-1891 ... **NCLC 2, 90**
 See also AMWS 1; CDALB 1640-1865; DLB 1, 11, 64, 79, 189, 235; RGAL 4
Lowell, Robert (Traill Spence, Jr.) 1917-1977 **CLC 1, 2, 3, 4, 5, 8, 9, 11, 15, 37, 124; PC 3; WLC 4**
 See also AMW; AMWC 2; AMWR 2; CA 9-12R; 73-76; CABS 2; CAD; CANR 26, 60; CDALBS; CP 1, 2; DA; DA3; DAB; DAC; DAM MST, NOV; DLB 5, 169; EWL 3; MAL 5; MTCW 1, 2; MTFW 2005; PAB; PFS 6, 7; RGAL 4; WP
Lowenthal, Michael (Francis) 1969- **CLC 119**
 See also CA 150; CANR 115
Lowndes, Marie Adelaide (Belloc) 1868-1947 **TCLC 12**
 See also CA 107; CMW 4; DLB 70; RHW
Lowry, (Clarence) Malcolm 1909-1957 **SSC 31; TCLC 6, 40**
 See also BPFB 2; BRWS 3; CA 105; 131; CANR 62, 105; CDBLB 1945-1960; DLB 15; EWL 3; MTCW 1, 2; MTFW 2005; RGAL 2
Lowry, Mina Gertrude 1882-1966
 See Loy, Mina
 See also CA 113
Lowry, Sam
 See Soderbergh, Steven
Loxsmith, John
 See Brunner, John (Kilian Houston)
Loy, Mina **CLC 28; PC 16**
 See Lowry, Mina Gertrude
 See also DAM POET; DLB 4, 54; PFS 20
Loyson-Bridet
 See Schwob, Marcel (Mayer Andre)
Lucan 39-65 **CMLC 33**
 See also AW 2; DLB 211; EFS 2; RGWL 2, 3
Lucas, Craig 1951- **CLC 64**
 See also CA 137; CAD; CANR 71, 109, 142; CD 5, 6; GLL 2; MTFW 2005
Lucas, E(dward) V(errall) 1868-1938 **TCLC 73**
 See also CA 176; DLB 98, 149, 153; SATA 20
Lucas, George 1944- **CLC 16**
 See also AAYA 1, 23; CA 77-80; CANR 30; SATA 56
Lucas, Hans
 See Godard, Jean-Luc
Lucas, Victoria
 See Plath, Sylvia

Lucian c. 125-c. 180 **CMLC 32**
 See also AW 2; DLB 176; RGWL 2, 3
Lucilius c. 180B.C.-102B.C. **CMLC 82**
 See also DLB 211
Lucretius c. 94B.C.-c. 49B.C. **CMLC 48**
 See also AW 2; CDWLB 1; DLB 211; EFS 2; RGWL 2, 3; WLIT 8
Ludlam, Charles 1943-1987 **CLC 46, 50**
 See also CA 85-88; 122; CAD; CANR 72, 86; DLB 266
Ludlum, Robert 1927-2001 **CLC 22, 43**
 See also AAYA 10, 59; BEST 89:1, 90:3; BPFB 2; CA 33-36R; 195; CANR 25, 41, 68, 105, 131; CMW 4; CPW; DA3; DAM NOV, POP; DLBY 1982; MSW; MTCW 1, 2; MTFW 2005
Ludwig, Ken 1950- **CLC 60**
 See also CA 195; CAD; CD 6
Ludwig, Otto 1813-1865 **NCLC 4**
 See also DLB 129
Lugones, Leopoldo 1874-1938 **HLCS 2; TCLC 15**
 See also CA 116; 131; CANR 104; DLB 283; EWL 3; HW 1; LAW
Lu Hsun **SSC 20; TCLC 3**
 See Shu-Jen, Chou
 See also EWL 3
Lukacs, George **CLC 24**
 See Lukacs, Gyorgy (Szegeny von)
Lukacs, Gyorgy (Szegeny von) 1885-1971
 See Lukacs, George
 See also CA 101; 29-32R; CANR 62; CDWLB 4; DLB 215, 242; EW 10; EWL 3; MTCW 1, 2
Luke, Peter (Ambrose Cyprian) 1919-1995 **CLC 38**
 See also CA 81-84; 147; CANR 72; CBD; CD 5, 6; DLB 13
Lunar, Dennis
 See Mungo, Raymond
Lurie, Alison 1926- **CLC 4, 5, 18, 39, 175**
 See also BPFB 2; CA 1-4R; CANR 2, 17, 50, 88; CN 1, 2, 3, 4, 5, 6, 7; DLB 2; MAL 5; MTCW 1; SATA 46, 112; TCLE 1:1
Lustig, Arnost 1926- **CLC 56**
 See also AAYA 3; CA 69-72; CANR 47, 102; CWW 2; DLB 232, 299; EWL 3; RGHL; SATA 56
Luther, Martin 1483-1546 **LC 9, 37**
 See also CDWLB 2; DLB 179; EW 2; RGWL 2, 3
Luxemburg, Rosa 1870(?)-1919 **TCLC 63**
 See also CA 118
Luzi, Mario (Egidio Vincenzo) 1914-2005 **CLC 13**
 See also CA 61-64; 236; CANR 9, 70; CWW 2; DLB 128; EWL 3
L'vov, Arkady **CLC 59**
Lydgate, John c. 1370-1450(?) **LC 81**
 See also BRW 1; DLB 146; RGEL 2
Lyly, John 1554(?)-1606 **DC 7; LC 41**
 See also BRW 1; DAM DRAM; DLB 62, 167; RGEL 2
L'Ymagier
 See Gourmont, Remy(-Marie-Charles) de
Lynch, B. Suarez
 See Borges, Jorge Luis
Lynch, David (Keith) 1946- **CLC 66, 162**
 See also AAYA 55; CA 124; 129; CANR 111
Lynch, James
 See Andreyev, Leonid (Nikolaevich)
Lyndsay, Sir David 1485-1555 **LC 20**
 See also RGEL 2
Lynn, Kenneth S(chuyler) 1923-2001 **CLC 50**
 See also CA 1-4R; 196; CANR 3, 27, 65

Lynx
 See West, Rebecca
Lyons, Marcus
 See Blish, James (Benjamin)
Lyotard, Jean-Francois 1924-1998 **TCLC 103**
 See also DLB 242; EWL 3
Lyre, Pinchbeck
 See Sassoon, Siegfried (Lorraine)
Lytle, Andrew (Nelson) 1902-1995 ... **CLC 22**
 See also CA 9-12R; 150; CANR 70; CN 1, 2, 3, 4, 5, 6; CSW; DLB 6; DLBY 1995; RGAL 4; RHW
Lyttelton, George 1709-1773 **LC 10**
 See also RGEL 2
Lytton of Knebworth, Baron
 See Bulwer-Lytton, Edward (George Earle Lytton)
Maas, Peter 1929-2001 **CLC 29**
 See also CA 93-96; 201; INT CA-93-96; MTCW 2; MTFW 2005
Mac A'Ghobhainn, Iain
 See Smith, Iain Crichton
Macaulay, Catherine 1731-1791 **LC 64**
 See also DLB 104
Macaulay, (Emilie) Rose 1881(?)-1958 **TCLC 7, 44**
 See also CA 104; DLB 36; EWL 3; RGEL 2; RHW
Macaulay, Thomas Babington 1800-1859 **NCLC 42**
 See also BRW 4; CDBLB 1832-1890; DLB 32, 55; RGEL 2
MacBeth, George (Mann) 1932-1992 **CLC 2, 5, 9**
 See also CA 25-28R; 136; CANR 61, 66; CP 1, 2, 3, 4, 5; DLB 40; MTCW 1; PFS 8; SATA 4; SATA-Obit 70
MacCaig, Norman (Alexander) 1910-1996 **CLC 36**
 See also BRWS 6; CA 9-12R; CANR 3, 34; CP 1, 2, 3, 4, 5, 6; DAB; DAM POET; DLB 27; EWL 3; RGEL 2
MacCarthy, Sir (Charles Otto) Desmond 1877-1952 **TCLC 36**
 See also CA 167
MacDiarmid, Hugh **CLC 2, 4, 11, 19, 63; PC 9**
 See Grieve, C(hristopher) M(urray)
 See also CDBLB 1945-1960; CP 1, 2; DLB 20; EWL 3; RGEL 2
MacDonald, Anson
 See Heinlein, Robert A(nson)
Macdonald, Cynthia 1928- **CLC 13, 19**
 See also CA 49-52; CANR 4, 44, 146; DLB 105
MacDonald, George 1824-1905 **TCLC 9, 113**
 See also AAYA 57; BYA 5; CA 106; 137; CANR 80; CLR 67; DLB 18, 163, 178; FANT; MAICYA 1, 2; RGEL 2; SATA 33, 100; SFW 4; SUFW; WCH
Macdonald, John
 See Millar, Kenneth
MacDonald, John D(ann) 1916-1986 **CLC 3, 27, 44**
 See also BPFB 2; CA 1-4R; 121; CANR 1, 19, 60; CMW 4; CPW; DAM NOV, POP; DLB 8, 306; DLBY 1986; MSW; MTCW 1, 2; MTFW 2005; SFW 4
Macdonald, John Ross
 See Millar, Kenneth
Macdonald, Ross **CLC 1, 2, 3, 14, 34, 41**
 See Millar, Kenneth
 See also AMWS 4; BPFB 2; CN 1, 2, 3; DLBD 6; MAL 5; MSW; RGAL 4
MacDougal, John
 See Blish, James (Benjamin)

MacDougal, John
See Blish, James (Benjamin)
MacDowell, John
See Parks, Tim(othy Harold)
MacEwen, Gwendolyn (Margaret)
1941-1987 **CLC 13, 55**
See also CA 9-12R; 124; CANR 7, 22; CP
1, 2, 3, 4; DLB 53, 251; SATA 50; SATA-
Obit 55
Macha, Karel Hynek 1810-1846 **NCLC 46**
Machado (y Ruiz), Antonio
1875-1939 **TCLC 3**
See also CA 104; 174; DLB 108; EW 9;
EWL 3; HW 2; PFS 23; RGWL 2, 3
Machado de Assis, Joaquim Maria
1839-1908 **BLC 2; HLCS 2; SSC 24;
TCLC 10**
See also CA 107; 153; CANR 91; DLB 307;
LAW; RGSF 2; RGWL 2, 3; TWA; WLIT
1
Machaut, Guillaume de c.
1300-1377 **CMLC 64**
See also DLB 208
Machen, Arthur **SSC 20; TCLC 4**
See Jones, Arthur Llewellyn
See also CA 179; DLB 156, 178; RGEL 2;
SUFW 1
Machiavelli, Niccolo 1469-1527 ... **DC 16; LC
8, 36; WLCS**
See also AAYA 58; DA; DAB; DAC; DAM
MST; EW 2; LAIT 1; LMFS 1; NFS 9;
RGWL 2, 3; TWA; WLIT 7
MacInnes, Colin 1914-1976 **CLC 4, 23**
See also CA 69-72; 65-68; CANR 21; CN
1, 2; DLB 14; MTCW 1, 2; RGEL 2;
RHW
MacInnes, Helen (Clark)
1907-1985 **CLC 27, 39**
See also BPFB 2; CA 1-4R; 117; CANR 1,
28, 58; CMW 4; CN 1, 2; CPW; DAM
POP; DLB 87; MSW; MTCW 1, 2;
MTFW 2005; SATA 22; SATA-Obit 44
Mackay, Mary 1855-1924
See Corelli, Marie
See also CA 118; 177; FANT; RHW
Mackay, Shena 1944- **CLC 195**
See also CA 104; CANR 88, 139; DLB 231,
319; MTFW 2005
Mackenzie, Compton (Edward Montague)
1883-1972 **CLC 18; TCLC 116**
See also CA 21-22; 37-40R; CAP 2; CN 1;
DLB 34, 100; RGEL 2
Mackenzie, Henry 1745-1831 **NCLC 41**
See also DLB 39; RGEL 2
Mackey, Nathaniel (Ernest) 1947- **PC 49**
See also CA 153; CANR 114; CP 6, 7; DLB
169
MacKinnon, Catharine A. 1946- **CLC 181**
See also CA 128; 132; CANR 73, 140; FW;
MTCW 2; MTFW 2005
Mackintosh, Elizabeth 1896(?)-1952
See Tey, Josephine
See also CA 110; CMW 4
MacLaren, James
See Grieve, C(hristopher) M(urray)
MacLaverty, Bernard 1942- **CLC 31**
See also CA 116; 118; CANR 43, 88; CN
5, 6, 7; DLB 267; INT CA-118; RGSF 2
MacLean, Alistair (Stuart)
1922(?)-1987 **CLC 3, 13, 50, 63**
See also CA 57-60; 121; CANR 28, 61;
CMW 4; CP 2, 3, 4, 5, 6, 7; CPW; DAM
POP; DLB 276; MTCW 1; SATA 23;
SATA-Obit 50; TCWW 2
Maclean, Norman (Fitzroy)
1902-1990 **CLC 78; SSC 13**
See also AMWS 14; CA 102; 132; CANR
49; CPW; DAM POP; DLB 206;
TCWW 2

MacLeish, Archibald 1892-1982 ... **CLC 3, 8,
14, 68; PC 47**
See also AMW; CA 9-12R; 106; CAD;
CANR 33, 63; CDALBS; CP 1, 2; DAM
POET; DFS 15; DLB 4, 7, 45; DLBY
1982; EWL 3; EXPP; MAL 5; MTCW 1,
2; MTFW 2005; PAB; PFS 5; RGAL 4;
TUS
MacLennan, (John) Hugh
1907-1990 **CLC 2, 14, 92**
See also CA 5-8R; 142; CANR 33; CN 1,
2, 3, 4; DAC; DAM MST; DLB 68; EWL
3; MTCW 1, 2; MTFW 2005; RGEL 2;
TWA
MacLeod, Alistair 1936- .. **CLC 56, 165; SSC
90**
See also CA 123; CCA 1; DAC; DAM
MST; DLB 60; MTCW 2; MTFW 2005;
RGSF 2; TCLE 1:2
Macleod, Fiona
See Sharp, William
See also RGEL 2; SUFW
MacNeice, (Frederick) Louis
1907-1963 **CLC 1, 4, 10, 53; PC 61**
See also BRW 7; CA 85-88; CANR 61;
DAB; DAM POET; DLB 10, 20; EWL 3;
MTCW 1, 2; MTFW 2005; RGEL 2
MacNeill, Dand
See Fraser, George MacDonald
Macpherson, James 1736-1796 **LC 29**
See Ossian
See also BRWS 8; DLB 109; RGEL 2
Macpherson, (Jean) Jay 1931- **CLC 14**
See also CA 5-8R; CANR 90; CP 1, 2, 3, 4,
6, 7; CWP; DLB 53
Macrobius fl. 430- **CMLC 48**
MacShane, Frank 1927-1999 **CLC 39**
See also CA 9-12R; 186; CANR 3, 33; DLB
111
Macumber, Mari
See Sandoz, Mari(e Susette)
Madach, Imre 1823-1864 **NCLC 19**
Madden, (Jerry) David 1933- **CLC 5, 15**
See also CA 1-4R; CAAS 3; CANR 4, 45;
CN 3, 4, 5, 6, 7; CSW; DLB 6; MTCW 1
Maddern, Al(an)
See Ellison, Harlan (Jay)
Madhubuti, Haki R. 1942- ... **BLC 2; CLC 6,
73; PC 5**
See Lee, Don L.
See also BW 2, 3; CA 73-76; CANR 24,
51, 73, 139; CP 6, 7; CSW; DAM MULT,
POET; DLB 5, 41; DLBD 8; EWL 3;
MAL 5; MTCW 2; MTFW 2005; RGAL
4
Madison, James 1751-1836 **NCLC 126**
See also DLB 37
Maepenn, Hugh
See Kuttner, Henry
Maepenn, K. H.
See Kuttner, Henry
Maeterlinck, Maurice 1862-1949 **TCLC 3**
See also CA 104; 136; CANR 80; DAM
DRAM; DLB 192; EW 8; EWL 3; GFL
1789 to the Present; LMFS 2; RGWL 2,
3; SATA 66; TWA
Maginn, William 1794-1842 **NCLC 8**
See also DLB 110, 159
Mahapatra, Jayanta 1928- **CLC 33**
See also CA 73-76; CAAS 9; CANR 15,
33, 66, 87; CP 4, 5, 6, 7; DAM MULT;
DLB 323
Mahfouz, Naguib (Abdel Aziz Al-Sabilgi)
1911(?)- **CLC 153; SSC 66**
See Mahfuz, Najib (Abdel Aziz al-Sabilgi)
See also AAYA 49; BEST 89:2; CA 128;
CANR 55, 101; DA3; DAM NOV;
MTCW 1, 2; MTFW 2005; RGWL 2, 3;
SSFS 9

Mahfuz, Najib (Abdel Aziz al-Sabilgi)
.. **CLC 52, 55**
See Mahfouz, Naguib (Abdel Aziz Al-
Sabilgi)
See also AFW; CWW 2; DLBY 1988; EWL
3; RGSF 2; WLIT 6
Mahon, Derek 1941- **CLC 27; PC 60**
See also BRWS 6; CA 113; 128; CANR 88;
CP 1, 2, 3, 4, 5, 6, 7; DLB 40; EWL 3
Maiakovskii, Vladimir
See Mayakovski, Vladimir (Vladimirovich)
See also IDTP; RGWL 2, 3
Mailer, Norman 1923- ... **CLC 1, 2, 3, 4, 5, 8,
11, 14, 28, 39, 74, 111**
See also AAYA 31; AITN 2; AMW; AMWC
2; AMWR 2; BPFB 2; CA 9-12R; CABS
1; CANR 28, 74, 77, 130; CDALB 1968-
1988; CN 1, 2, 3, 4, 5, 6, 7; CPW; DA;
DA3; DAB; DAC; DAM MST, NOV,
POP; DLB 2, 16, 28, 185, 278; DLBD 3;
DLBY 1980, 1983; EWL 3; MAL 5;
MTCW 1, 2; MTFW 2005; NFS 10;
RGAL 4; TUS
Mailer, Norman Kingsley
See Mailer, Norman
Maillet, Antonine 1929- **CLC 54, 118**
See also CA 115; 120; CANR 46, 74, 77,
134; CCA 1; CWW 2; DAC; DLB 60;
INT CA-120; MTCW 2; MTFW 2005
Maimonides, Moses 1135-1204 **CMLC 76**
See also DLB 115
Mais, Roger 1905-1955 **TCLC 8**
See also BW 1, 3; CA 105; 124; CANR 82;
CDWLB 3; DLB 125; EWL 3; MTCW 1;
RGEL 2
Maistre, Joseph 1753-1821 **NCLC 37**
See also GFL 1789 to the Present
Maitland, Frederic William
1850-1906 **TCLC 65**
Maitland, Sara (Louise) 1950- **CLC 49**
See also BRWS 11; CA 69-72; CANR 13,
59; DLB 271; FW
Major, Clarence 1936- **BLC 2; CLC 3, 19,
48**
See also AFAW 2; BW 2, 3; CA 21-24R;
CAAS 6; CANR 13, 25, 53, 82; CN 3, 4,
5, 6, 7; CP 2, 3, 4, 5, 6, 7; CSW; DAM
MULT; DLB 33; EWL 3; MAL 5; MSW
Major, Kevin (Gerald) 1949- **CLC 26**
See also AAYA 16; CA 97-100; CANR 21,
38, 112; CLR 11; DAC; DLB 60; INT
CANR-21; JRDA; MAICYA 1, 2; MAIC-
YAS 1; SATA 32, 82, 134; WYA; YAW
Maki, James
See Ozu, Yasujiro
Makine, Andrei 1957- **CLC 198**
See also CA 176; CANR 103; MTFW 2005
Malabaila, Damiano
See Levi, Primo
Malamud, Bernard 1914-1986 .. **CLC 1, 2, 3,
5, 8, 9, 11, 18, 27, 44, 78, 85; SSC 15;
TCLC 129; WLC 4**
See also AAYA 16; AMWS 1; BPFB 2;
BYA 15; CA 5-8R; 118; CABS 1; CANR
28, 62, 114; CDALB 1941-1968; CN 1, 2,
3, 4; CPW; DA; DA3; DAB; DAC; DAM
MST, NOV, POP; DLB 2, 28, 152; DLBY
1980, 1986; EWL 3; EXPS; LAIT 4;
LATS 1:1; MAL 5; MTCW 1, 2; MTFW
2005; NFS 4, 9; RGAL 4; RGHL; RGSF
2; SSFS 8, 13, 16; TUS
Malan, Herman
See Bosman, Herman Charles; Bosman,
Herman Charles
Malaparte, Curzio 1898-1957 **TCLC 52**
See also DLB 264
Malcolm, Dan
See Silverberg, Robert
Malcolm, Janet 1934- **CLC 201**
See also CA 123; CANR 89; NCFS 1

Malcolm X **BLC 2; CLC 82, 117; WLCS**
See Little, Malcolm
See also LAIT 5; NCFS 3

Malherbe, Francois de 1555-1628 **LC 5**
See also GFL Beginnings to 1789

Mallarme, Stephane 1842-1898 **NCLC 4, 41; PC 4**
See also DAM POET; DLB 217; EW 7; GFL 1789 to the Present; LMFS 2; RGWL 2, 3; TWA

Mallet-Joris, Francoise 1930- **CLC 11**
See also CA 65-68; CANR 17; CWW 2; DLB 83; EWL 3; GFL 1789 to the Present

Malley, Ern
See McAuley, James Phillip

Mallon, Thomas 1951- **CLC 172**
See also CA 110; CANR 29, 57, 92

Mallowan, Agatha Christie
See Christie, Agatha (Mary Clarissa)

Maloff, Saul 1922- **CLC 5**
See also CA 33-36R

Malone, Louis
See MacNeice, (Frederick) Louis

Malone, Michael (Christopher) 1942- ... **CLC 43**
See also CA 77-80; CANR 14, 32, 57, 114

Malory, Sir Thomas 1410(?)-1471(?) . **LC 11, 88; WLCS**
See also BRW 1; BRWR 2; CDBLB Before 1660; DA; DAB; DAC; DAM MST; DLB 146; EFS 2; RGEL 2; SATA 59; SATA-Brief 33; TEA; WLIT 3

Malouf, (George Joseph) David 1934- **CLC 28, 86**
See also CA 124; CANR 50, 76; CN 3, 4, 5, 6, 7; CP 1, 3, 4, 5, 6, 7; DLB 289; EWL 3; MTCW 2; MTFW 2005

Malraux, (Georges-)Andre 1901-1976 **CLC 1, 4, 9, 13, 15, 57**
See also BPFB 2; CA 21-22; 69-72; CANR 34, 58; CAP 2; DA3; DAM NOV; DLB 72; EW 12; EWL 3; GFL 1789 to the Present; MTCW 1, 2; MTFW 2005; RGWL 2, 3; TWA

Malthus, Thomas Robert 1766-1834 **NCLC 145**
See also DLB 107, 158; RGEL 2

Malzberg, Barry N(athaniel) 1939- ... **CLC 7**
See also CA 61-64; CAAS 4; CANR 16; CMW 4; DLB 8; SFW 4

Mamet, David 1947- .. **CLC 9, 15, 34, 46, 91, 166; DC 4, 24**
See also AAYA 3, 60; AMWS 14; CA 81-84; CABS 3; CAD; CANR 15, 41, 67, 72, 129; CD 5, 6; DA3; DAM DRAM; DFS 2, 3, 6, 12, 15; DLB 7; EWL 3; IDFW 4; MAL 5; MTCW 1, 2; MTFW 2005; RGAL 4

Mamet, David Alan
See Mamet, David

Mamoulian, Rouben (Zachary) 1897-1987 **CLC 16**
See also CA 25-28R; 124; CANR 85

Mandelshtam, Osip
See Mandelstam, Osip (Emilievich)
See also EW 10; EWL 3; RGWL 2, 3

Mandelstam, Osip (Emilievich) 1891(?)-1943(?) **PC 14; TCLC 2, 6**
See Mandelshtam, Osip
See also CA 104; 150; MTCW 2; TWA

Mander, (Mary) Jane 1877-1949 ... **TCLC 31**
See also CA 162; RGEL 2

Mandeville, Bernard 1670-1733 **LC 82**
See also DLB 101

Mandeville, Sir John fl. 1350- **CMLC 19**
See also DLB 146

Mandiargues, Andre Pieyre de **CLC 41**
See Pieyre de Mandiargues, Andre
See also DLB 83

Mandrake, Ethel Belle
See Thurman, Wallace (Henry)

Mangan, James Clarence 1803-1849 **NCLC 27**
See also RGEL 2

Maniere, J.-E.
See Giraudoux, Jean(-Hippolyte)

Mankiewicz, Herman (Jacob) 1897-1953 **TCLC 85**
See also CA 120; 169; DLB 26; IDFW 3, 4

Manley, (Mary) Delariviere 1672(?)-1724 **LC 1, 42**
See also DLB 39, 80; RGEL 2

Mann, Abel
See Creasey, John

Mann, Emily 1952- **DC 7**
See also CA 130; CAD; CANR 55; CD 5, 6; CWD; DLB 266

Mann, (Luiz) Heinrich 1871-1950 ... **TCLC 9**
See also CA 106; 164, 181; DLB 66, 118; EW 8; EWL 3; RGWL 2, 3

Mann, (Paul) Thomas 1875-1955 . **SSC 5, 80, 82; TCLC 2, 8, 14, 21, 35, 44, 60, 168; WLC 4**
See also BPFB 2; CA 104; 128; CANR 133; CDWLB 2; DA; DA3; DAB; DAC; DAM MST, NOV; DLB 66; EW 9; EWL 3; GLL 1; LATS 1:1; LMFS 1; MTCW 1, 2; MTFW 2005; NFS 17; RGSF 2; RGWL 2, 3; SSFS 4, 9; TWA

Mannheim, Karl 1893-1947 **TCLC 65**
See also CA 204

Manning, David
See Faust, Frederick (Schiller)

Manning, Frederic 1882-1935 **TCLC 25**
See also CA 124; 216; DLB 260

Manning, Olivia 1915-1980 **CLC 5, 19**
See also CA 5-8R; 101; CANR 29; CN 1, 2; EWL 3; FW; MTCW 1; RGEL 2

Mannyng, Robert c. 1264-c. 1340 .. **CMLC 83**
See also DLB 146

Mano, D. Keith 1942- **CLC 2, 10**
See also CA 25-28R; CAAS 6; CANR 26, 57; DLB 6

Mansfield, Katherine **SSC 9, 23, 38, 81; TCLC 2, 8, 39, 164; WLC 4**
See Beauchamp, Kathleen Mansfield
See also BPFB 2; BRW 7; DAB; DLB 162; EWL 3; EXPS; FW; GLL 1; RGEL 2; RGSF 2; SSFS 2, 8, 10, 11; WWE 1

Manso, Peter 1940- **CLC 39**
See also CA 29-32R; CANR 44

Mantecon, Juan Jimenez
See Jimenez (Mantecon), Juan Ramon

Mantel, Hilary (Mary) 1952- **CLC 144**
See also CA 125; CANR 54, 101; CN 5, 6, 7; DLB 271; RHW

Manton, Peter
See Creasey, John

Man Without a Spleen, A
See Chekhov, Anton (Pavlovich)

Manzano, Juan Franciso 1797(?)-1854 **NCLC 155**

Manzoni, Alessandro 1785-1873 ... **NCLC 29, 98**
See also EW 5; RGWL 2, 3; TWA; WLIT 7

Map, Walter 1140-1209 **CMLC 32**

Mapu, Abraham (ben Jekutiel) 1808-1867 **NCLC 18**

Mara, Sally
See Queneau, Raymond

Maracle, Lee 1950- **NNAL**
See also CA 149

Marat, Jean Paul 1743-1793 **LC 10**

Marcel, Gabriel Honore 1889-1973 . **CLC 15**
See also CA 102; 45-48; EWL 3; MTCW 1, 2

March, William **TCLC 96**
See Campbell, William Edward March
See also CA 216; DLB 9, 86, 316; MAL 5

Marchbanks, Samuel
See Davies, (William) Robertson
See also CCA 1

Marchi, Giacomo
See Bassani, Giorgio

Marcus Aurelius
See Aurelius, Marcus
See also AW 2

Marguerite
See de Navarre, Marguerite

Marguerite d'Angouleme
See de Navarre, Marguerite
See also GFL Beginnings to 1789

Marguerite de Navarre
See de Navarre, Marguerite
See also RGWL 2, 3

Margulies, Donald 1954- **CLC 76**
See also AAYA 57; CA 200; CD 6; DFS 13; DLB 228

Marie de France c. 12th cent. - **CMLC 8; PC 22**
See also DLB 208; FW; RGWL 2, 3

Marie de l'Incarnation 1599-1672 **LC 10**

Marier, Captain Victor
See Griffith, D(avid Lewelyn) W(ark)

Mariner, Scott
See Pohl, Frederik

Marinetti, Filippo Tommaso 1876-1944 **TCLC 10**
See also CA 107; DLB 114, 264; EW 9; EWL 3; WLIT 7

Marivaux, Pierre Carlet de Chamblain de 1688-1763 **DC 7; LC 4, 123**
See also DLB 314; GFL Beginnings to 1789; RGWL 2, 3; TWA

Markandaya, Kamala **CLC 8, 38**
See Taylor, Kamala (Purnaiya)
See also BYA 13; CN 1, 2, 3, 4, 5, 6, 7; DLB 323; EWL 3

Markfield, Wallace (Arthur) 1926-2002 **CLC 8**
See also CA 69-72; 208; CAAS 3; CN 1, 2, 3, 4, 5, 6, 7; DLB 2, 28; DLBY 2002

Markham, Edwin 1852-1940 **TCLC 47**
See also CA 160; DLB 54, 186; MAL 5; RGAL 4

Markham, Robert
See Amis, Kingsley (William)

Marks, J.
See Highwater, Jamake (Mamake)

Marks, J
See Highwater, Jamake (Mamake)

Marks-Highwater, J
See Highwater, Jamake (Mamake)

Marks-Highwater, J.
See Highwater, Jamake (Mamake)

Markson, David M(errill) 1927- **CLC 67**
See also CA 49-52; CANR 1, 91; CN 5, 6

Marlatt, Daphne (Buckle) 1942- **CLC 168**
See also CA 25-28R; CANR 17, 39; CN 6, 7; CP 4, 5, 6, 7; CWP; DLB 60; FW

Marley, Bob **CLC 17**
See Marley, Robert Nesta

Marley, Robert Nesta 1945-1981
See Marley, Bob
See also CA 107; 103

Marlowe, Christopher 1564-1593 . **DC 1; LC 22, 47, 117; PC 57; WLC 4**
See also BRW 1; BRWR 1; CDBLB Before 1660; DA; DA3; DAB; DAC; DAM DRAM, MST; DFS 1, 5, 13, 21; DLB 62; EXPP; LMFS 1; PFS 22; RGEL 2; TEA; WLIT 3

Marlowe, Stephen 1928- **CLC 70**
See Queen, Ellery
See also CA 13-16R; CANR 6, 55; CMW 4; SFW 4

Marmion, Shakerley 1603-1639 **LC 89**
See also DLB 58; RGEL 2

Marmontel, Jean-Francois 1723-1799 .. **LC 2**
See also DLB 314

Maron, Monika 1941- **CLC 165**
See also CA 201

Marquand, John P(hillips)
1893-1960 **CLC 2, 10**
See also AMW; BPFB 2; CA 85-88; CANR 73; CMW 4; DLB 9, 102; EWL 3; MAL 5; MTCW 2; RGAL 4

Marques, Rene 1919-1979 .. **CLC 96; HLC 2**
See also CA 97-100; 85-88; CANR 78; DAM MULT; DLB 305; EWL 3; HW 1, 2; LAW; RGSF 2

Marquez, Gabriel Garcia
See Garcia Marquez, Gabriel

Marquis, Don(ald Robert Perry)
1878-1937 **TCLC 7**
See also CA 104; 166; DLB 11, 25; MAL 5; RGAL 4

Marquis de Sade
See Sade, Donatien Alphonse Francois

Marric, J. J.
See Creasey, John
See also MSW

Marryat, Frederick 1792-1848 **NCLC 3**
See also DLB 21, 163; RGEL 2; WCH

Marsden, James
See Creasey, John

Marsh, Edward 1872-1953 **TCLC 99**

Marsh, (Edith) Ngaio 1895-1982 .. **CLC 7, 53**
See also CA 9-12R; CANR 6, 58; CMW 4; CN 1, 2, 3; CPW; DAM POP; DLB 77; MSW; MTCW 1, 2; RGEL 2; TEA

Marshall, Allen
See Westlake, Donald E(dwin)

Marshall, Garry 1934- **CLC 17**
See also AAYA 3; CA 111; SATA 60

Marshall, Paule 1929- .. **BLC 3; CLC 27, 72; SSC 3**
See also AFAW 1, 2; AMWS 11; BPFB 2; BW 2, 3; CA 77-80; CANR 25, 73, 129; CN 1, 2, 3, 4, 5, 6, 7; DA3; DAM MULT; DLB 33, 157, 227; EWL 3; LATS 1:2; MAL 5; MTCW 1, 2; MTFW 2005; RGAL 4; SSFS 15

Marshallik
See Zangwill, Israel

Marsten, Richard
See Hunter, Evan

Marston, John 1576-1634 **LC 33**
See also BRW 2; DAM DRAM; DLB 58, 172; RGEL 2

Martel, Yann 1963- **CLC 192**
See also AAYA 67; CA 146; CANR 114; DLB 326; MTFW 2005

Martens, Adolphe-Adhemar
See Ghelderode, Michel de

Martha, Henry
See Harris, Mark

Marti, Jose
See Marti (y Perez), Jose (Julian)
See also DLB 290

Marti (y Perez), Jose (Julian)
1853-1895 **HLC 2; NCLC 63**
See Marti, Jose
See also DAM MULT; HW 2; LAW; RGWL 2, 3; WLIT 1

Martial c. 40-c. 104 **CMLC 35; PC 10**
See also AW 2; CDWLB 1; DLB 211; RGWL 2, 3

Martin, Ken
See Hubbard, L. Ron

Martin, Richard
See Creasey, John

Martin, Steve 1945- **CLC 30, 217**
See also AAYA 53; CA 97-100; CANR 30, 100, 140; DFS 19; MTCW 1; MTFW 2005

Martin, Valerie 1948- **CLC 89**
See also BEST 90:2; CA 85-88; CANR 49, 89

Martin, Violet Florence 1862-1915 .. **SSC 56; TCLC 51**

Martin, Webber
See Silverberg, Robert

Martindale, Patrick Victor
See White, Patrick (Victor Martindale)

Martin du Gard, Roger
1881-1958 **TCLC 24**
See also CA 118; CANR 94; DLB 65; EWL 3; GFL 1789 to the Present; RGWL 2, 3

Martineau, Harriet 1802-1876 **NCLC 26, 137**
See also DLB 21, 55, 159, 163, 166, 190; FW; RGEL 2; YABC 2

Martines, Julia
See O'Faolain, Julia

Martinez, Enrique Gonzalez
See Gonzalez Martinez, Enrique

Martinez, Jacinto Benavente y
See Benavente (y Martinez), Jacinto

Martinez de la Rosa, Francisco de Paula
1787-1862 **NCLC 102**
See also TWA

Martinez Ruiz, Jose 1873-1967
See Azorin; Ruiz, Jose Martinez
See also CA 93-96; HW 1

Martinez Sierra, Gregorio
1881-1947 **TCLC 6**
See also CA 115; EWL 3

Martinez Sierra, Maria (de la O'LeJarraga)
1874-1974 **TCLC 6**
See also CA 115; EWL 3

Martinsen, Martin
See Follett, Ken(neth Martin)

Martinson, Harry (Edmund)
1904-1978 **CLC 14**
See also CA 77-80; CANR 34, 130; DLB 259; EWL 3

Martyn, Edward 1859-1923 **TCLC 131**
See also CA 179; DLB 10; RGEL 2

Marut, Ret
See Traven, B.

Marut, Robert
See Traven, B.

Marvell, Andrew 1621-1678 **LC 4, 43; PC 10; WLC 4**
See also BRW 2; BRWR 2; CDBLB 1660-1789; DA; DAB; DAC; DAM MST, POET; DLB 131; EXPP; PFS 5; RGEL 2; TEA; WP

Marx, Karl (Heinrich)
1818-1883 **NCLC 17, 114**
See also DLB 129; LATS 1:1; TWA

Masaoka, Shiki -1902 **TCLC 18**
See Masaoka, Tsunenori
See also RGWL 3

Masaoka, Tsunenori 1867-1902
See Masaoka, Shiki
See also CA 117; 191; TWA

Masefield, John (Edward)
1878-1967 **CLC 11, 47**
See also CA 19-20; 25-28R; CANR 33; CAP 2; CDBLB 1890-1914; DAM POET; DLB 10, 19, 153, 160; EWL 3; EXPP; FANT; MTCW 1, 2; PFS 5; RGEL 2; SATA 19

Maso, Carole 1955(?)- **CLC 44**
See also CA 170; CANR 148; CN 7; GLL 2; RGAL 4

Mason, Bobbie Ann 1940- ... **CLC 28, 43, 82, 154; SSC 4**
See also AAYA 5, 42; AMWS 8; BPFB 2; CA 53-56; CANR 11, 31, 58, 83, 125; CDALBS; CN 5, 6, 7; CSW; DA3; DLB 173; DLBY 1987; EWL 3; EXPS; INT CANR-31; MAL 5; MTCW 1, 2; MTFW 2005; NFS 4; RGAL 4; RGSF 2; SSFS 3, 8, 20; TCLE 1:2; YAW

Mason, Ernst
See Pohl, Frederik

Mason, Hunni B.
See Sternheim, (William Adolf) Carl

Mason, Lee W.
See Malzberg, Barry N(athaniel)

Mason, Nick 1945- **CLC 35**

Mason, Tally
See Derleth, August (William)

Mass, Anna **CLC 59**

Mass, William
See Gibson, William

Massinger, Philip 1583-1640 **LC 70**
See also BRWS 11; DLB 58; RGEL 2

Master Lao
See Lao Tzu

Masters, Edgar Lee 1868-1950 **PC 1, 36; TCLC 2, 25; WLCS**
See also AMWS 1; CA 104; 133; CDALB 1865-1917; DA; DAC; DAM MST, POET; DLB 54; EWL 3; EXPP; MAL 5; MTCW 1, 2; MTFW 2005; RGAL 4; TUS; WP

Masters, Hilary 1928- **CLC 48**
See also CA 25-28R; 217; CAAE 217; CANR 13, 47, 97; CN 6, 7; DLB 244

Mastrosimone, William 1947- **CLC 36**
See also CA 186; CAD; CD 5, 6

Mathe, Albert
See Camus, Albert

Mather, Cotton 1663-1728 **LC 38**
See also AMWS 2; CDALB 1640-1865; DLB 24, 30, 140; RGAL 4; TUS

Mather, Increase 1639-1723 **LC 38**
See also DLB 24

Mathers, Marshall Bruce
See Eminem

Matheson, Richard (Burton) 1926- .. **CLC 37**
See also AAYA 31; CA 97-100; CANR 88, 99; DLB 8, 44; HGG; INT CANR-97-100; SCFW 1, 2; SFW 4; SUFW 2

Mathews, Harry (Burchell) 1930- **CLC 6, 52**
See also CA 21-24R; CAAS 6; CANR 18, 40, 98; CN 5, 6, 7

Mathews, John Joseph 1894-1979 .. **CLC 84; NNAL**
See also CA 19-20; 142; CANR 45; CAP 2; DAM MULT; DLB 175; TCWW 1, 2

Mathias, Roland (Glyn) 1915- **CLC 45**
See also CA 97-100; CANR 19, 41; CP 1, 2, 3, 4, 5, 6, 7; DLB 27

Matsuo Basho 1644(?)-1694 **LC 62; PC 3**
See Basho, Matsuo
See also DAM POET; PFS 2, 7, 18

Mattheson, Rodney
See Creasey, John

Matthews, (James) Brander
1852-1929 **TCLC 95**
See also CA 181; DLB 71, 78; DLBD 13

Matthews, Greg 1949- **CLC 45**
See also CA 135

Matthews, William (Procter III)
1942-1997 **CLC 40**
See also AMWS 9; CA 29-32R; 162; CAAS 18; CANR 12, 57; CP 2, 3, 4, 5, 6; DLB 5

Matthias, John (Edward) 1941- **CLC 9**
See also CA 33-36R; CANR 56; CP 4, 5, 6, 7

Matthiessen, F(rancis) O(tto)
1902-1950 **TCLC 100**
See also CA 185; DLB 63; MAL 5
Matthiessen, Peter 1927- ... **CLC 5, 7, 11, 32, 64**
See also AAYA 6, 40; AMWS 5; ANW; BEST 90:4; BPFB 2; CA 9-12R; CANR 21, 50, 73, 100, 138; CN 1, 2, 3, 4, 5, 6, 7; DA3; DAM NOV; DLB 6, 173, 275; MAL 5; MTCW 1, 2; MTFW 2005; SATA 27
Maturin, Charles Robert
1780(?)-1824 **NCLC 6, 169**
See also BRWS 8; DLB 178; GL 3; HGG; LMFS 1; RGEL 2; SUFW
Matute (Ausejo), Ana Maria 1925- .. **CLC 11**
See also CA 89-92; CANR 129; CWW 2; DLB 322; EWL 3; MTCW 1; RGSF 2
Maugham, W. S.
See Maugham, W(illiam) Somerset
Maugham, W(illiam) Somerset
1874-1965 .. **CLC 1, 11, 15, 67, 93; SSC 8; WLC 4**
See also AAYA 55; BPFB 2; BRW 6; CA 5-8R; 25-28R; CANR 40, 127; CDBLB 1914-1945; CMW 4; DA; DA3; DAB; DAC; DAM DRAM, MST, NOV; DFS 22; DLB 10, 36, 77, 100, 162, 195; EWL 3; LAIT 3; MTCW 1, 2; MTFW 2005; NFS 23; RGEL 2; RGSF 2; SATA 54; SSFS 17
Maugham, William Somerset
See Maugham, W(illiam) Somerset
Maupassant, (Henri Rene Albert) Guy de
1850-1893 . **NCLC 1, 42, 83; SSC 1, 64; WLC 4**
See also BYA 14; DA; DA3; DAB; DAC; DAM MST; DLB 123; EW 7; EXPS; GFL 1789 to the Present; LAIT 2; LMFS 1; RGSF 2; RGWL 2, 3; SSFS 4, 21; SUFW; TWA
Maupin, Armistead (Jones, Jr.)
1944- .. **CLC 95**
See also CA 125; 130; CANR 58, 101; CPW; DA3; DAM POP; DLB 278; GLL 1; INT CA-130; MTCW 2; MTFW 2005
Maurhut, Richard
See Traven, B.
Mauriac, Claude 1914-1996 **CLC 9**
See also CA 89-92; 152; CWW 2; DLB 83; EWL 3; GFL 1789 to the Present
Mauriac, Francois (Charles)
1885-1970 **CLC 4, 9, 56; SSC 24**
See also CA 25-28; CAP 2; DLB 65; EW 10; EWL 3; GFL 1789 to the Present; MTCW 1, 2; MTFW 2005; RGWL 2, 3; TWA
Mavor, Osborne Henry 1888-1951
See Bridie, James
See also CA 104
Maxwell, William (Keepers, Jr.)
1908-2000 **CLC 19**
See also AMWS 8; CA 93-96; 189; CANR 54, 95; CN 1, 2, 3, 4, 5, 6, 7; DLB 218, 278; DLBY 1980; INT CA-93-96; MAL 5; SATA-Obit 128
May, Elaine 1932- **CLC 16**
See also CA 124; 142; CAD; CWD; DLB 44
Mayakovski, Vladimir (Vladimirovich)
1893-1930 **TCLC 4, 18**
See Maiakovskii, Vladimir; Mayakovsky, Vladimir
See also CA 104; 158; EWL 3; MTCW 2; MTFW 2005; SFW 4; TWA
Mayakovsky, Vladimir
See Mayakovski, Vladimir (Vladimirovich)
See also EW 11; WP
Mayhew, Henry 1812-1887 **NCLC 31**
See also DLB 18, 55, 190

Mayle, Peter 1939(?)- **CLC 89**
See also CA 139; CANR 64, 109
Maynard, Joyce 1953- **CLC 23**
See also CA 111; 129; CANR 64
Mayne, William (James Carter)
1928- .. **CLC 12**
See also AAYA 20; CA 9-12R; CANR 37, 80, 100; CLR 25; FANT; JRDA; MAICYA 1, 2; MAICYAS 1; SAAS 11; SATA 6, 68, 122; SUFW 2; YAW
Mayo, Jim
See L'Amour, Louis (Dearborn)
Maysles, Albert 1926- **CLC 16**
See also CA 29-32R
Maysles, David 1932-1987 **CLC 16**
See also CA 191
Mazer, Norma Fox 1931- **CLC 26**
See also AAYA 5, 36; BYA 1, 8; CA 69-72; CANR 12, 32, 66, 129; CLR 23; JRDA; MAICYA 1, 2; SAAS 1; SATA 24, 67, 105, 168; WYA; YAW
Mazzini, Guiseppe 1805-1872 **NCLC 34**
McAlmon, Robert (Menzies)
1895-1956 **TCLC 97**
See also CA 107; 168; DLB 4, 45; DLBD 15; GLL 1
McAuley, James Phillip 1917-1976 .. **CLC 45**
See also CA 97-100; CP 1, 2; DLB 260; RGEL 2
McBain, Ed
See Hunter, Evan
See also MSW
McBrien, William (Augustine)
1930- .. **CLC 44**
See also CA 107; CANR 90
McCabe, Patrick 1955- **CLC 133**
See also BRWS 9; CA 130; CANR 50, 90; CN 6, 7; DLB 194
McCaffrey, Anne 1926- **CLC 17**
See also AAYA 6, 34; AITN 2; BEST 89:2; BPFB 2; BYA 5; CA 25-28R, 227; CAAE 227; CANR 15, 35, 55, 96; CLR 49; CPW; DA3; DAM NOV, POP; DLB 8; JRDA; MAICYA 1, 2; MTCW 1, 2; MTFW 2005; SAAS 11; SATA 8, 70, 116, 152; SATA-Essay 152; SFW 4; SUFW 2; WYA; YAW
McCaffrey, Anne Inez
See McCaffrey, Anne
McCall, Nathan 1955(?)- **CLC 86**
See also AAYA 59; BW 3; CA 146; CANR 88
McCann, Arthur
See Campbell, John W(ood, Jr.)
McCann, Edson
See Pohl, Frederik
McCarthy, Charles, Jr. 1933-
See McCarthy, Cormac
See also CANR 42, 69, 101; CPW; CSW; DA3; DAM POP; MTCW 2; MTFW 2005
McCarthy, Cormac **CLC 4, 57, 101, 204**
See McCarthy, Charles, Jr.
See also AMWS 8; BPFB 2; CA 13-16R; CANR 10; CN 6, 7; DLB 6, 143, 256; EWL 3; LATS 1:2; MAL 5; TCLE 1:2; TCWW 2
McCarthy, Mary (Therese)
1912-1989 .. **CLC 1, 3, 5, 14, 24, 39, 59; SSC 24**
See also AMW; BPFB 2; CA 5-8R; 129; CANR 16, 50, 64; CN 1, 2, 3, 4; DA3; DLB 2; DLBY 1981; EWL 3; FW; INT CANR-16; MAL 5; MAWW; MTCW 1, 2; MTFW 2005; RGAL 4; TUS
McCartney, James Paul
See McCartney, Paul
McCartney, Paul 1942- **CLC 12, 35**
See also CA 146; CANR 111

McCauley, Stephen (D.) 1955- **CLC 50**
See also CA 141
McClaren, Peter **CLC 70**
McClure, Michael (Thomas) 1932- ... **CLC 6, 10**
See also BG 1:3; CA 21-24R; CAD; CANR 17, 46, 77, 131; CD 5, 6; CP 1, 2, 3, 4, 5, 6, 7; DLB 16; WP
McCorkle, Jill (Collins) 1958- **CLC 51**
See also CA 121; CANR 113; CSW; DLB 234; DLBY 1987
McCourt, Frank 1930- **CLC 109**
See also AAYA 61; AMWS 12; CA 157; CANR 97, 138; MTFW 2005; NCFS 1
McCourt, James 1941- **CLC 5**
See also CA 57-60; CANR 98, 152
McCourt, Malachy 1931- **CLC 119**
See also SATA 126
McCoy, Horace (Stanley)
1897-1955 **TCLC 28**
See also AMWS 13; CA 108; 155; CMW 4; DLB 9
McCrae, John 1872-1918 **TCLC 12**
See also CA 109; DLB 92; PFS 5
McCreigh, James
See Pohl, Frederik
McCullers, (Lula) Carson (Smith)
1917-1967 **CLC 1, 4, 10, 12, 48, 100; SSC 9, 24; TCLC 155; WLC 4**
See also AAYA 21; AMW; AMWC 2; BPFB 2; CA 5-8R; 25-28R; CABS 1, 3; CANR 18, 132; CDALB 1941-1968; DA; DA3; DAB; DAC; DAM MST, NOV; DFS 5, 18; DLB 2, 7, 173, 228; EWL 3; EXPS; FW; GLL 1; LAIT 3, 4; MAL 5; MAWW; MTCW 1, 2; MTFW 2005; NFS 6, 13; RGAL 4; RGSF 2; SATA 27; SSFS 5; TUS; YAW
McCulloch, John Tyler
See Burroughs, Edgar Rice
McCullough, Colleen 1937- **CLC 27, 107**
See also AAYA 36; BPFB 2; CA 81-84; CANR 17, 46, 67, 98, 139; CPW; DA3; DAM NOV, POP; MTCW 1, 2; MTFW 2005; RHW
McCunn, Ruthanne Lum 1946- **AAL**
See also CA 119; CANR 43, 96; DLB 312; LAIT 2; SATA 63
McDermott, Alice 1953- **CLC 90**
See also CA 109; CANR 40, 90, 126; CN 7; DLB 292; MTFW 2005; NFS 23
McElroy, Joseph 1930- **CLC 5, 47**
See also CA 17-20R; CANR 149; CN 3, 4, 5, 6, 7
McElroy, Joseph Prince
See McElroy, Joseph
McEwan, Ian (Russell) 1948- **CLC 13, 66, 169**
See also BEST 90:4; BRWS 4; CA 61-64; CANR 14, 41, 69, 87, 132; CN 3, 4, 5, 6, 7; DAM NOV; DLB 14, 194, 319, 326; HGG; MTCW 1, 2; MTFW 2005; RGSF 2; SUFW 2; TEA
McFadden, David 1940- **CLC 48**
See also CA 104; CP 1, 2, 3, 4, 5, 6, 7; DLB 60; INT CA-104
McFarland, Dennis 1950- **CLC 65**
See also CA 165; CANR 110
McGahern, John 1934-2006 **CLC 5, 9, 48, 156; SSC 17**
See also CA 17-20R; CANR 29, 68, 113; CN 1, 2, 3, 4, 5, 6, 7; DLB 14, 231, 319; MTCW 1
McGinley, Patrick (Anthony) 1937- . **CLC 41**
See also CA 120; 127; CANR 56; INT CA-127

McGinley, Phyllis 1905-1978 **CLC 14**
See also CA 9-12R; 77-80; CANR 19; CP 1, 2; CWRI 5; DLB 11, 48; MAL 5; PFS 9, 13; SATA 2, 44; SATA-Obit 24

McGinniss, Joe 1942- **CLC 32**
See also AITN 2; BEST 89:2; CA 25-28R; CANR 26, 70, 152; CPW; DLB 185; INT CANR-26

McGivern, Maureen Daly
See Daly, Maureen

McGrath, Patrick 1950- **CLC 55**
See also CA 136; CANR 65, 148; CN 5, 6, 7; DLB 231; HGG; SUFW 2

McGrath, Thomas (Matthew)
1916-1990 **CLC 28, 59**
See also AMWS 10; CA 9-12R; 132; CANR 6, 33, 95; CP 1, 2, 3, 4, 5; DAM POET; MAL 5; MTCW 1; SATA 41; SATA-Obit 66

McGuane, Thomas (Francis III)
1939- **CLC 3, 7, 18, 45, 127**
See also AITN 2; BPFB 2; CA 49-52; CANR 5, 24, 49, 94; CN 2, 3, 4, 5, 6, 7; DLB 2, 212; DLBY 1980; EWL 3; INT CANR-24; MAL 5; MTCW 1; MTFW 2005; TCWW 1, 2

McGuckian, Medbh 1950- **CLC 48, 174; PC 27**
See also BRWS 5; CA 143; CP 4, 5, 6, 7; CWP; DAM POET; DLB 40

McHale, Tom 1942(?)-1982 **CLC 3, 5**
See also AITN 1; CA 77-80; 106; CN 1, 2, 3

McHugh, Heather 1948- **PC 61**
See also CA 69-72; CANR 11, 28, 55, 92; CP 4, 5, 6, 7; CWP; PFS 24

McIlvanney, William 1936- **CLC 42**
See also CA 25-28R; CANR 61; CMW 4; DLB 14, 207

McIlwraith, Maureen Mollie Hunter
See Hunter, Mollie
See also SATA 2

McInerney, Jay 1955- **CLC 34, 112**
See also AAYA 18; BPFB 2; CA 116; 123; CANR 45, 68, 116; CN 5, 6, 7; CPW; DA3; DAM POP; DLB 292; INT CA-123; MAL 5; MTCW 2; MTFW 2005

McIntyre, Vonda N(eel) 1948- **CLC 18**
See also CA 81-84; CANR 17, 34, 69; MTCW 1; SFW 4; YAW

McKay, Claude **BLC 3; HR 1:3; PC 2; TCLC 7, 41; WLC 4**
See McKay, Festus Claudius
See also AFAW 1, 2; AMWS 10; DAB; DLB 4, 45, 51, 117; EWL 3; EXPP; GLL 2; LAIT 3; LMFS 2; MAL 5; PAB; PFS 4; RGAL 4; WP

McKay, Festus Claudius 1889-1948
See McKay, Claude
See also BW 1, 3; CA 104; 124; CANR 73; DA; DAC; DAM MST, MULT, NOV, POET; MTCW 1, 2; MTFW 2005; TUS

McKuen, Rod 1933- **CLC 1, 3**
See also AITN 1; CA 41-44R; CANR 40; CP 1

McLoughlin, R. B.
See Mencken, H(enry) L(ouis)

McLuhan, (Herbert) Marshall
1911-1980 **CLC 37, 83**
See also CA 9-12R; 102; CANR 12, 34, 61; DLB 88; INT CANR-12; MTCW 1, 2; MTFW 2005

McManus, Declan Patrick Aloysius
See Costello, Elvis

McMillan, Terry (L.) 1951- . **BLCS; CLC 50, 61, 112**
See also AAYA 21; AMWS 13; BPFB 2; BW 2, 3; CA 140; CANR 60, 104, 131; CN 7; CPW; DA3; DAM MULT, NOV, POP; MAL 5; MTCW 2; MTFW 2005; RGAL 4; YAW

McMurtry, Larry 1936- **CLC 2, 3, 7, 11, 27, 44, 127**
See also AAYA 15; AITN 2; AMWS 5; BEST 89:2; BPFB 2; CA 5-8R; CANR 19, 43, 64, 103; CDALB 1968-1988; CN 2, 3, 4, 5, 6, 7; CPW; CSW; DA3; DAM NOV, POP; DLB 2, 143, 256; DLBY 1980, 1987; EWL 3; MAL 5; MTCW 1, 2; MTFW 2005; RGAL 4; TCWW 1, 2

McMurtry, Larry Jeff
See McMurtry, Larry

McNally, Terrence 1939- ... **CLC 4, 7, 41, 91; DC 27**
See also AAYA 62; AMWS 13; CA 45-48; CAD; CANR 2, 56, 116; CD 5, 6; DA3; DAM DRAM; DFS 16, 19; DLB 7, 249; EWL 3; GLL 1; MTCW 2; MTFW 2005

McNally, Thomas Michael
See McNally, T.M.

McNally, T.M. 1961- **CLC 82**
See also CA 246

McNamer, Deirdre 1950- **CLC 70**

McNeal, Tom **CLC 119**

McNeile, Herman Cyril 1888-1937
See Sapper
See also CA 184; CMW 4; DLB 77

McNickle, (William) D'Arcy
1904-1977 **CLC 89; NNAL**
See also CA 9-12R; 85-88; CANR 5, 45; DAM MULT; DLB 175, 212; RGAL 4; SATA-Obit 22; TCWW 1, 2

McPhee, John (Angus) 1931- **CLC 36**
See also AAYA 61; AMWS 3; ANW; BEST 90:1; CA 65-68; CANR 20, 46, 64, 69, 121; CPW; DLB 185, 275; MTCW 1, 2; MTFW 2005; TUS

McPherson, James Alan 1943- . **BLCS; CLC 19, 77**
See also BW 1, 3; CA 25-28R; CAAS 17; CANR 24, 74, 140; CN 3, 4, 5, 6; CSW; DLB 38, 244; EWL 3; MTCW 1, 2; MTFW 2005; RGAL 4; RGSF 2; SSFS 23

McPherson, William (Alexander)
1933- ... **CLC 34**
See also CA 69-72; CANR 28; INT CANR-28

McTaggart, J. McT. Ellis
See McTaggart, John McTaggart Ellis

McTaggart, John McTaggart Ellis
1866-1925 **TCLC 105**
See also CA 120; DLB 262

Mead, George Herbert 1863-1931 . **TCLC 89**
See also CA 212; DLB 270

Mead, Margaret 1901-1978 **CLC 37**
See also AITN 1; CA 1-4R; 81-84; CANR 4; DA3; FW; MTCW 1, 2; SATA-Obit 20

Meaker, Marijane (Agnes) 1927-
See Kerr, M. E.
See also CA 107; CANR 37, 63, 145; INT CA-107; JRDA; MAICYA 1, 2; MAICYAS 1; MTCW 1; SATA 20, 61, 99, 160; SATA-Essay 111; YAW

Medoff, Mark (Howard) 1940- **CLC 6, 23**
See also AITN 1; CA 53-56; CAD; CANR 5; CD 5, 6; DAM DRAM; DFS 4; DLB 7; INT CANR-5

Medvedev, P. N.
See Bakhtin, Mikhail Mikhailovich

Meged, Aharon
See Megged, Aharon

Meged, Aron
See Megged, Aharon

Megged, Aharon 1920- **CLC 9**
See also CA 49-52; CAAS 13; CANR 1, 140; EWL 3; RGHL

Mehta, Deepa 1950- **CLC 208**

Mehta, Gita 1943- **CLC 179**
See also CA 225; CN 7; DNFS 2

Mehta, Ved (Parkash) 1934- **CLC 37**
See also CA 1-4R; 212; CAAE 212; CANR 2, 23, 69; DLB 323; MTCW 1; MTFW 2005

Melanchthon, Philipp 1497-1560 **LC 90**
See also DLB 179

Melanter
See Blackmore, R(ichard) D(oddridge)

Meleager c. 140B.C.-c. 70B.C. **CMLC 53**

Melies, Georges 1861-1938 **TCLC 81**

Melikow, Loris
See Hofmannsthal, Hugo von

Melmoth, Sebastian
See Wilde, Oscar (Fingal O'Flahertie Wills)

Melo Neto, Joao Cabral de
See Cabral de Melo Neto, Joao
See also CWW 2; EWL 3

Meltzer, Milton 1915- **CLC 26**
See also AAYA 8, 45; BYA 2, 6; CA 13-16R; CANR 38, 92, 107; CLR 13; DLB 61; JRDA; MAICYA 1, 2; SAAS 1; SATA 1, 50, 80, 128; SATA-Essay 124; WYA; YAW

Melville, Herman 1819-1891 **NCLC 3, 12, 29, 45, 49, 91, 93, 123, 157; SSC 1, 17, 46; WLC 4**
See also AAYA 25; AMW; AMWR 1; CDALB 1640-1865; DA; DA3; DAB; DAC; DAM MST, NOV; DLB 3, 74, 250, 254; EXPN; EXPS; GL 3; LAIT 1, 2; NFS 7, 9; RGAL 4; RGSF 2; SATA 59; SSFS 3; TUS

Members, Mark
See Powell, Anthony (Dymoke)

Membreno, Alejandro **CLC 59**

Menand, Louis 1952- **CLC 208**
See also CA 200

Menander c. 342B.C.-c. 293B.C. **CMLC 9, 51; DC 3**
See also AW 1; CDWLB 1; DAM DRAM; DLB 176; LMFS 1; RGWL 2, 3

Menchu, Rigoberta 1959- .. **CLC 160; HLCS 2**
See also CA 175; CANR 135; DNFS 1; WLIT 1

Mencken, H(enry) L(ouis)
1880-1956 **TCLC 13**
See also AMW; CA 105; 125; CDALB 1917-1929; DLB 11, 29, 63, 137, 222; EWL 3; MAL 5; MTCW 1, 2; MTFW 2005; NCFS 4; RGAL 4; TUS

Mendelsohn, Jane 1965- **CLC 99**
See also CA 154; CANR 94

Mendoza, Inigo Lopez de
See Santillana, Inigo Lopez de Mendoza, Marques de

Menton, Francisco de
See Chin, Frank (Chew, Jr.)

Mercer, David 1928-1980 **CLC 5**
See also CA 9-12R; 102; CANR 23; CBD; DAM DRAM; DLB 13, 310; MTCW 1; RGEL 2

Merchant, Paul
See Ellison, Harlan (Jay)

Meredith, George 1828-1909 .. **PC 60; TCLC 17, 43**
See also CA 117; 153; CANR 80; CDBLB 1832-1890; DAM POET; DLB 18, 35, 57, 159; RGEL 2; TEA

Meredith, William (Morris) 1919- **CLC 4, 13, 22, 55; PC 28**
See also CA 9-12R; CAAS 14; CANR 6, 40, 129; CP 1, 2, 3, 4, 5, 6, 7; DAM POET; DLB 5; MAL 5

Merezhkovsky, Dmitrii Sergeevich
See Merezhkovsky, Dmitry Sergeyevich
See also DLB 295

Merezhkovsky, Dmitry Sergeevich
See Merezhkovsky, Dmitry Sergeyevich
See also EWL 3

Merezhkovsky, Dmitry Sergeyevich
1865-1941 **TCLC 29**
See Merezhkovsky, Dmitrii Sergeyevich;
Merezhkovsky, Dmitry Sergeevich
See also CA 169

Merimee, Prosper 1803-1870 ... **NCLC 6, 65;**
SSC 7, 77
See also DLB 119, 192; EW 6; EXPS; GFL
1789 to the Present; RGSF 2; RGWL 2,
3; SSFS 8; SUFW

Merkin, Daphne 1954- **CLC 44**
See also CA 123

Merleau-Ponty, Maurice
1908-1961 **TCLC 156**
See also CA 114; 89-92; DLB 296; GFL
1789 to the Present

Merlin, Arthur
See Blish, James (Benjamin)

Mernissi, Fatima 1940- **CLC 171**
See also CA 152; FW

Merrill, James (Ingram) 1926-1995 .. **CLC 2,**
3, 6, 8, 13, 18, 34, 91; PC 28; TCLC
173
See also AMWS 3; CA 13-16R; 147; CANR
10, 49, 63, 108; CP 1, 2, 3, 4; DA3; DAM
POET; DLB 5, 165; DLBY 1985; EWL 3;
INT CANR-10; MAL 5; MTCW 1, 2;
MTFW 2005; PAB; PFS 23; RGAL 4

Merriman, Alex
See Silverberg, Robert

Merriman, Brian 1747-1805 **NCLC 70**

Merritt, E. B.
See Waddington, Miriam

Merton, Thomas (James)
1915-1968 . **CLC 1, 3, 11, 34, 83; PC 10**
See also AAYA 61; AMWS 8; CA 5-8R;
25-28R; CANR 22, 53, 111, 131; DA3;
DLB 48; DLBY 1981; MAL 5; MTCW 1,
2; MTFW 2005

Merwin, W(illiam) S(tanley) 1927- ... **CLC 1,**
2, 3, 5, 8, 13, 18, 45, 88; PC 45
See also AMWS 3; CA 13-16R; CANR 15,
51, 112, 140; CP 1, 2, 3, 4, 5, 6, 7; DA3;
DAM POET; DLB 5, 169; EWL 3; INT
CANR-15; MAL 5; MTCW 1, 2; MTFW
2005; PAB; PFS 5, 15; RGAL 4

Metastasio, Pietro 1698-1782 **LC 115**
See also RGWL 2, 3

Metcalf, John 1938- **CLC 37; SSC 43**
See also CA 113; CN 4, 5, 6, 7; DLB 60;
RGSF 2; TWA

Metcalf, Suzanne
See Baum, L(yman) Frank

Mew, Charlotte (Mary) 1870-1928 .. **TCLC 8**
See also CA 105; 189; DLB 19, 135; RGEL
2

Mewshaw, Michael 1943- **CLC 9**
See also CA 53-56; CANR 7, 47, 147;
DLBY 1980

Meyer, Conrad Ferdinand
1825-1898 **NCLC 81; SSC 30**
See also DLB 129; EW; RGWL 2, 3

Meyer, Gustav 1868-1932
See Meyrink, Gustav
See also CA 117; 190

Meyer, June
See Jordan, June

Meyer, Lynn
See Slavitt, David R(ytman)

Meyers, Jeffrey 1939- **CLC 39**
See also CA 73-76, 186; CAAE 186; CANR
54, 102; DLB 111

Meynell, Alice (Christina Gertrude
Thompson) 1847-1922 **TCLC 6**
See also CA 104; 177; DLB 19, 98; RGEL 2

Meyrink, Gustav **TCLC 21**
See Meyer, Gustav
See also DLB 81; EWL 3

Michaels, Leonard 1933-2003 **CLC 6, 25;**
SSC 16
See also CA 61-64; 216; CANR 21, 62, 119;
CN 3, 45, 6, 7; DLB 130; MTCW 1;
TCLE 1:2

Michaux, Henri 1899-1984 **CLC 8, 19**
See also CA 85-88; 114; DLB 258; EWL 3;
GFL 1789 to the Present; RGWL 2, 3

Micheaux, Oscar (Devereaux)
1884-1951 **TCLC 76**
See also BW 3; CA 174; DLB 50; TCWW
2

Michelangelo 1475-1564 **LC 12**
See also AAYA 43

Michelet, Jules 1798-1874 **NCLC 31**
See also EW 5; GFL 1789 to the Present

Michels, Robert 1876-1936 **TCLC 88**
See also CA 212

Michener, James A(lbert)
1907(?)-1997 .. **CLC 1, 5, 11, 29, 60, 109**
See also AAYA 27; AITN 1; BEST 90:1;
BPFB 2; CA 5-8R; 161; CANR 21, 45,
68; CN 1, 2, 3, 4, 5, 6; CPW; DA3; DAM
NOV, POP; DLB 6; MAL 5; MTCW 1, 2;
MTFW 2005; RHW; TCWW 1, 2

Mickiewicz, Adam 1798-1855 . **NCLC 3, 101;**
PC 38
See also EW 5; RGWL 2, 3

Middleton, (John) Christopher
1926- **CLC 13**
See also CA 13-16R; CANR 29, 54, 117;
CP 1, 2, 3, 4, 5, 6, 7; DLB 40

Middleton, Richard (Barham)
1882-1911 **TCLC 56**
See also CA 187; DLB 156; HGG

Middleton, Stanley 1919- **CLC 7, 38**
See also CA 25-28R; CAAS 23; CANR 21,
46, 81; CN 1, 2, 3, 4, 5, 6, 7; DLB 14,
326

Middleton, Thomas 1580-1627 **DC 5; LC**
33, 123
See also BRW 2; DAM DRAM, MST; DFS
18, 22; DLB 58; RGEL 2

Migueis, Jose Rodrigues 1901-1980 . **CLC 10**
See also DLB 287

Mikszath, Kalman 1847-1910 **TCLC 31**
See also CA 170

Miles, Jack **CLC 100**
See also CA 200

Miles, John Russiano
See Miles, Jack

Miles, Josephine (Louise)
1911-1985 **CLC 1, 2, 14, 34, 39**
See also CA 1-4R; 116; CANR 2, 55; CP 1,
2, 3, 4; DAM POET; DLB 48; MAL 5;
TCLE 1:2

Militant
See Sandburg, Carl (August)

Mill, Harriet (Hardy) Taylor
1807-1858 **NCLC 102**
See also FW

Mill, John Stuart 1806-1873 **NCLC 11, 58**
See also CDBLB 1832-1890; DLB 55, 190,
262; FW 1; RGEL 2; TEA

Millar, Kenneth 1915-1983 **CLC 14**
See Macdonald, Ross
See also CA 9-12R; 110; CANR 16, 63,
107; CMW 4; CPW; DA3; DAM POP;
DLB 2, 226; DLBD 6; DLBY 1983;
MTCW 1, 2; MTFW 2005

Millay, E. Vincent
See Millay, Edna St. Vincent

Millay, Edna St. Vincent 1892-1950 **PC 6,**
61; TCLC 4, 49, 169; WLCS
See Boyd, Nancy
See also AMW; CA 104; 130; CDALB
1917-1929; DA; DA3; DAB; DAC; DAM
MST, POET; DLB 45, 249; EWL 3;
EXPP; FL 1:6; MAL 5; MAWW; MTCW
1, 2; MTFW 2005; PAB; PFS 3, 17;
RGAL 4; TUS; WP

Miller, Arthur 1915-2005 **CLC 1, 2, 6, 10,**
15, 26, 47, 78, 179; DC 1; WLC 4
See also AAYA 15; AITN 1; AMW; AMWC
1; CA 1-4R; 236; CABS 3; CAD; CANR
2, 30, 54, 76, 132; CD 5, 6; CDALB
1941-1968; DA; DA3; DAB; DAC; DAM
DRAM, MST; DFS 1, 3, 8; DLB 7, 266;
EWL 3; LAIT 1, 4; LATS 1:2; MAL 5;
MTCW 1, 2; MTFW 2005; RGAL 4;
RGHL; TUS; WYAS 1

Miller, Henry (Valentine)
1891-1980 **CLC 1, 2, 4, 9, 14, 43, 84;**
WLC 4
See also AMW; BPFB 2; CA 9-12R; 97-
100; CANR 33, 64; CDALB 1929-1941;
CN 1, 2; DA; DA3; DAB; DAC; DAM
MST, NOV; DLB 4, 9; DLBY 1980; EWL
3; MAL 5; MTCW 1, 2; MTFW 2005;
RGAL 4; TUS

Miller, Hugh 1802-1856 **NCLC 143**
See also DLB 190

Miller, Jason 1939(?)-2001 **CLC 2**
See also AITN 1; CA 73-76; 197; CAD;
CANR 130; DFS 12; DLB 7

Miller, Sue 1943- **CLC 44**
See also AMWS 12; BEST 90:3; CA 139;
CANR 59, 91, 128; DA3; DAM POP;
DLB 143

Miller, Walter M(ichael, Jr.)
1923-1996 **CLC 4, 30**
See also BPFB 2; CA 85-88; CANR 108;
DLB 8; SCFW 1, 2; SFW 4

Millett, Kate 1934- **CLC 67**
See also AITN 1; CA 73-76; CANR 32, 53,
76, 110; DA3; DLB 246; FW; GLL 1;
MTCW 1, 2; MTFW 2005

Millhauser, Steven (Lewis) 1943- **CLC 21,**
54, 109; SSC 57
See also CA 110; 111; CANR 63, 114, 133;
CN 6, 7; DA3; DLB 2; FANT; INT CA-
111; MAL 5; MTCW 2; MTFW 2005

Millin, Sarah Gertrude 1889-1968 ... **CLC 49**
See also CA 102; 93-96; DLB 225; EWL 3

Milne, A. A. 1882-1956 **TCLC 6, 88**
See also BRWS 5; CA 104; 133; CLR 1,
26, 108; CMW 4; CWRI 5; DA3; DAB;
DAC; DAM MST; DLB 10, 77, 100, 160;
FANT; MAICYA 1, 2; MTCW 1, 2;
MTFW 2005; RGEL 2; SATA 100; WCH;
YABC 1

Milne, Alan Alexander
See Milne, A. A.

Milner, Ron(ald) 1938-2004 **BLC 3; CLC**
56
See also AITN 1; BW 1; CA 73-76; 230;
CAD; CANR 24, 81; CD 5, 6; DAM
MULT; DLB 38; MAL 5; MTCW 1

Milnes, Richard Monckton
1809-1885 **NCLC 61**
See also DLB 32, 184

Milosz, Czeslaw 1911-2004 **CLC 5, 11, 22,**
31, 56, 82; PC 8; WLCS
See also AAYA 62; CA 81-84; 230; CANR
23, 51, 91, 126; CDWLB 4; CWW 2;
DA3; DAM MST, POET; DLB 215; EW
13; EWL 3; MTCW 1, 2; MTFW 2005;
PFS 16; RGHL; RGWL 2, 3

Milton, John 1608-1674 **LC 9, 43, 92; PC**
19, 29; WLC 4
See also AAYA 65; BRW 2; BRWR 2; CD-
BLB 1660-1789; DA; DA3; DAB; DAC;

DAM MST, POET; DLB 131, 151, 281;
EFS 1; EXPP; LAIT 1; PAB; PFS 3, 17;
RGEL 2; TEA; WLIT 3; WP

Min, Anchee 1957- **CLC 86**
See also CA 146; CANR 94, 137; MTFW
2005

Minehaha, Cornelius
See Wedekind, Frank

Miner, Valerie 1947- **CLC 40**
See also CA 97-100; CANR 59; FW; GLL
2

Minimo, Duca
See D'Annunzio, Gabriele

Minot, Susan (Anderson) 1956- **CLC 44,
159**
See also AMWS 6; CA 134; CANR 118;
CN 6, 7

Minus, Ed 1938- **CLC 39**
See also CA 185

Mirabai 1498(?)-1550(?) **PC 48**
See also PFS 24

Miranda, Javier
See Bioy Casares, Adolfo
See also CWW 2

Mirbeau, Octave 1848-1917 **TCLC 55**
See also CA 216; DLB 123, 192; GFL 1789
to the Present

Mirikitani, Janice 1942- **AAL**
See also CA 211; DLB 312; RGAL 4

Mirk, John (?)-c. 1414 **LC 105**
See also DLB 146

Miro (Ferrer), Gabriel (Francisco Victor)
1879-1930 **TCLC 5**
See also CA 104; 185; DLB 322; EWL 3

Misharin, Alexandr **CLC 59**

Mishima, Yukio ... **CLC 2, 4, 6, 9, 27; DC 1;
SSC 4; TCLC 161; WLC 4**
See Hiraoka, Kimitake
See also AAYA 50; BPFB 2; GLL 1; MJW;
RGSF 2; RGWL 2, 3; SSFS 5, 12

Mistral, Frederic 1830-1914 **TCLC 51**
See also CA 122; 213; GFL 1789 to the
Present

Mistral, Gabriela
See Godoy Alcayaga, Lucila
See also DLB 283; DNFS 1; EWL 3; LAW;
RGWL 2, 3; WP

Mistry, Rohinton 1952- ... **CLC 71, 196; SSC
73**
See also BRWS 10; CA 141; CANR 86,
114; CCA 1; CN 6, 7; DAC; SSFS 6

Mitchell, Clyde
See Ellison, Harlan (Jay)

Mitchell, Emerson Blackhorse Barney
1945- ... **NNAL**
See also CA 45-48

Mitchell, James Leslie 1901-1935
See Gibbon, Lewis Grassic
See also CA 104; 188; DLB 15

Mitchell, Joni 1943- **CLC 12**
See also CA 112; CCA 1

Mitchell, Joseph (Quincy)
1908-1996 **CLC 98**
See also CA 77-80; 152; CANR 69; CN 1,
2, 3, 4, 5, 6; CSW; DLB 185; DLBY 1996

Mitchell, Margaret (Munnerlyn)
1900-1949 **TCLC 11, 170**
See also AAYA 23; BPFB 2; BYA 1; CA
109; 125; CANR 55, 94; CDALBS; DA3;
DAM NOV, POP; DLB 9; LAIT 2; MAL
5; MTCW 1, 2; MTFW 2005; NFS 9;
RGAL 4; RHW; TUS; WYAS 1; YAW

Mitchell, Peggy
See Mitchell, Margaret (Munnerlyn)

Mitchell, S(ilas) Weir 1829-1914 **TCLC 36**
See also CA 165; DLB 202; RGAL 4

Mitchell, W(illiam) O(rmond)
1914-1998 **CLC 25**
See also CA 77-80; 165; CANR 15, 43; CN
1, 2, 3, 4, 5, 6; DAC; DAM MST; DLB
88; TCLE 1:2

Mitchell, William (Lendrum)
1879-1936 **TCLC 81**
See also CA 213

Mitford, Mary Russell 1787-1855 ... **NCLC 4**
See also DLB 110, 116; RGEL 2

Mitford, Nancy 1904-1973 **CLC 44**
See also BRWS 10; CA 9-12R; CN 1; DLB
191; RGEL 2

Miyamoto, (Chujo) Yuriko
1899-1951 **TCLC 37**
See Miyamoto Yuriko
See also CA 170, 174

Miyamoto Yuriko
See Miyamoto, (Chujo) Yuriko
See also DLB 180

Miyazawa, Kenji 1896-1933 **TCLC 76**
See Miyazawa Kenji
See also CA 157; RGWL 3

Miyazawa Kenji
See Miyazawa, Kenji
See also EWL 3

Mizoguchi, Kenji 1898-1956 **TCLC 72**
See also CA 167

Mo, Timothy (Peter) 1950- **CLC 46, 134**
See also CA 117; CANR 128; CN 5, 6, 7;
DLB 194; MTCW 1; WLIT 4; WWE 1

Modarressi, Taghi (M.) 1931-1997 ... **CLC 44**
See also CA 121; 134; INT CA-134

Modiano, Patrick (Jean) 1945- **CLC 18,
218**
See also CA 85-88; CANR 17, 40, 115;
CWW 2; DLB 83, 299; EWL 3; RGHL

Mofolo, Thomas (Mokopu)
1875(?)-1948 **BLC 3; TCLC 22**
See also AFW; CA 121; 153; CANR 83;
DAM MULT; DLB 225; EWL 3; MTCW
2; MTFW 2005; WLIT 2

Mohr, Nicholasa 1938- **CLC 12; HLC 2**
See also AAYA 8, 46; CA 49-52; CANR 1,
32, 64; CLR 22; DAM MULT; DLB 145;
HW 1, 2; JRDA; LAIT 5; LLW; MAICYA
2; MAICYAS 1; RGAL 4; SAAS 8; SATA
8, 97; SATA-Essay 113; WYA; YAW

Moi, Toril 1953- **CLC 172**
See also CA 154; CANR 102; FW

Mojtabai, A(nn) G(race) 1938- **CLC 5, 9,
15, 29**
See also CA 85-88; CANR 88

Moliere 1622-1673 **DC 13; LC 10, 28, 64,
125, 127; WLC 4**
See also DA; DA3; DAB; DAC; DAM
DRAM, MST; DFS 13, 18, 20; DLB 268;
EW 3; GFL Beginnings to 1789; LATS
1:1; RGWL 2, 3; TWA

Molin, Charles
See Mayne, William (James Carter)

Molnar, Ferenc 1878-1952 **TCLC 20**
See also CA 109; 153; CANR 83; CDWLB
4; DAM DRAM; DLB 215; EWL 3;
RGWL 2, 3

Momaday, N(avarre) Scott 1934- **CLC 2,
19, 85, 95, 160; NNAL; PC 25; WLCS**
See also AAYA 11, 64; AMWS 4; ANW;
BPFB 2; BYA 12; CA 25-28R; CANR 14,
34, 68, 134; CDALBS; CN 2, 3, 4, 5, 6,
7; CPW; DA; DA3; DAB; DAC; DAM
MST, MULT, NOV, POP; DLB 143, 175,
256; EWL 3; EXPP; INT CANR-14;
LAIT 4; LATS 1:2; MAL 5; MTCW 1, 2;
MTFW 2005; NFS 10; PFS 2, 11; RGAL
4; SATA 48; SATA-Brief 30; TCWW 1,
2; WP; YAW

Monette, Paul 1945-1995 **CLC 82**
See also AMWS 10; CA 139; 147; CN 6;
GLL 1

Monroe, Harriet 1860-1936 **TCLC 12**
See also CA 109; 204; DLB 54, 91

Monroe, Lyle
See Heinlein, Robert A(nson)

Montagu, Elizabeth 1720-1800 **NCLC 7,
117**
See also FW

Montagu, Mary (Pierrepont) Wortley
1689-1762 **LC 9, 57; PC 16**
See also DLB 95, 101; FL 1:1; RGEL 2

Montagu, W. H.
See Coleridge, Samuel Taylor

Montague, John (Patrick) 1929- **CLC 13,
46**
See also CA 9-12R; CANR 9, 69, 121; CP
1, 2, 3, 4, 5, 6, 7; DLB 40; EWL 3;
MTCW 1; PFS 12; RGEL 2; TCLE 1:2

Montaigne, Michel (Eyquem) de
1533-1592 **LC 8, 105; WLC 4**
See also DA; DAB; DAC; DAM MST; EW
2; GFL Beginnings to 1789; LMFS 1;
RGWL 2, 3; TWA

Montale, Eugenio 1896-1981 ... **CLC 7, 9, 18;
PC 13**
See also CA 17-20R; 104; CANR 30; DLB
114; EW 11; EWL 3; MTCW 1; PFS 22;
RGWL 2, 3; TWA; WLIT 7

Montesquieu, Charles-Louis de Secondat
1689-1755 **LC 7, 69**
See also DLB 314; EW 3; GFL Beginnings
to 1789; TWA

Montessori, Maria 1870-1952 **TCLC 103**
See also CA 115; 147

Montgomery, (Robert) Bruce 1921(?)-1978
See Crispin, Edmund
See also CA 179; 104; CMW 4

Montgomery, L(ucy) M(aud)
1874-1942 **TCLC 51, 140**
See also AAYA 12; BYA 1; CA 108; 137;
CLR 8, 91; DA3; DAC; DAM MST; DLB
92; DLBD 14; JRDA; MAICYA 1, 2;
MTCW 2; MTFW 2005; RGEL 2; SATA
100; TWA; WCH; WYA; YABC 1

Montgomery, Marion H., Jr. 1925- **CLC 7**
See also AITN 1; CA 1-4R; CANR 3, 48;
CSW; DLB 6

Montgomery, Max
See Davenport, Guy (Mattison, Jr.)

Montherlant, Henry (Milon) de
1896-1972 **CLC 8, 19**
See also CA 85-88; 37-40R; DAM DRAM;
DLB 72, 321; EW 11; EWL 3; GFL 1789
to the Present; MTCW 1

Monty Python
See Chapman, Graham; Cleese, John
(Marwood); Gilliam, Terry (Vance); Idle,
Eric; Jones, Terence Graham Parry; Palin,
Michael (Edward)
See also AAYA 7

Moodie, Susanna (Strickland)
1803-1885 **NCLC 14, 113**
See also DLB 99

Moody, Hiram (F. III) 1961-
See Moody, Rick
See also CA 138; CANR 64, 112; MTFW
2005

Moody, Minerva
See Alcott, Louisa May

Moody, Rick **CLC 147**
See Moody, Hiram (F. III)

Moody, William Vaughan
1869-1910 **TCLC 105**
See also CA 110; 178; DLB 7, 54; MAL 5;
RGAL 4

Mooney, Edward 1951-
See Mooney, Ted
See also CA 130

Mooney, Ted **CLC 25**
See Mooney, Edward

Moorcock, Michael 1939- **CLC 5, 27, 58**
See Bradbury, Edward P.
See also AAYA 26; CA 45-48; CAAS 5;
CANR 2, 17, 38, 64, 122; CN 5, 6, 7;
DLB 14, 231, 261, 319; FANT; MTCW 1,
2; MTFW 2005; SATA 93, 166; SCFW 1,
2; SFW 4; SUFW 1, 2

Moorcock, Michael John
See Moorcock, Michael

Moore, Brian 1921-1999 ... **CLC 1, 3, 5, 7, 8, 19, 32, 90**
See Bryan, Michael
See also BRWS 9; CA 1-4R; 174; CANR 1,
25, 42, 63; CCA 1; CN 1, 2, 3, 4, 5, 6;
DAB; DAC; DAM MST; DLB 251; EWL
3; FANT; MTCW 1, 2; MTFW 2005;
RGEL 2

Moore, Edward
See Muir, Edwin
See also RGEL 2

Moore, G. E. 1873-1958 **TCLC 89**
See also DLB 262

Moore, George Augustus
1852-1933 **SSC 19; TCLC 7**
See also BRW 6; CA 104; 177; DLB 10,
18, 57, 135; EWL 3; RGEL 2; RGSF 2

Moore, Lorrie **CLC 39, 45, 68**
See Moore, Marie Lorena
See also AMWS 10; CN 5, 6, 7; DLB 234;
SSFS 19

Moore, Marianne (Craig)
1887-1972 **CLC 1, 2, 4, 8, 10, 13, 19, 47; PC 4, 49; WLCS**
See also AMW; CA 1-4R; 33-36R; CANR
3, 61; CDALB 1929-1941; CP 1; DA;
DA3; DAB; DAC; DAM MST, POET;
DLB 45; DLBD 7; EWL 3; EXPP; FL 1:6;
MAL 5; MAWW; MTCW 1, 2; MTFW
2005; PAB; PFS 14, 17; RGAL 4; SATA
20; TUS; WP

Moore, Marie Lorena 1957- **CLC 165**
See Moore, Lorrie
See also CA 116; CANR 39, 83, 139; DLB
234; MTFW 2005

Moore, Michael 1954- **CLC 218**
See also AAYA 53; CA 166; CANR 150

Moore, Thomas 1779-1852 **NCLC 6, 110**
See also DLB 96, 144; RGEL 2

Moorhouse, Frank 1938- **SSC 40**
See also CA 118; CANR 92; CN 3, 4, 5, 6,
7; DLB 289; RGSF 2

Mora, Pat(ricia) 1942- **HLC 2**
See also AMWS 13; CA 129; CANR 57,
81, 112; CLR 58; DAM MULT; DLB 209;
HW 1, 2; LLW; MAICYA 2; MTFW
2005; SATA 92, 134

Moraga, Cherríe 1952- **CLC 126; DC 22**
See also CA 131; CANR 66, 154; DAM
MULT; DLB 82, 249; FW; GLL 1; HW 1,
2; LLW

Morand, Paul 1888-1976 **CLC 41; SSC 22**
See also CA 184; 69-72; DLB 65; EWL 3

Morante, Elsa 1918-1985 **CLC 8, 47**
See also CA 85-88; 117; CANR 35; DLB
177; EWL 3; MTCW 1, 2; MTFW 2005;
RGHL; RGWL 2, 3; WLIT 7

Moravia, Alberto **CLC 2, 7, 11, 27, 46; SSC 26**
See Pincherle, Alberto
See also DLB 177; EW 12; EWL 3; MTCW
2; RGSF 2; RGWL 2, 3; WLIT 7

More, Hannah 1745-1833 **NCLC 27, 141**
See also DLB 107, 109, 116, 158; RGEL 2

More, Henry 1614-1687 **LC 9**
See also DLB 126, 252

More, Sir Thomas 1478(?)-1535 **LC 10, 32**
See also BRWC 1; BRWS 7; DLB 136, 281;
LMFS 1; RGEL 2; TEA

Moreas, Jean **TCLC 18**
See Papadiamantopoulos, Johannes
See also GFL 1789 to the Present

Moreton, Andrew Esq.
See Defoe, Daniel

Morgan, Berry 1919-2002 **CLC 6**
See also CA 49-52; 208; DLB 6

Morgan, Claire
See Highsmith, (Mary) Patricia
See also GLL 1

Morgan, Edwin (George) 1920- **CLC 31**
See also BRWS 9; CA 5-8R; CANR 3, 43,
90; CP 1, 2, 3, 4, 5, 6, 7; DLB 27

Morgan, (George) Frederick
1922-2004 **CLC 23**
See also CA 17-20R; 224; CANR 21, 144;
CP 2, 3, 4, 5, 6, 7

Morgan, Harriet
See Mencken, H(enry) L(ouis)

Morgan, Jane
See Cooper, James Fenimore

Morgan, Janet 1945- **CLC 39**
See also CA 65-68

Morgan, Lady 1776(?)-1859 **NCLC 29**
See also DLB 116, 158; RGEL 2

Morgan, Robin (Evonne) 1941- **CLC 2**
See also CA 69-72; CANR 29, 68; FW;
GLL 2; MTCW 1; SATA 80

Morgan, Scott
See Kuttner, Henry

Morgan, Seth 1949(?)-1990 **CLC 65**
See also CA 185; 132

Morgenstern, Christian (Otto Josef
Wolfgang) 1871-1914 **TCLC 8**
See also CA 105; 191; EWL 3

Morgenstern, S.
See Goldman, William

Mori, Rintaro
See Mori Ogai
See also CA 110

Mori, Toshio 1910-1980 **SSC 83**
See also CA 116; 244; DLB 312; RGSF 2

Moricz, Zsigmond 1879-1942 **TCLC 33**
See also CA 165; DLB 215; EWL 3

Morike, Eduard (Friedrich)
1804-1875 **NCLC 10**
See also DLB 133; RGWL 2, 3

Mori Ogai 1862-1922 **TCLC 14**
See Ogai
See also CA 164; DLB 180; EWL 3; RGWL
3; TWA

Moritz, Karl Philipp 1756-1793 **LC 2**
See also DLB 94

Morland, Peter Henry
See Faust, Frederick (Schiller)

Morley, Christopher (Darlington)
1890-1957 **TCLC 87**
See also CA 112; 213; DLB 9; MAL 5;
RGAL 4

Morren, Theophil
See Hofmannsthal, Hugo von

Morris, Bill 1952- **CLC 76**
See also CA 225

Morris, Julian
See West, Morris L(anglo)

Morris, Steveland Judkins (?)-
See Wonder, Stevie

Morris, William 1834-1896 . **NCLC 4; PC 55**
See also BRW 5; CDBLB 1832-1890; DLB
18, 35, 57, 156, 178, 184; FANT; RGEL
2; SFW 4; SUFW

Morris, Wright (Marion) 1910-1998 . **CLC 1, 3, 7, 18, 37; TCLC 107**
See also AMW; CA 9-12R; 167; CANR 21,
81; CN 1, 2, 3, 4, 5, 6; DLB 2, 206, 218;
DLBY 1981; EWL 3; MAL 5; MTCW 1,
2; MTFW 2005; RGAL 4; TCWW 1, 2

Morrison, Arthur 1863-1945 **SSC 40; TCLC 72**
See also CA 120; 157; CMW 4; DLB 70,
135, 197; RGEL 2

Morrison, Chloe Anthony Wofford
See Morrison, Toni

Morrison, James Douglas 1943-1971
See Morrison, Jim
See also CA 73-76; CANR 40

Morrison, Jim **CLC 17**
See Morrison, James Douglas

Morrison, John Gordon 1904-1998 ... **SSC 93**
See also CA 103; CANR 92; DLB 260

Morrison, Toni 1931- **BLC 3; CLC 4, 10, 22, 55, 81, 87, 173, 194; WLC 4**
See also AAYA 1, 22, 61; AFAW 1, 2;
AMWC 1; AMWS 3; BPFB 2; BW 2, 3;
CA 29-32R; CANR 27, 42, 67, 113, 124;
CDALB 1968-1988; CLR 99; CN 3, 4, 5,
6, 7; CPW; DA; DA3; DAB; DAC; DAM
MST, MULT, NOV, POP; DLB 6, 33, 143;
DLBY 1981; EWL 3; EXPN; FL 1:6; FW;
GL 3; LAIT 2, 4; LATS 1:2; LMFS 2;
MAL 5; MAWW; MTCW 1, 2; MTFW
2005; NFS 1, 6, 8, 14; RGAL 4; RHW;
SATA 57, 144; SSFS 5; TCLE 1:2; TUS;
YAW

Morrison, Van 1945- **CLC 21**
See also CA 116; 168

Morrissy, Mary 1957- **CLC 99**
See also CA 205; DLB 267

Mortimer, John (Clifford) 1923- **CLC 28, 43**
See also CA 13-16R; CANR 21, 69, 109;
CBD; CD 5, 6; CDBLB 1960 to Present;
CMW 4; CN 5, 6, 7; CPW; DA3; DAM
DRAM, POP; DLB 13, 245, 271; INT
CANR-21; MSW; MTCW 1, 2; MTFW
2005; RGEL 2

Mortimer, Penelope (Ruth)
1918-1999 **CLC 5**
See also CA 57-60; 187; CANR 45, 88; CN
1, 2, 3, 4, 5, 6

Mortimer, Sir John
See Mortimer, John (Clifford)

Morton, Anthony
See Creasey, John

Morton, Thomas 1579(?)-1647(?) **LC 72**
See also DLB 24; RGEL 2

Mosca, Gaetano 1858-1941 **TCLC 75**

Moses, Daniel David 1952- **NNAL**
See also CA 186

Mosher, Howard Frank 1943- **CLC 62**
See also CA 139; CANR 65, 115

Mosley, Nicholas 1923- **CLC 43, 70**
See also CA 69-72; CANR 41, 60, 108; CN
1, 2, 3, 4, 5, 6, 7; DLB 14, 207

Mosley, Walter 1952- **BLCS; CLC 97, 184**
See also AAYA 57; AMWS 13; BPFB 2;
BW 2; CA 142; CANR 57, 92, 136; CMW
4; CN 7; CPW; DA3; DAM MULT, POP;
DLB 306; MSW; MTCW 2; MTFW 2005

Moss, Howard 1922-1987 . **CLC 7, 14, 45, 50**
See also CA 1-4R; 123; CANR 1, 44; CP 1,
2, 3, 4; DAM POET; DLB 5

Mossgiel, Rab
See Burns, Robert

Motion, Andrew (Peter) 1952- **CLC 47**
See also BRWS 7; CA 146; CANR 90, 142;
CP 4, 5, 6, 7; DLB 40; MTFW 2005

Motley, Willard (Francis)
1909-1965 **CLC 18**
See also BW 1; CA 117; 106; CANR 88;
DLB 76, 143

Motoori, Norinaga 1730-1801 **NCLC 45**

Mott, Michael (Charles Alston)
1930- **CLC 15, 34**
See also CA 5-8R; CAAS 7; CANR 7, 29

Mountain Wolf Woman 1884-1960 . **CLC 92; NNAL**
See also CA 144; CANR 90

Moure, Erin 1955- **CLC 88**
See also CA 113; CP 5, 6, 7; CWP; DLB 60

Mourning Dove 1885(?)-1936 **NNAL**
See also CA 144; CANR 90; DAM MULT; DLB 175, 221

Mowat, Farley (McGill) 1921- **CLC 26**
See also AAYA 1, 50; BYA 2; CA 1-4R; CANR 4, 24, 42, 68, 108; CLR 20; CPW; DAC; DAM MST; DLB 68; INT CANR-24; JRDA; MAICYA 1, 2; MTCW 1, 2; MTFW 2005; SATA 3, 55; YAW

Mowatt, Anna Cora 1819-1870 **NCLC 74**
See also RGAL 4

Moyers, Bill 1934- **CLC 74**
See also AITN 2; CA 61-64; CANR 31, 52, 148

Mphahlele, Es'kia
See Mphahlele, Ezekiel
See also AFW; CDWLB 3; CN 4, 5, 6; DLB 125, 225; RGSF 2; SSFS 11

Mphahlele, Ezekiel 1919- ... **BLC 3; CLC 25, 133**
See Mphahlele, Es'kia
See also BW 2, 3; CA 81-84; CANR 26, 76; CN 1, 2, 3; DA3; DAM MULT; EWL 3; MTCW 2; MTFW 2005; SATA 119

Mqhayi, S(amuel) E(dward) K(rune Loliwe) 1875-1945 **BLC 3; TCLC 25**
See also CA 153; CANR 87; DAM MULT

Mrozek, Slawomir 1930- **CLC 3, 13**
See also CA 13-16R; CAAS 10; CANR 29; CDWLB 4; CWW 2; DLB 232; EWL 3; MTCW 1

Mrs. Belloc-Lowndes
See Lowndes, Marie Adelaide (Belloc)

Mrs. Fairstar
See Horne, Richard Henry Hengist

M'Taggart, John M'Taggart Ellis
See McTaggart, John McTaggart Ellis

Mtwa, Percy (?)- **CLC 47**
See also CD 6

Mueller, Lisel 1924- **CLC 13, 51; PC 33**
See also CA 93-96; CP 6, 7; DLB 105; PFS 9, 13

Muggeridge, Malcolm (Thomas)
1903-1990 **TCLC 120**
See also AITN 1; CA 101; CANR 33, 63; MTCW 1, 2

Muhammad 570-632 **WLCS**
See also DA; DAB; DAC; DAM MST; DLB 311

Muir, Edwin 1887-1959 . **PC 49; TCLC 2, 87**
See Moore, Edward
See also BRWS 6; CA 104; 193; DLB 20, 100, 191; EWL 3; RGEL 2

Muir, John 1838-1914 **TCLC 28**
See also AMWS 9; ANW; CA 165; DLB 186, 275

Mujica Lainez, Manuel 1910-1984 ... **CLC 31**
See Lainez, Manuel Mujica
See also CA 81-84; 112; CANR 32; EWL 3; HW 1

Mukherjee, Bharati 1940- **AAL; CLC 53, 115; SSC 38**
See also AAYA 46; BEST 89:2; CA 107, 232; CAAE 232; CANR 45, 72, 128; CN 5, 6, 7; DAM NOV; DLB 60, 218, 323; DNFS 1, 2; EWL 3; FW; MAL 5; MTCW 1, 2; MTFW 2005; RGAL 4; RGSF 2; SSFS 7; TUS; WWE 1

Muldoon, Paul 1951- **CLC 32, 72, 166**
See also BRWS 4; CA 113; 129; CANR 52, 91; CP 2, 3, 4, 5, 6, 7; DAM POET; DLB 40; INT CA-129; PFS 7, 22; TCLE 1:2

Mulisch, Harry (Kurt Victor)
1927- .. **CLC 42**
See also CA 9-12R; CANR 6, 26, 56, 110; CWW 2; DLB 299; EWL 3

Mull, Martin 1943- **CLC 17**
See also CA 105

Muller, Wilhelm **NCLC 73**

Mulock, Dinah Maria
See Craik, Dinah Maria (Mulock)
See also RGEL 2

Multatuli 1820-1881 **NCLC 165**
See also RGWL 2, 3

Munday, Anthony 1560-1633 **LC 87**
See also DLB 62, 172; RGEL 2

Munford, Robert 1737(?)-1783 **LC 5**
See also DLB 31

Mungo, Raymond 1946- **CLC 72**
See also CA 49-52; CANR 2

Munro, Alice (Anne) 1931- **CLC 6, 10, 19, 50, 95, 222; SSC 3; WLCS**
See also AITN 2; BPFB 2; CA 33-36R; CANR 33, 53, 75, 114; CCA 1; CN 1, 2, 3, 4, 5, 6, 7; DA3; DAC; DAM MST, NOV; DLB 53; EWL 3; MTCW 1, 2; MTFW 2005; RGEL 2; RGSF 2; SATA 29; SSFS 5, 13, 19; TCLE 1:2; WWE 1

Munro, H(ector) H(ugh) 1870-1916
See Saki
See also AAYA 56; CA 104; 130; CANR 104; CDBLB 1890-1914; DA; DA3; DAB; DAC; DAM MST, NOV; DLB 34, 162; EXPS; MTCW 1, 2; MTFW 2005; RGEL 2; SSFS 15

Murakami, Haruki 1949- **CLC 150**
See Murakami Haruki
See also CA 165; CANR 102, 146; MJW; RGWL 3; SFW 4; SSFS 23

Murakami Haruki
See Murakami, Haruki
See also CWW 2; DLB 182; EWL 3

Murasaki, Lady
See Murasaki Shikibu

Murasaki Shikibu 978(?)-1026(?) .. **CMLC 1, 79**
See also EFS 2; LATS 1:1; RGWL 2, 3

Murdoch, (Jean) Iris 1919-1999 ... **CLC 1, 2, 3, 4, 6, 8, 11, 15, 22, 31, 51; TCLC 171**
See also BRWS 1; CA 13-16R; 179; CANR 8, 43, 68, 103, 142; CBD; CDBLB 1960 to Present; CN 1, 2, 3, 4, 5, 6; CWD; DA3; DAB; DAC; DAM MST, NOV; DLB 14, 194, 233, 326; EWL 3; INT CANR-8; MTCW 1, 2; MTFW 2005; NFS 18; RGEL 2; TCLE 1:2; TEA; WLIT 4

Murfree, Mary Noailles 1850-1922 .. **SSC 22; TCLC 135**
See also CA 122; 176; DLB 12, 74; RGAL 4

Murnau, Friedrich Wilhelm
See Plumpe, Friedrich Wilhelm

Murphy, Richard 1927- **CLC 41**
See also BRWS 5; CA 29-32R; CP 1, 2, 3, 4, 5, 6, 7; DLB 40; EWL 3

Murphy, Sylvia 1937- **CLC 34**
See also CA 121

Murphy, Thomas (Bernard) 1935- ... **CLC 51**
See Murphy, Tom
See also CA 101

Murphy, Tom
See Murphy, Thomas (Bernard)
See also DLB 310

Murray, Albert L. 1916- **CLC 73**
See also BW 2; CA 49-52; CANR 26, 52, 78; CN 7; CSW; DLB 38; MTFW 2005

Murray, James Augustus Henry
1837-1915 **TCLC 117**

Murray, Judith Sargent
1751-1820 **NCLC 63**
See also DLB 37, 200

Murray, Les(lie Allan) 1938- **CLC 40**
See also BRWS 7; CA 21-24R; CANR 11, 27, 56, 103; CP 1, 2, 3, 4, 5, 6, 7; DAM POET; DLB 289; DLBY 2001; EWL 3; RGEL 2

Murry, J. Middleton
See Murry, John Middleton

Murry, John Middleton
1889-1957 **TCLC 16**
See also CA 118; 217; DLB 149

Musgrave, Susan 1951- **CLC 13, 54**
See also CA 69-72; CANR 45, 84; CCA 1; CP 2, 3, 4, 5, 6, 7; CWP

Musil, Robert (Edler von)
1880-1942 **SSC 18; TCLC 12, 68**
See also CA 109; CANR 55, 84; CDWLB 2; DLB 81, 124; EW 9; EWL 3; MTCW 2; RGSF 2; RGWL 2, 3

Muske, Carol **CLC 90**
See Muske-Dukes, Carol (Anne)

Muske-Dukes, Carol (Anne) 1945-
See Muske, Carol
See also CA 65-68, 203; CAAE 203; CANR 32, 70; CWP; PFS 24

Musset, Alfred de 1810-1857 . **DC 27; NCLC 7, 150**
See also DLB 192, 217; EW 6; GFL 1789 to the Present; RGWL 2, 3; TWA

Musset, Louis Charles Alfred de
See Musset, Alfred de

Mussolini, Benito (Amilcare Andrea)
1883-1945 **TCLC 96**
See also CA 116

Mutanabbi, Al-
See al-Mutanabbi, Ahmad ibn al-Husayn Abu al-Tayyib al-Jufi al-Kindi
See also WLIT 6

My Brother's Brother
See Chekhov, Anton (Pavlovich)

Myers, L(eopold) H(amilton)
1881-1944 **TCLC 59**
See also CA 157; DLB 15; EWL 3; RGEL 2

Myers, Walter Dean 1937- .. **BLC 3; CLC 35**
See also AAYA 4, 23; BW 2; BYA 6, 8, 11; CA 33-36R; CANR 20, 42, 67, 108; CLR 4, 16, 35, 110; DAM MULT, NOV; DLB 33; INT CANR-20; JRDA; LAIT 5; MAICYA 1, 2; MAICYAS 1; MTCW 2; MTFW 2005; SAAS 2; SATA 41, 71, 109, 157; SATA-Brief 27; WYA; YAW

Myers, Walter M.
See Myers, Walter Dean

Myles, Symon
See Follett, Ken(neth Martin)

Nabokov, Vladimir (Vladimirovich)
1899-1977 **CLC 1, 2, 3, 6, 8, 11, 15, 23, 44, 46, 64; SSC 11, 86; TCLC 108; WLC 4**
See also AAYA 45; AMW; AMWC 1; AMWR 1; BPFB 2; CA 5-8R; 69-72; CANR 20, 102; CDALB 1941-1968; CN 1, 2; CP 2; DA; DA3; DAB; DAC; DAM MST, NOV; DLB 2, 244, 278, 317; DLBD 3; DLBY 1980, 1991; EWL 3; EXPS; LATS 1:2; MAL 5; MTCW 1, 2; MTFW 2005; NCFS 4; NFS 9; RGAL 4; RGSF 2; SSFS 6, 15; TUS

Naevius c. 265B.C.-201B.C. **CMLC 37**
See also DLB 211

Nagai, Kafu **TCLC 51**
See Nagai, Sokichi
See also DLB 180

Nagai, Sokichi 1879-1959
See Nagai, Kafu
See also CA 117

Nagy, Laszlo 1925-1978 **CLC 7**
See also CA 129; 112

Naidu, Sarojini 1879-1949 **TCLC 80**
See also EWL 3; RGEL 2

Naipaul, Shiva(dhar Srinivasa)
1945-1985 **CLC 32, 39; TCLC 153**
See also CA 110; 112; 116; CANR 33; CN
2, 3; DA3; DAM NOV; DLB 157; DLBY
1985; EWL 3; MTCW 1, 2; MTFW 2005

Naipaul, V(idiadhar) S(urajprasad)
1932- **CLC 4, 7, 9, 13, 18, 37, 105,
199; SSC 38**
See also BPFB 2; BRWS 1; CA 1-4R;
CANR 1, 33, 51, 91, 126; CDBLB 1960
to Present; CDWLB 3; CN 1, 2, 3, 4, 5,
6, 7; DA3; DAB; DAC; DAM MST,
NOV; DLB 125, 204, 207, 326; DLBY
1985, 2001; EWL 3; LATS 1:2; MTCW
1, 2; MTFW 2005; RGEL 2; RGSF 2;
TWA; WLIT 4; WWE 1

Nakos, Lilika 1903(?)-1989 **CLC 29**

Napoleon
See Yamamoto, Hisaye

Narayan, R(asipuram) K(rishnaswami)
1906-2001 **CLC 7, 28, 47, 121, 211;
SSC 25**
See also BPFB 2; CA 81-84; 196; CANR
33, 61, 112; CN 1, 2, 3, 4, 5, 6, 7; DA3;
DAM NOV; DLB 323; DNFS 1; EWL 3;
MTCW 1, 2; MTFW 2005; RGEL 2;
RGSF 2; SATA 62; SSFS 5; WWE 1

Nash, (Frediric) Ogden 1902-1971 . **CLC 23;
PC 21; TCLC 109**
See also CA 13-14; 29-32R; CANR 34, 61;
CAP 1; CP 1; DAM POET; DLB 11;
MAICYA 1, 2; MAL 5; MTCW 1, 2;
RGAL 4; SATA 2, 46; WP

Nashe, Thomas 1567-1601(?) **LC 41, 89**
See also DLB 167; RGEL 2

Nathan, Daniel
See Dannay, Frederic

Nathan, George Jean 1882-1958 **TCLC 18**
See Hatteras, Owen
See also CA 114; 169; DLB 137; MAL 5

Natsume, Kinnosuke
See Natsume, Soseki

Natsume, Soseki 1867-1916 **TCLC 2, 10**
See Natsume Soseki; Soseki
See also CA 104; 195; RGWL 2, 3; TWA

Natsume Soseki
See Natsume, Soseki
See also DLB 180; EWL 3

Natti, (Mary) Lee 1919-
See Kingman, Lee
See also CA 5-8R; CANR 2

Navarre, Marguerite de
See de Navarre, Marguerite

Naylor, Gloria 1950- **BLC 3; CLC 28, 52,
156; WLCS**
See also AAYA 6, 39; AFAW 1, 2; AMWS
8; BW 2, 3; CA 107; CANR 27, 51, 74,
130; CN 4, 5, 6, 7; CPW; DA; DA3;
DAC; DAM MST, MULT, NOV, POP;
DLB 173; EWL 3; FW; MAL 5; MTCW
1, 2; MTFW 2005; NFS 4, 7; RGAL 4;
TCLE 1:2; TUS

Neal, John 1793-1876 **NCLC 161**
See also DLB 1, 59, 243; FW; RGAL 4

Neff, Debra .. **CLC 59**

Neihardt, John Gneisenau
1881-1973 **CLC 32**
See also CA 13-14; CANR 65; CAP 1; DLB
9, 54, 256; LAIT 2; TCWW 1, 2

Nekrasov, Nikolai Alekseevich
1821-1878 **NCLC 11**
See also DLB 277

Nelligan, Emile 1879-1941 **TCLC 14**
See also CA 114; 204; DLB 92; EWL 3

Nelson, Willie 1933- **CLC 17**
See also CA 107; CANR 114

Nemerov, Howard (Stanley)
1920-1991 **CLC 2, 6, 9, 36; PC 24;
TCLC 124**
See also AMW; CA 1-4R; 134; CABS 2;
CANR 1, 27, 53; CN 1, 2, 3; CP 1, 2, 3,
4, 5; DAM POET; DLB 5, 6; DLBY 1983;
EWL 3; INT CANR-27; MAL 5; MTCW
1, 2; MTFW 2005; PFS 10, 14; RGAL 4

Neruda, Pablo 1904-1973 .. **CLC 1, 2, 5, 7, 9,
28, 62; HLC 2; PC 4, 64; WLC 4**
See also CA 19-20; 45-48; CANR 131; CAP
2; DA; DA3; DAB; DAC; DAM MST,
MULT, POET; DLB 283; DNFS 2; EWL
3; HW 1; LAW; MTCW 1, 2; MTFW
2005; PFS 11; RGWL 2, 3; TWA; WLIT
1; WP

Nerval, Gerard de 1808-1855 ... **NCLC 1, 67;
PC 13; SSC 18**
See also DLB 217; EW 6; GFL 1789 to the
Present; RGSF 2; RGWL 2, 3

Nervo, (Jose) Amado (Ruiz de)
1870-1919 **HLCS 2; TCLC 11**
See also CA 109; 131; DLB 290; EWL 3;
HW 1; LAW

Nesbit, Malcolm
See Chester, Alfred

Nessi, Pio Baroja y
See Baroja, Pio

Nestroy, Johann 1801-1862 **NCLC 42**
See also DLB 133; RGWL 2, 3

Netterville, Luke
See O'Grady, Standish (James)

Neufeld, John (Arthur) 1938- **CLC 17**
See also AAYA 11; CA 25-28R; CANR 11,
37, 56; CLR 52; MAICYA 1, 2; SAAS 3;
SATA 6, 81, 131; SATA-Essay 131; YAW

Neumann, Alfred 1895-1952 **TCLC 100**
See also CA 183; DLB 56

Neumann, Ferenc
See Molnar, Ferenc

Neville, Emily Cheney 1919- **CLC 12**
See also BYA 2; CA 5-8R; CANR 3, 37,
85; JRDA; MAICYA 1, 2; SAAS 2; SATA
1; YAW

Newbound, Bernard Slade 1930-
See Slade, Bernard
See also CA 81-84; CANR 49; CD 5; DAM
DRAM

Newby, P(ercy) H(oward)
1918-1997 **CLC 2, 13**
See also CA 5-8R; 161; CANR 32, 67; CN
1, 2, 3, 4, 5, 6; DAM NOV; DLB 15, 326;
MTCW 1; RGEL 2

Newcastle
See Cavendish, Margaret Lucas

Newlove, Donald 1928- **CLC 6**
See also CA 29-32R; CANR 25

Newlove, John (Herbert) 1938- **CLC 14**
See also CA 21-24R; CANR 9, 25; CP 1, 2,
3, 4, 5, 6, 7

Newman, Charles 1938-2006 **CLC 2, 8**
See also CA 21-24R; CANR 84; CN 3, 4,
5, 6

Newman, Charles Hamilton
See Newman, Charles

Newman, Edwin (Harold) 1919- **CLC 14**
See also AITN 1; CA 69-72; CANR 5

Newman, John Henry 1801-1890 . **NCLC 38,
99**
See also BRWS 7; DLB 18, 32, 55; RGEL
2

Newton, (Sir) Isaac 1642-1727 **LC 35, 53**
See also DLB 252

Newton, Suzanne 1936- **CLC 35**
See also BYA 7; CA 41-44R; CANR 14;
JRDA; SATA 5, 77

New York Dept. of Ed. **CLC 70**

Nexo, Martin Andersen
1869-1954 **TCLC 43**
See also CA 202; DLB 214; EWL 3

Nezval, Vitezslav 1900-1958 **TCLC 44**
See also CA 123; CDWLB 4; DLB 215;
EWL 3

Ng, Fae Myenne 1957(?)- **CLC 81**
See also BYA 11; CA 146

Ngema, Mbongeni 1955- **CLC 57**
See also BW 2; CA 143; CANR 84; CD 5,
6

Nguei, James T(hiong'o) . **CLC 3, 7, 13, 182**
See Ngugi wa Thiong'o
See also CN 1, 2

Ngugi wa Thiong'o
See Ngugi wa Thiong'o
See also CD 3, 4, 5, 6, 7; DLB 125; EWL 3

Ngugi wa Thiong'o 1938- ... **BLC 3; CLC 36,
182**
See Ngugi, James T(hiong'o); Ngugi wa
Thiong'o
See also AFW; BRWS 8; BW 2; CA 81-84;
CANR 27, 58; CDWLB 3; DAM MULT,
NOV; DNFS 2; MTCW 1, 2; MTFW
2005; RGEL 2; WWE 1

Niatum, Duane 1938- **NNAL**
See also CA 41-44R; CANR 21, 45, 83;
DLB 175

Nichol, B(arrie) P(hillip) 1944-1988 . **CLC 18**
See also CA 53-56; CP 1, 2, 3, 4; DLB 53;
SATA 66

Nicholas of Cusa 1401-1464 **LC 80**
See also DLB 115

Nichols, John (Treadwell) 1940- **CLC 38**
See also AMWS 13; CA 9-12R, 190; CAAE
190; CAAS 2; CANR 6, 70, 121; DLBY
1982; LATS 1:2; MTFW 2005; TCWW 1,
2

Nichols, Leigh
See Koontz, Dean R.

Nichols, Peter (Richard) 1927- **CLC 5, 36,
65**
See also CA 104; CANR 33, 86; CBD; CD
5, 6; DLB 13, 245; MTCW 1

Nicholson, Linda ed. **CLC 65**

Ni Chuilleanain, Eilean 1942- **PC 34**
See also CA 126; CANR 53, 83; CP 5, 6, 7;
CWP; DLB 40

Nicolas, F. R. E.
See Freeling, Nicolas

Niedecker, Lorine 1903-1970 **CLC 10, 42;
PC 42**
See also CA 25-28; CAP 2; DAM POET;
DLB 48

Nietzsche, Friedrich (Wilhelm)
1844-1900 **TCLC 10, 18, 55**
See also CA 107; 121; CDWLB 2; DLB
129; EW 7; RGWL 2, 3; TWA

Nievo, Ippolito 1831-1861 **NCLC 22**

Nightingale, Anne Redmon 1943-
See Redmon, Anne
See also CA 103

Nightingale, Florence 1820-1910 ... **TCLC 85**
See also CA 188; DLB 166

Nijo Yoshimoto 1320-1388 **CMLC 49**
See also DLB 203

Nik. T. O.
See Annensky, Innokenty (Fyodorovich)

Nin, Anais 1903-1977 **CLC 1, 4, 8, 11, 14,
60, 127; SSC 10**
See also AITN 2; AMWS 10; BPFB 2; CA
13-16R; 69-72; CANR 22, 53; CN 1, 2;
DAM NOV, POP; DLB 2, 4, 152; EWL
3; GLL 2; MAL 5; MAWW; MTCW 1, 2;
MTFW 2005; RGAL 4; RGSF 2

Nisbet, Robert A(lexander)
1913-1996 **TCLC 117**
See also CA 25-28R; 153; CANR 17; INT
CANR-17

Nishida, Kitaro 1870-1945 **TCLC 83**
Nishiwaki, Junzaburo 1894-1982 **PC 15**
 See Junzaburo, Nishiwaki
 See also CA 194; 107; MJW; RGWL 3
Nissenson, Hugh 1933- **CLC 4, 9**
 See also CA 17-20R; CANR 27, 108, 151;
 CN 5, 6; DLB 28
Nister, Der
 See Der Nister
 See also EWL 3
Niven, Larry 1938-
 See Niven, Lawrence VanCott
 See also CA 21-24R, 207; CAAE 207;
 CAAS 12; CANR 14, 44, 66, 113; CPW;
 DAM POP; MTCW 1, 2; SATA 95, 171;
 SFW 4
Niven, Lawrence VanCott **CLC 8**
 See Niven, Larry
 See also AAYA 27; BPFB 2; BYA 10; DLB
 8; SCFW 1, 2
Nixon, Agnes Eckhardt 1927- **CLC 21**
 See also CA 110
Nizan, Paul 1905-1940 **TCLC 40**
 See also CA 161; DLB 72; EWL 3; GFL
 1789 to the Present
Nkosi, Lewis 1936- **BLC 3; CLC 45**
 See also BW 1, 3; CA 65-68; CANR 27,
 81; CBD; CD 5, 6; DAM MULT; DLB
 157, 225; WWE 1
Nodier, (Jean) Charles (Emmanuel)
 1780-1844 **NCLC 19**
 See also DLB 119; GFL 1789 to the Present
Noguchi, Yone 1875-1947 **TCLC 80**
Nolan, Christopher 1965- **CLC 58**
 See also CA 111; CANR 88
Noon, Jeff 1957- **CLC 91**
 See also CA 148; CANR 83; DLB 267;
 SFW 4
Norden, Charles
 See Durrell, Lawrence (George)
Nordhoff, Charles Bernard
 1887-1947 **TCLC 23**
 See also CA 108; 211; DLB 9; LAIT 1;
 RHW 1; SATA 23
Norfolk, Lawrence 1963- **CLC 76**
 See also CA 144; CANR 85; CN 6, 7; DLB
 267
Norman, Marsha (Williams) 1947- . **CLC 28,
 186; DC 8**
 See also CA 105; CABS 3; CAD; CANR
 41, 131; CD 5, 6; CSW; CWD; DAM
 DRAM; DFS 2; DLB 266; DLBY 1984;
 FW; MAL 5
Normyx
 See Douglas, (George) Norman
Norris, (Benjamin) Frank(lin, Jr.)
 1870-1902 **SSC 28; TCLC 24, 155**
 See also AAYA 57; AMW; AMWC 2; BPFB
 2; CA 110; 160; CDALB 1865-1917; DLB
 12, 71, 186; LMFS 2; MAL 5; NFS 12;
 RGAL 4; TCWW 1, 2; TUS
Norris, Leslie 1921-2006 **CLC 14**
 See also CA 11-12; CANR 14, 117; CAP 1;
 CP 1, 2, 3, 4, 5, 6, 7; DLB 27, 256
North, Andrew
 See Norton, Andre
North, Anthony
 See Koontz, Dean R.
North, Captain George
 See Stevenson, Robert Louis (Balfour)
North, Captain George
 See Stevenson, Robert Louis (Balfour)
North, Milou
 See Erdrich, Louise
Northrup, B. A.
 See Hubbard, L. Ron
North Staffs
 See Hulme, T(homas) E(rnest)
Northup, Solomon 1808-1863 **NCLC 105**

Norton, Alice Mary
 See Norton, Andre
 See also MAICYA 1; SATA 1, 43
Norton, Andre 1912-2005 **CLC 12**
 See Norton, Alice Mary
 See also AAYA 14; BPFB 2; BYA 4, 10,
 12; CA 1-4R; 237; CANR 2, 31, 68, 108,
 149; CLR 50; DLB 8, 52; JRDA; MAI-
 CYA 2; MTCW 1; SATA 91; SUFW 1, 2;
 YAW
Norton, Caroline 1808-1877 **NCLC 47**
 See also DLB 21, 159, 199
Norway, Nevil Shute 1899-1960
 See Shute, Nevil
 See also CA 102; 93-96; CANR 85; MTCW
 2
Norwid, Cyprian Kamil
 1821-1883 **NCLC 17**
 See also RGWL 3
Nosille, Nabrah
 See Ellison, Harlan (Jay)
Nossack, Hans Erich 1901-1978 **CLC 6**
 See also CA 93-96; 85-88; DLB 69; EWL 3
Nostradamus 1503-1566 **LC 27**
Nosu, Chuji
 See Ozu, Yasujiro
Notenburg, Eleanora (Genrikhovna) von
 See Guro, Elena (Genrikhovna)
Nova, Craig 1945- **CLC 7, 31**
 See also CA 45-48; CANR 2, 53, 127
Novak, Joseph
 See Kosinski, Jerzy (Nikodem)
Novalis 1772-1801 **NCLC 13**
 See also CDWLB 2; DLB 90; EW 5; RGWL
 2, 3
Novick, Peter 1934- **CLC 164**
 See also CA 188
Novis, Emile
 See Weil, Simone (Adolphine)
Nowlan, Alden (Albert) 1933-1983 ... **CLC 15**
 See also CA 9-12R; CANR 5; CP 1, 2, 3;
 DAC; DAM MST; DLB 53; PFS 12
Noyes, Alfred 1880-1958 **PC 27; TCLC 7**
 See also CA 104; 188; DLB 20; EXPP;
 FANT; PFS 4; RGEL 2
Nugent, Richard Bruce
 1906(?)-1987 **HR 1:3**
 See also BW 1; CA 125; DLB 51; GLL 2
Nunn, Kem **CLC 34**
 See also CA 159
Nussbaum, Martha Craven 1947- .. **CLC 203**
 See also CA 134; CANR 102
Nwapa, Flora (Nwanzuruaha)
 1931-1993 **BLCS; CLC 133**
 See also BW 2; CA 143; CANR 83; CD-
 WLB 3; CWRI 5; DLB 125; EWL 3;
 WLIT 2
Nye, Robert 1939- **CLC 13, 42**
 See also BRWS 10; CA 33-36R; CANR 29,
 67, 107; CN 1, 2, 3, 4, 5, 6, 7; CP 1, 2, 3,
 4, 5, 6, 7; CWRI 5; DAM NOV; DLB 14,
 271; FANT; HGG; MTCW 1; RHW;
 SATA 6
Nyro, Laura 1947-1997 **CLC 17**
 See also CA 194
Oates, Joyce Carol 1938- .. **CLC 1, 2, 3, 6, 9,
 11, 15, 19, 33, 52, 108, 134; SSC 6, 70;
 WLC 4**
 See also AAYA 15, 52; AITN 1; AMWS 2;
 BEST 89:2; BPFB 2; BYA 11; CA 5-8R;
 CANR 25, 45, 74, 113, 129; CDALB
 1968-1988; CN 1, 2, 3, 4, 5, 6, 7; CP 5,
 6, 7; CPW; CWP; DA; DA3; DAB; DAC;
 DAM MST, NOV, POP; DLB 2, 5, 130;
 DLBY 1981; EWL 3; EXPS; FL 1:6; FW;
 GL 3; HGG; INT CANR-25; LAIT 4;
 MAL 5; MAWW; MTCW 1, 2; MTFW
 2005; NFS 8; RGAL 4; RGSF 2; SATA
 159; SSFS 1, 8, 17; SUFW 2; TUS

O'Brian, E. G.
 See Clarke, Arthur C(harles)
O'Brien, Patrick 1914-2000 **CLC 152**
 See also AAYA 55; CA 144; 187; CANR
 74; CPW; MTCW 2; MTFW 2005; RHW
O'Brien, Darcy 1939-1998 **CLC 11**
 See also CA 21-24R; 167; CANR 8, 59
O'Brien, Edna 1932- **CLC 3, 5, 8, 13, 36,
 65, 116; SSC 10, 77**
 See also BRWS 5; CA 1-4R; CANR 6, 41,
 65, 102; CDBLB 1960 to Present; CN 1,
 2, 3, 4, 5, 6, 7; DA3; DAM NOV; DLB
 14, 231, 319; EWL 3; FW; MTCW 1, 2;
 MTFW 2005; RGSF 2; WLIT 4
O'Brien, Fitz-James 1828-1862 **NCLC 21**
 See also DLB 74; RGAL 4; SUFW
O'Brien, Flann **CLC 1, 4, 5, 7, 10, 47**
 See O Nuallain, Brian
 See also BRWS 2; DLB 231; EWL 3;
 RGEL 2
O'Brien, Richard 1942- **CLC 17**
 See also CA 124
O'Brien, (William) Tim(othy) 1946- . **CLC 7,
 19, 40, 103, 211; SSC 74**
 See also AAYA 16; AMWS 5; CA 85-88;
 CANR 40, 58, 133; CDALBS; CN 5, 6,
 7; CPW; DA3; DAM POP; DLB 152;
 DLBD 9; DLBY 1980; LATS 1:2; MAL
 5; MTCW 2; MTFW 2005; RGAL 4;
 SSFS 5, 15; TCLE 1:2
Obstfelder, Sigbjoern 1866-1900 **TCLC 23**
 See also CA 123
O'Casey, Sean 1880-1964 **CLC 1, 5, 9, 11,
 15, 88; DC 12; WLCS**
 See also BRW 7; CA 89-92; CANR 62;
 CBD; CDBLB 1914-1945; DA3; DAB;
 DAC; DAM DRAM, MST; DFS 19; DLB
 10; EWL 3; MTCW 1, 2; MTFW 2005;
 RGEL 2; TEA; WLIT 4
O'Cathasaigh, Sean
 See O'Casey, Sean
Occom, Samson 1723-1792 **LC 60; NNAL**
 See also DLB 175
Occomy, Marita (Odette) Bonner
 1899(?)-1971
 See Bonner, Marita
 See also BW 2; CA 142; DFS 13; DLB 51,
 228
Ochs, Phil(ip David) 1940-1976 **CLC 17**
 See also CA 185; 65-68
O'Connor, Edwin (Greene)
 1918-1968 **CLC 14**
 See also CA 93-96; 25-28R; MAL 5
O'Connor, (Mary) Flannery
 1925-1964 **CLC 1, 2, 3, 6, 10, 13, 15,
 21, 66, 104; SSC 1, 23, 61, 82; TCLC
 132; WLC 4**
 See also AAYA 7; AMW; AMWR 2; BPFB
 3; BYA 16; CA 1-4R; CANR 3, 41;
 CDALB 1941-1968; DA; DA3; DAB;
 DAC; DAM MST, NOV; DLB 2, 152;
 DLBD 12; DLBY 1980; EWL 3; EXPS;
 LAIT 5; MAL 5; MAWW; MTCW 1, 2;
 MTFW 2005; NFS 3, 21; RGAL 4; RGSF
 2; SSFS 2, 7, 10, 19; TUS
O'Connor, Frank **CLC 23; SSC 5**
 See O'Donovan, Michael Francis
 See also DLB 162; EWL 3; RGSF 2; SSFS
 5
O'Dell, Scott 1898-1989 **CLC 30**
 See also AAYA 3, 44; BPFB 3; BYA 1, 2,
 3, 5; CA 61-64; 129; CANR 12, 30, 112;
 CLR 1, 16; DLB 52; JRDA; MAICYA 1,
 2; SATA 12, 60, 134; WYA; YAW
Odets, Clifford 1906-1963 **CLC 2, 28, 98;
 DC 6**
 See also AMWS 2; CA 85-88; CAD; CANR
 62; DAM DRAM; DFS 3, 17, 20; DLB 7,
 26; EWL 3; MAL 5; MTCW 1, 2; MTFW
 2005; RGAL 4; TUS

Author Index

O'Doherty, Brian 1928- **CLC 76**
See also CA 105; CANR 108
O'Donnell, K. M.
See Malzberg, Barry N(athaniel)
O'Donnell, Lawrence
See Kuttner, Henry
O'Donovan, Michael Francis
1903-1966 **CLC 14**
See O'Connor, Frank
See also CA 93-96; CANR 84
Oe, Kenzaburo 1935- .. **CLC 10, 36, 86, 187;**
SSC 20
See Oe Kenzaburo
See also CA 97-100; CANR 36, 50, 74, 126;
DA3; DAM NOV; DLB 182; DLBY 1994;
LATS 1:2; MJW; MTCW 1, 2; MTFW
2005; RGSF 2; RGWL 2, 3
Oe Kenzaburo
See Oe, Kenzaburo
See also CWW 2; EWL 3
O'Faolain, Julia 1932- **CLC 6, 19, 47, 108**
See also CA 81-84; CAAS 2; CANR 12,
61; CN 2, 3, 4, 5, 6, 7; DLB 14, 231, 319;
FW; MTCW 1; RHW
O'Faolain, Sean 1900-1991 **CLC 1, 7, 14,**
32, 70; SSC 13; TCLC 143
See also CA 61-64; 134; CANR 12, 66; CN
1, 2, 3, 4; DLB 15, 162; MTCW 1, 2;
MTFW 2005; RGEL 2; RGSF 2
O'Flaherty, Liam 1896-1984 **CLC 5, 34;**
SSC 6
See also CA 101; 113; CANR 35; CN 1, 2,
3; DLB 36, 162; DLBY 1984; MTCW 1,
2; MTFW 2005; RGEL 2; RGSF 2; SSFS
5, 20
Ogai
See Mori Ogai
See also MJW
Ogilvy, Gavin
See Barrie, J(ames) M(atthew)
O'Grady, Standish (James)
1846-1928 **TCLC 5**
See also CA 104; 157
O'Grady, Timothy 1951- **CLC 59**
See also CA 138
O'Hara, Frank 1926-1966 **CLC 2, 5, 13,**
78; PC 45
See also CA 9-12R; 25-28R; CANR 33;
DA3; DAM POET; DLB 5, 16, 193; EWL
3; MAL 5; MTCW 1, 2; MTFW 2005;
PFS 8, 12; RGAL 4; WP
O'Hara, John (Henry) 1905-1970 . **CLC 1, 2,**
3, 6, 11, 42; SSC 15
See also AMW; BPFB 3; CA 5-8R; 25-28R;
CANR 31, 60; CDALB 1929-1941; DAM
NOV; DLB 9, 86, 324; DLBD 2; EWL 3;
MAL 5; MTCW 1, 2; MTFW 2005; NFS
11; RGAL 4; RGSF 2
O'Hehir, Diana 1929- **CLC 41**
See also CA 245
Ohiyesa
See Eastman, Charles A(lexander)
Okada, John 1923-1971 **AAL**
See also BYA 14; CA 212; DLB 312
Okigbo, Christopher 1930-1967 **BLC 3;**
CLC 25, 84; PC 7; TCLC 171
See also AFW; BW 1, 3; CA 77-80; CANR
74; CDWLB 3; DAM MULT, POET; DLB
125; EWL 3; MTCW 1, 2; MTFW 2005;
RGEL 2
Okigbo, Christopher Ifenayichukwu
See Okigbo, Christopher
Okri, Ben 1959- **CLC 87, 223**
See also AFW; BRWS 5; BW 2, 3; CA 130;
138; CANR 65, 128; CN 5, 6, 7; DLB
157, 231, 319, 326; EWL 3; INT CA-138;
MTCW 2; MTFW 2005; RGSF 2; SSFS
20; WLIT 2; WWE 1

Olds, Sharon 1942- .. **CLC 32, 39, 85; PC 22**
See also AMWS 10; CA 101; CANR 18,
41, 66, 98, 135; CP 5, 6, 7; CPW; CWP;
DAM POET; DLB 120; MAL 5; MTCW
2; MTFW 2005; PFS 17
Oldstyle, Jonathan
See Irving, Washington
Olesha, Iurii
See Olesha, Yuri (Karlovich)
See also RGWL 2
Olesha, Iurii Karlovich
See Olesha, Yuri (Karlovich)
See also DLB 272
Olesha, Yuri (Karlovich) 1899-1960 . **CLC 8;**
SSC 69; TCLC 136
See Olesha, Iurii; Olesha, Iurii Karlovich;
Olesha, Yury Karlovich
See also CA 85-88; EW 11; RGWL 3
Olesha, Yury Karlovich
See Olesha, Yuri (Karlovich)
See also EWL 3
Oliphant, Mrs.
See Oliphant, Margaret (Oliphant Wilson)
See also SUFW
Oliphant, Laurence 1829(?)-1888 .. **NCLC 47**
See also DLB 18, 166
Oliphant, Margaret (Oliphant Wilson)
1828-1897 **NCLC 11, 61; SSC 25**
See Oliphant, Mrs.
See also BRWS 10; DLB 18, 159, 190;
HGG; RGEL 2; RGSF 2
Oliver, Mary 1935- **CLC 19, 34, 98**
See also AMWS 7; CA 21-24R; CANR 9,
43, 84, 92, 138; CP 4, 5, 6, 7; CWP; DLB
5, 193; EWL 3; MTFW 2005; PFS 15
Olivier, Laurence (Kerr) 1907-1989 . **CLC 20**
See also CA 111; 150; 129
Olsen, Tillie 1912- ... **CLC 4, 13, 114; SSC 11**
See also AAYA 51; AMWS 13; BYA 11;
CA 1-4R; CANR 1, 43, 74, 132;
CDALBS; CN 2, 3, 4, 5, 6, 7; DA; DA3;
DAB; DAC; DAM MST; DLB 28, 206;
DLBY 1980; EWL 3; EXPS; FW; MAL
5; MTCW 1, 2; MTFW 2005; RGAL 4;
RGSF 2; SSFS 1; TCLE 1:2; TCWW 2;
TUS
Olson, Charles (John) 1910-1970 .. **CLC 1, 2,**
5, 6, 9, 11, 29; PC 19
See also AMWS 2; CA 13-16; 25-28R;
CABS 2; CANR 35, 61; CAP 1; CP 1;
DAM POET; DLB 5, 16, 193; EWL 3;
MAL 5; MTCW 1, 2; RGAL 4; WP
Olson, Toby 1937- **CLC 28**
See also CA 65-68; CANR 9, 31, 84; CP 3,
4, 5, 6, 7
Olyesha, Yuri
See Olesha, Yuri (Karlovich)
Olympiodorus of Thebes c. 375-c.
430 ... **CMLC 59**
Omar Khayyam
See Khayyam, Omar
See also RGWL 2, 3
Ondaatje, Michael 1943- **CLC 14, 29, 51,**
76, 180; PC 28
See also AAYA 66; CA 77-80; CANR 42,
74, 109, 133; CN 5, 6, 7; CP 1, 2, 3, 4, 5,
6, 7; DA3; DAB; DAC; DAM MST; DLB
60, 323, 326; EWL 3; LATS 1:2; LMFS
2; MTCW 2; MTFW 2005; NFS 23; PFS
8, 19; TCLE 1:2; TWA; WWE 1
Ondaatje, Philip Michael
See Ondaatje, Michael
Oneal, Elizabeth 1934-
See Oneal, Zibby
See also CA 106; CANR 28, 84; MAICYA
1, 2; SATA 30, 82; YAW
Oneal, Zibby **CLC 30**
See Oneal, Elizabeth
See also AAYA 5, 41; BYA 13; CLR 13;
JRDA; WYA

O'Neill, Eugene (Gladstone)
1888-1953 ... **DC 20; TCLC 1, 6, 27, 49;**
WLC 4
See also AAYA 54; AITN 1; AMW; AMWC
1; CA 110; 132; CAD; CANR 131;
CDALB 1929-1941; DA; DA3; DAB;
DAC; DAM DRAM, MST; DFS 2, 4, 5,
6, 9, 11, 12, 16, 20; DLB 7; EWL 3; LAIT
3; LMFS 2; MAL 5; MTCW 1, 2; MTFW
2005; RGAL 4; TUS
Onetti, Juan Carlos 1909-1994 ... **CLC 7, 10;**
HLCS 2; SSC 23; TCLC 131
See also CA 85-88; 145; CANR 32, 63; CD-
WLB 3; CWW 2; DAM MULT, NOV;
DLB 113; EWL 3; HW 1, 2; LAW;
MTCW 1, 2; MTFW 2005; RGSF 2
O Nuallain, Brian 1911-1966
See O'Brien, Flann
See also CA 21-22; 25-28R; CAP 2; DLB
231; FANT; TEA
Ophuls, Max 1902-1957 **TCLC 79**
See also CA 113
Opie, Amelia 1769-1853 **NCLC 65**
See also DLB 116, 159; RGEL 2
Oppen, George 1908-1984 **CLC 7, 13, 34;**
PC 35; TCLC 107
See also CA 13-16R; 113; CANR 8, 82; CP
1, 2, 3; DLB 5, 165
Oppenheim, E(dward) Phillips
1866-1946 **TCLC 45**
See also CA 111; 202; CMW 4; DLB 70
Opuls, Max
See Ophuls, Max
Orage, A(lfred) R(ichard)
1873-1934 **TCLC 157**
See also CA 122
Origen c. 185-c. 254 **CMLC 19**
Orlovitz, Gil 1918-1973 **CLC 22**
See also CA 77-80; 45-48; CN 1; CP 1, 2;
DLB 2, 5
O'Rourke, P(atrick) J(ake) 1947- .. **CLC 209**
See also CA 77-80; CANR 13, 41, 67, 111;
CPW; DAM POP; DLB 185
Orris
See Ingelow, Jean
Ortega y Gasset, Jose 1883-1955 **HLC 2;**
TCLC 9
See also CA 106; 130; DAM MULT; EW 9;
EWL 3; HW 1, 2; MTCW 1, 2; MTFW
2005
Ortese, Anna Maria 1914-1998 **CLC 89**
See also DLB 177; EWL 3
Ortiz, Simon J(oseph) 1941- ... **CLC 45, 208;**
NNAL; PC 17
See also AMWS 4; CA 134; CANR 69, 118;
CP 3, 4, 5, 6, 7; DAM MULT, POET;
DLB 120, 175, 256; EXPP; MAL 5; PFS
4, 16; RGAL 4; TCWW 2
Orton, Joe **CLC 4, 13, 43; DC 3; TCLC**
157
See Orton, John Kingsley
See also BRWS 5; CBD; CDBLB 1960 to
Present; DFS 3, 6; DLB 13, 310; GLL 1;
RGEL 2; TEA; WLIT 4
Orton, John Kingsley 1933-1967
See Orton, Joe
See also CA 85-88; CANR 35, 66; DAM
DRAM; MTCW 1, 2; MTFW 2005
Orwell, George **SSC 68; TCLC 2, 6, 15,**
31, 51, 128, 129; WLC 4
See Blair, Eric (Arthur)
See also BPFB 3; BRW 7; BYA 5; CDBLB
1945-1960; CLR 68; DAB; DLB 15, 98,
195, 255; EWL 3; EXPN; LAIT 4, 5;
LATS 1:1; NFS 3, 7; RGEL 2; SCFW 1,
2; SFW 4; SSFS 4; TEA; WLIT 4; YAW
Osborne, David
See Silverberg, Robert
Osborne, George
See Silverberg, Robert

Osborne, John (James) 1929-1994 **CLC 1, 2, 5, 11, 45; TCLC 153; WLC 4**
See also BRWS 1; CA 13-16R; 147; CANR 21, 56; CBD; CDBLB 1945-1960; DA; DAB; DAC; DAM DRAM, MST; DFS 4, 19; DLB 13; EWL 3; MTCW 1, 2; MTFW 2005; RGEL 2

Osborne, Lawrence 1958- **CLC 50**
See also CA 189; CANR 152

Osbourne, Lloyd 1868-1947 **TCLC 93**

Osgood, Frances Sargent
 1811-1850 **NCLC 141**
See also DLB 250

Oshima, Nagisa 1932- **CLC 20**
See also CA 116; 121; CANR 78

Oskison, John Milton
 1874-1947 **NNAL; TCLC 35**
See also CA 144; CANR 84; DAM MULT; DLB 175

Ossian c. 3rd cent. - **CMLC 28**
See Macpherson, James

Ossoli, Sarah Margaret (Fuller)
 1810-1850 **NCLC 5, 50**
See Fuller, Margaret; Fuller, Sarah Margaret
See also CDALB 1640-1865; FW; LMFS 1; SATA 25

Ostriker, Alicia (Suskin) 1937- **CLC 132**
See also CA 25-28R; CAAS 24; CANR 10, 30, 62, 99; CWP; DLB 120; EXPP; PFS 19

Ostrovsky, Aleksandr Nikolaevich
See Ostrovsky, Alexander
See also DLB 277

Ostrovsky, Alexander 1823-1886 .. **NCLC 30, 57**
See Ostrovsky, Aleksandr Nikolaevich

Otero, Blas de 1916-1979 **CLC 11**
See also CA 89-92; DLB 134; EWL 3

O'Trigger, Sir Lucius
See Horne, Richard Henry Hengist

Otto, Rudolf 1869-1937 **TCLC 85**

Otto, Whitney 1955- **CLC 70**
See also CA 140; CANR 120

Otway, Thomas 1652-1685 ... **DC 24; LC 106**
See also DAM DRAM; DLB 80; RGEL 2

Ouida ... **TCLC 43**
See De la Ramee, Marie Louise (Ouida)
See also DLB 18, 156; RGEL 2

Ouologuem, Yambo 1940- **CLC 146**
See also CA 111; 176

Ousmane, Sembene 1923- ... **BLC 3; CLC 66**
See Sembene, Ousmane
See also BW 1, 3; CA 117; 125; CANR 81; CWW 2; MTCW 1

Ovid 43B.C.-17 **CMLC 7; PC 2**
See also AW 2; CDWLB 1; DA3; DAM POET; DLB 211; PFS 22; RGWL 2, 3; WLIT 8; WP

Owen, Hugh
See Faust, Frederick (Schiller)

Owen, Wilfred (Edward Salter)
 1893-1918 ... **PC 19; TCLC 5, 27; WLC 4**
See also BRW 6; CA 104; 141; CDBLB 1914-1945; DA; DAB; DAC; DAM MST, POET; DLB 20; EWL 3; EXPP; MTCW 2; MTFW 2005; PFS 10; RGEL 2; WLIT 4

Owens, Louis (Dean) 1948-2002 **NNAL**
See also CA 137, 179; 207; CAAE 179; CAAS 24; CANR 71

Owens, Rochelle 1936- **CLC 8**
See also CA 17-20R; CAAS 2; CAD; CANR 39; CD 5, 6; CP 1, 2, 3, 4, 5, 6, 7; CWD; CWP

Oz, Amos 1939- **CLC 5, 8, 11, 27, 33, 54; SSC 66**
See also CA 53-56; CANR 27, 47, 65, 113, 138; CWW 2; DAM NOV; EWL 3; MTCW 1, 2; MTFW 2005; RGHL; RGSF 2; RGWL 3; WLIT 6

Ozick, Cynthia 1928- **CLC 3, 7, 28, 62, 155; SSC 15, 60**
See also AMWS 5; BEST 90:1; CA 17-20R; CANR 23, 58, 116; CN 3, 4, 5, 6, 7; CPW; DA3; DAM NOV, POP; DLB 28, 152, 299; DLBY 1982; EWL 3; EXPS; INT CANR-23; MAL 5; MTCW 1, 2; MTFW 2005; RGAL 4; RGHL; RGSF 2; SSFS 3, 12

Ozu, Yasujiro 1903-1963 **CLC 16**
See also CA 112

Pabst, G. W. 1885-1967 **TCLC 127**

Pacheco, C.
See Pessoa, Fernando (Antonio Nogueira)

Pacheco, Jose Emilio 1939- **HLC 2**
See also CA 111; 131; CANR 65; CWW 2; DAM MULT; DLB 290; EWL 3; HW 1, 2; RGSF 2

Pa Chin ... **CLC 18**
See Jin, Ba
See also EWL 3

Pack, Robert 1929- **CLC 13**
See also CA 1-4R; CANR 3, 44, 82; CP 1, 2, 3, 4, 5, 6, 7; DLB 5; SATA 118

Padgett, Lewis
See Kuttner, Henry

Padilla (Lorenzo), Heberto
 1932-2000 **CLC 38**
See also AITN 1; CA 123; 131; 189; CWW 2; EWL 3; HW 1

Page, James Patrick 1944-
See Page, Jimmy
See also CA 204

Page, Jimmy 1944- **CLC 12**
See Page, James Patrick

Page, Louise 1955- **CLC 40**
See also CA 140; CANR 76; CBD; CD 5, 6; CWD; DLB 233

Page, P(atricia) K(athleen) 1916- **CLC 7, 18; PC 12**
See Cape, Judith
See also CA 53-56; CANR 4, 22, 65; CP 1, 2, 3, 4, 5, 6, 7; DAC; DAM MST; DLB 68; MTCW 1; RGEL 2

Page, Stanton
See Fuller, Henry Blake

Page, Stanton
See Fuller, Henry Blake

Page, Thomas Nelson 1853-1922 **SSC 23**
See also CA 118; 177; DLB 12, 78; DLBD 13; RGAL 4

Pagels, Elaine
See Pagels, Elaine Hiesey

Pagels, Elaine Hiesey 1943- **CLC 104**
See also CA 45-48; CANR 2, 24, 51, 151; FW; NCFS 4

Paget, Violet 1856-1935
See Lee, Vernon
See also CA 104; 166; GLL 1; HGG

Paget-Lowe, Henry
See Lovecraft, H. P.

Paglia, Camille (Anna) 1947- **CLC 68**
See also CA 140; CANR 72, 139; CPW; FW; GLL 2; MTCW 2; MTFW 2005

Paige, Richard
See Koontz, Dean R.

Paine, Thomas 1737-1809 **NCLC 62**
See also AMWS 1; CDALB 1640-1865; DLB 31, 43, 73, 158; LAIT 1; RGAL 4; RGEL 2; TUS

Pakenham, Antonia
See Fraser, Antonia (Pakenham)

Palamas, Costis
See Palamas, Kostes

Palamas, Kostes 1859-1943 **TCLC 5**
See Palamas, Kostis
See also CA 105; 190; RGWL 2, 3

Palamas, Kostis
See Palamas, Kostes
See also EWL 3

Palazzeschi, Aldo 1885-1974 **CLC 11**
See also CA 89-92; 53-56; DLB 114, 264; EWL 3

Pales Matos, Luis 1898-1959 **HLCS 2**
See Pales Matos, Luis
See also DLB 290; HW 1; LAW

Paley, Grace 1922- .. **CLC 4, 6, 37, 140; SSC 8**
See also AMWS 6; CA 25-28R; CANR 13, 46, 74, 118; CN 2, 3, 4, 5, 6, 7; CPW; DA3; DAM POP; DLB 28, 218; EWL 3; EXPS; FW; INT CANR-13; MAL 5; MAWW; MTCW 1, 2; MTFW 2005; RGAL 4; RGSF 2; SSFS 3, 20

Palin, Michael (Edward) 1943- **CLC 21**
See Monty Python
See also CA 107; CANR 35, 109; SATA 67

Palliser, Charles 1947- **CLC 65**
See also CA 136; CANR 76; CN 5, 6, 7

Palma, Ricardo 1833-1919 **TCLC 29**
See also CA 168; LAW

Pamuk, Orhan 1952- **CLC 185**
See also CA 142; CANR 75, 127; CWW 2; WLIT 6

Pancake, Breece Dexter 1952-1979
See Pancake, Breece D'J
See also CA 123; 109

Pancake, Breece D'J **CLC 29; SSC 61**
See Pancake, Breece Dexter
See also DLB 130

Panchenko, Nikolai **CLC 59**

Pankhurst, Emmeline (Goulden)
 1858-1928 **TCLC 100**
See also CA 116; FW

Panko, Rudy
See Gogol, Nikolai (Vasilyevich)

Papadiamantis, Alexandros
 1851-1911 **TCLC 29**
See also CA 168; EWL 3

Papadiamantopoulos, Johannes 1856-1910
See Moreas, Jean
See also CA 117; 242

Papini, Giovanni 1881-1956 **TCLC 22**
See also CA 121; 180; DLB 264

Paracelsus 1493-1541 **LC 14**
See also DLB 179

Parasol, Peter
See Stevens, Wallace

Pardo Bazan, Emilia 1851-1921 **SSC 30**
See also EWL 3; FW; RGSF 2; RGWL 2, 3

Pareto, Vilfredo 1848-1923 **TCLC 69**
See also CA 175

Paretsky, Sara 1947- **CLC 135**
See also AAYA 30; BEST 90:3; CA 125; 129; CANR 59, 95; CMW 4; CPW; DA3; DAM POP; DLB 306; INT CA-129; MSW; RGAL 4

Parfenie, Maria
See Codrescu, Andrei

Parini, Jay (Lee) 1948- **CLC 54, 133**
See also CA 97-100, 229; CAAE 229; CAAS 16; CANR 32, 87

Park, Jordan
See Kornbluth, C(yril) M.; Pohl, Frederik

Park, Robert E(zra) 1864-1944 **TCLC 73**
See also CA 122; 165

Parker, Bert
See Ellison, Harlan (Jay)

Parker, Dorothy (Rothschild)
1893-1967 . **CLC 15, 68; PC 28; SSC 2;
TCLC 143**
See also AMWS 9; CA 19-20; 25-28R; CAP
2; DA3; DAM POET; DLB 11, 45, 86;
EXPP; FW; MAL 5; MAWW; MTCW 1,
2; MTFW 2005; PFS 18; RGAL 4; RGSF
2; TUS

Parker, Robert B. 1932- **CLC 27**
See also AAYA 28; BEST 89:4; BPFB 3;
CA 49-52; CANR 1, 26, 52, 89, 128;
CMW 4; CPW; DAM NOV, POP; DLB
306; INT CANR-26; MSW; MTCW 1;
MTFW 2005

Parker, Robert Brown
See Parker, Robert B.

Parkin, Frank 1940- **CLC 43**
See also CA 147

Parkman, Francis, Jr. 1823-1893 .. **NCLC 12**
See also AMWS 2; DLB 1, 30, 183, 186,
235; RGAL 4

Parks, Gordon 1912-2006 **BLC 3; CLC 1,
16**
See also AAYA 36; AITN 2; BW 2, 3; CA
41-44R; CANR 26, 66, 145; DA3; DAM
MULT; DLB 33; MTCW 2; MTFW 2005;
SATA 8, 108

Parks, Gordon Alexander Buchanan
See Parks, Gordon

Parks, Suzan-Lori 1964(?)- **DC 23**
See also AAYA 55; CA 201; CAD; CD 5,
6; CWD; DFS 22; RGAL 4

Parks, Tim(othy Harold) 1954- **CLC 147**
See also CA 126; 131; CANR 77, 144; CN
7; DLB 231; INT CA-131

Parmenides c. 515B.C.-c.
450B.C. **CMLC 22**
See also DLB 176

Parnell, Thomas 1679-1718 **LC 3**
See also DLB 95; RGEL 2

Parr, Catherine c. 1513(?)-1548 **LC 86**
See also DLB 136

Parra, Nicanor 1914- ... **CLC 2, 102; HLC 2;
PC 39**
See also CA 85-88; CANR 32; CWW 2;
DAM MULT; DLB 283; EWL 3; HW 1;
LAW; MTCW 1

Parra Sanojo, Ana Teresa de la
1890-1936 **HLCS 2**
See de la Parra, (Ana) Teresa (Sonojo)
See also LAW

Parrish, Mary Frances
See Fisher, M(ary) F(rances) K(ennedy)

Parshchikov, Aleksei 1954- **CLC 59**
See Parshchikov, Aleksei Maksimovich

Parshchikov, Aleksei Maksimovich
See Parshchikov, Aleksei
See also DLB 285

Parson, Professor
See Coleridge, Samuel Taylor

Parson Lot
See Kingsley, Charles

Parton, Sara Payson Willis
1811-1872 **NCLC 86**
See also DLB 43, 74, 239

Partridge, Anthony
See Oppenheim, E(dward) Phillips

Pascal, Blaise 1623-1662 **LC 35**
See also DLB 268; EW 3; GFL Beginnings
to 1789; RGWL 2, 3; TWA

Pascoli, Giovanni 1855-1912 **TCLC 45**
See also CA 170; EW 7; EWL 3

Pasolini, Pier Paolo 1922-1975 .. **CLC 20, 37,
106; PC 17**
See also CA 93-96; 61-64; CANR 63; DLB
128, 177; EWL 3; MTCW 1; RGWL 2, 3

Pasquini
See Silone, Ignazio

Pastan, Linda (Olenik) 1932- **CLC 27**
See also CA 61-64; CANR 18, 40, 61, 113;
CP 3, 4, 5, 6, 7; CSW; CWP; DAM
POET; DLB 5; PFS 8

Pasternak, Boris (Leonidovich)
1890-1960 **CLC 7, 10, 18, 63; PC 6;
SSC 31; WLC 4**
See also BPFB 3; CA 127; 116; DA; DA3;
DAB; DAC; DAM MST, NOV, POET;
DLB 302; EW 10; MTCW 1, 2; MTFW
2005; RGSF 2; RGWL 2, 3; TWA; WP

Patchen, Kenneth 1911-1972 **CLC 1, 2, 18**
See also BG 1:3; CA 1-4R; 33-36R; CANR
3, 35; CN 1; CP 1; DAM POET; DLB 16,
48; EWL 3; MAL 5; MTCW 1; RGAL 4

Pater, Walter (Horatio) 1839-1894 . **NCLC 7,
90, 159**
See also BRW 5; CDBLB 1832-1890; DLB
57, 156; RGEL 2; TEA

Paterson, A(ndrew) B(arton)
1864-1941 **TCLC 32**
See also CA 155; DLB 230; RGEL 2; SATA
97

Paterson, Banjo
See Paterson, A(ndrew) B(arton)

Paterson, Katherine 1932- **CLC 12, 30**
See also AAYA 1, 31; BYA 1, 2, 7; CA 21-
24R; CANR 28, 59, 111; CLR 7, 50;
CWRI 5; DLB 52; JRDA; LAIT 4; MAI-
CYA 1, 2; MAICYAS 1; MTCW 1; SATA
13, 53, 92, 133; WYA; YAW

Paterson, Katherine Womeldorf
See Paterson, Katherine

Patmore, Coventry Kersey Dighton
1823-1896 **NCLC 9; PC 59**
See also DLB 35, 98; RGEL 2; TEA

Paton, Alan (Stewart) 1903-1988 **CLC 4,
10, 25, 55, 106; TCLC 165; WLC 4**
See also AAYA 26; AFW; BPFB 3; BRWS
2; BYA 1; CA 13-16; 125; CANR 22;
CAP 1; CN 1, 2, 3, 4; DA; DA3; DAB;
DAC; DAM MST, NOV; DLB 225;
DLBD 17; EWL 3; EXPN; LAIT 4;
MTCW 1, 2; MTFW 2005; NFS 3, 12;
RGEL 2; SATA 11; SATA-Obit 56; TWA;
WLIT 2; WWE 1

Paton Walsh, Gillian 1937- **CLC 35**
See Paton Walsh, Jill; Walsh, Jill Paton
See also AAYA 11; CANR 38, 83; CLR 2,
65; DLB 161; JRDA; MAICYA 1, 2;
SAAS 3; SATA 4, 72, 109; YAW

Paton Walsh, Jill
See Paton Walsh, Gillian
See also AAYA 47; BYA 1, 8

Patsauq, Markoosie 1942- **NNAL**
See also CA 101; CLR 23; CWRI 5; DAM
MULT

Patterson, (Horace) Orlando (Lloyd)
1940- **BLCS**
See also BW 1; CA 65-68; CANR 27, 84;
CN 1, 2, 3, 4, 5, 6

Patton, George S(mith), Jr.
1885-1945 **TCLC 79**
See also CA 189

Paulding, James Kirke 1778-1860 ... **NCLC 2**
See also DLB 3, 59, 74, 250; RGAL 4

Paulin, Thomas Neilson 1949-
See Paulin, Tom
See also CA 123; 128; CANR 98

Paulin, Tom **CLC 37, 177**
See Paulin, Thomas Neilson
See also CP 3, 4, 5, 6, 7; DLB 40

Pausanias c. 1st cent. - **CMLC 36**

Paustovsky, Konstantin (Georgievich)
1892-1968 **CLC 40**
See also CA 93-96; 25-28R; DLB 272;
EWL 3

Pavese, Cesare 1908-1950 **PC 13; SSC 19;
TCLC 3**
See also CA 104; 169; DLB 128, 177; EW
12; EWL 3; PFS 20; RGSF 2; RGWL 2,
3; TWA; WLIT 7

Pavic, Milorad 1929- **CLC 60**
See also CA 136; CDWLB 4; CWW 2; DLB
181; EWL 3; RGWL 3

Pavlov, Ivan Petrovich 1849-1936 . **TCLC 91**
See also CA 118; 180

Pavlova, Karolina Karlovna
1807-1893 **NCLC 138**
See also DLB 205

Payne, Alan
See Jakes, John (William)

Payne, Rachel Ann
See Jakes, John (William)

Paz, Gil
See Lugones, Leopoldo

Paz, Octavio 1914-1998 . **CLC 3, 4, 6, 10, 19,
51, 65, 119; HLC 2; PC 1, 48; WLC 4**
See also AAYA 50; CA 73-76; 165; CANR
32, 65, 104; CWW 2; DA; DA3; DAB;
DAC; DAM MST, MULT, POET; DLB
290; DLBY 1990, 1998; DNFS 1; EWL
3; HW 1, 2; LAW; LAWS 1; MTCW 1, 2;
MTFW 2005; PFS 18; RGWL 2, 3; SSFS
13; TWA; WLIT 1

p'Bitek, Okot 1931-1982 **BLC 3; CLC 96;
TCLC 149**
See also AFW; BW 2, 3; CA 124; 107;
CANR 82; CP 1, 2, 3; DAM MULT; DLB
125; EWL 3; MTCW 1, 2; MTFW 2005;
RGEL 2; WLIT 2

Peabody, Elizabeth Palmer
1804-1894 **NCLC 169**
See also DLB 1, 223

Peacham, Henry 1578-1644(?) **LC 119**
See also DLB 151

Peacock, Molly 1947- **CLC 60**
See also CA 103; CAAS 21; CANR 52, 84;
CP 5, 6, 7; CWP; DLB 120, 282

Peacock, Thomas Love
1785-1866 **NCLC 22**
See also BRW 4; DLB 96, 116; RGEL 2;
RGSF 2

Peake, Mervyn 1911-1968 **CLC 7, 54**
See also CA 5-8R; 25-28R; CANR 3; DLB
15, 160, 255; FANT; MTCW 1; RGEL 2;
SATA 23; SFW 4

Pearce, Philippa
See Christie, Philippa
See also CA 5-8R; CANR 4, 109; CWRI 5;
FANT; MAICYA 2

Pearl, Eric
See Elman, Richard (Martin)

Pearson, T. R. 1956- **CLC 39**
See also CA 120; 130; CANR 97, 147;
CSW; INT CA-130

Pearson, Thomas Reid
See Pearson, T. R.

Peck, Dale 1967- **CLC 81**
See also CA 146; CANR 72, 127; GLL 2

Peck, John (Frederick) 1941- **CLC 3**
See also CA 49-52; CANR 3, 100; CP 4, 5,
6, 7

Peck, Richard (Wayne) 1934- **CLC 21**
See also AAYA 1, 24; BYA 1, 6, 8, 11; CA
85-88; CANR 19, 38, 129; CLR 15; INT
CANR-19; JRDA; MAICYA 1, 2; SAAS
2; SATA 18, 55, 97, 110, 158; SATA-
Essay 110; WYA; YAW

Peck, Robert Newton 1928- **CLC 17**
See also AAYA 3, 43; BYA 1, 6; CA 81-84,
182; CAAE 182; CANR 31, 63, 127; CLR
45; DA; DAC; DAM MST; JRDA; LAIT
3; MAICYA 1, 2; SAAS 1; SATA 21, 62,
111, 156; SATA-Essay 108; WYA; YAW

Peckinpah, David Samuel
See Peckinpah, Sam
Peckinpah, Sam 1925-1984 **CLC 20**
See also CA 109; 114; CANR 82
Pedersen, Knut 1859-1952
See Hamsun, Knut
See also CA 104; 119; CANR 63; MTCW 1, 2
Peele, George 1556-1596 **DC 27; LC 115**
See also BRW 1; DLB 62, 167; RGEL 2
Peeslake, Gaffer
See Durrell, Lawrence (George)
Peguy, Charles (Pierre)
1873-1914 **TCLC 10**
See also CA 107; 193; DLB 258; EWL 3; GFL 1789 to the Present
Peirce, Charles Sanders
1839-1914 **TCLC 81**
See also CA 194; DLB 270
Pellicer, Carlos 1897(?)-1977 **HLCS 2**
See also CA 153; 69-72; DLB 290; EWL 3; HW 1
Pena, Ramon del Valle y
See Valle-Inclan, Ramon (Maria) del
Pendennis, Arthur Esquir
See Thackeray, William Makepeace
Penn, Arthur
See Matthews, (James) Brander
Penn, William 1644-1718 **LC 25**
See also DLB 24
PEPECE
See Prado (Calvo), Pedro
Pepys, Samuel 1633-1703 ... **LC 11, 58; WLC 4**
See also BRW 2; CDBLB 1660-1789; DA; DA3; DAB; DAC; DAM MST; DLB 101, 213; NCFS 4; RGEL 2; TEA; WLIT 3
Percy, Thomas 1729-1811 **NCLC 95**
See also DLB 104
Percy, Walker 1916-1990 **CLC 2, 3, 6, 8, 14, 18, 47, 65**
See also AMWS 3; BPFB 3; CA 1-4R; 131; CANR 1, 23, 64; CN 1, 2, 3, 4; CPW; CSW; DA3; DAM NOV, POP; DLB 2; DLBY 1980, 1990; EWL 3; MAL 5; MTCW 1, 2; MTFW 2005; RGAL 4; TUS
Percy, William Alexander
1885-1942 **TCLC 84**
See also CA 163; MTCW 2
Perec, Georges 1936-1982 **CLC 56, 116**
See also CA 141; DLB 83, 299; EWL 3; GFL 1789 to the Present; RGHL; RGWL 3
Pereda (y Sanchez de Porrua), Jose Maria de 1833-1906 **TCLC 16**
See also CA 117
Pereda y Porrua, Jose Maria de
See Pereda (y Sanchez de Porrua), Jose Maria de
Peregoy, George Weems
See Mencken, H(enry) L(ouis)
Perelman, S(idney) J(oseph)
1904-1979 .. **CLC 3, 5, 9, 15, 23, 44, 49; SSC 32**
See also AITN 1, 2; BPFB 3; CA 73-76; 89-92; CANR 18; DAM DRAM; DLB 11, 44; MTCW 1, 2; MTFW 2005; RGAL 4
Peret, Benjamin 1899-1959 **PC 33; TCLC 20**
See also CA 117; 186; GFL 1789 to the Present
Peretz, Isaac Leib
See Peretz, Isaac Loeb
See also CA 201
Peretz, Isaac Loeb 1851(?)-1915 **SSC 26; TCLC 16**
See Peretz, Isaac Leib
See also CA 109

Peretz, Yitzkhok Leibush
See Peretz, Isaac Loeb
Perez Galdos, Benito 1843-1920 **HLCS 2; TCLC 27**
See Galdos, Benito Perez
See also CA 125; 153; EWL 3; HW 1; RGWL 2, 3
Peri Rossi, Cristina 1941- .. **CLC 156; HLCS 2**
See also CA 131; CANR 59, 81; CWW 2; DLB 145, 290; EWL 3; HW 1, 2
Perlata
See Peret, Benjamin
Perloff, Marjorie G(abrielle)
1931- **CLC 137**
See also CA 57-60; CANR 7, 22, 49, 104
Perrault, Charles 1628-1703 **LC 2, 56**
See also BYA 4; CLR 79; DLB 268; GFL Beginnings to 1789; MAICYA 1, 2; RGWL 2, 3; SATA 25; WCH
Perry, Anne 1938- **CLC 126**
See also CA 101; CANR 22, 50, 84, 150; CMW 4; CN 6, 7; CPW; DLB 276
Perry, Brighton
See Sherwood, Robert E(mmet)
Perse, St.-John
See Leger, (Marie-Rene Auguste) Alexis Saint-Leger
Perse, Saint-John
See Leger, (Marie-Rene Auguste) Alexis Saint-Leger
See also DLB 258; RGWL 3
Persius 34-62 **CMLC 74**
See also AW 2; DLB 211; RGWL 2, 3
Perutz, Leo(pold) 1882-1957 **TCLC 60**
See also CA 147; DLB 81
Peseenz, Tulio F.
See Lopez y Fuentes, Gregorio
Pesetsky, Bette 1932- **CLC 28**
See also CA 133; DLB 130
Peshkov, Alexei Maximovich 1868-1936
See Gorky, Maxim
See also CA 105; 141; CANR 83; DA; DAC; DAM DRAM, MST, NOV; MTCW 2; MTFW 2005
Pessoa, Fernando (Antonio Nogueira)
1888-1935 **HLC 2; PC 20; TCLC 27**
See also CA 125; 183; DAM MULT; DLB 287; EW 10; EWL 3; RGWL 2, 3; WP
Peterkin, Julia Mood 1880-1961 **CLC 31**
See also CA 102; DLB 9
Peters, Joan K(aren) 1945- **CLC 39**
See also CA 158; CANR 109
Peters, Robert L(ouis) 1924- **CLC 7**
See also CA 13-16R; CAAS 8; CP 1, 5, 6, 7; DLB 105
Petofi, Sandor 1823-1849 **NCLC 21**
See also RGWL 2, 3
Petrakis, Harry Mark 1923- **CLC 3**
See also CA 9-12R; CANR 4, 30, 85; CN 1, 2, 3, 4, 5, 6, 7
Petrarch 1304-1374 **CMLC 20; PC 8**
See also DA3; DAM POET; EW 2; LMFS 1; RGWL 2, 3; WLIT 7
Petronius c. 20-66 **CMLC 34**
See also AW 2; CDWLB 1; DLB 211; RGWL 2, 3; WLIT 8
Petrov, Evgeny **TCLC 21**
See Kataev, Evgeny Petrovich
Petry, Ann (Lane) 1908-1997 .. **CLC 1, 7, 18; TCLC 112**
See also AFAW 1, 2; BPFB 3; BW 1, 3; BYA 2; CA 5-8R; 157; CAAS 6; CANR 4, 46; CLR 12; CN 1, 2, 3, 4, 5, 6; DLB 76; EWL 3; JRDA; LAIT 1; MAICYA 1, 2; MAICYAS 1; MTCW 1; RGAL 4; SATA 5; SATA-Obit 94; TUS
Petursson, Halligrimur 1614-1674 **LC 8**

Peychinovich
See Vazov, Ivan (Minchov)
Phaedrus c. 15B.C.-c. 50 **CMLC 25**
See also DLB 211
Phelps (Ward), Elizabeth Stuart
See Phelps, Elizabeth Stuart
See also FW
Phelps, Elizabeth Stuart
1844-1911 **TCLC 113**
See Phelps (Ward), Elizabeth Stuart
See also CA 242; DLB 74
Philips, Katherine 1632-1664 . **LC 30; PC 40**
See also DLB 131; RGEL 2
Philipson, Morris H. 1926- **CLC 53**
See also CA 1-4R; CANR 4
Phillips, Caryl 1958- **BLCS; CLC 96, 224**
See also BRWS 5; BW 2; CA 141; CANR 63, 104, 140; CBD; CD 5, 6; CN 5, 6, 7; DA3; DAM MULT; DLB 157; EWL 3; MTCW 2; MTFW 2005; WLIT 4; WWE 1
Phillips, David Graham
1867-1911 **TCLC 44**
See also CA 108; 176; DLB 9, 12, 303; RGAL 4
Phillips, Jack
See Sandburg, Carl (August)
Phillips, Jayne Anne 1952- **CLC 15, 33, 139; SSC 16**
See also AAYA 57; BPFB 3; CA 101; CANR 24, 50, 96; CN 4, 5, 6, 7; CSW; DLBY 1980; INT CANR-24; MTCW 1, 2; MTFW 2005; RGAL 4; RGSF 2; SSFS 4
Phillips, Richard
See Dick, Philip K.
Phillips, Robert (Schaeffer) 1938- **CLC 28**
See also CA 17-20R; CAAS 13; CANR 8; DLB 105
Phillips, Ward
See Lovecraft, H. P.
Philostratus, Flavius c. 179-c.
244 **CMLC 62**
Piccolo, Lucio 1901-1969 **CLC 13**
See also CA 97-100; DLB 114; EWL 3
Pickthall, Marjorie L(owry) C(hristie)
1883-1922 **TCLC 21**
See also CA 107; DLB 92
Pico della Mirandola, Giovanni
1463-1494 **LC 15**
See also LMFS 1
Piercy, Marge 1936- **CLC 3, 6, 14, 18, 27, 62, 128; PC 29**
See also BPFB 3; CA 21-24R, 187; CAAE 187; CAAS 1; CANR 13, 43, 66, 111; CN 3, 4, 5, 6, 7; CP 1, 2, 3, 4, 5, 6, 7; CWP; DLB 120, 227; EXPP; FW; MAL 5; MTCW 1, 2; MTFW 2005; PFS 9, 22; SFW 4
Piers, Robert
See Anthony, Piers
Pieyre de Mandiargues, Andre 1909-1991
See Mandiargues, Andre Pieyre de
See also CA 103; 136; CANR 22, 82; EWL 3; GFL 1789 to the Present
Pilnyak, Boris 1894-1938 . **SSC 48; TCLC 23**
See Vogau, Boris Andreyevich
See also EWL 3
Pinchback, Eugene
See Toomer, Jean
Pincherle, Alberto 1907-1990 **CLC 11, 18**
See Moravia, Alberto
See also CA 25-28R; 132; CANR 33, 63, 142; DAM NOV; MTCW 1; MTFW 2005
Pinckney, Darryl 1953- **CLC 76**
See also BW 2, 3; CA 143; CANR 79

Pindar 518(?)B.C.-438(?)B.C. **CMLC 12; PC 19**
See also AW 1; CDWLB 1; DLB 176; RGWL 2

Pineda, Cecile 1942- **CLC 39**
See also CA 118; DLB 209

Pinero, Arthur Wing 1855-1934 **TCLC 32**
See also CA 110; 153; DAM DRAM; DLB 10; RGEL 2

Pinero, Miguel (Antonio Gomez)
1946-1988 **CLC 4, 55**
See also CA 61-64; 125; CAD; CANR 29, 90; DLB 266; HW 1; LLW

Pinget, Robert 1919-1997 **CLC 7, 13, 37**
See also CA 85-88; 160; CWW 2; DLB 83; EWL 3; GFL 1789 to the Present

Pink Floyd
See Barrett, (Roger) Syd; Gilmour, David; Mason, Nick; Waters, Roger; Wright, Rick

Pinkney, Edward 1802-1828 **NCLC 31**
See also DLB 248

Pinkwater, D. Manus
See Pinkwater, Daniel Manus

Pinkwater, Daniel
See Pinkwater, Daniel Manus

Pinkwater, Daniel M.
See Pinkwater, Daniel Manus

Pinkwater, Daniel Manus 1941- **CLC 35**
See also AAYA 1, 46; BYA 9; CA 29-32R; CANR 12, 38, 89, 143; CLR 4; CSW; FANT; JRDA; MAICYA 1, 2; SAAS 3; SATA 8, 46, 76, 114, 158; SFW 4; YAW

Pinkwater, Manus
See Pinkwater, Daniel Manus

Pinsky, Robert 1940- **CLC 9, 19, 38, 94, 121, 216; PC 27**
See also AMWS 6; CA 29-32R; CAAS 4; CANR 58, 97, 138; CP 3, 4, 5, 6, 7; DA3; DAM POET; DLBY 1982, 1998; MAL 5; MTCW 2; MTFW 2005; PFS 18; RGAL 4; TCLE 1:2

Pinta, Harold
See Pinter, Harold

Pinter, Harold 1930- .. **CLC 1, 3, 6, 9, 11, 15, 27, 58, 73, 199; DC 15; WLC 4**
See also BRWR 1; BRWS 1; CA 5-8R; CANR 33, 65, 112, 145; CBD; CD 5, 6; CDBLB 1960 to Present; CP 1; DA; DA3; DAB; DAC; DAM DRAM, MST; DFS 3, 5, 7, 14; DLB 13, 310; EWL 3; IDFW 3, 4; LMFS 2; MTCW 1, 2; MTFW 2005; RGEL 2; RGHL; TEA

Piozzi, Hester Lynch (Thrale)
1741-1821 **NCLC 57**
See also DLB 104, 142

Pirandello, Luigi 1867-1936 .. **DC 5; SSC 22; TCLC 4, 29, 172; WLC 4**
See also CA 104; 153; CANR 103; DA; DA3; DAB; DAC; DAM DRAM, MST; DFS 4, 9; DLB 264; EW 8; EWL 3; MTCW 2; MTFW 2005; RGSF 2; RGWL 2, 3; WLIT 7

Pirsig, Robert M(aynard) 1928- ... **CLC 4, 6, 73**
See also CA 53-56; CANR 42, 74; CPW 1; DA3; DAM POP; MTCW 1, 2; MTFW 2005; SATA 39

Pisarev, Dmitrii Ivanovich
See Pisarev, Dmitry Ivanovich
See also DLB 277

Pisarev, Dmitry Ivanovich
1840-1868 **NCLC 25**
See Pisarev, Dmitrii Ivanovich

Pix, Mary (Griffith) 1666-1709 **LC 8**
See also DLB 80

Pixerecourt, (Rene Charles) Guilbert de
1773-1844 **NCLC 39**
See also DLB 192; GFL 1789 to the Present

Plaatje, Sol(omon) T(shekisho)
1878-1932 **BLCS; TCLC 73**
See also BW 2, 3; CA 141; CANR 79; DLB 125, 225

Plaidy, Jean
See Hibbert, Eleanor Alice Burford

Planche, James Robinson
1796-1880 **NCLC 42**
See also RGEL 2

Plant, Robert 1948- **CLC 12**

Plante, David 1940- **CLC 7, 23, 38**
See also CA 37-40R; CANR 12, 36, 58, 82, 152; CN 2, 3, 4, 5, 6, 7; DAM NOV; DLBY 1983; INT CANR-12; MTCW 1

Plante, David Robert
See Plante, David

Plath, Sylvia 1932-1963 **CLC 1, 2, 3, 5, 9, 11, 14, 17, 50, 51, 62, 111; PC 1, 37; WLC 4**
See also AAYA 13; AMWR 2; AMWS 1; BPFB 3; CA 19-20; CANR 34, 101; CAP 2; CDALB 1941-1968; DA; DA3; DAB; DAC; DAM MST, POET; DLB 5, 6, 152; EWL 3; EXPN; EXPP; FL 1:6; FW; LAIT 4; MAL 5; MAWW; MTCW 1, 2; MTFW 2005; NFS 1; PAB; PFS 1, 15; RGAL 4; SATA 96; TUS; WP; YAW

Plato c. 428B.C.-347B.C. **CMLC 8, 75; WLCS**
See also AW 1; CDWLB 1; DA; DA3; DAB; DAC; DAM MST; DLB 176; LAIT 1; LATS 1:1; RGWL 2, 3; WLIT 8

Platonov, Andrei
See Klimentov, Andrei Platonovich

Platonov, Andrei Platonovich
See Klimentov, Andrei Platonovich
See also DLB 272

Platonov, Andrey Platonovich
See Klimentov, Andrei Platonovich
See also EWL 3

Platt, Kin 1911- **CLC 26**
See also AAYA 11; CA 17-20R; CANR 11; JRDA; SAAS 17; SATA 21, 86; WYA

Plautus c. 254B.C.-c. 184B.C. **CMLC 24; DC 6**
See also AW 1; CDWLB 1; DLB 211; RGWL 2, 3; WLIT 8

Plick et Plock
See Simenon, Georges (Jacques Christian)

Plieksans, Janis
See Rainis, Janis

Plimpton, George (Ames)
1927-2003 **CLC 36**
See also AITN 1; CA 21-24R; 224; CANR 32, 70, 103, 133; DLB 185, 241; MTCW 1, 2; MTFW 2005; SATA 10; SATA-Obit 150

Pliny the Elder c. 23-79 **CMLC 23**
See also DLB 211

Pliny the Younger c. 61-c. 112 **CMLC 62**
See also AW 2; DLB 211

Plomer, William Charles Franklin
1903-1973 **CLC 4, 8**
See also AFW; BRWS 11; CA 21-22; CANR 34; CAP 2; CN 1; CP 1, 2; DLB 20, 162, 191, 225; EWL 3; MTCW 1; RGEL 2; RGSF 2; SATA 24

Plotinus 204-270 **CMLC 46**
See also CDWLB 1; DLB 176

Plowman, Piers
See Kavanagh, Patrick (Joseph)

Plum, J.
See Wodehouse, P(elham) G(renville)

Plumly, Stanley (Ross) 1939- **CLC 33**
See also CA 108; 110; CANR 97; CP 3, 4, 5, 6, 7; DLB 5, 193; INT CA-110

Plumpe, Friedrich Wilhelm
1888-1931 **TCLC 53**
See also CA 112

Plutarch c. 46-c. 120 **CMLC 60**
See also AW 2; CDWLB 1; DLB 176; RGWL 2, 3; TWA; WLIT 8

Po Chu-i 772-846 **CMLC 24**

Podhoretz, Norman 1930- **CLC 189**
See also AMWS 8; CA 9-12R; CANR 7, 78, 135

Poe, Edgar Allan 1809-1849 **NCLC 1, 16, 55, 78, 94, 97, 117; PC 1, 54; SSC 1, 22, 34, 35, 54, 88; WLC 4**
See also AAYA 14; AMW; AMWC 1; AMWR 2; BPFB 2; BYA 5, 11; CDALB 1640-1865; CMW 4; DA; DA3; DAB; DAC; DAM MST, POET; DLB 3, 59, 73, 74, 248, 254; EXPP; EXPS; GL 3; HGG; LAIT 2; LATS 1:1; LMFS 1; MSW; PAB; PFS 1, 3, 9; RGAL 4; RGSF 2; SATA 23; SCFW 1, 2; SFW 4; SSFS 2, 4, 7, 8, 16; SUFW; TUS; WP; WYA

Poet of Titchfield Street, The
See Pound, Ezra (Weston Loomis)

Poggio Bracciolini, Gian Francesco
1380-1459 **LC 125**

Pohl, Frederik 1919- **CLC 18; SSC 25**
See also AAYA 24; CA 61-64, 188; CAAE 188; CAAS 1; CANR 11, 37, 81, 140; CN 1, 2, 3, 4, 5, 6; DLB 8; INT CANR-11; MTCW 1, 2; MTFW 2005; SATA 24; SCFW 1, 2; SFW 4

Poirier, Louis 1910-
See Gracq, Julien
See also CA 122; 126; CANR 141

Poitier, Sidney 1927- **CLC 26**
See also AAYA 60; BW 1; CA 117; CANR 94

Pokagon, Simon 1830-1899 **NNAL**
See also DAM MULT

Polanski, Roman 1933- **CLC 16, 178**
See also CA 77-80

Poliakoff, Stephen 1952- **CLC 38**
See also CA 106; CANR 116; CBD; CD 5, 6; DLB 13

Police, The
See Copeland, Stewart (Armstrong); Summers, Andrew James

Polidori, John William 1795-1821 . **NCLC 51**
See also DLB 116; HGG

Poliziano, Angelo 1454-1494 **LC 120**
See also WLIT 7

Pollitt, Katha 1949- **CLC 28, 122**
See also CA 120; 122; CANR 66, 108; MTCW 1, 2; MTFW 2005

Pollock, (Mary) Sharon 1936- **CLC 50**
See also CA 141; CANR 132; CD 5; CWD; DAC; DAM DRAM, MST; DFS 3; DLB 60; FW

Pollock, Sharon 1936- **DC 20**
See also CD 6

Polo, Marco 1254-1324 **CMLC 15**
See also WLIT 7

Polonsky, Abraham (Lincoln)
1910-1999 **CLC 92**
See also CA 104; 187; DLB 26; INT CA-104

Polybius c. 200B.C.-c. 118B.C. **CMLC 17**
See also AW 1; DLB 176; RGWL 2, 3

Pomerance, Bernard 1940- **CLC 13**
See also CA 101; CAD; CANR 49, 134; CD 5, 6; DAM DRAM; DFS 9; LAIT 2

Ponge, Francis 1899-1988 **CLC 6, 18**
See also CA 85-88; 126; CANR 40, 86; DAM POET; DLBY 2002; EWL 3; GFL 1789 to the Present; RGWL 2, 3

Poniatowska, Elena 1933- . **CLC 140; HLC 2**
See also CA 101; CANR 32, 66, 107; CDWLB 3; CWW 2; DAM MULT; DLB 113; EWL 3; HW 1, 2; LAWS 1; WLIT 1

Pontoppidan, Henrik 1857-1943 **TCLC 29**
See also CA 170; DLB 300

Ponty, Maurice Merleau
See Merleau-Ponty, Maurice

Poole, Josephine **CLC 17**
See Helyar, Jane Penelope Josephine
See also SAAS 2; SATA 5

Popa, Vasko 1922-1991 . **CLC 19; TCLC 167**
See also CA 112; 148; CDWLB 4; DLB
181; EWL 3; RGWL 2, 3

Pope, Alexander 1688-1744 **LC 3, 58, 60,
64; PC 26; WLC 5**
See also BRW 3; BRWC 1; BRWR 1; CD-
BLB 1660-1789; DA; DA3; DAB; DAC;
DAM MST, POET; DLB 95, 101, 213;
EXPP; PAB; PFS 12; RGEL 2; WLIT 3;
WP

Popov, Evgenii Anatol'evich
See Popov, Yevgeny
See also DLB 285

Popov, Yevgeny **CLC 59**
See Popov, Evgenii Anatol'evich

Poquelin, Jean-Baptiste
See Moliere

Porete, Marguerite (?)-1310 **CMLC 73**
See also DLB 208

Porphyry c. 233-c. 305 **CMLC 71**

Porter, Connie (Rose) 1959(?)- **CLC 70**
See also AAYA 65; BW 2, 3; CA 142;
CANR 90, 109; SATA 81, 129

Porter, Gene(va Grace) Stratton .. **TCLC 21**
See Stratton-Porter, Gene(va Grace)
See also BPFB 3; CA 112; CWRI 5; RHW

Porter, Katherine Anne 1890-1980 ... **CLC 1,
3, 7, 10, 13, 15, 27, 101; SSC 4, 31, 43**
See also AAYA 42; AITN 2; AMW; BPFB
3; CA 1-4R; 101; CANR 1, 65; CDALBS;
CN 1, 2; DA; DA3; DAB; DAC; DAM
MST, NOV; DLB 4, 9, 102; DLBD 12;
DLBY 1980; EWL 3; EXPS; LAIT 3;
MAL 5; MAWW; MTCW 1, 2; MTFW
2005; NFS 14; RGAL 4; RGSF 2; SATA
39; SATA-Obit 23; SSFS 1, 8, 11, 16, 23;
TCWW 2; TUS

Porter, Peter (Neville Frederick)
1929- **CLC 5, 13, 33**
See also CA 85-88; CP 1, 2, 3, 4, 5, 6, 7;
DLB 40, 289; WWE 1

Porter, William Sydney 1862-1910
See Henry, O.
See also CA 104; 131; CDALB 1865-1917;
DA; DA3; DAB; DAC; DAM MST; DLB
12, 78, 79; MTCW 1, 2; MTFW 2005;
TUS; YABC 2

Portillo (y Pacheco), Jose Lopez
See Lopez Portillo (y Pacheco), Jose

Portillo Trambley, Estela 1927-1998 .. **HLC 2**
See Trambley, Estela Portillo
See also CANR 32; DAM MULT; DLB
209; HW 1

Posey, Alexander (Lawrence)
1873-1908 **NNAL**
See also CA 144; CANR 80; DAM MULT;
DLB 175

Posse, Abel .. **CLC 70**

Post, Melville Davisson
1869-1930 **TCLC 39**
See also CA 110; 202; CMW 4

Potok, Chaim 1929-2002 ... **CLC 2, 7, 14, 26,
112**
See also AAYA 15, 50; AITN 1, 2; BPFB 3;
BYA 1; CA 17-20R; 208; CANR 19, 35,
64, 98; CLR 92; CN 4, 5, 6; DA3; DAM
NOV; DLB 28, 152; EXPN; INT CANR-
19; LAIT 4; MTCW 1, 2; MTFW 2005;
NFS 4; RGHL; SATA 33, 106; SATA-Obit
134; TUS; YAW

Potok, Herbert Harold -2002
See Potok, Chaim

Potok, Herman Harold
See Potok, Chaim

Potter, Dennis (Christopher George)
1935-1994 **CLC 58, 86, 123**
See also BRWS 10; CA 107; 145; CANR
33, 61; CBD; DLB 233; MTCW 1

Pound, Ezra (Weston Loomis)
1885-1972 .. **CLC 1, 2, 3, 4, 5, 7, 10, 13,
18, 34, 48, 50, 112; PC 4; WLC 5**
See also AAYA 47; AMW; AMWR 1; CA
5-8R; 37-40R; CANR 40; CDALB 1917-
1929; CP 1; DA; DA3; DAB; DAC; DAM
MST, POET; DLB 4, 45, 63; DLBD 15;
EFS 2; EWL 3; EXPP; LMFS 2; MAL 5;
MTCW 1, 2; MTFW 2005; PAB; PFS 2,
8, 16; RGAL 4; TUS; WP

Povod, Reinaldo 1959-1994 **CLC 44**
See also CA 136; 146; CANR 83

Powell, Adam Clayton, Jr.
1908-1972 **BLC 3; CLC 89**
See also BW 1, 3; CA 102; 33-36R; CANR
86; DAM MULT

Powell, Anthony (Dymoke)
1905-2000 **CLC 1, 3, 7, 9, 10, 31**
See also BRW 7; CA 1-4R; 189; CANR 1,
32, 62, 107; CDBLB 1945-1960; CN 1, 2,
3, 4, 5, 6; DLB 15; EWL 3; MTCW 1, 2;
MTFW 2005; RGEL 2; TEA

Powell, Dawn 1896(?)-1965 **CLC 66**
See also CA 5-8R; CANR 121; DLBY 1997

Powell, Padgett 1952- **CLC 34**
See also CA 126; CANR 63, 101; CSW;
DLB 234; DLBY 01

Powell, (Oval) Talmage 1920-2000
See Queen, Ellery
See also CA 5-8R; CANR 2, 80

Power, Susan 1961- **CLC 91**
See also BYA 14; CA 160; CANR 135; NFS
11

Powers, J(ames) F(arl) 1917-1999 **CLC 1,
4, 8, 57; SSC 4**
See also CA 1-4R; 181; CANR 2, 61; CN
1, 2, 3, 4, 5, 6; DLB 130; MTCW 1;
RGAL 4; RGSF 2

Powers, John J(ames) 1945-
See Powers, John R.
See also CA 69-72

Powers, John R. **CLC 66**
See Powers, John J(ames)

Powers, Richard (S.) 1957- **CLC 93**
See also AMWS 9; BPFB 3; CA 148;
CANR 80; CN 6, 7; MTFW 2005; TCLE
1:2

Pownall, David 1938- **CLC 10**
See also CA 89-92, 180; CAAS 18; CANR
49, 101; CBD; CD 5, 6; CN 4, 5, 6, 7;
DLB 14

Powys, John Cowper 1872-1963 ... **CLC 7, 9,
15, 46, 125**
See also CA 85-88; CANR 106; DLB 15,
255; EWL 3; FANT; MTCW 1, 2; MTFW
2005; RGEL 2; SUFW

Powys, T(heodore) F(rancis)
1875-1953 **TCLC 9**
See also BRWS 8; CA 106; 189; DLB 36,
162; EWL 3; FANT; RGEL 2; SUFW

Pozzo, Modesta
See Fonte, Moderata

Prado (Calvo), Pedro 1886-1952 ... **TCLC 75**
See also CA 131; DLB 283; HW 1; LAW

Prager, Emily 1952- **CLC 56**
See also CA 204

Pratchett, Terry 1948- **CLC 197**
See also AAYA 19, 54; BPFB 3; CA 143;
CANR 87, 126; CLR 64; CN 6, 7; CPW;
CWRI 5; FANT; MTFW 2005; SATA 82,
139; SFW 4; SUFW 2

Pratolini, Vasco 1913-1991 **TCLC 124**
See also CA 211; DLB 177; EWL 3; RGWL
2, 3

Pratt, E(dwin) J(ohn) 1883(?)-1964 . **CLC 19**
See also CA 141; 93-96; CANR 77; DAC;
DAM POET; DLB 92; EWL 3; RGEL 2;
TWA

Premchand **TCLC 21**
See Srivastava, Dhanpat Rai
See also EWL 3

Prescott, William Hickling
1796-1859 **NCLC 163**
See also DLB 1, 30, 59, 235

Preseren, France 1800-1849 **NCLC 127**
See also CDWLB 4; DLB 147

Preussler, Otfried 1923- **CLC 17**
See also CA 77-80; SATA 24

Prevert, Jacques (Henri Marie)
1900-1977 **CLC 15**
See also CA 77-80; 69-72; CANR 29, 61;
DLB 258; EWL 3; GFL 1789 to the
Present; IDFW 3, 4; MTCW 1; RGWL 2,
3; SATA-Obit 30

Prevost, (Antoine Francois)
1697-1763 .. **LC 1**
See also DLB 314; EW 4; GFL Beginnings
to 1789; RGWL 2, 3

Price, (Edward) Reynolds 1933- ... **CLC 3, 6,
13, 43, 50, 63, 212; SSC 22**
See also AMWS 6; CA 1-4R; CANR 1, 37,
57, 87, 128; CN 1, 2, 3, 4, 5, 6, 7; CSW;
DAM NOV; DLB 2, 218, 278; EWL 3;
INT CANR-37; MAL 5; MTFW 2005;
NFS 18

Price, Richard 1949- **CLC 6, 12**
See also CA 49-52; CANR 3, 147; CN 7;
DLBY 1981

Prichard, Katharine Susannah
1883-1969 **CLC 46**
See also CA 11-12; CANR 33; CAP 1; DLB
260; MTCW 1; RGEL 2; RGSF 2; SATA
66

Priestley, J(ohn) B(oynton)
1894-1984 **CLC 2, 5, 9, 34**
See also BRW 7; CA 9-12R; 113; CANR
33; CDBLB 1914-1945; CN 1, 2, 3; DA3;
DAM DRAM, NOV; DLB 10, 34, 77,
100, 139; DLBY 1984; EWL 3; MTCW
1, 2; MTFW 2005; RGEL 2; SFW 4

Prince 1958- **CLC 35**
See also CA 213

Prince, F(rank) T(empleton)
1912-2003 **CLC 22**
See also CA 101; 219; CANR 43, 79; CP 1,
2, 3, 4, 5, 6, 7; DLB 20

Prince Kropotkin
See Kropotkin, Peter (Aleksieievich)

Prior, Matthew 1664-1721 **LC 4**
See also DLB 95; RGEL 2

Prishvin, Mikhail 1873-1954 **TCLC 75**
See Prishvin, Mikhail Mikhailovich

Prishvin, Mikhail Mikhailovich
See Prishvin, Mikhail
See also DLB 272; EWL 3

Pritchard, William H(arrison)
1932- **CLC 34**
See also CA 65-68; CANR 23, 95; DLB
111

Pritchett, V(ictor) S(awdon)
1900-1997 ... **CLC 5, 13, 15, 41; SSC 14**
See also BPFB 3; BRWS 3; CA 61-64; 157;
CANR 31, 63; CN 1, 2, 3, 4, 5, 6; DA3;
DAM NOV; DLB 15, 139; EWL 3;
MTCW 1, 2; MTFW 2005; RGEL 2;
RGSF 2; TEA

Private 19022
See Manning, Frederic

Probst, Mark 1925- **CLC 59**
See also CA 130

Procaccino, Michael
See Cristofer, Michael

Proclus c. 412-c. 485 **CMLC 81**

Prokosch, Frederic 1908-1989 **CLC 4, 48**
　　See also CA 73-76; 128; CANR 82; CN 1,
　　2, 3, 4; CP 1, 2, 3, 4; DLB 48; MTCW 2

Propertius, Sextus c. 50B.C.-c.
　　16B.C. **CMLC 32**
　　See also AW 2; CDWLB 1; DLB 211;
　　RGWL 2, 3; WLIT 8

Prophet, The
　　See Dreiser, Theodore

Prose, Francine 1947- **CLC 45**
　　See also CA 109; 112; CANR 46, 95, 132;
　　DLB 234; MTFW 2005; SATA 101, 149

Protagoras c. 490B.C.-420B.C. **CMLC 85**
　　See also DLB 176

Proudhon
　　See Cunha, Euclides (Rodrigues Pimenta)
　　da

Proulx, Annie
　　See Proulx, E. Annie

Proulx, E. Annie 1935- **CLC 81, 158**
　　See also AMWS 7; BPFB 3; CA 145;
　　CANR 65, 110; CN 6, 7; CPW 1; DA3;
　　DAM POP; MAL 5; MTCW 2; MTFW
　　2005; SSFS 18, 23

Proulx, Edna Annie
　　See Proulx, E. Annie

Proust, (Valentin-Louis-George-Eugene)
　　Marcel 1871-1922 **SSC 75; TCLC 7,**
　　13, 33; WLC 5
　　See also AAYA 58; BPFB 3; CA 104; 120;
　　CANR 110; DA; DA3; DAB; DAC; DAM
　　MST, NOV; DLB 65; EW 8; EWL 3; GFL
　　1789 to the Present; MTCW 1, 2; MTFW
　　2005; RGWL 2, 3; TWA

Prowler, Harley
　　See Masters, Edgar Lee

Prudentius, Aurelius Clemens 348-c.
　　405 .. **CMLC 78**
　　See also EW 1; RGWL 2, 3

Prus, Boleslaw 1845-1912 **TCLC 48**
　　See also RGWL 2, 3

Pryor, Aaron Richard
　　See Pryor, Richard

Pryor, Richard 1940-2005 **CLC 26**
　　See also CA 122; 152; 246

Pryor, Richard Franklin Lenox Thomas
　　See Pryor, Richard

Przybyszewski, Stanislaw
　　1868-1927 **TCLC 36**
　　See also CA 160; DLB 66; EWL 3

Pteleon
　　See Grieve, C(hristopher) M(urray)
　　See also DAM POET

Puckett, Lute
　　See Masters, Edgar Lee

Puig, Manuel 1932-1990 **CLC 3, 5, 10, 28,**
　　65, 133; HLC 2
　　See also BPFB 3; CA 45-48; CANR 2, 32,
　　63; CDWLB 3; DA3; DAM MULT; DLB
　　113; DNFS 1; EWL 3; GLL 1; HW 1, 2;
　　LAW; MTCW 1, 2; MTFW 2005; RGWL
　　2, 3; TWA; WLIT 1

Pulitzer, Joseph 1847-1911 **TCLC 76**
　　See also CA 114; DLB 23

Purchas, Samuel 1577(?)-1626 **LC 70**
　　See also DLB 151

Purdy, A(lfred) W(ellington)
　　1918-2000 **CLC 3, 6, 14, 50**
　　See also CA 81-84; 189; CAAS 17; CANR
　　42, 66; CP 1, 2, 3, 4, 5, 6, 7; DAC; DAM
　　MST, POET; DLB 88; PFS 5; RGEL 2

Purdy, James (Amos) 1923- **CLC 2, 4, 10,**
　　28, 52
　　See also AMWS 7; CA 33-36R; CAAS 1;
　　CANR 19, 51, 132; CN 1, 2, 3, 4, 5, 6, 7;
　　DLB 2, 218; EWL 3; INT CANR-19;
　　MAL 5; MTCW 1; RGAL 4

Pure, Simon
　　See Swinnerton, Frank Arthur

Pushkin, Aleksandr Sergeevich
　　See Pushkin, Alexander (Sergeyevich)
　　See also DLB 205

Pushkin, Alexander (Sergeyevich)
　　1799-1837 **NCLC 3, 27, 83; PC 10;**
　　SSC 27, 55; WLC 5
　　See Pushkin, Aleksandr Sergeevich
　　See also DA; DA3; DAB; DAC; DAM
　　DRAM, MST, POET; EW 5; EXPS; RGSF
　　2; RGWL 2, 3; SATA 61; SSFS 9; TWA

P'u Sung-ling 1640-1715 **LC 49; SSC 31**

Putnam, Arthur Lee
　　See Alger, Horatio, Jr.

Puttenham, George 1529(?)-1590 **LC 116**
　　See also DLB 281

Puzo, Mario 1920-1999 **CLC 1, 2, 6, 36,**
　　107
　　See also BPFB 3; CA 65-68; 185; CANR 4,
　　42, 65, 99, 131; CN 1, 2, 3, 4, 5, 6; CPW;
　　DA3; DAM NOV, POP; DLB 6; MTCW
　　1, 2; MTFW 2005; NFS 16; RGAL 4

Pygge, Edward
　　See Barnes, Julian

Pyle, Ernest Taylor 1900-1945
　　See Pyle, Ernie
　　See also CA 115; 160

Pyle, Ernie **TCLC 75**
　　See Pyle, Ernest Taylor
　　See also DLB 29; MTCW 2

Pyle, Howard 1853-1911 **TCLC 81**
　　See also AAYA 57; BYA 2, 4; CA 109; 137;
　　CLR 22; DLB 42, 188; DLBD 13; LAIT
　　1; MAICYA 1, 2; SATA 16, 100; WCH;
　　YAW

Pym, Barbara (Mary Crampton)
　　1913-1980 **CLC 13, 19, 37, 111**
　　See also BPFB 3; BRWS 2; CA 13-14; 97-
　　100; CANR 13, 34; CAP 1; DLB 14, 207;
　　DLBY 1987; EWL 3; MTCW 1, 2; MTFW
　　2005; RGEL 2; TEA

Pynchon, Thomas (Ruggles, Jr.)
　　1937- **CLC 2, 3, 6, 9, 11, 18, 33, 62,**
　　72, 123, 192, 213; SSC 14, 84; WLC 5
　　See also AMWS 2; BEST 90:2; BPFB 3;
　　CA 17-20R; CANR 22, 46, 73, 142; CN
　　1, 2, 3, 4, 5, 6, 7; CPW 1; DA; DA3;
　　DAB; DAC; DAM MST, NOV, POP;
　　DLB 2, 173; EWL 3; MAL 5; MTCW 1,
　　2; MTFW 2005; NFS 23; RGAL 4; SFW
　　4; TCLE 1:2; TUS

Pythagoras c. 582B.C.-c. 507B.C. . **CMLC 22**
　　See also DLB 176

Q
　　See Quiller-Couch, Sir Arthur (Thomas)

Qian, Chongzhu
　　See Ch'ien, Chung-shu

Qian, Sima 145B.C.-c. 89B.C. **CMLC 72**

Qian Zhongshu
　　See Ch'ien, Chung-shu
　　See also CWW 2

Qroll
　　See Dagerman, Stig (Halvard)

Quarles, Francis 1592-1644 **LC 117**
　　See also DLB 126; RGEL 2

Quarrington, Paul (Lewis) 1953- **CLC 65**
　　See also CA 129; CANR 62, 95

Quasimodo, Salvatore 1901-1968 **CLC 10;**
　　PC 47
　　See also CA 13-16; 25-28R; CAP 1; DLB
　　114; EW 12; EWL 3; MTCW 1; RGWL
　　2, 3

Quatermass, Martin
　　See Carpenter, John (Howard)

Quay, Stephen 1947- **CLC 95**
　　See also CA 189

Quay, Timothy 1947- **CLC 95**
　　See also CA 189

Queen, Ellery **CLC 3, 11**
　　See also Dannay, Frederic; Davidson, Avram
　　(James); Deming, Richard; Fairman, Paul
　　W.; Flora, Fletcher; Hoch, Edward
　　D(entinger); Kane, Henry; Lee, Manfred
　　B.; Marlowe, Stephen; Powell, (Oval) Tal-
　　mage; Sheldon, Walter J(ames); Sturgeon,
　　Theodore (Hamilton); Tracy, Don(ald
　　Fiske); Vance, Jack
　　See also BPFB 3; CMW 4; MSW; RGAL 4

Queen, Ellery, Jr.
　　See Dannay, Frederic; Lee, Manfred B.

Queneau, Raymond 1903-1976 **CLC 2, 5,**
　　10, 42
　　See also CA 77-80; 69-72; CANR 32; DLB
　　72, 258; EW 12; EWL 3; GFL 1789 to
　　the Present; MTCW 1, 2; RGWL 2, 3

Quevedo, Francisco de 1580-1645 **LC 23**

Quiller-Couch, Sir Arthur (Thomas)
　　1863-1944 **TCLC 53**
　　See also CA 118; 166; DLB 135, 153, 190;
　　HGG; RGEL 2; SUFW 1

Quin, Ann 1936-1973 **CLC 6**
　　See also CA 9-12R; 45-48; CANR 148; CN
　　1; DLB 14, 231

Quin, Ann Marie
　　See Quin, Ann

Quincey, Thomas de
　　See De Quincey, Thomas

Quindlen, Anna 1953- **CLC 191**
　　See also AAYA 35; CA 138; CANR 73, 126;
　　DA3; DLB 292; MTCW 2; MTFW 2005

Quinn, Martin
　　See Smith, Martin Cruz

Quinn, Peter 1947- **CLC 91**
　　See also CA 197; CANR 147

Quinn, Peter A.
　　See Quinn, Peter

Quinn, Simon
　　See Smith, Martin Cruz

Quintana, Leroy V. 1944- **HLC 2; PC 36**
　　See also CA 131; CANR 65, 139; DAM
　　MULT; DLB 82; HW 1, 2

Quintilian c. 40-c. 100 **CMLC 77**
　　See also AW 2; DLB 211; RGWL 2, 3

Quintillian 0035-0100 **CMLC 77**

Quiroga, Horacio (Sylvestre)
　　1878-1937 ... **HLC 2; SSC 89; TCLC 20**
　　See also CA 117; 131; DAM MULT; EWL
　　3; HW 1; LAW; MTCW 1; RGSF 2;
　　WLIT 1

Quoirez, Francoise 1935-2004 **CLC 9**
　　See Sagan, Francoise
　　See also CA 49-52; 231; CANR 6, 39, 73;
　　MTCW 1, 2; MTFW 2005; TWA

Raabe, Wilhelm (Karl) 1831-1910 . **TCLC 45**
　　See also CA 167; DLB 129

Rabe, David (William) 1940- .. **CLC 4, 8, 33,**
　　200; DC 16
　　See also CA 85-88; CABS 3; CAD; CANR
　　59, 129; CD 5, 6; DAM DRAM; DFS 3,
　　8, 13; DLB 7, 228; EWL 3; MAL 5

Rabelais, Francois 1494-1553 **LC 5, 60;**
　　WLC 5
　　See also DA; DAB; DAC; DAM MST; EW
　　2; GFL Beginnings to 1789; LMFS 1;
　　RGWL 2, 3; TWA

Rabi'a al-'Adawiyya c. 717-c.
　　801 ... **CMLC 83**
　　See also DLB 311

Rabinovitch, Sholem 1859-1916
　　See Aleichem, Sholom
　　See also CA 104

Rabinyan, Dorit 1972- **CLC 119**
　　See also CA 170; CANR 147

Rachilde
　　See Vallette, Marguerite Eymery; Vallette,
　　Marguerite Eymery
　　See also EWL 3

Racine, Jean 1639-1699 **LC 28, 113**
See also DA3; DAB; DAM MST; DLB 268;
EW 3; GFL Beginnings to 1789; LMFS
1; RGWL 2, 3; TWA

Radcliffe, Ann (Ward) 1764-1823 ... **NCLC 6, 55, 106**
See also DLB 39, 178; GL 3; HGG; LMFS
1; RGEL 2; SUFW; WLIT 3

Radclyffe-Hall, Marguerite
See Hall, (Marguerite) Radclyffe

Radiguet, Raymond 1903-1923 **TCLC 29**
See also CA 162; DLB 65; EWL 3; GFL
1789 to the Present; RGWL 2, 3

Radnoti, Miklos 1909-1944 **TCLC 16**
See also CA 118; 212; CDWLB 4; DLB
215; EWL 3; RGHL; RGWL 2, 3

Rado, James 1939- **CLC 17**
See also CA 105

Radvanyi, Netty 1900-1983
See Seghers, Anna
See also CA 85-88; 110; CANR 82

Rae, Ben
See Griffiths, Trevor

Raeburn, John (Hay) 1941- **CLC 34**
See also CA 57-60

Ragni, Gerome 1942-1991 **CLC 17**
See also CA 105; 134

Rahv, Philip **CLC 24**
See Greenberg, Ivan
See also DLB 137; MAL 5

Raimund, Ferdinand Jakob
1790-1836 **NCLC 69**
See also DLB 90

Raine, Craig (Anthony) 1944- .. **CLC 32, 103**
See also CA 108; CANR 29, 51, 103; CP 3,
4, 5, 6, 7; DLB 40; PFS 7

Raine, Kathleen (Jessie) 1908-2003 .. **CLC 7, 45**
See also CA 85-88; 218; CANR 46, 109;
CP 1, 2, 3, 4, 5, 6, 7; DLB 20; EWL 3;
MTCW 1; RGEL 2

Rainis, Janis 1865-1929 **TCLC 29**
See also CA 170; CDWLB 4; DLB 220;
EWL 3

Rakosi, Carl **CLC 47**
See Rawley, Callman
See also CA 228; CAAS 5; CP 1, 2, 3, 4, 5,
6, 7; DLB 193

Ralegh, Sir Walter
See Raleigh, Sir Walter
See also BRW 1; RGEL 2; WP

Raleigh, Richard
See Lovecraft, H. P.

Raleigh, Sir Walter 1554(?)-1618 **LC 31, 39; PC 31**
See Ralegh, Sir Walter
See also CDBLB Before 1660; DLB 172;
EXPP; PFS 14; TEA

Rallentando, H. P.
See Sayers, Dorothy L(eigh)

Ramal, Walter
See de la Mare, Walter (John)

Ramana Maharshi 1879-1950 **TCLC 84**

Ramoacn y Cajal, Santiago
1852-1934 **TCLC 93**

Ramon, Juan
See Jimenez (Mantecon), Juan Ramon

Ramos, Graciliano 1892-1953 **TCLC 32**
See also CA 167; DLB 307; EWL 3; HW 2;
LAW; WLIT 1

Rampersad, Arnold 1941- **CLC 44**
See also BW 2, 3; CA 127; 133; CANR 81;
DLB 111; INT CA-133

Rampling, Anne
See Rice, Anne
See also GLL 2

Ramsay, Allan 1686(?)-1758 **LC 29**
See also DLB 95; RGEL 2

Ramsay, Jay
See Campbell, (John) Ramsey

Ramuz, Charles-Ferdinand
1878-1947 **TCLC 33**
See also CA 165; EWL 3

Rand, Ayn 1905-1982 **CLC 3, 30, 44, 79; WLC 5**
See also AAYA 10; AMWS 4; BPFB 3;
BYA 12; CA 13-16R; 105; CANR 27, 73;
CDALBS; CN 1, 2, 3; CPW; DA; DA3;
DAC; DAM MST, NOV, POP; DLB 227,
279; MTCW 1, 2; MTFW 2005; NFS 10,
16; RGAL 4; SFW 4; TUS; YAW

Randall, Dudley (Felker) 1914-2000 . **BLC 3; CLC 1, 135**
See also BW 1, 3; CA 25-28R; 189; CANR
23, 82; CP 1, 2, 3, 4, 5; DAM MULT;
DLB 41; PFS 5

Randall, Robert
See Silverberg, Robert

Ranger, Ken
See Creasey, John

Rank, Otto 1884-1939 **TCLC 115**

Ransom, John Crowe 1888-1974 .. **CLC 2, 4, 5, 11, 24; PC 61**
See also AMW; CA 5-8R; 49-52; CANR 6,
34; CDALBS; CP 1, 2; DA3; DAM POET;
DLB 45, 63; EWL 3; EXPP; MAL 5;
MTCW 1, 2; MTFW 2005; RGAL 4; TUS

Rao, Raja 1908-2006 **CLC 25, 56**
See also CA 73-76; CANR 51; CN 1, 2, 3,
4, 5, 6; DAM NOV; DLB 323; EWL 3;
MTCW 1, 2; MTFW 2005; RGEL 2;
RGSF 2

Raphael, Frederic (Michael) 1931- ... **CLC 2, 14**
See also CA 1-4R; CANR 1, 86; CN 1, 2,
3, 4, 5, 6, 7; DLB 14, 319; TCLE 1:2

Ratcliffe, James P.
See Mencken, H(enry) L(ouis)

Rathbone, Julian 1935- **CLC 41**
See also CA 101; CANR 34, 73, 152

Rattigan, Terence (Mervyn)
1911-1977 **CLC 7; DC 18**
See also BRWS 7; CA 85-88; 73-76; CBD;
CDBLB 1945-1960; DAM DRAM; DFS
8; DLB 13; IDFW 3, 4; MTCW 1, 2;
MTFW 2005; RGEL 2

Ratushinskaya, Irina 1954- **CLC 54**
See also CA 129; CANR 68; CWW 2

Raven, Simon (Arthur Noel)
1927-2001 **CLC 14**
See also CA 81-84; 197; CANR 86; CN 1,
2, 3, 4, 5, 6; DLB 271

Ravenna, Michael
See Welty, Eudora

Rawley, Callman 1903-2004
See Rakosi, Carl
See also CA 21-24R; 228; CANR 12, 32,
91

Rawlings, Marjorie Kinnan
1896-1953 **TCLC 4**
See also AAYA 20; AMWS 10; ANW;
BPFB 3; BYA 3; CA 104; 137; CANR 74;
CLR 63; DLB 9, 22, 102; DLBD 17;
JRDA; MAICYA 1, 2; MAL 5; MTCW 2;
MTFW 2005; RGAL 4; SATA 100; WCH;
YABC 1; YAW

Ray, Satyajit 1921-1992 **CLC 16, 76**
See also CA 114; 137; DAM MULT

Read, Herbert Edward 1893-1968 **CLC 4**
See also BRW 6; CA 85-88; 25-28R; DLB
20, 149; EWL 3; PAB; RGEL 2

Read, Piers Paul 1941- **CLC 4, 10, 25**
See also CA 21-24R; CANR 38, 86, 150;
CN 2, 3, 4, 5, 6, 7; DLB 14; SATA 21

Reade, Charles 1814-1884 **NCLC 2, 74**
See also DLB 21; RGEL 2

Reade, Hamish
See Gray, Simon (James Holliday)

Reading, Peter 1946- **CLC 47**
See also BRWS 8; CA 103; CANR 46, 96;
CP 5, 6, 7; DLB 40

Reaney, James 1926- **CLC 13**
See also CA 41-44R; CAAS 15; CANR 42;
CD 5, 6; CP 1, 2, 3, 4, 5, 6, 7; DAC;
DAM MST; DLB 68; RGEL 2; SATA 43

Rebreanu, Liviu 1885-1944 **TCLC 28**
See also CA 165; DLB 220; EWL 3

Rechy, John 1934- **CLC 1, 7, 14, 18, 107; HLC 2**
See also CA 5-8R; 195; CAAE 195; CAAS
4; CANR 6, 32, 64, 152; CN 1, 2, 3, 4, 5,
6, 7; DAM MULT; DLB 122, 278; DLBY
1982; HW 1, 2; INT CANR-6; LLW;
MAL 5; RGAL 4

Rechy, John Francisco
See Rechy, John

Redcam, Tom 1870-1933 **TCLC 25**

Reddin, Keith 1956- **CLC 67**
See also CAD; CD 6

Redgrove, Peter (William)
1932-2003 **CLC 6, 41**
See also BRWS 6; CA 1-4R; 217; CANR 3,
39, 77; CP 1, 2, 3, 4, 5, 6, 7; DLB 40;
TCLE 1:2

Redmon, Anne **CLC 22**
See Nightingale, Anne Redmon
See also DLBY 1986

Reed, Eliot
See Ambler, Eric

Reed, Ishmael (Scott) 1938- . **BLC 3; CLC 2, 3, 5, 6, 13, 32, 60, 174; PC 68**
See also AFAW 1, 2; AMWS 10; BPFB 3;
BW 2, 3; CA 21-24R; CANR 25, 48, 74,
128; CN 1, 2, 3, 4, 5, 6, 7; CP 1, 2, 3, 4,
5, 6, 7; CSW; DA3; DAM MULT; DLB
2, 5, 33, 169, 227; DLBD 8; EWL 3;
LMFS 2; MAL 5; MSW; MTCW 1, 2;
MTFW 2005; PFS 6; RGAL 4; TCWW 2

Reed, John (Silas) 1887-1920 **TCLC 9**
See also CA 106; 195; MAL 5; TUS

Reed, Lou **CLC 21**
See Firbank, Louis

Reese, Lizette Woodworth 1856-1935 . **PC 29**
See also CA 180; DLB 54

Reeve, Clara 1729-1807 **NCLC 19**
See also DLB 39; RGEL 2

Reich, Wilhelm 1897-1957 **TCLC 57**
See also CA 199

Reid, Christopher (John) 1949- **CLC 33**
See also CA 140; CANR 89; CP 4, 5, 6, 7;
DLB 40; EWL 3

Reid, Desmond
See Moorcock, Michael

Reid Banks, Lynne 1929-
See Banks, Lynne Reid
See also AAYA 49; CA 1-4R; CANR 6, 22,
38, 87; CLR 24; CN 1, 2, 3, 7; JRDA;
MAICYA 1, 2; SATA 22, 75, 111, 165;
YAW

Reilly, William K.
See Creasey, John

Reiner, Max
See Caldwell, (Janet Miriam) Taylor
(Holland)

Reis, Ricardo
See Pessoa, Fernando (Antonio Nogueira)

Reizenstein, Elmer Leopold
See Rice, Elmer (Leopold)
See also EWL 3

Remarque, Erich Maria 1898-1970 . **CLC 21**
See also AAYA 27; BPFB 3; CA 77-80; 29-
32R; CDWLB 2; DA; DA3; DAB; DAC;
DAM MST, NOV; DLB 56; EWL 3;
EXPN; LAIT 3; MTCW 1, 2; MTFW
2005; NFS 4; RGHL; RGWL 2, 3

Remington, Frederic S(ackrider)
　　1861-1909 **TCLC 89**
　　See also CA 108; 169; DLB 12, 186, 188;
　　SATA 41; TCWW 2

Remizov, A.
　　See Remizov, Aleksei (Mikhailovich)

Remizov, A. M.
　　See Remizov, Aleksei (Mikhailovich)

Remizov, Aleksei (Mikhailovich)
　　1877-1957 **TCLC 27**
　　See Remizov, Alexey Mikhaylovich
　　See also CA 125; 133; DLB 295

Remizov, Alexey Mikhaylovich
　　See Remizov, Aleksei (Mikhailovich)
　　See also EWL 3

Renan, Joseph Ernest 1823-1892 . **NCLC 26, 145**
　　See also GFL 1789 to the Present

Renard, Jules(-Pierre) 1864-1910 .. **TCLC 17**
　　See also CA 117; 202; GFL 1789 to the
　　Present

Renart, Jean fl. 13th cent. - **CMLC 83**

Renault, Mary **CLC 3, 11, 17**
　　See Challans, Mary
　　See also BPFB 3; BYA 2; CN 1, 2, 3;
　　DLBY 1983; EWL 3; GLL 1; LAIT 1;
　　RGEL 2; RHW

Rendell, Ruth (Barbara) 1930- .. **CLC 28, 48**
　　See Vine, Barbara
　　See also BPFB 3; BRWS 9; CA 109; CANR
　　32, 52, 74, 127; CN 5, 6, 7; CPW; DAM
　　POP; DLB 87, 276; INT CANR-32;
　　MSW; MTCW 1, 2; MTFW 2005

Renoir, Jean 1894-1979 **CLC 20**
　　See also CA 129; 85-88

Resnais, Alain 1922- **CLC 16**

Revard, Carter 1931- **NNAL**
　　See also CA 144; CANR 81, 153; PFS 5

Reverdy, Pierre 1889-1960 **CLC 53**
　　See also CA 97-100; 89-92; DLB 258; EWL
　　3; GFL 1789 to the Present

Rexroth, Kenneth 1905-1982 **CLC 1, 2, 6, 11, 22, 49, 112; PC 20**
　　See also BG 1:3; CA 5-8R; 107; CANR 14,
　　34, 63; CDALB 1941-1968; CP 1, 2, 3;
　　DAM POET; DLB 16, 48, 165, 212;
　　DLBY 1982; EWL 3; INT CANR-14;
　　MAL 5; MTCW 1, 2; MTFW 2005;
　　RGAL 4

Reyes, Alfonso 1889-1959 **HLCS 2; TCLC 33**
　　See also CA 131; EWL 3; HW 1; LAW

Reyes y Basoalto, Ricardo Eliecer Neftali
　　See Neruda, Pablo

Reymont, Wladyslaw (Stanislaw)
　　1868(?)-1925 **TCLC 5**
　　See also CA 104; EWL 3

Reynolds, John Hamilton
　　1794-1852 **NCLC 146**
　　See also DLB 96

Reynolds, Jonathan 1942- **CLC 6, 38**
　　See also CA 65-68; CANR 28

Reynolds, Joshua 1723-1792 **LC 15**
　　See also DLB 104

Reynolds, Michael S(hane)
　　1937-2000 **CLC 44**
　　See also CA 65-68; 189; CANR 9, 89, 97

Reznikoff, Charles 1894-1976 **CLC 9**
　　See also AMWS 14; CA 33-36; 61-64; CAP
　　2; CP 1, 2; DLB 28, 45; RGHL; WP

Rezzori, Gregor von
　　See Rezzori d'Arezzo, Gregor von

Rezzori d'Arezzo, Gregor von
　　1914-1998 **CLC 25**
　　See also CA 122; 136; 167

Rhine, Richard
　　See Silverstein, Alvin; Silverstein, Virginia
　　B(arbara Opshelor)

Rhodes, Eugene Manlove
　　1869-1934 **TCLC 53**
　　See also CA 198; DLB 256; TCWW 1, 2

R'hoone, Lord
　　See Balzac, Honore de

Rhys, Jean 1890-1979 **CLC 2, 4, 6, 14, 19, 51, 124; SSC 21, 76**
　　See also BRWS 2; CA 25-28R; 85-88;
　　CANR 35, 62; CDBLB 1945-1960; CD-
　　WLB 3; CN 1, 2; DA3; DAM NOV; DLB
　　36, 117, 162; DNFS 2; EWL 3; LATS 1:1;
　　MTCW 1, 2; MTFW 2005; NFS 19;
　　RGEL 2; RGSF 2; RHW; TEA; WWE 1

Ribeiro, Darcy 1922-1997 **CLC 34**
　　See also CA 33-36R; 156; EWL 3

Ribeiro, Joao Ubaldo (Osorio Pimentel)
　　1941- **CLC 10, 67**
　　See also CA 81-84; CWW 2; EWL 3

Ribman, Ronald (Burt) 1932- **CLC 7**
　　See also CA 21-24R; CAD; CANR 46, 80;
　　CD 5, 6

Ricci, Nino (Pio) 1959- **CLC 70**
　　See also CA 137; CANR 130; CCA 1

Rice, Anne 1941- **CLC 41, 128**
　　See Rampling, Anne
　　See also AAYA 9, 53; AMWS 7; BEST
　　89:2; BPFB 3; CA 65-68; CANR 12, 36,
　　53, 74, 100, 133; CN 6, 7; CPW; CSW;
　　DA3; DAM POP; DLB 292; GL 3; GLL
　　2; HGG; MTCW 2; MTFW 2005; SUFW
　　2; YAW

Rice, Elmer (Leopold) 1892-1967 **CLC 7, 49**
　　See Reizenstein, Elmer Leopold
　　See also CA 21-22; 25-28R; CAP 2; DAM
　　DRAM; DFS 12; DLB 4, 7; IDTP; MAL
　　5; MTCW 1, 2; RGAL 4

Rice, Tim(othy Miles Bindon)
　　1944- ... **CLC 21**
　　See also CA 103; CANR 46; DFS 7

Rich, Adrienne (Cecile) 1929- ... **CLC 3, 6, 7, 11, 18, 36, 73, 76, 125; PC 5**
　　See also AAYA 69; AMWR 2; AMWS 1;
　　CA 9-12R; CANR 20, 53, 74, 128;
　　CDALBS; CP 1, 2, 3, 4, 5, 6, 7; CSW;
　　CWP; DA3; DAM POET; DLB 5, 67;
　　EWL 3; EXPP; FL 1:6; FW; MAL 5;
　　MAWW; MTCW 1, 2; MTFW 2005;
　　PAB; PFS 15; RGAL 4; RGHL; WP

Rich, Barbara
　　See Graves, Robert (von Ranke)

Rich, Robert
　　See Trumbo, Dalton

Richard, Keith **CLC 17**
　　See Richards, Keith

Richards, David Adams 1950- **CLC 59**
　　See also CA 93-96; CANR 60, 110; CN 7;
　　DAC; DLB 53; TCLE 1:2

Richards, I(vor) A(rmstrong)
　　1893-1979 **CLC 14, 24**
　　See also BRWS 2; CA 41-44R; 89-92;
　　CANR 34, 74; CP 1, 2; DLB 27; EWL 3;
　　MTCW 2; RGEL 2

Richards, Keith 1943-
　　See Richard, Keith
　　See also CA 107; CANR 77

Richardson, Anne
　　See Roiphe, Anne

Richardson, Dorothy Miller
　　1873-1957 **TCLC 3**
　　See also CA 104; 192; DLB 36; EWL 3;
　　FW; RGEL 2

**Richardson (Robertson), Ethel Florence
　　Lindesay** 1870-1946
　　See Richardson, Henry Handel
　　See also CA 105; 190; DLB 230; RHW

Richardson, Henry Handel **TCLC 4**
　　See Richardson (Robertson), Ethel Florence
　　Lindesay
　　See also DLB 197; EWL 3; RGEL 2; RGSF
　　2

Richardson, John 1796-1852 **NCLC 55**
　　See also CCA 1; DAC; DLB 99

Richardson, Samuel 1689-1761 **LC 1, 44; WLC 5**
　　See also BRW 3; CDBLB 1660-1789; DA;
　　DAB; DAC; DAM MST, NOV; DLB 39;
　　RGEL 2; TEA; WLIT 3

Richardson, Willis 1889-1977 **HR 1:3**
　　See also BW 1; CA 124; DLB 51; SATA 60

Richler, Mordecai 1931-2001 **CLC 3, 5, 9, 13, 18, 46, 70, 185**
　　See also AITN 1; CA 65-68; 201; CANR
　　31, 62, 111; CCA 1; CLR 17; CN 1, 2, 3,
　　4, 5, 7; CWRI 5; DAC; DAM MST, NOV;
　　DLB 53; EWL 3; MAICYA 1, 2; MTCW
　　1, 2; MTFW 2005; RGEL 2; RGHL;
　　SATA 44, 98; SATA-Brief 27; TWA

Richter, Conrad (Michael)
　　1890-1968 **CLC 30**
　　See also AAYA 21; BYA 2; CA 5-8R; 25-
　　28R; CANR 23; DLB 9, 212; LAIT 1;
　　MAL 5; MTCW 1, 2; MTFW 2005;
　　RGAL 4; SATA 3; TCWW 1, 2; TUS;
　　YAW

Ricostranza, Tom
　　See Ellis, Trey

Riddell, Charlotte 1832-1906 **TCLC 40**
　　See Riddell, Mrs. J. H.
　　See also CA 165; DLB 156

Riddell, Mrs. J. H.
　　See Riddell, Charlotte
　　See also HGG; SUFW

Ridge, John Rollin 1827-1867 **NCLC 82; NNAL**
　　See also CA 144; DAM MULT; DLB 175

Ridgeway, Jason
　　See Marlowe, Stephen

Ridgway, Keith 1965- **CLC 119**
　　See also CA 172; CANR 144

Riding, Laura **CLC 3, 7**
　　See Jackson, Laura (Riding)
　　See also CP 1, 2, 3, 4, 5; RGAL 4

Riefenstahl, Berta Helene Amalia 1902-2003
　　See Riefenstahl, Leni
　　See also CA 108; 220

Riefenstahl, Leni **CLC 16, 190**
　　See Riefenstahl, Berta Helene Amalia

Riffe, Ernest
　　See Bergman, (Ernst) Ingmar

Riggs, (Rolla) Lynn
　　1899-1954 **NNAL; TCLC 56**
　　See also CA 144; DAM MULT; DLB 175

Riis, Jacob A(ugust) 1849-1914 **TCLC 80**
　　See also CA 113; 168; DLB 23

Riley, James Whitcomb 1849-1916 **PC 48; TCLC 51**
　　See also CA 118; 137; DAM POET; MAI-
　　CYA 1, 2; RGAL 4; SATA 17

Riley, Tex
　　See Creasey, John

Rilke, Rainer Maria 1875-1926 **PC 2; TCLC 1, 6, 19**
　　See also CA 104; 132; CANR 62, 99; CD-
　　WLB 2; DA3; DAM POET; DLB 81; EW
　　9; EWL 3; MTCW 1, 2; MTFW 2005;
　　PFS 19; RGWL 2, 3; TWA; WP

Rimbaud, (Jean Nicolas) Arthur
　　1854-1891 ... **NCLC 4, 35, 82; PC 3, 57; WLC 5**
　　See also DA; DA3; DAB; DAC; DAM
　　MST, POET; DLB 217; EW 7; GFL 1789
　　to the Present; LMFS 2; RGWL 2, 3;
　　TWA; WP

Rinehart, Mary Roberts
1876-1958 **TCLC 52**
See also BPFB 3; CA 108; 166; RGAL 4;
RHW
Ringmaster, The
See Mencken, H(enry) L(ouis)
Ringwood, Gwen(dolyn Margaret) Pharis
1910-1984 **CLC 48**
See also CA 148; 112; DLB 88
Rio, Michel 1945(?)- **CLC 43**
See also CA 201
Rios, Alberto (Alvaro) 1952- **PC 57**
See also AAYA 66; AMWS 4; CA 113;
CANR 34, 79, 137; CP 6, 7; DLB 122;
HW 2; MTFW 2005; PFS 11
Ritsos, Giannes
See Ritsos, Yannis
Ritsos, Yannis 1909-1990 **CLC 6, 13, 31**
See also CA 77-80; 133; CANR 39, 61; EW
12; EWL 3; MTCW 1; RGWL 2, 3
Ritter, Erika 1948(?)- **CLC 52**
See also CD 5, 6; CWD
Rivera, Jose Eustasio 1889-1928 ... **TCLC 35**
See also CA 162; EWL 3; HW 1, 2; LAW
Rivera, Tomas 1935-1984 **HLCS 2**
See also CA 49-52; CANR 32; DLB 82;
HW 1; LLW; RGAL 4; SSFS 15; TCWW
2; WLIT 1
Rivers, Conrad Kent 1933-1968 **CLC 1**
See also BW 1; CA 85-88; DLB 41
Rivers, Elfrida
See Bradley, Marion Zimmer
See also GLL 1
Riverside, John
See Heinlein, Robert A(nson)
Rizal, Jose 1861-1896 **NCLC 27**
Roa Bastos, Augusto 1917-2005 **CLC 45;
HLC 2**
See also CA 131; 238; CWW 2; DAM
MULT; DLB 113; EWL 3; HW 1; LAW;
RGSF 2; WLIT 1
Roa Bastos, Augusto Jose Antonio
See Roa Bastos, Augusto
Robbe-Grillet, Alain 1922- **CLC 1, 2, 4, 6,
8, 10, 14, 43, 128**
See also BPFB 3; CA 9-12R; CANR 33,
65, 115; CWW 2; DLB 83; EW 13; EWL
3; GFL 1789 to the Present; IDFW 3, 4;
MTCW 1, 2; MTFW 2005; RGWL 2, 3;
SSFS 15
Robbins, Harold 1916-1997 **CLC 5**
See also BPFB 3; CA 73-76; 162; CANR
26, 54, 112; DA3; DAM NOV; MTCW 1,
2
Robbins, Thomas Eugene 1936-
See Robbins, Tom
See also CA 81-84; CANR 29, 59, 95, 139;
CN 7; CPW; CSW; DA3; DAM NOV,
POP; MTCW 1, 2; MTFW 2005
Robbins, Tom **CLC 9, 32, 64**
See Robbins, Thomas Eugene
See also AAYA 32; AMWS 10; BEST 90:3;
BPFB 3; CN 3, 4, 5, 6, 7; DLBY 1980
Robbins, Trina 1938- **CLC 21**
See also CA 128; CANR 152
Roberts, Charles G(eorge) D(ouglas)
1860-1943 **SSC 91; TCLC 8**
See also CA 105; 188; CLR 33; CWRI 5;
DLB 92; RGEL 2; RGSF 2; SATA 88;
SATA-Brief 29
Roberts, Elizabeth Madox
1886-1941 **TCLC 68**
See also CA 111; 166; CLR 100; CWRI 5;
DLB 9, 54, 102; RGAL 4; RHW; SATA
33; SATA-Brief 27; TCWW 2; WCH
Roberts, Kate 1891-1985 **CLC 15**
See also CA 107; 116; DLB 319

Roberts, Keith (John Kingston)
1935-2000 **CLC 14**
See also BRWS 10; CA 25-28R; CANR 46;
DLB 261; SFW 4
Roberts, Kenneth (Lewis)
1885-1957 **TCLC 23**
See also CA 109; 199; DLB 9; MAL 5;
RGAL 4; RHW
Roberts, Michele (Brigitte) 1949- ... **CLC 48,
178**
See also CA 115; CANR 58, 120; CN 6, 7;
DLB 231; FW
Robertson, Ellis
See Ellison, Harlan (Jay); Silverberg, Rob-
ert
Robertson, Thomas William
1829-1871 **NCLC 35**
See Robertson, Tom
See also DAM DRAM
Robertson, Tom
See Robertson, Thomas William
See also RGEL 2
Robeson, Kenneth
See Dent, Lester
Robinson, Edwin Arlington
1869-1935 **PC 1, 35; TCLC 5, 101**
See also AMW; CA 104; 133; CDALB
1865-1917; DA; DAC; DAM MST,
POET; DLB 54; EWL 3; EXPP; MAL 5;
MTCW 1, 2; MTFW 2005; PAB; PFS 4;
RGAL 4; WP
Robinson, Henry Crabb
1775-1867 **NCLC 15**
See also DLB 107
Robinson, Jill 1936- **CLC 10**
See also CA 102; CANR 120; INT CA-102
Robinson, Kim Stanley 1952- **CLC 34**
See also AAYA 26; CA 126; CANR 113,
139; CN 6, 7; MTFW 2005; SATA 109;
SCFW 2; SFW 4
Robinson, Lloyd
See Silverberg, Robert
Robinson, Marilynne 1944- **CLC 25, 180**
See also AAYA 69; CA 116; CANR 80, 140;
CN 4, 5, 6, 7; DLB 206; MTFW 2005
Robinson, Mary 1758-1800 **NCLC 142**
See also DLB 158; FW
Robinson, Smokey **CLC 21**
See Robinson, William, Jr.
Robinson, William, Jr. 1940-
See Robinson, Smokey
See also CA 116
Robison, Mary 1949- **CLC 42, 98**
See also CA 113; 116; CANR 87; CN 4, 5,
6, 7; DLB 130; INT CA-116; RGSF 2
Roches, Catherine des 1542-1587 **LC 117**
Rochester
See Wilmot, John
See also RGEL 2
Rod, Edouard 1857-1910 **TCLC 52**
Roddenberry, Eugene Wesley 1921-1991
See Roddenberry, Gene
See also CA 110; 135; CANR 37; SATA 45;
SATA-Obit 69
Roddenberry, Gene **CLC 17**
See Roddenberry, Eugene Wesley
See also AAYA 5; SATA-Obit 69
Rodgers, Mary 1931- **CLC 12**
See also BYA 5; CA 49-52; CANR 8, 55,
90; CLR 20; CWRI 5; INT CANR-8;
JRDA; MAICYA 1, 2; SATA 8, 130
Rodgers, W(illiam) R(obert)
1909-1969 **CLC 7**
See also CA 85-88; DLB 20; RGEL 2
Rodman, Eric
See Silverberg, Robert
Rodman, Howard 1920(?)-1985 **CLC 65**
See also CA 118

Rodman, Maia
See Wojciechowska, Maia (Teresa)
Rodo, Jose Enrique 1871(?)-1917 **HLCS 2**
See also CA 178; EWL 3; HW 2; LAW
Rodolph, Utto
See Ouologuem, Yambo
Rodriguez, Claudio 1934-1999 **CLC 10**
See also CA 188; DLB 134
Rodriguez, Richard 1944- **CLC 155; HLC
2**
See also AMWS 14; CA 110; CANR 66,
116; DAM MULT; DLB 82, 256; HW 1,
2; LAIT 5; LLW; MTFW 2005; NCFS 3;
WLIT 1
Roelvaag, O(le) E(dvart) 1876-1931
See Rolvaag, O(le) E(dvart)
See also CA 117; 171
Roethke, Theodore (Huebner)
1908-1963 **CLC 1, 3, 8, 11, 19, 46,
101; PC 15**
See also AMW; CA 81-84; CABS 2;
CDALB 1941-1968; DA3; DAM POET;
DLB 5, 206; EWL 3; EXPP; MAL 5;
MTCW 1, 2; PAB; PFS 3; RGAL 4; WP
Rogers, Carl R(ansom)
1902-1987 **TCLC 125**
See also CA 1-4R; 121; CANR 1, 18;
MTCW 1
Rogers, Samuel 1763-1855 **NCLC 69**
See also DLB 93; RGEL 2
Rogers, Thomas Hunton 1927- **CLC 57**
See also CA 89-92; INT CA-89-92
Rogers, Will(iam Penn Adair)
1879-1935 **NNAL; TCLC 8, 71**
See also CA 105; 144; DA3; DAM MULT;
DLB 11; MTCW 2
Rogin, Gilbert 1929- **CLC 18**
See also CA 65-68; CANR 15
Rohan, Koda
See Koda Shigeyuki
Rohlfs, Anna Katharine Green
See Green, Anna Katharine
Rohmer, Eric **CLC 16**
See Scherer, Jean-Marie Maurice
Rohmer, Sax **TCLC 28**
See Ward, Arthur Henry Sarsfield
See also DLB 70; MSW; SUFW
Roiphe, Anne 1935- **CLC 3, 9**
See also CA 89-92; CANR 45, 73, 138;
DLBY 1980; INT CA-89-92
Roiphe, Anne Richardson
See Roiphe, Anne
Rojas, Fernando de 1475-1541 ... **HLCS 1, 2;
LC 23**
See also DLB 286; RGWL 2, 3
Rojas, Gonzalo 1917- **HLCS 2**
See also CA 178; HW 2; LAWS 1
Roland (de la Platiere), Marie-Jeanne
1754-1793 **LC 98**
See also DLB 314
**Rolfe, Frederick (William Serafino Austin
Lewis Mary)** 1860-1913 **TCLC 12**
See Al Siddik
See also CA 107; 210; DLB 34, 156; RGEL
2
Rolland, Romain 1866-1944 **TCLC 23**
See also CA 118; 197; DLB 65, 284; EWL
3; GFL 1789 to the Present; RGWL 2, 3
Rolle, Richard c. 1300-c. 1349 **CMLC 21**
See also DLB 146; LMFS 1; RGEL 2
Rolvaag, O(le) E(dvart) **TCLC 17**
See Roelvaag, O(le) E(dvart)
See also DLB 9, 212; MAL 5; NFS 5;
RGAL 4
Romain Arnaud, Saint
See Aragon, Louis

Romains, Jules 1885-1972 **CLC 7**
　See also CA 85-88; CANR 34; DLB 65,
　321; EWL 3; GFL 1789 to the Present;
　MTCW 1
Romero, Jose Ruben 1890-1952 **TCLC 14**
　See also CA 114; 131; EWL 3; HW 1; LAW
Ronsard, Pierre de 1524-1585 . **LC 6, 54; PC
11**
　See also EW 2; GFL Beginnings to 1789;
　RGWL 2, 3; TWA
Rooke, Leon 1934- **CLC 25, 34**
　See also CA 25-28R; CANR 23, 53; CCA
　1; CPW; DAM POP
Roosevelt, Franklin Delano
　1882-1945 **TCLC 93**
　See also CA 116; 173; LAIT 3
Roosevelt, Theodore 1858-1919 **TCLC 69**
　See also CA 115; 170; DLB 47, 186, 275
Roper, William 1498-1578 **LC 10**
Roquelaure, A. N.
　See Rice, Anne
Rosa, Joao Guimaraes 1908-1967 ... **CLC 23;
HLCS 1**
　See Guimaraes Rosa, Joao
　See also CA 89-92; DLB 113, 307; EWL 3;
　WLIT 1
Rose, Wendy 1948- . **CLC 85; NNAL; PC 13**
　See also CA 53-56; CANR 5, 51; CWP;
　DAM MULT; DLB 175; PFS 13; RGAL
　4; SATA 12
Rosen, R. D.
　See Rosen, Richard (Dean)
Rosen, Richard (Dean) 1949- **CLC 39**
　See also CA 77-80; CANR 62, 120; CMW
　4; INT CANR-30
Rosenberg, Isaac 1890-1918 **TCLC 12**
　See also BRW 6; CA 107; 188; DLB 20,
　216; EWL 3; PAB; RGEL 2
Rosenblatt, Joe **CLC 15**
　See Rosenblatt, Joseph
　See also CP 3, 4, 5, 6, 7
Rosenblatt, Joseph 1933-
　See Rosenblatt, Joe
　See also CA 89-92; CP 1, 2; INT CA-89-92
Rosenfeld, Samuel
　See Tzara, Tristan
Rosenstock, Sami
　See Tzara, Tristan
Rosenstock, Samuel
　See Tzara, Tristan
Rosenthal, M(acha) L(ouis)
　1917-1996 **CLC 28**
　See also CA 1-4R; 152; CAAS 6; CANR 4,
　51; CP 1, 2, 3, 4, 5, 6; DLB 5; SATA 59
Ross, Barnaby
　See Dannay, Frederic; Lee, Manfred B.
Ross, Bernard L.
　See Follett, Ken(neth Martin)
Ross, J. H.
　See Lawrence, T(homas) E(dward)
Ross, John Hume
　See Lawrence, T(homas) E(dward)
Ross, Martin 1862-1915
　See Martin, Violet Florence
　See also DLB 135; GLL 2; RGEL 2; RGSF
　2
Ross, (James) Sinclair 1908-1996 ... **CLC 13;
SSC 24**
　See also CA 73-76; CANR 81; CN 1, 2, 3,
　4, 5, 6; DAC; DAM MST; DLB 88;
　RGEL 2; RGSF 2; TCWW 1, 2
Rossetti, Christina 1830-1894 ... **NCLC 2, 50,
66; PC 7; WLC 5**
　See also AAYA 51; BRW 5; BYA 4; DA;
　DA3; DAB; DAC; DAM MST, POET;
　DLB 35, 163, 240; EXPP; FL 1:3; LATS
　1:1; MAICYA 1, 2; PFS 10, 14; RGEL 2;
　SATA 20; TEA; WCH

Rossetti, Christina Georgina
　See Rossetti, Christina
Rossetti, Dante Gabriel 1828-1882 . **NCLC 4,
77; PC 44; WLC 5**
　See also AAYA 51; BRW 5; CDBLB 1832-
　1890; DA; DAB; DAC; DAM MST,
　POET; DLB 35; EXPP; RGEL 2; TEA
Rossi, Cristina Peri
　See Peri Rossi, Cristina
Rossi, Jean-Baptiste 1931-2003
　See Japrisot, Sebastien
　See also CA 201; 215
Rossner, Judith 1935-2005 **CLC 6, 9, 29**
　See also AITN 2; BEST 90:3; CA
　17-20R; 242; CANR 18, 51, 73; CN 4, 5,
　6, 7; DLB 6; INT CANR-18; MAL 5;
　MTCW 1, 2; MTFW 2005
Rossner, Judith Perelman
　See Rossner, Judith
Rostand, Edmond (Eugene Alexis)
　1868-1918 **DC 10; TCLC 6, 37**
　See also CA 104; 126; DA; DA3; DAB;
　DAC; DAM DRAM, MST; DFS 1; DLB
　192; LAIT 1; MTCW 1; RGWL 2, 3;
　TWA
Roth, Henry 1906-1995 **CLC 2, 6, 11, 104**
　See also AMWS 9; CA 11-12; 149; CANR
　38, 63; CAP 1; CN 1, 2, 3, 4, 5, 6; DA3;
　DLB 28; EWL 3; MAL 5; MTCW 1, 2;
　MTFW 2005; RGAL 4
Roth, (Moses) Joseph 1894-1939 ... **TCLC 33**
　See also CA 160; DLB 85; EWL 3; RGWL
　2, 3
Roth, Philip 1933- ... **CLC 1, 2, 3, 4, 6, 9, 15,
22, 31, 47, 66, 86, 119, 201; SSC 26;
WLC 5**
　See also AAYA 67; AMWR 2; AMWS 3;
　BEST 90:3; BPFB 3; CA 1-4R; CANR 1,
　22, 36, 55, 89, 132; CDALB 1968-1988;
　CN 3, 4, 5, 6, 7; CPW 1; DA; DA3; DAB;
　DAC; DAM MST, NOV, POP; DLB 2,
　28, 173; DLBY 1982; EWL 3; MAL 5;
　MTCW 1, 2; MTFW 2005; RGAL 4;
　RGHL; RGSF 2; SSFS 12, 18; TUS
Roth, Philip Milton
　See Roth, Philip
Rothenberg, Jerome 1931- **CLC 6, 57**
　See also CA 45-48; CANR 1, 106; CP 1, 2,
　3, 4, 5, 6, 7; DLB 5, 193
Rotter, Pat ed. **CLC 65**
Roumain, Jacques (Jean Baptiste)
　1907-1944 **BLC 3; TCLC 19**
　See also BW 1; CA 117; 125; DAM MULT;
　EWL 3
Rourke, Constance Mayfield
　1885-1941 **TCLC 12**
　See also CA 107; 200; MAL 5; YABC 1
Rousseau, Jean-Baptiste 1671-1741 **LC 9**
Rousseau, Jean-Jacques 1712-1778 **LC 14,
36, 122; WLC 5**
　See also DA; DA3; DAB; DAC; DAM
　MST; DLB 314; EW 4; GFL Beginnings
　to 1789; LMFS 1; RGWL 2, 3; TWA
Roussel, Raymond 1877-1933 **TCLC 20**
　See also CA 117; 201; EWL 3; GFL 1789
　to the Present
Rovit, Earl (Herbert) 1927- **CLC 7**
　See also CA 5-8R; CANR 12
Rowe, Elizabeth Singer 1674-1737 **LC 44**
　See also DLB 39, 95
Rowe, Nicholas 1674-1718 **LC 8**
　See also DLB 84; RGEL 2
Rowlandson, Mary 1637(?)-1678 **LC 66**
　See also DLB 24, 200; RGAL 4
Rowley, Ames Dorrance
　See Lovecraft, H. P.
Rowley, William 1585(?)-1626 ... **LC 100, 123**
　See also DFS 22; DLB 58; RGEL 2

Rowling, J. K. 1966- **CLC 137, 217**
　See also AAYA 34; BYA 11, 13, 14; CA
　173; CANR 128; CLR 66, 80, 112; MAI-
　CYA 2; MTFW 2005; SATA 109; SUFW
　2
Rowling, Joanne Kathleen
　See Rowling, J. K.
Rowson, Susanna Haswell
　1762(?)-1824 **NCLC 5, 69**
　See also AMWS 15; DLB 37, 200; RGAL 4
Roy, Arundhati 1960(?)- **CLC 109, 210**
　See also CA 163; CANR 90, 126; CN 7;
　DLB 323, 326; DLBY 1997; EWL 3;
　LATS 1:2; MTFW 2005; NFS 22; WWE
　1
Roy, Gabrielle 1909-1983 **CLC 10, 14**
　See also CA 53-56; 110; CANR 5, 61; CCA
　1; DAB; DAC; DAM MST; DLB 68;
　EWL 3; MTCW 1; RGWL 2, 3; SATA
　104; TCLE 1:2
Royko, Mike 1932-1997 **CLC 109**
　See also CA 89-92; 157; CANR 26, 111;
　CPW
Rozanov, Vasilii Vasil'evich
　See Rozanov, Vassili
　See also DLB 295
Rozanov, Vasily Vasilyevich
　See Rozanov, Vassili
　See also EWL 3
Rozanov, Vassili 1856-1919 **TCLC 104**
　See Rozanov, Vasilii Vasil'evich; Rozanov,
　Vasily Vasilyevich
Rozewicz, Tadeusz 1921- **CLC 9, 23, 139**
　See also CA 108; CANR 36, 66; CWW 2;
　DA3; DAM POET; DLB 232; EWL 3;
　MTCW 1, 2; MTFW 2005; RGHL;
　RGWL 3
Ruark, Gibbons 1941- **CLC 3**
　See also CA 33-36R; CAAS 23; CANR 14,
　31, 57; DLB 120
Rubens, Bernice (Ruth) 1923-2004 . **CLC 19,
31**
　See also CA 25-28R; 232; CANR 33, 65,
　128; CN 1, 2, 3, 4, 5, 6, 7; DLB 14, 207,
　326; MTCW 1
Rubin, Harold
　See Robbins, Harold
Rudkin, (James) David 1936- **CLC 14**
　See also CA 89-92; CBD; CD 5, 6; DLB 13
Rudnik, Raphael 1933- **CLC 7**
　See also CA 29-32R
Ruffian, M.
　See Hasek, Jaroslav (Matej Frantisek)
Ruiz, Jose Martinez **CLC 11**
　See Martinez Ruiz, Jose
Ruiz, Juan c. 1283-c. 1350 **CMLC 66**
Rukeyser, Muriel 1913-1980 . **CLC 6, 10, 15,
27; PC 12**
　See also AMWS 6; CA 5-8R; 93-96; CANR
　26, 60; CP 1, 2, 3; DA3; DAM POET;
　DLB 48; EWL 3; FW; GLL 2; MAL 5;
　MTCW 1, 2; PFS 10; RGAL 4; SATA-
　Obit 22
Rule, Jane (Vance) 1931- **CLC 27**
　See also CA 25-28R; CAAS 18; CANR 12,
　87; CN 4, 5, 6, 7; DLB 60; FW
Rulfo, Juan 1918-1986 .. **CLC 8, 80; HLC 2;
SSC 25**
　See also CA 85-88; 118; CANR 26; CD-
　WLB 3; DAM MULT; DLB 113; EWL 3;
　HW 1, 2; LAW; MTCW 1, 2; RGSF 2;
　RGWL 2, 3; WLIT 1
Rumi, Jalal al-Din 1207-1273 **CMLC 20;
PC 45**
　See also AAYA 64; RGWL 2, 3; WLIT 6;
　WP
Runeberg, Johan 1804-1877 **NCLC 41**

Runyon, (Alfred) Damon
1884(?)-1946 **TCLC 10**
See also CA 107; 165; DLB 11, 86, 171;
MAL 5; MTCW 2; RGAL 4
Rush, Norman 1933- **CLC 44**
See also CA 121; 126; CANR 130; INT CA-
126
Rushdie, (Ahmed) Salman 1947- **CLC 23,**
31, 55, 100, 191; SSC 83; WLCS
See also AAYA 65; BEST 89:3; BPFB 3;
BRWS 4; CA 108; 111; CANR 33, 56,
108, 133; CN 4, 5, 6, 7; CPW 1; DA3;
DAB; DAC; DAM MST, NOV, POP;
DLB 194, 323, 326; EWL 3; FANT; INT
CA-111; LATS 1:2; LMFS 2; MTCW 1,
2; MTFW 2005; NFS 22, 23; RGEL 2;
RGSF 2; TEA; WLIT 4
Rushforth, Peter 1945-2005 **CLC 19**
See also CA 101; 243
Rushforth, Peter Scott
See Rushforth, Peter
Ruskin, John 1819-1900 **TCLC 63**
See also BRW 5; BYA 5; CA 114; 129; CD-
BLB 1832-1890; DLB 55, 163, 190;
RGEL 2; SATA 24; TEA; WCH
Russ, Joanna 1937- **CLC 15**
See also BPFB 3; CA 25-28; CANR 11, 31,
65; CN 4, 5, 6, 7; DLB 8; FW; GLL 1;
MTCW 1; SCFW 1, 2; SFW 4
Russ, Richard Patrick
See O'Brian, Patrick
Russell, George William 1867-1935
See A.E.; Baker, Jean H.
See also BRWS 8; CA 104; 153; CDBLB
1890-1914; DAM POET; EWL 3; RGEL
2
Russell, Jeffrey Burton 1934- **CLC 70**
See also CA 25-28R; CANR 11, 28, 52
Russell, (Henry) Ken(neth Alfred)
1927- .. **CLC 16**
See also CA 105
Russell, William Martin 1947-
See Russell, Willy
See also CA 164; CANR 107
Russell, Willy **CLC 60**
See Russell, William Martin
See also CBD; CD 5, 6; DLB 233
Russo, Richard 1949- **CLC 181**
See also AMWS 12; CA 127; 133; CANR
87, 114
Rutherford, Mark **TCLC 25**
See White, William Hale
See also DLB 18; RGEL 2
Ruysbroeck, Jan van 1293-1381 ... **CMLC 85**
Ruyslinck, Ward **CLC 14**
See Belser, Reimond Karel Maria de
Ryan, Cornelius (John) 1920-1974 **CLC 7**
See also CA 69-72; 53-56; CANR 38
Ryan, Michael 1946- **CLC 65**
See also CA 49-52; CANR 109; DLBY
1982
Ryan, Tim
See Dent, Lester
Rybakov, Anatoli (Naumovich)
1911-1998 **CLC 23, 53**
See Rybakov, Anatolii (Naumovich)
See also CA 126; 135; 172; SATA 79;
SATA-Obit 108
Rybakov, Anatolii (Naumovich)
See Rybakov, Anatoli (Naumovich)
See also DLB 302; RGHL
Ryder, Jonathan
See Ludlum, Robert
Ryga, George 1932-1987 **CLC 14**
See also CA 101; 124; CANR 43, 90; CCA
1; DAC; DAM MST; DLB 60
S. H.
See Hartmann, Sadakichi

S. S.
See Sassoon, Siegfried (Lorraine)
Sa'adawi, al- Nawal
See El Saadawi, Nawal
See also AFW; EWL 3
Saadawi, Nawal El
See El Saadawi, Nawal
See also WLIT 2
Saba, Umberto 1883-1957 **TCLC 33**
See also CA 144; CANR 79; DLB 114;
EWL 3; RGWL 2, 3
Sabatini, Rafael 1875-1950 **TCLC 47**
See also BPFB 3; CA 162; RHW
Sabato, Ernesto (R.) 1911- **CLC 10, 23;**
HLC 2
See also CA 97-100; CANR 32, 65; CD-
WLB 3; CWW 2; DAM MULT; DLB 145;
EWL 3; HW 1, 2; LAW; MTCW 1, 2;
MTFW 2005
Sa-Carneiro, Mario de 1890-1916 . **TCLC 83**
See also DLB 287; EWL 3
Sacastru, Martin
See Bioy Casares, Adolfo
See also CWW 2
Sacher-Masoch, Leopold von
1836(?)-1895 **NCLC 31**
Sachs, Hans 1494-1576 **LC 95**
See also CDWLB 2; DLB 179; RGWL 2, 3
Sachs, Marilyn 1927- **CLC 35**
See also AAYA 2; BYA 6; CA 17-20R;
CANR 13, 47, 150; CLR 2; JRDA; MAI-
CYA 1, 2; SAAS 2; SATA 3, 68, 164;
SATA-Essay 110; WYA; YAW
Sachs, Marilyn Stickle
See Sachs, Marilyn
Sachs, Nelly 1891-1970 **CLC 14, 98**
See also CA 17-18; 25-28R; CANR 87;
CAP 2; EWL 3; MTCW 2; MTFW 2005;
PFS 20; RGHL; RGWL 2, 3
Sackler, Howard (Oliver)
1929-1982 **CLC 14**
See also CA 61-64; 108; CAD; CANR 30;
DFS 15; DLB 7
Sacks, Oliver 1933- **CLC 67, 202**
See also CA 53-56; CANR 28, 50, 76, 146;
CPW; DA3; INT CANR-28; MTCW 1, 2;
MTFW 2005
Sacks, Oliver Wolf
See Sacks, Oliver
Sackville, Thomas 1536-1608 **LC 98**
See also DAM DRAM; DLB 62, 132;
RGEL 2
Sadakichi
See Hartmann, Sadakichi
Sa'dawi, Nawal al-
See El Saadawi, Nawal
See also CWW 2
Sade, Donatien Alphonse Francois
1740-1814 **NCLC 3, 47**
See also DLB 314; EW 4; GFL Beginnings
to 1789; RGWL 2, 3
Sade, Marquis de
See Sade, Donatien Alphonse Francois
Sadoff, Ira 1945- **CLC 9**
See also CA 53-56; CANR 5, 21, 109; DLB
120
Saetone
See Camus, Albert
Safire, William 1929- **CLC 10**
See also CA 17-20R; CANR 31, 54, 91, 148
Sagan, Carl (Edward) 1934-1996 **CLC 30,**
112
See also AAYA 2, 62; CA 25-28R; 155;
CANR 11, 36, 74; CPW; DA3; MTCW 1,
2; MTFW 2005; SATA 58; SATA-Obit 94
Sagan, Francoise **CLC 3, 6, 9, 17, 36**
See Quoirez, Francoise
See also CWW 2; DLB 83; EWL 3; GFL
1789 to the Present; MTCW 2

Sahgal, Nayantara (Pandit) 1927- **CLC 41**
See also CA 9-12R; CANR 11, 88; CN 1,
2, 3, 4, 5, 6, 7; DLB 323
Said, Edward W. 1935-2003 **CLC 123**
See also CA 21-24R; 220; CANR 45, 74,
107, 131; DLB 67; MTCW 2; MTFW
2005
Saint, H(arry) F. 1941- **CLC 50**
See also CA 127
St. Aubin de Teran, Lisa 1953-
See Teran, Lisa St. Aubin de
See also CA 118; 126; CN 6, 7; INT CA-
126
Saint Birgitta of Sweden c.
1303-1373 **CMLC 24**
Sainte-Beuve, Charles Augustin
1804-1869 **NCLC 5**
See also DLB 217; EW 6; GFL 1789 to the
Present
Saint-Exupery, Antoine de
1900-1944 **TCLC 2, 56, 169; WLC**
See also AAYA 63; BPFB 3; BYA 3; CA
108; 132; CLR 10; DA3; DAM NOV;
DLB 72; EW 12; EWL 3; GFL 1789 to
the Present; LAIT 3; MAICYA 1, 2;
MTCW 1, 2; MTFW 2005; RGWL 2, 3;
SATA 20; TWA
Saint-Exupery, Antoine Jean Baptiste Marie
Roger de
See Saint-Exupery, Antoine de
St. John, David
See Hunt, E(verette) Howard, (Jr.)
St. John, J. Hector
See Crevecoeur, Michel Guillaume Jean de
Saint-John Perse
See Leger, (Marie-Rene Auguste) Alexis
Saint-Leger
See also EW 10; EWL 3; GFL 1789 to the
Present; RGWL 2
Saintsbury, George (Edward Bateman)
1845-1933 **TCLC 31**
See also CA 160; DLB 57, 149
Sait Faik .. **TCLC 23**
See Abasiyanik, Sait Faik
Saki **SSC 12; TCLC 3; WLC 5**
See Munro, H(ector) H(ugh)
See also BRWS 6; BYA 11; LAIT 2; RGEL
2; SSFS 1; SUFW
Sala, George Augustus 1828-1895 . **NCLC 46**
Saladin 1138-1193 **CMLC 38**
Salama, Hannu 1936- **CLC 18**
See also CA 244; EWL 3
Salamanca, J(ack) R(ichard) 1922- .. **CLC 4,**
15
See also CA 25-28R; 193; CAAE 193
Salas, Floyd Francis 1931- **HLC 2**
See also CA 119; CAAS 27; CANR 44, 75,
93; DAM MULT; DLB 82; HW 1, 2;
MTCW 2; MTFW 2005
Sale, J. Kirkpatrick
See Sale, Kirkpatrick
Sale, John Kirkpatrick
See Sale, Kirkpatrick
Sale, Kirkpatrick 1937- **CLC 68**
See also CA 13-16R; CANR 10, 147
Salinas, Luis Omar 1937- ... **CLC 90; HLC 2**
See also AMWS 13; CA 131; CANR 81,
153; DAM MULT; DLB 82; HW 1, 2
Salinas (y Serrano), Pedro
1891(?)-1951 **TCLC 17**
See also CA 117; DLB 134; EWL 3
Salinger, J(erome) D(avid) 1919- .. **CLC 1, 3,**
8, 12, 55, 56, 138; SSC 2, 28, 65; WLC
5
See also AAYA 2, 36; AMW; AMWC 1;
BPFB 3; CA 5-8R; CANR 39, 129;
CDALB 1941-1968; CLR 18; CN 1, 2, 3,
4, 5, 6, 7; CPW 1; DA; DA3; DAB; DAC;
DAM MST, NOV, POP; DLB 2, 102, 173;

EWL 3; EXPN; LAIT 4; MAICYA 1, 2;
 MAL 5; MTCW 1, 2; MTFW 2005; NFS
 1; RGAL 4; RGSF 2; SATA 67; SSFS 17;
 TUS; WYA; YAW

Salisbury, John
 See Caute, (John) David

Sallust c. 86B.C.-35B.C. **CMLC 68**
 See also AW 2; CDWLB 1; DLB 211;
 RGWL 2, 3

Salter, James 1925- .. **CLC 7, 52, 59; SSC 58**
 See also AMWS 9; CA 73-76; CANR 107;
 DLB 130

Saltus, Edgar (Everton) 1855-1921 . **TCLC 8**
 See also CA 105; DLB 202; RGAL 4

Saltykov, Mikhail Evgrafovich
 1826-1889 **NCLC 16**
 See also DLB 238:

Saltykov-Shchedrin, N.
 See Saltykov, Mikhail Evgrafovich

Samarakis, Andonis
 See Samarakis, Antonis
 See also EWL 3

Samarakis, Antonis 1919-2003 **CLC 5**
 See Samarakis, Andonis
 See also CA 25-28R; 224; CAAS 16; CANR
 36

Sanchez, Florencio 1875-1910 **TCLC 37**
 See also CA 153; DLB 305; EWL 3; HW 1;
 LAW

Sanchez, Luis Rafael 1936- **CLC 23**
 See also CA 128; DLB 305; EWL 3; HW 1;
 WLIT 1

Sanchez, Sonia 1934- **BLC 3; CLC 5, 116,
 215; PC 9**
 See also BW 2, 3; CA 33-36R; CANR 24,
 49, 74, 115; CLR 18; CP 2, 3, 4, 5, 6, 7;
 CSW; CWP; DA3; DAM MULT; DLB 41;
 DLBD 8; EWL 3; MAICYA 1, 2; MAL 5;
 MTCW 1, 2; MTFW 2005; SATA 22, 136;
 WP

Sancho, Ignatius 1729-1780 **LC 84**

Sand, George 1804-1876 **NCLC 2, 42, 57;
 WLC 5**
 See also DA; DA3; DAB; DAC; DAM
 MST, NOV; DLB 119, 192; EW 6; FL 1:3;
 FW; GFL 1789 to the Present; RGWL 2,
 3; TWA

Sandburg, Carl (August) 1878-1967 . **CLC 1,
 4, 10, 15, 35; PC 2, 41; WLC 5**
 See also AAYA 24; AMW; BYA 1, 3; CA
 5-8R; 25-28R; CANR 35; CDALB 1865-
 1917; CLR 67; DA; DA3; DAB; DAC;
 DAM MST, POET; DLB 17, 54, 284;
 EWL 3; EXPP; LAIT 2; MAICYA 1, 2;
 MAL 5; MTCW 1, 2; MTFW 2005; PAB;
 PFS 3, 6, 12; RGAL 4; SATA 8; TUS;
 WCH; WP; WYA

Sandburg, Charles
 See Sandburg, Carl (August)

Sandburg, Charles A.
 See Sandburg, Carl (August)

Sanders, (James) Ed(ward) 1939- **CLC 53**
 See Sanders, Edward
 See also BG 1:3; CA 13-16R; CAAS 21;
 CANR 13, 44, 78; CP 1, 2, 3, 4, 5, 6, 7;
 DAM POET; DLB 16, 244

Sanders, Edward
 See Sanders, (James) Ed(ward)
 See also DLB 244

Sanders, Lawrence 1920-1998 **CLC 41**
 See also BEST 89:4; BPFB 3; CA 81-84;
 165; CANR 33, 62; CMW 4; CPW; DA3;
 DAM POP; MTCW 1

Sanders, Noah
 See Blount, Roy (Alton), Jr.

Sanders, Winston P.
 See Anderson, Poul (William)

Sandoz, Mari(e Susette) 1900-1966 .. **CLC 28**
 See also CA 1-4R; 25-28R; CANR 17, 64;
 DLB 9, 212; LAIT 2; MTCW 1, 2; SATA
 5; TCWW 1, 2

Sandys, George 1578-1644 **LC 80**
 See also DLB 24, 121

Saner, Reg(inald Anthony) 1931- **CLC 9**
 See also CA 65-68; CP 3, 4, 5, 6, 7

Sankara 788-820 **CMLC 32**

Sannazaro, Jacopo 1456(?)-1530 **LC 8**
 See also RGWL 2, 3; WLIT 7

Sansom, William 1912-1976 . **CLC 2, 6; SSC
 21**
 See also CA 5-8R; 65-68; CANR 42; CN 1,
 2; DAM NOV; DLB 139; EWL 3; MTCW
 1; RGEL 2; RGSF 2

Santayana, George 1863-1952 **TCLC 40**
 See also AMW; CA 115; 194; DLB 54, 71,
 246, 270; DLBD 13; EWL 3; MAL 5;
 RGAL 4; TUS

Santiago, Danny **CLC 33**
 See James, Daniel (Lewis)
 See also DLB 122

**Santillana, Inigo Lopez de Mendoza,
 Marques de** 1398-1458 **LC 111**
 See also DLB 286

Santmyer, Helen Hooven
 1895-1986 **CLC 33; TCLC 133**
 See also CA 1-4R; 118; CANR 15, 33;
 DLBY 1984; MTCW 1; RHW

Santoka, Taneda 1882-1940 **TCLC 72**

Santos, Bienvenido N(uqui)
 1911-1996 ... **AAL; CLC 22; TCLC 156**
 See also CA 101; 151; CANR 19, 46; CP 1;
 DAM MULT; DLB 312; EWL; RGAL 4;
 SSFS 19

Sapir, Edward 1884-1939 **TCLC 108**
 See also CA 211; DLB 92

Sapper .. **TCLC 44**
 See McNeile, Herman Cyril

Sapphire
 See Sapphire, Brenda

Sapphire, Brenda 1950- **CLC 99**

Sappho fl. 6th cent. B.C.- ... **CMLC 3, 67; PC
 5**
 See also CDWLB 1; DA3; DAM POET;
 DLB 176; FL 1:1; PFS 20; RGWL 2, 3;
 WLIT 8; WP

Saramago, Jose 1922- **CLC 119; HLCS 1**
 See also CA 153; CANR 96; CWW 2; DLB
 287; EWL 3; LATS 1:2; SSFS 23

Sarduy, Severo 1937-1993 **CLC 6, 97;
 HLCS 2; TCLC 167**
 See also CA 89-92; 142; CANR 58, 81;
 CWW 2; DLB 113; EWL 3; HW 1, 2;
 LAW

Sargeson, Frank 1903-1982 **CLC 31**
 See also CA 25-28R; 106; CANR 38, 79;
 CN 1, 2, 3; EWL 3; GLL 2; RGEL 2;
 RGSF 2; SSFS 20

Sarmiento, Domingo Faustino
 1811-1888 **HLCS 2; NCLC 123**
 See also LAW; WLIT 1

Sarmiento, Felix Ruben Garcia
 See Dario, Ruben

Saro-Wiwa, Ken(ule Beeson)
 1941-1995 **CLC 114**
 See also BW 2; CA 142; 150; CANR 60;
 DLB 157

Saroyan, William 1908-1981 ... **CLC 1, 8, 10,
 29, 34, 56; SSC 21; TCLC 137; WLC 5**
 See also AAYA 66; CA 5-8R; 103; CAD;
 CANR 30; CDALBS; CN 1, 2; DA; DA3;
 DAB; DAC; DAM DRAM, MST, NOV;
 DFS 17; DLB 7, 9, 86; DLBY 1981; EWL
 3; LAIT 4; MAL 5; MTCW 1, 2; MTFW
 2005; RGAL 4; RGSF 2; SATA 23; SATA-
 Obit 24; SSFS 14; TUS

Sarraute, Nathalie 1900-1999 **CLC 1, 2, 4,
 8, 10, 31, 80; TCLC 145**
 See also BPFB 3; CA 9-12R; 187; CANR
 23, 66, 134; CWW 2; DLB 83; 321; EW
 12; EWL 3; GFL 1789 to the Present;
 MTCW 1, 2; MTFW 2005; RGWL 2, 3

Sarton, (Eleanor) May 1912-1995 **CLC 4,
 14, 49, 91; PC 39; TCLC 120**
 See also AMWS 8; CA 1-4R; 149; CANR
 1, 34, 55, 116; CN 1, 2, 3, 4, 5, 6; CP 1,
 2, 3, 4, 5, 6; DAM POET; DLB 48; DLBY
 1981; EWL 3; FW; INT CANR-34; MAL
 5; MTCW 1, 2; MTFW 2005; RGAL 4;
 SATA 36; SATA-Obit 86; TUS

Sartre, Jean-Paul 1905-1980 . **CLC 1, 4, 7, 9,
 13, 18, 24, 44, 50, 52; DC 3; SSC 32;
 WLC 5**
 See also AAYA 62; CA 9-12R; 97-100;
 CANR 21; DA; DA3; DAB; DAC; DAM
 DRAM, MST, NOV; DFS 5; DLB 72,
 296, 321; EW 12; EWL 3; GFL 1789 to
 the Present; LMFS 2; MTCW 1, 2; MTFW
 2005; NFS 21; RGHL; RGSF 2; RGWL
 2, 3; SSFS 9; TWA

Sassoon, Siegfried (Lorraine)
 1886-1967 **CLC 36, 130; PC 12**
 See also BRW 6; CA 104; 25-28R; CANR
 36; DAB; DAM MST, NOV, POET; DLB
 20, 191; DLBD 18; EWL 3; MTCW 1, 2;
 MTFW 2005; PAB; RGEL 2; TEA

Satterfield, Charles
 See Pohl, Frederik

Satyremont
 See Peret, Benjamin

Saul, John (W. III) 1942- **CLC 46**
 See also AAYA 10, 62; BEST 90:4; CA 81-
 84; CANR 16, 40, 81; CPW; DAM NOV,
 POP; HGG; SATA 98

Saunders, Caleb
 See Heinlein, Robert A(nson)

Saura (Atares), Carlos 1932-1998 **CLC 20**
 See also CA 114; 131; CANR 79; HW 1

Sauser, Frederic Louis
 See Sauser-Hall, Frederic

Sauser-Hall, Frederic 1887-1961 **CLC 18**
 See Cendrars, Blaise
 See also CA 102; 93-96; CANR 36, 62;
 MTCW 1

Saussure, Ferdinand de
 1857-1913 **TCLC 49**
 See also DLB 242

Savage, Catharine
 See Brosman, Catharine Savage

Savage, Richard 1697(?)-1743 **LC 96**
 See also DLB 95; RGEL 2

Savage, Thomas 1915-2003 **CLC 40**
 See also CA 126; 132; 218; CAAS 15; CN
 6, 7; INT CA-132; SATA-Obit 147;
 TCWW 2

Savan, Glenn 1953-2003 **CLC 50**
 See also CA 225

Sax, Robert
 See Johnson, Robert

Saxo Grammaticus c. 1150-c.
 1222 **CMLC 58**

Saxton, Robert
 See Johnson, Robert

Sayers, Dorothy L(eigh) 1893-1957 . **SSC 71;
 TCLC 2, 15**
 See also BPFB 3; BRWS 3; CA 104; 119;
 CANR 60; CDBLB 1914-1945; CMW 4;
 DAM POP; DLB 10, 36, 77, 100; MSW;
 MTCW 1, 2; MTFW 2005; RGEL 2;
 SSFS 12; TEA

Sayers, Valerie 1952- **CLC 50, 122**
 See also CA 134; CANR 61; CSW

Sayles, John (Thomas) 1950- **CLC 7, 10,
 14, 198**
 See also CA 57-60; CANR 41, 84; DLB 44

Scammell, Michael 1935- **CLC 34**
See also CA 156
Scannell, Vernon 1922- **CLC 49**
See also CA 5-8R; CANR 8, 24, 57, 143;
CN 1, 2; CP 1, 2, 3, 4, 5, 6, 7; CWRI 5;
DLB 27; SATA 59
Scarlett, Susan
See Streatfeild, (Mary) Noel
Scarron 1847-1910
See Mikszath, Kalman
Scarron, Paul 1610-1660 **LC 116**
See also GFL Beginnings to 1789; RGWL
2, 3
Schaeffer, Susan Fromberg 1941- **CLC 6,
11, 22**
See also CA 49-52; CANR 18, 65; CN 4, 5,
6, 7; DLB 28, 299; MTCW 1, 2; MTFW
2005; SATA 22
Schama, Simon (Michael) 1945- **CLC 150**
See also BEST 89:4; CA 105; CANR 39,
91
Schary, Jill
See Robinson, Jill
Schell, Jonathan 1943- **CLC 35**
See also CA 73-76; CANR 12, 117
Schelling, Friedrich Wilhelm Joseph von
1775-1854 **NCLC 30**
See also DLB 90
Scherer, Jean-Marie Maurice 1920-
See Rohmer, Eric
See also CA 110
Schevill, James (Erwin) 1920- **CLC 7**
See also CA 5-8R; CAAS 12; CAD; CD 5,
6; CP 1, 2, 3, 4, 5
Schiller, Friedrich von 1759-1805 **DC 12;
NCLC 39, 69, 166**
See also CDWLB 2; DAM DRAM; DLB
94; EW 5; RGWL 2, 3; TWA
Schisgal, Murray (Joseph) 1926- **CLC 6**
See also CA 21-24R; CAD; CANR 48, 86;
CD 5, 6; MAL 5
Schlee, Ann 1934- **CLC 35**
See also CA 101; CANR 29, 88; SATA 44;
SATA-Brief 36
Schlegel, August Wilhelm von
1767-1845 **NCLC 15, 142**
See also DLB 94; RGWL 2, 3
Schlegel, Friedrich 1772-1829 **NCLC 45**
See also DLB 90; EW 5; RGWL 2, 3; TWA
Schlegel, Johann Elias (von)
1719(?)-1749 **LC 5**
Schleiermacher, Friedrich
1768-1834 **NCLC 107**
See also DLB 90
Schlesinger, Arthur M(eier), Jr.
1917- ... **CLC 84**
See also AITN 1; CA 1-4R; CANR 1, 28,
58, 105; DLB 17; INT CANR-28; MTCW
1, 2; SATA 61
Schlink, Bernhard 1944- **CLC 174**
See also CA 163; CANR 116; RGHL
Schmidt, Arno (Otto) 1914-1979 **CLC 56**
See also CA 128; 109; DLB 69; EWL 3
Schmitz, Aron Hector 1861-1928
See Svevo, Italo
See also CA 104; 122; MTCW 1
Schnackenberg, Gjertrud (Cecelia)
1953- **CLC 40; PC 45**
See also AMWS 15; CA 116; CANR 100;
CP 5, 6, 7; CWP; DLB 120, 282; PFS 13
Schneider, Leonard Alfred 1925-1966
See Bruce, Lenny
See also CA 89-92
Schnitzler, Arthur 1862-1931 **DC 17; SSC
15, 61; TCLC 4**
See also CA 104; CDWLB 2; DLB 81, 118;
EW 8; EWL 3; RGSF 2; RGWL 2, 3

Schoenberg, Arnold Franz Walter
1874-1951 **TCLC 75**
See also CA 109; 188
Schonberg, Arnold
See Schoenberg, Arnold Franz Walter
Schopenhauer, Arthur 1788-1860 . **NCLC 51,
157**
See also DLB 90; EW 5
Schor, Sandra (M.) 1932(?)-1990 **CLC 65**
See also CA 132
Schorer, Mark 1908-1977 **CLC 9**
See also CA 5-8R; 73-76; CANR 7; CN 1,
2; DLB 103
Schrader, Paul (Joseph) 1946- . **CLC 26, 212**
See also CA 37-40R; CANR 41; DLB 44
Schreber, Daniel 1842-1911 **TCLC 123**
Schreiner, Olive (Emilie Albertina)
1855-1920 **TCLC 9**
See also AFW; BRWS 2; CA 105; 154;
DLB 18, 156, 190, 225; EWL 3; FW;
RGEL 2; TWA; WLIT 2; WWE 1
Schulberg, Budd (Wilson) 1914- .. **CLC 7, 48**
See also BPFB 3; CA 25-28R; CANR 19,
87; CN 1, 2, 3, 4, 5, 6, 7; DLB 6, 26, 28;
DLBY 1981, 2001; MAL 5
Schulman, Arnold
See Trumbo, Dalton
Schulz, Bruno 1892-1942 .. **SSC 13; TCLC 5,
51**
See also CA 115; 123; CANR 86; CDWLB
4; DLB 215; EWL 3; MTCW 2; MTFW
2005; RGSF 2; RGWL 2, 3
Schulz, Charles M. 1922-2000 **CLC 12**
See also AAYA 39; CA 9-12R; 187; CANR
6, 132; INT CANR-6; MTFW 2005;
SATA 10; SATA-Obit 118
Schulz, Charles Monroe
See Schulz, Charles M.
Schumacher, E(rnst) F(riedrich)
1911-1977 **CLC 80**
See also CA 81-84; 73-76; CANR 34, 85
Schumann, Robert 1810-1856 **NCLC 143**
Schuyler, George Samuel 1895-1977 . **HR 1:3**
See also BW 2; CA 81-84; 73-76; CANR
42; DLB 29, 51
Schuyler, James Marcus 1923-1991 .. **CLC 5,
23**
See also CA 101; 134; CP 1, 2, 3, 4, 5;
DAM POET; DLB 5, 169; EWL 3; INT
CA-101; MAL 5; WP
Schwartz, Delmore (David)
1913-1966 ... **CLC 2, 4, 10, 45, 87; PC 8**
See also AMWS 2; CA 17-18; 25-28R;
CANR 35; CAP 2; DLB 28, 48; EWL 3;
MAL 5; MTCW 1, 2; MTFW 2005; PAB;
RGAL 4; TUS
Schwartz, Ernst
See Ozu, Yasujiro
Schwartz, John Burnham 1965- **CLC 59**
See also CA 132; CANR 116
Schwartz, Lynne Sharon 1939- **CLC 31**
See also CA 103; CANR 44, 89; DLB 218;
MTCW 2; MTFW 2005
Schwartz, Muriel A.
See Eliot, T(homas) S(tearns)
Schwarz-Bart, Andre 1928- **CLC 2, 4**
See also CA 89-92; CANR 109; DLB 299;
RGHL
Schwarz-Bart, Simone 1938- . **BLCS; CLC 7**
See also BW 2; CA 97-100; CANR 117;
EWL 3
Schwerner, Armand 1927-1999 **PC 42**
See also CA 9-12R; 179; CANR 50, 85; CP
2, 3, 4, 5, 6; DLB 165
**Schwitters, Kurt (Hermann Edward Karl
Julius)** 1887-1948 **TCLC 95**
See also CA 158

Schwob, Marcel (Mayer Andre)
1867-1905 **TCLC 20**
See also CA 117; 168; DLB 123; GFL 1789
to the Present
Sciascia, Leonardo 1921-1989 .. **CLC 8, 9, 41**
See also CA 85-88; 130; CANR 35; DLB
177; EWL 3; MTCW 1; RGWL 2, 3
Scoppettone, Sandra 1936- **CLC 26**
See Early, Jack
See also AAYA 11, 65; BYA 8; CA 5-8R;
CANR 41, 73; GLL 1; MAICYA 2; MAI-
CYAS 1; SATA 9, 92; WYA; YAW
Scorsese, Martin 1942- **CLC 20, 89, 207**
See also AAYA 38; CA 110; 114; CANR
46, 85
Scotland, Jay
See Jakes, John (William)
Scott, Duncan Campbell
1862-1947 **TCLC 6**
See also CA 104; 153; DAC; DLB 92;
RGEL 2
Scott, Evelyn 1893-1963 **CLC 43**
See also CA 104; 112; CANR 64; DLB 9,
48; RHW
Scott, F(rancis) R(eginald)
1899-1985 **CLC 22**
See also CA 101; 114; CANR 87; CP 1, 2,
3, 4; DLB 88; INT CA-101; RGEL 2
Scott, Frank
See Scott, F(rancis) R(eginald)
Scott, Joan .. **CLC 65**
Scott, Joanna 1960- **CLC 50**
See also CA 126; CANR 53, 92
Scott, Paul (Mark) 1920-1978 **CLC 9, 60**
See also BRWS 1; CA 81-84; 77-80; CANR
33; CN 1, 2; DLB 14, 207, 326; EWL 3;
MTCW 1; RGEL 2; RHW; WWE 1
Scott, Ridley 1937- **CLC 183**
See also AAYA 13, 43
Scott, Sarah 1723-1795 **LC 44**
See also DLB 39
Scott, Sir Walter 1771-1832 **NCLC 15, 69,
110; PC 13; SSC 32; WLC 5**
See also AAYA 22; BRW 4; BYA 2; CD-
BLB 1789-1832; DA; DAB; DAC; DAM
MST, NOV, POET; DLB 93, 107, 116,
144, 159; GL 3; HGG; LAIT 1; RGEL 2;
RGSF 2; SSFS 10; SUFW 1; TEA; WLIT
3; YABC 2
Scribe, (Augustin) Eugene 1791-1861 . **DC 5;
NCLC 16**
See also DAM DRAM; DLB 192; GFL
1789 to the Present; RGWL 2, 3
Scrum, R.
See Crumb, R.
Scudery, Georges de 1601-1667 **LC 75**
See also GFL Beginnings to 1789
Scudery, Madeleine de 1607-1701 .. **LC 2, 58**
See also DLB 268; GFL Beginnings to 1789
Scum
See Crumb, R.
Scumbag, Little Bobby
See Crumb, R.
Seabrook, John
See Hubbard, L. Ron
Seacole, Mary Jane Grant
1805-1881 **NCLC 147**
See also DLB 166
Sealy, I(rwin) Allan 1951- **CLC 55**
See also CA 136; CN 6, 7
Search, Alexander
See Pessoa, Fernando (Antonio Nogueira)
Sebald, W(infried) G(eorg)
1944-2001 **CLC 194**
See also BRWS 8; CA 159; 202; CANR 98;
MTFW 2005; RGHL
Sebastian, Lee
See Silverberg, Robert

Sebastian Owl
See Thompson, Hunter S(tockton)
Sebestyen, Igen
See Sebestyen, Ouida
Sebestyen, Ouida 1924- **CLC 30**
See also AAYA 8; BYA 7; CA 107; CANR 40, 114; CLR 17; JRDA; MAICYA 1, 2; SAAS 10; SATA 39, 140; WYA; YAW
Sebold, Alice 1963(?)- **CLC 193**
See also AAYA 56; CA 203; MTFW 2005
Second Duke of Buckingham
See Villiers, George
Secundus, H. Scriblerus
See Fielding, Henry
Sedges, John
See Buck, Pearl S(ydenstricker)
Sedgwick, Catharine Maria
1789-1867 **NCLC 19, 98**
See also DLB 1, 74, 183, 239, 243, 254; FL 1:3; RGAL 4
Seelye, John (Douglas) 1931- **CLC 7**
See also CA 97-100; CANR 70; INT CA-97-100; TCWW 1, 2
Seferiades, Giorgos Stylianou 1900-1971
See Seferis, George
See also CA 5-8R; 33-36R; CANR 5, 36; MTCW 1
Seferis, George **CLC 5, 11; PC 66**
See Seferiades, Giorgos Stylianou
See also EW 12; EWL 3; RGWL 2, 3
Segal, Erich (Wolf) 1937- **CLC 3, 10**
See also BEST 89:1; BPFB 3; CA 25-28R; CANR 20, 36, 65, 113; CPW; DAM POP; DLBY 1986; INT CANR-20; MTCW 1
Seger, Bob 1945- **CLC 35**
Seghers, Anna **CLC 7**
See Radvanyi, Netty
See also CDWLB 2; DLB 69; EWL 3
Seidel, Frederick (Lewis) 1936- **CLC 18**
See also CA 13-16R; CANR 8, 99; CP 1, 2, 3, 4, 5, 6, 7; DLBY 1984
Seifert, Jaroslav 1901-1986 . **CLC 34, 44, 93; PC 47**
See also CA 127; CDWLB 4; DLB 215; EWL 3; MTCW 1, 2
Sei Shonagon c. 966-1017(?) **CMLC 6**
Sejour, Victor 1817-1874 **DC 10**
See also DLB 50
Sejour Marcou et Ferrand, Juan Victor
See Sejour, Victor
Selby, Hubert, Jr. 1928-2004 **CLC 1, 2, 4, 8; SSC 20**
See also CA 13-16R; 226; CANR 33, 85; CN 1, 2, 3, 4, 5, 6, 7; DLB 2, 227; MAL 5
Selzer, Richard 1928- **CLC 74**
See also CA 65-68; CANR 14, 106
Sembene, Ousmane
See Ousmane, Sembene
See also AFW; EWL 3; WLIT 2
Senancour, Etienne Pivert de
1770-1846 **NCLC 16**
See also DLB 119; GFL 1789 to the Present
Sender, Ramon (Jose) 1902-1982 **CLC 8; HLC 2; TCLC 136**
See also CA 5-8R; 105; CANR 8; DAM MULT; DLB 322; EWL 3; HW 1; MTCW 1; RGWL 2, 3
Seneca, Lucius Annaeus c. 4B.C.-c. 65 **CMLC 6; DC 5**
See also AW 2; CDWLB 1; DAM DRAM; DLB 211; RGWL 2, 3; TWA; WLIT 8
Senghor, Leopold Sedar 1906-2001 ... **BLC 3; CLC 54, 130; PC 25**
See also AFW; BW 2; CA 116; 125; 203; CANR 47, 74, 134; CWW 2; DAM MULT, POET; DNFS 2; EWL 3; GFL 1789 to the Present; MTCW 1, 2; MTFW 2005; TWA

Senior, Olive (Marjorie) 1941- **SSC 78**
See also BW 3; CA 154; CANR 86, 126; CN 6; CP 6, 7; CWP; DLB 157; EWL 3; RGSF 2
Senna, Danzy 1970- **CLC 119**
See also CA 169; CANR 130
Serling, (Edward) Rod(man)
1924-1975 **CLC 30**
See also AAYA 14; AITN 1; CA 162; 57-60; DLB 26; SFW 4
Serna, Ramon Gomez de la
See Gomez de la Serna, Ramon
Serpieres
See Guillevic, (Eugene)
Service, Robert
See Service, Robert W(illiam)
See also BYA 4; DAB; DLB 92
Service, Robert W(illiam)
1874(?)-1958 ... **PC 70; TCLC 15; WLC 5**
See Service, Robert
See also CA 115; 140; CANR 84; DA; DAC; DAM MST, POET; PFS 10; RGEL 2; SATA 20
Seth, Vikram 1952- **CLC 43, 90**
See also BRWS 10; CA 121; 127; CANR 50, 74, 131; CN 6, 7; CP 5, 6, 7; DA3; DAM MULT; DLB 120, 271, 282, 323; EWL 3; INT CA-127; MTCW 2; MTFW 2005; WWE 1
Seton, Cynthia Propper 1926-1982 .. **CLC 27**
See also CA 5-8R; 108; CANR 7
Seton, Ernest (Evan) Thompson
1860-1946 **TCLC 31**
See also ANW; BYA 3; CA 109; 204; CLR 59; DLB 92; DLBD 13; JRDA; SATA 18
Seton-Thompson, Ernest
See Seton, Ernest (Evan) Thompson
Settle, Mary Lee 1918-2005 **CLC 19, 61**
See also BPFB 3; CA 89-92; 243; CAAS 1; CANR 44, 87, 126; CN 6, 7; CSW; DLB 6; INT CA-89-92
Seuphor, Michel
See Arp, Jean
Sevigne, Marie (de Rabutin-Chantal)
1626-1696 **LC 11**
See Sevigne, Marie de Rabutin Chantal
See also GFL Beginnings to 1789; TWA
Sevigne, Marie de Rabutin Chantal
See Sevigne, Marie (de Rabutin-Chantal)
See also DLB 268
Sewall, Samuel 1652-1730 **LC 38**
See also DLB 24; RGAL 4
Sexton, Anne (Harvey) 1928-1974 **CLC 2, 4, 6, 8, 10, 15, 53, 123; PC 2; WLC 5**
See also AMWS 2; CA 1-4R; 53-56; CABS 2; CANR 3, 36; CDALB 1941-1968; CP 1, 2; DA; DA3; DAB; DAC; DAM MST, POET; DLB 5, 169; EWL 3; EXPP; FL 1:6; FW; MAL 5; MAWW; MTCW 1, 2; MTFW 2005; PAB; PFS 4, 14; RGAL 4; RGHL; SATA 10; TUS
Shaara, Jeff 1952- **CLC 119**
See also AAYA 70; CA 163; CANR 109; CN 7; MTFW 2005
Shaara, Michael (Joseph, Jr.)
1929-1988 **CLC 15**
See also AAYA 71; AITN 1; BPFB 3; CA 102; 125; CANR 52, 85; DAM POP; DLBY 1983; MTFW 2005
Shackleton, C. C.
See Aldiss, Brian W(ilson)
Shacochis, Bob **CLC 39**
See Shacochis, Robert G.
Shacochis, Robert G. 1951-
See Shacochis, Bob
See also CA 119; 124; CANR 100; INT CA-124

Shadwell, Thomas 1641(?)-1692 **LC 114**
See also DLB 80; IDTP; RGEL 2
Shaffer, Anthony (Joshua)
1926-2001 **CLC 19**
See also CA 110; 116; 200; CBD; CD 5, 6; DAM DRAM; DFS 13; DLB 13
Shaffer, Peter (Levin) 1926- .. **CLC 5, 14, 18, 37, 60; DC 7**
See also BRWS 1; CA 25-28R; CANR 25, 47, 74, 118; CBD; CD 5, 6; CDBLB 1960 to Present; DA3; DAB; DAM DRAM, MST; DFS 5, 13; DLB 13, 233; EWL 3; MTCW 1, 2; MTFW 2005; RGEL 2; TEA
Shakespeare, William 1564-1616 **WLC 5**
See also AAYA 35; BRW 1; CDBLB Before 1660; DA; DA3; DAB; DAC; DAM DRAM, MST, POET; DFS 20, 21; DLB 62, 172, 263; EXPP; LAIT 1; LATS 1:1; LMFS 1; PAB; PFS 1, 2, 3, 4, 5, 8, 9; RGEL 2; TEA; WLIT 3; WP; WS; WYA
Shakey, Bernard
See Young, Neil
Shalamov, Varlam (Tikhonovich)
1907-1982 **CLC 18**
See also CA 129; 105; DLB 302; RGSF 2
Shamloo, Ahmad
See Shamlu, Ahmad
Shamlou, Ahmad
See Shamlu, Ahmad
Shamlu, Ahmad 1925-2000 **CLC 10**
See also CA 216; CWW 2
Shammas, Anton 1951- **CLC 55**
See also CA 199
Shandling, Arline
See Berriault, Gina
Shange, Ntozake 1948- .. **BLC 3; CLC 8, 25, 38, 74, 126; DC 3**
See also AAYA 9, 66; AFAW 1, 2; BW 2; CA 85-88; CABS 3; CAD; CANR 27, 48, 74, 131; CD 5, 6; CP 5, 6, 7; CWD; CWP; DA3; DAM DRAM, MULT; DFS 2, 11; DLB 38, 249; FW; LAIT 4, 5; MAL 5; MTCW 1, 2; MTFW 2005; NFS 11; RGAL 4; SATA 157; YAW
Shanley, John Patrick 1950- **CLC 75**
See also AMWS 14; CA 128; 133; CAD; CANR 83, 154; CD 5, 6; DFS 23
Shapcott, Thomas W(illiam) 1935- .. **CLC 38**
See also CA 69-72; CANR 49, 83, 103; CP 1, 2, 3, 4, 5, 6, 7; DLB 289
Shapiro, Jane 1942- **CLC 76**
See also CA 196
Shapiro, Karl (Jay) 1913-2000 **CLC 4, 8, 15, 53; PC 25**
See also AMWS 2; CA 1-4R; 188; CAAS 6; CANR 1, 36, 66; CP 1, 2, 3, 4, 5, 6; DLB 48; EWL 3; EXPP; MAL 5; MTCW 1, 2; MTFW 2005; PFS 3; RGAL 4
Sharp, William 1855-1905 **TCLC 39**
See Macleod, Fiona
See also CA 160; DLB 156; RGEL 2
Sharpe, Thomas Ridley 1928-
See Sharpe, Tom
See also CA 114; 122; CANR 85; INT CA-122
Sharpe, Tom **CLC 36**
See Sharpe, Thomas Ridley
See also CN 4, 5, 6, 7; DLB 14, 231
Shatrov, Mikhail **CLC 59**
Shaw, Bernard
See Shaw, George Bernard
See also DLB 10, 57, 190
Shaw, G. Bernard
See Shaw, George Bernard
Shaw, George Bernard 1856-1950 **DC 23; TCLC 3, 9, 21, 45; WLC 5**
See Shaw, Bernard
See also AAYA 61; BRW 6; BRWC 1; BRWR 2; CA 104; 128; CDBLB 1914-1945; DA; DA3; DAB; DAC; DAM

DRAM, MST; DFS 1, 3, 6, 11, 19, 22;
EWL 3; LAIT 3; LATS 1:1; MTCW 1, 2;
MTFW 2005; RGEL 2; TEA; WLIT 4

Shaw, Henry Wheeler 1818-1885 .. **NCLC 15**
See also DLB 11; RGAL 4

Shaw, Irwin 1913-1984 **CLC 7, 23, 34**
See also AITN 1; BPFB 3; CA 13-16R; 112;
CANR 21; CDALB 1941-1968; CN 1, 2,
3; CPW; DAM DRAM, POP; DLB 6,
102; DLBY 1984; MAL 5; MTCW 1, 21;
MTFW 2005

Shaw, Robert (Archibald)
1927-1978 **CLC 5**
See also AITN 1; CA 1-4R; 81-84; CANR
4; CN 1, 2; DLB 13, 14

Shaw, T. E.
See Lawrence, T(homas) E(dward)

Shawn, Wallace 1943- **CLC 41**
See also CA 112; CAD; CD 5, 6; DLB 266

Shaykh, al- Hanan
See al-Shaykh, Hanan
See also CWW 2; EWL 3

Shchedrin, N.
See Saltykov, Mikhail Evgrafovich

Shea, Lisa 1953- **CLC 86**
See also CA 147

Sheed, Wilfrid (John Joseph) 1930- . **CLC 2,
4, 10, 53**
See also CA 65-68; CANR 30, 66; CN 1, 2,
3, 4, 5, 6, 7; DLB 6; MAL 5; MTCW 1,
2; MTFW 2005

Sheehy, Gail 1937- **CLC 171**
See also CA 49-52; CANR 1, 33, 55, 92;
CPW; MTCW 1

Sheldon, Alice Hastings Bradley
1915(?)-1987
See Tiptree, James, Jr.
See also CA 108; 122; CANR 34; INT CA-
108; MTCW 1

Sheldon, John
See Bloch, Robert (Albert)

Sheldon, Walter J(ames) 1917-1996
See Queen, Ellery
See also AITN 1; CA 25-28R; CANR 10

Shelley, Mary Wollstonecraft (Godwin)
1797-1851 **NCLC 14, 59, 103, 170;
SSC 92; WLC 5**
See also AAYA 20; BPFB 3; BRW 3;
BRWC 2; BRWS 3; BYA 5; CDBLB
1789-1832; DA; DA3; DAB; DAC; DAM
MST, NOV; DLB 110, 116, 159, 178;
EXPN; FL 1:3; GL 3; HGG; LAIT 1;
LMFS 1, 2; NFS 1; RGEL 2; SATA 29;
SCFW 1, 2; SFW 4; TEA; WLIT 3

Shelley, Percy Bysshe 1792-1822 .. **NCLC 18,
93, 143; PC 14, 67; WLC 5**
See also AAYA 61; BRW 4; BRWR 1; CD-
BLB 1789-1832; DA; DA3; DAB; DAC;
DAM MST, POET; DLB 96, 110, 158;
EXPP; LMFS 1; PAB; PFS 2; RGEL 2;
TEA; WLIT 3; WP

Shepard, James R. **CLC 36**
See also CA 137; CANR 59, 104; SATA 90,
164

Shepard, Jim
See Shepard, James R.

Shepard, Lucius 1947- **CLC 34**
See also CA 128; 141; CANR 81, 124;
HGG; SCFW 2; SFW 4; SUFW 2

Shepard, Sam 1943- **CLC 4, 6, 17, 34, 41,
44, 169; DC 5**
See also AAYA 1, 58; AMWS 3; CA 69-72;
CABS 3; CAD; CANR 22, 120, 140; CD
5, 6; DA3; DAM DRAM; DFS 3, 6, 7,
14; DLB 7, 212; EWL 3; IDFW 3, 4;
MAL 5; MTCW 1, 2; MTFW 2005;
RGAL 4

Shepherd, Jean (Parker)
1921-1999 **TCLC 177**
See also AAYA 69; AITN 2; CA 77-80; 187

Shepherd, Michael
See Ludlum, Robert

Sherburne, Zoa (Lillian Morin)
1912-1995 **CLC 30**
See also AAYA 13; CA 1-4R; 176; CANR
3, 37; MAICYA 1, 2; SAAS 18; SATA 3;
YAW

Sheridan, Frances 1724-1766 **LC 7**
See also DLB 39, 84

Sheridan, Richard Brinsley
1751-1816 . **DC 1; NCLC 5, 91; WLC 5**
See also BRW 3; CDBLB 1660-1789; DA;
DAB; DAC; DAM DRAM, MST; DFS
15; DLB 89; WLIT 3

Sherman, Jonathan Marc 1968- **CLC 55**
See also CA 230

Sherman, Martin 1941(?)- **CLC 19**
See also CA 116; 123; CAD; CANR 86;
CD 5, 6; DFS 20; DLB 228; GLL 1;
IDTP; RGHL

Sherwin, Judith Johnson
See Johnson, Judith (Emlyn)
See also CANR 85; CP 2, 3, 4, 5; CWP

Sherwood, Frances 1940- **CLC 81**
See also CA 146, 220; CAAE 220

Sherwood, Robert E(mmet)
1896-1955 **TCLC 3**
See also CA 104; 153; CANR 86; DAM
DRAM; DFS 11, 15, 17; DLB 7, 26, 249;
IDFW 3, 4; MAL 5; RGAL 4

Shestov, Lev 1866-1938 **TCLC 56**

Shevchenko, Taras 1814-1861 **NCLC 54**

Shiel, M(atthew) P(hipps)
1865-1947 **TCLC 8**
See Holmes, Gordon
See also CA 106; 160; DLB 153; HGG;
MTCW 2; MTFW 2005; SCFW 1, 2;
SFW 4; SUFW

Shields, Carol (Ann) 1935-2003 **CLC 91,
113, 193**
See also AMWS 7; CA 81-84; 218; CANR
51, 74, 98, 133; CCA 1; CN 6, 7; CPW;
DA3; DAC; MTCW 2; MTFW 2005; NFS
23

Shields, David (Jonathan) 1956- **CLC 97**
See also CA 124; CANR 48, 99, 112

Shiga, Naoya 1883-1971 **CLC 33; SSC 23;
TCLC 172**
See Shiga Naoya
See also CA 101; 33-36R; MJW; RGWL 3

Shiga Naoya
See Shiga, Naoya
See also DLB 180; EWL 3; RGWL 3

Shilts, Randy 1951-1994 **CLC 85**
See also AAYA 19; CA 115; 127; 144;
CANR 45; DA3; GLL 1; INT CA-127;
MTCW 2; MTFW 2005

Shimazaki, Haruki 1872-1943
See Shimazaki Toson
See also CA 105; 134; CANR 84; RGWL 3

Shimazaki Toson **TCLC 5**
See Shimazaki, Haruki
See also DLB 180; EWL 3

Shirley, James 1596-1666 **DC 25; LC 96**
See also DLB 58; RGEL 2

Sholokhov, Mikhail (Aleksandrovich)
1905-1984 **CLC 7, 15**
See also CA 101; 112; DLB 272; EWL 3;
MTCW 1, 2; MTFW 2005; RGWL 2, 3;
SATA-Obit 36

Shone, Patric
See Hanley, James

Showalter, Elaine 1941- **CLC 169**
See also CA 57-60; CANR 58, 106; DLB
67; FW; GLL 2

Shreve, Susan
See Shreve, Susan Richards

Shreve, Susan Richards 1939- **CLC 23**
See also CA 49-52; CAAS 5; CANR 5, 38,
69, 100; MAICYA 1, 2; SATA 46, 95, 152;
SATA-Brief 41

Shue, Larry 1946-1985 **CLC 52**
See also CA 145; 117; DAM DRAM; DFS
7

Shu-Jen, Chou 1881-1936
See Lu Hsun
See also CA 104

Shulman, Alix Kates 1932- **CLC 2, 10**
See also CA 29-32R; CANR 43; FW; SATA
7

Shuster, Joe 1914-1992 **CLC 21**
See also AAYA 50

Shute, Nevil **CLC 30**
See Norway, Nevil Shute
See also BPFB 3; DLB 255; NFS 9; RHW;
SFW 4

Shuttle, Penelope (Diane) 1947- **CLC 7**
See also CA 93-96; CANR 39, 84, 92, 108;
CP 3, 4, 5, 6, 7; CWP; DLB 14, 40

Shvarts, Elena 1948- **PC 50**
See also CA 147

Sidhwa, Bapsi 1939-
See Sidhwa, Bapsy (N.)
See also CN 6, 7; DLB 323

Sidhwa, Bapsy (N.) 1938- **CLC 168**
See Sidhwa, Bapsi
See also CA 108; CANR 25, 57; FW

Sidney, Mary 1561-1621 **LC 19, 39**
See Sidney Herbert, Mary

Sidney, Sir Philip 1554-1586 . **LC 19, 39; PC
32**
See also BRW 1; BRWR 2; CDBLB Before
1660; DA; DA3; DAB; DAC; DAM MST,
POET; DLB 167; EXPP; PAB; RGEL 2;
TEA; WP

Sidney Herbert, Mary
See Sidney, Mary
See also DLB 167

Siegel, Jerome 1914-1996 **CLC 21**
See Siegel, Jerry
See also CA 116; 169; 151

Siegel, Jerry
See Siegel, Jerome
See also AAYA 50

Sienkiewicz, Henryk (Adam Alexander Pius)
1846-1916 **TCLC 3**
See also CA 104; 134; CANR 84; EWL 3;
RGSF 2; RGWL 2, 3

Sierra, Gregorio Martinez
See Martinez Sierra, Gregorio

Sierra, Maria (de la O'LeJarraga) Martinez
See Martinez Sierra, Maria (de la
O'LeJarraga)

Sigal, Clancy 1926- **CLC 7**
See also CA 1-4R; CANR 85; CN 1, 2, 3,
4, 5, 6, 7

Siger of Brabant 1240(?)-1284(?) . **CMLC 69**
See also DLB 115

Sigourney, Lydia H.
See Sigourney, Lydia Howard (Huntley)
See also DLB 73, 183

Sigourney, Lydia Howard (Huntley)
1791-1865 **NCLC 21, 87**
See Sigourney, Lydia H.; Sigourney, Lydia
Huntley
See also DLB 1

Sigourney, Lydia Huntley
See Sigourney, Lydia Howard (Huntley)
See also DLB 42, 239, 243

Siguenza y Gongora, Carlos de
1645-1700 **HLCS 2; LC 8**
See also LAW

Sigurjonsson, Johann
See Sigurjonsson, Johann

Sigurjonsson, Johann 1880-1919 ... **TCLC 27**
See also CA 170; DLB 293; EWL 3

Sikelianos, Angelos 1884-1951 **PC 29; TCLC 39**
See also EWL 3; RGWL 2, 3

Silkin, Jon 1930-1997 **CLC 2, 6, 43**
See also CA 5-8R; CAAS 5; CANR 89; CP 1, 2, 3, 4, 5, 6; DLB 27

Silko, Leslie (Marmon) 1948- **CLC 23, 74, 114, 211; NNAL; SSC 37, 66; WLCS**
See also AAYA 14; AMWS 4; ANW; BYA 12; CA 115; 122; CANR 45, 65, 118; CN 4, 5, 6, 7; CP 4, 5, 6, 7; CPW 1; CWP; DA; DA3; DAC; DAM MST, MULT, POP; DLB 143, 175, 256, 275; EWL 3; EXPP; EXPS; LAIT 4; MAL 5; MTCW 2; MTFW 2005; NFS 4; PFS 9, 16; RGAL 4; RGSF 2; SSFS 4, 8, 10, 11; TCWW 1, 2

Sillanpaa, Frans Eemil 1888-1964 ... **CLC 19**
See also CA 129; 93-96; EWL 3; MTCW 1

Sillitoe, Alan 1928- .. **CLC 1, 3, 6, 10, 19, 57, 148**
See also AITN 1; BRWS 5; CA 9-12R, 191; CAAE 191; CAAS 2; CANR 8, 26, 55, 139; CDBLB 1960 to Present; CN 1, 2, 3, 4, 5, 6; CP 1, 2, 3, 4, 5; DLB 14, 139; EWL 3; MTCW 1, 2; MTFW 2005; RGEL 2; RGSF 2; SATA 61

Silone, Ignazio 1900-1978 **CLC 4**
See also CA 25-28; 81-84; CANR 34; CAP 2; DLB 264; EW 12; EWL 3; MTCW 1; RGSF 2; RGWL 2, 3

Silone, Ignazione
See Silone, Ignazio

Silver, Joan Micklin 1935- **CLC 20**
See also CA 114; 121; INT CA-121

Silver, Nicholas
See Faust, Frederick (Schiller)

Silverberg, Robert 1935- **CLC 7, 140**
See also AAYA 24; BPFB 3; BYA 7, 9; CA 1-4R, 186; CAAE 186; CAAS 3; CANR 1, 20, 36, 85, 140; CLR 59; CN 6, 7; CPW; DAM POP; DLB 8; INT CANR-20; MAICYA 1, 2; MTCW 1, 2; MTFW 2005; SATA 13, 91; SATA-Essay 104; SCFW 1, 2; SFW 4; SUFW 2

Silverstein, Alvin 1933- **CLC 17**
See also CA 49-52; CANR 2; CLR 25; JRDA; MAICYA 1, 2; SATA 8, 69, 124

Silverstein, Shel(don Allan)
1932-1999 **PC 49**
See also AAYA 40; BW 3; CA 107; 179; CANR 47, 74, 81; CLR 5, 96; CWRI 5; JRDA; MAICYA 1, 2; MTCW 2; MTFW 2005; SATA 33, 92; SATA-Brief 27; SATA-Obit 116

Silverstein, Virginia B(arbara Opshelor)
1937- ... **CLC 17**
See also CA 49-52; CANR 2; CLR 25; JRDA; MAICYA 1, 2; SATA 8, 69, 124

Sim, Georges
See Simenon, Georges (Jacques Christian)

Simak, Clifford D(onald) 1904-1988 . **CLC 1, 55**
See also CA 1-4R; 125; CANR 1, 35; DLB 8; MTCW 1; SATA-Obit 56; SCFW 1, 2; SFW 4

Simenon, Georges (Jacques Christian)
1903-1989 **CLC 1, 2, 3, 8, 18, 47**
See also BPFB 3; CA 85-88; 129; CANR 35; CMW 4; DA3; DAM POP; DLB 72; DLBY 1989; EW 12; EWL 3; GFL 1789 to the Present; MSW; MTCW 1, 2; MTFW 2005; RGWL 2, 3

Simic, Charles 1938- **CLC 6, 9, 22, 49, 68, 130; PC 69**
See also AMWS 8; CA 29-32R; CAAS 4; CANR 12, 33, 52, 61, 96, 140; CP 2, 3, 4, 5, 6, 7; DA3; DAM POET; DLB 105; MAL 5; MTCW 2; MTFW 2005; PFS 7; RGAL 4; WP

Simmel, Georg 1858-1918 **TCLC 64**
See also CA 157; DLB 296

Simmons, Charles (Paul) 1924- **CLC 57**
See also CA 89-92; INT CA-89-92

Simmons, Dan 1948- **CLC 44**
See also AAYA 16, 54; CA 138; CANR 53, 81, 126; CPW; DAM POP; HGG; SUFW 2

Simmons, James (Stewart Alexander)
1933- **CLC 43**
See also CA 105; CAAS 21; CP 1, 2, 3, 4, 5, 6, 7; DLB 40

Simms, William Gilmore
1806-1870 **NCLC 3**
See also DLB 3, 30, 59, 73, 248, 254; RGAL 4

Simon, Carly 1945- **CLC 26**
See also CA 105

Simon, Claude 1913-2005 ... **CLC 4, 9, 15, 39**
See also CA 89-92; 241; CANR 33, 117; CWW 2; DAM NOV; DLB 83; EW 13; EWL 3; GFL 1789 to the Present; MTCW 1

Simon, Claude Eugene Henri
See Simon, Claude

Simon, Claude Henri Eugene
See Simon, Claude

Simon, Marvin Neil
See Simon, Neil

Simon, Myles
See Follett, Ken(neth Martin)

Simon, Neil 1927- **CLC 6, 11, 31, 39, 70; DC 14**
See also AAYA 32; AITN 1; AMWS 4; CA 21-24R; CAD; CANR 26, 54, 87, 126; CD 5, 6; DA3; DAM DRAM; DFS 2, 6, 12, 18; DLB 7, 266; LAIT 4; MAL 5; MTCW 1, 2; MTFW 2005; RGAL 4; TUS

Simon, Paul 1941(?)- **CLC 17**
See also CA 116; 153; CANR 152

Simon, Paul Frederick
See Simon, Paul

Simonon, Paul 1956(?)- **CLC 30**

Simonson, Rick ed. **CLC 70**

Simpson, Harriette
See Arnow, Harriette (Louisa) Simpson

Simpson, Louis (Aston Marantz)
1923- **CLC 4, 7, 9, 32, 149**
See also AMWS 9; CA 1-4R; CAAS 4; CANR 1, 61, 140; CP 1, 2, 3, 4, 5, 6, 7; DAM POET; DLB 5; MAL 5; MTCW 1, 2; MTFW 2005; PFS 7, 11, 14; RGAL 4

Simpson, Mona 1957- **CLC 44, 146**
See also CA 122; 135; CANR 68, 103; CN 6, 7; EWL 3

Simpson, Mona Elizabeth
See Simpson, Mona

Simpson, N(orman) F(rederick)
1919- **CLC 29**
See also CA 13-16R; CBD; DLB 13; RGEL 2

Sinclair, Andrew (Annandale) 1935- . **CLC 2, 14**
See also CA 9-12R; CAAS 5; CANR 14, 38, 91; CN 1, 2, 3, 4, 5, 6, 7; DLB 14; FANT; MTCW 1

Sinclair, Emil
See Hesse, Hermann

Sinclair, Iain 1943- **CLC 76**
See also CA 132; CANR 81; CP 5, 6, 7; HGG

Sinclair, Iain MacGregor
See Sinclair, Iain

Sinclair, Irene
See Griffith, D(avid Lewelyn) W(ark)

Sinclair, Mary Amelia St. Clair 1865(?)-1946
See Sinclair, May
See also CA 104; HGG; RHW

Sinclair, May **TCLC 3, 11**
See Sinclair, Mary Amelia St. Clair
See also CA 166; DLB 36, 135; EWL 3; RGEL 2; SUFW

Sinclair, Roy
See Griffith, D(avid Lewelyn) W(ark)

Sinclair, Upton 1878-1968 **CLC 1, 11, 15, 63; TCLC 160; WLC 5**
See also AAYA 63; AMWS 5; BPFB 3; BYA 2; CA 5-8R; 25-28R; CANR 7; CDALB 1929-1941; DA; DA3; DAB; DAC; DAM MST, NOV; DLB 9; EWL 3; INT CANR-7; LAIT 3; MAL 5; MTCW 1, 2; MTFW 2005; NFS 6; RGAL 4; SATA 9; TUS; YAW

Sinclair, Upton Beall
See Sinclair, Upton

Singe, (Edmund) J(ohn) M(illington)
1871-1909 **WLC**

Singer, Isaac
See Singer, Isaac Bashevis

Singer, Isaac Bashevis 1904-1991 .. **CLC 1, 3, 6, 9, 11, 15, 23, 38, 69, 111; SSC 3, 53, 80; WLC 5**
See also AAYA 32; AITN 1, 2; AMW; AMWR 2; BPFB 3; BYA 1, 4; CA 1-4R; 134; CANR 1, 39, 106; CDALB 1941-1968; CLR 1; CN 1, 2, 3, 4; CWRI 5; DA; DA3; DAB; DAC; DAM MST, NOV; DLB 6, 28, 52, 278; DLBY 1991; EWL 3; EXPS; HGG; JRDA; LAIT 3; MAICYA 1, 2; MAL 5; MTCW 1, 2; MTFW 2005; RGAL 4; RGHL; RGSF 2; SATA 3, 27; SATA-Obit 68; SSFS 2, 12, 16; TUS; TWA

Singer, Israel Joshua 1893-1944 **TCLC 33**
See also CA 169; EWL 3

Singh, Khushwant 1915- **CLC 11**
See also CA 9-12R; CAAS 9; CANR 6, 84; CN 1, 2, 3, 4, 5, 6, 7; DLB 323; EWL 3; RGEL 2

Singleton, Ann
See Benedict, Ruth

Singleton, John 1968(?)- **CLC 156**
See also AAYA 50; BW 2, 3; CA 138; CANR 67, 82; DAM MULT

Siniavskii, Andrei
See Sinyavsky, Andrei (Donatevich)
See also CWW 2

Sinjohn, John
See Galsworthy, John

Sinyavsky, Andrei (Donatevich)
1925-1997 **CLC 8**
See Siniavskii, Andrei; Sinyavsky, Andrey Donatovich; Tertz, Abram
See also CA 85-88; 159

Sinyavsky, Andrey Donatovich
See Sinyavsky, Andrei (Donatevich)
See also EWL 3

Sirin, V.
See Nabokov, Vladimir (Vladimirovich)

Sissman, L(ouis) E(dward)
1928-1976 **CLC 9, 18**
See also CA 21-24R; 65-68; CANR 13; CP 2; DLB 5

Sisson, C(harles) H(ubert)
1914-2003 **CLC 8**
See also BRWS 11; CA 1-4R; 220; CAAS 3; CANR 3, 48, 84; CP 1, 2, 3, 4, 5, 6, 7; DLB 27

Sitting Bull 1831(?)-1890 **NNAL**
See also DA3; DAM MULT

Sitwell, Dame Edith 1887-1964 **CLC 2, 9, 67; PC 3**
See also BRW 7; CA 9-12R; CANR 35; CDBLB 1945-1960; DAM POET; DLB 20; EWL 3; MTCW 1, 2; MTFW 2005; RGEL 2; TEA

Siwaarmill, H. P.
See Sharp, William

Sjoewall, Maj 1935- **CLC 7**
See Sjowall, Maj
See also CA 65-68; CANR 73

Sjowall, Maj
See Sjoewall, Maj
See also BPFB 3; CMW 4; MSW

Skelton, John 1460(?)-1529 **LC 71; PC 25**
See also BRW 1; DLB 136; RGEL 2

Skelton, Robin 1925-1997 **CLC 13**
See Zuk, Georges
See also AITN 2; CA 5-8R; 160; CAAS 5;
CANR 28, 89; CCA 1; CP 1, 2, 3, 4, 5, 6;
DLB 27, 53

Skolimowski, Jerzy 1938- **CLC 20**
See also CA 128

Skram, Amalie (Bertha)
1847-1905 **TCLC 25**
See also CA 165

Skvorecky, Josef (Vaclav) 1924- **CLC 15,
39, 69, 152**
See also CA 61-64; CAAS 1; CANR 10,
34, 63, 108; CDWLB 4; CWW 2; DA3;
DAC; DAM NOV; DLB 232; EWL 3;
MTCW 1, 2; MTFW 2005

Slade, Bernard 1930- **CLC 11, 46**
See Newbound, Bernard Slade
See also CAAS 9; CCA 1; CD 6; DLB 53

Slaughter, Carolyn 1946- **CLC 56**
See also CA 85-88; CANR 85; CN 5, 6, 7

Slaughter, Frank G(ill) 1908-2001 ... **CLC 29**
See also AITN 2; CA 5-8R; 197; CANR 5,
85; INT CANR-5; RHW

Slavitt, David R(ytman) 1935- **CLC 5, 14**
See also CA 21-24R; CAAS 3; CANR 41,
83; CN 1, 2; CP 1, 2, 3, 4, 5, 6, 7; DLB
5, 6

Slesinger, Tess 1905-1945 **TCLC 10**
See also CA 107; 199; DLB 102

Slessor, Kenneth 1901-1971 **CLC 14**
See also CA 102; 89-92; DLB 260; RGEL
2

Slowacki, Juliusz 1809-1849 **NCLC 15**
See also RGWL 3

Smart, Christopher 1722-1771 . **LC 3; PC 13**
See also DAM POET; DLB 109; RGEL 2

Smart, Elizabeth 1913-1986 **CLC 54**
See also CA 81-84; 118; CN 4; DLB 88

Smiley, Jane (Graves) 1949- **CLC 53, 76,
144**
See also AAYA 66; AMWS 6; BPFB 3; CA
104; CANR 30, 50, 74, 96; CN 6, 7; CPW
1; DA3; DAM POP; DLB 227, 234; EWL
3; INT CANR-30; MAL 5; MTFW 2005;
SSFS 19

Smith, A(rthur) J(ames) M(arshall)
1902-1980 **CLC 15**
See also CA 1-4R; 102; CANR 4; CP 1, 2,
3; DAC; DLB 88; RGEL 2

Smith, Adam 1723(?)-1790 **LC 36**
See also DLB 104, 252; RGEL 2

Smith, Alexander 1829-1867 **NCLC 59**
See also DLB 32, 55

Smith, Anna Deavere 1950- **CLC 86**
See also CA 133; CANR 103; CD 5, 6; DFS
2, 22

Smith, Betty (Wehner) 1904-1972 **CLC 19**
See also BPFB 3; BYA 3; CA 5-8R; 33-
36R; DLBY 1982; LAIT 3; RGAL 4;
SATA 6

Smith, Charlotte (Turner)
1749-1806 **NCLC 23, 115**
See also DLB 39, 109; RGEL 2; TEA

Smith, Clark Ashton 1893-1961 **CLC 43**
See also CA 143; CANR 81; FANT; HGG;
MTCW 2; SCFW 1, 2; SFW 4; SUFW

Smith, Dave **CLC 22, 42**
See Smith, David (Jeddie)
See also CAAS 7; CP 3, 4, 5, 6, 7; DLB 5

Smith, David (Jeddie) 1942-
See Smith, Dave
See also CA 49-52; CANR 1, 59, 120;
CSW; DAM POET

Smith, Iain Crichton 1928-1998 **CLC 64**
See also BRWS 9; CA 21-24R; 171; CN 1,
2, 3, 4, 5, 6; CP 1, 2, 3, 4, 5, 6; DLB 40,
139, 319; RGSF 2

Smith, John 1580(?)-1631 **LC 9**
See also DLB 24, 30; TUS

Smith, Johnston
See Crane, Stephen (Townley)

Smith, Joseph, Jr. 1805-1844 **NCLC 53**

Smith, Kevin 1970- **CLC 223**
See also AAYA 37; CA 166; CANR 131

Smith, Lee 1944- **CLC 25, 73**
See also CA 114; 119; CANR 46, 118; CN
7; CSW; DLB 143; DLBY 1983; EWL 3;
INT CA-119; RGAL 4

Smith, Martin
See Smith, Martin Cruz

Smith, Martin Cruz 1942- **CLC 25; NNAL**
See also BEST 89:4; BPFB 3; CA 85-88;
CANR 6, 23, 43, 65, 119; CMW 4; CPW;
DAM MULT, POP; HGG; INT CANR-
23; MTCW 2; MTFW 2005; RGAL 4

Smith, Patti 1946- **CLC 12**
See also CA 93-96; CANR 63

Smith, Pauline (Urmson)
1882-1959 **TCLC 25**
See also DLB 225; EWL 3

Smith, Rosamond
See Oates, Joyce Carol

Smith, Sheila Kaye
See Kaye-Smith, Sheila

Smith, Stevie 1902-1971 **CLC 3, 8, 25, 44;
PC 12**
See also BRWS 2; CA 17-18; 29-32R;
CANR 35; CAP 2; CP 1; DAM POET;
DLB 20; EWL 3; MTCW 1, 2; PAB; PFS
3; RGEL 2; TEA

Smith, Wilbur (Addison) 1933- **CLC 33**
See also CA 13-16R; CANR 7, 46, 66, 134;
CPW; MTCW 1, 2; MTFW 2005

Smith, William Jay 1918- **CLC 6**
See also AMWS 13; CA 5-8R; CANR 44,
106; CP 1, 2, 3, 4, 5, 6, 7; CSW; CWRI
5; DLB 5; MAICYA 1, 2; SAAS 22;
SATA 2, 68, 154; SATA-Essay 154; TCLE
1:2

Smith, Woodrow Wilson
See Kuttner, Henry

Smith, Zadie 1975- **CLC 158**
See also AAYA 50; CA 193; MTFW 2005

Smolenskin, Peretz 1842-1885 **NCLC 30**

Smollett, Tobias (George) 1721-1771 ... **LC 2,
46**
See also BRW 3; CDBLB 1660-1789; DLB
39, 104; RGEL 2; TEA

Snodgrass, W(illiam) D(e Witt)
1926- **CLC 2, 6, 10, 18, 68**
See also AMWS 6; CA 1-4R; CANR 6, 36,
65, 85; CP 1, 2, 3, 4, 5, 6, 7; DAM POET;
DLB 5; MAL 5; MTCW 1, 2; MTFW
2005; RGAL 4; TCLE 1:2

Snorri Sturluson 1179-1241 **CMLC 56**
See also RGWL 2, 3

Snow, C(harles) P(ercy) 1905-1980 ... **CLC 1,
4, 6, 9, 13, 19**
See also BRW 7; CA 5-8R; 101; CANR 28;
CDBLB 1945-1960; CN 1, 2; DAM NOV;
DLB 15, 77; DLBD 17; EWL 3; MTCW
1, 2; MTFW 2005; RGEL 2; TEA

Snow, Frances Compton
See Adams, Henry (Brooks)

Snyder, Gary (Sherman) 1930- . **CLC 1, 2, 5,
9, 32, 120; PC 21**
See also AMWS 8; ANW; BG 1:3; CA 17-
20R; CANR 30, 60, 125; CP 1, 2, 3, 4, 5,
6, 7; DA3; DAM POET; DLB 5, 16, 165,
212, 237, 275; EWL 3; MAL 5; MTCW
2; MTFW 2005; PFS 9, 19; RGAL 4; WP

Snyder, Zilpha Keatley 1927- **CLC 17**
See also AAYA 15; BYA 1; CA 9-12R;
CANR 38; CLR 31; JRDA; MAICYA 1,
2; SAAS 2; SATA 1, 28, 75, 110, 163;
SATA-Essay 112, 163; YAW

Soares, Bernardo
See Pessoa, Fernando (Antonio Nogueira)

Sobh, A.
See Shamlu, Ahmad

Sobh, Alef
See Shamlu, Ahmad

Sobol, Joshua 1939- **CLC 60**
See Sobol, Yehoshua
See also CA 200; RGHL

Sobol, Yehoshua 1939-
See Sobol, Joshua
See also CWW 2

Socrates 470B.C.-399B.C. **CMLC 27**

Soderberg, Hjalmar 1869-1941 **TCLC 39**
See also DLB 259; EWL 3; RGSF 2

Soderbergh, Steven 1963- **CLC 154**
See also AAYA 43; CA 243

Soderbergh, Steven Andrew
See Soderbergh, Steven

Sodergran, Edith (Irene) 1892-1923
See Soedergran, Edith (Irene)
See also CA 202; DLB 259; EW 11; EWL
3; RGWL 2, 3

Soedergran, Edith (Irene)
1892-1923 **TCLC 31**
See Sodergran, Edith (Irene)

Softly, Edgar
See Lovecraft, H. P.

Softly, Edward
See Lovecraft, H. P.

Sokolov, Alexander V(sevolodovich) 1943-
See Sokolov, Sasha
See also CA 73-76

Sokolov, Raymond 1941- **CLC 7**
See also CA 85-88

Sokolov, Sasha **CLC 59**
See Sokolov, Alexander V(sevolodovich)
See also CWW 2; DLB 285; EWL 3; RGWL
2, 3

Solo, Jay
See Ellison, Harlan (Jay)

Sologub, Fyodor **TCLC 9**
See Teternikov, Fyodor Kuzmich
See also EWL 3

Solomons, Ikey Esquir
See Thackeray, William Makepeace

Solomos, Dionysios 1798-1857 **NCLC 15**

Solwoska, Mara
See French, Marilyn

Solzhenitsyn, Aleksandr I. 1918- .. **CLC 1, 2,
4, 7, 9, 10, 18, 26, 34, 78, 134; SSC 32;
WLC 5**
See Solzhenitsyn, Aleksandr Isayevich
See also AAYA 49; AITN 1; BPFB 3; CA
69-72; CANR 40, 65, 116; DA; DA3;
DAB; DAC; DAM MST, NOV; DLB 302;
EW 13; EXPS; LAIT 4; MTCW 1, 2;
MTFW 2005; NFS 6; RGSF 2; RGWL 2,
3; SSFS 9; TWA

Solzhenitsyn, Aleksandr Isayevich
See Solzhenitsyn, Aleksandr I.
See also CWW 2; EWL 3

Somers, Jane
See Lessing, Doris (May)

Somerville, Edith Oenone
1858-1949 **SSC 56; TCLC 51**
See also CA 196; DLB 135; RGEL 2; RGSF 2

Somerville & Ross
See Martin, Violet Florence; Somerville, Edith Oenone

Sommer, Scott 1951- **CLC 25**
See also CA 106

Sommers, Christina Hoff 1950- **CLC 197**
See also CA 153; CANR 95

Sondheim, Stephen (Joshua) 1930- . **CLC 30, 39, 147; DC 22**
See also AAYA 11, 66; CA 103; CANR 47, 67, 125; DAM DRAM; LAIT 4

Sone, Monica 1919- **AAL**
See also DLB 312

Song, Cathy 1955- **AAL; PC 21**
See also CA 154; CANR 118; CWP; DLB 169, 312; EXPP; FW; PFS 5

Sontag, Susan 1933-2004 ... **CLC 1, 2, 10, 13, 31, 105, 195**
See also AMWS 3; CA 17-20R; 234; CANR 25, 51, 74, 97; CN 1, 2, 3, 4, 5, 6, 7; CPW; DA3; DAM POP; DLB 2, 67; EWL 3; MAL 5; MAWW; MTCW 1, 2; MTFW 2005; RGAL 4; RHW; SSFS 10

Sophocles 496(?)B.C.-406(?)B.C. **CMLC 2, 47, 51; DC 1; WLCS**
See also AW 1; CDWLB 1; DA; DA3; DAB; DAC; DAM DRAM, MST; DFS 1, 4, 8; DLB 176; LAIT 1; LATS 1:1; LMFS 1; RGWL 2, 3; TWA; WLIT 8

Sordello 1189-1269 **CMLC 15**

Sorel, Georges 1847-1922 **TCLC 91**
See also CA 118; 188

Sorel, Julia
See Drexler, Rosalyn

Sorokin, Vladimir **CLC 59**
See Sorokin, Vladimir Georgievich

Sorokin, Vladimir Georgievich
See Sorokin, Vladimir
See also DLB 285

Sorrentino, Gilbert 1929-2006 **CLC 3, 7, 14, 22, 40**
See also CA 77-80; CANR 14, 33, 115; CN 3, 4, 5, 6, 7; CP 1, 2, 3, 4, 5, 6, 7; DLB 5, 173; DLBY 1980; INT CANR-14

Soseki
See Natsume, Soseki
See also MJW

Soto, Gary 1952- ... **CLC 32, 80; HLC 2; PC 28**
See also AAYA 10, 37; BYA 11; CA 119; 125; CANR 50, 74, 107; CLR 38; CP 4, 5, 6, 7; DAM MULT; DLB 82; EWL 3; EXPP; HW 1, 2; INT CA-125; JRDA; LLW; MAICYA 2; MAICYAS 1; MAL 5; MTCW 2; MTFW 2005; PFS 7; RGAL 4; SATA 80, 120; WYA; YAW

Soupault, Philippe 1897-1990 **CLC 68**
See also CA 116; 147; 131; EWL 3; GFL 1789 to the Present; LMFS 2

Souster, (Holmes) Raymond 1921- **CLC 5, 14**
See also CA 13-16R; CAAS 14; CANR 13, 29, 53; CP 1, 2, 3, 4, 5, 6, 7; DA3; DAC; DAM POET; DLB 88; RGEL 2; SATA 63

Southern, Terry 1924(?)-1995 **CLC 7**
See also AMWS 11; BPFB 3; CA 1-4R; 150; CANR 1, 55, 107; CN 1, 2, 3, 4, 5, 6; DLB 2; IDFW 3, 4

Southerne, Thomas 1660-1746 **LC 99**
See also DLB 80; RGEL 2

Southey, Robert 1774-1843 **NCLC 8, 97**
See also BRW 4; DLB 93, 107, 142; RGEL 2; SATA 54

Southwell, Robert 1561(?)-1595 **LC 108**
See also DLB 167; RGEL 2; TEA

Southworth, Emma Dorothy Eliza Nevitte
1819-1899 **NCLC 26**
See also DLB 239

Souza, Ernest
See Scott, Evelyn

Soyinka, Wole 1934- .. **BLC 3; CLC 3, 5, 14, 36, 44, 179; DC 2; WLC 5**
See also AFW; BW 2, 3; CA 13-16R; CANR 27, 39, 82, 136; CD 5, 6; CDWLB 3; CN 6, 7; CP 1, 2, 3, 4, 5, 6 ,7; DA; DA3; DAB; DAC; DAM DRAM, MST, MULT; DFS 10; DLB 125; EWL 3; MTCW 1, 2; MTFW 2005; RGEL 2; TWA; WLIT 2; WWE 1

Spackman, W(illiam) M(ode)
1905-1990 **CLC 46**
See also CA 81-84; 132

Spacks, Barry (Bernard) 1931- **CLC 14**
See also CA 154; CANR 33, 109; CP 3, 4, 5, 6, 7; DLB 105

Spanidou, Irini 1946- **CLC 44**
See also CA 185

Spark, Muriel (Sarah) 1918-2006 . **CLC 2, 3, 5, 8, 13, 18, 40, 94; PC 72; SSC 10**
See also BRWS 1; CA 5-8R; CANR 12, 36, 76, 89, 131; CDBLB 1945-1960; CN 1, 2, 3, 4, 5, 6, 7; CP 1, 2, 3, 4, 5, 6, 7; DA3; DAB; DAC; DAM MST, NOV; DLB 15, 139; EWL 3; FW; INT CANR-12; LAIT 4; MTCW 1, 2; MTFW 2005; NFS 22; RGEL 2; TEA; WLIT 4; YAW

Spaulding, Douglas
See Bradbury, Ray (Douglas)

Spaulding, Leonard
See Bradbury, Ray (Douglas)

Speght, Rachel 1597-c. 1630 **LC 97**
See also DLB 126

Spence, J. A. D.
See Eliot, T(homas) S(tearns)

Spencer, Anne 1882-1975 **HR 1:3**
See also BW 2; CA 161; DLB 51, 54

Spencer, Elizabeth 1921- **CLC 22; SSC 57**
See also CA 13-16R; CANR 32, 65, 87; CN 1, 2, 3, 4, 5, 6, 7; CSW; DLB 6, 218; EWL 3; MTCW 1; RGAL 4; SATA 14

Spencer, Leonard G.
See Silverberg, Robert

Spencer, Scott 1945- **CLC 30**
See also CA 113; CANR 51, 148; DLBY 1986

Spender, Stephen (Harold)
1909-1995 .. **CLC 1, 2, 5, 10, 41, 91; PC 71**
See also BRWS 2; CA 9-12R; 149; CANR 31, 54; CDBLB 1945-1960; CP 1, 2, 3, 4, 5, 6; DA3; DAM POET; DLB 20; EWL 3; MTCW 1, 2; MTFW 2005; PAB; PFS 23; RGEL 2; TEA

Spengler, Oswald (Arnold Gottfried)
1880-1936 **TCLC 25**
See also CA 118; 189

Spenser, Edmund 1552(?)-1599 **LC 5, 39, 117; PC 8, 42; WLC 5**
See also AAYA 60; BRW 1; CDBLB Before 1660; DA; DA3; DAB; DAC; DAM MST, POET; DLB 167; EFS 2; EXPP; PAB; RGEL 2; TEA; WLIT 3; WP

Spicer, Jack 1925-1965 **CLC 8, 18, 72**
See also BG 1:3; CA 85-88; DAM POET; DLB 5, 16, 193; GLL 1; WP

Spiegelman, Art 1948- **CLC 76, 178**
See also AAYA 10, 46; CA 125; CANR 41, 55, 74, 124; DLB 299; MTCW 2; MTFW 2005; RGHL; SATA 109, 158; YAW

Spielberg, Peter 1929- **CLC 6**
See also CA 5-8R; CANR 4, 48; DLBY 1981

Spielberg, Steven 1947- **CLC 20, 188**
See also AAYA 8, 24; CA 77-80; CANR 32; SATA 32

Spillane, Frank Morrison **CLC 3, 13**
See Spillane, Mickey
See also BPFB 3; CMW 4; DLB 226; MSW

Spillane, Mickey 1918-2006
See Spillane, Frank Morrison
See also CA 25-28R; CANR 28, 63, 125; DA3; MTCW 1, 2; MTFW 2005; SATA 66

Spinoza, Benedictus de 1632-1677 .. **LC 9, 58**

Spinrad, Norman (Richard) 1940- ... **CLC 46**
See also BPFB 3; CA 37-40R, 233; CAAE 233; CAAS 19; CANR 20, 91; DLB 8; INT CANR-20; SFW 4

Spitteler, Carl (Friedrich Georg)
1845-1924 **TCLC 12**
See also CA 109; DLB 129; EWL 3

Spivack, Kathleen (Romola Drucker)
1938- **CLC 6**
See also CA 49-52

Spofford, Harriet (Elizabeth) Prescott
1835-1921 **SSC 87**
See also CA 201; DLB 74, 221

Spoto, Donald 1941- **CLC 39**
See also CA 65-68; CANR 11, 57, 93

Springsteen, Bruce 1949- **CLC 17**
See also CA 111

Springsteen, Bruce F.
See Springsteen, Bruce

Spurling, Hilary 1940- **CLC 34**
See also CA 104; CANR 25, 52, 94

Spurling, Susan Hilary
See Spurling, Hilary

Spyker, John Howland
See Elman, Richard (Martin)

Squared, A.
See Abbott, Edwin A.

Squires, (James) Radcliffe
1917-1993 **CLC 51**
See also CA 1-4R; 140; CANR 6, 21; CP 1, 2, 3, 4, 5

Srivastava, Dhanpat Rai 1880(?)-1936
See Premchand
See also CA 118; 197

Stacy, Donald
See Pohl, Frederik

Stael
See Stael-Holstein, Anne Louise Germaine Necker
See also EW 5; RGWL 2, 3

Stael, Germaine de
See Stael-Holstein, Anne Louise Germaine Necker
See also DLB 119, 192; FL 1:3; FW; GFL 1789 to the Present; TWA

Stael-Holstein, Anne Louise Germaine Necker 1766-1817 **NCLC 3, 91**
See Stael; Stael, Germaine de

Stafford, Jean 1915-1979 .. **CLC 4, 7, 19, 68; SSC 26, 86**
See also CA 1-4R; 85-88; CANR 3, 65; CN 1, 2; DLB 2, 173; MAL 5; MTCW 1, 2; MTFW 2005; RGAL 4; RGSF 2; SATA-Obit 22; SSFS 21; TCWW 1, 2; TUS

Stafford, William (Edgar)
1914-1993 **CLC 4, 7, 29; PC 71**
See also AMWS 11; CA 5-8R; 142; CAAS 3; CANR 5, 22; CP 1, 2, 3, 4, 5; DAM POET; DLB 5, 206; EXPP; INT CANR-22; MAL 5; PFS 2, 8, 16; RGAL 4; WP

Stagnelius, Eric Johan 1793-1823 . **NCLC 61**

Staines, Trevor
See Brunner, John (Kilian Houston)

Stairs, Gordon
See Austin, Mary (Hunter)

Stalin, Joseph 1879-1953 **TCLC 92**

Stampa, Gaspara c. 1524-1554 .. **LC 114; PC 43**
See also RGWL 2, 3; WLIT 7
Stampflinger, K. A.
See Benjamin, Walter
Stancykowna
See Szymborska, Wislawa
Standing Bear, Luther
1868(?)-1939(?) **NNAL**
See also CA 113; 144; DAM MULT
Stanislavsky, Konstantin (Sergeivich)
1863(?)-1938 **TCLC 167**
See also CA 118
Stannard, Martin 1947- **CLC 44**
See also CA 142; DLB 155
Stanton, Elizabeth Cady
1815-1902 **TCLC 73**
See also CA 171; DLB 79; FL 1:3; FW
Stanton, Maura 1946- **CLC 9**
See also CA 89-92; CANR 15, 123; DLB 120
Stanton, Schuyler
See Baum, L(yman) Frank
Stapledon, (William) Olaf
1886-1950 **TCLC 22**
See also CA 111; 162; DLB 15, 255; SCFW 1, 2; SFW 4
Starbuck, George (Edwin)
1931-1996 **CLC 53**
See also CA 21-24R; 153; CANR 23; CP 1, 2, 3, 4, 5, 6; DAM POET
Stark, Richard
See Westlake, Donald E(dwin)
Staunton, Schuyler
See Baum, L(yman) Frank
Stead, Christina (Ellen) 1902-1983 ... **CLC 2, 5, 8, 32, 80**
See also BRWS 4; CA 13-16R; 109; CANR 33, 40; CN 1, 2, 3; DLB 260; EWL 3; FW; MTCW 1, 2; MTFW 2005; RGEL 2; RGSF 2; WWE 1
Stead, William Thomas
1849-1912 **TCLC 48**
See also CA 167
Stebnitsky, M.
See Leskov, Nikolai (Semyonovich)
Steele, Richard 1672-1729 **LC 18**
See also BRW 3; CDBLB 1660-1789; DLB 84, 101; RGEL 2; WLIT 3
Steele, Timothy (Reid) 1948- **CLC 45**
See also CA 93-96; CANR 16, 50, 92; CP 5, 6, 7; DLB 120, 282
Steffens, (Joseph) Lincoln
1866-1936 **TCLC 20**
See also CA 117; 198; DLB 303; MAL 5
Stegner, Wallace (Earle) 1909-1993 .. **CLC 9, 49, 81; SSC 27**
See also AITN 1; AMWS 4; ANW; BEST 90:3; BPFB 3; CA 1-4R; 141; CAAS 9; CANR 1, 21, 46; CN 1, 2, 3, 4, 5; DAM NOV; DLB 9, 206, 275; DLBY 1993; EWL 3; MAL 5; MTCW 1, 2; MTFW 2005; RGAL 4; TCWW 1, 2; TUS
Stein, Gertrude 1874-1946 **DC 19; PC 18; SSC 42; TCLC 1, 6, 28, 48; WLC 5**
See also AAYA 64; AMW; AMWC 2; CA 104; 132; CANR 108; CDALB 1917-1929; DA; DA3; DAB; DAC; DAM MST, NOV, POET; DLB 4, 54, 86, 228; DLBD 15; EWL 3; EXPS; FL 1:6; GLL 1; MAL 5; MAWW; MTCW 1, 2; MTFW 2005; NCFS 4; RGAL 4; RGSF 2; SSFS 5; TUS; WP
Steinbeck, John (Ernst) 1902-1968 ... **CLC 1, 5, 9, 13, 21, 34, 45, 75, 124; SSC 11, 37, 77; TCLC 135; WLC 5**
See also AAYA 12; AMW; BPFB 3; BYA 2, 3, 13; CA 1-4R; 25-28R; CANR 1, 35; CDALB 1929-1941; DA; DA3; DAB;

DAC; DAM DRAM, MST, NOV; DLB 7, 9, 212, 275, 309; DLBD 2; EWL 3; EXPS; LAIT 3; MAL 5; MTCW 1, 2; MTFW 2005; NFS 1, 5, 7, 17, 19; RGAL 4; RGSF 2; RHW; SATA 9; SSFS 3, 6; TCWW 1, 2; TUS; WYA; YAW
Steinem, Gloria 1934- **CLC 63**
See also CA 53-56; CANR 28, 51, 139; DLB 246; FW; MTCW 1, 2; MTFW 2005
Steiner, George 1929- **CLC 24, 221**
See also CA 73-76; CANR 31, 67, 108; DAM NOV; DLB 67, 299; EWL 3; MTCW 1, 2; MTFW 2005; RGHL; SATA 62
Steiner, K. Leslie
See Delany, Samuel R(ay), Jr.
Steiner, Rudolf 1861-1925 **TCLC 13**
See also CA 107
Stendhal 1783-1842 .. **NCLC 23, 46; SSC 27; WLC 5**
See also DA; DA3; DAB; DAC; DAM MST, NOV; DLB 119; EW 5; GFL 1789 to the Present; RGWL 2, 3; TWA
Stephen, Adeline Virginia
See Woolf, (Adeline) Virginia
Stephen, Sir Leslie 1832-1904 **TCLC 23**
See also BRW 5; CA 123; DLB 57, 144, 190
Stephen, Sir Leslie
See Stephen, Sir Leslie
Stephen, Virginia
See Woolf, (Adeline) Virginia
Stephens, James 1882(?)-1950 **SSC 50; TCLC 4**
See also CA 104; 192; DLB 19, 153, 162; EWL 3; FANT; RGEL 2; SUFW
Stephens, Reed
See Donaldson, Stephen R(eeder)
Steptoe, Lydia
See Barnes, Djuna
See also GLL 1
Sterchi, Beat 1949- **CLC 65**
See also CA 203
Sterling, Brett
See Bradbury, Ray (Douglas); Hamilton, Edmond
Sterling, Bruce 1954- **CLC 72**
See also CA 119; CANR 44, 135; CN 7; MTFW 2005; SCFW 2; SFW 4
Sterling, George 1869-1926 **TCLC 20**
See also CA 117; 165; DLB 54
Stern, Gerald 1925- **CLC 40, 100**
See also AMWS 9; CA 81-84; CANR 28, 94; CP 3, 4, 5, 6, 7; DLB 105; RGAL 4
Stern, Richard (Gustave) 1928- ... **CLC 4, 39**
See also CA 1-4R; CANR 1, 25, 52, 120; CN 1, 2, 3, 4, 5, 6, 7; DLB 218; DLBY 1987; INT CANR-25
Sternberg, Josef von 1894-1969 **CLC 20**
See also CA 81-84
Sterne, Laurence 1713-1768 **LC 2, 48; WLC 5**
See also BRW 3; BRWC 1; CDBLB 1660-1789; DA; DAB; DAC; DAM MST, NOV; DLB 39; RGEL 2; TEA
Sternheim, (William Adolf) Carl
1878-1942 **TCLC 8**
See also CA 105; 193; DLB 56, 118; EWL 3; IDTP; RGWL 2, 3
Stevens, Margaret Dean
See Aldrich, Bess Streeter
Stevens, Mark 1951- **CLC 34**
See also CA 122
Stevens, Wallace 1879-1955 . **PC 6; TCLC 3, 12, 45; WLC 5**
See also AMW; AMWR 1; CA 104; 124; CDALB 1929-1941; DA; DA3; DAB; DAC; DAM MST, POET; DLB 54; EWL 3; EXPP; MAL 5; MTCW 1, 2; PAB; PFS 13, 16; RGAL 4; TUS; WP

Stevenson, Anne (Katharine) 1933- .. **CLC 7, 33**
See also BRWS 6; CA 17-20R; CAAS 9; CANR 9, 33, 123; CP 3, 4, 5, 6, 7; CWP; DLB 40; MTCW 1; RHW
Stevenson, Robert Louis (Balfour)
1850-1894 **NCLC 5, 14, 63; SSC 11, 51; WLC 5**
See also AAYA 24; BPFB 3; BRW 5; BRWC 1; BRWR 1; BYA 1, 2, 4, 13; CD-BLB 1890-1914; CLR 10, 11, 107; DA; DA3; DAB; DAC; DAM MST, NOV; DLB 18, 57, 141, 156, 174; DLBD 13; GL 3; HGG; JRDA; LAIT 1, 3; MAICYA 1, 2; NFS 11, 20; RGEL 2; RGSF 2; SATA 100; SUFW; TEA; WCH; WLIT 4; WYA; YABC 2; YAW
Stewart, J(ohn) I(nnes) M(ackintosh)
1906-1994 **CLC 7, 14, 32**
See Innes, Michael
See also CA 85-88; 147; CAAS 3; CANR 47; CMW 4; CN 1, 2, 3, 4, 5; MTCW 1, 2
Stewart, Mary (Florence Elinor)
1916- **CLC 7, 35, 117**
See also AAYA 29; BPFB 3; CA 1-4R; CANR 1, 59, 130; CMW 4; CPW; DAB; FANT; RHW; SATA 12; YAW
Stewart, Mary Rainbow
See Stewart, Mary (Florence Elinor)
Stifle, June
See Campbell, Maria
Stifter, Adalbert 1805-1868 .. **NCLC 41; SSC 28**
See also CDWLB 2; DLB 133; RGSF 2; RGWL 2, 3
Still, James 1906-2001 **CLC 49**
See also CA 65-68; 195; CAAS 17; CANR 10, 26; CSW; DLB 9; DLBY 01; SATA 29; SATA-Obit 127
Sting 1951-
See Sumner, Gordon Matthew
See also CA 167
Stirling, Arthur
See Sinclair, Upton
Stitt, Milan 1941- **CLC 29**
See also CA 69-72
Stockton, Francis Richard 1834-1902
See Stockton, Frank R.
See also AAYA 68; CA 108; 137; MAICYA 1, 2; SATA 44; SFW 4
Stockton, Frank R. **TCLC 47**
See Stockton, Francis Richard
See also BYA 4, 13; DLB 42, 74; DLBD 13; EXPS; SATA-Brief 32; SSFS 3; SUFW; WCH
Stoddard, Charles
See Kuttner, Henry
Stoker, Abraham 1847-1912
See Stoker, Bram
See also CA 105; 150; DA; DA3; DAC; DAM MST, NOV; HGG; MTFW 2005; SATA 29
Stoker, Bram . **SSC 62; TCLC 8, 144; WLC 6**
See Stoker, Abraham
See also AAYA 23; BPFB 3; BRWS 3; BYA 5; CDBLB 1890-1914; DAB; DLB 304; GL 3; LATS 1:1; NFS 18; RGEL 2; SUFW; TEA; WLIT 4
Stolz, Mary (Slattery) 1920- **CLC 12**
See also AAYA 8; AITN 1; CA 5-8R; CANR 13, 41, 112; JRDA; MAICYA 1, 2; SAAS 3; SATA 10, 71, 133; YAW
Stone, Irving 1903-1989 **CLC 7**
See also AITN 1; BPFB 3; CA 1-4R; 129; CAAS 3; CANR 1, 23; CN 1, 2, 3, 4; CPW; DA3; DAM POP; INT CANR-23; MTCW 1, 2; MTFW 2005; RHW; SATA 3; SATA-Obit 64

Stone, Oliver (William) 1946- **CLC 73**
　See also AAYA 15, 64; CA 110; CANR 55, 125

Stone, Robert (Anthony) 1937- ... **CLC 5, 23, 42, 175**
　See also AMWS 5; BPFB 3; CA 85-88; CANR 23, 66, 95; CN 4, 5, 6, 7; DLB 152; EWL 3; INT CANR-23; MAL 5; MTCW 1; MTFW 2005

Stone, Ruth 1915- **PC 53**
　See also CA 45-48; CANR 2, 91; CP 5, 6, 7; CSW; DLB 105; PFS 19

Stone, Zachary
　See Follett, Ken(neth Martin)

Stoppard, Tom 1937- ... **CLC 1, 3, 4, 5, 8, 15, 29, 34, 63, 91; DC 6; WLC 6**
　See also AAYA 63; BRWC 1; BRWR 2; BRWS 1; CA 81-84; CANR 39, 67, 125; CBD; CD 5, 6; CDBLB 1960 to Present; DA; DA3; DAB; DAC; DAM DRAM, MST; DFS 2, 5, 8, 11, 13, 16; DLB 13, 233; DLBY 1985; EWL 3; LATS 1:2; MTCW 1, 2; MTFW 2005; RGEL 2; TEA; WLIT 4

Storey, David (Malcolm) 1933- . **CLC 2, 4, 5, 8**
　See also BRWS 1; CA 81-84; CANR 36; CBD; CD 5, 6; CN 1, 2, 3, 4, 5, 6; DAM DRAM; DLB 13, 14, 207, 245, 326; EWL 3; MTCW 1; RGEL 2

Storm, Hyemeyohsts 1935- ... **CLC 3; NNAL**
　See also CA 81-84; CANR 45; DAM MULT

Storm, (Hans) Theodor (Woldsen)
　1817-1888 **NCLC 1; SSC 27**
　See also CDWLB 2; DLB 129; EW; RGSF 2; RGWL 2, 3

Storni, Alfonsina 1892-1938 . **HLC 2; PC 33; TCLC 5**
　See also CA 104; 131; DAM MULT; DLB 283; HW 1; LAW

Stoughton, William 1631-1701 **LC 38**
　See also DLB 24

Stout, Rex (Todhunter) 1886-1975 **CLC 3**
　See also AITN 2; BPFB 3; CA 61-64; CANR 71; CMW 4; CN 2; DLB 306; MSW; RGAL 4

Stow, (Julian) Randolph 1935- ... **CLC 23, 48**
　See also CA 13-16R; CANR 33; CN 1, 2, 3, 4, 5, 6, 7; CP 1, 2, 3, 4; DLB 260; MTCW 1; RGEL 2

Stowe, Harriet (Elizabeth) Beecher
　1811-1896 **NCLC 3, 50, 133; WLC 6**
　See also AAYA 53; AMWS 1; CDALB 1865-1917; DA; DA3; DAB; DAC; DAM MST, NOV; DLB 1, 12, 42, 74, 189, 239, 243; EXPN; FL 1:3; JRDA; LAIT 2; MAICYA 1, 2; NFS 6; RGAL 4; TUS; YABC 1

Strabo c. 64B.C.-c. 25 **CMLC 37**
　See also DLB 176

Strachey, (Giles) Lytton
　1880-1932 **TCLC 12**
　See also BRWS 2; CA 110; 178; DLB 149; DLBD 10; EWL 3; MTCW 2; NCFS 4

Stramm, August 1874-1915 **PC 50**
　See also CA 195; EWL 3

Strand, Mark 1934- .. **CLC 6, 18, 41, 71; PC 63**
　See also AMWS 4; CA 21-24R; CANR 40, 65, 100; CP 1, 2, 3, 4, 5, 6, 7; DAM POET; DLB 5; EWL 3; MAL 5; PAB; PFS 9, 18; RGAL 4; SATA 41; TCLE 1:2

Stratton-Porter, Gene(va Grace) 1863-1924
　See Porter, Gene(va Grace) Stratton
　See also ANW; CA 137; CLR 87; DLB 221; DLBD 14; MAICYA 1, 2; SATA 15

Straub, Peter 1943- **CLC 28, 107**
　See also BEST 89:1; BPFB 3; CA 85-88; CANR 28, 65, 109; CPW; DAM POP; DLBY 1984; HGG; MTCW 1, 2; MTFW 2005; SUFW 2

Straub, Peter Francis
　See Straub, Peter

Strauss, Botho 1944- **CLC 22**
　See also CA 157; CWW 2; DLB 124

Strauss, Leo 1899-1973 **TCLC 141**
　See also CA 101; 45-48; CANR 122

Streatfeild, (Mary) Noel
　1897(?)-1986 **CLC 21**
　See also CA 81-84; 120; CANR 31; CLR 17, 83; CWRI 5; DLB 160; MAICYA 1, 2; SATA 20; SATA-Obit 48

Stribling, T(homas) S(igismund)
　1881-1965 **CLC 23**
　See also CA 189; 107; CMW 4; DLB 9; RGAL 4

Strindberg, (Johan) August
　1849-1912 ... **DC 18; TCLC 1, 8, 21, 47; WLC 6**
　See also CA 104; 135; DA; DA3; DAB; DAC; DAM DRAM, MST; DFS 4, 9; DLB 259; EW 7; EWL 3; IDTP; LMFS 2; MTCW 2; MTFW 2005; RGWL 2, 3; TWA

Stringer, Arthur 1874-1950 **TCLC 37**
　See also CA 161; DLB 92

Stringer, David
　See Roberts, Keith (John Kingston)

Stroheim, Erich von 1885-1957 **TCLC 71**

Strugatskii, Arkadii (Natanovich)
　1925-1991 **CLC 27**
　See Strugatsky, Arkadii Natanovich
　See also CA 106; 135; SFW 4

Strugatskii, Boris (Natanovich)
　1933- **CLC 27**
　See Strugatsky, Boris (Natanovich)
　See also CA 106; SFW 4

Strugatsky, Arkadii Natanovich
　See Strugatskii, Arkadii (Natanovich)
　See also DLB 302

Strugatsky, Boris (Natanovich)
　See Strugatskii, Boris (Natanovich)
　See also DLB 302

Strummer, Joe 1952-2002 **CLC 30**

Strunk, William, Jr. 1869-1946 **TCLC 92**
　See also CA 118; 164; NCFS 5

Stryk, Lucien 1924- **PC 27**
　See also CA 13-16R; CANR 10, 28, 55, 110; CP 1, 2, 3, 4, 5, 6, 7

Stuart, Don A.
　See Campbell, John W(ood, Jr.)

Stuart, Ian
　See MacLean, Alistair (Stuart)

Stuart, Jesse (Hilton) 1906-1984 ... **CLC 1, 8, 11, 14, 34; SSC 31**
　See also CA 5-8R; 112; CANR 31; CN 1, 2, 3; DLB 9, 48, 102; DLBY 1984; SATA 2; SATA-Obit 36

Stubblefield, Sally
　See Trumbo, Dalton

Sturgeon, Theodore (Hamilton)
　1918-1985 **CLC 22, 39**
　See Queen, Ellery
　See also AAYA 51; BPFB 3; BYA 9, 10; CA 81-84; 116; CANR 32, 103; DLB 8; DLBY 1985; HGG; MTCW 1, 2; MTFW 2005; SCFW 4; SFW 4; SUFW

Sturges, Preston 1898-1959 **TCLC 48**
　See also CA 114; 149; DLB 26

Styron, William 1925- **CLC 1, 3, 5, 11, 15, 60; SSC 25**
　See also AMW; AMWC 2; BEST 90:4; BPFB 3; CA 5-8R; CANR 6, 33, 74, 126; CDALB 1968-1988; CN 1, 2, 3, 4, 5, 6, 7; CPW; CSW; DA3; DAM NOV, POP;
DLB 2, 143, 299; DLBY 1980; EWL 3; INT CANR-6; LAIT 2; MAL 5; MTCW 1, 2; MTFW 2005; NCFS 1; NFS 22; RGAL 4; RGHL; RHW; TUS

Su, Chien 1884-1918
　See Su Man-shu
　See also CA 123

Suarez Lynch, B.
　See Bioy Casares, Adolfo; Borges, Jorge Luis

Suassuna, Ariano Vilar 1927- **HLCS 1**
　See also CA 178; DLB 307; HW 2; LAW

Suckert, Kurt Erich
　See Malaparte, Curzio

Suckling, Sir John 1609-1642 . **LC 75; PC 30**
　See also BRW 2; DAM POET; DLB 58, 126; EXPP; PAB; RGEL 2

Suckow, Ruth 1892-1960 **SSC 18**
　See also CA 193; 113; DLB 9, 102; RGAL 4; TCWW 2

Sudermann, Hermann 1857-1928 .. **TCLC 15**
　See also CA 107; 201; DLB 118

Sue, Eugene 1804-1857 **NCLC 1**
　See also DLB 119

Sueskind, Patrick 1949- **CLC 44, 182**
　See Suskind, Patrick

Suetonius c. 70-c. 130 **CMLC 60**
　See also AW 2; DLB 211; RGWL 2, 3; WLIT 8

Sukenick, Ronald 1932-2004 **CLC 3, 4, 6, 48**
　See also CA 25-28R; 209; 229; CAAE 209; CAAS 8; CANR 32, 89; CN 3, 4, 5, 6, 7; DLB 173; DLBY 1981

Suknaski, Andrew 1942- **CLC 19**
　See also CA 101; CP 3, 4, 5, 6, 7; DLB 53

Sullivan, Vernon
　See Vian, Boris

Sully Prudhomme, Rene-Francois-Armand
　1839-1907 **TCLC 31**
　See also GFL 1789 to the Present

Su Man-shu **TCLC 24**
　See Su, Chien
　See also EWL 3

Sumarokov, Aleksandr Petrovich
　1717-1777 **LC 104**
　See also DLB 150

Summerforest, Ivy B.
　See Kirkup, James

Summers, Andrew James 1942- **CLC 26**

Summers, Andy
　See Summers, Andrew James

Summers, Hollis (Spurgeon, Jr.)
　1916- **CLC 10**
　See also CA 5-8R; CANR 3; CN 1, 2, 3; CP 1, 2, 3, 4; DLB 6; TCLE 1:2

Summers, (Alphonsus Joseph-Mary Augustus) Montague
　1880-1948 **TCLC 16**
　See also CA 118; 163

Sumner, Gordon Matthew **CLC 26**
　See Police, The; Sting

Sun Tzu c. 400B.C.-c. 320B.C. **CMLC 56**

Surrey, Henry Howard 1517-1574 ... **LC 121; PC 59**
　See also BRW 1; RGEL 2

Surtees, Robert Smith 1805-1864 .. **NCLC 14**
　See also DLB 21; RGEL 2

Susann, Jacqueline 1921-1974 **CLC 3**
　See also AITN 1; BPFB 3; CA 65-68; 53-56; MTCW 1, 2

Su Shi
　See Su Shih
　See also RGWL 2, 3

Su Shih 1036-1101 **CMLC 15**
　See Su Shi

Suskind, Patrick **CLC 182**
 See Sueskind, Patrick
 See also BPFB 3; CA 145; CWW 2

Sutcliff, Rosemary 1920-1992 **CLC 26**
 See also AAYA 10; BYA 1, 4; CA 5-8R;
 139; CANR 37; CLR 1, 37; CPW; DAB;
 DAC; DAM MST, POP; JRDA; LATS
 1:1; MAICYA 1, 2; MAICYAS 1; RHW;
 SATA 6, 44, 78; SATA-Obit 73; WYA;
 YAW

Sutro, Alfred 1863-1933 **TCLC 6**
 See also CA 105; 185; DLB 10; RGEL 2

Sutton, Henry
 See Slavitt, David R(ytman)

Suzuki, D. T.
 See Suzuki, Daisetz Teitaro

Suzuki, Daisetz T.
 See Suzuki, Daisetz Teitaro

Suzuki, Daisetz Teitaro
 1870-1966 **TCLC 109**
 See also CA 121; 111; MTCW 1, 2; MTFW
 2005

Suzuki, Teitaro
 See Suzuki, Daisetz Teitaro

Svevo, Italo **SSC 25; TCLC 2, 35**
 See Schmitz, Aron Hector
 See also DLB 264; EW 8; EWL 3; RGWL
 2, 3; WLIT 7

Swados, Elizabeth (A.) 1951- **CLC 12**
 See also CA 97-100; CANR 49; INT CA-
 97-100

Swados, Harvey 1920-1972 **CLC 5**
 See also CA 5-8R; 37-40R; CANR 6; CN
 1; DLB 2; MAL 5

Swan, Gladys 1934- **CLC 69**
 See also CA 101; CANR 17, 39; TCLE 1:2

Swanson, Logan
 See Matheson, Richard (Burton)

Swarthout, Glendon (Fred)
 1918-1992 **CLC 35**
 See also AAYA 55; CA 1-4R; 139; CANR
 1, 47; CN 1, 2, 3, 4, 5; LAIT 5; SATA 26;
 TCWW 1, 2; YAW

Swedenborg, Emanuel 1688-1772 **LC 105**

Sweet, Sarah C.
 See Jewett, (Theodora) Sarah Orne

Swenson, May 1919-1989 **CLC 4, 14, 61,**
 106; PC 14
 See also AMWS 4; CA 5-8R; 130; CANR
 36, 61, 131; CP 1, 2, 3, 4; DA; DAB;
 DAC; DAM MST, POET; DLB 5; EXPP;
 GLL 2; MAL 5; MTCW 1, 2; MTFW
 2005; PFS 16; SATA 15; WP

Swift, Augustus
 See Lovecraft, H. P.

Swift, Graham (Colin) 1949- **CLC 41, 88**
 See also BRWC 2; BRWS 5; CA 117; 122;
 CANR 46, 71, 128; CN 4, 5, 6, 7; DLB
 194, 326; MTCW 2; MTFW 2005; NFS
 18; RGSF 2

Swift, Jonathan 1667-1745 **LC 1, 42, 101;**
 PC 9; WLC 6
 See also AAYA 41; BRW 3; BRWC 1;
 BRWR 1; BYA 5, 14; CDBLB 1660-1789;
 CLR 53; DA; DA3; DAB; DAC; DAM
 MST, NOV, POET; DLB 39, 95, 101;
 EXPN; LAIT 1; NFS 6; RGEL 2; SATA
 19; TEA; WCH; WLIT 3

Swinburne, Algernon Charles
 1837-1909 ... **PC 24; TCLC 8, 36; WLC**
 6
 See also BRW 5; CA 105; 140; CDBLB
 1832-1890; DA; DA3; DAB; DAC; DAM
 MST, POET; DLB 35, 57; PAB; RGEL 2;
 TEA

Swinfen, Ann **CLC 34**
 See also CA 202

Swinnerton, Frank (Arthur)
 1884-1982 **CLC 31**
 See also CA 202; 108; CN 1, 2, 3; DLB 34

Swinnerton, Frank Arthur
 1884-1982 **CLC 31**
 See also CA 108; DLB 34

Swithen, John
 See King, Stephen

Sylvia
 See Ashton-Warner, Sylvia (Constance)

Symmes, Robert Edward
 See Duncan, Robert (Edward)

Symonds, John Addington
 1840-1893 **NCLC 34**
 See also DLB 57, 144

Symons, Arthur 1865-1945 **TCLC 11**
 See also CA 107; 189; DLB 19, 57, 149;
 RGEL 2

Symons, Julian (Gustave)
 1912-1994 **CLC 2, 14, 32**
 See also CA 49-52; 147; CAAS 3; CANR
 3, 33, 59; CMW 4; CN 1, 2, 3, 4, 5; CP 1,
 3, 4; DLB 87, 155; DLBY 1992; MSW;
 MTCW 1

Synge, (Edmund) J(ohn) M(illington)
 1871-1909 **DC 2; TCLC 6, 37**
 See also BRW 6; BRWR 1; CA 104; 141;
 CDBLB 1890-1914; DAM DRAM; DFS
 18; DLB 10, 19; EWL 3; RGEL 2; TEA;
 WLIT 4

Syruc, J.
 See Milosz, Czeslaw

Szirtes, George 1948- **CLC 46; PC 51**
 See also CA 109; CANR 27, 61, 117; CP 4,
 5, 6, 7

Szymborska, Wislawa 1923- ... **CLC 99, 190;**
 PC 44
 See also CA 154; CANR 91, 133; CDWLB
 4; CWP; CWW 2; DA3; DLB 232; DLBY
 1996; EWL 3; MTCW 2; MTFW 2005;
 PFS 15; RGHL; RGWL 3

T. O., Nik
 See Annensky, Innokenty (Fyodorovich)

Tabori, George 1914- **CLC 19**
 See also CA 49-52; CANR 4, 69; CBD; CD
 5, 6; DLB 245; RGHL

Tacitus c. 55-c. 117 **CMLC 56**
 See also AW 2; CDWLB 1; DLB 211;
 RGWL 2, 3; WLIT 8

Tagore, Rabindranath 1861-1941 **PC 8;**
 SSC 48; TCLC 3, 53
 See also CA 104; 120; DA3; DAM DRAM,
 POET; DLB 323; EWL 3; MTCW 1, 2;
 MTFW 2005; PFS 18; RGEL 2; RGSF 2;
 RGWL 2, 3; TWA

Taine, Hippolyte Adolphe
 1828-1893 **NCLC 15**
 See also EW 7; GFL 1789 to the Present

Talayesva, Don C. 1890-(?) **NNAL**

Talese, Gay 1932- **CLC 37**
 See also AITN 1; CA 1-4R; CANR 9, 58,
 137; DLB 185; INT CANR-9; MTCW 1,
 2; MTFW 2005

Tallent, Elizabeth (Ann) 1954- **CLC 45**
 See also CA 117; CANR 72; DLB 130

Tallmountain, Mary 1918-1997 **NNAL**
 See also CA 146; 161; DLB 193

Tally, Ted 1952- **CLC 42**
 See also CA 120; 124; CAD; CANR 125;
 CD 5, 6; INT CA-124

Talvik, Heiti 1904-1947 **TCLC 87**
 See also EWL 3

Tamayo y Baus, Manuel
 1829-1898 **NCLC 1**

Tammsaare, A(nton) H(ansen)
 1878-1940 **TCLC 27**
 See also CA 164; CDWLB 4; DLB 220;
 EWL 3

Tam'si, Tchicaya U
 See Tchicaya, Gerald Felix

Tan, Amy (Ruth) 1952- . **AAL; CLC 59, 120,**
 151
 See also AAYA 9, 48; AMWS 10; BEST
 89:3; BPFB 3; CA 136; CANR 54, 105,
 132; CDALBS; CN 6, 7; CPW 1; DA3;
 DAM MULT, NOV, POP; DLB 173, 312;
 EXPN; FL 1:6; FW; LAIT 3, 5; MAL 5;
 MTCW 2; MTFW 2005; NFS 1, 13, 16;
 RGAL 4; SATA 75; SSFS 9; YAW

Tandem, Felix
 See Spitteler, Carl (Friedrich Georg)

Tanizaki, Jun'ichiro 1886-1965 ... **CLC 8, 14,**
 28; SSC 21
 See Tanizaki Jun'ichiro
 See also CA 93-96; 25-28R; MJW; MTCW
 2; MTFW 2005; RGSF 2; RGWL 2

Tanizaki Jun'ichiro
 See Tanizaki, Jun'ichiro
 See also DLB 180; EWL 3

Tannen, Deborah 1945- **CLC 206**
 See also CA 118; CANR 95

Tannen, Deborah Frances
 See Tannen, Deborah

Tanner, William
 See Amis, Kingsley (William)

Tao Lao
 See Storni, Alfonsina

Tapahonso, Luci 1953- **NNAL; PC 65**
 See also CA 145; CANR 72, 127; DLB 175

Tarantino, Quentin (Jerome)
 1963- **CLC 125**
 See also AAYA 58; CA 171; CANR 125

Tarassoff, Lev
 See Troyat, Henri

Tarbell, Ida M(inerva) 1857-1944 . **TCLC 40**
 See also CA 122; 181; DLB 47

Tarkington, (Newton) Booth
 1869-1946 **TCLC 9**
 See also BPFB 3; BYA 3; CA 110; 143;
 CWRI 5; DLB 9, 102; MAL 5; MTCW 2;
 RGAL 4; SATA 17

Tarkovskii, Andrei Arsen'evich
 See Tarkovsky, Andrei (Arsenyevich)

Tarkovsky, Andrei (Arsenyevich)
 1932-1986 **CLC 75**
 See also CA 127

Tartt, Donna 1964(?)- **CLC 76**
 See also AAYA 56; CA 142; CANR 135;
 MTFW 2005

Tasso, Torquato 1544-1595 **LC 5, 94**
 See also EFS 2; EW 2; RGWL 2, 3; WLIT
 7

Tate, (John Orley) Allen 1899-1979 .. **CLC 2,**
 4, 6, 9, 11, 14, 24; PC 50
 See also AMW; CA 5-8R; 85-88; CANR
 32, 108; CN 1, 2; CP 1, 2; DLB 4, 45, 63;
 DLBD 17; EWL 3; MAL 5; MTCW 1, 2;
 MTFW 2005; RGAL 4; RHW

Tate, Ellalice
 See Hibbert, Eleanor Alice Burford

Tate, James (Vincent) 1943- **CLC 2, 6, 25**
 See also CA 21-24R; CANR 29, 57, 114;
 CP 1, 2, 3, 4, 5, 6, 7; DLB 5, 169; EWL
 3; PFS 10, 15; RGAL 4; WP

Tate, Nahum 1652(?)-1715 **LC 109**
 See also DLB 80; RGEL 2

Tauler, Johannes c. 1300-1361 **CMLC 37**
 See also DLB 179; LMFS 1

Tavel, Ronald 1940- **CLC 6**
 See also CA 21-24R; CAD; CANR 33; CD
 5, 6

Taviani, Paolo 1931- **CLC 70**
 See also CA 153

Taylor, Bayard 1825-1878 **NCLC 89**
 See also DLB 3, 189, 250, 254; RGAL 4

Taylor, C(ecil) P(hilip) 1929-1981 **CLC 27**
 See also CA 25-28R; 105; CANR 47; CBD

Taylor, Edward 1642(?)-1729 . **LC 11; PC 63**
See also AMW; DA; DAB; DAC; DAM MST, POET; DLB 24; EXPP; RGAL 4; TUS

Taylor, Eleanor Ross 1920- **CLC 5**
See also CA 81-84; CANR 70

Taylor, Elizabeth 1912-1975 **CLC 2, 4, 29**
See also CA 13-16R; CANR 9, 70; CN 1, 2; DLB 139; MTCW 1; RGEL 2; SATA 13

Taylor, Frederick Winslow
1856-1915 **TCLC 76**
See also CA 188

Taylor, Henry (Splawn) 1942- **CLC 44**
See also CA 33-36R; CAAS 7; CANR 31; CP 6, 7; DLB 5; PFS 10

Taylor, Kamala (Purnaiya) 1924-2004
See Markandaya, Kamala
See also CA 77-80; 227; MTFW 2005; NFS 13

Taylor, Mildred D(elois) 1943- **CLC 21**
See also AAYA 10, 47; BW 1; BYA 3, 8; CA 85-88; CANR 25, 115, 136; CLR 9, 59, 90; CSW; DLB 52; JRDA; LAIT 3; MAICYA 1, 2; MTFW 2005; SAAS 5; SATA 135; WYA; YAW

Taylor, Peter (Hillsman) 1917-1994 .. **CLC 1, 4, 18, 37, 44, 50, 71; SSC 10, 84**
See also AMWS 5; BPFB 3; CA 13-16R; 147; CANR 9, 50; CN 1, 2, 3, 4, 5; CSW; DLB 218, 278; DLBY 1981, 1994; EWL 3; EXPS; INT CANR-9; MAL 5; MTCW 1, 2; MTFW 2005; RGSF 2; SSFS 9; TUS

Taylor, Robert Lewis 1912-1998 **CLC 14**
See also CA 1-4R; 170; CANR 3, 64; CN 1, 2; SATA 10; TCWW 1, 2

Tchekhov, Anton
See Chekhov, Anton (Pavlovich)

Tchicaya, Gerald Felix 1931-1988 .. **CLC 101**
See Tchicaya U Tam'si
See also CA 129; 125; CANR 81

Tchicaya U Tam'si
See Tchicaya, Gerald Felix
See also EWL 3

Teasdale, Sara 1884-1933 **PC 31; TCLC 4**
See also CA 104; 163; DLB 45; GLL 1; PFS 14; RGAL 4; SATA 32; TUS

Tecumseh 1768-1813 **NNAL**
See also DAM MULT

Tegner, Esaias 1782-1846 **NCLC 2**

Teilhard de Chardin, (Marie Joseph) Pierre
1881-1955 **TCLC 9**
See also CA 105; 210; GFL 1789 to the Present

Temple, Ann
See Mortimer, Penelope (Ruth)

Tennant, Emma (Christina) 1937- .. **CLC 13, 52**
See also BRWS 9; CA 65-68; CAAS 9; CANR 10, 38, 59, 88; CN 3, 4, 5, 6, 7; DLB 14; EWL 3; SFW 4

Tenneshaw, S. M.
See Silverberg, Robert

Tenney, Tabitha Gilman
1762-1837 **NCLC 122**
See also DLB 37, 200

Tennyson, Alfred 1809-1892 ... **NCLC 30, 65, 115; PC 6; WLC 6**
See also AAYA 50; BRW 4; CDBLB 1832-1890; DA; DA3; DAB; DAC; DAM MST, POET; DLB 32; EXPP; PAB; PFS 1, 2, 4, 11, 15, 19; RGEL 2; TEA; WLIT 4; WP

Teran, Lisa St. Aubin de **CLC 36**
See St. Aubin de Teran, Lisa

Terence c. 184B.C.-c. 159B.C. **CMLC 14; DC 7**
See also AW 1; CDWLB 1; DLB 211; RGWL 2, 3; TWA; WLIT 8

Teresa de Jesus, St. 1515-1582 **LC 18**

Teresa of Avila, St.
See Teresa de Jesus, St.

Terkel, Louis **CLC 38**
See Terkel, Studs
See also AAYA 32; AITN 1; MTCW 2; TUS

Terkel, Studs 1912-
See Terkel, Louis
See also CA 57-60; CANR 18, 45, 67, 132; DA3; MTCW 1, 2; MTFW 2005

Terry, C. V.
See Slaughter, Frank G(ill)

Terry, Megan 1932- **CLC 19; DC 13**
See also CA 77-80; CABS 3; CAD; CANR 43; CD 5, 6; CWD; DFS 18; DLB 7, 249; GLL 2

Tertullian c. 155-c. 245 **CMLC 29**

Tertz, Abram
See Sinyavsky, Andrei (Donatevich)
See also RGSF 2

Tesich, Steve 1943(?)-1996 **CLC 40, 69**
See also CA 105; 152; CAD; DLBY 1983

Tesla, Nikola 1856-1943 **TCLC 88**

Teternikov, Fyodor Kuzmich 1863-1927
See Sologub, Fyodor
See also CA 104

Tevis, Walter 1928-1984 **CLC 42**
See also CA 113; SFW 4

Tey, Josephine **TCLC 14**
See Mackintosh, Elizabeth
See also DLB 77; MSW

Thackeray, William Makepeace
1811-1863 **NCLC 5, 14, 22, 43, 169; WLC 6**
See also BRW 5; BRWC 2; CDBLB 1832-1890; DA; DA3; DAB; DAC; DAM MST, NOV; DLB 21, 55, 159, 163; NFS 13; RGEL 2; SATA 23; TEA; WLIT 3

Thakura, Ravindranatha
See Tagore, Rabindranath

Thames, C. H.
See Marlowe, Stephen

Tharoor, Shashi 1956- **CLC 70**
See also CA 141; CANR 91; CN 6, 7

Thelwall, John 1764-1834 **NCLC 162**
See also DLB 93, 158

Thelwell, Michael Miles 1939- **CLC 22**
See also BW 2; CA 101

Theobald, Lewis, Jr.
See Lovecraft, H. P.

Theocritus c. 310B.C.- **CMLC 45**
See also AW 1; DLB 176; RGWL 2, 3

Theodorescu, Ion N. 1880-1967
See Arghezi, Tudor
See also CA 116

Theriault, Yves 1915-1983 **CLC 79**
See also CA 102; CANR 150; CCA 1; DAC; DAM MST; DLB 88; EWL 3

Theroux, Alexander (Louis) 1939- **CLC 2, 25**
See also CA 85-88; CANR 20, 63; CN 4, 5, 6, 7

Theroux, Paul (Edward) 1941- **CLC 5, 8, 11, 15, 28, 46**
See also AAYA 28; AMWS 8; BEST 89:4; BPFB 3; CA 33-36R; CANR 20, 45, 74, 133; CDALBS; CN 1, 2, 3, 4, 5, 6, 7; CP 1; CPW 1; DA3; DAM POP; DLB 2, 218; EWL 3; HGG; MAL 5; MTCW 1, 2; MTFW 2005; RGAL 4; SATA 44, 109; TUS

Thesen, Sharon 1946- **CLC 56**
See also CA 163; CANR 125; CP 5, 6, 7; CWP

Thespis fl. 6th cent. B.C.- **CMLC 51**
See also LMFS 1

Thevenin, Denis
See Duhamel, Georges

Thibault, Jacques Anatole Francois
1844-1924
See France, Anatole
See also CA 106; 127; DA3; DAM NOV; MTCW 1, 2; TWA

Thiele, Colin (Milton) 1920- **CLC 17**
See also CA 29-32R; CANR 12, 28, 53, 105; CLR 27; CP 1, 2; DLB 289; MAICYA 1, 2; SAAS 2; SATA 14, 72, 125; YAW

Thistlethwaite, Bel
See Wetherald, Agnes Ethelwyn

Thomas, Audrey (Callahan) 1935- **CLC 7, 13, 37, 107; SSC 20**
See also AITN 2; CA 21-24R, 237; CAAE 237; CAAS 19; CANR 36, 58; CN 2, 3, 4, 5, 6, 7; DLB 60; MTCW 1; RGSF 2

Thomas, Augustus 1857-1934 **TCLC 97**
See also MAL 5

Thomas, D(onald) M(ichael) 1935- . **CLC 13, 22, 31, 132**
See also BPFB 3; BRWS 4; CA 61-64; CAAS 11; CANR 17, 45, 75; CDBLB 1960 to Present; CN 4, 5, 6, 7; CP 1, 2, 3, 4, 5, 6, 7; DA3; DLB 40, 207, 299; HGG; INT CANR-17; MTCW 1, 2; MTFW 2005; RGHL; SFW 4

Thomas, Dylan (Marlais) 1914-1953 **PC 2, 52; SSC 3, 44; TCLC 1, 8, 45, 105; WLC 6**
See also AAYA 45; BRWS 1; CA 104; 120; CANR 65; CDBLB 1945-1960; DA; DA3; DAB; DAC; DAM DRAM, MST, POET; DLB 13, 20, 139; EWL 3; EXPP; LAIT 3; MTCW 1, 2; MTFW 2005; PAB; PFS 1, 3, 8; RGEL 2; RGSF 2; SATA 60; TEA; WLIT 4; WP

Thomas, (Philip) Edward 1878-1917 . **PC 53; TCLC 10**
See also BRW 6; BRWS 3; CA 106; 153; DAM POET; DLB 19, 98, 156, 216; EWL 3; PAB; RGEL 2

Thomas, Joyce Carol 1938- **CLC 35**
See also AAYA 12, 54; BW 2, 3; CA 113; 116; CANR 48, 114, 135; CLR 19; DLB 33; INT CA-116; JRDA; MAICYA 1, 2; MTCW 1, 2; MTFW 2005; SAAS 7; SATA 40, 78, 123, 137; SATA-Essay 137; WYA; YAW

Thomas, Lewis 1913-1993 **CLC 35**
See also ANW; CA 85-88; 143; CANR 38, 60; DLB 275; MTCW 1, 2

Thomas, M. Carey 1857-1935 **TCLC 89**
See also FW

Thomas, Paul
See Mann, (Paul) Thomas

Thomas, Piri 1928- **CLC 17; HLCS 2**
See also CA 73-76; HW 1; LLW

Thomas, R(onald) S(tuart)
1913-2000 **CLC 6, 13, 48**
See also CA 89-92; 189; CAAS 4; CANR 30; CDBLB 1960 to Present; CP 1, 2, 3, 4, 5, 6, 7; DAB; DAM POET; DLB 27; EWL 3; MTCW 1; RGEL 2

Thomas, Ross (Elmore) 1926-1995 .. **CLC 39**
See also CA 33-36R; 150; CANR 22, 63; CMW 4

Thompson, Francis (Joseph)
1859-1907 **TCLC 4**
See also BRW 5; CA 104; 189; CDBLB 1890-1914; DLB 19; RGEL 2; TEA

Thompson, Francis Clegg
See Mencken, H(enry) L(ouis)

Thompson, Hunter S(tockton)
1937(?)-2005 **CLC 9, 17, 40, 104**
See also AAYA 45; BEST 89:1; BPFB 3; CA 17-20R; 236; CANR 23, 46, 74, 77, 111, 133; CPW; CSW; DA3; DAM POP; DLB 185; MTCW 1, 2; MTFW 2005; TUS

Thompson, James Myers
See Thompson, Jim (Myers)
Thompson, Jim (Myers)
1906-1977(?) **CLC 69**
See also BPFB 3; CA 140; CMW 4; CPW;
DLB 226; MSW
Thompson, Judith (Clare Francesca)
1954- ... **CLC 39**
See also CA 143; CD 5, 6; CWD; DFS 22
Thomson, James 1700-1748 **LC 16, 29, 40**
See also BRWS 3; DAM POET; DLB 95;
RGEL 2
Thomson, James 1834-1882 **NCLC 18**
See also DAM POET; DLB 35; RGEL 2
Thoreau, Henry David 1817-1862 .. **NCLC 7,
21, 61, 138; PC 30; WLC 6**
See also AAYA 42; AMW; ANW; BYA 3;
CDALB 1640-1865; DA; DA3; DAB;
DAC; DAM MST; DLB 1, 183, 223, 270,
298; LAIT 2; LMFS 1; NCFS 3; RGAL
4; TUS
Thorndike, E. L.
See Thorndike, Edward L(ee)
Thorndike, Edward L(ee)
1874-1949 **TCLC 107**
See also CA 121
Thornton, Hall
See Silverberg, Robert
Thorpe, Adam 1956- **CLC 176**
See also CA 129; CANR 92; DLB 231
Thubron, Colin (Gerald Dryden)
1939- ... **CLC 163**
See also CA 25-28R; CANR 12, 29, 59, 95;
CN 5, 6, 7; DLB 204, 231
Thucydides c. 455B.C.-c. 395B.C. . **CMLC 17**
See also AW 1; DLB 176; RGWL 2, 3;
WLIT 8
Thumboo, Edwin Nadason 1933- **PC 30**
See also CA 194; CP 1
Thurber, James (Grover)
1894-1961 .. **CLC 5, 11, 25, 125; SSC 1,
47**
See also AAYA 56; AMWS 1; BPFB 3;
BYA 5; CA 73-76; CANR 17, 39; CDALB
1929-1941; CWRI 5; DA; DA3; DAB;
DAC; DAM DRAM; DLB 4,
11, 22, 102; EWL 3; EXPS; FANT; LAIT
3; MAICYA 1, 2; MAL 5; MTCW 1, 2;
MTFW 2005; RGAL 4; RGSF 2; SATA
13; SSFS 1, 10, 19; SUFW; TUS
Thurman, Wallace (Henry)
1902-1934 **BLC 3; HR 1:3; TCLC 6**
See also BW 1, 3; CA 104; 124; CANR 81;
DAM MULT; DLB 51
Tibullus c. 54B.C.-c. 18B.C. **CMLC 36**
See also AW 2; DLB 211; RGWL 2, 3;
WLIT 8
Ticheburn, Cheviot
See Ainsworth, William Harrison
Tieck, (Johann) Ludwig
1773-1853 **NCLC 5, 46; SSC 31**
See also CDWLB 2; DLB 90; EW 5; IDTP;
RGSF 2; RGWL 2, 3; SUFW
Tiger, Derry
See Ellison, Harlan (Jay)
Tilghman, Christopher 1946- **CLC 65**
See also CA 159; CANR 135, 151; CSW;
DLB 244
Tillich, Paul (Johannes)
1886-1965 **CLC 131**
See also CA 5-8R; 25-28R; CANR 33;
MTCW 1, 2
Tillinghast, Richard (Williford)
1940- ... **CLC 29**
See also CA 29-32R; CAAS 23; CANR 26,
51, 96; CP 2, 3, 4, 5, 6, 7; CSW
Timrod, Henry 1828-1867 **NCLC 25**
See also DLB 3, 248; RGAL 4

Tindall, Gillian (Elizabeth) 1938- **CLC 7**
See also CA 21-24R; CANR 11, 65, 107;
CN 1, 2, 3, 4, 5, 6, 7
Tiptree, James, Jr. **CLC 48, 50**
See Sheldon, Alice Hastings Bradley
See also DLB 8; SCFW 1, 2; SFW 4
Tirone Smith, Mary-Ann 1944- **CLC 39**
See also CA 118; 136; CANR 113; SATA
143
Tirso de Molina 1580(?)-1648 **DC 13;
HLCS 2; LC 73**
See also RGWL 2, 3
Titmarsh, Michael Angelo
See Thackeray, William Makepeace
**Tocqueville, Alexis (Charles Henri Maurice
Clerel Comte) de** 1805-1859 .. **NCLC 7,
63**
See also EW 6; GFL 1789 to the Present;
TWA
Toer, Pramoedya Ananta
1925-2006 **CLC 186**
See also CA 197; RGWL 3
Toffler, Alvin 1928- **CLC 168**
See also CA 13-16R; CANR 15, 46, 67;
CPW; DAM POP; MTCW 1, 2
Toibin, Colm 1955- **CLC 162**
See also CA 142; CANR 81, 149; CN 7;
DLB 271
Tolkien, J(ohn) R(onald) R(euel)
1892-1973 **CLC 1, 2, 3, 8, 12, 38;
TCLC 137; WLC 6**
See also AAYA 10; AITN 1; BPFB 3;
BRWC 2; BRWS 2; CA 17-18; 45-48;
CANR 36, 134; CAP 2; CDBLB 1914-
1945; CLR 56; CN 1; CPW 1; CWRI 5;
DA; DA3; DAB; DAC; DAM MST, NOV,
POP; DLB 15, 160, 255; EFS 2; EWL 3;
FANT; JRDA; LAIT 1; LATS 1:2; LMFS
2; MAICYA 1, 2; MTCW 1, 2; MTFW
2005; NFS 8; RGEL 2; SATA 2, 32, 100;
SATA-Obit 24; SFW 4; SUFW; TEA;
WCH; WYA; YAW
Toller, Ernst 1893-1939 **TCLC 10**
See also CA 107; 186; DLB 124; EWL 3;
RGWL 2, 3
Tolson, M. B.
See Tolson, Melvin B(eaunorus)
Tolson, Melvin B(eaunorus)
1898(?)-1966 **BLC 3; CLC 36, 105**
See also AFAW 1, 2; BW 1, 3; CA 124; 89-
92; CANR 80; DAM MULT, POET; DLB
48, 76; MAL 5; RGAL 4
Tolstoi, Aleksei Nikolaevich
See Tolstoy, Alexey Nikolaevich
Tolstoi, Lev
See Tolstoy, Leo (Nikolaevich)
See also RGSF 2; RGWL 2, 3
Tolstoy, Aleksei Nikolaevich
See Tolstoy, Alexey Nikolaevich
See also DLB 272
Tolstoy, Alexey Nikolaevich
1882-1945 **TCLC 18**
See Tolstoy, Aleksei Nikolaevich
See also CA 107; 158; EWL 3; SFW 4
Tolstoy, Leo (Nikolaevich)
1828-1910 . **SSC 9, 30, 45, 54; TCLC 4,
11, 17, 28, 44, 79, 173; WLC 6**
See Tolstoi, Lev
See also AAYA 56; CA 104; 123; DA; DA3;
DAB; DAC; DAM MST, NOV; DLB 238;
EFS 2; EW 7; EXPS; IDTP; LAIT 2;
LATS 1:1; LMFS 1; NFS 10; SATA 26;
SSFS 5; TWA
Tolstoy, Count Leo
See Tolstoy, Leo (Nikolaevich)
Tomalin, Claire 1933- **CLC 166**
See also CA 89-92; CANR 52, 88; DLB
155

Tomasi di Lampedusa, Giuseppe 1896-1957
See Lampedusa, Giuseppe (Tomasi) di
See also CA 111; DLB 177; EWL 3; WLIT
7
Tomlin, Lily **CLC 17**
See Tomlin, Mary Jean
Tomlin, Mary Jean 1939(?)-
See Tomlin, Lily
See also CA 117
Tomline, F. Latour
See Gilbert, W(illiam) S(chwenck)
Tomlinson, (Alfred) Charles 1927- **CLC 2,
4, 6, 13, 45; PC 17**
See also CA 5-8R; CANR 33; CP 1, 2, 3, 4,
5, 6, 7; DAM POET; DLB 40; TCLE 1:2
Tomlinson, H(enry) M(ajor)
1873-1958 **TCLC 71**
See also CA 118; 161; DLB 36, 100, 195
Tonna, Charlotte Elizabeth
1790-1846 **NCLC 135**
See also DLB 163
Tonson, Jacob fl. 1655(?)-1736 **LC 86**
See also DLB 170
Toole, John Kennedy 1937-1969 **CLC 19,
64**
See also BPFB 3; CA 104; DLBY 1981;
MTCW 2; MTFW 2005
Toomer, Eugene
See Toomer, Jean
Toomer, Eugene Pinchback
See Toomer, Jean
Toomer, Jean 1894-1967 .. **BLC 3; CLC 1, 4,
13, 22; HR 1:3; PC 7; SSC 1, 45;
TCLC 172; WLCS**
See also AFAW 1, 2; AMWS 3, 9; BW 1;
CA 85-88; CDALB 1917-1929; DA3;
DAM MULT; DLB 45, 51; EWL 3; EXPP;
EXPS; LMFS 2; MAL 5; MTCW 1, 2;
MTFW 2005; NFS 11; RGAL 4; RGSF 2;
SSFS 5
Toomer, Nathan Jean
See Toomer, Jean
Toomer, Nathan Pinchback
See Toomer, Jean
Torley, Luke
See Blish, James (Benjamin)
Tornimparte, Alessandra
See Ginzburg, Natalia
Torre, Raoul della
See Mencken, H(enry) L(ouis)
Torrence, Ridgely 1874-1950 **TCLC 97**
See also DLB 54, 249; MAL 5
Torrey, E(dwin) Fuller 1937- **CLC 34**
See also CA 119; CANR 71
Torsvan, Ben Traven
See Traven, B.
Torsvan, Benno Traven
See Traven, B.
Torsvan, Berick Traven
See Traven, B.
Torsvan, Berwick Traven
See Traven, B.
Torsvan, Bruno Traven
See Traven, B.
Torsvan, Traven
See Traven, B.
Tourneur, Cyril 1575(?)-1626 **LC 66**
See also BRW 2; DAM DRAM; DLB 58;
RGEL 2
Tournier, Michel 1924- **CLC 6, 23, 36, 95;
SSC 88**
See also CA 49-52; CANR 3, 36, 74, 149;
CWW 2; DLB 83; EWL 3; GFL 1789 to
the Present; MTCW 1, 2; SATA 23
Tournier, Michel Edouard
See Tournier, Michel
Tournimparte, Alessandra
See Ginzburg, Natalia

Towers, Ivar
See Kornbluth, C(yril) M.
Towne, Robert (Burton) 1936(?)- **CLC 87**
See also CA 108; DLB 44; IDFW 3, 4
Townsend, Sue **CLC 61**
See Townsend, Susan Lilian
See also AAYA 28; CA 119; 127; CANR
65, 107; CBD; CD 5, 6; CPW; CWD;
DAB; DAC; DAM MST; DLB 271; INT
CA-127; SATA 55, 93; SATA-Brief 48;
YAW
Townsend, Susan Lilian 1946-
See Townsend, Sue
Townshend, Pete
See Townshend, Peter (Dennis Blandford)
Townshend, Peter (Dennis Blandford)
1945- **CLC 17, 42**
See also CA 107
Tozzi, Federigo 1883-1920 **TCLC 31**
See also CA 160; CANR 110; DLB 264;
EWL 3; WLIT 7
Tracy, Don(ald Fiske) 1905-1970(?)
See Queen, Ellery
See also CA 1-4R; 176; CANR 2
Trafford, F. G.
See Riddell, Charlotte
Traherne, Thomas 1637(?)-1674 .. **LC 99; PC
70**
See also BRW 2; BRWS 11; DLB 131;
PAB; RGEL 2
Traill, Catharine Parr 1802-1899 .. **NCLC 31**
See also DLB 99
Trakl, Georg 1887-1914 **PC 20; TCLC 5**
See also CA 104; 165; EW 10; EWL 3;
LMFS 2; MTCW 2; RGWL 2, 3
Trambley, Estela Portillo **TCLC 163**
See Portillo Trambley, Estela
See also CA 77-80; RGAL 4
Tranquilli, Secondino
See Silone, Ignazio
Transtroemer, Tomas Gosta
See Transtromer, Tomas (Goesta)
Transtromer, Tomas (Gosta)
See Transtromer, Tomas (Goesta)
See also CWW 2
Transtromer, Tomas (Goesta)
1931- **CLC 52, 65**
See Transtromer, Tomas (Gosta)
See also CA 117; 129; CAAS 17; CANR
115; DAM POET; DLB 257; EWL 3; PFS
21
Transtromer, Tomas Gosta
See Transtromer, Tomas (Goesta)
Traven, B. 1882(?)-1969 **CLC 8, 11**
See also CA 19-20; 25-28R; CAP 2; DLB
9, 56; EWL 3; MTCW 1; RGAL 4
Trediakovsky, Vasilii Kirillovich
1703-1769 **LC 68**
See also DLB 150
Treitel, Jonathan 1959- **CLC 70**
See also CA 210; DLB 267
Trelawny, Edward John
1792-1881 **NCLC 85**
See also DLB 110, 116, 144
Tremain, Rose 1943- **CLC 42**
See also CA 97-100; CANR 44, 95; CN 4,
5, 6, 7; DLB 14, 271; RGSF 2; RHW
Tremblay, Michel 1942- **CLC 29, 102, 225**
See also CA 116; 128; CCA 1; CWW 2;
DAC; DAM MST; DLB 60; EWL 3; GLL
1; MTCW 1, 2; MTFW 2005
Trevanian ... **CLC 29**
See Whitaker, Rod
Trevor, Glen
See Hilton, James

Trevor, William .. **CLC 7, 9, 14, 25, 71, 116;
SSC 21, 58**
See Cox, William Trevor
See also BRWS 4; CBD; CD 5, 6; CN 1, 2,
3, 4, 5, 6, 7; DLB 14, 139; EWL 3; LATS
1:2; RGEL 2; RGSF 2; SSFS 10; TCLE
1:2
Trifonov, Iurii (Valentinovich)
See Trifonov, Yuri (Valentinovich)
See also DLB 302; RGWL 2, 3
Trifonov, Yuri (Valentinovich)
1925-1981 **CLC 45**
See Trifonov, Iurii (Valentinovich); Tri-
fonov, Yury Valentinovich
See also CA 126; 103; MTCW 1
Trifonov, Yury Valentinovich
See Trifonov, Yuri (Valentinovich)
See also EWL 3
Trilling, Diana (Rubin) 1905-1996 . **CLC 129**
See also CA 5-8R; 154; CANR 10, 46; INT
CANR-10; MTCW 1, 2
Trilling, Lionel 1905-1975 **CLC 9, 11, 24;
SSC 75**
See also AMWS 3; CA 9-12R; 61-64;
CANR 10, 105; CN 1, 2; DLB 28, 63;
EWL 3; INT CANR-10; MAL 5; MTCW
1, 2; RGAL 4; TUS
Trimball, W. H.
See Mencken, H(enry) L(ouis)
Tristan
See Gomez de la Serna, Ramon
Tristram
See Housman, A(lfred) E(dward)
Trogdon, William (Lewis) 1939-
See Heat-Moon, William Least
See also AAYA 66; CA 115; 119; CANR
47, 89; CPW; INT CA-119
Trollope, Anthony 1815-1882 **NCLC 6, 33,
101; SSC 28; WLC 6**
See also BRW 5; CDBLB 1832-1890; DA;
DA3; DAB; DAC; DAM MST, NOV;
DLB 21, 57, 159; RGEL 2; RGSF 2;
SATA 22
Trollope, Frances 1779-1863 **NCLC 30**
See also DLB 21, 166
Trollope, Joanna 1943- **CLC 186**
See also CA 101; CANR 58, 95, 149; CN
7; CPW; DLB 207; RHW
Trotsky, Leon 1879-1940 **TCLC 22**
See also CA 118; 167
Trotter (Cockburn), Catharine
1679-1749 **LC 8**
See also DLB 84, 252
Trotter, Wilfred 1872-1939 **TCLC 97**
Trout, Kilgore
See Farmer, Philip Jose
Trow, George W. S. 1943- **CLC 52**
See also CA 126; CANR 91
Troyat, Henri 1911- **CLC 23**
See also CA 45-48; CANR 2, 33, 67, 117;
GFL 1789 to the Present; MTCW 1
Trudeau, Garry B. **CLC 12**
See Trudeau, G.B.
See also AAYA 10; AITN 2
Trudeau, G.B. 1948-
See Trudeau, Garry B.
See also AAYA 60; CA 81-84; CANR 31;
SATA 35, 168
Truffaut, Francois 1932-1984 ... **CLC 20, 101**
See also CA 81-84; 113; CANR 34
Trumbo, Dalton 1905-1976 **CLC 19**
See also CA 21-24R; 69-72; CANR 10; CN
1, 2; DLB 26; IDFW 3, 4; YAW
Trumbull, John 1750-1831 **NCLC 30**
See also DLB 31; RGAL 4
Trundlett, Helen B.
See Eliot, T(homas) S(tearns)
Truth, Sojourner 1797(?)-1883 **NCLC 94**
See also DLB 239; FW; LAIT 2

Tryon, Thomas 1926-1991 **CLC 3, 11**
See also AITN 1; BPFB 3; CA 29-32R; 135;
CANR 32, 77; CPW; DA3; DAM POP;
HGG; MTCW 1
Tryon, Tom
See Tryon, Thomas
Ts'ao Hsueh-ch'in 1715(?)-1763 **LC 1**
Tsushima, Shuji 1909-1948
See Dazai Osamu
See also CA 107
Tsvetaeva (Efron), Marina (Ivanovna)
1892-1941 **PC 14; TCLC 7, 35**
See also CA 104; 128; CANR 73; DLB 295;
EW 11; MTCW 1, 2; RGWL 2, 3
Tuck, Lily 1938- **CLC 70**
See also CA 139; CANR 90
Tu Fu 712-770 .. **PC 9**
See Du Fu
See also DAM MULT; TWA; WP
Tunis, John R(oberts) 1889-1975 **CLC 12**
See also BYA 1; CA 61-64; CANR 62; DLB
22, 171; JRDA; MAICYA 1, 2; SATA 37;
SATA-Brief 30; YAW
Tuohy, Frank **CLC 37**
See Tuohy, John Francis
See also CN 1, 2, 3, 4, 5, 6, 7; DLB 14,
139
Tuohy, John Francis 1925-
See Tuohy, Frank
See also CA 5-8R; 178; CANR 3, 47
Turco, Lewis (Putnam) 1934- **CLC 11, 63**
See also CA 13-16R; CAAS 22; CANR 24,
51; CP 1, 2, 3, 4, 5, 6, 7; DLBY 1984;
TCLE 1:2
Turgenev, Ivan (Sergeevich)
1818-1883 **DC 7; NCLC 21, 37, 122;
SSC 7, 57; WLC 6**
See also AAYA 58; DA; DAB; DAC; DAM
MST, NOV; DFS 6; DLB 238, 284; EW
6; LATS 1:1; NFS 16; RGSF 2; RGWL 2,
3; TWA
Turgot, Anne-Robert-Jacques
1727-1781 **LC 26**
See also DLB 314
Turner, Frederick 1943- **CLC 48**
See also CA 73-76; 227; CAAE 227; CAAS
10; CANR 12, 30, 56; DLB 40, 282
Turton, James
See Crace, Jim
Tutu, Desmond M(pilo) 1931- .. **BLC 3; CLC
80**
See also BW 1, 3; CA 125; CANR 67, 81;
DAM MULT
Tutuola, Amos 1920-1997 **BLC 3; CLC 5,
14, 29**
See also AFW; BW 2, 3; CA 9-12R; 159;
CANR 27, 66; CDWLB 3; CN 1, 2, 3, 4,
5, 6; DA3; DAM MULT; DLB 125; DNFS
2; EWL 3; MTCW 1, 2; MTFW 2005;
RGEL 2; WLIT 2
Twain, Mark **SSC 6, 26, 34, 87; TCLC 6,
12, 19, 36, 48, 59, 161; WLC 6**
See Clemens, Samuel Langhorne
See also AAYA 20; AMW; AMWC 1; BPFB
3; BYA 2, 3, 11, 14; CLR 58, 60, 66; DLB
11; EXPN; EXPS; FANT; LAIT 2; MAL
5; NCFS 4; NFS 1, 6; RGAL 4; RGSF 2;
SFW 4; SSFS 1, 7, 16, 21; SUFW; TUS;
WCH; WYA; YAW
Tyler, Anne 1941- . **CLC 7, 11, 18, 28, 44, 59,
103, 205**
See also AAYA 18, 60; AMWS 4; BEST
89:1; BPFB 3; BYA 12; CA 9-12R; CANR
11, 33, 53, 109, 132; CDALBS; CN 1, 2,
3, 4, 5, 6, 7; CPW; CSW; DAM NOV,
POP; DLB 6, 143; DLBY 1982; EWL 3;
EXPN; LATS 1:2; MAL 5; MAWW;
MTCW 1, 2; MTFW 2005; NFS 2, 7, 10;
RGAL 4; SATA 7, 90; SSFS 17; TCLE
1:2; TUS; YAW

Tyler, Royall 1757-1826 **NCLC 3**
See also DLB 37; RGAL 4

Tynan, Katharine 1861-1931 **TCLC 3**
See also CA 104; 167; DLB 153, 240; FW

Tyndale, William c. 1484-1536 **LC 103**
See also DLB 132

Tyutchev, Fyodor 1803-1873 **NCLC 34**

Tzara, Tristan 1896-1963 **CLC 47; PC 27; TCLC 168**
See also CA 153; 89-92; DAM POET; EWL 3; MTCW 2

Uchida, Yoshiko 1921-1992 **AAL**
See also AAYA 16; BYA 2, 3; CA 13-16R; 139; CANR 6, 22, 47, 61; CDALBS; CLR 6, 56; CWRI 5; DLB 312; JRDA; MAI-CYA 1, 2; MTCW 1, 2; MTFW 2005; SAAS 1; SATA 1, 53; SATA-Obit 72

Udall, Nicholas 1504-1556 **LC 84**
See also DLB 62; RGEL 2

Ueda Akinari 1734-1809 **NCLC 131**

Uhry, Alfred 1936- **CLC 55**
See also CA 127; 133; CAD; CANR 112; CD 5, 6; CSW; DA3; DAM DRAM, POP; DFS 11, 15; INT CA-133; MTFW 2005

Ulf, Haerved
See Strindberg, (Johan) August

Ulf, Harved
See Strindberg, (Johan) August

Ulibarri, Sabine R(eyes)
1919-2003 **CLC 83; HLCS 2**
See also CA 131; 214; CANR 81; DAM MULT; DLB 82; HW 1, 2; RGSF 2

Unamuno (y Jugo), Miguel de
1864-1936 .. **HLC 2; SSC 11, 69; TCLC 2, 9, 148**
See also CA 104; 131; CANR 81; DAM MULT, NOV; DLB 108, 322; EW 8; EWL 3; HW 1, 2; MTCW 1, 2; MTFW 2005; RGSF 2; RGWL 2, 3; SSFS 20; TWA

Uncle Shelby
See Silverstein, Shel(don Allan)

Undercliffe, Errol
See Campbell, (John) Ramsey

Underwood, Miles
See Glassco, John

Undset, Sigrid 1882-1949 .. **TCLC 3; WLC 6**
See also CA 104; 129; DA; DA3; DAB; DAC; DAM MST, NOV; DLB 293; EW 9; EWL 3; FW; MTCW 1, 2; MTFW 2005; RGWL 2, 3

Ungaretti, Giuseppe 1888-1970 ... **CLC 7, 11, 15; PC 57**
See also CA 19-20; 25-28R; CAP 2; DLB 114; EW 10; EWL 3; PFS 20; RGWL 2, 3; WLIT 7

Unger, Douglas 1952- **CLC 34**
See also CA 130; CANR 94

Unsworth, Barry (Forster) 1930- **CLC 76, 127**
See also BRWS 7; CA 25-28R; CANR 30, 54, 125; CN 6, 7; DLB 194, 326

Updike, John 1932- . **CLC 1, 2, 3, 5, 7, 9, 13, 15, 23, 34, 43, 70, 139, 214; SSC 13, 27; WLC 6**
See also AAYA 36; AMW; AMWC 1; AMWR 1; BPFB 3; BYA 12; CA 1-4R; CABS 1; CANR 4, 33, 51, 94, 133; CDALB 1968-1988; CN 1, 2, 3, 4, 5, 6, 7; CP 1, 2, 3, 4, 5, 6, 7; CPW 1; DA; DA3; DAB; DAC; DAM MST, NOV, POET, POP; DLB 2, 5, 143, 218, 227; DLBD 3; DLBY 1980, 1982, 1997; EWL 3; EXPP; HGG; MAL 5; MTCW 1, 2; MTFW 2005; NFS 12; RGAL 4; RGSF 2; SSFS 3, 19; TUS

Updike, John Hoyer
See Updike, John

Upshaw, Margaret Mitchell
See Mitchell, Margaret (Munnerlyn)

Upton, Mark
See Sanders, Lawrence

Upward, Allen 1863-1926 **TCLC 85**
See also CA 117; 187; DLB 36

Urdang, Constance (Henriette)
1922-1996 **CLC 47**
See also CA 21-24R; CANR 9, 24; CP 1, 2, 3, 4, 5, 6; CWP

Uriel, Henry
See Faust, Frederick (Schiller)

Uris, Leon (Marcus) 1924-2003 ... **CLC 7, 32**
See also AITN 1, 2; BEST 89:2; BPFB 3; CA 1-4R; 217; CANR 1, 40, 65, 123; CN 1, 2, 3, 4, 5, 6; CPW 1; DA3; DAM NOV, POP; MTCW 1, 2; MTFW 2005; RGHL; SATA 49; SATA-Obit 146

Urista (Heredia), Alberto (Baltazar)
1947- ... **HLCS 1**
See Alurista
See also CA 182; CANR 2, 32; HW 1

Urmuz
See Codrescu, Andrei

Urquhart, Guy
See McAlmon, Robert (Menzies)

Urquhart, Jane 1949- **CLC 90**
See also CA 113; CANR 32, 68, 116; CCA 1; DAC

Usigli, Rodolfo 1905-1979 **HLCS 1**
See also CA 131; DLB 305; EWL 3; HW 1; LAW

Usk, Thomas (?)-1388 **CMLC 76**
See also DLB 146

Ustinov, Peter (Alexander)
1921-2004 **CLC 1**
See also AITN 1; CA 13-16R; 225; CANR 25, 51; CBD; CD 5, 6; DLB 13; MTCW 2

U Tam'si, Gerald Felix Tchicaya
See Tchicaya, Gerald Felix

U Tam'si, Tchicaya
See Tchicaya, Gerald Felix

Vachss, Andrew 1942- **CLC 106**
See also CA 118, 214; CAAE 214; CANR 44, 95, 153; CMW 4

Vachss, Andrew H.
See Vachss, Andrew

Vachss, Andrew Henry
See Vachss, Andrew

Vaculik, Ludvik 1926- **CLC 7**
See also CA 53-56; CANR 72; CWW 2; DLB 232; EWL 3

Vaihinger, Hans 1852-1933 **TCLC 71**
See also CA 116; 166

Valdez, Luis (Miguel) 1940- **CLC 84; DC 10; HLC 2**
See also CA 101; CAD; CANR 32, 81; CD 5, 6; DAM MULT; DFS 5; DLB 122; EWL 3; HW 1; LAIT 4; LLW

Valenzuela, Luisa 1938- **CLC 31, 104; HLCS 2; SSC 14, 82**
See also CA 101; CANR 32, 65, 123; CD-WLB 3; CWW 2; DAM MULT; DLB 113; EWL 3; FW; HW 1, 2; LAW; RGSF 2; RGWL 3

Valera y Alcala-Galiano, Juan
1824-1905 **TCLC 10**
See also CA 106

Valerius Maximus fl. 20- **CMLC 64**
See also DLB 211

Valery, (Ambroise) Paul (Toussaint Jules)
1871-1945 **PC 9; TCLC 4, 15**
See also CA 104; 122; DA3; DAM POET; DLB 258; EW 8; EWL 3; GFL 1789 to the Present; MTCW 1, 2; MTFW 2005; RGWL 2, 3; TWA

Valle-Inclan, Ramon (Maria) del
1866-1936 **HLC 2; TCLC 5**
See del Valle-Inclan, Ramon (Maria)
See also CA 106; 153; CANR 80; DAM MULT; DLB 134; EW 8; EWL 3; HW 2; RGSF 2; RGWL 2, 3

Vallejo, Antonio Buero
See Buero Vallejo, Antonio

Vallejo, Cesar (Abraham)
1892-1938 **HLC 2; TCLC 3, 56**
See also CA 105; 153; DAM MULT; DLB 290; EWL 3; HW 1; LAW; RGWL 2, 3

Valles, Jules 1832-1885 **NCLC 71**
See also DLB 123; GFL 1789 to the Present

Vallette, Marguerite Eymery
1860-1953 **TCLC 67**
See Rachilde
See also CA 182; DLB 123, 192

Valle Y Pena, Ramon del
See Valle-Inclan, Ramon (Maria) del

Van Ash, Cay 1918-1994 **CLC 34**
See also CA 220

Vanbrugh, Sir John 1664-1726 **LC 21**
See also BRW 2; DAM DRAM; DLB 80; IDTP; RGEL 2

Van Campen, Karl
See Campbell, John W(ood, Jr.)

Vance, Gerald
See Silverberg, Robert

Vance, Jack 1916-
See Queen, Ellery; Vance, John Holbrook
See also CA 29-32R; CANR 17, 65, 154; CMW 4; MTCW 1

Vance, John Holbrook **CLC 35**
See Vance, Jack
See also DLB 8; FANT; SCFW 1, 2; SFW 4; SUFW 1, 2

Van Den Bogarde, Derek Jules Gaspard
Ulric Niven 1921-1999 **CLC 14**
See Bogarde, Dirk
See also CA 77-80; 179

Vandenburgh, Jane **CLC 59**
See also CA 168

Vanderhaeghe, Guy 1951- **CLC 41**
See also BPFB 3; CA 113; CANR 72, 145; CN 7

van der Post, Laurens (Jan)
1906-1996 **CLC 5**
See also AFW; CA 5-8R; 155; CANR 35; CN 1, 2, 3, 4, 5, 6; DLB 204; RGEL 2

van de Wetering, Janwillem 1931- ... **CLC 47**
See also CA 49-52; CANR 4, 62, 90; CMW 4

Van Dine, S. S. **TCLC 23**
See Wright, Willard Huntington
See also DLB 306; MSW

Van Doren, Carl (Clinton)
1885-1950 **TCLC 18**
See also CA 111; 168

Van Doren, Mark 1894-1972 **CLC 6, 10**
See also CA 1-4R; 37-40R; CANR 3; CN 1; CP 1; DLB 45, 284; MAL 5; MTCW 1, 2; RGAL 4

Van Druten, John (William)
1901-1957 **TCLC 2**
See also CA 104; 161; DLB 10; MAL 5; RGAL 4

Van Duyn, Mona (Jane) 1921-2004 .. **CLC 3, 7, 63, 116**
See also CA 9-12R; 234; CANR 7, 38, 60, 116; CP 1, 2, 3, 4, 5, 6, 7; CWP; DAM POET; DLB 5; MAL 5; MTFW 2005; PFS 20

Van Dyne, Edith
See Baum, L(yman) Frank

van Itallie, Jean-Claude 1936- **CLC 3**
See also CA 45-48; CAAS 2; CAD; CANR 1, 48; CD 5, 6; DLB 7

Van Loot, Cornelius Obenchain
See Roberts, Kenneth (Lewis)

van Ostaijen, Paul 1896-1928 **TCLC 33**
See also CA 163

Van Peebles, Melvin 1932- **CLC 2, 20**
See also BW 2, 3; CA 85-88; CANR 27,
67, 82; DAM MULT

van Schendel, Arthur(-Francois-Emile)
1874-1946 **TCLC 56**
See also EWL 3

Vansittart, Peter 1920- **CLC 42**
See also CA 1-4R; CANR 3, 49, 90; CN 4,
5, 6, 7; RHW

Van Vechten, Carl 1880-1964 ... **CLC 33; HR**
1:3
See also AMWS 2; CA 183; 89-92; DLB 4,
9, 51; RGAL 4

van Vogt, A(lfred) E(lton) 1912-2000 . **CLC 1**
See also BPFB 3; BYA 13, 14; CA 21-24R;
190; CANR 28; DLB 8, 251; SATA 14;
SATA-Obit 124; SCFW 1, 2; SFW 4

Vara, Madeleine
See Jackson, Laura (Riding)

Varda, Agnes 1928- **CLC 16**
See also CA 116; 122

Vargas Llosa, Jorge Mario Pedro
See Vargas Llosa, Mario

Vargas Llosa, Mario 1936- .. **CLC 3, 6, 9, 10,**
15, 31, 42, 85, 181; HLC 2
See Llosa, Jorge Mario Pedro Vargas
See also BPFB 3; CA 73-76; CANR 18, 32,
42, 67, 116, 140; CDWLB 3; CWW 2;
DA; DA3; DAB; DAC; DAM MST,
MULT, NOV; DLB 145; DNFS 2; EWL
3; HW 1, 2; LAIT 5; LATS 1:2; LAW;
LAWS 1; MTCW 1, 2; MTFW 2005;
RGWL 2; SSFS 14; TWA; WLIT 1

Varnhagen von Ense, Rahel
1771-1833 **NCLC 130**
See also DLB 90

Vasari, Giorgio 1511-1574 **LC 114**

Vasilikos, Vasiles
See Vassilikos, Vassilis

Vasiliu, George
See Bacovia, George

Vasiliu, Gheorghe
See Bacovia, George
See also CA 123; 189

Vassa, Gustavus
See Equiano, Olaudah

Vassilikos, Vassilis 1933- **CLC 4, 8**
See also CA 81-84; CANR 75, 149; EWL 3

Vaughan, Henry 1621-1695 **LC 27**
See also BRW 2; DLB 131; PAB; RGEL 2

Vaughn, Stephanie **CLC 62**

Vazov, Ivan (Minchov) 1850-1921 . **TCLC 25**
See also CA 121; 167; CDWLB 4; DLB
147

Veblen, Thorstein B(unde)
1857-1929 **TCLC 31**
See also AMWS 1; CA 115; 165; DLB 246;
MAL 5

Vega, Lope de 1562-1635 ... **HLCS 2; LC 23,**
119
See also EW 2; RGWL 2, 3

Veldeke, Heinrich von c. 1145-c.
1190 **CMLC 85**

Vendler, Helen (Hennessy) 1933- ... **CLC 138**
See also CA 41-44R; CANR 25, 72, 136;
MTCW 1, 2; MTFW 2005

Venison, Alfred
See Pound, Ezra (Weston Loomis)

Ventsel, Elena Sergeevna 1907-2002
See Grekova, I.
See also CA 154

Verdi, Marie de
See Mencken, H(enry) L(ouis)

Verdu, Matilde
See Cela, Camilo Jose

Verga, Giovanni (Carmelo)
1840-1922 **SSC 21, 87; TCLC 3**
See also CA 104; 123; CANR 101; EW 7;
EWL 3; RGSF 2; RGWL 2, 3; WLIT 7

Vergil 70B.C.-19B.C. ... **CMLC 9, 40; PC 12;**
WLCS
See Virgil
See also AW 2; DA; DA3; DAB; DAC;
DAM MST, POET; EFS 1; LMFS 1

Vergil, Polydore c. 1470-1555 **LC 108**
See also DLB 132

Verhaeren, Emile (Adolphe Gustave)
1855-1916 **TCLC 12**
See also CA 109; EWL 3; GFL 1789 to the
Present

Verlaine, Paul (Marie) 1844-1896 .. **NCLC 2,**
51; PC 2, 32
See also DAM POET; DLB 217; EW 7;
GFL 1789 to the Present; LMFS 2; RGWL
2, 3; TWA

Verne, Jules (Gabriel) 1828-1905 ... **TCLC 6,**
52
See also AAYA 16; BYA 4; CA 110; 131;
CLR 88; DA3; DLB 123; GFL 1789 to
the Present; JRDA; LAIT 2; LMFS 2;
MAICYA 1, 2; MTFW 2005; RGWL 2, 3;
SATA 21; SCFW 1, 2; SFW 4; TWA;
WCH

Verus, Marcus Annius
See Aurelius, Marcus

Very, Jones 1813-1880 **NCLC 9**
See also DLB 1, 243; RGAL 4

Vesaas, Tarjei 1897-1970 **CLC 48**
See also CA 190; 29-32R; DLB 297; EW
11; EWL 3; RGWL 3

Vialis, Gaston
See Simenon, Georges (Jacques Christian)

Vian, Boris 1920-1959(?) **TCLC 9**
See also CA 106; 164; CANR 111; DLB
72, 321; EWL 3; GFL 1789 to the Present;
MTCW 2; RGWL 2, 3

Viaud, (Louis Marie) Julien 1850-1923
See Loti, Pierre
See also CA 107

Vicar, Henry
See Felsen, Henry Gregor

Vicente, Gil 1465-c. 1536 **LC 99**
See also DLB 318; IDTP; RGWL 2, 3

Vicker, Angus
See Felsen, Henry Gregor

Vidal, Eugene Luther Gore
See Vidal, Gore

Vidal, Gore 1925- **CLC 2, 4, 6, 8, 10, 22,**
33, 72, 142
See Box, Edgar
See also AAYA 64; AITN 1; AMWS 4;
BEST 90:2; BPFB 3; CA 5-8R; CAD;
CANR 13, 45, 65, 100, 132; CD 5, 6;
CDALBS; CN 1, 2, 3, 4, 5, 6, 7; CPW;
DA3; DAM NOV, POP; DFS 2; DLB 6,
152; EWL 3; INT CANR-13; MAL 5;
MTCW 1, 2; MTFW 2005; RGAL 4;
RHW; TUS

Viereck, Peter 1916-2006 **CLC 4; PC 27**
See also CA 1-4R; CANR 1, 47; CP 1, 2, 3,
4, 5, 6, 7; DLB 5; MAL 5; PFS 9, 14

Viereck, Peter Robert Edwin
See Viereck, Peter

Vigny, Alfred (Victor) de
1797-1863 **NCLC 7, 102; PC 26**
See also DAM POET; DLB 119, 192, 217;
EW 5; GFL 1789 to the Present; RGWL
2, 3

Vilakazi, Benedict Wallet
1906-1947 **TCLC 37**
See also CA 168

Villa, Jose Garcia 1914-1997 ... **AAL; PC 22;**
TCLC 176
See also CA 25-28R; CANR 12, 118; CP 1,
2, 3, 4; DLB 312; EWL 3; EXPP

Villard, Oswald Garrison
1872-1949 **TCLC 160**
See also CA 113; 162; DLB 25, 91

Villarreal, Jose Antonio 1924- **HLC 2**
See also CA 133; CANR 93; DAM MULT;
DLB 82; HW 1; LAIT 4; RGAL 4

Villaurrutia, Xavier 1903-1950 **TCLC 80**
See also CA 192; EWL 3; HW 1; LAW

Villaverde, Cirilo 1812-1894 **NCLC 121**
See also LAW

Villehardouin, Geoffroi de
1150(?)-1218(?) **CMLC 38**

Villiers, George 1628-1687 **LC 107**
See also DLB 80; RGEL 2

Villiers de l'Isle Adam, Jean Marie Mathias
Philippe Auguste 1838-1889 ... **NCLC 3;**
SSC 14
See also DLB 123, 192; GFL 1789 to the
Present; RGSF 2

Villon, Francois 1431-1463(?) . **LC 62; PC 13**
See also DLB 208; EW 2; RGWL 2, 3;
TWA

Vine, Barbara **CLC 50**
See Rendell, Ruth (Barbara)
See also BEST 90:4

Vinge, Joan (Carol) D(ennison)
1948- **CLC 30; SSC 24**
See also AAYA 32; BPFB 3; CA 93-96;
CANR 72; SATA 36, 113; SFW 4; YAW

Viola, Herman J(oseph) 1938- **CLC 70**
See also CA 61-64; CANR 8, 23, 48, 91;
SATA 126

Violis, G.
See Simenon, Georges (Jacques Christian)

Viramontes, Helena Maria 1954- **HLCS 2**
See also CA 159; DLB 122; HW 2; LLW

Virgil
See Vergil
See also CDWLB 1; DLB 211; LAIT 1;
RGWL 2, 3; WLIT 8; WP

Visconti, Luchino 1906-1976 **CLC 16**
See also CA 81-84; 65-68; CANR 39

Vitry, Jacques de
See Jacques de Vitry

Vittorini, Elio 1908-1966 **CLC 6, 9, 14**
See also CA 133; 25-28R; DLB 264; EW
12; EWL 3; RGWL 2, 3

Vivekananda, Swami 1863-1902 **TCLC 88**

Vizenor, Gerald Robert 1934- **CLC 103;**
NNAL
See also CA 13-16R, 205; CAAE 205;
CAAS 22; CANR 5, 21, 44, 67; DAM
MULT; DLB 175, 227; MTCW 2; MTFW
2005; TCWW 2

Vizinczey, Stephen 1933- **CLC 40**
See also CA 128; CCA 1; INT CA-128

Vliet, R(ussell) G(ordon)
1929-1984 **CLC 22**
See also CA 37-40R; 112; CANR 18; CP 2,
3

Vogau, Boris Andreyevich 1894-1938
See Pilnyak, Boris
See also CA 123; 218

Vogel, Paula A(nne) 1951- ... **CLC 76; DC 19**
See also CA 108; CAD; CANR 119, 140;
CD 5, 6; CWD; DFS 14; MTFW 2005;
RGAL 4

Voigt, Cynthia 1942- **CLC 30**
See also AAYA 3, 30; BYA 1, 3, 6, 7, 8;
CA 106; CANR 18, 37, 40, 94, 145; CLR
13, 48; INT CANR-18; JRDA; LAIT 5;
MAICYA 1, 2; MAICYAS 1; MTFW
2005; SATA 48, 79, 116, 160; SATA-Brief
33; WYA; YAW

Voigt, Ellen Bryant 1943- **CLC 54**
See also CA 69-72; CANR 11, 29, 55, 115;
CP 5, 6, 7; CSW; CWP; DLB 120; PFS
23

Voinovich, Vladimir 1932- .. **CLC 10, 49, 147**
See also CA 81-84; CAAS 12; CANR 33,
67, 150; CWW 2; DLB 302; MTCW 1

Voinovich, Vladimir Nikolaevich
See Voinovich, Vladimir

Vollmann, William T. 1959- **CLC 89**
See also CA 134; CANR 67, 116; CN 7;
CPW; DA3; DAM NOV, POP; MTCW 2;
MTFW 2005

Voloshinov, V. N.
See Bakhtin, Mikhail Mikhailovich

Voltaire 1694-1778 . **LC 14, 79, 110; SSC 12;**
WLC 6
See also BYA 13; DA; DA3; DAB; DAC;
DAM DRAM, MST; DLB 314; EW 4;
GFL Beginnings to 1789; LATS 1:1;
LMFS 1; NFS 7; RGWL 2, 3; TWA

von Aschendrof, Baron Ignatz
See Ford, Ford Madox

von Chamisso, Adelbert
See Chamisso, Adelbert von

von Daeniken, Erich 1935- **CLC 30**
See also AITN 1; CA 37-40R; CANR 17,
44

von Daniken, Erich
See von Daeniken, Erich

von Hartmann, Eduard
1842-1906 **TCLC 96**

von Hayek, Friedrich August
See Hayek, F(riedrich) A(ugust von)

von Heidenstam, (Carl Gustaf) Verner
See Heidenstam, (Carl Gustaf) Verner von

von Heyse, Paul (Johann Ludwig)
See Heyse, Paul (Johann Ludwig von)

von Hofmannsthal, Hugo
See Hofmannsthal, Hugo von

von Horvath, Odon
See von Horvath, Odon

von Horvath, Odon
See von Horvath, Odon

von Horvath, Odon 1901-1938 **TCLC 45**
See von Horvath, Oedoen
See also CA 118; 194; DLB 85, 124; RGWL
2, 3

von Horvath, Oedoen
See von Horvath, Odon
See also CA 184

von Kleist, Heinrich
See Kleist, Heinrich von

von Liliencron, (Friedrich Adolf Axel)
Detlev
See Liliencron, (Friedrich Adolf Axel) De-
tlev von

Vonnegut, Kurt, Jr.
See Vonnegut, Kurt

Vonnegut, Kurt 1922- ... **CLC 1, 2, 3, 4, 5, 8,**
12, 22, 40, 60, 111, 212; SSC 8; WLC 6
See also AAYA 6, 44; AITN 1; AMWS 2;
BEST 90:4; BPFB 3; BYA 3, 14; CA
1-4R; CANR 1, 25, 49, 75, 92; CDALB
1968-1988; CN 1, 2, 3, 4, 5, 6, 7; CPW 1;
DA; DA3; DAB; DAC; DAM MST, NOV,
POP; DLB 2, 8, 152; DLBD 3; DLBY
1980; EWL 3; EXPN; EXPS; LAIT 4;
LMFS 2; MAL 5; MTCW 1, 2; MTFW
2005; NFS 3; RGAL 4; SCFW; SFW 4;
SSFS 5; TUS; YAW

Von Rachen, Kurt
See Hubbard, L. Ron

von Sternberg, Josef
See Sternberg, Josef von

Vorster, Gordon 1924- **CLC 34**
See also CA 133

Vosce, Trudie
See Ozick, Cynthia

Voznesensky, Andrei (Andreievich)
1933- **CLC 1, 15, 57**
See Voznesensky, Andrey
See also CA 89-92; CANR 37; CWW 2;
DAM POET; MTCW 1

Voznesensky, Andrey
See Voznesensky, Andrei (Andreievich)
See also EWL 3

Wace, Robert c. 1100-c. 1175 **CMLC 55**
See also DLB 146

Waddington, Miriam 1917-2004 **CLC 28**
See also CA 21-24R; 225; CANR 12, 30;
CCA 1; CP 1, 2, 3, 4, 5, 6, 7; DLB 68

Wagman, Fredrica 1937- **CLC 7**
See also CA 97-100; INT CA-97-100

Wagner, Linda W.
See Wagner-Martin, Linda (C.)

Wagner, Linda Welshimer
See Wagner-Martin, Linda (C.)

Wagner, Richard 1813-1883 **NCLC 9, 119**
See also DLB 129; EW 6

Wagner-Martin, Linda (C.) 1936- **CLC 50**
See also CA 159; CANR 135

Wagoner, David (Russell) 1926- **CLC 3, 5,**
15; PC 33
See also AMWS 9; CA 1-4R; CAAS 3;
CANR 2, 71; CN 1, 2, 3, 4, 5, 6, 7; CP 1,
2, 3, 4, 5, 6, 7; DLB 5, 256; SATA 14;
TCWW 1, 2

Wah, Fred(erick James) 1939- **CLC 44**
See also CA 107; 141; CP 1, 6, 7; DLB 60

Wahloo, Per 1926-1975 **CLC 7**
See also BPFB 3; CA 61-64; CANR 73;
CMW 4; MSW

Wahloo, Peter
See Wahloo, Per

Wain, John (Barrington) 1925-1994 . **CLC 2,**
11, 15, 46
See also CA 5-8R; 145; CAAS 4; CANR
23, 54; CDBLB 1960 to Present; CN 1, 2,
3, 4, 5; CP 1, 2, 3, 4, 5; DLB 15, 27, 139,
155; EWL 3; MTCW 1, 2; MTFW 2005

Wajda, Andrzej 1926- **CLC 16, 219**
See also CA 102

Wakefield, Dan 1932- **CLC 7**
See also CA 21-24R; 211; CAAE 211;
CAAS 7; CN 4, 5, 6, 7

Wakefield, Herbert Russell
1888-1965 **TCLC 120**
See also CA 5-8R; CANR 77; HGG; SUFW

Wakoski, Diane 1937- **CLC 2, 4, 7, 9, 11,**
40; PC 15
See also CA 13-16R; 216; CAAE 216;
CAAS 1; CANR 9, 60, 106; CP 1, 2, 3, 4,
5, 6, 7; CWP; DAM POET; DLB 5; INT
CANR-9; MAL 5; MTCW 2; MTFW
2005

Wakoski-Sherbell, Diane
See Wakoski, Diane

Walcott, Derek (Alton) 1930- ... **BLC 3; CLC**
2, 4, 9, 14, 25, 42, 67, 76, 160; DC 7;
PC 46
See also BW 2; CA 89-92; CANR 26, 47,
75, 80, 130; CBD; CD 5, 6; CDWLB 3;
CP 1, 2, 3, 4, 5, 6, 7; DA3; DAB; DAC;
DAM MST, MULT, POET; DLB 117;
DLBY 1981; DNFS 1; EFS 1; EWL 3;
LMFS 2; MTCW 1, 2; MTFW 2005; PFS
6; RGEL 2; TWA; WWE 1

Waldman, Anne (Lesley) 1945- **CLC 7**
See also BG 1:3; CA 37-40R; CAAS 17;
CANR 34, 69, 116; CP 1, 2, 3, 4, 5, 6, 7;
CWP; DLB 16

Waldo, E. Hunter
See Sturgeon, Theodore (Hamilton)

Waldo, Edward Hamilton
See Sturgeon, Theodore (Hamilton)

Walker, Alice 1944- **BLC 3; CLC 5, 6, 9,**
19, 27, 46, 58, 103, 167; PC 30; SSC 5;
WLCS
See also AAYA 3, 33; AFAW 1, 2; AMWS
3; BEST 89:4; BPFB 3; BW 2, 3; CA 37-
40R; CANR 9, 27, 49, 66, 82, 131;
CDALB 1968-1988; CN 4, 5, 6, 7; CPW;
CSW; DA; DA3; DAB; DAC; DAM MST,
MULT, NOV, POET, POP; DLB 6, 33,
143; EWL 3; EXPN; EXPS; FL 1:6; FW;
INT CANR-27; LAIT 3; MAL 5; MAWW;
MTCW 1, 2; MTFW 2005; NFS 5; RGAL
4; RGSF 2; SATA 31; SSFS 2, 11; TUS;
YAW

Walker, Alice Malsenior
See Walker, Alice

Walker, David Harry 1911-1992 **CLC 14**
See also CA 1-4R; 137; CANR 1; CN 1, 2;
CWRI 5; SATA 8; SATA-Obit 71

Walker, Edward Joseph 1934-2004
See Walker, Ted
See also CA 21-24R; 226; CANR 12, 28,
53

Walker, George F(rederick) 1947- .. **CLC 44,**
61
See also CA 103; CANR 21, 43, 59; CD 5,
6; DAB; DAC; DAM MST; DLB 60

Walker, Joseph A. 1935-2003 **CLC 19**
See also BW 1, 3; CA 89-92; CAD; CANR
26, 143; CD 5, 6; DAM DRAM, MST;
DFS 12; DLB 38

Walker, Margaret (Abigail)
1915-1998 **BLC; CLC 1, 6; PC 20;**
TCLC 129
See also AFAW 1, 2; BW 2, 3; CA 73-76;
172; CANR 26, 54, 76, 136; CN 1, 2, 3,
4, 5, 6; CP 1, 2, 3, 4, 5, 6; CSW; DAM
MULT; DLB 76, 152; EXPP; FW; MAL
5; MTCW 1, 2; MTFW 2005; RGAL 4;
RHW

Walker, Ted **CLC 13**
See Walker, Edward Joseph
See also CP 1, 2, 3, 4, 5, 6, 7; DLB 40

Wallace, David Foster 1962- ... **CLC 50, 114;**
SSC 68
See also AAYA 50; AMWS 10; CA 132;
CANR 59, 133; CN 7; DA3; MTCW 2;
MTFW 2005

Wallace, Dexter
See Masters, Edgar Lee

Wallace, (Richard Horatio) Edgar
1875-1932 **TCLC 57**
See also CA 115; 218; CMW 4; DLB 70;
MSW; RGEL 2

Wallace, Irving 1916-1990 **CLC 7, 13**
See also AITN 1; BPFB 3; CA 1-4R; 132;
CAAS 1; CANR 1, 27; CPW; DAM NOV,
POP; INT CANR-27; MTCW 1, 2

Wallant, Edward Lewis 1926-1962 ... **CLC 5,**
10
See also CA 1-4R; CANR 22; DLB 2, 28,
143, 299; EWL 3; MAL 5; MTCW 1, 2;
RGAL 4; RGHL

Wallas, Graham 1858-1932 **TCLC 91**

Waller, Edmund 1606-1687 **LC 86; PC 72**
See also BRW 2; DAM POET; DLB 126;
PAB; RGEL 2

Walley, Byron
See Card, Orson Scott

Walpole, Horace 1717-1797 **LC 2, 49**
See also BRW 3; DLB 39, 104, 213; GL 3;
HGG; LMFS 1; RGEL 2; SUFW 1; TEA

Walpole, Hugh (Seymour)
1884-1941 **TCLC 5**
See also CA 104; 165; DLB 34; HGG;
MTCW 2; RGEL 2; RHW

Walrond, Eric (Derwent) 1898-1966 . **HR 1:3**
See also BW 1; CA 125; DLB 51

Walser, Martin 1927- **CLC 27, 183**
See also CA 57-60; CANR 8, 46, 145;
CWW 2; DLB 75, 124; EWL 3

Walser, Robert 1878-1956 **SSC 20; TCLC 18**
See also CA 118; 165; CANR 100; DLB 66; EWL 3

Walsh, Gillian Paton
See Paton Walsh, Gillian

Walsh, Jill Paton **CLC 35**
See Paton Walsh, Gillian
See also CLR 2, 65; WYA

Walter, Villiam Christian
See Andersen, Hans Christian

Walters, Anna L(ee) 1946- **NNAL**
See also CA 73-76

Walther von der Vogelweide c. 1170-1228 **CMLC 56**

Walton, Izaak 1593-1683 **LC 72**
See also BRW 2; CDBLB Before 1660; DLB 151, 213; RGEL 2

Wambaugh, Joseph (Aloysius), Jr. 1937- **CLC 3, 18**
See also AITN 1; BEST 89:3; BPFB 3; CA 33-36R; CANR 42, 65, 115; CMW 4; CPW 1; DA3; DAM NOV, POP; DLB 6; DLBY 1983; MSW; MTCW 1, 2

Wang Wei 699(?)-761(?) **PC 18**
See also TWA

Warburton, William 1698-1779 **LC 97**
See also DLB 104

Ward, Arthur Henry Sarsfield 1883-1959
See Rohmer, Sax
See also CA 108; 173; CMW 4; HGG

Ward, Douglas Turner 1930- **CLC 19**
See also BW 1; CA 81-84; CAD; CANR 27; CD 5, 6; DLB 7, 38

Ward, E. D.
See Lucas, E(dward) V(errall)

Ward, Mrs. Humphry 1851-1920
See Ward, Mary Augusta
See also RGEL 2

Ward, Mary Augusta 1851-1920 ... **TCLC 55**
See Ward, Mrs. Humphry
See also DLB 18

Ward, Nathaniel 1578(?)-1652 **LC 114**
See also DLB 24

Ward, Peter
See Faust, Frederick (Schiller)

Warhol, Andy 1928(?)-1987 **CLC 20**
See also AAYA 12; BEST 89:4; CA 89-92; 121; CANR 34

Warner, Francis (Robert le Plastrier) 1937- **CLC 14**
See also CA 53-56; CANR 11; CP 1, 2, 3, 4

Warner, Marina 1946- **CLC 59**
See also CA 65-68; CANR 21, 55, 118; CN 5, 6, 7; DLB 194; MTFW 2005

Warner, Rex (Ernest) 1905-1986 **CLC 45**
See also CA 89-92; 119; CN 1, 2, 3, 4; CP 1, 2, 3, 4; DLB 15; RGEL 2; RHW

Warner, Susan (Bogert) 1819-1885 **NCLC 31, 146**
See also DLB 3, 42, 239, 250, 254

Warner, Sylvia (Constance) Ashton
See Ashton-Warner, Sylvia (Constance)

Warner, Sylvia Townsend 1893-1978 .. **CLC 7, 19; SSC 23; TCLC 131**
See also BRWS 7; CA 61-64; 77-80; CANR 16, 60, 104; CN 1, 2; DLB 34, 139; EWL 3; FANT; FW; MTCW 1, 2; RGEL 2; RGSF 2; RHW

Warren, Mercy Otis 1728-1814 **NCLC 13**
See also DLB 31, 200; RGAL 4; TUS

Warren, Robert Penn 1905-1989 .. **CLC 1, 4, 6, 8, 10, 13, 18, 39, 53, 59; PC 37; SSC 4, 58; WLC 6**
See also AITN 1; AMW; AMWC 2; BPFB 3; BYA 1; CA 13-16R; 129; CANR 10, 47; CDALB 1968-1988; CN 1, 2, 3, 4; CP 1, 2, 3, 4; DA; DA3; DAB; DAC; DAM MST, NOV, POET; DLB 2, 48, 152, 320; DLBY 1980, 1989; EWL 3; INT CANR-10; MAL 5; MTCW 1, 2; MTFW 2005; NFS 13; RGAL 4; RGSF 2; RHW; SATA 46; SATA-Obit 63; SSFS 8; TUS

Warrigal, Jack
See Furphy, Joseph

Warshofsky, Isaac
See Singer, Isaac Bashevis

Warton, Joseph 1722-1800 ... **LC 128; NCLC 118**
See also DLB 104, 109; RGEL 2

Warton, Thomas 1728-1790 **LC 15, 82**
See also DAM POET; DLB 104, 109; RGEL 2

Waruk, Kona
See Harris, (Theodore) Wilson

Warung, Price **TCLC 45**
See Astley, William
See also DLB 230; RGEL 2

Warwick, Jarvis
See Garner, Hugh
See also CCA 1

Washington, Alex
See Harris, Mark

Washington, Booker T(aliaferro) 1856-1915 **BLC 3; TCLC 10**
See also BW 1; CA 114; 125; DA3; DAM MULT; LAIT 2; RGAL 4; SATA 28

Washington, George 1732-1799 **LC 25**
See also DLB 31

Wassermann, (Karl) Jakob 1873-1934 **TCLC 6**
See also CA 104; 163; DLB 66; EWL 3

Wasserstein, Wendy 1950-2006 . **CLC 32, 59, 90, 183; DC 4**
See also AMWS 15; CA 121; 129; 247; CABS 3; CAD; CANR 53, 75, 128; CD 5, 6; CWD; DA3; DAM DRAM; DFS 5, 17; DLB 228; EWL 3; FW; INT CA-129; MAL 5; MTCW 2; MTFW 2005; SATA 94

Waterhouse, Keith (Spencer) 1929- . **CLC 47**
See also CA 5-8R; CANR 38, 67, 109; CBD; CD 6; CN 1, 2, 3, 4, 5, 6, 7; DLB 13, 15; MTCW 1, 2; MTFW 2005

Waters, Frank (Joseph) 1902-1995 ... **CLC 88**
See also CA 5-8R; 149; CAAS 13; CANR 3, 18, 63, 121; DLB 212; DLBY 1986; RGAL 4; TCWW 1, 2

Waters, Mary C. **CLC 70**

Waters, Roger 1944- **CLC 35**

Watkins, Frances Ellen
See Harper, Frances Ellen Watkins

Watkins, Gerrold
See Malzberg, Barry N(athaniel)

Watkins, Gloria Jean
See hooks, bell

Watkins, Paul 1964- **CLC 55**
See also CA 132; CANR 62, 98

Watkins, Vernon Phillips 1906-1967 **CLC 43**
See also CA 9-10; 25-28R; CAP 1; DLB 20; EWL 3; RGEL 2

Watson, Irving S.
See Mencken, H(enry) L(ouis)

Watson, John H.
See Farmer, Philip Jose

Watson, Richard F.
See Silverberg, Robert

Watts, Ephraim
See Horne, Richard Henry Hengist

Watts, Isaac 1674-1748 **LC 98**
See also DLB 95; RGEL 2; SATA 52

Waugh, Auberon (Alexander) 1939-2001 **CLC 7**
See also CA 45-48; 192; CANR 6, 22, 92; CN 1, 2, 3; DLB 14, 194

Waugh, Evelyn (Arthur St. John) 1903-1966 .. **CLC 1, 3, 8, 13, 19, 27, 44, 107; SSC 41; WLC 6**
See also BPFB 3; BRW 7; CA 85-88; 25-28R; CANR 22; CDBLB 1914-1945; DA; DA3; DAB; DAC; DAM MST, NOV, POP; DLB 15, 162, 195; EWL 3; MTCW 1, 2; MTFW 2005; NFS 13, 17; RGEL 2; RGSF 2; TEA; WLIT 4

Waugh, Harriet 1944- **CLC 6**
See also CA 85-88; CANR 22

Ways, C. R.
See Blount, Roy (Alton), Jr.

Waystaff, Simon
See Swift, Jonathan

Webb, Beatrice (Martha Potter) 1858-1943 **TCLC 22**
See also CA 117; 162; DLB 190; FW

Webb, Charles (Richard) 1939- **CLC 7**
See also CA 25-28R; CANR 114

Webb, Frank J. **NCLC 143**
See also DLB 50

Webb, James H(enry), Jr. 1946- **CLC 22**
See also CA 81-84

Webb, Mary Gladys (Meredith) 1881-1927 **TCLC 24**
See also CA 182; 123; DLB 34; FW

Webb, Mrs. Sidney
See Webb, Beatrice (Martha Potter)

Webb, Phyllis 1927- **CLC 18**
See also CA 104; CANR 23; CCA 1; CP 1, 2, 3, 4, 5, 6, 7; CWP; DLB 53

Webb, Sidney (James) 1859-1947 .. **TCLC 22**
See also CA 117; 163; DLB 190

Webber, Andrew Lloyd **CLC 21**
See Lloyd Webber, Andrew
See also DFS 7

Weber, Lenora Mattingly 1895-1971 **CLC 12**
See also CA 19-20; 29-32R; CAP 1; SATA 2; SATA-Obit 26

Weber, Max 1864-1920 **TCLC 69**
See also CA 109; 189; DLB 296

Webster, John 1580(?)-1634(?) **DC 2; LC 33, 84, 124; WLC 6**
See also BRW 2; CDBLB Before 1660; DA; DAB; DAC; DAM DRAM, MST; DFS 17, 19; DLB 58; IDTP; RGEL 2; WLIT 3

Webster, Noah 1758-1843 **NCLC 30**
See also DLB 1, 37, 42, 43, 73, 243

Wedekind, Benjamin Franklin
See Wedekind, Frank

Wedekind, Frank 1864-1918 **TCLC 7**
See also CA 104; 153; CANR 121, 122; CDWLB 2; DAM DRAM; DLB 118; EW 8; EWL 3; LMFS 2; RGWL 2, 3

Wehr, Demaris **CLC 65**

Weidman, Jerome 1913-1998 **CLC 7**
See also AITN 2; CA 1-4R; 171; CAD; CANR 1; CD 1, 2, 3, 4, 5; DLB 28

Weil, Simone (Adolphine) 1909-1943 **TCLC 23**
See also CA 117; 159; EW 12; EWL 3; FW; GFL 1789 to the Present; MTCW 2

Weininger, Otto 1880-1903 **TCLC 84**

Weinstein, Nathan
See West, Nathanael

Weinstein, Nathan von Wallenstein
See West, Nathanael

Weir, Peter (Lindsay) 1944- **CLC 20**
See also CA 113; 123

Weiss, Peter (Ulrich) 1916-1982 .. **CLC 3, 15, 51; TCLC 152**
See also CA 45-48; 106; CANR 3; DAM DRAM; DFS 3; DLB 69, 124; EWL 3; RGHL; RGWL 2, 3

Weiss, Theodore (Russell)
1916-2003 **CLC 3, 8, 14**
See also CA 9-12R, 189; 216; CAAE 189; CAAS 2; CANR 46, 94; CP 1, 2, 3, 4, 5, 6, 7; DLB 5; TCLE 1:2

Welch, (Maurice) Denton
1915-1948 **TCLC 22**
See also BRWS 8, 9; CA 121; 148; RGEL 2

Welch, James (Phillip) 1940-2003 **CLC 6, 14, 52; NNAL; PC 62**
See also CA 85-88; 219; CANR 42, 66, 107; CN 5, 6, 7; CP 2, 3, 4, 5, 6, 7; CPW; DAM MULT, POP; DLB 175, 256; LATS 1:1; NFS 23; RGAL 4; TCWW 1, 2

Weldon, Fay 1931- . **CLC 6, 9, 11, 19, 36, 59, 122**
See also BRWS 4; CA 21-24R; CANR 16, 46, 63, 97, 137; CDBLB 1960 to Present; CN 3, 4, 5, 6, 7; CPW; DAM POP; DLB 14, 194, 319; EWL 3; FW; HGG; INT CANR-16; MTCW 1, 2; MTFW 2005; RGEL 2; RGSF 2

Wellek, Rene 1903-1995 **CLC 28**
See also CA 5-8R; 150; CAAS 7; CANR 8; DLB 63; EWL 3; INT CANR-8

Weller, Michael 1942- **CLC 10, 53**
See also CA 85-88; CAD; CD 5, 6

Weller, Paul 1958- **CLC 26**

Wellershoff, Dieter 1925- **CLC 46**
See also CA 89-92; CANR 16, 37

Welles, (George) Orson 1915-1985 .. **CLC 20, 80**
See also AAYA 40; CA 93-96; 117

Wellman, John McDowell 1945-
See Wellman, Mac
See also CA 166; CD 5

Wellman, Mac **CLC 65**
See Wellman, John McDowell; Wellman, John McDowell
See also CAD; CD 6; RGAL 4

Wellman, Manly Wade 1903-1986 ... **CLC 49**
See also CA 1-4R; 118; CANR 6, 16, 44; FANT; SATA 6; SATA-Obit 47; SFW 4; SUFW

Wells, Carolyn 1869(?)-1942 **TCLC 35**
See also CA 113; 185; CMW 4; DLB 11

Wells, H(erbert) G(eorge) 1866-1946 . **SSC 6, 70; TCLC 6, 12, 19, 133; WLC 6**
See also AAYA 18; BPFB 3; BRW 6; CA 110; 121; CDBLB 1914-1945; CLR 64; DA; DA3; DAB; DAC; DAM MST, NOV; DLB 34, 70, 156, 178; EWL 3; EXPS; HGG; LAIT 3; LMFS 2; MTCW 1, 2; MTFW 2005; NFS 17, 20; RGEL 2; RGSF 2; SATA 20; SCFW 1, 2; SFW 4; SSFS 3; SUFW; TEA; WCH; WLIT 4; YAW

Wells, Rosemary 1943- **CLC 12**
See also AAYA 13; BYA 7, 8; CA 85-88; CANR 48, 120; CLR 16, 69; CWRI 5; MAICYA 1, 2; SAAS 1; SATA 18, 69, 114, 156; YAW

Wells-Barnett, Ida B(ell)
1862-1931 **TCLC 125**
See also CA 182; DLB 23, 221

Welsh, Irvine 1958- **CLC 144**
See also CA 173; CANR 146; CN 7; DLB 271

Welty, Eudora 1909-2001 **CLC 1, 2, 5, 14, 22, 33, 105, 220; SSC 1, 27, 51; WLC 6**
See also AAYA 48; AMW; AMWR 1; BPFB 3; CA 9-12R; 199; CABS 1; CANR 32, 65; CDALB 1941-1968; CN 1, 2, 3, 4, 5, 6, 7; CSW; DA; DA3; DAB; DAC;

DAM MST, NOV; DLB 2, 102, 143; DLBD 12; DLBY 1987, 2001; EWL 3; EXPS; HGG; LAIT 3; MAL 5; MAWW; MTCW 1, 2; MTFW 2005; NFS 13, 15; RGAL 4; RGSF 2; RHW; SSFS 2, 10; TUS

Welty, Eudora Alice
See Welty, Eudora

Wen I-to 1899-1946 **TCLC 28**
See also EWL 3

Wentworth, Robert
See Hamilton, Edmond

Werfel, Franz (Viktor) 1890-1945 ... **TCLC 8**
See also CA 104; 161; DLB 81, 124; EWL 3; RGWL 2, 3

Wergeland, Henrik Arnold
1808-1845 **NCLC 5**

Wersba, Barbara 1932- **CLC 30**
See also AAYA 2, 30; BYA 6, 12, 13; CA 29-32R, 182; CAAE 182; CANR 16, 38; CLR 3, 78; DLB 52; JRDA; MAICYA 1, 2; SAAS 2; SATA 1, 58; SATA-Essay 103; WYA; YAW

Wertmueller, Lina 1928- **CLC 16**
See also CA 97-100; CANR 39, 78

Wescott, Glenway 1901-1987 .. **CLC 13; SSC 35**
See also CA 13-16R; 121; CANR 23, 70; CN 1, 2, 3, 4; DLB 4, 9, 102; MAL 5; RGAL 4

Wesker, Arnold 1932- **CLC 3, 5, 42**
See also CA 1-4R; CAAS 7; CANR 1, 33; CBD; CD 5, 6; CDBLB 1960 to Present; DAB; DAM DRAM; DLB 13, 310, 319; EWL 3; MTCW 1; RGEL 2; TEA

Wesley, Charles 1707-1788 **LC 128**
See also DLB 95; RGEL 2

Wesley, John 1703-1791 **LC 88**
See also DLB 104

Wesley, Richard (Errol) 1945- **CLC 7**
See also BW 1; CA 57-60; CAD; CANR 27; CD 5, 6; DLB 38

Wessel, Johan Herman 1742-1785 **LC 7**
See also DLB 300

West, Anthony (Panther)
1914-1987 **CLC 50**
See also CA 45-48; 124; CANR 3, 19; CN 1, 2, 3, 4; DLB 15

West, C. P.
See Wodehouse, P(elham) G(renville)

West, Cornel (Ronald) 1953- **BLCS; CLC 134**
See also CA 144; CANR 91; DLB 246

West, Delno C(loyde), Jr. 1936- **CLC 70**
See also CA 57-60

West, Dorothy 1907-1998 **HR 1:3; TCLC 108**
See also BW 2; CA 143; 169; DLB 76

West, (Mary) Jessamyn 1902-1984 ... **CLC 7, 17**
See also CA 9-12R; 112; CANR 27; CN 1, 2, 3; DLB 6; DLBY 1984; MTCW 1, 2; RGAL 4; RHW; SATA-Obit 37; TCWW 2; TUS; YAW

West, Morris L(anglo) 1916-1999 **CLC 6, 33**
See also BPFB 3; CA 5-8R; 187; CANR 24, 49, 64; CN 1, 2, 3, 4, 5, 6; CPW; DLB 289; MTCW 1, 2; MTFW 2005

West, Nathanael 1903-1940 .. **SSC 16; TCLC 1, 14, 44**
See also AMW; AMWR 2; BPFB 3; CA 104; 125; CDALB 1929-1941; DA3; DLB 4, 9, 28; EWL 3; MAL 5; MTCW 1, 2; MTFW 2005; NFS 16; RGAL 4; TUS

West, Owen
See Koontz, Dean R.

West, Paul 1930- **CLC 7, 14, 96, 226**
See also CA 13-16R; CAAS 7; CANR 22, 53, 76, 89, 136; CN 1, 2, 3, 4, 5, 6, 7; DLB 14; INT CANR-22; MTCW 2; MTFW 2005

West, Rebecca 1892-1983 ... **CLC 7, 9, 31, 50**
See also BPFB 3; BRWS 3; CA 5-8R; 109; CANR 19; CN 1, 2, 3; DLB 36; DLBY 1983; EWL 3; FW; MTCW 1, 2; MTFW 2005; NCFS 4; RGEL 2; TEA

Westall, Robert (Atkinson)
1929-1993 **CLC 17**
See also AAYA 12; BYA 2, 6, 7, 8, 9, 15; CA 69-72; 141; CANR 18, 68; CLR 13; FANT; JRDA; MAICYA 1, 2; MAICYAS 1; SAAS 2; SATA 23, 69; SATA-Obit 75; WYA; YAW

Westermarck, Edward 1862-1939 . **TCLC 87**

Westlake, Donald E(dwin) 1933- . **CLC 7, 33**
See also BPFB 3; CA 17-20R; CAAS 13; CANR 16, 44, 65, 94, 137; CMW 4; CPW; DAM POP; INT CANR-16; MSW; MTCW 2; MTFW 2005

Westmacott, Mary
See Christie, Agatha (Mary Clarissa)

Weston, Allen
See Norton, Andre

Wetcheek, J. L.
See Feuchtwanger, Lion

Wetering, Janwillem van de
See van de Wetering, Janwillem

Wetherald, Agnes Ethelwyn
1857-1940 **TCLC 81**
See also CA 202; DLB 99

Wetherell, Elizabeth
See Warner, Susan (Bogert)

Whale, James 1889-1957 **TCLC 63**

Whalen, Philip (Glenn) 1923-2002 **CLC 6, 29**
See also BG 1:3; CA 9-12R; 209; CANR 5, 39; CP 1, 2, 3, 4, 5, 6, 7; DLB 16; WP

Wharton, Edith (Newbold Jones)
1862-1937 ... **SSC 6, 84; TCLC 3, 9, 27, 53, 129, 149; WLC 6**
See also AAYA 25; AMW; AMWC 2; AMWR 1; BPFB 3; CA 104; 132; CDALB 1865-1917; DA; DA3; DAB; DAC; DAM MST, NOV; DLB 4, 9, 12, 78, 189; DLBD 13; EWL 3; EXPS; FL 1:6; GL 3; HGG; LAIT 2, 3; LATS 1:1; MAL 5; MAWW; MTCW 1, 2; MTFW 2005; NFS 5, 11, 15, 20; RGAL 4; RGSF 2; RHW; SSFS 6, 7; SUFW; TUS

Wharton, James
See Mencken, H(enry) L(ouis)

Wharton, William (a pseudonym)
1925- **CLC 18, 37**
See also CA 93-96; CN 4, 5, 6, 7; DLBY 1980; INT CA-93-96

Wheatley (Peters), Phillis
1753(?)-1784 ... **BLC 3; LC 3, 50; PC 3; WLC 6**
See also AFAW 1, 2; CDALB 1640-1865; DA; DA3; DAC; DAM MST, MULT, POET; DLB 31, 50; EXPP; FL 1:1; PFS 13; RGAL 4

Wheelock, John Hall 1886-1978 **CLC 14**
See also CA 13-16R; 77-80; CANR 14; CP 1, 2; DLB 45; MAL 5

Whim-Wham
See Curnow, (Thomas) Allen (Monro)

Whitaker, Rod 1931-2005
See Trevanian
See also CA 29-32R; 246; CANR 45, 153; CMW 4

White, Babington
See Braddon, Mary Elizabeth

White, E. B. 1899-1985 **CLC 10, 34, 39**
See also AAYA 62; AITN 2; AMWS 1; CA 13-16R; 116; CANR 16, 37; CDALBS; CLR 1, 21, 107; CPW; DA3; DAM POP; DLB 11, 22; EWL 3; FANT; MAICYA 1, 2; MAL 5; MTCW 1, 2; MTFW 2005; NCFS 5; RGAL 4; SATA 2, 29, 100; SATA-Obit 44; TUS

White, Edmund (Valentine III)
1940- **CLC 27, 110**
See also AAYA 7; CA 45-48; CANR 3, 19, 36, 62, 107, 133; CN 5, 6, 7; DA3; DAM POP; DLB 227; MTCW 1, 2; MTFW 2005

White, Elwyn Brooks
See White, E. B.

White, Hayden V. 1928- **CLC 148**
See also CA 128; CANR 135; DLB 246

White, Patrick (Victor Martindale)
1912-1990 **CLC 3, 4, 5, 7, 9, 18, 65, 69; SSC 39; TCLC 176**
See also BRWS 1; CA 81-84; 132; CANR 43; CN 1, 2, 3, 4; DLB 260; EWL 3; MTCW 1; RGEL 2; RGSF 2; RHW; TWA; WWE 1

White, Phyllis Dorothy James 1920-
See James, P. D.
See also CA 21-24R; CANR 17, 43, 65, 112; CMW 4; CN 7; CPW; DA3; DAM POP; MTCW 1, 2; MTFW 2005; TEA

White, T(erence) H(anbury)
1906-1964 **CLC 30**
See also AAYA 22; BPFB 3; BYA 4, 5; CA 73-76; CANR 37; DLB 160; FANT; JRDA; LAIT 1; MAICYA 1, 2; RGEL 2; SATA 12; SUFW 1; YAW

White, Terence de Vere 1912-1994 ... **CLC 49**
See also CA 49-52; 145; CANR 3

White, Walter
See White, Walter F(rancis)

White, Walter F(rancis) 1893-1955 ... **BLC 3; HR 1:3; TCLC 15**
See also BW 1; CA 115; 124; DAM MULT; DLB 51

White, William Hale 1831-1913
See Rutherford, Mark
See also CA 121; 189

Whitehead, Alfred North
1861-1947 **TCLC 97**
See also CA 117; 165; DLB 100, 262

Whitehead, E(dward) A(nthony)
1933- ... **CLC 5**
See Whitehead, Ted
See also CA 65-68; CANR 58, 118; CBD; CD 5; DLB 310

Whitehead, Ted
See Whitehead, E(dward) A(nthony)
See also CD 6

Whiteman, Roberta J. Hill 1947- **NNAL**
See also CA 146

Whitemore, Hugh (John) 1936- **CLC 37**
See also CA 132; CANR 77; CBD; CD 5, 6; INT CA-132

Whitman, Sarah Helen (Power)
1803-1878 **NCLC 19**
See also DLB 1, 243

Whitman, Walt(er) 1819-1892 .. **NCLC 4, 31, 81; PC 3; WLC 6**
See also AAYA 42; AMW; AMWR 1; CDALB 1640-1865; DA; DA3; DAB; DAC; DAM MST, POET; DLB 3, 64, 224, 250; EXPP; LAIT 2; LMFS 1; PAB; PFS 2, 3, 13, 22; RGAL 4; SATA 20; TUS; WP; WYAS 1

Whitney, Phyllis A(yame) 1903- **CLC 42**
See also AAYA 36; AITN 2; BEST 90:3; CA 1-4R; CANR 3, 25, 38, 60; CLR 59; CMW 4; CPW; DA3; DAM POP; JRDA; MAICYA 1, 2; MTCW 2; RHW; SATA 1, 30; YAW

Whittemore, (Edward) Reed, Jr.
1919- ... **CLC 4**
See also CA 9-12R, 219; CAAE 219; CAAS 8; CANR 4, 119; CP 1, 2, 3, 4, 5, 6, 7; DLB 5; MAL 5

Whittier, John Greenleaf
1807-1892 **NCLC 8, 59**
See also AMWS 1; DLB 1, 243; RGAL 4

Whittlebot, Hernia
See Coward, Noel (Peirce)

Wicker, Thomas Grey 1926-
See Wicker, Tom
See also CA 65-68; CANR 21, 46, 141

Wicker, Tom ... **CLC 7**
See Wicker, Thomas Grey

Wideman, John Edgar 1941- ... **BLC 3; CLC 5, 34, 36, 67, 122; SSC 62**
See also AFAW 1, 2; AMWS 10; BPFB 4; BW 2, 3; CA 85-88; CANR 14, 42, 67, 109, 140; CN 4, 5, 6, 7; DAM MULT; DLB 33, 143; MAL 5; MTCW 2; MTFW 2005; RGAL 4; RGSF 2; SSFS 6, 12; TCLE 1:2

Wiebe, Rudy (Henry) 1934- .. **CLC 6, 11, 14, 138**
See also CA 37-40R; CANR 42, 67, 123; CN 1, 2, 3, 4, 5, 6, 7; DAC; DAM MST; DLB 60; RHW; SATA 156

Wieland, Christoph Martin
1733-1813 **NCLC 17**
See also DLB 97; EW 4; LMFS 1; RGWL 2, 3

Wiene, Robert 1881-1938 **TCLC 56**

Wieners, John 1934- **CLC 7**
See also BG 1:3; CA 13-16R; CP 1, 2, 3, 4, 5, 6, 7; DLB 16; WP

Wiesel, Elie 1928- **CLC 3, 5, 11, 37, 165; WLCS**
See also AAYA 7, 54; AITN 1; CA 5-8R; CAAS 4; CANR 8, 40, 65, 125; CDALBS; CWW 2; DA; DA3; DAB; DAC; DAM MST, NOV; DLB 83, 299; DLBY 1987; EWL 3; INT CANR-8; LAIT 4; MTCW 1, 2; MTFW 2005; NCFS 4; NFS 4; RGHL; RGWL 3; SATA 56; YAW

Wiesel, Eliezer
See Wiesel, Elie

Wiggins, Marianne 1947- **CLC 57**
See also AAYA 70; BEST 89:3; CA 130; CANR 60, 139; CN 7

Wigglesworth, Michael 1631-1705 **LC 106**
See also DLB 24; RGAL 4

Wiggs, Susan .. **CLC 70**
See also CA 201

Wight, James Alfred 1916-1995
See Herriot, James
See also CA 77-80; SATA 55; SATA-Brief 44

Wilbur, Richard (Purdy) 1921- **CLC 3, 6, 9, 14, 53, 110; PC 51**
See also AMWS 3; CA 1-4R; CABS 2; CANR 2, 29, 76, 93, 139; CDALBS; CP 1, 2, 3, 4, 5, 6, 7; DA; DAB; DAC; DAM MST, POET; DLB 5, 169; EWL 3; EXPP; INT CANR-29; MAL 5; MTCW 1, 2; MTFW 2005; PAB; PFS 11, 12, 16; RGAL 4; SATA 9, 108; WP

Wild, Peter 1940- **CLC 14**
See also CA 37-40R; CP 1, 2, 3, 4, 5, 6, 7; DLB 5

Wilde, Oscar (Fingal O'Flahertie Wills)
1854(?)-1900 **DC 17; SSC 11, 77; TCLC 1, 8, 23, 41, 175; WLC 6**
See also AAYA 49; BRW 5; BRWC 1, 2; BRWR 2; BYA 15; CA 104; 119; CANR 112; CDBLB 1890-1914; DA; DA3; DAB; DAC; DAM DRAM, MST, NOV; DFS 4, 8, 9, 21; DLB 10, 19, 34, 57, 141,

156, 190; EXPS; FANT; GL 3; LATS 1:1; NFS 20; RGEL 2; RGSF 2; SATA 24; SSFS 7; SUFW; TEA; WCH; WLIT 4

Wilder, Billy .. **CLC 20**
See Wilder, Samuel
See also AAYA 66; DLB 26

Wilder, Samuel 1906-2002
See Wilder, Billy
See also CA 89-92; 205

Wilder, Stephen
See Marlowe, Stephen

Wilder, Thornton (Niven)
1897-1975 .. **CLC 1, 5, 6, 10, 15, 35, 82; DC 1, 24; WLC 6**
See also AAYA 29; AITN 2; AMW; CA 13-16R; 61-64; CAD; CANR 40, 132; CDALBS; CN 1, 2; DA; DA3; DAB; DAC; DAM DRAM, MST, NOV; DFS 1, 4, 16; DLB 4, 7, 9, 228; DLBY 1997; EWL 3; LAIT 3; MAL 5; MTCW 1, 2; MTFW 2005; RGAL 4; RHW; WYAS 1

Wilding, Michael 1942- **CLC 73; SSC 50**
See also CA 104; CANR 24, 49, 106; CN 4, 5, 6, 7; DLB 325; RGSF 2

Wiley, Richard 1944- **CLC 44**
See also CA 121; 129; CANR 71

Wilhelm, Kate ... **CLC 7**
See Wilhelm, Katie (Gertrude)
See also AAYA 20; BYA 16; CAAS 5; DLB 8; INT CANR-17; SCFW 2

Wilhelm, Katie (Gertrude) 1928-
See Wilhelm, Kate
See also CA 37-40R; CANR 17, 36, 60, 94; MTCW 1; SFW 4

Wilkins, Mary
See Freeman, Mary E(leanor) Wilkins

Willard, Nancy 1936- **CLC 7, 37**
See also BYA 5; CA 89-92; CANR 10, 39, 68, 107, 152; CLR 5; CP 2, 3, 4, 5; CWP; CWRI 5; DLB 5, 52; FANT; MAICYA 1, 2; MTCW 1; SATA 37, 71, 127; SATA-Brief 30; SUFW 2; TCLE 1:2

William of Malmesbury c. 1090B.C.-c. 1140B.C. **CMLC 57**

William of Ockham 1290-1349 **CMLC 32**

Williams, Ben Ames 1889-1953 **TCLC 89**
See also CA 183; DLB 102

Williams, C(harles) K(enneth)
1936- **CLC 33, 56, 148**
See also CA 37-40R; CAAS 26; CANR 57, 106; CP 1, 2, 3, 4, 5, 6, 7; DAM POET; DLB 5; MAL 5

Williams, Charles
See Collier, James Lincoln

Williams, Charles (Walter Stansby)
1886-1945 **TCLC 1, 11**
See also BRWS 9; CA 104; 163; DLB 100, 153, 255; FANT; RGEL 2; SUFW 1

Williams, Ella Gwendolen Rees
See Rhys, Jean

Williams, (George) Emlyn
1905-1987 **CLC 15**
See also CA 104; 123; CANR 36; DAM DRAM; DLB 10, 77; IDTP; MTCW 1

Williams, Hank 1923-1953 **TCLC 81**
See Williams, Hiram King

Williams, Helen Maria
1761-1827 **NCLC 135**
See also DLB 158

Williams, Hiram Hank
See Williams, Hank

Williams, Hiram King
See Williams, Hank
See also CA 188

Williams, Hugo (Mordaunt) 1942- ... **CLC 42**
See also CA 17-20R; CANR 45, 119; CP 1, 2, 3, 4, 5, 6, 7; DLB 40

Williams, J. Walker
See Wodehouse, P(elham) G(renville)

Williams, John A(lfred) 1925- . **BLC 3; CLC 5, 13**
See also AFAW 2; BW 2, 3; CA 53-56, 195; CAAE 195; CAAS 3; CANR 6, 26, 51, 118; CN 1, 2, 3, 4, 5, 6, 7; CSW; DAM MULT; DLB 2, 33; EWL 3; INT CANR-6; MAL 5; RGAL 4; SFW 4

Williams, Jonathan (Chamberlain) 1929- .. **CLC 13**
See also CA 9-12R; CAAS 12; CANR 8, 108; CP 1, 2, 3, 4, 5, 6, 7; DLB 5

Williams, Joy 1944- **CLC 31**
See also CA 41-44R; CANR 22, 48, 97

Williams, Norman 1952- **CLC 39**
See also CA 118

Williams, Roger 1603(?)-1683 **LC 129**
See also DLB 24

Williams, Sherley Anne 1944-1999 ... **BLC 3; CLC 89**
See also AFAW 2; BW 2, 3; CA 73-76; 185; CANR 25, 82; DAM MULT, POET; DLB 41; INT CANR-25; SATA 78; SATA-Obit 116

Williams, Shirley
See Williams, Sherley Anne

Williams, Tennessee 1911-1983 . **CLC 1, 2, 5, 7, 8, 11, 15, 19, 30, 39, 45, 71, 111; DC 4; SSC 81; WLC 6**
See also AAYA 31; AITN 1, 2; AMW; AMWC 1; CA 5-8R; 108; CABS 3; CAD; CANR 31, 132; CDALB 1941-1968; CN 1, 2, 3; DA; DA3; DAB; DAC; DAM DRAM, MST; DFS 17; DLB 7; DLBD 4; DLBY 1983; EWL 3; GLL 1; LAIT 4; LATS 1:2; MAL 5; MTCW 1, 2; MTFW 2005; RGAL 4; TUS

Williams, Thomas (Alonzo) 1926-1990 **CLC 14**
See also CA 1-4R; 132; CANR 2

Williams, William C.
See Williams, William Carlos

Williams, William Carlos 1883-1963 **CLC 1, 2, 5, 9, 13, 22, 42, 67; PC 7; SSC 31; WLC 6**
See also AAYA 46; AMW; AMWR 1; CA 89-92; CANR 34; CDALB 1917-1929; DA; DA3; DAB; DAC; DAM MST, POET; DLB 4, 16, 54, 86; EWL 3; EXPP; MAL 5; MTCW 1, 2; MTFW 2005; NCFS 4; PAB; PFS 1, 6, 11; RGAL 4; RGSF 2; TUS; WP

Williamson, David (Keith) 1942- **CLC 56**
See also CA 103; CANR 41; CD 5, 6; DLB 289

Williamson, Ellen Douglas 1905-1984
See Douglas, Ellen
See also CA 17-20R; 114; CANR 39

Williamson, Jack **CLC 29**
See Williamson, John Stewart
See also CAAS 8; DLB 8; SCFW 1, 2

Williamson, John Stewart 1908-
See Williamson, Jack
See also CA 17-20R; CANR 23, 70, 153; SFW 4

Willie, Frederick
See Lovecraft, H. P.

Willingham, Calder (Baynard, Jr.) 1922-1995 **CLC 5, 51**
See also CA 5-8R; 147; CANR 3; CN 1, 2, 3, 4, 5; CSW; DLB 2, 44; IDFW 3, 4; MTCW 1

Willis, Charles
See Clarke, Arthur C(harles)

Willy
See Colette, (Sidonie-Gabrielle)

Willy, Colette
See Colette, (Sidonie-Gabrielle)
See also GLL 1

Wilmot, John 1647-1680 **LC 75; PC 66**
See Rochester
See also BRW 2; DLB 131; PAB

Wilson, A(ndrew) N(orman) 1950- .. **CLC 33**
See also BRWS 6; CA 112; 122; CN 4, 5, 6, 7; DLB 14, 155, 194; MTCW 2

Wilson, Angus (Frank Johnstone) 1913-1991 . **CLC 2, 3, 5, 25, 34; SSC 21**
See also BRWS 1; CA 5-8R; 134; CANR 21; CN 1, 2, 3, 4; DLB 15, 139, 155; EWL 3; MTCW 1, 2; MTFW 2005; RGEL 2; RGSF 2

Wilson, August 1945-2005 .. **BLC 3; CLC 39, 50, 63, 118, 222; DC 2; WLCS**
See also AAYA 16; AFAW 2; AMWS 8; BW 2, 3; CA 115; 122; 244; CAD; CANR 42, 54, 76, 128; CD 5, 6; DA; DA3; DAB; DAC; DAM DRAM, MST, MULT; DFS 3, 7, 15, 17; DLB 228; EWL 3; LAIT 4; LATS 1:2; MAL 5; MTCW 1, 2; MTFW 2005; RGAL 4

Wilson, Brian 1942- **CLC 12**

Wilson, Colin (Henry) 1931- **CLC 3, 14**
See also CA 1-4R; CAAS 5; CANR 1, 22, 33, 77; CMW 4; CN 1, 2, 3, 4, 5, 6; DLB 14, 194; HGG; MTCW 1; SFW 4

Wilson, Dirk
See Pohl, Frederik

Wilson, Edmund 1895-1972 .. **CLC 1, 2, 3, 8, 24**
See also AMW; CA 1-4R; 37-40R; CANR 1, 46, 110; CN 1; DLB 63; EWL 3; MAL 5; MTCW 1, 2; MTFW 2005; RGAL 4; TUS

Wilson, Ethel Davis (Bryant) 1888(?)-1980 **CLC 13**
See also CA 102; CN 1, 2; DAC; DAM POET; DLB 68; MTCW 1; RGEL 2

Wilson, Harriet
See Wilson, Harriet E. Adams
See also DLB 239

Wilson, Harriet E.
See Wilson, Harriet E. Adams
See also DLB 243

Wilson, Harriet E. Adams 1827(?)-1863(?) **BLC 3; NCLC 78**
See Wilson, Harriet; Wilson, Harriet E.
See also DAM MULT; DLB 50

Wilson, John 1785-1854 **NCLC 5**

Wilson, John (Anthony) Burgess 1917-1993
See Burgess, Anthony
See also CA 1-4R; 143; CANR 2, 46; DA3; DAC; DAM NOV; MTCW 1, 2; MTFW 2005; NFS 15; TEA

Wilson, Lanford 1937- .. **CLC 7, 14, 36, 197; DC 19**
See also CA 17-20R; CABS 3; CAD; CANR 45, 96; CD 5, 6; DAM DRAM; DFS 4, 9, 12, 16, 20; DLB 7; EWL 3; MAL 5; TUS

Wilson, Robert M. 1941- **CLC 7, 9**
See also CA 49-52; CAD; CANR 2, 41; CD 5, 6; MTCW 1

Wilson, Robert McLiam 1964- **CLC 59**
See also CA 132; DLB 267

Wilson, Sloan 1920-2003 **CLC 32**
See also CA 1-4R; 216; CANR 1, 44; CN 1, 2, 3, 4, 5, 6

Wilson, Snoo 1948- **CLC 33**
See also CA 69-72; CBD; CD 5, 6

Wilson, William S(mith) 1932- **CLC 49**
See also CA 81-84

Wilson, (Thomas) Woodrow 1856-1924 **TCLC 79**
See also CA 166; DLB 47

Wilson and Warnke eds. **CLC 65**

Winchilsea, Anne (Kingsmill) Finch 1661-1720
See Finch, Anne
See also RGEL 2

Winckelmann, Johann Joachim 1717-1768 **LC 129**
See also DLB 97

Windham, Basil
See Wodehouse, P(elham) G(renville)

Wingrove, David (John) 1954- **CLC 68**
See also CA 133; SFW 4

Winnemucca, Sarah 1844-1891 **NCLC 79; NNAL**
See also DAM MULT; DLB 175; RGAL 4

Winstanley, Gerrard 1609-1676 **LC 52**

Wintergreen, Jane
See Duncan, Sara Jeannette

Winters, Arthur Yvor
See Winters, Yvor

Winters, Janet Lewis **CLC 41**
See Lewis, Janet
See also DLBY 1987

Winters, Yvor 1900-1968 **CLC 4, 8, 32**
See also AMWS 2; CA 11-12; 25-28R; CAP 1; DLB 48; EWL 3; MAL 5; MTCW 1; RGAL 4

Winterson, Jeanette 1959- **CLC 64, 158**
See also BRWS 4; CA 136; CANR 58, 116; CN 5, 6, 7; CPW; DA3; DAM POP; DLB 207, 261; FANT; FW; GLL 1; MTCW 2; MTFW 2005; RHW

Winthrop, John 1588-1649 **LC 31, 107**
See also DLB 24, 30

Wirth, Louis 1897-1952 **TCLC 92**
See also CA 210

Wiseman, Frederick 1930- **CLC 20**
See also CA 159

Wister, Owen 1860-1938 **TCLC 21**
See also BPFB 3; CA 108; 162; DLB 9, 78, 186; RGAL 4; SATA 62; TCWW 1, 2

Wither, George 1588-1667 **LC 96**
See also DLB 121; RGEL 2

Witkacy
See Witkiewicz, Stanislaw Ignacy

Witkiewicz, Stanislaw Ignacy 1885-1939 **TCLC 8**
See also CA 105; 162; CDWLB 4; DLB 215; EW 10; EWL 3; RGWL 2, 3; SFW 4

Wittgenstein, Ludwig (Josef Johann) 1889-1951 **TCLC 59**
See also CA 113; 164; DLB 262; MTCW 2

Wittig, Monique 1935-2003 **CLC 22**
See also CA 116; 135; 212; CANR 143; CWW 2; DLB 83; EWL 3; FW; GLL 1

Wittlin, Jozef 1896-1976 **CLC 25**
See also CA 49-52; 65-68; CANR 3; EWL 3

Wodehouse, P(elham) G(renville) 1881-1975 . **CLC 1, 2, 5, 10, 22; SSC 2; TCLC 108**
See also AAYA 65; AITN 2; BRWS 3; CA 45-48; 57-60; CANR 3, 33; CDBLB 1914-1945; CN 1, 2; CPW 1; DA3; DAB; DAC; DAM NOV; DLB 34, 162; EWL 3; MTCW 1, 2; MTFW 2005; RGEL 2; RGSF 2; SATA 22; SSFS 10

Woiwode, L.
See Woiwode, Larry (Alfred)

Woiwode, Larry (Alfred) 1941- ... **CLC 6, 10**
See also CA 73-76; CANR 16, 94; CN 3, 4, 5, 6, 7; DLB 6; INT CANR-16

Wojciechowska, Maia (Teresa) 1927-2002 **CLC 26**
See also AAYA 8, 46; BYA 3; CA 9-12R; 183; 209; CAAE 183; CANR 4, 41; CLR 1; JRDA; MAICYA 1, 2; SAAS 1; SATA 1, 28, 83; SATA-Essay 104; SATA-Obit 134; YAW

Wojtyla, Karol (Josef)
See John Paul II, Pope

Wojtyla, Karol (Jozef)
See John Paul II, Pope

Wolf, Christa 1929- **CLC 14, 29, 58, 150**
See also CA 85-88; CANR 45, 123; CD-WLB 2; CWW 2; DLB 75; EWL 3; FW; MTCW 1; RGWL 2, 3; SSFS 14

Wolf, Naomi 1962- **CLC 157**
See also CA 141; CANR 110; FW; MTFW 2005

Wolfe, Gene 1931- **CLC 25**
See also AAYA 35; CA 57-60; CAAS 9; CANR 6, 32, 60, 152; CPW; DAM POP; DLB 8; FANT; MTCW 2; MTFW 2005; SATA 118, 165; SCFW 2; SFW 4; SUFW 2

Wolfe, Gene Rodman
See Wolfe, Gene

Wolfe, George C. 1954- **BLCS; CLC 49**
See also CA 149; CAD; CD 5, 6

Wolfe, Thomas (Clayton)
1900-1938 **SSC 33; TCLC 4, 13, 29, 61; WLC 6**
See also AMW; BPFB 3; CA 104; 132; CANR 102; CDALB 1929-1941; DA; DA3; DAB; DAC; DAM MST, NOV; DLB 9, 102, 229; DLBD 2, 16; DLBY 1985, 1997; EWL 3; MAL 5; MTCW 1, 2; NFS 18; RGAL 4; SSFS 18; TUS

Wolfe, Thomas Kennerly, Jr.
1931- ... **CLC 147**
See Wolfe, Tom
See also CA 13-16R; CANR 9, 33, 70, 104; DA3; DAM POP; DLB 185; EWL 3; INT CANR-9; MTCW 1, 2; MTFW 2005; TUS

Wolfe, Tom **CLC 1, 2, 9, 15, 35, 51**
See Wolfe, Thomas Kennerly, Jr.
See also AAYA 8, 67; AITN 2; AMWS 3; BEST 89:1; BPFB 3; CN 5, 6, 7; CPW; CSW; DLB 152; LAIT 5; RGAL 4

Wolff, Geoffrey 1937- **CLC 41**
See also CA 29-32R; CANR 29, 43, 78, 154

Wolff, Geoffrey Ansell
See Wolff, Geoffrey

Wolff, Sonia
See Levitin, Sonia (Wolff)

Wolff, Tobias (Jonathan Ansell)
1945- **CLC 39, 64, 172; SSC 63**
See also AAYA 16; AMWS 7; BEST 90:2; BYA 12; CA 114; 117; CAAS 22; CANR 54, 76, 96; CN 5, 6, 7; CSW; DA3; DLB 130; EWL 3; INT CA-117; MTCW 2; MTFW 2005; RGAL 4; RGSF 2; SSFS 4, 11

Wolfram von Eschenbach c. 1170-c.
1220 ... **CMLC 5**
See Eschenbach, Wolfram von
See also CDWLB 2; DLB 138; EW 1; RGWL 2

Wolitzer, Hilma 1930- **CLC 17**
See also CA 65-68; CANR 18, 40; INT CANR-18; SATA 31; YAW

Wollstonecraft, Mary 1759-1797 **LC 5, 50, 90**
See also BRWS 3; CDBLB 1789-1832; DLB 39, 104, 158, 252; FL 1:1; FW; LAIT 1; RGEL 2; TEA; WLIT 3

Wonder, Stevie 1950- **CLC 12**
See also CA 111

Wong, Jade Snow 1922-2006 **CLC 17**
See also CA 109; CANR 91; SATA 112

Woodberry, George Edward
1855-1930 **TCLC 73**
See also CA 165; DLB 71, 103

Woodcott, Keith
See Brunner, John (Kilian Houston)

Woodruff, Robert W.
See Mencken, H(enry) L(ouis)

Woolf, (Adeline) Virginia 1882-1941 .. **SSC 7, 79; TCLC 1, 5, 20, 43, 56, 101, 123, 128; WLC 6**
See also AAYA 44; BPFB 3; BRW 7; BRWC 2; BRWR 1; CA 104; 130; CANR 64, 132; CDBLB 1914-1945; DA; DA3; DAB; DAC; DAM MST, NOV; DLB 36, 100, 162; DLBD 10; EWL 3; EXPS; FL 1:6; FW; LAIT 3; LATS 1:1; LMFS 2; MTCW 1, 2; MTFW 2005; NCFS 2; NFS 8, 12; RGEL 2; RGSF 2; SSFS 4, 12; TEA; WLIT 4

Woollcott, Alexander (Humphreys)
1887-1943 **TCLC 5**
See also CA 105; 161; DLB 29

Woolrich, Cornell **CLC 77**
See Hopley-Woolrich, Cornell George
See also MSW

Woolson, Constance Fenimore
1840-1894 **NCLC 82; SSC 90**
See also DLB 12, 74, 189, 221; RGAL 4

Wordsworth, Dorothy 1771-1855 . **NCLC 25, 138**
See also DLB 107

Wordsworth, William 1770-1850 .. **NCLC 12, 38, 111, 166; PC 4, 67; WLC 6**
See also AAYA 70; BRW 4; BRWC 1; CD-BLB 1789-1832; DA; DA3; DAB; DAC; DAM MST, POET; DLB 93, 107; EXPP; LATS 1:1; LMFS 1; PAB; PFS 2; RGEL 2; TEA; WLIT 3; WP

Wotton, Sir Henry 1568-1639 **LC 68**
See also DLB 121; RGEL 2

Wouk, Herman 1915- **CLC 1, 9, 38**
See also BPFB 2, 3; CA 5-8R; CANR 6, 33, 67, 146; CDALBS; CN 1, 2, 3, 4, 5, 6; CPW; DA3; DAM NOV, POP; DLBY 1982; INT CANR-6; LAIT 4; MAL 5; MTCW 1, 2; MTFW 2005; NFS 7; TUS

Wright, Charles (Penzel, Jr.) 1935- .. **CLC 6, 13, 28, 119, 146**
See also AMWS 5; CA 29-32R; CAAS 7; CANR 23, 36, 62, 88, 135; CP 3, 4, 5, 6, 7; DLB 165; DLBY 1982; EWL 3; MTCW 1, 2; MTFW 2005; PFS 10

Wright, Charles Stevenson 1932- **BLC 3; CLC 49**
See also BW 1; CA 9-12R; CANR 26; CN 1, 2, 3, 4, 5, 6, 7; DAM MULT, POET; DLB 33

Wright, Frances 1795-1852 **NCLC 74**
See also DLB 73

Wright, Frank Lloyd 1867-1959 **TCLC 95**
See also AAYA 33; CA 174

Wright, Jack R.
See Harris, Mark

Wright, James (Arlington)
1927-1980 **CLC 3, 5, 10, 28; PC 36**
See also AITN 2; AMWS 3; CA 49-52; 97-100; CANR 4, 34, 64; CDALBS; CP 1, 2; DAM POET; DLB 5, 169; EWL 3; EXPP; MAL 5; MTCW 1, 2; MTFW 2005; PFS 7, 8; RGAL 4; TUS; WP

Wright, Judith (Arundell)
1915-2000 **CLC 11, 53; PC 14**
See also CA 13-16R; 188; CANR 31, 76, 93; CP 1, 2, 3, 4, 5, 6, 7; CWP; DLB 260; EWL 3; MTCW 1, 2; MTFW 2005; PFS 8; RGEL 2; SATA 14; SATA-Obit 121

Wright, L(aurali) R. 1939- **CLC 44**
See also CA 138; CMW 4

Wright, Richard (Nathaniel)
1908-1960 ... **BLC 3; CLC 1, 3, 4, 9, 14, 21, 48, 74; SSC 2; TCLC 136, 180; WLC 6**
See also AAYA 5, 42; AFAW 1, 2; AMW; BPFB 3; BW 1; BYA 2; CA 108; CANR 64; CDALB 1929-1941; DA; DA3; DAB; DAC; DAM MST, MULT, NOV; DLB 76, 102; DLBD 2; EWL 3; EXPN; LAIT 3;

4; MAL 5; MTCW 1, 2; MTFW 2005; NCFS 1; NFS 1, 7; RGAL 4; RGSF 2; SSFS 3, 9, 15, 20; TUS; YAW

Wright, Richard B(ruce) 1937- **CLC 6**
See also CA 85-88; CANR 120; DLB 53

Wright, Rick 1945- **CLC 35**

Wright, Rowland
See Wells, Carolyn

Wright, Stephen 1946- **CLC 33**
See also CA 237

Wright, Willard Huntington 1888-1939
See Van Dine, S. S.
See also CA 115; 189; CMW 4; DLBD 16

Wright, William 1930- **CLC 44**
See also CA 53-56; CANR 7, 23, 154

Wroth, Lady Mary 1587-1653(?) **LC 30; PC 38**
See also DLB 121

Wu Ch'eng-en 1500(?)-1582(?) **LC 7**

Wu Ching-tzu 1701-1754 **LC 2**

Wulfstan c. 10th cent. -1023 **CMLC 59**

Wurlitzer, Rudolph 1938(?)- **CLC 2, 4, 15**
See also CA 85-88; CN 4, 5, 6, 7; DLB 173

Wyatt, Sir Thomas c. 1503-1542 . **LC 70; PC 27**
See also BRW 1; DLB 132; EXPP; RGEL 2; TEA

Wycherley, William 1640-1716 **LC 8, 21, 102**
See also BRW 2; CDBLB 1660-1789; DAM DRAM; DLB 80; RGEL 2

Wyclif, John c. 1330-1384 **CMLC 70**
See also DLB 146

Wylie, Elinor (Morton Hoyt)
1885-1928 **PC 23; TCLC 8**
See also AMWS 1; CA 105; 162; DLB 9, 45; EXPP; MAL 5; RGAL 4

Wylie, Philip (Gordon) 1902-1971 ... **CLC 43**
See also CA 21-22; 33-36R; CAP 2; CN 1; DLB 9; SFW 4

Wyndham, John **CLC 19**
See Harris, John (Wyndham Parkes Lucas) Beynon
See also DLB 255; SCFW 1, 2

Wyss, Johann David Von
1743-1818 **NCLC 10**
See also CLR 92; JRDA; MAICYA 1, 2; SATA 29; SATA-Brief 27

Xenophon c. 430B.C.-c. 354B.C. ... **CMLC 17**
See also AW 1; DLB 176; RGWL 2, 3; WLIT 8

Xingjian, Gao 1940-
See Gao Xingjian
See also CA 193; DFS 21; RGWL 3

Yakamochi 718-785 **CMLC 45; PC 48**

Yakumo Koizumi
See Hearn, (Patricio) Lafcadio (Tessima Carlos)

Yamada, Mitsuye (May) 1923- **PC 44**
See also CA 77-80

Yamamoto, Hisaye 1921- **AAL; SSC 34**
See also CA 214; DAM MULT; DLB 312; LAIT 4; SSFS 14

Yamauchi, Wakako 1924- **AAL**
See also CA 214; DLB 312

Yanez, Jose Donoso
See Donoso (Yanez), Jose

Yanovsky, Basile S.
See Yanovsky, V(assily) S(emenovich)

Yanovsky, V(assily) S(emenovich)
1906-1989 **CLC 2, 18**
See also CA 97-100; 129

Yates, Richard 1926-1992 **CLC 7, 8, 23**
See also AMWS 11; CA 5-8R; 139; CANR 10, 43; CN 1, 2, 3, 4, 5; DLB 2, 234; DLBY 1981, 1992; INT CANR-10

Yau, John 1950- **PC 61**
See also CA 154; CANR 89; CP 4, 5, 6, 7;
DLB 234, 312

Yeats, W. B.
See Yeats, William Butler

Yeats, William Butler 1865-1939 . **PC 20, 51;**
TCLC 1, 11, 18, 31, 93, 116; WLC 6
See also AAYA 48; BRW 6; BRWR 1; CA
104; 127; CANR 45; CDBLB 1890-1914;
DA; DA3; DAB; DAC; DAM DRAM,
MST, POET; DLB 10, 19, 98, 156; EWL
3; EXPP; MTCW 1, 2; MTFW 2005;
NCFS 3; PAB; PFS 1, 2, 5, 7, 13, 15;
RGEL 2; TEA; WLIT 4; WP

Yehoshua, A(braham) B. 1936- .. **CLC 13, 31**
See also CA 33-36R; CANR 43, 90, 145;
CWW 2; EWL 3; RGHL; RGSF 2; RGWL
3; WLIT 6

Yellow Bird
See Ridge, John Rollin

Yep, Laurence Michael 1948- **CLC 35**
See also AAYA 5, 31; BYA 7; CA 49-52;
CANR 1, 46, 92; CLR 3, 17, 54; DLB 52,
312; FANT; JRDA; MAICYA 1; MAI-
CYAS 1; SATA 7, 69, 123; WYA; YAW

Yerby, Frank G(arvin) 1916-1991 **BLC 3;**
CLC 1, 7, 22
See also BPFB 3; BW 1, 3; CA 9-12R; 136;
CANR 16, 52; CN 1, 2, 3, 4, 5; DAM
MULT; DLB 76; INT CANR-16; MTCW
1; RGAL 4; RHW

Yesenin, Sergei Alexandrovich
See Esenin, Sergei (Alexandrovich)

Yesenin, Sergey
See Esenin, Sergei (Alexandrovich)
See also EWL 3

Yevtushenko, Yevgeny (Alexandrovich)
1933- **CLC 1, 3, 13, 26, 51, 126; PC**
40
See Evtushenko, Evgenii Aleksandrovich
See also CA 81-84; CANR 33, 54; DAM
POET; EWL 3; MTCW 1; RGHL

Yezierska, Anzia 1885(?)-1970 **CLC 46**
See also CA 126; 89-92; DLB 28, 221; FW;
MTCW 1; RGAL 4; SSFS 15

Yglesias, Helen 1915- **CLC 7, 22**
See also CA 37-40R; CAAS 20; CANR 15,
65, 95; CN 4, 5, 6, 7; INT CANR-15;
MTCW 1

Yokomitsu, Riichi 1898-1947 **TCLC 47**
See also CA 170; EWL 3

Yonge, Charlotte (Mary)
1823-1901 **TCLC 48**
See also CA 109; 163; DLB 18, 163; RGEL
2; SATA 17; WCH

York, Jeremy
See Creasey, John

York, Simon
See Heinlein, Robert A(nson)

Yorke, Henry Vincent 1905-1974 **CLC 13**
See Green, Henry
See also CA 85-88; 49-52

Yosano, Akiko 1878-1942 ... **PC 11; TCLC 59**
See also CA 161; EWL 3; RGWL 3

Yoshimoto, Banana **CLC 84**
See Yoshimoto, Mahoko
See also AAYA 50; NFS 7

Yoshimoto, Mahoko 1964-
See Yoshimoto, Banana
See also CA 144; CANR 98; SSFS 16

Young, Al(bert James) 1939- ... **BLC 3; CLC**
19
See also BW 2, 3; CA 29-32R; CANR 26,
65, 109; CN 2, 3, 4, 5, 6, 7; CP 1, 2, 3, 4,
5, 6, 7; DAM MULT; DLB 33

Young, Andrew (John) 1885-1971 **CLC 5**
See also CA 5-8R; CANR 7, 29; CP 1;
RGEL 2

Young, Collier
See Bloch, Robert (Albert)

Young, Edward 1683-1765 **LC 3, 40**
See also DLB 95; RGEL 2

Young, Marguerite (Vivian)
1909-1995 **CLC 82**
See also CA 13-16; 150; CAP 1; CN 1, 2,
3, 4, 5, 6

Young, Neil 1945- **CLC 17**
See also CA 110; CCA 1

Young Bear, Ray A. 1950- ... **CLC 94; NNAL**
See also CA 146; DAM MULT; DLB 175;
MAL 5

Yourcenar, Marguerite 1903-1987 ... **CLC 19,**
38, 50, 87
See also BPFB 3; CA 69-72; CANR 23, 60,
93; DAM NOV; DLB 72; DLBY 1988;
EW 12; EWL 3; GFL 1789 to the Present;
GLL 1; MTCW 1, 2; MTFW 2005;
RGWL 2, 3

Yuan, Chu 340(?)B.C.-278(?)B.C. . **CMLC 36**

Yurick, Sol 1925- **CLC 6**
See also CA 13-16R; CANR 25; CN 1, 2,
3, 4, 5, 6, 7; MAL 5

Zabolotsky, Nikolai Alekseevich
1903-1958 **TCLC 52**
See Zabolotsky, Nikolay Alekseevich
See also CA 116; 164

Zabolotsky, Nikolay Alekseevich
See Zabolotsky, Nikolai Alekseevich
See also EWL 3

Zagajewski, Adam 1945- **PC 27**
See also CA 186; DLB 232; EWL 3

Zalygin, Sergei -2000 **CLC 59**

Zalygin, Sergei (Pavlovich)
1913-2000 **CLC 59**
See also DLB 302

Zamiatin, Evgenii
See Zamyatin, Evgeny Ivanovich
See also RGSF 2; RGWL 2, 3

Zamiatin, Evgenii Ivanovich
See Zamyatin, Evgeny Ivanovich
See also DLB 272

Zamiatin, Yevgenii
See Zamyatin, Evgeny Ivanovich

Zamora, Bernice (B. Ortiz) 1938- .. **CLC 89;**
HLC 2
See also CA 151; CANR 80; DAM MULT;
DLB 82; HW 1, 2

Zamyatin, Evgeny Ivanovich
1884-1937 **SSC 89; TCLC 8, 37**
See Zamiatin, Evgenii; Zamiatin, Evgenii
Ivanovich; Zamyatin, Yevgeny Ivanovich
See also CA 105; 166; SFW 4

Zamyatin, Yevgeny Ivanovich
See Zamyatin, Evgeny Ivanovich
See also EW 10; EWL 3

Zangwill, Israel 1864-1926 ... **SSC 44; TCLC**
16
See also CA 109; 167; CMW 4; DLB 10,
135, 197; RGEL 2

Zanzotto, Andrea 1921- **PC 65**
See also CA 208; CWW 2; DLB 128; EWL
3

Zappa, Francis Vincent, Jr. 1940-1993
See Zappa, Frank
See also CA 108; 143; CANR 57

Zappa, Frank **CLC 17**
See Zappa, Francis Vincent, Jr.

Zaturenska, Marya 1902-1982 **CLC 6, 11**
See also CA 13-16R; 105; CANR 22; CP 1,
2, 3

Zayas y Sotomayor, Maria de 1590-c.
1661 **LC 102**
See also RGSF 2

Zeami 1363-1443 **DC 7; LC 86**
See also DLB 203; RGWL 2, 3

Zelazny, Roger (Joseph) 1937-1995 . **CLC 21**
See also AAYA 7, 68; BPFB 3; CA 21-24R;
148; CANR 26, 60; CN 6; DLB 8; FANT;
MTCW 1, 2; MTFW 2005; SATA 57;
SATA-Brief 39; SCFW 1, 2; SFW 4;
SUFW 1, 2

Zhang Ailing
See Chang, Eileen
See also CWW 2; RGSF 2

Zhdanov, Andrei Alexandrovich
1896-1948 **TCLC 18**
See also CA 117; 167

Zhukovsky, Vasilii Andreevich
See Zhukovsky, Vasily (Andreevich)
See also DLB 205

Zhukovsky, Vasily (Andreevich)
1783-1852 **NCLC 35**
See Zhukovsky, Vasilii Andreevich

Ziegenhagen, Eric **CLC 55**

Zimmer, Jill Schary
See Robinson, Jill

Zimmerman, Robert
See Dylan, Bob

Zindel, Paul 1936-2003 **CLC 6, 26; DC 5**
See also AAYA 2, 37; BYA 2, 3, 8, 11, 14;
CA 73-76; 213; CAD; CANR 31, 65, 108;
CD 5, 6; CDALBS; CLR 3, 45, 85; DA;
DA3; DAB; DAC; DAM DRAM, MST,
NOV; DFS 12; DLB 7, 52; JRDA; LAIT
5; MAICYA 1, 2; MTCW 1, 2; MTFW
2005; NFS 14; SATA 16, 58, 102; SATA-
Obit 142; WYA; YAW

Zinn, Howard 1922- **CLC 199**
See also CA 1-4R; CANR 2, 33, 90

Zinov'Ev, A.A.
See Zinoviev, Alexander

Zinov'ev, Aleksandr
See Zinoviev, Alexander
See also DLB 302

Zinoviev, Alexander 1922-2006 **CLC 19**
See Zinov'ev, Aleksandr
See also CA 116; 133; CAAS 10

Zinoviev, Alexander Aleksandrovich
See Zinoviev, Alexander

Zizek, Slavoj 1949- **CLC 188**
See also CA 201; MTFW 2005

Zoilus
See Lovecraft, H. P.

Zola, Emile (Edouard Charles Antoine)
1840-1902 .. **TCLC 1, 6, 21, 41; WLC 6**
See also CA 104; 138; DA; DA3; DAB;
DAC; DAM MST, NOV; DLB 123; EW
7; GFL 1789 to the Present; IDTP; LMFS
1, 2; RGWL 2; TWA

Zoline, Pamela 1941- **CLC 62**
See also CA 161; SFW 4

Zoroaster 628(?)B.C.-551(?)B.C. ... **CMLC 40**

Zorrilla y Moral, Jose 1817-1893 **NCLC 6**

Zoshchenko, Mikhail (Mikhailovich)
1895-1958 **SSC 15; TCLC 15**
See also CA 115; 160; EWL 3; RGSF 2;
RGWL 3

Zuckmayer, Carl 1896-1977 **CLC 18**
See also CA 69-72; DLB 56, 124; EWL 3;
RGWL 2, 3

Zuk, Georges
See Skelton, Robin
See also CCA 1

Zukofsky, Louis 1904-1978 ... **CLC 1, 2, 4, 7,**
11, 18; PC 11
See also AMWS 3; CA 9-12R; 77-80;
CANR 39; CP 1, 2; DAM POET; DLB 5,
165; EWL 3; MAL 5; MTCW 1; RGAL 4

Zweig, Paul 1935-1984 **CLC 34, 42**
See also CA 85-88; 113

Zweig, Stefan 1881-1942 **TCLC 17**
See also CA 112; 170; DLB 81, 118; EWL
3; RGHL

Zwingli, Huldreich 1484-1531 **LC 37**
See also DLB 179

Literary Criticism Series
Cumulative Topic Index

This index lists all topic entries in Thompson Gale's *Children's Literature Review* (CLR), *Classical and Medieval Literature Criticism* (CMLC), *Contemporary Literary Criticism* (CLC), *Drama Criticism* (DC), *Literature Criticism from 1400 to 1800* (LC), *Nineteenth-Century Literature Criticism* (NCLC), *Short Story Criticism* (SSC), and *Twentieth-Century Literary Criticism* (TCLC). The index also lists topic entries in the Gale Critical Companion Collection, which includes the following publications: *The Beat Generation* (BG), *Feminism in Literature* (FL), *Gothic Literature* (GL), and *Harlem Renaissance* (HR).

Abbey Theatre in the Irish Literary Renaissance TCLC 154: 1-114
origins and development, 2-14
major figures, 14-30
plays and controversies, 30-59
artistic vision and significance, 59-114

Abolitionist Literature of Cuba and Brazil, Nineteenth-Century NCLC 132: 1-94
overviews, 2-11
origins and development, 11-23
sociopolitical concerns, 23-39
poetry, 39-47
prose, 47-93

The Aborigine in Nineteenth-Century Australian Literature NCLC 120: 1-88
overviews, 2-27
representations of the Aborigine in Australian literature, 27-58
Aboriginal myth, literature, and oral tradition, 58-88

The Aesopic Fable LC 51: 1-100
the British Aesopic Fable, 1-54
the Aesopic tradition in non-English-speaking cultures, 55-66
political uses of the Aesopic fable, 67-88
the evolution of the Aesopic fable, 89-99

African-American Folklore and Literature TCLC 126: 1-67
African-American folk tradition, 1-16
representative writers, 16-34
hallmark works, 35-48
the study of African-American literature and folklore, 48-64

Age of al-Andalus CMLC 81: 1-174
overviews, 1-48
history, society, and culture, 48-127
Andalusī poetry, 127-73

Age of Johnson LC 15: 1-87
Johnson's London, 3-15
aesthetics of neoclassicism, 15-36
"age of prose and reason," 36-45
clubmen and bluestockings, 45-56
printing technology, 56-62
periodicals: "a map of busy life," 62-74
transition, 74-86

The Age of King Alfred the Great CMLC 79: 1-141
overviews and historical background, 4-17

the Alfredian translations, 17-43
King Alfred's prefaces, 43-84
Alfred and Boethius, 84-140

Age of Spenser LC 39: 1-70
overviews and general studies, 2-21
literary style, 22-34
poets and the crown, 34-70

AIDS in Literature CLC 81: 365-416

Alcohol and Literature TCLC 70: 1-58
overview, 2-8
fiction, 8-48
poetry and drama, 48-58

American Abolitionism NCLC 44: 1-73
overviews and general studies, 2-26
abolitionist ideals, 26-46
the literature of abolitionism, 46-72

American Autobiography TCLC 86: 1-115
overviews and general studies, 3-36
American authors and autobiography, 36-82
African-American autobiography, 82-114

American Black Humor Fiction TCLC 54: 1-85
characteristics of black humor, 2-13
origins and development, 13-38
black humor distinguished from related literary trends, 38-60
black humor and society, 60-75
black humor reconsidered, 75-83

American Civil War in Literature NCLC 32: 1-109
overviews and general studies, 2-20
regional perspectives, 20-54
fiction popular during the war, 54-79
the historical novel, 79-108

American Frontier in Literature NCLC 28: 1-103
definitions, 2-12
development, 12-17
nonfiction writing about the frontier, 17-30
frontier fiction, 30-45
frontier protagonists, 45-66
portrayals of Native Americans, 66-86
feminist readings, 86-98
twentieth-century reaction against frontier literature, 98-100

American Humor Writing NCLC 52: 1-59
overviews and general studies, 2-12

the Old Southwest, 12-42
broader impacts, 42-5
women humorists, 45-58

American Naturalism in Short Fiction SSC 77: 1-103
overviews and general studies, 2-30
major authors of American literary Naturalism, 30-102
Ambrose Bierce, 30
Stephen Crane, 30-53
Theodore Dreiser, 53-65
Jack London, 65-80
Frank Norris, 80-9
Edith Wharton, 89-102

American Novel of Manners TCLC 130: 1-42
history of the Novel of Manners in America, 4-10
representative writers, 10-18
relevancy of the Novel of Manners, 18-24
hallmark works in the Novel of Manners, 24-36
Novel of Manners and other media, 36-40

American Mercury, The TCLC 74: 1-80

American Popular Song, Golden Age of TCLC 42: 1-49
background and major figures, 2-34
the lyrics of popular songs, 34-47

American Proletarian Literature TCLC 54: 86-175
overviews and general studies, 87-95
American proletarian literature and the American Communist Party, 95-111
ideology and literary merit, 111-17
novels, 117-36
Gastonia, 136-48
drama, 148-54
journalism, 154-9
proletarian literature in the United States, 159-74

American Realism NCLC 120: 89-246
overviews, 91-112
background and sources, 112-72
social issues, 172-223
women and realism, 223-45

American Renaissance SSC 64: 46-193
overviews and general studies, 47-103
major authors of short fiction, 103-92

American Romanticism NCLC 44: 74-138
overviews and general studies, 74-84
sociopolitical influences, 84-104
Romanticism and the American frontier, 104-15
thematic concerns, 115-37

American Western Literature TCLC 46: 1-100
definition and development of American Western literature, 2-7
characteristics of the Western novel, 8-23
Westerns as history and fiction, 23-34
critical reception of American Western literature, 34-41
the Western hero, 41-73
women in Western fiction, 73-91
later Western fiction, 91-9

American Writers in Paris TCLC 98: 1-156
overviews and general studies, 2-155

Anarchism NCLC 84: 1-97
overviews and general studies, 2-23
the French anarchist tradition, 23-56
Anglo-American anarchism, 56-68
anarchism: incidents and issues, 68-97

Angry Young Men TCLC 166: 1-80
overviews, 2-18
major figures, 18-58
themes and style, 58-79

Animals in Literature TCLC 106: 1-120
overviews and general studies, 2-8
animals in American literature, 8-45
animals in Canadian literature, 45-57
animals in European literature, 57-100
animals in Latin American literature, 100-06
animals in women's literature, 106-20

Antebellum South, Literature of the NCLC 112:1-188
overviews, 4-55
culture of the Old South, 55-68
antebellum fiction: pastoral and heroic romance, 68-120
role of women: a subdued rebellion, 120-59
slavery and the slave narrative, 159-85

Anti-Americanism TCLC 158: 1-98
overviews and general studies, 3-18
literary and intellectual perspectives, 18-36
social and political reactions, 36-98

Anti-Apartheid TCLC 162: 1-121
overviews, 3-45
major authors, 45-74
anti-apartheid literature and the liberal tradition, 74-101
writing under apartheid: historical views, 101-20

The Apocalyptic Movement TCLC 106: 121-69

Aristotle CMLC 31:1-397
philosophy, 3-100
poetics, 101-219
rhetoric, 220-301
science, 302-397

Art and Literature TCLC 54: 176-248
overviews and general studies, 176-93
definitions, 193-219
influence of visual arts on literature, 219-31
spatial form in literature, 231-47

Arthurian Literature CMLC 10: 1-127
historical context and literary beginnings, 2-27
development of the legend through Malory, 27-64
development of the legend from Malory to the Victorian Age, 65-81
themes and motifs, 81-95
principal characters, 95-125

Arthurian Revival NCLC 36: 1-77
overviews and general studies, 2-12
Tennyson and his influence, 12-43
other leading figures, 43-73
the Arthurian legend in the visual arts, 73-6

The Audience and Nineteenth-Century Literature NCLC 160: 1-158
overviews, 3-35
race, class, gender, 35-89
America, 89-102
Britain and Europe, 102-30
genre and audience, 130-57

Australian Cultural Identity in Nineteenth-Century Literature NCLC 124: 1-164
overviews and general studies, 4-22
poetry, 22-67
fiction, 67-135
role of women writers, 135-64

Australian Literature TCLC 50: 1-94
origins and development, 2-21
characteristics of Australian literature, 21-33
historical and critical perspectives, 33-41
poetry, 41-58
fiction, 58-76
drama, 76-82
Aboriginal literature, 82-91

Aztec Myths and Literature LC 122: 1-182
Overviews and General Studies, 3-68
Cosmology, 68-136
Language and Literature, 136-81

The Beat Generation BG 1:1-562
the Beat Generation: an overview, 1-137
primary sources, 3-32
overviews and general studies, 32-47
Beat Generation as a social phenomenon, 47-65
drugs, inspiration, and the Beat Generation, 65-92
religion and the Beat Generation, 92-124
women of the Beat Generation, 124-36
Beat "scene": East and West, 139-259
primary sources, 141-77
Beat scene in the East, 177-218
Beat scene in the West, 218-59
Beat Generation publishing: periodicals, small presses, and censorship, 261-349
primary sources, 263-74
overview, 274-88
Beat periodicals: "little magazines," 288-311
Beat publishing: small presses, 311-24
Beat battles with censorship, 324-49
performing arts and the Beat Generation, 351-417
primary sources, 353-58
Beats and film, 358-81
Beats and music, 381-415
visual arts and the Beat Generation, 419-91
primary sources, 421-24
critical commentary, 424-90

Beat Generation, Literature of the TCLC 42: 50-102
overviews and general studies, 51-9
the Beat generation as a social phenomenon, 59-62
development, 62-5
Beat literature, 66-96
influence, 97-100

The Bell Curve Controversy CLC 91: 281-330

***Bildungsroman* in Nineteenth-Century Literature** NCLC 20: 92-168
surveys, 93-113
in Germany, 113-40
in England, 140-56
female *Bildungsroman*, 156-67
NCLC 152: 1-129
overview, 3-16

definition and issues, 16-52
female *Bildungsromane* , 52-83
ideology and nationhood, 83-128

Black Humor, Contemporary CLC 196: 1-128
overviews and general studies, 2-18
black humor in American fiction, 18-28
development and history, 29-62
major authors, 62-115
technique and narrative, 115-127

The Bloomsbury Group TCLC 34: 1-73
history and major figures, 2-13
definitions, 13-7
influences, 17-27
thought, 27-40
prose, 40-52
and literary criticism, 52-4
political ideals, 54-61
response to, 61-71

The Bloomsbury Group TCLC 138: 1-59
representative members of the Bloomsbury Group, 9-24
literary relevance of the Bloomsbury Group, 24-36
Bloomsbury's hallmark works, 36-48
other modernists studied with the Bloomsbury Group, 48-54

The Blues in Literature TCLC 82: 1-71

Bly, Robert, *Iron John: A Book about Men and Men's Work* CLC 70: 414-62

The Book of J CLC 65: 289-311

The Book of Common Prayer LC 118: 1-76
overviews, 2-43
translation and diffusion, 44-63
influence of the Prayer Book, 63-76

Brazilian Literature TCLC 134: 1-126
overviews and general studies, 3-33
Brazilian poetry, 33-48
contemporary Brazilian writing, 48-76
culture, politics, and race in Brazilian writing, 76-100
modernism and postmodernism in Brazil, 100-25

British Ephemeral Literature LC 59: 1-70
overviews and general studies, 1-9
broadside ballads, 10-40
chapbooks, jestbooks, pamphlets, and newspapers, 40-69

Buddhism and Literature TCLC 70: 59-164
eastern literature, 60-113
western literature, 113-63

Buddhism in the Nineteenth-Century Western World NCLC 164: 1-88
overviews, 3-47
Buddhism and Western Philosophers, 47-74
Buddhism in Western Literature, 74-88

The *Bulletin* and the Rise of Australian Literary Nationalism NCLC 116: 1-121
overviews, 3-32
legend of the nineties, 32-55
Bulletin style, 55-71
Australian literary nationalism, 71-98
myth of the bush, 98-120

Businessman in American Literature TCLC 26: 1-48
portrayal of the businessman, 1-32
themes and techniques in business fiction, 32-47

The Calendar LC 55: 1-92
overviews and general studies, 2-19
measuring time, 19-28
calendars and culture, 28-60
calendar reform, 60-92

Captivity Narratives LC 82: 71-172
overviews, 72-107
captivity narratives and Puritanism, 108-34

captivity narratives and Native Americans, 134-49
influence on American literature, 149-72

Caribbean Literature TCLC 138: 60-135
overviews and general studies, 61-9
ethnic and national identity, 69-107
expatriate Caribbean literature, 107-23
literary histoiography, 123-35

Catholicism in Nineteenth-Century American Literature NCLC 64: 1-58
overviews, 3-14
polemical literature, 14-46
Catholicism in literature, 47-57

Cavalier Poetry and Drama LC 107: 1-71
overviews, 2-36
Cavalier drama, 36-48
major figures, 48-70

Celtic Mythology CMLC 26: 1-111
overviews and general studies, 2-22
Celtic myth as literature and history, 22-48
Celtic religion: Druids and divinities, 48-80
Fionn MacCuhaill and the Fenian cycle, 80-111

Celtic Twilight See Irish Literary Renaissance

Censorship and Contemporary World Literature CLC 194: 1-80
overviews and general studies, 2-19
notorious cases, 19-59
censorship in the global context, 59-79

Censorship of the Press in the Nineteenth Century NCLC 156: 1-133
overviews, 3-29
censorship in Austria, Germany, and Russia, 29-87
censorship in France and Spain, 87-120
censorship in England and America, 120-33

Censorship in Twentieth-Century Literature TCLC 154: 115-238
overviews and general studies, 117-25
censorship and obscenity trials, 125-61
censorship and sexual politics, 161-81
censorship and war, 181-207
political censorship and the state, 207-28
censorship and the writer, 228-38

The Chartist Movement and Literature NCLC 60: 1-84
overview: nineteenth-century working-class fiction, 2-19
Chartist fiction and poetry, 19-73
the Chartist press, 73-84

The Chicago Renaissance TCLC 154: 239-341
overviews and general studies, 240-60
definitions and growth, 260-82
the language debate, 282-318
major authors, 318-40

Chicano/a Literature, Contemporary CLC 205: 82-181
overviews, 84-124
Chicana studies, 124-40
some representative works, 140-80

Chick-Lit and Lad-Lit CLC 210: 115-64
overviews, 117-25
the debate over Chick Lit, 125-46
representative authors, 146-64

Child Labor in Nineteenth-Century Literature NCLC 108: 1-133
overviews, 3-10
climbing boys and chimney sweeps, 10-16
the international traffic in children, 16-45
critics and reformers, 45-82
fictional representations of child laborers, 83-132

Childhood in Nineteenth-Century Literature NCLC 172: 1-140
overviews, 2-20
Romanticism and childhood, 20-46
childhood in the works of William Wordsworth, 46-72
childhood in the works of Charles Dickens, 72-106
childhood in the works of Leo Tolstoy, 106-29
childhood in the works of Emily Dickinson, 129-39

Children's Literature, Nineteenth-Century NCLC 52: 60-135
overviews and general studies, 61-72
moral tales, 72-89
fairy tales and fantasy, 90-119
making men/making women, 119-34

Christianity in Twentieth-Century Literature TCLC 110: 1-79
overviews and general studies, 2-31
Christianity in twentieth-century fiction, 31-78

Chronicle Plays LC 89: 1-106
development of the genre, 2-33
historiography and literature, 33-56
genre and performance, 56-88
politics and ideology, 88-106

The City and Literature TCLC 90: 1-124
overviews and general studies, 2-9
the city in American literature, 9-86
the city in European literature, 86-124

City Comedy LC 118: 77-211
origins and development, 79-113
economic issues, 113-32
women and city comedy, 132-82
the plays of Thomas Middleton, 182-211

Civic Critics, Russian NCLC 20: 402-46
principal figures and background, 402-9
and Russian Nihilism, 410-6
aesthetic and critical views, 416-45

The Cockney School NCLC 68: 1-64
overview, 2-7
Blackwood's Magazine and the contemporary critical response, 7-24
the political and social import of the Cockneys and their critics, 24-63

Colonial America: The Intellectual Background LC 25: 1-98
overviews and general studies, 2-17
philosophy and politics, 17-31
early religious influences in Colonial America, 31-60
consequences of the Revolution, 60-78
religious influences in post-revolutionary America, 78-87
colonial literary genres, 87-97

Colonialism in Victorian English Literature NCLC 56: 1-77
overviews and general studies, 2-34
colonialism and gender, 34-51
monsters and the occult, 51-76

Columbus, Christopher, Books on the Quincentennial of His Arrival in the New World CLC 70: 329-60

Comic Books TCLC 66: 1-139
historical and critical perspectives, 2-48
superheroes, 48-67
underground comix, 67-88
comic books and society, 88-122
adult comics and graphic novels, 122-36

Comedy of Manners LC 92: 1-75
overviews, 2-21
comedy of manners and society, 21-47
comedy of manners and women, 47-74

Commedia dell'Arte LC 83: 1-147
overviews, 2-7
origins and development, 7-23
characters and actors, 23-45
performance, 45-62
texts and authors, 62-100
influence in Europe, 100-46

Conduct Books in Nineteenth-Century Literature NCLC 152: 130-229
women's education, 131-68
feminist revisions, 168-82
American behavioral literature: cultivating national identity, 182-209
English behavioral literature: defining a middle class, 209-27

Connecticut Wits NCLC 48: 1-95
overviews and general studies, 2-40
major works, 40-76
intellectual context, 76-95

Crime Fiction, Contemporary CLC 209: 34-192
overviews, 37-61
ethnicity and race in crime fiction, 61-105
literary traditions and crime fiction, 105-43
themes, 143-81
representative authors, 181-92

Crime in Literature TCLC 54: 249-307
evolution of the criminal figure in literature, 250-61
crime and society, 261-77
literary perspectives on crime and punishment, 277-88
writings by criminals, 288-306

Crime-Mystery-Detective Stories SSC 59:89-226
overviews and general studies, 90-140
origins and early masters of the crime-mystery-detective story, 140-73
hard-boiled crime-mystery-detective fiction, 173-209
diversity in the crime-mystery-detective story, 210-25

The Crusades CMLC 38: 1-144
history of the Crusades, 3-60
literature of the Crusades, 60-116
the Crusades and the people: attitudes and influences, 116-44

Cuban Exile Literature, Contemporary CLC 207: 1-100
overviews, 2-20
Cubana writers and exile, 20-48
some representative works, 48-100

Cyberpunk TCLC 106: 170-366
overviews and general studies, 171-88
feminism and cyberpunk, 188-230
history and cyberpunk, 230-70
sexuality and cyberpunk, 270-98
social issues and cyberpunk, 299-366

Cyberpunk Short Fiction SSC 60: 44-108
overviews and general studies, 46-78
major writers of cyberpunk fiction, 78-81
sexuality and cyberpunk fiction, 81-97
additional pieces, 97-108

Czechoslovakian Literature of the Twentieth Century TCLC 42:103-96
through World War II, 104-35
de-Stalinization, the Prague Spring, and contemporary literature, 135-72
Slovak literature, 172-85
Czech science fiction, 185-93

Dadaism TCLC 46: 101-71
background and major figures, 102-16
definitions, 116-26
manifestos and commentary by Dadaists, 126-40

theater and film, 140-58
nature and characteristics of Dadaist writing, 158-70

Danish Literature See Twentieth-Century Danish Literature

Darwinism and Literature NCLC 32: 110-206
background, 110-31
direct responses to Darwin, 131-71
collateral effects of Darwinism, 171-205

Death in American Literature NCLC 92: 1-170
overviews and general studies, 2-32
death in the works of Emily Dickinson, 32-72
death in the works of Herman Melville, 72-101
death in the works of Edgar Allan Poe, 101-43
death in the works of Walt Whitman, 143-70

Death in Nineteenth-Century British Literature NCLC 68: 65-142
overviews and general studies, 66-92
responses to death, 92-102
feminist perspectives, 103-17
striving for immortality, 117-41

Death in Literature TCLC 78: 1-183
fiction, 2-115
poetry, 115-46
drama, 146-81

Decadence in Nineteenth-Century Literature NCLC 164: 90-191
overviews, 90-132
Decadent literary subjects, 132-44
Decadence in British literature, 144-57
Decadence in French literature, 158-79
women writers and Decadence, 179-90

Deconstruction TCLC 138: 136-256
overviews and general studies, 137-83
deconstruction and literature, 183-221
deconstruction in philosophy and history, 221-56

de Man, Paul, Wartime Journalism of CLC 55: 382-424

Depictions of Islam in Modern Literature TCLC 166: 81-198
overviews, 82-115
literature in the Muslim world, 115-56
Western interpretations, 156-82
women, Islam, and literature, 182-97

Detective Fiction, Nineteenth-Century NCLC 36: 78-148
origins of the genre, 79-100
history of nineteenth-century detective fiction, 101-33
significance of nineteenth-century detective fiction, 133-46
NCLC 148: 1-161
overviews, 3-26
origins and influences, 26-63
major authors, 63-134
Freud and detective fiction, 134-59

Detective Fiction, Twentieth-Century TCLC 38: 1-96
genesis and history of the detective story, 3-22
defining detective fiction, 22-32
evolution and varieties, 32-77
the appeal of detective fiction, 77-90

Detective Story See Crime-Mystery-Detective Stories

Dime Novels NCLC 84: 98-168
overviews and general studies, 99-123
popular characters, 123-39
major figures and influences, 139-52
socio-political concerns, 152-167

Disease and Literature TCLC 66: 140-283
overviews and general studies, 141-65
disease in nineteenth-century literature, 165-81
tuberculosis and literature, 181-94
women and disease in literature, 194-221
plague literature, 221-53
AIDS in literature, 253-82

El Dorado, The Legend of See The Legend of El Dorado

The Double in Nineteenth-Century Literature NCLC 40: 1-95
genesis and development of the theme, 2-15
the double and Romanticism, 16-27
sociological views, 27-52
psychological interpretations, 52-87
philosophical considerations, 87-95

Dramatic Realism NCLC 44: 139-202
overviews and general studies, 140-50
origins and definitions, 150-66
impact and influence, 166-93
realist drama and tragedy, 193-201

Drugs and Literature TCLC 78: 184-282
overviews and general studies, 185-201
pre-twentieth-century literature, 201-42
twentieth-century literature, 242-82

Dystopias in Contemporary Literature CLC 168: 1-91
overviews and general studies, 2-52
dystopian views in Margaret Atwood's *The Handmaid's Tale* (1985), 52-71
feminist readings of dystopias, 71-90

Eastern Mythology CMLC 26: 112-92
heroes and kings, 113-51
cross-cultural perspective, 151-69
relations to history and society, 169-92

Ecocriticism and Nineteenth-Century Literature NCLC 140: 1-168
overviews, 3-20
American literature: Romantics and Realists, 20-76
American explorers and naturalists, 76-123
English literature: Romantics and Victorians, 123-67

Ecofeminism and Nineteenth-Century Literature NCLC 136: 1-110
overviews, 2-24
the local landscape, 24-72
travel writing, 72-109

Eighteenth-Century British Periodicals LC 63: 1-123
rise of periodicals, 2-31
impact and influence of periodicals, 31-64
periodicals and society, 64-122

Eighteenth-Century Travel Narratives LC 77: 252-355
overviews and general studies, 254-79
eighteenth-century European travel narratives, 279-334
non-European eighteenth-century travel narratives, 334-55

Electronic "Books": Hypertext and Hyperfiction CLC 86: 367-404
books vs. CD-ROMS, 367-76
hypertext and hyperfiction, 376-95
implications for publishing, libraries, and the public, 395-403

Eliot, T. S., Centenary of Birth CLC 55: 345-75

Elizabethan Drama LC 22: 140-240
origins and influences, 142-67
characteristics and conventions, 167-83
theatrical production, 184-200
histories, 200-12
comedy, 213-20
tragedy, 220-30

Elizabethan Prose Fiction LC 41: 1-70
overviews and general studies, 1-15
origins and influences, 15-43
style and structure, 43-69

The Emergence of the Short Story in the Nineteenth Century NCLC 140: 169-279
overviews, 171-74
the American short story, 174-214
the short story in Great Britain and Ireland, 214-235
stories by women in English, 235-45
the short story in France and Russia, 245-66
the Latin American short story, 266-77

Enclosure of the English Common NCLC 88: 1-57
overviews and general studies, 1-12
early reaction to enclosure, 12-23
nineteenth-century reaction to enclosure, 23-56

The Encyclopedists LC 26: 172-253
overviews and general studies, 173-210
intellectual background, 210-32
views on esthetics, 232-41
views on women, 241-52

English Abolitionist Literature of the Nineteenth Century NCLC 136: 111-235
overview, 112-35
origins and development, 135-42
poetry, 142-58
prose, 158-80
sociopolitical concerns, 180-95
English abolitionist literature and feminism, 195-233

English Caroline Literature LC 13: 221-307
background, 222-41
evolution and varieties, 241-62
the Cavalier mode, 262-75
court and society, 275-91
politics and religion, 291-306

English Decadent Literature of the 1890s NCLC 28: 104-200
fin de siècle: the Decadent period, 105-19
definitions, 120-37
major figures: "the tragic generation," 137-50
French literature and English literary Decadence, 150-7
themes, 157-61
poetry, 161-82
periodicals, 182-96

English Emblem Books LC 125: 1-99
overviews, 2-27
background and contexts, 27-63
major emblem writers, 63-83
religion and emblem books, 83-99

English Essay, Rise of the LC 18: 238-308
definitions and origins, 236-54
influence on the essay, 254-69
historical background, 269-78
the essay in the seventeenth century, 279-93
the essay in the eighteenth century, 293-307

English Mystery Cycle Dramas LC 34: 1-88
overviews and general studies, 1-27
the nature of dramatic performances, 27-42
the medieval worldview and the mystery cycles, 43-67
the doctrine of repentance and the mystery cycles, 67-76
the fall from grace in the mystery cycles, 76-88

The English Realist Novel, 1740-1771 LC 51: 102-98
overviews and general studies, 103-22
from Romanticism to Realism, 123-58
women and the novel, 159-175
the novel and other literary forms, 176-197

English Revolution, Literature of the LC 43: 1-58
overviews and general studies, 2-24
pamphlets of the English Revolution, 24-38
political sermons of the English Revolution, 38-48
poetry of the English Revolution, 48-57

English Romantic Hellenism NCLC 68: 143-250
overviews and general studies, 144-69
historical development of English Romantic Hellenism, 169-91
influence of Greek mythology on the Romantics, 191-229
influence of Greek literature, art, and culture on the Romantics, 229-50

English Romantic Poetry NCLC 28: 201-327
overviews and reputation, 202-37
major subjects and themes, 237-67
forms of Romantic poetry, 267-78
politics, society, and Romantic poetry, 278-99
philosophy, religion, and Romantic poetry, 299-324

The Epistolary Novel LC 59: 71-170
overviews and general studies, 72-96
women and the Epistolary novel, 96-138
principal figures: Britain, 138-53
principal figures: France, 153-69

Espionage Literature TCLC 50: 95-159
overviews and general studies, 96-113
espionage fiction/formula fiction, 113-26
spies in fact and fiction, 126-38
the female spy, 138-44
social and psychological perspectives, 144-58

European Debates on the Conquest of the Americas LC 67: 1-129
overviews and general studies, 3-56
major Spanish figures, 56-98
English perceptions of Native Americans, 98-129

European Romanticism NCLC 36: 149-284
definitions, 149-77
origins of the movement, 177-82
Romantic theory, 182-200
themes and techniques, 200-23
Romanticism in Germany, 223-39
Romanticism in France, 240-61
Romanticism in Italy, 261-4
Romanticism in Spain, 264-8
impact and legacy, 268-82

Exile in Literature TCLC 122: 1-129
overviews and general studies, 2-33
exile in fiction, 33-92
German literature in exile, 92-129

Exile in Nineteenth-Century European and American Literature NCLC 172: 141-248
overview, 143-51
exile in French literature, 151-81
exile in British literature, 181-202
exile in American literature, 202-27
women and exile, 227-47

Existentialism and Literature TCLC 42: 197-268
overviews and definitions, 198-209
history and influences, 209-19
Existentialism critiqued and defended, 220-35
philosophical and religious perspectives, 235-41
Existentialist fiction and drama, 241-67

Ezra Pound Controversy TCLC 150: 1-132
politics of Ezra Pound, 3-42
anti-semitism of Ezra Pound, 42-57
the Bollingen Award controversy, 57-76
Pound's later writing, 76-104
criticism of *The Pisan Cantos,* 104-32

Familiar Essay NCLC 48: 96-211
definitions and origins, 97-130
overview of the genre, 130-43
elements of form and style, 143-59
elements of content, 159-73
the Cockneys: Hazlitt, Lamb, and Hunt, 173-91
status of the genre, 191-210

Fantasy in Contemporary Literature CLC 193: 137-250
overviews and general studies, 139-57
language, form, and theory, 157-91
major writers, 191-230
women writers and fantasy, 230-50

Fashion in Nineteenth-Century Literature NCLC 128: 104-93
overviews and general studies, 105-38
fashion and American literature, 138-46
fashion and English literature, 146-74
fashion and French literature, 174-92

The Faust Legend LC 47: 1-117

Fear in Literature TCLC 74: 81-258
overviews and general studies, 81
pre-twentieth-century literature, 123
twentieth-century literature, 182

Feminism in the 1990s: Commentary on Works by Naomi Wolf, Susan Faludi, and Camille Paglia CLC 76: 377-415

Feminist Criticism, Contemporary CLC 180: 1-103
overviews and general studies, 2-59
modern French feminist theory, 59-102

Feminist Criticism in 1990 CLC 65: 312-60

Feminism in Literature FL 1: 1-279; 2: 1-295; 4: 1-626
women and women's writings from antiquity through the middle ages, 1:1-99
primary sources, 1:4-12
women in the ancient world, 1:12-34
women in the medieval world, 1:34-56
women in classical art and literature, 1:56-74
classical and medieval women writers, 1:74-96
women in the 16th, 17th, and 18th centuries: an overview, 1:101-91
primary sources, 1:104-11
overviews, 1:112-32
society, 1:132-64
politics, 1:164-77
women in literature, 1:177-90
women's literature in the 16th, 17th, and 18th centuries 1:193-279
primary sources, 1:195-201
overviews, 1:202-39
women's literature in the 16th, 17th, and 18th centuries, 1:239-78
women in the 19th century: an overview, 2:1-88
primary sources, 2:3-15
overviews, 2:15-50
early feminists, 2:50-67
representations of women in literature and art in the 19th century, 2:67-86
women's literature in the 19th century, 2:89-206
primary sources, 2:91-9
overviews, 2:99-140
American women writers, 2:141-77
British women writers, 2:177-204
United States suffrage movement in the 19th century, 2:207-95
primary sources, 2:209-29
overviews, 2:229-39
the civil war and its effect on suffrage, 2:239-53
suffrage: issues and individuals, 2:253-94
women in the early to mid-20th century (1900-1960): an overview, 4:1-126

primary sources, 4:1-14
overviews, 4:14-48
social and economic conditions, 4:48-67
women and the arts, 4:67-125
suffrage in the 20th century, 4:127-234
primary sources, 4:129-36
overviews, 4:136-77
major figures and organizations, 4:177-214
women and law, 4:214-32
women's literature from 1900 to 1960, 4:235-344
primary sources, 4:238-41
overviews, 4:241-61
impact of the world wars, 4:261-304
women and the dramatic tradition, 4:304-39
Asian American influences, 4:339-42
the feminist movement in the 20th century, 4:345-443
primary sources, 4:347-58
overviews, 4:358-403
feminist legal battles, 4:403-34
third-wave feminism, 4:434-42
women's literature from 1960 to the present, 4:445-536
primary sources, 4:448-60
overviews, 4:460-83
women authors of color, 4:483-97
feminist literary theory, 4:497-511
modern lesbian literature, 4:511-534

Fifteenth-Century English Literature LC 17: 248-334
background, 249-72
poetry, 272-315
drama, 315-23
prose, 323-33

Fifteenth-Century Spanish Poetry LC 100: 82-173
overviews and general studies, 83-101
the Cancioneros, 101-57
major figures, 157-72

The Figure of La Malinche in Mexican Literature LC 127: 91-172
Overview 92-108
The Historical Malinche 108-33
Malinche Reinvented 133-72

Film and Literature TCLC 38: 97-226
overviews and general studies, 97-119
film and theater, 119-34
film and the novel, 134-45
the art of the screenplay, 145-66
genre literature/genre film, 167-79
the writer and the film industry, 179-90
authors on film adaptations of their works, 190-200
fiction into film: comparative essays, 200-23

Finance and Money as Represented in Nineteenth-Century Literature NCLC 76: 1-69
historical perspectives, 2-20
the image of money, 20-37
the dangers of money, 37-50
women and money, 50-69

Folklore and Literature TCLC 86: 116-293
overviews and general studies, 118-144
Native American literature, 144-67
African-American literature, 167-238
folklore and the American West, 238-57
modern and postmodern literature, 257-91

Food in Literature TCLC 114: 1-133
food and children's literature, 2-14
food as a literary device, 14-32
rituals invloving food, 33-45
food and social and ethnic identity, 45-90
women's relationship with food, 91-132

Food in Nineteenth-Century Literature
NCLC 108: 134-288
 overviews, 136-74
 food and social class, 174-85
 food and gender, 185-219
 food and love, 219-31
 food and sex, 231-48
 eating disorders, 248-70
 vegetarians, carnivores, and cannibals,
 270-87

French Drama in the Age of Louis XIV LC
28: 94-185
 overview, 95-127
 tragedy, 127-46
 comedy, 146-66
 tragicomedy, 166-84

French Enlightenment LC 14: 81-145
 the question of definition, 82-9
 le siècle des lumières, 89-94
 women and the salons, 94-105
 censorship, 105-15
 the philosophy of reason, 115-31
 influence and legacy, 131-44

French New Novel TCLC 98: 158-234
 overviews and general studies, 158-92
 influences, 192-213
 themes, 213-33

French Realism NCLC 52: 136-216
 origins and definitions, 137-70
 issues and influence, 170-98
 realism and representation, 198-215

French Revolution and English Literature
NCLC 40: 96-195
 history and theory, 96-123
 romantic poetry, 123-50
 the novel, 150-81
 drama, 181-92
 children's literature, 192-5

French Symbolist Poetry NCLC 144: 1-107
 overviews, 2-14
 Symbolist aesthetics, 14-47
 the Symbolist lyric, 47-60
 history and influence, 60-105

Futurism TCLC 166: 199-338
 overviews, 200-10
 poetry, 210-23
 theater, 223-32
 music, 232-46
 Futurism and Fascism, 246-312
 women Futurist writers, 312-37

Futurism, Italian TCLC 42: 269-354
 principles and formative influences, 271-9
 manifestos, 279-88
 literature, 288-303
 theater, 303-19
 art, 320-30
 music, 330-6
 architecture, 336-9
 and politics, 339-46
 reputation and significance, 346-51

Gaelic Revival See Irish Literary Renaissance

**Gates, Henry Louis, Jr., and African-
American Literary Criticism** CLC 65: 361-
405

Gaucho Literature TCLC 158: 99-195
 overviews and general studies, 101-43
 major works, 143-95

Gambling in Nineteenth-Century Literature
NCLC 168: 1-84
 overview, 2-7
 gambling in American literature, 7-39
 gambling in British literature, 39-57
 gambling in Russian literature, 57-84

Gay and Lesbian Literature CLC 76: 416-39

Gay and Lesbian Literature, Contemporary
CLC 171: 1-130
 overviews and general studies, 2-43
 contemporary gay literature, 44-95
 lesbianism in contemporary literature, 95-
 129

Gender in Nineteenth-Century Literature
NCLC 168: 192-352
 overviews, 195-256
 gender and race, 256-83
 gender and men, 283-309
 gender and class, 309-20
 gender and the text, 320-51

The Generation of 1927 TCLC 178: 1-109
 overviews 2-17
 literary and thematic assessments 17-59
 major authors 59-108

Generation of 1898 Short Fiction SSC 75:
182-287
 overviews and general studies, 182-210
 major short story writers of the Generation
 of 1898, 210-86
 Azorín, 210-16
 Emilia Pardo Bazán, 216-34
 Vicente Blasco Ibáñez, 234-36
 Gabriel Miró, 236-43
 Miguel de Unamuno, 243-68
 Ramon del Valle-Inclán, 268-86

German Exile Literature TCLC 30: 1-58
 the writer and the Nazi state, 1-10
 definition of, 10-4
 life in exile, 14-32
 surveys, 32-50
 Austrian literature in exile, 50-2
 German publishing in the United States,
 52-7

German Expressionism TCLC 34: 74-160
 history and major figures, 76-85
 aesthetic theories, 85-109
 drama, 109-26
 poetry, 126-38
 film, 138-42
 painting, 142-7
 music, 147-53
 and politics, 153-8

The Ghost Story SSC 58: 1-142
 overviews and general studies, 1-21
 the ghost story in American literature,
 21-49
 the ghost story in Asian literature, 49-53
 the ghost story in European and English
 literature, 54-89
 major figures, 89-141

The Gilded Age NCLC 84: 169-271
 popular themes, 170-90
 Realism, 190-208
 Aestheticism, 208-26
 socio-political concerns, 226-70

***Glasnost* and Contemporary Soviet Litera-
ture** CLC 59: 355-97

***Gone with the Wind* as Cultural Phenomenon**
TCLC 170: 1-103
 overviews, 2-60
 race, gender, and class in *Gone with the
 Wind,* 60-102

Gothic Drama NCLC 132: 95-198
 overviews, 97-125
 sociopolitical contexts, 125-58
 Gothic playwrights, 158-97

Gothic Literature GL 1: 1-577
 Gothic Literature: an overview, 1-106
 primary sources, 4-16
 overviews, 16-40
 origins of the Gothic, 40-57
 American Gothic, 57-74
 European Gothic, 74-104
 society, culture, and the Gothic, 107-229

 primary sources, 110-27
 overviews, 127-80
 race and the Gothic, 180-210
 women and the Gothic, 210-28
gothic themes, settings, and figures, 231-
 387
 primary sources, 236-49
 overviews, 249-64
 haunted dwellings and the supernatural,
 264-301
 psychology and the Gothic, 301-42
 vampires, 342-85
performing arts and the Gothic, 389-474
 primary sources, 394-401
 drama, 401-15
 film, 415-52
 television, 452-60
 music, 461-73
visual arts and the Gothic, 475-526
 primary sources, 477-80
 overviews, 480-86
 architecture, 486-506
 art, 506-525

Gothic Novel NCLC 28: 328-402
 development and major works, 328-34
 definitions, 334-50
 themes and techniques, 350-78
 in America, 378-85
 in Scotland, 385-91
 influence and legacy, 391-400

**The Governess in Nineteenth-Century Lit-
erature** NCLC 104: 1-131
 overviews and general studies, 3-28
 social roles and economic conditions, 28-86
 fictional governesses, 86-131

**The Grail Theme in Twentieth-Century Lit-
erature** TCLC 142: 1-89
 overviews and general studies, 2-20
 major works, 20-89

Graphic Narratives CLC 86: 405-32
 history and overviews, 406-21
 the "Classics Illustrated" series, 421-2
 reviews of recent works, 422-32

Graphic Novels CLC 177: 163-299
 overviews and general studies, 165-198
 critical readings of major works, 198-286
 reviews of recent graphic novels, 286-299

Graveyard Poets LC 67: 131-212
 origins and development, 131-52
 major figures, 152-75
 major works, 175-212

Greek Historiography CMLC 17: 1-49

Greek Lyric Poetry, The Rise of CMLC 77:
226-329
 overviews, 229-46
 literary history, 246-72
 themes and style, 272-302
 representative authors, 302-28

Greek Mythology CMLC 26: 193-320
 overviews and general studies, 194-209
 origins and development of Greek mythol-
 ogy, 209-29
 cosmogonies and divinities in Greek my-
 thology, 229-54
 heroes and heroines in Greek mythology,
 254-80
 women in Greek mythology, 280-320

Greek Theater CMLC 51: 1-58
 criticism, 2-58

Hard-Boiled Fiction TCLC 118: 1-109
 overviews and general studies, 2-39
 major authors, 39-76
 women and hard-boiled fiction, 76-109

The Harlem Renaissance HR 1: 1-563
 overviews and general studies of the Har-
 lem Renaissance, 1-137
 primary sources, 3-12

overviews, 12-38
background and sources of the Harlem
Renaissance, 38-56
the New Negro aesthetic, 56-91
patrons, promoters, and the New York
Public Library, 91-121
women of the Harlem Renaissance,
121-37
social, economic, and political factors that
influenced the Harlem Renaissance,
139-240
primary sources, 141-53
overviews, 153-87
social and economic factors, 187-213
Black intellectual and political thought,
213-40
publishing and periodicals during the Har-
lem Renaissance, 243-339
primary sources, 246-52
overviews, 252-68
African American writers and main-
stream publishers, 268-91
anthologies: *The New Negro* and others,
291-309
African American periodicals and the
Harlem Renaissance, 309-39
performing arts during the Harlem Renais-
sance, 341-465
primary sources, 343-48
overviews, 348-64
drama of the Harlem Renaissance,
364-92
influence of music on Harlem Renais-
sance writing, 437-65
visual arts during the Harlem Renaissance,
467-563
primary sources, 470-71
overviews, 471-517
painters, 517-36
sculptors, 536-58
photographers, 558-63

Harlem Renaissance TCLC 26: 49-125
principal issues and figures, 50-67
the literature and its audience, 67-74
theme and technique in poetry, fiction, and
drama, 74-115
and American society, 115-21
achievement and influence, 121-2

Havel, Václav, Playwright and President CLC
65: 406-63

Heroic Drama LC 91: 249-373
definitions and overviews, 251-78
politics and heroic drama, 278-303
early plays: Dryden and Orrery, 303-51
later plays: Lee and Otway, 351-73

Historical Fiction, Nineteenth-Century NCLC
48: 212-307
definitions and characteristics, 213-36
Victorian historical fiction, 236-65
American historical fiction, 265-88
realism in historical fiction, 288-306

Hollywood and Literature TCLC 118: 110-
251
overviews and general studies, 111-20
adaptations, 120-65
socio-historical and cultural impact, 165-
206
theater and hollywood, 206-51

**Holocaust and the Atomic Bomb: Fifty Years
Later** CLC 91: 331-82
the Holocaust remembered, 333-52
Anne Frank revisited, 352-62
the atomic bomb and American memory,
362-81

Holocaust Denial Literature TCLC 58: 1-110
overviews and general studies, 1-30
Robert Faurisson and Noam Chomsky,
30-52

Holocaust denial literature in America,
52-71
library access to Holocaust denial litera-
ture, 72-5
the authenticity of Anne Frank's diary,
76-90
David Irving and the "normalization" of
Hitler, 90-109

Holocaust, Literature of the TCLC 42: 355-
450
historical overview, 357-61
critical overview, 361-70
diaries and memoirs, 370-95
novels and short stories, 395-425
poetry, 425-41
drama, 441-8

**Homosexuality in Nineteenth-Century Lit-
erature** NCLC 56: 78-182
defining homosexuality, 80-111
Greek love, 111-44
trial and danger, 144-81

Humors Comedy LC 85: 194-324
overviews, 195-251
major figures: Ben Jonson, 251-93
major figures: William Shakespeare, 293-
324

**Hungarian Literature of the Twentieth Cen-
tury** TCLC 26: 126-88
surveys of, 126-47
Nyugat and early twentieth-century litera-
ture, 147-56
mid-century literature, 156-68
and politics, 168-78
since the 1956 revolt, 178-87

Hysteria in Nineteenth-Century Literature
NCLC 64: 59-184
the history of hysteria, 60-75
the gender of hysteria, 75-103
hysteria and women's narratives, 103-57
hysteria in nineteenth-century poetry,
157-83

Image of the Noble Savage in Literature LC
79: 136-252
overviews and development, 136-76
the Noble Savage in the New World, 176-
221
Rousseau and the French Enlightenment's
view of the noble savage, 221-51

Imagism TCLC 74: 259-454
history and development, 260
major figures, 288
sources and influences, 352
Imagism and other movements, 397
influence and legacy, 431

**Immigrants in Nineteenth-Century Litera-
ture, Representation of** NCLC 112: 188-298
overview, 189-99
immigrants in America, 199-223
immigrants and labor, 223-60
immigrants in England, 260-97

**Incest in Nineteenth-Century American Lit-
erature** NCLC 76: 70-141
overview, 71-88
the concern for social order, 88-117
authority and authorship, 117-40

Incest in Victorian Literature NCLC 92: 172-
318
overviews and general studies, 173-85
novels, 185-276
plays, 276-84
poetry, 284-318

Indian Literature in English TCLC 54: 308-
406
overview, 309-13
origins and major figures, 313-25
the Indo-English novel, 325-55
Indo-English poetry, 355-67

Indo-English drama, 367-72
critical perspectives on Indo-English litera-
ture, 372-80
modern Indo-English literature, 380-9
Indo-English authors on their work, 389-
404

The Industrial Revolution in Literature
NCLC 56: 183-273
historical and cultural perspectives, 184-
201
contemporary reactions to the machine,
201-21
themes and symbols in literature, 221-73

The Influence of Ernest Hemingway TCLC
162: 122-259
overviews, 123-43
writers on Hemingway, 143-58
Hemingway's evocation of place, 158-84
gender and identity, 184-229
Hemingway and the quest for meaning,
229-58

The Influence of William Faulkner TCLC
170: 104-255
overviews, 105-16
Faulkner and narrative, 116-60
Faulkner and psychology, 160-80
Faulkner and race, 180-219
impact on contemporary culture, 219-43
Faulkner and women, 243-54

**The Irish Famine as Represented in
Nineteenth-Century Literature** NCLC 64:
185-261
overviews and general studies, 187-98
historical background, 198-212
famine novels, 212-34
famine poetry, 234-44
famine letters and eye-witness accounts,
245-61

Irish Literary Renaissance TCLC 46: 172-
287
overview, 173-83
development and major figures, 184-202
influence of Irish folklore and mythology,
202-22
Irish poetry, 222-34
Irish drama and the Abbey Theatre, 234-56
Irish fiction, 256-86

Irish Nationalism and Literature NCLC 44:
203-73
the Celtic element in literature, 203-19
anti-Irish sentiment and the Celtic response,
219-34
literary ideals in Ireland, 234-45
literary expressions, 245-73

The Irish Novel NCLC 80: 1-130
overviews and general studies, 3-9
principal figures, 9-22
peasant and middle class Irish novelists,
22-76
aristocratic Irish and Anglo-Irish novelists,
76-129

Israeli Literature TCLC 94: 1-137
overviews and general studies, 2-18
Israeli fiction, 18-33
Israeli poetry, 33-62
Israeli drama, 62-91
women and Israeli literature, 91-112
Arab characters in Israeli literature, 112-36

Italian Futurism See Futurism, Italian

Italian Humanism LC 12: 205-77
origins and early development, 206-18
revival of classical letters, 218-23
humanism and other philosophies, 224-39
humanism and humanists, 239-46
the plastic arts, 246-57
achievement and significance, 258-76

Italian Romanticism NCLC 60: 85-145
origins and overviews, 86-101
Italian Romantic theory, 101-25
the language of Romanticism, 125-45

Jacobean Drama LC 33: 1-37
the Jacobean worldview: an era of transition, 2-14
the moral vision of Jacobean drama, 14-22
Jacobean tragedy, 22-3
the Jacobean masque, 23-36

Jazz and Literature TCLC 102: 3-124

Jewish-American Fiction TCLC 62: 1-181
overviews and general studies, 2-24
major figures, 24-48
Jewish writers and American life, 48-78
Jewish characters in American fiction, 78-108
themes in Jewish-American fiction, 108-43
Jewish-American women writers, 143-59
the Holocaust and Jewish-American fiction, 159-81

Jews in Literature TCLC 118: 252-417
overviews and general studies, 253-97
representing the Jew in literature, 297-351
the Holocaust in literature, 351-416

The Journals of Lewis and Clark NCLC 100: 1-88
overviews and general studies, 4-30
journal-keeping methods, 30-46
Fort Mandan, 46-51
the Clark journal, 51-65
the journals as literary texts, 65-87

Kabuki LC 73: 118-232
overviews and general studies, 120-40
the development of Kabuki, 140-65
major works, 165-95
Kabuki and society, 195-231

King Alfred the Great, The Age of See The Age of King Alfred the Great

The Kit-Kat Club LC 71: 66-112
overviews and general studies, 67-88
major figures, 88-107
attacks on the Kit-Kat Club, 107-12

The Knickerbocker Group NCLC 56: 274-341
overviews and general studies, 276-314
Knickerbocker periodicals, 314-26
writers and artists, 326-40

Künstlerroman TCLC 150: 133-260
overviews and general studies, 135-51
major works, 151-212
feminism in the *Künstlerroman*, 212-49
minority *Künstlerroman*, 249-59

The Lake Poets NCLC 52: 217-304
characteristics of the Lake Poets and their works, 218-27
literary influences and collaborations, 227-66
defining and developing Romantic ideals, 266-84
embracing Conservatism, 284-303

Language Poets TCLC 126: 66-172
overviews and general studies, 67-122
selected major figures in language poetry, 122-72

Larkin, Philip, Controversy CLC 81: 417-64

Latin American Literature, Twentieth-Century TCLC 58: 111-98
historical and critical perspectives, 112-36
the novel, 136-45
the short story, 145-9
drama, 149-60
poetry, 160-7
the writer and society, 167-86

Native Americans in Latin American literature, 186-97

Law and Literature TCLC 126: 173-347
overviews and general studies, 174-253
fiction critiquing the law, 253-88
literary responses to the law, 289-346

The Legend of El Dorado LC 74: 248-350
overviews, 249-308
major explorations for El Dorado, 308-50

The Legend of Pope Joan LC 123: 1-88
overviews and general studies, 3-87

The Levellers LC 51: 200-312
overviews and general studies, 201-29
principal figures, 230-86
religion, political philosophy, and pamphleteering, 287-311

The Lilith Legend in Modern Literature TCLC 170: 256-319
overviews, 257-67
historical and literary background, 267-89
the Lilith legend in twentieth-century literature, 289-319

Literary Criticism in the Nineteenth Century, American NCLC 128: 1-103
overviews and general studies, 2-44
the trancendentalists, 44-65
"young America," 65-71
James Russell Lowell, 71-9
Edgar Allan Poe, 79-97
Walt Whitman, 97-102

Literary Expressionism TCLC 142: 90-185
overviews and general studies, 91-138
themes in literary expressionism, 138-61
expressionism in Germany, 161-84

The Literary Marketplace Nineteenth-Century NCLC 128: 194-368
overviews and general studies, 197-228
British literary marketplace, 228-66
French literary marketplace, 266-82
American literary marketplace, 282-323
Women in the literary marketplace, 323-67

Literary Prizes TCLC 122: 130-203
overviews and general studies, 131-34
the Nobel Prize in Literature, 135-83
the Pulitzer Prize, 183-203

Literature and Millenial Lists CLC 119: 431-67
The Modern Library list, 433
The Waterstone list, 438-439

Literature in Response to the September 11 Attacks CLC 174: 1-46
Major works about September 11, 2001, 2-22
Critical, artistic, and journalistic responses, 22-45

Literature of the American Cowboy NCLC 96: 1-60
overview, 3-20
cowboy fiction, 20-36
cowboy poetry and songs, 36-59

Literature of the California Gold Rush NCLC 92: 320-85
overviews and general studies, 322-24
early California Gold Rush fiction, 324-44
Gold Rush folklore and legend, 344-51
the rise of Western local color, 351-60
social relations and social change, 360-385

Literature of the Counter-Reformation LC 109: 213-56
overviews and general studies, 214-33
influential figures, 233-56

The Living Theatre DC 16: 154-214

The Lost Generation See Writers of the Lost Generation

Luddism in Nineteenth-Century Literature NCLC 140: 280-365
overviews, 281-322
the literary response, 322-65

Lynching in Nineteenth-Century Literature NCLC 148: 162-247
lynching in literature and music, 163-92
Ida B. Wells-Barnett and the anti-lynching movement, 192-221
resistance to lynching in society and the press, 221-46

Madness in Nineteenth-Century Literature NCLC 76: 142-284
overview, 143-54
autobiography, 154-68
poetry, 168-215
fiction, 215-83

Madness in Twentieth-Century Literature TCLC 50: 160-225
overviews and general studies, 161-71
madness and the creative process, 171-86
suicide, 186-91
madness in American literature, 191-207
madness in German literature, 207-13
madness and feminist artists, 213-24

Magic Realism TCLC 110: 80-327
overviews and general studies, 81-94
magic realism in African literature, 95-110
magic realism in American literature, 110-32
magic realism in Canadian literature, 132-46
magic realism in European literature, 146-66
magic realism in Asian literature, 166-79
magic realism in Latin-American literature, 179-223
magic realism in Israeli literature and the novels of Salman Rushdie, 223-38
magic realism in literature written by women, 239-326

The Martin Marprelate Tracts LC 101: 165-240
criticism, 166-240

Marxist Criticism TCLC 134: 127-57
overviews and general studies, 128-67
Marxist interpretations, 167-209
cultural and literary Marxist theory, 209-49
Marxism and feminist critical theory, 250-56

The Masque LC 63: 124-265
development of the masque, 125-62
sources and structure, 162-220
race and gender in the masque, 221-64

Medical Writing LC 55: 93-195
colonial America, 94-110
enlightenment, 110-24
medieval writing, 124-40
sexuality, 140-83
vernacular, 185-95

Memoirs of Trauma CLC 109: 419-466
overview, 420
criticism, 429

Memoirs, Truth in CLC 226: 253-88
arguments for and against fictionalization, 254-69
reaction to James Frey's *A Million Little Pieces,* 269-80
other suspected and proven memoir hoaxes, 280-88

Metafiction TCLC 130: 43-228
overviews and general studies, 44-85

Spanish metafiction, 85-117
studies of metafictional authors and works, 118-228

Metaphysical Poets LC 24: 356-439
early definitions, 358-67
surveys and overviews, 367-92
cultural and social influences, 392-406
stylistic and thematic variations, 407-38

Metrical Psalms LC 129: 85-180
overviews, 87-180

Missionaries in the Nineteenth-Century, Literature of NCLC 112: 299-392
history and development, 300-16
uses of ethnography, 316-31
sociopolitical concerns, 331-82
David Livingstone, 382-91

The Modern Essay TCLC 58: 199-273
overview, 200-7
the essay in the early twentieth century, 207-19
characteristics of the modern essay, 219-32
modern essayists, 232-45
the essay as a literary genre, 245-73

Modern French Literature TCLC 122: 205-359
overviews and general studies, 207-43
French theater, 243-77
gender issues and French women writers, 277-315
ideology and politics, 315-24
modern French poetry, 324-41
resistance literature, 341-58

Modern Irish Literature TCLC 102: 125-321
overview, 129-44
dramas, 144-70
fiction, 170-247
poetry, 247-321

Modern Japanese Literature TCLC 66: 284-389
poetry, 285-305
drama, 305-29
fiction, 329-61
western influences, 361-87

Modernism TCLC 70: 165-275
definitions, 166-84
Modernism and earlier influences, 184-200
stylistic and thematic traits, 200-29
poetry and drama, 229-42
redefining Modernism, 242-75

Monasticism and Literature CMLC 74: 88-294
major figures, 89-132
secular influences, 132-54
monastic principles and literary practices, 154-232
women and monasticism, 232-93

Muckraking Movement in American Journalism TCLC 34: 161-242
development, principles, and major figures, 162-70
publications, 170-9
social and political ideas, 179-86
targets, 186-208
fiction, 208-19
decline, 219-29
impact and accomplishments, 229-40

Multiculturalism CLC 189: 167-254
overviews and general studies, 168-93
the effects of multiculturalism on global literature, 193-213
multicultural themes in specific contemporary works, 213-53

Multiculturalism in Literature and Education CLC 70: 361-413

Music and Modern Literature TCLC 62: 182-329
overviews and general studies, 182-211
musical form/literary form, 211-32
music in literature, 232-50
the influence of music on literature, 250-73
literature and popular music, 273-303
jazz and poetry, 303-28

Mystery Story See Crime-Mystery-Detective Stories

Native American Literature CLC 76: 440-76

Natural School, Russian NCLC 24: 205-40
history and characteristics, 205-25
contemporary criticism, 225-40

Naturalism NCLC 36: 285-382
definitions and theories, 286-305
critical debates on Naturalism, 305-16
Naturalism in theater, 316-32
European Naturalism, 332-61
American Naturalism, 361-72
the legacy of Naturalism, 372-81

Negritude TCLC 50: 226-361
origins and evolution, 227-56
definitions, 256-91
Negritude in literature, 291-343
Negritude reconsidered, 343-58

Negritude TCLC 158: 196-280
overviews and general studies, 197-208
major figures, 208-25
Negritude and humanism, 225-29
poetry of Negritude, 229-47
politics of Negritude, 247-68
the Negritude debate, 268-79

New Criticism TCLC 34: 243-318
development and ideas, 244-70
debate and defense, 270-99
influence and legacy, 299-315

New Criticism TCLC 146: 1-108
overviews and general studies, 3-19
defining New Criticism, 19-28
place in history, 28-51
poetry and New Criticism, 51-78
major authors, 78-108

The New Humanists TCLC 162: 260-341
overviews, 261-92
major figures, 292-310
New Humanism in education and literature, 310-41

New South, Literature of the NCLC 116: 122-240
overviews, 124-66
the novel in the New South, 166-209
myth of the Old South in the New, 209-39

The New Woman in Nineteenth-Century Literature NCLC 156: 134-281
overview, 136-39
historical and social context, 139-57
contemporary descriptions of the new woman, 157-65
the new woman and popular fiction, 165-86
the new woman and the decadents, 187-207
the new woman and the theater, 207-48
Henry James, Bram Stoker, and Others, 248-80

The New World in Renaissance Literature LC 31: 1-51
overview, 1-18
utopia vs. terror, 18-31
explorers and Native Americans, 31-51

New York Intellectuals and *Partisan Review* TCLC 30: 117-98
development and major figures, 118-28
influence of Judaism, 128-39
Partisan Review, 139-57
literary philosophy and practice, 157-75
political philosophy, 175-87
achievement and significance, 187-97

The New Yorker TCLC 58: 274-357
overviews and general studies, 274-95
major figures, 295-304
New Yorker style, 304-33
fiction, journalism, and humor at *The New Yorker*, 333-48
the new *New Yorker*, 348-56

Newgate Novel NCLC 24: 166-204
development of Newgate literature, 166-73
Newgate Calendar, 173-7
Newgate fiction, 177-95
Newgate drama, 195-204

New Zealand Literature TCLC 134: 258-368
overviews and general studies, 260-300
Maori literature, 300-22
New Zealand drama, 322-32
New Zealand fiction, 332-51
New Zealand poetry, 351-67

Nigerian Literature of the Twentieth Century TCLC 30: 199-265
surveys of, 199-227
English language and African life, 227-45
politics and the Nigerian writer, 245-54
Nigerian writers and society, 255-62

Nihilism and Literature TCLC 110: 328-93
overviews and general studies, 328-44
European and Russian nihilism, 344-73
nihilism in the works of Albert Camus, Franz Kafka, and John Barth, 373-92

Nineteenth-Century Captivity Narratives NCLC 80:131-218
overview, 132-37
the political significance of captivity narratives, 137-67
images of gender, 167-96
moral instruction, 197-217

Nineteenth-Century Euro-American Literary Representations of Native Americans NCLC 104: 132-264
overviews and general studies, 134-53
Native American history, 153-72
the Indians of the Northeast, 172-93
the Indians of the Southeast, 193-212
the Indians of the West, 212-27
Indian-hater fiction, 227-43
the Indian as exhibit, 243-63

Nineteenth-Century Native American Autobiography NCLC 64: 262-389
overview, 263-8
problems of authorship, 268-81
the evolution of Native American autobiography, 281-304
political issues, 304-15
gender and autobiography, 316-62
autobiographical works during the turn of the century, 362-88

Nineteenth-Century Pornography NCLC 144: 108-202
nineteenth-century pornographers, 110-64
pornography and literature, 164-91
pornography and censorship, 191-201

Nineteenth-Century Western Literature in Japan NCLC 156: 282-352
overviews, 283-305
European literature in Japan, 305-28
American literature in Japan, 328-52

Noh Drama LC 103: 189-270
overviews, 190-94
origins and development, 194-214
structure, 214-28
types of plays, 228-45
masks in Noh drama, 245-57
Noh drama and the audience, 257-69

Norse Mythology CMLC 26: 321-85
history and mythological tradition, 322-44

Eddic poetry, 344-74
Norse mythology and other traditions, 374-85

Northern Humanism LC 16: 281-356
background, 282-305
precursor of the Reformation, 305-14
the Brethren of the Common Life, the Devotio Moderna, and education, 314-40
the impact of printing, 340-56

The Novel of Manners NCLC 56: 342-96
social and political order, 343-53
domestic order, 353-73
depictions of gender, 373-83
the American novel of manners, 383-95

Novels of the Ming and Early Ch'ing Dynasties LC 76: 213-356
overviews and historical development, 214-45
major works—overview, 245-85
genre studies, 285-325
cultural and social themes, 325-55

Nuclear Literature: Writings and Criticism in the Nuclear Age TCLC 46: 288-390
overviews and general studies, 290-301
fiction, 301-35
poetry, 335-8
nuclear war in Russo-Japanese literature, 338-55
nuclear war and women writers, 355-67
the nuclear referent and literary criticism, 367-88

Occultism in Modern Literature TCLC 50: 362-406
influence of occultism on literature, 363-72
occultism, literature, and society, 372-87
fiction, 387-96
drama, 396-405

Opium and the Nineteenth-Century Literary Imagination NCLC 20:250-301
original sources, 250-62
historical background, 262-71
and literary society, 271-9
and literary creativity, 279-300

Orientalism NCLC 96: 149-364
overviews and general studies, 150-98
Orientalism and imperialism, 198-229
Orientalism and gender, 229-59
Orientalism and the nineteenth-century novel, 259-321
Orientalism in nineteenth-century poetry, 321-63

The Oxford Movement NCLC 72: 1-197
overviews and general studies, 2-24
background, 24-59
and education, 59-69
religious responses, 69-128
literary aspects, 128-178
political implications, 178-196

The Parnassian Movement NCLC 72: 198-241
overviews and general studies, 199-231
and epic form, 231-38
and positivism, 238-41

Pastoral Literature of the English Renaissance LC 59: 171-282
overviews and general studies, 172-214
principal figures of the Elizabethan period, 214-33
principal figures of the later Renaissance, 233-50
pastoral drama, 250-81

Periodicals, Nineteenth-Century American NCLC 132: 199-374
overviews, chronology, and development, 200-41
literary periodicals, 241-83
regional periodicals, 283-317

women's magazines and gender issues, 317-47
minority periodicals, 347-72

Periodicals, Nineteenth-Century British NCLC 24: 100-65
overviews and general studies, 100-30
in the Romantic Age, 130-41
in the Victorian era, 142-54
and the reviewer, 154-64

Picaresque Literature of the Sixteenth and Seventeenth Centuries LC 78: 223-355
context and development, 224-71
genre, 271-98
the picaro, 299-326
the picara, 326-53

Plath, Sylvia, and the Nature of Biography CLC 86: 433-62
the nature of biography, 433-52
reviews of *The Silent Woman,* 452-61

Political Theory from the 15th to the 18th Century LC 36: 1-55
overview, 1-26
natural law, 26-42
empiricism, 42-55

Polish Romanticism NCLC 52: 305-71
overviews and general studies, 306-26
major figures, 326-40
Polish Romantic drama, 340-62
influences, 362-71

Politics and Literature TCLC 94: 138-61
overviews and general studies, 139-96
Europe, 196-226
Latin America, 226-48
Africa and the Caribbean, 248-60

Popular Literature TCLC 70: 279-382
overviews and general studies, 280-324
"formula" fiction, 324-336
readers of popular literature, 336-351
evolution of popular literature, 351-382

The Portrayal of Jews in Nineteenth-Century English Literature NCLC 72: 242-368
overviews and general studies, 244-77
Anglo-Jewish novels, 277-303
depictions by non-Jewish writers, 303-44
Hebraism versus Hellenism, 344-67

The Portrayal of Mormonism NCLC 96: 61-148
overview, 63-72
early Mormon literature, 72-100
Mormon periodicals and journals, 100-10
women writers, 110-22
Mormonism and nineteenth-century literature, 122-42
Mormon poetry, 142-47

Post-apartheid Literature CLC 187: 284-382
overviews and general studies, 286-318
the post-apartheid novel, 318-65
post-apartheid drama, 365-81

Postcolonial African Literature TCLC 146: 110-239
overviews and general studies, 111-45
ideology and theory, 145-62
postcolonial testimonial literature, 162-99
major authors, 199-239

Postcolonialism TCLC 114: 134-239
overviews and general studies, 135-153
African postcolonial writing, 153-72
Asian/Pacific literature, 172-78
postcolonial literary theory, 178-213
postcolonial women's writing, 213-38

Postmodernism TCLC 90:125-307
overview, 126-166
criticism, 166-224
fiction, 224-282
poetry, 282-300
drama, 300-307

Pragmatism in Nineteenth-Century Literature NCLC 168: 85-209
overviews, 86-133
pragmatism and literature, 133-52
Charles Sanders Peirce, 152-65
William James, 165-208

Pre-Raphaelite Movement NCLC 20: 302-401
overview, 302-4
genesis, 304-12
Germ and *Oxford and Cambridge Magazine,* 312-20
Robert Buchanan and the "Fleshly School of Poetry," 320-31
satires and parodies, 331-4
surveys, 334-51
aesthetics, 351-75
sister arts of poetry and painting, 375-94
influence, 394-9

Pre-romanticism LC 40: 1-56
overviews and general studies, 2-14
defining the period, 14-23
new directions in poetry and prose, 23-45
the focus on the self, 45-56

The Presentation of Literature in the Nineteenth Century NCLC 160: 159-226
book design, 160-71
gift books, 172-91
serial novels, 191-214
dime novels, 214-226

Pre-Socratic Philosophy CMLC 22: 1-56
overviews and general studies, 3-24
the Ionians and the Pythagoreans, 25-35
Heraclitus, the Eleatics, and the Atomists, 36-47
the Sophists, 47-55

The Prison in Nineteenth-Century Literature NCLC 116: 241-357
overview, 242-60
romantic prison, 260-78
domestic prison, 278-316
America as prison, 316-24
physical prisons and prison authors, 324-56

Protestant Hagiography and Martyrology LC 84: 106-217
overview, 106-37
John Foxe's *Book of Martyrs,* 137-97
martyrology and the feminine perspective, 198-216

Protestant Reformation, Literature of the LC 37: 1-83
overviews and general studies, 1-49
humanism and scholasticism, 49-69
the reformation and literature, 69-82

Psychoanalysis and Literature TCLC 38: 227-338
overviews and general studies, 227-46
Freud on literature, 246-51
psychoanalytic views of the literary process, 251-61
psychoanalytic theories of response to literature, 261-88
psychoanalysis and literary criticism, 288-312
psychoanalysis as literature/literature as psychoanalysis, 313-34

The Quarrel between the Ancients and the Moderns LC 63: 266-381
overviews and general studies, 267-301
Renaissance origins, 301-32
Quarrel between the Ancients and the Moderns in France, 332-58
Battle of the Books in England, 358-80

Racism in Literature TCLC 138: 257-373
overviews and general studies, 257-326
racism and literature by and about African Americans, 292-326
theme of racism in literature, 326-773

Rap Music CLC 76: 477-50

Reader-Response Criticism TCLC 146: 240-357
 overviews and general studies, 241-88
 critical approaches to reader response, 288-342
 reader-response interpretation, 342-57

Realism in Short Fiction SSC 63: 128-57
 overviews and general studies, 129-37
 realist short fiction in France, 137-62
 realist short fiction in Russia, 162-215
 realist short fiction in England, 215-31
 realist short fiction in the United States, 231-56

Regionalism and Local Color in Short Fiction SSC 65: 160-289
 overviews and general studies, 163-205
 regionalism/local color fiction of the west, 205-42
 regionalism/local color fiction of the midwest, 242-57
 regionalism/local color fiction of the south, 257-88

Renaissance Natural Philosophy LC 27: 201-87
 cosmology, 201-28
 astrology, 228-54
 magic, 254-86

Representations of Africa in Nineteenth-Century Literature NCLC 148: 248-351
 overview, 251-66
 Northeast and Central Africa, 266-76
 South Africa, 276-301
 West Africa, 301-49

Representations of the Devil in Nineteenth-Century Literature NCLC 100: 89-223
 overviews and general studies, 90-115
 the Devil in American fiction, 116-43
 English Romanticism: the satanic school, 143-89
 Luciferian discourse in European literature, 189-222

Restoration Drama LC 21: 184-275
 general overviews and general studies, 185-230
 Jeremy Collier stage controversy, 230-9
 other critical interpretations, 240-75

Revenge Tragedy LC 71: 113-242
 overviews and general studies, 113-51
 Elizabethan attitudes toward revenge, 151-88
 the morality of revenge, 188-216
 reminders and remembrance, 217-41

Revising the Literary Canon CLC 81: 465-509

Revising the Literary Canon TCLC 114: 240-84
 overviews and general studies, 241-85
 canon change in American literature, 285-339
 gender and the literary canon, 339-59
 minority and third-world literature and the canon, 359-84

Revolutionary Astronomers LC 51: 314-65
 overviews and general studies, 316-25
 principal figures, 325-51
 Revolutionary astronomical models, 352-64

Robin Hood, Legend of LC 19: 205-58
 origins and development of the Robin Hood legend, 206-20
 representations of Robin Hood, 220-44
 Robin Hood as hero, 244-56

Romance Fiction, Contemporary CLC 206: 178-271
 overviews, 180-93
 literary conventions, 193-215

 opposing viewpoints, 215-20
 reader response to Romance literature, 220-37
 Romance literature in the world, 237-70

Romantic Literary Criticism NCLC 144: 203-357
 background and overviews, 205-30
 literary reviews, 230-38
 the German Romantics, 238-81
 Wordsworth and Coleridge, 281-326
 variations on Romantic critical theory, 326-56

Rushdie, Salman, *Satanic Verses* Controversy CLC 55: 214-63; 59:404-56

Russian Nihilism NCLC 28: 403-47
 definitions and overviews, 404-17
 women and Nihilism, 417-27
 literature as reform: the Civic Critics, 427-33
 Nihilism and the Russian novel: Turgenev and Dostoevsky, 433-47

Russian Thaw TCLC 26: 189-247
 literary history of the period, 190-206
 theoretical debate of socialist realism, 206-11
 Novy Mir, 211-7
 Literary Moscow, 217-24
 Pasternak, *Zhivago,* and the Nobel prize, 224-7
 poetry of liberation, 228-31
 Brodsky trial and the end of the Thaw, 231-6
 achievement and influence, 236-46

Salem Witch Trials LC 38: 1-145
 overviews and general studies, 2-30
 historical background, 30-65
 judicial background, 65-78
 the search for causes, 78-115
 the role of women in the trials, 115-44

Salinger, J. D., Controversy Surrounding *In Search of J. D. Salinger* CLC 55: 325-44

Samizdat Literature TCLC 150: 261-342
 overviews and general studies, 262-64
 history and development, 264-309
 politics and Samizdat, 309-22
 voices of Samizdat, 322-42

Sanitation Reform, Nineteenth-Century NCLC 124: 165-257
 overviews and general studies, 166
 primary texts, 186-89
 social context, 189-221
 public health in literature, 221-56

Science and Modern Literature TCLC 90: 308-419
 overviews and general studies, 295-333
 fiction, 333-95
 poetry, 395-405
 drama, 405-19

Science in Nineteenth-Century Literature NCLC 100: 224-366
 overviews and general studies, 225-65
 major figures, 265-336
 sociopolitical concerns, 336-65

Science Fiction, Nineteenth-Century NCLC 24: 241-306
 background, 242-50
 definitions of the genre, 251-56
 representative works and writers, 256-75
 themes and conventions, 276-305

Scottish Chaucerians LC 20: 363-412

Scottish Poetry, Eighteenth-Century LC 29: 95-167
 overviews and general studies, 96-114
 the Scottish Augustans, 114-28
 the Scots Vernacular Revival, 132-63
 Scottish poetry after Burns, 163-66

The Sea in Literature TCLC 82: 72-191
 drama, 73-9
 poetry, 79-119
 fiction, 119-91

The Sea in Nineteenth-Century English and American Literature NCLC 104: 265-362
 overviews and general studies, 267-306
 major figures in American sea fiction—Cooper and Melville, 306-29
 American sea poetry and short stories, 329-45
 English sea literature, 345-61

The Sensation Novel NCLC 80: 219-330
 overviews and general studies, 221-46
 principal figures, 246-62
 nineteenth-century reaction, 262-91
 feminist criticism, 291-329

The Sentimental Novel NCLC 60: 146-245
 overviews and general studies, 147-58
 the politics of domestic fiction, 158-79
 a literature of resistance and repression, 179-212
 the reception of sentimental fiction, 213-44

September 11 Attacks See Literature in Response to the September 11 Attacks

Sex and Literature TCLC 82: 192-434
 overviews and general studies, 193-216
 drama, 216-63
 poetry, 263-87
 fiction, 287-431

Sherlock Holmes Centenary TCLC 26: 248-310
 Doyle's life and the composition of the Holmes stories, 248-59
 life and character of Holmes, 259-78
 method, 278-79
 Holmes and the Victorian world, 279-92
 Sherlockian scholarship, 292-301
 Doyle and the development of the detective story, 301-07
 Holmes's continuing popularity, 307-09

Short Science Fiction, Golden Age of, 1938-1950 SSC 73: 1-145
 overviews and general studies, 3-48
 publishing history of Golden Age Short Science Fiction, 48-65
 major Golden Age Short Science Fiction authors and editors
 Isaac Asimov, 65-77
 Ray Bradbury, 77-92
 John W. Campbell, 92-106
 Arthur C. Clarke, 106-15
 Robert A. Heinlein, 115-29
 Damon Knight, 129-40
 Frederik Pohl, 141-43

Short-Short Fiction SSC 61: 311-36
 overviews and general studies, 312-19
 major short-short fiction writers, 319-35

The Silver Fork Novel NCLC 88: 58-140
 criticism, 59-139

Slave Narratives, American NCLC 20: 1-91
 background, 2-9
 overviews and general studies, 9-24
 contemporary responses, 24-7
 language, theme, and technique, 27-70
 historical authenticity, 70-5
 antecedents, 75-83
 role in development of Black American literature, 83-8

The Slave Trade in British and American Literature LC 59: 283-369
 overviews and general studies, 284-91
 depictions by white writers, 291-331
 depictions by former slaves, 331-67

Social Conduct Literature LC 55: 196-298
 overviews and general studies, 196-223

prescriptive ideology in other literary forms, 223-38
role of the press, 238-63
impact of conduct literature, 263-87
conduct literature and the perception of women, 287-96
women writing for women, 296-98

Social Protest Literature of Victorian England NCLC 160: 227-359
overviews: protest in Victorian literature, 229-62
woman question, 262-304
condition-of-England novel, 304-58

Social Protest Literature Outside England, Nineteenth-Century NCLC 124: 258-350
overviews and general studies, 259-72
oppression revealed, 272-306
literature to incite or prevent reform, 306-50

Socialism NCLC 88: 141-237
origins, 142-54
French socialism, 154-83
Anglo-American socialism, 183-205
Socialist-Feminism, 205-36

Southern Gothic Literature TCLC 142: 186-270
overviews and general studies, 187-97
major authors in southern Gothic literature, 197-230
structure and technique in southern Gothic literature, 230-50
themes in southern Gothic literature, 250-70

Southern Literature, Contemporary CLC 167: 1-132
criticism, 2-131

Southern Literature of the Reconstruction NCLC 108: 289-369
overview, 290-91
reconstruction literature: the consequences of war, 291-321
old south to new: continuities in southern culture, 321-68

Southwestern Humor SSC 81: 105-248
overviews, 106-83
Mark Twain, 183-97
George Washington Harris, 197-208
other major figures, 208-46

Spanish Civil War Literature TCLC 26: 311-85
topics in, 312-33
British and American literature, 333-59
French literature, 359-62
Spanish literature, 362-73
German literature, 373-75
political idealism and war literature, 375-83

Spanish Golden Age Literature LC 23: 262-332
overviews and general studies, 263-81
verse drama, 281-304
prose fiction, 304-19
lyric poetry, 319-31

Sparta in Literature CMLC 70: 145-271
overviews, 147-61
Spartan poetry, 161-72
the Spartan myth, 172-200
historical background, 200-27
Spartan society and culture, 227-69

Spasmodic School of Poetry NCLC 24: 307-52
history and major figures, 307-21
the Spasmodics on poetry, 321-7
Firmilian and critical disfavor, 327-39
theme and technique, 339-47
influence, 347-51

Sports in Literature TCLC 86: 294-445
overviews and general studies, 295-324
major writers and works, 324-402
sports, literature, and social issues, 402-45

Steinbeck, John, Fiftieth Anniversary of *The Grapes of Wrath* CLC 59: 311-54

The Stream-of-Consciousness Novel TCLC 178: 110-95
style and development 111-43
representative authors 134-95

Sturm und Drang NCLC 40: 196-276
definitions, 197-238
poetry and poetics, 238-58
drama, 258-75

Supernatural Fiction in the Nineteenth Century NCLC 32: 207-87
major figures and influences, 208-35
the Victorian ghost story, 236-54
the influence of science and occultism, 254-66
supernatural fiction and society, 266-86

Supernatural Fiction, Modern TCLC 30: 59-116
evolution and varieties, 60-74
"decline" of the ghost story, 74-86
as a literary genre, 86-92
technique, 92-101
nature and appeal, 101-15

Surrealism TCLC 30: 334-406
history and formative influences, 335-43
manifestos, 343-54
philosophic, aesthetic, and political principles, 354-75
poetry, 375-81
novel, 381-6
drama, 386-92
film, 392-8
painting and sculpture, 398-403
achievement, 403-5

Surrealism in Children's Literature CLR 103: 127-200
overviews and general studies, 130-52
critical analysis of surrealist children's authors and works, 152-99

Sylvia Beach and Company TCLC 158: 281-370
overviews and general studies, 282-97
Shakespeare and Company, 297-314
the business of publishing, 315-40
Sylvia Beach and James Joyce, 341-70

Symbolism, Russian TCLC 30: 266-333
doctrines and major figures, 267-92
theories, 293-8
and French Symbolism, 298-310
themes in poetry, 310-4
theater, 314-20
and the fine arts, 320-32

Symbolist Movement, French NCLC 20: 169-249
background and characteristics, 170-86
principles, 186-91
attacked and defended, 191-7
influences and predecessors, 197-211
and Decadence, 211-6
theater, 216-26
prose, 226-33
decline and influence, 233-47

Television and Literature TCLC 78: 283-426
television and literacy, 283-98
reading vs. watching, 298-341
adaptations, 341-62
literary genres and television, 362-90
television genres and literature, 390-410
children's literature/children's television, 410-25

Theater of the Absurd TCLC 38: 339-415
"The Theater of the Absurd," 340-7
major plays and playwrights, 347-58
and the concept of the absurd, 358-86
theatrical techniques, 386-94

predecessors of, 394-402
influence of, 402-13

Tin Pan Alley See American Popular Song, Golden Age of

Tobacco Culture LC 55: 299-366
social and economic attitudes toward tobacco, 299-344
tobacco trade between the old world and the new world, 344-55
tobacco smuggling in Great Britain, 355-66

Transcendentalism, American NCLC 24: 1-99
overviews and general studies, 3-23
contemporary documents, 23-41
theological aspects of, 42-52
and social issues, 52-74
literature of, 74-96

Travel Narratives in Contemporary Literature CLC 204: 260-351
overviews, 261-76
major authors, 276-311
modern travel writing, 311-31
women writers and travel, 331-51

Travel Writing in the Nineteenth Century NCLC 44: 274-392
the European grand tour, 275-303
the Orient, 303-47
North America, 347-91
NCLC 168: 210-347
overviews, 212-43
women's travel writing, 243-311
other notable travel writers and their works, 312-47

Travel Writing in the Twentieth Century TCLC 30: 407-56
conventions and traditions, 407-27
and fiction writing, 427-43
comparative essays on travel writers, 443-54

Treatment of Death in Children's Literature CLR 101: 152-201
overviews and general studies, 155-80
analytical and bibliographical reviews of death in children's literature, 180-97
death of animals in children's literature, 197-200

Tristan and Isolde Legend CMLC 42: 311-404

Troubadours CMLC 66: 244-383
overviews, 245-91
politics, economics, history, and the troubadours, 291-344
troubadours and women, 344-82

True-Crime Literature CLC 99: 333-433
history and analysis, 334-407
reviews of true-crime publications, 407-23
writing instruction, 424-29
author profiles, 429-33

Twentieth-Century Danish Literature TCLC 142: 271-344
major works, 272-84
major authors, 284-344

***Ulysses* and the Process of Textual Reconstruction** TCLC 26:386-416
evaluations of the new *Ulysses,* 386-94
editorial principles and procedures, 394-401
theoretical issues, 401-16

Unconventional Family in Children's Literature CLR 102: 146-213
overviews and general studies, 149-79
analytical and bibliographical reviews, 179-97
types of unconventional families: foster, adopted, homosexual, 197-212

Urban Life in Nineteenth-Century Literature NCLC 172: 249-334

overviews, 250-77
urban poetry, 277-304
urban life and individual identity, 304-34

Utilitarianism NCLC 84: 272-340
J. S. Mill's Utilitarianism: liberty, equality, justice, 273-313
Jeremy Bentham's Utilitarianism: the science of happiness, 313-39

Utopianism NCLC 88: 238-346
overviews: Utopian literature, 239-59
Utopianism in American literature, 259-99
Utopianism in British literature, 299-311
Utopianism and Feminism, 311-45

Utopian Literature, Nineteenth-Century NCLC 24: 353-473
definitions, 354-74
overviews and general studies, 374-88
theory, 388-408
communities, 409-26
fiction, 426-53
women and fiction, 454-71

Utopian Literature, Renaissance LC 32: 1-63
overviews and general studies, 2-25
classical background, 25-33
utopia and the social contract, 33-9
origins in mythology, 39-48
utopia and the Renaissance country house, 48-52
influence of millenarianism, 52-62

Vampire in Literature TCLC 46: 391-454
origins and evolution, 392-412
social and psychological perspectives, 413-44
vampire fiction and science fiction, 445-53

Vernacular Bibles LC 67: 214-388
overviews and general studies, 215-59
the English Bible, 259-355
the German Bible, 355-88

Victorian Autobiography NCLC 40: 277-363
development and major characteristics, 278-88
themes and techniques, 289-313
the autobiographical tendency in Victorian prose and poetry, 313-47
Victorian women's autobiographies, 347-62
NCLC 152: 230-365
overviews and general studies, 232-61
autobiography and the self, 261-93
autobiography and gender, 293-307
autobiography and class, 307-36
autobiography and fiction, 336-64

Victorian Critical Theory NCLC 136: 236-379
overviews and general studies, 237-86
Matthew Arnold, 286-324
Walter Pater and aestheticism, 324-36
other Victorian critics, 336-78

Victorian Fantasy Literature NCLC 60: 246-384
overviews and general studies, 247-91
major figures, 292-366
women in Victorian fantasy literature, 366-83

Victorian Hellenism NCLC 68: 251-376
overviews and general studies, 252-78

the meanings of Hellenism, 278-335
the literary influence, 335-75

Victorian Illustrated Fiction NCLC 120: 247-356
overviews and development, 128-76
technical and material aspects of book illustration, 276-84
Charles Dickens and his illustrators, 284-320
William Makepeace Thackeray, 320-31
George Eliot and Frederic Leighton, 331-51
Lewis Carroll and John Tenniel, 351-56

Victorian Novel NCLC 32: 288-454
development and major characteristics, 290-310
themes and techniques, 310-58
social criticism in the Victorian novel, 359-97
urban and rural life in the Victorian novel, 397-406
women in the Victorian novel, 406-25
Mudie's Circulating Library, 425-34
the late-Victorian novel, 434-51

Vietnamese Literature TCLC 102: 322-386

Vietnam War in Literature and Film CLC 91: 383-437
overview, 384-8
prose, 388-412
film and drama, 412-24
poetry, 424-35

The Vietnam War in Short Fiction SSC 79: 83-177
overviews and general studies, 84-93
women authors of Vietnam War short fiction, 93-116
Robert Olen Butler: *A Good Scent from a Strange Mountain* (1992), 116-31
Barry Hannah: *Airships* (1978), 131-50
Tim O'Brien: *The Things They Carried* (1990), 150-65
Tobias Wolff: *Back in the World* (1985), 165-69
other authors and works, 169-76

Violence in Literature TCLC 98: 235-358
overviews and general studies, 236-74
violence in the works of modern authors, 274-358

Vorticism TCLC 62: 330-426
Wyndham Lewis and Vorticism, 330-8
characteristics and principles of Vorticism, 338-65
Lewis and Pound, 365-82
Vorticist writing, 382-416
Vorticist painting, 416-26

The Well-Made Play NCLC 80: 331-370
overviews and general studies, 332-45
Scribe's style, 345-56
the influence of the well-made play, 356-69

Women's Autobiography, Nineteenth-Century NCLC 76: 285-368
overviews and general studies, 287-300
autobiographies concerned with religious and political issues, 300-15
autobiographies by women of color, 315-38

autobiographies by women pioneers, 338-51
autobiographies by women of letters, 351-68

Women's Diaries, Nineteenth-Century NCLC 48: 308-54
overview, 308-13
diary as history, 314-25
sociology of diaries, 325-34
diaries as psychological scholarship, 334-43
diary as autobiography, 343-8
diary as literature, 348-53

Women in Modern Literature TCLC 94: 262-425
overviews and general studies, 263-86
American literature, 286-304
other national literatures, 304-33
fiction, 333-94
poetry, 394-407
drama, 407-24

Women Writers, Seventeenth-Century LC 30: 2-58
overview, 2-15
women and education, 15-9
women and autobiography, 19-31
women's diaries, 31-9
early feminists, 39-58

World War I Literature TCLC 34: 392-486
overview, 393-403
English, 403-27
German, 427-50
American, 450-66
French, 466-74
and modern history, 474-82

World War I Short Fiction SSC 71: 187-347
overviews and general studies, 187-206
female short fiction writers of World War I, 206-36
Central Powers
Czechoslovakian writers of short fiction, 236-44
German writers of short fiction, 244-61
Entente/Allied Alliance
Australian writers of short fiction, 261-73
English writers of short fiction, 273-305
French writers of short fiction, 305-11
Associated Power: American writers of short fiction, 311-46

Writers of the Lost Generation TCLC 178: 196-369
overviews 197-225
major figures 225-98
women of the Lost Generation 298-341
expatriate writers and Paris 341-68

Yellow Journalism NCLC 36: 383-456
overviews and general studies, 384-96
major figures, 396-413

Yiddish Literature TCLC 130: 229-364
overviews and general studies, 230-54
major authors, 254-305
Yiddish literature in America, 305-34
Yiddish and Judaism, 334-64

Young Playwrights Festival
1988 CLC 55: 376-81
1989 CLC 59: 398-403
1990 CLC 65: 444-8

NCLC Cumulative Nationality Index

AMERICAN

Adams, John **106**
Alcott, Amos Bronson **1, 167**
Alcott, Louisa May **6, 58, 83**
Alger, Horatio Jr. **8, 83**
Allston, Washington **2**
Apess, William **73**
Audubon, John James **47**
Barlow, Joel **23**
Bartram, William **145**
Beecher, Catharine Esther **30**
Bellamy, Edward **4, 86, 147**
Bird, Robert Montgomery **1**
Boker, George Henry **125**
Boyesen, Hjalmar Hjorth **135**
Brackenridge, Hugh Henry **7**
Brentano, Clemens (Maria) **1**
Brown, Charles Brockden **22, 74, 122**
Brown, William Wells **2, 89**
Brownson, Orestes Augustus **50**
Bryant, William Cullen **6, 46**
Calhoun, John Caldwell **15**
Channing, William Ellery **17**
Child, Francis James **173**
Child, Lydia Maria **6, 73**
Chivers, Thomas Holley **49**
Cooke, John Esten **5**
Cooke, Rose Terry **110**
Cooper, James Fenimore **1, 27, 54**
Cooper, Susan Fenimore **129**
Cranch, Christopher Pearse **115**
Crèvecoeur, Michel Guillaume Jean de **105**
Crockett, David **8**
Cummins, Maria Susanna **139**
Dana, Richard Henry Sr. **53**
Delany, Martin Robinson **93**
Dickinson, Emily (Elizabeth) **21, 77, 171**
Douglass, Frederick **7, 55, 141**
Dunlap, William **2**
Dwight, Timothy **13**
Emerson, Mary Moody **66**
Emerson, Ralph Waldo **1, 38, 98**
Field, Eugene **3**
Foster, Hannah Webster **99**
Foster, Stephen Collins **26**
Frederic, Harold **10**
Freneau, Philip Morin **1, 111**
Garrison, William Lloyd **149**
Hale, Sarah Josepha (Buell) **75**
Halleck, Fitz-Greene **47**
Hamilton, Alexander **49**
Hammon, Jupiter **5**
Harris, George Washington **23, 165**
Hawthorne, Nathaniel **2, 10, 17, 23, 39, 79, 95, 158, 171**
Hawthorne, Sophia Peabody **150**
Hayne, Paul Hamilton **94**
Holmes, Oliver Wendell **14, 81**
Horton, George Moses **87**
Irving, Washington **2, 19, 95**
Jackson, Helen Hunt **90**
Jacobs, Harriet A(nn) **67, 162**

James, Henry Sr. **53**
Jefferson, Thomas **11, 103**
Kennedy, John Pendleton **2**
Kirkland, Caroline M. **85**
Lanier, Sidney **6, 118**
Lazarus, Emma **8, 109**
Lincoln, Abraham **18**
Longfellow, Henry Wadsworth **2, 45, 101, 103**
Longstreet, Augustus Baldwin **159**
Lowell, James Russell **2, 90**
Madison, James **126**
Melville, Herman **3, 12, 29, 45, 49, 91, 93, 123, 157**
Mowatt, Anna Cora **74**
Murray, Judith Sargent **63**
Neal, John **161**
Osgood, Frances Sargent **141**
Parkman, Francis Jr. **12**
Parton, Sara Payson Willis **86**
Paulding, James Kirke **2**
Peabody, Elizabeth Palmer **169**
Pinkney, Edward **31**
Poe, Edgar Allan **1, 16, 55, 78, 94, 97, 117**
Prescott, William Hickling **163**
Rowson, Susanna Haswell **5, 69**
Sedgwick, Catharine Maria **19, 98**
Shaw, Henry Wheeler **15**
Sigourney, Lydia Howard (Huntley) **21, 87**
Simms, William Gilmore **3**
Smith, Joseph Jr. **53**
Solomon, Northup **105**
Southworth, Emma Dorothy Eliza Nevitte **26**
Stowe, Harriet (Elizabeth) Beecher **3, 50, 133**
Taylor, Bayard **89**
Tenney, Tabitha Gilman **122**
Thoreau, Henry David **7, 21, 61, 138**
Timrod, Henry **25**
Trumbull, John **30**
Truth, Sojourner **94**
Tyler, Royall **3**
Very, Jones **9**
Warner, Susan (Bogert) **31, 146**
Warren, Mercy Otis **13**
Webster, Noah **30**
Webb, Frank J. **143**
Whitman, Sarah Helen (Power) **19**
Whitman, Walt(er) **4, 31, 81**
Whittier, John Greenleaf **8, 59**
Wilson, Harriet E. Adams **78**
Winnemucca, Sarah **79**

ARGENTINIAN

Echeverria, (Jose) Esteban (Antonino) **18**
Hernández, José **17**
Sarmiento, Domingo Faustino **123**

AUSTRALIAN

Adams, Francis **33**
Clarke, Marcus (Andrew Hislop) **19**
Gordon, Adam Lindsay **21**

Harpur, Charles **114**
Kendall, Henry **12**

AUSTRIAN

Grillparzer, Franz **1, 102**
Lenau, Nikolaus **16**
Nestroy, Johann **42**
Raimund, Ferdinand Jakob **69**
Sacher-Masoch, Leopold von **31**
Stifter, Adalbert **41**

BRAZILIAN

Alencar, Jose de **157**

CANADIAN

Crawford, Isabella Valancy **12, 127**
De Mille, James **123**
Haliburton, Thomas Chandler **15, 149**
Lampman, Archibald **25**
Moodie, Susanna (Strickland) **14, 113**
Richardson, John **55**
Traill, Catharine Parr **31**

CHINESE

Li Ju-chen **137**

COLOMBIAN

Isaacs, Jorge Ricardo **70**
Silva, José Asunción **114**

CUBAN

Avellaneda, Gertrudis Gómez de **111**
Casal, Julián del **131**
Manzano, Juan Francisco **155**
Martí (y Pérez), José (Julian) **63**
Villaverde, Cirilo **121**

CZECH

Macha, Karel Hynek **46**

DANISH

Andersen, Hans Christian **7, 79**
Grundtvig, Nicolai Frederik Severin **1, 158**
Jacobsen, Jens Peter **34**
Kierkegaard, Søren **34, 78, 125**

DUTCH

Multatuli (Eduard Douwes Dekker) **165**

ENGLISH

Ainsworth, William Harrison **13**
Arnold, Matthew **6, 29, 89, 126**
Arnold, Thomas **18**
Austen, Jane **1, 13, 19, 33, 51, 81, 95, 119, 150**
Bagehot, Walter **10**
Barbauld, Anna Laetitia **50**
Barham, Richard Harris **77**
Barnes, William **75**

Beardsley, Aubrey **6**
Beckford, William **16**
Beddoes, Thomas Lovell **3, 154**
Bentham, Jeremy **38**
Blake, William **13, 37, 57, 127, 173**
Bloomfield, Robert **145**
Borrow, George (Henry) **9**
Bowles, William Lisle **103**
Brontë, Anne **4, 71, 102**
Brontë, Charlotte **3, 8, 33, 58, 105, 155**
Brontë, Emily (Jane) **16, 35, 165**
Brontë, (Patrick) Branwell **109**
Browning, Elizabeth Barrett **1, 16, 61, 66, 170**
Browning, Robert **19, 79**
Bulwer-Lytton, Edward (George Earle Lytton) **1, 45**
Burney, Fanny **12, 54, 107**
Burton, Richard F(rancis) **42**
Byron, George Gordon (Noel) **2, 12, 109, 149**
Carlyle, Thomas **22, 70**
Carroll, Lewis **2, 53, 139**
Clare, John **9, 86**
Clough, Arthur Hugh **27, 163**
Cobbett, William **49**
Coleridge, Hartley **90**
Coleridge, Samuel Taylor **9, 54, 99, 111**
Coleridge, Sara **31**
Collins, (William) Wilkie **1, 18, 93**
Cowper, William **8, 94**
Crabbe, George **26, 121**
Craik, Dinah Maria (Mulock) **38**
Cumberland, Richard **167**
Dacre, Charlotte **151**
Darwin, Charles **57**
Darwin, Erasmus **106**
De Quincey, Thomas **4, 87**
Dickens, Charles (John Huffam) **3, 8, 18, 26, 37, 50, 86, 105, 113, 161**
Disraeli, Benjamin **2, 39, 79**
Dobell, Sydney Thompson **43**
Du Maurier, George **86**
Dyer, George **129**
Eden, Emily **10**
Eliot, George **4, 13, 23, 41, 49, 89, 118**
FitzGerald, Edward **9, 153**
Forster, John **11**
Froude, James Anthony **43**
Gaskell, Elizabeth Cleghorn **5, 70, 97, 137**
Gilpin, William **30**
Godwin, William **14, 130**
Gore, Catherine **65**
Hallam, Arthur Henry **110**
Hamilton, Elizabeth **153**
Haydon, Benjamin Robert **146**
Hays, Mary **114**
Hazlitt, William **29, 82**
Hemans, Felicia **29, 71**
Holcroft, Thomas **85**
Hood, Thomas **16**
Hopkins, Gerard Manley **17**
Horne, Richard Hengist **127**
Hunt, (James Henry) Leigh **1, 70**
Huxley, T(homas) H(enry) **67**
Inchbald, Elizabeth **62**
Ingelow, Jean **39, 107**
Jefferies, (John) Richard **47**
Jerrold, Douglas William **2**
Jewsbury, Geraldine (Endsor) **22**
Keats, John **8, 73, 121**
Keble, John **87**
Kemble, Fanny **18**
Kingsley, Charles **35**
Kingsley, Henry **107**
Lamb, Charles **10, 113**
Lamb, Lady Caroline **38**
Lamb, Mary **125**
Landon, Letitia Elizabeth **15**
Landor, Walter Savage **14**
Lear, Edward **3**
Lennox, Charlotte Ramsay **23, 134**

Lewes, George Henry **25**
Lewis, Matthew Gregory **11, 62**
Linton, Eliza Lynn **41**
Macaulay, Thomas Babington **42**
Malthus, Thomas Robert **145**
Marryat, Frederick **3**
Martineau, Harriet **26, 137**
Mayhew, Henry **31**
Mill, Harriet (Hardy) Taylor **102**
Mill, John Stuart **11, 58**
Mitford, Mary Russell **4**
Montagu, Elizabeth **117**
More, Hannah **27, 141**
Morris, William **4**
Newman, John Henry **38, 99**
Norton, Caroline **47**
Oliphant, Laurence **47**
Opie, Amelia **65**
Paine, Thomas **62**
Pater, Walter (Horatio) **7, 90, 159**
Patmore, Coventry Kersey Dighton **9**
Peacock, Thomas Love **22**
Percy, Thomas **95**
Piozzi, Hester Lynch (Thrale) **57**
Planché, James Robinson **42**
Polidori, John William **51**
Radcliffe, Ann (Ward) **6, 55, 106**
Reade, Charles **2, 74**
Reeve, Clara **19**
Reynolds, John Hamilton **146**
Robertson, Thomas William **35**
Robinson, Henry Crabb **15**
Robinson, Mary **142**
Rogers, Samuel **69**
Rossetti, Christina (Georgina) **2, 50, 66**
Rossetti, Dante Gabriel **4, 77**
Sala, George Augustus **46**
Shelley, Mary Wollstonecraft (Godwin) **14, 59, 103, 170**
Shelley, Percy Bysshe **18, 93, 143**
Smith, Charlotte (Turner) **23, 115**
Southey, Robert **8, 97**
Surtees, Robert Smith **14**
Symonds, John Addington **34**
Tennyson, Alfred **30, 65, 115**
Thackeray, William Makepeace **5, 14, 22, 43, 169**
Thelwall, John **162**
Tonna, Charlotte Elizabeth **135**
Trelawny, Edward John **85**
Trollope, Anthony **6, 33, 101**
Trollope, Frances **30**
Warton, Joseph **118**
Williams, Helen Maria **135**
Wordsworth, Dorothy **25, 138**
Wordsworth, William **12, 38, 111, 166**

FILIPINO

Rizal, José **27**

FINNISH

Kivi, Aleksis **30**
Lonnrot, Elias **53**
Runeberg, Johan **41**

FRENCH

Augier, Emile **31**
Balzac, Honoré de **5, 35, 53, 153**
Banville, Théodore (Faullain) de **9**
Barbey d'Aurevilly, Jules-Amédée **1**
Baudelaire, Charles **6, 29, 55, 155**
Becque, Henri **3**
Beranger, Pierre Jean de **34**
Bertrand, Aloysius **31**
Borel, Pétrus **41**
Chamisso, Adelbert von **82**
Chateaubriand, François René de **3, 134**
Comte, Auguste **54**
Constant (de Rebecque), (Henri) Benjamin **6**
Corbière, Tristan **43**
Crèvecoeur, Michel Guillaume Jean de **105**

Daudet, (Louis Marie) Alphonse **1**
Delacroix, Eugene **133**
Desbordes-Valmore, Marceline **97**
Dumas, Alexandre (fils) **9**
Dumas, Alexandre (pere) **11, 71**
Duras, Claire de **154**
Feuillet, Octave **45**
Flaubert, Gustave **2, 10, 19, 62, 66, 135**
Fourier, Charles **51**
Fromentin, Eugène (Samuel Auguste) **10, 125**
Gaboriau, émile **14**
Gautier, Théophile **1, 59**
Genlis, Stéphanie-Félicité de **166**
Gobineau, Joseph-Arthur **17**
Goncourt, Edmond (Louis Antoine Huot) de **7**
Goncourt, Jules (Alfred Huot) de **7**
Hugo, Victor (Marie) **3, 10, 21, 161**
Joubert, Joseph **9**
Kock, Charles Paul de **16**
Laclos, Pierre Ambroise François **4, 87**
Laforgue, Jules **5, 53**
Lamartine, Alphonse (Marie Louis Prat) de **11**
Lautréamont **12**
Leconte de Lisle, Charles-Marie-René **29**
Maistre, Joseph **37**
Mallarmé, Stéphane **4, 41**
Maupassant, (Henri René Albert) Guy de **1, 42, 83**
Mérimée, Prosper **6, 65**
Michelet, Jules **31**
Musset, (Louis Charles) Alfred de **7, 150**
Nerval, Gérard de **1, 67**
Nodier, (Jean) Charles (Emmanuel) **19**
Pixérécourt, (René Charles) Guilbert de **39**
Renan, Joseph Ernest **26, 145**
Rimbaud, (Jean Nicolas) Arthur **4, 35, 82**
Sade, Donatien Alphonse François **3, 47**
Sainte-Beuve, Charles Augustin **5**
Sand, George **2, 42, 57**
Scribe, (Augustin) Eugène **16**
Senancour, Etienne Pivert de **16**
Staël-Holstein, Anne Louise Germaine Necker **3**
Stendhal **23, 46**
Sue, Eugene **1**
Taine, Hippolyte Adolphe **15**
Tocqueville, Alexis (Charles Henri Maurice Clérel Comte) de **7, 63**
Vallès, Jules **71**
Verlaine, Paul (Marie) **2, 51**
Vigny, Alfred (Victor) de **7, 102**
Villiers de l'Isle Adam, Jean Marie Mathias Philippe Auguste **3**

GERMAN

Arnim, Achim von (Ludwig Joachim von Arnim) **5, 159**
Arnim, Bettina von **38, 123**
Auerbach, Berthold **171**
Bonaventura **35**
Büchner, (Karl) Georg **26, 146**
Chamisso, Adelbert von **82**
Claudius, Matthias **75**
Droste-Hülshoff, Annette Freiin von **3, 133**
Eichendorff, Joseph **8**
Engels, Friedrich **85, 114**
Feuerbach, Ludwig **139**
Fichte, Johann Gottlieb **62**
Fontane, Theodor **26, 163**
Fouqué, Friedrich (Heinrich Karl) de la Motte **2**
Freytag, Gustav **109**
Goethe, Johann Wolfgang von **4, 22, 34, 90, 154**
Grabbe, Christian Dietrich **2**
Grimm, Jacob Ludwig Karl **3, 77**
Grimm, Wilhelm Karl **3, 77**
Hebbel, Friedrich **43**
Hegel, Georg Wilhelm Friedrich **46, 151**

Heine, Heinrich **4, 54, 147**
Herder, Johann Gottfried von **8**
Hoffmann, E(rnst) T(heodor) A(madeus) **2**
Hölderlin, (Johann Christian) Friedrich **16**
Humboldt, Alexander von **170**
Humboldt, Wilhelm von **134**
Immermann, Karl (Lebrecht) **4, 49**
Jean Paul **7**
Kant, Immanuel **27, 67**
Kleist, Heinrich von **2, 37**
Klinger, Friedrich Maximilian von **1**
Klopstock, Friedrich Gottlieb **11**
Kotzebue, August (Friedrich Ferdinand) von **25**
La Roche, Sophie von **121**
Ludwig, Otto **4**
Marx, Karl (Heinrich) **17, 114**
Mörike, Eduard (Friedrich) **10**
Novalis **13**
Schelling, Friedrich Wilhelm Joseph von **30**
Schiller, Friedrich von **39, 69, 166**
Schlegel, August Wilhelm von **15, 142**
Schlegel, Friedrich **45**
Schleiermacher, Friedrich **107**
Schopenhauer, Arthur **51, 157**
Schumann, Robert **143**
Storm, (Hans) Theodor (Woldsen) **1**
Tieck, (Johann) Ludwig **5, 46**
Varnhagen, Rahel **130**
Wagner, Richard **9, 119**
Wieland, Christoph Martin **17**

GREEK

Foscolo, Ugo **8, 97**
Solomos, Dionysios **15**

HUNGARIAN

Arany, Janos **34**
Madach, Imre **19**
Petofi, Sándor **21**

INDIAN

Chatterji, Bankim Chandra **19**
Dutt, Michael Madhusudan **118**
Dutt, Toru **29**

IRISH

Allingham, William **25**
Banim, John **13**
Banim, Michael **13**
Boucicault, Dion **41**
Carleton, William **3**
Croker, John Wilson **10**
Darley, George **2**
Edgeworth, Maria **1, 51, 158**
Ferguson, Samuel **33**
Griffin, Gerald **7**
Jameson, Anna **43**
Le Fanu, Joseph Sheridan **9, 58**
Lever, Charles (James) **23**
Maginn, William **8**
Mangan, James Clarence **27**
Maturin, Charles Robert **6, 169**
Merriman, Brian **70**
Moore, Thomas **6, 110**
Morgan, Lady **29**
O'Brien, Fitz-James **21**

Sheridan, Richard Brinsley **5, 91**

ITALIAN

Alfieri, Vittorio **101**
Collodi, Carlo **54**
Foscolo, Ugo **8, 97**
Gozzi, (Conte) Carlo **23**
Leopardi, Giacomo **22, 129**
Manzoni, Alessandro **29, 98**
Mazzini, Guiseppe **34**
Nievo, Ippolito **22**

JAMAICAN

Seacole, Mary Jane Grant **147**

JAPANESE

Akinari, Ueda **131**
Ichiyō, Higuchi **49**
Motoori, Norinaga **45**

LITHUANIAN

Mapu, Abraham (ben Jekutiel) **18**

MEXICAN

Lizardi, Jose Joaquin Fernandez de **30**
Najera, Manuel Gutierrez **133**

NORWEGIAN

Collett, (Jacobine) Camilla (Wergeland) **22**
Wergeland, Henrik Arnold **5**

POLISH

Fredro, Aleksander **8**
Krasicki, Ignacy **8**
Krasiński, Zygmunt **4**
Mickiewicz, Adam **3, 101**
Norwid, Cyprian Kamil **17**
Slowacki, Juliusz **15**

ROMANIAN

Eminescu, Mihail **33, 131**

RUSSIAN

Aksakov, Sergei Timofeyvich **2**
Bakunin, Mikhail (Alexandrovich) **25, 58**
Baratynsky, Evgenii Abramovich **103**
Bashkirtseff, Marie **27**
Belinski, Vissarion Grigoryevich **5**
Bestuzhev, Aleksandr Aleksandrovich **131**
Chernyshevsky, Nikolay Gavrilovich **1**
Dobrolyubov, Nikolai Alexandrovich **5**
Dostoevsky, Fedor Mikhailovich **2, 7, 21, 33, 43, 119, 167**
Gogol, Nikolai (Vasilyevich) **5, 15, 31, 162**
Goncharov, Ivan Alexandrovich **1, 63**
Granovsky, Timofei Nikolaevich **75**
Griboedov, Aleksandr Sergeevich **129**
Herzen, Aleksandr Ivanovich **10, 61**
Karamzin, Nikolai Mikhailovich **3, 173**
Krylov, Ivan Andreevich **1**
Lermontov, Mikhail Yuryevich **5, 47, 126**
Leskov, Nikolai (Semyonovich) **25**
Nekrasov, Nikolai Alekseevich **11**
Ostrovsky, Alexander **30, 57**
Pavlova, Karolina Karlovna **138**

Pisarev, Dmitry Ivanovich **25**
Pushkin, Alexander (Sergeyevich) **3, 27, 83**
Saltykov, Mikhail Evgrafovich **16**
Smolenskin, Peretz **30**
Turgenev, Ivan **21, 37, 122**
Tyutchev, Fyodor **34**
Zhukovsky, Vasily (Andreevich) **35**

SCOTTISH

Baillie, Joanna **2, 151**
Beattie, James **25**
Blair, Hugh **75**
Campbell, Thomas **19**
Carlyle, Thomas **22, 70**
Ferrier, Susan (Edmonstone) **8**
Galt, John **1, 110**
Hogg, James **4, 109**
Jeffrey, Francis **33**
Lockhart, John Gibson **6**
Mackenzie, Henry **41**
Miller, Hugh **143**
Oliphant, Margaret (Oliphant Wilson) **11, 61**
Scott, Walter **15, 69, 110**
Stevenson, Robert Louis (Balfour) **5, 14, 63**
Thomson, James **18**
Wilson, John **5**
Wright, Frances **74**

SERBIAN

Karadžić, Vuk Stefanović **115**

SLOVENIAN

Kopitar, Jernej **117**
Prešeren, Francè **127**

SPANISH

Alarcon, Pedro Antonio de **1**
Bécquer, Gustavo Adolfo **106**
Caballero, Fernan **10**
Castro, Rosalia de **3, 78**
Espronceda, Jose de **39**
Larra (y Sanchez de Castro), Mariano Jose de **17, 130**
Martínez de la Rosa, Francisco de Paula **102**
Tamayo y Baus, Manuel **1**
Zorrilla y Moral, Jose **6**

SWEDISH

Almqvist, Carl Jonas Love **42**
Bremer, Fredrika **11**
Stagnelius, Eric Johan **61**
Tegner, Esaias **2**

SWISS

Amiel, Henri Frederic **4**
Burckhardt, Jacob (Christoph) **49**
Charriere, Isabelle de **66**
Gotthelf, Jeremias **117**
Keller, Gottfried **2**
Lavater, Johann Kaspar **142**
Meyer, Conrad Ferdinand **81**
Wyss, Johann David Von **10**

UKRAINIAN

Shevchenko, Taras **54**

VENEZUELAN

Bello, Andrés **131**

NCLC-173 Title Index

"An Aberration" (Karamzin)
 See "Strannost"
"Afinskaia zhizn" (Karamzin) **173**:309, 323
"Alina" (Karamzin) **173**:266
All Religions Are One (Blake) **173**:9
America: A Prophecy (Blake) **173**:152, 157
"Anecdote" (Karamzin)
 See "Anekdot"
"Anekdot" (Karamzin) **173**:268
"Annotations to Reynold's *Discourses* "
 (Blake) **173**:90, 149
"Athenian Life" (Karamzin)
 See "Afinskaia zhizn"
"Auguries of Innocence" (Blake) **173**:69
"Ballad Books" (Child) **173**:224
"Ballad Poetry" (Child) **173**:176, 183, 195-96,
 212-13, 218, 220-21, 224, 233, 235
Ballads (Child)
 See *English and Scottish Ballads*
"Bard's Song" (Blake) **173**:5, 11, 17-18, 59-63,
 65, 69, 89-90, 92-95, 98-101, 106, 113, 122,
 151
"Bednaya Liza" (Karamzin) **173**:279, 283, 296,
 309, 347-48, 350
"Bird of Paradise" (Karamzin)
 See "Rayskaya ptichka"
" *Bishop Percy's Folio Manuscript* " (Child)
 173:224, 229
"Blagodeyaniye" (Karamzin) **173**:284
"Blake's Cottage at Felpham" (Blake) **173**:64
"The Book of Ahania" (Blake) **173**:81
The Book of Los (Blake) **173**:61
The Book of Thel (Blake) **173**:108
Book of Urizen (Blake)
 See *The First Book of Urizen*
"Bornholm Island" (Karamzin)
 See "Ostrov Borngol'm"
British Poets (Child) **173**:167, 169, 171-72,
 189, 198, 208-9, 225-27, 244
"Chto nuzhno avtoru" (Karamzin) **173**:350
"Chuvstvitel'nyy i kholodnyy" (Karamzin)
 See "Cuvstvitel'nyj i xolodnyj, dva xarak-
 tera"
*The Complete Poetry and Prose of William
 Blake* (Blake) **173**:23, 36, 70, 98, 136
"Conversation about Happiness" (Karamzin)
 See "Razgover o shchastii"
"The Crystal Cabinet" (Blake) **173**:109, 111,
 117
"Cuvstvitel'nyj i xolodnyj, dva xaraktera"
 (Karamzin) **173**:268, 280, 312
*A Descriptive Catalogue of Pictures, Poetical
 and Historical Inventions, Painted by
 William Blake in Water Colours, being
 the Ancient Method of Fresco Painting
 Restored: And Drawing for Public
 Inspection, etc.* (Blake) **173**:48, 52, 70,
 143
"A Dialogue On Happiness" (Karamzin)
 See "Razgover o shchastii"

"Dissertation on Old and New Styles of the
 Russian Language" (Karamzin)
 See "Rassuždenie o starom i novom sloge
 rossijskogo jazyka"
"The Divine Image" (Blake) **173**:16
"The Emotional and the Cold, Two Characters"
 (Karamzin)
 See "Cuvstvitel'nyj i xolodnyj, dva xarak-
 tera"
English and Scottish Ballads (Child) **173**:166-
 70, 172-73, 178-80, 183, 189-91, 193-95,
 198-200, 209, 211, 226-29, 232-35, 238,
 244
The English and Scottish Popular Ballads
 (Child) **173**:169-72, 175-79, 186-87, 189,
 194, 197-98, 201, 204-6, 209-12, 223-24,
 226-28, 232-35, 238, 244
English Poets (Child)
 See *British Poets*
Europe: A Prophecy (Blake) **173**:147, 152, 157
"Filalet k Melodor" (Karamzin) **173**:277, 309,
 323
The First Book of Urizen (Blake) **173**:25, 40,
 61, 147
"Four Old Plays. Three Interludes: *Thersytes,
 Jack Jugler,* and Heywood's *Pardoner
 and Frere:* and *Jocaste, a Tragedy* by
 Gascoigne and Kinwelmarsh" (Child)
 173:167, 198, 207-8, 225
*The Four Zoas: The Torments of Love and
 Jealousy in the Death and Judgment of
 Albion* (Blake) **173**:10-11, 13-15, 37, 41,
 56-58, 61-62, 65, 74, 79-80, 86, 96-97, 111-
 12, 138
"Frol Silin" (Karamzin) **173**:309
The Gates of Paradise (Blake) **173**:16
"Gimm gluptsam" (Karamzin) **173**:280
"Good Deeds" (Karamzin)
 See "Blagodeyaniye"
"The Graveyard" (Karamzin)
 See "Kladbishche"
Historical Panegyric to Catherine II
 (Karamzin)
 See "Istoricheskoye pokhval'noye slovo
 Yekaterine II"
History of the Russian State (Karamzin)
 See *Istoriya gosudarstva Rossiiskogo*
"The Human Abstract" (Blake) **173**:16
"Hymn to Fools" (Karamzin)
 See "Gimm gluptsam"
"Il'ya Muromets" (Karamzin) **173**:283
"Information on Martha the Burgomistress
 from the Life of St Zosima" (Karamzin)
 See "Izvestiye o Marfe Posadnitse, vzya-
 toye iz zhitiya Zosimy"
"The Island of Bornholm" (Karamzin)
 See "Ostrov Borngol'm"
"Istoricheskoye pokhval'noye slovo Yekaterine
 II" (Karamzin) **173**:285-86, 288
Istoriya gosudarstva Rossiiskogo (Karamzin)
 173:255-60, 262-63, 280, 298, 301, 308,
 310, 312, 329-37, 343-46

"Izvestiye o Marfe Posadnitse, vzyatoye iz
 zhitiya Zosimy" (Karamzin) **173**:283
Jerusalem: The Emanation of the Giant Albion
 (Blake) **173**:4, 10-16, 18-19, 36-37, 46,
 50, 52, 61, 65-66, 70, 73, 82, 94, 96-98,
 108, 152-53, 157
"A Journey around Moscow" (Karamzin)
 173:284
"K dobrodeteli" (Karamzin) **173**:280
"K milosti" (Karamzin) **173**:266
"K solov'iu" (Karamzin) **173**:351
*Karamzin's Memoir on Ancient and Modern
 Russia: A Translation and Analysis*
 (Karamzin)
 See *O drevnei i novoi Rossii v ee
 politicheskom i grazhdanskom otnosheni-
 iakh*
"Kladbishche" (Karamzin) **173**:347
"A Knight of Our Time" (Karamzin)
 See "Rytsar nashego vremeni"
"The Laocoön" (Blake) **173**:153, 157
"The Lass of the Pamunky" (Child) **173**:210
"Letter of a Country Dweller" (Karamzin)
 See "Pis'mo sel'skago žitelja"
Letters of a Russian Traveler (Karamzin)
 See *Pis'ma Russkogo puteshestvennika*
"Liodor" (Karamzin) **173**:290
"The Man of Feeling and the Cold-Blooded
 Man" (Karamzin)
 See "Cuvstvitel'nyj i xolodnyj, dva xarak-
 tera"
"Marfa-posadnitsa" (Karamzin) **173**:280, 283,
 296, 312, 333
The Marriage of Heaven and Hell (Blake)
 173:8, 10, 39, 44, 52, 56-57, 66, 73, 78-79,
 84, 112, 116
"Martha" (Karamzin)
 See "Marfa-posadnitsa"
"Melancholy" (Karamzin)
 See "Melankholiya"
"Melankholiya" (Karamzin) **173**:280
"Melodor k Filalet" (Karamzin) **173**:277, 323,
 352
Memoir on Ancient and Modern Russia
 (Karamzin)
 See *O drevnei i novoi Rossii v ee
 politicheskom i grazhdanskom otnosheni-
 iakh*
Memorandum on Old and New Russia
 (Karamzin)
 See *O drevnei i novoi Rossii v ee
 politicheskom i grazhdanskom otnosheni-
 iakh*
Milton (Blake) **173**:1-163
"Mneniye russkogo grazhdanina" (Karamzin)
 173:286
"Moja ispoved" (Karamzin) **173**:268, 280, 285,
 312, 322-26
"The Moral View of Plato as Unfolded in the
 Gorgias" (Child) **173**:207
"Un mot sur la littérature russe" (Karamzin)
 173:267

"Moya ispoved" (Karamzin)
 See "Moja ispoved"
"My Confession" (Karamzin)
 See "Moja ispoved"
"Mysli ob istinnoy svobode" (Karamzin)
 173:286
"Na puti k Troitse" (Karamzin) **173**:342
"Natal'ya, boyarskaya doch" (Karamzin)
 173:279, 283, 295-96, 313-14, 333, 350-51
"Nathalie, the Boyar's Daughter" (Karamzin)
 See "Natal'ya, boyarskaya doch"
"Nechto o naukakh, isskustvakh i
 prosveshchenii" (Karamzin) **173**:309,
 323-25
"Nezhnost' druzhby v nizkom sostoianii"
 (Karamzin) **173**:309
"O Bogdanoviche i yego sochineniyakh"
 (Karamzin) **173**:281
*O drevnei i novoi Rossii v ee politicheskom i
 grazhdanskom otnosheniiakh* (Karamzin)
 173:254, 258, 269, 286, 300-302, 304, 310
"O lvubvi k otechestvu i narodnoy gordosti"
 (Karamzin) **173**:282
"O lyogkoy odezhde modnykh drasavits XIX
 veka" (Karamzin) **173**:288
"O sluchayakh i kharaterakh v rossiyskoy
 istorii, kotoryye mogut byt' predmetom
 khudozhestv" (Karamzin) **173**:283
"Observations on the Language of Chaucer"
 (Child) **173**:168-69, 171, 189, 209, 226
*Observations on the Language of Gower's
 Confessio Amantis* (Child) **173**:168-69,
 171-72, 189, 209
"On Bogdanovich and his Works" (Karamzin)
 See "O Bogdanoviche i yego soch-
 ineniyakh"
"On Homer's Poetry" (Blake) **173**:157
"On Love of One's Country and National
 Pride" (Karamzin)
 See "O lvubvi k otechestvu i narodnoy gor-
 dosti"
"On the Incidents and Characters in Russian
 History, Which May Provide Subjects for
 the Arts" (Karamzin)
 See "O sluchayakh i kharaterakh v
 rossiyskoy istorii, kotoryye mogut byt'
 predmetom khudozhestv"
"On the Light Dress of Fashionable Beauties"
 (Karamzin)
 See "O lyogkoy odezhde modnykh drasav-
 its XIX veka"
"On the Moscow Earthquake of 1802"
 (Karamzin) **173**:284
"On the Moscow Revolt in the Reign of
 Aleksey Mikhaylovich" (Karamzin)
 173:284
"On the Secret Chancellery" (Karamzin)
 173:284
"On the Way to Trinity Monastery"
 (Karamzin)
 See "Na puti k Troitse"
"On Virgil" (Blake) **173**:157

"Opinion of a Russian Citizen" (Karamzin)
 See "Mneniye russkogo grazhdanina"
"Ostrov Borngol'm" (Karamzin) **173**:342, 348,
 350-54
"Ot chego v Rossii malo avtorskikh talantov"
 (Karamzin) **173**:282
"Philalet to Melodor" (Karamzin)
 See "Filalet k Melodor"
Pis'ma Russkogo puteshestvennika (Karamzin)
 173:251, 254, 267, 272-76, 278-79, 308,
 325-26, 333, 348, 353-54
"Pis'mo sel'skago žitelja" (Karamzin) **173**:268,
 286
"Pleasing Prospects, Hopes and Desires of the
 Present Time" (Karamzin)
 See "Priyatnyye vidy, nadezhdy i zhelaniya
 nyneshego vremeni"
*Poems of Religious Sorrow, Comfort, Counsel
 and Aspiration* (Child) **173**:167
Poems of Sorrow and Comfort (Child)
 See *Poems of Religious Sorrow, Comfort,
 Counsel and Aspiration*
The Poetical Works of Edmund Spenser (Child)
 173:167, 169, 171, 189, 208, 225
The Poetry and Prose of William Blake (Blake)
 See *The Complete Poetry and Prose of Wil-
 liam Blake*
"A Poison Tree" (Blake) **173**:90
"Poor Liza" (Karamzin)
 See "Bednaya Liza"
*The Popular Ballads of the English Race by
 Professor F. J. Child* (Child)
 See *The English and Scottish Popular Bal-
 lads*
"Priyatnyye vidy, nadezhdy i zhelaniya
 nyneshego vremeni" (Karamzin) **173**:285
"Professor Child's Appeal" (Child) **173**:233
"Raisa" (Karamzin) **173**:266
"Rassuždenie o starom i novom sloge
 rossijskogo jazyka" (Karamzin) **173**:269
"Rayskaya ptichka" (Karamzin) **173**:283
"Razgover o shchastii" (Karamzin) **173**:309,
 323-25
"Rec, proiznesënnaja na toržestvennom
 sobranii imperatorskoj Rossijskoj
 akademii" (Karamzin) **173**:294
"Recovery" (Karamzin)
 See "Vyzdorovlenie"
"Reply to my Friend, who Wanted Me to Write
 an Ode to Catherine the Great"
 (Karamzin) **173**:309
"Rytsar nashego vremeni" (Karamzin) **173**:280,
 295, 311-13, 316-20
"Sel'skii prazdnik i svad'ba" (Karamzin)
 173:309
"The Sick Rose" (Blake) **173**:105
"Sierra-Morena" (Karamzin) **173**:342
"Something about the Sciences, Arts and
 Enlightenment" (Karamzin)
 See "Nechto o naukakh, isskustvakh i pros-
 veshchenii"

"Song" (Blake)
 See "Bard's Song"
The Song of Los (Blake) **173**:9
"The Song of Los" (Blake) **173**:81
"Song of the Bard" (Blake)
 See "Bard's Song"
"Songs of Beulah" (Blake) **173**:111
Songs of Experience (Blake)
 See *Songs of Innocence and of Experience:
 Shewing the Two Contrary States of the
 Human Soul*
Songs of Innocence (Child) **173**:108
*Songs of Innocence and of Experience:
 Shewing the Two Contrary States of the
 Human Soul* (Blake) **173**:10, 16-17, 28,
 108
"Strannost" (Karamzin) **173**:285
"Tender Friendship in the Lower Estate"
 (Karamzin)
 See "Nezhnost' druzhby v nizkom sostoia-
 nii"
There Is No Natural Religion (Blake) **173**:9
"Thoughts on True Freedom" (Karamzin)
 See "Mysli ob istinnoy svobode"
Tiriel (Blake) **173**:128
"To a Nightingale" (Karamzin)
 See "K solov'iu"
"To Mercy" (Karamzin)
 See "K milosti"
"To Tirzah" (Blake) **173**:28
"To Virtue" (Karamzin)
 See "K dobrodeteli"
*Travels from Moscow through Prussia,
 Germany, Switzerland, France, and
 England* (Karamzin)
 See *Pis'ma Russkogo puteshestvennika*
Vala (Blake)
 See *The Four Zoas: The Torments of Love
 and Jealousy in the Death and Judgment
 of Albion*
"A Village Holiday and Wedding" (Karamzin)
 See "Sel'skii prazdnik i svad'ba"
A Vision of the Last Judgment (Blake) **173**:8,
 18, 47, 51, 104, 120-21, 123, 132-33, 153
*Visions of the Daughters of Albion: The Eye
 Sees More than the Heart Knows* (Blake)
 173:42, 61, 105, 152, 157
"Voice of the Ancient Bard" (Blake) **173**:17
"Vyzdorovlenie" (Karamzin) **173**:347
War-songs for Freemen (Child) **173**:210
"What does an Author need?" (Karamzin)
 See "Chto nuzhno avtoru"
"Why Are There Few Writers of Talent in
 Russia?" (Karamzin)
 See "Ot chego v Rossii malo avtorskikh ta-
 lantov"
Zapiska o drevnej i novoj rossii (Karamzin)
 See *O drevnei i novoi Rossii v ee
 politicheskom i grazhdanskom otnosheni-
 iakh*

ISBN-13: 978-0-7876-8657-4
ISBN-10: 0-7876-8657-3